Lecture Notes in Computer Science 16360

Founding Editors

Gerhard Goos

Juris Hartmanis

The series Lecture Notes in Computer Science (LNCS), including its subseries Lecture Notes in Artificial Intelligence (LNAI) and Lecture Notes in Bioinformatics (LNBI), has established itself as a medium for the publication of new developments in computer science and information technology research, teaching, and education.

LNCS enjoys close cooperation with the computer science R & D community, the series counts many renowned academics among its volume editors and paper authors, and collaborates with prestigious societies. Its mission is to serve this international community by providing an invaluable service, mainly focused on the publication of conference and workshop proceedings and postproceedings. LNCS commenced publication in 1973.

Wei Jia · Lu Leng · Jie Gui · Xiangbo Shu ·
Xianye Ben · Zhenan Sun · Yuming Fang ·
Weidong Min · Jun Chu
Editors

Biometric Recognition

19th Chinese Conference, CCBR 2025
Nanchang, China, November 21–23, 2025
Proceedings

 Springer

Editors
Wei Jia
Hefei University of Technology
Hefei, China

Jie Gui
Southeast University
Jiangsu, China

Xianye Ben
Shandong University
Shandong, China

Yuming Fang
Jiangxi University of Finance and Economics
Nanchang, China

Jun Chu
Nanchang Hangkong University
Nanchang, China

Lu Leng
Nanchang Hangkong University
Nanchang, China

Xiangbo Shu
Nanjing University of Science
and Technology
Jiangsu, China

Zhenan Sun
Institute of Automation Chinese Academy
of Sciences
Beijing, China

Weidong Min
Nanchang Hangkong University
Nanchang, China

ISSN 0302-9743   ISSN 1611-3349 (electronic)
Lecture Notes in Computer Science
ISBN 978-981-95-6122-3   ISBN 978-981-95-6123-0 (eBook)
https://doi.org/10.1007/978-981-95-6123-0

This Springer imprint is published by the registered company Springer Nature Singapore Pte Ltd.
The registered company address is: 152 Beach Road, #21-01/04 Gateway East, Singapore 189721, Singapore

If disposing of this product, please recycle the paper.

Preface

Biometric technologies, which enable automatic person identification or verification based on physiological or behavioral traits, such as face, fingerprint, iris, gait, or signature, find extensive applications in modern society. In recent years, biometric recognition systems have been widely deployed globally, spanning across law enforcement, government, and consumer sectors. Developing diverse and reliable approaches for trustworthy biometric applications has become imperative. In China, the proliferation of the Internet and smartphones among its vast population, coupled with substantial government investments in security and privacy protection, has led to the rapid growth of the biometric market. Consequently, biometric research in the country has garnered increasing attention. Researchers have been actively addressing various scientific challenges in biometrics, exploring diverse biometric techniques, and making significant contributions to the field. The Chinese Conference on Biometric Recognition (CCBR), an annual event held in China, serves as a pivotal platform for biometric researchers. It provides an excellent opportunity to exchange knowledge, share progress, and discuss ideas related to the development and applications of biometric theory, technology, and systems.

CCBR 2025 took place in Nanchang from November 21–23, marking the 19th edition in a series of successful conferences held in prominent cities such as Nanjing, Beijing, Hangzhou, Xi'an, Guangzhou, Jinan, Shenyang, Tianjin, Chengdu, Shenzhen, Urumqi, Zhuzhou, Shanghai, and Xuzhou since 2000. The conference received 90 submissions, each meticulously reviewed by a minimum of three experts from the Program Committee. Following a rigorous double-blind peer-review process, 62 papers were chosen for presentation (68.9% acceptance rate). These papers comprise this volume of the CCBR 2025 conference proceedings, which covers a wide range of topics: Fingerprint, Palmprint, and Vein Recognition; Face Detection, Recognition, and Tracking; Affective Computing and Human-Computer Interface; Gait, Iris, and Other Biometrics; Trustworthiness, Privacy, and Personal Data Security; Medical and Other Applications.

We would like to thank all the authors, reviewers, invited speakers, volunteers, and organizing committee members, without whom CCBR 2025 would not have been successful. We also wish to acknowledge the support of the China Society of Image and

Graphics, the Chinese Association for Artificial Intelligence, the Institute of Automation of the Chinese Academy of Sciences, Springer, Nanchang Hangkong University, and Jiangxi University of Finance and Economics for sponsoring this conference.

December 2025

Zhenan Sun
Yuming Fang
Weidong Min
Jun Chu
Wei Jia
Lu Leng
Jie Gui
Xiangbo Shu
Xianye Ben

Organization

Academic Advisory Committee

Anil K. Jain	Michigan State University, USA
Tieniu Tan	Nanjing University, China
David Zhang	Chinese University of Hong Kong (Shenzhen), China
Massimo Tistarelli	University of Sassari, Italy

Industry Advisory Committee

Zhifei Wang	Information Center of the Ministry of Human Resources and Social Security, China
Hongchuan Hou	First Research Institute of the Ministry of Public Security, China
Zhe Li	Ant Digital Technology, China
Cong Liu	Iflytek Co., Ltd., China

General Chairs

Zhenan Sun	Institute of Automation, Chinese Academy of Sciences, China
Yuming Fang	Jiangxi University of Finance and Economics, China
Weidong Min	Nanchang University, China
Jun Chu	Nanchang Hangkong University, China

Program Committee Chairs

Wei Jia	Hefei University of Technology, China
Lu Leng	Nanchang Hangkong University, China
Jie Gui	Southeast University, China
Xiangbo Shu	Nanjing University of Science and Technology, China
Xianye Ben	Shandong University, China

Organizing Committee Chairs

Zhaofeng He	Beijing University of Posts and Telecommunications, China
Jianjiang Feng	Tsinghua University, China
Congxuan Zhang	Nanchang Hangkong University, China
Jun Wang	China University of Mining and Technology, China
Mao Ye	Wuhan University, China

Publicity Chairs

Nan Su	Harbin Engineering University, China
Shiqi Yu	Southern University of Science and Technology, China
Wenxiong Kang	South China University of Technology, China

Sponsorship Chairs

Lunke Fei	Guangdong University of Technology, China

Publication Chairs

Qijun Zhao	Sichuan University, China
Dan Zeng	Sun Yat-sen University, China

Forum Chairs

Qi Li	Institute of Automation, Chinese Academy of Sciences, China
Dexing Zhong	Xi'an Jiaotong University, China
Hao Liu	Ningxia University, China
Zhe Jin	Anhui University, China
Huafeng Qin	Chongqing Technology and Business University, China
Ying Chen	Nanchang Hangkong University, China

Jinrong Cui	South China Agricultural University, China
Shuping Zhao	Guangdong University of Technology, China
Zitong Yu	Great Bay University, China

Contents

**Human-Centric AIGC (Face Synthesis, Speech Synthesis, Gesture
Generation, Human Motion Generation, etc.)**

Gait, Footprint

Face Related

Anti-spoofing, Presentation Attack Detection

Human-Related Understanding

Basic Theory of Biometric Recognition

Gesture, Action

Individual Characterization and Human-Computer Interaction

Adversarial Attack and Proactive Defense

Template Protection and Cryptosystems

Datasets, Evaluation, Benchmarking, Performance Modelling and Prediction

Others

Fingerprint, Palmprint and Vein Recognition

EC-PVGAN: Affine-Equivariant Generative Adversarial Data Augmentation for Palm-Vein Identification

Hulei Deng, Haiyang Li, Hailong Hu, and Huafeng Qin[(✉)]

Chongqing Technology and Business University, Chongqing, India
`huhailong@ctbu.edu.cn`, `14_dhl@163.com`

Abstract. Palm-vein identification has emerged as a research hotspot in high-security authentication, due to the unique vascular texture and its resistance to spoofing. However, the scarcity of high-quality palm-vein image samples often restricts the performance and generalization capabilities of deep learning models. To address this challenge, we propose EC-PVGAN, an adversarial generative data augmentation method that leverages affine-equivariant constraints to synthesize realistic and diverse palm-vein samples while preserving structural fidelity. The EC-PVGAN begins by applying random affine transformations to binary vein masks extracted by a segmentation model. These transformed masks are then fed into a Pix2Pix-based generator to produce augmented samples. The equivariance similarity loss and commutativity loss are designed to establish a linear equivalence between the affine transformation and image synthesis, thereby guiding the generator to produce affine-equivariant images. Experimental results on two palm-vein datasets demonstrate that our proposed EC-PVGAN significantly improves the identification accuracy and equal error rates across eight vein classifiers, outperforming classic data augmentation methods.

Keywords: Affine-equivariant adversarial augmentation · Palm-vein identification · Generative adversarial network

1 Introduction

As digitalization progresses, information security challenges have become increasingly severe. Traditional authentication methods exhibit inherent shortcomings: passwords are easily forgotten and vulnerable to brute-force attacks; access control cards might be lost or duplicated at any time; identity documents may be forged or compromised due to physical wear and degradation. To overcome these limitations, biometric authentication technologies have emerged as an alternative and are broadly classified into two main categories: behavioral biometrics, such as gait [25] and voice [13]), and physiological biometrics, including

W. Jia et al. (Eds.): CCBR 2025, LNCS 16360, pp. 3–13, 2026.
https://doi.org/10.1007/978-981-95-6123-0_1

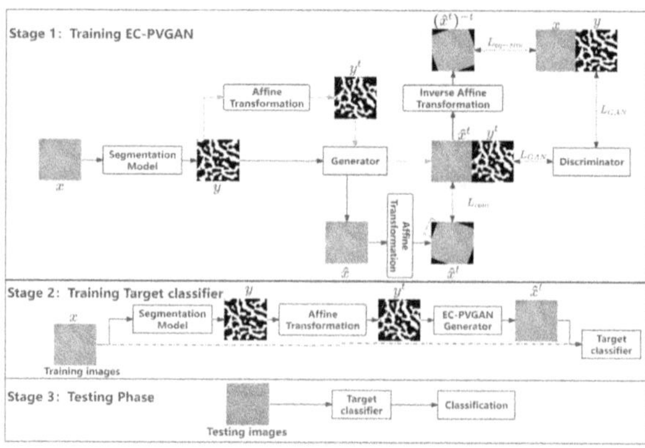

Fig. 1. Overview of the EC-PVGAN palm-vein identification system.

fingerprint [7] and face [12]. Although behavioral biometrics can enhance security to some extent, their dependence on high-precision sensing equipment and complex algorithms limits their practical adoption. In contrast, physiological biometrics have attracted considerable attention due to their relative stability and operational efficiency.

In physiological biometrics, external features (e.g., fingerprints [7]) are widely used due to ease of acquisition but are also prone to replication or tampering. In contrast, internal features, such as palm-vein [14], reside beneath the skin and can only be captured from living subjects, making them difficult to forge while also enabling effective liveness detection, thereby offering unique advantages in security and privacy protection [20]. As requirements for the security and reliability of identity authentication continue to rise, palm-vein based identification has become a focal point of research and application in recent years and is widely regarded as a practical solution to the limitations of traditional methods.

However, the samples are limited for vein recognition tasks. Specifically, there are no more than twenty samples [5] for each class in most existing vein databases, which significantly restricts the performance of deep learning-based classifiers. Although classic data augmentation approaches, such as rotation and scaling, can create huge samples with large diversity based on limited samples, they are prone to disrupting data distribution, resulting in poor consistency. For example, the augmented samples include black-border artifacts, as marked with the red box in Fig. 1. By contrast, the generative adversarial networks (GANs) can generate samples with good consistency because they learns the real data distribution by training it on huge samples. However, there are slight variations such as illuminations and local distributions in the generated images, resulting in poor diversity. In addition, the GANs as a deep learning model generally require a large amount of samples for training, so it is difficult to achieve robust data augmentation on a small dataset.

To address these problems, in this paper, we propose EC-PVGAN—an affine-equivariant adversarial augmentation method that combines the diversity of affine transformations with the distribution fidelity of GANs, enabling the synthesis of diverse palm-vein images while preserving the structural integrity and texture of the original vein patterns. As shown in Fig. 1, in the training process of the EC-PVGAN (i.e. stage 1), we first employ a segmentation model to extract the binary vein mask y from the original image x. A random affine transformation is then applied to y, and the transformed mask is passed to the generator to synthesize the augmented image $\hat{x}^t$. The generator is jointly optimized using a combination of adversarial loss, equivariance similarity loss, and commutativity loss to enhance the realism of generated samples while guaranteeing affine equivariance. Once the generator is trained (stage 2), it is employed to augment the training set, and a target classifier is trained jointly on both the original and augmented images. During the testing phase (stage 3), the trained classifier is directly applied to unseen test images to evaluate the performance improvements achieved by the EC-PVGAN augmentation method. Our contributions are summarized as follows:

- We propose the EC-PVGAN to achieve adversarial generative data augmentation for palm-vein datasets. The proposed approach combines the advantages of classical data augmentation and GAN, so as to generate samples with good diversity and consistency.
- The equivariance similarity loss and commutativity loss are proposed to learn the affine-equivariance.
- We conduct extensive experiments on two public palm-vein datasets, demonstrating that EC-PVGAN significantly improves the identification accuracy of existing vein classifiers.

2   Related Work

Traditional Feature Extraction Methods. The Local Binary Pattern (LBP) [8] generates binary features by comparing the gray-level difference between a pixel and its neighborhood, thereby effectively characterizing vein texture. To better capture the linear morphology of vascular structures, the Local Line Binary Pattern (LLBP) [18] enhances sensitivity to vessel orientation during encoding, thereby improving the discriminability of vein patterns.

Another category of methods models the vein network as a set of linear gray-level valleys and extracts vessel paths via geometric analysis or filtering techniques. The Repeated Line Tracking method [11] incrementally traces the vessel centerline along the depth of gray-level valleys, thereby preserving path continuity even under complex background conditions. In contrast, the Wide Line Detector (WLD) method [5] enhances the visibility of vein lines by extracting texture responses across multiple scales and orientations.

Deep Learning Based Feature Extraction Methods. In recent years, deep learning methods have emerged as the dominant paradigm in vein recognition, due to their effectiveness in overcoming the limitations of traditional feature extraction methods [23]. Convolutional neural networks (CNNs) are particularly effective at capturing local texture features in vein images and have been widely employed for finger vein and palm vein representation and classification tasks [1]. In addition, more advanced work, such as ALE-IVT [16], integrates multi-branch attention interaction and attention-based label distribution strategy to further enhance the discriminative capabilities of vein features. Furthermore, Luo et al. propose AMPVNet, a lightweight convolutional network architecture tailored for vein texture representation, which leverages online data augmentation and an adaptive margin loss to achieve robust palm vein recognition [9].

Generative Adversarial Networks Based Augmentation. Classic augmentation methods based on geometric and color transformations can increase sample diversity, but cannot replicate the complex texture and structural variations in real-world environments [17]. Generative Adversarial Networks (GANs) address this limitation by adversarially training a generator and a discriminator to learn the underlying data distribution and synthesize images that are nearly indistinguishable from real samples. Common GANs include the original GAN [3], the conditional GAN (cGAN) [10], and the Pix2Pix image-to-image translator [6]. Building upon these foundations, recent studies have proposed a conditional DCGAN [17], which introduces an adversarial framework between the generator and a fixed classifier to enhance the classifier's feature representation.

3 Methodology

In this section, we present the EC-PVGAN, a data augmentation framework for palm-vein image synthesis. As illustrated in Fig. 1 (stage 1), the method first uses a segmentation model to extract a binary mask from the input image. A random affine transformation is then applied to the mask, and the transformed mask is fed into a Pix2Pix-based generator to synthesize the corresponding image. To enforce the structural consistency of palm-vein images, the EC-PVGAN incorporates an equivariance similarity loss and a commutativity loss. These losses ensure that, after applying the inverse transformation, the generated image remains structurally consistent with the original and preserves class-specific features. Finally, adversarial training with a discriminator is utilized to improve the visual realism and distributional fidelity of the generated images.

3.1 Feature Segmentation

Building on prior work [30], we employ multiple baseline methods to annotate veins and background in palm-vein images. Specifically, we segment each image using three distinct baseline techniques: mean curvature [9], repeated line tracking [14], and the wide line detector [15]. The resulting binary masks from these methods are summed to obtain a probability map, which is subsequently binarized to produce the final label, as formalized in Eq. (1):

$$L(i,j) = \begin{cases} 1 & \text{if } \sum_{m=1}^{M} l_m(i,j) \geq \frac{M}{2}, \\ 0 & \text{if } \sum_{m=1}^{M} l_m(i,j) < \frac{M}{2}, \end{cases} \tag{1}$$

In Eq. (1), a pixel value of 0 indicates the background and a pixel value of 1 indicates a vein. The M represents the total number of baseline methods (here $M = 3$). $L_m(i,j)$ denotes the segmentation result of the m_{th} baseline method at pixel (i,j), and $L(i,j)$ denotes the final ground-truth label of the pixel (i,j).

To improve segmentation accuracy and generalization, we adopt the method proposed in [22], where LoRA layers are inserted into the query and key projection matrices of each self-attention module in SAM's image encoder. Only these added parameters are fine-tuned, keeping the rest of the model fixed. Leveraging raw palm-vein images as input, the previously described handcrafted labels for supervision, we generate the final segmentation masks.

3.2 Affine-Equivariant Enhancement Based on Pix2Pix

To address the artifacts introduced by classic geometric transformations, our work adopts a mask-to-image mapping based on the Pix2Pix framework [6]. The Pix2Pix is an image-to-image translation model that learns the joint distribution of paired inputs and outputs, transforming binary masks into realistic vein images. Compared to applying affine transformations directly in the image domain, leveraging Pix2Pix fully exploits the learning capacity of the network to inpaint edge pixels while maintaining the continuity of the vascular structure. Specifically, the Pix2Pix consists of three core components: the generator, discriminator, and adversarial loss, each described in detail below.

Generator: The generator in the Pix2Pix uses a U-Net architecture, comprising a seven-level downsampling encoder and a symmetric upsampling decoder. The input is the binary vein mask $y \in \mathbb{R}^{C_{in} \times W \times H}$. The encoder progressively reduces spatial resolution while increasing the number of feature channels up to the bottleneck. The decoder then symmetrically restores spatial resolution and merges encoder feature maps via skip connections. Finally, the network projects the decoded features into C_{out} channels, producing the high-fidelity reconstructed image $\hat{x}^t$ at the same resolution as the original mask.

Discriminator: The discriminator consists of five convolutional layers and takes as input a tensor $z \in \mathbb{R}^{(C_{in}+C_{out}) \times W \times H}$, and outputs a local real-vs-fake probability map $P \in \mathbb{R}^{W' \times H'}$. The first three layers utilize 4×4 convolutions with a stride of 2 to downsample the input and progressively increase feature channels. The fourth layer employs a 4×4 convolution with a stride of 1, preserving spatial resolution while integrating deeper features. The final layer applies another 4×4 convolution to produce a single-channel prediction map, where each entry indicates the probability that the corresponding image patch is real.

Adversarial Loss: Let the generator and discriminator be denoted by G and D, respectively. Given a genuine maskimage pair (x, y), and an affine-transformed maskimage pair $(\hat{x}^t, y^t)$, the adversarial loss is defined as shown in Eq. (2).

$$\mathcal{L}_{\mathrm{GAN}}(D, G) = \mathbb{E}_{x,y}\big[\log D(x \mid y)\big] + \mathbb{E}_{x,y,t}\big[\log\big(1 - D(\hat{x}^t \mid y^t)\big)\big]. \qquad (2)$$

Here, the first term encourages D to correctly classify real samples, while the second term drives G to synthesize images realistic enough to deceive D.

Although directly applying a random affine transformation to the binary segmentation mask can effectively remove black-border artifacts, the generated image $\hat{x}^t = G(y^t)$ often fails to remain consistent with the original image x in both venous texture and geometric structure. To address this, we introduce the equivariance similarity loss and the commutativity loss to establish a linear equivalence between affine transformation and image generation. The Equivariance Similarity Loss is defined in Eq. (3):

$$L_{\text{eq-sim}} = \mathbb{E}_{x,t}\big\|x - (\hat{x}^t)^{-t}\big\|_1. \qquad (3)$$

This loss first applies the inverse affine transformation to the generated image $\hat{x}^t$, yielding $(\hat{x}^t)^{-t}$, and compares it with the original image x at the pixel level. This ensures that the reconstructed result remains consistent with the original in both venous texture and geometric structure.

Next, to guarantee linear alignment between the two processing pathways: affine-then-generate and generate-then-affine, we introduce the commutativity loss, formally defined in Eq. (4):

$$L_{\text{com}} = \mathbb{E}_{x,t}\big\|\hat{x}^t - (\hat{x})^t\big\|_1. \qquad (4)$$

Here, $\hat{x} = G(y)$ denotes the image generated directly from the original mask y. $\hat{x}^t$ denotes the image generated from the transformed mask y^t, and $(\hat{x})^t$ denotes the result of applying the same affine transformation to $\hat{x}$. This loss term enforces consistency between the two pathways by aligning their outputs geometrically, thereby ensuring that the generation process is equivariant to affine operations. Finally, the adversarial loss is defined as shown in Eq. (5):

$$L_{\text{adv}}(D, G) = L_{\mathrm{GAN}}(D, G) + \lambda_{\text{eq}}\, L_{\text{eq-sim}} + \lambda_{\text{com}}\, L_{\text{com}}. \qquad (5)$$

Here, λ_{eq} and λ_{com} control the weights of the equivariance similarity loss and the commutativity loss, respectively.

3.3   Adversarial Enhancement

Within the EC-PVGAN, the generator $G_\phi(\cdot)$ and the discriminator $D_\theta(\cdot)$ are alternately optimized in an adversarial manner. Let ϕ denote the generator's parameters. While preserving geometric consistency, the generator is trained to deceive the discriminator by ensuring that the pair $(\hat{x}^t, y^t)$ is classified as a real sample. Specifically, the generator's parameters ϕ^* are optimized by solving the minimization problem in Eq. (6):

$$\phi^* = \arg \min_{\phi} \left\{ \mathbb{E}_{x,y,t} \left[\log\left(1 - D_\theta(\hat{x}^t, y^t)\right) \right] + \lambda_{\text{eq}} L_{\text{eq-sim}} + \lambda_{\text{com}} L_{\text{com}} \right\}. \qquad (6)$$

The generator's parameters are updated at each iteration based on Eq. (7):

$$\phi \leftarrow \phi - \eta_G \nabla_\phi \left\{ \mathbb{E}_{x,y,t} \left[\log\left(1 - D_\theta(\hat{x}^t, y^t)\right) \right] + \lambda_{\text{eq}} L_{\text{eq-sim}} + \lambda_{\text{com}} L_{\text{com}} \right\}, \qquad (7)$$

where η_G denotes the generator's learning rate.

Correspondingly, let the discriminator's parameters be denoted by θ. The discriminator aims to distinguish the authenticity of imagemask pairs. Therefore, the discriminator's parameters are optimized by Eq. (8):

$$\theta^* = \arg \max_{\theta} \left\{ \mathbb{E}_{x,y} \left[\log D_\theta(x, y) \right] + \mathbb{E}_{x,y,t} \left[\log\left(1 - D_\theta(\hat{x}^t, y^t)\right) \right] \right\}. \qquad (8)$$

The parameters are updated by Eq. (9):

$$\theta \leftarrow \theta + \eta_D \nabla_\theta \left\{ \mathbb{E}_{x,y} \left[\log D_\theta(x, y) \right] + \mathbb{E}_{x,y,t} \left[\log\left(1 - D_\theta(\hat{x}^t, y^t)\right) \right] \right\}. \qquad (9)$$

Here, η_D denotes the discriminator's learning rate. During training, the generator and discriminator are updated alternately.

4   Experiments

4.1   Experimental Settings

To validate the proposed method, experiments were conducted on two public palm-vein datasets: the VERA PalmVein dataset [21] (dataset A) and the Tongji University palmprint dataset [26] (dataset B). When evaluating the performance of the EC-PVGAN, we adopted eight classifiers as baselines—including ResNet18 [4], FV-CNN [1], PV-CNN [14], FVRAS-Net [24], LWCNN [19], IVT [15], AG-NAS [2], and AMPVNet [9]. These classifiers were integrated into the EC-PVGAN to assess the improvement in classification performance achieved through the proposed data augmentation methods.

All experiments were implemented in the PyTorch framework and executed on a high-performance computing platform equipped with an NVIDIA GeForce GTX 4090 GPU. For dataset A, both the training set and the test set comprise 1,100 images (5 images per palm sample, for a total of 220 samples). For dataset B, the training set contains 6,000 images (10 images per palm sample, for a total of 600 samples), and the test set also contains 6,000 images. We utilized Equal Error Rate (EER) and accuracy to evaluate our method's performance. The EER is defined as the verification error rate at which the False Acceptance Rate (FAR) equals the False Rejection Rate (FRR).

The affine transformation for data augmentation consists of three operations: rotation (range 15° to 15°, probability 0.6), translation (range 10 pixels to 10 pixels, probability 0.2), and scaling (range 0.9 to 1.1, probability 0.2).

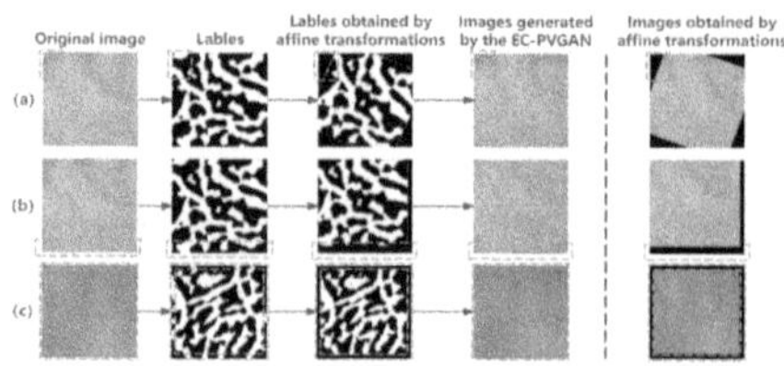

Fig. 2. Visual comparison between EC-PVGAN and affine transformations: (a) rotation; (b) translation; (c) scaling.

4.2   Visual Assessment

As illustrated in Fig. 2, EC-PVGAN effectively eliminates transformation-induced artifacts while preserving vein-feature consistency. When affine transformations (including rotation, translation, and scaling) are applied to segmentation masks, they produce noticeable black border artifacts at their edges, as shown in the fifth column ("Images obtained by affine transformations") of Fig. 2. In contrast, as depicted in the fourth column ("Images generated by the EC-PVGAN") of Fig. 2, the EC-PVGAN not only reconstructs the vein's texture and geometry but also inpaints the affine-induced black-border regions.

4.3   Identification Performance

After extracting binary vein masks and applying random affine transformations, the trained generator synthesizes augmented images, which are subsequently combined with the original samples to train the target classifier. In this subsection, we evaluate and compare the identification performance of the proposed method against classical augmentation methods. Table 1 and Table 2 show that our proposed EC-PVGAN significantly outperforms classical methods in identification performance. Classical methods generally include geometric

Table 1. Identification performance on dataset A

Method	Without augmentation		Classic methods		EC-PVGAN	
	Acc (%)	EER (%)	Acc (%)	EER (%)	Acc (%)	EER (%)
Resnet18 [4]	79.45	4.89	90.82	2.45	**97.91**	**1.07**
FVCNN [1]	88.45	4.33	89.68	3.59	**93.27**	**2.07**
PVCNN [14]	83.18	2.97	90.05	2.27	**96.59**	**1.02**
IVT [15]	92.86	1.90	95.14	1.19	**97.91**	**0.57**
AG-NAS [2]	92.64	1.72	94.45	1.97	**97.86**	**0.73**
FVRAS-NET [24]	94.45	1.70	96.32	0.91	**98.77**	**0.73**
LWCNN [19]	80.45	4.00	89.32	3.26	**94.14**	**1.90**
AMPVNet [9]	95.55	1.27	96.41	0.88	**98.05**	**0.60**

transformations—such as rotation, scaling, and translation—as well as color-based transformations, including adjustments to contrast, brightness, quantization, and saturation. However, geometric transformations often introduce black border artifacts at image edges and disrupt the original palm vein texture distribution. For fair comparison, in this work, we choose color-based transformations. While the dataset augmented through color-based transformations leads to improved identification accuracy, its performance remains consistently inferior to that achieved by our proposed EC-PVGAN method.

Table 2. Identification performance on dataset B

Method	Without augmentation		Classic methods		EC-PVGAN	
	Acc (%)	EER (%)	Acc (%)	EER (%)	Acc (%)	EER (%)
Resnet18 [4]	79.92	4.07	86.98	3.02	**92.36**	**1.97**
FVCNN [1]	90.91	5.77	91.41	3.85	**92.43**	**3.15**
PVCNN [14]	86.07	3.42	87.29	3.93	**90.33**	**2.55**
IVT [15]	79.15	5.08	88.01	3.45	**91.23**	**1.97**
AG-NAS [2]	93.63	1.80	94.53	1.22	**95.85**	**1.13**
FVRAS-NET [24]	91.88	1.60	95.03	1.50	**97.80**	**0.50**
LWCNN [19]	82.23	4.35	89.88	2.34	**94.57**	**1.65**
AMPVNet [9]	96.82	0.83	97.44	0.38	**98.64**	**0.28**

5 Conclusion

This work proposes EC-PVGAN, an adversarial generative framework for data augmentation in palm-vein identification. Unlike traditional augmentation methods that often produce black-border artifacts due to affine transformation, EC-PVGAN incorporates the equivariance similarity loss and similarity loss to establish a linear equivalence between the affine transformation and image synthesis. Experimental results on two public palm-vein datasets demonstrate that EC-PVGAN significantly improves the identification accuracy, outperforming classical data augmentation methods.

Acknowledgments. This work was supported in part by the Natural Science Foundation of Chongqing under Grant CSTB2024NSCQ-MSX1118, the Chongqing Municipal Education Commission under Grants KJZD-M202500804 and KJQN202500812, and by the Chongqing Technology and Business University under Grant 2556007.

References

1. Das, R., Piciucco, E., Maiorana, E., Campisi, P.: Convolutional neural network for finger-vein-based biometric identification. IEEE Trans. Inf. Forensics Secur. **14**(2), 360–373 (2018)
2. Deng, S., Fan, C., Li, Y., Qin, H., El Yacoubi, M., Zhou, G.: Gru-based neural architecture search for finger-vein identification. In: International Conference on Computer Communications and Networks (ICCCN) (2023)
3. Goodfellow, I.J., et al.: Generative adversarial nets. In: Advances in Neural Information Processing Systems (NeurIPS) (2014)
4. He, K., Zhang, X., Ren, S., Sun, J.: Deep residual learning for image recognition. In: IEEE Conference on Computer Vision and Pattern Recognition (CVPR), pp. 770–778 (2016)
5. Huang, B., Dai, Y., Li, R., Tang, D., Li, W.: Finger-vein authentication based on wide line detector and pattern normalization. In: International Conference on Pattern Recognition, pp. 1269–1272. IEEE (2010)
6. Isola, P., Zhu, J.Y., Zhou, T., Efros, A.A.: Image-to-image translation with conditional adversarial networks. In: IEEE Conference on Computer Vision and Pattern Recognition, pp. 1125–1134 (2017)
7. Jain, A., Hong, L., Bolle, R.: On-line fingerprint verification. IEEE Trans. Pattern Anal. Mach. Intell. **19**(4), 302–314 (1997)
8. Kang, W., Wu, Q.: Contactless palm vein recognition using a mutual foreground-based local binary pattern. IEEE Trans. Inf. Forensics Secur. **9**(11), 1974–1985 (2014)
9. Luo, D., Qiao, Y., Xie, D., Zhang, S., Kang, W.: Palm vein recognition under unconstrained and weak-cooperative conditions. IEEE Trans. Inf. Forensics Secur. (2024)
10. Mirza, M., Osindero, S.: Conditional generative adversarial nets. arXiv preprint arXiv:1411.1784 (2014)
11. Miura, N., Nagasaka, A., Miyatake, T.: Feature extraction of finger-vein patterns based on repeated line tracking and its application to personal identification. Mach. Vis. Appl. **15**, 194–203 (2004)
12. Parkhi, O., Vedaldi, A., Zisserman, A.: Deep face recognition. In: British Machine Vision Conference (BMVC). British Machine Vision Association (2015)
13. Perrachione, T.K., Del Tufo, S.N., Gabrieli, J.D.: Human voice recognition depends on language ability. Science **333**(6042), 595–595 (2011)
14. Qin, H., El-Yacoubi, M.A., Li, Y., Liu, C.: Multi-scale and multi-direction gan for cnn-based single palm-vein identification. IEEE Trans. Inf. Forensics Secur. **16**, 2652–2666 (2021)
15. Qin, H., Gong, C., Li, Y., El-Yacoubi, M.A., Gao, X., Wang, J.: Attention label learning to enhance interactive vein transformer for palm-vein recognition. IEEE Trans. Biometr. Behav. Identity Sci. (2024)
16. Qin, H., Gong, C., Li, Y., Gao, X., El-Yacoubi, M.A.: Label enhancement-based multiscale transformer for palm-vein recognition. IEEE Trans. Instrum. Meas. **72**, 1–17 (2023)
17. Qin, H., Xi, H., Li, Y., El-Yacoubi, M.A., Wang, J., Gao, X.: Adversarial learning-based data augmentation for palm-vein identification. IEEE Trans. Circuits Syst. Video Technol. **34**(6), 4325–4341 (2023)
18. Rosdi, B.A., Shing, C.W., Suandi, S.A.: Finger vein recognition using local line binary pattern. Sensors **11**(12), 11357–11371 (2011)

19. Shen, J., Liu, N., Xu, C., Sun, H., Xiao, Y., Li, D., Zhang, Y.: Finger vein recognition algorithm based on lightweight deep convolutional neural network. IEEE Trans. Instrum. Meas. **71**, 1–13 (2021)
20. Tanaka, T., Kubo, N.: Biometric authentication by hand vein patterns. In: SICE Annual Conference. vol. 1, pp. 249–253. IEEE (2004)
21. Tome, P., Marcel, S.: On the vulnerability of palm vein recognition to spoofing attacks. In: International Conference on Biometrics (ICB), pp. 319–325. IEEE (2015)
22. Wang, C., Chen, X., Ning, H., Li, S.: Sam-octa: a fine-tuning strategy for applying foundation model octa image segmentation tasks. In: IEEE International Conference on Acoustics, Speech and Signal Processing (ICASSP), pp. 1771–1775. IEEE (2024)
23. Wang, P., Fan, E., Wang, P.: Comparative analysis of image classification algorithms based on traditional machine learning and deep learning. Pattern Recogn. Lett. **141**, 61–67 (2021)
24. Yang, W., Luo, W., Kang, W., Huang, Z., Wu, Q.: Fvras-net: an embedded finger-vein recognition and antispoofing system using a unified cnn. IEEE Trans. Instrum. Meas. **69**(11), 8690–8701 (2020)
25. Zhang, C., Liu, W., Ma, H., Fu, H.: Siamese neural network based gait recognition for human identification. In: IEEE International Conference on Acoustics, Speech and Signal Processing (ICASSP), pp. 2832–2836. IEEE (2016)
26. Zhang, L., Cheng, Z., Shen, Y., Wang, D.: Palmprint and palmvein recognition based on dcnn and a new large-scale contactless palmvein dataset. Symmetry **10**(4), 78 (2018)

A Cloud-Edge-End Federated Learning Secret Sharing Scheme for Finger Vein Recognition System

Guang Chen[1,2], Hui Huang[1], Tianming Xie[1], Jianliang Hu[3], Arif Mahmood[4], and Wenxiong Kang[1(✉)]

[1] School of Automation Science and Engineering, South China University of Technology, Guangzhou 510641, China
jidiangaopeichen@126.com
[2] GRGBanking Equipment Co., Ltd., Guangzhou 510663, China
[3] Guangzhou GRG Intelligent Technology Solution Co., Ltd, Guangzhou 510663, China
[4] Department of Computer Science, Information Technology, University, Lahore, Pakistan

Abstract. Federated learning (FL) is increasingly adopted for training finger vein recognition models to address client-level data scarcity while preserving privacy. However, as biometric data involves sensitive personal information, higher security guarantees are imperative for FL systems. This paper proposes a novel cloud-edge-end federated learning framework specifically designed for finger vein recognition, incorporating a Multi-dimensional Secret Sharing (MSS) scheme to secure model aggregation. MSS strategically integrates client additive secret sharing and edge Newton interpolation-based secret sharing, establishing a strict security threshold. Crucially, the framework guarantees secure aggregation under the non-collusion of at least a predefined number of edge servers, preventing compromise even if multiple clients or a single edge server are compromised. Evaluations demonstrate that the proposed framework not only provides robust security against collusion attacks but also improves finger vein model accuracy under challenging conditions of non-IID (non-independent and identically distributed) and class-imbalanced data. Furthermore, its effectiveness extends to multi-modal biometric systems (e.g., iris, face recognition), maintaining comparable accuracy to FedAvg while significantly enhancing aggregation security.

Keywords: Federal learning · Secret sharing · Biometric recognition system · Cloud edge

---

This work was partially supported by the International Science and Technology Cooperation Project of Guangzhou Economic and Technological Development District(No.2023GH16).

W. Jia et al. (Eds.): CCBR 2025, LNCS 16360, pp. 14–24, 2026.
https://doi.org/10.1007/978-981-95-6123-0_2

1   Introduction

When vein recognition technology is applied in practical financial device scenarios, a large number of devices and models from different vendors are deployed on the same system. This configuration presents several significant challenges, including security risks associated with integrating models across different vendors, the potential leakage of registration templates due to cross-vendor interoperability, and the increased complexity of encryption during real-world implementation. Furthermore, the system may be vulnerable to attacks from semi-honest adversaries. Federated Learning (FL) enables multiple data owners to collaboratively train a machine learning model without disclosing their respective private datasets. To address the issue of information leakage, previous studies have explored techniques such as differential privacy [1,2] and secure multi-party computation [3,4]. Decentralized multi-party computation avoids introducing additional biases to the results and can enhance the accuracy of federated models. Representative techniques in decentralized MPC (Secure Multi-Party Computation) include garbled circuits, secret sharing, and homomorphic encryption [5]. The primary advantage of integrating MPC protocols into FL lies in its scalability to a large number of users and relatively low computational overhead [6–8]. However, a key limitation of generic MPC protocols based on secret sharing is their substantial communication costs [9].

In this paper, we introduce a secure federated learning framework for cloud-edge-end applications, based on the Secret Sharing Cloud-Edge-End Security Federated Learning Framework (SSFL). This framework utilizes a combination of additive secret sharing and Newton interpolation to safeguard the privacy and security of model parameters from the participating parties in cloud-edge-end applications of smart devices, even in the presence of semi-honest collaborators. It prevents the server of a semi-honest collaborator from training according to the protocol and from inferring other collaborators' private information through the data they access. This enhances the privacy and security of the training process while ensuring the efficiency of the computational transmission of model confidential parameters. The framework involves participants at different levels, including clients, edge servers, and central parameter servers.

The main contributions of this paper are as follows:

(1) This paper proposes a security federated learning framework based on secret sharing for cloud-edge-end applications (SSFL), enabling the layered integration of secure federated learning training for intelligent device systems.
(2) This paper introduces a multi-dimensional secret-hiding security sharing method, which provides dual security guarantees for model parameter sharing while enhancing processing efficiency.
(3) The theoretical analysis and experimental validation of the SSFL framework are presented. The findings demonstrate that the proposed framework ensures improved security protection while maintaining the accuracy of the lightweight finger vein model.

2 Design of the Framework

This section proposes a method implemented within the finite field F. As shown in Fig. 1, it assumes the presence of a central parameter server C, which coordinates model aggregation and secure computation, and distributes models. Additionally, there is a group of n honest but curious edge servers E, responsible for receiving secret shared model parameters from clients. Furthermore, there are m clients P, each holding a local private dataset Di, (where $i \in 1, ..., m$), to perform local model training and personalized adjustments.

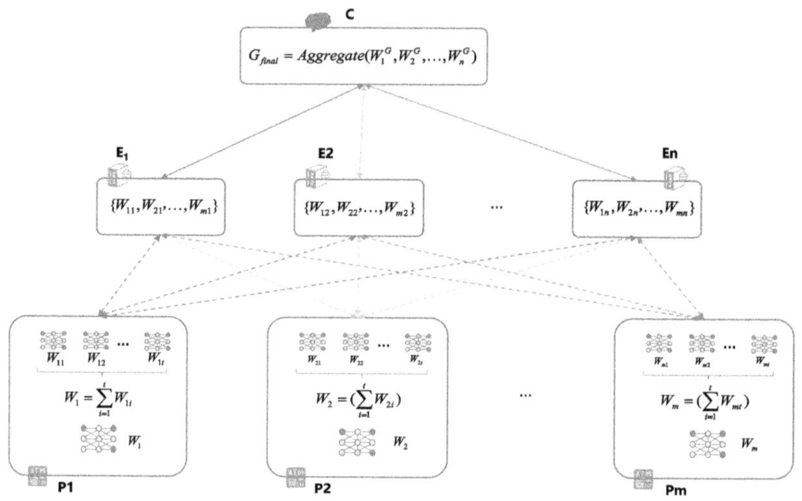

Fig. 1. Schematic diagram of SSFL framework

2.1 Local Training and Secret Sharing of the Client

Based on the basic security requirements that data does not leave the local client, the client does not transmit the original finger vein data to other clients, edge terminals and central services, but only transmits the parameters after local model training and their related totals. The specific process is as follows:

1. Client local model training

The client uses the local finger vein data for local iterative training, divides the local data into N_b batches, and forms P_i the local model parameters W_i of the client training after each local training.

2. Client model parameter segmentation

Select the local model W_i parameters as, and divide the model parameters into m shares for additive secret sharing segmentation. The sum of these secret shares is equal to the original parameters:

Algorithm 1. Federated learning of end-edge-cloud

1: **function** FederatedLearningInEdgeCloud(devices, edge_servers, cloud, n, t)
2:   *// device: List of client devices*
3:   *// edge servers: List of edge servers*
4:   *// cloud: Central server*
5:   *// n: Total number of participants (including client devices and edge servers)*
6:   *// t: At least t participants submit shares to restore the model parameters*
7:
8:   *// Client devices perform local training and share shares*
9: **for** each device in devices **do**
10:     Local_data ← device.GetData() *// Get local data*
11:     Model ← cloud.GetGlobalModel() *// Get the global model*
12:     DeviceTrainingAndSharing(local_data, model, n) *// Share the edge server equipment for recovery and consolidation*
13: **end for**
14:
15: **for** each edge_server in edge_servers **do**
16:     Shares_list ← ReceiveSharesFromDevices(devices)
17:     Edge_server.ProcessReceivedShares(shares_list, t)
18: **end for**
19:
20: *// Global model update of the central server*
21: Global_update_from_edges ← ReceiveGlobalUpdatesFromEdges(edge_servers)
22: Cloud.CloudLayerProcessing(global_update_from_edges)
23:
24: *// Return the updated global model*
25: cloud.SendUpdatedGlobalModelToEdge(edge_servers)
26: **end function**

$$W_i = W_{i1} + W_{i2} + \cdots + W_{it} \tag{1}$$

For each secret W_i, the device generates m-1 random $\omega_i^1, \omega_i^2, \cdots, \omega_i^{m-1}$ parameters and calculates the last share.

$$W_{it} = W_i - \sum_{j}^{m-1} \omega_{ij} \tag{2}$$

For each secret W_i, construct a polynomial $f_i(x)_{r-1}$ of degree with constant term equal to W_{ir}, that is: among them ω_i^k, r-1 random parameters are generated when the additive secret sharing is performed for the device end $f_i(x) = W_{ir} + \omega_i^1 x + \omega_i^2 x^2 + \cdots + \omega_i^{r-1} x^{r-1}$.

Each device selects r different $f_i(x)$ interpolation points $x_1, x_2, \cdots, x_r$ for each polynomial and calculates the corresponding function value:

$$f_i(x_j) = W_{ir} + \sum_{k=1}^{r-1} \omega_i^k x_j^k \quad (j = 1, 2, \ldots, n) \tag{3}$$

Each device upload $\{x_j, f_i(x_j)\}$ to the edge server as a share.

2.2 Model Recovery of Edge Server and Aggregation of Middle Layer

The edge server collects the shares uploaded by client devices.

1. Receive the share of client devices

The edge server can only recover the share when it receives at least t shares uploaded by participants from client $\{(x_1, f_1(x_1)), (x_2, f_2(x_2)), \cdots, (x_t, f_t(x_t))\}$ devices. The resulting share set includes the identifier of the edge server's device. Here, each client's uploaded share represents a part of the model parameters, which is the randomized value obtained through additive secret sharing.

2. Edge parameter collection

The edge server collects parameters from multiple end devices and sends them to the cloud for final aggregation.

2.3 The Central Server Finally Updates the Global Model

The central server is responsible for aggregating the intermediate model update results uploaded by multiple edge servers to obtain the final global model.

1. Newton interpolation to restore model parameters

The central server uses Newton interpolation to efficiently recover the model parameters through the above shares. In Newton interpolation, the secret is decomposed into all the coefficients of the polynomial, rather than just the constant term. Let's define Newton interpolation formula:

$$P(x) = a_0 + a_1(x - x_0)(x - x_1) + \cdots + a_{i-1}(x - x_0) \cdots (x - x_{i-2}) \quad (4)$$

Among them $a_0, a_1, \cdots, a_{i-1}$, the difference quotient coefficient is calculated from the known share data. The target secret is the sum of the polynomial constant term and the class coefficient.

$$W_i = a_0 + a_1 + \cdots + a_{t-1} \quad (5)$$

2. Update of the global model

After the central server receives the local update parameters from each edge server, it further performs global merging operations:

$$G_{final} = \text{Aggregate}(W_1^G, W_2^G, \cdots, W_n^G) \quad (6)$$

After the central server completes the merger, it returns the global updated model parameters to the edge layer and further feeds back to the client device.

2.4 Client Update Process

After the client obtains the updated global model from the central server, it carries out a new round of local training and parameter update. The above process is repeated to gradually improve the accuracy and generalization performance of the model.

3   Experimental Setup and Analysis

3.1   Experimental Configuration

The hardware environment used in the experiment is as follows: NVIDIA GeForce GTX 1080 Ti, CUDA version: 12.7. In the distributed computing environment, the related parameter configuration is as follows: total number of devices: num devices = 5.Total number of servers: num servers = 6.

1. Basic model

Pre-training model: Utilizing the lightweight MobileNetV2 [10] convolutional neural network architecture and the official pre-trained weights from PyTorch, this model leverages deep separable convolutions to achieve efficient feature extraction capabilities, making it suitable for deployment in resource-constrained environments. The model's input size is fixed at 224×224, and it uses the standardized parameters of the ImageNet pre-trained weights. For the classification layer adjustment, considering the total number of categories 5000, the original model's fully connected layer at the end was removed and replaced with a new trainable classification layer (nn.Linear(in features = 1280, out features=num classes = 5000)).

2. Attention Module

SEBlock channel configuration: the channel attention mechanism Squeeze-and-Excitation Block (SEBlock) is embedded after the last layer of convolution output in MobileNetV2. The channel number is set to 1280, which is strictly consistent with the channel dimension of the end feature map in MobileNetV2.

3. Loss Function

Main loss function: Crossentropyloss is used as the optimization objective function, and its formula is defined as:

$$L_{CE} = -\sum_{i=1}^{N} y_i \log(p_i) \tag{7}$$

Among these y_i, is the real label is encoded, p_i represents the category probability distribution predicted by the model. To address the issue of class imbalance, a category weight adjustment strategy is introduced: based on the statistical results from the training set, higher weight coefficients are assigned to less frequent categories (weight = total number of samples/number of samples in the category). Additionally, label smoothing ($\varepsilon = 0.1$) is employed to prevent overfitting of the model to the training data (Table 1).

This configuration combines lightweight backbone network, dynamic channel attention, and robust loss function design to improve the discriminant ability of the model for fine-grained classification tasks while ensuring the calculation efficiency.

Table 1. Model Settings Table

Module	Parameter/Component	Technical Detail
Pre-training model	MobileNetV2 [10]	Freeze the first 80% layer and fine-tune the end feature extraction layer
Attention mechanism	SEBlock	The compression ratio is $r = 16$, the channel dimension matching is 1280
Loss function	CrossEntropyLoss	label smoothing ($\epsilon = 0.1$)

3.2 Safety Analysis

By integrating the Shamir threshold mechanism with additive secret sharing, this approach establishes a dynamically adjustable threshold mechanism, enabling the system to flexibly calibrate security and efficiency based on practical requirements. The introduced difference distribution technique further strengthens the defense capabilities, particularly in mitigating joint attacks among edge servers. Traditional Shamir secret sharing mechanisms typically rely on fixed thresholds and constant terms, where attackers only need to obtain a sufficient number of secret shares (e.g., exceeding the threshold) to recover the secret. In contrast, this method divides the secret into distinct "difference shares," requiring attackers to acquire all the different shares simultaneously to reconstruct the complete secret, rather than simply cracking a single constant term. This mechanism effectively thwarts collaborative attacks among edge servers, as attackers must obtain all independent shares without cooperation.

Furthermore, compared to methods such as FedShare [7] and SCOTCH [8], this approach offers superior adaptability in dynamic threshold adjustments, allowing the system to adjust flexibly according to environmental conditions and requirements, thereby providing enhanced security. During the dynamic threshold adjustment process, attackers are unable to predict the system's threshold in advance, significantly increasing the difficulty of successful attacks, particularly in scenarios involving frequently changing and complex environments, such as those encountered in intelligent device applications. This ensures the system maintains a higher level of security (Table 2).

Table 2. Comparison of safety analysis

Method	Dynamic threshold adjustment	Conspiracy attack
Additive secret sharing	×	stronger
Traditional Shamir secret sharing	✓	weak
Multi-dimensional secrets are hidden and shared	✓	stronger

3.3   Performance Analysis

In this paper, the performance experiments use three finger vein datasets: USM [11], SDUMLA [12], and SCUT [13], where 80% of the data is randomly selected for model training, while 20% is reserved for testing. The method focuses on enhancing the model's security while ensuring the accuracy of the training process.

Performance Comparison Experiment: This experiment compares the performance of three methods of federated learning across three finger vein datasets. During the experiment, the number of epochs set on the client side is 5, the number of epochs on the edge server side is 5, and the number of epochs on the central server side is 6. As shown in Fig. 2, the three methods tested in this paper all converged within the first 20 iterations. As the training rounds increased, the accuracy and equal error rate (EER) of all three methods improved across the three datasets.

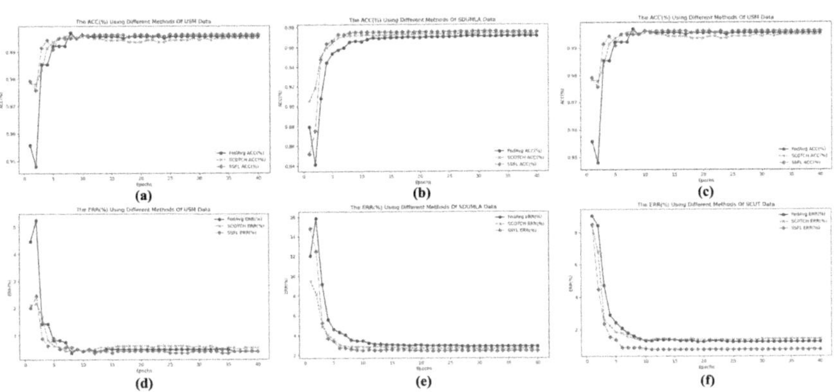

Fig. 2. Illustrates the equal error rate and accuracy rate of the training rounds for the model. (a) ACC (%) of the three models on USM dataset. (b) ACC (%) of the three models on SDUMLA dataset. (c) ACC (%) of the three models on SCUT dataset. (d) ERR (%) of the three models on USM dataset. (e) ERR (%) of the three models on SDUMLA dataset. (f) ERR (%) of the three models on SCUT dataset.

Table 3. The equal error rate and accuracy effect of different rounds of model training

dataset	method	iterations	ACC(%)	EER(%)
USM	FedAvg	Rounds = 10/20/40	99.63/99.56/99.56	0.41/0.48/0.41
	SCOTCH	Rounds = 10/20/40	99.56/99.35/99.49	0.41/0.61/0.54
	SSFL	Rounds = 10/20/40	99.63/99.63/99.63	0.41/0.41/0.41
SDUMLA	FedAvg	Rounds = 10/20/40	96.56/96.98/97.14	3.41/2.99/2.89
	SCOTCH	Rounds = 10/20/40	97.19/97.35/97.35	2.83/2.68/2.62
	SSFL	Rounds = 10/20/40	97.51/97.56/97.56	2.47/2.41/2.41
SCUT	FedAvg	Rounds = 10/20/40	98.67/98.79/98.79	1.29/1.24/1.24
	SCOTCH	Rounds = 10/20/40	98.67/98.61/98.55	1.36/1.36/1.42
	SSFL	Rounds = 10/20/40	99.20/99.26/99.26	0.83/0.77/0.77

Table 4. Effect of this method on the error rate and accuracy when increasing the number of edge servers

Nums of servers	4	5	6
EER(%)	1.00	1.00	0.77
ACC(%)	98.97	99.03	99.26

In the comparison of accuracy (ACC,(%)) and EER(,(%)) (Table 3), the proposed method SSFL outperforms FedAvg [14] and SCOTCH across three datasets. The comparison is based on the average ACC and average ERR at the 40th round of model training convergence for each dataset. Specifically, FedAvg achieves an accuracy of 98.50%, SCOTCH 98.46%, and our SSFL 99.82%. Overall, the ACC accuracy has improved by 1.32% and 1.36%, respectively. For the equal error rate, FedAvg is 1.51%, SCOTCH 1.53%, and SSFL 1.20%. Overall, the ERR has decreased by 0.31% and 0.33%, respectively. This experiment demonstrates that our method can enhance model performance while ensuring the security of federated training (Table 5).

The experiment also examines how performance changes with different numbers of edge servers. We use SCUT dataset and set the configuration parameter threshold to 4. The Table 4 shows that increasing the number of edge servers

Table 5. Comparison of accuracy of this method extended to fingerprints, iris and face

method	Fingerprint mode FVC2004 data set	Iris modalities CASIA-iris-Thousand data set	Face modalities AgeDB data set
FedAvg	91.33%	99.10%	82.17%
SSFL	90.25%	98.17%	81.79%

does not significantly impact training performance when using this method. The error rate (ERR) remains stable at an average of 0.92 across different numbers of edge servers. Similarly, the accuracy rate (ACC) also remains stable at an average of 99.09 across different numbers of edge servers.

Extended Validation Experiment: Our proposed method can also be extended to other modalities of biometric recognition. We expand the scope to include fingerprint, iris, and face recognition, using the FVC2004 dataset, the CASIA-iris-Thousand dataset, and the AgeDB dataset, respectively. Compared to FedAvg, our method showed improved security but a 1.08% decrease in fingerprint accuracy, an 0.84% decrease in iris accuracy, and a 0.38% decrease in face recognition accuracy.

4   Conclusion

In this work paper a security federated learning framework (SSFL) is proposed, utilizing the secret sharing method in secure multi-party computation to ensure the security and privacy of models between clients, edge servers, and central servers. This approach effectively balances privacy protection and accuracy in biometric recognition model training. Our experiments on various data types, including finger vein, fingerprint, iris, and face, clearly demonstrate that using SSFL does not significantly impact accuracy. It ensures strong adaptability while maintaining security. In more applications, it can be combined with methods like homomorphic encryption to broaden its applicability.

References

1. Geyer, R.C., Klein, T., Nabi, M.: Differentially private federated learning: a client level perspective (2017). arXiv preprint arXiv:1712.07557
2. Ruan, W., Xu, M., Fang, W., Wang, L., Wang, L., Han, W.: Private, efficient, and accurate: Protecting models trained by multi-party learning with differential privacy. In: In: 2023 IEEE Symposium on Security and Privacy (SP), pp. 1926–1943. IEEE (2023)
3. Bonawitz, K., et al.: Practical secure aggregation for privacy-preserving machine learning. In: Proceedings of the 2017 ACM SIGSAC Conference on Computer and Communications Security, pp. 1175–1191 (2017)
4. Sav, S., et al.: Poseidon: privacy-preserving federated neural network learning (2020). arXiv preprint arXiv:2009.00349
5. Zhao, C., et al.: Secure multi-party computation: theory, practice and applications. Inf. Sci. **476**, 357–372 (2019)
6. Kai, H., Gong, S., Zhang, Q., Seng, C., Xia, M., Jiang, S.: An overview of implementing security and privacy in federated learning. Artif. Intell. Rev. **57**(8), 204 (2024)
7. Khojir, H.F., Alhadidi, D., Rouhani, S., Mohammed, N.: Fedshare: secure aggregation based on additive secret sharing in federated learning. In: Proceedings of the 27th International Database Engineered Applications Symposium, pp. 25–33 (2023)

8. More, Y., Ramachandran, P., Panda, P., Mondal, A., Virk, H., Gupta, D.: Scotch: an efficient secure computation framework for secure aggregation (2022). arXiv preprint arXiv:2201.07730
9. Liu, F., Zheng, Z., Shi, Y., Tong, Y., Zhang, Y.: A survey on federated learning: a perspective from multi-party computation. Front. Comp. Sci. **18**(1), 181336 (2024)
10. Sandler, M., Howard, A., Zhu, M., Zhmoginov, A., Chen, L.C.: Mobilenetv2: inverted residuals and linear bottlenecks. In: Proceedings of the IEEE Conference on Computer Vision and Pattern Recognition, pp. 4510–4520 (2018)
11. Asaari, M.S.M., Suandi, S.A., Rosdi, B.A.: Fusion of band limited phase only correlation and width centroid contour distance for finger based biometrics. Expert Syst. Appl. **41**(7), 3367–3382 (2014)
12. Yin, Y., Liu, L., Sun, X.: SDUMLA-HMT: a multimodal biometric database. In: Sun, Z., Lai, J., Chen, X., Tan, T. (eds.) CCBR 2011. LNCS, vol. 7098, pp. 260–268. Springer, Heidelberg (2011). https://doi.org/10.1007/978-3-642-25449-9_33
13. Zhang, Z., Zhong, F., Kang, W.: Study on reflection-based imaging finger vein recognition. IEEE Trans. Inf. Forensics Secur. **17**, 2298–2310 (2021)
14. McMahan, H.B., Moore, E., Ramage, D., Hampson, S., Arcas, B.A.: Communication-efficient learning of deep networks from decentralized data. In: International Conference on Artificial Intelligence and Statistics (2016)

Toward Abandoning Tedious ROI Alignment for Unconstrained Palmprint Recognition

Longfa Liu[1], Qichao Xiong[1], Hanhui Zhan[2], Lunke Fei[1(✉)], Shuping Zhao[1], and Shaohua Teng[1]

[1] School of Computer Science and Technology,
Guangdong University of Technology, Guangzhou, China
`flksxm@126.com`
[2] Faculty of Computer Science, Beijing Normal-Hong Kong Baptist University,
Zhuhai, China

Abstract. Unconstrained palmprint recognition has shown great potential for practical applications due to its safety, convenience, and hygiene. However, unconstrained palmprint recognition often has difficulties in existing region of interest (ROI) and robust feature descriptor. In this paper, we propose a vision transformer network MDHs-ViT for unconstrained palmprint recognition based on defining the enlarged ROI (EROI) of palmprint images. Firstly, EROI breaks the limitation of traditional small ROI extraction of palmprint, that is, without aligning, EROI can still bring better performance for unconstrained palmprint recognition. Then, according to the inherent traits of EROI, the proposed MDHs-ViT fully learns discriminative features by multi-scale feature learning and dense attention heads transformer. Extensive experimental results on three public datasets demonstrate the effectiveness of the defined EROI and the proposed MDHs-ViT.

Keywords: Biometrics · Unconstrained palmprint recognition · Enlarged palmprint ROI · Vision transformer

1 Introduction

Biometric recognition has become an integral part of modern society due to its uniqueness and user convenience [1]. Among various biometric modalities, palmprint recognition has attracted increasing attention in recent years, particularly in both academic and industrial domains, such as Amazon [2]. Most existing studies have focused on constrained palmprint recognition. However, as the demand for more flexible and convenient user experiences continues to grow, unconstrained palmprint recognition is emerging as a forward-looking and challenging research direction. In this paper, we focus on addressing the problem of palmprint recognition under unconstrained conditions.

© The Author(s), under exclusive license to Springer Nature Singapore Pte Ltd. 2026
W. Jia et al. (Eds.): CCBR 2025, LNCS 16360, pp. 25–35, 2026.
https://doi.org/10.1007/978-981-95-6123-0_3

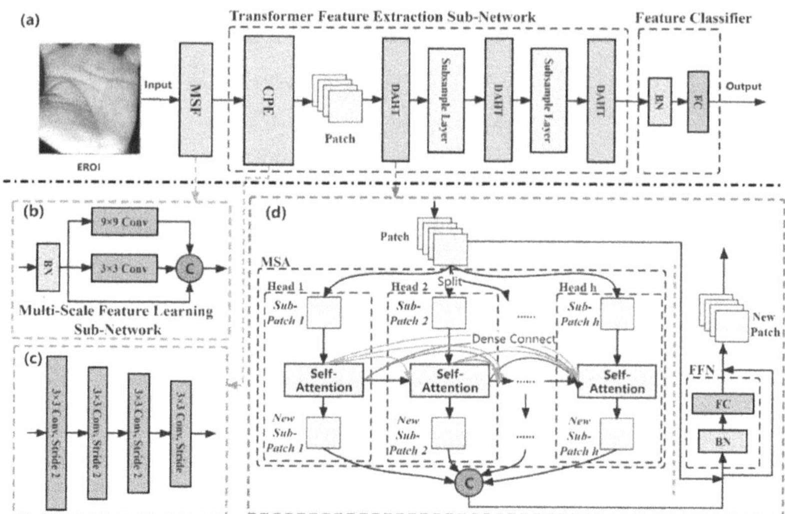

Fig. 1. Overview of proposed MDHs-ViT. (a) Architecture of MDHs-ViT. (b) Multi-scale feature learning sub-network (MSF). (c) Convolutional patch embedding (CPE). (d) Dense attention heads transformer (DAHT).

According to the acquisition conditions, palmprint recognition can be roughly divided into constrained and unconstrained. The constrained palmprint recognition means that the palm needs to be fixed for recognition. Many traditional methods leverage line-based [3] and orientation-based [4] features to achieve impressive performance in such settings. However, in unconstrained scenarios, palmprints often suffer from misalignment, deformation, and varying poses (e.g., bending or tilting), making existing constrained methods ineffective. To address these challenges, several robust feature extraction techniques have been proposed. For example, SIFT-based methods [5] align palmprints before extracting invariant features, while handcrafted descriptors, such as ALDC [7], attempt to encode deformation-tolerant representations. Nonetheless, their reliance on shallow features limits their performance under complex variations.So, the deep learning-based methods extract deep robust features well for unconstrained palmprint recognition, such as Palm-ID [6].

As aforementioned, robust feature extraction from deformed palmprints is a concern of unconstrained palmprint recognition. In this paper, we define a palmprint enlarged ROI (EROI), which is worth mentioning that some other hand features existing in the EROI are regarded as the potential palmprint spatial information to narrow the misaligned palmprint intra-class gap. Based on this, we propose a multi-scale feature-based dense attention heads vision transformer (MDHs-ViT) for unconstrained palmprint recognition, as shown in Fig. 1. The proposed MDHs-ViT first extracts the different scale features of palmprint EROI by a multi-scale features learning sub-network. Then, the discriminative palmprint feature descriptor is learned by the transformer feature extraction sub-network. Finally, the palmprint category is identified by the feature classifier. Experimental results on three unconstrained palmprint datasets demonstrate the promising effectiveness of the defined EROI and the proposed MDHs-ViT.

2   Related Work

Over the decades, unconstrained palmprint ROI extraction has evolved with application scenarios and can be broadly divided into contactless extraction under simple and complex backgrounds. Under a simple background, Zhang et al. [8] have used the maximum inscribed circle (MIC) to extract the palmprint ROI, reducing the palmprint intra-class gap. However, under the complex background, the ROI localization effect of these methods is greatly discounted by the influence of complex background noise. To solve this, some deep learning-based palmprint ROI extraction methods have been propose. For example, Liu et al. [9] tailored the Faster R-CNN based ROI extractor for palmprints. Liang et al. [10] designed a key point detection network to effectively detect the finger-valley key points, and then extract the palmprint ROI. These methods still cannot achieve satisfactory extraction results under complex backgrounds.

The extraction of palmprint traditional ROI (TROI) is shown in Fig. 2 (a). First, the original palmprint image is input. Then, two finger-valley key points are detected by binary thresholding and a boundary tracking algorithm. Third, TROI is located according to the perpendicular bisector of the line segment between the two finger-valley key points. Finally, the localized TROI is cropped from the original palmprint image. It can be seen that most existing palmprint ROI extraction methods usually define the small central region of palmprint images as the ROI, which usually ignores much information of a palm. Moreover, it is hard to clearly detect the finger-valley points under unconstrained scenarios such as an unopen palm and complex background, as shown in Fig. 2 (b), making it hard to correctly detect the ROI of palmprint images. In this paper, we introduce a new enlarged palmprint ROI for large-scale unconstrained palmprint recognition using a deep-learning network.

3   Proposed Methods

3.1   Enlarged Region of Interest of Palmprint Images

It is seen that existing palmprint ROI extraction methods usually require clear finger-valley points as the landmarks to crop the small central region as the ROI of a palmprint image, which misses much informative boundary region of the palmprint. To address this, we define an enlarged ROI (EROI) by bounding a complete palm region of the palmprint within a suitable rectangle, as shown in Fig. 3. The defined EROI has three characteristics as follows:

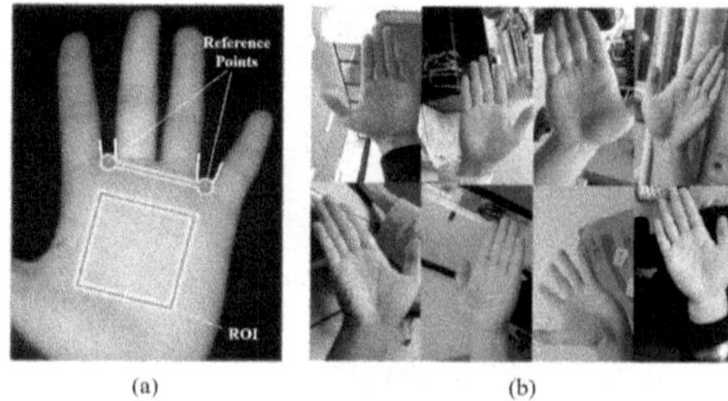

(a)   (b)

Fig. 2. The samples of palmprint TROI. (a) The extraction sample of palmprint TROI. (b) undetectable samples of palmprint TROI.

Convenient Extraction: Due to the large obvious palm regions, the EROI can be easily detected by using the existing object detection networks such as Faster R-CNN and YOLO [11]. In this study, we train a Faster R-CNN network based on 2000 labeled palm images for EROI extraction. Figure 3 shows some typical examples of EROI extraction, from which we can see that EROI can be correctly detected for unconstrained palmprint images.

Sufficient Features: The EROI contains more information about a palmprint than the conventional small ROI for reliable biometric recognition.

Unneeded Alignment: It is worth mentioning that some other hand features in EROI can be considered as potential palmprint spatial information, which can reduce palmprint intra-class gaps under palmprint misalignment.

For the three traits, EROI is suitable for unconstrained palmprint recognition. In the following, we propose a simple yet effective attention-based learning network for palmprint recognition based on the EROI of palmprint images.

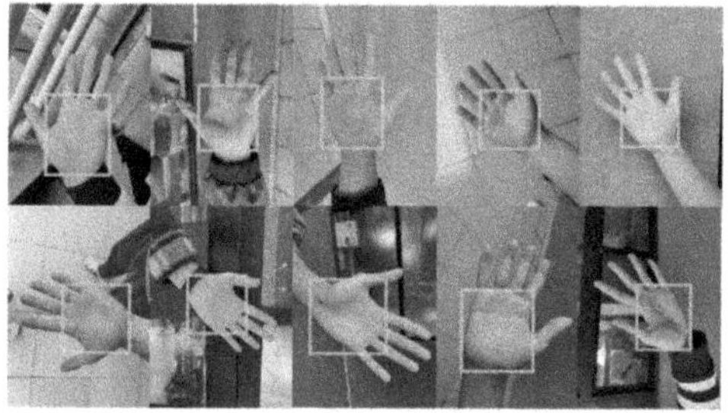

Fig. 3. The typical EROI samples of palmprint images detected by using a pre-trained Faster R-CNN.

3.2 Multi-scale Feature Based Dense Attention Heads Vision Transformer

Compared with small ROI, EROI contains multiple types of characteristics such as more texture patterns, lines, hand edges and finger seams. To extensively exploit the discriminative features from EROI, we propose a multi-scale feature based dense attention heads vision transformer (MDHs-ViT) network (as shown in Fig. 1), which consists of a multi-scale feature learning sub-network, a transformer feature extraction sub-network, and a feature classifier. In the following, we introduce the main components and the learning procedure of the proposed MDHs-ViT.

Multi-scale Feature Learning Sub-network (MSF). As shown in Fig. 1(b), the MSF aims to extract multi type features of the palmprints via a Batch Normalization (BN) layer connecting with three parallel learning branches, including a 3×3 convolutional layer, a 9×9 convolutional layer and a residual connection. Let $X \in \Re^{H \times W \times C}$ be the palmprint EROI samples, where $H \times W$ and C denote the spatial dimension and channel of the samples, respectively. The multi-scale feature learning process can be formulated as follows:

$$\tilde{X} = Concat\left(f_{BN}\left(X\right) * T_1, f_{BN}\left(X\right) * T_2, f_{BN}\left(X\right)\right), \tag{1}$$

where $f_{BN}\left(.\right)$ is Batch Normalization. $T_1 \in \Re^{9 \times 9 \times C}$ and $T_2 \in \Re^{3 \times 3 \times C}$ represent the 3×3 and 9×9 convolutional kernels, respectively. $Concat\left(.\right)$ represents concatenation operation. By doing this, the three parallel learning results can be concatenated into a multi-scale feature map, referred to as $\tilde{X} \in \Re^{H \times W \times (3 \times C)}$, with the channel expanding to $3 \times C$. In addition, the BN layer can accelerate the convergence of the multi-scale feature learning.

Transformer Feature Extraction Sub-network. Inspired by the fact that the transformer can capture long-range information and excels at modeling global context and spatial dependencies, we further design a transformer-based feature learning sub-network to learn palmprint-specific discriminant features for recognition. Figure 1(a) shows the basic architecture of the transformer feature extraction sub-network, which mainly consists of the convolutional patch embedding layer and a couple of Dense Attention Heads Transformer blocks (DAHT). First, we convert the multi-scale feature $\tilde{X}$ into a patch via the convolutional patch embedding layer (CPE) as follows:

$$Z^{in} = H_{emb}\left(\tilde{X}\right), \tag{2}$$

where $H_{emb}\left(.\right)$ is convolutional patch embedding layer, consisting of four 3×3 convolutions with the stride of 2. $Z^{in} \in \Re^{H^{in} \times W^{in} \times C^{in}}$ denotes the patch with the spatial dimension of $H^{in} \times W^{in}$ and the channel of C^{in}. Via the convolution operation, Z^{in} can better preserve the local information of the palmprint during patch embedding.

Having obtained the patch representation, we employ a three-layer DAHT block to learn the deep discriminant feature representation of palmprint images. To obtain fine-grained high-level palmprint features, a subsampling layer is embedded into each pair of two DAHTs. Therefore, the deep feature learning of DAHT can be expressed as:

$$Z^{out} = D_{DAHT}\left\{ f_{sub} \left\{ D_{DAHT} \left[f_{sub} \left[D_{DAHT} \left(Z^{in} \right) \right] \right] \right\} \right\}, \tag{3}$$

where $D_{DAHT}(\cdot)$ denotes the DAHT block. $f_{sub}(\cdot)$ represents the subsampling layer, which consists of a 3×3 convolution with a stride of 2 and a BN layer. Through the subsampling layer, the network can learn deeper features and reduce the cost of calculation.

Feature Classifier. Lastly, a feature classifier, which consists of a BN layer and a fully connected layer, is used to perform palmprint recognition. The process can be expressed as:

$$Y = f_{FC}\left(f_{BN}\left(Z^{out} \right) \right), \tag{4}$$

where $f_{FC}(\cdot)$ denotes fully connected layer. The $f_{FC}(\cdot)$ aims to convert Z^{out} into a m-dimensional feature vector $Y \in \Re^{1 \times m}$, indicating the class label of a palmprint sample.

3.3   Dense Attention Heads Transformer

To learn the discriminative information from different-scale palmprint features, we develop a dense attention head transformer (DAHT). Figure 1 (d) shows the basic architecture of the DAHT, which consists of a multi-head self-attention block (MSA) and a feed-forward network (FNN). Given an input feature patch $Q^{in} \in \Re^{H \times W \times C}$, it is divided into h feature sub-patches $\left[q_1^{in}, q_2^{in}, ..., q_h^{in} \right] \in \Re^{H \times W \times (C/h)}$, where h denotes the number of self-attention heads of the DAHT. Let the feature sub-patches are the input of the self-attention blocks for learning the new feature sub-patches $[A_1, A_2, ..., A_h] \in \Re^{H \times W \times (C/h)}$. The MSA aims to learn the new feature sub-patches, which can be formulated as follows:

$$A^j = \begin{cases} f_{SA}(q_j^{in}), & j = 1 \\ f_{SA}\left(\sum_{i=1}^{j} q_i^{in} + \sum_{k=1}^{j-1} A_k \right), & 2 \leq j \leq h \end{cases}, \tag{5}$$

where $f_{SA}(\cdot)$ is the self-attention blocks, which are the basic component of transformer [23]. Having obtained the new feature sub-patches, the FNN, which consists of a BN layer and an FC layer, aims to learn the nonlinear relationship between different scales of palmprint features. The feature learning of FNN can be expressed as follows:

$$\hat{Q} = \text{Concat}(A_1, A_2, \ldots, A_h) + Q^{in},$$
$$Q^{out} = f_{FC}(f_{BN}(\hat{Q})) + \hat{Q}, \tag{6}$$

where $\hat{Q} \in \Re^{H \times W \times C}$ is the input of the FNN, and the new feature patches $Q^{out} \in \Re^{H \times W \times C}$ are learned.

4   Experiments

In this section, we conduct comparative experiments on three unconstrained palmprint image databases, including the CASIA, IITD and XJTU-UP, to evaluate the our method. All the experiments are conducted based on the Pytorch framework in the Ubuntu 18.04 system. The hardware includes the NVIDIA GPU RTX3060Ti with 8 GB and the Intel CPU i7-12700F with 12 cores.

4.1   Database

CASIA Database [14]: The CASIA palmprint image database contains $5,501$ unconstrained palmprint images collected from 312 different subjects with both the left and right palms, and each palm provided about 8 to 17 samples.

IITD Database [15]: The IITD database consists of $2,601$ palmprint images acquired from both the left and right palms of 230 volunteers, and each palm provided 5–7 images via the normal camera in a contactless manner.

XJTU-UP Database [16]: The XJTU-UP database collects $2,000$ palmprint images from the left and right hands of 100 volunteers using the iPhone 6 s under natural and flash illuminations, respectively. For each hand, 10 samples were captured under each illumination, such that each hand provided 20 samples under the two illuminations.

Figure 4 shows some typical examples selected from the CASIA, IITD and XJTU-UP databases, respectively, including the original palmprint images, EROI images and ROI images.

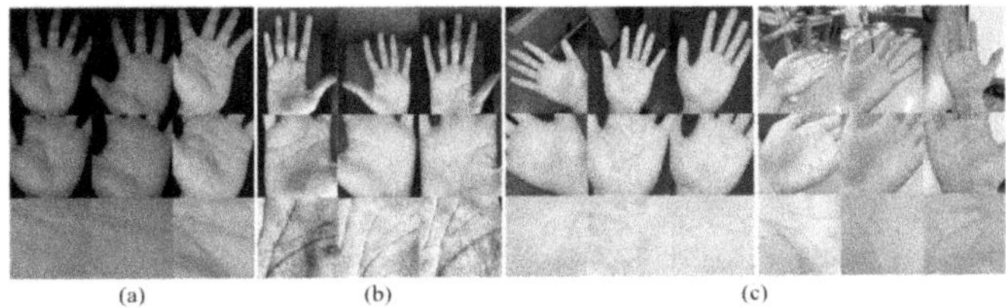

Fig. 4. The typical palmprint images from the (a) CASIA, (b) IITD, and (c) XJTU-UP databases, respectively. The first to third rows correspond to the original palmprint images, EROI and ROI, respectively.

4.2   Palmprint Recognition Results of MDHs-ViT

To better evaluate the proposed MDHs-ViT, we conduct both palmprint identification and verification experiments on the CASIA, IITD and XJTU-UP databases, and compare the proposed method with the state-of-the-art learning networks, including the ResNet18 [17], DenseNet [18], shufflenetV2 [19], and

EfficientViT [12]. For each database, half of the images of each subject are used as training sets, and the rest are used as the test set. It is worth mentioning that the experiments were performed on the EROI of the three databases. The palmprint identification adopts a one-to-many way to calculate recognition rank-one accuracy, and the best result in 100 epochs is shown in Table 1. We can see that our proposed method outperforms the state-of-the-art methods. This is because the proposed MDHs-ViT can make full use of the different scale features of palmprint EROI and develop the powerful global learning ability of transformer to learn palmprint discriminative information.

Moreover, we drew the receiver operating characteristic (ROC) for the palmprint verification, as shown in Fig. 5. From the ROC curves, the proposed method MDHs-ViT is more stable for palmprint verification than the other comparison methods. This is because the self-attention heads in the transformer are densely connected, which makes the intra-class palmprint more closely associated, such that a more robust feature descriptor can be learn.

Table 1. The average identification accuracies on EROI of three databases respectively.

Methods	Params(M)	CASIA	IITD	XJTU-UP	
				Flash	Nature
ShufflenetV2	**6.611**	94.11	88.86	92.63	88.69
DenseNet	7.587	95.06	87.39	92.42	81.83
EfficientViT	12.326	95.87	92.55	95.54	89.17
ResNet18	21.602	94.99	84.60	94.54	81.36
MDHs-ViT (ours)	10.610	**96.93**	**92.88**	**96.06**	**90.44**

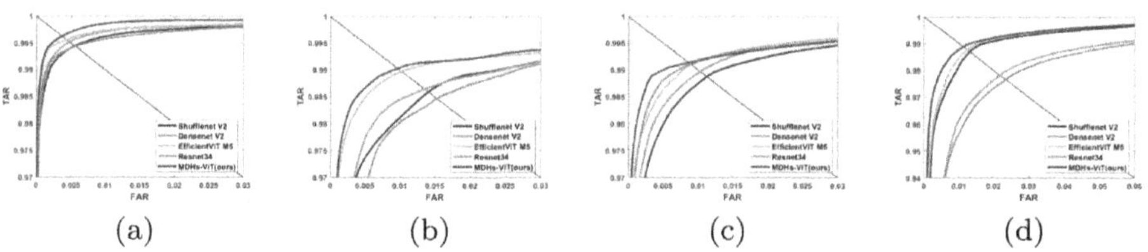

Fig. 5. The ROCs of different methods on the (a) CASIA, (b) IITD, (c) Flash and (d) Nature of XJTU-UP datasets, respectively.

4.3   Effectiveness of EROI

In order to verify the effectiveness of EROI on the CASIA, IITD and XJTU-UP palmprint databases, we introduce the hand-crafted palmprint descriptors: ALDC [7], and LCMFC [20] and learning-based networks: Resnet50 [17],

MobilenetV3 [21], and EfficientnetV2 [22] to perform palmprint recognition experiments under original palmprint images (Original), TROI and EROI respectively. We take the best result in 200 epochs, as shown in Table 2.

Table 2. Results (**accuracy/equal error rate**) of palmprint recognition on TROI and EROI of three databases respectively.

Methods	Params(M)	Type	CASIA	IITD	XJTU-UP	
					Flash	Nature
ALDC	0.066	Original	37.98/23.16	61.90/10.86	24.78/37.78	20.61/42.88
		TROI	**50.01/18.63**	**62.92/19.01**	**88.74/15.03**	**82.51/17.11**
		EROI	47.20/20.95	50.27/28.16	39.84/25.16	56.65/29.80
LCMFC	0.099	Original	37.92/25.34	48.41/28.40	25.89/27.46	33.05/31.17
		TROI	**44.53/22.92**	**53.70/22.75**	**77.58/13.82**	**75.65/15.74**
		EROI	36.83/23.87	45.15/31.81	37.07/24.55	54.27/28.84
MobileNetV3	4.994	Original	95.10/0.29	83.78/0.98	88.80/1.39	80.82/2.15
		TROI	95.36/0.48	84.84/1.97	92.96/1.22	75.84/3.76
		EROI	**96.82/0.29**	**88.37/1.16**	**93.20/1.21**	**89.84/1.21**
ResNet50	24.774	Original	97.59/0.29	92.14/0.94	94.97/0.79	82.77/1.95
		TROI	97.22/0.40	89.59/1.32	95.61/0.82	82.34/1.74
		EROI	**98.06/0.22**	**92.55/0.90**	**95.82/0.73**	**92.53/0.94**
EfficientNetV2	20.969	Original	97.26/0.37	92.22/0.87	95.68/0.64	90.24/1.01
		TROI	96.64/0.48	90.16/1.03	97.04/0.56	87.31/1.79
		EROI	**98.02/0.33**	**92.63/0.82**	**97.55/0.36**	**95.63/0.47**

Regarding the experimental results in Table 2, we can see the three observations: 1) the EROI performs better than the TROI and the original palmprint image in deep learning palmprint recognition on three databases. The reason for this may be that the palmprint features contained from EROI are more comprehensive, so the feature descriptor is more discriminative and more robust. 2) the EROI exhibits inefficiency in non-deep learning methods for palmprint recognition. This is because the method needs to learn discriminative features in EROI of misaligned palmprint and complex background, which requires a powerful and deep learning capabilities-based method to learn palmprint discriminative information. 3) The recognition results of EROI in the relatively clear palmprint images are only slightly improved. The reason behind this is that the highly clear palmprint texture features carried by TROI is enough to provide palmprint discriminative information, so the comprehensive palmprint features of EROI are not fully utilized.

5   Conclusion

In this paper, to solve the existing problems in unconstrained palmprint recognition, we define EROI and propose a vision transformer network MDHs-ViT for unconstrained palmprint recognition. First, the defined EROI shows tolerance and is convenient for extracting ROIs from complex scenes. Then, the MDHs-ViT is proposed for unconstrained palmprint recognition. Through multi-scale feature learning and dense attention heads transformer, MDHs-ViT learns discriminative and robust features from EROI for unconstrained palmprint recognition. Experimental results on three public palmprint databases show that the defined EROI can achieve excellent recognition performance without palmprint alignment. Meanwhile, experiments also show that the proposed MDHs-ViT outperforms the state-of-the-art methods for unconstrained palmprint recognition. For the future, how to make full use of EROI to complete more robust palmprint recognition is a question worth exploring.

Acknowledgments. This work was supported in part by the National Natural Science Foundation of China under Grant 62576112, and in part by the Natural Science Foundation of Guangdong Province under Grant 2023A1515012717.

References

1. Wang, H., Jia, W.: Enhance the performance of directional feature-based palmprint recognition by directional response stability measurement. Mach. Intell. Res. **21**(3), 597–614 (2024)
2. Amazon One. https://one.amazon.com
3. Han, C.-C., Cheng, H.-L., Lin, C.-L., Fan, K.-C.: Personal authentication using palm-print features. Pattern Recogn. **36**(2), 371–381 (2003)
4. Fei, L., Xu, Y., Tang, W., Zhang, D.: Double-orientation code and nonlinear matching scheme for palmprint recognition. Pattern Recogn. **49**, 89–101 (2016)
5. Zhao, Q., Bu, W., Wu, X.: SIFT-based image alignment for contactless palmprint verification. In: International Conference on Biometrics, pp. 1–6. IEEE Press, New York (2013)
6. Grosz, S.A., Jain, A.K.: Mobile contactless palmprint recognition: use of multiscale, multimodel embeddings. IEEE Trans. Inf. Forensics Secur. **19**, 8428–8440 (2024)
7. Brown, D., Bradshaw, K.: Deep palmprint recognition with alignment and augmentation of limited training samples. SN Comput. Sci. **3**, 1–17 (2022)
8. Zhang, D.: Palmprint segmentation by key point features. In: Palmprint Authentication, pp. 73–83. Springer, Heidelberg (2004). https://doi.org/10.1007/1-4020-8097-2_6
9. Liu, Y., Kumar, A.: Contactless palmprint identification using deeply learned residual features. IEEE Trans. Biom. Behav. Identity Sci. **2**(2), 172–181 (2020)
10. Liang, X., Fan, D., Yang, J., Jia, W., Lu, G., Zhang, D.: PKLNet: keypoint localization neural network for touchless palmprint recognition based on edge-aware regression. IEEE J. Sel. Topics Signal Process. **17**(1), 1–15 (2023)
11. Redmon, J., Farhadi, A.: YOLOv3: an incremental improvement. arXiv preprint arXiv:1804.02767 (2018)
12. Liu, X., Peng, H., Zheng, N., Yang, Y., Hu, H., Yuan, Y.: EfficientViT: memory efficient vision transformer with cascaded group attention. In: Proceedings of IEEE Conference on Computer Vision and Pattern Recognition, pp. 14420–14430 (2023)
13. Vaswani, A., Shazeer, N., Parmar, N., Jones, L., Gomez, A.N., Kaiser, Ł.: Attention is all you need. Adv. Neural Inf. Process. Syst. 5998–6008 (2017)

14. Sun, Z., Tan, T., Wang, Y., Li, S.: Ordinal palmprint representation for personal identification. In: Proceedings of IEEE Conference on Computer Vision and Pattern Recognition, vol. 1, pp. 279–284. IEEE Press, New York (2005)
15. IITD Touchless Palmprint Database. http://www4.comp.polyu.edu.hk/~csajaykr/IITD/Database_Palm.htm
16. Shao, H., Zhong, D., Du, X.: Deep distillation hashing for unconstrained palmprint recognition. IEEE Trans. Instrum. Meas. **70**, 1–13 (2021)
17. He, K., Zhang, X., Ren, S., Sun, J.: Deep residual learning for image recognition. In: Proceedings of IEEE Conference on Computer Vision and Pattern Recognition, pp. 770–778 (2016)
18. Huang, G., Liu, Z., Weinberger, K.Q.: Densely connected convolutional networks. In: Proceedings of IEEE Conference on Computer Vision and Pattern Recognition, pp. 4700–4708 (2017)
19. Ma, N., Zhang, X., Zheng, H.-T.: ShuffleNet V2: practical guidelines for efficient CNN architecture design. In: Proceedings of European Conference on Computer Vision, pp. 122–138 (2018)
20. Fei, L., Zhang, B., Zhang, L., Jia, W., Wen, J., Wu, J.: Learning compact multifeature codes for palmprint recognition from a single training image per palm. IEEE Trans. Multimedia **23**, 2930–2942 (2021)
21. Howard, A., et al.: Searching for MobileNetV3. In: Proceedings of IEEE International Conference on Computer Vision, pp. 1314–1324 (2019)
22. Tan, M., Le, Q.: EfficientNet: rethinking model scaling for convolutional neural networks. In: Proceedings of International Conference on Machine Learning, pp. 6105–6114 (2019)

Contact-to-Contactless Fingerprint Generation with Content Consistency

Hangle Sun, Zhe Cui$^{(\boxtimes)}$, and Fei Su

Beijing Key Laboratory of Network System and Network Culture,
Beijing University of Posts and Telecommunications, Beijing, China
`cuizhe@bupt.edu.cn`

Abstract. As one of the most established biometric modalities, fingerprint recognition plays a crucial role in personal authentication and security systems, with fingerprints captured through contact-based or contactless acquisition. However, contactless fingerprint data remains relatively scarce compared to contact-based data, posing challenges for both intra-domain and cross-domain matching. To address these issues, we propose a contact-to-contactless fingerprint generation approach, which integrates a GAN-based fingerprint transfer module with a Unified Fingerprint Enhancement (UFE) module to maintain content consistency and preserve identity information. Extensive experiments on the NIST SD14 database, including both quantitative and qualitative evaluations, demonstrate the effectiveness of the proposed method.

Keywords: Contactless Fingerprint · Fingerprint Generation · Fingerprint Enhancement · Content Consistency

1 Introduction

Fingerprint recognition is a widely used biometric technology for personal identity verification and security [1,2]. Fingerprint images are typically acquired using contact-based or contactless methods, relying on different sensors such as optical, capacitive, or even ultrasonic types [3,4]. Contact-based sensing requires direct physical contact between the finger and the sensor, and has been well studied during the past century, supported by a wide range of publicly available datasets. In contrast, contactless acquisition employs cameras or other non-contact devices, thereby avoiding issues such as finger distortion and hygiene concerns [5]. However, it also presents challenges, including variations in lighting, finger positioning, and background interference. Consequently, contactless fingerprint datasets remain relatively scarce compared to their contact-based counterparts, which restricts the development of accurate recognition algorithms.

With the development of deep learning techniques, generative method has been adopted for generating synthetic fingerprints from existing databases, as collecting large-scale fingerprint data is privacy-sensitive and challenging. Unlike

W. Jia et al. (Eds.): CCBR 2025, LNCS 16360, pp. 36–46, 2026.
https://doi.org/10.1007/978-981-95-6123-0_4

general image generation tasks, fingerprint generation requires maintaining fine-grained ridge structures and preserving identity information, which necessitates additional constraints during the training procedure. To this end, we are further inspired by the work of FingerGAN [6], which enhances latent fingerprints while preserving their skeleton maps and orientation fields. Notably, their training samples are generated by applying Total Variation decomposition [7,8] to contact-based rolled fingerprints, with the skeleton maps of the rolled fingerprints serving as the ground-truth enhanced fingerprints. This observation motivates us to integrate these components and fine-tune specific parameters to develop a content-constrained loss tailored for contactless fingerprint synthesis.

In this paper, we propose a contact-to-contactless fingerprint generation method, which synthesizes contactless fingerprint images from existing contact-based datasets. Our method introduces a Unified Fingerprint Enhancement (UFE) module that simultaneously enhances contact-based and contactless fingerprints to generate skeleton maps with a consistent style. By computing a reconstruction loss between the two enhanced fingerprints, the method effectively enforces content consistency and preserves minutiae-level identity information. Figure 1 illustrates a contactless fingerprint (right) synthesized from a real contact-based fingerprint (left). This method not only increases the availability of contactless fingerprint data but also generates paired samples that facilitate the training of cross-modal recognition models, thereby eliminating the need for manually collected paired data [9].

The rest of this paper is organized as follows. Section 2 reviews related works. Section 3 introduces the details of the proposed method. Section 4 presents the experimental results. Finally, Sect. 5 concludes the paper.

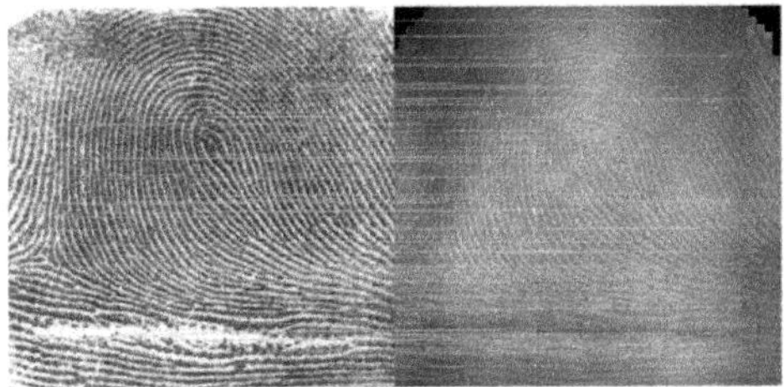

Fig. 1. Generation example of our proposed method. Minutiae points are shown in red, with 105 matched pairs connected by green lines. (Color figure online)

2   Related Work

Various approaches have been proposed for fingerprint generation, primarily encompassing feature-statistics alignment methods, attention-based techniques, and GAN-based models. Emerging methods such as Variational Autoencoders

(VAEs) and diffusion models remain relatively underexplored and are beyond the scope of this work.

For feature-statistics alignment methods, Huang et al. [10] proposed Adaptive Instance Normalization (AdaIN), a style transfer method that effectively transfers style by aligning the channel-wise mean and variance of the content features to those of the style image. Gajawada et al. [11] and Chugh et al. [12] employed AdaIN-based style transfer to generate synthetic fingerprints, which were subsequently used to train spoof detectors, thus improving their generalizability. Extending AdaIN, Joshi et al. [13] utilized AdaAttn [14], which incorporates an attention mechanism, to generate latent fingerprints. Specifically, a pre-trained encoder is leveraged to extract fingerprint features from both source and target domains, thereby enforcing content consistency by minimizing a reconstruction loss defined over the extracted representations.

Generative Adversarial Networks (GANs), trained adversarially between a generator and discriminator, were widely adopted for synthetic fingerprint generation [15,16]. Engelsma et al. [17] used several GANs along with style transfer and image warping to produce highly realistic fingerprints. Cheng et al. [18] proposed a cross-sensor fingerprint recognition approach that utilized Cycle-GAN [19] to unify fingerprint styles collected from different sensors, followed by a series of enhancement techniques and similarity computation. Zhu et al. [6] formulated latent fingerprint enhancement as a constrained generation task within a GAN framework. Their model was trained using both skeleton maps and orientation fields derived from the FOMFE method [20], enforcing that the generated fingerprint preserves the original structural details while effectively transferring the style. Wone [21] proposed a multi-domain style transfer approach based on MWGAN [22] to generate synthetic fingerprints, improving the robustness of spoof detection systems.

Most existing fingerprint generation works focus on spoof detection, fingerprint enhancement, and cross-sensor fingerprint matching, while the preservation of identity information remains a challenging problem. To our knowledge, we are the first to leverage a GAN-based method to generate content-consistent and identity-preserving contactless fingerprints from existing contact-based samples.

3   Proposed Method

In this section, we first present the overall framework of the proposed method. Next, we provide a detailed description of the Unified Fingerprint Enhancement (UFE) module. Finally, we describe the design of the loss functions.

3.1   Network Architecture

The overall architecture of our method is illustrated in Fig. 2. A CycleGAN-based network (Fig. 2 Left) is employed to perform fingerprint transfer, where contact fingerprints correspond to the source domain X, and contactless fingerprints correspond to the target domain Y. G and F denote the generators for the source and target domains, respectively. D_X and D_Y represent their corresponding discriminators. Given an unpaired inputs x_{real} and y_{real}, synthetic images y_{fake} and x_{fake} are generated. Real and fake images within the same domain are further distinguished by the discriminators. During the inference time, only the generator G is used.

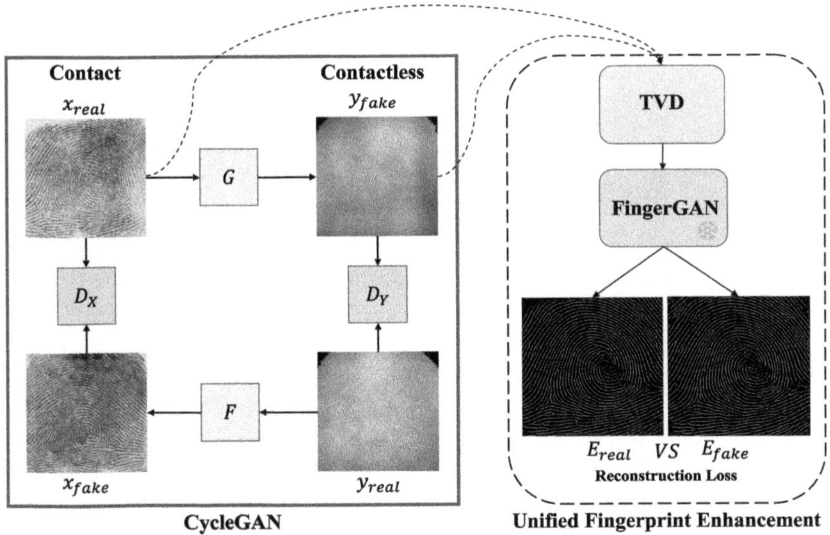

Fig. 2. Overall Architecture of our proposed method

3.2   Unified Fingerprint Enhancement

The right dashed box in Fig. 2 highlights the Unified Fingerprint Enhancement (UFE) module, which is designed to maintain the ridge structures of fingerprints. The process comprises two main steps: texture extraction via TVD, followed by fingerprint enhancement.

We adopt the algorithm proposed in [8], which is based on Total Variation decomposition [7], a widely used method in image processing for separating an image into cartoon and texture components. In our implementation, we set the parameters to $\sigma = 6$ (Gaussian smoothing strength), $ksize = 27$ (Gaussian kernel size), and $n_{iter} = 5$ (number of filtering iterations). This module is incorporated into the end-to-end training framework to extract fingerprint textures.

Since the resulting texture values often fall outside the normalized range [0,1], we apply several normalization strategies to remap the texture values into the [0,1] interval. We first employ min-max normalization (Eq. (1)), and then experiment with a combination of z-score normalization, followed by a sigmoid function (Eq. (2)), providing a smoother and more statistically stable mapping.

Here, μ and σ denote the mean and std of texture component, ϵ denotes a small constant to avoid numerical problems.

$$T_{mm} = \frac{T - \min(T)}{\max(T) - \min(T) + \epsilon} \tag{1}$$

$$T_{zs} = \text{Sigmoid}\left(\frac{T - \mu}{\sigma + \epsilon}\right) \tag{2}$$

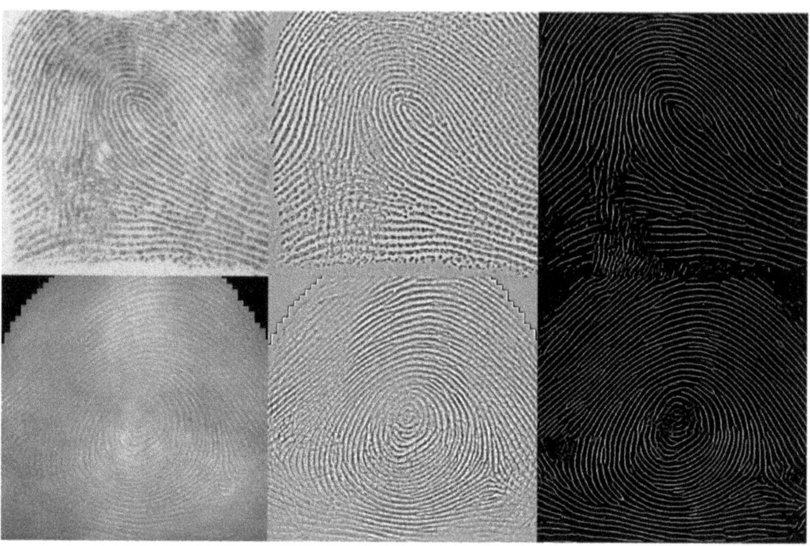

Fig. 3. Examples of Unified Fingerprint Enhancement. The top row shows contact fingerprint, while the bottom row shows contactless fingerprint. The three columns correspond to the original images, texture components, and enhanced images.

The pre-trained FingerGAN [6] model is adopted as a fingerprint enhancement model to generate skeleton maps E from texture components T extracted by TVD. It follows a patch-based enhancement strategy with a sliding window size of 192. The stride is set to 96 to balance processing efficiency and enhancement accuracy. Given an input resolution of 480 × 480, the image is divided into 16 patches for individual enhancement, which are subsequently merged to form the final output. Enhancement examples are presented in Fig. 3.

3.3   Loss Function

Our network uses adversarial, cycle consistency, and identity losses from Cycle-GAN, along with an additional fingerprint content loss. We briefly describe these losses below, with emphasis on our proposed content loss. For details on the CycleGAN losses, please refer to the original paper.

The adversarial loss (Eq. (4)) sums two GAN losses, encouraging the generator to produce realistic images that fool the discriminator.

$$\mathcal{L}_{\text{GAN}}(G, D_Y) = \log D_Y(y) + \log(1 - D_Y(G(x))) \tag{3}$$

$$\mathcal{L}_{\text{adv}} = \mathcal{L}_{\text{GAN}}(G, D_Y) + \mathcal{L}_{\text{GAN}}(F, D_X) \tag{4}$$

Cycle consistency loss (Eq. (5)) enforces that translating a sample to the other domain and back reconstructs the original input.

$$\mathcal{L}_{\text{cyc}}(G, F) = \|F(G(x)) - x\|_1 + \|G(F(y)) - y\|_1 \tag{5}$$

Identity loss (Eq. (6) encourages the generator to behave as an identity mapping when the input belongs to the target domain.

$$\mathcal{L}_{\text{identity}}(G, F) = \|G(y) - y\|_1 + \|F(x) - x\|_1 \tag{6}$$

We introduce an extra content loss (Eq.(7)) in our method to explicitly enforce content consistency during synthesis. As illustrated in Fig. 2, images x_{real} and y_{fake} are fed into the UFE module to produce enhanced fingerprint skeleton maps E_{real} and E_{fake}, The content loss, calculated as the L_1 distance between these two outputs, serves as an additional constraint to better preserve domain-invariant features during generation.

$$\mathcal{L}_{\text{content}} = \|E_{\text{real}} - E_{\text{fake}}\|_1 \tag{7}$$

Finally, our model is trained with a combined loss (Eq. (8)). The weights λ_{cyc}, $\lambda_{\text{identity}}$ and λ_{content} are set to 10, 0.5 and 10.

$$\mathcal{L}(G, F, D_X, D_Y) = \mathcal{L}_{\text{adv}} + \lambda_{\text{cyc}}\mathcal{L}_{\text{cyc}} + \lambda_{\text{identity}}\mathcal{L}_{\text{identity}} + \lambda_{\text{content}}\mathcal{L}_{\text{content}} \tag{8}$$

4   Experiments

4.1   Experimental Setup

Databases. 4,000 contact fingerprints from NIST SD4 database [23] and 1,332 contactless fingerprints from UWA Benchmark 3D Fingerprint Database [24] are used to train the model. 54,000 contact fingerprints from NIST SD14 [25] are used to test the model. All images are cropped into a square region of interest (ROI) at 480×480.

Implementation Details. We set the input and output channels of Cycle-GAN to one. The generator and discriminator architectures follow the original CycleGAN design, with a ResNet generator containing 9 residual blocks and a 70×70 PatchGAN discriminator. A pre-trained FingerGAN model is employed as the enhancement backbone, with its parameters kept frozen during training. The model is trained for 150 epochs with a batch size of 1. The initial learning rate is set to 0.0002, which remains constant for the first 100 epochs and linearly decays to zero over the next 50 epochs. All experiments are conducted on a NVIDIA RTX 4090 GPU with 24 GB of memory.

4.2   Experimental Results

Minutiae Performance. A total of 200 contact fingerprints are selected from the NIST SD14 database and transformed into contactless fingerprints using our proposed method. Subsequently, minutiae points are extracted from these 200 fingerprint pairs using Verifinger. To verify content consistency between genuine and synthetic fingerprints, minutiae matching between corresponding fingerprints is performed with location and orientation tolerances of 12 pixels and 20°, respectively. The average precision, recall, and F1 scores are presented in Table 1. 'FG' denotes FingerGAN, 'MM' and 'ZS' denote the two normalization methods described in Eqs. (1) and (2).

Table 1. Minutiae Matching Performance (%) between 200 pairs of contact fingerprints and synthetic contactless fingerprints on NIST SD14

Method	MM	ZS	FG	Precision	Recall	F1 Score
Baseline (CycleGAN)	–	–	–	47.4	45.6	45.9
Ours (FG only)	–	–	✓	49.3	49.7	48.9
Ours (MM + FG)	✓	–	✓	65.6	71.0	67.6
Ours (ZS + FG)	–	✓	✓	**73.7**	**79.8**	**76.3**

As shown in Table 1, directly applying FG(FingerGAN) to enhance fingerprints leads to only a small improvement, likely because it was originally

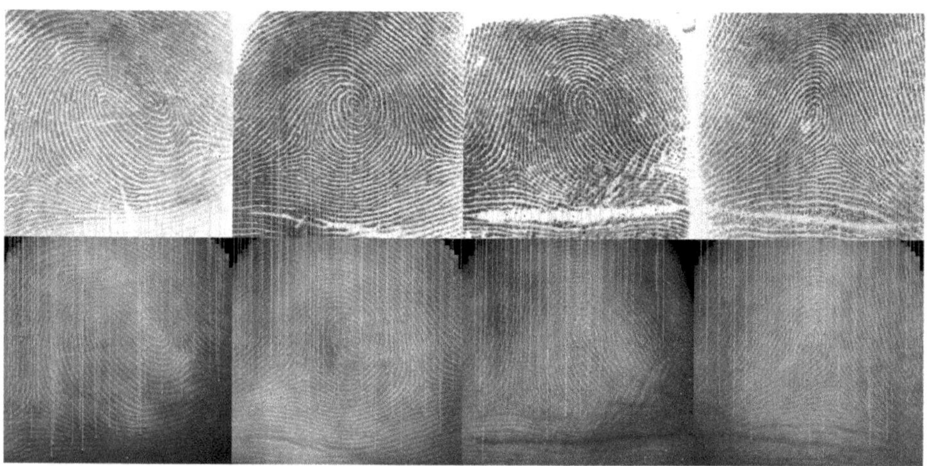

Fig. 4. Qualitative results on NIST SD14. The top row shows four contact-based fingerprints from the NIST SD14 database, and the bottom row presents their corresponding synthetic contactless fingerprints. Minutiae points are marked in red, with matched correspondences indicated by green lines. The numbers of matching minutiae points are 88, 111, 72, and 99, respectively. (Color figure online)

designed for latent fingerprint enhancement. The UFE module with normalization achieves a significant improvement, while 'MM' normalization results in substantial gains. The 'ZS' normalization method yields the best performance, with a matching precision of 73.7%. We present qualitative results of our best model (ZS + FG) in Fig. 4. These experimental results demonstrate that our model effectively preserves a substantial portion of minutiae information and retains content consistency during fingerprint transfer.

Recognition Performance. We further utilize 54,000 contact-based fingerprints from NIST SD14 database, forming 27,000 pairs, with each pair originating from the same finger. For each pair, one fingerprint is assigned to the probe set and the other to the gallery set. After applying our contactless fingerprint generation method, we generate contactless (i.e., synthetic) versions of both the probe and gallery fingerprints, resulting in four groups of probe-gallery combinations for evaluation. Matching is performed using Verifinger, and recognition performance is evaluated using top Rank-k metrics. The results for all four comparison scenarios are summarized in Table 2. 'C' denotes contact-based fingerprints, while 'CL' denotes contactless fingerprints.

Table 2. Fingerprint Recognition Performance (%) on NIST SD14

Probe-Gallery	Rank-1	Rank-5	Rank-10
C-C	**99.09**	**99.30**	**99.34**
C-CL(synthetic)	98.07	98.55	98.67
CL(synthetic)-C	97.54	98.09	98.27
CL(synthetic)-CL(synthetic)	97.02	97.58	97.81

As shown in Table 2, matching performance is highest when both the probe and gallery sets consist of real data (C-C). Introducing synthetic data into either the probe (CL-C) or gallery (C-CL) slightly reduces performance, with the lowest results observed when both are synthetic (CL-CL). Despite this, Rank-k remains steadily high across all settings, demonstrating that our synthetic fingerprints are compatible with real data and preserve key identity features.

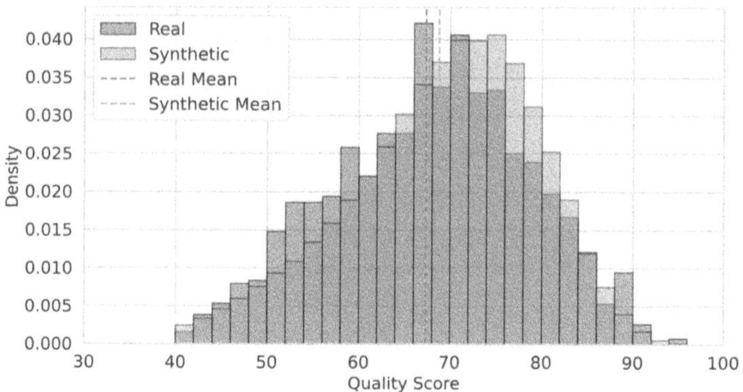

Fig. 5. Quality Distribution Comparison

Generated Fingerprint Quality. We evaluate fingerprint quality using the Verifinger quality score. Figure 5 shows the quality score distributions of 1,332 real and 54,000 synthetic contactless fingerprints. The two distributions are largely similar, with the synthetic fingerprints exhibiting a slightly higher average quality (from 67.3 to 68.8). This indicates that our method produces high-quality samples with a distribution closely aligned with the original data, highlighting the fidelity and realism of our synthesis approach.

5   Conclusion

In this paper, we propose a contact-to-contactless fingerprint generation framework that integrates a GAN-based fingerprint transfer module with the Unified Fingerprint Enhancement (UFE) module to maintain content consistency, thereby facilitating the preservation of identity information. The UFE module is implemented in an end-to-end manner to enhance both contact and contactless fingerprint images, and our proposed content loss, calculated based on the enhanced results, explicitly and effectively constrains alterations to fingerprint content during the generation process.

Quantitative and qualitative experimental results validate the effectiveness of the proposed framework in fingerprint translation and identity preservation. Moreover, the UFE module has the potential to serve as a unified encoder for matching contact and contactless fingerprints, which warrants further investigation. Additionally, by leveraging the bidirectional nature of CycleGAN and replicating the UFE module, the framework enables style conversion in both directions, demonstrating promise for contactless-to-contact fingerprint synthesis.

Acknowledgments.. This work is supported in part by the National Natural Science Foundation of China under Grants 62206026.

References

1. Pankanti, S., Prabhakar, S., Jain, A.K.: On the individuality of fingerprints. IEEE Trans. Pattern Anal. Mach. Intell. **24**(8), 1010–1025 (2002)
2. Yoon, S., Jain, A.K.: Longitudinal study of fingerprint recognition. Proc. Natl. Acad. Sci. **112**(28), 8555–8560 (2015)
3. Lugini, L., Marasco, E., Cukic, B., Gashi, I.: Interoperability in fingerprint recognition: a large-scale empirical study. In: 2013 43rd Annual IEEE/IFIP Conference on Dependable Systems and Networks Workshop (DSN-W), pp. 1–6. IEEE (2013)
4. AlShehri, H., Hussain, M., AboAlSamh, H., AlZuair, M.: A large-scale study of fingerprint matching systems for sensor interoperability problem. Sensors **18**(4), 1008 (2018)
5. Okereafor, K., Ekong, I., Markson, I.O., Enwere, K., et al.: Fingerprint biometric system hygiene and the risk of covid-19 transmission. JMIR Biomed. Eng. **5**(1), e19623 (2020)
6. Zhu, Y., Yin, X., Hu, J.: Fingergan: a constrained fingerprint generation scheme for latent fingerprint enhancement. IEEE Trans. Pattern Anal. Mach. Intell. **45**(7), 8358–8371 (2023)
7. Buades, A., Le, T.M., Morel, J.M., Vese, L.A.: Fast cartoon+ texture image filters. IEEE Trans. Image Process. **19**(8), 1978–1986 (2010)
8. Buades, A., Le, T., Morel, J.M., Vese, L.: Cartoon+Texture image decomposition. Image Process. On Line **1**, 200–207 (2011). https://doi.org/10.5201/ipol.2011.blmv_ct
9. Grosz, S.A., Engelsma, J.J., Liu, E., Jain, A.K.: C2CL: contact to contactless fingerprint matching. IEEE Trans. Inf. Forensics Secur. **17**, 196–210 (2021)
10. Huang, X., Belongie, S.: Arbitrary style transfer in real-time with adaptive instance normalization. In: Proceedings of the IEEE International Conference on Computer Vision, pp. 1501–1510 (2017)
11. Gajawada, R., Popli, A., Chugh, T., Namboodiri, A., Jain, A.K.: Universal material translator: towards spoof fingerprint generalization. In: 2019 International Conference on Biometrics (ICB), pp. 1–8. IEEE (2019)
12. Chugh, T., Jain, A.K.: Fingerprint spoof detector generalization. IEEE Trans. Inf. Forensics Secur. **16**, 42–55 (2020)
13. Joshi, A.S., Dabouei, A., Nasrabadi, N.M., Dawson, J.: Synthetic latent fingerprint generation using style transfer. In: 2023 International Conference of the Biometrics Special Interest Group (BIOSIG), pp. 1–6. IEEE (2023)
14. Liu, S., et al.: Adaattn: revisit attention mechanism in arbitrary neural style transfer. In: Proceedings of the IEEE/CVF International Conference on Computer Vision, pp. 6649–6658 (2021)
15. Wyzykowski, A.B.V., Segundo, M.P., de Paula Lemes, R.: Level three synthetic fingerprint generation. In: 2020 25th International Conference on Pattern Recognition (ICPR), pp. 9250–9257. IEEE (2021)
16. Bahmani, K., Plesh, R., Johnson, P., Schuckers, S., Swyka, T.: High fidelity fingerprint generation: quality, uniqueness, and privacy. In: 2021 IEEE International Conference on Image Processing (ICIP), pp. 3018–3022. IEEE (2021)
17. Engelsma, J.J., Grosz, S., Jain, A.K.: Printsgan: synthetic fingerprint generator. IEEE Trans. Pattern Anal. Mach. Intell. **45**(5), 6111–6124 (2022)
18. Cheng, C., Yu, J., Niu, L., Cao, Z., Zhao, H.: Cross-sensor fingerprint recognition based on style transfer network and score fusion. In: Chinese Conference on Biometric Recognition, pp. 85–95. Springer, Heidelberg (2023). https://doi.org/10.1007/978-981-99-8565-4_9

19. Zhu, J.Y., Park, T., Isola, P., Efros, A.A.: Unpaired image-to-image translation using cycle-consistent adversarial networks. In: Proceedings of the IEEE International Conference on Computer Vision, pp. 2223–2232 (2017)
20. Wang, Y., Hu, J., Phillips, D.: A fingerprint orientation model based on 2d fourier expansion (fomfe) and its application to singular-point detection and fingerprint indexing. IEEE Trans. Pattern Anal. Mach. Intell. **29**(4), 573–585 (2007)
21. Wone, A., Di Manno, J., Charrier, C., Rosenberger, C.: Fingerprint spoof generation using style transfer. IEEE Trans. Biometr. Behav. Identity Sci. (2025)
22. Cao, J., Mo, L., Zhang, Y., Jia, K., Shen, C., Tan, M.: Multi-marginal wasserstein gan. Adv. Neural Inf. Process. Syst. **32** (2019)
23. Watson, C.I., Wilson, C.L.: Nist special database 4. Fingerprint Database, National Institute of Standards and Technology **17**(77), 5 (1992)
24. Zhou, W., Hu, J., Petersen, I., Wang, S., Bennamoun, M.: A benchmark 3d fingerprint database. In: 2014 11th International Conference on Fuzzy Systems and Knowledge Discovery (FSKD), pp. 935–940. IEEE (2014)
25. Watson, C.I., et al.: Nist special database 14. Fingerprint Database, US National Institute of Standards and Technology (1993)

UMR-Net: Unified Multimodal Representation Network for Multimodal Biometric Recognition with Missing Modality

Yan Gu, Yi Yu, Shuangtia Jiang, Zaiyu Pan$^{(\boxtimes)}$, and Jun Wang

China University of Mining and Technology, Xuzhou, China
`pzycumt@163.com`

Abstract. Most existing multimodal biometric recognition algorithms require test samples with complete multimodal data. However, it often encounters the problem of missing modality data and thus suffers severe performance degradation in practical scenarios. Also, most existing multimodal biometric recognition methods mainly employ multiple separate feature extraction networks for multimodal biometrics, which increased inference time and hindered the widespread employment of multimodal biometric recognition in embedded devices for autonomous systems. To this end, we proposed a Unified Multimodal Representation Network (UMR-Net) for multimodal biometric recognition based on palmvein and palmprint modalities. Firstly, an Image-Level Adaptive Fusion (ILAF) module is proposed to achieve the dynamic fusion of palmprint and palmvein images in pixel space. Secondly, a single-stream feature encoder is designed to jointly learn the unified representations of unimodal or multimodal inputs. Specifically, the palmVein-aware Feature Alignment (VFA) module and palmPrint-aware Feature Alignment (PFA) module are presented to guarantee that the multimodal biometric features contain the semantic information of each modality. Besides, a Cross-modal Semantic Consistency (CSC) loss is designed to sure that the unimodal biometric features generated by a single-stream feature encoder do not exhibit modality bias. Extensive experiments conducted on three public benchmark datasets demonstrate the effectiveness of the proposed UMR-Net.

1 Introduction

Multimodal biometric recognition technology is currently one of the most secure identity recognition technologies, and it adopts two or more biometric features for identity recognition, which effectively leverage the complementary advantages of multiple biometric information. In recent years, most researchers have proposed numerous multimodal biometric fusion methods, effectively improving the recognition accuracy of multimodal biometric recognition models. For example, Li et al. [1] proposed a high discriminative joint sparse coding model, which can fully explore the relevant information between different modalities and achieve joint representation of fingerprint and finger joint print or palmprint and palmvein.

W. Jia et al. (Eds.): CCBR 2025, LNCS 16360, pp. 47–56, 2026.
https://doi.org/10.1007/978-981-95-6123-0_5

Although the above multimodal biometric recognition algorithms has achieved excellent performance, there are still two shortcomings when deployed to real-world applications.

Firstly, the existing multimodal biometric recognition models assume that test samples contain complete multimodal data, and ignore the problem of missing modality in testing process. Figure 1(a) illustrates the configurations of complete multimodal biometric recognition and incomplete multimodal biometric recognition. For complete multimodal biometric recognition, it is assumed that both paired and full multimodal data are available in both the training and testing datasets. For multimodal biometric recognition with missing modalities, the multimodal samples in the training set are paired, while in the testing set, multimodal samples may have missing modalities. Therefore, multimodal biometric recognition models for paired testing sets mostly suffer from performance degradation when evaluated on testing set with missing modality.

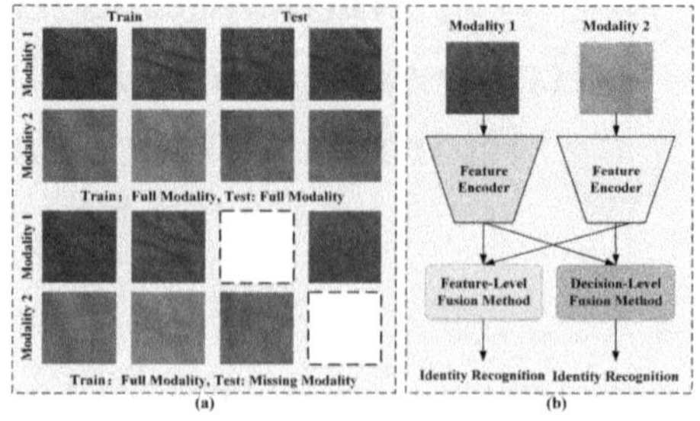

Fig. 1. The disadvantage description of current multimodal biometric recognition methods: (a) Complete and incomplete multimodal biometric recognition, (b) Existing multimodal biometric recognition framework.

Secondly, current multimodal biometric recognition methods primarily focus on model performance while overlooking the complexity of the models themselves. As shown in Fig. 1(b), most existing multimodal biometric systems utilize multiple separate feature extraction networks, resulting in inference times that are nearly several times longer than those of a single-stream feature extraction network. This increase in inference time hinders the widespread application of multimodal biometric recognition in embedded devices for autonomous systems.

To address the above problems, in this paper, a Unified Multimodal Representation Network (UMR-Net) for multimodal biometric recognition based on palmvein and palmprint modalities is proposed to jointly learn unified features of unimodal and multimodal input images and decrease model complexity. In contrast to existing multimodal biometric recognition models, the proposed method prioritizes addressing the issue of missing modality in multimodal biometric recognition tasks. In addition, Compared to existing lightweight multimodal models, we utilize a single-stream feature extraction network instead of a multi- stream feature network to achieve the representation fusion of multimodal biometric traits, thereby reducing model complexity. The detailed procedure of the designed UMR-Net is as follows: Firstly, an Image-Level Adaptive Fusion (ILAF) module is proposed to achieve the dynamic fusion of palmprint and palmvein images in pixel space, and then the fuse images, palmvein and palmprint images are respectively inputted into a single-stream feature encoder for identity recognition. Secondly, to ensure that the single-stream feature encoder can learn the representation of unimodal and multimodal biometric images, the palmVein-aware Feature Alignment (VFA) module and palmPrint-aware Feature Alignment (PFA) module are presented. Besides, a Cross-modal Semantic Consistency (CSC) loss is proposed to sure that the unimodal biometric features generated by a single-stream feature encoder do not exhibit modality bias. Finally, the unimodal and multimodal representations are respectively fed into unimodal recognition head and multimodal fusion recognition head for identity recognition.

Overall, the main contributions of this paper are summarized as follows:

- We propose a Unified Multimodal Representation Network (UMR-Net) for multimodal biometric recognition based on palmvein and palmprint modalities to jointly learn unified features of unimodal and multimodal input images and decrease model complexity.
- The palmVein-aware Feature Alignment (VFA) module and palmPrint-aware Feature Alignment (PFA) module are presented to guarantee that the multimodal biometric features contain the semantic information of each modality.
- A Cross-modal Semantic Consistency (CSC) loss is proposed to sure that the unimodal biometric features generated by a single-stream feature encoder do not exhibit modality bias.
- Extensive experiments conducted on three public benchmark datasets demonstrate the effectiveness of our proposed framework.

2   Related Work

2.1   Multimodal Biometric Recognition

Deep learning-based MBR has gained widespread attention. MBR can effectively handle common and complementary features between different modalities, offering stronger generalization capabilities. For example, Ren et al. [2] proposed FPV-Net, which utilized an attention mechanism to perform weighted fusion of shallow and deep features from fingerprints and finger veins, significantly improving information interaction and feature representation. Yang et al. [3] innovatively decoupled multimodal features of the finger into shared and private features, reducing correlations between different modalities to enhance identity information complementarity and fusion recognition accuracy.

2.2   Incomplete Multimodal Learning

At present, incomplete multi-modal learning can be summarized into two categories: generative models and unified models. The method in this paper belongs to the unified models, so only the unified models will be introduced in this paper. Unified model: This method mainly obtained unified features under random missing modality by designing a dynamic multimodal fusion model. For example, Ding et al. [4] proposed a multimodal brain tumor medical image segmentation based on region-aware fusion network and designed a segmentation

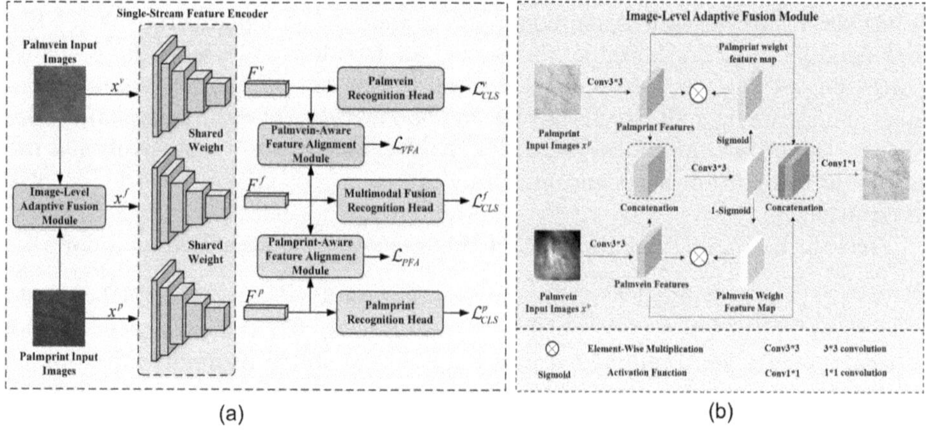

Fig. 2. (a): The framework of the proposed UMR-Net, (b): The structure parameters of our designed image-level adaptive fusion module.

based regularization to solve the problem of missing modality in multimodal segmentation process. Zhao et al. [5] proposed a multimodal emotion recognition model with missing modality based on an imagination network. Pan et al. [6] proposed cross-modal neural image generation based on hybrid generative adversarial networks, which solves the problem of robust recognition of brain diseases under missing modality and Wang et al. [7] constructed a multimodal shared-specific feature decoupling framework.

3   Methods

The proposed methods mainly contains image-level adaptive fusion module, unified multimodal representation learning and loss function, which is shown in Fig. 2.

3.1   Image-Level Adaptive Fusion Module

Previous multimodal biometric recognition models utilized multiple independent feature extraction networks to obtain the representations of each modality, and then performed late fusion for identity recognition, leading to inference times that are nearly several times longer than those of a single-stream feature extraction network. Therefore, this paper adopts a simple multimodal biometric fusion framework based on early fusion strategy and single-stream feature encoder network. The single-stream feature encoder network adopts the ResNet18 without full connected layers as backbone, and is used to extract the deep features of fusion images. The image-level adaptive fusion module is designed based on the self-attention mechanism, and it can achieve the dynamic fusion of palmprint and palmvein images in pixel space. The detailed process is illustrated as follows.

Given a multimodal biometric dataset $D = \{(x^p, x^v), y\}$, where x^p represents the input images of palmprint modality, x^v denotes the input images of palmvein modality and y is label information of input images of palmprint and palmvein modalities. The image-level adaptive fusion module is firstly used to fuse the palmvein and the palmprint input images, which can be defined as:

$$x^f = F(x^p, x^v) \tag{1}$$

where x^f denotes the fused images and F represents the image-level adaptive fusion module, and its structure parameters are shown in Fig. 2(b). Specifically, we first obtain the low-level features of each modality:

$$f_p = \text{Conv}_{3\times3}(x^p), \quad f_v = \text{Conv}_{3\times3}(x^v) \tag{2}$$

Then, we use the fused features to generate different modality weights:

$$W_p = \text{Sigmoid}\left(\text{Conv}_{3\times3}\left([f_p, f_v]\right)\right) \quad \text{and} \quad W_v = 1 - W_p \tag{3}$$

where $[\ ]$ represents the concat operation. Then, we use the modality weigths to obtain the fused images:

$$x^f = \text{Conv}_{1\times1}\left([f_p \cdot W_p, f_v \cdot W_v]\right) \tag{4}$$

Then, the fused images are fed into the single-stream feature encoder network E to obtain the multimodal fused features F^f, which can be represented as:

$$F^f = E(x^f) \tag{5}$$

To ensure that the single-stream feature encoder network can learn the representations of unimodal and multimodal biometric input images, we designed a unified multimodal representation learning framework, which is illustrated in Sect. 3.2.

3.2   Unified Multimodal Representation Learning

As shown in Fig. 3, the proposed unified multimodal representation learning includes palmVein-aware Feature Alignment (VFA) module and palmPrint-aware Feature Alignment (PFA) module, which is utilized to guarantee that the single-stream feature encoder network learns rich multimodal fused feature contained complete information of each modality.

Palmvein-Aware Feature Alignment Module. Given the deep features F^v of palmvein images extracted by the single-stream feature encoder network, we employ a multi-layer perceptron to construct the palmvein-aware feature

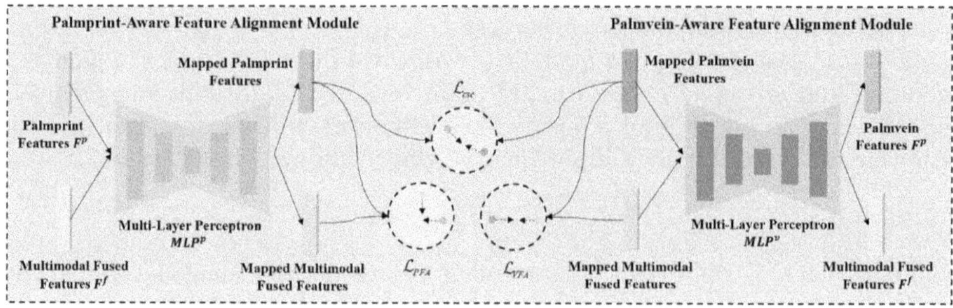

Fig. 3. The framework of VFA and PFA modules

alignment module, and to ensure that the multimodal fused feature F^f contains feature information of palmvein modality, we aim to minimize its ℓ_2 distance from the single-modal palmvein features, which can be defined as:

$$L_{VFA} = \|MLP^v(F^v) - MLP^v(F^f)\|_2 \tag{6}$$

where MLP^v represents a multi-layer perceptron and it is utilized to achieve the palmvein semantic alignment between multimodal fused features and single-modal palmvein features. Subsequently, the single-modal palmvein feature is fed into the palmvein recognition head for supervised learning, which can guarantee that the single-stream feature encoder network learns specific information of palmvein images. In the palmvein recognition head, we utilize the cross-entropy loss function for supervised learning, which can be defined as:

$$L_{CLS}^v = \sum_{i=1}^{N} y_i^v \log(\hat{y}_i^v) \tag{7}$$

where y_i' denotes the label information of single-modal palmvein features, and $\hat{y}_i'$ represents the prediction results of single-modal palmvein features.

Palmprint-Aware Feature Alignment Module. Given the deep features F^p of palmprint images extracted by the single-stream feature encoder network, similar to the construction of the VFA module, we also employ a multi-layer perceptron to construct the palmprint-aware feature alignment module, and the ℓ-function is utilized to minimize the distance between multimodal fused features and single-modal palmprint features, which aims to ensure that multimodal fused features can contain feature information of palmprint images. The corresponding loss is defined as:

$$L_{PFA} = \|MLP^p(F^p) - MLP^p(F^f)\|_2 \tag{8}$$

where MLP^p denotes a multi-layer perceptron, which is used to realize the palmprint semantic alignment between multimodal fused features and single-modal palmprint features. Subsequently, the single-modal palmprint feature is fed into the palmprint recognition head for supervised learning, which can guarantee that the single-stream feature encoder network learns specific information of palmprint images. In the palmprint recognition head, the cross-entropy loss is adopted as the objective function for supervised learning, which can be represented as:

$$L_{CLS}^{p} = \sum_{i=1}^{N} y_i^p \log(\hat{y}_i^p) \tag{9}$$

where y_i^p denotes the label information of single-modal palmprint features, and $\hat{y}_i^p$ represents the prediction results of single-modal palmprint features.

Although the proposed VFA and PFA can guarantee that the single-stream feature encoder network learns rich multimodal fused features, it cannot avoid modality bias for palmvein and palmprint modalities. Therefore, to address this issue, a Cross-modal Semantic Consistency (CSC) loss is designed, which can be defined as:

$$L_{csc} = \|F^v - F^p\|_2 \tag{10}$$

As mentioned above, the total loss function of our proposed UMR-Net is represented as follows:

$$L_{total} = \lambda_1(L_{CLS}^{f} + L_{CLS}^{v} + L_{CLS}^{p}) + \lambda_2(L_{VFA} + L_{PFA}) + \lambda_3 L_{csc} \tag{11}$$

where L_{CLS}^{f} denotes the cross-entropy loss function for supervised learning in multimodal fused recognition head, and $\lambda_1, \lambda_2, \lambda_3$ are the balance parameters.

4   Experiments and Results

4.1   Dataset

We select the three multimodal biometric benchmark datasets including CUMT Palmprint and Palmvein Dataset (CUMT), Tongji University Contactless Palmprint and Palmvein Dataset (Tongji), and Tsinghua Palmprint and Palmvein Dataset(Tsinghua) to evaluate the performance of our proposed LMBR-Net.

4.2   Implementation Details

For the Tongji dataset, the training set and the test set each contain 6,000 palmvein images and 6,000 palmprint images. For CUMT, both sets contain 1,450 palmvein images and 1,450 palmprint images. For Tsinghua, both sets contain 3,000 palmvein images and 3,000 palmprint images.

During the training process of the designed network, SGD optimization algorithm is employed to optimize the proposed model. The initial learning rate is set to 0.0001, the weight decay is set to 0.005, the batch size is set to 4, the dropout is set to 0.5, and the input image size is set to 224×224. λ_1, λ_2, and λ_3 are set to 1, 10, and 14, respectively. Our experiments are performed by using NVIDIA GeForce GTX 2080 Ti GPU

The Effectiveness of Image-Level Adaptive Fusion Module. We compare two simple image-level fusion methods including concatenation operation and sum operation to verify the effectiveness of the proposed image-level adaptive fusion module. The experimental results are illustrated in Table 1. The proposed model with ILAF module preeminent performance compared to other simple image-level fusion methods.

Table 1. Performance comparison

Dataset	Methods		
	Concat	Sum	ILAF
CUMT	97.80	98.85	**100**
Tongji	98.69	99.51	**99.85**
Tsinghua	99.05	99.63	**99.93**

The Effectiveness of Unified Multimodal Representation Learning. In our experiments, we adopts the designed ILAF module as image-level fusion method and the ResNet18 model as single-stream feature encoder network. Table 2 shows the experimental results on three multimodal biometric datasets. After removing different modules, the model's robustness decreased to varying degrees. Therefore, it can be concluded that the designed UMR-Net can enable the single-stream feature extraction network to obtain rich multimodal fused information and complete specific information of each modality.

Table 2. Ablation experiments under complete missing of palmprint

L_{VFA}	L_{PFA}	L_{csc}	Tongji	CUMT	Tsinghua
×	✓	✓	96.30	89.98	90.25
✓	×	✓	98.40	96.69	87.03
✓	✓	×	96.33	70.21	64.13
✓	✓	✓	99.63	100	99.73

Table 3. Performance comparison on differenct datasets

Modality combinations	Methods					
	ShaSpecNet	MMANet	DrFuse	DMRNet	SSFD-Net	UMR-Net
CUMT						
{Print}	44.90	98.15	86.43	98.53	99.45	**100**
{Vein}	80.69	97.81	95.47	98.57	99.24	**100**
{Vein, Print}	98.76	99.93	99.38	99.90	99.78	**100**
Tongji						
{Print}	80.67	98.98	93.65	97.94	**99.88**	99.63
{Vein}	44.17	98.67	98.53	98.55	99.23	**99.65**
{Vein, Print}	99.07	99.28	99.70	99.35	**99.97**	99.85
Tsinghua						
{Print}	63.27	99.30	80.33	99.35	99.58	**99.73**
{Vein}	57.50	99.13	95.13	98.37	99.28	**99.90**
{Vein, Print}	99.43	99.50	99.53	99.70	99.78	**99.93**

4.3 Comparison with Incomplete Multimodal Image Classification Models

We adopt six multimodal learning with missing modality methods including DENet [8], MFD [9], ShaSpecNet [7], MMANet [10], DrFuse [11] and DMR-Net [12] as comparison models to evaluate the performance of our proposed UMR-Net. In our experiments, {Vein} represents the test samples only exist plamvein modality, {Print} represents the test samples only exist plamprint modality and {Vein, Print} represents the complete modality. The experimental results show in Table 3, which denoting UMR-Net achieves the best robustness across different datasets. It is worth noting that although SSFD-Net outperforms UMR-Net in some aspects at Tongji, it is a reconstruction model, and its number of model parameters is much larger than that of UMR-Net.

4.4 Model Complexity and Running Time

We conduct an experiment to analyze the model complexity and time consumption of different multimodal learning models. Table 4 shows the experimental results of each model. The proposed model achieves faster runtime which demonstrates the fact that the proposed method can obtain pleasing recognition results with a low computation cost.

Table 4. Comparison of model size and running time

Models	Running Time (ms)	Model Size (M)
MFD	**6.73**	15.34
ShaSpecNet	14.62	89.16
MMANet	7.13	32.10
DrFuse	11.85	137.42
DMRNet	10.19	61.61
SSFD-Net	8.79	59.88
MKDNet	6.31	**14.39**

5 Conclusion

In this paper, we propose the UMR-Net. Firstly, an Image-Level Adaptive Fusion (ILAF) module is proposed to achieve the dynamic fusion of palmprint and palmvein images in pixel space, and then the fuse images, palmvein and palmprint images are respectively inputted into a single-stream modality-agnostic encoder for identity recognition. Secondly, the palmVein-aware Feature Alignment (VFA) module and palmPrint-aware Feature Alignment (PFA) module are presented to ensure that the single-stream modality encoder can learn the representation of unimodal biometric images.

Acknowledgements. This work was supported in part by the National Natural Science Foundation of China under Grant 62403470.

References

1. Li, Y., Yuan, L., Vasconcelos, N.: Bidirectional learning for domain adaptation of semantic segmentation. In: Proceedings of the IEEE/CVF Conference on Computer Vision and Pattern Recognition, pp. 6936–6945 (2019)
2. Ren, D., Zuo, W., Hu, Q., Zhu, P., Meng, D.: Progressive image deraining networks: a better and simpler baseline. In: Proceedings of the IEEE/CVF Conference on Computer Vision and Pattern Recognition, pp. 3937–3946 (2019)
3. Yang, W., Huang, J., Luo, D., Kang, W.: Efficient disentangled representation learning for multi-modal finger biometrics. Pattern Recogn. **145**, 109944 (2024)
4. Ding, Y., Yu, X., Yang, Y.: Rfnet: region-aware fusion network for incomplete multi-modal brain tumor segmentation. In: Proceedings of the IEEE/CVF International Conference on Computer Vision, pp. 3975–3984 (2021)
5. Zhao, J., Li, R., Jin, Q.: Missing modality imagination network for emotion recognition with uncertain missing modalities. In: Proceedings of the 59th Annual Meeting of the Association for Computational Linguistics and the 11th International Joint Conference on Natural Language Processing, vol. 1: Long Papers, pp. 2608–2618 (2021)
6. Pan, Y., Liu, M., Lian, C., Xia, Y., Shen, D.: Spatially-constrained fisher representation for brain disease identification with incomplete multi-modal neuroimages. IEEE Trans. Med. Imaging **39**(9), 2965–2975 (2020)
7. Wang, H., Chen, Y., Ma, C., Avery, A., Hull, L., Carneiro, G.: Multi-modal learning with missing modality via shared-specific feature modelling. In: Proceedings of the IEEE/CVF Conference on Computer Vision and Pattern Recognition, pp. 15878–15887 (2023)
8. Aihua Zheng, Ziling He, Zi Wang, Chenglong Li, and Jin Tang. Dynamic enhancement network for partial multi-modality person re-identification. *arXiv preprint* arXiv:2305.15762, 2023
9. Kang, M., Ting, F.F., Phan, R.C.W., Ge, Z., Ting, C.M.: A multimodal feature distillation with cnn-transformer network for brain tumor segmentation with incomplete modalities. arXiv preprint arXiv:2404.14019 (2024)
10. Wei, S., Luo, C., Luo, Y.: Mmanet: margin-aware distillation and modality-aware regularization for incomplete multimodal learning. In: Proceedings of the IEEE/CVF Conference on Computer Vision and Pattern Recognition, pp. 20039–20049 (2023)
11. Yao, W., Yin, K., Cheung, W.K., Liu, J., Qin, J.: Drfuse: learning disentangled representation for clinical multi-modal fusion with missing modality and modal inconsistency. In: Proceedings of the AAAI Conference on Artificial Intelligence, vol. 38, pp. 16416–16424 (2024)
12. Wei, S., Luo, Y., Wang, Y., Luo, C.: Robust multimodal learning via representation decoupling. In: European Conference on Computer Vision, pp. 38–54. Springer, Heidelberg (2024). https://doi.org/10.1007/978-3-031-72946-1_3

Enhanced Contactless Palmprint Backdoor Attack with Invisible Sample-Specific Triggers

Yonghan Chen[1], Shuping Zhao[1(✉)], Lunke Fei[1], Tingting Chai[2], Jinrong Cui[3], and Qi Lai[4]

[1] Guangdong University of Technology, Guangzhou, China
`yb77458@um.edu.mo`
[2] Harbin Institute of Technology, Harbin, China
[3] South China Agricultural University, Guangzhou, China
[4] Shenzhen Institute of Advanced Technology, Chinese Academy of Sciences, Guangdong, China

Abstract. In current years, with the widespread commercial application of contactless palmprint recognition based on deep learning, the unique backdoor defect of deep neural networks (DNN) is seriously threatening its security. The attacker tries to embed hidden backdoors in DNN, ensuring the model performs correctly on clean data but outputs manipulated results when triggered by predefined inputs. However, existing palmprint backdoor attack methods usually adopt the same texture/principal line-based triggers for all palmprint samples, which makes the attacks easily detectable and mitigated by existing backdoor defenses. To tackle these issues, in this paper, we proposed an enhanced contactless palmprint backdoor attack method with invisible sample-specific triggers (ECPBA_SST). Specifically, the proposed ECPBA_SST explored an encoder-decoder architecture to generate the additive noise trigger fused with palmprint features. To this end, an asymmetric label poisoning strategy with non-uniform poisoning tactics is designed to avoid the latent space separation. Experimental results on a number of contactless palmprrint datasests demonstrate that the proposed ECPBA_SST not only outperforms mainstream methods in attack effectiveness, but also exhibits exceptional stealthiness.

Keywords: Contactless palmprint recognition · Backdoor attack · Invisible triggers

1 Introduction

Currently, contactless palmprint recognition technology has been widely applied to identity authentication due to its user-friendliness and high recognition accuracy [1,2]. Over the past decades, palmprint recognition methodologies have evolved significantly from early approaches reliant on handcrafted features (e.g.,

W. Jia et al. (Eds.): CCBR 2025, LNCS 16360, pp. 57–67, 2026.
https://doi.org/10.1007/978-981-95-6123-0_6

line-based, orientation-based, texture analysis, and subspace learning [1]) to the current deep learning-dominated paradigm [2]. However, despite the performance gains offered by deep neural networks (DNN), they remain vulnerable to security threats, notably adversarial attacks and backdoor attacks [3]. While existing research has primarily focused on adversarial attacks targeting palmprint systems [4], investigations into their susceptibility to backdoor attacks remain notably scarce.

Extensive research exists on backdoor attacks, which can be categorized based on attacker capability into data poisoning based attacks (e.g., BadNets [5]) and training controllable base attacks (e.g., WaNet [6]). The former operates by implanting visible or invisible triggers into training data to induce misclassification, while the latter entails not only manipulating training data but also exerting control over the training process itself. Crucially, data poisoning based attacks present greater practical challenges in real-world scenarios, and the use of invisible triggers significantly enhances both stealth and attack efficacy. Consequently, this work focuses on imperceptible, data poisoning based backdoor attacks against palmprint recognition models to rigorously evaluate their contemporary security posture.

Motivated by the steganography techniques, we design a novel palmprint attack paradigm, which generates an invisible, additive noise trigger by encoding the target label into the palmprint image, thereby incorporating inherent palmprint characteristics into the trigger pattern (Fig. 1). When a victim model is trained on the poisoned dataset, palmprint images embedded with this trigger will consistently misclassify any input to the attacker-specified target label. Furthermore, we introduce a novel poisoning strategy that combines palmprint-specific trigger design with asymmetric poisoning to evade latent space separation detection. Extensive experiments conducted on multiple palmprint datasets validate the stealthiness and effectiveness of our proposed method.

The main contributions of this work are briefly summarized as follows:

1) Different from the other related works, we propose an enhanced invisible and sample-specific additive noise trigger for contactless palmprint backdoor attack, which exploits the inherent palmprint features while maintaining visual stealth to avoid the problem that traditional visual triggers are easy to detect.
2) We propose and design an enhanced novel poisoning method, conducting extensive experiments on multiple palmprint datasets to validate the stealthiness and effectiveness of our approach.

2 Related Works

2.1 Backdoor Attack

While backdoor attacks fall into *data poisoning based* and *training controllable base* categories, this work focuses exclusively on the data-poisoning threat model (attacker manipulates only training data). Representative methods under

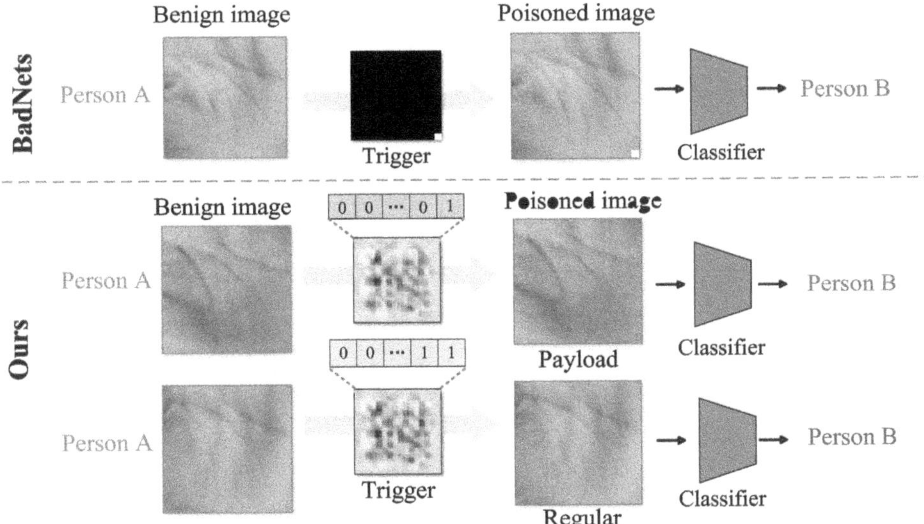

Fig. 1. Trigger comparison: BadNets vs. our palmprint-generated triggers. Our method produces label-specific triggers for both regularization and payload samples. (Triggers normalized to [0,255] for visualization; actual near-black triggers shown in Fig. 4)

this paradigm include: BadNet [5] (visible patch triggers), Blended [15] (alpha-blended imperceptible triggers), and ISSBA [7] (steganography-based sample-specific triggers). Additional approaches leverage physical phenomena as triggers, such as natural reflections, human-imperceptible noise, and image perturbations [8].

In the field of biometric recognition, existing research on backdoor attacks predominantly targets facial verification systems, with mainstream approaches being perturbation-based attacks [9] for high stealth and visible-feature modification [10] for physical realizability. Critically, backdoor attacks against modalities like palmprint, fingerprint, and iris remain unexplored, posing significant risks to high-stakes deployments such as financial security.

2.2   Poisoning Frameworks

Early frameworks employ uniform random selection with dirty-label settings (e.g., [5,7]). While simple, they exhibit limited stealth: label contamination facilitates detection, and poisoned samples form clusters in latent space [12,13]. Clean-label frameworks [11,14] preserve original labels but require sophisticated sample selection and feature alignment. Emerging frameworks adopt fine-grained scheduling: extending contamination to dual-label strategies with trigger diversification and asymmetric trigger intensity (e.g., Adaptive-Blend/Patch [13]). These evade latent space separation detection via data-level optimization without training process intervention.

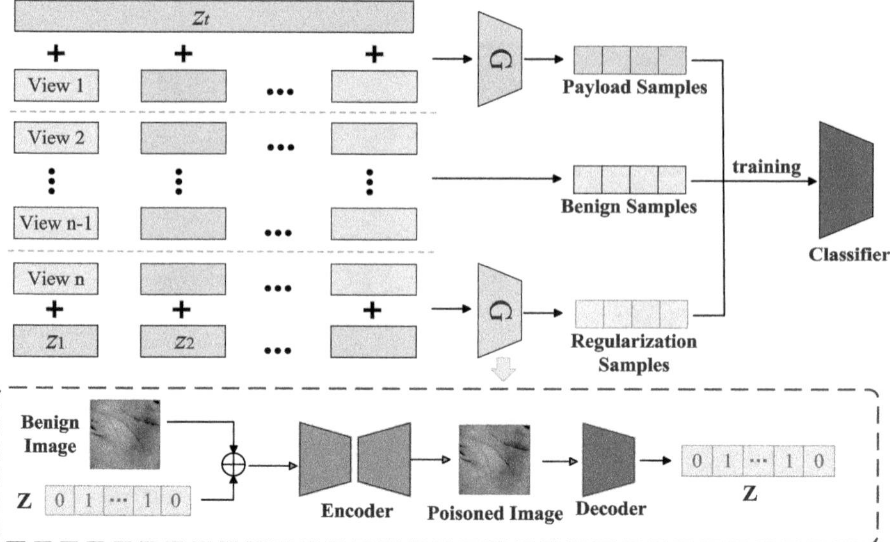

Fig. 2. Overview of the ECPBA_SST Attack Methodology. Trigger generator model G (encoder-decoder) creates adversarial samples: payload samples (z_t: target label) and regularization samples ($z_i \neq z_t$). During training, benign, payload, and regularization samples are jointly trained to implant the backdoor.

3   The Proposed Method

3.1   Threat Model

Our core approach employs a pre-trained encoder-decoder model to generate invisible triggers conditioned on palmprint features. These triggers are embedded into a poisoned training set. The poisoned set, alongside benign samples, is then used to train the recognition model via the Adaptive-Blend poisoning framework [13], achieving backdoor implantation. Figure 2 illustrates the overall framework.

Symbol Definition. Let $D_{train} = (x_i, y_i)_{i=1}^{N}$ be the clean training dataset, where $x_i \in X = \{0, 1, ..., 255\}^{C \times W \times H}$ represents an image and i$y_i \in Y = \{1, 2, ..., K\}$ is the corresponding label, with K being the number of classes. Given a training dataset, the core of a backdoor attack lies in generating poisoned samples D_p. Specifically, D_p is a subset selected from D_{train} with a poisoning rate p, while D_b denotes the remaining benign samples. $D_p = \{(x_i', y_t)|x_i' = T(x_i), x_i \in X\}$, where $T(\cdot)$ is the backdoor transformation function and y_t is the attacker-specified target label. Within the Adapt-Blend [13] poisoning framework, poisoned samples are further categorized into payload samples D_a and regularization samples D_r, defined as $D_a = \{(x_i', y_t)|x_i' = T(x_i), x_i \in X\}$ (labeled with the attacker-specified target) and $D_r = \{(x_i', y_i)|x_i' = T'(x_i), x_i \in X\}$ (retaining its original label). For a given dataset D_{train}, the attacker attempts to train a backdoored model f using the poisoned training set $D'_{train} = D_b \cup D_a \cup D_r$, such that for any $x \in D'_{train}$, f predicts the corresponding label associated with x.

The Target of Backdoor Attack. Backdoor attacks aim to implant a hidden backdoor into a DNN model through data poisoning. When the backdoored model encounters a specific trigger, it will misclassify the input to the attacker-specified target label. Specifically, the attacker has two primary objectives: effectiveness and stealthiness. Effectiveness refers to the attacker's attempt to train a backdoored model with a high Attack Success Rate (ASR), while ensuring that the Benign Accuracy (BA) does not significantly decline. Stealthiness means that samples containing the trigger should be sufficiently concealed, and there should be no clear separation between poisoned samples and clean samples in the latent space.

3.2   Implementation of Palmprint Backdoor Attack

Design of the Paplmprint Trigger. In this subsection, we detail the specific implementation of the palmprint-based invisible backdoor attack. We first learn an encoder-decoder model as the palmprint trigger generator G to embed distinct label information into palmprint images for trigger generation. These palmprint triggers are imperceptible additive residuals. For a palmprint image x_i, we multiply the residual $G(x_i, z)$ by a coefficient a to obtain the poisoned palmprint image, where z denotes the label information selected for embedding. Specifically, when generating payload samples, the poisoned image should be:

$$x'_i = x_i + a \cdot G(x_i, z_t) \tag{1}$$

When generating regularization samples, the poisoned image should be:

$$x'_i = x_i + a \cdot G(x_i, z_i) \tag{2}$$

For the embedded label information z, it may differ from the actual classification label y, but must satisfy the following two properties: the regularization label z_i differs from the payload label z_t; and regularization labels z_i for distinct classes are mutually distinct.

For the trigger generator G, our method requires optimization of two objectives. First, to ensure effectiveness in generating palmprint triggers, we need to recover the embedded label information z' at the decoder end and minimize the cross-entropy loss of the label information, thereby obtaining palmprint triggers containing stable hidden information. The specific optimization goal is as follows:

$$\mathcal{L}_z = \mathcal{L}(z_t, z'_t) + \mathcal{L}(z_i, z'_i) \tag{3}$$

where $\mathcal{L}(\cdot)$ denotes the cross-entropy loss function. Second, for the stealthiness of palmprint triggers, we achieve this by minimizing both the perceptual difference $\mathcal{L}_p$ between the original and poisoned images and the color space loss $\mathcal{L}_c$. The total loss function for the trigger generator G is as follows:

$$\mathcal{L}_{total} = \mathcal{L}_z + \mathcal{L}_p + \mathcal{L}_c \tag{4}$$

To achieve more stable training outcomes, we exclusively employ $\mathcal{L}_z$ for optimization during the initial training steps. Once $\mathcal{L}_z$ stabilizes, we then switch to optimizing the model using $\mathcal{L}_{total}$.

Design of Asymmetric Poisoning. Within the Adapt-Blend framework [13], regularization samples D_r enhance backdoor stealthiness in latent space by forcing the DNN to jointly learn palmprint features and trigger features. However, this simultaneously penalizes the backdoor association, reducing Attack Success Rate (ASR). To mitigate this, we implement specialized label processing and propose an asymmetric poisoning strategy: applying a small residual coefficient ($a = 0.2$) during training to weaken triggers, while using a larger coefficient ($a = 2$) during inference to activate the backdoor. This approach effectively minimizes the negative impact of D_r while enhancing stealthiness and attack efficacy.

4   Experiments and Analysis

4.1   Datasets

In this section, we evaluated the performance of the proposed method on two contactless palmprint datasets, i.e., Mobile_PV1 [17] and TJI [18], as well as one palm-vein dataset of PolyU Multi-Spectral (PolyU-MS) [19], where theh ResNet18 [16] was chosen as the baseline DNN architecture. The Mobile_PV1 dataset comprises 11,768 Region of Interest (ROI) images from 370 palm classes (left/right hands of 185 subjects), captured in unconstrained open environments without palm fixation. The TJI dataset contains 907 palmprint ROI images across 100 classes, with $\leq$ 10 samples per class. To satisfy poisoning attack requirements (minimum 6 samples per class), 95 classes were retained after filtering. For PolyU-MS (24,000 multi-spectral images), we utilized a subset of 6,000 Near-Infrared (NIR) spectral ROI images, representing the most discriminative band. Benign and poisoned samples are illustrated in Fig. 3 for enhanced visualization of dataset characteristics and attack effects.

4.2   Experimental Settings

We benchmark against three representative backdoor attacks–BadNets [5], Blended [15], and ISSBA [7]–using identical poisoning sample counts and training configurations (SGD optimizer, initial LR = 0.001, decayed by 0.1 after epochs 20/25). BadNets and Blended employ a bottom-right 10×10 white trigger (Blended transparency: 0.2). ISSBA shares our encoder architecture to validate our poisoning strategy's evasion of latent space separation. Detailed settings are in Table 1.

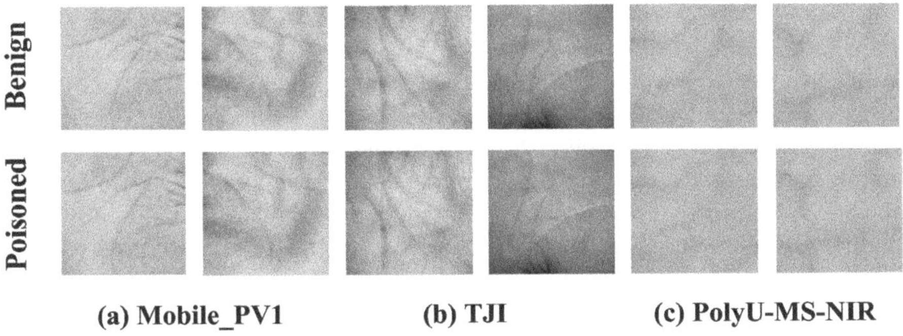

Fig. 3. Palmprint Dataset Samples and Poisoning Effects.

Table 1. Datasets Settings.

Dataset	Input Size	Classes	Train		Test	
			Benign	Poisoned	Benign	Poisoned
Mobile_PV1	$3 \times 128 \times 128$	370	5848	740	2590	2590
TJI	$3 \times 128 \times 128$	95	340	190	181	181
PolyU-MS-NIR	$1 \times 128 \times 128$	500	3000	1000	1500	1500

The effectiveness of the proposed method is validated using Attack Success Rate (ASR) and Benign Accuracy (BA). Stealthiness is evaluated via three metrics, including Peak Signal-to-Noise Ratio (PSNR), Structural Similarity Index (SSIM), and Inception Score (IS).

4.3 Experimental Results

Attack Effectiveness. To evaluate the effectiveness of the ECPBA_SST method, we compared its performance in Attack Success Rate (ASR) and Benign Accuracy (BA) against three baseline methods (BadNets, Blended, and ISSBA).

Table 2. Attack performance comparison between ECPBA_SST and three other attack methods. The best and the second-best results are highlighted and underlined, respectively.

Method	Mobile_PV1		TJI		PolyU-MS-NIR	
	BA ↑	ASR ↑	BA ↑	ASR ↑	BA ↑	ASR ↑
No attack	99.25	–	99.45	–	99.63	–
BadNets	98.38	100	98.90	100	98.84	100
Blended	97.84	96	97.24	96.69	97.67	98
ISSBA	**98.76**	100	**99.45**	100	98.80	100
Ours	98.38	100	**99.45**	100	**99.60**	100

As shown in Table 2, our attack method achieved 100% ASR across all three palmprint datasets. Other methods also attained 100% ASR, with the exception of Blended. Regarding the impact on Benign Accuracy (BA), our method exhibited an impact on the Mobile_PV1 dataset that was merely 0.38% points higher than the optimal baseline, while demonstrating the lowest impact on the remaining datasets. These results indicate that Deep Neural Network (DNN) models for palmprint recognition exhibit significant security vulnerabilities to backdoor attacks, enabling attackers to achieve precise targeted attacks with minimal degradation to normal functionality.

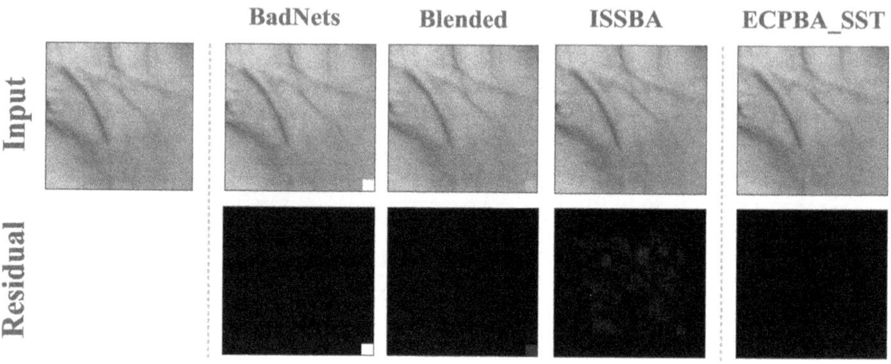

Fig. 4. Comparison of examples generated by four backdoor attacks. For each attack, we show the poisoned sample (top) and the magnified (×5) residual (bottom).

Table 3. Attack stealthiness comparison (PSNR, SSIM and IS metrics)

Attack	Mobile_PV1			TJI			PolyU-MS-NIR		
	PSNR ↑	SSIM ↑	IS ↓	PSNR ↑	SSIM ↑	IS ↓	PSNR ↑	SSIM ↑	IS ↓
No attack	INF	1.0000	0.0000	INF	1.0000	0.0000	INF	1.0000	0.0000
BadNets	29.03	0.9941	0.0595	27.06	0.9938	0.0911	28.90	0.9942	0.0508
Blended	43.17	0.9970	0.0308	41.16	**0.9966**	0.0560	43.03	0.9968	**0.0015**
ISSBA	39.97	0.9833	0.1797	31.63	0.9586	0.1374	45.67	0.9883	0.0166
Ours	**47.70**	**0.9982**	**0.0030**	**42.87**	0.9934	0.0835	**50.45**	**0.9972**	0.0076

Attack Stealthiness. Figure 4 compares poisoned samples generated by different attacks and their corresponding residual maps (×5 magnification). The figure reveals that our method produces the smallest residuals, leaving only subtle shadow-like artifacts, which effectively evade human inspection. Furthermore, we evaluated the stealthiness of various attack methods using three metrics: Peak Signal-to-Noise Ratio (PSNR), Structural Similarity Index (SSIM), and Inception Score (IS). Detailed results are presented in Table 3. Our method achieved superior results across all metrics on the Mobile_PV1 dataset. On the TJI dataset, its SSIM was approximately 0.003 lower than Blended, while on the PolyU-MS-NIR palmprints dataset, its IS was approximately 0.006 higher than Blended.

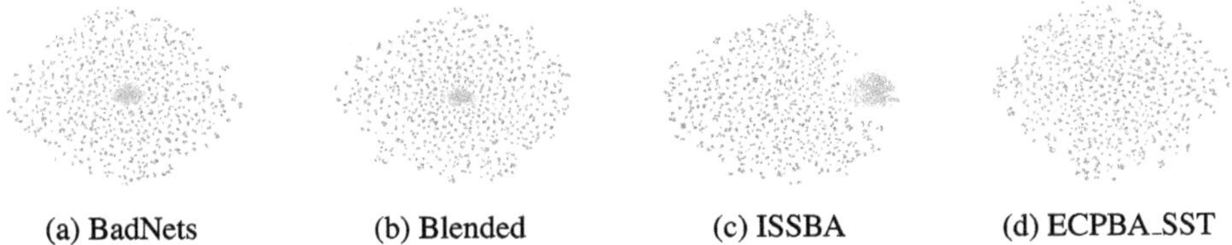

(a) BadNets   (b) Blended   (c) ISSBA   (d) ECPBA_SST

Fig. 5. The t-SNE of feature vectors in the latent space under different attacks on Mobile_PV1. We use red and blue points to denote poisoned and benign samples, respectively, where each point in the plots corresponds to a training sample from the target label. (Color figure online)

We selected the Mobile_pv1 dataset (with a poisoning rate of 11.23%) as the attack target, extracted the latent representations of poisoned and clean samples under different attacks, and visualized them using t-SNE (Van der Maaten & Hinton, 2008). As illustrated in Fig. 5, the poisoned samples generated by the BadNets and Blended methods form distinct clusters but contain outliers. ISSBA exhibits perfectly separated clusters. In contrast, the poisoned samples generated by ECPBA_SST (marked in red) and the benign samples (marked in blue) demonstrate a uniformly mixed distribution without forming separable cluster structures. This result validates that our method effectively evades detection mechanisms based on the latent space separation hypothesis, further confirming its advantage in stealthiness.

5   Conclusions

This work pioneers an invisible backdoor attack (ECPBA_SST) against palmprint recognition systems. The proposed method leverages an encoder-decoder architecture to generate feature-fused invisible triggers and employs unequal label assignments and asymmetric poisoning strategies, achieving high attack success rates and strong stealthiness while preserving benign recognition accuracy. Experimental results demonstrate that ECPBA_SST consistently achieves 100% attack success rates across three palmprint datasets, with minimal degradation in benign accuracy ($\leq 0.5\%$). In multi-dimensional stealthiness evaluations (PSNR, SSIM, Inception Score), the proposed ECPBA_SST significantly outperforms mainstream backdoor attacks. T-SNE visualizations of latent space further confirm ECPBA_SST ability to avoid cluster separation of poisoned samples. Future work will explore backdoor attacks for additional biometric modalities and investigate defense frameworks to strengthen security in biometric systems.

Acknowledgments. This research is sponsored by the National Natural Science Foundation of China (Grant no. 62106052), and the Natural Science Foundation of Guangdong Province (Grant no. 2024A1515011647).

References

1. Zhao, S., Zhang, B.: Learning salient and discriminative descriptor for palmprint feature extraction and identification. IEEE Trans. Neural Netw. Learn. Syst. **31**(12), 5219–5230 (2020)
2. Genovese, A., Piuri, V., Plataniotis, K.N., Scotti, F.: PalmNet: GaborPCA convolutional networks for touchless palmprint recognition. IEEE Trans. Inf. Forensics Secur. **14**(12), 3160–3174 (2019)
3. Goldblum, M., Tsipras, D., Xie, C., et al.: Dataset security for machine learning: Data poisoning, backdoor attacks, and defenses. IEEE Trans. Pattern Anal. Mach. Intell. **45**(2), 1563–1580 (2022)
4. Yang, J., Wong, W.K., Fei, L., Zhao, S., Wen, J., Teng, S.: Decoupling visual and identity features for adversarial palm-vein image attack. Neural Netw. **180**, 106693 (2024)
5. Gu, T., Liu, K., Dolan-Gavitt, B., Garg, S.: Badnets: evaluating backdooring attacks on deep neural networks. IEEE Access **7**, 47230–47244 (2019)
6. Nguyen, T.A., Tran, A.T.: Wanet – imperceptible warping-based backdoor attack. In: International Conference on Learning Representations (2021)
7. Li, Y., Li, Y., Wu, B., Li, L., He, R., Lyu, S.: Invisible backdoor attack with sample-specific triggers. In: Proceedings of IEEE/CVF International Conference on Computer Vision (2021)
8. Wenger, E., Passananti, J., Bhagoji, A.N., et al.: Backdoor attacks against deep learning systems in the physical world. In: Proceedings of the IEEE/CVF Conference on Computer Vision and Pattern Recognition, pp. 6206–6215 (2021)
9. Pasquini, C., Böhme, R.: Trembling triggers: exploring the sensitivity of backdoors in DNN-based face recognition. EURASIP J. Inf. Secur. **2020**(1), 12 (2020)
10. Xue, M., He, C., Wang, J., Liu, W.: Backdoors hidden in facial features: a novel invisible backdoor attack against face recognition systems. Peer-to-Peer Network. Appl. **14**, 1458–1474 (2021)
11. Souri, H., Fowl, L., Chellappa, R., et al.: Sleeper agent: scalable hidden trigger backdoors for neural networks trained from scratch. Adv. Neural. Inf. Process. Syst. **35**, 19165–19178 (2022)
12. Chen, B., et al.: Detecting backdoor attacks on deep neural networks by activation clustering. In: AAAI Workshop (2019)
13. Qi, X., Xie, T., Li, Y., Mahloujifar, S., Mittal, P.: Revisiting the assumption of latent separability for backdoor defenses. In: Proceedings of the International Conference on Learning Representations (ICLR) (2023)

14. Zhao, S., Ma, X., Zheng, X., et al.: Clean-label backdoor attacks on video recognition models. In: Proceedings of the IEEE/CVF Conference on Computer Vision and Pattern Recognition, pp. 14443–14452 (2020)
15. Chen, X., Liu, C., Li, B., Lu, K., Song, D.: Targeted backdoor attacks on deep learning systems using data poisoning, arXiv preprint arXiv:1712.05526 (2017)
16. He, K., Zhang, X., Ren, S., Sun, J.: Deep residual learning for image recognition. In: Proceedings of the IEEE/CVF Conference on Computer Vision and Pattern Recognition (CVPR), pp. 770–778 (2016)
17. Zhao, S., Fei, L., Zhang, B., et al.: Towards mobile palmprint recognition via multi-view hierarchical graph learning. IEEE Trans. Inf. Forensics Secur. (2024)
18. Zhang, L., Li, L., Yang, A., et al.: Towards contactless palmprint recognition: a novel device, a new benchmark, and a collaborative representation based identification approach. Pattern Recogn. **69**, 199–212 (2017)
19. Zhang, D., Guo, Z., Lu, G., et al.: An online system of multispectral palmprint verification. IEEE Trans. Instrum. Meas. **59**(2), 480–490 (2009)

Progressive Adversarial Learning for Multi-modality Biometric Recognition with Missing Modality

Hai Yuan, Xiao Yang, Jun Wang$^{(\boxtimes)}$, Zhengwen Shen, and Zaiyu Pan

School of Information and Control Engineering, China University of Mining and Technology, Xuzhou 221000, Jiangsu, China
jrobot@126.com

Abstract. Multimodal biometric recognition technology has garnered significant attention in recent years owing to its benefits in security and recognition precision compared to traditional single biometric recognition methods, the fusion of multiple biometric features can effectively mitigate the constraints of individual features, reducing issues such as recognition failure caused by forgery or inability to capture a single biometric trait. Given that scenarios including missing modalities may occur, most approaches primarily address missing modalities as independent tasks, ignoring the interrelationships among different combinations of missing modalities and insufficiently adapting to varied input modalities. Thus, we introduce a progressive adversarial learning framework that enables the joint utilization of various missing modality combinations. Specifically, a semantic consistency learning is developed, employing an adversarial technique for arbitrarily missing modality combinations. Additionally, a progressive modality completion learning network is utilized, incorporating arbitrary combinations of missing modalities with complete modality combinations for adversarial learning. This progressively modifies the interrelation across modality combinations, enabling the model to acquire multi-modal semantic information that resembles a complete modality combination. Extensive experiments have been performed to validate the effectiveness of the proposed method.

Keywords: Progressive adversarial learning · Missing modality · Semantic consistency learning · Progressive modality completion learning

1 Introduction

With growing demands for convenience and security, biometric recognition technology has emerged as a focus in research and practical applications [1,2]. This technology involves the automatic recognition and verification of persons by examining their physiological or behavioral traits via intelligent systems. Typical biometric modalities encompass fingerprints, iris patterns, facial features, palmprints, and palm vein scans. Recognition systems reliant on a single biometric

W. Jia et al. (Eds.): CCBR 2025, LNCS 16360, pp. 68–78, 2026.
https://doi.org/10.1007/978-981-95-6123-0_7

characteristic [3] encounter difficulties, including vulnerability to environmental influences, resulting in diminished recognition accuracy and an inability to satisfy the escalating security requirements and intricate application demands. Consequently, multi-modal biometric recognition technology has been developed [4]. This method improves recognition accuracy and strengthens system resilience by integrating biometric characteristics for identity authentication.

However, multi-modality fusion methods can improve resilience to environmental interference, but the issue of missing modalities still arises in the real world. Existing approaches primarily treat missing modalities as independent tasks, neglecting the relationships among various combinations of missing modalities. As the number of modalities increases, these methods often struggle to adapt effectively to different input modalities, leading to a decline in the model's adaptability and robustness in the presence of missing modalities.

To overcome the challenges mentioned above, we propose a progressive adversarial learning approach that progressively explores the interdependencies among various combinations of missing modalities. This strategy facilitates the joint use of arbitrarily combination of missing modalities. Specifically, we incorporate semantic consistency learning to capture the semantically invariant information across different modality combinations. Additionally, we introduce a progressive modality completion learning that enhances the representation ability of multimodal information by utilizing adversarial learning between the combinations of missing modalities and complete modalities. This method strengthens the model's robustness in its recognition of missing modalities and improves its overall adaptability, increasing its effectiveness in real-world situations.

We summarize our main contributions as follows:

- We introduce a novel progressive adversarial learning that facilitates multimodal biometric feature recognition, even in scenarios when certain modalities are missing.
- A semantic consistency learning is presented, employing adversarial learning with different missing modality combinations to acquire semantically invariant unified features.
- A progressive modal completion learning is proposed, allowing the model to progressively acquire complete multi-modal semantic information.

2   Related Work

To tackle the issue of missing modality in real-world situations, current research may be mainly classified into two methods: generative reconstruction models and unified models.

2.1   Generative Models

Wang et al. [5] proposed the Shared-Specific Feature Modelling (ShaSpec) method to address the missing modality issue in multi-modal tasks. ShaSpec learns shared and specific features using auxiliary tasks and a residual feature fusion procedure, enabling easy adaptation to both classification and segmentation tasks. Chen et al. [6] proposed ActionMAE, a robust model for multimodal action recognition under missing modality conditions. They explored training regularization techniques, such as data augmentation, and found that transformer-based fusion methods outperform traditional summation or concatenation for handling missing modalities. ActionMAE learns missing modality prediction by randomly dropping modality features and reconstructing them from the remaining features, achieving state-of-the-art performance across multiple benchmarks, even with missing modalities.

2.2 Unified Models

Unified models: Zhang et al. [7] proposed multimodal Medical Transformer for incomplete multimodal learning, consisting of hybrid modality-specific encoders, an inter-modal Transformer, and a decoder. The model captures local and global context within each modality, aligns cross-modality correlations, and performs robust segmentation through progressive up-sampling. Auxiliary regularizers are introduced to enhance robustness against incomplete modalities. Yao et al. [8] presented DrFuse, an approach addressing missing modalities and discrepancies in clinical predictions by separating shared features from modality-specific features. The methodology integrates a disease-specific attention layer to prioritize modalities according to the attributes of the patient and the disease.

However, these approaches neglect the interrelations across diverse combinations of missing modalities, hence constraining the model's capacity to proficiently adjust to varying input modalities. This consequently undermines its overall resilience and adaptability.

3   Methods

3.1   Overview

To tackle the issue of arbitrarily missing modalities in real-world scenarios and improve the robustness of multi-modal fusion, we propose a progressive adversarial learning (PAL) approach, as illustrated in Fig. 1. This method consists of two stages: the first stage employs adversarial learning with various missing modality combinations to capture the semantically invariant information across modalities. The second stage progressively strengthens the representation capability of multi-modal information by applying adversarial learning between combinations of missing modalities and complete modalities.

3.2   Semantic Consistency Learning (SCL)

We define modality indicator (MID) as an indicator for identifying missing modalities. The inputs to the PAL framework are denoted as $\{x_m, MID_m\}_{m=1}^M$, where x_m represents the data input for the m-th modality, and M is the total

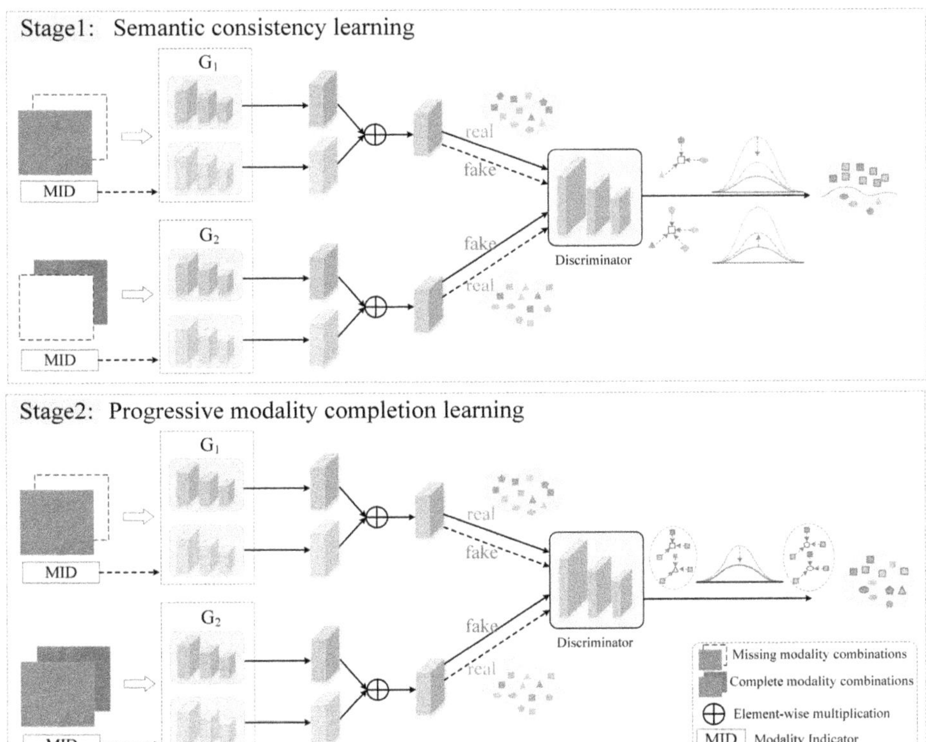

Fig. 1. Architecture of the Progressive Adversarial Learning framework. In Stage 1 (SCL), features from randomly missing combinations are aligned through Generators G1 and G2, along with dual Discriminators. In Stage 2 (PMCL), incomplete and complete features are matched to progressively restore missing modality information.

number of modalities. Initially, a shared latent space is constructed, where adversarial learning is applied with various combinations of missing modalities to extract semantically invariant unified features across different missing modality scenarios. We define the complete multi-modal dataset as M_s, where M_u represents the missing modality combinations.

During training, two subsets are randomly chosen from the missing modality combinations. For instance, let M_{u1} and M_{u2} be selected; these are subsequently fed into G_1 and G_2, respectively, utilising the VGG16 architecture for feature extraction under missing modality conditions. This results in the fused features $F_{M_{u1}}$ and $F_{M_{u2}}$, as shown below:

$$F_{M_{u1}} = G_1(M_{u1}; MID_{u1}), \tag{1}$$

$$F_{M_{u2}} = G_2(M_{u2}; MID_{u2})), \tag{2}$$

where MID_{u1} and MID_{u2} represent the missing modality states.

The fused feature $F_{M_{u1}}$ and the missing modality combination M_{u2} are passed through G_2, where their feature representations undergo adversarial learning via the discriminator D_1. In the same way, the missing modality combination M_{u1} and the fused feature $F_{M_{u2}}$ are processed through G_1, with their feature representations subjected to adversarial learning through the discriminator D_2. The model employs dual discriminators for adversarial learning of features derived from various combinations of missing modalities, promoting the acquisition of unified features that maintain semantic invariance within the feature space. The adversarial loss is expressed as follows:

$$L_{D_1}^{\text{stage1}} = E\left[\log D_1(F_{M_{u1}})\right] + E\left[\log(1 - D_1(G_2(M_{u2})))\right], \tag{3}$$

$$L_{D_2}^{\text{stage1}} = E\left[\log D_2(F_{M_{u2}})\right] + E\left[\log(1 - D_2(G_1(M_{u1})))\right], \tag{4}$$

$$L_{\text{Adv}}^{\text{stage1}} = L_{D_1}^{\text{stage1}} + L_{D_2}^{\text{stage1}}. \tag{5}$$

Additionally, a supervised loss is applied to the predicted outputs of the modality subsets M_{u1} and M_{u2}, along with their corresponding labels, as shown below:

$$L_{u1}^{\text{stage1}} = -\sum_{p1=1}^{n} y_{p1} \cdot \log(\hat{y}_{p1}), \tag{6}$$

$$L_{u2}^{\text{stage1}} = -\sum_{p2=1}^{n} y_{p2} \cdot \log(\hat{y}_{p2}), \tag{7}$$

where $\hat{y}_{p1}$ and $\hat{y}_{p2}$ represent the classification outputs from the fully connected layer, while y_{p1} and y_{p2} denote the labels corresponding to the input images.

By combining adversarial feature learning with label supervision, the model's recognition performance is improved through joint training. This method enhances the model's robustness when confronting diverse combinations of missing modalities. The total loss function is delineated as follows:

$$L_{\text{total}}^{\text{stage1}} = L_{\text{Adv}}^{\text{stage1}} + L_{u1}^{\text{stage1}} + L_{u2}^{\text{stage1}}. \tag{8}$$

3.3   Progressive Modality Completion Learning (PMCL)

Following the analysis of consistency within the semantic feature space of various combinations of missing modalities, this stage employs arbitrary combinations of missing modalities with complete modality combinations for adversarial learning. This stage progressively enhances the interaction among modality combinations, enabling the model to gradually acquire multi-modal semantic information that closely approximates the complete modality combination.

In this stage, using M_{u3} as an example of arbitrarily missing modality combinations, both M_{u3} and the complete modality combinations M_S are fed into the progressive modality completion learning network. The resulting combined features are presented as follows:

$$F_{M_{u3}} = G_1(M_{u3}; MID_{u3}), \tag{9}$$

$$F_{M_S} = G_2(M_S; MID_S), \tag{10}$$

where MID_{u3} and MID_S represent states of missing modalities. Progressive learning constructs feature representations by converting incomplete modalities into complete forms. The fused features are denoted as $F_{M_{u3}}$ and F_{M_S}.

A dual discriminator is then employed to facilitate adversarial learning between features derived from both missing and complete modality combinations, helping the model to learn features that closely resemble those from the complete modality. The adversarial loss is as follows:

$$L_{D_1}^{\text{stage2}} = E\left[\log D_1(F_{M_{u3}})\right] + E\left[\log(1 - D_1(G_2(M_S)))\right], \tag{11}$$

$$L_{D_2}^{\text{stage2}} = E\left[\log D_2(F_{M_S})\right] + E\left[\log(1 - D_2(G_1(M_{u3})))\right], \tag{12}$$

$$L_{\text{Adv}}^{\text{stage2}} = L_{D_1}^{\text{stage2}} + L_{D_2}^{\text{stage2}}. \tag{13}$$

Furthermore, a supervised loss is calculated for predicted outputs of the modality subsets M_{u3} and M_S, along with their labels, as shown below:

$$L_{u3}^{\text{stage2}} = -\sum_{q1=1}^{n} y_{q1} \cdot \log(\hat{y}_{q1}), \tag{14}$$

$$L_S^{\text{stage2}} = -\sum_{q2=1}^{n} y_{q2} \cdot \log(\hat{y}_{q2}). \tag{15}$$

We use adversarial loss and label loss as the objective functions for progressive modality completion learning. The overall loss function is defined as follows:

$$L_{\text{total}}^{\text{stage2}} = L_{\text{Adv}}^{\text{stage2}} + L_{u3}^{\text{stage2}} + L_S^{\text{stage2}}. \tag{16}$$

4   Experiments and Results

4.1   Dataset and Experiment Settings

We use two publicly accessible datasets in our experiment: The Tongji Dataset [9], which comprises 24,000 pictures of 600 palms taken by 300 participants. A total of 40 pictures were captured per individual, with 10 pictures taken of each palm over the two data collecting sessions, encompassing both palm vein and palmprint modalities. The 90,000 ROI pictures from 250 people, including 500 palms, make up the Tsinghua Dataset [10]. Each palm is captured in 12 images across 15 spectral bands, encompassing RGB and infrared. We use pictures of palm veins and palmprints from these spectral bands for our research.

To maintain consistency throughout the tests, all of the pictures in this study are resized to 224×224 pixels. A 1:1 ratio is used to separate each dataset into training and testing sets. The PyTorch framework and Python 3.7.16 are used in the experiments, which are conducted on an NVIDIA GeForce GTX 2080 GPU. The SGD optimiser is used to train the model for 100 epochs, with 1×10^{-4} and 1×10^{-5} for the learning rate and weight decay, respectively.

4.2 Ablation Study

To evaluate the distinct contributions of each module within the proposed architecture, we conducted a series of ablation experiments, as detailed in Table 1. We specifically introduced the SCL and PMCL, assessing their accuracy under different random missing rates, specifically 0%, 10%, 20%, 50%, 80%, and 100%.

Table 1. Ablation study results on Tongji dataset.

SCL	PMCL	Missing Ratio (%)					
		0	10	20	50	80	100
		99.66	95.08	91.27	81.13	69.35	60.83
✓		99.41	98.95	98.74	98.34	97.65	97.13
✓	✓	**99.88**	**99.85**	**99.82**	**99.80**	**99.78**	**99.75**

To evaluate module efficacy, we used VGG16 as the baseline in ablation tests on the TongJi dataset, applying a "zero-padding" method to simulate missing feature channels. The accuracy of VGG16 decreased from 99.66% (0% missing modalities) to 60.83% (100% missing). This highlights the importance of accounting for modality missingness in multi-modality recognition tasks. To address this, we proposed the first-stage SCL, which improves accuracy by 36.30% when 100% of modalities are missing, demonstrating its effectiveness in handling missing data. However, SCL does not fully utilize complete modality information during training and testing.

Thus, we constructed PMCL to progressively approximate complete modality information, enabling the model to utilize available data. The accuracy reached 99.88% with no missing modalities and dropped slightly to 99.75% with 100% missing, showing a minor decline of 0.13%. This represents a 2.62% improvement over SCL, highlighting PMCL's enhanced ability to handle missing data and perform better in situations with frequent modality loss.

4.3 Comparison with State-of-the-Art Methods

In following section, we compared the suggested approach to a number of advanced algorithms created especially to address the problem of missing modalities, including DENet [11], MFD [12], ShaSpecNet [5], MMANet [13], DrFuse [8],

Table 2. The recognition results of methods under different missing rates on the Tongji dataset.

Method	Modality Combination	Missing Ratio (%)					
		0	10	20	50	80	100
DENet [11]	[p*,v]	99.72	90.00	80.00	53.00	42.17	30.17
	[p,v*]	99.72	89.17	79.17	59.67	49.83	30.17
	[Avg]	99.72	89.59	79.59	56.34	46.00	30.17
MFD [12]	[p*,v]	98.28	97.48	95.92	91.47	86.92	83.63
	[p,v*]	98.28	94.87	92.85	80.92	70.30	68.42
	[Avg]	98.28	96.18	94.39	86.20	78.61	76.03
ShaSpecNet [5]	[p*,v]	99.07	93.00	86.82	70.82	54.67	44.17
	[p,v*]	99.07	89.17	88.33	87.33	85.83	80.67
	[Avg]	99.07	91.09	87.58	79.08	70.25	62.42
MMANet [13]	[p*,v]	99.28	99.25	99.16	99.05	98.70	98.67
	[p,v*]	99.28	99.26	99.25	99.20	99.15	98.98
	[Avg]	99.28	99.26	99.21	99.13	98.93	98.83
DrFuse [8]	[p*,v]	99.70	99.35	99.17	98.93	98.73	98.53
	[p,v*]	99.70	98.82	98.35	96.13	94.65	93.65
	[Avg]	99.70	99.09	98.76	97.53	96.69	96.09
DMRNet [14]	[p*,v]	99.35	99.25	99.13	98.88	98.67	98.55
	[p,v*]	99.35	99.25	99.02	98.72	98.36	97.94
	[Avg]	99.35	99.25	99.08	98.80	98.52	98.25
Proposed	[p*,v]	99.88	99.84	99.79	99.75	99.72	99.70
	[p,v*]	99.88	99.81	99.76	99.70	99.68	99.65
	[Avg]	99.88	99.83	99.78	99.73	99.70	99.68
	[AM]	**99.88**	**99.85**	**99.82**	**99.80**	**99.78**	**99.75**

and DMRNet [14], to evaluate its overall performance and efficacy, as indicated in Tables 2 and 3.

In the experimental setup, the palm vein modality is accessible, as indicated by [p*, v], while the palmprint modality has a fixed missing rate ranging from 0% to 100%. On the other hand, [p, v*] indicates that the palmprint modality is accessible, whereas the palm vein modality has a consistent missing rate that falls between 0% and 100%. The average Correct Recognition Rate (CRR) for the two distinct missing modality scenarios [p*, v] and [p, v*] is denoted by the word "Avg". "AM" indicates how well the suggested approach performs in situations where modalities might be omitted at random.

The findings show a decline in recognition rates for DENet, MFD, and ShaSpecNet, indicating a high sensitivity to missing data. MMANet, DrFuse, and DMRNet, on the other hand, provide comparatively consistent recognition performance under various missing situations. However, there is still room for

Table 3. The recognition results of methods under different missing rates on the Tsinghua dataset.

Method	Modality Combination	Missing Ratio (%)					
		0	10	20	50	80	100
DENet [11]	[p*,v]	98.73	89.50	79.73	59.93	48.76	41.89
	[p,v*]	98.73	90.05	80.00	60.20	46.76	32.89
	[Avg]	98.73	89.78	79.87	60.07	47.76	37.39
MFD [12]	[p*,v]	97.13	92.73	86.40	69.80	52.19	40.30
	[p,v*]	97.13	93.29	91.20	80.55	70.57	64.13
	[Avg]	97.13	93.01	88.80	75.18	61.38	52.22
ShaSpecNet [5]	[p*,v]	99.43	95.90	91.43	78.70	66.17	57.50
	[p,v*]	99.43	96.43	93.53	81.77	70.37	63.27
	[Avg]	99.43	96.17	92.48	80.24	68.27	60.39
MMANet [13]	[p*,v]	99.50	99.40	99.36	99.26	99.23	99.13
	[p,v*]	99.50	99.46	99.43	99.40	99.33	99.30
	[Avg]	99.50	99.43	99.40	99.33	99.28	99.22
DrFuse [8]	[p*,v]	99.53	97.97	97.83	96.73	95.73	95.13
	[p,v*]	99.53	96.70	94.53	88.30	83.30	80.33
	[Avg]	99.53	97.34	96.18	92.52	89.52	87.73
DMRNet [14]	[p*,v]	99.70	99.42	99.42	98.40	99.38	99.37
	[p,v*]	99.70	99.44	99.42	99.41	99.37	99.35
	[Avg]	99.70	99.43	99.42	98.91	99.38	99.36
Proposed	[p*,v]	99.89	99.85	99.80	99.72	99.68	99.65
	[p,v*]	99.89	99.86	99.84	99.82	99.78	99.75
	[Avg]	99.89	99.86	99.82	99.77	99.73	99.70
	[AM]	**99.89**	**99.88**	**99.84**	**99.80**	**99.77**	**99.73**

improvement in terms of accuracy in situations where modality is missing. By contrast, our PMCL approach outperforms the average accuracy of these methods in AM experiments, demonstrating stronger information flow and a more comprehensive semantic representation.

5   Conclusion

To address the challenge of missing modalities in real-world applications, we propose a progressive adversarial learning approach that leverages various combinations of missing modalities, enabling the joint utilization of arbitrarily missing modality combinations. Specifically, we introduce a progressive adversarial framework to create a shared space for different combinations of missing modalities, progressively capturing multi-modal semantic information that closely approximates the complete modality. The effectiveness of this progressive adversarial learning approach was validated on two public datasets. In the future, we aim to conduct an exhaustive investigation into the interaction mechanisms between modality features under missing modality conditions, with the goal of exploring potential information complementarity across available modalities.

Acknowledgements. This work was supported by the Graduate Innovation Program of China University of Mining and Technology (2024WLKXJ088), the Fundamental Research Funds for the Central Universities (2024XSCX015), and the Postgraduate Research & Practice Innovation Program of Jiangsu Province (KYCX24_2776).

References

1. Khodadoust, J., Medina-Pérez, M.A., Monroy, R., Khodadoust, A.M., Mirkamali, S.S.: A multibiometric system based on the fusion of fingerprint, finger-vein, and finger-knuckle-print. Expert Syst. Appl. **176**, 114687 (2021)
2. Alrawili, R., AlQahtani, A.A.S., Khan, M.K.: Comprehensive survey: biometric user authentication application, evaluation, and discussion. Comput. Electr. Eng. **119**, 109485 (2024)
3. Ren, H., Sun, L., Guo, J., Han, C., Cao, Y.: A high compatibility finger vein image quality assessment system based on deep learning. Expert Syst. Appl. **196**, 116603 (2022)
4. Heidari, H., Chalechale, A.: Biometric authentication using a deep learning approach based on different level fusion of finger knuckle print and fingernail. Expert Syst. Appl. **191**, 116278 (2022)
5. Wang, H., Chen, Y., Ma, C., Avery, J., Hull, L., Carneiro, G.: Multi-modal learning with missing modality via shared-specific feature modelling. In: Proceedings of the IEEE/CVF Conference on Computer Vision and Pattern Recognition, pp. 15878–15887 (2023)
6. Woo, S., Lee, S., Park, Y., Nugroho, M.A., Kim, C.: Towards good practices for missing modality robust action recognition. In: Proceedings of the AAAI Conference on Artificial Intelligence, vol. 37, pp. 2776–2784 (2023)
7. Zhang, Y., et al.: mmformer: multimodal medical transformer for incomplete multimodal learning of brain tumor segmentation. In: International Conference on Medical Image Computing and Computer-Assisted Intervention, pp. 107–117. Springer (2022)
8. Yao, W., Yin, K., Cheung, W. K., Liu, J., Qin, J.: Drfuse: learning disentangled representation for clinical multi-modal fusion with missing modality and modal inconsistency. In: Proceedings of the AAAI Conference on Artificial Intelligence, vol. 38, pp. 16416–16424 (2024)
9. Zhang, L., Li, L., Yang, A., Shen, Y., Yang, M.: Towards contactless palmprint recognition: a novel device, a new benchmark, and a collaborative representation based identification approach. Pattern Recogn. **69**, 199–212 (2017)
10. Xie, Z., Guo, Z., Qian, C.: Palmprint gender classification by convolutional neural network. IET Comput. Vision **12**(4), 476–483 (2018)
11. Zheng, A., He, Z., Wang, Z., Li, C., Tang, J.: Dynamic enhancement network for partial multi-modality person re-identification. arXiv preprint arXiv:2305.15762 (2023)

12. Kang, M., Ting, F.F., Phan, R.C.-W., Ge, Z., Ting, C.-M.: A multimodal feature distillation with CNN-transformer network for brain tumor segmentation with incomplete modalities. arXiv preprint arXiv:2404.14019 (2024)
13. Wei, S., Luo, C., Luo, Y.: Mmanet: margin-aware distillation and modality-aware regularization for incomplete multimodal learning. In: Proceedings of the IEEE/CVF Conference on Computer Vision and Pattern Recognition, pp. 20039–20049 (2023)
14. Wei, S., Luo, Y., Wang, Y., Luo, C.: Robust multimodal learning via representation decoupling. In: European Conference on Computer Vision, pp. 38–54. Springer (2024)

Learning Without Borders: A Domain-Adapted and Federated Approach to Palmprint Recognition

Congcong Jia[1], Shiyu Gu[1], Hanyu Wang[1], Qingguo Meng[1], Zhe Jin[1(✉)], Lianqiang Yang[1], Xingbo Dong[1], and Junduan Huang[2]

[1] Anhui Provincial Key Laboratory of Secure Artificial Intelligence, Anhui Provincial International Joint Research Center for Advanced Technology in Medical Imaging, School of Artificial Intelligence, Anhui University, Hefei 230093, China
`jinzhe@ahu.edu.cn`
[2] South China Normal University, Guangzhou, Guangdong, China

Abstract. Deep learning based palmprint recognition has gained wide adoption in identity authentication and security systems owing to its unique and stable biometric features. However, conventional methods rely on centralized data storage, where multi-source datasets are aggregated to train deep learning models, raising significant privacy leakage and security concerns. To mitigate these risks, we propose DAFL-Palm, a novel Federated Learning framework for palmprint recognition enhanced with Domain Adaptation (DA). DAFL-Palm employs a distributed training paradigm, allowing clients to retain raw data locally while leveraging a single-source domain adaptation technique that aligns feature distributions at both pixel and frequency levels. The framework generates a global model and an anchor model through federated aggregation, followed by joint optimization to boost recognition performance. Experimental results demonstrate that DAFL-Palm significantly improves accuracy while robustly preserving user privacy and data security.

Keywords: Palmprint Recognition · Privacy Protection · Federated Learning · Domain Adaptation

1 Introduction

Palmprint recognition, as an important research direction in the field of biometrics, have achieved remarkable progress recently [12]. Due to the uniqueness, stability, and strong anti-spoofing capability of palmprints, palmprint recognition has been widely applied in various fields such as identity authentication, financial payment, and security monitoring applications [10].

With the introduction of deep learning, methods like GaborNet [1], CO3Net [28], PDFG [21], and CCNet [25] have achieved high accuracy on multispectral palmprint datasets, sometimes reaching 99% [25]. However, they rely on centralized training, requiring all data to be uploaded to one server, which raises privacy and security risks due to centralized biometric storage [19,20].

W. Jia et al. (Eds.): CCBR 2025, LNCS 16360, pp. 79–89, 2026.
https://doi.org/10.1007/978-981-95-6123-0_8

To address privacy concerns, Federated Learning (FL) enables collaborative training by sharing model updates instead of local data, protecting user privacy [8]. FL has shown promise in biometric recognition, including palmprint. For example, Dong et al. improved cross-spectral robustness with distributed hashing learning [3], and Yang et al. proposed PSFed-Palm using physics-based spectral consistency loss to handle feature inconsistencies [26]. However, these methods overlook performance drops when generalizing to new palmprint data.

Federated palmprint recognition systems face significant challenges from domain gaps caused by varying client devices, capture conditions, and sensor characteristics, which create heterogeneous data distributions that degrade performance [6,11]. Current federated optimization methods exhibit a critical limitation: although FL can process heterogeneous data by aggregating model parameters or gradients from all clients to learn a generalized global model, it fails to adequately address the enhancement of individual clients' model generalization capabilities, neglecting client-specific optimization opportunities [7].

To address these issues, we propose DAFL-Palm, a framework combining client-side domain adaptation with FL. It uses spectral-grouped anchor models and a global consensus model, enforcing spectral consistency via Fourier alignment and histogram matching. A multi-loss scheme reduces domain shifts and model drift, enabling robust cross-device recognition while preserving privacy by avoiding raw data sharing. The main contributions are:

1. We propose DAFL-Palm, combining domain adaptation and FL with anchor models and spectral alignment for accurate, privacy-preserving cross-device palmprint recognition.
2. We use Fourier alignment and histogram matching to reduce domain gaps and apply a multi-loss strategy to address non-IID data and model drift in federated learning.
3. We conduct extensive experiments on public datasets, demonstrating our framework outperforms existing FL methods in recognition accuracy.

2   Related Work

2.1   Palmprint Recognition

Early palmprint recognition used handcrafted features like PalmCode [18] and Competitive Code [23], but lacked robustness. Fei et al. [5] proposed Palm-GAN to reduce cross-spectral feature differences and improve accuracy.

Deep learning methods like CompNet [16] improve texture modeling, while CO3Net and CCNet [25,28] enhance robustness with contrastive and multi-scale learning. Jia et al.'s PalmRSS improves generalization by exchanging low-frequency components and aligning spectral features via histogram matching [11]. However, most methods rely on centralized training, raising privacy risks [19,20], and domain gaps from sensors and lighting limit federated learning performance [6,11].

2.2   Federated Learning

FL enables privacy-preserving model training via local updates and aggregation [18], with improvements such as contrastive learning [28], FedNova [14], and FedPer [22]. These advances have also benefited palmprint recognition, where FL reduces spectral differences [4] and enhances feature consistency through grouped spectra and anchor models [26].

However, challenges persist: (1) most FL methods assume uniform client data [7]; (2) spectral and device domain gaps are underexplored. Bridging these is key for accurate, privacy-preserving palmprint recognition in real-world settings.

3   Methodology

The proposed DAFL-Palm framework is agnostic to the underlying FL aggregation strategy and can be seamlessly integrated with existing FL frameworks, as shown in Fig. 1. To validate its compatibility, we implemented DAFL-Palm using many widely-adopted FL approaches in our experiments, such as FedAvg [18], FedProx [14], FedBN [15], pFedLA [17] and so on.

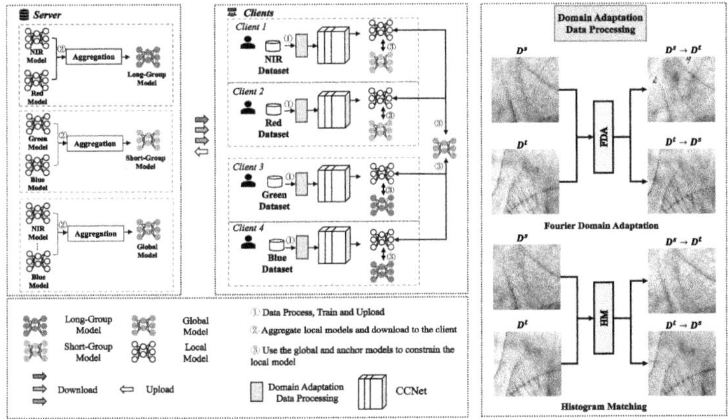

Fig. 1. The framework of the proposed method DAFL-Palm, including data processing, consists of FDA (Fourier Domain Adaptation) and HM (Histogram Matching).

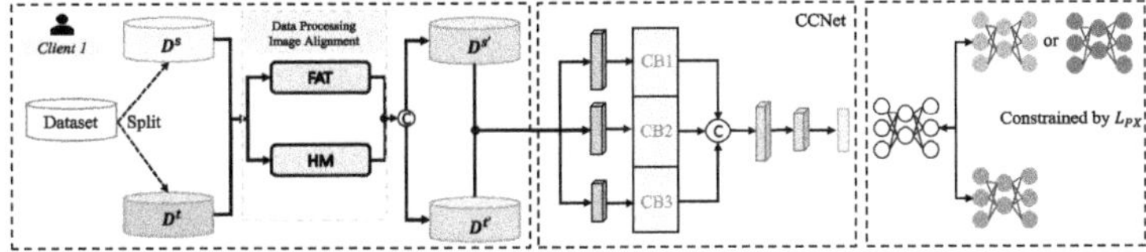

Fig. 2. The optimization process of data training on a single client involves CCNet, which is composed of three competitive blocks and three Gabor layers of different sizes.

3.1   Domain Adaptation Data Processing

Although FL avoids sharing raw data, each client's limited data makes it hard for the model to generalize. To address this, SSDA techniques like Fourier alignment and adversarial training help clients learn features that work across different devices—without leaking privacy [11].

By combining SSDA with FL, DAFL-Palm reduces client overfitting and model drift, allowing the global model to perform well on unseen devices while strictly protecting user privacy—crucial for real-world biometric applications.

Following [11], we split each client's data into training and testing sets (D^s and D^t). Inspired by FDA [24], we apply Fourier Alignment Transform (FAT) to exchange low-frequency components between samples and align spectral patterns.

Let x represents a palmprint image with height H and width W (typically $H = W = 128$ pixels), x_{D^s} and x_{D^t} denote images randomly sampled from subsets D^s and D^t. FAT swaps low-frequency amplitude spectra between images while preserving phase:

$$\mathcal{F}(x)(m,n) = \sum_{h=1}^{H}\sum_{w=1}^{W} x(h,w)e^{-j2\pi\left(\frac{h}{H}m+\frac{w}{W}n\right)}, \tag{1}$$

where $\mathcal{F}(x)(m,n)$ represents the transformed output, $x(h,w)$ is the pixel intensity of the input image, and m and n are the coordinates in the frequency domain. and $M_\beta(h,w) = \mathbb{1}_{(h,w)\in[-\beta H:\beta H,-\beta W:\beta W]}$ ($\beta = 0.1$) masks the central low-frequency region.

$$x_{D^s\to D^t} = \mathcal{F}^{-1}\left(\underbrace{\left[M_\beta \circ \mathcal{F}^A(x_{D^t}) + (1-M_\beta)\circ \mathcal{F}^A(x_{D^s})\right]}_{\text{Amplitude alignment}}, \underbrace{\mathcal{F}^P(x_{D^s})}_{\text{Phase preservation}}\right) \tag{2}$$

where $\mathcal{F}^A$ and $\mathcal{F}^P$ represent the amplitude and phase components of $\mathcal{F}(\cdot)$, respectively. $\mathcal{F}^{-1}$ denotes the inverse transformation of Fourier transform $\mathcal{F}(\cdot)$, namely the inverse Fourier transform (iFFT).

Additionally, we employ direct histogram matching (HM) to align pixel intensity distributions. HM aligns pixel intensity distributions by mapping the CDF of x_{D^s} to x_{D^t}:

$$C_{D^s}(i) = \sum_{j=0}^{i} h_{D^s}(j), \quad C_{D^t}(i) = \sum_{j=0}^{i} h_{D^t}(j), \tag{3}$$

$$x_{D^s\to D^t}(h,w) = T(x_{D^s}(h,w)), \quad T(i) = C_{D^t}^{-1}(C_{D^s}(i)). \tag{4}$$

The aligned images $F_s = \text{FAT}(x_{D^s}, x_{D^t})$ and $F_t = \text{HM}(x_{D^s}, x_{D^t})$ are concatenated:

$$F_{\text{cat}} = \text{Concat}(F_s, F_t). \tag{5}$$

Combining frequency and spatial-domain alignment (Fig. 1) with adversarial training allows clients to learn robust, domain-invariant features while maintaining data privacy, since all processing is local and no raw data is shared. The dataset split (D^s/D^t) simulates domain shifts during local training, enhancing model generalization for federated aggregation.

3.2 Federated Learning Framework for Spectral Palmprint Recognition

As shown in Fig. 1, after client-side domain adaptation, trained model parameters are uploaded to the server, which aggregates local models to generate a new global model and anchor models via the strategy in [26]. This aggregation enables knowledge integration across clients for global performance optimization.

Local Model Upload and Aggregation at the Server: Taking the multispectral (MS) dataset as an example, we denote the spectral datasets as D_{NIR}, D_R, D_G (near-infrared, red, green, blue), with corresponding locally trained models M_{NIR}, M_R, M_G, and M_B with parameters θ_{NIR}, θ_R, θ_G, and θ_B.

Based on spectral wavelength characteristics, we group the four spectra into: i) Short-Spectrum Group: $G_S = \{M_G, M_B\}$; ii) Long-Spectrum Group: $G_L = \{M_R, M_{\mathrm{NIR}}\}$. The server performs weighted aggregation within each group to generate a short-spectrum anchor model M_S (parameters θ_S), Long-spectrum anchor model M_L (parameters θ_L) and Global model M_{Global} (parameters θ_{Global}), following:

$$\theta_S = \frac{\theta_G + \theta_B}{2}, \theta_L = \frac{\theta_{\mathrm{NIR}} + \theta_R}{2}, \theta_{\mathrm{Global}} = \frac{\theta_S + \theta_L}{2}. \tag{6}$$

Model Distribution from Server: Then clients receive the global model M_{Global} and the anchor model from their complementary spectral group. Specifically, long-spectrum clients (M_R, M_{NIR}) receive M_S and short-spectrum clients (M_G, M_B) receive M_L.

Local Training Protocol: Each client k optimizes its model M_k using its local data D_k, the global model M_{Global} and the complementary anchor model (M_S or M_L). The training update rules are:

$$\text{Long-spectrum:} \quad \theta_R = \mathcal{T}(D_R, \theta_{\mathrm{Global}}, \theta_S); \theta_{\mathrm{NIR}} = \mathcal{T}(D_{\mathrm{NIR}}, \theta_{\mathrm{Global}}, \theta_S); \tag{7}$$

$$\text{Short-spectrum:} \quad \theta_G = \mathcal{T}(D_G, \theta_{\mathrm{Global}}, \theta_L); \theta_B = \mathcal{T}(D_B, \theta_{\mathrm{Global}}, \theta_L); \tag{8}$$

where $\mathcal{T}$ represents the local training procedure that preserves data privacy while incorporating knowledge from both global and anchor models. The optimization method is given in the below subsection.

Unlike the FL-based palmprint method [20] that requires sharing common data between clients and the server (which may risk privacy leakage), DAFL-Palm avoids any data sharing. Although PSFed [26] also avoids data sharing, it focuses on physics-based consistency and does not use domain adaptation. Its experiments are limited to multispectral datasets.

In contrast, DAFL-Palm combines domain adaptation with FL to improve generalization while strictly protecting privacy—each client keeps its own data, and no data transfer occurs during training.

3.3 Local Model Optimization

The local model is trained on each dataset on top of the domain adaptive data processing. The total loss is defined as:

$$\mathcal{L} = w_{\mathrm{d}} * \mathcal{L}_{cda} + w_{\mathrm{t}} * \mathcal{L}_{tsk} + w_{\mathrm{m}} * \mathcal{L}_{mse} + w_{\mathrm{p}} * \mathcal{L}_{\mathcal{PX}}, \tag{9}$$

where $\mathcal{L}_{mse}$ is the L2 loss that ensures prediction alignment between the local and auxiliary models. $w_{\mathrm{d}} = 1$, $w_{\mathrm{t}} = 1$, $w_{\mathrm{m}} = 100$, and $w_{\mathrm{p}} = 1$ are weighting hyperparameters. $\mathcal{L}_{cda}$ integrates adversarial training to improve cross-domain robustness:

$$\mathcal{L}_{cda} = -\mathbb{E}_{v_s \sim \mathcal{D}^s}[\log(A(v_s))] - \mathbb{E}_{v_t \sim \mathcal{D}^t}[\log(1 - A(v_t))]. \tag{10}$$

where $A(\cdot)$ denotes the domain discriminator, which is responsible for predicting whether a given feature representation originates from the source or target domain. The variables v_s and v_t correspond to the embedded features extracted from the subsets D^s and D^t, respectively.

The task loss ($\mathcal{L}_{tsk}$) is defined as the sum of three components:

$$\mathcal{L}_{tsk} = \mathcal{L}_{ce} + \mathcal{L}_{con} + \mathcal{L}_{sim}, \tag{11}$$

where $\mathcal{L}_{ce}$ is the standard cross-entropy loss for classification. $\mathcal{L}_{con}$ is the supervised contrastive loss, which encourages samples with the same label to be close in the feature space and those with different labels to be separated, improving representation discriminability. $\mathcal{L}_{sim}$ is the feature similarity loss, which minimizes the distance between original and augmented feature pairs, promoting robustness and reducing intra-class variation.

Surrogate loss ($\mathcal{L}_{\mathcal{PX}}$) prevents model drift by constraining the local model's parameters θ_x to stay close to the global (θ_{global}) and auxiliary (θ_{aux}) models:

$$\mathcal{L}_{\mathcal{PX}} = \frac{\mu}{2}\|\theta_x - \theta_{\mathrm{global}}\|_2^2 + \frac{\mu}{2}\|\theta_x - \theta_{\mathrm{aux}}\|_2^2. \tag{12}$$

As shown in Fig. 2, data is first split into source and target sets following [11]. Each client applies domain adaptation using FAT and HM to align spectral and intensity distributions, then trains a local model with a multi-objective loss.

After local training, clients upload model parameters for aggregation, updating global and anchor models. These are redistributed for continued training, enabling privacy-preserving, device-independent palmprint recognition with consistent and robust performance across domains.

4   Experiments

4.1   Experiment Settings

To evaluate DAFL-Palm, multiple public palmprint and palm vein datasets are used following the grouping strategy in [26]. Group details and sample sizes are listed in Table 1. For CasiaM, three groupings (CaM1, CaM2, CaM3) examine the impact of wavelength-based grouping on domain adaptation. Dataset sizes are balanced for fair training. For other groupings (e.g., CaM13, TPI12, TVP), training follows the same protocol as MS, with Group 2 using a single dataset serving as both local and anchor model.

Table 1. Grouping of Different Palmprint Datasets.

Settings	Group1	Group2	Numbers
Multi-Spectral (MS) [29]	Red, NIR	Green, Blue	$500 \times 12 \times 4$
CaM1 [9]	460,700	850	$200 \times 6 \times 3$
CaM2 [9]	460,850	700	$200 \times 6 \times 3$
CaM3 [9]	700,850	460	$200 \times 6 \times 3$
TPI1	Tongji [31], PolyU [30]	IITD [13]	$378 \times 5 \times 3$
TPI2	Tongji [31], IITD [13]	PolyU [30]	$378 \times 5 \times 3$
TVP	Tongji [31], Tongji-PV [31]	PolyU [30]	$378 \times 20 \times 3$

*Numbers = Number of IDs $\times$ Samples per ID $\times$ Number of spectral/modalities

We use Equal Error Rate (EER) and recognition accuracy as evaluation metrics. The model is trained on D_s and D_t using DAFL-Palm and tested on D_t. EER is computed based on features from D_t using cosine distance, following [11]. We compare various FL aggregation methods, including FedAvg [18], FedProx [14], FedBN [15], pFedLA [17], FedPer [22], FedProto [2], HyperFed [27], and those used in PSFed [26].

We use CCNet [25] as DAFL-Palm's network architecture. We also compare DAFL-Palm with PSFed, which employs a specific network and aggregation method, as detailed in Sect. 4.2.

4.2   Performance Evaluation

Performance of Various Dataset Groupings. Firstly, for the MS scenario, two federated learning aggregation strategies are evaluated, with results in Table 2. The proposed DAFL-Palm method consistently achieves the lowest EER compared to other strategies and PSFed. Additionally, FedAvg outperforms PSFed, indicating improved domain generalization.

Secondly, Table 3 shows results for different scenarios and aggregation strategies on the CasiaM dataset. Under the same strategy, different groupings yield

Table 2. EER(%) under different groupings of the MS.

Method $\diagdown^{D_t}_{D_s}$	NIR	Red	Green	Blue	NIR	Red	Green	Blue
Ours NIR	0.0011	0	0	0	0.0067	0	0.2182	0.3451
Red	0.0111	0	0	0	0.0078	0	0	0
Green	0	0	0	0	0.0423	0	0	0
Blue	0	0	0	0	0.0924	0	0	0
PSFed NIR	0.0400	0.0245	0.1071	0.1000	0.0900	0.7792	12.3400	15.2900
Red	0.0500	0.0200	0.0600	0.0449	0.5300	0.0095	0.8829	1.3056
Green	0.1500	0.0526	0.0300	0.0400	12.2570	0.8500	0.0400	0.1100
Blue	0.1600	0.0500	0.0371	0.0211	17.5500	1.5200	0.1107	0.0800

varied performance. The grouping in the table achieves the lowest EER, suggesting that grouping wavelengths with higher similarity improves model stability and performance. Aggregation strategies have limited impact on this dataset.

Table 3. Average EER of CasiaM in Different Scenarios (%) and TVP EER (%)

Method	FedAvg			FedBN	pFedLA	Method	FedAvg			FedProx		
$D_s \diagdown^{SE}$	CaM1	CaM2	CaM3	CaM1	CaM1	$D_s \diagdown^{D_t}$	Tongji	Tongji-PV	PolyU	Tongji	Tongji-PV	PolyU
460	0.5408	0.5615	0.5076	0.5674	0.5089	Tongji	0.0351	0.1799	0.0529	0.0518	0.1878	0.0529
700	0.4992	0.5000	0.4626	0.5359	0.5311	Tongji-PV	0.1032	0.1806	0.0529	0.1280	0.2347	0.0503
850	0.5272	0.5370	0.5000	0.5921	0.5267	PolyU	0.0767	0.1496	0.0472	0.0794	0.1852	0.0385

We evaluate the performance of TVP and TPI datasets under various scenarios and aggregation strategies. Results in Table 3 and Table 4 show that both datasets achieve low EER across different strategies, confirming the effectiveness of our method.

4.3   Ablation Study

Table 5 evaluates component effectiveness: single transforms cause performance degradation due to limited spatial/frequency feature extraction. Pairwise combinations yield marginal improvements but lack adequate constraint. Bold results with all components achieve optimal performance, validating synergistic effectiveness.

Table 4. EER of the TPI (%).

Method	TPI1 Ours FedAvg			TPI1 Ours pFedLA			TPI2 Ours FedAvg			TPI2 Ours pFedLA		
D_t D_s	Tongji	PolyU	IITD	Tongji	PolyU	IITD	Tongji	PolyU	IITD	Tongji	PolyU	IITD
Tongji	0.2654	0.0079	2.5794	0.1984	0.0142	2.5132	0.2137	0.0032	2.4471	0.1665	0.0028	2.5532
PolyU	0.2546	0.0042	2.7848	0.2646	0.0002	2.5132	0.2646	0.0044	2.5269	0.2646	0	2.7822
IITD	0.3968	0.0104	2.3245	0.3968	0.0079	1.7857	0.3307	0.0040	2.2487	0.3968	0.0081	1.7196

Table 5. Ablation Results of Different Components under the $FedAvg$ Aggregation Strategy Based on $CaM3$ grouping setting.

HM	FAT	$\mathcal{L}_{cda}$	EER(%)
✓	✗	✗	0.5831
✗	✓	✗	0.5512
✗	✗	✓	0.5141
✓	✓	✗	0.5139
✓	✗	✓	0.6165
✗	✓	✓	0.6061
✓	✓	✓	**0.4901**

5 Conclusion

In this work, we propose DAFL-Palm, a privacy-preserving palmprint recognition framework that integrates domain adaptation with federated learning (FL). By keeping raw palmprint data local and only sharing model updates, it avoids privacy leakage risks from direct data transmission. To address cross-device domain gaps caused by varying devices and capture conditions, the framework incorporates client-side Fourier alignment and histogram matching for domain-invariant feature learning, paired with a multi-loss scheme to prevent model drift—ensuring competitive recognition accuracy despite communication-related information loss. Notably, DAFL-Palm is not limited to palmprint recognition; its design can be extended to other biometric modalities (e.g., fingerprint, finger-vein) where privacy-preserving distributed learning is critical, offering broad application potential.

Acknowledgments. This work was supported by the National Natural Science Foundation of China (Nos. 62376003) and Anhui Provincial Natural Science Foundation (No. 2308085MF200)

References

1. Alekseev, A., Bobe, A.: Gabornet: gabor filters with learnable parameters in deep convolutional neural network. In: 2019 International Conference on Engineering and Telecommunication (EnT), pp. 1–4. IEEE (2019)
2. Dai, Y., Chen, Z., Li, J., Heinecke, S., Sun, L., Xu, R.: Tackling data heterogeneity in federated learning with class prototypes. In: Proceedings of the AAAI Conference on Artificial Intelligence, vol. 37, pp. 7314–7322 (2023)
3. Dong, X., Khan, M.K., Leng, L., Teoh, A.B.J.: Co-learning to hash palm biometrics for flexible IoT deployment. IEEE Internet Things J. **9**(23), 23786–23794 (2022)
4. Dong, X., Khan, M.K., Leng, L., Teoh, A.B.J.: Co-learning to hash palm biometrics for flexible iot deployment. IEEE Internet Things J. **9**(23), 23786–23794 (2022)
5. Fei, L., Wong, W.K., Zhao, S., Wen, J., Zhu, J., Xu, Y.: Learning spectrum-invariance representation for cross-spectral palmprint recognition. IEEE Trans. Syst. Man Cybern. Syst. **53**(6), 3868–3879 (2023)
6. Fei, L., Zhang, B., Jia, W., Wen, J., Zhang, D.: Feature extraction for 3-D palmprint recognition: a survey. IEEE Trans. Instrum. Meas. **69**(3), 645–656 (2020)
7. Fu, L., Zhang, H., Gao, G., Zhang, M., Liu, X.: Client selection in federated learning: principles, challenges, and opportunities. IEEE Internet Things J. **10**(24), 21811–21819 (2023)
8. Guendouzi, B.S., Ouchani, S., Assaad, H.E., Zaher, M.E.: A systematic review of federated learning: challenges, aggregation methods, and development tools. J. Netw. Comput. Appl. **220**, 103714 (2023)
9. Hao, Y., Sun, Z., Tan, T., Ren, C.: Multispectral palm image fusion for accurate contact-free palmprint recognition. In: 2008 15th IEEE International Conference on Image Processing, pp. 281–284. IEEE (2008)
10. Jain, A.K., Deb, D., Engelsma, J.J.: Biometrics: trust, but verify. IEEE Trans. Biometrics Behavior Identity Sci. **4**(3), 303–323 (2021)
11. Jia, C., et al.: Single source domain generalization for palm biometrics. Pattern Recognit. 111620 (2025)
12. Jia, W., et al.: Palmprint recognition based on complete direction representation. IEEE Trans. Image Process. **26**(9), 4483–4498 (2017)
13. Kumar, A., Shekhar, S.: Personal identification using multibiometrics rank-level fusion. IEEE Trans. Syst. Man Cybern. Part C (Appl. Rev.) **41**(5), 743–752 (2010)
14. Li, T., Sahu, A.K., Zaheer, M., Sanjabi, M., Talwalkar, A., Smith, V.: Federated optimization in heterogeneous networks. Proc. Mach. Learn. Syst. **2**, 429–450 (2020)
15. Li, X., Jiang, M., Zhang, X., Kamp, M., Dou, Q.: Fedbn: federated learning on non-IID features via local batch normalization. In: 9th International Conference on Learning Representations, ICLR 2021, Virtual Event, Austria, 3–7 May 2021. OpenReview.net (2021). https://openreview.net/forum?id=6YEQUn0QICG
16. Liang, X., Yang, J., Lu, G., Zhang, D.: Compnet: competitive neural network for palmprint recognition using learnable gabor kernels. IEEE Signal Process. Lett. **28**, 1739–1743 (2021)
17. Ma, X., Zhang, J., Guo, S., Xu, W.: Layer-wised model aggregation for personalized federated learning. In: Proceedings of the IEEE/CVF Conference on Computer Vision and Pattern Recognition, pp. 10092–10101 (2022)
18. McMahan, B., Moore, E., Ramage, D., Hampson, S., y Arcas, B.A.: Communication-efficient learning of deep networks from decentralized data. In: Artificial Intelligence and Statistics, pp. 1273–1282. PMLR (2017)

19. Nandakumar, K., Jain, A.K.: Biometric template protection: bridging the performance gap between theory and practice. IEEE Signal Process. Mag. **32**(5), 88–100 (2015)
20. Shao, H., Zhong, D.: Towards privacy palmprint recognition via federated hash learning. Electron. Lett. **56**(25), 1418–1420 (2020)
21. Shao, H., Zou, Y., Liu, C., Guo, Q., Zhong, D.: Learning to generalize unseen dataset for cross-dataset palmprint recognition. IEEE Trans. Inf. Forensics Secur. (2024)
22. Dinh, C.T., Tran, N., Nguyen, J.: Personalized federated learning with moreau envelopes. Adv. Neural Inf. Process. Syst. **33**, 21394–21405 (2020)
23. Xu, Y., Fei, L., Wen, J., Zhang, D.: Discriminative and robust competitive code for palmprint recognition. IEEE Trans. Syst. Man Cybern. Syst. **48**(2), 232–241 (2016)
24. Yang, Y., Soatto, S.: FDA: fourier domain adaptation for semantic segmentation. In: Proceedings of the IEEE/CVF Conference on Computer Vision and Pattern Recognition, pp. 4085–4095 (2020)
25. Yang, Z., Huangfu, H., Leng, L., Zhang, B., Teoh, A.B.J., Zhang, Y.: Comprehensive competition mechanism in palmprint recognition. IEEE Trans. Inf. Forensics Secur. **18**, 5160–5170 (2023)
26. Yang, Z., Teoh, A.B.J., Zhang, B., Leng, L., Zhang, Y.: Physics-driven spectrum-consistent federated learning for palmprint verification. Int. J. Comput. Vision 1–16 (2024)
27. Yang, Z., Xia, W., Lu, Z., Chen, Y., Li, X., Zhang, Y.: Hypernetwork-based physics-driven personalized federated learning for CT imaging. IEEE Trans. Neural Netw. Learn. Syst. (2023)
28. Yang, Z., et al.: Co3net: coordinate-aware contrastive competitive neural network for palmprint recognition. IEEE Trans. Instrum. Meas. **72**, 1–14 (2023)
29. Zhang, D., Guo, Z., Lu, G., Zhang, L., Zuo, W.: An online system of multispectral palmprint verification. IEEE Trans. Instrum. Meas. **59**(2), 480–490 (2009)
30. Zhang, D., Kong, W.K., You, J., Wong, M.: Online palmprint identification. IEEE Trans. Pattern Anal. Mach. Intell. **25**(9), 1041–1050 (2003)
31. Zhang, L., Li, L., Yang, A., Shen, Y., Yang, M.: Towards contactless palmprint recognition: a novel device, a new benchmark, and a collaborative representation based identification approach. Pattern Recogn. **69**, 199–212 (2017)

Cross-Domain Palmprint Cryptosystems via Image Alignment and Neural Error Correction

Yanhong Qian, Xinyue Liu, Fuyou Leng, Hui Zhang, Xingbo Dong, and Zhe Jin[✉]

Anhui Provincial Key Laboratory of Secure Artificial Intelligence, Anhui Provincial International Joint Research Center for Advanced Technology in Medical Imaging, School of Artificial Intelligence, Anhui University, Hefei 230093, China
`jinzhe@ahu.edu.cn`

Abstract. To address the challenges of feature instability and domain shift in palmprint key generation under cross-dataset and open-set scenarios, this paper proposes the PalmOKey framework. The framework extracts discriminative and domain-invariant features through a Single-Source Domain Generalization (SSDG)-enhanced Comprehensive Competition Network (CCNet) and combines a fuzzy commitment scheme based on Neural Low-Density Parity-Check (LDPC) codes to achieve reliable key generation. Experimental results show that PalmOKey performs excellently in cross-dataset key generation tasks: when MS_Blue is used as the source dataset and Tongji as the target dataset, the True Acceptance Rate (TAR) at a False Acceptance Rate (FAR) of 0% reaches 99.97%; the Equal Error Rate (EER) on the Tongji dataset is as low as 0.0000, significantly outperforming existing methods.

Keywords: Biometrics · Key generation · Palmprint Recognition · Single-Source Domain Generalization · CCNet · Fuzzy Commitment

1 Introduction

Biometric technology has become an ideal alternative to traditional authentication methods [1]. Among various biometrics, palmprints hold great potential in high-security applications due to their large surface area, rich features, and easy acquisition [2]. However, like other biometric traits, palmprint templates face severe security risks if unprotected. Unauthorized access to these templates may enable attackers to reconstruct original palmprint patterns or forge traits to bypass authentication, thus threatening user privacy and system security. Biometric template protection (BTP) mechanisms provide an effective solution to this problem [3]. They secure palmprint data without impairing authentication functionality: by transforming or encrypting templates, BTP retains the critical features necessary for valid identity verification, while ensuring that even leaked

W. Jia et al. (Eds.): CCBR 2025, LNCS 16360, pp. 90–100, 2026.
https://doi.org/10.1007/978-981-95-6123-0_9

protected data cannot be reversed to recover original palmprints or used for forgery, making it a key safeguard for palmprint recognition systems.

Despite the protection offered by BTP, generating stable cryptographic keys from palmprints remains challenging due to two core issues: First, feature instability: palmprint features are susceptible to physiological changes and acquisition variations, making it difficult to bridge the noise gap between biometric features and cryptographic keys [4]. Second is the domain shift problem: models trained on single-source data exhibit significant performance degradation in cross-dataset and open-set scenarios, struggling to adapt to device and environmental diversity in practical applications [5].

To tackle these issues, this paper proposes the PalmOKey framework, which addresses the above challenges through two core innovations. On the one hand, PalmOKey adopts a Comprehensive Competition Network (CCNet) that enhances the comprehensive single source domain generalization (SSDG) [8] to extract domain-invariant discriminative features, improving the generalization ability between domains. On the other hand, PalmOKey designs a fuzzy commitment scheme based on a neural low-density parity-check (LDPC) code, using a neural decoder to adaptively correct noise and ensure the stability of key generation. Based on these innovations, the main contributions of this paper are threefold.

1. We propose a new cross-domain palmprint cryptosystem, PalmOKey. It handles feature instability and domain shift in cross-dataset and open-set palmprint key generation, enabling more reliable practical security applications.
2. PalmOKey constructs a domain-adaptive palmprint feature extraction pipeline that integrates single-source domain generalization technology with a comprehensive competition network.
3. We innovatively applies the neural LDPC code-based fuzzy commitment scheme to palmprint biocryptosystems, optimizing error correction performance through the adaptive learning ability of the Neural-Min-Sum (NMS) decoder.

The following sections will elaborate on the method design, experimental setup and results, followed by a concluding discussion and outlook.

2   Related Work

Palmprint recognition has become an important research direction in the field of biometrics, with biometric template protection (BTP) and secure key generation as the core pillars of its security architecture. According to the ISO/IEC 24745 standard [6], BTP has three clear security requirements: irreversibility, revocability, and unlinkability. These standards are deeply related to secure key generation, as cryptographic keys derived from palmprint features must comply with BTP requirements to balance security and practicality. Existing studies [9, 16–18] have explored feature processing and key generation, but they struggle to meet all three BTP standards simultaneously.

In terms of feature transformation and encryption, early methods attempted to balance effectiveness and BTP compliance but had limitations. Leng et al.'s dual-key method [9] protected features through dual-key-binding chaotic scrambling, but its reliance on handcrafted features limited discriminability and hindered strict irreversibility. Similarly, Wang et al.'s one-factor method [16] used Orthogonal Index of Maximum (OIOM) hashing and Minimum Signature Hash (MSH) to enhance protection. Though it avoided external tokens by generating pseudonymous identifiers directly from features, its fixed feature mappings undermined unlinkability, and its cross-domain adaptability remained unvalidated.

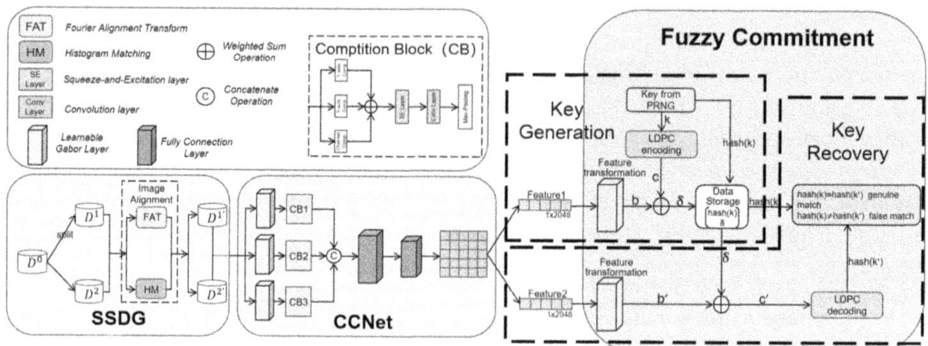

Fig. 1. Overview of the *PalmOKey*. The figure illustrates the proposed model framework, integrating three core modules. First, SSDG partitions the single-source dataset and aligns images via FAT and HM. Then, CCNet extracts comprehensive competitive features. Finally, Fuzzy Commitment generates keys from the features.

Secure key generation within the BTP framework faces the challenge of aligning biometric features with cryptographic keys. Liu et al.'s PalmKeyNet [17] utilized deep CNNs to map palmprint and palm vein features into a unified key space and combined them with LDPC coding for error correction. While it improved key discriminability, its fixed architecture required full model retraining for template updates, violating BTP's revocability requirement. Meanwhile, Liu et al.'s PalmSecMatch [18] enhanced security through random transformation but relied on raw features, introducing irreversibility risks, as raw features could potentially be reverse-engineered to reconstruct original biometrics and undermine a core pillar of BTP.

3   Proposed Method

3.1   Overview

Figure 1 presents the overall framework of the proposed model, which integrates three key components: Single Source Domain Generalization (SSDG) technology, the Comprehensive Competitive Network (CCNet [8]), and fuzzy commitment key generation technology. CCNet enhances feature discriminability by extracting multi-scale and multi-order palmprint textures through combined channel and spatial competition mechanisms, and it is designed to achieve high-accuracy palmprint recognition using learnable Gabor filters and hybrid loss optimization to capture comprehensive texture information for robust identity verification.

3.2 Single Source Domain Generalization (SSDG)

The core idea of **SSDG** is to train a model using only data from a single source domain, enabling it to effectively generalize to unseen target domains. To achieve this goal, SSDG adopts an innovative strategy: the single-source dataset D^0 is divided into two subsets D^1 and D^2. By simulating domain shifts, the single-source generalization problem is transformed into a more manageable domain generalization framework, thereby enhancing the model's adaptability to unknown target domains.

To achieve effective alignment between subsets, SSDG integrates two key image alignment techniques. First, **Fourier Alignment Transform (FAT)** is employed in the spectral domain: images from D^1 and D^2 are respectively subjected to the Fast Fourier Transform (FFT) to obtain amplitude and phase components. The low-frequency amplitude components of images in D^1 are replaced with the corresponding components from D^2 using a mask, followed by image reconstruction via the Inverse Fast Fourier Transform (iFFT). This process effectively aligns the low-frequency statistics of different subsets, reducing spectral domain shifts caused by imaging differences.

Second, **Histogram Matching (HM)** is used in the spatial domain: by calculating the Cumulative Distribution Functions (CDFs) of pixel intensities for D^1 and D^2, a mapping function is constructed to adjust the pixel values of D^1 images to match the histogram distribution of D^2. This aligns the pixel-level statistical properties between subsets, further mitigating domain shifts in the spatial domain and ensuring stable model performance when processing diverse datasets.

3.3 Fuzzy Commitment

In bio-encryption, this paper employs a fuzzy commitment scheme to generate cryptographic keys from extracted palmprint features. This scheme ensures key consistency and biometric privacy despite acquisition noise and feature variations. Its core principle is to bind the secret key with biometric data through Error Correction Codes (ECC), enabling reliable reconstruction of the original key in noisy environments. The entire process is divided into the enrollment stage and the verification stage.

During the enrollment stage, discriminative palmprint features from input images are first processed through the AdaMTrans pipeline from [10]: real-valued features are quantized into integers, converted into a binary template via linearly separable subcode binarization (LSSC) [11], and then an adaptive random mask [10] is applied. This step precisely aligns the Bit Error Rate (BER) generated by biometric data with the error-correcting capability of the selected Low-Density Parity-Check (LDPC) encoder, narrowing the noise gap between biometric variations and the ECC correction margin. After generating the binary template b, a random secret key k is generated and converted into a codeword c using a 5G NR LDPC encoder. Finally, the commitment $\delta = b \oplus c$ and the hash of k (e.g., SHA-3) are computed and stored, ensuring the stored commitment does not reveal the original key or template.

In the verification stage, upon receiving a user's query image, a new binary template b' is generated through the same AdaMTrans pipeline. Using the stored δ, the candidate codeword $c' = b' \oplus \delta$ is recovered and input into the supervised learning-driven Neural-Min-Sum (NMS) [12] decoder designed in this paper. By optimizing normalization parameters and offset factors, this decoder can more robustly correct errors in c' to recover the original codeword c, requiring fewer iterations than traditional hard-decision decoders. If the decoded codeword matches the stored content, authentication succeeds and the key k is recovered; otherwise, authentication fails.

4 Experiments and Results

4.1 Datasets and Experimental Setup

This paper adopts four public palmprint datasets: **PolyU** [7], **Multi-Spectral (MS)** [13], **Tongji** [14], and **CasiaM** [15] with acquisition methods covering contact-based (**PolyU**), multi-spectral (**MS**), and contactless (**Tongji**, **CasiaM**)to simulate diverse practical scenarios. For the experiment, specific bands and sample sizes are selected from each dataset: the **MS** dataset uses 1200 images from the blue band, the **CasiaM** dataset uses 1200 images from the 460nm band, and the remaining datasets participate in the experiment with their complete sample distributions. These datasets provide a rich benchmark for evaluating the robustness and generalization ability of the method. Dataset partitioning follows the standard strategy for SSDG, with each dataset split into a training set (D^1) and a test set (D^2) in a 1:1 ratio. In terms of implementation, PalmOKey is built on the PyTorch framework, and the experimental environment is as follows: Intel(R) Xeon(R) CPU E5-2680 v4 @ 2.40GHz, 24 GB internal storage, and RTX 2080Ti graphics card.

4.2 Evaluation Metrics

The key evaluation metrics include the **Equal Error Rate (EER)**, which refers to the point where the False Acceptance Rate (FAR) is equal to the

False Rejection Rate (FRR); a lower EER indicates better discriminative performance of the model. Another metric is the **True Accept Rate at a given FAR (TAR@FAR)**, representing the proportion of genuine samples correctly accepted under a predefined FAR threshold.

Table 1. Cross-Dataset EERs

Source	Target			
	Tongji	PolyU	CasiaM_460	MS_Blue
Tongji	0.0000	0.0273	0.0753	0.0157
PolyU	0.0747	0.0047	0.1233	0.0303
CasiaM_460	0.0330	0.0350	0.0013	0.0153
MS_Blue	0.0593	0.0450	0.1267	0.0037

Table 2. Key Generation Performance Based on NMS decoder (TAR@FAR = 0%)

Source	Target			
	Tongji	PolyU	CasiaM_460	MS_Blue
Tongji	-	98.63	96.40	98.43
PolyU	99.20	-	97.69	99.77
CasiaM_460	97.67	99.39	-	97.53
MS_Blue	99.97	96.50	90.13	-

Table 3. Decoder Comparison (TAR@FAR = 0%)

Scenario	MS	SP	NMS
PolyU → Tongji	99.25	99.20	**99.27**
CasiaM460 → Tongji	97.99	97.67	**98.07**
MS_Blue → Tongji	99.85	99.97	**99.97**

4.3   Experiments

To verify the model's recognition performance in cross dataset scenarios, we conducted experiments using palmprint features extracted by CCNet. We selected four datasets: Tongji, PolyU, CasiaM_460, and MS_Blue. We set up different combinations of source domains (Source) and target domains (Target) to calculate the EER. The results are presented in Table 1. Main diagonal data like Tongji→Tongji (0.0000) and PolyU→PolyU (0.0047) near 0 confirm CCNet enables precise same-domain recognition. Off-diagonal data such as Tongji→PolyU (0.0273) and PolyU→Tongji (0.0747) show SSDG enhances cross-domain adaptation, making the experiment a comprehensive test of generalization.

To verify cross-dataset key generation performance, we used the NMS decoder (TAR@FAR = 0%) on the same four datasets. As shown in the results in Table 2, MS_Blue→Tongji achieves 99.97% TAR (optimal), and PolyU→MS_Blue reaches 99.77%, showing the method's reliability and advantages in practical cross-dataset key generation.

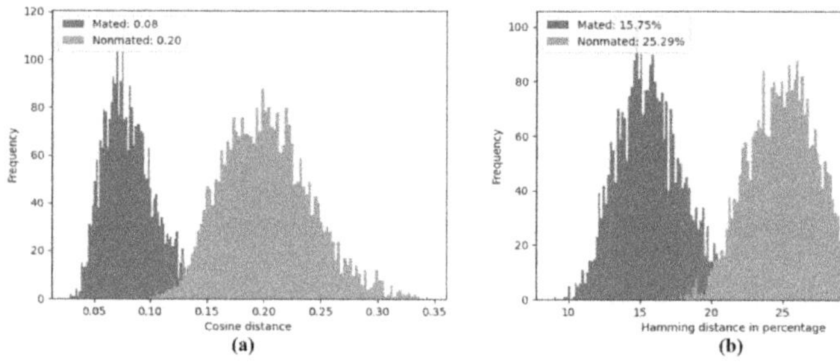

Fig. 2. Distance distributions of mated and nonmated pairs for SSDG-enhanced CCNet features using the NMS decoder. (a) Cosine distance distributions. (b) Hamming distance distributions (in percentage).

We tested the combination of SSDG-enhanced CCNet and the NMS decoder, using PolyU as the source dataset and Tongji as the target dataset to analyze the distance distributions of mated and non-mated pairs. Figure 2(a) shows that the distribution of mated pairs peaks sharply, with approximately 8% of pairs concentrated within a very small cosine distance interval near zero, while the distribution of non-mated pairs is much broader, with about 20% spread over a larger range of distances, Fig. 2(b) shows that the Hamming distances of mated pairs are concentrated within a range that falls under the error-correction capability of the LDPC code. This result reflects the core role of the NMS decoder: it effectively reduces intra-class distances and expands inter-class differences during the iterative update of information between variable nodes and check nodes, which is consistent with its design goal of enhancing error correction capability through optimizing the iterative update mechanism.

4.4   Ablation Studies

To verify the advantages of neural LDPC decoders in handling cross-domain noise and biometric variations, this section conducts ablation studies to analyze the impact of different decoders on key generation performance. The experiments use PolyU, CasiaM_460, and MS_Blue as source domains, with the Tongji dataset as the target domain, comparing the key generation performance (evaluated by $TAR@FAR = 0\%$) of the standard Sum-Product (SP) [19], traditional Min-Sum (MS) [20], and NMS decoders in cross-dataset scenarios. As shown in Table 3, NMS achieves the best performance in all scenarios. This advantage is derived from NMS optimizing normalization parameters and offset factors through supervised learning, allowing adaptive correction of complex errors caused by domain shifts and biometric noise. In contrast, SP and MS rely on fixed parameters and struggle to handle dynamic variations.

Table 4. Comparison of Palmprint Template Protection Methods

Method	Feature Extractor	Key Generation/Protection	EER (Dataset:Tongji)
Dual-key [9]	Gabor filters, handcrafted features	Dual-key chaotic scrambling with BCH error correction	0.3020
One-Factor [16]	CompCode features, orthogonal GRP	OIOM hash+MSH; XOR with random string for helper data; pseudonymous identifiers via MSH	0.0032
PalmKeyNet [17] (EfficientNet-B5)	EfficientNet-B5	Multi-modal shared key via dual sub-networks	0.0330
PalmKeyNet [17] (ResNet18)	ResNet18	Multi-modal shared key via dual sub-networks	0.0420
PalmKeyNet [17] (MobileNetV2)	MobileNetV2	Multi-modal shared key via dual sub-networks	0.0830
PalmSecMatch [18]	Original palmprint feature vector	Data self-encryption + shuffle basis + checksum + functional encryption	0.0002
PalmOKey (Ours)	SSDG + CCNet	NMS LDPC Fuzzy Commitment	0.0000

4.5   Comparison with State-of-the-Art Methods

To fully demonstrate the advantages of the proposed PalmOKey method in palmprint template protection and key generation tasks, this section compares it with four mainstream palmprint template protection methods under consistent experimental conditions. As shown in Table 4, we compare the performance of the proposed PalmOKey method with four mainstream palmprint template protection methods (Dual-key [9], One-Factor [16], PalmKeyNet [17], and PalmSecMatch [18]). All methods are evaluated on the Tongji dataset, focusing on three core dimensions: feature extractor, key generation/protection mechanism, and EER.

In contrast, the proposed PalmOKey achieves an EER value of 0.0000 on the Tongji dataset, which demonstrates significant performance advantages. This dataset is specifically selected because EER on Tongji is a unified evaluation metric consistently reported in the literature for all compared methods. Its core strengths are reflected in three aspects: first, high efficiency in feature extraction, as the combination of SSDG and CCNet reduces computational complexity while ensuring feature discriminability; second, a more reliable key protection mechanism, where NMS LDPC fuzzy commitment technology effectively enhances the key's anti-attack capability; third, better comprehensive performance, as the zero EER value verifies its ability to balance palmprint recognition accuracy and template security, providing an efficient and feasible new solution for palmprint template protection tasks.

5   Security Analysis

The PalmOKey framework achieves significant improvements in multi-dimensional security through a fuzzy commitment-based biometric cryptosystem, which adopts a neural LDPC decoding scheme and an adaptive masking strategy. In terms of irreversibility, the cryptographic key generation process relies on binarized palmprint features processed through the AdaMTrans pipeline. This transformation ensures that even if stored commitments are compromised, attackers cannot reverse-engineer the original palmprint patterns. For unlinkability, each user is assigned a unique random mask during registration. This mask is applied to the binary template before generating the commitment, ensuring that encrypted outputs from different applications cannot be linked to the same user. Even if multiple encrypted commitments are obtained, attackers cannot establish user identity links across scenarios, thereby protecting cross-application privacy. Regarding revocability, the system supports seamless template updates without re-collecting palmprints. When a security breach occurs, users can generate new masks and keys to create new commitments, avoiding re-registration while invalidating leaked data. In summary, through the integrated design of feature transformation, neural error correction, and random masking, PalmOKey meets the three core security requirements of ISO/IEC 24745 [6], balances the uniqueness of biometric features with cryptographic security, and lays a solid foundation for a highly reliable palmprint key generation system.

6   Conclusion

The core innovations of this framework lie in the organic integration of two key technologies: on one hand, a SSDG-based feature extraction pipeline is built, which simulates domain shifts through FAT and HM, effectively enhancing CCNet's ability to discriminate cross-domain features; on the other hand, a neural LDPC fuzzy commitment scheme is designed, which utilizes the NMS decoder to adaptively correct biometric noise, controlling the key recovery error within the LDPC error-correction range and significantly improving the stability of key generation.

Experimental verification shows that PalmOKey achieves state-of-the-art performance in multi-dataset evaluations: EER on the Tongji dataset reaches 0.0000, significantly outperforming existing methods; the maximum TAR@FAR$=0\%$ in cross-dataset scenarios reaches 99.97% (MS_Blue$\rightarrow$Tongji). Further ablation experiments confirm that compared with traditional SP and MS decoders, the NMS decoder can increase TAR by 0.02%-0.3% in cross-domain scenarios, fully verifying the effectiveness of each component.

Acknowledgments. This work was supported by the National Natural Science Foundation of China (No. 62376003) and Anhui Provincial Natural Science Foundation (No. 2308085MF200).

References

1. Uludag, U., Pankanti, S., Prabhakar, S., et al.: Biometric cryptosystems: issues and challenges. Proc. IEEE **92**(6), 948–960 (2004)
2. Gao, C., Yang, Z., Jia, W., Leng, L., Zhang, B., Teoh, A.B.J.: Deep Learning in Palmprint Recognition-A Comprehensive Survey. arXiv preprint arXiv:2501.01166 (2025)
3. Kim, S., Paik, S., Hwang, C., Kim, D., Shin, J., Seo, J.H.: IDFace: Face Template Protection for Efficient and Secure Identification. arXiv (2025). https://arxiv.org/abs/2507.12050
4. Qiu, J., Li, H., Zhao, C.: Cancelable palmprint templates based on random measurement and noise data for security and privacy-preserving authentication. Comput. Secur. **82**, 1–14 (2019)
5. Ganin, Y., Lempitsky, V.: Unsupervised domain adaptation by backpropagation. In: Proceedings of the 32nd International Conference on Machine Learning, in Proceedings of Machine Learning Research, vol. 37, pp. 1180–1189 (2015). https://proceedings.mlr.press/v37/ganin15.html
6. International Organization for Standardization: Information security, cybersecurity and privacy protection — biometric information protection. Standard, ISO 24745:22, International Organization for Standardization, Geneva, CH (2022)
7. Zhang, D., Kong, W.-K., You, J., Wong, M.: Online palmprint identification. IEEE Trans. Pattern Anal. Mach. Intell. **25**(9), 1041–1050 (2003)
8. Yang, Z., Huangfu, H., Leng, L., Zhang, B., Teoh, A.B.J., Zhang, Y.: Comprehensive competition mechanism in palmprint recognition. IEEE Trans. Inf. Forensics Secur. (2023)
9. Leng, L., Zhang, J.: Dual-key-binding cancelable palmprint cryptosystem for palmprint protection and information security. J. Netw. Comput. Appl. **34**(6), 1979–1989 (2011)
10. Dong, X., et al.: WiFaKey: generating cryptographic keys from face in the wild. IEEE Trans. Instrum. Meas. **73**, 1–16 (2024)

11. Lim, M.-H., Teoh, A.B.J.: A novel encoding scheme for effective biometric discretization: linearly separable subcode. IEEE Trans. Pattern Anal. Mach. Intell. **35**(2), 300–313 (2013)
12. Dai, J., et al.: Learning to decode protograph LDPC codes. IEEE J. Sel. Areas Commun. **39**(7), 1983–1999 (2021)
13. Zhang, D., Guo, Z., Lu, G., Zhang, L., Zuo, W.: An online system of multispectral palmprint verification. IEEE Trans. Instrum. Meas. **59**(2), 480–490 (2010)
14. Zhang, L., Li, L., Yang, A., Shen, Y., Yang, M.: Towards contactless palmprint recognition: a novel device, a new benchmark, and a collaborative collaborative representation based identification approach. Pattern Recognit. **69**, 199–212 (2017)
15. Hao, Y., Sun, Z., Tan, T., Ren, C.: Multispectral palm image fusion for accurate contact-free palmprint recognition. In: 15th IEEE International Conference on Image Processing, pp. 281–284. IEEE (2008)
16. Wang, X., Li, H.: One-factor cancellable palmprint recognition scheme based on OIOM and minimum signature hash. IEEE Access **7**, 131338–131354 (2019)
17. Liu, X., Wang, H., Wang, M., et al.: PalmKeyNet: palm template protection based on multi-modal shared key. In: Chinese Conference on Pattern Recognition and Computer Vision (PRCV), pp. 110–121. Springer, Singapore (2023)
18. Liu, C., Shao, H., Zhong, D.: PalmSecMatch: a data-centric template protection method for palmprint recognition. Displays **84**, 102771 (2024)
19. Kschischang, F.R., Frey, B.J., Loeliger, H.-A.: Factor graphs and the sum-product algorithm. IEEE Trans. Inf. Theory **47**(2), 498–519 (2001)
20. Lugosch, L., Gross, W.J.: Neural offset min-sum decoding. In: 2017 IEEE International Symposium on Information Theory (ISIT), Aachen, Germany, pp. 1361–1365 (2017)

TSCAN: Teacher-Student Co-Learning Adaptive Network for Cross-Device Palmprint Recognition

Huayang Li[1], Huikai Shao[1,2,3], Yani Ren[1], and Dexing Zhong[1,4,5]($\boxtimes$)

[1] School of Automation Science and Engineering, Xi'an Jiaotong University, Xi'an 710049, Shaanxi, China
bell@xjtu.edu.cn
[2] State Key Lab. for Novel Software Technology, Nanjing University, NanJing 210000, Jiangsu, China
[3] Sichuan Digital Economy Industry Development Research Institute, Chengdu 610084, Sichuan, China
[4] Pazhou Lab, Guangzhou 510335, China
[5] Research Institute of Xi'an Jiaotong University, Zhejiang 311215, China

Abstract. With the rapid development of biometrics, palmprint recognition, due to uniqueness, non-contact and high security, is a core intelligent authentication technology. However, cross-device domain shift from hardware differences and complex environments degrades recognition accuracy and stability. To address this, we propose TSCAN, a teacher-student co-learning network for cross- device palmprint recognition. It introduces adaface loss to adjust classification boundaries, tackling poor discriminability in low-quality images. A teacher- student framework with pseudo-label transmission and EMA updates enables learning unlabeled target domain data. Adversarial learning combined with GRL aligns source and target feature distributions. Experiments on XJTU-UP show that TSCAN improves recognition accuracy by 7.5% in four cross-device scenarios and reduces EER by 8.5% compared to the baseline, and excellent generalization across target domains, validating its practical value in intelligent authentication.

Keyword: Cross-Device Recognition · Domain Adaptation · Co-Learning

1 Introduction

With the rise of mobile and IoT technologies, palmprint recognition is widely used in intelligent authentication scenarios like financial payment and access control [1]. Compared with biometric features like fingerprints and faces, palmprints possess unique advantages including rich texture information, high stability, and non-contact acquisition, exhibiting greater competitiveness in accuracy and user acceptance [2]. However, in practical applications, palmprint data collection relies on diverse devices such as various smartphones and dedicated scanners. Differences in hardware parameters of different

W. Jia et al. (Eds.): CCBR 2025, LNCS 16360, pp. 101–111, 2026.
https://doi.org/10.1007/978-981-95-6123-0_10

devices and fluctuations in acquisition environments can lead to significant feature differences in palmprint images of the same user. This "cross-device domain shift" can cause a sudden drop in model recognition performance, becoming a core bottleneck restricting technology implementation.

In existing cross-device recognition studies, filtering strategies for low-quality images (e.g., blurred, overexposed) reduce data utilization. Additionally, traditional methods struggle to balance feature discriminability and domain invariance in domain alignment, limiting model generalization [3]. To address these, this paper proposes a teacher-student co-learning network (TSCAM), which achieves cross-device adaptation via teacher network initialization based on adaface loss, combined with teacher-student co-learning and adversarial networks.

The main contributions can be summarized as follows:

(1) Introduce adaface loss to dynamically adjust classification boundaries based on image quality, enhancing feature utilization of low-quality samples and addressing the quality sensitivity of traditional loss functions.
(2) Combine a domain discriminator with Gradient Reversal Layer (GRL) to align feature distributions between source and target domains while preserving palmprint identity discriminative information.
(3) Construct a co-learning mechanism of "teacher generates pseudo-labels and student updates teacher in reverse", combined with Exponential Moving Average (EMA) to reduce pseudo-label noise, enabling efficient transfer of unsupervised target domain knowledge.

2   Related Work

2.1   Palmprint Recognition

The core process of palmprint recognition includes three stages: image preprocessing, feature extraction, and matching [4], among which the core stages are palmprint feature extraction and matching. Palmprint image feature extraction algorithms mainly consist of structure-based, coding-based, and subspace-based feature extraction algorithms [5]. Traditional cross-device recognition methods rely on local feature representations such as LBP and SIFT, but these features are sensitive to device differences and exhibit insufficient robustness in complex scenarios [6]. After the application of convolutional neural networks [7], CNNs eliminate the need for manually designing feature extraction processes and enhance feature discriminability through end-to-end learning.

2.2   Domain Adaptation

Domain adaptation alleviates this by aligning source and target domain feature distributions. Early methods like Maximum Mean Discrepancy (MMD) [8] align shallow features by measuring distribution distances but miss deep semantic differences. Adversarial methods like DANN ignore class discriminability [9]. Pseudo-label methods generate target domain pseudo-labels via source domain models for semi-supervised learning [10], but face high pseudo-label noise. Recently, teacher-student co-learning frameworks have been used in domain adaptation [11], improving pseudo-label quality via smooth teacher model updates.

3   Method

The proposed Teacher-Student Co-learning Adaptation Network (TSCAN) aims to improve the performance of cross-device palmprint recognition. Its architecture is shown in Fig. 1, which mainly includes three core modules: a teacher model, a student model, and a domain discriminator. The training process is divided into two stages: (1) Initialization of the teacher model: training the palmprint recognition network using source domain data; (2) Teacher-student co-learning: optimizing the generalization of the student model by combining adversarial learning, and updating the teacher model via EMA [12].

3.1   Teacher Network Initialization

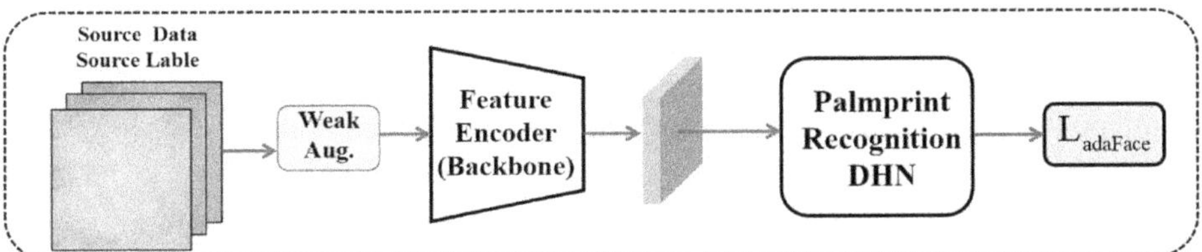

Fig. 1. Teacher Network Initialization Schematic Diagram

Teacher network initialization is shown in the Fig. 1. It adopts ResNet18 as the backbone, followed by a linear layer and a hash layer, with supervised training on the source domain. The input is a 112×112 palmprint ROI image, and the network extracts a 128-dimensional feature vector for identity matching. To enhance feature discriminability, AdaFaceLoss [13]—which dynamically adjusts classification boundaries based on sample quality—is introduced. Its formula is:

$$L_{AdaFace} = -log\left(\frac{e^{s(cos(\theta_{y_i}+m(\|z_i\|)))}}{e^{s(cos(\theta_{y_i}+m(\|z_i\|)))}+\sum_{j\neq y_i}e^{scos\theta_j}}\right)$$

where θ_{y_i} is the angle between the feature vector z_i and the center of the target class, s is the scaling factor, and $m(\|z_i\|)$ is the adaptive margin based on the feature norm $\|z_i\|$. Experiments demonstrate that the feature norm $\|z_i\|$ can reflect sample quality. The design of the adaptive margin $m(\|z_i\|)$ follows these principles: high-quality samples adopt a larger margin to enhance inter-class differences, while low-quality samples use a smaller margin to avoid excessive penalty. This paper sets:

$$m(\|z_i\|) = max\left(m_{min}, m_0 - \frac{\|z_i\| - t}{max\_norm - t} \cdot m_0\right)$$

where $m_0 = 0.5$ is the base margin, $m_{min} = 0.25$ is the minimum margin, t is the mean of feature norms, and max_norm is the maximum feature norm. When the sample quality

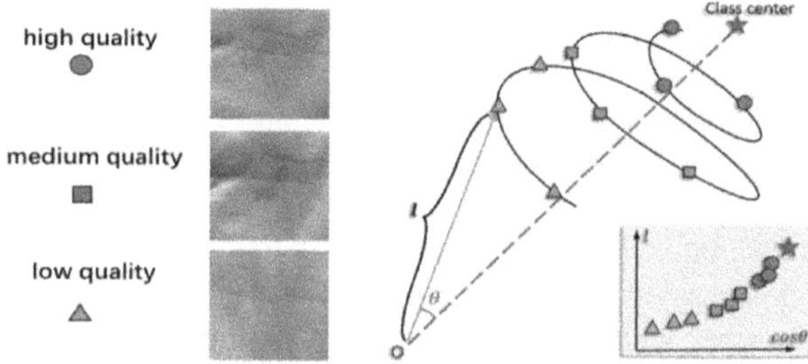

Fig. 2. Schematic Diagram of Palmprint Image Clustering Distribution

is below the threshold, the margin gradually decreases to m_{min}; when the sample quality is above the threshold, the margin increases with improved quality to enhance inter-class separability.

This mechanism not only enhances the model's recognition capability but also prevents overfitting on low-quality noisy samples. As shown in Fig. 2, feature points of high-quality images are pulled toward class centers, forming compact clusters; while feature points of low-quality images are distributed near class boundaries.

3.2 Cross-Domain Adaptation Based on Teacher-Student Co-Learning

The cross-domain adaptive training stage achieves the transfer of source domain knowledge to the target domain through teacher-student co-learning and adversarial domain alignment [14]. Its data flow is shown in Fig. 3: source domain and target domain strongly augmented images are input to the student model, while target domain weakly augmented images are input to the teacher model to generate pseudo-labels; the student model is optimized via a joint loss function, and the teacher model is dynamically updated through EMA.

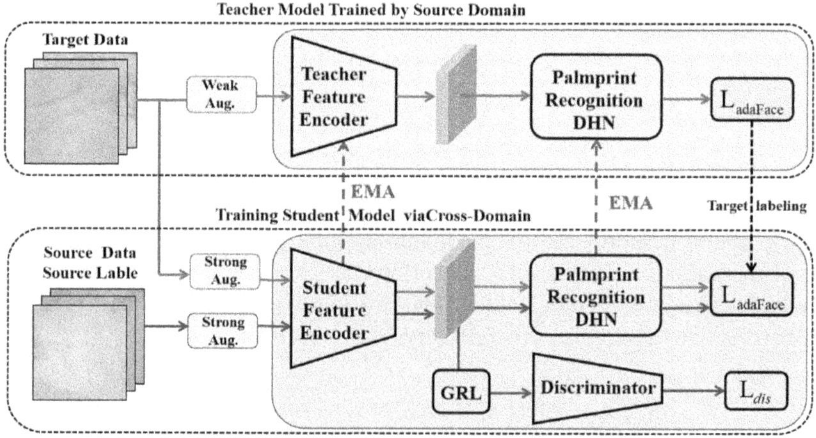

Fig. 3. Schematic Diagram of TSCAN Algorithm Flow.

3.2.1 Preprocessing Module

Preprocessing simulates cross-device acquisition differences through data augmentation, while providing differentiated inputs (strong or weak augmentation) for teacher and student models [15]. The specific strategies are as follows:

Weak augmentation is used for the teacher model to generate pseudo-labels, aiming to maintain the domain style of images and ensure the reliability of pseudo-labels. The process includes: (1) palmprint ROI extraction; (2) resizing to 124 × 124; (3) random cropping to 112 × 112; (4) random horizontal flipping; (5) random rotation.

Strong augmentation is applied to train the student model, with the purpose of expanding the sample distribution range and forcing the model to learn core textures. On the basis of weak augmentation, it adds: (1) random color; (2) contrast adjustment; (3) Gaussian blur; (4) random grayscale; (5) Gaussian noise.

3.2.2 Pseudo-Label Generation Module

In cross-device scenarios, the lack of label information in target domain data is a key issue restricting model performance. Traditional pseudo-label methods directly generate labels using source domain models, suffering from severe domain shift problems; while simple self-training methods tend to introduce high-noise pseudo-labels in the early training stage. To address these issues, TSCAN designs an independent teacher network and an Exponential Moving Average (EMA) update mechanism as shown in Fig. 4, enabling effective utilization of target domain data.

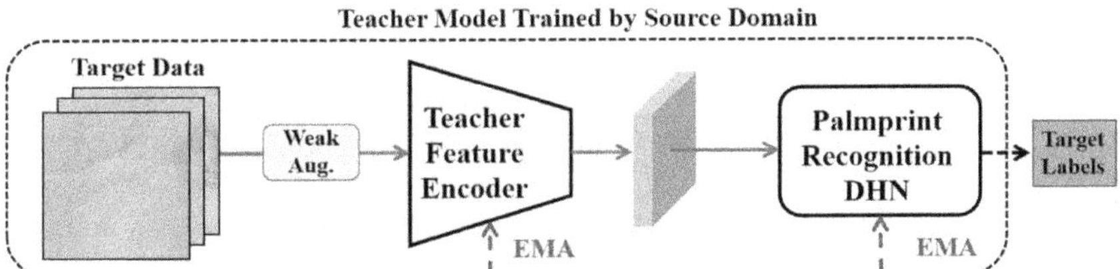

Fig. 4. Schematic Diagram of Teacher Network Update Process.

In the cross-domain training phase, the teacher network generates pseudo-labels for target domain data. Specifically, the initialized teacher network avoids pseudo-label generation from scratch. Target domain images first undergo weak augmentation, then are input to the teacher network and converted into a probability distribution p1 via the Softmax function. Only when the highest predicted probability exceeds the confidence threshold of 0.8 is the corresponding class taken as the pseudo-label yt. To further improve the quality of pseudo-labels, teacher network parameters are smoothly updated via the EMA mechanism [16]:

$$\theta_{teacher} \leftarrow \lambda\theta_{teacher} + (1 - \lambda)\theta_{student}$$

where $\lambda = 0.99$ is the decay coefficient, and $\theta_{student}$ is the parameter of the student network. This mechanism has dual advantages: the teacher network absorbs new target domain knowledge from the student network, and exponential smoothing suppresses training fluctuations to stabilize pseudo-labels.

3.2.3 Student Model Adaptive Training Module

The training objective of the student network is to adapt to target domain distribution characteristics while maintaining source domain discriminative ability. To this end, this paper designs a multi-task loss function that integrates supervised learning, self-supervised learning, and adversarial learning.

The student network adopts the same structure and training strategy as the teacher network to ensure good discriminative ability on source domain data; meanwhile, it uses pseudo-labels generated by the teacher network for self-supervised learning on target domain data, enabling the student network to gradually adapt to target domain feature distributions.

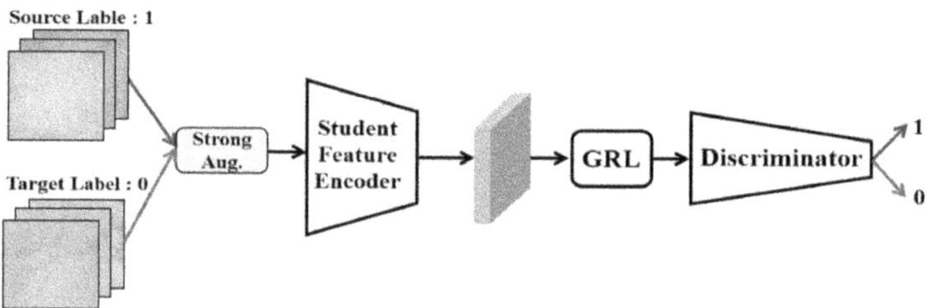

Fig. 5. Schematic Diagram of Adversarial Network Adaptation.

In addition, a domain discriminator with a Gradient Reversal Layer (GRL) (as shown in Fig. 5) is introduced to force the student network to extract domain-invariant features. Specifically, GRL reverses the gradient sign, enabling the feature extractor to implicitly minimize the distribution difference between source and target domains while minimizing classification loss, with the formula as follows:

$$L_{dis} = \frac{1}{N+M} \sum_{i=1}^{N+M} [d_i log\,(q_i) + (1-d)\,log\,(1-q_i)]$$

where d_i denotes the domain label (*0* for the source domain, *1* for the target domain), and q_i represents the predicted probability of the domain classifier. The binary discriminator distinguishes whether features originate from the source or target domain, while the student network learns domain-invariant representations by maximizing the discriminator's classification errors. Therefore, the total loss of the student network consists of three components:

$$L_{student} = \alpha L_{sup} + \beta L_{unsup} + \gamma L_{dis}$$

where α, β and γ are balance coefficients with values of 1, 0.8, 0.3 respectively, controlling the weights of source domain supervision, target domain self-supervision, and domain adversarial learning.

4   Experiments and Results

4.1   Palmprint Dataset

The experiment uses the XJTU-UP palmprint dataset [17], which contains left and right palm images of approximately 100 volunteers. These images were captured using 5 devices (LG G4, iPhone 6S, MI8, Samsung Galaxy Note5, Huawei Mate8) under natural light (N) and flash (F) conditions, forming 10 sub-datasets (e.g., HN: Huawei under natural light, HF: Huawei under flash). All images were processed into 280×280 ROI regions with background and redundant information removed, and typical palmprint samples are shown in Fig. 6.

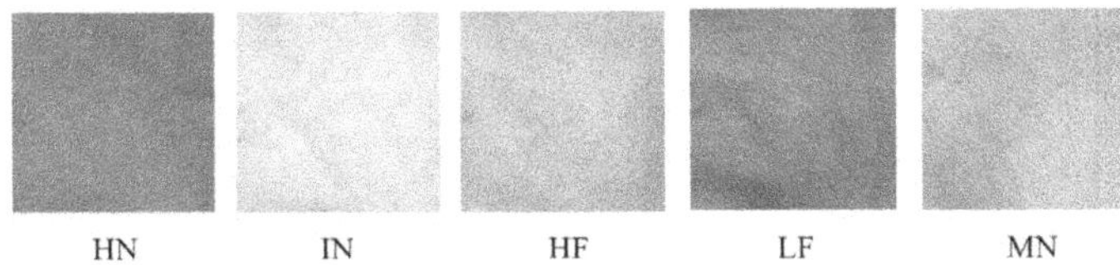

Fig. 6. ROIs of XJTU-UP Dataset.

To simulate cross-device scenarios from a single source domain to a single target domain, the experiment sets 4 test schemes (see Table 1), covering combinations of different devices and lighting conditions:

Table 1. Selection Scheme of Source Domain and Target Domain

Testing Protocols	Source--Target Domain	Palm ID	Number of Palm ROIs	Scence Description
I	HN--IN	1–200	2000	Natural light, Cross-device
I	HF--IF	1–200	2000	Flash, Cross-device
II	HN--HF	1–200	2000	Same device, Cross-scene
IIII	HN--MF	1–200	2000	Cross-scene,Cross-device

4.2   Implementation Details

To accurately quantify identity matching performance in palmprint recognition, this paper selects Accuracy (ACC), Equal Error Rate (EER), and True Acceptance Rate at a specific False Acceptance Rate (TAR@FAR $= 0.1$) as core evaluation metrics.

In palmprint identity matching, sample pairs are divided into positive pairs and negative pairs. Based on predictions vs. true labels, they fall into TP (correctly predicted positive pairs), TN (correctly predicted negative pairs), FP (negative pairs falsely predicted as positive), and FN (positive pairs falsely predicted as negative).

ACC is the proportion of correctly classified pairs, measuring recognition accuracy; a higher value indicates better performance, with the formula as follows:

$$ACC = \frac{TP + TN}{TP + TN + FP + FN}$$

False Acceptance Rate (FAR) is the proportion of negative pairs falsely predicted as "match", with the formula as follows:

$$FAR = \frac{FP}{FP + TN}$$

False Rejection Rate (FRR) is the proportion of positive pairs falsely predicted as "non-match," with the formula as follows:

$$FRR = \frac{FN}{TP + FN}$$

True Acceptance Rate (TAR) is the proportion of positive pairs correctly judged as "match," with the formula as follows:

$$TAR = \frac{TP}{TP + FN}$$

4.3　Experimental Results

Table 2. Performance on different domains.

Domains	Acc(%)	EER(%)	TAR@FAR $= 0.1$(%)	TAR@FAR $= 0.01$(%)
Source-HN	97.52	3.20	98.59	94.05
Target-IN	89.68	7.50	86.21	73.55
Target-HF	68.38	31.58	51.00	23.00
Target-MH	78.57	29.16	64.88	27.38

Experiments in this paper are conducted on the XJTU-UP database. In the first stage, HN data is to train the teacher model, which is then tested on different target domains, with results shown in Table 2. The pre-trained teacher model performs poorly on target domains; among them, performance across devices under the same natural light is relatively better, while flash has a greater impact on the model.

Table 3. Performance of different rotocols

Testing Protocols	Acc(%)	EER(%)	TAR@FAR = 0.1(%)	TAR@FAR = 0.01(%)
I - Source	92.86	5.62	94.14	87.61
I - Target	93.70	5.82	94.51	85.16
II - Source	94.74	8.47	95.04	85.32
II - Target	87.86	17.21	86.25	62.35
III - Source	87.92	17.4	86.33	63.88
III - Target	78.02	21.7	70.11	54.44
IIII - Source	95.65	5.37	96.22	86.88
IIII - Target	97.35	2.65	98.17	95.5

Four adaptive networks are obtained through training TSCAN in four cross-domain scenarios. These networks are tested on the corresponding domains and target domains respectively, with the experimental results shown in Table 3. The ACC of palmprint recognition is approximately 91.26%, which is an average increase of 7.5%. The average EER is about 10.4%, which is a decrease of 8.5%. The cross-domain generalization performance of HN-HF is slightly poor, indicating that different ambient light conditions on the same device have a greater impact on the model.

Table 4. The average performance of different methods

Protocols	Methods	Acc(%)	EER(%)	TAR@FAR = 0.1(%)	TAR@FAR = 0.01(%)
I-S-T	MMD-ResNet	92.32	6.42	**94.40**	**86.50**
	DANN	89.17	8.81	92.10	83.20
	TSCAN	**93.28**	**5.72**	94.33	86.39
II-S-T	MMD-ResNet	88.38	19.63	84.50	68.20
	DANN	90.47	13.31	88.80	71.50
	TSCAN	**91.30**	**12.84**	**90.65**	**73.84**
III-S-T	MMD-ResNet	75.78	24.72	72.30	52.50
	DANN	79.79	27.36	76.10	56.80
	TSCAN	**82.97**	**19.55**	**78.22**	**59.16**
IIII-S-T	MMD-ResNet	83.59	16.37	89.80	74.20
	DANN	92.63	8.12	95.90	87.60
	TSCAN	**96.50**	**4.01**	**97.20**	**91.19**

The average performance comparison experiments are shown in Table 4. In scenarios with small differences, the performance of this method is close to that of MMD; in scenarios with large differences, it achieves significant improvement [18]. Overall, the

TSCAN algorithm has achieved good results in the cross-device palmprint recognition task, with improvements compared to the other two methods, and is more suitable for cases with large Domain Shift.

5 Conclusion

To tackle unstable cross-device palmprint recognition, this paper proposes TSCAN, a teacher-student co-learning cross-domain adaptive network. TSCAN initializes the teacher network with adaface loss, dynamically adjusting classification boundaries via feature norms to boost low-quality feature. It employs a teacher-student co-learning framework—with the teacher generating high-confidence pseudo-labels and updating parameters via exponential moving average to leverage unlabeled target data, and aligns domain feature distributions via adversarial learning to reduce domain bias. Experiments on the XJTU-UP dataset show that the accuracy of TSCAN in cross-device scenarios has increased by 7.5%, and the EER has decreased by 8.5%,, demonstrating strong effectiveness and generalization.

Acknowledgments. This work was supported in part by National Natural Science Foundation of China under Grant 62376211 and Grant 62206218, in part by Key Research and Development Program of Shaanxi under Grant 2024GX-YBXM-158, in part by Sichuan Science and Technology Program under Grant 2025ZNSFSC1494, in part by Zhejiang Provincial Natural Science Foundation of China under Grant LTGG23F030006, in part by Shaanxi Postdoctoral Research Project Funding, and in part by Fundamental Research Funds for the Central Universities under Grant xzy012023061.

References

1. Zhao, S., Fei, L., Wen, J.: Multiview-learning-based generic palmprint recognition: a literature review. Mathematics **11**(5), 1261 (2023)
2. Du, X., Zhong, D., Shao, H.: Cross-domain palmprint recognition via regularized adversarial domain adaptive hashing. IEEE Trans. Circuits Syst. Video Technol. **31**(6), 2372–2385 (2020)
3. Singhal, P., Walambe, R., Ramanna, S., et al.: Domain adaptation: challenges, methods, datasets, and applications. IEEE Access **11**, 6973–7020 (2023)
4. Guo, Q., Shao, H., Liu, C., et al.: Homomorphic encryption-based privacy protection for palmprint recognition. In: Chinese Conference on Biometric Recognition, pp. 363–371. Springer Nature Singapore, Singapore (2023)
5. Zhong, D., Du, X., Zhong, K.: Decade progress of palmprint recognition: a brief survey. Neurocomputing **328**, 16–28 (2019)
6. Amrouni, N., Benzaoui, A., Zeroual, A.: Palmprint recognition: extensive exploration of databases, methodologies, comparative assessment, and future directions. Appl. Sci.-Basel **14**(1), 34 (2024)
7. Salehi, A.W., Khan, S., Gupta, G., et al.: A study of CNN and transfer learning in medical imaging: advantages, challenges, future scope. Sustainability **15**(7), 5930 (2023)
8. Borgwardt, K.M., Gretton, A., Rasch, M.J., et al.: Integrating structured biological data by Kernel maximum mean discrepancy. Bioinformatics **22**(14), e49–e57 (2006)

9. Ganin, Y., Lempitsky, V.: Unsupervised domain adaptation by backpropagation. In: International Conference on Machine Learning, pp. 1180–1189. PMLR (2015)
10. Lee, D.H.: Pseudo-label: the simple and efficient semi-supervised learning method for deep neural networks. In: Workshop on Challenges in Representation Learning, ICML, vol. 3(2), p. 896 (2013)
11. Xiao, R., Liu, Z., Wu, B.: Teacher-student competition for unsupervised domain adaptation. In: 2020 25th International Conference on Pattern Recognition (ICPR), pp. 8291–8298. IEEE Press, New York (2021)
12. Deng, J., Guo, J., Yang, J., et al.: ArcFace: additive angular margin loss for deep face recognition. IEEE Trans. Pattern Anal. Mach. Intell. (2021)
13. Kim, M., Jain, A.K., Liu, X.: AdaFace: quality adaptive margin for face recognition (2022)
14. Tian, J., Zhang, J., Jiang, Y., et al.: A novel generalized source-free domain adaptation approach for cross-domain industrial fault diagnosis. Reliab. Eng. Syst. Saf. **243**, 109891 (2024)
15. Wang, J., He, Y., Li, K., et al.: MDANet: a multi-stage domain adaptation framework for generalizable low-light image enhancement. Neurocomputing **627**, 129572 (2025)
16. Qian, K., Zhu, D., Wu, Y., et al.: TransIST: transformer based infrared small target tracking using multi-scale feature and exponential moving average learning. Infrared Phys. Technol. **145**, 105674 (2025)
17. Shao, H., Zhong, D., Du, X.: Deep distillation hashing for unconstrained palmprint recognition. IEEE Trans. Instrum. Meas. **70**, 1–13 (2021)
18. Li, J., Yu, Z., Du, Z., et al.: A comprehensive survey on source-free domain adaptation. IEEE Trans. Pattern Anal. Mach. Intell. **46**(8), 5743–5762 (2024)

Internal Fingerprint Imaging System Based on Full Field Optical Coherence Tomography

Wei Li, Haixia Wang[✉], Haohao Sun, Yilong Zhang, Peng Chen, Nan Gao, and Yuanjie Dang

College of Computer Science and Technology, Zhejiang University of Technology, Hangzhou 310023, China
hxwang@zjut.edu.cn

Abstract. Fingerprints is one of the most widely used biometric features, but its performance is affected by unstable quality and vulnerability to counterfeiting. Internal fingerprints from active epidermal layer can supplement external ones better, which captured by optical coherence tomography (OCT). But its point-scanning method limits imaging speed. Full-field optical coherence tomography (FF-OCT), evolved from OCT, can capture full-surface information in one scan. In order to obtain fingerprints that can be used for high anti-counterfeiting, we propose an internal fingerprint imaging system based on FF-OCT, which uses differences in scattering intensity within finger internal structures to perform layer-by-layer tomography and rapidly acquire internal fingerprints. By improving the optical path and system, we obtained information on the internal structure of the finger. Combined with corresponding scanning and processing algorithms, we can quickly generate internal fingerprint images. This work lays a foundation for the subsequent application of FF-OCT in fingerprint recognition and anti-counterfeiting.

Keywords: FF-OCT · external fingerprints · coherence

1 Introduction

With the rapid advancement of information technology, biometric technologies have found increasingly widespread applications in fields such as financial payments, access control security, and forensic authentication [1]. Among various biometric methods, fingerprint recognition stands as the most mature biometric technique due to its uniqueness, stability, and operational convenience. However, traditional surface fingerprint recognition faces critical issues, it is prone to environmental factors such as dirt, wear and moisture, which can reduce accuracy, and it is also vulnerable to forgery, such as fingerprint membranes, silicone molds and 3D printing. These challenges urgently necessitate technological innovations to enhance the reliability and security of fingerprint recognition. Finger skin has multiple layers. Internal fingerprints in the viable epidermis retain complete ridge details and resist forgery due to their subsurface location, offering a new direction for advancing fingerprint recognition and anti-counterfeiting.

© The Author(s), under exclusive license to Springer Nature Singapore Pte Ltd. 2026
W. Jia et al. (Eds.): CCBR 2025, LNCS 16360, pp. 112–121, 2026.
https://doi.org/10.1007/978-981-95-6123-0_11

In exploring internal fingerprint imaging, Optical Coherence Tomography (OCT) excels in biomedical imaging for high resolution, non-invasiveness, and real-time capabilities [3]. It reconstructs internal structures via low-coherence interferometry of backscattered light, leveraging tissue layer scattering differences [4]. Derived from OCT, FF-OCT uses a planar light source and area-array camera (instead of point scanning) to split and interfere laser beams, overcoming slow imaging speed to rapidly acquire 2D planar interference images, with strong biomedical potential [5].

Despite this, FF-OCT faces challenges in internal fingerprint imaging. First, multi-layer heterogeneous finger skin causes significant light attenuation; limited by camera sensitivity and light source distribution [6], deep viable epidermis fingerprint details are hard to capture, leading to low-contrast, blurred images. Second, conventional FF-OCT treats fingers as homogeneous, using "carpet-style" full-volume scanning that reduces efficiency and generates redundant data. Since internal fingerprints lie in the viable epidermis, lacking precise depth positioning includes invalid non-fingerprint data, wasting resources.

To address these, this study presents an FF-OCT-based internal fingerprint system. Optimized optics filter stray light, boost deep tissue signal collection, and enhance subsurface fingerprint detection. It uses automatic positioning and dynamic acquisition: multi-step phase-shifting algorithms and texture detection pinpoint viable epidermis depth, eliminating redundant data and enabling automatic focus. Post-processing optimizes data, markedly improving imaging efficiency and quality. Integrating hardware and algorithm optimizations, the system resolves deep signal capture and data efficiency issues, offering a practical solution for internal fingerprint imaging.

2 Related Works

Traditional fingerprint recognition relies on surface imaging techniques that capture epidermal ridge patterns. However, its susceptibility to surface contamination, abrasion, and spoofing attacks has driven researchers toward deep-layer imaging of dermal fingerprints. Optical coherence tomography, with its non-scanning capability and high resolution, has become a critical tool for tomographic imaging of biological tissues, with its technological evolution closely tied to biomedical applications.

In 2004, Dubois et al. [7] pioneered full-field OCT (FF-OCT), achieving scan-free micron-resolution 3D imaging of living tissues via low-coherence interferometry and an area-array camera, though early systems had high in vivo noise due to source instability. In 2007, Jain et al. [8] proposed using near-infrared light to penetrate the epidermis for dermal fingerprint detection, indirectly inferring subcutaneous ridge structures via multispectral imaging, but it suffered from resolution limits and high sensitivity to skin tone variations. Boccara et al. [9] introduced dynamic FF-OCT in 2012, extracting subcellular motion via temporal speckle fluctuations to enable label-free functional imaging in neuroscience, laying groundwork for dynamic tissue monitoring. In 2013, Rowe et al. [10] used high-frequency ultrasound for direct 80 μm imaging of dermal-epidermal junction fingerprints, though requiring coupling gel (compromising non-invasiveness). That year, Liu et al. [11] first reconstructed dermal fingerprints with Fourier-domain OCT (FD-OCT) but failed to resolve motion artifacts from finger tremors due to slow lateral scanning.

To balance speed and resolution, Auksorius et al. [12] explored FF-OCT for finger imaging in 2016, eliminating mechanical scanning to reduce 3D imaging time to milliseconds, yet insufficient SNR persisted due to scattering from sweat glands and vasculature. Concurrently, Zhang et al. [13] developed a multimodal system combining OCT and photoacoustic imaging, enhancing dermal vascular contrast via photoacoustic signals, but system complexity increased significantly with resolution constrained by ultrasound detectors. Thouvenin et al. [14] optimized FF-OCT optics in 2017, replacing halogen lamps with LED broadband sources to boost imaging speed to 30 Hz, demonstrating dynamic corneal endothelial cell observation. In 2021, Cheng et al. [15] developed an FF-OCT prototype for internal fingerprint imaging, achieving scan-free 3D imaging but struggling to reliably extract deep ridge details due to multilayer scattering noise. Chen et al. [16] applied FF-OCT to in vivo finger vein imaging in 2022, enabling identity authentication via dermal vascular network reconstruction, though fingerprint ridge extraction was unaddressed. Wang et al. [17] introduced dynamic speckle analysis in 2023 to suppress motion artifacts, achieving 25 Hz in vivo imaging rates and preliminarily validating motion artifact mitigation at high frame rates, yet signal attenuation at the dermal-hypodermal junction remained unresolved.

As a novel modality for internal fingerprint acquisition, full-field optical coherence tomography holds significant promise for complementing surface fingerprints and advancing anti-counterfeiting technologies.

3   System

The core of FF-OCT internal fingerprint acquisition system is to utilize the low-coherence interference of light to achieve tomographic imaging of the internal structures of the finger. The superposition of two coherent light beams in space creates a non-uniform intensity distribution within their overlapping region, a phenomenon known as optical interference [18]. To ensure interference occurs exclusively at positions of equal optical path length, we employ weakly coherent laser sources split into two beams. The short coherence length inherent to broadband light sources enables high-precision tomographic localization. When near-infrared laser light illuminates the fingertip, reflections and scattering arise from distinct layers within the dermal structure. While the sample light inherently contains multi-layered tissue reflections and backscattered signals, the FF-OCT system inherently suppresses non-equal-path contributions due to the broadband source's coherence properties, thereby effectively capturing contour information from the active epidermal layer.

This study establishes an FF-OCT-based internal fingerprint acquisition system built upon a Michelson interferometer framework. While Fig. 1(a) illustrates the optical schematic and Fig. 1(b) shows the physical implementation. The system integrates beam splitter prisms, blazed grating, imaging lenses, and apertures, augmented by a piezoelectric ceramic (PZT) actuator, a single-axis motorized stage, an infrared area-array camera, an 850 nm near-infrared laser, and a laser collimator. Uniform Köhler-illuminated laser light enters the beam splitter prism, generating two beams directed into reference and sample arms. Depth-resolved scanning at equal optical path positions is achieved through axial displacement of the reference arm via synchronized PZT and motorized stage actuation.

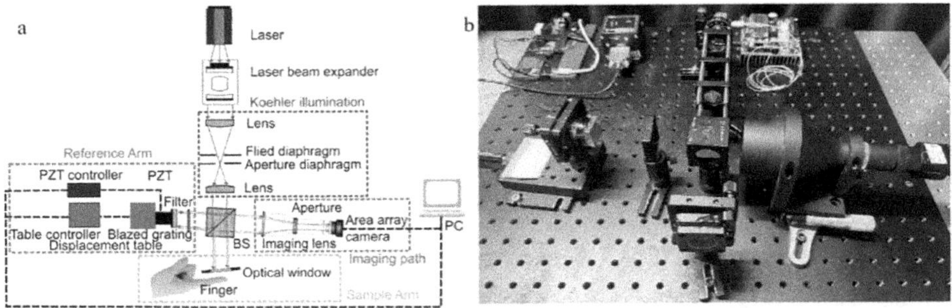

Fig. 1. (a) Optical structure diagram; (b) Physical system diagram. A laser, after passing through a beam expander, enters a Kohler illumination structure to form a uniform surface light source. It is split 50:50 by a beam splitter (BS) into reference and sample arms. Light in the reference arm is reflected by a blazed grating, attenuated by a filter, then returns to the BS and enters the imaging path. Light in the sample arm hits the sample, scatters back to the BS, and enters the imaging path. Finally, the image is recorded by an area array camera and transmitted to PC.

The first point worth noting is that the reference arm and imaging path are intentionally tilted to redirect secondary reflections generated at the beam splitter interface and prism glass surfaces. Subsequent imaging optics employ reduced apertures to block these stray light paths, effectively eliminating parasitic interference.

The second point worth noting is that the sample arm's optical window is tilted at $5.2°$ to suppress direct glass surface reflections—far stronger than dermal backscattering, which would otherwise dominate the camera's dynamic range. This tilt allows longer exposure without saturation, boosting weak scattering signal SNR significantly. To match this tilted interference surface, the reference beam uses an identically tilted blazed grating. As shown in Fig. 2, the grating's angles align reference and sample planes to the same tilt with equal optical paths across the plane. Though the reference surface has small undulating steps, coherence length makes it equivalent to a continuous surface. Thus, oblique matching captures structural information from the sample's surface to interior.

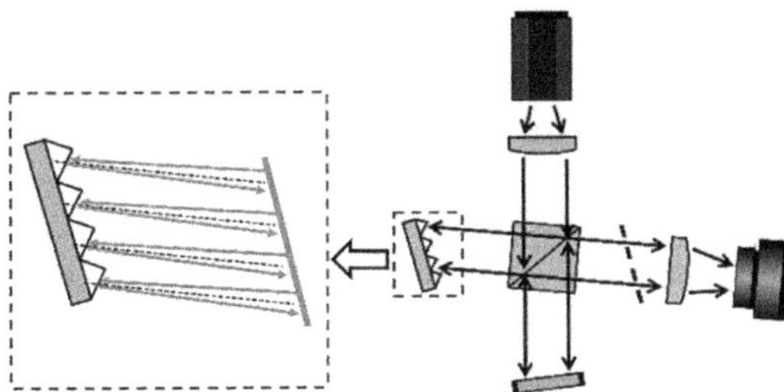

Fig. 2. Schematic diagram of interference surface. The blazed grating and optical window are tilted at the same angle, and the stepped equal path surface is regarded as a plane.

The third point worth noting is that a neutral density filter (70% transmittance) is incorporated in the reference arm to balance light intensities between the two interferometric paths. Given that dermal backscattering typically retains only about 5% of the incident near-infrared intensity, matching reference arm intensity to sample arm scattering optimizes interference contrast and further enhancing SNR.

4 Data Processing

On the basis of the system described in the previous section, in order to extract the internal fingerprints of the finger, a series of algorithmic processes are required, including interference analysis, imaging depth positioning, fingerprint extraction and other processes. Interference analysis is used to analyze the interference image at the current depth. The four two-dimensional plane images obtained by the system are finely analyzed and calculated based on phase to obtain the internal structure plane image at that depth. Imaging depth positioning is used to quickly locate the starting depth of internal fingerprints. As the equidistant interference position is scanned from the outside to the inside, the interference image obtained from the aforementioned interference analysis is used to determine whether the interference position has reached the depth of the internal fingerprint, reducing unnecessary tomographic steps. Three-dimensional correction is used to correct the continuous two-dimensional tomographic images obtained. Due to the use of a tilted interference plane, we need to correct the tilted plane back to the front. Fingerprint extraction is to use multiple continuous tomographic images to synthesize internal fingerprints, so as to obtain the fingerprint images in the general sense.

4.1 Interference Analysis

We use the four-step phase-shifting method to solve the interference images. The light intensity distribution of dual beam interference can be derived from the Maxwell equations based on the light intensity at a certain point recorded by the system array camera:

$$I = I_R + I_S + 2\sqrt{I_R I_S}\cos(\varphi_1 - \varphi_2) \tag{1}$$

In Formula 1, I_R represents the light intensity distribution of the reference arm, I_S represents the light intensity distribution of the sample arm at the interference position, carrying the structural information of that position, and $\varphi_1 - \varphi_2$ represents the phase difference between the reference light and the sample light at this position.

We drive a small movement of PZT to change the optical path of the reference arm, which is equivalent to introducing a phase shift term in formula 1 and representing it in another form:

$$I_i(x, y) = A(x, y) + B(x, y)\cos[\phi(x, y) + \varphi] \tag{2}$$

In formula 2, $A(x, y)$ represents the sum of I_1 and I_2, which is the constant term. $\cos[.]$ is the interference term, which varies with the phase difference of $P(x, y)$. $B(x, y)$ is the coherent term image information. $\phi(x, y)$ is the initial phase, and φ is the introduced phase shift.

Therefore, by introducing four phase shifts ranging from 0 to 2π, we can obtain four equations I_1, I_2, I_3, and I_4 that are related to the phase shift. Based on formula 2, we can solve for the relevant term information of each point:

$$\begin{cases} \phi(x, y) = \arctan\delta \\ \delta = \frac{(I_1-I_3)(cos\varphi_2-cos\varphi_4)-(I_2-I_4)(cos\varphi_1-cos\varphi_3)}{(I_1-I_3)(sin\varphi_2-sin\varphi_4)-(I_2-I_4)(sin\varphi_1-sin\varphi_3)} \\ B(x, y) = \frac{(I_1-I_3)}{cos(\delta+\varphi_1)-cos(\delta+\varphi_3)} \\ A(x, y) = \frac{I_3cos(\delta+\varphi_1)-I_1cos(\delta+\varphi_3)}{cos(\delta+\varphi_1)-cos(\delta+\varphi_3)} \end{cases} \tag{3}$$

Therefore, we can finally obtain I_s, that is, the scattering intensity of this layer inside the finger, which represents the information about the undulation of the internal contour:

$$I_S = 0.5 * (A - \sqrt{(A^2 - B^2)}) \tag{4}$$

By using this four-step phase shift operation, and then moving the reference mirror with a fixed stepping depth through the motorized displacement stage, the system can cooperate with the area array camera to obtain the tomographic structure information at each depth within the effective range.

4.2 Imaging Depth Positioning

Imaging depth positioning is conducive to quickly locating the position of the internal fingerprint that we are interested in. Through the tomographic images obtained by analyzing the interference images, we can determine whether we have reached the starting depth of the internal fingerprint by observing the changes in the overall or block brightness of these images. This is because the structure between the stratum corneum of the finger and the viable epidermis layer is relatively uniform. Apart from the presence of sweat glands, there is no texture information, which is reflected in the image as the absence of large patches of pixel brightness. Therefore, by using an algorithm to capture the images in which large patches of brightness appear, we can determine that the scanning depth has reached the internal fingerprint structure. So that we can directly start the collection from the internal fingerprint area.

4.3 Fingerprint Extraction

Due to fingertip skin structure, internal fingerprint contours undulate slightly (100–200 μm) in 3D depth. With the system's 10 μm longitudinal resolution, over a dozen textured images from different layers are captured. As shown in Fig. 3, firstly we register all images via features like ridge direction and bifurcation points, ensuring spatial consistency across layers. Then, using grayscale and texture similarity, we adopt a weighted average fusion strategy to smooth transitions in overlapping areas. Finally, we perform simple enhancement on the fingerprint area to further optimize the synthesized image's contrast and clarity.

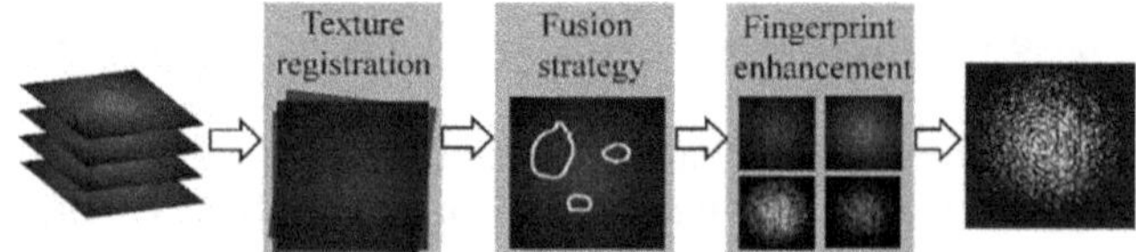

Fig. 3. Fingerprint extraction process diagram. We register and align the corrected image according to texture features, and then combine the texture information of multiple fingerprint images to fill in and fuse the missing areas of internal fingerprint texture. Finally, we perform fingerprint enhancement to increase contrast and reduce noise.

5   Experiments

To comprehensively verify the FF-OCT internal fingerprint imaging system's performance and reliability, we designed a series of experiments. First, we used the USFA-1951 plate to quantitatively evaluate the system's optical resolution, determining its ability to distinguish tiny structures. Second, we imaged a coin's surface to verify depth-direction tomographic capability. Then, we performed layer-by-layer scanning of a complete finger to confirm the device can capture internal tomographic structures, using image synthesis to reconstruct layer data into a 3D visualization model, intuitively showing internal spatial distribution. Finally, we activated the system's automated acquisition program to obtain finger internal fingerprint information.

5.1   Imaging Experiment

We measured the imaging resolution of the system using the internationally standardized USFA-1951 plate. The laser light source adopted by the system has a central wavelength of 850 nm and a bandwidth of 60 nm. Therefore, it can be calculated that the coherence length of the light source is approximately 5.3 um. Considering that the displacement accuracy of the motorized displacement stage used for depth scanning is 0.01 mm, the longitudinal resolution of the system is approximately 10 um. As shown in Fig. 4, it is the imaging result of the standard resolution plate. According to the line groups that can be resolved in the figure, by referring to the reference table, the resolution of this image can be obtained as approximately 13.9 um. Taking into account that the minimum resolution of the imaging lens is 12.6 um, the resolution of the area array camera is 2.4 um, so the lateral resolution of the system is approximately 14 um.

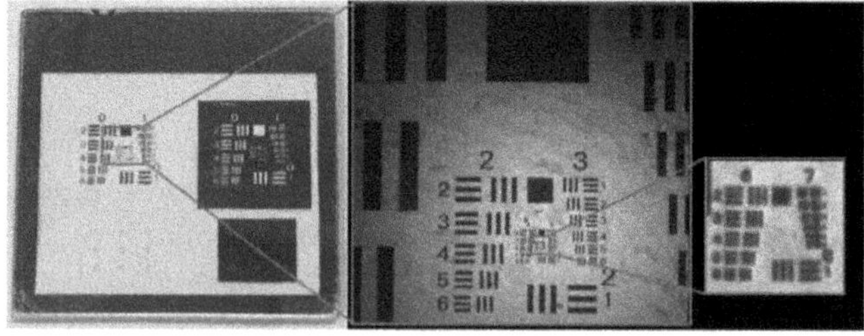

Fig. 4. Imaging results of USFA-1951 board resolution.

5.2 Coin Experiment

We conducted interferometric imaging tests on the surface of the coin, and the results are shown in Fig. 5. Due to the fact that coins are not purely flat and have some undulating patterns on the surface, we can use different interference depth positions to distinguish between the concave and convex parts. The imaging experiment results on the surface indicate that the system has tomographic capability in the depth direction.

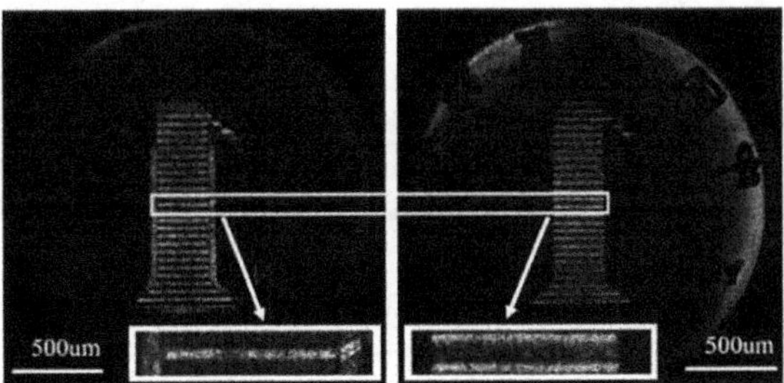

Fig. 5. Interference imaging image of coin surface. It can be clearly seen that the uneven patterns on the surface of the coin exhibit brightness and darkness at different interference depths.

5.3 Scanning Experiment

As shown in Fig. 6, the depth scanning effect of the finger from the surface to the internal structure can be observed. The scanning starts at a certain distance from the surface of the finger and gradually proceeds into the interior until it reaches a depth below the contour of the dermis layer.

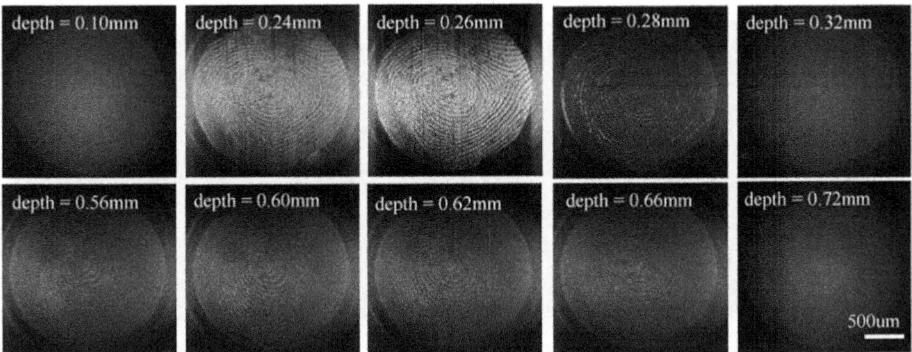

Fig. 6. Finger tomographic structure diagram. Tomographic planar images are arranged by depth, covering 0.10–0.72 mm. Each small image is marked with depth info at the top left. Successively visible are: information-free surface, glass reflection surface, surface fingerprint, sweat glands, internal fingerprint, and finally depth layers below the dermis contour.

We also performed 3D visualization to display the tomographic imaging results of the finger's internal structure, as shown in Fig. 7. The figure clearly shows the tomographic structures from the finger's surface to a certain depth within, including fingerprint textures and sweat gland structures.

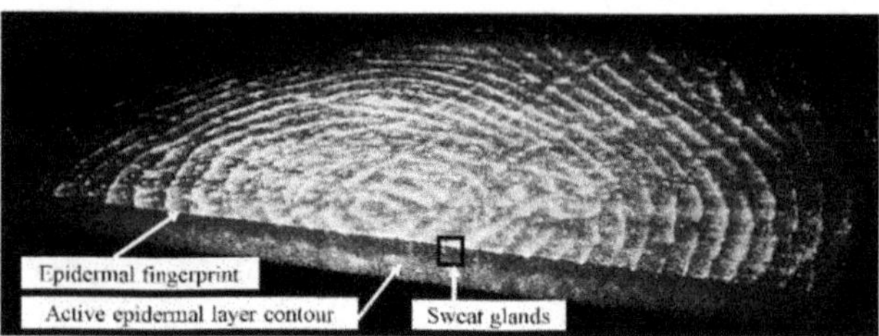

Fig. 7. 3D visualization of the finger's internal tomographic structure. We stack a set of finger depth tomography images in depth order into a three-dimensional display, displaying the tomography structure from an oblique direction. From the figure, information such as the epidermal fingerprint, the contour of the active epidermal layer, and sweat glands can be seen.

5.4 Internal Fingerprint Experiment

We directly used this system to image the finger and generate the internal fingerprint, and selected the internal fingerprint obtained by this system for comparison with the epidermal fingerprint, as shown in Fig. 8. The images reveal numerous similarities and a few differences between epidermal and internal fingerprints, since both essentially represent the same fingerprint, naturally formed by the upward growth of the inner epidermal layer contour. Based on these results, we conclude that the system possesses the imaging capability for internal finger fingerprints.

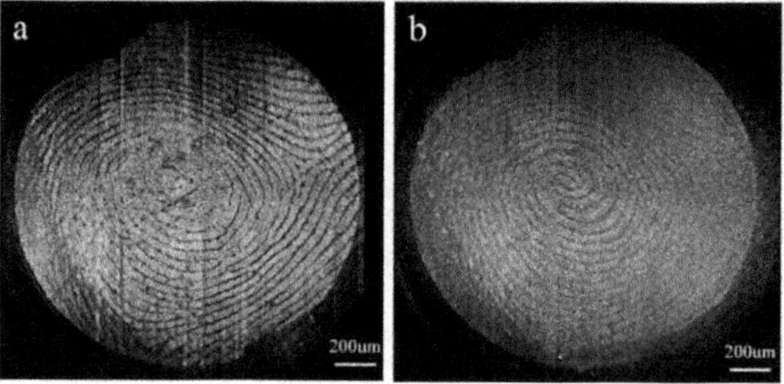

Fig. 8. Images of epidermal and internal fingerprints. The image on the left is the epidermal fingerprint, and the image on the right is the internal fingerprint.

6 Conclusions

Our internal finger fingerprint imaging system utilizes low-coherence interferometry, processes multi-frame depth images in real time to synthesize internal finger structures, and paves the way for FF-OCT in fingerprint recognition and anti-counterfeiting. However, this study has a limitation. Though internal fingerprints were captured, clear internal structures were lacking. The images only support anti-counterfeiting through traditional recognition, revealing the systems insufficient ability to extract deeper finger structures, which is our next research direction.

Acknowledgments. This work was supported in part by Zhejiang Provincial Natural Science Foundation of China under Grant NoLR24F030003 and Grant LD24F020005, National Natural Science Foundation of China under Grant 62376250, Grant 62276236 and Grant 62406283.

References

1. Jain, A.K., Ross, A., Prabhakar, S.: Biometrics: a review of current trends and future directions. IEEE Trans. Biometrics, Behav. Identity Sci. **2**, 1–18 (2020)
2. Yu, Y., Wang, H., Zhang, Y., Liang, R., Chen, P.: Methods and applications of fingertip subcutaneous biometrics based on optical coherence tomography. IEEE Trans. Biometrics, Behav. Identity Sci. **5**, 126—250 (2023)
3. Kirfel, A., Scheer, T., Jung, N., Busch, C.: Robust identification and segmentation of the outer skin layers in volumetric fingerprint data. Sensors **22**(21), 17(2022)
4. Chinn, S.R., Fujimoto, J.G., Swanson, E.A.: Optical coherence tomography using a frequency-domain technique. Opt. Lett. **22**(11), 783–785 (1997)
5. Wang, L., Fu, R., Xu, C., Xu, M.: Methods and applications of full-field optical coherence tomography: a review. J. Biomed. Opt. **27**(5), 050901 (2022)
6. Vasudevan, V.S., et al.: Finite element multilayer skin model for applications in diffuse optical spectroscopy. Asian J. Phys. **29**(1), 115–127 (2020)
7. Dubois, A., Vabre, L., Boccara, A.C., Beaurepaire, E.: High-resolution full-field optical coherence tomography with a Linnik microscope. Appl. Opt. **41**(4), 805–812 (2002)
8. Jain, A.K., et al.: Multispectral fingerprint imaging for spoof detection and biometric authentication. IEEE Trans. Pattern Anal. Mach. Intell. **29**(8), 1363–1369 (2007)
9. Beaurepaire, E., Supatto, W., Boccara, A.C.: Full-field optical coherence microscopy for dynamic live-cell imaging. Opt. Express **20**(21), 23613–23624 (2012)
10. Rowe, R. K., Smith, L. A., Jones, M. T.: High-frequency ultrasound for subsurface fingerprint imaging. In: 2013 IEEE International Conference on Biometrics: Theory, Applications and Systems (BTAS). pp. 1–8 (2013)
11. Liu, G., et al.: Vascular fingerprint recognition based on optical coherence tomography. Appl. Opt. **52**(22), 5473–5477 (2013)
12. Auksorius, E., Boccara, A.C.: Full-field optical coherence tomography with a high-speed CMOS camera for dynamic fingerprint imaging. Opt. Express **24**, 17102–17113 (2016)
13. Zhang, Y., et al.: Multimodal optical coherence tomography and photoacoustic imaging for in vivo dermal vascular visualization. Biomed. Opt. Express **7**(10), 4022–4035 (2016)
14. Thouvenin, O., Leclercq, L., Boccara, A.C.: High-speed full-field optical coherence tomography with LED illumination for in vivo imaging of corneal endothelium. Opt. Express **25**(19), 22645–22657 (2017)
15. Cheng, Y., Wang, N., Tang, S.: Scan-free 3D internal fingerprint imaging using full-field optical coherence tomography. Biomed. Opt. Express **12**(5), 3012–3024 (2021)
16. Wei, C., Liang, S., David, D.S.: In vivo finger vein imaging using full-field optical coherence tomography for biometric authentication. Biomed. Opt. Express **13**(9), 5210–5223 (2022)
17. Wang, H., et al.: Dynamic speckle analysis for motion artifact suppression in high-speed full-field OCT: in vivo imaging at 25 Hz. Biomed. Opt. Express **14**(6), 3452–3465 (2023)
18. Born, M., Wolf, E.: Principles of Optics: Electromagnetic Theory of Propagation, Interference and Diffraction of Light, 7th ed. Cambridge University, Cambridge, pp. 271–332 (1999)

A Review on Palmprint Image-Level Attacks

Qiuli Zhang[1], Kaihua Zheng[1], Jinhui Xu[1], Yong Xu[2,3], and Jinrong Cui[1,2(✉)]

[1] College of Mathematics and Informatics, South China Agricultural University, Guangzhou, China
tweety1028@163.com

[2] Guangdong Provincial Key Laboratory of Novel Security Intelligence Technologies, Shenzhen, China

[3] Department of Computer Science and Technology, Harbin Institute of Technology, Shenzhen, China

Abstract. With the popularization of biometric recognition technology, palmprint recognition has attracted widespread attention because of its high uniqueness and non-replicability. However, recent studies have shown that various image-level attacks on palmprint recognition systems can interfere with the decision-making process of the model, leading to a decline in both the accuracy and security of the system. In this paper, we first summarize the applications of palmprint recognition technology and then describe two main types of image-level attacks: adversarial attacks and reconstruction attacks. Finally, we summarize existing works on image-level attacks targeting palmprint recognition, highlighting key methods and strategies.

Keywords: Palmprint Recognition · Adversarial Attack · Reconstruction Attack · Security

1 Introduction

Since the information society has grown so quickly, identity authentication has become an indispensable part of all walks of life [1]. Although traditional identity authentication methods, such as those based on passwords and ID cards, have guaranteed the function of identity authentication to a certain extent, there are still many security risks. Problems such as easy loss and easy forgetting have become major hidden dangers to user safety. To address the limitations of conventional verification methods, biometric recognition technology has emerged. For example, fingerprints, palmprints, and faces are used for identity authentication. Their high uniqueness and non-replicability make them more secure and reliable. Among them, Palmprint recognition is generally considered superior to other biometric methods due to its low intrusion and convenient user experience [2]. The palmprint images contain rich feature information [3] and palms have excellent recognition capabilities because they have more surface features

W. Jia et al. (Eds.): CCBR 2025, LNCS 16360, pp. 122–130, 2026.
https://doi.org/10.1007/978-981-95-6123-0_12

than fingerprints while remaining stable [4]. These characteristics make palmprint recognition an important technology that can provide high accuracy in the field of personal authentication and identity recognition.

As shown in Fig. 1, the fundamental palmprint identification procedure consists of image acquisition, image preprocessing, feature extraction, and matching. The collection methods can be categorized into contact palmprint recognition and non-contact palmprint recognition. The preprocessing process is mainly to extract ROI and then extract the unique features of the palmprint from the processed image in a global or local range. Finally, these features are compared with the palmprint data in the database to complete the identity verification process.

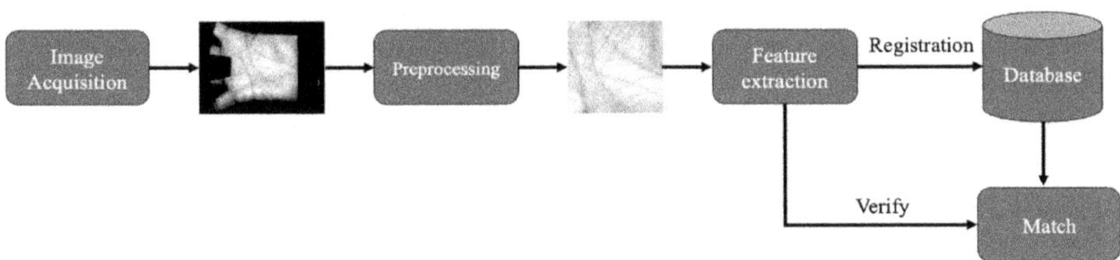

Fig. 1. The basic palmprint recognition process

Although palmprint recognition technology is becoming increasingly mature, attack methods have become more sophisticated and are no longer limited to simple deception. For example, attackers can generate adversarial examples by making subtle but imperceptible modifications to the original input, which will lead to the model generating inaccurate predictions [5] [6]. White-box and black-box attacks are two categories of adversarial attacks. In white-box attacks, the attacker has full access to the internal workings of the system and can design effective attacks against model vulnerabilities. For example, Fast Gradient Sign Method (FGSM) [6] generates adversarial examples by calculating the gradient of the loss function with respect to the input. Black box attacks, on the other hand, are limited to attacking input and output data. A notable example of a black-box attack is the transferability-based attack [7], where adversarial examples designed for one model are used to deceive another model without having direct access to the parameters of the second model. In addition to adversarial attacks, another type of image-level attack is reconstruction attacks. Reconstruction attacks are attacks that attempt to restore the original data by accessing or analyzing part of the information or data. In the field of data security, attackers attempt to reconstruct private information by obtaining processed data samples and applying specific algorithms or models.

The rest of the article is organized as follows. Section 2 will give a summary of the basic concepts of palmprint recognition and image-level attack; Sect. 3 will discuss the latest advances in image-level attacks in the field of palmprint recognition and we conclude in Sect. 4.

2   Background

This section explores the evolution of palmprint recognition technology, from early approaches to contemporary deep learning-based methods, and introduces the landscape of image-level attacks and corresponding defenses

2.1   Palmprint Recognition

Palmprint recognition has made significant progress, and new feature extraction algorithms continue to emerge. PalmCode [8] uses 2D Gabor phase coding scheme for palmprint representation. Compared with the traditional single feature extraction method, Kong and Zhang [9] proposed to use multiple two-dimensional Gabor filters to extract direction information from palmprint images and combined it with Competitive Coding method to improve recognition accuracy and robustness.

The technology for palmprint identification has advanced quickly with the advent of deep learning. By combining deep neural networks, researchers can more accurately extract features from complex palmprint images. PalmNet [10] is a novel technique for using Gabor filters in CNN, which has excellent recognition accuracy in different databases. Veigas [11] introduced a fuzzy SVM classification method for palmprint recognition using transfer learning and fine-tuning the Alexnet model for feature extraction. Zhao and Zhang [12] proposed deep discriminative representation (DDR), which represents high-level discriminative features for multi-scenario palmprint recognition. GANs can generate realistic palmprint images and help build more diverse training datasets. These generated images can not only increase the number of samples but also cover different environmental changes, thereby improving the generalization ability of models. Wang et al. [13] generate high-quality palmprint images through improved deep convolutional GAN (DCGAN). Minaee et al. [14] added a regularization to the loss function to ensure that the main lines are connected. Chowdhary et al. [15]introduced the utilization of the "Style-based generator", StyleGAN2-ADA, from the StyleGAN series, renowned for generating high-quality images. Chen et al. [16] developed a GAN-based palmprint recognition model that can effectively handle noise and retain more directional information.

In conclusion, through the development of various feature extraction methods and the integration of deep learning technology, palmprint recognition has made great progress and improved the accuracy, robustness and generalization ability of the palmprint recognition model.

2.2   Image-Level Attack and Defense

The primary goals of attacking the biometric recognition system is to deceive the system verification, steal information, and seriously threaten the privacy and security of users. In this section, we will introduce two main image-level attacks and their applications: adversarial attack and reconstruction attack.

Adversarial attacks involve subtle modifications to images, aiming to mislead models into making erroneous predictions. These perturbations are typically imperceptible to the human eye but can drastically affect model performance. As shown in Fig. 2, the palmprint image is attacked by FGSM. The Basic Iterative Method (BIM) [17], an extension of FGSM, iteratively refines this perturbation, resulting in a more precise adversarial attack. Projected Gradient Descent (PGD) [18] uses multiple iterations of calculations, taking a small step each time, and each iteration projects the disturbance into a specified range. Optimization-based attacks, such as the C&W attack [19], introduce a set of targeted adversarial attacks and search for the minimum perturbation within the range of three different metrics. Su et al. [20] proposed a new method to generate single-pixel adversarial perturbations similar to black-box attacks. Generative-based attacks are inspired by game theory and consist of two parts: the generator and the discriminator. These two components engage in a game with each other, eventually reaching an equilibrium. Xiao et al. [21] proposed AdvGAN to learn and approximate the distribution of the original instances.

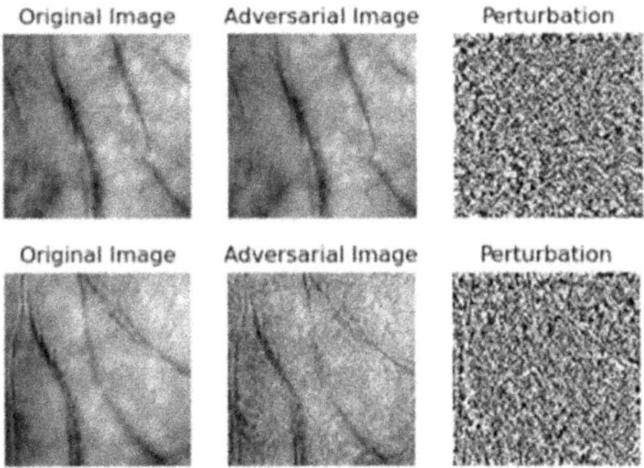

Fig. 2. The adversarial examples of palmprint image attacked by FGSM

In addition to adversarial attacks, there are also reconstruction attacks, where an attacker can use the leaked feature template to recover the user's biometric image. These images usually contain the user's unique biometric information, such as fingerprints, palmprints, or facial features. Once reconstructed, the attacker can forge these features and bypass the system's authentication. Such attacks not only threaten the user's privacy security but also pose a serious challenge to the reliability of the biometric system. In the application of fingerprints, Hill et al. [22] proposed a general method for developing camouflaged artifacts based on the information contained in the stored template. Galbally et al. [23] proposed a neighborly de-convolutional neural network (NbNet) to reconstruct face images from their deep templates and the experimental results show a high True Acceptance Rate. Shahreza et al. [24] proposed a novel method (dubbed GaFaR) to reconstruct 3D faces from facial templates.

To reduce the potential harm, defense mechanisms against image-level attacks have emerged. Adversarial defense aims to protect machine learning models from adversarial attacks by reducing their sensitivity to small and imperceptible perturbations in the input data. By adding adversarial examples to train the model, the model becomes robust to adversarial samples [25]. In terms of model optimization, Hinton et al. [26] proposed distillation, and it transformed complex networks into simple networks and introduced an ensemble model consisting of full models and many expert models. Cohen et al. [27] trained an adversarial detector using the k-NN ranks and distances, and the adversarial examples were successfully distinguished.

In conclusion, the security of biometric recognition systems is threatened by reconstruction and adversarial attacks. In addition, many defense mechanisms for image-level attacks have been proposed to improve the model's robustness.

3 Palmprint Image-Level Attacks

Palmprint recognition systems are facing more and more security threats, especially the challenge of image-level attacks. In this section, we will introduce some recent research on palmprint image-level attacks in two parts: adversarial attacks (AA) and reconstruction attacks (RA). The recent palmprint image-level attacks are summarized in Table 1.

Table 1. Recent palmprint image-level attacks

Ref.	Year	Type	Methodology
[28]	2023	AA	Combine Correlation Perturbation and Discriminative Perturbation to generate adversarial examples
[29]	2020	RA	Palmprint images generated by GANs for false acceptance attack
[30]	2022	RA	Reinforcement strategy
[31]	2023	RA	Two novel style-transfer methods
[32]	2024	RA	Incorporated the dropout mechanism into the generator of ProGAN

3.1 Palmprint Adversarial Attacks

Palmprint adversarial attacks generate adversarial examples of palmprints to deceive palmprint recognition systems, thereby threatening user security. Although the research on adversarial attacks on biometric systems has received extensive attention in recent years, there are relatively few studies on adversarial attacks on palmprint modalities. We will introduce in detail a representative palmprint adversarial attack. As shown in Fig. 3, Zhu et al. [28] proposed a novel multi-spectral palmprint attack. This method combines two types of perturbations: Correlation Perturbation and Discriminative Perturbation. Specifically,

DGCCA is used to capture the multi-view deep common features of the input view, and the loss function is used to calculate the loss gradient to obtain the Correlation Perturbation. The samples are projected into the difference subspace to determine the difference discriminant information. The adversarial region concept is then used to produce discriminative perturbations. The generated palmprint adversarial examples are more difficult to detect.

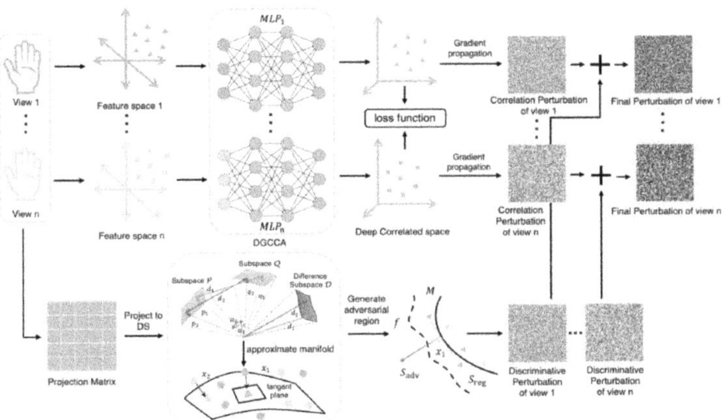

Fig. 3. The multi-spectral palmprints joint attack and defense framework [28]

3.2 Palmprint Reconstruction Attacks

Palmprint reconstruction attacks exploit vulnerabilities in palmprint recognition systems to reconstruct original palmprint data, threatening personal privacy and system security. As shown in Fig. 4, Wang et al. [29] proposed false acceptance attack (FAA). FAA does not require real palmprint images, but uses generated images. Specifically, they selected DCGAN to generate the fake palmprint images. When a forged image is able to impersonate the target user, the FAA succeeds. However, since it is very time-consuming to generate palmprint images through GANs, Yue et al. [30] proposed Modification Constraint within Neighborhood (MCwN) to reduce the modification extent and Batch Member Selection (BMS) to decide how to select the members of the batch. Yang et al. [31] proposed two novel style-transfer methods to reconstruct a high-quality image. Yan et al. [32] proposed a black-box palmprint template reconstruction method based on the modified Progressive GAN (ProGAN) and they incorporate the dropout mechanism into the generator of ProGAN.

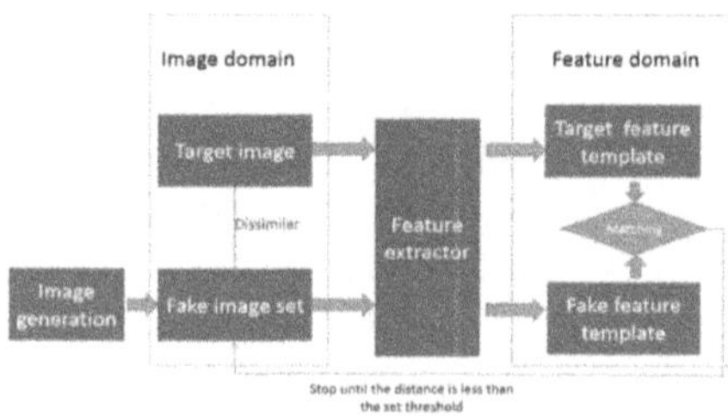

Fig. 4. The architecture diagram of FAA. [29]

4   Conclusion

In conclusion, while palmprint recognition offers a promising biometric authentication solution due to its unique characteristics, it is susceptible to image-level attacks. This paper reviewed two major types of image-level attacks: adversarial and reconstruction attacks. Adversarial attacks manipulate palmprint images to deceive recognition systems, making them a serious threat to security. A representative method, proposed by Zhu et al. [28], combines two perturbations, correlation perturbation and discriminative perturbation, to generate palmprint adversarial examples that are harder to detect. On the other hand, reconstruction attacks exploit vulnerabilities in the system to reconstruct original palmprint data, threatening personal privacy. For instance, Wang et al. [29] proposed a false acceptance attack (FAA) using generated palmprint images without the need for real ones. In the future, designing more effective attack methods remains an important area for palmprint recognition. At the same time, developing more powerful defense mechanisms is also crucial to ensure the robustness and security of palmprint recognition systems.

Acknowledgment. This research was financially supported by Guangdong Provincial Key Laboratory of Novel SecurityIntelligence Technologies (Grant No.2022B1212010005). We thank the anonymous reviewers for their constructive comments.

References

1. Amrouni, N., Benzaoui, A., Zeroual, A.: Palmprint recognition: extensive exploration of databases, methodologies, comparative assessment, and future directions. Appl. Sci. **14**(1), 153 (2023)
2. Gao, C., Yang, Z., Jia, W., et al.: Deep learning in palmprint recognition-a comprehensive survey. arXiv preprint: arXiv:2501.01166 (2025)
3. Trabelsi, S., Samai, D., Dornaika, F., et al.: Efficient palmprint biometric identification systems using deep learning and feature selection methods. Neural Comput. Appl. **34**(14), 12119–12141 (2022)

4. El-Tarhouni, W., Boubchir, L., Elbendak, M., et al.: Multispectral palmprint recognition using Pascal coefficients-based LBP and PHOG descriptors with random sampling. Neural Comput. Appl. **31**(2), 593–603 (2019)
5. Szegedy, C., Zaremba, W., Sutskever, I., et al. Intriguing properties of neural networks. arXiv preprint: arXiv:1312.6199 (2013)
6. Goodfellow, I.J., Shlens, J., Szegedy, C.: Explaining and harnessing adversarial examples. arXiv preprint: arXiv:1412.6572 (2014)
7. Papernot, N., McDaniel, P., Goodfellow, I.: Transferability in machine learning: from phenomena to black-box attacks using adversarial samples. arXiv preprint: arXiv:1605.07277 (2016)
8. Zhang, D., Kong, W.K., You, J., et al.: Online palmprint identification. IEEE Trans. Pattern Anal. Mach. Intell. **25**(9), 1041–1050 (2003)
9. Kong, A.W.K., Zhang, D.: Competitive coding scheme for palmprint verification. In: Proceedings of the 17th International Conference on Pattern Recognition, 2004, ICPR 2004, vol. 1, pp. 520–523. IEEE (2004)
10. Genovese, A., Piuri, V., Plataniotis, K.N., et al.: PalmNet: Gabor-PCA convolutional networks for touchless palmprint recognition. IEEE Trans. Inf. Forensics Secur. **14**(12), 3160–3174 (2019)
11. Veigas, J.P., Kumari, M.S.: Deep learning approach for touchless palmprint recognition based on AlexNet and fuzzy support vector machine. Int. J. Electr. Comput. Eng. Syst. **13**(7), 551–559 (2022)
12. Zhao, S., Zhang, B.: Deep discriminative representation for generic palmprint recognition. Pattern Recogn. **98**, 107071 (2020)
13. Wang, G., Kang, W., Wu, Q., et al.: Generative adversarial network (GAN) based data augmentation for palmprint recognition. In: 2018 Digital Image Computing: Techniques and Applications (DICTA), pp. 1–7. IEEE (2018)
14. Minaee, S., Minaei, M., Abdolrashidi, A.A.: Palm-GAN: generating realistic palmprint images using total-variation regularized GAN. arXiv preprint: arXiv:2003.10834 (2020)
15. Chowdhury, A.M.M., Khondkar, M.J.A., Imtiaz, M.H.: Advancements in synthetic generation for contactless palmprint biometrics using StyleGAN2-ADA and StyleGAN3 (2023)
16. Chen, S., Chen, S., Guo, Z., et al.: Low-resolution palmprint image denoising by generative adversarial networks. Neurocomputing **358**, 275–284 (2019)
17. Kurakin, A., Goodfellow, I.J., Bengio, S.: Adversarial examples in the physical world. In: Artificial Intelligence Safety and Security, pp. 99–112. Chapman and Hall/CRC (2018)
18. Madry, A., Makelov, A., Schmidt, L., Tsipras, D., Vladu, A.: Towards deep learning models resistant to adversarial attacks. STAT **1050**(9) (2017)
19. Carlini, N., Wagner, D.: Towards evaluating the robustness of neural networks. In: IEEE Symposium on Security and Privacy (SP), pp. 39–57. IEEE (2017)
20. Su, J., Vargas, D.V., Sakurai, K.: One pixel attack for fooling deep neural networks. IEEE Trans. Evol. Comput. **23**(5), 828–841 (2019)
21. Xiao, C., Li, B., Zhu, J.Y., et al.: Generating adversarial examples with adversarial networks. arXiv preprint: arXiv:1801.02610 (2018)
22. Hill, C.J.: Risk of masquerade arising from the storage of biometrics. Bachelor of Science thesis, The Department of Computer Science, Australian National University (2001)
23. Mai, G., Cao, K., Yuen, P.C., et al.: On the reconstruction of face images from deep face templates. IEEE Trans. Pattern Anal. Mach. Intell. **41**(5), 1188–1202 (2018)

24. Shahreza, H.O., Marcel, S.: Template inversion attack against face recognition systems using 3D face reconstruction. In: Proceedings of the IEEE/CVF International Conference on Computer Vision, pp. 19662–19672 (2023)
25. Liang, H., He, E., Zhao, Y., et al.: Adversarial attack and defense: a survey. Electronics **11**(8), 1283 (2022)
26. Hinton, G., Vinyals, O., Dean, J.: Distilling the knowledge in a neural network (2015). arXiv:1503.02531
27. Cohen, G., Sapiro, G., Giryes, R.: Detecting adversarial samples using influence functions and nearest neighbors. In: Proceedings of the IEEE/CVF Conference on Computer Vision and Pattern Recognition, Seattle, WA, USA, pp. 14453–14462 (2020)
28. Zhu, Q., Zhou, Y., Fei, L., et al.: Multi-spectral palmprints joint attack and defense with adversarial examples learning. IEEE Trans. Inf. Forensics Secur. **18**, 1789–1799 (2023)
29. Wang, F., Leng, L., Teoh, A.B.J., et al.: Palmprint false acceptance attack with a generative adversarial network (GAN). Appl. Sci. **10**(23), 8547 (2020)
30. Sun, Y., Leng, L., Jin, Z., et al.: Reinforced palmprint reconstruction attacks in biometric systems. Sensors **22**(2), 591 (2022)
31. Yang, Z., Leng, L., Zhang, B., et al.: Two novel style-transfer palmprint reconstruction attacks. Appl. Intell. **53**(6), 6354–6371 (2023)
32. Yan, L., Wang, F., Leng, L., et al.: Toward comprehensive and effective palmprint reconstruction attack. Pattern Recogn. **155**, 110655 (2024)

Topographic Feature-Based Vein Biometric Recognition

Xueshuang Li$^{(\boxtimes)}$, Xu Gao, and Guodong Zhao

Saint Deem, Hangzhou 310053, Zhejiang, China
lxsilu@163.com

Abstract. Finger vein recognition have emerged as promising biometric technologies. Traditional algorithms often directly extract features from vein images, which can be heavily impacted by image segmentation techniques and contain unnecessary information. This study proposes a novel topographically-based vein recognition technique to address these issues. Terrain features are extracted based on the Digital Elevation Model (DEM), focusing on the concavo-convex characteristics of the surface. The similarity between vein codes is then measured by computing the structure similarity of the feature matrix. Extensive experiments on various vein datasets demonstrate that the proposed method achieves favorable accuracy and outperforms existing techniques. The contribution of this work lies in the introduction of the direct extraction of topographic features from gray-scale vein images, leading to more robust and efficient vein recognition.

Keywords: topographic attributes · feature code · optimized matching · vein recognition

1 Introduction

Compared to traditional identification systems (password or token-based), biometrics-based automated human identification has been extensively deployed in various civilian applications (e.g. access control, verification devices, and financial-related applications). However, the widely used biometrics, such as fingerprint, face, and iris, are exposed to the public and may cause sensor-level spoof attacks. As an alternative, the subcutaneous vein patterns captured by near-infrared (NIR) illuminator and NIR camera are deemed to be secure. At present, the camera on the vein image acquisition device is close to the light source, which may lead to problems such as too much noise, intensity inhomogeneity, and obscured vein images. These problems will decrease the discriminability between different vein images, making it difficult to extract robust features [1]. To eliminate the influence of illuminants on the recognition results, the existing technologies generally enhance image contrast by adjusting the gray level of the vein image [2]. A number of studies on improving the quality of the vein images have been conducted recently [3–5].

Additionally, for low-quality finger vein image recognition, a simple and effective feature extraction method is also important. Inspired by the human brain, deep learning

W. Jia et al. (Eds.): CCBR 2025, LNCS 16360, pp. 131–141, 2026.
https://doi.org/10.1007/978-981-95-6123-0_13

methods, such as convolution neural networks (CNNs), can be used to learn hierarchical features from data [1]. Compared to the handcrafted-based method, the deep-learning-based method achieves higher performance but needs longer processing time [6]. Moreover, the promising performance of deep-learning-based methods also needs a large-scale finger-vein database for training, high hardware requirements and high costs, thus making it difficult for the recognition models trained by deep learning to be quickly published and applied to terminal recognition devices. Aside from the deep-learning-based methods mentioned above, one more effective approach [7–13] can skip training to extract vein topographic features directly, and can avoid loss of feature information. Digital Elevation Model (DEM) is a solid model that uses a set of ordered numerical arrays to represent the ground elevation and has been widely used in many digital terrain analysis fields, such as terrain feature extraction, and watershed drainage system analysis [7, 8]. The terrain feature lines (ridge line, valley line) are the main framework of terrain and geomorphology. Automatic and efficient extraction of terrain feature lines has always been an important research content of digital terrain analysis. The hidden information in geographic data can be intensely mined and the geomorphic morphology can be classified by DEM. Primaet et al. [9]. And Iwahashiet et al. [10]. Use DEM to extract various terrain surface factors based on regular statistics unit, and design supervised and unsupervised geomorphic classification methods, respectively. Kakoliet et al. [11]. Used object-oriented thinking to realize landform classification.

The extraction of terrain features based on DEM has made progress in the related categories and technical methods [12–14]. However, the disadvantage of such traditional processing is that some features will be lost inevitably during the vein pattern segmentation and binarization stage, affecting performance in the following processing stages [15]. In order to overcome this problem, a new approach is explored in this paper which can extract topographic features directly from gray-scale vein images without binarization processing. Firstly, the data of regular grid DEM is regarded as a grid image. Then, the grid size corresponds to the image pixel size, while the elevation value corresponds to the gray value. The extracted terrain feature lines correspond to the blood vessel trend of the finger vein. Ridge lines and valley lines are the line features in the DEM image, and various feature extraction methods in image processing can be used to obtain terrain features. The terrain features of the image are extracted based on the DEM, mainly according to the concavo-convex characteristic of the surface where the feature points are located in different directions. This scheme extracts 8-dimensional finger vein information, while existing techniques only extract 1 or 2 dimensions, providing significant advantages.

The contribution of this paper is to propose the extraction of topographic features from gray scale vein images. The vein terrain feature extraction and feature code are performed on the enhanced image, which effectively improves the recognition performance.

The remainder of this paper is organized as follows: Sect. 2 introduces the DEM. a new scheme for extracting vein topographic features are reported in Sect. 3. Section 4 reports the experimental results. Finally, the conclusion and suggestions for future work are given in Sect. 5.

2 Preliminaries

2.1 Digital Elevation Model

Digital terrain model (DTM) is a digital representation of terrain morphological attribute information, and a digital description with spatial location features and terrain features [16]. DEM is the most basic part of DTM, which is a discrete mathematical expression of the earth's surface topography [15]. DEM represents the finite sequence of three-dimensional vectors on area D, which is described as follows:

$$V_i = (X_i, Y_i, Z_i), i = 1, 2, \ldots, n. \tag{1}$$

where, $(X_i, Y_i) \in D$ are plane coordinate values, Z_i are elevation values corresponding to (X_i, Y_i).

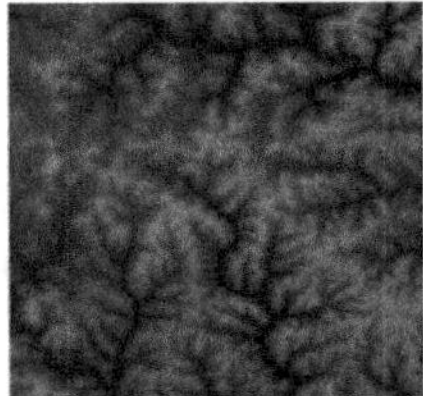

Fig. 1. Example map of grayscale terrain data.

Grid DEM is a kind of elevation matrix. The elevation data can be directly obtained by the analytical stereo plotter, or can be generated by regular or irregular discrete data interpolation. The grayscale terrain data map after visualizing DEM data is shown in Fig. 1, with a pixel of 600×600, the size of its gray value corresponds to different elevation values in DEM data.

3 Proposed Method

In this section, the main contribution of this paper is the incorporation of Gaussian Filter combined with terrain features to obtain a robust descriptor. Subsequently, a feature encoding algorithm for matching is described. Finally, the coefficient of structure similarity based on the feature matrix is employed to perform the feature matching. The proposed recognition framework is illustrated in Fig. 2.

3.1 Extraction of Terrain Features

The terrain features of the image are extracted based on the DEM, mainly according to the concavo-convex characteristic of the surface where the feature points are located in different directions. The method of slipping window is applied to calculate the first and second derivative values of each grid point, and then judge the type of feature points by the positive and negative derivatives. The main steps include:

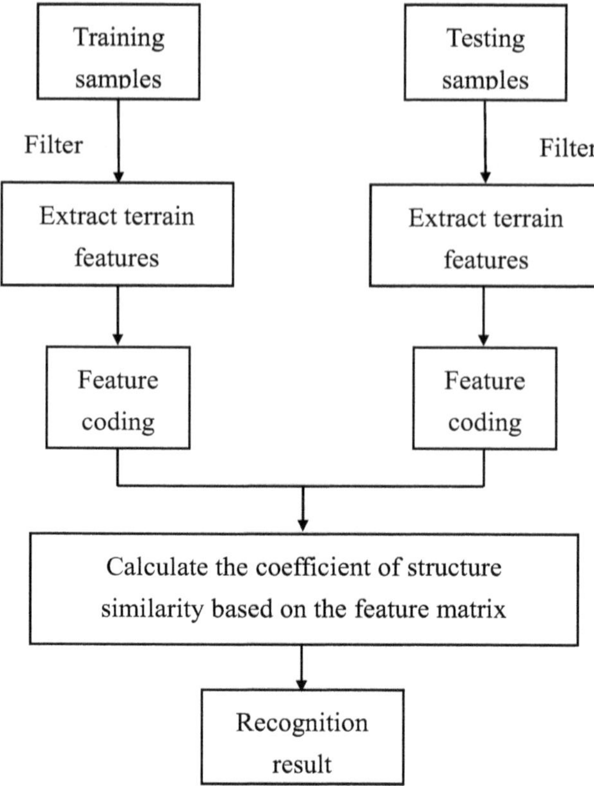

Fig. 2. The flowchart of the proposed method.

Step 1: The boundary of the input finger-vein image is expanded with 0. The size of expanded image is $(i + 2, j + 2)$, where i and j represent the number of rows and columns of the original image, respectively.

Step 2: Set a 3×3 size of slipping window, the pixels in the grid window are numbered sequentially. The encoding method is shown in Fig. 3.

8	1	2
7	0	3
6	5	4

Fig. 3. The encoding method of slipping window.

Vectors V_i in the neighborhood are calculated by Eq. (2).

$$V_i = (x_i - x_0, y_i - y_0, f_i - f_0).\tag{2}$$

where, x_i, y_i, f_i are respectively the number of rows, columns, gray values of each point in the neighborhood of the center point, x_0, y_0, f_0 are the number of rows, columns and gray values of the center pixel point, respectively.

Step 3: The second derivative of the vector V_i with respect to the elevation Z in the x-direction and y-direction is obtained;

Step 4: The positive and negative combination of the second derivative of elevation Z is used for feature coding. The coding method is as follows:

$$\begin{cases} \frac{\partial^2 z}{\partial x^2} \le 0 \ \& \ \frac{\partial^2 z}{\partial y^2} \le 0, \ V(x,y) = 0 \\ \frac{\partial^2 z}{\partial x^2} > 0 \ \& \ \frac{\partial^2 z}{\partial y^2} > 0, \ V(x,y) = 1 \\ \frac{\partial^2 z}{\partial x^2} < 0 \ \& \ \frac{\partial^2 z}{\partial y^2} = 0, \ V(x,y) = 2 \\ \frac{\partial^2 z}{\partial x^2} = 0 \ \& \ \frac{\partial^2 z}{\partial y^2} < 0, \ V(x,y) = 3 \\ \frac{\partial^2 z}{\partial x^2} > 0 \ \& \ \frac{\partial^2 z}{\partial y^2} = 0, \ V(x,y) = 4 \\ \frac{\partial^2 z}{\partial x^2} = 0 \ \& \ \frac{\partial^2 z}{\partial y^2} > 0, \ V(x,y) = 5 \\ \frac{\partial^2 z}{\partial x^2} < 0 \ \& \ \frac{\partial^2 z}{\partial y^2} > 0, \ V(x,y) = 6 \\ \frac{\partial^2 z}{\partial x^2} > 0 \ \& \ \frac{\partial^2 z}{\partial y^2} < 0, \ V(x,y) = 7 \end{cases}\tag{3}$$

where, $V(x, y)$ is the value of feature encoding, $\frac{\partial^2 z}{\partial x^2}, \frac{\partial^2 z}{\partial y^2}$ are the second derivative of elevation Z in the x-direction and y-direction, respectively.

Eight types of features can be extracted by the encoded topographic patterns. The examples of feature coding are shown in Fig. 4.

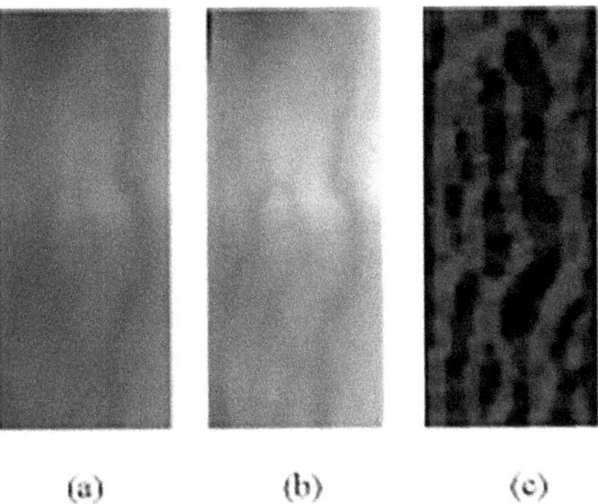

Fig. 4. Examples of terrain feature coding: (a) shows the original image, (b) shows the corrected image of (a), (c) is the encoded feature map of (b).

3.2 Feature Matching

In this paper, the specific steps for feature matching of vein images can be described as follows:

Step 1: Sort the similarity of the features to be matched. The specific steps of sorting are:

Step 1.1: If the number of features to be matched is 1, skip Step 1 and go to step 2 directly. If the number of features to be matched is greater than 1, go to Step 1.2;

Step 1.2: The bilinear interpolation method is used to scale the image matrix to be matched and the original template to a quarter of the original image;

Step 1.3: The structure similarity coefficient of feature matrix is calculated by Eq. (4):

$$S = \frac{(2u_a u_b + c_1)(\delta_{ab} + c_2)}{\left(u_a^2 + u_b^2 + c_1\right)\left(\delta_a^2 + \delta_b^2 + c_2\right)}. \tag{4}$$

where, S is the calculated structure similarity, a and b represent two vein characteristic matrices, respectively. u_a and u_b represents the average gray value of the characteristic matrix a and b, respectively. δ_a and δ_b represents the standard deviation. δ_{ab} represents the covariance of two characteristic matrices a and b. c_1 and c_2 are constants.

Step 1.4: Sort the matched features by the calculated the value of similarity;

Step 2: The first feature to be matched in the queue is precisely compared with the template feature. The specific steps are as follows:

Step 2.1: Calculate the value of similarity between the feature to be matched and the template feature in the sliding window. The calculation formula is as follows:

$$TS = \sum_{m=1}^{H-H_w, St=Hs} \sum_{n=1}^{W-W_w, St=Ws} (Ta(f(p, q))). \tag{5}$$

where, TS is the value of similarity, St is the step size, H is the maximum number of lines in the window, and H_w is the number of window rows, W is the maximum number of window columns, W_w is the number of window columns, Hs is the step size in the window along row direction, Ws is the step size of the window along column direction, $f(p, q)$ is the feature to be matched, m, n are the row and column coordinates, Ti is the similarity calculation table of the feature to be matched and the template feature, Ti is expressed as:

$$Ti = \begin{bmatrix} x_{00} & x_{01} & \cdots & x_{08} \\ x_{10} & x_{11} & \cdots & x_{18} \\ \vdots & \vdots & \vdots & \vdots \\ x_{80} & x_{81} & \cdots & x_{88} \end{bmatrix}. \tag{6}$$

where, $x_{00} \sim x_{88}$ are the parameters of the model, and $Ti = Ti^T$.

Step 2.2: Rotate the features to be matched by $0°$, $\pm 2°$ and $\pm 4°$, respectively. Then match them with the template features one by one to obtain multiple matching values. Select the smallest value from the multiple matching values as the final matching result of the two features to be matched;

Step 2.3: Calculate the inter class and intra class results of venous images, obtain the data curve, determine the threshold value according to the curve, and finally judge whether the venous images belong to the same or different category according to the threshold value.

4   Experimental Results and Analysis

To verify the effectiveness of the proposed method, different methods for image enhancement and vein recognition were implemented for comparison. All the experiments were performed on four available finger vein datasets (SDUMLA [17], FV_USM [18], SD_FV and SD_DDV), using MATLAB (R2018b) on a computer with an Intel Core i5-8300H and 8 GB of RAM. All the finger-vein images have been segmented with accurate ROI (region of interest) extraction algorithm, and thus can be directly used to test the performance.

4.1   Datasets

The SDUMLA dataset was created by the Machine Learning and Data Mining Laboratory of Shandong University. It was captured from 106 individuals, each of whom contributed 36 images from the index, middle and ring finger of both hands, with 6 images of each finger. Consequently, it is composed of 3816 images in total. The size of the cropped ROI image is 250 * 100 pixels.

The FV_USM dataset was created by the Malaysian Polytechnic University. It was captured from 123 individuals, each of whom contributed 24 images from the index and middle finger of both hands, with 6 images of each finger. As a consequence, it is composed of 2952 images in total. The size of the cropped ROI image is 300 * 100 pixels.

We made two self-acquired finger vein dataset and dorsal digital vein dataset, namely the SaintDeem Finger Vein dataset (SD_FV) and SaintDeem Dorsal Digital Vein dataset (SD_DDV). It was captured from 50 individuals, each of whom contributed 60 images from the index, middle and ring finger of both hands, with 10 images of each finger. In consequence, it is composed of 3000 images in total. The size of the cropped ROI image is 250 * 100 pixels.

Sample images of four datasets are shown in Fig. 5.

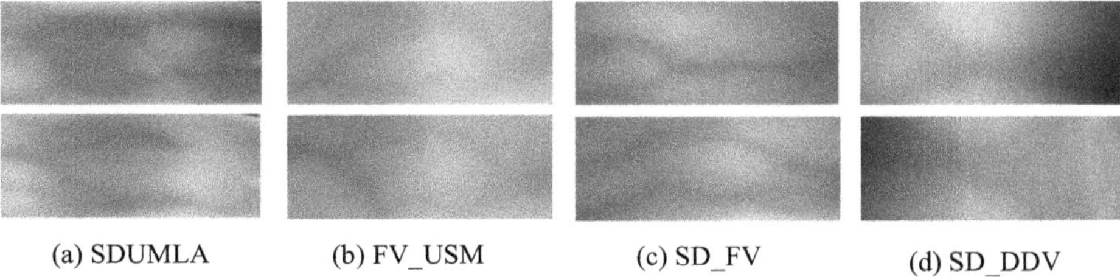

Fig. 5. The ROI images of the finger-vein.

4.2 Evaluation Index of Vein Recognition Performance

Several experiments, which were mentioned in the above section, were designed to validate the proposed method. The matching performance is evaluated by the equal error rate (EER) and the recognition rate. The EER is the error rate when the false acceptance rate (FAR) is equal to the false rejection rate (FRR). In all experiments, each finger was considered as an individual. On four databases, one of six images per finger is selected as the training set, and others are used as the testing set, which is repeated six times.

4.3 Performance Comparison of Image Feature Extraction and Matching

4.3.1 Comparison of Different Security Levels

In this section, terrain features are adopted for feature extraction. As the experiment designed in Sect. 4.3.1, the FRR value was adopted to evaluate the matching accuracy and further to illustrate effectiveness of the image enhancement methods. The security levels of FAR 1, 2, 3, 4, and 5 in the figure represent FAR values of 0, 0.0000001, 0.000001, 0.00001, and 0.0001, respectively. The experimental results are shown in Fig. 6.

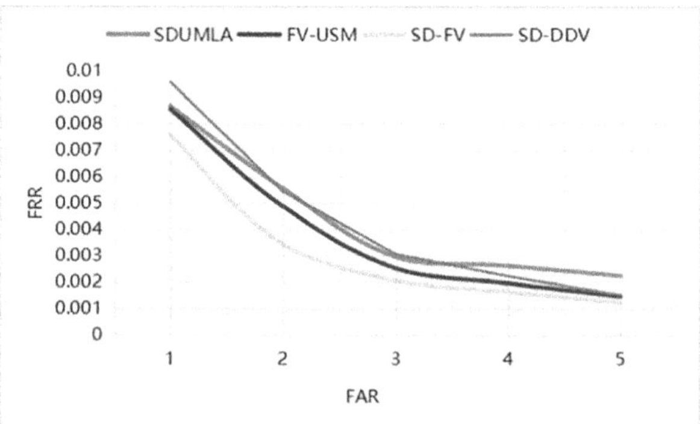

Fig. 6. The FRR values achieved using terrain features based on different security levels.

It can be seen from Fig. 6 that the finger vein feature extraction and recognition algorithm based on digital elevation model (DEM)-based terrain concavity-convexity features proposed in this paper achieves the optimal performance. Moreover, the false rejection rate (FRR) varies very little with the change in FAR, which demonstrates the excellent robustness of the recognition algorithm proposed in this paper.

4.3.2 Comparison with State-of-the-Art Methods

In this section, several classic and advanced vein recognition methods were selected to compare with the proposed method. In this experiment, we adopted the first four finger vein images of each class as the test images and randomly selected on finger vein image from the remaining three images of each class as samples. The rank of each probe is acquired by calculating the ranking of its true class matching score. We repeated the experiment ten times in order to obtain an unbiased result. The average Rank-1 recognition rates are shown in Table 1. We also compare the computational costs of all involved feature extraction methods. The feature extraction durations of all images per database are given in Table 2.

Table 1. Identification performance by different methods on SDUMLA, FV-USM, SD-FV and SD-DDV database.

Algorithms	Rank-1 recognition rate			
	SDUMLA	FV-USM	SD-FV	SD-DDV
Proposed method	99.98%	99.98%	99.99%	99.96%
Gabor + SURF [19]	99.94%	–	99.96%	99.91%
LDC + SIFT [20]	99.97%	–	99.98%	99.93%
CLAHE + AT [21]	98.84%	–	98.95%	98.32%
CLAHE + 2DPCA [22]	97.61%	97.02%	96.64%	95.15%
VDC [23]	99.01%	99.93%	99.95%	98.69%
VF-DCN [24]	99.96%	99.97%	99.94%	99.95%
FV-DDC [25]	98.74%	99.80%	98.93%	98.75%

Table 2. Time duration of feature extraction stages of all finger vein images per database.

Algorithms	Time (Seconds)			
	SDUMLA	FV-USM	SD-FV	SD-DDV
Proposed method	2.63	1.19	6.88	6.51
SURF [19]	3.85	2.38	8.56	8.32
SIFT [20]	8.16	9.52	14.00	14.15
AT [21]	7.25	8.46	12.57	12.24
Elliptical sampling + 2DPCA [22]	9.74	10.61	16.39	16.38
VDC [23]	2.98	1.55	7.24	7.15
VF [24]	6.57	5.89	9.34	9.58
FVTN [25]	4.51	3.55	8.13	8.28

As shown in Table 1, the recognition rates of the proposed method on the four image databases are 99.98%, 99.98%, 99.99% and 99.96% respectively, which rendering it the best performer amongst the selected solutions. From the results, it is obvious that our recognition system achieved slightly better recognition rates than other methods. As shown in Table 2, the experimental results show that the proposed method not only effectively improves recognition performance, but also takes the shortest time for feature extraction. Another interesting observation is that our computationally efficient topographic extractor was able to capture true invariant features and achieve comparable results with well-known methods like SURF or SIFT. The advantage of our method on the feature extraction efficiency is mainly attributed to the simple and fast threshold-based direction encoding.

5 Conclusions

In the process of vein image acquisition, there may be different degrees of problems, such as scale shift, overexposure, and blurring of background and finger areas caused by excessive noise. In this paper, we presented a finger vein recognition system based on terrain features extractor play a crucial role. To improve the feature robustness and recognition performance, a recognition model based on image terrain features is proposed. Based on the valley shaped terrain of finger veins, a vein skeleton line is designed to detect vein features. In this way, blurry vein lines and thinner vein lines as well as legible vein lines can be extracted. After improved feature coding, the model not only reduces the time for feature extraction, but also improves the recognition accuracy. Compared with the state-of-the-art methods on three datasets, the experimental results show that our recognition system is feasible and effective for finger vein recognition.

For future works, We will extend our method to palm vein biometrics to explore its effectiveness and generalization.

References

1. Ren, H.Y., Sun, L.J., Guo, J., Han, C., Cao, Y.: A high compatibility finger vein image quality assessment system based on deep learning". Expert Syst. Appl. **196**, 116603 (2022)
2. Kashif, S., Qureshi, I.: A hybrid proposed image quality assessment and enhancement framework for finger vein recognition. Multimed Tools Appl. **83**, 1536–15388 (2024)
3. Huang, X.: Moving object detection in low-luminance images. Visual Comput. **39**(1), 183–195 (2023)
4. Meng, X.J., Zheng, J.W., Xi, X.M., Zhang, Q., Yin, Y.L.: Finger vein recognition based on zone-based minutia matching. Neurocomputing **423**, 110–123 (2021)
5. Yang, W., Wang, S., Hu, J., Tao, X. Li, Y.: Feature extraction and learning approaches for cancellable biometrics: a survey. CAAI Trans. Intell. Technol. **9**(1) (2024)
6. Hou, B.R., Zhang, H.J., Yan, R.Q.: Finger-vein biometric recognition: a review. IEEE Trans. Instrum. Meas. **71**, 5020426 (2022)
7. Pham, H.T., Marshall, L., Johnson, F., Sharma, A.: A method for combining SRTM DEM and ASTER GDEM2 to improve topography estimation in regions without reference data. Remote Sens. Environ. **210**, 229–241 (2018)
8. Saint-Laurent, D., Paradis, R., Drouin, A., Gervais-Beaulac, V.: Impacts of floods on organic carbon concentrations in alluvial soils along hydrological gradients using a digital elevation model (DEM). Water **8**(5), 208 (2016)
9. Prima, O.D.A., Echigo, A., Yokoyama, R., Yoshida, T.: Supervised landform classification of Northeast Honshu from DEM-derived thematic maps. Geomorphology **78**(3–4), 373–386 (2006)
10. Iwahashi, J., Pike, R.J.: Automated classifications of topography from DEMs by an unsupervised nested-means algorithm and a three-part geometric signature. Geomorphology **86**(3–4), 409–440 (2007)

11. Saha, K., Wells, N.A., Munro-Stasiuk, M.: An object-oriented approach to automated landform mapping: a case study of drumlins. Comput. Geosci. **37**(9), 1324–1336 (2011)
12. Zhao, L.S., Hou, R., Wu, F.Q.: Effect of DEM grid size on microrelief indexes estimation for sloping lands after reservoir tillage. Soil Tillage Res. **196**, 104451 (2020)
13. Mukherjee, S., Garg, R.D., Bhardwaj, A., Raju, P.L.N.: Evaluation of topographic index in relation to terrain roughness and DEM grid spacing. J. Earth Syst. Sci. **122**(3), 869–886 (2013)
14. Kang, W.X., Li, H.S., Deng, F.Q.: Direct gray-scale extraction of topographic features for vein recognition. Science China Inf. Sci. **53**(10), 2062–2074 (2010)
15. Woodrow, K., Lindsay, J.B., Berg, A.A.: Evaluating DEM conditioning techniques, elevation source data, and grid resolution for field-scale hydrological parameter extraction. J. Hydrol. **540**, 1022–1029 (2016)
16. Amirkolaee, H.A., Arefi, H., Ahmadlou, M., Raikwar, V.: DTM extraction from DSM using a multi-scale DTM fusion strategy based on deep learning. Remote Sens. Environ. **274**, 113014 (2022)
17. Yin, Y.L., Liu, L.L., Sun, X.W.: SDUMLA-HMT: a multimodal biometric database. In: 6th Chinese Conference on Biometric Recognition, pp. 260–268 (2011)
18. Asaari, M.S.M., Suandi, S.A., Rosdi, B.A.: Fusion of band limited phase only correlation and width centroid contour distance for finger based biometrics. Expert Syst. Appl. **41**(7), 3367–3382 (2014)
19. Kovac, I., Marak, P.: Finger vein recognition: utilization of adaptive gabor filters in the enhancement stage combined with SIFT/SURF-based feature extraction. SIViP **17**, 635–641 (2022)
20. Meng, X.J., Xi, X.M., Yang, G.P., Yin, Y.L.: Finger vein recognition based on deformation information. Science China Inf. Sci. **61**(5), 052103 (2018)
21. Banerjee, A., Basu, S., Nasipuri, M.: ARTeM: a new system for human authentication using finger vein images. Multimedia Tools Appl. **77**(5), 5857–5884 (2018)
22. Qiu, S.Q., Liu, Y.Q., Zhou, Y.J., Huang, J., Nie, Y.X.: Finger-vein recognition based on dual-sliding window localization and pseudo-elliptical transformer. Expert Syst. Appl. **64**, 618–632 (2016)
23. Yang, L., Yang, G.P., Xi, X.M., Su, K., Chen, Q., Yin, Y.L.: Finger vein code: from indexing to matching. IEEE Trans. Inf. Forensics Secur. **14**(5), 1210–1223 (2019)
24. Yao, Q., Song, D., Xu, X., Zou, K.: Visual feature-guided diamond convolutional network for finger vein recognition. Sensors. **24**(18), 6097 (2024)
25. Ren, H., Sun, L., Ren, J., Cao, Y.: FV-DDC: a novel finger-vein recognition model with deformation detection and correction. Biomed. Sig. Process. Control **100** (2025)

RSANet Multi-level Fusion Dual-Modal Recognition Network

Jinglong Zhang and Hui Ma[✉]

School of Electronic Engineering, Heilongjiang University, Heilongjiang, China
`mahui929@126.com`

Abstract. In recent years, multi-modal recognition has attracted extensive attention due to its security and high accuracy. However, existing dual-modal fusion methods are limited, and simple fusion strategies fail to meet the requirements of recognition tasks. To address this issue, this paper proposes an Attention-guided Multi-level Fusion Module (AFM), which integrates both shallow and deep features from two modalities through collaborative learning rather than simple concatenation or addition. This fusion approach maximizes the complementary characteristics of fingerprint and finger-vein information, enhancing the discriminative power of the fused features. Additionally, we introduce the RSANet with attention mechanisms. Experimental results demonstrate that RSANet achieves 98.4% identification accuracy on the SDUMLA dataset, 100% on the FVC-HKPU dataset, and 99.5% on the NUPT-FPV dataset. These results validate the effectiveness of the proposed method. Ablation studies on the AFM module further confirm that the multi-level fusion significantly improves recognition performance.

Keywords: Multi-modal Biometric Recognition · Deep Learning · Feature Fusion · Attention Mechanism · Feature Extraction

1   Introduction

Biometric recognition technology [1] identifies and verifies individuals by measuring and analyzing unique biological characteristics, which include but are not limited to fingerprints, handwriting, gait, voiceprints, palm prints, and veins. Compared with traditional token-based or password-based authentication methods [2], biometrics offers reliable and efficient authentication by leveraging the uniqueness of physiological or behavioral traits. This technology has been widely applied in daily life. Furthermore, with the advancement of science and technology, biometric recognition is increasingly integrated into intelligent electronic products for device unlocking and payment verification.

However, despite its widespread applications across various fields, unimodal biometric recognition has certain limitations, such as low robustness and sensitivity to external factors like light, temperature, and humidity. Moreover, some individuals may lack unimodal feature information, which directly restricts the applicability of biometric recognition. Additionally, security issues may arise as single biometric traits can be

W. Jia et al. (Eds.): CCBR 2025, LNCS 16360, pp. 142–149, 2026.
https://doi.org/10.1007/978-981-95-6123-0_14

easily replicated or forged. Therefore, multi-modal biometric recognition has attracted significant attention from researchers in recent years.

Currently, mainstream multi-modal feature fusion methods can be categorized into pixel-level fusion [3], feature-level fusion [4], score-level fusion [5], and decision-level fusion [6]. Compared with other fusion approaches, feature-level fusion integrates multi-modal features such as textures and edges, thereby complementing the limitations of single-modal features. Furthermore, this fusion method only requires a single classifier to recognize the fused features, making it a commonly used approach in multi-modal feature fusion recognition. Nevertheless, existing feature-level fusion methods mostly rely on simple concatenation or addition. Although such simple fusion strategies can enhance feature representation to some extent, they tend to lose partial useful information, which impairs model performance. In scenarios requiring higher recognition rates, simple fusion methods usually fail to meet the requirements.

To address the issues of information loss and incomplete fusion in the process of modal fusion, this paper presents the following work:

1 RSANet: Inspired by the ResNet [7] architecture, this paper proposes RSANet, a residual network integrated with the SimAM attention mechanism. The residual connections in RSANet mitigate the risk of overfitting, while the SimAM [8] attention mechanism enables the network to focus on both channel-wise and spatial information simultaneously.
2 Multi-level Fusion Strategy: We design an Attention-guided Fusion Module (AFM) that enhances feature representation by integrating shallow global information with deep local information. This strategy improves the effectiveness of subsequent classification tasks.
3 Experimental Evaluation: The proposed RSANet model is compared with state-of-the-art methods on the SDUMLA, HKPU, and NUPT datasets. Results demonstrate that RSANet outperforms existing models, achieving superior recognition accuracy.

2 Methods

2.1 Network Architecture

Traditional residual networks reduce the spatial dimensions of feature maps through multiple downsampling operations. While this strategy expands the receptive field to capture global features, it often leads to the loss of fine-grained details, thereby affecting subsequent recognition accuracy. To address this issue, we propose RSANet, a novel architecture that effectively balances global and local feature attention, enabling the extraction of discriminative feature representations.

RSANet consists of dual branches for fingerprint and finger-vein feature extraction. Each branch begins with an Image Preprocessing Module that captures salient features and reduces computational overhead. Subsequently, three groups of Basic Blocks extract key features from the preprocessed inputs. The extracted features then undergo multi-level fusion through the proposed AFM (Attention-guided Fusion Module), which integrates fingerprint and finger-vein features to generate a comprehensive representation.

Finally, a classification module leverages these fused features to perform the identification task, ensuring the model fully utilizes multi-modal information for reliable recognition. The architecture of RSANet is illustrated in Fig. 1.

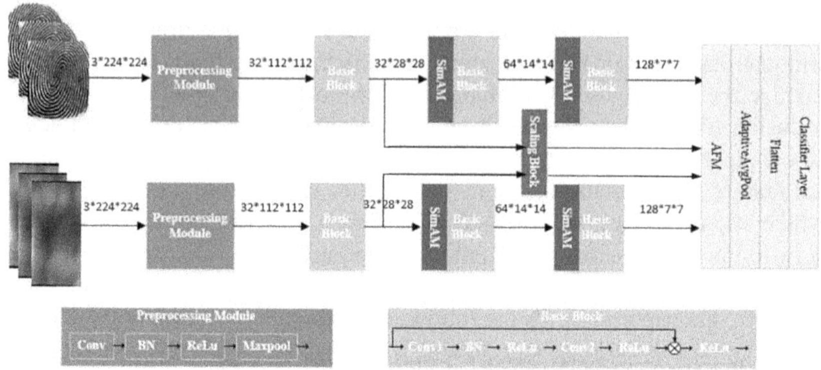

Fig. 1. Overall Network Architecture of RSANet

2.2 Multi-level Fusion Strategy

The key challenge in multi-modal biometric recognition lies in integrating complementary information across different modalities. Our approach employs an attention-based feature fusion module to combine features from varying depths within the same modality. Specifically, we denote the features to be fused as F1,F2 $\in$ R$^{C \times H \times W}$ The fusion module consists of three main components:

1) Calculate the local and global features of F1 and F2, and use two branches of different scales to extract the local and global information of the features.

   Among them, one branch directly uses point-wise convolution to extract the channel attention of the local feature Local(F1 + F2), and the other branch uses global average pooling based on point-wise convolution to extract the channel attention of the global feature Global(F1 + F2), as follows:

$$\mathrm{Local}(F_1 + F_2) = \beta(\mathrm{Conv2}(\delta(\beta(\mathrm{Conv1}(F_1 + F_2))))) \tag{1}$$

$$\mathrm{Global}(F_1 + F_2) = \mathrm{GAP}(\beta(\mathrm{Conv2}(\delta \times (\beta(\mathrm{Conv1}(F_1 + F_2)))))) \tag{2}$$

   Where Conv1 and Conv2 are both 1×1 point - wise convolutions, β is batch normalization, δ is ReLU, and GAP is global average pooling.

2) We aggregate the local and global features of F1 and F2. Subsequently, we combine the local and global features using element-wise addition and apply the sigmoid function to constrain the values within the range (0, 1), yielding the aggregated feature M(F1 + F2) as follows:

$$M(F_1 + F_2) = \sigma(\mathrm{Local}(F_1 + F_2) + \mathrm{Global}(F_1 + F_2)) \tag{3}$$

3) M(F1 + F2) is used to interact with individual modalities to obtain the fused feature Fm, as follows:

$$F_m = M\left(F_1 + F_2\right) \otimes F_1 + \left(1 - M\left(F_1 + F_2\right)\right) \otimes F_2 \tag{4}$$

Here, $\otimes$ denotes element-wise multiplication, and σ represents the sigmoid function. Notably, the aggregated feature M(F1 + F2) consists of real numbers between 0 and 1.

The term 1 - M(F1 + F2) follows the same principle, enabling the network to perform soft selection or weighted averaging between the two modalities, thereby enhancing information interaction. The overall fusion module is illustrated in Fig. 2.

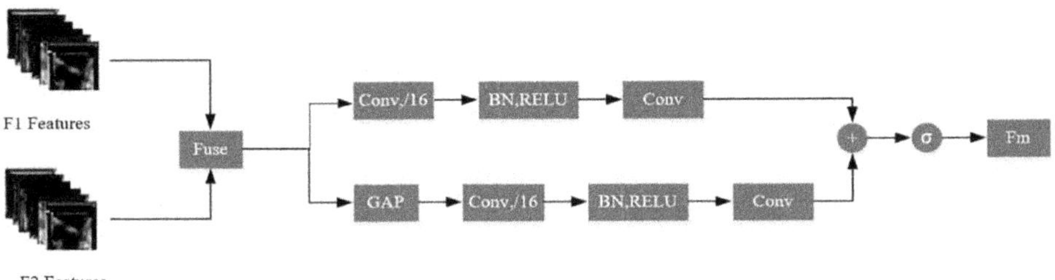

Fig. 2. Multi-level Fusion Module

3 Experiment

In this section, we design multiple steps to comprehensively evaluate the performance of RSANet. In the first part of the experiments, we test RSANet under both unimodal and multimodal settings. The structure of the unimodal network is identical to a single branch of the multimodal network, adopting the same feature extraction and classification methods.

In further experiments, we conduct ablation studies on the Attention-guided Fusion Module (AFM). By removing or replacing the AFM module, we observe its impact on feature extraction and overall performance, thereby validating the critical role of AFM in the entire network.

Finally, we compare the performance of RSANet with state-of-the-art (SOTA) recognition methods. Under the same experimental conditions, RSANet outperforms SOTA methods in evaluation metrics. These results clearly demonstrate that RSANet has significant advantages in improving recognition performance.

In the hyperparameter configuration of the finger vein recognition model, this study sets the learning rate to 0.002, the input resolution of network images to 224×224, the batch size to 16, and the training epochs to 70. Both the training set and validation set of the dataset are experimented with at a 1:1 ratio. To optimize model weights, AdamW is adopted as the optimizer, and cosine annealing is employed to adjust the learning rate during training. The experimental platform consists of a computer running the Windows system with an NVIDIA RTX1650 GPU, PyTorch version 1.12, and CUDA version 11.3.

3.1 Dataset

1) *SDUMLA-HMT*

SDUMLA-HMT [9] (Shandong University Multi-modal Biometric Database) contains fingerprint and finger-vein images from 106 distinct individuals. The database includes images of the left and right index, middle, and ring fingers from these 106 individuals. Each finger was imaged six times, resulting in a total of 3,816 images across 636 classes for both fingerprint and finger-vein modalities. Each image has a resolution of 320 × 240 pixels.

2) *FVC-HKPU*

The FVC-HKPU [10] multi-modal dataset is a recombination of the FVC 2006 fingerprint dataset and the HKPU finger-vein dataset. The FVC 2006 dataset was originally used for fingerprint verification competitions. In this study, we utilize the DB2 subset collected by an optical sensor from FVC 2006, which contains 150 finger samples with 12 images per finger. The finger-vein dataset was collected by The Hong Kong Polytechnic University, featuring 6 images per finger from 150 finger samples. By combining these fingerprint and finger-vein datasets, the testing dataset consists of Region of Interest (ROI) extracted images with a resolution of 300 × 100 pixels.

3) *NUPT-FPV*

The NUPT-FPV [11] Dataset is a significant dataset collected and constructed by Nanjing University of Posts and Telecommunications (NUPT) for multi-modal biometric recognition research. This dataset was compiled from 140 volunteers of diverse genders, including 108 female students and 32 male volunteers. Fingerprint and finger-vein images were captured from the index, middle, and ring fingers of each volunteer's hands, amounting to 840 fingers in total. Each finger was imaged 10 times, resulting in 8,400 fingerprint images and 8,400 finger-vein images. The finger-vein images in the dataset are sized at 300 × 450 pixels, while the fingerprint images are 200 × 400 pixels.

3.2 Cross-Modal Efficiency Comparison of RSANet

To validate the stability of the proposed multi-modal system, we designed a set of experiments aimed at evaluating the role of RSANet in enhancing recognition performance through cross-modal fusion. Specifically, we conducted unimodal feature recognition using individual branches of RSANet and compared their performance against the full multi-modal model.

The experimental results, as shown in Table 1, demonstrate that the multi-modal fusion model consistently outperforms unimodal counterparts. On the SDUMLA-HMT, FVC-HKPU, and NUPT-FPV datasets, our method achieved recognition rates of 98.4%, 100%, and 99.5%, respectively, significantly improving upon the unimodal baselines of 82.9%, 95.9%, and 95.9% (for fingerprint) and 99%, 98.8%, and 97.3% (for finger-vein). These results conclusively validate the superiority of the multi-modal approach in biometric recognition tasks.

Table 1. Comparison with the recognition performance of single-modal recognition systems

Model	SDUMLA-HMT	FVC-HKPU	NUPT-FPV
	ACC(%)	ACC(%)	ACC(%)
FP	82.9	99.0	95.9
FV	95.9	98.8	97.3
FP + FV	**98.4**	**100**	**99.5**

3.3 Effectiveness of the AFM-Block Method

This paper presents a novel multi-level feature fusion method to enhance the recognition performance of multi-modal networks. We conducted comparative experiments against the current mainstream fusion methods, Concat and Add. As shown in Table 2, our proposed method outperforms these baseline approaches, validating its effectiveness in feature fusion.

Table 2. Compares with common fusion methods

Fusion method	SDUMLA-HMT	FVC-HKPU	NUPT-FPV
	ACC(%)	ACC(%)	ACC(%)
Add	97.2	99.8	98.9
Concat	97.6	**100**	99.3
Ours	**98.4**	**100**	**99.5**

3.4 Comparison with Other SOTA Methods

To demonstrate the superiority of RSANet, we conducted comparative experiments between RSANet and recently proposed bimodal recognition networks on three finger-print and finger-vein bimodal datasets. The results in Table 3 fully validate the effectiveness and superiority of the proposed network. RSANet exhibits significant improvements across all performance metrics, showcasing broad prospects and potential in the field of image processing.

Table 3. Comparative analysis among HDCNET and other SOTA methods

Methods	SDUMLA-HMT	FVC-HKPU	NUPT-FPV
	ACC(%)	ACC(%)	ACC(%)
FPV-Net [11]	96.2	92.8	99.0
Efficient-Net [12]	95.2	98.8	98.4

(continued)

Table 3. (*continued*)

Methods	SDUMLA-HMT	FVC-HKPU	NUPT-FPV
	ACC(%)	ACC(%)	ACC(%)
FAB-AEF [13]	95.8	97.6	96.6
NL-Net [14]	97.7	99.7	99.1
Ours	**98.4**	**100**	**99.5**

4   Conclusion

This paper proposes a novel network RSANet for fingerprint and finger vein recognition, which adopts a new feature fusion method and can effectively integrate the key information of images.

RSANet reduces the risk of network overfitting through residual connections. On the other hand, by introducing the SimAM attention mechanism, the network can focus on both channel information and spatial information to extract more effective feature information. Subsequently, the AFM block enhances the feature representation ability by fusing global and local features. Finally, we evaluated RSANet on three datasets. The recognition accuracy on the SDUMLA dataset reached 98.4%, 100% on the FVC-HKPU dataset, and 99.5% on the NUPT-FPV dataset. In the future, we expect to propose a more secure and convenient multi-modal recognition model by combining other biometric features such as face and voiceprint.

References

1. Yang, X., Jia, X., Gong, D., Yan, D.-M., Li, Z., Liu, W.: LARNeXt: end-to-end lie algebra residual network for face recognition. IEEE Trans. Pattern Anal. Mach. Intell. **45**(10), 11961–11976 (2023). https://doi.org/10.1109/TPAMI.2023.3279378
2. Boutros, F., Damer, N., Kirchbuchner, F., Kuijper, A.: ElasticFace: elastic margin loss for deep face recognition. In: 2022 IEEE/CVF Conference on Computer Vision and Pattern Recognition Workshops (CVPRW), pp. 1154–1163. IEEE (2022). https://doi.org/10.1109/CVPRW56347.2022.00164
3. Liu, J., Dian, R., Li, S., Liu, H.: SGFusion: a saliency guided deep - learning framework for pixel - level image fusion. Inf. Fus. **91**, 205–214 (2023). ISSN 1566-3535
4. Yuan, C., Jiao, S., Sun, X., Wu, Q.M.J.: MFFFLD: a Multimodal - feature - fusion - based fingerprint liveness detection. IEEE Trans. Cogn. Dev. Syst. **14**(2), 648–661 (2022)
5. Aizi, K., Ouslim, M.: Score level fusion in multi - biometric identification based on zones of interest. J. King Saud Univ. Comput. Inf. Sci. **34**(1), 1498–1509 (2022). ISSN 1319–1578
6. Pradhan, A., He, J., Jiang, N.: Score, rank, and decision - level fusion strategies of multicode electromyogram - based verification and identification biometrics. IEEE J. Biomed. Health Inf. **26**(3), 1068–1079 (2022)
7. He, K., Zhang, X., Ren, S., Sun, J.: Deep residual learning for image recognition. In: Proceedings of the IEEE Conference on Computer Vision and Pattern Recognition, pp. 770–778 (2016)

8. Liu, Y., et al.: SimAM: a simple, parameter - free attention module for convolutional neural networks. IEEE Trans. Neural Netw. Learn. Syst. **34**(5), 2567–2578 (2023)

9. Yin, Y., Liu, L., Sun, X.: SDUMLA - HMT: a multimodal biometric database. In: Sun, Z., Lai, J., Chen, X., Tan, T. (eds.) Biometric Recognition (Lecture Notes in Computer Science, vol. 7098, pp. 260–268. Springer Berlin Heidelberg (2011). https://doi.org/10.1007/978-3-642-25449-9_33

10. Kumar, A., Zhou, Y.: Human identification using finger images. IEEE Trans. Image Process. **21**(4), 2228–2244 (2012). https://doi.org/10.1109/TIP.2011.2171697

11. Ren, H., Sun, L., Guo, J., Han, C.: A dataset and benchmark for multimodal biometric recognition based on fingerprint and finger vein. IEEE Trans. Inf. Forensics Secur. **17**, 2030–2043 (2022)

12. Tan,M., Le, Q.V.: EfficientNet: rethinking model scaling for convolutional neural networks. CoRR, abs/1905.11946 (2019)

13. Huang, Y., Ma, H., Wang, M.: Multimodal finger recognition based on asymmetric networks with fused similarity. IEEE Access **11**, 17497–17509 (2023). https://doi.org/10.1109/ACCESS.2023.3242984

14. Guo, Z., Ma, H., Liu, J.: NLNet: a narrow - channel lightweight network for finger multimodal recognition. Dig. Sig. Process. **150**, 104517 (2024). https://doi.org/10.1016/j.dsp.2024.104517

Dynamic Selective Distillation Network Based on Quality-Aware Fusion for Multimodal Biometric Recognition

Hai Yuan, Xiao Yang, Jinpeng Guan, Zaiyu Pan, and Jun Wang$^{(\boxtimes)}$

School of Information and Control Engineering, China University of Mining and Technology, Xuzhou 221000, Jiangsu, China
jrobot@126.com

Abstract. Multimodal biometric recognition has been widely applied in various fields in recent years due to its advantages in enhancing the security and convenience of identity verification. However, traditional multimodal systems face the challenge of information redundancy. Existing methods rely on static teacher models for self-distillation and neglect the quality differences in inter- and intra- modalities, which hinder their overall performance. To address these issues, we propose a dynamic selective distillation network (DSD-Network) that integrates the early exit mechanism with dynamic selective self-distillation to optimize the performance and computational efficiency of multimodal biometric recognition frameworks. Specifically, we introduce a selective distillation strategy based on entropy-based to regulate the application of distillation. Subsequently, a dynamic distillation factor is employed to adaptively adjust the distillation process according to the learning status of each layer. The integration enables early-stage predictions by transferring knowledge from deeper layers to shallow layers, thereby further enhancing the model's performance and efficiency. Additionally, a Modality Quality-Aware Fusion (MQAF) approach is introduced, which incorporates intra-modality confidence and inter-modality energy uncertainty weighting. This module leverages an inter-modality energy uncertainty evaluation strategy to calibrate intra-modality feature weights, fully exploiting the complementarity and correlation among modalities. Extensive experiments have been conducted to validate the effectiveness of the proposed method.

Keywords: multi-modality biometric recognition · dynamic selective distillation · modality quality-aware fusion · dynamic distillation factor

1 Introduction

Recent advances in computer technology have increased the demand for secure and convenient identity verification. Biometric recognition, which verifies identity via unique physiological or behavioral traits, is widely used in electronic payments, financial security, border control, and smart cities [1]. Unimodal systems face challenges like incomplete data, poor sampling, and limited accuracy.

W. Jia et al. (Eds.): CCBR 2025, LNCS 16360, pp. 150–160, 2026.
https://doi.org/10.1007/978-981-95-6123-0_15

Multimodal biometrics overcome these by integrating multiple traits, improving accuracy, security, robustness, and anti-spoofing [2]. Hand-based systems, using features like palmprints and palmveins, are especially promising due to their high uniqueness and stability.

However, there are two main challenges in multimodal biometric recognition methods: (1) Different modalities data typically have high dimensionality and heterogeneity, which often leads to information redundancy. Furthermore, as the layers of a CNN deepen, the computational complexity grows exponentially. Existing lightweight methods rely on static teacher models for self-distillation, overlooking differences in knowledge transfer across layers and the dynamic variation in the influence of teacher layer on the student model. (2) Existing multimodal biometric fusion methods primarily focus on the individual quality differences across modalities, ignoring the global relationship and complementarity between modalities. This limitation leads to the underutilization of high-quality modalities, while the interference of low-quality modalities may weaken the overall fusion performance.

To solve the above problem: (1) We propose a dynamic selective distillation network (DSD-Network) that adjusts the distillation process based on the learning progress between the teacher and student layers. By incorporating inter-layer selection modeling and a dynamic distillation module, the strategy takes into account the importance of the teacher model and adaptively adjusts the distillation intensity based on the learning progress of the student layers. This approach facilitates effective knowledge transfer across layers, ultimately enhancing the performance of the student model. (2) A Modality Quality-Aware Fusion (MQAF) is introduced, which calibrates the uncertainty weights in intra-modality by using global inter-modality energy scores. Specifically, a multi-layer perceptron (MLP) is employed to calculate intra-modality weights, dynamically evaluating the quality of modality features. Subsequently, energy scores are utilized to generate global inter-modality weights, allowing for the weighted calibration of intra-modality weights, thereby prioritizing the utilization of high-quality modalities while effectively suppressing low-quality modalities.

We summarize our main contributions as follows:

- A dynamic selective distillation network is introduced, which leverages a selective distillation strategy and a dynamic distillation module to enhance cross-layer knowledge transfer.

- A Modality Quality-Aware Fusion is proposed, dynamically adjusting modality feature weights to fully leverage the potential correlations and complementarities between modalities.

2   Related Work

Multimodal biometric recognition technology made significant progress in enhancing multimodal system robustness and accuracy. With the advancement of deep learning, various levels of fusion methods emerged, such as feature-level, score-level, and decision-level fusion.

In feature-level fusion, Riaz et al. [3] fused CSC-LBP features of dorsal crease and knuckle print at the feature level and classified with SVM, achieving significantly superior performance over unimodal approaches. Sengar et al. [4] introduced a feature-level fusion method of fingerprint and palmprint, first extracting features with Gabor filters, followed by a deep neural network (DNN) for recognition. These feature-level fusion methods retain more original information, achieving outstanding performance in complex biometric recognition scenarios.

In score-level fusion, Peng et al. [5] employed a score-level fusion method based on the triangular rule to integrate fingerprint, finger vein, finger shape, and knuckle print, distinguishing the score distributions of genuine users and impostors, thus achieving a lower error rate. Almaymuni et al. [6] proposed MBEAS, merging iris, face, hand, speech, signature, handwriting, fingerprint and keystroke from BiosecurID via modified score-level fusion and matching templates with a CNN-RNN-BiLSTM TriBlendNN. These methods improved the accuracy of recognition systems by integrating biometric features from different modalities at the score level.

In decision-level fusion, Iloanusi et al. [7] integrated decision information from five fingerprints for gender recognition, showing multi-fingerprint fusion improves classification accuracy. Zhu et al. [8] used an AND rule to combine finger geometry, knuckle texture, and palmprint features for more accurate recognition. These decision-level fusion techniques combine decisions from multiple modalities to enhance performance and reliability of biometric recognition systems.

The above methods implement multimodal fusion at various levels, primarily emphasizing the independent optimization of intra-modal features. However, they overlook the global relationships and complementarities between modalities, resulting in limitations in the fusion effectiveness.

3   Methods

3.1   Overall Framework

We propose dynamic selective distillation network based on quality-aware fusion to improve multimodal hand biometrics recognition, as shown in Fig. 1. First, multimodal data are input into the VGG16 network for feature extraction. A Modality Quality-Aware Fusion mechanism is then introduced to handle modality quality differences. Next, a dynamic inference strategy with internal classifiers (IC) and confidence-driven early exit is applied. Additionally, dynamic selective distillation is used to guide earlier layers with refined features from later layers, enabling cross-layer knowledge transfer and adaptive inference path selection.

3.2   Modality Quality-Aware Fusion

In multimodal fusion tasks, the data quality of different modalities varies significantly. To ensure that high-quality modalities are prioritized and the impact of low-quality modalities is mitigated during the fusion process, we designed a Modality Quality-Aware Fusion (MQAF). This module dynamically adjusts

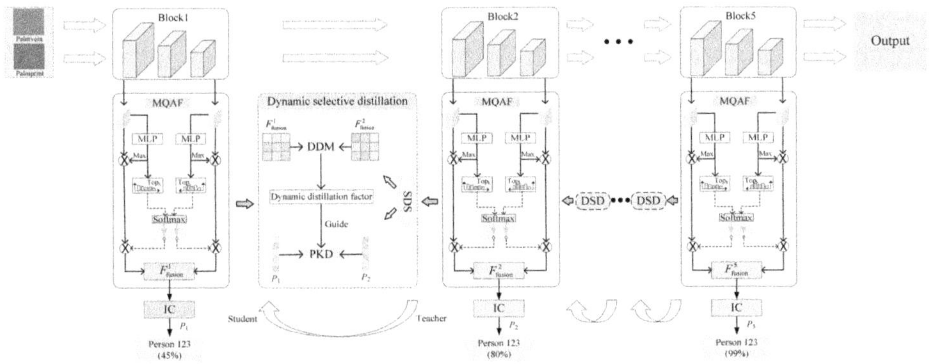

Fig. 1. Dynamic selective distillation framework based on quality-aware fusion.

intra-class confidence weights using inter-class energy uncertainty, fully exploiting the potential correlations and complementarity between modalities.

Firstly, the intra-modal confidence $intra\,{}^{(i)}_m$ of each modality is calculated to quantify the importance of features within the modality.

$$intra\,{}^{(i)}_m = \mathrm{Max}(S_{\mathrm{MLP}}(x^{(i)}_m)), \tag{1}$$

where $x^{(i)}_m$ represents the output features of modality m at layer i, where $m = 1, 2, \ldots, M$, and S_{MLP} denotes the logits produced by the MLP and softmax operations. The Max() function selects the maximum value as the confidence score for the corresponding modality.

To further enhance the perception of different modality qualities, we introduce inter-modality energy uncertainty scores to dynamically adjust intra-modality confidence. Specifically, the inter-modality energy score $\mathrm{Energy}(x^{(i)}_m)$ for each modality is first calculated. A higher inter-modality energy score indicates greater confidence of the model in certain categories among the top N classes. The formula is as follows,

$$\mathrm{Energy}(x^{(i)}_m) = \mathrm{Top}_N \left(\log \sum_{n=1}^{N} e^{z_n} \right), \tag{2}$$

where $z_n = S_{\mathrm{MLP}}(x^{(i)}_m)$, represents predicted probability for the n-th class. Top_N refers to the top N classes with highest confidence scores among the modalities.

Then, the inter-modality energy score is utilized to calculate the inter-modality weight for each modality, enabling the weighted adjustment of intra-modality features during the fusion process. The formula is as follows,

$$inter\,{}^{(i)}_m = \frac{\exp(\mathrm{Energy}(x^{(i)}_m))}{\sum_{m=1}^{M} \exp(\mathrm{Energy}(x^{(i)}_m))}. \tag{3}$$

Next, the intra-modality confidence $intra_m^{(i)}$ is multiplied by the inter-modality weight $inter_m^{(i)}$ to obtain the final modality quality-aware weight $w_m^{(i)}$, as follows,

$$w_m^{(i)} = intra_m^{(i)} \cdot inter_m^{(i)}. \tag{4}$$

Finally, the quality-aware weight $w_m^{(i)}$ is multiplied with modality features $x_m^{(i)}$ to generate weighted features. These weighted features from all modalities are then concatenated to form the fused feature $F_{\text{fusion}}^{(i)}$, as follows,

$$F_{\text{fusion}}^{(i)} = \text{Concat}(w_1^{(i)} \cdot x_1^{(i)}, \ldots, w_m^{(i)} \cdot x_m^{(i)}), \quad m = 1, 2, \ldots, M. \tag{5}$$

3.3 Dynamic Selective Distillation

To enhance the efficiency of the distillation process and reduce information redundancy, we propose a dynamic selective distillation network (DSD-network). This approach introduces an entropy-based selective distillation strategy (SDS) and a dynamic distillation module (DDM), which adaptively adjusts the distillation intensity based on the learning progress between the teacher and student models across layers, optimizing the knowledge transfer process.

(1) Selective distillation strategy (SDS)

The selective distillation strategy determines whether to apply the distillation process based on the calculation of entropy. The entropy value reflects the level of uncertainty in the model's output. By calculating the entropy values of the teacher model outputs, we assess whether the current distillation is meaningful for the student model. Specifically, for each layer of the teacher's output, we calculate the entropy value:

$$H(P) = -\sum_{i=1}^{C} H(P_i) \log(H(P_i) + \epsilon), \tag{6}$$

where $H(P_i) = \frac{e^{P_i}}{\sum_{j=1}^{C} e^{P_j}}$ is the probability output of the softmax, C represents the number of categories, and ϵ is a small constant used to avoid computational errors during the logarithm operation.

The SDS is applied to calculate the entropy value $H(P_l)$ of the teacher model's output. Based on a threshold τ, it dynamically determines whether to apply distillation. If the entropy of the teacher's layer is below the predefined threshold τ, the layer is selected for distillation to the student layer. Otherwise, distillation is skipped to avoid unnecessary computational overhead.

(2) Dynamic distillation module (DDM)

To further optimize the distillation process, we introduce a dynamic distillation module, which calculates the correlation between the teacher and student layers and adaptively adjusts the distillation intensity based on the learning state of the student layer. By dynamically adjusting the distillation factor, the distillation intensity for each layer can be finely controlled according to the model's actual learning progress. The dynamic distillation factor δ is defined as follows:

$$\delta = \frac{F_{\text{fusion}}^{(i)} \cdot F_{\text{fusion}}^{(i+1)}}{\| F_{\text{fusion}}^{(i)} \| \| F_{\text{fusion}}^{(i+1)} \|}, \tag{7}$$

where $F_{\text{fusion}}^{(i)}$ and $F_{\text{fusion}}^{(i+1)}$ represent the normalized feature vectors of the student and teacher layers, respectively. The δ is then normalized to ensure its range lies between 0 and 1.

Then, we incorporate the DDF into the distillation loss. The distillation loss for layer i is defined as the Kullback-Leibler (KL) divergence between the soft predictions of the i-th layer and the target soft labels from the deeper layer L_{i+1}:

$$L_{distillation}(L_i) = \delta_i \cdot D_{KL}(P_i, P_{i+1}), \tag{8}$$

where P_i is the probability distribution predicted by the i-th layer. P_{i+1} is the probability distribution of the target from the deeper layer L_{i+1}, typically from the next layer or the final output layer.

3.4   Dynamic Inference

To optimize both efficiency and accuracy during model inference, a dynamic inference mechanism is proposed. This mechanism embeds an internal classifier at each block of the model to evaluate intermediate features and predict confidence scores. Based on these scores, the mechanism adaptively determines whether to exit early or continue to deeper layers, optimizing computational cost.

Each IC consists of a feature reduction layer and a softmax output layer. The IC evaluates the feature representation at the current layer and computes a exit confidence score $p_{\max}(L_i)$ as follows:

$$p_{\max}(L_i) = \text{Max}\left(\text{softmax}\left(W_i \cdot F_{\text{fusion}}^{(i)} + b_i\right)\right), \tag{9}$$

where W_i and b_i denote the weight matrix and bias vector, respectively. The symbol $F_{\text{fusion}}^{(i)}$ represents the fused feature map at the current layer L_i.

Each internal classifier is assigned a confidence threshold θ_i to determine whether to exit early at the current layer. If the output $p_{\max}(L_i)$ of an internal classifier exceeds this threshold, the prediction result is directly returned as the final output, terminating further inference. Otherwise, the sample is passed to the next layer for evaluation,

$$\text{Output}(L_i) = \begin{cases} \text{Predict}(L_i), & \text{if } p_{\max}(L_i) \geq \theta_i, \\ \text{Pass}(L_{i+1}), & \text{otherwise}, \end{cases} \tag{10}$$

where $\text{Output}(L_i)$ represents the output result of the current layer, $\text{Predict}(L_i)$ denotes the predicted class of the current classifier, and $\text{Pass}(L_{i+1})$ indicates that the sample is passed to the next layer.

3.5 Loss Function

The loss function is defined as the sum of the classification loss and the distillation loss for each layer in the network:

$$L_{\text{total}} = \sum_{i=1}^{L} \left(\alpha_i \cdot L_{\text{CE}}(L_i) + \beta_i \cdot L_{\text{distillation}}(L_i) \right), \tag{11}$$

where $L_{\text{CE}}(L_i)$ represents the classification loss for the i-th layer, $L_{\text{distillation}}(L_i)$ is the distillation loss for the i-th layer, with α_i and β_i [9] denoting the weights of the classification loss and distillation loss for the i-th layer, respectively.

4 Experiments

4.1 Dataset and Experiment Settings

The CASIA Multi-Spectral Palmprint Image Dataset V1.0 [10] contains 7,200 palm images from 100 participants covering 200 palms. Palmprint and palmvein images at 460nm and 850nm wavelengths with extracted ROIs were used. Tongji Dataset [11] contains 24,000 images from 300 participants and 600 palms, with extracted ROIs for experiments. The Tsinghua IC-LAB Dataset [12] provides 90,000 ROI images from 250 subjects (500 palms) with RGB and infrared palmprint and palmvein images. The CUMT Dataset [13] provides right palmprint, palmvein, and dorsal vein images from 290 participants; palmprint and palmvein ROIs were used.

In our experiments, all images were resized to 224 × 224 pixels to ensure input consistency across experiments. Each dataset was split into a 1:1 ratio for training and testing. The experiments were carried out using an NVIDIA GeForce GTX 2080 GPU and implemented in Python 3.7.16 with the PyTorch framework. In the evaluation experiments for the proposed method, the model was trained for 100 epochs using the SGD optimizer. The learning rate and weight decay were set to 1×10^{-5}.

4.2 Ablation Study

To validate each module, we conducted ablation experiments on the Tsinghua dataset, as shown in Table 1, progressively introducing early exit, MQAF, self-distillation, and DSD. The baseline VGG16 achieved 99.48% accuracy with 29.959M parameters and a runtime of 0.0077 s. Introducing early exit reduced the parameters to 19.388M and the runtime to 0.0068 s, but slightly lowered accuracy. MQAF compensated for lost deep features, raising accuracy to 99.60% while cutting parameters to 16.033M and runtime to 0.0064 s

Next, self-distillation is introduced, where teacher features from later layers guide the student features of the current layer, facilitating cross-layer knowledge transfer, improving accuracy to 99.88%. However, the absence of dynamic selection during distillation limits the further performance enhancement. To address

Table 1. Ablation study results on accuracy, params, and running time.

Early Exit	MQAF	Self Distillation	DSD	Accuracy (%)	Params (M)	Running Time (S)
				99.48	29.959	0.0077
✓				99.40	19.388	0.0068
✓	✓			99.60	16.033	0.0064
✓	✓	✓		99.88	13.542	0.0061
✓	✓		✓	**99.92**	**12.347**	**0.0059**

this limitation, we propose Dynamic Selective Distillation (DSD), which adjusts the distillation process based on the learning progress between the teacher and student layers. Experimental results show that DSD achieves optimal performance, with accuracy increasing to 99.92%, parameters reduced to 12.347M, and running time shortened to 0.0059 s.

4.3   Comparison With State-of-the-Art Methods

This section compares our method with state-of-the-art algorithms on four datasets, as shown in Table 2. The "-fusion" method concatenates features from three modalities. FPV-NET [18] enhances intermodal representations but lacks hierarchical feature optimization. TAI [20] leverages triple attention to achieve 93.83% on CASIA and 99.80% on Tsinghua, but fails to fully capture global relationships and modality complementarity.

In contrast, we introduce the Dynamic Selective Distillation Network Based on Quality-Aware Fusion. This network combines the early exit mechanism with dynamic selective self-distillation, allowing the model to make more accurate early exit decisions based on guidance from deeper layers that capture finer features. Experimental results show that the recognition rates on the CASIA, Tongji, Tsinghua, and CUMT datasets are 96.67%, 99.94%, 99.92%, and 99.76%, respectively, achieving optimal performance.

Table 2. Recognition accuracy of multi-modality method and the proposed method.

Method	CASIA (%)	Tongji (%)	Tsinghua (%)	CUMT (%)
AlexNet-fusion [14]	84.50	99.00	99.10	98.90
MobileNet-fusion [15]	86.00	99.27	99.20	99.12
VGG16-fusion [16]	94.50	99.66	99.48	99.46
CSAFM [17]	95.00	99.80	99.83	99.62
FPV-NET [18]	96.17	99.86	99.37	99.66
MMRACR [19]	92.83	99.61	99.70	99.52
TAI [20]	93.83	99.90	99.80	99.59
Our method	**96.67**	**99.94**	**99.92**	**99.76**

4.4 The Evaluation of Params and Running Time

We compared the proposed method with several mainstream multimodal recognition algorithms, focusing on the number of parameters and running time on the Tsinghua dataset. Table 3 reveals that the running times of CSAFM and FPV-NET are significantly higher, primarily due to the additional computational overhead introduced by their complex fusion modules. MMRACR and TAI reduce the number of parameters, but their running times increase to 0.0085 s and 0.0109 s, respectively, indicating that their lightweight designs do not effectively balance parameter size and inference speed. The proposed method achieves 12.347M parameters and 0.0059 s runtime, demonstrating superior efficiency.

Table 3. Comparison results of different methods on the number of parameters and running time.

Dataset	Params (M)	Running Time (S)
CSAFM	59.182	0.0078
FPV-NET	59.859	0.0077
MMRACR	21.607	0.0085
TAI	22.988	0.0109
Our method	**12.347**	**0.0059**

5 Conclusion

This paper presents an innovative approach to enhancing multimodal biometric recognition systems. We introduce a DSD-Network, which adopts a selective distillation strategy and a dynamic distillation module to adaptively adjust the distillation process based on the learning progress of each layer. This enables early predictions by distilling deeper layer information to the current shallow layer, enhancing the accuracy of early exits while reducing computational complexity. Furthermore, The MQAF dynamically calibrates intra-modality feature weights based on intra-modality confidence evaluation and inter-modality uncertainty-driven weighting, fully leveraging high-quality modality features. Experimental results the proposed method significantly outperforms state-of-the-art multimodal fusion recognition algorithms. In the future, we will further optimize the DSD network by incorporating more refined inter-layer relationship modeling and a smarter dynamic adjustment mechanism to enhance the effectiveness of cross-layer knowledge transfer.

Acknowledgements. This work was supported by the Graduate Innovation Program of China University of Mining and Technology (2024WLKXJ088), the Fundamental Research Funds for the Central Universities (2024XSCX015), and the Postgraduate Research & Practice Innovation Program of Jiangsu Province (KYCX24_2776).

References

1. Zhang, Y., Mu, Z., Yuan, L., Yu, C., Liu, Q.: USTB-Helloear: a large database of ear images photographed under uncontrolled conditions. In: Zhao, Y., Kong, X., Taubman, D. (eds.) ICIG 2017. LNCS, vol. 10667, pp. 405–416. Springer, Cham (2017). https://doi.org/10.1007/978-3-319-71589-6_35

2. Harshvardhan, A.S., et al.: Anti-spoofing: a bio finger print recognition method using pattern matching algorithm. In: 2025 IEEE International Students' Conference on Electrical, Electronics and Computer Science (SCEECS). IEEE (2025)

3. Riaz, I., et al.: Multimodal biometric recognition system based on feature-level fusion of dorsal finger crease and finger knuckle print. IEEE Trans. Artif. Intell., 1–13 (2025)

4. Sengar, S., et al.: Multimodal biometric authentication system using deep learning method. In: Proc. Int. Conf. Emerg. Smart Comput. Inform, pp. 309–312. IEEE (2020)

5. Peng, J., Abd El-Latif, A.A., Li, Q., et al.: Multimodal biometric authentication based on score level fusion of finger biometrics. Optik **125**(23), 6891–6897 (2014)

6. Almaymuni, A.Z., et al.: Multimodal biometric enrolment and authentication system (MBEAS) with modified score-level fusion and TriBlendNN-based template matching. Adv. Appl. Discrete Math. **42**(2), 113–149 (2025)

7. Iloanusi, O., Ejiogu, U.: Gender classification from fused multi-fingerprint types. Inf. Secur. J. Glob. Perspect. **29**(5), 209–219 (2020)

8. Zhu, L., et al.: Multimodal biometric identification system based on finger geometry, knuckle print and palm print. Pattern Recognit. Lett. **31**(12), 1641–1649 (2010)

9. Kaya, Y., et al.: Shallow-deep networks: understanding and mitigating network overthinking. In: International Conference on Machine Learning, pp. 3301–3310. PMLR (2019)

10. Hao, Y., et al.: Multispectral palm image fusion for accurate contact-free palmprint recognition. In: Proc. 15th IEEE Int. Conf. Image Process., pp. 281–284 (2008)

11. Zhang, L., Li, L., Yang, A., Shen, Y., Yang, M.: Towards contactless palmprint recognition: a novel device, a new benchmark, and a collaborative representation based identification approach. Pattern Recognit. **69**, 199–212 (2017)

12. Xie, Z., Guo, Z., Qian, C.: Palmprint gender classification by convolutional neural network (CNN). IET Comput. Vis. **12**(4), 476–483 (2018)

13. Pan, Z., et al.: Palmprint and palm vein recognition method based on modal information evaluation strategy. CAAI Trans. Intell. Syst. **19**(5), 1136–1148 (2024)

14. Krizhevsky, A., Sutskever, I., Hinton, G.E.: ImageNet classification with deep convolutional neural networks. In: Advances in Neural Information Processing Systems, vol. 25 (2012)

15. Howard, A.G.: MobileNets: efficient convolutional neural networks for mobile vision applications. arXiv preprint: arXiv:1704.04861 (2017)

16. Simonyan, K.: Very deep convolutional networks for large-scale image recognition. arXiv preprint: arXiv:1409.1556 (2014)

17. Ren, H., et al.: A dataset and benchmark for multimodal biometric recognition based on fingerprint and finger vein. IEEE Trans. Inf. Forensics Secur. **17**, 2030–2043 (2022)

18. Guo, J., et al.: Finger multimodal feature fusion and recognition based on channel spatial attention. arXiv preprint: arXiv:2209.02368 (2022)

19. Yang, X., et al.: Multi-modality relation attention network for breast tumor classification. Comput. Biol. Med. **150**, 106210 (2022)
20. Yang, X., et al.: Triple-attention interaction network for breast tumor classification based on multi-modality images. Pattern Recognit. **139**, 109526 (2023)

LACE: Learnable Adaptive Cross-Entropy Loss for Vein Recognition

Xianghuai Liu, Haiyang Li, Hailong Hu$^{(\boxtimes)}$, and Huafeng Qin

Chongqing Technology and Business University, Chongqing, China
`2023313024@ctbu.edu.cn`, `huhailong94@163.com`

Abstract. Vein recognition, valued for its contactless, anti-counterfeiting, and interference-resistant properties, has become a key focus in identity authentication. In deep learning-based vein recognition, the loss function plays a vital role in guiding model optimization and achieving high recognition accuracy. However, existing methods, such as Poly-1, rely on fixed, manually tuned hyperparameters, which limit their adaptability to different data distributions and network architectures. To address this issue, this paper proposes LACE (Learnable Adaptive Cross-Entropy Loss), a novel adaptive loss function based on the Taylor expansion of the standard cross-entropy, which incorporates learnable parameters to dynamically optimize the polynomial coefficients. Unlike Poly-1, LACE automatically adjusts its parameters during training, better adapting to diverse scenarios. Experiments on three vein datasets and nine deep learning models demonstrate that LACE consistently improves recognition performance, reducing the average equal error rates by 0.15%, 0.16%, and 0.37% on FV_USM, TJU_PV600, and VERA_PV200, respectively.

Keywords: Learnable adaptive cross-entropy loss function · Deep learning optimization · Vein recognition

1 Introduction

With the rapid advancement of digitalization, the demand for high-security identity authentication has experienced explosive growth. In this context, vein recognition has emerged as a promising solution for sensitive scenarios, leveraging its unique advantages of liveness detection, contactless acquisition, and resistance to environmental interference [1,14].

Deep learning based methods have substantially advanced vein recognition by overcoming the inherent limitations of traditional handcrafted feature extraction [4,9,15,18,22]. For example, Das et al. [4] propose optimizing the architecture of convolutional neural networks (CNNs) to effectively capture both local

---

Supplementary Information The online version contains supplementary material available at https://doi.org/10.1007/978-981-95-6123-0_16.

W. Jia et al. (Eds.): CCBR 2025, LNCS 16360, pp. 161–170, 2026.
https://doi.org/10.1007/978-981-95-6123-0_16

and global vascular patterns, achieving superior performance on finger vein datasets. Furthermore, Qin et al. [15] extend CNNs to palm vein recognition by integrating multi-scale and multi-directional generative adversarial networks, thereby enriching data diversity and improving model generalization. Despite the remarkable progress made by the powerful representation capabilities of deep neural networks, the loss function, one of the critical components of deep learning models [19], continues to pose challenges that limit overall performance in vein recognition [20]. On the one hand, traditional loss functions such as the cross-entropy [13] struggle to adapt to the non-uniform distribution characteristics of vein images, often resulting in imbalanced learning between blood vessels and tissues [8]. On the other hand, the fixed hyperparameters of traditional loss functions are inadequate for adapting to the dynamic changes during training, as the difficulty of learning various features evolves across different training stages [2]. This mismatch between fixed loss functions and the evolving demands of model learning has driven the development of more adaptive and flexible loss functions to enhance vein recognition performance further.

Several studies have explored the design of loss functions from different perspectives. In the direction of parameterized loss design, Barron et al. [3] propose the General Adaptive Loss that can adaptively choose L1 or L2 norms. Lin et al. [12] develop the Focal Loss with dynamic modulation factors to address sample imbalance issues. In the direction of automated loss function search, Li et al. [11] propose the AM-LFS framework, which enables the automatic search for loss function forms. Gonzalez et al. [5] utilize genetic algorithms to find the optimal structures of loss functions. In the direction of polynomial reconstruction of loss functions, Leng et al. [10] propose the PolyLoss, which enables fine-grained control over polynomial coefficients through vertical adjustment mechanisms. The core variant, Poly-1 (only the first hyperparameter term, ϵ_1, is adjusted), has been shown to improve model performance significantly. Although these methods have laid a solid foundation for adaptive loss function design, they are not well-suited to vein recognition.

Specifically, existing loss functions face two key challenges in vein recognition scenarios. First, fixed hyperparameters fail to maintain consistent performance across diverse vein datasets. They cannot adapt to training-phase specific features, thereby limiting the model's ability to learn critical discriminative characteristics [3,10,12]. Second, methods based on automatic search or genetic algorithms require dataset-specific search configurations, which are time-consuming and lack principled optimization strategies [5,11]. Overall, these limitations highlight the critical need for a dynamically adaptive loss mechanism that can respond to both data-specific characteristics and training dynamics.

In this paper, we propose the Learnable Adaptive Cross-Entropy (LACE) loss function to address challenges as mentioned above. Our contributions are twofold. 1 A learnable loss function LACE is designed, which can universally improve the performance and robustness of deep learning models across various vein datasets. 2 Extensive experiments demonstrate the superior performance of

LACE compared to both the traditional cross-entropy and the improved Poly-1 [10] loss functions.

2   Methodology

2.1   Cross-Entropy Loss (CE)

Cross-Entropy (CE) loss is a fundamental loss function in classification and recognition tasks. Given the ground truth distribution Q and the predicted distribution P, the loss function of CE is defined as [13]:

$$\mathcal{L}_{CE} = -\sum_{t=1}^{N} Q_t \log(P_t) \tag{1}$$

where $Q_t \in \{0,1\}$ denotes the true probability (one-hot encoded ground truth) for class t, $P_t \in [0,1]$ represents the predicted probability for class t, and N is the total number of classes.

2.2   Poly-1 Loss (PCE)

The Taylor expansion of the CE loss is as follows [10]:

$$\mathcal{L}_{CE} = -\log\left(P_t\right) = \sum_{j=1}^{\infty} \frac{1}{j}\left(1-P_t\right)^j = \left(1-P_t\right) + \frac{1}{2}\left(1-P_t\right)^2 + \cdots \tag{2}$$

It can be observed that taking the gradient of the loss $\mathcal{L}_{CE}$ concerning P_t results in a series of polynomial terms, where the first-order term contributes the most to the overall gradient, followed by higher-order terms with diminishing impact. This indicates that within the cross-entropy formulation, the first polynomial term plays a dominant role in driving the optimization process. Based on this observation, Leng et al. [10] propose Poly-1 that selectively adjusts the first-order term of the cross-entropy expansion, which is defined as:

$$\begin{aligned} \mathcal{L}_{\text{Poly}-1} &= \mathcal{L}_{CE} + \epsilon_1 \left(1-P_t\right) \\ &= \left(\epsilon_1 + 1\right)\left(1-P_t\right) + \frac{1}{2}\left(1-P_t\right)^2 + \cdots + \frac{1}{N}\left(1-P_t\right)^N + \cdots \end{aligned} \tag{3}$$

However, this method still exhibits particular subjectivity and limitations. Manually adjusting the polynomial coefficients remains a form of hyperparameter tuning, and the complexity increases with the number of adjustable factors, leading to significant time costs for parameter optimization.

Therefore, we propose a learnable adaptive loss function that dynamically optimizes these hyperparameters.

2.3   Learnable Adaptive Cross-Entropy Loss (LACE)

Building upon CE loss and inspired by the work of Leng et al. [10], we propose a learnable adaptive loss function, LACE. It optimizes the Taylor expansion of the CE loss term by term, allowing the model to automatically learn the optimal coefficients (hyperparameters) of the polynomial components.

The mathematical formulation of LACE is as follows:

$$\mathcal{L}_{\text{ACE}} = \mathcal{L}_{\text{CE}} + \sum_{k=1}^{N} \epsilon_k (1 - P_t)^k = (\epsilon_1 + 1)(1 - P_t)$$

$$+ \left(\epsilon_2 + \frac{1}{2}\right)(1 - P_t)^2 + \cdots + \left(\epsilon_n + \frac{1}{N}\right)(1 - P_t)^N + \cdots \tag{4}$$

where $N \in \mathbb{N}^+$, ϵ_k is the k-th learnable independent parameter, and $P_t \in [0, 1]$ denotes the model's predicted probability. The series needs to converge when $|1 - P_t| < 1$.

Unlike traditional loss functions, LACE introduces learnable adjustment factors for each polynomial term, allowing the loss to be automatically adapted to different models and datasets. First, by incorporating and optimizing the influence of higher-order polynomial terms beyond a fixed truncation point, LACE maximizes the expressive capacity of the loss function without manual intervention. Second, this design eliminates the need for labor-intensive coefficient tuning, significantly reducing the time required for hyperparameter optimization. Indeed, its adaptive nature ensures consistent and robust performance across a variety of experimental settings, as illustrated in Sect. 3.4.

Figure 1 illustrates the architectural design of the LACE. To optimize the learnable parameters, a gradient-based optimization approach is employed. Consistent with the common practice of utilizing gradient descent for model weight updates in deep learning, we adopt the same strategy for LACE. Specifically, the update rule for the learnable parameters in LACE can be derived from Equation (4). For parameter updates, we consider the simplified case where $N = 1$. The refined update formulas are presented as follows.

$$W = W + \eta \cdot (\epsilon_1 + 1) \times \frac{\partial P_t}{\partial W} \tag{5}$$

$$\epsilon_1 = \epsilon_1 - \eta \cdot (1 - P_t) \tag{6}$$

This simplified version focuses on learning only the most influential factor ϵ_1 to enable rapid validation of the effectiveness of the method. In our experimental evaluation, we apply Equations (5) and (6) on three vein data sets. The detailed derivation is provided in the **supplementary material**.

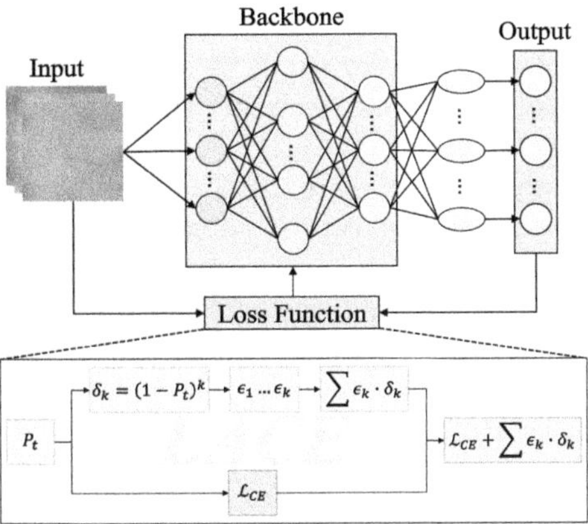

Fig. 1. The overview of LACE. **Top:** the backbone network receives a vein image as input and produces a predicted probability distribution through a neural network. **Bottom:** the loss module takes the predicted probability P_t, computes the deviation $\delta_k = (1 - P_t)^k$, then, using a set of learnable parameters $\{\epsilon_k\}_{k=1}^{K}$, constructs a dynamic weighting term $\sum_{k=1}^{K} \epsilon_k \delta_k$. Finally, the standard cross-entropy loss $\mathcal{L}_{\mathrm{CE}}$ is augmented to yield the novel loss $\mathcal{L}_{\mathrm{ACE}} = \mathcal{L}_{\mathrm{CE}} + \sum_{k=1}^{K} \epsilon_k \delta_k$.

3   Experiments

3.1   Datasets

The proposed method, LACE, is evaluated on three vein datasets, including two palm vein datasets (VERA_PV220, TJU_PV600) and one finger vein dataset (FV_USM).

VERA_PV220 comprises palm vein images from 110 subjects. For each subject, both hands are imaged in two separate sessions with five captures per hand, yielding a total of 1,100 images. The original image resolution of 480×680 pixels is resized to 200×200 pixels during preprocessing.

TJU_PV600 contains palm vein images from 300 participants. Each hand was captured 10 times per session over two sessions, totalling 20 images per hand. This results in 6,000 images. The original resolution of 800×600 pixels is down-sampled to 128×128 for analysis.

FV_USM is a finger vein dataset collected from 123 volunteers. Four fingers per subject were scanned, with three captures per finger in each of the two sessions, totaling 2,952 images. After extracting the vein region from the original 640×480 images, each is resized to 100×300 and then stitched into 300×300 images for training.

3.2   Experimental Configurations

For all three datasets, we conduct comprehensive experiments using nine different model architectures: CMT [6], FV CNN [4], FVRAS Net [21], IVT [16],

Lightweight CNN [18], MSVT [17], PV CNN [15], ResNet18 [7], and ResNet50 [7]. Each model is trained and evaluated using three loss functions: CE, Poly-1, and LACE. As a result, a total of 27 experiments (9 models × three loss functions) are conducted for each dataset.

Different training configurations are used. For palm vein data sets, the batch size is set at 10 and the learning rate is set to 5×10^{-4}, while for the finger vein dataset, the batch size is set to 4 and the learning rate is set to 10^{-3}. The AdamW optimizer is used to update the model weight parameters in all experiments. For the learnable parameters ϵ_k within the LACE loss function, we also use the AdamW optimizer for updates. The initial value ϵ_1 is set to 2.0, and its learning rate is set to 10^{-6}.

3.3   Evaluation Metrics

We employ three metrics to assess recognition performance.

Accuracy (ACC): the proportion of correctly recognized samples over the total number of trials.

Equal Error Rate (EER): the error rate at the operating point where the false acceptance rate (FAR) equals the false rejection rate (FRR).

True Accept Rate at FAR = 0.1% (TAR@FAR=0.1%): the proportion of genuine attempts correctly accepted when the system's false acceptance rate is restricted to 0.1%.

3.4   Experimental Results

Performance on the FV_USM Dataset. As shown in Table 1, LACE consistently improves performance on the FV_USM dataset. Compared with CE, it achieves an average increase of 1.10% in ACC, a reduction of 0.17% in EER, and an improvement of 0.87% in TAR@FAR=0.1%. The most notable gains appear in models with lower baselines; for example, PV-CNN improves from 69.11% to 70.66% in ACC and from 72.90% to 76.29% in TAR@FAR=0.1%, demonstrating the effectiveness of LACE in enhancing weaker models.

Performance on the TJU_PV600 Dataset. On the TJU_PV600 dataset (Table 2), LACE also shows consistent advantages over CE. It reduces the average EER by 0.23%, increases the ACC by 0.91%, and raises the TAR@FAR=0.1% by 0.87%. The LWDCNN model benefits significantly, with its EER reduced to 0.57% and TAR@FAR=0.1% reaching 98.30%, highlighting the robustness of LACE in high-precision biometric recognition tasks.

Performance on the VERA_PV220 Dataset. On the VERA_PV220 dataset (Table 3), LACE achieves the most substantial improvements. Compared with CE, the average ACC increases by 2.34%, the EER decreases by 0.35%, and the TAR@FAR=0.1% improves by 3.06%. In particular, the baseline ResNet-50 model, which originally shows lower performance, achieves significant gains, with ACC rising by 7.46% and TAR increasing by 9.09%, demonstrating that

Table 1. Performance Comparison on FV_USM Dataset

Model	ACC(%)			EER(%)			TAR@FAR=0.1(%)		
	CE	PCE	OURS	CE	PCE	OURS	CE	PCE	OURS
CMT	96.00	96.14	**96.75**	0.72	0.50	**0.41**	99.05	99.05	**99.05**
FVCNN	84.08	83.94	**84.82**	3.25	3.35	**3.05**	**89.43**	88.62	89.36
FVRASNet	94.17	94.51	**95.33**	0.68	0.79	**0.68**	97.56	97.63	**97.70**
IVT	93.43	94.04	**94.78**	0.76	0.84	**0.61**	97.15	98.17	**98.51**
LWDCNN	92.48	93.36	**93.36**	1.14	**0.88**	0.95	95.87	**96.88**	96.75
MSVT	85.98	87.06	**88.41**	1.91	1.61	**1.44**	92.14	93.22	**94.17**
PVCNN	69.11	**70.80**	70.66	3.83	4.14	**3.58**	72.90	76.08	**76.29**
ResNet18	**98.58**	98.37	98.51	0.16	**0.15**	0.16	99.73	**99.80**	99.73
ResNet50	97.15	97.70	**98.31**	**0.31**	0.33	0.34	99.25	99.32	**99.39**
Avg	90.11	90.66	**91.21**	1.42	1.40	**1.25**	93.68	94.31	**94.55**

Table 2. Performance Comparison on TJU_PV600 Dataset

Model	ACC(%)			EER(%)			TAR@FAR=0.1(%)		
	CE	PCE	OURS	CE	PCE	OURS	CE	PCE	OURS
CMT	92.00	91.67	**93.53**	0.77	0.91	**0.65**	96.70	96.20	**97.87**
FVCNN	83.50	84.47	**84.63**	3.04	**2.71**	2.83	88.13	**89.83**	89.63
FVRASNet	**89.73**	86.80	89.47	1.55	1.53	**1.37**	94.57	92.43	**94.73**
IVT	90.67	**91.40**	91.27	1.23	**0.84**	1.11	95.53	96.43	**96.47**
LWDCNN	94.20	93.83	**94.30**	1.08	0.90	**0.57**	97.53	97.77	**98.30**
MSVT	83.20	81.17	**83.97**	1.97	2.39	**1.95**	**90.70**	88.03	90.07
PVCNN	72.43	74.47	**75.23**	3.60	3.57	**3.20**	78.63	81.00	**81.83**
ResNet18	89.63	89.97	**90.67**	1.33	**1.13**	1.23	94.87	**95.27**	95.10
ResNet50	88.40	87.33	**88.87**	1.60	1.57	**1.24**	93.57	92.90	**94.07**
Avg	87.08	86.79	**87.99**	1.80	1.73	**1.57**	92.25	92.21	**93.12**

LACE effectively mitigates performance bottlenecks under conditions of limited or low-quality data.

ROC Curves on Different Datasets. As illustrated in Fig. 2, models trained with the LACE loss function (solid lines) consistently outperform those trained with CE and Poly-1 Cross-Entropy (PCE) loss functions across various architectures. The ROC curves for LACE are consistently closer to the top-left corner, with particularly significant improvements observed in regions of low false positive rate. This performance advantage is especially critical in strict security scenarios, confirming LACE's effectiveness in reducing false acceptance risks.

Table 3. Performance Comparison on VERA_PV220 Dataset

Model	ACC(%)			EER(%)			TAR@FAR=0.1(%)		
	CE	PCE	OURS	CE	PCE	OURS	CE	PCE	OURS
CMT	75.82	75.45	**78.18**	5.10	4.73	**4.37**	74.73	74.91	**78.91**
FVCNN	93.09	93.09	**93.45**	1.57	1.49	**1.37**	96.36	95.64	**96.55**
FVRASNet	89.27	89.64	**90.91**	1.48	1.81	1.81	94.36	93.09	**94.55**
IVT	87.09	88.00	**89.82**	**2.05**	2.18	2.22	89.45	90.18	**92.55**
LWDCNN	94.00	92.73	**94.55**	1.10	1.61	**1.00**	96.55	95.82	**97.09**
MSVT	84.36	85.09	**85.82**	2.93	2.69	**2.28**	86.00	88.18	**89.09**
PVCNN	73.09	**75.82**	74.36	4.52	4.40	**4.36**	71.45	**76.36**	74.00
ResNet18	82.73	84.00	**86.00**	3.28	3.29	**2.71**	84.36	85.27	**88.91**
ResNet50	76.18	77.64	**83.64**	4.19	4.15	**2.91**	76.00	78.91	**85.09**
Avg	83.96	84.61	**86.30**	2.91	2.93	**2.56**	85.47	86.48	**88.53**

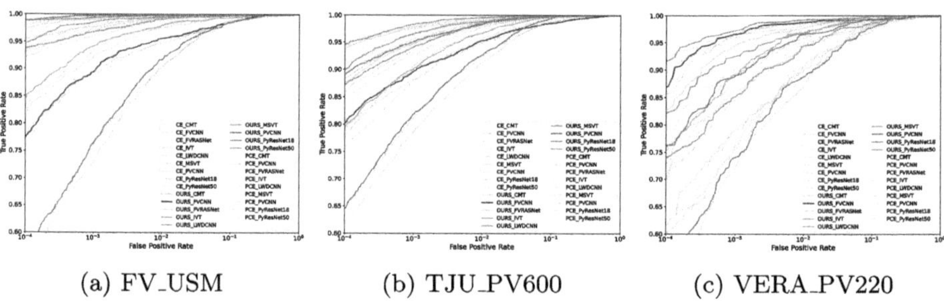

(a) FV_USM   (b) TJU_PV600   (c) VERA_PV220

Fig. 2. ROC Curves: (a) FV_USM dataset; (b) TJU_PV600 dataset; (c) VERA_PV220 dataset. Different colors represent different models, and different line styles represent different loss functions.

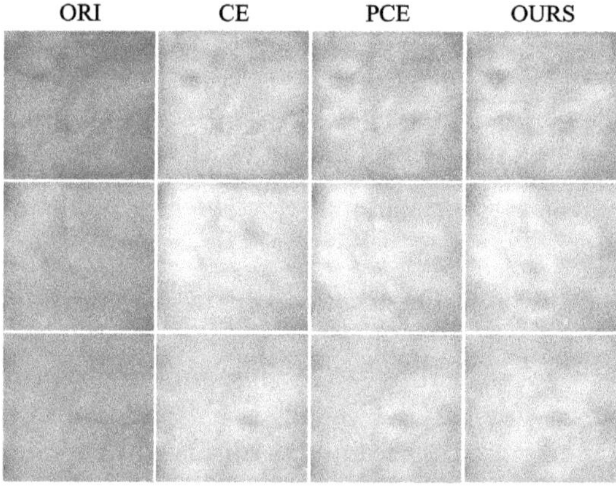

Fig. 3. Heatmap comparisons. ORI shows the original vein image. CE, PCE, and OURS represent the heatmaps generated by models trained with the corresponding loss functions.

Heatmap Visualizations. Figure 3 presents heatmap visualizations that elucidate the optimization mechanism of the LACE loss function. Compared to CE and PCE, those trained with LACE exhibit more complete and continuous activation patterns corresponding to vein structures. This indicates that LACE, through its dynamic loss adjustment strategy, effectively guides the model to learn more discriminative and anatomically meaningful features, rather than focusing solely on localized strong responses. Such enhanced feature representation contributes to the observed improvements in generalization performance.

4 Conclusion

This paper proposes the Learnable Adaptive Cross-Entropy (LACE) loss function, an innovative extension of the PolyLoss framework that transforms key polynomial coefficients into learnable parameters. By introducing a co-optimization mechanism, LACE enables real-time and synchronous adaptation between loss function parameters and model weights during training. Experimental results on three vein datasets demonstrate that LACE significantly improves recognition accuracy and reduces error rates, all without requiring manual hyperparameter tuning. ROC curve analyses reveal that models trained with LACE consistently achieve superior discrimination performance, particularly in regions with low false favorable rates, which are critical for biometric security. Furthermore, heatmap visualizations indicate that LACE guides models to learn more comprehensive and anatomically meaningful vein feature representations, contributing to enhanced generalization. In future work, we will focus on theoretical analyses of LACE's convergence properties, extend its applicability to diverse biometric modalities and model architectures, and enhance its adaptability through meta-learning techniques.

Acknowledgments. This work was supported in part by the Natural Science Foundation of Chongqing under Grant CSTB2024NSCQ-MSX1118, the Chongqing Municipal Education Commission under Grants KJZD-M202500804 and KJQN202500812, and by the Chongqing Technology and Business University under Grant 2556007.

References

1. Al-Tamimi, M.: A survey on the vein biometric recognition systems: trends and challenges. J. Theor. Appl. Inf. Technol. **97**(2), 551–568 (2019)
2. Baldock, R., Maennel, H., Neyshabur, B.: Deep learning through the lens of example difficulty. In: Advances in Neural Information Processing Systems, vol. 34, pp. 10876–10889. Curran Associates, Inc. (2021)
3. Barron, J.T.: A general and adaptive robust loss function. In: IEEE/CVF Conference on Computer Vision and Pattern Recognition (CVPR), pp. 4326–4334. IEEE (2019)
4. Das, R., Piciucco, E., Maiorana, E., Campisi, P.: Convolutional neural network for finger-vein-based biometric identification. IEEE Trans. Inf. Forensics Secur. **14**(2), 360–373 (2019)

5. Gonzalez, S., Miikkulainen, R.: Improved training speed, accuracy, and data utilization through loss function optimization. In: IEEE Congress on Evolutionary Computation (CEC), pp. 1–8. IEEE (2020)
6. Guo, J., et al.: CMT: convolutional neural networks meet vision transformers. In: IEEE/CVF Conference on Computer Vision and Pattern Recognition (CVPR), pp. 12165–12175. IEEE (2022)
7. He, K., Zhang, X., Ren, S., Sun, J.: Deep residual learning for image recognition. In: IEEE Conference on Computer Vision and Pattern Recognition (CVPR), pp. 770–778. IEEE (2016)
8. Khaniabadi, S.M., Khaniabadi, F.M., Huqqani, I.A., Saleh, S.A.M., Teoh, S.S., Ibrahim, H.: Addressing imbalanced data challenges in blood vessel image segmentation: a comprehensive review. In: IEEE Control and System Graduate Research Colloquium (ICSGRC), pp. 302–307. IEEE (2024)
9. Lefkovits, S., Lefkovits, L., Szilágyi, L.: Applications of different CNN architectures for palm vein identification. In: Modeling Decisions for Artificial Intelligence: 16th International Conference, pp. 295–306. Springer (2019)
10. Leng, Z., et al.: PolyLoss: a polynomial expansion perspective of classification loss functions. In: International Conference on Learning Representations (ICLR), pp. 1–16. OpenReview.net (2022)
11. Li, C., et al.: AM-LFS: AutoML for loss function search. In: IEEE/CVF International Conference on Computer Vision (ICCV), pp. 8409–8418. IEEE (2019)
12. Lin, T.Y., Goyal, P., Girshick, R., He, K., Dollár, P.: Focal loss for dense object detection. IEEE Trans. Pattern Anal. Mach. Intell. **42**(2), 318–327 (2020)
13. Mao, A., Mohri, M., Zhong, Y.: Cross-entropy loss functions: theoretical analysis and applications. In: International conference on Machine learning, pp. 23803–23828. PMLR (2023)
14. Pattnaik, K., Mishra, B.S.P., Sarangi, P.P.: Recent advancements in finger vein biometrics: a review. In: IEEE International Conference on Cybernetics, Cognition and Machine Learning Applications (ICCCMLA), pp. 91–98. IEEE (2022)
15. Qin, H., El-Yacoubi, M.A., Li, Y., Liu, C.: Multi-scale and multi-direction GAN for CNN-based single palm-vein identification. IEEE Trans. Inf. Forensics Secur. **16**, 2652–2666 (2021)
16. Qin, H., Gong, C., Li, Y., El-Yacoubi, M.A., Gao, X., Wang, J.: Attention label learning to enhance interactive vein transformer for palm-vein recognition. IEEE Trans. Biometrics, Behav., Identity Sci. **6**(3), 341–351 (2024)
17. Qin, H., Gong, C., Li, Y., Gao, X., El-Yacoubi, M.A.: Label enhancement-based multiscale transformer for palm-vein recognition. IEEE Trans. Instrum. Meas. **72**, 1–17 (2023)
18. Shen, J., Liu, N., Xu, C., Sun, H., Xiao, Y., Li, D., Zhang, Y.: Finger vein recognition algorithm based on lightweight deep convolutional neural network. IEEE Trans. Instrum. Meas. **71**, 1–13 (2022)
19. Terven, J., Cordova-Esparza, D.M., Romero-González, J.A., Ramírez-Pedraza, A., Chávez-Urbiola, E.: A comprehensive survey of loss functions and metrics in deep learning. Artif. Intell. Rev. **58**(7), 195 (2025)
20. Wang, Q., Ma, Y., Zhao, K., Tian, Y.: A comprehensive survey of loss functions in machine learning. Ann. Data Sci. **9**(2), 187–212 (2022)
21. Yang, W., Luo, W., Kang, W., Huang, Z., Wu, Q.: FVRAS-Net: an embedded finger-vein recognition and AntiSpoofing system using a unified CNN. IEEE Trans. Instrum. Meas. **69**(11), 8690–8701 (2020)
22. Yin, Y., et al.: Artificial neural networks for finger vein recognition: a survey. Eng. Appl. Artif. Intell. **150**, 110586 (2025)

Human-Centric AIGC (Face Synthesis, Speech Synthesis, Gesture Generation, Human Motion Generation, etc.)

EmoPrompt+: Emotional Image Content Generation via Emotion-Driven Prompting and Multi-Level Emotional Guidance in Stable Diffusion

Junheng Lin and Ya Li[✉]

School of Computer Science and Cyber Engineering, Guangzhou University, Guangzhou 510006, China
liya@gzhu.edu.cn

Abstract. Recently, text-to-image generation tasks have achieved remarkable progress, enabling the production of appropriate images from natural language descriptions. Although existing models can generate images that align with textual prompts, they still face significant limitations when dealing with abstract emotions. Thus, the EmoGen method introduces the task of Emotional Image Content Generation (EICG) for the first time. In this paper, we propose EmoPrompt+, a novel approach designed for the task of EICG. Specifically, we employ prefix language modeling to train an emotion-only text decoder, and we use dedicated emotion residual blocks to enhance the CLIP text encoder, improving its sensitivity to emotional content. This design endows abstract emotional concepts with richer semantics and enhances their intrinsic emotional representations. Experimental results demonstrate that our approach can effectively generate emotional image content and substantially outperforms existing state-of-the-art methods.

Keywords: Emotional Image Content Generation · Diffusion Model · CLIP Model

1 Introduction

Visual media serve as a vessel for emotional expression, offering an intuitive, vivid and readily resonant means of communication. From the prehistoric cave paintings at Lascaux to the masterpieces of the Renaissance, humans have always been adept at using visual imagery to convey emotion.

With the advent of the digital age, images and videos have increasingly become the primary medium for everyday emotional exchange. This has given rise to the field of visual emotion analysis, which is dedicated to uncovering the emotional cues within visual content. As visual emotion analysis has flourished, it has found diverse applications, ranging from advertising design [1,2]

W. Jia et al. (Eds.): CCBR 2025, LNCS 16360, pp. 173–182, 2026.
https://doi.org/10.1007/978-981-95-6123-0_17

Fig. 1. The performance of our method on Emotional Image Content Generation (EICG). It can generate highly realistic images that evoke the corresponding emotion when given an emotion category.

and social media monitoring [3,4] to psychological health assessment [5]. Concurrently, text-to-image generation technologies, particularly those based on diffusion models [6–8], have achieved an almost perfect mapping between natural language descriptions and high-fidelity image generation. These methods not only comprehend complex semantic content but also produce remarkable detail in terms of lighting, atmosphere and material textures, thereby opening unprecedented possibilities in fields such as art, design and entertainment.

At this point, an interesting and challenging question arises: What kind of innovations can emerge when human emotions meet advanced image generation technologies? Therefore, Yang *et al.* [9] first introduce the Emotional Image Content Generation (EICG) task. Their EmoGen method introduces an emotional space that clusters similar emotions and distinguishes distinct ones, aligning this space with the semantically rich CLIP embedding space through a learned mapping network. This enables abstract emotions to acquire concrete semantic representations. Nonetheless, EmoGen approach maps emotion embeddings to a single pseudo-token embedding while keeping the CLIP text encoder's parameters fixed. This design causes the resulting text embeddings to drift from the original embedding distribution, yielding generated images that are visually less realistic and, in some cases, suffer from content distortions.

Recognizing that natural language intrinsically conveys the compositional details of an entire image, we train an emotion-only text decoder to generate emotional content prompts, thereby mitigating drift from the CLIP text embedding distribution, thereby producing more realistic images. Additionally, we found that the original CLIP text encoder struggles to determine which semantic information is relevant to the given emotion during the encoding process. As a result, it may mistakenly treat local semantic information that does not align with the emotion as the main content, leading to a mismatch between the generated image content and the intended emotion. To address this, we add lightweight emotion residual blocks to the original CLIP text encoder, allowing for multi-level emotion-guided semantic fine-tuning to obtain text embeddings that are highly aligned with the given emotion. This enables Stable Diffusion to generate image content that is more faithful to and realistic in conveying the intended emotion, as shown in Fig. 1.

Our major contributions are as follows:

1. We propose an emotion-only text decoder that generates emotional content prompts conditioned on the given emotion category.
2. We propose a lightweight emotion residual block that enables the CLIP text encoder to perform semantic fine-tuning during the encoding process, enhancing its sensitivity to emotional content.
3. Through extensive experiments, we demonstrate that our approach produces higher-quality, more emotionally resonant images, significantly outperforming existing methods.

2 Related Work

2.1 Visual Emotion Analysis

Visual Emotion Analysis (VEA) aims to discover and quantify emotional information from visual content. Machajdik *et al.* [10] introduce color, texture and composition features grounded in psychological and artistic theory for image emotion classification. Subsequently, Borth *et al.* [11] develop a large-scale Visual Sentiment Ontology and the SentiBank detection framework centered on adjectivenoun pairs, significantly enhancing the detection of mid-level semantic emotional concepts. With the advent of deep learning, You *et al.* [12] design a convolutional neural network architecture that, together with progressive training and domain transfer strategies, achieves robust emotion classification on millions of web images. More recently, Xu *et al.* [13] propose a Multi-level Dependent Attention Network, which employs hierarchical bottom-up and top-down attention modules to more effectively capture emotional cues and semantic relationships at different layers of an image.

Despite significant progress in classification accuracy, most VEA research remains at a passive level, focusing on mapping images to emotions, and lacks controllable synthesis of emotions into images. This gap has given rise to emerging research in emotion-driven image generation and editing.

2.2 Emotional Image Content Generation

Given the limited research on generating images capable of evoking specific emotions, Yang *et al.* [9] are the first to introduce the Emotional Image Content Generation (EICG) task. Their method maps the emotion space into the CLIP semantic space and employs both an attribute loss and emotion-confidence scores to ensure that generated images exhibit emotional fidelity and content diversity.

However, this approach causes the text embeddings to deviate from their original distribution, which in turn degrades the quality of the generated images. Recently, He *et al.* [14] propose EmotiCrafter, a method based on the continuous Valence-Arousal (V-A) emotional model. It embeds V-A values into text features to achieve Continuous Emotional Image Content Generation (C-EICG) driven by textual prompts. While V-A coordinates offer nuanced emotional expression, it remains challenging to pre-define text prompts relevant to the desired emotion, particularly considering the established view that visual emotions are triggered by specific semantics [15,16].

Our approach uses the emotion embedding as a prefix to the input of an emotion-only text decode, producing emotional content prompts that effectively mitigate distributional shift. Additionally, we added emotion residual blocks to the CLIP text encoder, which enhances the sensitivity of the CLIP text encoder to emotional content through semantic fine-tuning.

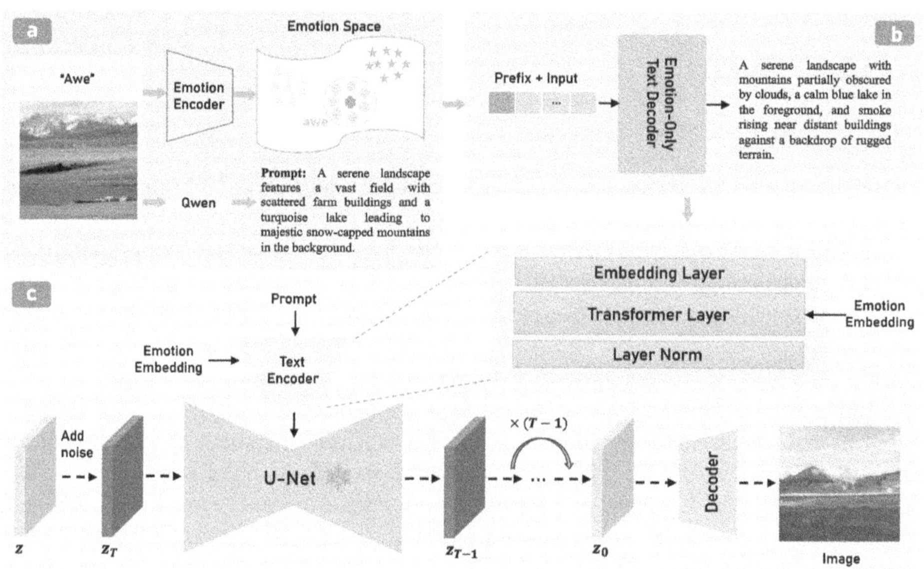

Fig. 2. Overview of our method. (a) We retain the emotion space from the EmoGen method, while using a pretrained large vision-language model to generate captions for each image. (b) Next, we use the emotion embedding as a prefix input to the emotion-only text decoder to generate the emotional content prompt. (c) Ultimately, we use a text encoder enhanced with emotion residual blocks to obtain text embeddings, enabling Stable Diffusion to generate emotional image content.

3   Methods

3.1   Overview

As shown in Fig. 2, our method adopts the emotion space proposed by Yang *et al.* [9], which effectively clusters similar emotions together while separating dissimilar ones. After obtaining the emotion embedding corresponding to a specific category, our method feeds it into the text decoder as a prefix to generate emotional content prompts. Furthermore, to enhance the emotional relevance of the generated images, we employ the CLIP text encoder augmented with emotion residual blocks to encode the prompt, thereby producing emotionally faithful and visually realistic content.

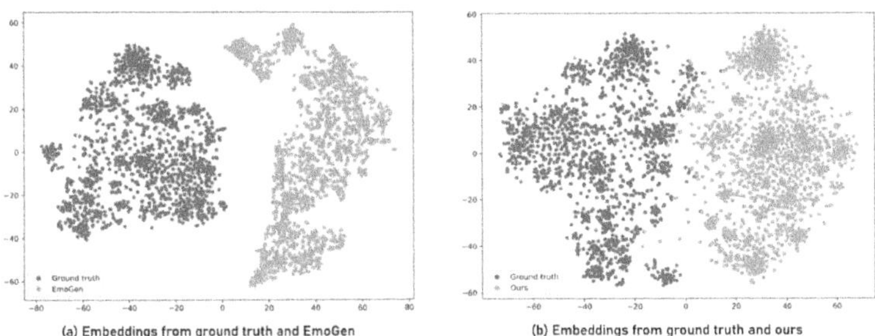

(a) Embeddings from ground truth and EmoGen   (b) Embeddings from ground truth and ours

Fig. 3. Visualization of embeddings in 2D space by t-SNE. We sampled 2,000 embeddings from each of the following sources for visualization: the CLIP text embeddings generated by the EmoGen method, the CLIP text embeddings obtained from the ground-truth text, and the CLIP text embeddings produced by our method.

3.2   Emotion-Only Text Decoder

Existing approaches [9] map an emotion embedding to the embedding of a single pseudo-token and then feed it into a frozen text encoder. Because the encoder's parameters remain fixed, the resulting text embeddings tend to drift away from their original distribution, as shown in Fig. 3(a), which can cause the diffusion model to generate warped or even distorted images. To mitigate this, our method treats the emotion embedding as a prefix and trains an autoregressive transformer language model P_θ from scratch using prefix language modeling. Given an image caption $T = \{w_1, w_2, \dots, w_t\}$, the prefix language model P_θ reconstructs T under the specified emotional condition e. Formally, the objective is defined as:

$$\mathcal{L}(\theta) = -\frac{1}{t}\sum_{i=1}^{t} \log P_\theta(w_i|w_{<i}, e). \tag{1}$$

After training, the text decoder can generate prompts solely from the emotion embedding and then feed them into the text encoder, thereby effectively alleviating the distribution-shift problem, as illustrated in Fig. 3(b).

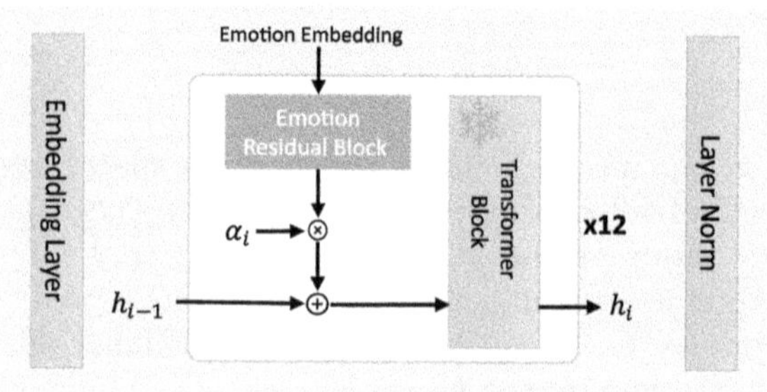

Fig. 4. Structure of the emotion residual block.

3.3   Emotion Residual Blocks

To incorporate emotional guidance into the text-to-image generation process, we modify the CLIP text encoder by introducing a emotion residual block(ERB) before each transformer layer. This design enables the encoder to integrate emotional information through semantic fine-tuning. As shown in Fig. 4, ERB is a lightweight module implemented as a two-layer MLP, designed to inject emotion information into the encoding process and increase the encoder's sensitivity to emotional signals. For the i-th transformer layer, let h_{i-1} denote the original input hidden state. Given an emotion embedding e, the emotion-enhanced input hidden state h'_{i-1} is computed as follows:

$$h'_{i-1} = h_{i-1} + \alpha_i \cdot ERB(e), \tag{2}$$

where α_i is a learnable weight. This mechanism ensures that emotional information is gradually integrated across all layers of the CLIP text encoder, guiding the text embedding to remain highly consistent with the given emotional category through semantic fine-tuning.

Existing text-to-image diffusion models typically optimize using the Latent Diffusion Model (LDM) loss. Accordingly, in this work we also employ the LDM loss to optimize the ERBs within text encoder φ_{ERB}:

$$\mathcal{L}_{LDM} = \mathbb{E}_{z,x,\epsilon,t,e} \left[\|\epsilon - \epsilon_\theta \left(z_t, t, \varphi_{ERB} \left(x, e \right) \right)\|_2^2 \right], \tag{3}$$

where ϵ denotes the real added noise, ϵ_θ represents the denoising network and z_t is the latent noise at time step t.

The learning objective of the ERBs is to steer the text encoder toward encoding emotion-relevant features. However, in the absence of explicit emotion supervision, optimizing the ERBs with the LDM loss alone is ineffective. To address this, and leveraging CLIP's image-text alignment property, we first pretrain an emotion classifier CLS_{emo} in the CLIP image-text aligned embedding space. We then use CLIP's linear projection layer to map text embeddings into its shared multimodal space and apply the pretrained classifier CLS_{emo} to these projected text embeddings to compute an emotion loss. Formally, the optimization objective is defined as follows:

$$\mathcal{L}_{emo} = -\sum_{j=1}^{C} y_{emo} \log \frac{\exp(CLS_{emo}(LP(\varphi_{\mathrm{ERB}}(x,e))))}{\sum_{j=1}^{C} \exp(CLS_{emo}(LP(\varphi_{ERB}(x,e))))}, \qquad (4)$$

where y_{emo} denotes the ground-truth emotion label, $LP(\cdot)$ is the CLIP model's linear projection layer, and C is the number of emotion categories.

In addition, to prevent excessive emotion guidance from causing the encoded outputs to deviate from the original semantics, we introduce a semantic regularization term:

$$\mathcal{L}_{reg} = 1 - f(\varphi_{ERB}(x,e), \varphi_{raw}(x)), \qquad (5)$$

$$f(p,q) = \frac{p \cdot q}{\|p\|\|q\|}, \qquad (6)$$

where φ_{raw} denotes the original text encoder. Finally, we perform joint training using the following loss function to optimize the ERBs within φ_{ERB}:

$$\mathcal{L} = \mathcal{L}_{LDM} + \mathcal{L}_{emo} + \lambda_{reg} \cdot \mathcal{L}_{reg}, \qquad (7)$$

where λ_{reg} denotes the weight of the regularization term.

Fig. 5. Qualitative comparisons with state-of-the-art text-to-image generation methods and an ablation study of our approach.

4 Experiments

4.1 Data Processing

EmoSet [17] is a large-scale visual emotion dataset, and EmoSet-118K is a high-quality subset annotated with the eight emotion categories from the Mikels emotion model. We note that not every image in EmoSet-118K comes with scene or object descriptions, nor are there accompanying textual captions. To address this, we leveraged the visual question-answering capabilities of the pre-trained large language model Qwen 2.5 [18] to generate descriptive text for each image, thereby ensuring an accurate depiction of each image's content.

4.2 Comparisons

Because our method builds on and improves the EmoGen approach that first introduces the EICG task, we adopt EmoGen's experimental setup and directly compare against it. Moreover, since there has been relatively little work on the EICG task to date, we also evaluate our method against the most relevant and state-of-the-art text-to-image generation techniques: Stable Diffusion, Textual Inversion and DreamBooth. Notably, Textual Inversion and DreamBooth represent leading methods in personalized text-to-image generation.

Qualitative Comparisons. In Fig. 1, we demonstrate our method's capability to generate emotion-faithful and realistic images across eight emotion categories. Figure 5 compares our method with other state-of-the-art approaches, specifically evaluating the generation results for the emotion categories of awe, anger and contentment. Images produced by previous methods often exhibit a darker tone and commonly suffer from distortion or a lack of realism. Although the EmoGen method outperforms earlier approaches in generating emotion-faithful images, it still encounters issues with content distortion. Additionally, we observe that EmoGen tends to produce repetitive content, such as frequently generating scenes of grass or lakes for the contentment category. In contrast, our method generates more realistic images that accurately reflect the specified emotion while significantly reducing content distortion.

Table 1. Comparisons with the state-of-the-art methods and ablation studies on emotional image content generation task, involving five metrics.

Method	FID↓	LPIPS↑	Emo-A↑	Sem-C↑	Sem-D↑
Stable Diffusion [7]	44.05	0.687	70.77%	0.608	0.0199
Textual Inversion [19]	50.51	0.702	74.87%	0.605	0.0282
DreamBooth [20]	46.89	0.661	70.50%	0.614	0.0178
EmoGen [9]	41.6	0.717	76.25%	0.633	**0.0335**
Ours	**28.06**	**0.784**	**84.35%**	**0.635**	0.0303
w/o ERB	28.72	0.782	70.59%	0.625	0.0271

Quantitative Comparisons. We use the EICG task-specific evaluation metrics proposed in the EmoGen [9] method to evaluate the performance of our approach, namely emotion accuracy (Emo-A), semantic clarity (Sem-C) and semantic diversity (Sem-D). Additionally, to comprehensively assess the quality of the generated images, we also employ the commonly used metrics Fréchet Inception Distance (FID) and Learned Perceptual Image Patch Similarity (LPIPS).

As shown in Table 1, although our method experiences a slight decrease in the Sem-D metric, it remains within a moderate range. On the other four evaluation metrics, our method outperforms existing methods, with a particularly significant improvement in the FID metric and Emo-A metric. This indicates that the images generated by our method are more similar to real images while remaining faithful to the emotions, which is a direct manifestation of alleviating the distribution shift issue present in previous methods.

4.3   Ablation Study

In this section, we primarily validate the effectiveness of the ERB. As shown in Table 1, removing the ERB directly leads to a decrease in Emo-A, indicating that the model struggles to generate image content strongly correlated with the given emotion. Furthermore, as illustrated in Fig. 5, the absence of an ERB can lead to image content that does not match the given emotion, such as "riding a bike" for the emotion "awe" and "car" for the emotion "anger". Therefore, only by incorporating the ERB can the model generate images capable of eliciting specific target emotions.

5   Conclusion

In this paper, we propose EmoPrompt+, a novel approach for emotional image content generation. EmoPrompt+ first trains an emotion-only text decoder to produce emotional content prompts. To further enhance the CLIP text encoder's sensitivity to emotional content, we introduce an emotion residual block before each transformer layer of the text encoder, thereby aligning the resulting text embeddings more closely with the target emotion categories. Experimental results demonstrate that our method significantly outperforms existing state-of-the-art techniques.

References

1. Anglay, H.M.: Emotion in visual design: a review. ShodhKosh: J. Vis. Perform. Arts **4**(1), 443–452 (2023)
2. Guo, W., Ye, H.: Emotional analysis and expression in advertising art design based on deep learning algorithms. Comput.-Aided Design Appl. 147–162 (2023)
3. Al-Tameemi, I.K.S., Feizi-Derakhshi, M.R., Pashazadeh, S., Asadpour, M.: A comprehensive review of visual-textual sentiment analysis from social media networks. J. Comput. Soc. Sci. **7**(3), 2767–2838 (2024)
4. Chandrasekaran, G., Antoanela, N., Andrei, G., Monica, C., Hemanth, J.: Visual sentiment analysis using deep learning models with social media data. Appl. Sci. **12**(3), 1030 (2022)

5. Marczak-Czajka, A., Redgrave, T., Mitcheff, M., Villano, M., Czajka, A.: Assessment of human emotional reactions to visual stimuli "deep-dreamed" by artificial neural networks. Front. Psychol. **15**, 1509392 (2024)
6. Dhariwal, P., Nichol, A.: Diffusion models beat GANs on image synthesis. Adv. Neural. Inf. Process. Syst. **34**, 8780–8794 (2021)
7. Rombach, R., Blattmann, A., Lorenz, D., Esser, P., Ommer, B.: High-resolution image synthesis with latent diffusion models. In: Proceedings of the IEEE/CVF Conference on Computer Vision and Pattern Recognition, pp. 10684–10695 (2022)
8. Nichol, A.Q., et al.: GLIDE: towards photorealistic image generation and editing with text-guided diffusion models. In: International Conference on Machine Learning, pp. 16784–16804. PMLR (2022)
9. Yang, J., Feng, J., Huang, H.: EmoGen: emotional image content generation with text-to-image diffusion models. In: Proceedings of the IEEE/CVF Conference on Computer Vision and Pattern Recognition, pp. 6358–6368 (2024)
10. Machajdik, J., Hanbury, A.: Affective image classification using features inspired by psychology and art theory. In: Proceedings of the 18th ACM International Conference on Multimedia, pp. 83–92 (2010)
11. Borth, D., Ji, R., Chen, T., Breuel, T., Chang, S.F.: Large-scale visual sentiment ontology and detectors using adjective noun pairs. In: Proceedings of the 21st ACM International Conference on Multimedia, pp. 223–232 (2013)
12. You, Q., Luo, J., Jin, H., Yang, J.: Robust image sentiment analysis using progressively trained and domain transferred deep networks. In: Proceedings of the AAAI Conference on Artificial Intelligence, vol. 29 (2015)
13. Xu, L., Wang, Z., Wu, B., Lui, S.: MDAN: multi-level dependent attention network for visual emotion analysis. In: Proceedings of the IEEE/CVF Conference on Computer Vision and Pattern Recognition, pp. 9479–9488 (2022)
14. He, Y., Dang, S., Ling, L., Qian, Z., Zhao, N., Cao, N.: EmotiCrafter: text-to-emotional-image generation based on valence-arousal model. arXiv preprint arXiv:2501.05710 (2025)
15. Borth, D., Chen, T., Ji, R., Chang, S.F.: SentiBank: large-scale ontology and classifiers for detecting sentiment and emotions in visual content. In: Proceedings of the 21st ACM International Conference on Multimedia, pp. 459–460 (2013)
16. Brosch, T., Pourtois, G., Sander, D.: The perception and categorisation of emotional stimuli: a review. Cogn. Emot. **24**(3), 377–400 (2010)
17. Yang, J., Huang, Q., Ding, T., Lischinski, D., Cohen-Or, D., Huang, H.: EmoSet: a large-scale visual emotion dataset with rich attributes. In: Proceedings of the IEEE/CVF International Conference on Computer Vision, pp. 20383–20394 (2023)
18. Bai, S., et al.: Qwen2. 5-VL technical report. arXiv preprint arXiv:2502.13923 (2025)
19. Gal, R., et al.: An image is worth one word: personalizing text-to-image generation using textual inversion. arXiv preprint arXiv:2208.01618 (2022)
20. Ruiz, N., Li, Y., Jampani, V., Pritch, Y., Rubinstein, M., Aberman, K.: DreamBooth: fine tuning text-to-image diffusion models for subject-driven generation. In: Proceedings of the IEEE/CVF Conference on Computer Vision and Pattern Recognition, pp. 22500–22510 (2023)

Online Emotion-Driven Generation of Multiple Appropriate Facial Reactions

Jiajian Huang[1], Siyang Song[2], Xiangyu Kong[2], Weicheng Xie[3], Linlin Shen[3], and Zitong Yu[1(✉)]

[1] School of Computing and Information Technology, Great Bay University, Dongguan, China
yuzitong@gbu.edu.cn
[2] Department of Computer Science, University of Exeter, Exeter, China
[3] College of Computer Science and Software Engineering, Shenzhen University, Shenzhen, China

Abstract. The multiple appropriate facial reaction online generation task aims to generate real-time, appropriate, and diverse facial reactions for virtual listeners in response to audio-visual behaviours expressed by a human speaker. While recent approaches have focused on improving reaction diversity and coarse synchronicity, they often fail to capture emotionally coherent responses that align with both the emotion type and intensity level of the speaker. In this work, we propose an emotion-driven framework that treats the speaker's emotional state as the core driving force behind listener behavior. Our framework integrates a pre-trained audio emotion encoder (PAEE) and visual emotion encoder (PVEE) to extract fine-grained emotional representations from speech and facial expressions. We further design a lightweight, online-capable Motion Representation Module (MRM), optimized for real-time generation, that captures emotional intensity through facial motion amplitude and variation, enabling our system to dynamically modulate the strength of listener reactions with low latency. Besides, an Unpredictable Motion Generator (UMG) further introduces minor, stochastic perturbations, making the generated reactions more lifelike and individualized. Extensive experiments demonstrate that our method achieves significant improvements in reaction appropriateness and diversity, while maintaining real-time performance. The codes are available at this link.

Keywords: Online facial reaction generation · Emotion-driven modeling

1 Introduction

With the rapid development of human-computer interaction technologies, generating real-time, appropriate, and diverse facial reactions from virtual listeners has become increasingly important [1], which enables engaging, empathetic, and socially intelligent systems in bidirectional communication [2,3].

Recent years have witnessed significant progress in generating listener facial reactions from speaker inputs, driven by advances in multimodal learning and

© The Author(s), under exclusive license to Springer Nature Singapore Pte Ltd. 2026
W. Jia et al. (Eds.): CCBR 2025, LNCS 16360, pp. 183–194, 2026.
https://doi.org/10.1007/978-981-95-6123-0_18

generative modeling. Existing methods can be broadly categorized into several paradigms: alignment-based strategies [4,5], unsupervised representation learning [6], and generative models [7–10] such as diffusion and latent variable frameworks. These approaches have demonstrated promising results in generating multiple appropriate facial reactions. However, most existing methods lack explicit modeling of emotional alignment, fine-grained control over expression intensity, and disentanglement of sporadic and unpredictable motions from emotion-driven motions.

To address these challenges, we propose an online emotion-driven framework that explicitly models the speaker's emotional state with both its type and intensity as the core driving force behind listener behavior generation. Our approach integrates pre-trained emotion encoders for both audio and visual modalities to extract fine-grained affective cues from the speaker's input. To further characterize the emotional intensity, the Motion Representation Module (MRM) is proposed with a lightweight, online-capable architecture to model facial motion dynamics as a proxy for reflecting the speaker's emotional intensity, enabling reactions scaled to the strength of the expressed emotion. To enhance individuality, we incorporate an Unpredictable Motion Generator (UMG) to introduce unpredictable micro-variations in facial expressions. Our method produces appropriate and diverse facial reactions, enhancing the naturalness of virtual listeners online behaviors. Extensive experiments on benchmark datasets demonstrate that our framework outperforms existing state-of-the-art approaches across multiple metrics. Our main contributions are summarized as follows:

- An online emotion-driven framework that treats the speaker's emotional state–both category and intensity–as the core signal for guiding listener reaction generation.
- A lightweight Motion Representation Module (MRM) that characterizes emotional intensity through facial motion amplitude and variation, enabling adaptive modulation of listener expression strength during real-time generation.
- An Unpredictable Motion Generator (UMG) that introduces fine-grained variations to enhance the individuality of generated reactions.
- Our method consistently outperforms state-of-the-art approaches across a wide range of metrics on multiple benchmark datasets, including React2024 and the newly introduced React2025 datasets.

2   Related Works

Recent works have made significant progress in generating online listener behaviors from speaker visual-audio inputs. Some methods focus on cross-modal alignment and temporal coherence: BEAMER [4] aligns speaker and listener representations via contrastive learning, and ReactFace [5] models temporal dynamics using spatio-temporal attention. Others leverage large-scale pre-training to learn universal mappings between speech rhythms and facial motion, such as UniFaRN [6], which improves robustness and generalization. To enhance response diversity and generation efficiency, several approaches explore latent-structure modeling and diffusion-based techniques. FRDiff [7] accelerates diffusion models via feature reuse, while VQD [8] combines vector quantization with diffusion to better balance quality and diversity. Liu et al. [9] introduce discrete latent variables to model diverse reactions, Nguyen et al. [10] propose a latent behavior diffusion framework, and Nguyen et al. [11] employ a multimodal VAE with Gaussian mixture modeling for context-aware variation. ReactDiff [12] further integrates multi-modality Transformers with latent-space diffusion, and Lv et al. [13] decouple 3D identity from expression to improve temporal coherence and diversity.

Despite these advances, most methods lack explicit emotional alignment, fine-grained control over expression intensity, and effective disentanglement of unpredictable motion variations from emotion-driven dynamics. In contrast, our method explicitly conditions reaction generation on the speaker's emotional state–both category and intensity–enabling more appropriate, diverse, and synchronized listener behaviors.

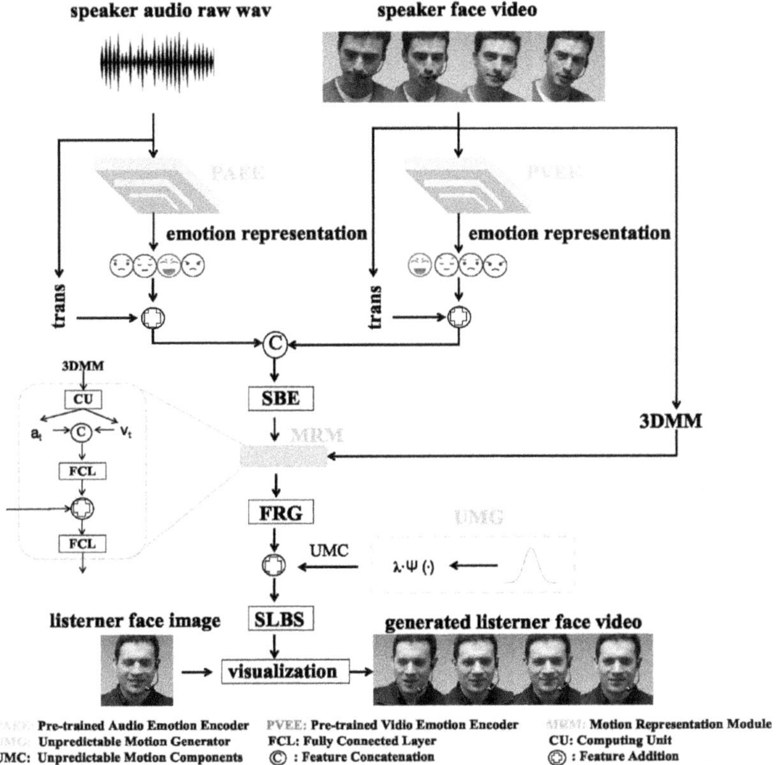

Fig. 1. Overview of the proposed framework. It integrates multimodal cues from speech (PAEE) [14], visual expressions (PVEE) [15], and motion dynamics (MRM) to guide listener reaction generation. In addition, an Unpredictable Motion Generator (UMG) is introduced to inject stochastic and spontaneous motions, enhancing the naturalness and variability of synthesized reactions. The other modules, namely Speaker Behavior Encoding (SBE), Facial Reaction Generation (FRG), and Speaker-Listener Behavior Synchronization (SLBS), are described in detail in [5].

3   Methodology

Figure 1 illustrates our overall online emotion-driven framework for generating facial reactions in virtual listeners. Our approach leverages both pre-trained audio and visual emotion encoders (PAEE [14] and PVEE [15]) to extract fine-grained affective cues from the speaker's speech and facial expressions. A lightweight Motion Representation Module (MRM) is further introduced to model the intensity of emotional expressions through facial motion amplitude and variation. Finally, an Unpredictable Motion Generator (UMG) enriches the diversity and individuality of generated reactions by introducing subtle variations.

3.1   Emotion Representation

To capture the emotional content of the speaker, we separately extract emotional features from the audio and video signals using two emotion-specific pre-trained models. Specifically, for the audio modality, we employ *emotion2vec-finetune* [14] to extract fine-grained, frame-level emotional features from the speaker's speech signal. This model has demonstrated strong performance in encoding emotionally salient information at a high temporal resolution.

Given an audio segment $\mathcal{A} = \{a_t | t = 1, \ldots, T\}$, where a_t denotes the acoustic feature at time step t, we obtain the corresponding emotional representation as:

$$\mathbf{E}_a = \Phi_a(\mathcal{A}), \tag{1}$$

where $\Phi_a(\cdot)$ represents the forward pass through the *emotion2vec-finetune* model, yielding a sequence of frame-level emotional embeddings $\mathbf{E}_a = [\mathbf{e}_{a_1}, \mathbf{e}_{a_2}, \ldots, \mathbf{e}_{a_T}] \in \mathbb{R}^{T \times d_a}$.

For the video modality, we utilize the Context-Aware Emotion Embedding (CEE) network [15] to extract segment-level emotional embeddings. CEE captures both local facial expressions and global contextual cues, enabling robust emotional representation across short video segments.

Given a video clip v, the corresponding emotional embedding $\mathbf{e}_v$ is obtained via:

$$\mathbf{e}_v = \Phi_v(v), \tag{2}$$

where $\Phi_v(\cdot)$ denotes the CEE network and $\mathbf{e}_v \in \mathbb{R}^{d_v}$.

Given that the extracted emotional features reside in a distinct semantic space compared to the converted video and audio representations (e.g., geometry coefficients or acoustic features), we adopt a simple yet effective fusion strategy: the emotional embeddings are projected through a lightweight fully connected layer and then added element-wise to the corresponding modality-specific representations. Formally, for each modality, we perform:

$$\mathbf{h}'_m = \mathbf{h}_m + \mathrm{FC}_m(\mathbf{e}_m), \quad m \in \{a, v\}, \tag{3}$$

where $\mathbf{h}_m$ is the original modality-specific representation (e.g., motion or acoustic features), $\mathbf{e}_m$ is the corresponding emotional embedding, $\mathrm{FC}_m(\cdot)$ denotes a learnable projection layer, and $\mathbf{h}'_m$ is the emotion-enhanced representation.

This ensures that the downstream neural components are conditioned not only on the speaker's physical behavior but also on their underlying emotional state. As a result, it enhances the expressiveness and contextual appropriateness of the synthesized listener responses, promoting more natural and emotionally coherent interactions.

3.2   Motion Representation Module

To better capture the intensity of the speaker's emotional expressions, we design a Motion Representation Module (MRM) that models fine-grained facial dynamics through the temporal evolution of facial movements. Rather than relying on complex, pre-trained motion encoders or optical flow estimation—which are computationally heavy and often incompatible with online deployment—we adopt a lightweight and interpretable representation. Specially, our method computes dynamic motion cues by estimating the first-order (velocity) and second-order (acceleration) temporal derivatives across consecutive frames based on 3D Morphable Model (3DMM) coefficients:

$$v_t = \Delta\mathbf{p}_t = \mathbf{p}_t - \mathbf{p}_{t-1}, \quad a_t = \Delta^2\mathbf{p}_t = v_t - v_{t-1}, \tag{4}$$

where $\mathbf{p}_t$ denotes the 3DMM coefficients at frame t, and v_t, a_t represent the corresponding velocity and acceleration vectors, respectively.

These motion cues provide valuable information about the intensity and variation of facial expressions over time. We further encode these dynamic features using a fully connected neural network to obtain an intermediate conditioning vector, which is used to modulate the listener reaction generation process. This allows the model to adapt the strength and timing of listener responses according to the speaker's emotional intensity, thereby improving the emotional coherence and naturalness of synthesized reactions.

3.3   Unpredictable Motion Generator

Although our framework effectively aligns listener reactions with the speaker's emotional state and motion dynamics, real-world listener behaviors also contain small, non-deterministic variations that are not directly driven by the speaker. These include micro-expressions, idiosyncratic gestures, and other subtle facial movements that contribute significantly to the perceived naturalness and individuality of the listener.

To account for this inherent variability, we propose an Unpredictable Motion Generator (UMG), which synthesizes fine-grained, stochastic motion deviations and incorporates them into the generated 3D Morphable Model (3DMM) coefficients. Formally, let $\mathcal{F} = \{\mathbf{f}_t \in \mathbb{R}^{d_f} | t = 1, \dots, T\}$ denote the sequence of emotion-driven facial features produced by our deterministic listener behavior generation process. The UMG introduces a latent stochastic component $\Delta\mathcal{F} = \{\Delta\mathbf{f}_t \in \mathbb{R}^{d_f} | t = 1, \dots, T\}$, modeled as:

$$\Delta \mathbf{f}_t = \Psi(\mathbf{z}_t), \tag{5}$$

where $\mathbf{z}_t \sim \mathcal{N}(0, \mathbf{I})$ is a random noise vector sampled independently at each time step, and $\Psi(\cdot)$ denotes the neural function implemented by the UMG module.

The final output sequence $\hat{\mathcal{F}} = \{\hat{\mathbf{f}}_t \in \mathbb{R}^{d_f}\}$ is obtained via:

$$\hat{\mathbf{f}}_t = \mathbf{f}_t + \lambda \cdot \Delta \mathbf{f}_t, \tag{6}$$

where $\lambda = 0.02$ is a scaling factor that controls the intensity of the injected variation, ensuring that the resulting motion remains plausible and contextually appropriate.

This stochastic generation mechanism enhances the naturalness and individuality of the listener's facial behavior, enabling the synthesis of socially rich and emotionally coherent interactions while preserving speaker-listener alignment.

Table 1. Quantitative results comparison between the our method and other state-of-the-art methods on **React2024 datasets**. The best result in each column is marked in bold. Higher values are better for FRDvs, FRVar, FRDiv, and FRCorr; lower values are better for FRSyn.

	Source	FRDvs ($\uparrow$)	FRVar ($\uparrow$)	FRDiv ($\uparrow$)	FRCorr ($\uparrow$)	FRSyn ($\downarrow$)
GT [16]	FG'24	0.2483	0.0724	0.0000	8.73	47.69
Trans-AE [16]	FG'24	0.0009	0.0012	0.0064	0.07	**44.65**
BeLFusion(k=1) [16]	FG'24	0.0103	0.0079	0.0083	0.12	45.17
BeLFusion(k=10) [16]	FG'24	0.0120	0.0082	0.0112	0.12	44.89
BeLFusion (k=10)+ Binarized AUs [16]	FG'24	0.0397	0.0248	0.0379	0.12	49.00
REGNN [17]	TAFFC'24	0.0342	0.0061	0.0007	0.19	47.66
ReactFace [5]	TVCG'24	0.0334	0.0133	0.0328	0.15	47.37
Ours	ours	**0.0523**	**0.0839**	**0.0520**	**0.52**	46.25

Table 2. Quantitative comparison on the **React2025 dataset**. The best result among advanced methods in each column is in bold. Higher values are better for FRVar, FRDiv, and FRCorr; lower values are preferred for FRSyn and FRDist. Few advanced methods have yet to publish results on this newly released dataset with restricted test access.

	Source	FRVar ($\uparrow$)	FRDiv ($\uparrow$)	FRCorr ($\uparrow$)	FRDist ($\downarrow$)	FRSyn ($\downarrow$)
GT	MM'25	0.0669	0.187	10	0.00	48.66
Heuristic Strategies						
Random [18]	MM'25	0.1671	0.3342	0.03	474.68	46.64
Mime [18]	MM'25	0.0766	0.0000	0.52	206.02	43.70
MeanFr [18]	MM'25	0.0000	0.0000	0.00	205.65	49.00
Advance Method						
Trans-VAE-25 [18]	MM'25	0.0564	0.1082	0.25	**212.22**	48.20
Ours	ours	**0.0925**	**0.1747**	**0.30**	220.37	**47.52**

4   Experiments

4.1   Dataset and Metrics

The dataset we use is the React2024 [16] and React2025 [18][1] Challenge dataset. The React2024 Challenge dataset is composed of two publicly available datasets NoXI [19] and RECOLA [20]. It contains a total of 2962 audio-visual speaker-listener interaction clip pairs, with each clip lasting 30 s. Among them, 1594 pairs are used as the training set, 562 pairs form the validation set, and the remaining 806 pairs constitute the test set. React2024 adopts the evaluation framework proposed in [21], which comprehensively assesses three key properties: appropriateness, diversity, and synchrony. Appropriateness measures how well the generated facial reaction aligns with an appropriate real-world response. This is quantified using the Concordance Correlation Coefficient (CCC) between the generated sequence and the most correlated ground-truth reaction, referred to as FRCorr. Diversity evaluates the listener reaction variation across different speakers and within a conversation of the same speaker. It is measured through three metrics introduced in [1]: FRVar evaluates the variance of each generated facial reaction; FRDiv evaluates generated facial reactions in response to each input speaker behavior; and FRDvs evaluates the diversity of the generated facial reactions in response to different speaker behaviors. Synchrony assesses temporal alignment between the generated facial reaction and the corresponding speaker's behavior. We compute the time-lagged cross-correlation (TLCC) between these two modalities to quantify this property, denoted as FRSyn.

The React2025 Challenge introduces the Multi-modal Multiple Appropriate Reaction in Social Dyads (MARS) dataset, the first multi-modal dataset designed for this task. It contains 137 dyadic interaction clips involving 23 speakers and 137 listeners, resulting in 270 multi-modal recordings (each 2035 min). Each recording includes audio, video, and EEG data from both speaker and listener, split into 3,105 session pairs across five topics: cultural differences, movie sharing, policy changes, quizzes/games, and interviews. The React2025 dataset also improves the evaluation metrics by removing the diversity-related metric FRDvs and introducing FRDist based on Dynamic Time Warping (DTW), aiming to reduce redundancy among metrics and enhance the measurement of appropriateness.

---

[1] https://sites.google.com/view/react2025.

Table 3. Ablation Study of Emotion Representation (ER), Unpredictable Motion Generator(UMG), and Motion Representation Module (MRM) on Facial Reaction Generation Performance.

ER	UMG	MRM	FRDvs (↑)	FRVar (↑)	FRDiv (↑)	FRCorr(↑)	FRSyn (↓)
			0.0334	0.0133	0.0328	0.15	47.37
✓			0.0402	0.0395	0.0400	0.41	46.77
	✓		0.0366	0.0349	0.0355	0.77	46.57
		✓	0.0320	0.0403	0.0257	0.59	46.71
✓	✓		0.0409	0.0369	0.0408	0.68	46.88
	✓	✓	0.0484	0.0524	0.0424	0.70	45.82
✓		✓	0.0486	0.0756	0.0484	0.71	46.26
✓	✓	✓	0.0523	0.0839	0.0520	0.52	46.25

Table 4. Ablation of first-order motion information (FMI) and second-order motion information(SMI) on Facial Reaction Generation Performance.

FMI	SMI	FRDvs (↑)	FRVar (↑)	FRDiv (↑)	FRCorr(↑)	FRSyn (↓)
		0.0334	0.0133	0.0328	0.15	47.37
✓		0.0411	0.0388	0.0409	0.56	47.02
	✓	0.0441	0.0511	0.0439	0.39	47.03
✓	✓	0.0523	0.0839	0.0520	0.52	46.25

4.2   Comparison with State-of-the-Art Methods

We evaluate our method on both the React2024 and React2025 datasets, with results summarized in Table 1 and Table 2, respectively.

Evaluation on React2024: As shown in Table 1, our method achieves the best performance across almost all metrics. Our method achieves a score of 0.52 on content consistency (FRCorr), significantly outperforming the best compared method (0.19). It also achieves the highest values in all expression diversity metrics (FRVar = 0.0839, FRDvs = 0.0523, FRDiv = 0.520). While ReactFace performs better in synchronization (43.94 vs. 46.25), its content consistency is very low, suggesting that it generates synchronized but emotionless reactions. In contrast, our method maintains reasonable synchronization while generating expressive and emotionally coherent responses.

In addition to achieving state-of-the-art performance in generation quality, the framework also exhibits favorable efficiency. It takes only 31.117 s to process a 750-frame input video and generate a corresponding 750-frame output video.

Evaluation on React2025: In addition to the initial benchmark, we evaluate our method on the React2025 dataset, which represents the latest and highest-quality dataset available for this domain. As shown in Table 2, we include several heuristic strategies–*Random, Mime,* and *MeanFr*–for reference, which reflect simple generation principles such as random sampling, speaker mimicry, and static averaging. As expected, *Random* achieves high variability but poor correlation (FRCorr = 0.03), while *Mime* yields smooth motion (FRSyn = 43.70) but zero diversity (FRDiv = 0.0000). Due to the recent release of React2025 dataset and the requirement for test set access approval, only a few advanced methods have published results on it to date. We compare our approach against Trans-VAE-25 [18], a representative and publicly available advanced baseline. Our method achieves superior performance in diversity (FRVar = 0.0925, FRDiv = 0.1747) and synchrony (FRSyn = 47.52), and sets a new state-of-the-art in appropriateness as measured by reaction alignment (FRCorr = 0.30). While Trans-VAE-25 achieves a slightly lower reaction distance (FRDist: 212.22 vs. 220.37), our approach demonstrates a highly competitive performance across all dimensions. This balanced and strong performance, particularly excelling in diversity and temporal coherence, highlights the effectiveness of our framework in generating expressive and contextually appropriate listener reactions.

4.3   Ablation Study

To validate the effectiveness of each component in our framework, we conduct ablation studies on three core modules on the React2024 dataset[2]: the Emotion Representation (ER), the Unpredictable Motion Generator (UMG), and the Motion Representation Module (MRM). We also analyze the impact of incorporating first-order motion information (FMI) and second-order motion information (SMI) within MRM. As shown in Table 3, removing any of the three key components leads to performance degradation across all metrics. Notably, disabling ER results in a significant drop in the diversity of generated reactions. This may be because ER enables listeners to generate distinct reactions tailored to the emotional states of individual speakers. Moreover, throughout the conversation, the listener can exhibit richer and more varied responses in response to the speaker's evolving emotional expressions. Removing UMG leads to reduced expression diversity (e.g., FRVar drops from 0.0839 to 0.0756), highlighting its importance in generating individualized and spontaneous responses. Disabling MRM not only reduces FRVar but also degrades synchronization (FRSyn up to 46.88), indicating that motion intensity modeling contributes to both expressiveness and contextual synchronization. Further analysis of motion dynamics in Table 4 reveals that combining FMI and SMI yields the best performance in terms of FRDvs (0.0523), FRVar (0.0839), FRDiV (0.0520), and FRSyn (46.25), demonstrating that both velocity and acceleration are essential for capturing nuanced facial variations. These findings support our design choices and demonstrate that each module contributes uniquely to generating emotionally coherent, temporally synchronized, and individually expressive listener reactions.

---

[2] We use React2024 for ablation studies due to its readily accessible test set.

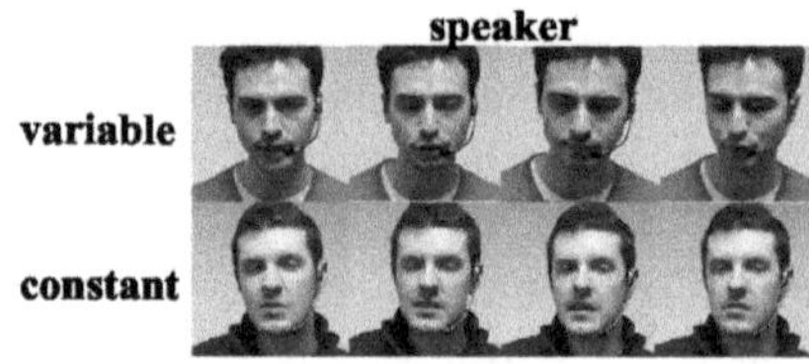
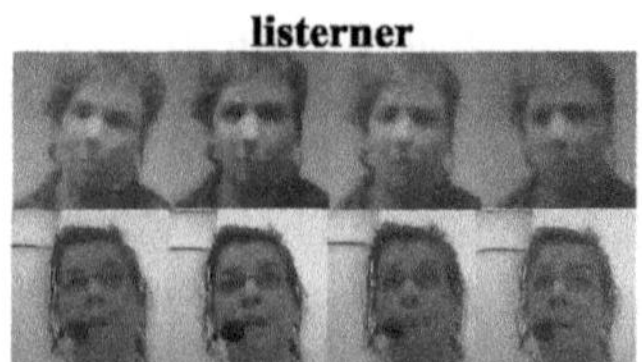

Fig. 2. Listener Reactions under Varying Emotional Dynamics of the Speaker. The left column shows the speaker's dynamic expressions, while the right column displays the corresponding listener reactions. When the speaker exhibits varied facial expressions (top left), the listener generates diverse and temporally synchronized reactions (top right). Conversely, when the speaker's expression remains static (bottom left), the listener's response stays stable and contextually appropriate (bottom right). These results highlight the effectiveness of our method in modeling reaction diversity, temporal synchrony, and contextual appropriateness.

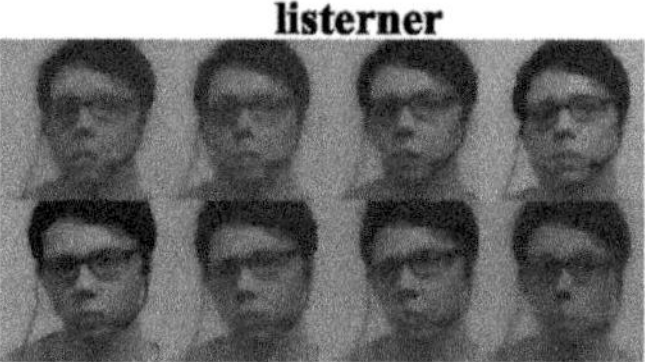

Fig. 3. Listener Reactions under Different Emotional Categories of the Speaker. In the first row, the speaker exhibits a calm emotional state (top left), and the listener responds with a similarly tranquil reaction (top right). Conversely, in the second row, when the speaker conveys a serious, and heavy emotional state (bottom left), the listener's response reflects this weight, appearing visibly subdued or startled (bottom right).

4.4   Visualization Analysis

We conducted two sets of visualizations to analyze the generated listener's reactions. In the first set, as shown in Fig. 2, we compare the listener responses generated by speakers with varying levels of emotional expressiveness. It can be observed that when the speaker displays rich emotional changes, the corresponding listener reactions also exhibit a high degree of variation and dynamic engagement. The second set, as shown in Fig. 3, focuses on the same speaker-listener pair under different emotional contexts. Here, we observe that when the speaker adopts a calm tone, the listener's response remains gentle and aligned, whereas when the speaker conveys a serious and heavy state, the listener's reaction shifts to a more subdued or startled demeanor, reflecting the emotional weight. These findings highlight three important characteristics of listener behavior: reaction diversity, temporal synchrony, and contextual appropriateness.

5 Conclusion

In this study, we propose an online framework for listener reaction generation that integrates speaker emotion states, emotional intensity dynamics, and stochastic facial variations, achieving superior appropriateness and diversity. In the future, we plan to combine more advanced generative techniques such as [22] to further improve the generation quality.

References

1. Song, S., Spitale, M., Luo, Y., et al.: Multiple appropriate facial reaction generation in dyadic interaction settings: what, why and how? arXiv (2023)
2. Wang, I., Ruiz, J.: Examining the use of nonverbal communication in virtual agents. IJHCI (2021)
3. Aburumman, N., Gillies, M., Ward, J., Hamilton, A.: Nonverbal communication in virtual reality: nodding as a social signal in virtual interactions. IJHCS (2022)
4. Hoque, X., Mann, A., Sharma, G., Dhall, A.: Beamer: behavioral encoder to generate multiple appropriate facial reactions. In: ACM MM (2023)
5. Luo, C., Song, S., Xie, W., et al.: ReactFace: online multiple appropriate facial reaction generation in dyadic interactions. IEEE TVCG (2024)
6. Liang, C., Wang, J., Zhang, H., et al.: UniFaRN: unified transformer for facial reaction generation. In: ACM MM (2023)
7. Yu, J., Zhao, J., Xie, G., et al.: Leveraging the latent diffusion models for offline facial multiple appropriate reactions generation. In: ACM MM (2023)
8. Nguyen, M., Yang, H., Ho, N., Kim, S., et al.: Vector quantized diffusion models for multiple appropriate reactions generation. In: FG (2024)
9. Liu, Z., Liang, C., Wang, J., et al.: One-to-many appropriate reaction mapping modeling with discrete latent variable. In: FG (2024)
10. Nguyen, M., Yang, H., Kim, S., Shin, J., Kim, S.: Latent behavior diffusion for sequential reaction generation in dyadic setting. In: ICPR (2024)
11. Nguyen, D., Paudel, P., Kim, S., et al.: Multiple facial reaction generation using gaussian mixture of models and multimodal bottleneck transformer. In: FG (2024)
12. Li, J., Wang, S., Wang, X., et al.: ReactDiff: latent diffusion for facial reaction generation. NN (2025)
13. Lv, Q., Liu, X., Li, J., et al.: Hierarchical multimodal decoupling-fusion framework for offline multiple appropriate facial reaction generation. In: ICASSP (2025)
14. Ma, Z., Zheng, Z., Ye, J., et al.: Emotion2vec: self-supervised pre-training for speech emotion representation. In: ACL 2024 Findings (2024)
15. Savchenko, A., Savchenko, L., Makarov, I.: Classifying emotions and engagement in online learning based on a single facial expression recognition neural network. IEEE TAFFC (2022)
16. Song, S., Spitale, M., Luo, C., et al.: REACT 2024: the second multiple appropriate facial reaction generation challenge. In: FG (2024)
17. Xu, T., Spitale, M., Tang, H., et al.: Reversible graph neural network-based reaction distribution learning for multiple appropriate facial reactions generation. IEEE TAFFC (2024)
18. Song, S., Micol, S., Kong, X., et al.: REACT 2025: the third multiple appropriate facial reaction generation challenge. In: ACM MM (2025)

19. Cafaro, A., Wagner, J., Baur, T., et al.: The noxi database: multimodal recordings of mediated novice-expert interactions. In: ACM MM (2017)
20. Ringeval, F., Sonderegger, A., Sauer, J., Lalanne, D.: Introducing the RECOLA multimodal corpus of remote collaborative and affective interactions. In: FG (2013)
21. Song, S., Spitale, M., Luo, C., et al.: REACT2023: the first multiple appropriate facial reaction generation challenge. In: ACM MM (2023)
22. Xie, X., Cui, Y., Tan, T., et al.: FusionMamba: dynamic feature enhancement for multimodal image fusion with mamba. Vis. Intell. (2024)

HairEditor: Diffusion-Guided Supervision for StyleGAN-Based Hair Editing in Real-World Portraits

Jijie Li[1,2], Xiangyu Zhu[1,2(✉)], Xiaoyu Zhu[1,2], and Zhen Lei[1,2,3,4]

[1] School of Artificial Intelligence, University of Chinese Academy of Sciences, Beijing, China
[2] MAIS, Institute of Automation, Chinese Academy of Sciences, Beijing, China
`xiangyu.zhu@ia.ac.cn`
[3] CAIR, HKISI, Chinese Academy of Sciences, Beijing, China
[4] School of Computer Science and Engineering, the Faculty of Innovation Engineering, M.U.S.T, Macau, China

Abstract. With the rapid advancement of social media and virtual reality technologies, the demand for personalized hair editing has significantly increased. However, achieving high-fidelity and real-time hair editing in practical applications remains challenging due to the lack of diverse high-quality portrait datasets and the computational constraints of existing editing frameworks. To tackle these challenges, we propose HairEditor, a novel framework designed for efficient and high-quality hair modifications in real-world scenarios. First, we leverage the generative capabilities of Stable Diffusion to construct a large-scale dataset comprising real portraits, bald images, and the corresponding hairstyle and hair color exemplars, addressing the issue of data scarcity. Second, we design a lightweight yet powerful editing network based on the StyleGAN latent space, enabling precise hair manipulation with minimal computational cost. Furthermore, we extend hair editing beyond standard aligned headshots to loosely aligned upper-body portraits, significantly enhancing its applicability in diverse real-world settings. Extensive experiments using real human portraits as users and AI-generated images as hairstyle references demonstrate that HairEditor outperforms existing methods in visual quality, identity preservation, and editing precision, while maintaining high efficiency. We will release our code to support future research in this field.

Keywords: Conditional image generation · Image Editing · StyleGAN

1 Introduction

With the advancement of generative artificial intelligence, hairstyle editing has emerged as an intriguing yet challenging problem. The goal is to modify a portrait's hair based on a reference while preserving the subject's identity. This task has broad applications but is hindered by the limitations of current methods.

W. Jia et al. (Eds.): CCBR 2025, LNCS 16360, pp. 195–203, 2026.
https://doi.org/10.1007/978-981-95-6123-0_19

Existing approaches primarily rely on StyleGAN [1,2] or Stable Diffusion [4]. StyleGAN-based methods [5–10] are restricted to standardized, aligned head-shots, making them unsuitable for real-world upper-body portraits. Conversely, Stable Diffusion-based methods [12,28,29] struggle with decoupling hairstyle and color editing and suffer from high computational costs. To address these limitations, we introduce HairEditor, a framework that integrates the interpretability of StyleGAN with the generative power of Stable Diffusion to achieve superior editing quality and efficiency for upper-body portraits. Our primary contribution is a novel data construction pipeline that uses Stable Diffusion to create a comprehensive, high-resolution dataset of upper-body portraits, corresponding bald images, and hairstyle exemplars. This dataset enables us to train a lightweight yet powerful StyleGAN-based editing network that extends hair editing beyond simple headshots to more realistic, non-aligned upper-body images while maintaining real-time performance. Our evaluation, which simulates real-world use cases with AI-generated models, confirms that HairEditor significantly outperforms existing techniques in quality, identity preservation, and efficiency (Fig. 1).

Fig. 1. Hairstyle and hair color editing results by HairEditor. Our method transfers hairstyles from AI-generated virtual models to real portraits and enables RGB-based hair color manipulation.

2 Methodology

2.1 Overview

Our goal is to achieve high-quality hair editing by transforming a target portrait to adopt a reference hairstyle and a specified hair color. The process involves three steps: bald head editing, hairstyle transfer, and hair color editing (Fig. 2). For GAN inversion, we adopt the E4E [17] encoder, which operates in the W+ space to ensure a balance between editability and reconstruction quality for upper-body portraits, where hair occupies a smaller image area. First, we synthesize a large dataset of bald half-body portraits to train a supervised network for removing the original hair. Next, for hairstyle transfer, we construct a *source-bald-model* dataset and train a feature fusion network to merge facial information from the bald image with hairstyle details from a reference model. Finally, for hair color editing, we train a network that takes the portrait's latent code and a target RGB value to produce the desired hair color. The final edited portrait is generated by seamlessly blending the edited hair region with the bald image using Laplacian pyramid fusion to preserve the original identity and background.

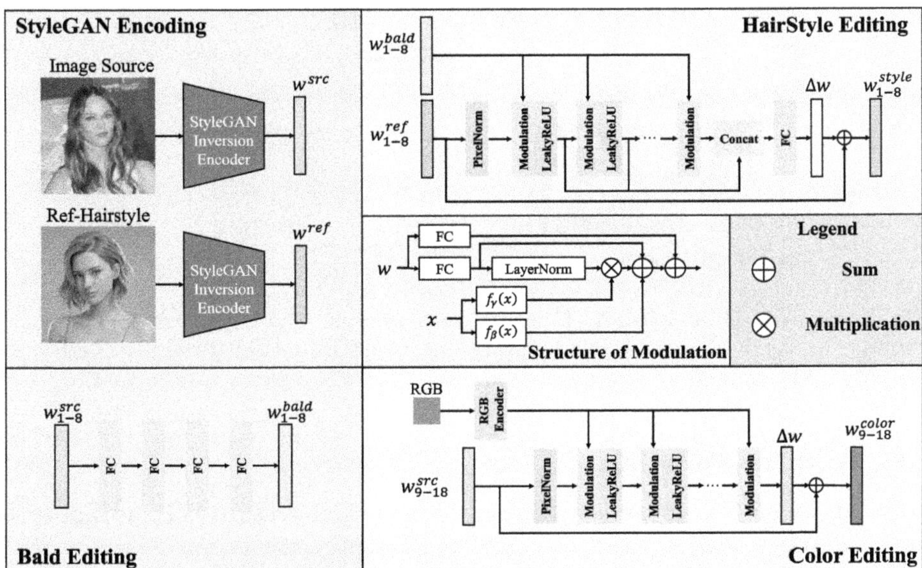

Fig. 2. The Structure of Hair Editing Models. The StyleGAN Inversion Encoder uses E4E, and the network structure of BaldEditing is the same as HairMapper, with the fully connected layer structure similar to the one that converts the latent code z to the w+ space in StyleGAN network.

2.2   Dataset Construction

We constructed a high-resolution (1024×1024) dataset from the Matting Human Dataset [38], using Stable Diffusion outpainting for upscaling. Bald portraits were synthesized by applying HairMapper [11] to cropped headshots and using SDXL Inpainting to refine the results on the full upper-body image. Hairstyle and hair color labels were generated through data augmentation and color space transformations, resulting in a comprehensive *sourcebaldmodel* data pipeline (Fig. 3) for training.

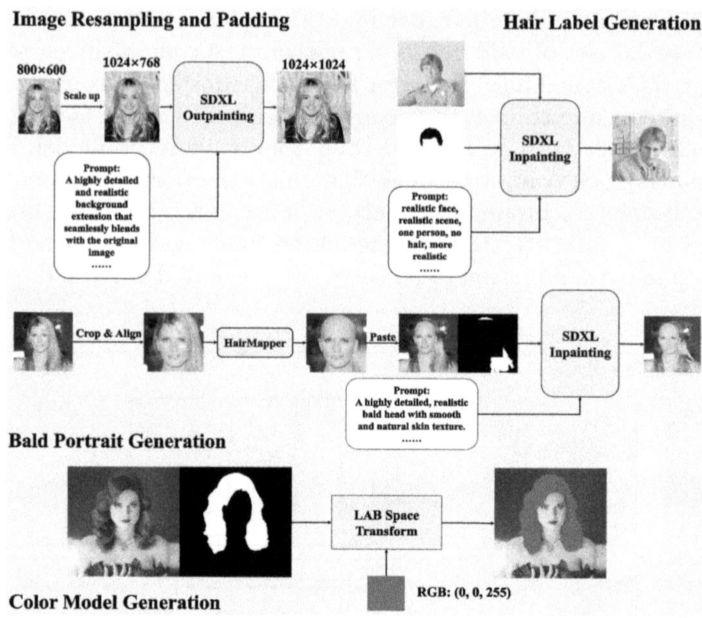

Fig. 3. Source-Bald-Model Data Construction Process. The source, bald, hairstyle model data are constructed using the extended functionalities of SDXL, while the hair color model data is generated via RGBLAB color space transformations.

2.3   Bald Head Editing

We train a *BaldMapper* network, using the same architecture as HairMapper, to map the source image's latent code $\mathbf{w}^{\mathrm{src}}$ to a bald representation. The network is trained on our synthesized source-bald image pairs ($I^{\mathrm{src}}, I^{\mathrm{btg}}$) by first encoding them into the W+ space using a retrained E4E encoder E.

$$\mathbf{w}^{\mathrm{src}} = E(I^{\mathrm{src}}), \tag{1}$$

$$\mathbf{w}^{\mathrm{btg}} = E(I^{\mathrm{btg}}). \tag{2}$$

The network modifies the first 8 style layers to produce the bald representation $\mathbf{w}^{\mathrm{bald}}_{1-8}$.

$$\mathbf{w}^{\mathrm{bald}}_{1-8} = \mathbf{w}^{\mathrm{src}}_{1-8} + \alpha \cdot \mathrm{BaldMapper}(\mathbf{w}^{\mathrm{src}}_{1-8}), \tag{3}$$

The generated image $I^{\mathrm{bald}}_{\mathrm{pix}}$ is produced by the StyleGAN generator G.

$$I^{\mathrm{bald}}_{\mathrm{pix}} = G(\mathrm{concat}(\mathbf{w}^{\mathrm{bald}}_{1-8}, \mathbf{w}^{\mathrm{src}}_{9-18})). \tag{4}$$

The network is trained using a combination of pixel-space hair loss L_{hair}, latent space loss L_{latent}, CLIP-based semantic loss L_{clip}, ArcFace ID loss L_{id} [19], and perceptual loss L_{lpips} [20]. To avoid color shifts common with Poisson blending on upper-body portraits, we use Laplacian pyramid blending to seamlessly integrate the generated bald head onto the source image.

2.4 Hairstyle Transfer

The *StyleMapper* network fuses the latent code of the bald portrait w^{bald} with a reference hairstyle w^{ref} to produce the target style. To improve generalization across different genders and hair lengths, we incorporate a weak supervision signal using a randomly sampled image w^{rand} during training. The network operates on the first 8 style layers to deform the hairstyle while preserving the original hair color information from layers 9-18.

$$\mathbf{w}^{\text{style}}_{1-8} = \text{StyleMapper}(\mathbf{w}^{\text{bald}}_{1-8}, \mathbf{w}^{\text{ref}}_{1-8}), \tag{5}$$

$$\mathbf{w}^{\text{blend}}_{1-18} = \text{concat}(\mathbf{w}^{\text{style}}_{1-8}, \mathbf{w}^{\text{src}}_{9-18}), \tag{6}$$

$$I^{\text{style}}_{\text{pix}} = G(\mathbf{w}^{\text{blend}}_{1-18}). \tag{7}$$

The network is trained with a combination of style loss L_{style} [27], perceptual loss L_{lpips} [20], keypoint loss L_{kp} for facial alignment, and latent space losses L_{latent}, L_{reg}. As with bald editing, the final result is composited using Laplacian Pyramid Blending for a natural transition.

2.5 Hair Color Editing

We propose a user-friendly approach based on direct RGB value input, avoiding the need for reference images. We construct a supervised dataset by transforming images into the LAB color space, modifying the chromatic channels, and converting back to RGB. A *ColorMapper* network is then trained to map the source latent code and target RGB value to the desired colored output.

$$\mathbf{w}^{\text{color}}_{9-18} = \text{ColorMapper}(\mathbf{w}^{\text{src}}_{9-18}), \tag{8}$$

$$I^{\text{color}} = G(\text{concat}(\mathbf{w}^{\text{src}}_{1-8}, \mathbf{w}^{\text{color}}_{9-18})). \tag{9}$$

The model is optimized using a CLIP-based loss function that prioritizes natural, perceptually plausible transformations over rigid pixel-wise color fidelity.

2.6 Final Image Synthesis

The final edited latent code, $\mathbf{w}^{\text{edit}}$, combines the new hairstyle and/or hair color information. For joint editing, this is:

$$\mathbf{w}^{\text{edit}}_{\text{dual}} = \text{concat}(\mathbf{w}^{\text{style}}_{1-8}, \mathbf{w}^{\text{color}}_{9-18}), \tag{10}$$

This latent code is decoded by the generator G to produce the edited image I^{edit}. Finally, Laplacian pyramid fusion is used to obtain the final output I^{output}, which preserves the original identity and background.

Fig. 4. Visual comparison with PbE [34]**, Anydoor** [35]**, HairFusion** [28] **and our HairEditor.** Our method demonstrates superior performance in both hairstyle matching and visual naturalness. Additionally, by employing a Laplacian pyramid blending strategy between bald images and the edited hairstyles, our approach introduces minimal changes to facial and background regions. This ensures exceptional preservation of identity-irrelevant areas before and after editing.

3   Experiments

We retrained StyleGAN2 and the E4E encoder on our extended MattingHuman dataset (1024 × 1024). Training was performed on NVIDIA RTX 4090 GPUs. Learning rates were set to 1×10^{-2} (bald), 1×10^{-4} (hairstyle), and 1×10^{-4} (color).

3.1   Quantitative and Qualitative Comparison

We evaluated HairEditor against state-of-the-art methods Paint-by-Example [34], AnyDoor [35], and HairFusion [28] using SSIM [30], PSNR [31], FID [32], and FID-CLIP [33] metrics on a test set of 4,000 portraits. As shown in Table 1, HairEditor achieves superior performance across all metrics, particularly in FID and FID-CLIP, while using significantly fewer parameters. Qualitative results in Fig. 4 demonstrate our method's superior hairstyle matching and identity preservation with minimal background alteration.

3.2   Ablation Study

To validate our supervised data construction, we performed an ablation study by removing label-dependent losses L_{latent} and L_{lpips} from the hairstyle editing

Table 1. Quantitative comparison for HairEditing. We apply the same agnostic mask generation strategy provided by HairFusion to the other three methods, using it as the inpainting region mask. The params of HairEditor consists of two components: the *StyleMapper* and the StyleGAN generator G.

Model	SSIM ↑	PSNR ↑	FID ↓	FID-CLIP ↓	Params(M) ↓
PbE [34]	0.92	17.43	34.19	20.91	1249.45
Anydoor [35]	0.91	16.56	32.88	18.13	2338.26
HairFusion [28]	0.88	15.38	23.40	9.35	1755.72
HairEditor (Ours)	**0.94**	**21.53**	**9.32**	**3.50**	**64.41**

stage. The results in Table 2 show that while weak supervision is effective, our full method with strong label supervision yields significantly better FID and FID-CLIP scores, confirming the value of our data pipeline.

Table 2. Ablation Study for Hair Editing. *w/o label* means that we remove the strict label supervision loss and train the StyleMapper using only weak supervision.

Model	SSIM ↑	PSNR ↑	FID ↓	FID-CLIP ↓
Ours(w/o label)	**0.94**	20.52	11.50	5.11
Ours	**0.94**	**21.53**	**9.32**	**3.50**

4   Conclusion

In summary, our source-bald-model data construction pipeline successfully extends StyleGAN-based hair editing to non-aligned, upper-body portraits, enhancing robustness and applicability for real-world scenarios. By simulating use cases with AI-generated virtual avatars, we also address growing privacy concerns, arguing that prioritizing the use of AI-synthesized data in algorithm development is a meaningful and forward-looking approach.

Acknowledgments. This work was supported in part by Beijing Natural Science Foundation L242092, Chinese National Natural Science Foundation Projects U23B2054, 62276254, 62206280, 62376265, the Beijing Science and Technology Plan Project Z231100005923033, the Science and Technology Development Fund of Macau Project 0140/2024/AGJ, and InnoHK program.

References

1. Karras, T., Laine, S., Aila, T.: A style-based generator architecture for generative adversarial networks. In: CVPR, pp. 4401–4410 (2019)
2. Karras, T., Laine, S., Aittala, M., Hellsten, J., Lehtinen, J., Aila, T.: Analyzing and improving the image quality of StyleGAN. In: CVPR, pp. 8107–8116 (2020)
3. Karras, T., Aila, T., Laine, S., Lehtinen, J.: Progressive growing of GANs for improved quality, stability, and variation. arXiv preprint arXiv:1710.10196 (2017)
4. Rombach, R., Blattmann, A., Lorenz, D., Esser, P., Ommer, B.: High-resolution image synthesis with latent diffusion models. In: CVPR, pp. 10684–10695 (2022)
5. Zhu, P., Abdal, R., Femiani, J., Wonka, P.: Barbershop: GAN-based image compositing using segmentation masks. arXiv:2106.01505 (2021)
6. Kim, T., Chung, C., Kim, Y., Park, S., Kim, K., Choo, J.: Style your hair: latent optimization for pose-invariant hairstyle transfer via local-style-aware hair alignment. In: ECCV, pp. 188–203. Springer, Cham (2022)
7. Khwanmuang, S., Phongthawee, P., Sangkloy, P., Suwajanakorn, S.: StyleGAN salon: multi-view latent optimization for pose-invariant hairstyle transfer. In: CVPR (2023)
8. Wei, T., et al.: HairCLIP: design your hair by text and reference image. In: CVPR (2022)
9. Wei, T., et al.: HairCLIPV2: unifying hair editing via proxy feature blending. In: ICCV (2023)
10. Nikolaev, M., Kuznetsov, M., Vetrov, D., Alanov, A.: HairFastGAN: realistic and robust hair transfer with a fast encoder-based approach. arXiv preprint arXiv:2404.01094 (2024)
11. Wu, Y., Yang, Y.-L., Jin, X.: HairMapper: removing hair from portraits using GANs. In: CVPR, pp. 4227–4236 (2022)
12. Zhang, Y., Zhang, Q., Song, Y., Liu, J.: Stable-hair: real-world hair transfer via diffusion model. arXiv preprint arXiv:2407.14078 (2024)
13. Zhang, L., Rao, A., Agrawala, M.: Adding conditional control to text-to-image diffusion models. In: ICCV, pp. 3836–3847 (2023)
14. Patashnik, O., Wu, Z., Shechtman, E., Cohen-Or, D., Lischinski, D.: StyleCLIP: text-driven manipulation of StyleGAN imagery. In: ICCV, pp. 2085–2094 (2021)
15. Yao, X., Newson, A., Gousseau, Y., Hellier, P.: A style-based GAN encoder for high fidelity reconstruction of images and videos. In: ECCV (2022)
16. Bobkov, D., Titov, V., Alanov, A., Vetrov, D.: StyleFeatureEditor for detail-rich StyleGAN inversion and high quality image editing. In: CVPR, pp. 9337–9346 (2024)
17. Tov, O., Alaluf, Y., Nitzan, Y., Patashnik, O., Cohen-Or, D.: Designing an encoder for StyleGAN image manipulation. arXiv preprint arXiv:2102.02766 (2021)
18. Lyu, Y., Lin, T., Li, F., He, D., Dong, J., Tan, T.: DeltaEdit: exploring text-free training for text-driven image manipulation. In: CVPR (2023)
19. Deng, J., Guo, J., Xue, N., Zafeiriou, S.: ArcFace: additive angular margin loss for deep face recognition. In: CVPR, pp. 4690–4699 (2019)
20. Zhang, R., Isola, P., Efros, A.A., Shechtman, E., Wang, O.: The unreasonable effectiveness of deep features as a perceptual metric. In: CVPR (2018)
21. Simonyan, K., Zisserman, A.: Very deep convolutional networks for large-scale image recognition. In: ICLR (2015)
22. Yu, C., Wang, J., Peng, C., Gao, C., Yu, G., Sang, N.: BiSeNet: bilateral segmentation network for real-time semantic segmentation. In: ECCV, pp. 334–349 (2018)

23. Yu, C., Gao, C., Wang, J., Yu, G., Shen, C., Sang, N.: BiSeNet V2: bilateral network with guided aggregation for real-time semantic segmentation. Int. J. Comput. Vision **129**(11), 3051–3068 (2021). https://doi.org/10.1007/s11263-021-01515-2
24. Suvorov, R., et al.: Resolution-robust large mask inpainting with Fourier convolutions. arXiv preprint arXiv:2109.07161 (2021)
25. Radford, A., et al.: Learning transferable visual models from natural language supervision. arXiv preprint arXiv:2103.00020 (2021)
26. Bulat, A., Tzimiropoulos, G.: How far are we from solving the 2D & 3D face alignment problem? In: ICCV (2017)
27. Gatys, L.A., Ecker, A.S., Bethge, M.: A neural algorithm of artistic style. arXiv preprint arXiv:1508.06576 (2015)
28. Chung, C., Park, S., Kim, J., Choo, J.: HairFusion: faithful, identity-preserving diffusion-based hairstyle transfer. In: AAAI (2025)
29. Zeng, Y., et al.: HairDiffusion: vivid multi-colored hair editing via latent diffusion. In: NeurIPS, pp. 5048–5073 (2024)
30. Wang, Z., Bovik, A.C., Sheikh, H.R., Simoncelli, E.P.: Image quality assessment: from error visibility to structural similarity. IEEE Trans. Image Process. **13**(4), 600–612 (2004)
31. Horé, A., Ziou, D.: Image quality metrics: PSNR vs. SSIM. In: ICPR, pp. 2366–2369 (2010)
32. Heusel, M., Ramsauer, H., Unterthiner, T., Nessler, B., Hochreiter, S.: GANs trained by a two time-scale update rule converge to a local nash equilibrium. In: NeurIPS, vol. 30 (2017)
33. Kynkäänniemi, T., Karras, T., Aittala, M., Aila, T., Lehtinen, J.: The role of ImageNet classes in Fréchet inception distance. In: ICLR (2023)
34. Yang, B., et al.: Paint by example: exemplar-based image editing with diffusion models. In: CVPR, pp. 18381–18391 (2023)
35. Chen, X., et al.: AnyDoor: zero-shot object-level image customization. In: CVPR, pp. 6593–6602 (2024)
36. Hu, E.J., et al.: LoRA: low-rank adaptation of large language models. In: ICLR (2022)
37. Vaswani, A., et al.: Attention is all you need. In: NeurIPS, vol. 30 (2017)
38. Chen, Q., et al: Semantic human matting. In: MM (2018)

Conservation-Informed Neural Network for Human Motion Prediction

Yangyang Hu, Ping Ye$^{(\boxtimes)}$, Xiangjuan Wu, and Hao Liu

School of Information Engineering, Ningxia University, Ningxia, China
`yeping@nxu.edu.cn`

Abstract. In this paper, we propose a conservation-informed end-to-end learning framework to achieve accurate human motion prediction based on conservation laws. Existing methods, which rely purely on data-driven approaches, often produce physically implausible results due to their neglect of the physical principles of human movement. This shortcoming often leads to prediction results that are not applicable to real-world scenarios. To address these challenges, our proposed Conservation-informed Neural Network (CiNN) treats the human body as an independent spatiotemporal dynamical system. By solving the conservation equations that describe the rules of human motion, CiNN calculates the next frame of human movement. The physical constraints provided by the conservation laws effectively mitigate the inherent cumulative error problem in human motion prediction. Extensive experiments demonstrate that our proposed conservation framework generates results that are more in line with physical laws and shows significant performance improvement in long-term prediction.

Keywords: Human Motion Prediction · Spatiotemporal Dynamics · Conservation Law

1 Introduction

Human motion prediction aims to forecast future human motion sequences based on observed historical motion sequences, which plays a crucial role in many real-world applications, such as human–robot interaction, autonomous driving, and behavior analysis. Although existing methods have made significant efforts to learn complex human dynamics from data distributions, their performance in unconstrained real-world environments remains unsatisfactory. This limitation primarily stems from neglecting the physical consistency required for the human body as a complex dynamical system, making it impractical to predict human motions that conform to real-world physical laws. Therefore, this challenge motivates us to develop a human motion prediction method guided by physical priors to ensure the physical consistency of human motion prediction in unconstrained environments.

Traditional human motion prediction methods treat human motion prediction as a vanilla temporal prediction issue, utilizing different types of neural

W. Jia et al. (Eds.): CCBR 2025, LNCS 16360, pp. 204–214, 2026.
https://doi.org/10.1007/978-981-95-6123-0_20

networks to process sequential data [1]. In addition, the excellent performance of generative models has attracted widespread attention from researchers. For example, Deepak et al. [2] used bidirectional generative adversarial networks to recursively predict human pose sequences and Chen et al. [3] proposed a motion diffusion model that generates motions from random noise. Although these methods have demonstrated the potential to learn complex kinematics from data distributions, they adopt purely data-driven strategies. The motion features learned by these methods lack physical information and are susceptible to data noise, making it difficult to handle complex real-world environments.

Recently, some studies have attempted to predict human motion based on physical dynamics. Yue et al. [4] simplified the human body as a single-pendulum model and used single-pendulum dynamics to learn human motion. Zhang et al. [16] calculated the next moment of human motion by solving the Euler-Lagrange equations. Chen et al. [5] modeled keypoints as independent Hamiltonian mechanical systems and used symplectic integration to predict motion trajectories. These works have demonstrated that physical information can effectively compensate for the deficiencies of purely data-driven methods. However, these methods, despite incorporating physical dynamics, primarily focus on specific mechanical equations (e.g., single-pendulum dynamics, Euler-Lagrange equations) and fail to integrate fundamental conservation laws (such as angular momentum conservation) as intrinsic constraints. This partiality in physical modeling leads to the inability to preserve key conserved quantities during human motion evolution, making it hard to maintain long-term physical consistency in predictions–especially in complex multi-joint movements where inter-body part interactions rely heavily on conserved physical properties.

In this paper, our method aims to integrate the laws of conservation into the motion prediction model. We propose an end-to-end learning framework that complies with the laws of conservation, called the Conservation-informed Neural Network (CiNN), to learn the spatiotemporal dynamics of human motion. Inspired by Noether's theorem, we describe the conservation of angular momentum of the human body based on the fundamental principles of symmetry to constrain the model to conform to physical laws. Specifically, we design a conservation-informed module for learning conservation feature representations. This module models the angular dynamics in the process of joint motion. The training process employs a dual-dynamics design, with angular dynamics forward propagation implemented based on Euler's equations. Meanwhile, to enhance the stability of long-term prediction, we use a data-driven model to capture long-term dependencies and guide motion prediction through the conservation-preserving module, thereby reducing the inherent cumulative errors in motion prediction. Extensive experiments have proven that our model effectively improves the performance of long-term prediction and provides stronger physical interpretability.

2   Approach

The architecture of our proposed CiNN is depicted in Fig. 1, comprising two key components: a data - driven model and a conservation - informed model.

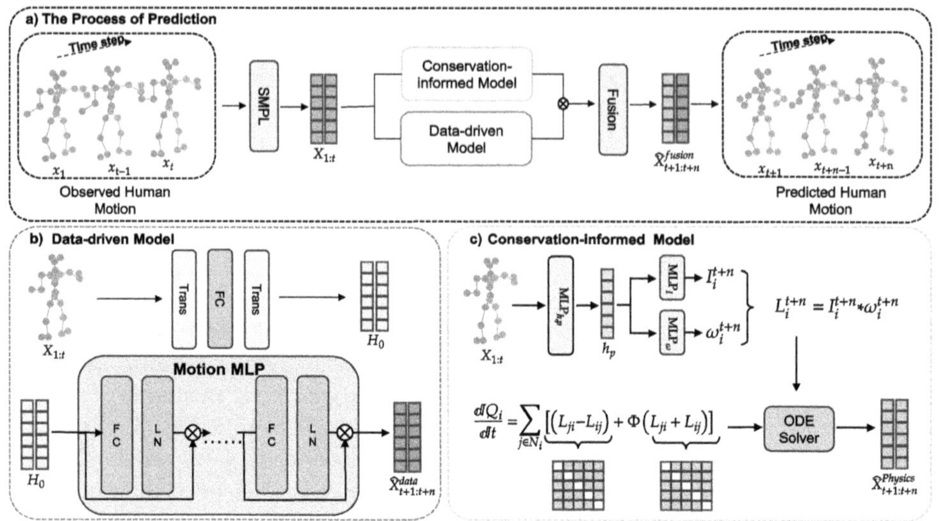

Fig. 1. The framework of our proposed CiNN. In Figure a, we present the overall process of our method, which first applies SMPL forward dynamics to preprocess human motion data. The transformed SMPL parameters are then used as inputs for both the data-driven model and the conservation information model, ultimately predicting future human motions by integrating data prediction results and conservation information guidance. Figure b illustrates the data-driven model implemented based on MLP. Figure c shows the specific details of the conservation information model, where we construct predictions that adhere to mathematical properties and physical laws.

2.1   Problem Formulation

Human motion prediction aims to forecast future human poses given an observed sequence of body postures. Specifically, given the observed motion sequence $\mathbf{X} = [\mathbf{x}_1, \mathbf{x}_2, \ldots, \mathbf{x}_t]$, the objective is to predict the future motion sequence $\hat{\mathbf{X}} = [\mathbf{x}_{t+1}, \mathbf{x}_{t+2}, \ldots, \mathbf{x}_{t+n}]$, where t and n denote the numbers of observed and predicted frames, respectively. Formally, we learn a predictor $\mathcal{F}$ that establishes the mapping between the observed sequence and the future sequence. In this paper, our work can be formulated as follows:

$$\hat{X} = D(X, CiNN(X)) \tag{1}$$

where $CiNN$ refers to the conservation-informed neural network that we propose, and D denotes the data-driven model.

To the best of our knowledge, existing human motion prediction methods mostly rely on sophisticated deeplearning models to directly learn motion patterns from observed data while neglecting inherent physical laws in human motion, such as the conservation of angular momentum. Although such approaches can achieve satisfactory predictions in some scenarios, they frequently fall short of a profound comprehension of motion dynamics and exhibit limited generalizability. Inspired by Physics-Informed Neural Networks (PINNs) [6–8], we recognize that the human body, as a spatiotemporal dynamical system, should obey numerous conservation laws, e.g., the conservation of angular momentum. In general, the universal form of conservation laws in physics can be expressed by the continuity equation as follows:

$$\frac{\partial \mathbf{u}}{\partial t} + \nabla \cdot \mathbf{F}(\mathbf{u}) = \mathbf{s}(\mathbf{u}; \mathbf{x}, t) \tag{2}$$

where $\mathbf{u}(\mathbf{x}, t) \in \mathbb{R}^d$ denotes the system state variable vector composed of d components, $\mathbf{x} \in \mathbb{R}^m$ the m-dimensional spatial coordinate, t denotes time, ∇ denotes the Nabla operator, $\mathbf{F}(\cdot) \in \mathbb{R}^{m \times d}$ denotes the flux function, and $\mathbf{s}(\cdot) \in \mathbb{R}^d$ denotes the source term. This equation models the evolution of the system state $\mathbf{u}(\mathbf{x}, t)$ over time as the composition of a local flux term and the source term.

$$\frac{\mathrm{d}Q_i}{\mathrm{d}t} = \sum_{j \in \mathcal{N}_i} \Big[\underbrace{(L_{ji} - L_{ij})}_{\text{skew-symmetric}} + \Phi \underbrace{(L_{ji} + L_{ij})}_{\text{symmetric}} \Big]. \tag{3}$$

where Q denotes angular momentum and L_{ij} denotes the angular-momentum flux flowing from joint i to joint j; the angular momentum is computed as follows.

$$\mathbf{L} = \mathbf{I} \cdot \boldsymbol{\omega} \tag{4}$$

where I denotes the moment of inertia and $\boldsymbol{\omega}$ denotes the angular-velocity vector.

2.2 Data-Driven Model

We utilize the Skinned Multi-Person Linear Model (SMPL) [9] model to represent human motion. Specifically, this model represents the human body as a 3D mesh composed of 6,890 vertices and describes the body posture and shape using a set of low - dimensional parameters. The posture parameters $\boldsymbol{\theta} \in \mathbb{R}^{43 \times 3}$ include the rotation angles of 23 individual joints and a root rotation, defining the joint positions and poses of the human body. The shape parameters $\boldsymbol{\beta} \in \mathbb{R}^{10}$ are coefficients that control variations in body attributes such as width and height. By leveraging the kinematic constraints provided by the SMPL model, we ensure the rationality of the generated samples.

Part (b) of Fig. 1 illustrates the specific design of the data - driven model. First, we input the transformed 63 - dimensional SMPL parameters. Considering the heterogeneity between joints, we employ a multi - scale spatial modeling strategy. For each joint, we use the Discrete Cosine Transform (DCT) to ensure that each joint independently learns a temporal model. Additionally, we utilize a spatial fully connected layer to transform features H_0 in the spatial dimension, capturing detailed structural information between local and non - local regions.

Based on the model proposed in [14], we further develop a data - driven human motion prediction model using a Multi - Layer Perceptron (MLP) to perform temporal modeling of human motion and generate future motion predictions. The core module of the data - driven model, Motion MLP, is implemented with 48 layers of siMLPe modules. Each module consists of a Temporal Fully Connected Layer (FC) and Spatial Layer Normalization (LN), with residual connections applied between each module, as follows:

$$\mathbf{H}_{l+1} = \mathbf{H}_l + \mathrm{LN}(\mathrm{FC}(\mathbf{H}_l)) \tag{5}$$

The Temporal FC layer performs linear transformations in the sequence dimension, effectively capturing temporal dependencies between frames. After deep feature extraction, the network outputs the predicted increments $\Delta \mathbf{Y}_{t+1:t+n}$. The final predictions are generated via residual connections:

$$\hat{\mathbf{X}}^{data}_{t+1:t+n} = \Delta \mathbf{Y}_{t+1:t+n} + \mathbf{X}_{1:t} \tag{6}$$

where $n = 25$ is the number of predicted frames. This residual learning strategy effectively mitigates the vanishing gradient problem in long - sequence predictions, enhancing training stability. The entire data - driven branch outputs the complete motion sequence $\hat{\mathbf{X}}^{data}_{t+1:t+n} \in \mathbb{R}^{50 \times 63}$, providing a data - driven prediction basis for subsequent conservation - informed constraints.

For the training process of the data-driven model, we adopt the following loss functions:

$$\mathcal{L}_{data} = \sum_{t+1}^{t+n} \left\| \mathbf{X}_T - \hat{\mathbf{X}}^{data}_T \right\| + \lambda \sum_{t+1}^{t+n} \left\| \mathbf{K}_T - \hat{\mathbf{K}}^{data}_T \right\| \tag{7}$$

where X represents the parameters of the SMPL model, K denotes the positions of the 3D keypoints, and λ signifies the weight of the keypoint loss.

2.3   Conservation-Informed Model

In our approach, the conservation information model is utilized to guide the data - driven model in generating human motions that comply with the law of conservation of angular momentum. As shown in part (c) of Fig. 1, the conservation information model takes the historical motion sequence as input to predict the motion state increments for the next $t + n$ frames. Given the transformed SMPL model parameters, our conservation information model estimates the changes in physical parameters such as the moment of inertia and angular velocity through a neural network. Specifically, we first employ a multilayer perceptron to extract features $\mathbf{h}_p$ related to the physical properties from the human motion sequence.

$$\mathbf{h}_p = \mathrm{MLP}_{h,p} \left(\{ \mathbf{X}^T \}_1^t \right) \tag{8}$$

Then, we use two additional MLPs to respectively predict the physical parameters in Eq. 4.

$$\mathbf{I}_i^{t+n} = \text{MLP}_I(\mathbf{h}_p), \tag{9}$$

$$\omega_i^{t+n} = \text{MLP}_\omega(\mathbf{h}_p), \tag{10}$$

We design the model to fully leverage the powerful data - processing capabilities of neural networks while ensuring that the model strictly adheres to physical laws. Inspired by Noether's theorem, we further develop a symmetric information - passing mechanism to ensure that our network strictly follows conservation laws. Specifically, considering the propagation of angular momentum between nodes, we process high - dimensional physical features through an iterative process. In each iteration, each node exchanges information with its neighbors. Moreover, we regard this iterative process as a potential time - evolution process and introduce residual connections between iterations to enhance the stability and accuracy of the model. The symmetric information - passing mechanism is formalized as Eq. 3.

Based on the predicted physical parameters, we employ an Ordinary Differential Equation (ODE) neural solver to forecast changes in motion states $\mathbf{X}_{t+1:t+n}^{physics}$, and utilize an additional fusion neural network to estimate a fusion weight. This fusion process combines the conservation information with the predictions from the data model to produce the final prediction output, as follows:

$$\hat{\mathbf{X}}_{t+1:t+n}^{fusion} = (1 - \hat{w}^t)\hat{\mathbf{X}}_{t+1:t+n}^{physics} + \hat{w}^t\hat{\mathbf{X}}_{t+1:t+n}^{data}, \tag{11}$$

where $\hat{w}^t$ is a scalar fusion weight.

For the training process, we rely on the following loss to minimize the physical information loss.

$$\mathcal{L}_{physics} = \sum_{t+1}^{t+n} \left\|\mathbf{X}_T - \hat{\mathbf{X}}_T^{physics}\right\| + \lambda_1 \sum_{t+1}^{t+n} \left\|\mathbf{K}_T - \hat{\mathbf{K}}_T^{physics}\right\| + \lambda_2 \sum_{t+1}^{t+n} \left\|\mathbf{L}_{T+1}^i - \mathbf{L}_T^i\right\| \tag{12}$$

where $\mathbf{L}_{T+1}^i$ represents the angular momentum of the i-th joint at time $T+1$, $\mathbf{L}_T^i$ represents the angular momentum of the i-th joint at time T, and λ_2 represents the weight for the angular momentum loss.

3   Experiments

3.1   Datasets and Implementation Details

Dataset. We evaluated our model on Human3.6M [10]. To ensure a fair comparison, we followed the same dataset partition settings as in prior works [17].

Implementation Details. For Human3.6M, we fix the input history and the output prediction horizon to 25 frames, and parameterize the data via the SMPL model. Data-driven baseline: We adopted a 48-layer MLP backbone with residual connections after every layer to ensure stable feature learning. The model is trained for 5 epochs with an initial learning rate of 3×10^{-4} and a batch size of 64. Conservation-informed Neural Network (CiNN): Optimization is performed with Adam (weight decay $= 1\times10^{-4}$). The initial learning rate is set to 3×10^{-4} and is decayed by a factor of 0.9 every 500 gradient steps. Training lasts 3 epochs with a batch size of 64. All experiments are conducted on two NVIDIA RTX 4090 GPUs.

3.2 Metrics and Baselines

Following prior work [17], we adopted Mean Per-Joint Position Error (MPJPE) as the primary metric. After root-alignment, MPJPE is defined as the average ℓ_2 Euclidean distance between the predicted 3D joint positions and their ground-truth counterparts, providing a direct measure of motion-prediction quality. We conduct evaluations on the Human3.6M dataset and benchmark our method against leading approaches including ST-DGCN [12], siMLPe [14], EqMotion [15], and PhysMoP [16].

3.3 Quantitative Results

Short- and long-term motion prediction. By reporting the Mean Per-Joint Position Error (MPJPE) at multiple horizons, we demonstrate CiNN's superiority over prior art in both short-term (<400 ms) and long-term (>400 ms) human motion forecasting. Extensive evaluations on Human3.6M show consistent improvements over existing methods, while an additional action-classification assessment on Human3.6M further underscores CiNN's outstanding long-term predictive performance.

On the Human3.6M dataset, we adopted the widely-used Protocol 1 (H3.6M-P1) and evaluated at the target frames [12–14]. Under this protocol, the current state-of-the-art achieves 37.0 mm and 80.1 mm MPJPE for short- and long-term horizons, respectively. Our CiNN further reduces these errors, delivering a substantial leap in performance. The per-action results in Table 1 reveal that CiNN excels not only on simple motions such as Walking but also on irregular, complex actions like Greeting across both short and long horizons. This highlights CiNN's strength in long-term prediction, where the conservation-informed design—embedding the law of angular-momentum conservation as a physical prior—constrains the otherwise purely data-driven model, supplying the missing regularity that drastically suppresses accumulated error over time. The results on Human3.6M (Table 1) showed that CiNN was slightly inferior to prior methods at very short horizons (e.g., 80 ms on "Directions"), but quickly surpassed all competitors as the forecast horizon increased. The performance drop at 80 ms is attributed to the unnecessary rigidity introduced by enforcing angular-momentum conservation in such a short window.

3.4 Qualitative Results

In Fig. 2, we visualized representative motion sequences to present qualitative comparisons. This figure visualizes the Walking action from the Human3.6M test

Table 1. Performance evaluation (in MPJPE) on the H3.6 m dataset. The best results are highlighted in bold.

	Directions				Greeting				Phoning				Posing			
Time (ms)	80	160	320	400	80	160	320	400	80	160	320	400	80	160	320	400
ST-DGCN [13]	7.2	17.6	40.9	51.5	15.2	34.1	71.6	87.1	8.3	18.3	38.7	48.4	10.7	25.7	60.0	76.6
siMLPe [14]	6.5	–	–	55.8	12.4	–	–	77.3	8.1	–	–	48.6	8.8	–	–	73.8
EqMotion [15]	6.3	15.8	38.9	50.1	–	–	–	–	7.4	16.7	36.9	47.0	8.2	18.9	43.4	57.5
PhysMoP [16]	**1.6**	**6.0**	23.8	37.6	2.9	10.2	37.0	56.1	**1.7**	**6.2**	23.6	37.0	2.2	8.1	30.0	46.3
Ours	2.2	6.3	**17.7**	**23.9**	**2.0**	**5.2**	**25.1**	**42.6**	2.4	6.4	**17.3**	**23.4**	**1.7**	**4.7**	**21.4**	**33.2**

	Walking				Eating				Smoking				Discussion			
Time (ms)	80	160	320	400	80	160	320	400	80	160	320	400	80	160	320	400
ST-DGCN [13]	10.2	19.8	34.5	40.3	7.0.2	15.1	30.6	38.1	6.6.3	14.1	28.2	34.7	10.0	23.8	53.6	66.7
siMLPe [14]	9.9.6	–	–	39.6	5.9	–	–	36.1	6.5	–	–	36.3	9.4	-	-	64.3
EqMotion [15]	9.0	17.5	32.6	39.2	6.3	13.6	28.9	36.5	5.5	11.3	23.0	29.3	8.2	18.9	42.1	53.9
PhysMoP [16]	2.6	9.0	29.0	42.4	**1.3**	**4.9**	**19.9**	31.1	**1.3**	4.9	19.5	31.6	**2.0**	7.6	31.0	48.3
Ours	**1.4**	**3.7**	**19.2**	**31.9**	2.6	7.5	20.9	**28.1**	1.6	**4.7**	**13.6**	**22.7**	2.7	**7.3**	**19.7**	**36.4**

	Purchases				Sitting				Sittingdown				Takingphoto			
Time (ms)	80	160	320	400	80	160	320	400	80	160	320	400	80	160	320	400
ST-DGCN [13]	12.5	28.7	60.1	73.3	8.8	19.2	42.2	53.8	13.9	27.9	57.4	71.5	8.4	18.9	42.0	53.3
siMLPe [14]	11.7	–	–	72.4	8.6	–	–	55.2	13.6	–	–	70.8	7.8	–	–	50.8
EqMotion [15]	–	–	–	–	8.1	18.0	41.2	52.9	13.0	26.5	56.2	70.7	–	–	–	–
PhysMoP [16]	**2.5**	9.1	36.0	56.1	**1.7**	**6.2**	**23.7**	37.4	2.7	9.6	31.6	46.8	1.6	6.0	24.4	38.3
Ours	3.2	**9.1**	**24.0**	**41.7**	3.4	9.8	25.5	**33.6**	**1.5**	**4.1**	**21.1**	**35.0**	**1.5**	**3.5**	**16.2**	**28.7**

	Waiting				Walkingdog				Walkingtogether				Average			
Time (ms)	80	160	320	400	80	160	320	400	80	160	320	400	80	160	320	400
ST-DGCN [13]	8.9	20.1	43.6	54.3	18.8	39.3	73.7	86.4	8.7	18.6	34.4	41.0	10.3	22.7	47.4	58.5
siMLPe [14]	7.8	–	–	53.2	18.2	–	–	83.6	8.4	–	–	41.2	9.6	21.7	46.3	57.3
EqMotion [15]	7.6	17.4	39.9	51.1	–	–	–	–	7.8	16.1	30.6	37.1	9.1	20.1	43.7	55.0
PhysMoP [16]	1.9	7.0	25.8	39.8	3.6	12.5	45.0	68.9	**2.1**	**7.2**	**25.4**	39.5	**2.1**	7.6	28.4	43.8
Ours	**1.9**	**4.9**	**17.0**	**28.5**	**1.9**	**4.8**	**33.1**	**53.2**	3.8	11.0	28.4	**36.7**	2.3	**6.2**	**21.6**	**33.3**

set at several key time steps. While previous methods tend to converge to static, motionless poses during long-term prediction, our CiNN consistently preserves natural motion dynamics and plausible trends over extended horizons.

3.5   Ablation Study

We evaluated the advantages of the CiNN through an ablation study. Specifically, Table 2 compares the performance of a model that is purely data-driven without the guidance of conservation laws, and that of the complete CiNN. The results show that the data-driven baseline performs poorly on both short- and long-term motion prediction. By contrast, CiNN incorporates the law of conservation of angular momentum, enabling it to synergize the strengths of data-driven learning

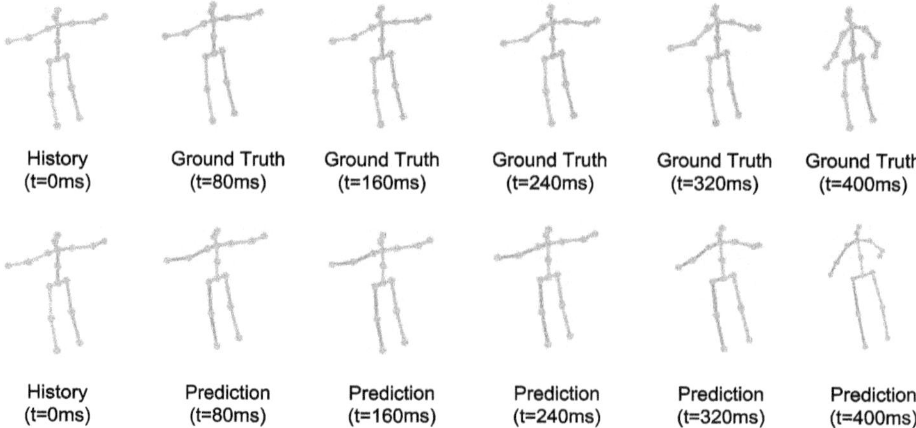

Fig. 2. Result visualizations on the Walking action in the Human3.6 m dataset up to 400 ms.

Table 2. Ablation studies on the impact of different components on Human3.6M.

Data-driven	CiNN	80	160	320	400	1000
✓	×	6.6	12.9	32.4	36.7	58.5
✓	✓	**2.3**	**6.2**	**21.6**	**33.3**	**56.8**

and physics-based regularization, and thus achieves strong performance across all prediction horizons.

4   Conclusion

We propose a Conservation-informed Neural Network (CiNN) that integrates conservation laws to enhance the physical plausibility of human motion prediction. By incorporating a symmetric information-passing module, CiNN ensures the propagation of angular momentum conservation across body parts, thereby addressing the issue of physical consistency in predictions. Experiments on Human3.6M show CiNN outperforms state-of-the-art methods, with notable MPJPE reductions in long-term prediction, and the results further demonstrate that our model is superior to existing methods in both accuracy and robustness, maintaining stable performance even in complex motion prediction processes where existing methods often struggle. The predictions, which demonstrate the value of merging physical principles with neural networks for reliable human motion prediction.

Acknowledgments. This work was supported by grants from the National Science Foundation of China (62476147), Ningxia Leaders in Innovation Fellowships (2024GKL-RLX17), and the Open Fund of the Key Laboratory of the Ministry of Education on Artificial Intelligence in Equipment (AAIE-2023-0403).

References

1. Lucas, T., Baradel, F., Weinzaepfel, P., Rogez, G.: PoseGPT: quantization-based 3D human motion generation and forecasting. In: European Conference on Computer Vision, pp. 417–435. Springer (2022)
2. Jain, D.K., Zareapoor, M., Jain, R., Kathuria, A., Bachhety, S.: GAN-poser: an improvised bidirectional GAN model for human motion prediction. Neural Comput. Appl. **32**(18), 14579–14591 (2020)
3. Chen, L.-H., Zhang, J., Li, Y., Pang, Y., Xia, X., Liu, T.: HumanMAC: masked motion completion for human motion prediction. In: Proceedings of the IEEE/CVF International Conference on Computer Vision (ICCV), pp. 9544–9555 (2023)
4. Yue, J., Li, B., Pettré, J., Seyfried, A., Wang, H.: Human motion prediction under unexpected perturbation. In: Proceedings of the IEEE/CVF Conference on Computer Vision and Pattern Recognition (CVPR), pp. 1501–1511 (2024)
5. Chen, H., Lyu, K., Liu, Z., Yin, Y., Yang, X., Lyu, Y.: Rethinking human motion prediction with symplectic integral. In: Proceedings of the IEEE/CVF Conference on Computer Vision and Pattern Recognition (CVPR), pp. 2134–2143 (2024)
6. Raissi, M., Perdikaris, P., Karniadakis, G.E.: Physics-informed neural networks: a deep learning framework for solving forward and inverse problems involving nonlinear partial differential equations. J. Comput. Phys. **378**, 686–707 (2019)
7. Ren, P., Rao, C., Chen, S., Wang, J.-X., Sun, H., Liu, Y.: SeismicNet: physics-informed neural networks for seismic wave modeling in semi-infinite domain. Comput. Phys. Commun. **295**, 109010 (2024)
8. Mi, Y., et al.: Conservation-informed graph learning for spatiotemporal dynamics prediction. In: Proceedings of the 31st ACM SIGKDD Conference on Knowledge Discovery and Data Mining, vol. 1, pp. 1056–1067 (2025)
9. Loper, M., Mahmood, N., Romero, J., Pons-Moll, G., Black, M.J.: SMPL: a skinned multi-person linear model. In: Seminal Graphics Papers: Pushing the Boundaries, vol. 2, pp. 851–866 (2023)
10. Ionescu, C., Papava, D., Olaru, V., Sminchisescu, C.: Human3.6M: large scale datasets and predictive methods for 3D human sensing in natural environments. IEEE Trans. Pattern Anal. Mach. Intell. **36**(7), 1325–1339 (2013)
11. von Marcard, T., Henschel, R., Black, M.J., Rosenhahn, B., Pons-Moll, G.: Recovering accurate 3D human pose in the wild using IMUs and a moving camera. In: Ferrari, V., Hebert, M., Sminchisescu, C., Weiss, Y. (eds.) ECCV 2018. LNCS, vol. 11214, pp. 614–631. Springer, Cham (2018). https://doi.org/10.1007/978-3-030-01249-6_37
12. Mao, W., Liu, M., Salzmann, M.: History repeats itself: human motion prediction via motion attention. In: European Conference on Computer Vision, pp. 474–489. Springer (2020)
13. Ma, T., Nie, Y., Long, C., Zhang, Q., Li, G.: Progressively generating better initial guesses towards next stages for high-quality human motion prediction. In: Proceedings of the IEEE/CVF Conference on Computer Vision and Pattern Recognition, pp. 6437–6446 (2022)
14. Guo, W., Du, Y., Shen, X., Lepetit, V., Alameda-Pineda, X., Moreno-Noguer, F.: Back to MLP: a simple baseline for human motion prediction. In: Proceedings of the IEEE/CVF Winter Conference on Applications of Computer Vision, pp. 4809–4819 (2023)
15. Xu, C., et al.: EqMotion: equivariant multi-agent motion prediction with invariant interaction reasoning. In: Proceedings of the IEEE/CVF Conference on Computer Vision and Pattern Recognition, pp. 1410–1420 (2023)

16. Zhang, Y., Kephart, J.O., Ji, Q.: Incorporating physics principles for precise human motion prediction. In: Proceedings of the IEEE/CVF Winter Conference on Applications of Computer Vision, pp. 6164–6174 (2024)
17. Zhong, C., Hu, L., Zhang, Z., Ye, Y., Xia, S.: Spatio-temporal gating-adjacency GCN for human motion prediction. In: Proceedings of the IEEE/CVF Conference on Computer Vision and Pattern Recognition (CVPR), pp. 6447–6456 (2022)

High-Low Feature Fusion Generative Adversarial Network for the Inpainting of Irregularly Occluded Iris Images

Junkang Deng, Zhijie Chen, Ying Chen$^{(\boxtimes)}$, Changle He, and Xiaodong Zhu

School of Software, Nanchang Hangkong University, Jiangxi, China
c_y2008@nchu.edu.cn

Abstract. Iris images inpainting is an effective means to reduce the impact of low-quality iris images in recognition. To improve the recognition rate of low-quality iris image, this paper proposes a High-Low Feature Fusion Generative Adversarial Network (HLFG) to restore irregularly occluded iris images. HLFG designs hierarchical attention to capture long-distance dependencies and enhance context delivery, and designs feature fusion up-sampling modules in skip connections to fuse local details and global structure. The experimental results based on three iris datasets, CASIA-Iris-Interval, IITD and ND-IRIS-0405, show that the PNSR of repaired iris images increased by 20.2521dB, 19.4234dB and 26.0561dB respectively; SSIM increased by 0.0897, 0.1090 and 0.1542, respectively; TAR increased by 27.13%, 8.94% and 53.55%, respectively; EER decreased by 4.6337%, 1.8876% and 12.8380%, respectively and the above results fully validate the effectiveness of the HLFG.

Keywords: Iris images inpainting · Generative adversarial network · Hierarchical attention · Feature fusion

1 Introduction

The iris is a highly secure biometric identifier due to its complexity, uniqueness, stability, and resistance to forgery. Iris images are commonly captured under near infrared (NIR) or visible light (VIS) conditions, and low-quality images often occur during acquisition. These low-quality images reduce the effective region ratio, thereby degrading recognition accuracy. Traditional patch-based inpainting methods perform well on simple structures but struggle with complex textures. Deep generative models for image inpainting still perform poorly on iris images with complex topology and high-entropy random textures. Existing iris images inpainting frameworks are complex, slow in inference, and less applicable. Therefore, developing efficient iris inpainting algorithms is crucial for improving recognition performance. This paper proposes a high-low feature fusion generative adversarial network for inpainting irregularly occluded iris images, enhancing inpainting quality while preserving both global structure and local texture consistency.

In summary, the main contributions of this paper are as follows: (1) HLFG is proposed for the inpainting of irregularly occluded iris images. (2) Proposed hierarchical attention

W. Jia et al. (Eds.): CCBR 2025, LNCS 16360, pp. 215–225, 2026.
https://doi.org/10.1007/978-981-95-6123-0_21

and feature fusion up-sampling. (3) Excellent inpainting on CASIA-Iris-Interval, IITD, and ND-IRIS-0405 datasets for improved recognition rates.

2   Related Work

2.1   Patch-Based Methods

Patch-based methods accomplish image inpainting by partitioning the data into local patches and conducting feature extraction on these patches. Yu et al. [1] utilized attention weights to dynamically select matching blocks in the source region, effectively solving the long-distance dependency problem. Xu et al. [2] proposed a deep inpainting method that incorporates patch distribution loss and sample block techniques to enable texture memory retrieval. Cheng et al. [3] proposed an inpainting method based on patch denoising diffusion model, which can effectively repair severe weather degraded images. Patch-based methods struggle to achieve accurate matching using available information when inpainting images with complex textures and structures.

2.2   Neural Network-Based Methods

Neural network-based methods include both diffusion-based approaches and generative adversarial network (GAN)-based techniques. Lugmayr et al. [4] proposed an alternative sampling strategy based on DDPM to enhance contextual consistency in diffusion model. Corneanu et al. [5] employed diffusion models for image i in potential space, enabling rapid inference without domain-specific training. However, reducing computational costs during the inference and sampling stages remains a key challenge for diffusion models. GAN achieve image inpainting through a competitive interaction between generators and discriminators. Zeng et al. [6] proposed the Progressive PGGAN iris inpainting network for repairing regularly blurred iris images. Chen et al. [7] proposed a two-stage deep residual attention generative adversarial network for repairing iris textures obscured by eyelids. Chen et al. [8] proposed a two-stage dual-discriminator generative adversarial network for repairing irregularly occluded iris images.

Unlike existing approaches, this paper proposes a high-low feature fusion generative adversarial network for irregularly occluded iris inpainting.

3   Proposed Methods

As shown in Fig. 1, HLFG consists of a generator and a discriminator. The generator adopts an encoder-decoder structure with a 256×256 input size. Ordinary convolutions have limited receptive fields, when most of the receptive field falls within the occluded region, acquiring and transmitting effective information becomes challenging. To address this issue, the generator incorporates gated convolutions [9] to adaptively learn and focus on the masked region, thereby effectively suppressing the transmission of irrelevant information. To further enhance restoration quality, hierarchical attention is designed in intermediate layers to strengthen information flow. Additionally, feature fusion up-sampling is applied the decoding phase to enable joint optimization of global structure and local details, resulting in more realistic iris images.

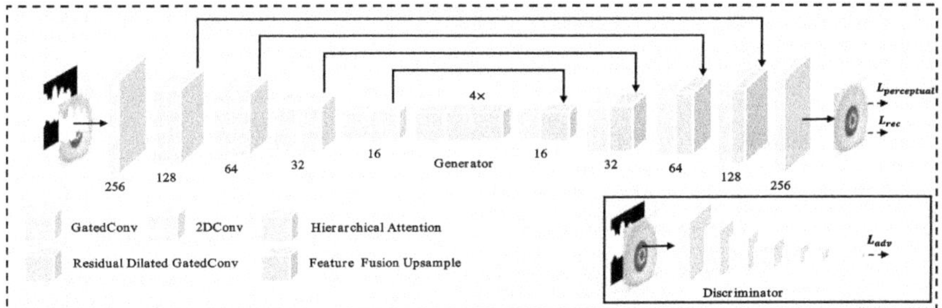

Fig. 1. Framework of high-low feature fusion generative adversarial network

3.1 Hierarchical Attention

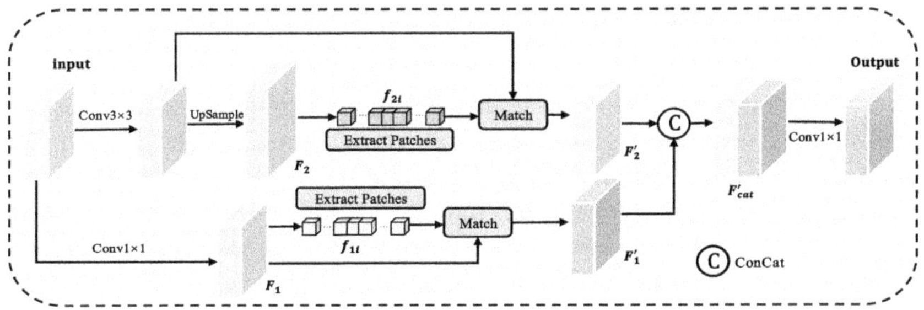

Fig. 2. Framework of hierarchical attention

Irregular occlusion disrupts the continuity of iris features, while convolutional networks are constrained by their limited receptive fields, making it difficult to capture long-range complementary cues and leading to boundary artifacts. To better restore texture continuity and help the model learn iris features across multiple scales, hierarchical attention is proposed. As shown in Fig. 2, it consists of two branches that divide the feature map into blocks. These branches separately compute attention weights for local blocks and cross-scale local blocks. The calculation process is as in Eqs. (1).

$$a_{i,j} = softmax\left(\langle \frac{f_i}{\|f_i\|_2}, \frac{f_j}{\|f_j\|_2} \rangle\right) \tag{1}$$

Here, f_i and f_j represent the i th and j th blocks in the two feature maps and N is the total number of blocks in the feature map.

After computing the attention weights, the two branches adjust the output features accordingly. These features are then concatenated and fused through a 1×1 gated convolution to enable cross-layer feature interactions. Calculation process is as in Eqs. (2) to (3).

$$q_i = \sum_j a_{i,j} b_j \tag{2}$$

$$Output = Conv^{1 \times 1}\left(Concat\left(F_1', F_2'\right)\right) \tag{3}$$

Here, b_j represents the j th input feature block extracted. q_i represents i th output feature after attention weight matching, *Concat* is the splicing operation.

3.2 Feature Fusion Up-Sampling

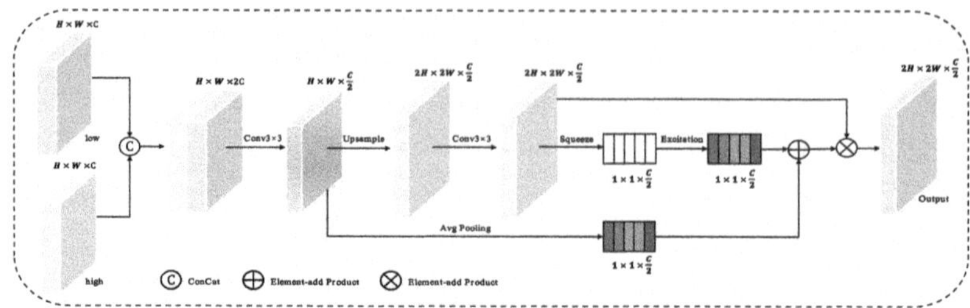

Fig. 3. Framework of feature fusion up-sampling

When the encoder extracts high-level semantic features through layer-by-layer convolutions, it loses local texture and global structural information. Since the decoder struggles to recover this lost information, a feature fusion up-sampling module is proposed. As shown in Fig. 3, the module concatenates high-level and low-level semantic features via skip connections and performs initial fusion using a 3×3 convolution. To mitigate detail loss during up-sampling, the SE module [10] introduces channel attention to strengthen the key feature information.

3.3 Loss Function

HLFG contains reconstruction loss, perception loss and adversarial loss.

The reconstruction loss promotes pixel-wise reconstruction by computing the L1 distance, as shown in Eq. (4).

$$L_{rec} = \frac{1}{N} \| I_{gt} - I_{out} \| \tag{4}$$

Here, I_{gt} represents the original image and I_{out} represents the restored image, N represents the number of elements in I_{gt}.

Perceptual loss uses VGG-19 to bring the restoration results closer to real semantic content, as shown in Eq. (5).

$$L_{percep} = \sum_{p=1}^{P} \frac{\| \phi_p^{I_{gt}} - \phi_p^{I_{out}} \|}{N_p^{I_{gt}}} \tag{5}$$

Here, P represents the number of output layers selected by VGG19, $\varphi_p^{I_{gt}}$ and $\varphi_p^{I_{out}}$ represent the features of the real image and the output image at the p th layer, $N_p^{I_{gt}}$ represents the total number of elements of I_{gt}.

Adversarial loss as shown in Eqs. (6)–(7).

$$L_{adv, D} = E_{x \sim P_x(x)} \left[\text{ReLU} \left(1 - D \left(I_{gt}, m \right) \right) \right] + \left[\text{ReLU} (1 + D(G(x), m)) \right] \tag{6}$$

$$L_G = -E_{x \sim P_x(x)}[-D(G(x), m)] \tag{7}$$

Here, G is the generator, D is the discriminator, x is the input image, I_{gt} represents the real image and m represents the mask.

The total loss functions are shown in equations. (8)–(9).

$$L_G = \lambda_{rec}L_{rec} + \lambda_{percep}L_{percep} + \lambda_{adv}L_{adv,G} \tag{8}$$

$$L_D = L_{adv,D} \tag{9}$$

Here, λ_{rec} is set to 5 to ensure fidelity, λ_{percep} is set to 0.4 to balance texture and training, λ_{adv} is set to 0.2 to stabilize adversarial learning.

4 Experiments and Results

4.1 Preparation of Iris Image Dataset

Iris images captured under NIR light exhibit clearer textures, making them more appropriate for iris image inpainting. The experiment employed three representative NIR iris image datasets, which are described in detail below: (1) The CASIA-Iris-Interval iris dataset [11], collected by the Institute of Automation, Chinese Academy of Sciences (IAAS), contains 2,639 iris images from 249 subjects. (2) The IITD dataset [12], provided by IITD Delhi, India, includes 2240 iris images from 224 subjects. (3) The ND-IRIS-0405 dataset [13], acquired using an LG 2200 sensor, consists of 64,980 iris images from 365 subjects. In this study, 288 classes comprising a total of 10,080 images that are suitable for both inpainting and recognition are selected.

Table 1. Information on the iris image dataset used for all experiments

Datasets	Categories	Total numbers	Numbers of training	Numbers of testing
CASIA-Iris-Interval	249	2639	2042	597
IITD	224	2240	1792	448
ND-IRIS-0405	288	10080	7200	2880

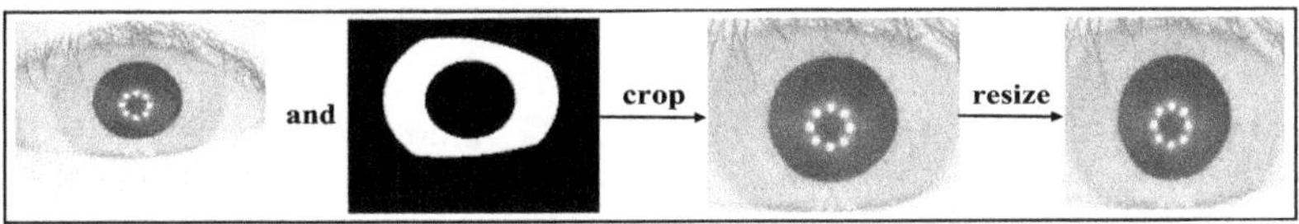

Fig. 4. Process of iris images preprocessing

Three datasets were randomly split into training and testing sets at an 8:2 ratio, and the details of the iris datasets used in the experiment are summarized in Table 1. Preprocessing the masked iris image is necessary to improve restoration efficiency. As shown in Fig. 4, The GT algorithm is employed to extract the iris boundary, crop the region within the boundary, and resize it to 256 × 256.

4.2 Experimental Environment and Parameters

All experiments employed a single Nvidia RTX 3090 GPU. The generator and discriminator were optimized using the Adam optimizer. A low learning rate was adopted to ensure stable model training, with the learning rates for the generator and discriminator set to 1e-5 and 1e-6, respectively. The batch size was 16, and 100 training epochs were sufficient for the model to converge. The network used for recognition experiments was MobileViT [14], with a learning rate of 2e-4, a batch size of 16, and 200 training epochs to ensure comprehensive model training.

4.3 Iris Image Inpainting Effect Analysis

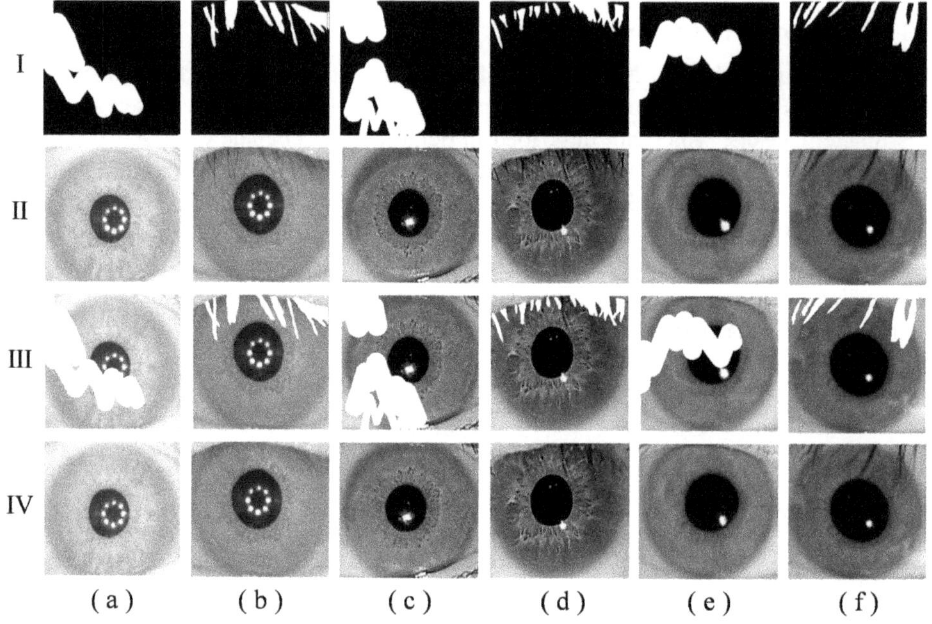

Fig. 5. Inpainting result of CASIA-Iris-Interval, IITD, and ND-IRIS-0405 datasets

The inpainting results are shown in Fig. 5. HLFG demonstrates superior performance on irregularly occluded iris images across the three datasets, generating realistic and coherent textures. In (a), (b), and (c), the network not only reconstructs structurally consistent iris textures but also restores plausible inner boundary morphology. In (b), (d), and (f), the network effectively reduces the impact of eyelash occlusion while preserving the structural rationality of the outer boundary.

The restoration experiments utilized occluded masks with a coverage rate ranging from 10% to 40%. As shown in Table 2, the SSIM and PSNR of the restored images are higher than those of the occluded images. Compared with the occluded images, the PSNR increases by 20.2521 dB, 19.4234 dB, and 26.0561 dB, while the SSIM improves by

Table 2. Comparison of PSNR, SSIM, EER, TAR on CASIA-Iris-Interval, IITD, and ND-IRIS-0405 datasets

Dataset	Method	PSNR ↑	SSIM ↑	EER ↓	TAR ↑
CASIA-Iris-Interval	Occluded images	14.0128	0.8604	4.9687	72.53
	Inpainting images	**34.2649**	**0.9501**	**0.3350**	**99.66**
IITD	Occluded images	10.5005	0.8143	2.0730	90.84
	Inpainting images	**29.9239**	**0.9233**	**0.1854**	**99.78**
ND-IRIS-0405	Occluded images	10.1928	0.8212	13.4473	44.90
	Inpainting images	**36.2489**	**0.9754**	**0.6093**	**98.45**

0.0897, 0.1090, and 0.1542, respectively. These results confirm the superior performance of HLFG on the NIR iris dataset.

4.4 Comparative Experiments

As shown in Fig. 6, the experiment employed common occlusion rates of 10–40% and large occlusion rates of 40–60% to evaluate subjective inpainting effectiveness. Under 10–40% occlusion (I, III, and V) DeepFillv2 and CTSDG improved objective metrics but exhibited noticeable artifacts. TT-GAN reduces these artifacts yet lacks sufficient texture details. In contrast, HLFG restored richer textures while preserving the global structure. Under 40–60% occlusion (II, IV, and VI), iris image information is severely limited, which significantly increases the inpainting difficulty. HLFG effectively reconstructs plausible boundaries by leveraging the limited image information available under extensive occlusion, thereby significantly reducing artifacts.

This paper compare TT-GAN [8], DeepFillv2 [9], and CTSDG [15], all methods use the original network structure. The objective results are shown in Table 3. HLFG significantly reduces the model size compared to other methods while achieving superior performance under the same occlusion conditions. At occlusion rates of 10–40%, FID scores decreased by 5.87, 6.11, and 0.65; PSNR increased by 1.37 dB, 0.65 dB, and 0.26 dB; SSIM improved by 0.020, 0.014, and 0.003; EER decreased by 0.1675%, 0.3262%, and 0.0504%; and TAR increased by 0.16%, 0.73%, and 0.25%. At occlusion rates of 40–60%, FID scores decreased by 10.99, 1.86, and 1.16; PSNR increased by 0.39 dB, 0.04 dB on CASIA-Iris-Interval and IITD, but was 0.26 dB lower than the optimal method on ND-IRIS-0405; SSIM improved by 0.007, 0.001, and 0.0002; EER decreased by 0.9971%, 1.8291%, and 0.5823%; and TAR increased by 6.41%, 12.14%, and 3.49.

This paper presents recognition experiments conducted using MobileViT [14] on three datasets. As shown in Fig. 7, (a) the ROC curves of various methods under occlusion rates ranging from 10% to 40% indicate that HLFG achieves the highest recognition accuracy. (b) The ROC curves under occlusion rates of 40% to 60% further demonstrate HLFG's strong capability in identity feature recovery. Given the challenges associated with texture reconstruction under large-area occlusions, alternative methods tend to

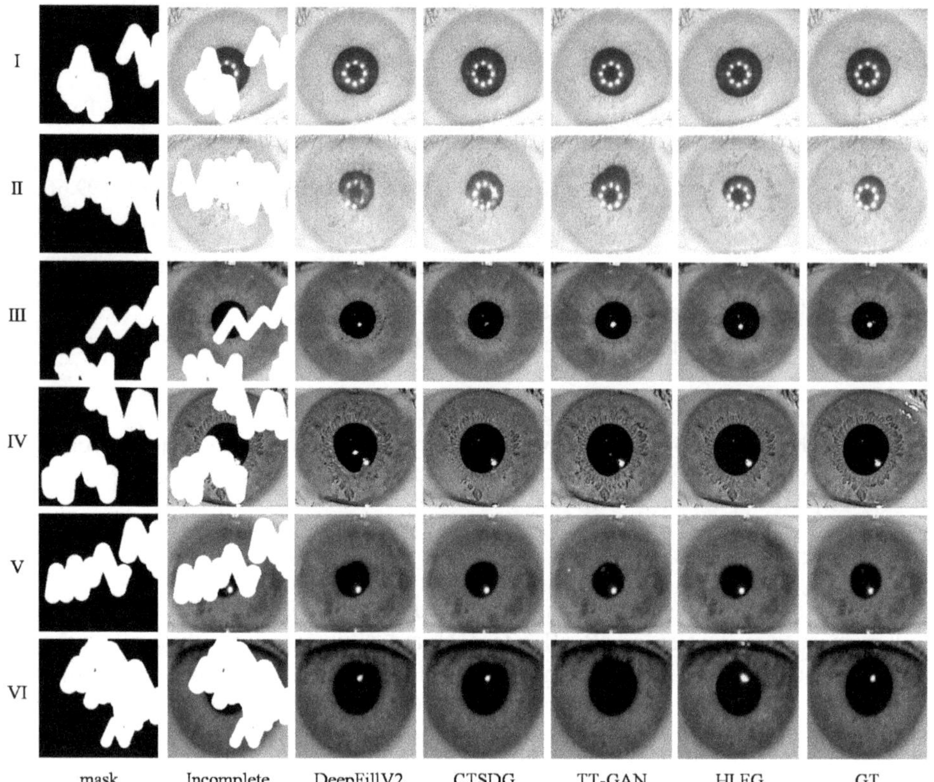

Fig. 6. Inpainting results of different methods on CASIA-Iris-Interval, IITD, and ND-IRIS-0405 datasets

generate artifacts in their restoration results. In fact, their true acceptance rates even fall below those of the original occluded images, indicating that restoration fails to enhance recognition performance. In contrast, HLFG effectively preserves identity information under such challenging conditions.

4.5 Ablation Experiments

To verify each module's effectiveness, ablation experiments were conducted on the ND-IRIS-0405 dataset with mask rates ranging at 10–40%, As shown in Table 4, the ablation study focuses on the effectiveness of Hierarchical Attention (HA) and Feature Fusion Up-sampling (FFU), as well as the differences between ordinary convolutions (Conv) and gated convolutions (Gconv). Data shows that Gconv significantly improves objective metrics compared to Conv. Moreover, Best outperforms HA and Base in terms of FID, PSNR, and SSIM, confirming the effectiveness of the HLFG algorithm.

Table 3. Comparison of FID, PSNR, SSIM, EER, and TAR from different methods on CASIA-Iris-Interval, IITD, and ND-IRIS-0405 datasets

Rates	Dataset	Method	Model Size(MB)	FID ↓	PSNR ↑	SSIM ↑	EER ↓	TAR ↑
10–40%	CASIA-Iris-Interval	DeepFillV2 [9]	114.56	17.9621	31.0991	0.9301	1.0820	97.32
		CTSDG [15]	220.31	12.6811	32.8925	0.9269	0.5025	98.58
		TT-GAN [8]	216.59	15.4596	31.9111	0.8965	0.5025	99.50
		HLFG	**93.81**	**6.8106**	**34.2649**	**0.9501**	**0.3350**	**99.66**
	IITD	DeepFillV2 [9]	114.56	18.8450	28.0017	0.9094	0.6278	99.11
		CTSDG [15]	220.31	15.4163	29.2774	0.9011	0.4216	99.05
		TT-GAN [8]	216.59	16.7316	27.5751	0.8560	0.4515	99.01
		HLFG	**93.81**	**9.3018**	**29.9239**	**0.9233**	**0.1854**	**99.78**
	ND-IRIS-0405	DeepFillV2 [9]	114.56	4.7556	34.1481	0.9667	1.1741	95.15
		CTSDG [15]	220.31	5.8006	35.9895	0.9703	0.9387	96.48
		TT-GAN [8]	216.59	2.4027	35.7652	0.9729	0.6597	98.20
		HLFG	**93.81**	**1.7519**	**36.2489**	**0.9754**	**0.6093**	**98.45**
40–60%	CASIA-Iris-Interval	DeepFillV2 [9]	114.56	33.3583	27.4272	0.8625	6.8884	62.34
		CTSDG [15]	220.31	34.1397	27.5714	0.8573	4.6257	71.76
		TT-GAN [8]	216.59	30.8127	28.1470	0.8327	2.3371	86.75
		HLFG	**93.81**	**19.8147**	**28.5381**	**0.8697**	**1.3400**	**93.16**
	IITD	DeepFillV2 [9]	114.56	49.7306	23.1637	0.7750	7.9336	54.70
		CTSDG [15]	220.31	37.3395	25.4067	0.8024	4.6477	71.76

(continued)

Table 3. (*continued*)

Rates	Dataset	Method	Model Size(MB)	FID ↓	PSNR ↑	SSIM ↑	EER ↓	TAR ↑
		TT-GAN [8]	216.59	27.7494	24.4944	0.7704	3.6148	75.88
		HLFG	**93.81**	**25.8858**	**25.4473**	**0.8034**	**1.7857**	**88.02**
	ND-IRIS-0405	DeepFillV2 [9]	114.56	12.4762	29.6612	0.9335	5.0443	66.87
		CTSDG [15]	220.31	18.3167	**31.0954**	0.9410	4.4139	68.41
		TT-GAN [8]	216.59	5.8123	30.5746	0.9403	2.3364	85.22
		HLFG	**93.81**	**4.6424**	30.8290	**0.9412**	**1.7541**	**88.71**

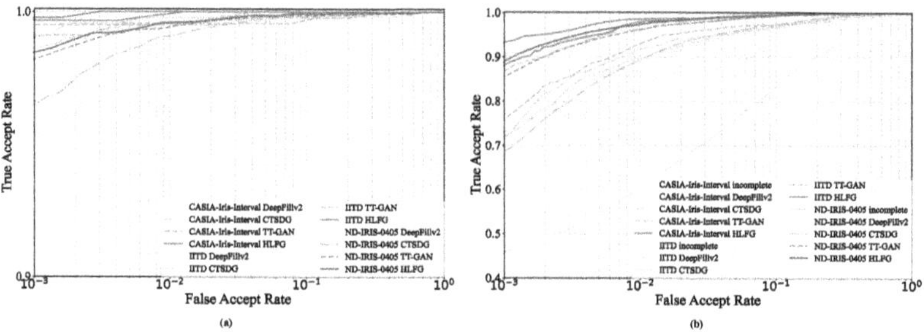

Fig. 7. ROC curves for CASIA-Iris-Interval, IITD, and ND-IRIS-0405 datasets on different methods

Table 4. Ablation experiments on the ND-IRIS-0405 dataset

Method	Cat	HA	FFU	Conv	Gconv	FID ↓	PSNR ↑	SSIM ↑
Base	✗	✗	✗	✗	✔	2.3024	34.7697	0.9703
HA	✔	✔	✗	✗	✔	2.0326	35.6028	0.9745
Conv	✔	✔	✔	✔	✗	4.2237	30.6905	0.9595
Best	✔	✔	✔	✗	✔	**1.7519**	**36.2489**	**0.9754**

5 Conclusion and Future Work

This paper proposes a high-low feature fusion-based generative adversarial network (HLFG) for repairing irregularly masked iris images. It incorporates gated convolutional feature learning, fuses high- and low-level features through hierarchical attention and skip connections, and achieves accurate restoration of complex iris textures and fine structures. HLFG performs well in inpainting random occlusions and mitigating eyelash interference, but still relies on pre-generated masks, which increases computational overhead. Future work will explore autonomous masked region learning and the integration of identity information to guide inpainting, enabling joint optimization of image reconstruction quality and downstream recognition performance, thereby enhancing the efficiency and practicality of restoration models.

Acknowledgements. This work was supported by the Natural Science Foundation of Jiangxi Province (Grant No. 20242BAB26015 and Grant No. 20232BAB206129).

References

1. Yu, J., Lin, Z., Yang, J., et al.: Generative image inpainting with contextual attention. In: Proceedings of the IEEE Conference on Computer Vision and Pattern Recognition (CVPR), pp. 5505–5514 (2018)
2. Xu, R., Guo, M., Wang, J., et al.: Texture memory-augmented deep patch-based image inpainting. IEEE Trans. Image Process. **30**, 9112–9124 (2021)
3. Cheng, B., Li, J., Shi, J., et al.: Weafu: Weather-informed image blind restoration via multi-weather distribution diffusion. IEEE Trans. Circuits Syst. Video Technol. **34**, 13530–13542 (2024)
4. Lugmayr, A., Danelljan, M., Romero, A., et al.: Repaint: inpainting using denoising diffusion probabilistic models. In: Proceedings of the IEEE/CVF Conference on Computer Vision and Pattern Recognition (CVPR), pp. 11461–11471 (2022)
5. Corneanu, C., Gadde, R., Martinez, A.M.: Latentpaint: image inpainting in latent space with diffusion models. In: Proceedings of the IEEE/CVF Winter Conference on Applications of Computer Vision (WACV), pp. 4334–4343 (2024)
6. Zeng, Y., Chen, Y., Gan, H., et al.: Incomplete texture repair of iris based on generative adversarial networks. In: Proceedings of the 15th Chinese Conference on Biometric Recognition (CCBR), pp. 335–345 (2021)
7. Chen, Y., Zeng, Y., Xu, L., Guo, S., et al.: From coarse to fine: two-stage deep residual attention generative adversarial network for repair of iris textures obscured by eyelids and eyelashes. iScience **26**(7), 107169 (2023)
8. Chen, Y., Xu, L., Chen, H., et al.: Two-Stage and Two-Discriminator generative adversarial network for the inpainting of irregularly incomplete iris images. Displays **82**, 102626 (2024)
9. Yu, J., Lin, Z., Yang, J., et al.: Free-form image inpainting with gated convolution. In: Proceedings of the IEEE/CVF International Conference on Computer Vision (ICCV), pp. 4471–4480 (2019)
10. Hu, J., Shen, L., Sun, G.: Squeeze-and-excitation networks. In: Proceedings of the IEEE Conference on Computer Vision and Pattern Recognition (CVPR), pp. 7132–7141 (2018)
11. BIT. http://biometrics.idealtest.org/#/datasetDetail/4. Accessed 23 July 2025
12. IIT Delhi Iris Database. https://web.comp.polyu.edu.hk/csajaykr/IITD/Database_Iris.htm. Accessed 23 July 2025
13. Bowyer, K., Flynn, P.: The ND-IRIS-0405 iris image dataset. arXiv preprint arXiv:1606.04853 (2016)
14. Mehta, S., Rastegari, M.: Mobilevit: light-weight, general-purpose, and mobile-friendly vision transformer. arXiv preprint arXiv:2110.02178 (2021)
15. Guo, X., Yang, H., Huang, D.: Image inpainting via conditional texture and structure dual generation. In: Proceedings of the IEEE/CVF International Conference on Computer Vision (ICCV), pp. 14134–14143 (2021)

FP-Director: Direction-Guided Latent Code Refinement for Facial-Preference Alignment in Text-to-Image Diffusion

Yue Jiang[1,2], Yueming Lyu[3], Tianxiang Ma[1,2], Bo Peng[1], and Jing Dong[1(✉)]

[1] NLPR, MAIS, Institute of Automation, Chinese Academy of Sciences,
Beijing 100190, China
[2] University of Chinese Academy of Sciences, Beijing 100190, China
[3] Nanjing University, Suzhou 215163, China

Abstract. Recent text-conditioned image generation models have demonstrated an exceptional capacity to produce diverse and creative imagery with high visual quality. However, when trained on billion-scale datasets randomly collected from the Internet, where human aesthetic preferences are inadequately learned, these models often generate facial images that deviate from mainstream aesthetics, particularly across different racial groups. While some existing methods attempt to address this issue by fine-tuning models on large-scale, manually annotated facial datasets, such approaches incur substantial annotation and computational costs. To overcome these limitations, we propose a framework called FP-Director, which learns a facial-preference direction in the latent space and updates latent codes to refine the generated results. This alignment process is applied during inference and does not require fine-tuning of the original model or access to large-scale datasets. Extensive empirical evaluations demonstrate that FP-Director significantly improves both overall quality and aesthetics of generated faces.

Keywords: Text-to image diffusion model · Human preference alignment · Inference-time refinement

1 Introduction

In recent years, text-conditioned generative diffusion models [1–4] have demonstrated remarkable capabilities and shown great potential for a wide range of downstream applications [5–9]. However, as these models are trained on large-scale, unfiltered datasets [10], which often contain undesired or low-quality content [11], they may exhibit problematic generative behaviors [12,13]. In particular, when generating facial-oriented outputs, especially for different racial groups,

---

Y. Jiang—Please note that the LNCS Editorial assumes that all authors have used the western naming convention, with given names preceding surnames. This determines the structure of the names in the running heads and the author index.

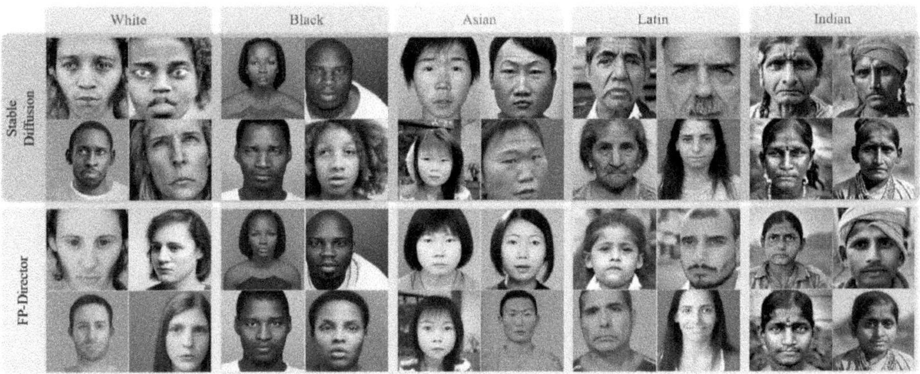

Fig. 1. Compared to the results generated by Stable Diffusion [1], FP-Director achieves notable improvements in facial appearance quality across different racial groups, generating images that are more realistic and better aligned with human aesthetic preferences.

these models often produce unnatural and unpleasant results [14]. As shown in Fig. 1, SD generates facial images for Asian individuals that frequently exhibit features like small eyes and high cheekbones, while those for Latin and Indian individuals often show excessive wrinkling. These generated results frequently display group-specific visual patterns that reinforce narrow representations and display noticeable aesthetic deviations from authentic human preferences, potentially undermining the performance of downstream face-related applications.

To improve human preference alignment in diffusion models, some approaches construct large-scale, human-labeled datasets to train reward models [15,16], and apply various reinforcement learning algorithms to fine-tune the original model [8,9,17]. However, since these reward models are trained on diverse image-text datasets, they often perform unsatisfactorily in evaluating the rationality and aesthetic appeal of generated facial images [14]. FaceScore [14] proposes a human-oriented quality evaluation metric, but it typically requires thousands of preference-labeled samples, resulting in substantial annotation overhead and increased training costs. Other methods that fine-tune diffusion models using limited data [5,7,18] can learn meaningful features from small-scale examples, but they are highly prone to overfitting to specific visual characteristics.

To address this problem while avoiding the need to construct large-scale datasets or exhaustively fine-tune the original model, we propose an effective method named FP-Director to refine the preference of latent diffusion models. Our main objective is to obtain a preference prior in the latent space and leverage it to adjust latent codes for preference-aligned image generation. To this end, we first learn to distinguish between low-quality model-generated images and preferred facial images within the latent space. We then optimize and obtain the latent prior using a contrastive learning approach, which requires only a few hundred training images and significantly reduces the overall data requirement.

Subsequently, the obtained latent prior is applied during inference to guide the latent code update toward a preference-aligned direction. With our approach, the generated facial outputs are substantially refined and display improved quality. As shown in Fig. 1, the facial appearances of individuals across different racial groups are notably enhanced.

To summarize, our contributions are as follows:

- We analyze the facial outputs of latent diffusion models across different racial groups, highlighting the prevalence of unnatural and unpleasant facial images that diverge from authentic human aesthetic preferences.
- We introduce an effective framework called FP-Director to refine the facial preference embedded in the original model. Our approach focuses on learning a preference prior in the latent space and updating the latent code to produce improved facial outputs. Notably, our method requires significantly less training data and does not modify the original model.
- Extensive qualitative and quantitative experiments demonstrate that our method effectively refines facial preference. The results generated by FP-Director exhibit high plausibility and enhanced quality in terms of facial aesthetics.

2 Related Work

2.1 LDMs Alignment and Fine-Tuning

Recently, text-to-image diffusion models have achieved more impressive and high-quality results, with higher super-resolution and a more stable training process [1]. Aligning the latent diffusion models(LDMs) with human preferences can further improve model performance not only in terms of text-to-image alignment but also in aesthetics, distortion control, and the avoidance of inappropriate content. Recent works [15,16] introduce large-scale human preference datasets and train reward models based on them. Leveraging these datasets and reward models, latent diffusion models can be fine-tuned using reinforcement learning approaches to better align with human preferences [8,9,17]. However, these datasets are not specifically tailored for facial image generation and therefore offer limited effectiveness in evaluating facial outputs [14]. FaceScore [14] addresses this limitation by introducing thousands of high-quality facial images and proposing a dedicated metric for facial aesthetic evaluation. Nevertheless, it still depends on large-scale datasets for fine-tuning, which limits its practicality in scenarios with high computational costs or constrained resources. Other fine-tuning-based methods focus on learning specific concepts or styles from a small number of samples [5–7,18]. DreamBooth [5] is a representative example, designed to learn a new concept from just a few images by fine-tuning the entire model to generate a sequence of high-fidelity, concept-specific outputs. Textual Inversion [18] encodes new concepts into a single word embedding without modifying the main components of the diffusion model. However, these

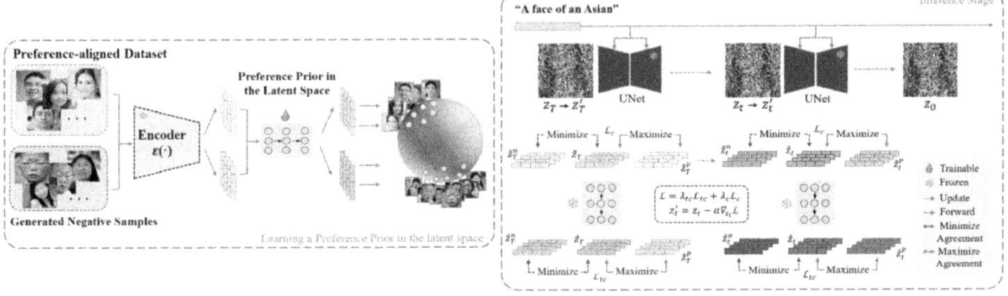

Fig. 2. Overview of FP-Director. Given a preference-aligned dataset and generated negative samples, we establish a preference prior in the latent space and employ it to guide the refinement of the latent code, cooperating with direct preference guidance.

text-conditioned models are prone to overfitting, especially when trained on limited data, often leading to repetitive facial features such as fixed expressions or unnatural attributes (Fig. 2).

3 Method

3.1 FP-Director

In this section, we introduce the proposed **FP-Director**, which aims to refine generated results without fine-tuning the original model. The key idea is to obtain a preference prior in the latent space and iteratively update the latent code to produce preference-aligned outputs. This entire process is conducted during the inference stage, eliminating the need for any modification to the original model.

To acquire the latent preference, we first construct a preference prior in the latent space that captures the most distinguishable representations between preferred samples and undesired results generated by the original model. This latent prior is then employed during inference to guide the refinement of the latent code toward the preference direction. To further enhance this process, we introduce a direct preference guidance mechanism that coherently refines the latent code. These two components work in tandem to steer the latent code toward representations that closely align with human preferences.

Learning a Preference Prior in the Latent Space. To refine undesired results during inference, we identify the most distinctive representations of preferred and undesired images in the latent space and use them to construct a preference prior.

For a set of preferred images I_p, which are considered to be "positive", and model-generated undesired images I_n are regarded as "negative". The two types of images are sent to the image encoder $\mathcal{E}$ of SD for latent representation $z_0^p = \mathcal{E}(I_p)$ and $z_0^n = \mathcal{E}(I_n)$ to guarantee spatial consistency in the latent space. Our goal is to conduct a preference prior F for z_0^p and z_0^n. In order to enhance the extraction of discerning features and facilitate the computation of contrastive similarity, the latent representations $z \in R^{B \times C \times H \times W}$ of four dimensions is first flattened to $R^{B \times (C \times H \times W)}$ of two dimensions [19]. Additionally, as feature normalization is crucial for feature combination and classification [20], the flattened representations are then normed to a unit vector $\tilde{z}$ as follows:

$$\tilde{z}_0^{\{p,n\}} = Norm(flatten(\mathcal{E}(I_{\{p,n\}}))), \tag{1}$$

The latent prior is conducted by adding a projector to the image encoder $\mathcal{E}$ as $F(\tilde{z})$, which only consists of a single fully connected layer. New unit vectors $\hat{z}_p$, $\hat{z}_n$ is obtained as $\hat{z}_p = F(\tilde{z}_0^p), \hat{z}_n = F(\tilde{z}_0^p)$. The projector is trained by maximizing the agreement between positive pairs and minimizing the agreement between negative pairs [19] as follows:

$$\mathcal{L}_F = -log\frac{\hat{s}_p^{i,j}}{\hat{s}_p^{i,j} + \sum_m \hat{s}_n^{i,m}} \tag{2}$$

where $\hat{s}_p^{i,j} = exp(sim(\hat{z}_p^i, \hat{z}_p^j)/\tau)$, and $\hat{s}_n^{i,m} = exp(sim(\hat{z}_p^i, \hat{z}_n^m)/\tau)$. τ is a temperature parameter and $sim(\cdot, \cdot)$ is the similarity function, which is the dot product in this work.

The trained projector serves as a preference prior to guide the refinement of the latent code toward better alignment with authentic human aesthetic preferences. Notably, the projector requires only a few hundred images for training, rather than thousands, thus significantly reducing computational overhead.

Obtaining a Direct Preference Guidance. To further guide the refinement of the latent code, we employ a direct contrastive constraint during the inference stage. For a latent code z_i, we randomly select a positive sample I_p and a negative sample I_n and obtain their latent representation $z_0^p = \mathcal{E}(I_p)$, $z_0^n = \mathcal{E}(I_n)$. The noisy version z_t^p, z_t^n of z_0^p, z_0^n at timestep t can be directly sampled as follows:

$$z_t^{\{p,n\}} = \sqrt{\alpha_t} \cdot z_0^{\{p,n\}} + \sqrt{1 - \alpha_t} \cdot z_0^{\{p,n\}} \epsilon, \tag{3}$$

where α_t is a fixed scale factor, and ϵ is a Gaussian noise. After being flattened and normalized, the similarity between $\tilde{z}_t$ and $\tilde{z}_t^p$ in a unit hypersphere is obtained by a traditional contrastive loss as follows:

$$\mathcal{L}_c = -log\frac{\tilde{s}_p^{t,p}}{\tilde{s}_p^{t,p} + \tilde{s}_n^{t,n}}, \tag{4}$$

where $\tilde{s}_p^{t,p} = exp(sim(\tilde{z}_t, \tilde{z}_t^p)/\tau')$ and $\tilde{s}_n^{t,n} = exp(sim(\tilde{z}_t, \tilde{z}_t^n)/\tau')$. τ' is a different temperature parameter to τ in Eq. 2.

The purpose of both losses is to instruct the refinement of the latent code towards the direction of similarity with positive samples in the latent space.

In the inference stage, the pretrained prior F is utilized to obtain prior constraint as follows:

$$\mathcal{L}_{tc} = -log\frac{\hat{s}_p^{t,p}}{\hat{s}_p^{t,p} + \hat{s}_n^{t,n}}, \tag{5}$$

where $\hat{s}_p^{t,p}$ is calculated similar to $\tilde{s}_p^{t,p}$ in Eq. 4, but with the use of projected variables $\hat{z}_t = F(\tilde{z}^t)$, $\hat{z}_t^p = F(\tilde{z}_t^p)$. $\hat{s}_n^{t,n}$ is calculate in like manner. The overall objective consists of the above two losses:

$$\mathcal{L} = \lambda_{tc}\mathcal{L}_{tc} + \lambda_c\mathcal{L}_c. \tag{6}$$

Finally, the latent code is updated as follows during the inference stage:

$$z_t' = \epsilon_\theta(z_t, \mathcal{P}, t) - \eta\nabla_{z_t}\mathcal{L}, \tag{7}$$

where $\mathcal{P}$ is the conditional textual prompt, t is the denoising timestep, and η is the optimzation step size.

4   Experiments

4.1   Experimental Setups

Datasets. We filter and re-annotate the facial images in LAION-5B [10], considering racial groups of White, Black, Asian, Latin, and Indian. The conditioned textual prompts include "a face of a Race person". We utilize a pre-trained face detection model libface[1] to identify and extract facial images from LAION-5B, which are subsequently labeled by CLIP [21] roughly. Following the initial labeling, each image undergoes verification by human workers for more precise annotation and preference selection. Images in the preference-aligned dataset are utilized in our approach as positive samples.

Implementation Details. The projector $F(\cdot)$ is trained for 4 epochs using a batch size of 4 and a temperature parameter $\tau = 0.1$, with 100 positive and 100 negative samples. During inference, we empirically set the hyperparameters to $\lambda_{tc} = 9$ and $\lambda_c = 150$. The latent code is updated over timesteps ranging from $t_i = 30$ to $t_k = 26$ (out of 30 total timesteps), using an optimization step size $\eta = 2$. All experiments are conducted on a single Tesla V100 GPU.

Evaluation Metrics. Traditional preference-based metrics [15,16] often fail to effectively assess the rationality and aesthetic appeal of generated facial images [14]. Therefore, we adopt a combination of a user study and the Face++ API[2] for aesthetic evaluation. Our evaluation framework encompasses the following two aspects: (i) User Study: Participants were tasked with selecting images that appeared the least distorted or unpleasant, aligning with authentic human aesthetic preferences, and avoiding images with racial prejudice, discrimination,

---

[1] https://github.com/ShiqiYu/libfacedetection.
[2] https://www.faceplusplus.com.

Fig. 3. Qualitative comparison of generated results for different racial groups. For each racial group, we exhibit three images generated by comparing methods, where the generation seed is the same.

Table 1. User study. The results show the average preference across five racial groups for different methods. The best results are in **bold**.

Method	Stable Diffusion	Textual Inversion	DreamBooth	Attend-and-Excite	FP-Director
Preference ($\uparrow$)	10.88%	8.32 %	13.28%	6.24%	**61.28%**

or vilification. (ii) Facial Aesthetics: This includes assessments of the skin condition by Face++ API, aiming to evaluate whether specific racial groups are portrayed in a degraded or unhealthy manner, with attention to potential racial stigmatization and vilification.

4.2   Qualitative Analysis

Since human-preference alignment methods typically require large-scale datasets [15,16], we conduct evaluations using latent diffusion models that are either fine-tuned on smaller datasets or used without fine-tuning. These models include Stable Diffusion [1] and its derivatives: Textual Inversion [18], DreamBooth [5], and Attend-and-Excite [22]. For consistency, both Textual Inversion and Dream-Booth are fine-tuned on our preference-aligned dataset. Attend-and-Excite modifies the latent code during inference and does not require fine-tuning.

Generated results for different racial groups are shown in Fig. 3. As observed, Stable Diffusion tends to depict individuals from the Asian group with disproportionately small eyes, single eyelids, and excessively high cheekbones. These features not only lack aesthetic appeal but also raise concerns about potential racial stereotyping and discrimination. For the Latin and Indian groups, Stable Diffusion often produces faces with more pronounced wrinkles, sagging skin, and discoloration, indicating a deviation from human subjective preferences. For the Black group, the generated results tend to be distorted and less visually appealing. For the White group, Stable Diffusion frequently generates mismatched racial features. Textual Inversion and DreamBooth, which fine-tune the base model, produce images that differ from those generated by Stable Dif-

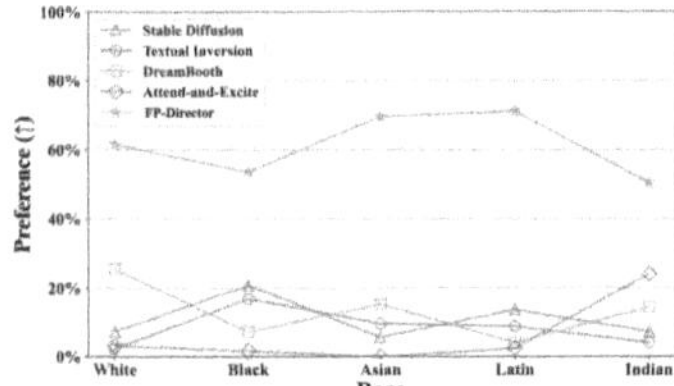

| Metric | Skin Health (↑) | | | | | Skin Defects (↓) | | | | | Time(s) |
Race	White	Black	Asian	Latin	Indian	White	Black	Asian	Latin	Indian	(↓)
Stable Diffusion	18.223	13.598	32.214	12.050	5.253	20.310	20.249	12.426	27.396	52.975	6.277
Textual Inversion	20.086	6.439	27.186	28.412	**15.055**	22.896	35.708	11.037	17.649	**27.791**	9.190
DreamBooth	14.924	17.462	25.726	8.295	7.681	21.903	13.487	15.033	28.160	44.208	29.618
Attend-and-Excite	16.315	20.739	29.554	11.807	8.406	27.475	24.673	17.770	39.332	50.445	15.700
FP-Director	**49.805**	**33.639**	**53.852**	**34.372**	11.534	**7.290**	**7.406**	**6.808**	**10.271**	38.816	**7.964**

Fig. 4. User preference results across racial groups.

Fig. 5. Facial Aesthetics evaluation and inference time comparison between FP-Director and others.

fusion. However, their outputs still suffer from noticeable distortions, blurriness, and unnatural facial expressions. These limitations are likely due to the models' design, which targets style or concept learning from a few samples. Attend-and-Excite tends to display stylistic features rather than authentic ones. The generated authentic results are similar to those in Stable Diffusion, inheriting the same less-preferred visual characteristics. In contrast, FP-Director demonstrates significant improvements in both aesthetic quality and realism. The generated faces appear more visually pleasing, natural, and aligned with human preferences.

4.3   Quantitative Analysis

User Study. We conducted a survey with 25 participants to assess the preferences for generated images of each method. A total of 625 votes were collected from the participants, representing assessments across five racial groups. The preferences across five racial groups for each method are illustrated in Fig. 4, and the average preferences of different racial groups are presented in Table 1. In both cases, our method outperforms the others, demonstrating superior performance in generating natural and aesthetically pleasing facial images, as confirmed by human evaluations.

Facial Aesthetics. In Table 5, we present measurements of facial aesthetic. Compared to other methods, FP-Director achieves the best performance in most cases across all the racial groups. Textual Inversion and DreamBooth exhibit inconsistent improvements in face aesthetics, as their disrupted results may introduce additional defects, attenuating the overall performance. Attend-and-Excite is hard to yield authentic images, and their skin status scores are also suboptimal. FP-Director achieves the best facial aesthetics performance in terms of different skin statuses. It is worth noting that the generated results for the Indian group sometimes include cultural or religious ornaments, such as facial paint and feathers, which may influence the skin status scores for this group (Fig. 5).

Inference Efficiency. quad We also evaluated the inference time of different methods in Table 5. FP-Director exhibits superior efficiency. Additionally, there

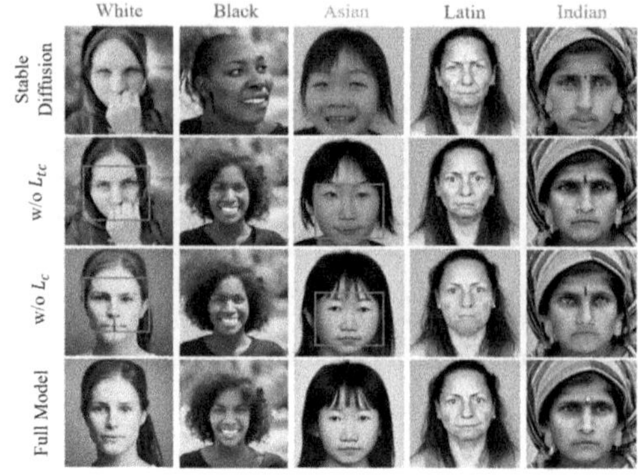

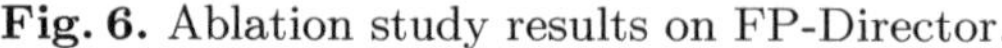

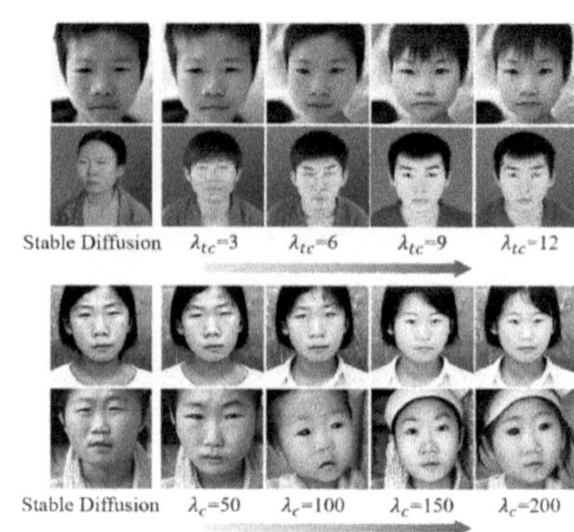

Fig. 6. Ablation study results on FP-Director.

Fig. 7. Visual comparisons of FP-Director and its variants.

is only a marginal increase in the inference time compared to the baseline SD model. This is because we only update the latent code during a limited number of timesteps. In contrast, other models necessitate more intricate computational processes and a greater number of inference timesteps, resulting in lower efficiency during inference.

4.4   Ablation Study

We show the ablation study of different latent constraints in Fig. 6. The preference prior in the latent space $\mathcal{L}_{tc}$ effectively guides the refinement in the overall structure of the original image, while the direct preference guidance $\mathcal{L}_c$ refines facial features to enhanced aesthetic appeal while likely to maintain the structure of the original image. However, the full model demonstrates the best performance on facial appearance. To further understand how these constraints affect the refinement process of the latent code, we separately conduct experiments for different configurations of each loss in Fig. 7. As the hyper-parameters increase, the refinement induced by the corresponding constraints on the final result becomes more pronounced and satisfying. However, when the increase exceeds a certain limit, the effectiveness begins to diminish.

5   Conclusion

In this paper, we introduce a simple yet effective framework, FP-Director, for refining facial preferences in latent diffusion models. By learning a preference prior and applying contrastive guidance with both preferred and undesired samples, our method improves facial aesthetics without fine-tuning and requires less training data. A limitation is that the method may introduce systematic preference shifts originating from the selected preference data and negative examples, leading the aligned aesthetics to reflect subjective specific values.

Acknowledgments. This work is supported by the National Natural Science Foundation of China (NSFC) under Grant 62272460, Jiangsu Provincial Science and Technology Major Project under Grant BG2024042, Natural Science Foundation of Jiangsu Province under Grant SBK20250401282 and National Natural Science Foundation of China under Grants 62502200.

References

1. Rombach, R., Blattmann, A., Lorenz, D., Esser, P., Ommer, B.: High-resolution image synthesis with latent diffusion models. In: CVPR (2022)
2. Ramesh, A., Dhariwal, P., Nichol, A., Chu, C., Chen, M.: Hierarchical text-conditional image generation with clip latents. arXiv preprint arXiv:2204.06125 (2022)
3. Hu, E.J., et al.: Lora: low-rank adaptation of large language models. arXiv preprint arXiv:2106.09685 (2021)
4. Kawar, B., et al.: Imagic: text-based real image editing with diffusion models. In: CVPR, pp. 6007–6017 (2023)
5. Ruiz, N., Li, Y., Jampani, V., Pritch, Y., Rubinstein, M., Aberman, K.: Dreambooth: fine tuning text-to-image diffusion models for subject-driven generation. In: CVPR, pp. 22500–22510 (2023)
6. Ruiz, N., et al.: Hyperdreambooth: hypernetworks for fast personalization of text-to-image models. arXiv preprint arXiv:2307.06949 (2023)
7. Kumari, N., Zhang, B., Zhang, R., Shechtman, E., Zhu, J.Y.: Multi-concept customization of text-to-image diffusion. In: CVPR (2023)
8. Black, K., Janner, M., Du, Y., Kostrikov, I., Levine, S.: Training diffusion models with reinforcement learning. arXiv preprint arXiv:2305.13301 (2023)
9. Fan, Y., et al.: Dpok: reinforcement learning for fine-tuning text-to-image diffusion models. Adv. Neural. Inf. Process. Syst. **36**, 79858–79885 (2023)
10. Schuhmann, C., et al.: Laion-5b: an open large-scale dataset for training next generation image-text models. Adv. Neural Inf. Process. Syst. (2022)
11. Birhane, A., Prabhu, V.U., Kahembwe, E.: Multimodal datasets: misogyny, pornography, and malignant stereotypes. arXiv preprint arXiv:2110.01963 (2021)
12. Schramowski, P., Brack, M., Deiseroth, B., Kersting, K.: Safe latent diffusion: mitigating inappropriate degeneration in diffusion models. In: CVPR (2023)
13. Howard, P., Madasu, A., Le, T., Moreno, G.L., Lal, V.: Probing intersectional biases in vision-language models with counterfactual examples. arXiv preprint arXiv:2310.02988 (2023)
14. Liao, Z., Xie, Q., Chen, C., Lu, H., Deng, Z.: Facescore: benchmarking and enhancing face quality in human generation. arXiv preprint arXiv:2406.17100 (2024)
15. Xu, J., et al.: Imagereward: learning and evaluating human preferences for text-to-image generation. Adv. Neural Inf. Process. Syst. (2023)
16. Wu, X., Sun, K., Zhu, F., Zhao, R., Li, H.: Better aligning text-to-image models with human preference. arXiv preprint arXiv:2303.14420 **1**(3) (2023)
17. Cai, M., et al.: Dspo: direct semantic preference optimization for real-world image super-resolution. arXiv preprint arXiv:2504.15176 (2025)
18. Gal, R., et al.: An image is worth one word: personalizing text-to-image generation using textual inversion. arXiv preprint arXiv:2208.01618 (2022)
19. Oord, A.V.D., Li, Y., Vinyals, O.: Representation learning with contrastive predictive coding. arXiv preprint arXiv:1807.03748 (2018)

20. Wang, T., Isola, P.: Understanding contrastive representation learning through alignment and uniformity on the hypersphere. In: International Conference on Machine Learning, pp. 9929–9939. PMLR (2020)
21. Radford, A., et al.: Learning transferable visual models from natural language supervision. In: International Conference on Machine Learning. (2021)
22. Chefer, H., Alaluf, Y., Vinker, Y., Wolf, L., Cohen-Or, D.: Attend-and-excite: attention-based semantic guidance for text-to-image diffusion models. ACM Trans. Graph. (TOG) **42**(4), 1–10 (2023)

Hand Motion Retargeting Based on Graph Attention Residual Perception

Zhiyuan Wang[✉], Xiao Hu, and Wei Jia

School of Computer Science and Information Engineering,
Hefei University of Technology, Hefei 230601, China
2023110506@mail.hfut.edu.cn

Abstract. Motion retargeting refers to the efficient transfer of motion across models with different proportions by decoupling motion data from specific character topologies. However, existing research mainly focuses on retargeting torso movements of the human body, with insufficient attention given to hand motion. Our work focuses on hand motion retargeting and proposes a novel retargeting algorithm based on graph attention residual perception. To enhance the model's generalization capability, we conduct cross-domain training using both the Mixamo animation dataset and the InterHand2.6M real-world hand dataset. Our method employs an extended hand model and innovatively incorporates a Graph Attention Network (GAT), which effectively captures the biomechanical priors between finger joints while preserving fine-grained motion details at the frame level. Quantitative and qualitative experiments on public datasets demonstrate that our model achieves superior performance in the task of hand motion retargeting.

Keywords: Hand Motion Retargeting · Graph Attention Network · Computer Animation

1 Introduction

Motion retargeting is the process of mapping motion from a source character to a target character without sacrificing motion plausibility. It is a longstanding problem in the fields of computer vision and computer graphics. With wide applications in the game and animation industries, motion retargeting also serves as a foundational technology for digital avatars and the metaverse.

However, existing mature solutions for motion retargeting typically overlook hand motion, which introduces several significant challenges [1–4]. Firstly, compared to torso joints, hand motion exhibits significantly higher complexity. In addition, the limitations of existing datasets present further challenges, as commonly used large-scale datasets often lack the paired data necessary for precise motion retargeting tasks. Moreover, mesh penetration frequently occurs in interactive scenarios, further complicating practical applications [5].

W. Jia et al. (Eds.): CCBR 2025, LNCS 16360, pp. 237–246, 2026.
https://doi.org/10.1007/978-981-95-6123-0_23

Hand motion retargeting inherits the inherent challenges of traditional retargeting tasks while also introducing additional complexity due to the fine-grained structure and articulation of the human hand. In response to the current lack of effective hand motion retargeting solutions, this work proposes a Graph Attention Residual Perception Network for hand motion retargeting. We conduct cross-domain training on both the Mixamo and InterHand2.6M hand motion datasets, significantly enhancing the model's generalization capability. The proposed method achieves superior retargeting performance and demonstrates robust cross-dataset applicability. The main contributions of this paper are as follows:

- We propose a graph attention-based residual perception framework for hand motion retargeting, enabling semantically meaningful transfer of hand motion across skeletal models of varying scales in cross-domain scenarios.
- We design a novel hand topology structure, leveraging Graph Attention Networks to explicitly model semantic relationships between fingers and the palm.
- Compared to current state-of-the-art open-source retargeting methods, our approach achieves improved performance across multiple evaluation metrics.

2   Related Work

2.1   Motion Retargeting Based on Traditional Methods

Early motion retargeting techniques relied on classical approaches such as motion editing and spatiotemporal constraint solving [6,7]. Lee and Shin [8] later decomposed the spatiotemporal constraints into intra-frame and inter-frame components, reducing complexity. Popović and Witkin [9] proposed a dynamic method introducing physical constraints for natural, controllable motion transfer.

In 2000, Choi and Ko [10] developed an online approach enabling real-time retargeting via feedback, while Borno [11] designed a nonlinear feedback control strategy allowing accurate trajectory tracking without relying on inverse kinematics.

2.2   Motion Retargeting Based on Deep Learning

Villegas et al. [1] proposed Neural Kinematic Networks (NKN), one of the earliest unsupervised deep learning frameworks for motion retargeting. Given an initial pose and a sequence of joint rotations, NKN infers the spatial coordinates of each end-effector through forward kinematics. Aberman et al. [2] introduced Skeleton-Aware Networks (SAN) for unpaired cross-domain translation, enabling retargeting between heterogeneous but homeomorphic skeletons. Later works [3,4] employed Transformer-based architectures to extract motion features invariant to skeletal topology, achieving heterogeneous model motion retargeting via denoising, joint sampling, or pose-aware latent feature sharing.

Recent studies have begun to focus on hand-specific motion generation. Inter-HandGen [12] proposes a cascaded diffusion framework for two-hand interaction synthesis, while PromptFDDM [13] introduces a prompt-driven approach for future hand motion prediction. While these works highlight growing interest in hand motion modeling, they do not directly address hand motion retargeting with parametric models such as MANO under weak supervision.

Most existing motion retargeting methods focus on full-body motion and rely on task-specific assumptions or skeletal topologies. Even recent hand-specific motion generation methods target hand motion synthesis rather than retargeting using parametric models like MANO. Consequently, dedicated baselines for fine-grained hand motion retargeting remain lacking. Motivated by this gap, we propose a Graph Attention Residual Perception framework tailored for hand motion retargeting, which preserves single-frame motion details while leveraging biomechanical priors among finger joints.

3   Method

The proposed Graph Attention Residual Perception framework for hand motion retargeting is illustrated in Fig. 1. The initial hand motion sequence Q_A of the source character A and the static skeleton information γ_A, γ_B of the target character B's hand model serve as inputs to the entire module. First, the Kinematics-based Hand Descriptor Generator adjusts Q_A to produce a feature matrix D_A that incorporates inter-finger and palm-finger features. Subsequently, D_A and γ_B are fed into the Skeletal-Aware Residual Module ΔF_s to perform the first stage of hand motion retargeting. Within ΔF_s, the Static Skeleton Encoder ΔF_e is utilized to fully integrate the target model's static hand skeleton information, yielding a preliminary retargeting result Q'_B. Thereafter, a second-stage retargeting is performed using a Graph Attention Network incorporating biomechanical priors, which refines Q'_B into the final retargeting result Q_B.

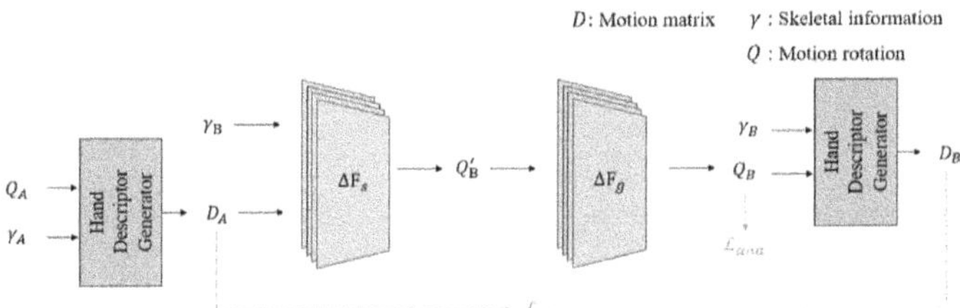

Fig. 1. Overview and schematic diagram of the proposed graph-attention residual perception framework.

3.1   Kinematics-Based Hand Descriptor Generator

Common hand models consist of five fingers and a wrist joint, with each finger comprising three joints and one virtual fingertip joint. Inspired by the work of

Yang et al. [5], we extend the standard hand model by interpolating 10 virtual palm joints along the connection lines between the wrist and the base joints of each finger. These additional joints serve to convey the semantic structure of the palm, thereby constructing an extended palm model.

Assuming that at time step t, the global coordinate of the k-th finger joint is denoted as $\mathbf{X}_k \in \mathbb{R}^3$, and $\mathbf{M}_k$ represents the Euler rotation matrix of joint k in the global coordinate system. The inter-joint (finger-to-finger) feature between joint k and joint m in the local coordinate system is defined as $\delta_{k,m} = \mathbf{M}_k (\mathbf{X}_m - \mathbf{X}_k)$, and the palm-to-finger feature between joint k and the n-th palm joint is defined as $\delta_{k,p_n} = \mathbf{M}_k (\mathbf{X}_{p_n} - \mathbf{X}_k)$, where $\mathbf{X}_{p_n}$ denotes the global coordinate of the n-th palm joint. We construct the feature matrix of joint k as:

$$\mathbf{D}_k = [\delta_{k,1}, \delta_{k,2}, \ldots, \delta_{k,19}, \delta_{k,p_1}, \delta_{k,p_2}, \ldots, \delta_{k,p_{10}}] \in \mathbb{R}^{29 \times 3}. \tag{1}$$

The feature tensor $\mathbf{D}_A$ is composed of the fingerfinger and fingerpalm features of all 20 finger joints:

$$\mathbf{D}_A = [\mathbf{D}_1, \mathbf{D}_2, \ldots, \mathbf{D}_{20}] \in \mathbb{R}^{20 \times 29 \times 3}. \tag{2}$$

3.2 Skeletal-Aware Residual Module

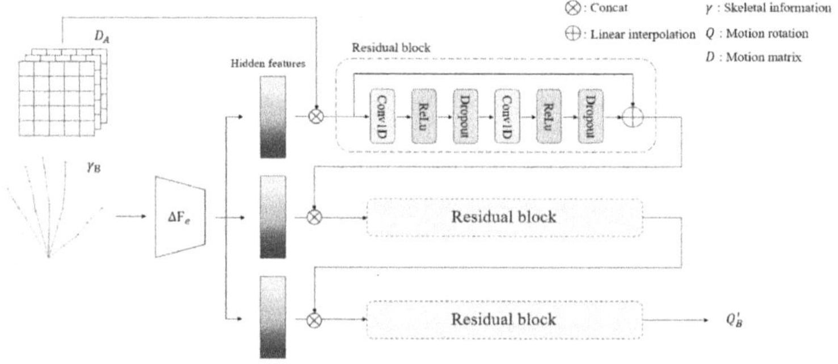

Fig. 2. The detailed architecture of the proposed Skeletal-Aware Residual Module.

As previous end-to-end motion retargeting methods often underperform without supervision from the target model's static information [14], we introduce a static feature supervision mechanism, as shown in Fig. 2.

The static encoding module ΔF_e encodes the static hand skeleton information γ_B of the target character B by combining convolutional layers with multi-head self-attention layers. The convolutional layers extract local features from the static skeleton representation, which are then fed into the multi-head self-attention module to further capture global dependencies. This process produces the static hand feature $\Delta F_e(\gamma_B)$, as illustrated in Fig. 3. ΔF_e effectively

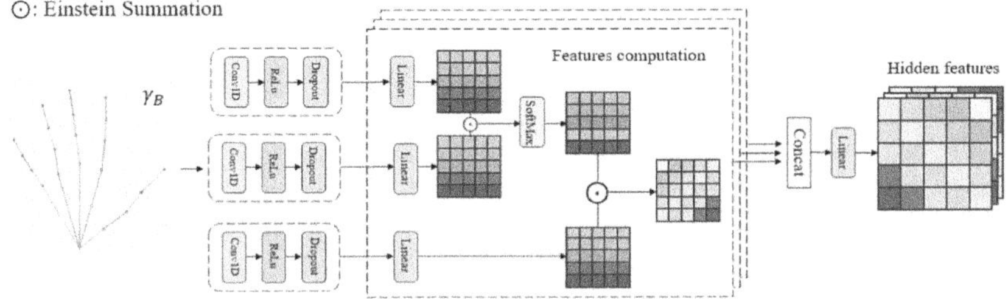

Fig. 3. Detailed structure of the Static Skeleton Encoder.

extracts deep static features of the target model and provides crucial skeletal-aware supervision for the residual network training. Finally, the source character A's hand feature matrix D_A is concatenated with $\Delta F_e(\gamma_B)$ and fed into the residual network for inference. The output of each residual block is concatenated again with $\Delta F_e(\gamma_B)$ and passed as input to the next residual block. This design ensures that the target skeleton features are preserved throughout the deep network, thereby enhancing the adaptability of the final output. The preliminary retargeting result Q'_B is thus obtained.

3.3   Graph Attention Network

Graph Attention Networks are specialized neural architectures designed to process graph-structured data, leveraging attention mechanisms to learn edge weights between adjacent nodes and thereby capture the overall semantic information within the graph. The proposed graph attention module ΔF_g consists of three layers of graph attention convolution. The design of the graph structure fully leverages the anatomical priors of the human hand, incorporating four types of inter-joint relationships.

- **Finger-chain connectivity:** This connects the four joints along each finger sequentially, simulating the biomechanical chain structure and motion propagation inherent to finger articulation.
- **Palm-to-finger linkage:** Each palm joint, located at the intersection between the wrist and the base of a finger, is connected to the four joints of the corresponding finger, capturing the control dependencies between the palm and fingers.
- **Intra-palm connectivity:** The ten palm joints are interconnected in both horizontal and vertical directions, forming a mesh-like structure that reflects the anatomical continuity across the palm.
- **Cross-finger tendon constraints:** Inspired by biomechanical tendon constraints, specific connections are established between joints across different fingers to simulate the coordinated movement induced by inter-finger tendons.

3.4 Losses

We design three loss functions as conditional constraints tailored for the hand motion retargeting task.

To ensure semantic consistency between the retargeted and source motion sequences, we define a semantic similarity loss based on the processed hand motion sequence feature matrices. Specifically, the similarity loss L_{sem} between D_A and D_B is formulated as a weighted cosine similarity between the two matrices, as shown in Eq. (3).

$$L_{\text{sem}} = \frac{1}{T} \sum_{t=1}^{T} \sum_{j=1}^{20} \sum_{k=1}^{29} \omega_{jk} \cdot \frac{D_A^{j,t,k} \cdot D_B^{j,t,k}}{\|D_A^{j,t,k}\|_2 \cdot \|D_B^{j,t,k}\|_2} \tag{3}$$

$$\omega_{jk} = \begin{cases} 1 + \dfrac{\exp\left(-\|D_A^{j,t,k}\|_2\right)}{\sum\limits_{m=1}^{20} \exp\left(-\|D_A^{j,t,m}\|_2\right)}, & \text{if } k \in \{1, 2, \ldots, 20\} \\[2ex] 1, & \text{if } k \in \{21, 22, \ldots, 29\}. \end{cases} \tag{4}$$

In addition, based on biomechanical and anatomical principles of the human hand, joint movements are modeled within the Euler rotation coordinate system. Anatomical constraints L_{ana} are applied between finger joints, as defined in Eq. (5), where ϕ_{roll}, ϕ_{yaw}, and ϕ_{pitch} represent the rotation angles around the three axes in the Euler coordinate system, respectively.

$$\begin{aligned} L_{\text{ana}} = \frac{1}{T} \sum_{t=1}^{T} \sum_{j \in \text{all}} &\left(\left|\phi_{\text{roll}}^{t,j}\right|^2 + \sum_{j \notin \text{knuckle}} \left|\phi_{\text{yaw}}^{t,j}\right|^2 \right. \\ &+ \sum_{j \in \text{knuckle}} \max\left(\left|\phi_{\text{yaw}}^{t,j}\right| - \frac{\pi}{18}, 0 \right)^2 \\ &\left. + \sum_{j \in \text{all}} \max\left(\phi_{\text{pitch}}^{t,j} - \frac{\pi}{2}, 0 \right)^2 + \sum_{j \in \text{all}} \min\left(\phi_{\text{pitch}}^{t,j}, 0 \right)^2 \right). \end{aligned} \tag{5}$$

The aforementioned loss functions are primarily applied in motion retargeting tasks between different hand models. During training, some experiments are conducted on motion retargeting between identical hand models to further enhance and validate model performance. The reconstruction loss is used in such scenarios and is defined over the motion rotations Q_A and Q_B of the source character A and the target character B, respectively, as shown in Eq. (6).

$$L_{\text{recon}} = 1_{A=B} \cdot \text{MSE}(Q_A, Q_B). \tag{6}$$

By combining the above three loss functions, the final loss is defined as shown in Equation (3.15), where λ_{recon}, λ_{sem}, and λ_{ana} denote the weighting coefficients of each respective loss term.

$$L_{\text{total}} = \lambda_{\text{recon}} L_{\text{recon}} - \lambda_{\text{sem}} L_{\text{sem}} + \lambda_{\text{ana}} L_{\text{ana}}. \tag{7}$$

4   Experiments

Datasets: We conduct experimental evaluations on the Mixamo [15] and Inter-Hand2.6M [16] datasets. The Mixamo dataset provides over 150 pre-rigged 3D humanoid character models of varying genders, body types, and artistic styles. The InterHand2.6M dataset is currently the largest and most comprehensively annotated multi-view 3D hand interaction dataset, containing over 2.6 million frames of real-world dual-hand interaction images.

Implementation Details: The Skeletal-Aware Residual Module ΔF_s and the Static Encoding Module ΔF_e are each composed of three layers, with ΔF_e containing two convolutional layers internally. We use the Adam optimizer [17] with a learning rate of 0.0001 and a batch size of 128. The hyperparameters λ_{recon}, λ_{sem}, and λ_{ana} are set to 1.0, 1.0, and 0.1, respectively. The model runs at around 10 frames per second (FPS) on an NVIDIA RTX 3070 8GB GPU, and with lightweight optimization, the speed increases to 1520 FPS, approaching real-time performance suitable for practical applications.

Evaluation Metrics: To quantitatively evaluate the performance of hand motion retargeting, two metrics are employed depending on the availability of ground-truth data. When ground-truth joint positions of the target hand model are available, the Mean Per-Joint Position Error (MPJPE) is used. For datasets without ground-truth annotations, the Mean Cosine Similarity (MCS) is adopted to measure structural consistency.

Baseline Limitations: Most existing motion retargeting methods are designed for full-body motion and rely on task-specific assumptions, making them unsuitable for MANO-based hand retargeting. We attempted to adapt models such as NKN [1], but their full-body assumptions caused convergence issues, so results are not reported to avoid misleading comparisons. Consequently, we only include SAN [2] as a baseline, since it supports cross-domain retargeting between heterogeneous skeletons and can be partially applied to hand motion. This highlights the lack of dedicated baselines and motivates our evaluation.

4.1   Quantitative Results

We compare our proposed hand motion retargeting method based on Graph Attention Residual Perception with currently available state-of-the-art open-source motion retargeting methods. Among these methods, R^2ET [9] is constrained by its reliance on the SMPL human body model, making it inapplicable to the MANO [18] hand model and thus unsuitable for direct comparison in our experiments.

As shown in Table 1, compared with SAN [2], which has demonstrated strong performance in human pose motion retargeting tasks, our method achieves a

Table 1. Comparison with the state-of-the-art methods. MCS_{palm} and MCS_{finger} denote the average cosine similarity between finger joints and palm joints, and between finger joints themselves, respectively. Ours/L_{sem}, Ours/L_{ana}, and Ours/ΔF_g refer to our method without the similarity loss, without the anatomical loss, and without the graph attention module, respectively.

	MPJPE ↓	MCS_{palm}^{Ih2Mx} ↑	MCS_{finger}^{Ih2Mx} ↑	MCS_{palm}^{Mx2Ih} ↑	MCS_{finger}^{Mx2Ih} ↑
Copy	**4.76e-12**	0.923	0.851	0.941	0.872
SAN [2]	3.134	0.866	0.820	0.034	0.475
Ours/L_{sem}	0.531	0.971	0.924	0.899	0.807
Ours/L_{ana}	1.133	0.967	0.916	0.973	0.920
Ours/ΔF_g	0.515	0.800	0.828	0.871	0.827
Ours	0.407	**0.972**	**0.925**	**0.980**	**0.930**

significant reduction of 87.01% in MPJPE. After removing the semantic similarity loss L_{sem} and the anatomical constraint loss L_{ana} separately, the MPJPE increases by 23.35% and 64.08%, respectively, compared to the full version of our method. This validates the effectiveness of both loss functions in our framework. Furthermore, in cross-domain retargeting tasks, our approach achieves the best performance in terms of the MCS metric compared with other hand motion retargeting methods, demonstrating its superior capability in preserving the spatial relationships among finger joints.

In addition, Table 1 compares the performance gap with and without the ΔF_g module. As shown in the table, the introduction of the ΔF_g graph attention module significantly improves the overall performance: MPJPE decreases by 20.97%, and MCS increases by 14.46%. These results demonstrate the positive contribution of the graph attention neural network in our proposed method.

4.2   Qualitative Results

In the qualitative comparison experiments, three challenging motion sequences were selected to evaluate cross-domain retargeting between the InterHand model and the Mixamo model. Figure 4 shows the hand motion retargeting results under different conditions. The motion sequence of the source hand model and the copy-control experiment is denoted as Q_A, while the motion sequences for the SAN baseline and our method are the retargeted Q_B.

Based on the model performance shown in Fig. 4, although the Copy baseline achieves the lowest MSE, it fails to effectively preserve the semantic information of the source motion in terms of visual appearance. This result not only demonstrates the necessity of hand motion retargeting techniques, but also underscores the importance of the proposed MCS evaluation metric. Compared with SAN, which is also designed for motion retargeting, our method achieves higher accuracy in reconstructing fine finger details, and the smoother overall motion leads to more coherent video sequences.

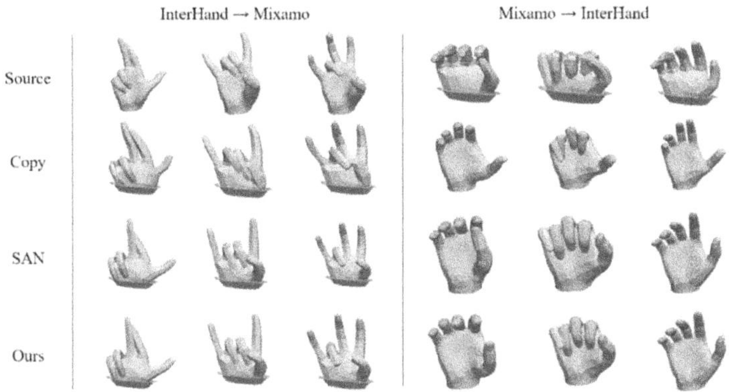

Fig. 4. Visualized retargeting results of different experimental groups.

5   Conclusion

To address the absence of dedicated algorithms for hand motion retargeting in the current research landscape, we propose a graph attention-based residual-aware retargeting method that enables cross-domain training while effectively handling the challenges posed by high-degree-of-freedom hand motion retargeting. The proposed method enables cross-domain training while tackling various challenges associated with high-degree-of-freedom hand retargeting. It adopts an extended hand model that captures palm semantics by associating finger joints with palm joints. Compared with existing works, our method innovatively integrates a Graph Attention Network, which preserves per-frame motion details while effectively leveraging biomechanical priors among finger joints. Furthermore, the attention mechanism enables more efficient extraction of global features. The effectiveness of the proposed model is ultimately validated through both quantitative and qualitative experiments.

References

1. Villegas, R., et al.: Neural kinematic networks for unsupervised motion retargetting. In: Proceedings of the IEEE Conference on Computer Vision and Pattern Recognition, pp. 8639–8648 (2018)
2. Aberman, K., et al.: Skeleton-aware networks for deep motion retargeting. ACM Trans. Graph. (TOG) **39**(4), 62–1 (2020)
3. Mourot, L., et al.: HuMoT: human motion representation using topology- agnostic transformers for character animation retargeting. arXiv preprint arXiv:2305.18897 (2023)
4. Hu, L., et al.: Pose-aware attention network for flexible motion retargeting by body part. IEEE Trans. Visualization Comput. Graph. (2023)
5. Yang, L., et al.: CPF: learning a contact potential field to model the hand-object interaction. In: Proceedings of the IEEE/CVF International Conference on Computer Vision, pp. 11097–11106 (2021)

6. Perlin, K.: Real time responsive animation with personality. IEEE Trans. Visualization Comput. Graph. **1**(1), 5–15 (2002)
7. Witkin, A., Kass, M.: Spacetime constraints. ACM SIGGRAPH Comput. Graph. **22**(4), 159–168 (1988)
8. Lee, J., Shin, S.Y.: A hierarchical approach to interactive motion editing for human-like figures. In: Proceedings of the 26th Annual Conference on Computer Graphics and Interactive Techniques, pp. 39–48 (1999)
9. Popović, Z., Witkin, A.: Physically based motion transformation. In: Proceedings of the 26th Annual Conference on Computer Graphics and Interactive Techniques, pp. 11–20 (1999)
10. Choi, K.-J., Ko, H.-S.: Online motion retargetting. J. Visualization Comput. Animation **11**(5), 223–235 (2000)
11. Al Borno, M., et al.: Robust physics-based motion retargeting with realistic body shapes. Comput. Graph. Forum **37**(8), 81–92 (2018)
12. Lee, J., et al.: Interhandgen: two-hand interaction generation via cascaded reverse diffusion. In: Proceedings of the IEEE/CVF Conference on Computer Vision and Pattern Recognition, pp. 527–537 (2024)
13. Tang, B., et al.: Prompting future driven diffusion model for hand motion prediction. In: European Conference on Computer Vision, pp. 169–186. Springer, Cham (2024)
14. Savenko, A., Clapworthy, G.: Using motion analysis techniques for motion retargeting. In: Proceedings Sixth International Conference on Information Visualisation, pp. 110–115. IEEE (2002)
15. Adobe. Mixamo (2024). https://www.mixamo.com/. Accessed 12 Sept 2023
16. Moon, G., et al.: InterHand2.6M: a dataset and baseline for 3D interacting hand pose estimation from a single RGB image. In: European Conference on Computer Vision, pp. 548–564. Springer, Cham (2020)
17. Gleicher, M., Litwinowicz, P.: Constraint-based motion adaptation. J. Visualization Comput. Animation **9**(2), 65–94 (1998)
18. Romero, J., Tzionas, D., Black, M.J.: Embodied hands: modeling and capturing hands and bodies together. arXiv preprint arXiv:2201.02610 (2022)

Gait, Footprint

SMEGNet: A Lightweight MLP-Enhanced Architecture for Cross-View Gait Recognition

Kaihui Xu[1], Shaoxiong Zhang[2(✉)], and Zongpeng Li[1]

[1] School of Automation, Hangzhou Dianzi University, Hangzhou, China
[2] School of Communication Engineering, Hangzhou Dianzi University, Hangzhou, China
`zhangsx@hdu.edu.cn`

Abstract. Recent advances in deep learning have substantially enhanced gait recognition performance. However, the increasing parameter size of large-scale models has become a major limitation, hindering further progress. Since binary silhouette sequences used in gait recognition are typically of variable length and contain considerable redundancy, it is essential to develop efficient and lightweight methods for their effective processing. To this end, we propose SMEGNet, a lightweight MLP-based framework for variable-length gait sequences. Specifically, SMEGNet introduces a proposed Fixed-Length Sequence Truncation method to standardize input sequence lengths. Furthermore, it incorporates a Cross-Dimensional Attention module to capture comprehensive spatial, channel, and temporal dependencies, as well as a Block-wise MLP module to enhance spatiotemporal feature modeling through structured tensor partitioning. Extensive experimental results demonstrate that the proposed method achieves competitive recognition accuracy while significantly reducing the number of parameters compared to existing methods.

Keywords: Gait recognition · convolutional neural network · multi-layer perception · variable-length sequences

1 Introduction

Gait is a biometric for identifying individuals by analyzing their walking patterns. Compared to other biometric recognition methods, gait exhibits distinct advantages such as non-contact acquisition, long-range sensing, and robustness against forgery. These advantages render it particularly suitable for a wide range of applications in security surveillance [1,2].

In recent years, by utilizing powerful deep learning architectures, gait recognition has achieved substantial progress in identifying individuals under challenging conditions. For example, DeepGaitV2 [3] and BigGait [4] have significantly improved recognition performance by increasing network depth, expanding feature extraction dimensions, and incorporating additional data modalities. However, the recognition accuracy improvements achieved by large models tend to exhibit diminishing marginal returns. This presents a key challenge: achieving comparable recognition accuracy with models of lower parameter complexity and computational cost. Unfortunately, research on the efficiency of gait recognition models remains limited. Previous studies have seldom addressed the challenge of reducing model parameters and computational cost while preserving recognition accuracy.

It is noteworthy that the silhouette images commonly employed in gait recognition are binary, with each pixel representing either foreground or background, thereby lacking high-frequency information such as texture and color. Compared to natural images, gait silhouettes are visually simpler and frequently contain redundant information (see Fig. 1). Meanwhile, although CNNs are known for their translational invariance, this property may be less essential in gait recognition tasks, where input images are generally preprocessed to center the subject. As a result, the strong invariance to spatial shifts, crucial in natural image recognition tasks, offers limited additional benefit in this context. Thus, we believe it is necessary to explore alternative deep learning architectures that enable low-parameter, high-efficiency extraction of gait features.

Multi-Layer Perceptron (MLP)-based architectures have demonstrated strong capabilities in capturing global features. Compared to CNN-based models, MLPs are more effective in capturing global spatial relationships and can offer improved computational efficiency, particularly in tasks involving structured or preprocessed inputs [5]. For example, MorphMLP [6] extends MLP-based architectures to video feature extraction tasks, showing that such architectures can achieve a favorable trade-off between accuracy and efficiency while significantly reducing computational overhead. However, MorphMLP is limited to input sequences with a fixed number of frames. In gait recognition tasks, input sequences typically vary in length, which presents a key challenge to the direct application of existing MLP-based architectures.

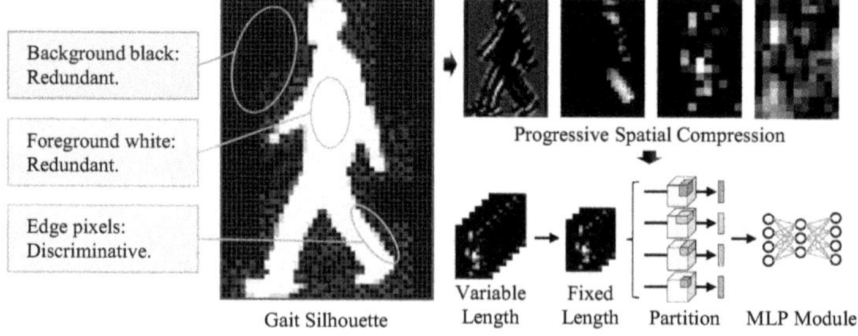

Fig. 1. Illustration of the spatial redundancy of gait silhouettes and the motivation of our proposed method.

Based on the aforementioned insights, we propose a lightweight model for gait recognition, termed the **Sequence-aware MLP-enhanced Gait Network (SMEGNet)**. SMEGNet is designed to learn efficient and discriminative spatiotemporal representations, as illustrated in Fig. 1. In the spatial domain, progressive compression reduces spatial information and computational cost before feature extraction. In the temporal domain, variable-length sequences are divided into fixed-length segments, enabling MLP-based modules to capture fine-grained features. The Cross-Dimensional Attention (CDA) and Block-wise MLP (B-MLP) modules jointly extract spatiotemporal features, alleviating the burden of four-dimensional modeling and achieving efficient inference with competitive recognition performance.

To summarize, our main contributions are as follows:

1. We propose a novel lightweight framework, termed SMEGNet, which effectively handles variable-length gait sequences through fixed-length transformation and MLP-based modeling.
2. We introduce two core modules: the Cross-Dimensional Attention module, which captures interactions across spatial, channel, and temporal dimensions; and the Block-wise MLP module, which enhances spatiotemporal dependency modeling through structured tensor partitioning.
3. Experiments on CASIA-B and OU-MVLP demonstrate that our method achieves competitive recognition performance with significantly fewer parameters compared to existing approaches.

2   Related Work

2.1   Gait Recognition

Several novel convolutional neural network (CNN)-based gait models [7–10] have been proposed to address this task. These approaches employ convolutional layers to capture both global visual representations and fine-grained local details, thereby substantially enhancing feature extraction performance. Additionally, other deep models, such as Transformers [3], have also been proposed. By modeling long-range dependencies through self-attention mechanisms, these methods have attracted significant attention in the field of gait recognition [11,12]. Although gait models substantially improve recognition performance, their large parameter sizes hinder computational efficiency and practical deployment.

2.2   Multilayer Perceptron

Besides CNN- and Transformer-based architectures, multilayer perceptron (MLP)-based models have also been extensively employed in various computer vision tasks [13]. This popularity is attributed to their architectural simplicity and strong capability to approximate complex nonlinear functions. For example, MLP-Mixer [14] established a baseline for pure MLP-based vision backbones. Subsequently, several MLP-based architectures have been proposed for image recognition, including AS-MLP [15], Hire-MLP [16], and CycleMLP [17]. As for video recognition, MorphMLP [6] further incorporates a morphology-inspired spatial branch and an in-channel Temporal MLP to enhance fine-grained spatial detail and pseudo-temporal dependencies. However, MorphMLP is limited to videos with a fixed number of frames, whereas gait recognition tasks require processing gait silhouette sequences of arbitrary lengths.

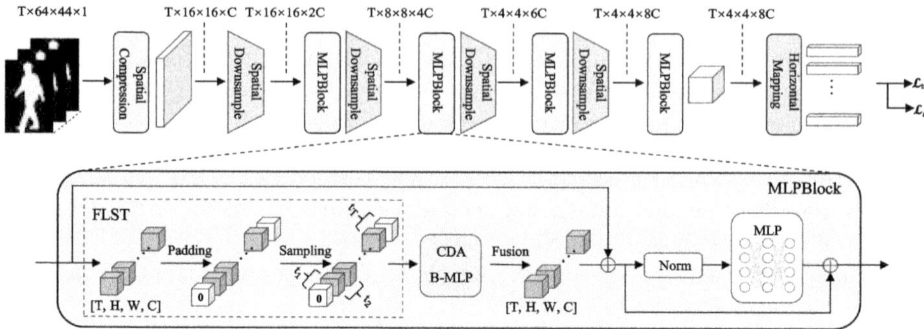

Fig. 2. Pipeline of the proposed Sequence-aware MLP-enhanced Gait Network (SMEG-Net). The model consists of a Spatial Compression module, four Spatial Downsampling and MLPBlocks, and a Horizontal Mapping module.

3   Proposed Method

We propose a lightweight gait recognition framework, SMEGNet as illustrated in Fig. 2. We will describe each component in the following subsections.

3.1   Spatial Compression Module

Binary silhouettes are commonly used in gait recognition tasks, with features distributed across the spatial domain and each pixel conveying only limited information. Since convolution simultaneously extracts local edge features and rapidly reduces spatial resolution, we apply three convolutions to reduce the spatial dimensions of the input image. Given the unequal height and width of the input image, we employ convolutional kernels with sizes of $(3, 3)$, $(3, 5)$, and $(3, 5)$, accompanied by strides of $(1, 1)$, $(2, 2)$, and $(2, 1)$, along with padding sizes of $(1, 1)$, $(1, 0)$, and $(1, 0)$. Finally, the image is compressed to a spatial resolution of 16×16.

3.2   Spatial Downsampling

The spatial downsampling layers use 3×3 convolutional kernels with a padding of 1 to perform both spatial and channel transformations. The second and third downsampling layers have a stride of 2, halving the spatial dimensions of the input image, reducing computational complexity, and aggregating local information. The first and fourth layers have a stride of 1, maintaining the spatial dimensions while only changing the channel count.

3.3   MLPBlock

Each MLPBlock comprises four components: Fixed-Length Sequence Truncation (FLST), Cross-Dimensional Attention (CDA), Block-wise MLP (B-MLP), and Multi-Branch Integration Module (Fig. 3).

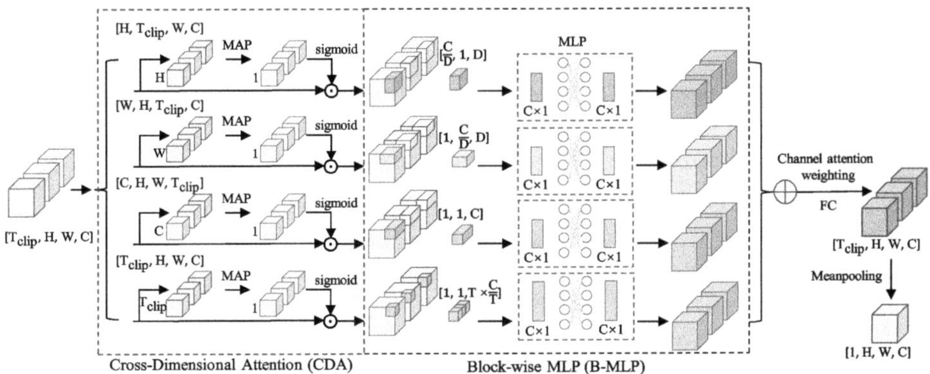

Fig. 3. The detailed structure of CDA and B-MLP.

Fixed-Length Sequence Truncation. To address the challenge of variable-length sequences commonly encountered in gait recognition tasks, we propose a simple yet effective method, inspired by the sliding convolution window, to transform variable-length sequences into fixed-length representations. This method is termed Fixed-length Sequence Truncation (FLST). Given an gait silhouette sequence $X \in \mathbb{R}^{T \times H \times W \times C}$, we select a window with a fixed length t and apply zero-padding of $\frac{t-1}{2}$ on both sides of the temporal dimension. This padding ensures that the output feature maps retain the same temporal length as the input. Subsequently, we slide a fixed-size window along the temporal axis and concatenate the resulting features along the temporal dimension to construct the final fixed-length feature map:

$$X_{\text{clip}} = \{X[i : i + t - 1] \mid i = 1, 2, \ldots, T\} \tag{1}$$

where i represents the starting position of the window.

Cross-Dimensional Attention. Inspired by existing attention design methods [18], we propose a module called Cross-Dimensional Attention (CDA), which emphasizes the importance of cross-dimensional interactions. It is designed to capture the relationships between the spatial dimensions (H, W), the channel dimension (C), and the temporal dimension (T) within the input tensor.

CDA has four branches, each with the same input and output shape. Given an input tensor $X \in \mathbb{R}^{T_{\text{clip}} \times H \times W \times C}$, in the interaction branch between the height and time dimensions, we first transform the dimensions to obtain $X' \in \mathbb{R}^{H \times T_{\text{clip}} \times W \times C}$. Then, X' is passed through the MAP layer, followed by a sigmoid activation function to generate attention weights. Finally, these weights are applied to X, and the result is reshaped back to the original dimensions. The MAP function is:

$$MAP = \text{MLP}(MaxPool_{d0}(X) + AvgPool_{d0}(X)), \tag{2}$$

where d0 denotes the 0th dimension over which the max and average pooling operations are applied. The other three branches follow a similar procedure, with the last branch not requiring any dimensional transformation.

Block-Wise MLP. To enhance the modeling of complex spatiotemporal dependencies, we adopt a block-wise MLP architecture to process the four representational branches derived from the CDA module, corresponding to the height, width, channel, and temporal dimensions. For the height dimension branch, the channel C is partitioned into segments of length D, and the height H is divided into segments of length $\frac{C}{D}$, resulting in $T \times H \times W$ blocks of size $\frac{C}{D} \times 1 \times D$. Similarly, the width branch is divided into $T \times H \times W$ blocks of size $1 \times \frac{C}{D} \times D$; the channel branch is divided into $T \times H \times W$ blocks of size $1 \times 1 \times C$; and the temporal branch is divided along the channel dimension C, with features at the same position in the temporal dimension concatenated, yielding $H \times W \times T$ blocks of size $1 \times 1 \times (T \times \frac{C}{T})$. Then, each branch's feature map is flattened into $C \times 1$ tensors and passed through MLPs for feature transformation. The outputs are then reshaped back to their original spatial configurations, yielding the refined feature representations for each of the four semantic dimensions.

Multi-branch Integration Module. To integrate multi-branch information, we first perform element-wise summation across the four branches, followed by spatial pooling. A fully connected layer is then used to compute channel-wise weights. Subsequently, a weighted average of the four branches is performed based on the learned weights. Finally, temporal average pooling is applied to obtain the feature representation of a single window.

3.4   Horizontal Pooling

Based on the design of the Horizontal Pyramid Mapping module [10,19], we simplified it by dividing the feature map according to its minimum height, followed by feature extraction using global max pooling, global average pooling, and a fully connected layer.

3.5   Loss Function

To achieve the best performance, we adopt Triplet Loss L_{Triplet} and Cross-Entropy Loss L_{CE} to supervise the identity learning process based on features extracted from the training set. The final loss function is $L_{\text{Triplet}} + 0.1 L_{\text{CE}}$.

4   Experiments

4.1   Datasets and Implementation Details

We conduct experiments on two popular datasets. **CASIA-B** [20] contains gait sequences of 124 subjects. We follow the standard protocol described in [7]; the first 74 sequences are used for training. **OU-MVLP** [21] contains gait sequences of 10,307 subjects. According to the protocol in [21], 5153 subjects are assigned to the training set, while the remaining 5154 subjects are used for testing.

All datasets are resized to 64×44. We adopt batch size [P, K] and the number of iterations, [8, 16], 60K for CASIA-B, and [32, 16], 120K for OU-MVLP. We sample 30 frames of each gait sequence in the training stage, and all frames are used for inference. We adopt the SGD optimizer with a momentum of 0.9 and a weight decay of 0.0005. For the CASIA-B dataset, the initial learning rate is set to 0.1 and is reduced by a factor of 10 at the 20k, 40k, and 50k iterations. For the OU-MVLP dataset, the initial learning rate is set to 0.01 and decays by a factor of 10 at the 60k, 80k, and 100k iterations.

4.2   Main Results

Comparison of Model Size and Performance. We first conduct a comprehensive comparison of the proposed SMEGNet with six classical gait recognition models in terms of model size and performance, as summarized in Table 1. SMEGNet achieves a mean Rank-1 accuracy of 90.0% on CASIA-B and 91.1% on OU-MVLP, ranking third on OU-MVLP and only slightly lower than GaitGL on CASIA-B. Considering that SMEGNet substantially reduces the number of model parameters (3.47M) and computational cost (2.54 GFLOPs), it demonstrates superior efficiency while maintaining competitive recognition performance. In particular, SMEGNet reduces the computational cost compared to classical gait recognition models, clearly demonstrating the efficiency of our model design.

Comparison with the State-of-the-Art. To further evaluate the performance of lightweight models, we compare SMEGNet with the latest state-of-the-art results on the OU-MVLP dataset, listed in Table 2. It is worth noting that most State-of-the-art methods do not provide model size parameters or release their source code, making it difficult to conduct a comprehensive comparison of model

Table 1. Comparison with the representative methods on CASIA-B and OU-MVLP datasets in terms of Rank-1 accuracy (%).

Methods	Venue	Params (M)	GFLOPs	CASIA-B				OU-MVLP
				NM	BG	CL	Mean	Mean
GaitSet [7]	AAAI2019	6.3	25.9	95.0	87.2	70.4	84.2	87.1
GaitPart [8]	CVPR2020	4.8	16.0	96.2	91.5	78.7	88.8	88.7
GaitGL [9]	ICCV2021	11.2	117.1	97.4	94.5	83.7	91.8	89.7
GaitBase [10]	CVPR2023	7.0	70.7	97.6	94.0	77.4	89.7	90.8
DGaitV2-3D [3]	arXiv-2023	27.5	6.8	-	-	-	89.6	92.0
DGaitV2-P3D [3]	arXiv-2023	11.1	2.9	-	-	-	89.6	91.9
SMEGNet	(Ours)	**3.47**	**2.54**	97.4	93.9	78.7	90.0	91.1

size and performance. Therefore, we only present their performance results to demonstrate the effectiveness of our approach in Table 2. Overall, SMEGNet achieves a competitive recognition accuracy as a lightweight gait recognition model.

Table 2. Comparison with the state-of-the-art methods on OU-MVLP datasets in terms of Rank-1 accuracy (%).

Methods	Venue	OU-MVLP
GaitMPL [22]	TIP2022	90.6
GaitGCI [9]	CVPR2023	92.1
DANet [23]	CVPR2023	89.8
IGPS [24]	T-BIOM2023	89.8
CLASH [25]	TIP2024	91.9
GaitW [12]	ACCV2024	92.9
GaitDAN [26]	TCSVT2024	90.2
CLTD [27]	ECCV2024	92.3
LMGCS [28]	TCSVT2024	90.9
SMEGNet	(Ours)	91.1

4.3 Ablation Study

To evaluate the effectiveness of the proposed modules, we conducted an ablation study on the OU-MVLP dataset. As shown in Table 3, the integration of each module leads to consistent performance improvements. The FLST module contributes to recognition accuracy, with a window length of $t = 7$ yielding better results. Compared to the baseline, FLST provides an average improvement of

1.1% on OU-MVLP. Incorporating the B-MLP module further enhances performance, resulting in a 3.8% gain. Additionally, introducing the CDA module enables the model to achieve the highest mean accuracy of 91.1%. These results clearly demonstrate the complementary nature and effectiveness of the proposed components.

Table 3. Performance of ablation study on OU-MVLP.

Module				Rank-1 Accuracy (%)
FLST		B-MLP	CDA	
$t = 5$	$t = 7$			
$\times$	$\times$	$\times$	$\times$	86.0
$\checkmark$	$\times$	$\times$	$\times$	86.8
$\times$	$\checkmark$	$\times$	$\times$	87.1
$\times$	$\checkmark$	$\checkmark$	$\times$	90.9
$\times$	$\checkmark$	$\checkmark$	$\checkmark$	91.1

5 Conclusion

In this paper, we present a novel and lightweight MLP-based deep framework, SMEGNet, designed to efficiently process variable-length gait sequences. The proposed Cross-Dimensional Attention and Block-wise MLP modules enhance the model's representational capacity while significantly reducing the number of parameters. Experimental results on the CASIA-B and OU-MVLP datasets demonstrate that SMEGNet achieves competitive recognition performance despite its significantly reduced model size, highlighting its potential for deployment in resource-constrained scenarios.

Acknowledgement. This work was supported by the Scientific Research Foundation of Hangzhou Dianzi University (Grant No. KYS085625281).

References

1. Sivarathinabala, M., Abirami, S., Baskaran, R.: A study on security and surveillance system using gait recognition. In: Dey, N., Santhi, V. (eds.) Intelligent Techniques in Signal Processing for Multimedia Security. SCI, vol. 660, pp. 227–252. Springer, Cham (2017). https://doi.org/10.1007/978-3-319-44790-2_11
2. Shen, C., Yu, S., Wang, J., Huang, G.Q., Wang, L.: A comprehensive survey on deep gait recognition: algorithms, datasets, and challenges. IEEE TBBIS (2024)
3. Fan, C., Hou, S., Huang, Y., Yu, S.: Exploring deep models for practical gait recognition. arXiv (2023)

4. Ye, D., Fan, C., Ma, J., Liu, X., Yu, S.: Biggait: learning gait representation you want by large vision models. In: CVPR, pp. 200–210 (2024)
5. Aman, N., Islam, Md.R., Ahamed, Md.F., Ahsan, M.: Performance evaluation of various deep learning models in gait recognition using the Casia-b dataset. Technologies **12**(12), 264 (2024)
6. Zhang, D.J., et al.: MorphMLP: an efficient MLP-like backbone for spatial-temporal representation learning. In: Avidan, S., Brostow, G., Cissé, M., Farinella, G.M., Hassner, T. (eds.) ECCV 2022. LNCS, vol. 13695, pp. 230–248. Springer, Cham (2022). https://doi.org/10.1007/978-3-031-19833-5_14
7. Chao, H., He, Y., Zhang, J., Feng, J.: Gaitset: regarding gait as a set for cross-view gait recognition. In: AAAI, vol. 33, pp. 8126–8133 (2019)
8. Fan, C., et al.: Gaitpart: temporal part-based model for gait recognition. In: CVPR, pp. 14225–14233 (2020)
9. Lin, B., Zhang, S., Wang, M., Li, L., Yu, X.: Gaitgl: learning discriminative global-local feature representations for gait recognition. arXiv (2022)
10. Fan, C., Liang, J., Shen, C., Hou, S., Huang, Y., Yu, S.: Opengait: revisiting gait recognition towards better practicality. In: CVPR, pp. 9707–9716 (2023)
11. Zhu, D., et al.: Multi-scale context-aware network with transformer for gait recognition. arXiv (2022)
12. Thapar, D., Chaudhari, J., Manchanda, S., Nigam, A., Arora, C.: Gaitw: enhancing gait recognition in the wild using dynamic information. In: ACCV, pp. 268–285 (2024)
13. Yang, J., Yang, J., Yu, X., Qiu, P., Prajapat, S.: D2-MLP: dynamic decomposed MLP mixer for medical image segmentation. In: ICASSP, pp. 1–5. IEEE (2025)
14. Tolstikhin, I.O., et al.: MLP-mixer: an all-MLP architecture for vision. In: NeurIPS, vol. 34, pp. 24261–24272 (2021)
15. Lian, D., Yu, Z., Sun, X., Gao, S.: As-MLP: an axial shifted MLP architecture for vision. arXiv (2021)
16. Guo, J., et al.: Hire-MLP: vision MLP via hierarchical rearrangement. In: CVPR, pp. 826–836 (2022)
17. Chen, S., Xie, E., Ge, C., Chen, R., Liang, D., Luo, P.: Cyclemlp: a MLP-like architecture for dense visual predictions. IEEE TPAMI **45**(12), 14284–14300 (2023)
18. Misra, D., Nalamada, T., Arasanipalai, A.U., Hou, Q.: Rotate to attend: convolutional triplet attention module. In: WACV, pp. 3139–3148 (2021)
19. Fu, Y., et al.: Cut out the middleman: revisiting pose-based gait recognition. In: Leonardis, A., Ricci, E., Roth, S., Russakovsky, O., Sattler, T., Varol, G. (eds.) ECCV 2024. LNCS, vol. 15089, pp. 112–128. Springer, Cham (2025). https://doi.org/10.1007/978-3-031-72751-1_7
20. Yu, S., Tan, D., Tan, T.: A framework for evaluating the effect of view angle, clothing and carrying condition on gait recognition. In: ICPR, vol. 4, pp. 441–444. IEEE (2006)
21. Takemura, N., Makihara, Y., Muramatsu, D., Echigo, T., Yagi, Y.: Multi-view large population gait dataset and its performance evaluation for cross-view gait recognition. IPSJ Trans. Comput. Vis. Appl. **10**(1), 1–14 (2018). https://doi.org/10.1186/s41074-018-0039-6
22. Dou, H., Zhang, P., Zhao, Y., Dong, L., Qin, Z., Li, X.: Gaitmpl: gait recognition with memory-augmented progressive learning. IEEE TIP **33**, 1464–1475 (2022)
23. Ma, K., Fu, Y., Zheng, D., Cao, C., Hu, X., Huang, Y.: Dynamic aggregated network for gait recognition. In: CVPR, pp. 22076–22085 (2023)
24. Wang, R., et al.: Gait recognition via gait period set. IEEE TBBIS **5**(2), 183–195 (2023)

25. Dou, H., Zhang, P., Zhao, Y., Jin, L., Li, X.: Clash: complementary learning with neural architecture search for gait recognition. IEEE TIP (2024)
26. Huang, T., Ben, X., Gong, C., Xu, W., Wu, Q., Zhou, H.: Gaitdan: cross-view gait recognition via adversarial domain adaptation. IEEE TCSVT (2024)
27. Xiong, H., Feng, B., Wang, X., Liu, W.: Causality-inspired discriminative feature learning in triple domains for gait recognition. In: Leonardis, A., Ricci, E., Roth, S., Russakovsky, O., Sattler, T., Varol, G. (eds.) ECCV 2024. LNCS, vol. 15112, pp. 251–270. Springer, Cham (2025). https://doi.org/10.1007/978-3-031-72949-2_15
28. Zhai, W., Li, H., Zheng, C., Xing, X.: Multi-view gait recognition with joint local multi-scale and global contextual spatio-temporal features. IEEE TCSVT (2024)

Revisiting Euclidean Triplet Loss for Gait Recognition

Guozhen Peng, Ruiyi Zhan, Annan Li$^{(\boxtimes)}$, and Yunhong Wang$^{(\boxtimes)}$

State Key Laboratory of Virtual Reality Technology and Systems, School of Computer Science and Engineering, Beihang University, Beijing 100191, China
{guozhen_peng,zry,liannan,yhwang}@buaa.edu.cn

Abstract. Triplet loss, a widely utilized function in deep gait recognition, optimizes embedding spaces by pulling features of the same identity while pushing those of different identities. However, we found that the *Euclidean* distance, which is frequently adopted in triplet loss, inherently limits the optimization process in the later stage of training. Through gradient decomposition analysis, a key limitation is recognized, i.e. as samples approach positive anchors, the dominance of their radial gradient components diminishes, hindering convergence. To address this issue, we propose the **A**ngle-guided **T**riplet **L**oss (ATL), which incorporates a geometrically inspired rotation function that re-calibrates gradient directions based on the between-sample angles. ATL effectively enhances radial guidance from positive samples, thereby accelerating convergence and improving the discriminative power. Extensive experiments demonstrate the superiority of ATL, as it consistently outperforms state-of-the-art methods across various model scales and loss functions on challenging in-the-wild datasets.

Keywords: Gait recognition · Triplet loss · Euclidean metric · Gradients analysis

1   Introduction

Gait recognition, a non-intrusive biometric modality, identifies individuals by analyzing distinctive body shapes and motion patterns. Unlike cooperative modalities such as fingerprint, iris and face, gait silhouettes can be acquired at a distance without cooperation. This inherent advantage of distant feature capture positions gait recognition as a promising solution for surveillance applications, including identity verification and behavioral analysis, contributing to its increasing research prominence.

Recent research has seen numerous metric learning approaches applied to gait recognition. Yu et al. [1] design weighting strategies for hard samples, CTL [2]

G. Peng and R. Zhan—Equal contribution.

W. Jia et al. (Eds.): CCBR 2025, LNCS 16360, pp. 260–270, 2026.
https://doi.org/10.1007/978-981-95-6123-0_25

reduces intra-class variance by leveraging class-centers to guide positive samples, while QATriplet [3] integrates quality assessment mechanisms into triplet loss. However, these methods primarily focus on sample selection or weighting, with perspectives limited to the final distribution in latent space and overlooking the gradient-based optimization process. Therefore, we rethink the standard triplet loss with Euclidean metric and develop refinements through rigorous analysis of its gradient-driven optimization process.

During optimization with Euclidean distance based triplet loss, gradients of positive and negative samples can be decomposed into tangential and radial directional components (see Fig. 1 (a)). The tangential component consistently directs samples toward the positive sample throughout training. As training goes on, diminishing distance to the positive sample reduces angular separation between samples, causing the positive sample's gradient contribution to become decreasingly dominated by its radial component (see Fig. 1 (b)). Conversely, growing distance to negative samples increases their angular separation, leading negative samples to contribute predominantly radial gradient components. Critically, since the Euclidean metric yields gradients of constant magnitude, the radial component from negative samples progressively exceeds that from positive samples in later training stage. This radial gradient disparity impedes convergence toward positive samples along the radial dimension during optimization.

To address these limitations, we propose **A**ngle-guided **T**riplet **L**oss (ATL), a novel loss function that enhances conventional Euclidean-based triplet loss through angular constraints with directional bias. ATL adjusts gradient vectors of positive and negative samples via angular transformation, effectively accelerating radial convergence toward positive samples during later training stage. Concurrently, ATL adaptively modulates gradient contributions by mitigating influence from negative samples while amplifying guidance from positive samples throughout training. This dual-gradient modulation promotes greater intra-class compactness, ultimately enhancing model stability and discriminative power. Finally, experimental results demonstrate that ATL consistently improves the performance of existing gait recognition frameworks, outperforming state-of-the-art approaches on in-the-wild datasets.

The main contributions are summarized as follows:

- We conduct a theoretical analysis of the optimization process using Euclidean triplet loss, characterizing the dynamic impact of positive and negative sample gradients across training stages.
- We propose **A**ngle-guided **T**riplet **L**oss to mitigate late-stage radial gradient convergence difficulties while optimizing the embedding distribution through enhancing intra-class compactness, thereby improving model stability.
- Extensive experiments demonstrate the effectiveness when integrating ATL into existing gait recognition frameworks, with performance surpassing state-of-the-art methods on in-the-wild datasets.

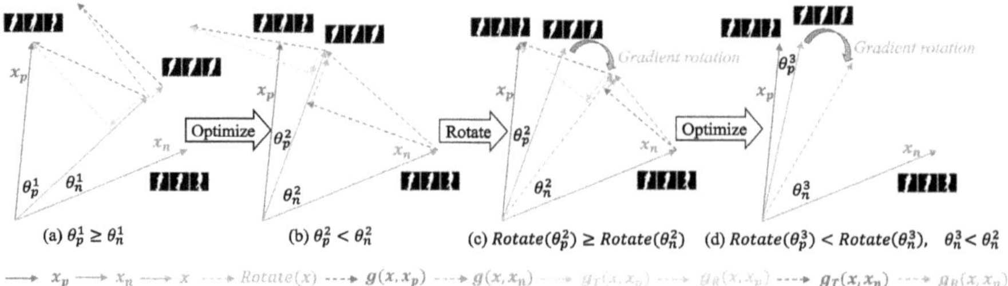

Fig. 1. Gradient of x and its decomposition in radial and tangential direction. As formulated in Equation (4), the optimization direction of radial gradient depends on size of θ_p and θ_n. The proposed ATL rotates x only for the calculation of gradients, which moves x closer to x_p in radial direction.

2   Related Works

2.1   Gait Recognition

Model-based Methods leverage the physical structure of the human body by utilizing pose representations as input. PoseGait [4] extracts spatio-temporal features from body poses using convolutional networks; LidarGait [5] generates gait point clouds from LiDAR data. However, these methods are inherently constrained by pose estimation, limiting practical deployment in reality due to computational complexity and generalization challenges.

Appearance-based Methods learn body representations without explicit structural modeling, predominantly utilizing silhouette sequences [13–16] as input. These approaches employ deep neural networks [17,18] to extract features, performing recognition through cross-sequence similarity comparisons. While achieving strong performance in controlled laboratory settings [13–15], recent in-the-wild benchmarks (e.g., Gait3D [7], GREW [8]) reveal significant challenges. Then, some methods [2,3,9–12] are proposed to employ precise gait recognition in wild scenarios. DyGait [12] extracts feature dynamically with automated part learning. GaitBase [11] proposes efficient ResNet-inspired frameworks while DGaitV2 [10] extends it via architectural scaling. Compared to model-based methods, appearance-based approaches offer greater deployment flexibility due to easier data acquisition but exhibit reduced robustness with variations [6].

2.2   Triplet Loss in Gait Recognition

Recent advancements in gait recognition have witnessed extensive adoption of Euclidean distance-based triplet loss. Several strategies have emerged to enhance this framework. Yu et al. [1] design weight allocation mechanisms to distinguish hard samples, adjusting weights for hard samples. CTL [2] leverages cluster centers of positive samples to guide sample distribution. QATriplet [3] incorporates quality assessment into triplet loss to modulate the optimization process. However, these methods predominantly focus on sample selection or weight assignment, paying lack attention to the gradient-based optimization process. Consequently, we conduct dynamic analysis on the Euclidean-based triplet loss and propose ATL to the gradient-driven optimization mechanism.

3   Method

In this section, we first present a theoretical analysis of the Euclidean metric in triplet loss minimization/optimization. Then, we propose the ATL and detail its formulation and integration mechanism. As shown is Fig. 2, ATL is integrated into gait recognition pipeline in the loss function.

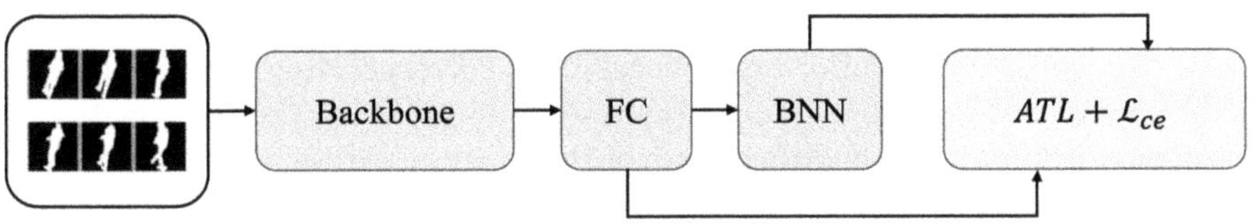

Fig. 2. Pipeline of gait recognition with ATL. FC is the fully connected layer to map features, while BNN refers BNNeck [21] for calculation of cross-entropy loss ($\mathcal{L}_{ce}$).

3.1   Euclidean Triplet Loss

Triplet Loss. Given the input x, x_p and x_n, the triplet loss $\mathcal{L}_{tri}$ can be formulated as

$$\mathcal{L}_{tri}(x) = ReLU(\mathcal{D}(x, x_p) - \mathcal{D}(x, x_n) + m), \tag{1}$$

where $\mathcal{D}(\cdot, \cdot)$ calculates the distance, x is the anchor sample, x_p is the positive sample, x_n is the negative sample, m is the margin. Specifically, the ReLU activation ensures $\mathcal{L}_{tri} \geq 0$ throughout our analysis, simplifying theoretical examination. Using *Euclidean* distance $\mathcal{D}(\cdot, \cdot)$ as metric, the triplet loss $\mathcal{L}_{tri}^{euc}$ can be formally defined as

$$\mathcal{L}_{tri}^{euc}(x) = \|x - x_p\|_2 - \|x - x_n\|_2 + m, \tag{2}$$

where $\| \cdot \|_2$ indicates ℓ_2-norm. Triplet loss aims to decrease the intra-class distance by minimizing $\|x - x_p\|_2$ to pull positive pairs (x, x_p) closer, and increase the inter-class distance by maximizing $\|x - x_n\|_2$ to push negative pairs (x, x_n) far away.

To optimize the gait recognition model by $\mathcal{L}_{tri}^{euc}(x)$, we first compute the gradient of x in $\mathcal{D}(x, y)$, noted as $\mathcal{G}(x, y)$, which is formulated as:

$$\mathcal{G}(x, y) = \frac{\partial \mathcal{D}(x, y)}{\partial x} = \frac{\partial \|x - y\|_2}{\partial x} = \sum_j \frac{\partial [\sum_i (x_i - y_i)^2)]^{\frac{1}{2}}}{\partial x_j}$$

$$= \sum_j \frac{x_j - y_j}{[\sum_i (x_i - y_i)^2]^{\frac{1}{2}}} = \frac{x - y}{\mathcal{D}(x, y)}. \tag{3}$$

Here $\boldsymbol{x} = (\boldsymbol{x_1}, \boldsymbol{x_2}, \cdots, \boldsymbol{x_k})$ and $\boldsymbol{y} = (\boldsymbol{y_1}, \boldsymbol{y_2}, \cdots, \boldsymbol{y_k})$, k is the dimension of $\boldsymbol{x}$ and $\boldsymbol{y}$. Then, it is easy to find that the gradient remains constant at unit norm. As illustrated in Fig. 1, the gradient $\mathcal{G}(\boldsymbol{x}, \boldsymbol{y})$ can be decomposed into tangential and radial directional components $\mathcal{G}_T(\boldsymbol{x}, \boldsymbol{y}) = \mathcal{G}(\boldsymbol{x}, \boldsymbol{y}) \cdot cos(\angle(\boldsymbol{x}, \boldsymbol{y}))$ and $\mathcal{G}_R(\boldsymbol{x}, \boldsymbol{y}) = \mathcal{G}(\boldsymbol{x}, \boldsymbol{y}) \cdot sin(\angle(\boldsymbol{x}, \boldsymbol{y}))$. Finally, the gradient of Euclidean triplet loss can be formulated as

$$\frac{\partial \mathcal{L}_{tri}^{euc}(\boldsymbol{x})}{\partial \boldsymbol{x}} = [\mathcal{G}_T(\boldsymbol{x}, \boldsymbol{x_p}) - \mathcal{G}_T(\boldsymbol{x}, \boldsymbol{x_n})] + [\mathcal{G}_R(\boldsymbol{x}, \boldsymbol{x_p}) - \mathcal{G}_R(\boldsymbol{x}, \boldsymbol{x_n})]. \tag{4}$$

During optimization, two primary stages emerge based on angular relationships: 1) $\theta_p \geq \theta_n$ and 2) $\theta_p < \theta_n$, where θ_p is the angle between $\boldsymbol{x}$ and $\boldsymbol{x_p}$ while θ_n is the angle between $\boldsymbol{x}$ and $\boldsymbol{x_n}$. As the angular relationships differs in two stages, the radial direction of gradient changes correspondingly.

In early training stage, characterized by random parameter initialization and consequent arbitrary embedding distributions, the distribution of samples are corresponds to Fig. 1 **(a)**. As optimization progresses and samples $\boldsymbol{x}$ converge toward $\boldsymbol{x_p}$, the system transitions to the second stage in Fig. 1 **(b)**. This transition induces a critical gradient imbalance, i.e. $\|\mathcal{G}_R(\boldsymbol{x}, \boldsymbol{x_n})\|_2 > \|\mathcal{G}_R(\boldsymbol{x}, \boldsymbol{x_p})\|_2$, which impedes further radial convergence toward $\boldsymbol{x_p}$.

As a result, the core optimization challenge emerges in the later stage $(\theta_p < \theta_n)$. Specifically, the radial gradient component from $\boldsymbol{x_n}$ dominates the direction in the radial dimension, opposing the convergence toward $\boldsymbol{x_p}$.

3.2   Angle-Guided Triplet Loss

We propose an **A**ngle-guided **T**riplet **L**oss (ATL) to address the aforementioned problem. ATL rotates the gradient $\mathcal{G}(\boldsymbol{x}, \boldsymbol{y})$ by inserting the designed $\mathcal{R}(\boldsymbol{x}, \boldsymbol{y})$ to the angle between $\boldsymbol{x}$ and $\boldsymbol{y}$. In the training stage, $\mathcal{G}_R(\boldsymbol{x}, \boldsymbol{x_p})$ is amplified through the rotation, while $\mathcal{G}_R(\boldsymbol{x}, \boldsymbol{x_n})$ is reduced in the same time. This directional re-weighting facilitates the accelerated convergence toward in radial dimension throughout training. Furthermore, ATL increases gradient toward $\boldsymbol{x_p}$, which helps enhancing intra-class compactness.

Angle-guided triplet loss is proposed based on $\mathcal{L}_{tri}^{euc}$ in Equation (2). We first design a angle rotation function $\mathcal{R}(\boldsymbol{x}, \boldsymbol{y})$ as

$$\mathcal{R}(\boldsymbol{x}, \boldsymbol{y}) = 2 \cdot r \cdot \|\boldsymbol{x}\|_2 \cdot \|\boldsymbol{y}\|_2, \tag{5}$$

where r is a hyperparameter for the rotation strength. Then, the *Euclidean* distance can be refined as

$$\mathcal{D}_\mathcal{R}(\boldsymbol{x}, \boldsymbol{y}) = [\boldsymbol{x} \cdot \boldsymbol{x}^T + \boldsymbol{y} \cdot \boldsymbol{y}^T - 2 \cdot \|\boldsymbol{x}\|_2 \cdot \|\boldsymbol{y}\|_2 \cdot cos(\angle(\boldsymbol{x}, \boldsymbol{y})) + \mathcal{R}(\boldsymbol{x}, \boldsymbol{y})]^{\frac{1}{2}}$$

$$= [\boldsymbol{x} \cdot \boldsymbol{x}^T + \boldsymbol{y} \cdot \boldsymbol{y}^T - 2 \cdot \|\boldsymbol{x}\|_2 \cdot \|\boldsymbol{y}\|_2 \cdot (cos(\angle(\boldsymbol{x}, \boldsymbol{y})) - r)]^{\frac{1}{2}}. \tag{6}$$

After combining Equation (3) and (5), the combined gradient $\mathcal{G}_R(\boldsymbol{x}, \boldsymbol{y})$ can be formulated as:

$$\mathcal{G}_R(\boldsymbol{x}, \boldsymbol{y}) = \frac{\partial \mathcal{D}_R(\boldsymbol{x}, \boldsymbol{y})}{\partial \boldsymbol{x}} = \sum_j \frac{\partial[\sum_i(\boldsymbol{x}_i - \boldsymbol{y}_i)^2) + 2 \cdot r \cdot (\sum_i(\boldsymbol{x}_i)^2)^{\frac{1}{2}} \cdot \|\boldsymbol{y}\|_2]^{\frac{1}{2}}}{\partial \boldsymbol{x}_j}$$

$$= \frac{1}{\mathcal{D}_R(\boldsymbol{x}, \boldsymbol{y})} \cdot [(1 + r \cdot \frac{\|\boldsymbol{y}\|_2}{\|\boldsymbol{x}\|_2}) \cdot \boldsymbol{x} - \boldsymbol{y}]. \tag{7}$$

Furthermore, we rotate the gradient $\mathcal{G}(\boldsymbol{x}, \boldsymbol{x_p})$ and $\mathcal{G}(\boldsymbol{x}, \boldsymbol{x_n})$ with opposite direction toward $\boldsymbol{x}$, which means positive r in $\mathcal{R}(\boldsymbol{x}, \boldsymbol{x_p})$ and negative r in $\mathcal{R}(\boldsymbol{x}, \boldsymbol{x_n})$, respectively. As illustrated in Fig. 1 (c), the rotated gradients remains effective even in the stage where $\theta_p < \theta_n$, which helps the convergence toward $\boldsymbol{x_p}$ in the radial dimension. Finally, $D(\boldsymbol{x}, \boldsymbol{x_p})$ decreases while $D(\boldsymbol{x}, \boldsymbol{x_n})$ increases in Fig. 1 (d), which demonstrates the effectiveness of ATL in enhancing intra-class compactness.

There are several advantages for the proposed ATL: 1) The rotation strength $\mathcal{R}(\boldsymbol{x}, \boldsymbol{y})$ is a variable rather than a scalar, which adaptively fit the value of $\|\boldsymbol{x}\|_2$, $\|\boldsymbol{x_p}\|_2$ and $\|\boldsymbol{x_n}\|_2$. 2) The norm of $\mathcal{G}_R(\boldsymbol{x}, \boldsymbol{y})$ is limited, which prevent the optimization process from gradient explosion and maintain stable training gradients. 3) Specifically, $\mathcal{G}_R(\boldsymbol{x}, \boldsymbol{y})$ reaches $\sqrt{\frac{m}{2}}$ when $\boldsymbol{x}$ equals $\boldsymbol{y}$, reveals the possibility of convergence to $\boldsymbol{x_p}$.

4 Experiments

4.1 Datasets and Implementation Details

Gait3D contains 4,000 subjects, 25,309 sequences and 3,279,239 frame images. In practice, 3,000 subjects are compiled as the training set while the remaining 1,000 subjects form the test set. For the test phase, the probe comprises one sequence from each subject and the gallery consists of the rest sequences.

GREW is one of the largest gait datasets in the wild, which are collected from 882 cameras in large public areas, containing nearly 3,500 h of 1,920 $\times$ 1,080 streams. It has 26,345 subjects and 128,671 sequences, dividing into two parts with 20,000 and 6,000 subjects as training set and test set.

Implementation Details. In our experiments, the rotation strength r in $\mathcal{R}(\boldsymbol{x}, \boldsymbol{y})$ is set to 0.05. We partition the model size into two segments: Base (B) and Large (L), which is corresponding to DGaitV2 [10]. Both the base model and the large model share the same architectures except for the channels, which are (32, 64, 128, 256) and (64, 128, 256, 512) respectively. In the training stage, the input is a sequence of 30 silhouettes whose resolution are 64 $\times$ 44. The optimizer is Stochastic Gradient Descent (SGD), while the weight decay and the momentum are set to 0.0005 and 0.9. Then, we train the model with a batch size of 32 $\times$ 4 (4 sequences for each pedestrian, 32 pedestrians in total). 1) On Gait3D, the training iteration is 120k. The learning rate starts at 0.1 and is subsequently decreased by a factor of 0.1 at iterations (40k, 80k, 100k). 2) On GREW, the training iteration is 180k. The learning rate starts at 0.05 and is subsequently decreased by a factor of 0.2 at iterations (60k, 120k, 150k).

Table 1. Comparison of Rank-1, 5, 10 accuracy and mean Average Precision (%) on Gait3D and GREW.

Method	Triplet Loss	Gait3D			GREW		
		Rank-1	Rank-5	mAP	Rank-1	Rank-5	Rank-10
GaitSet [13]	$\mathcal{L}_{tri}^{euc}$	36.7	58.3	30.0	46.3	63.6	70.3
GaitPart [14]		28.2	47.6	21.6	44.0	60.7	67.3
GaitGL [15]		29.7	48.5	22.3	47.3	63.6	69.3
SMPLGait [7]		42.9	63.9	35.2	–	–	–
DyGait [12]		66.3	80.8	56.4	71.4	83.2	86.8
HSTL [16]		61.3	76.3	55.5	62.7	76.6	81.3
GaitGCI [9]		50.3	68.5	39.5	68.5	80.8	84.9
GaitBase [11]		64.3	79.6	55.5	59.1	74.5	78.9
DGaitV2-2D-B [10]		64.5	81.7	56.5	62.3	76.4	81.5
DGaitV2-2D-L [10]	$\mathcal{L}_{tri}^{euc}$	67.8	**83.9**	59.7	69.7	82.4	86.7
DGaitV2-2D-L [10]	ATL (Ours)	**69.1**	83.7	**61.1**	**71.0**	**83.7**	**87.3**
DGaitV2-P3D-L [10]	$\mathcal{L}_{tri}^{euc}$	74.2	86.9	67.1	78.3	88.5	91.4
DGaitV2-P3D-L [10]	ATL (Ours)	**76.8**	**87.4**	**68.5**	**79.2**	**88.7**	**91.5**

Table 2. Comparison of $\mathcal{D}(\boldsymbol{x}, \boldsymbol{x}_p)$, $\mathcal{D}(\boldsymbol{x}, \boldsymbol{x}_n)$, $\|\boldsymbol{x}\|_2$ and $\mathcal{L}_{tri}^{num}$ between ATL and $\mathcal{L}_{tri}^{euc}$ (120k iterations on Gait3D).

Method	Loss	Gait3D			
		$\mathcal{D}(\boldsymbol{x}, \boldsymbol{x}_p)$	$\mathcal{D}(\boldsymbol{x}, \boldsymbol{x}_n)$	$\|\boldsymbol{x}\|_2$	$\mathcal{L}_{tri}^{num}$
DGaitV2-P3D-L [10]	$\mathcal{L}_{tri}^{euc}$	1.558	3.849	1.394	116
	ATL (Ours)	**1.556**	**3.951**	**0.7043**	**85**

4.2　Performance Comparison

We integrate our proposed ATL with DGaitV2-P3D and compare it with other state-of-the-art methods for gait recognition on Gait3D and GREW datasets with Rank-1, 5, 10 accuracy and mean Average Precision.

Table 3. Comparison between different losses used for gait recognition on Gait3D with Rank-1 accuracy and mean Average Precision (%).

Method	Loss	Gait3D	
		Rank-1	mAP
DGaitV2-P3D-L [10]	ArcFace [19]	75.8	67.2
	CosFace [20]	75.2	67.8
	AdaFace [22]	75.8	68.0
	ATL (Ours)	**76.8**	**68.5**

Table 4. Comparison between different scales of the gait recognition model used on Gait3D with Rank-1 accuracy and mean Average Precision (%).

Method	Triplet Loss	Gait3D		
		Rank-1	Rank-5	mAP
DGaitV2-P3D-B [10]	$\mathcal{L}_{tri}^{euc}$	70.8	85.7	62.9
DGaitV2-P3D-B [10]	ATL (Ours)	**73.6**	**86.7**	**65.9**
DGaitV2-P3D-L [10]	$\mathcal{L}_{tri}^{euc}$	74.2	86.9	67.1
DGaitV2-P3D-L [10]	ATL (Ours)	**76.8**	**87.4**	**68.5**

Improvement on Metrics. As shown in Table 1, the experimental results confirm significant performance gains over both DGaitV2-2D-L [10] and DGaitV2-P3D-L [10]: Rank-1 accuracy increases by 1.3%–2.6% and 1.3%–1.1% on Gait3D and GREW, respectively. ATL effectively rotate the gradients derived from x_p and x_n. This rotation enhances the gradient component in the radial direction, aligning it closer to the direction of x_p. Table 2 demonstrates ATL reduces $\mathcal{D}(x, x_p)$ while increases $\mathcal{D}(x, x_n)$, pulling x_p closer and pushing x_n far away. The reduced $\|x\|_2$ can be attributed to correct direction of the radial gradient, which moves x to x_p. Furthermore, ATL yields fewer unconverged triplets ($\mathcal{L}_{tri}^{num}$) compared to $\mathcal{L}_{tri}^{euc}$, demonstrating superior optimization convergence. As a result, ATL facilitates improved convergence and superior overall performance.

Table 5. Ablation study of the rotation strength r inside $\mathcal{R}(\mathbf{x},\mathbf{y})$ on Gait3D with Rank-1, 5 accuracy and mean Average Precision (%).

Method	Triplet Loss	r	Gait3D		
			Rank-1	Rank-5	mAP
DGaitV2-P3D-L [10]	$\mathcal{L}_{tri}^{euc}$	–	74.2	86.9	67.1
	ATL (Ours)	0.02	74.7	87.2	67.9
		0.05	**76.8**	**87.4**	**68.5**
		0.10	74.7	87.1	67.4

Comparison with Other Losses. In addition, several other margin-loss functions are commonly used in human identification, such as ArcFace [19], CosFace [20] and AdaFace [22]. To further evaluate the effectiveness of the proposed ATL, we compare it against these losses on the Gait3D using DGaitV2-P3D-L [10] model. As shown in Table 3, ATL achieves the best performance among all compared methods, further demonstrating its superiority.

Effectiveness in Different Scale. To further validate the effectiveness of ATL across different model sizes, we conduct comparative experiments on DGaitV2-P3D [10]. The results in Table 4 show that ATL improves the Rank-1 accuracy of DGaitV2-P3D [10] by 2.8% and 2.6%, and mAP by 3.0% and 1.4% on the Base and Large model scales, respectively. These findings indicate that ATL consistently enhances performance across both small and large scale models, demonstrating its robustness and general applicability.

4.3   Ablation Study

In the context of ATL, rotation strength r is introduced as a hyperparameter in $\mathcal{R}(\boldsymbol{x}, \boldsymbol{y})$. This section presents ablation experiments conducted to explore its impact. As proved in Sect. 3.2, in the later stage of training a larger rotation strength indeed has the effect of delaying the point, where the radial gradient of positive samples is surpassed by that of negative samples. However, the rotation of gradient influences the optimization process during the earlier stage of training as well. A more substantial change of the gradient leads to increased challenges in the convergence of the training process during the early phase.

To comprehensively evaluate the influence of rotation strength, we compare various rotation strength settings in the Table 5. The experimental findings indicate that when the rotation strength is set at 0.05, the overall performance across all evaluation metrics attains an optimal state. Consequently, based on these experimental results, we set the rotation strength to 0.05 for achieving the best performance in ATL for both Gait3D and GREW.

5   Conclusion

In this paper, we analyze the limitations of Euclidean metric in triplet loss $\mathcal{L}_{tri}^{euc}$ for gait recognition from the perspective of gradient decomposition and rotation. As the radial component towards $\boldsymbol{x}_p$ diminishes in the later training stage, we rotate the direction of $\mathcal{G}(\boldsymbol{x}, \boldsymbol{y})$ to move $\boldsymbol{x}$ closer to $\boldsymbol{x}_p$ while far away from $\boldsymbol{x}_n$ in the radial direction. Experimental results demonstrate that our ATL outperforms state-of-the-art gait recognition methods using silhouette input and show superiority to other margin-loss functions.

Acknowledgment. This work is partly supported by the National Natural Science Foundation of China (82441024).

References

1. Yu, W., Yu, H., Huang, Y., Wang, L.: Generalized inter-class loss for gait recognition. In: Proceedings of the 30th ACM International Conference on Multimedia, pp. 141–150. ACM, New York (2022)
2. Peng, G., Wang, Y., Zhao, Y., Zhang, S., Li, A.: GLGait: a global-local temporal receptive field network for gait recognition in the wild. In: Proceedings of the 32nd ACM International Conference on Multimedia, pp. 826–835. ACM, New York (2024)
3. Wang, Z., et al.: QAGait: revisit gait recognition from a quality perspective. In: AAAI Conference on Artificial Intelligence, vol. 38, pp. 5785–5793. AAAI, Menlo Park (2024)
4. Liao, R., Yu, S., An, W., Huang, Y.: A model-based gait recognition method with body pose and human prior knowledge. Pattern Recogn. **98**, 107069 (2020)
5. Shen, C., Fan, C., Wu, W., Wang, R., Huang, Q.G., Yu, S.: Lidargait: benchmarking 3d gait recognition with point clouds. In: IEEE/CVF Conference on Computer Vision and Pattern Recognition, pp. 1054–1063. IEEE Computer Society, Piscataway (2023)
6. Sarkar, S., Phillips, P.J., Liu, Z., Vega, I.R., Grother, P., Bowyer, K.W.: The humanid gait challenge problem: data sets, performance, and analysis. IEEE Trans. Pattern Anal. Mach. Intell. **27**(2), 162–177 (2005)
7. Zheng, J., Liu, X., Liu, W., He, L., Yan, C., Mei, T.: Gait recognition in the wild with dense 3D representations and a benchmark. In: IEEE/CVF Conference on Computer Vision and Pattern Recognition, pp. 20228–20237. IEEE Computer Society, Piscataway (2022)
8. Zhu, Z., et al.: Gait recognition in the wild: a benchmark. In: IEEE/CVF International Conference on Computer Vision, pp. 14789–14799. IEEE Computer Society, Piscataway (2021)
9. Dou, H., Zhang, P., Su, W., Yu, Y., Lin, Y., Li, X.: GaitGCI: generative counterfactual intervention for gait recognition. In: IEEE/CVF Conference on Computer Vision and Pattern Recognition, pp. 5578–5588. IEEE Computer Society, Piscataway (2023)
10. Fan, C., Hou, S., Huang, Y., Yu, S.: Exploring deep models for practical gait recognition. arXiv preprint arXiv:2303.03301 (2023)
11. Fan, C., Liang, J., Shen, C., Hou, S., Huang, Y., Yu, S.: OpenGait: revisiting gait recognition towards better practicality. In: IEEE/CVF Conference on Computer Vision and Pattern Recognition, pp. 9707–9716. IEEE Computer Society, Piscataway (2023)
12. Wang, M., et al.: DyGait: exploiting dynamic representations for highperformance gait recognition. In: IEEE/CVF Conference on Computer Vision and Pattern Recognition, pp. 13424–13433. IEEE Computer Society, Piscataway (2023)
13. Chao, H., He, Y., Zhang, J., Feng, J.: Gaitset: regarding gait as a set for cross-view gait recognition. In: AAAI Conference on Artificial Intelligence, vol. 33, pp. 8126–8133. AAAI, Menlo Park (2019)
14. Fan, C., et al.: Gaitpart: temporal part-based model for gait recognition. In: IEEE/CVF Conference on Computer Vision and Pattern Recognition, pp. 14225–14233. IEEE Computer Society, Piscataway (2020)
15. Lin, B., Zhang, S., Yu, X.: Gait Recognition via Effective GlobalLocal Feature Representation and Local Temporal Aggregation. In: IEEE/CVF International Conference on Computer Vision, pp. 14648–14656. IEEE Computer Society, Piscataway (2021)

16. Wang, L., Liu, B., Liang, F., Wang, B.: Hierarchical spatio-temporal representation learning for gait recognition. In: IEEE/CVF International Conference on Computer Vision, pp. 19639–19649. IEEE Computer Society, Piscataway (2023)
17. He, K., Zhang, X., Ren, S., Sun, J.: Deep residual learning for image recognition. In: IEEE/CVF Conference on Computer Vision and Pattern Recognition, pp. 770–778. IEEE Computer Society, Piscataway (2016)
18. Qiu, Z., Yao, T., Mei, T.: Learning spatio-temporal representation with pseudo-3D residual networks. In: IEEE/CVF International Conference on Computer Vision, pp. 5534–5542. IEEE Computer Society, Piscataway (2017)
19. Deng, J., Guo, J., Xue, N., Zafeiriou, S.: Arcface: additive angular margin loss for deep face recognition. In: IEEE/CVF Conference on Computer Vision and Pattern Recognition, pp. 4690–4699. IEEE Computer Society, Piscataway (2019)
20. Wang, H., et al.: Cosface: large margin cosine loss for deep face recognition. In: IEEE/CVF Conference on Computer Vision and Pattern Recognition, pp. 5265–5274. IEEE Computer Society, Piscataway (2018)
21. Luo, H., Gu, Y., Liao, X., Lai, S., Jiang, W.: Bag of tricks and a strong baseline for deep person re-identification. In: IEEE/CVF Conference on Computer Vision and Pattern Recognition Workshops. IEEE Computer Society, Piscataway (2019)
22. Kim, M., Jain, A. K., Liu, X.: Adaface: quality adaptive margin for face recognition. In: IEEE/CVF Conference on Computer Vision and Pattern Recognition, pp. 18750–18759. IEEE Computer Society, Piscataway (2022)

Action-Agnostic Pose-Based Gait Recognition

Hongsong Wang[1], Yingjie Cheng[2], and Jie Gui[2,3,4(✉)]

[1] School of Computer Science and Engineering, Southeast University, Nanjing, China
[2] School of Cyber Science and Engineering, Southeast University, Nanjing, China
[3] Purple Mountain Laboratories, Nanjing, China
[4] Engineering Research Center of Blockchain Application, Supervision and Management (Southeast University), Ministry of Education, Nanjing, China
guijie@seu.edu.cn

Abstract. Gait recognition has emerged as a promising biometric identification technique due to its non-invasive nature and distance operability. However, existing approaches struggle with robustness against scenarios across different actions with varying walking patterns. To address this issue, we study action-agnostic gait recognition based on human skeletons. We propose a Multi-Granularity Spatio-Temporal Mixer (MG-STM), a novel pose-based gait recognition framework that hierarchically partitions skeletal data into joint, part, and body-level representations to capture multi-granularity motion patterns. The encoder integrates self-attention mechanisms with large-kernel convolutions to learn action-invariant spatio-temporal features at different hierarchical levels. Experimental results on NTU RGB+D and CASIA-B demonstrate substantial improvements of our approach over the SOTA methods, and the ability to identify the person based on gait across different actions.

Keywords: Gait recognition · Action-agnostic · Human skeletons

1 Introduction

Gait recognition is a biometric application that aims to identify pedestrians by their walking patterns [1]. As a vision-based person retrieval problem, it seeks to achieve human identification from gait sequences captured by visual cameras. Unlike conventional biometrics, such as fingerprints and iris scans, gait recognition offers distinct advantages: it is noninvasive, requires no direct contact or active subject cooperation, and can be performed at a distance [2]. These properties make it especially effective in scenarios that involve low-resolution imagery, long-range observation, and real-world surveillance or security applications.

Human gait represents a complex biomechanical process that involves coordinated movement of multiple body segments, joints, and muscles. This intricate locomotion pattern is influenced by various anatomical and physiological factors,

W. Jia et al. (Eds.): CCBR 2025, LNCS 16360, pp. 271–281, 2026.
https://doi.org/10.1007/978-981-95-6123-0_26

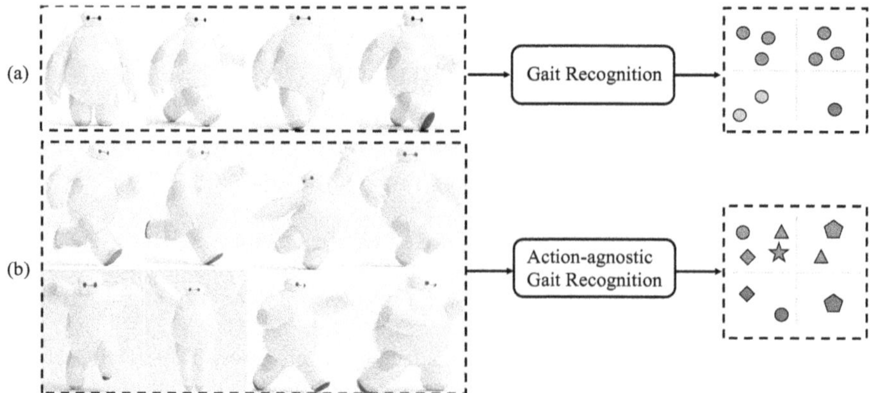

Fig. 1. Gait recognition vs. action-agnostic gait recognition. (a) Traditional silhouette-based gait recognition. (b) Our action-agnostic pose-based gait recognition which achieves robust person identification independent of specific walking behaviors. In the feature space, different colors denote different identifications, while different shapes represent different human actions.

including skeletal structure, muscle strength, joint flexibility, and neurological control mechanisms. Consequently, each individual exhibits a distinctive gait signature that remains relatively stable over time.

Most existing gait recognition methods primarily rely on silhouettes as input modality [3–5], which present inherent limitations: silhouettes contain only binary values, their quality depends heavily on extraction algorithms, and they may not capture sufficient discriminative information. In addition, conventional approaches often assume consistent walking behaviors. In fact, there are many types of forward-walking behaviors, such as running, jumping, dancing, or walking while waving the limbs. Existing gait recognition methods are limited in handling real-world scenarios where individuals may perform varying actions.

To overcome these limitations, we introduce a novel problem of action-agnostic pose-based gait recognition, as shown in Fig. 1. Accordingly, we propose Multi-Granularity Spatio-Temporal Mixer (MG-STM), which addresses the fundamental challenge of recognizing individuals regardless of their specific actions or behaviors, capturing richer structural information from skeletal data and making it more robust for practical applications. In the MG-STM, we introduce a hierarchical partitioning strategy that organizes skeletal data into joint, part, and body-level representations and propose a Spatial Convolutional Transformer Mixer (SCTM) module that integrates self-attention mechanisms and large-kernel convolutions to learn features across these hierarchical levels.

The main contributions are as follows: First, we introduce the problem of action-agnostic pose-based gait recognition and propose a Multi-Granularity Spatio-Temporal Mixer (MG-STM) to tackle it. Second, we propose a hierarchical partitioning strategy with joint, part, and body-level representations to capture motion correlations across multiple levels for gait recognition. Third, comprehensive experimental results demonstrate the robustness of our approach for gait recognition, highlighting its applicability in scenarios where individuals deliberately perform actions to conceal their natural gait.

2   Related Work

Pose-Based Gait Recognition: Pose-based gait recognition has gained popularity recently. It uses sequential human skeleton data instead of silhouettes. GaitGraph [6] employs spatial-temporal graph convolutional networks (ST-GCNs) and learns an adaptive adjacency matrix to capture motion features from skeleton sequences. GaitGraph2 [7] extends this idea with multi-branch graph modeling and achieves superior performance. SDHF-GCN [8] identifies redundant features in gait representations and improves learning efficiency by selectively suppressing them within the graph structure. Beyond graph-based approaches, PoseGait [9] uses 3D pose data to construct multi-feature vectors, which are processed by convolutional neural networks to learn spatial-temporal gait features. GaitHeat [10] introduces a heatmap-based representation of pose, replacing raw joint coordinates with multi-channel heatmaps. SkeletonGait [11] has also demonstrated promising results by mapping keypoints to heatmaps. With the advent of attention mechanisms [12], recent studies, including GaitTR [13] and GaitMixer [14], have employed self-attention to effectively capture long-range spatial dependencies. Additionally, these models incorporate large-kernel temporal convolutions to extract comprehensive temporal information, achieving robust performance in modeling global gait patterns. While previous methods are limited to handling normal walking, our method is more robust and capable of identifying individuals even when they are performing actions concurrently with walking.

IMU-Based Gait Recognition: Similar to pose-based gait recognition, IMU-based gait recognition also represents human gait as time-series data of joint movements. IMU-based gait recognition leverages the portability of inertial measurement units (IMUs) to capture unique gait patterns. Hong et al. [15] propose a mass vector representation combined with DTW to handle speed variations in silhouette-based gait sequences. Similarly, Sun et al. [16] propose an accelerometer-based method tailored for older adults. However, visual methods remain vulnerable to occlusion, viewpoint changes, and environmental noise, which limits their practical utility. To address these issues, researchers have explored alternative sensing modalities. For example, CL-Gait [17] introduce a cross-modality framework combining camera and LiDAR data. Likewise, occlusion-aware visual methods have been proposed by Gupta et al. [18], yet they still require clean visual input, which may not always be feasible. In addition, IMU-based gait recognition methods, particularly those using smartphones, have emerged as practical and robust alternatives. Andersson et al. [19] use smartphone IMUs to extract hip joint angles and achieved 88.9% precision using classical ML classifiers. Rana et al. [20] demonstrate that a single ankle-mounted smartphone can effectively support gait identification. Furthermore, IMU-based

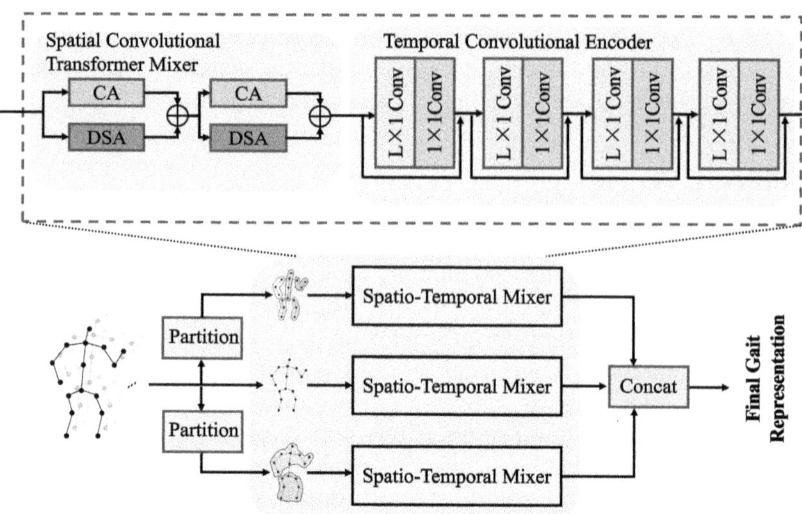

Fig. 2. Overview of the Multi-Granularity Spatio-Temporal Mixer. Input skeletal sequences are hierarchically partitioned into joint, part, and body levels. Each level is then processed by parallel Spatial Convolutional Transformer Mixers with CA and DSA, followed by Temporal Convolutional Encoders. Finally, multi-granularity features are concatenated to form the final gait representation.

human activity recognition (HAR) approaches have shown promise in biometric identification beyond gait-specific patterns. For example, Mekruksavanich et al. [21] apply CNN and LSTM models to wearable IMU data in daily activities, achieving a precision greater than 92%. Compared with visual biometrics, these behavioral signatures offer better privacy and adaptability for real-world deployment.

3   Multi-granularity Spatio-Temporal Mixer

We propose Multi-Granularity Spatio-Temporal Mixer (MG-STM) for pose-based gait recognition, as illustrated in Fig. 2. This method organizes skeletal data into joint, part, and body-level representations, facilitating the extraction of temporal and spatial features across multiple hierarchical levels. The MG-STM consists of a Spatial Convolutional Transformer Mixer (SCTM) and a temporal convolutional encoder, designed to learn spatial attention relationships and long-range temporal correlations at each hierarchical level.

3.1   Multi-granularity Partition

The human skeleton can be regarded as a structured system consisting of bones and their connecting joints. This structure partitions the body into distinct components, such as the limbs, and larger regions, such as the torso [22]. It is necessary to supplement the gait representation learning with detailed information on the specific parts of the body that influence movement expression. This allows for the correct identification of different individuals performing the same action and the recognition of the same individual across different actions. In addition, there are motion correlations between certain joints during limb movements. Recognizing these correlations, which are closely related to individual characteristics, is crucial for identity recognition tasks that are independent of behavior. To effectively capture both joint-level nuances and their motion correlations, we introduce a structured partitioning strategy along with a hierarchical multi-stage feature learning framework.

The raw data consists of joints that directly serve as the joint-level partition. As illustrated in Fig. 3, the data are further divided into body-level and part-level motion partitions. Since learning the spatial relationships between skeletons or body parts is necessary, all partitions are based on the spatial dimension, without division in the temporal dimension. For the part-level motion partition strategy, the human body is divided into five parts: head, torso, left arm, right arm, left leg, and right leg. For the body-level motion partition, the body is divided into the upper and lower body.

Following data partition based on the proposed strategy, we utilize the Spatial Convolutional Transformer Mixer (SCTM) module to capture motion relationships across three levels. The SCTM integrates a self-attention mechanism and large-kernel convolutions to independently learn spatio-temporal features for each level. These extracted features are concatenated to form a new vector that represents the current sequence.

Given an input skeletal sequence $A = \{a \in \mathbb{R}^{T_{in} \times V_{in} \times C_{in}}\}$, the data are partitioned according to the joint-level, part-level, and body-level strategies. The resulting sequences at each level $l \in \{k, p, b\}$, denoted as $A^{(k)}$, $A^{(p)}$, and $A^{(b)}$, respectively, are processed by three distinct SCTM modules. Each module employs independently learned parameters to minimize cross-granularity interference:

$$F^{(l)} = \text{SCTM}(A^{(l)}). \tag{1}$$

The learned features are then concatenated through a multi-feature fusion module to construct a comprehensive representation:

$$F_{final} = \mathcal{F}_c(F^{(k)}, F^{(p)}, F^{(b)}) = [F^{(k)} \parallel F^{(p)} \parallel F^{(b)}], \tag{2}$$

where $\parallel$ denotes channel-wise concatenation. Through the channel concatenation operation of the multi-level feature fusion module $\mathcal{F}_c$, the model achieves an organic fusion of cross-granularity features: high-frequency fine-grained features at the joint level complement low-frequency global features at the body level, while part-level limb coordination features serve as an intermediary. This hierarchical and complementary feature integration strategy ensures the completeness of the motion feature space, offering stronger feature representation capability compared to single-granularity approaches.

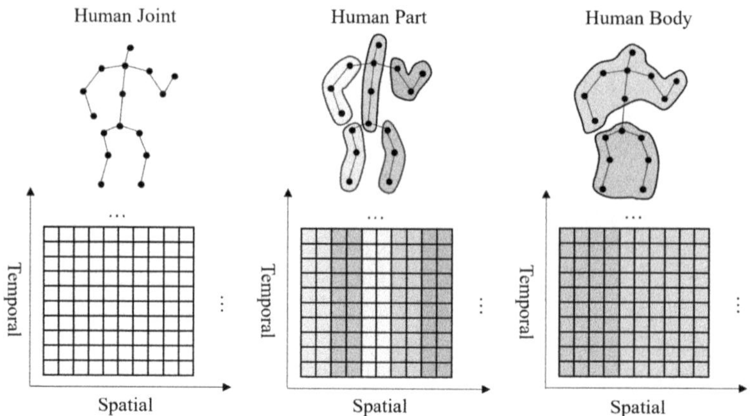

Fig. 3. Hierarchical Partitioning Strategy for Multi-Granularity Feature Learning. The framework organizes skeletal data into joint, part, and body levels. The joint level processes individual joints, part level groups joints into five anatomical regions (shown in different colors), and body level aggregates into upper/lower body regions. Each level captures motion correlations at different granularities.

3.2 Spatial Convolutional Transformer Mixer

The SCTM module consists of two attention sub-modules: Convolutional Attention (CA) and Dense Shift Attention (DSA). The CA module first performs a channel-wise spatial convolution on the mapped embedding vector $\mathbf{X} \in \mathbb{R}^{N \times T \times V \times C}$ to enhance local feature interactions within the sequence:

$$\mathbf{F}_{conv} = \sigma(\text{Conv1}\mathcal{D}(\mathbf{X}^{\top}; \mathbf{W}_c))^{\top} + \mathbf{X}, \tag{3}$$

where $\mathbf{W}_c \in \mathbb{R}^{k \times C \times C}$ is the kernel of 1D convolution, and σ is the ReLU activation function. Dilated convolution is utilized to capture local joint motion patterns, allowing the network to expand the receptive field without increasing the number of parameters.

Subsequently, multi-head self-attention is applied to the convolutional features $\mathbf{F}_{conv}$ to model long-range joint dependencies and global feature interactions:

$$\mathbf{F}_{attn} = \text{Softmax}\left(\frac{(\mathbf{F}_{conv}\mathbf{W}_Q)(\mathbf{F}_{conv}\mathbf{W}_K)^{\top}}{\sqrt{d}}\right)(\mathbf{F}_{conv}, \mathbf{W}_V), \tag{4}$$

where $\mathbf{W}_Q$, $\mathbf{W}_K$, and $\mathbf{W}_V \in \mathbb{R}^{C \times d}$ are the attention projection matrices. To facilitate information fusion, preserve original input, and enable cross-layer feature reuse while maintaining the continuity of original motion during global interaction, a residual skip connection is incorporated into the module. The final output of the CA module is formulated by:

$$\mathbf{X}_{out} = \text{MLP}(\text{LayerNorm}(\mathbf{F}_{attn} + \mathbf{X})). \tag{5}$$

The DSA module adopts a dual-branch structure, where each branch includes a multi-head self-attention layer and an MLP sub-layer. One branch corrects feature displacements through a learned displacement matrix to handle speed variations, while the other preserves original motion patterns. The first branch employs learnable displacement matrices with sparse sampling for motion speed robustness. The displacement operation is expressed as follows:

$$\mathbf{F}_{shift} = \mathbf{W}_2 \cdot \mathrm{ReLU}(\mathbf{W}_1 \cdot \mathbf{X}^\top) + \mathbf{X}^\top, \tag{6}$$

where $\mathbf{W}_1, \mathbf{W}_2 \in \mathbb{R}^{T \times T}$ are displacement matrices that learn feature alignment patterns under varying motion speeds through backpropagation. The sparse sampling mechanism ensures keyframe preservation, preventing the displacement operation from disrupting critical motion phases. The second branch shares parameters with the first in both the multi-head self-attention and MLP layers, projecting displaced and original features into a unified latent space to mitigate feature drift from different input transformations. Since variations stem exclusively from input transformations rather than model-induced bias, this design facilitates efficient complementary feature learning. The final output of the DSA module is obtained by integrating the features of both branches.

$$\mathbf{X}_{out} = \mathrm{Path}_1(\mathbf{F}_{shift}) + \mathrm{Path}_2(\mathbf{X}), \tag{7}$$

Finally, the outputs of the CA and DSA modules are integrated to extract salient spatial features from the input data:

$$\mathbf{y} = \mathrm{CA}(\mathbf{X}) + \mathrm{DSA}(\mathbf{X}). \tag{8}$$

3.3 Temporal Convolutional Encoder

The temporal convolutional encoder consists of a large-kernel convolution (L × 1), a 1 × 1 channel convolution, and a residual connection. The large kernel enables the model to capture long-range motion patterns within a single layer, alleviating information degradation caused by deep stacking. This cascaded design decouples feature learning into two orthogonal subspaces: the temporal dimension models joint trajectory continuity, while the channel dimension enhances cross-joint interaction and reduces dimensionality through the 1 × 1 convolution.

4 Experiment

4.1 Datasets and Experimental Setup

We conduct experiments on two widely used benchmarks for gait recognition: NTU RGB+D and CASIA-B.

NTU RGB+D is a large-scale dataset with 56,880 video samples from 40 subjects across 60 action classes, including daily activities, health-related actions, and interactions. Each sample provides synchronized data from three Kinect V2 sensors: RGB videos (1920 × 1080), depth maps, infrared videos (512 × 424), and 3D skeletal data with 25 joints per frame. This multi-modal diversity makes it ideal for evaluating gait recognition under real-world conditions.

CASIA-B, developed by the Chinese Academy of Sciences, contains gait sequences from 124 subjects captured across 11 view angles (0°–180°) under three conditions: normal walking (NM, 6 sequences), walking with bag (BG, 2 sequences), and walking with coat (CL, 2 sequences). The dataset uses binary silhouette frames, making it suitable for analyzing view-invariant and condition-robust gait features.

The model is trained for 100 epochs using Adam with a learning rate of 0.001, cosine annealing, and cross-entropy loss.

4.2 Performance Comparison

The proposed MG-STM method is evaluated on the NTU RGB+D and CASIA-B datasets for gait recognition.

Table 1. Results of gait recognition on the NTU RGB+D dataset.

Method	Rank-1
GaitMixer [14]	29.40
GPGait [23]	30.57
MG-STM (ours)	**42.50**

Table 2. Results of pose-based gait recognition on the CASIA-B dataset.

Method	NM	BG	CL	Mean
GaitMixer [14]	91.70	**80.74**	78.82	**83.82**
GPGait [23]	**94.07**	79.51	68.93	80.84
MG-STM (ours)	92.36	78.04	**79.42**	83.27

As shown in Table 1, we compare the performance of MG-STM with previous gait recognition methods. Our proposed method achieves the highest Rank-1 accuracy of 42.50% on the NTU RGB+D dataset(+12% on GPGait and +13.1% on GaitMixers), demonstrating superior performance. Furthermore, we present the results for the CASIA-B dataset in Table 2, which evaluates performance in three conditions of the dataset.

4.3 Ablation Study and Parameter Analysis

We conduct comprehensive ablation studies on the NTU RGB+D dataset to evaluate the effectiveness of each component in our proposed method. Specifically, we investigate the impact of hierarchical partitioning, spatial block configuration, and temporal block configuration.

As shown in Fig. 4(a), the complete model achieves a rank-1 accuracy of 42.5%. Removing features at the joint level leads to the most significant performance drop, reducing accuracy to 28. 9%, highlighting the critical importance of joint level information. Excluding part-level features results in a drop in 40. 2%, while removing body-level features decreases performance to 41.0%. These results demonstrate that all hierarchical levels contribute meaningfully to overall performance, with joint-level features being the most crucial.

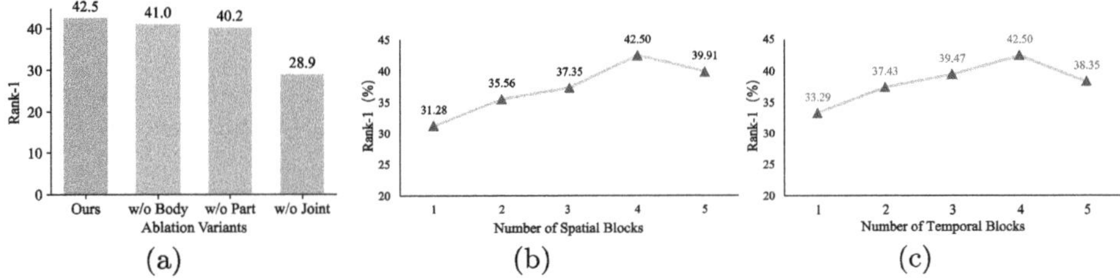

Fig. 4. Ablation Study. (a) Multi-granularity ablation study showing the contribution of each granularity level, (b) Impact of spatial block number on model performance, and (c) Impact of temporal block number on model performance.

Figure 4(b) and Fig. 4(c) show consistent trends for both spatial and temporal block configurations. Performance improves from approximately 3133% when using a single block to a peak of 42.5% with four blocks. Increasing the number of blocks to five leads to a performance decline of around 38- 40%, suggesting that the use of four blocks provides the best trade-off between model capacity and overfitting.

5   Conclusion

In this work, we study the problem of action-agnostic pose-based gait recognition and propose the Multi-Granularity Spatio-Temporal Mixer (MG-STM). The MG-STM features a hierarchical architecture with three decoding levels (joint, part, and body) and a spatio-temporal encoder, which together model spatial dependencies and long-range temporal relationships. Experiments on the NTU RGB+D dataset show the MG-STM achieves 42.5% rank-1 accuracy, surpassing state-of-the-art methods by 11.9%. These results validate the feasibility of action-agnostic pose-based gait recognition and its applicability in scenarios where individuals disguise their characteristic gait with concurrent body movements and actions.

Acknowledgments. This work was supported by the Jiangsu Science Foundation under Grant BK20230833, the National Natural Science Foundation of China under Grant 62302093 and 62172090, the Start-up Research Fund of Southeast University under Grant RF1028623097 and the Open Research Fund of the State Key Laboratory of Multimodal Artificial Intelligence Systems under Grant E5SP060116.

References

1. Sarkar, S., Phillips, P.J., Liu, Z., Vega, I.R., Grother, P., Bowyer, K.W.: The humanid gait challenge problem: data sets, performance, and analysis. IEEE TPAMI **27**(2), 162–177 (2005)
2. Nixon, M.S., Tan, T., Chellappa, R.: Human Identification Based on Gait, vol. 4. Springer, Cham (2010)
3. Chao, H., He, Y., Zhang, J., Feng, J.: Gaitset: regarding gait as a set for cross-view gait recognition. In: AAAI, vol. 33, pp. 8126–8133 (2019)
4. Fan, C., et al.: Gaitpart: temporal part-based model for gait recognition. In: CVPR, pp. 14225–14233 (2020)
5. Lin, B., Zhang, S., Yu, X.: Gait recognition via effective global-local feature representation and local temporal aggregation. In: ICCV, pp. 14648–14656 (2021)
6. Teepe, T., Khan, A., Gilg, J., Herzog, F., Hörmann, S., Rigoll, G.: Gaitgraph: graph convolutional network for skeleton-based gait recognition. In: IEEE International Conference on Image Processing, pp. 2314–2318. IEEE (2021)
7. Teepe, T., Gilg, J., Herzog, F., Hörmann, S., Rigoll, G.: Towards a deeper understanding of skeleton-based gait recognition. In: IEEE/CVF CVPR Workshops, pp. 1568–1576. IEEE (2022)
8. Liu, X., You, Z., He, Y., Bi, S., Wang, J.: Symmetry-driven hyper feature GCN for skeleton-based gait recognition. PR **125**, 108520 (2022)
9. Liao, R., Yu, S., An, W., Huang, Y.: A model-based gait recognition method with body pose and human prior knowledge. PR **98**, 107069 (2020)
10. Fu, Y., et al.: Cut out the middleman: Revisiting pose-based gait recognition. In: ECCV, pp. 112–128. Springer, Cham (2024)
11. Fan, C., Ma, J., Jin, D., Shen, C., Yu, S.: Skeletongait: gait recognition using skeleton maps. In: Proceedings of the AAAI Conference on Artificial Intelligence, vol. 38, pp. 1662–1669 (2024)
12. Vaswani, A., et al.: Attention is all you need. In: NeurIPS, vol. 30 (2017)
13. Zhang, C., Chen, X.P., Han, G.Q., Liu, X.J.: Spatial transformer network on skeleton-based gait recognition. Expert. Syst. **40**(6), e13244 (2023)
14. Pinyoanuntapong, E., Ali, A., Wang, P., Lee, M., Chen, C.: Gaitmixer: skeleton-based gait representation learning via wide-spectrum multi-axial mixer. In: ICASSP, pp. 1–5. IEEE (2023)
15. Hong, S., Lee, H., Nizami, I.F., An, S.J., Kim, E.: Human identification based on gait analysis. In: ICCAS, pp. 2234–2237. IEEE (2007)
16. Sun, F., Zang, W., Gravina, R., Fortino, G., Li, Y.: Gait-based identification for elderly users in wearable healthcare systems. Inf. Fusion **53**, 134–144 (2020)
17. Guo, W., Liang, Y., Pan, Z., Xi, Z., Feng, J., Zhou, J.: Camera-lidar cross-modality gait recognition. In: ECCV, pp. 439–455. Springer, Cham (2024)
18. Gupta, A., Chellappa, R.: You can run but not hide: improving gait recognition with intrinsic occlusion type awareness. In: Proceedings of the IEEE/CVF Winter Conference on Applications of Computer Vision, pp. 5893–5902 (2024)
19. Andersson, R., Bermejo-García, J., Agujetas, R., Cronhjort, M., Chilo, J.: Smartphone IMU sensors for human identification through hip joint angle analysis. Sensors **24**(15), 4769 (2024)
20. Talha, M., Soomro, H.A., Naeem, N., Ali, E., Kyrarini, M.: Human identification using a smartphone motion sensor and gait analysis. In: Proceedings of the 15th International Conference on PErvasive Technologies Related to Assistive Environments, pp. 197–202 (2022)

21. Mekruksavanich, S., Jitpattanakul, A.: Biometric user identification based on human activity recognition using wearable sensors: an experiment using deep learning models. Electronics **10**(3), 308 (2021)
22. Du, Y., Wang, W., Wang, L.: Hierarchical recurrent neural network for skeleton based action recognition. In: CVPR, pp. 1110–1118 (2015)
23. Fu, Y., Meng, S., Hou, S., Hu, X., Huang, Y.: Gpgait: generalized pose-based gait recognition. In: ICCV, pp. 19538–19547. IEEE (2023)

DeepSNNGait: A Spiking Neural Network Framework for Robust Gait Recognition

Kun Liu, Xiaochuan Liao, Zizhe Zhou, Wenxiong Kang, Weijie Sun, and M. Saad Shakeel[(✉)]

The School of Automation Science and Engineering,
South China University of Technology, Guangzhou 510641, China
`saadshakeel@scut.edu.cn`

Abstract. Gait recognition (GR) has emerged as a promising biometric technology due to its non-contact nature and long-range identification capabilities, offering transformative potential in surveillance, healthcare, and intelligent systems. Despite significant progress in gait biometrics, current GR algorithms continue to struggle against dynamic gait variations, such as diverse viewpoints, appearance changes, and occlusion. To alleviate the aforementioned issues, this work introduces a spiking neural networks (SNNs)-based deep architecture, designed to optimize spatio-temporal gait feature modeling. The proposed architecture features two principal innovations: (1) a novel gait recognition framework that leverages the sparse activation and event-driven processing of SNNs to model temporal dynamics directly from gait sequences, marking the first application of SNNs in silhouette-based gait recognition; and (2) an SNNBlock that integrates 3D convolution and Leaky Integrate-and-Fire (LIF) neurons in a parallel pathway, capturing gait periodicity and spatial correlations effectively via dual branch structure. Experimental evaluations on multiple outdoor gait datasets demonstrate that the threshold dynamics inherent to LIF neurons enable superior temporal encoding of gait patterns, while the SNNBlock's hierarchical spiking mechanism enhances regional perceptual weighting. This research not only establishes the novel framework for high-performing gait recognition but also advances the theoretical development of SNNs in computer vision, providing a scalable solution for real-world deployment.

Keywords: Gait recognition · Leaky Integrate-and-Fire (LIF) neuron · Spiking neural network · Spatio-temporal modeling · Pseudo-3D convolution

1 Introduction

Gait recognition (GR) has been established as a critical non-contact, long-range biometric modality, offering tremendous potential in public security, biomedical diagnostics, and intelligent transportation systems. Unlike conventional biometric approaches (e.g., fingerprint or facial recognition), GR demonstrates robustness to occlusion and low-light conditions while operating effectively at a distance

W. Jia et al. (Eds.): CCBR 2025, LNCS 16360, pp. 282–292, 2026.
https://doi.org/10.1007/978-981-95-6123-0_27

exceeding 50 m without requiring subject cooperation. Despite these advantages, prevailing methodologies exhibit significant limitations in real-world deployment scenarios, particularly under clothing variations, occlusions caused by carried objects, and dynamic environmental perturbations. These persistent challenges necessitate the development of robust and computationally efficient frameworks with discriminative feature learning capabilities.

Recent advancements in deep learning architectures have substantially advanced GR research where dominant approaches concentrates on learning features either from silhouettes or skeleton-based gait modalities. The silhouette-based GR methods [1–3] remain vulnerable to illumination variations and shadow artifacts, while skeleton-based alternatives [4,5] require precise joint localization that becomes problematic under low-resolution and motion blur conditions. A fundamental constraint in current frameworks involves isotropic processing of the complete gait silhouette, where convolutional operations apply uniform attention weights across all spatial regions. This approach contradicts biological evidence indicating spatial heterogeneity in discriminative gait information—limb motion patterns (e.g., knee flexion angles) and joint trajectories contribute three to four times more to identification accuracy than static torso regions. Notably, Takemura et al. [6] demonstrated that using thigh angular velocity variations alone can achieve 87% classification accuracy, whereas torso texture features contributes less than 12% in occluded environments.

To address these limitations, this study proposes *DeepSNNGait*, a novel GR framework based on spiking neural networks specifically engineered for silhouette-based GR applications. As the third-generation neural networks, SNNs [7] exploit sparse activation mechanisms and event-driven computation to model temporal dynamics with exceptional efficiency. While recent work like GaitSpike [8] has integrated SNNs with event cameras for motion, our proposed architecture introduces two key innovations: (1) the first deep learning model integrating SNNs for silhouette-based GR, leveraging their biologically inspired temporal encoding to directly capture motion patterns from sequential data without handcrafted time modules; (2) a specialized SNN unit with parallel feature pathways to capture gait periodicity and spatial correlations. By combining biologically plausible LIF dynamics with spatio-temporal feature decoupling, the SNNBlock enables hierarchical temporal encoding across abstraction levels—low-level neurons focus on local limb kinematics, while high-level ones synthesize global gait cycles. This design enhances occlusion/clothing robustness and reduces redundant feature interference via spike sparsity.

Comprehensive experimental evaluations on multiple benchmark gait datasets validate the superior capability of our method in addressing real-world GR complexities, particularly under dynamic occlusion and clothing variations.

2 Related Work

2.1 Appearance-Based Gait Recognition

The existing appearance-based gait recognition methods primarily rely on shape information derived from binary silhouette images or RGB sequences for feature learning. Notably, Chao et al. [1] revolutionized the field by treating gait sequences as unordered sets and employed max-pooling operation to compress frame-level spatial features, achieving remarkable performance through its elegant design. Fan et al. [2] extends this paradigm by exploring local silhouette details while explicitly modeling temporal dependencies. To address limitations in global feature modeling, Lin et al. [16] proposed a 3D-CNN based framework for jointly learning spatio-temporal representation from global and local perspectives. Huang et al. [3] proposed adaptive-scale 3D convolution operations for limb feature extraction and Wang et al. [20] proposed learning spatial-temporal representations from dynamic body segments. Fan et al. [21] introduced a residual learning-based backbone, GaitBase, to enhance performance on unconstrained datasets through network depth optimization. Later, a series of ResNet-based DeepGaitV2 architectures were introduced to explore the gait recognition performance in more challenging real-world conditions. These models validates the positive correlation between model depth and recognition accuracy. Statistical analyses demonstrate the dominance of appearance-based methods in GR research due to their capabilities of learning effective spatio-temporal feature representation.

2.2   Spiking Neural Networks

Recent research efforts have demonstrated significant advancements in spiking neural network (SNN) architectures. Zheng et al. [9] developed a threshold-dependent batch normalization (tdBN) method through spatiotemporal back-propagation, enabling effective training of deep SNN models containing up to 50 layers. Concurrently, Fang et al. [10] introduced the SEW ResNet framework for deep SNN residual learning to mitigate gradient vanishing issues. Subsequent work by the same group established a training algorithm that optimizes individual neuron thresholds to enhance SNN performance. In the domain of attention-integrated SNN development, Shi et al. [11] proposed a dual-layer attention mechanism to refine local feature extraction and implemented the SpikingResformer architecture based on ResNet principles. Wang et al. [12] further advanced this paradigm by integrating self-attention mechanism with feature pruning through stochastic spiking neural masking, effectively reducing computational costs while maintaining accuracy. These innovations have facilitated SNN deployment across diverse applications including medical diagnosis [13], optical flow estimation [14], and action recognition [15]. While our proposed method represents the initial integration of conventional SNN frameworks in appearance-based GR research, emerging advanced SNN architectures and training methodologies offer substantial opportunities for innovation in biometric identification systems.

3   Method

3.1   Overview

Our proposed network's architecture is based on ResNet-style that incorporates multi-level SNN blocks, as illustrated in Fig. 1. The initial feature extraction is performed through a standard 2D convolutional layer, with subsequent processing conducted through sequential feature extraction stages (i.e., Layer 1 to Layer 4). Layer 1 utilizes a pseudo-3D convolutional residual block to establish foundational feature representations. Layers 2 and 3 integrate conventional residual blocks with corresponding SNN block, creating a hybrid configuration comprising traditional convolutional operations and spiking activation mechanisms. Layer 4 exclusively employs non-spiking residual structures to consolidate high-level semantic features. The final feature representation is processed through hierarchical pyramid pooling (HPP), temporal pooling (TP), and classification heads to yield the final gait representation and recognition output, respectively.

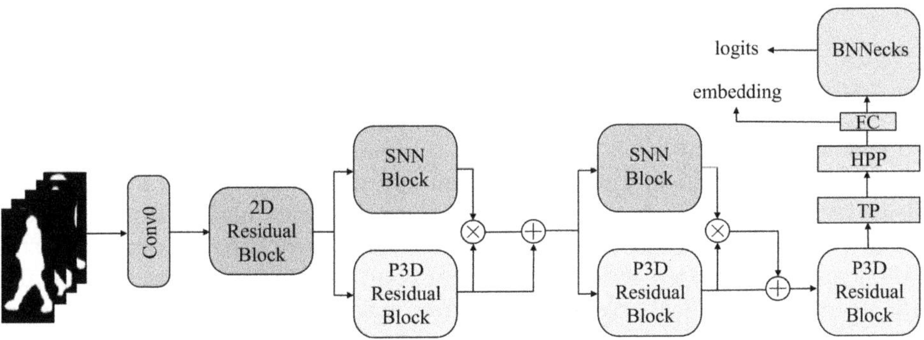

Fig. 1. The architecture of proposed DeepSNNGait. The SNNBlock and P3D blocks are connected in parallel, and their output features are weighted before being fused through a residual connection.

3.2   SNN-Based GR Framework

To overcome the limitations of single-branch architectures (i.e., DeepGaitV2-2D) in simultaneously capturing temporal dynamics and spatio-temporal correlations, we propose an SNN-based GR framework that integrates SNNs with pseudo-3D convolution operations to model dynamic motion patterns and static spatial correlations, Fig. 1 illustrates our proposed SNN-based GR framework. Specifically, the SNN component leverages the temporal encoding capabilities of LIF neurons to capture gait periodicity, while pseudo-3D convolutions extract spatio-temporal features through volumetric kernel decomposition. The learned complementary features are fused via an adaptive region-specific mechanism combining element-wise multiplication and additive attention, which emphasizes discriminative limb regions while suppressing non-informative static torso areas. This design enables hierarchical learning of dynamic motion patterns (via SNN temporal encoding) and static spatial correlations (via pseudo-3D convolutions), effectively addressing the limitations of uni-modal feature extraction approaches.

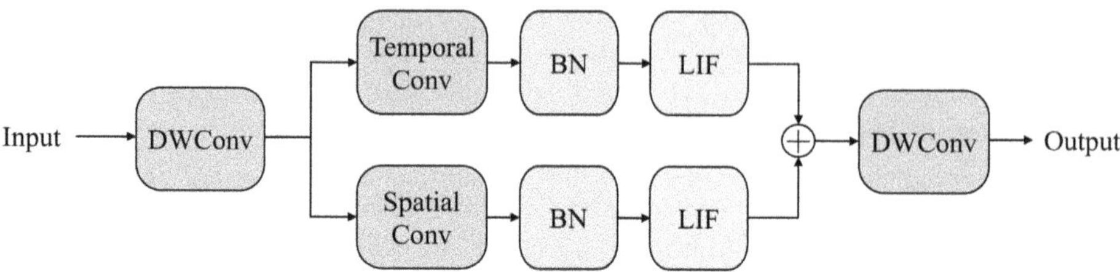

Fig. 2. SNNBlock architecture. The temporal and spatial features are processed separately within the module, and LIF neurons are employed to activate different temporal frames.

3.3 SNN Block

To enable adaptive saliency attention in complex gait recognition scenarios, we propose the SNN block (Fig. 2), which integrates bio-inspired dynamic mechanisms with spatio-temporal feature decoupling. The module implements a temporally memory-enhanced feature extraction framework through multi-timestep LIF neurons integrated with conventional convolution operations. Specifically, LIF neurons encode gait sequence dynamics into sparse spike signals via membrane potential accumulation and threshold-triggering mechanisms, effectively emulating biological nervous system processing of sequential information. This architecture enables direct capture of critical dynamic gait characteristics, including limb swing rhythms and joint trajectories without requiring manually engineered temporal modeling components.

At the feature extraction level, the SNNBlock employs a spatio-temporal decoupled convolution strategy that separates spatial feature extraction and temporal dependency modeling into sequential processing stages. The spatial convolution operation prioritize local edge and texture analysis of gait silhouettes, while temporal convolutions model inter-frame motion variations through sliding window mechanisms. This architectural decoupling enhances robustness against occlusions and clothing variations while minimizing redundant feature interference through spike signal sparsity.

The module further implements hierarchical spiking activation through cascaded multi-level LIF neuron networks. Each LIF layer maintains temporal modeling capabilities across abstraction levels, enabling adaptive learning of temporal patterns at different semantic depths. Lower-level LIF neurons demonstrate sensitivity to localized limb kinematics, while higher-order LIF layers synthesize global gait cycle characteristics through temporal integration. This hierarchical temporal encoding mechanism significantly enhances model robustness under challenging conditions such as low-frame-rate sequences or partial occlusion scenarios.

4   Experiment

4.1   Dataset

The diversity and scene adaptability of datasets impact the performance and application scope of algorithms. Keeping this in mind, we conducted experiments on three mainstream complex outdoor gait datasets, including SUSTech1K [17], Gait3D [19], and CCPG [18].

The SUSTech1K dataset collects gait data from 1,050 subjects in complex real-world scenarios, constructing over 200,000 synchronized multi-modal sequences through simultaneous deployment of RGB cameras and LiDAR sensors. It covers challenging test conditions including indoor-outdoor environments, low-lighting, diverse occlusion scenarios, and dynamic background interference.

The Gait3D dataset captures natural walking data from 4,000 subjects in a large-scale indoor supermarket environment, building an extensive collection of over 250,000 gait sequences. Its core value lies in capturing uncontrolled real-world complexities, including natural illumination variations, irregular walking speeds, frequent pedestrian occlusions, diverse carried objects, and dynamic background interference.

The CCPG dataset contains 200 subjects and over 16,000 sequences captured in both indoor and outdoor environments. The dataset is specifically designed to study gait recognition under three cloth changing settings, including full cloth changing (CL), Ups-changing (UP) and pants-changing (DN). In addition, objects carrying bag-packs (BG) are also included to make the testing scenario more realistic.

4.2   Implementation Details

Preprocessing. All silhouette images are first aligned using the size normalization method proposed in [6] and then resized to the dimension of 64×44.

Training Configurations. We implemented our proposed method using an open-source GR framework, OpenGait [21]. The DeepGaitV2-P3D served as the primary backbone in our method. For training, we utilized an SGD optimizer with an initial learning rate of 0.1 and weight decay of 0.0005. Table 1 presents the main training hyper-parameters for all the three datasets. We utilized the same spatial data augmentation strategy as proposed by OpenGait [21]. During training, a fixed-frame sequential sampling strategy is applied across all the experiment settings.

Evaluation Metrics. For the Gait3D dataset, we report the results in terms of three metrics: (1) rank-wise accuracy (i.e., Rank-1 (R1) and Rank-5 (R5)), mean average precision (mAP), and mean inverse negative penalty (mINP). For the SUSTech1K dataset, we report the individual rank-1 accuracy under different test scenarios (i.e., Normal, Bag, Clothing, etc.) along with the overall rank-1 and rank-5 accuracies for each scenario. Similarly, for the CCPG dataset, we reported both the individual recognition accuracy and their mean for all four categories (i.e., CL, UP, DN, and BG). All performance metrics were averaged across three independent experimental runs with different initialization seeds.

Table 1. Implementation details. The batch size is represented as (q, p, k) where q, p, and k indicates the IDs, sequences per ID, and frames per sequence, respectively.

DataSet	Batch Size	Milestones	Steps
Gait3D	(32, 4, 30)	(20k, 40k, 50k)	60k
SUSTech1K	(8, 8, 10)	(20k, 30k, 40k)	50k
CCPG	(8, 16, 30)	(20k, 40k, 50k)	60k

4.3   Comparative Analysis

To demonstrate the effectiveness of our proposed framework, we compare its performance with both shallow and deep GR methods. The comparative results are shown in Tables 2 and 3, respectively.

Results on SUSTech1K. As presented in Table 2, the attribute-specific performance analysis on the SUSTech1K dataset demonstrates the superior recognition capability of DeepSNNGait. Our method achieves an overall R1 accuracy of **83.00%** and R5 accuracy of **92.80%**, outperforming the current state-of-the-art DeepGaitV2 baseline by 2.1% and 0.9%, respectively. Specifically, our method achieves the noteworthy performance improvements under challenging environmental conditions: clothing variation scenarios (+5.6%), carried object configurations (+1.5%), and night-time illumination settings (+1.0%). These quantitative enhancements validate the robust temporal modeling capabilities of SNNBlock in handling occlusion-induced feature degradation and appearance variation challenges.

Results on CCPG. On the CCPG dataset, our framework achieves a mean recognition accuracy of **84.6%**, surpassing DeepGaitV2 by +1.3%. Specifically, our method achieves the performance improvement of 1.4%, 0.8%, 1.5%, and 1.4% in CL, UP, DN, and BG scenarios, respectively. This demonstrates the robustness of our method against substantial appearance changes caused by cloth changes and occlusion caused by different objects while preserving discriminative gait patterns. The corresponding results are shown in Table 3.

Results on Gait3D. For the large-scale Gait3D benchmark, DeepSNNGait achieves the highest R1, R5, mAP, and mINP scores of **75.5%**, 88.4%, 68.5%,

Table 2. Performance evaluation with different attributes on the SUSTech1K valid + test set. The bold values represent the best results.

Model	Publication	Normal	Bag	Clothing	Carrying	Umbrella	Uniform	Occlusion	Night	Overall R1	Overall R5
GaitSet [1]	AAAI2019	69.10	68.25	37.44	65.01	63.08	61.00	67.19	23.04	65.04	84.76
GaitPart [2]	CVPR2019	62.20	62.81	33.08	59.53	57.25	54.85	57.20	21.75	59.19	80.79
GaitGL [16]	ICCV2021	67.11	66.16	35.92	63.31	61.58	58.07	66.59	17.88	63.14	82.82
GaitBase [21]	CVPR2023	81.46	77.48	49.60	75.77	75.55	76.66	81.40	25.92	76.12	89.39
DeepGaitV2 [22]	Arxiv2023	86.5	82.8	49.2	80.4	83.3	81.9	86.0	28.0	80.9	91.9
DeepSNNGait	Ours	**88.22**	**84.15**	**55.24**	**81.86**	**87.43**	**85.98**	**89.19**	**29.01**	**83.00**	**92.80**

and 49.8%, respectively. This represents the performance gain of +1.1% in terms of R1 accuracy and +10.6% in terms of mINP compared to the runner-up (i.e., DeepGaitV2). Notably, the significant improvement in mINP demonstrates the superior ability of our method to handle hard samples, which is attributed to the hierarchical temporal encoding mechanism of the SNNBlock. The spiking activation function exhibit inherent sensitivity to subtle motion variations, which enables more effective discrimination of visually similar gait patterns under large intra-class variations.

Table 3. Performance comparison of different methods on the CCPG and Gait3D datasets.

Method	CCPG					Gait3D			
	CL	UP	DN	BG	Mean	R-1	R-5	mAP	mINP
GaitSet (Chao et al. 2019)	60.2	65.2	65.1	68.5	64.8	36.7	58.3	30.0	17.3
GaitPart (Fan et al. 2020)	64.3	67.8	68.6	71.7	68.1	28.2	47.6	21.6	12.4
GaitGL (Lin, Zhang, and Yu 2021)	61.7	67.3	64.2	69.1	65.6	29.7	48.5	22.3	13.6
GaitBase (Fan et al. 2023c)	71.6	75.0	76.8	78.6	75.5	64.6	-	-	-
DeepGaitV2 (Fan et al. 2023a)	78.6	84.8	80.7	89.2	83.3	74.4	88.0	65.8	39.2
DyGait (Wang et al. 2024)	-	-	-	-	-	66.3	80.8	56.4	37.3
DeepSNNGait (Ours)	**80.0**	**85.6**	**82.2**	**90.6**	**84.6**	**75.5**	**88.4**	**68.5**	**49.8**

4.4 Ablation Studies

To verify the effectiveness of our proposed SNN-Based GR Framework and the SNN block, we conducted several ablation experiments on the CCPG dataset and reported their results in Table 4. These ablation studies provides the systematic validation of our architectural design.

In the first ablation study, we integrate our proposed SNN branch into the GaitBase model, which consists of only 2D convolution layers. This results in the significant performance improvements across all four evaluation scenarios

Table 4. Comparison of different methods with various activation functions and integration strategies, along with their performance on the CCPG dataset.

Method	SNNBlock	Activation function			Fusion method			CCPG			
		Relu	Tanh	Lif	Add	Multi	Mult&Add	CL	UP	DN	BG
GaitBase								71.6	78.0	76.8	78.6
	✓			✓			✓	**75.4**	**81.2**	**80.2**	**88.9**
DeepGaitv2	✓	✓					✓	79.7	85.5	81.1	89.9
	✓		✓				✓	79.5	85.4	81.9	89.9
	✓			✓			✓	**80.0**	**85.6**	**82.2**	**90.6**
	✓			✓	✓			78.7	84.8	81.1	89.5
	✓			✓		✓		79.2	84.9	81.3	90.2

compared to the GaitBase baseline. This empirical evidence validates the superior capability of SNN-Based GR framework in terms of temporal information exploitation for gait pattern recognition. In the second ablation study, we substituted the inherent LIF neuron activation mechanism of SNNBlock with conventional ReLU or Tanh activation functions results, which results in moderate performance degradation, which demonstrates that the biologically plausible membrane potential accumulation and threshold-triggering dynamics of LIF neurons enable more effective temporal feature encoding compared to static activation functions. In the third ablation study, we replace our proposed fusion mechanism with direct element-wise feature addition/multiplication operations after the batch normalization layer, which results in inferior recognition accuracy. This confirms that our hierarchical fusion strategy, which implements adaptive feature weighting through region-specific attention followed by residual connection captures discriminative dynamic features while maintaining spatial specificity in gait motion analysis.

5   Conclusions

This research systematically investigates the innovative integration of SNNs into gait recognition paradigms, addressing the fundamental limitations of traditional CNNs in terms of temporal feature modeling and computational efficiency. The proposed framework is based on SNNs complementary spatio-temporal features through biologically interpretable dynamic mechanisms, while enhancing the perceptual weighting of discriminative limb regions. Experimental validation demonstrates significant performance improvements on challenging outdoor benchmarks, with particular robustness observed under dynamic occlusion scenarios and clothing variation conditions. These contributions establish a novel architectural paradigm for high-precision gait recognition while advancing SNN theory through the introduction of region-specific dynamic modeling mechanisms into computer vision applications. The work bridges the gap between neuromorphic computing principles and biometric recognition tasks, opening new avenues for energy-efficient temporal modeling in visual perception systems.

Acknowledgment. This work was supported in part by the National Natural Science Foundation of China Research Fund for International Young Scientists (RFIS-I) (No. W2433155) and in part by the Fundamental Research Funds for the Central Universities (No. 2024ZYGXZR104).

References

1. Chao, H., et al.: GaitSet: regarding gait as a set for cross-view gait recognition. In: AAAI Conference on Artificial Intelligence (2018)
2. Fan, C., et al.: GaitPart: temporal part-based model for gait recognition. In: 2020 IEEE/CVF Conference on Computer Vision and Pattern Recognition (CVPR), pp. 14213–14221 (2020)
3. Huang, Z., et al.: 3D local convolutional neural networks for gait recognition. In: Proceedings of the IEEE/CVF International Conference on Computer Vision (2021)
4. Fan, C., et al.: Skeletongait: gait recognition using skeleton maps. In: Proceedings of the AAAI Conference on Artificial Intelligence, vol. 38, no. 2, pp. 1662–1669 (2024)
5. Liao, R., Yu, S., An, W., Huang, Y.: A model-based gait recognition method with body pose and human prior knowledge. Pattern Recogn. **98**, 107069 (2020)
6. Takemura, N., et al.: Multi-view large population gait dataset and its performance evaluation for cross-view gait recognition. IPSJ Trans. Comput. Vis. Appl. **10**, 1–14 (2018)
7. Maass, W.: Networks of spiking neurons: the third generation of neural network models. Neural Netw. **10**(9), 1659–1671 (1997)
8. Tao, Y., Chang, C.H., Saïghi, S., et al.: GaitSpike: event-based gait recognition with spiking neural network. In: 2024 IEEE 6th International Conference on AI Circuits and Systems (AICAS), pp. 357–361 (2024)
9. Zheng, H., et al.: Going deeper with directly-trained larger spiking neural networks. In: Proceedings of the AAAI Conference on Artificial Intelligence, vol. 35, no. 12 (2021)
10. He, K., et al.: Deep residual learning for image recognition. In: Proceedings of the IEEE Conference on Computer Vision and Pattern Recognition (2016)
11. Shi, X., Hao, Z., Yu, Z.: SpikingResformer: bridging ResNet and vision transformer in spiking neural networks. In: Proceedings of the IEEE/CVF Conference on Computer Vision and Pattern Recognition (2024)
12. Wang, Z., et al.: Masked spiking transformer. In: Proceedings of the IEEE/CVF International Conference on Computer Vision (2023)
13. Yan, Z., Zhou, J., Wong, W.-F.: EEG classification with spiking neural network: smaller, better, more energy efficient. Smart Health **24**, 100261 (2022)
14. Chaney, K., et al.: Self-supervised optical flow with spiking neural networks and event based cameras. In: 2021 IEEE/RSJ International Conference on Intelligent Robots and Systems (IROS). IEEE (2021)
15. Banerjee, D., et al.: Application of spiking neural networks for action recognition from radar data. In: 2020 International Joint Conference on Neural Networks (IJCNN). IEEE (2020)

16. Lin, B., et al.: GaitGL: learning discriminative global-local feature representations for gait recognition. arXiv abs/2208.01380 (2022)
17. Shen, C., et al.: LidarGait: benchmarking 3D gait recognition with point clouds. In: 2023 IEEE/CVF Conference on Computer Vision and Pattern Recognition (CVPR), pp. 1054–1063 (2022)
18. Li, W., et al.: An in-depth exploration of person re-identification and gait recognition in cloth-changing conditions. In: Proceedings of the IEEE/CVF Conference on Computer Vision and Pattern Recognition (2023)
19. Zheng, J., et al.: Gait recognition in the wild with dense 3D representations and a benchmark. In: Proceedings of the IEEE/CVF Conference on Computer Vision and Pattern Recognition (2022)
20. Wang, M., et al.: Dygait: exploiting dynamic representations for high-performance gait recognition. In: Proceedings of the IEEE/CVF International Conference on Computer Vision (2023)
21. Fan, C., et al.: OpenGait: revisiting gait recognition toward better practicality. In: 2023 IEEE/CVF Conference on Computer Vision and Pattern Recognition (CVPR), pp. 9707–9716 (2022)
22. Fan, C., et al.: Exploring deep models for practical gait recognition. arXiv abs/2303.03301 (2023)

HealthGait-Uni: Health Assessment by Human Body Appearance and Motion from Videos

Shiwen Cao[1], Rafael Aguilar-Ortega[2], Dongyang Jin[1],
Manuel J. Marin-Jimenez[2], and Shiqi Yu[1(✉)]

[1] Department of Computer Science and Engineering, Southern University of Science
and Technology, Shenzhen, China
`yusq@sustech.edu.cn`
[2] Department of Computer Science and Artificial Intelligence, University of Córdoba,
Córdoba, Spain

Abstract. Some basic health information of the human body, such as age, weight, gender, etc., can be obtained through gait analysis. We propose a unified gait health analysis framework for multimodal and multiattribute prediction tasks. In the proposed framework, we integrate silhouette and optical flow modalities and employ a gait feature extractor to extract robust gait features. We also design a Mixture-of-Experts (MoE) fusion module to dynamically combine complementary static and dynamic information, enabling a shared representation for predicting multiple biometric and health-related attributes. The extensive experiments on the Health&Gait dataset show our proposed models outperform baseline single-modality methods across various prediction tasks, validating the effectiveness of multimodal gait analysis in practical health assessment scenarios.

Keywords: Gait Analysis · Health Assessment · Deep Learning

1 Introduction

As a distinctive dynamic biometric, gait is hard to disguise and remains identifiable even at a distance. Unlike other biometric traits such as face or fingerprint, gait can be captured unobtrusively without physical contact or wearable devices. These properties make it particularly suitable for long-range surveillance, crowded public spaces, and other scenarios where privacy and non-intrusive monitoring are important. Beyond identity recognition, gait analysis can also assess individual's health status. Some recent works indicate that gender, age, weight, and some health conditions can be estimated from gait [24,27]. For example, elderly individuals exhibit changes in gait cycles and stride length due to muscle degeneration; obese individuals often demonstrate shorter strides and reduced walking speeds; neurological disease patients, such as those with Parkinson's disease, typically show shuffling and rigid gait patterns. Clearly,

W. Jia et al. (Eds.): CCBR 2025, LNCS 16360, pp. 293–303, 2026.
https://doi.org/10.1007/978-981-95-6123-0_28

gait variations closely correlate with overall health. Several studies have shown significant progress in gait-based health prediction tasks such as gender classification [9], age estimation [27], and early disease screening [30,31]. Such remote health attribute assessment from gait is of great importance, especially in contexts where traditional medical testing is impractical or not feasible. For example, elderly individuals in undeveloped areas, patients under home care, or large-scale population monitoring in public health scenarios all benefit from non-contact, long-range, and privacy-preserving health assessment technologies. Compared to conventional diagnostic tools, gait-based analysis reduces patient burden while enabling continuous and unobtrusive monitoring, making it particularly suitable for large-scale early screening and long-term follow-up.

However, progress in gait-based health attribute prediction has long been limited by the lack of suitable datasets. Early studies relied on small datasets with few annotated attributes (e.g., gender, age), limiting complex prediction tasks, while recent large-scale multi-attribute datasets have advanced the field. These datasets contain diverse health-related labels such as gender, age, weight, and body composition, providing new opportunities for comprehensive gait-based health assessment. Despite these improvements in data availability, most existing methods still operate on a single modality, predominantly relying on silhouettes. While silhouette-based features are effective at capturing static morphological characteristics (e.g., body shape, limb length, walking posture), they often fail to exploit the temporal dynamics inherent in human motion fully. Except for silhouette, flow, as a motion-oriented modality, offers rich dynamic cues that may also reflect underlying health conditions—for instance, walking speed, joint flexibility, and gait rhythm, which are valuable for inferring physical fitness or detecting early signs of health decline.

To this end, we propose a **unified multimodal framework HealthGait-Uni** for gait-based health attribute prediction, which simultaneously leverages the static morphological information from silhouette sequences and the dynamic motion cues from optical flow. This unified approach enables the model to fully exploit both appearance and movement patterns related to human health. Experimental results demonstrate that our framework significantly outperforms single-modality baselines across multiple health-related prediction tasks, validating the effectiveness of multimodal gait analysis in practical health assessment scenarios. Our main contributions are summarized as follows:

- **Unified Multimodal-Multitask Framework:** We propose a unified framework that integrates silhouette and optical flow with a strong gait backbone to predict multiple health attributes, enabling comprehensive gait-based assessment.
- **Adaptive Feature Fusion via MoE:** We design a Mixture-of-Experts fusion module where expert branches capture diverse features, and a gating network adaptively weights them for input-aware multimodal integration.

2   Related Work

2.1   Gait Recognition and Analysis

Gait recognition has emerged as a fast-developing subfield of gait analysis, with numerous effective methods proposed in recent years. Traditional models [2] focus on learning spatial and temporal features from silhouette sequences. To enhance robustness against clothing changes, occlusion, and illumination, alternative modalities like skeleton maps, optical flow, and parsing maps have been explored [4,6,14,16,20,21,26]. To improve robustness under complex conditions, multimodal gait recognition has become increasingly popular. These approaches integrate complementary cues from multiple sources. UGaitNet [15] proposed a unified multimodal structure. SkeletonGait++ [6] fused silhouette and skeleton information. MultiGait++ [11] jointly incorporated silhouettes, optical flow, and human parsing maps via an advanced fusion strategy.

To facilitate research in this direction, OpenGait [5] was released as a comprehensive open-source platform that standardizes data preprocessing, model training, and evaluation. It supports multiple modalities and strong gait recognition models [12,13,17–19,22,23,29], offering modular and scalable tools for rapid development. In this work, we build upon OpenGait to construct our unified framework for multimodal gait-based health attribute prediction, leveraging its flexibility and reproducibility.

2.2   Health-Related Attribute Prediction

Gait data contains not only identity-discriminative features but also health-related attributes, including gender, age, weight, and body composition. Medical studies have shown strong correlations between gait patterns and physiological conditions. For example, aging can alter gait cycles and stride lengths; obesity may reduce walking speed and increase asymmetry; and neurodegenerative diseases like Parkinson's often manifest in rigid or shuffling gait [3,7]. Consequently, gait analysis offers a non-invasive and contactless approach to remote health assessment and early disease screening. The lack of large-scale datasets with rich labels hindered early research in gait-based health attribute prediction. Datasets such as OU-ISIR [8,10] provided foundational benchmarks, and models like those from Isaac et al. [9] and Zhang et al. [28] achieved promising results in gender and age estimation. However, these datasets typically offered limited modalities and coarse attribute annotations, restricting the scope and generalizability of further developments.

To address these limitations, Zafra-Palma et al. introduced the Health&Gait dataset [25], the most comprehensive resource to date for gait-based health analysis. It includes over ten health attributes and four gait modalities. The dataset offers high-quality annotations and diverse inputs, providing an ideal testbed for multimodal, multi-attribute learning. Building on this dataset, Aguilar-Ortega et al. [1] employed silhouette-based models GaitBase and DeepGaitV2 [4] and proposed a task-grouping strategy that achieved impressive results. However, their methods remained limited to single-modality inputs, underutilizing the rich multimodal structure of the dataset. In contrast, we propose to fully exploit the diverse modalities and abundant attribute labels in Health&Gait. By integrating both static silhouette features and dynamic optical flow cues, we aim to develop a unified multimodal-multitask learning framework capable of jointly predicting multiple health indicators, unlocking the full potential of gait analysis for intelligent healthcare.

3   Methodology

3.1   Framework of the Multimodal Multitask Model

To comprehensively evaluate the effectiveness of multimodal learning for multi-attribute gait analysis, we propose **HealthGait-Uni**, a unified multimodal and multiattribute gait analysis framework built upon the open-source OpenGait [5] codebase, as shown in Fig. 1. This framework is designed to jointly address a wide range of person-related prediction tasks by leveraging the complementary strengths of silhouettes and optical flow. The former is effective for capturing body shape and spatial structure, and the latter provides rich motion dynamics crucial for understanding temporal gait patterns.

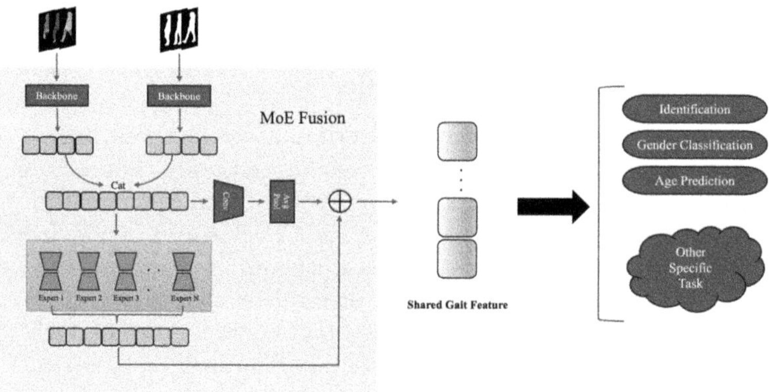

Fig. 1. The pipeline of our proposed multitask model HealthGait-Uni.

To extract modality-specific features, we adopt two widely-used gait recognition backbones: **GaitBase** and **DeepGaitV2**, which represent two mainstream convolutional paradigms in gait modeling. **GaitBase** leverages a *2D convolutional* structure, which is efficient and effective at capturing fine-grained spatial patterns from individual frames. In contrast, **DeepGaitV2** utilizes *P3D (Pseudo-3D) convolutions*, which jointly model spatial structure and short-term motion, offering stronger capabilities for capturing temporal dynamics. Based on these two backbones, we design two variants of our framework: **HealthGait-Uni-2d**, which adopts GaitBase to emphasize lightweight and robust spatial feature extraction, and **HealthGait-Uni-p3d**, which adopts DeepGaitV2 to enhance the modeling of spatiotemporal gait dynamics.

We also propose a Mixture-of-Experts (MoE) fusion module to integrate the features from different modalities. MoE is particularly well-suited to multimodal fusion, as it provides flexibility, scalability, and content-aware weighting, which are essential when dealing with heterogeneous and task-dependent cues from both static and motion modalities. Each fused feature vector is then fed into a set of task-specific heads to support ten representative tasks, such as identity recognition, gender classification, age estimation, weight prediction, and BMI regression.

3.2 MoE Fusion

The silhouettes capture the static shape and appearance of human gait, which are robust to noise and beneficial for recognizing identity and physical attributes. In contrast, optical flow emphasizes motion dynamics and temporal changes, providing valuable cues for understanding gait patterns and health-related metrics. These two modalities offer complementary perspectives, and their effective fusion can enhance the overall representation quality by jointly leveraging appearance and motion cues.

To achieve this, we adopt a Mixture-of-Experts (MoE) fusion strategy that enables adaptive integration of silhouette and optical flow features. Let the extracted silhouette and optical flow features be denoted as

$$\mathbf{f}_{\text{sil}} \in \mathbb{R}^D, \quad \mathbf{f}_{\text{flow}} \in \mathbb{R}^D,$$

where D is the feature dimension. We concatenate these features into a single representation

$$\mathbf{X} = [\mathbf{f}_{\text{sil}}, \mathbf{f}_{\text{flow}}] \in \mathbb{R}^{2D}.$$

We define M expert networks $\{\mathcal{E}_m(\cdot)\}_{m=1}^M$, each specializing in a distinct fusion pattern. The fused representation is computed as

$$\mathbf{f}_{\text{fused}} = \sum_{m=1}^{M} g_m(\mathbf{X}) \cdot \mathcal{E}_m(\mathbf{X}),$$

where $g_m(\mathbf{X})$ is the mixture weight of the m-th expert, obtained through a gating function:

$$g_m(\mathbf{X}) = \frac{\exp\left(\mathbf{w}_m^\top \phi(\mathbf{X}) + b_m\right)}{\sum_{j=1}^{M} \exp\left(\mathbf{w}_j^\top \phi(\mathbf{X}) + b_j\right)},$$

where $\phi(\cdot)$ denotes a transformation function (e.g., MLP or linear projection). The weights satisfy

$$\sum_{m=1}^{M} g_m(\mathbf{X}) = 1, \quad g_m(\mathbf{X}) \geq 0.$$

This design allows the MoE module to adaptively select the most informative expert(s) based on the combined silhouette and optical flow features. By doing so, the fusion can dynamically emphasize static or motion cues according to the input content, leading to a more flexible and discriminative multimodal representation.

3.3 Loss Function

Let $\mathcal{L}_i$ denote the loss of the i-th task. We use the cross-entropy loss for classification tasks and the mean squared error (MSE) loss for regression tasks:

$$\mathcal{L}_i = \begin{cases} \mathcal{L}_{\mathrm{CE}}(y_i, \hat{y}_i), & \text{if task } i \text{ is classification,} \\ \mathcal{L}_{\mathrm{MSE}}(y_i, \hat{y}_i), & \text{if task } i \text{ is regression,} \end{cases}$$

where y_i and $\hat{y}_i$ are the ground-truth label and the predicted output, respectively. The total loss is defined as a weighted sum of all task losses:

$$\mathcal{L}_{\text{total}} = \sum_{i=1}^{N} \lambda_i \mathcal{L}_i, \tag{1}$$

where λ_i is the weighting coefficient for the i-th task. This joint optimization encourages the backbone and MoE module to learn a unified gait representation that is beneficial across all tasks (see Fig. 1).

4 Experiments

4.1 Dataset

All experiments are conducted on the Health&Gait [25] multimodal gait health assessment dataset, which serves as a comprehensive and large-scale benchmark designed explicitly for gait-based health analysis. This dataset comprises 1,564 video sequences from 398 participants, capturing diverse real-world walking conditions, including different speeds, viewpoints, and simple clothing variations. It stands out in both scale and richness of annotations, making it a valuable resource for training and evaluating robust gait models in health-related applications. It provides four gait modalities—silhouettes, optical flow, human parsing maps, skeleton maps, and annotations for ten health-related attributes, such as gender, age, height, and so on. To ensure a subject-independent evaluation, we split the dataset into training and testing sets using a 3:1 ratio based on participant identities. No subject appears in both sets, ensuring that the model is evaluated on entirely unseen individuals.

4.2 Implementation Details

We apply cropping and alignment operations to both silhouette and optical flow inputs, after which all frames are resized to a fixed resolution of 64×44. The training is conducted using four A40 GPUs with a batch size of (8, 8, 30), representing 8 identities, each with 8 sequences, and each sequence containing

Table 1. Performance of different methods. MT1 and MT2 use GaitBase and Deep-GaitV2 as backbones, respectively. HGU-2d and HGU-p3d denote our HealthGait-Uni-2d and HealthGait-Uni-p3d. **Bold** indicates the best performance and <u>underline</u> is the second best.

Task	Metric	MT1 [1]	HGU-2d (Ours)	MT2 [1]	HGU-p3d (Ours)
Identity↑	Fast@R1 (%)	98.64	98.25	<u>99.48</u>	**99.71**
Age↓	MAE (years)	8.49	<u>7.94</u>	8.47	**7.53**
BMI↓	MAE (kg/m^2)	**2.61**	<u>3.61</u>	**2.61**	3.64
Height↓	MAE (cm)	<u>3.89</u>	**3.80**	4.65	4.96
HipC↓	MAE (cm)	15.55	**4.60**	16.63	<u>4.93</u>
L.Mass↓	MAE (kg)	5.56	**4.02**	6.19	<u>4.07</u>
NeckC↓	MAE (cm)	<u>1.64</u>	**1.58**	1.69	**1.58**
PA_level↑	Accuracy (%)	58.03	59.51	59.04	**61.55**
FatMass↓	MAE (%)	4.97	**3.63**	4.89	<u>3.64</u>
Gender↑	Accuracy (%)	94.78	<u>96.74</u>	94.48	**97.83**

30 frames. We use the AdamW optimizer with an initial learning rate of 0.001 and a weight decay of 0.001. The model is trained for 20,000 iterations, and the learning rate is decayed at 10,000, 15,000, and 18,000 iterations. To account for the varying complexity of different tasks, we assign task-specific weights to the loss functions. In particular, we set the weight of the identity recognition task to 1, while all other tasks (e.g., gender, age, BMI) are assigned a weight of 0.5. These hyperparameters were selected based on preliminary experiments that aimed to balance training stability and final performance.

4.3   Experimental Results

To evaluate the effectiveness of our proposed multimodal and multitask learning framework, we conduct extensive experiments on the Health&Gait dataset and compare our models with two strong unimodal baselines, **MT1** and **MT2**, both proposed in [1]. Specifically, MT1 combines GaitBase with silhouette input, while MT2 uses DeepGaitV2 with silhouette input. These models only leverage a single modality (silhouettes), which limits their ability to capture dynamic motion cues. In contrast, our proposed models, **HealthGait-Uni-2d (HGU-2d)** and **HealthGait-Uni-p3d (HGU-p3d)**, are unified multimodal multitask frameworks that integrate both silhouettes and optical flow through a Mixture-of-Experts fusion strategy, and jointly predict multiple biometric and health-related attributes within a single model. HealthGait-Uni-2d adopts GaitBase as its backbone, while HealthGait-Uni-p3d uses DeepGaitV2, allowing for a direct comparison with MT1 and MT2, respectively.

As shown in Table 1, our models consistently outperform the baselines across most tasks. Compared to MT1, **HealthGait-Uni-2d** achieves substantial improvements in age estimation (**7.94** vs. 8.49), hip circumference (**4.60** vs.

15.55), lean mass (**4.02** vs. 5.56), fat mass (**3.63** vs. 4.97), and gender classification (**96.74%** vs. 94.78%). Similarly, compared to MT2, **HealthGait-Uni-p3d** demonstrates superior performance in identity recognition (**99.71%** vs. 99.48%), age prediction (**7.53** vs. 8.47), physical activity level (**61.55%** vs. 59.04%), and gender classification (**97.83%** vs. 94.48%). These results clearly validate the advantages of our proposed method. By leveraging complementary static (silhouettes) and dynamic (optical flow) features, and optimizing multiple prediction tasks simultaneously within a unified architecture, HealthGait-Uni achieves more accurate and robust gait-based health attribute estimation.

4.4   Ablation Study

To evaluate the contribution of modality fusion, we compare the performance of our fused model (HealthGait-Uni-p3d) with its single-modality counterparts: DeepGaitV2-Silhouette (DGV2-S) and DeepGaitV2-Flow (DGV2-F). As shown in Table 2, the fused model consistently outperforms or matches the best results across all ten biometric and health-related metrics. Specifically, HealthGait-Uni-p3d achieves the highest accuracy in identity recognition (99.71%) and gender classification (97.83%), as well as the lowest errors in key health indicators such as age (7.53), lean mass (4.07), neck circumference (1.58), and fat mass (3.64). These improvements demonstrate that the fused model effectively captures complementary information from both static appearance and motion dynamics, thereby enhancing the quality of representation. Moreover, compared to DGV2-S and DGV2-F, the fused model shows a clear reduction in regression errors for most physiological attributes. This performance gain highlights the information synergy achieved through cross-modal fusion, validating the effectiveness of our MoE-based fusion strategy in multitask gait-based health analysis.

Table 2. Performance comparison among DeepGaitV2 (Silhouette and Flow) and HealthGait-Uni-p3d across biometric and health-related metrics.

Task	Metric	DeepGaitv2-S	DeepGaitv2-F	HealthGait-Uni
Identity↑	Fast@R1 (%)	99.48	95.61	**99.71**
Age↓	MAE (years)	8.47	8.77	**7.53**
BMI↓	MAE (kg/m^2)	**2.61**	3.80	3.64
Height↓	MAE (cm)	**4.65**	5.10	4.96
HipC↓	MAE (cm)	16.63	**4.90**	4.93
L.Mass↓	MAE (kg)	6.19	4.35	**4.07**
NeckC↓	MAE (cm)	1.69	1.64	**1.58**
PA_level↑	Accuracy (%)	59.04	60.60	**61.55**
P.FatMass↓	MAE (%)	4.89	3.82	**3.64**
Gender↑	Accuracy (%)	94.48	96.33	**97.83**

5 Conclusion and Future Work

In this paper, we propose a unified multimodal and multitask gait analysis framework for health attribute prediction. Leveraging the OpenGait platform, we integrate silhouette and optical flow modalities and employ a gait feature extractor to extract robust gait features. A Mixture-of-Experts (MoE) fusion module is designed to dynamically combine complementary static and dynamic information, enabling a shared representation for predicting multiple biometric and health-related attributes. We conduct extensive experiments on the Health&Gait dataset. Our proposed models, HealthGait-Uni-2d and HealthGait-Uni-p3d, outperform baseline single-modality methods across various prediction tasks, including identity recognition, age estimation, and more.

Acknowledgments. This work was supported by the National Natural Science Foundation of China (Grant 62476120) and partially supported by the Spanish project PID2023-147296NB-I00.

References

1. Aguilar-Ortega, R., Yu, S., Marin-Jimenez, N., Marin-Jimenez, M.J.: What does gait reveal about health? Investigating human motion as an indicator. In: The 21st International Conference in Computer Analysis of Images and Patterns (2025)
2. Chao, H., Wang, K., He, Y., Zhang, J., Feng, J.: Gaitset: cross-view gait recognition through utilizing gait as a deep set. IEEE Trans. Pattern Anal. Mach. Intell. **44**(7), 3467–3478 (2021)
3. Cho, C.W., Chao, W.H., Lin, S.H., Chen, Y.Y.: A vision-based analysis system for gait recognition in patients with Parkinson's disease. Expert Syst. Appl. **36**(3), 7033–7039 (2009)
4. Fan, C., et al.: Opengait: a comprehensive benchmark study for gait recognition towards better practicality. IEEE Trans. Pattern Anal. Mach. Intell. (2025)
5. Fan, C., Liang, J., Shen, C., Hou, S., Huang, Y., Yu, S.: Opengait: revisiting gait recognition towards better practicality. In: Proceedings of the IEEE/CVF Conference on Computer Vision and Pattern Recognition, pp. 9707–9716 (2023)
6. Fan, C., Ma, J., Jin, D., Shen, C., Yu, S.: Skeletongait: gait recognition using skeleton maps. In: Proceedings of the AAAI Conference on Artificial Intelligence, vol. 38, pp. 1662–1669 (2024)
7. Ge, Z., et al.: KDDA-balance: Knowledge-driven domain adaptation with correlated gait information for elderly balance assessment. Knowl. Based Syst. 114276 (2025)
8. Guo, X., et al.: Gait recognition in the wild: a large-scale benchmark and NAS-based baseline. IEEE Trans. Pattern Anal. Mach. Intell. (2025)
9. Isaac, E.R., Elias, S., Rajagopalan, S., Easwarakumar, K.: Multiview gait-based gender classification through pose-based voting. Pattern Recogn. Lett. **126**, 41–50 (2019)
10. Iwama, H., Okumura, M., Makihara, Y., Yagi, Y.: The OU-ISIR gait database comprising the large population dataset and performance evaluation of gait recognition. IEEE Trans. Inf. Forensics Secur. **7**(5), 1511–1521 (2012)

11. Jin, D., Fan, C., Chen, W., Yu, S.: Exploring more from multiple gait modalities for human identification. In: Proceedings of the AAAI Conference on Artificial Intelligence, vol. 39, pp. 4120–4128 (2025)
12. Jin, D., Fan, C., Ma, J., Zhou, J., Chen, W., Yu, S.: On denoising walking videos for gait recognition. In: Proceedings of the Computer Vision and Pattern Recognition Conference, pp. 12347–12357 (2025)
13. Ma, J., Ye, D., Fan, C., Yu, S.: Pedestrian attribute editing for gait recognition and anonymization. arXiv preprint arXiv:2303.05076 (2023)
14. Ma, J., Zhang, X., Yu, S.: An identity-preserved framework for human motion transfer. IEEE Trans. Inf. Forensics Secur. **19**, 3495–3509 (2024)
15. Marín-Jiménez, M.J., Castro, F.M., Delgado-Escaño, R., Kalogeiton, V., Guil, N.: Ugaitnet: multimodal gait recognition with missing input modalities. IEEE Trans. Inf. Forensics Secur. **16**, 5452–5462 (2021)
16. Shen, C., Fan, C., Wu, W., Wang, R., Huang, G.Q., Yu, S.: Lidargait: benchmarking 3d gait recognition with point clouds. In: Proceedings of the IEEE/CVF Conference on Computer Vision and Pattern Recognition, pp. 1054–1063 (2023)
17. Shen, C., Lin, B., Zhang, S., Yu, X., Huang, G.Q., Yu, S.: Gait recognition with mask-based regularization. In: 2023 IEEE International Joint Conference on Biometrics (IJCB), pp. 1–10. IEEE (2023)
18. Shen, C., Wang, R., Duan, L., Yu, S.: Lidargait++: learning local features and size awareness from lidar point clouds for 3d gait recognition. In: Proceedings of the Computer Vision and Pattern Recognition Conference, pp. 6627–6636 (2025)
19. Wang, R., Shen, C., Fan, C., Huang, G.Q., Yu, S.: Pointgait: boosting end-to-end 3d gait recognition with point clouds via spatiotemporal modeling. In: 2023 IEEE International Joint Conference on Biometrics (IJCB), pp. 1–10. IEEE (2023)
20. Wang, Z., Hou, S., Zhang, M., Liu, X., Cao, C., Huang, Y.: Gaitparsing: human semantic parsing for gait recognition. IEEE Trans. Multimedia **26**, 4736–4748 (2023)
21. Xu, R., et al.: Scalar: Scale-wise controllable visual autoregressive learning. arXiv preprint arXiv:2507.19946 (2025)
22. Ye, D., et al.: Biggergait: unlocking gait recognition with layer-wise representations from large vision models. arXiv preprint arXiv:2505.18132 (2025)
23. Ye, D., Fan, C., Ma, J., Liu, X., Yu, S.: Biggait: learning gait representation you want by large vision models. In: Proceedings of the IEEE/CVF Conference on Computer Vision and Pattern Recognition, pp. 200–210 (2024)
24. Yu, S., Tan, T., Huang, K., Jia, K., Wu, X.: A study on gait-based gender classification. IEEE Trans. Image Process. **18**(8), 1905–1910 (2009)
25. Zafra-Palma, J., Marín-Jiménez, N., Castro-Piñero, J., Cuenca-García, M., Muñoz-Salinas, R., Marín-Jiménez, M.J.: Health & gait: a dataset for gait-based analysis. Sci. Data **12**(1), 44 (2025)
26. Zeng, J., Song, D., Nie, W., Tian, H., Wang, T., Liu, A.A.: Cat-dm: controllable accelerated virtual try-on with diffusion model. In: Proceedings of the IEEE/CVF Conference on Computer Vision and Pattern Recognition, pp. 8372–8382 (2024)
27. Zhang, S., Wang, Y., Li, A.: Gait-based age estimation with deep convolutional neural network. In: 2019 International Conference on Biometrics (ICB), pp. 1–8. IEEE (2019)
28. Zhang, Y., Huang, Y., Wang, L., Yu, S.: A comprehensive study on gait biometrics using a joint CNN-based method. Pattern Recogn. **93**, 228–236 (2019)
29. Zhou, Q., et al.: Exploring generalized gait recognition: reducing redundancy and noise within indoor and outdoor datasets. arXiv preprint arXiv:2505.15176 (2025)

30. Zhou, Z., Liang, J., Peng, Z., Fan, C., An, F., Yu, S.: Gait patterns as biomarkers: a video-based approach for classifying scoliosis. In: International Conference on Medical Image Computing and Computer-Assisted Intervention, pp. 284–294. Springer, Cham (2024)
31. Zhou, Z., Peng, Z., Jin, D., Fan, C., An, F., Yu, S.: Pose as clinical prior: learning dual representations for scoliosis screening. arXiv preprint arXiv:2509.00872 (2025)

Face Related

DRAge: Dynamic Routing Mixture of Experts for Facial Age Estimation

Zhengyu Dou[1], Xiaomei Zhang[2,6], Ajian Liu[2,5], Fengmei Liang[1(✉)],
Hongsen Bi[3(✉)], and Zhen Lei[2,4,5,6]

[1] Taiyuan University of Technology, College of Electronic Information Engineering, Jinzhong, Shanxi, China
fm_liang@163.com
[2] MAIS, Institute of Automation, Chinese Academy of Science, Beijing, China
[3] Department of Plastic Surgery, Peking University Third Hospital, Beijing, China
313503068@qq.com
[4] CAIR, HKISI, Chinese Academy of Sciences, Hong Kong, China
[5] School of Computer Science and Engineering, the Faculty of Innovation Engineering, M.U.S.T, Macau, China
[6] School of Artificial Intelligence, University of Chinese Academy of Sciences, Beijing, China

Abstract. Most existing facial age estimation methods operate as isolated single-task systems, neglecting the potential synergies among correlated facial attributes. We propose Dynamic Routing Age (DRAge), a novel facial age estimation approach that integrates dynamic routing and multi-task collaboration. Our framework employs the Dynamic Routing Mixture of Experts (DRMoE) architecture, where features are dynamically routed to task-specific experts via cosine similarity between input representations and expert embeddings, ensuring adaptive feature selection. Additionally, we incorporate multiple task-specific subnets. We design a Cross-Attention Mechanism Feature Fusion (CAMFF) module within the facial analysis subnet, which strengthens feature representation through attention-driven interactions. To leverage pretrained features from related tasks while avoiding feature interference during multi-task optimization, we freeze other face analysis subnets during training and fine-tune specifically for age estimation. The effectiveness and feasibility of the proposed model was validated through extensive age estimation experiments on the FG-NET and CLAP2015 facial image datasets.

Keywords: Facial Age Estimation · Dynamic Routing Mixture of Experts · Cross-Attention Mechanism

1 Introduction

Facial age estimation has been an active research topic in the computer vision, for its important role in humancomputer interaction [1,2], facial attribute analysis [3], market analysis [3], and face anti-spoofing [4–6]. Many researchers have

W. Jia et al. (Eds.): CCBR 2025, LNCS 16360, pp. 307–317, 2026.
https://doi.org/10.1007/978-981-95-6123-0_29

made significant progress in this field by developing innovative network architectures [7–9], refining loss functions [10], and optimizing training strategies [11,12].

Deep learning-based age estimation methods can be broadly categorized into four main approaches: regression, classification, ranking, and distribution learning. The most direct approach to facial age estimation is regression, where age is treated as a continuous value. C3AE [13] enhances performance by using standard convolution for small-scale image processing, along with a cascaded model and multi-scale context regression. Classification-based methods treat age estimation as a multi-class classification problem. DEX [12] addresses this by defining age as one of 101 classes, while AL [8] improves accuracy by integrating ResNets/RoR with LSTM and employing an attention mechanism to extract age-sensitive features from specific regions of the face. Ranking-based methods, such as OR-CNN [9], approach age estimation as a ranking task, estimating age by comparing the relationships between different facial images. Finally, distribution learning methods treat age as a probability distribution rather than a single value. AGEn [10] extends classification-based approaches by incorporating label distribution learning to enhance prediction accuracy. Additionally, DRF [14] and DLDLF [15] connect split nodes to the final CNN layer, jointly learning input-dependent data partitions at split nodes and age distributions at leaf nodes to handle non-uniform data.

While existing methods show strong performance under specific conditions, they are typically designed solely for facial age estimation and fail to leverage the potential synergistic effects between facial attributes (such as gender, expression, etc.) and age estimation. Large-scale multi-task models [16], which can handle multiple related tasks simultaneously, offer the potential to capture these synergies. However, they often encounter practical challenges, including high computational costs and inefficient task processing. Furthermore, the significant differences in data distribution between tasks make it difficult to balance the learning process effectively and avoid negative transfer, presenting an ongoing challenge that must be addressed.

Inspired by multi-task collaboration, we propose Dynamic Routing Age (DRAge), a novel approach for facial age estimation. The key idea of DRAge is Dynamic Routing Mixture of Experts (DRMoE) that dynamically assigns features to experts based on their similarity. The method works by calculating the similarity between input features and each expert's embedding vector, enabling precise matching. To further improve the model's performance, we design a feature fusion module based on a cross-attention mechanism within the facial analysis subnet. Additionally, the framework incorporates multiple task analysis subnets to leverage the potential synergistic effects of various tasks on age estimation.

2 Method

2.1 Overall Architecture

As illustrated in Fig. 1, DRAge employs a shared backbone network to extract multi-level feature maps for all tasks. The input face image ($112 \times 112 \times 3$) is

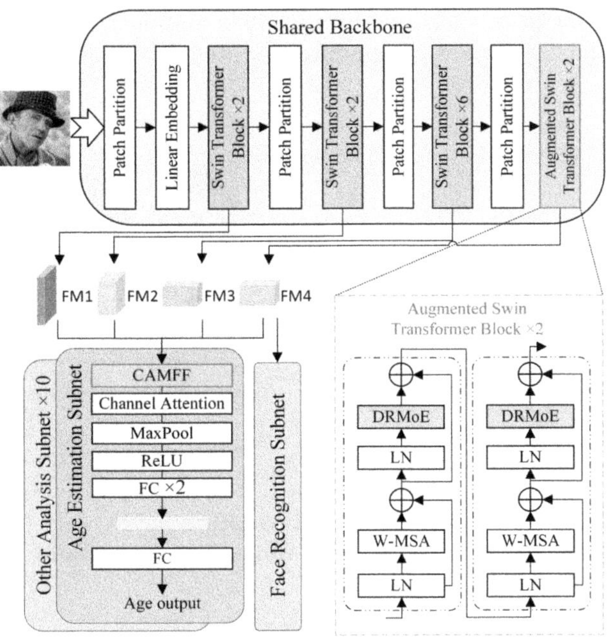

Fig. 1. Overall architecture of DRAge. The dashed region highlights the Swin Transformer Blocks augmented with our proposed DRMoE.

split into patches, linearly embedded into 96 dimensions, and processed through Swin Transformer blocks to generate hierarchical features (FM1FM4).

The face recognition subnet uses only FM4 to produce 512-D embedding features via Batch Normalization, following ArcFace [11]. For age estimation, the face analysis subnet incorporates a Cross-Attention Mechanism Feature Fusion (CAMFF) module to integrate multi-level features (FM1FM4), followed by channel attention, pooling, and fully connected layers. To leverage multi-task synergies, other face analysis subnets are frozen during age-specific fine-tuning.

2.2 Dynamic Routing Mixture of Experts

The Mixture of Experts framework processes inputs through three stages: routing computation, expert processing, and output aggregation. A gating network assigns probabilities to experts, which selectively process the input. Their outputs are combined via weighted summation, optimizing computational efficiency. In practical applications, some experts may be underutilized or not used at all. To address this challenge, we introduce a dynamic routing strategy based on similarity matching. This strategy replaces the original gating network with one that utilizes cosine similarity between input features and expert features. By employing this dynamic routing mechanism, the model can efficiently process facial features across various age groups, overcoming the limitations typically encountered when dealing with complex and diverse facial characteristics.

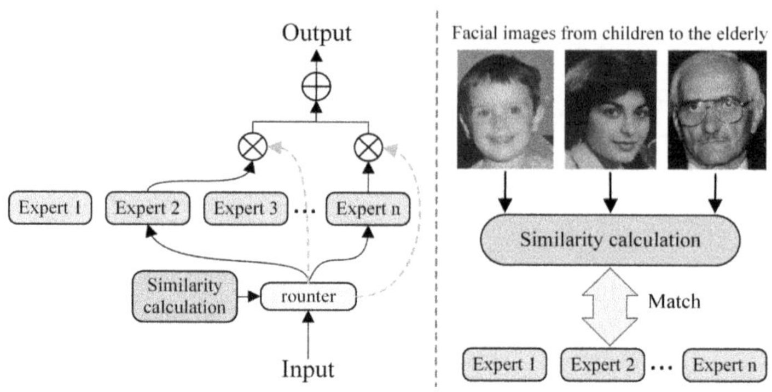

Fig. 2. Schematic diagram of Dynamic Routing Mixture of Experts. Our design enables task-specific feature specialization through similarity computation.

A schematic diagram of Dynamic Routing Mixture of Experts is shown in Fig. 2. The cosine similarity-based routing mechanism calculates the similarity between the input data and each expert's embedding vector, allowing the model to select the most suitable experts for the current input. Given an input vector x and a set of expert embedding vectors $E = \{e_1, e_2, ..., e_n\}$, where n represents the number of experts and e_i denotes the embedding vector of the i-th expert, we begin by performing l2 normalization on the input vector x. This step ensures that the direction of the vector is preserved, while its magnitude is disregarded. Similarly, all expert embedding vectors undergo the same l2 normalization process. Then, for each input vector x and expert vector e_i, we compute the cosine similarity between them using the following formula:

$$similarity(x, e_i) = \frac{x \cdot e_i}{\| x \|_2 \cdot \| e_i \|_2},\tag{1}$$

after l2 normalization, the denominator $\| x \|_2 \cdot \| e_i \|_2$ in this formula becomes equal to 1, simplifying the cosine similarity to the dot product between the input vector and the expert embedding vectors.

In the cosine similarity-based routing mechanism, we begin by calculating the similarity between the input vector and each expert embedding. The top k most similar experts are selected, with their corresponding similarity scores serving as weights. These weights are then used to compute a weighted sum of the expert outputs, which is subsequently normalized. Therefore, for each input x, the final output y can be expressed as:

$$y = \sum_{j \in top_k} \left(\frac{S_j}{\sum_{j' \in top_k} S_{j'}} \cdot E_j(x) \right),\tag{2}$$

where S_j represents the score of the j-th expert, and $E_j(x)$ represents the output of the j-th expert's processing of the input x.

2.3 Cross-Attention Mechanism Feature Fusion

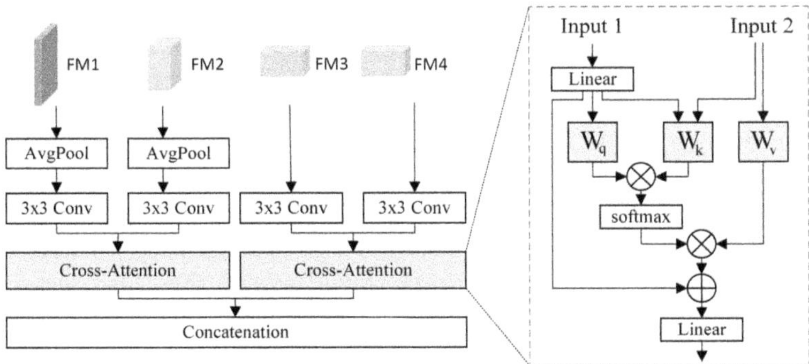

Fig. 3. Cross-Attention Mechanism Feature Fusion. In this module, we incorporate a residual connection that adds the original input to the attention output after weighted summation.

To allow the model to selectively focus on the most relevant features for age estimation, a cross-attention mechanism [17] is introduced to integrate feature maps across different levels. As shown in Fig. 3, the process starts with an average pooling layer applied to downsample FM1 and FM2, ensuring consistent proportions across feature maps at different levels. Next, four independent 3 × 3 convolutions are applied to FM1 through FM4 to reduce the number of channels proportionally. Subsequently, FM1 and FM2, as well as FM3 and FM4, are processed through separate cross-attention windows before being concatenated. This enables the model to learn the correlations and dependencies between features at different hierarchical levels.

The cross-attention fusion module computes separate query (Q), key (K), and value (V) matrices for both input features. It calculates attention scores using FM1 as Q and FM2 as both K and V. In a similar manner, FM2 is used as the query and FM1 as the key and value to generate a second set of attention scores. The resulting attention outputs from each feature map are then merged with the original feature maps. To enhance model capacity, we employ residual learning by adding the original input to the attention output. This process ensures that the new feature map preserves the information from the original input while also incorporating relevant details from the other feature map, thereby enhancing the model's ability to capture complex patterns.

3   Experiments

3.1   Datasets and Data Preprocessing

For face recognition, we use MS-Celeb-1M [18], containing 5.8M images of 85,742 identities. Facial expression recognition employs RAF-DB [19] with 12,271 training and 3,068 test images. Face attribute estimation utilizes CelebA [20] (162,770 training images). For age estimation, we utilize three datasets: IMDB+WIKI [21], Adience [22], and MORPH [23], for training. IMDB+WIKI, which contains 523K images in total, is the largest dataset for age estimation. Adience includes 26,580 images from 2,284 subjects, categorized into 8 distinct age groups. MORPH, the largest dataset with accurate age labels and ethnicity information, consists of approximately 55,000 facial images, with ages ranging from 16 to 77 years.

The experiments are conducted on the FG-NET [24] and CLAP2015 [25] datasets, which cover a broad spectrum of facial images. FG-NET is particularly suited for cross-age age estimation and facial recognition tasks. It comprises 1,002 images from 82 individuals, with ages spanning from 0 to 69 years, providing a 45-year age gap that is ideal for testing the model's cross-age recognition ability. The Chalearn challenge dataset focuses on apparent age estimation, containing 2,476 images for training, 1,136 for validation, and 1,079 for testing. This dataset also provides the standard deviation for each age label. After fine-tuning the age subnet, we evaluate the model's performance on the validation and test splits.

3.2   Implementation Details

The experiments are conducted on a 2080Ti GPU using the AdamW optimizer. The input images are resized to 112×112 pixels. The initial learning rate is set to 5×10^{-4}, with a weight decay of 0.05, a global batch size of 12, and a maximum of 80,000 training steps. For pretraining, we use a shared backbone and a facial recognition subnet to achieve a robust initialization for face recognition. This pretraining lasts for 40 epochs, utilizing a cosine decay learning rate scheduler with a 5-epoch linear warm-up. The batch size is set to 512, with the learning rates as follows: an initial learning rate of 5×10^{-4}, a warm-up learning rate of 5×10^{-7}, and a minimum learning rate of 5×10^{-6}.

For evaluation on the validation set, we use the training set to finetune the age subnet. For evaluation on the test set, we use the validation set, as well as the training set, to finetune the age subnet, as in [7,10,11,26]. The fine-tuning process lasts for 4,000 steps, without any warm-up phase, with the minimum learning rate set to 5×10^{-7}.

In the experiments, we quantitatively assess the performance of age estimation using three metrics: the Mean Absolute Error (MAE), Cumulative Score (CS) and ε-error. The MAE is defined as follows:

$$MAE = \frac{1}{N} \sum_{i=1}^{N} | y_i - \hat{y}_i |, \tag{3}$$

where y_i and $\hat{y}_i$ represent the predicted age value and the true age value of the i-th test sample. CS is the percentage of images whose absolute errors are less than or equal to a tolerance level l, we set $l = 5$. The ε-error is defined as $1 - \exp(-\frac{(\hat{a}-a)^2}{2\delta^2})$, where δ represents the standard deviation of the sample, $\hat{a}$ denotes the predicted age, and a signifies the ground truth age.

3.3 Main Results

Fig. 4. Success and failure cases of the proposed algorithm on FG-NET and CLAP2015.

We evaluate DRAge on the FG-NET and CLAP2015 to validate its effectiveness. The results are compared against several representative network architectures to assess performance. Some cases of the proposed algorithm in facial age estimation are shown in Fig. 4.

Comparison on FG-NET: As shown in Table 1, our proposed DRAge achieves superior performance on the FG-NET dataset, outperforming all compared methods in both MAE and CS. Specifically, DRAge attains an MAE of 2.17, which represents a 0.06 improvement over the previous best method (MWR). In terms of CS, our model achieves 91.5%, surpassing MWR by 0.4% and BridgeNet by 5.5%. Notably, methods like DRFs and AGEn, which rely on traditional regression or distribution learning, exhibit higher errors (MAE of 3.85 and 2.96, respectively), highlighting the advantages of our dynamic routing and multi-task collaboration framework. The consistent improvements across both metrics validate the effectiveness of DRMoE in capturing age-sensitive features and leveraging cross-task synergies.

Table 1. Comparison of MAE and CS(%) on FG-NET dataset.

Method	MAE	CS(%)
DEX [12]	3.09	-
DRFs [14]	3.85	80.6
AGEn [10]	2.96	85.0
C3AE [13]	2.95	-
MCGRL [27]	2.67	85.7
BridgeNet [7]	2.56	86.0
MWR [11]	2.23	91.1
DRAge (Ours)	**2.17**	**91.5**

Comparison on CLAP2015: Table 2 presents the results on the CLAP2015 dataset, where DRAge achieves an MAE of 2.29 (validation) and 2.26 (test), along with ε-errors of 0.18 and 0.20, respectively. These results significantly outperform SwinFace (MAE: 2.50, ε-error: 0.20) and MWR (MAE: 2.95, ε-error: 0.26). The 0.21 MAE reduction over SwinFace underscores the benefits of our cross-attention feature fusion and task-specific subnet freezing strategy. The lower ε-error further confirms the robustness of our model in handling apparent age estimation with noisy or ambiguous labels. These improvements are attributed to DRMoE's adaptive feature selection and the hierarchical integration of multi-level features via cross-attention.

Table 2. Comparison of MAE and ε-error on CLAP2015 dataset.

Method	Validatation		Test	
	MAE	ε-error	MAE	ε-error
AgeNet [28]	3.33	0.29	-	0.26
DEX [12]	3.25	0.28	-	0.26
AGEn [10]	3.21	0.28	2.94	0.26
AL-RoR [8]	3.14	0.27	-	0.25
BridgeNet [7]	2.98	0.26	2.87	0.26
MWR [11]	2.95	0.26	2.77	0.25
SwinFace [16]	2.50	0.20	2.47	0.22
DRAge (Ours)	**2.29**	**0.18**	**2.26**	**0.20**

The comparison results demonstrate that DRAge, through its integration of DRMoE and multi-task collaboration, establishes new state-of-the-art performance across both datasets. The improvements validate three key advantages: (1) DRMoE's dynamic routing mitigates feature interference via specialized expert allocation; (2) Cross-attention fusion enhances hierarchical feature utilization for subtle age patterns; (3) Task-specific subnet freezing isolates age-relevant features while preserving shared representations.

3.4 Ablation Study

We conduct an ablation study on CLAP2015 to validate the contributions of DRMoE and CAMFF modules. Table 3 summarizes the results.

Table 3. Ablation study of our proposed modules on CLAP2015 dataset.

Method	Validatation		Test	
	MAE	ε-error	MAE	ε-error
SwinFace [16]	2.50	0.20	2.47	0.22
SwinFace+CAMFF	2.39	0.19	2.37	0.21
SwinFace+DRMoE	2.35	0.19	2.32	0.21
SwinFace+DRMoE+CAMFF	**2.29**	**0.18**	**2.26**	**0.20**

Using SwinFace [16] as the baseline (MAE: 2.50, ε-error: 0.20), we first integrate CAMFF, which reduces MAE to 2.39 by enhancing hierarchical feature fusion via cross-attention. Adding DRMoE alone further lowers MAE to 2.35, demonstrating its efficacy in dynamic feature routing. The combined DRMoE+CAMFF model achieves the best performance (MAE: 2.29, ε-error: 0.18), highlighting the synergy between adaptive routing and attention-driven feature integration. Similar improvements are observed on the test set, confirming the robustness of our design.

4 Conclusion

In this work, we proposed DRAge, a novel facial age estimation approach that integrates dynamic routing and multi-task collaboration. We design a called DRMoE that dynamically routes facial features to appropriate experts in age estimation, significantly improving feature diversity and representation power. To further enhance the interaction between multiple tasks, we designed task-specific analysis subnets and introduced a feature fusion module using a cross-attention mechanism. This module enables effective feature integration at various levels within the face analysis subnet. To leverage potential synergies between tasks, we freeze other face analysis subnets while fine-tuning specifically for age estimation. We validate the effectiveness of our approach through main results and ablation study. Our method outperforms all existing baselines across metric, demonstrating its potential for facial age estimation.

Acknowledgement. This work was supported in part by Chinese National Natural Science Foundation Projects 62206280, U23B2054 and 62276254, 62376265, 62406320, Young Scientists Fund of The State Key Laboratory of Multimodal Artificial Intelligence Systems ES2P100113, Beijing Natural Science Foundation 7252151 and L221013, Science and Technology Development Fund of Macau Project 0140/2024/AGJ.

References

1. Fragopanagos, N., Taylor, J.G.: Emotion recognition in human-computer interaction. Neural Netw. **18**(4), 389–405 (2005)
2. Tang, J., Li, Z., Lai, H., Zhang, L., Yan, S., et al.: Personalized age progression with bi-level aging dictionary learning. IEEE Trans. Pattern Anal. Mach. Intell. **40**(4), 905–917 (2017)
3. Mérillou, S., Ghazanfarpour, D.: A survey of aging and weathering phenomena in computer graphics. Comput. Graph. **32**(2), 159–174 (2008)
4. Liu, A.: Ca-moeit: generalizable face anti-spoofing via dual cross-attention and semi-fixed mixture-of-expert. Int. J. Comput. Vis. 1–14 (2024)
5. Liu, A., et al.: Cfpl-fas: class free prompt learning for generalizable face anti-spoofing. In: Proceedings of the IEEE/CVF Conference on Computer Vision and Pattern Recognition (2024)
6. Liu, A., et al.: Fm-vit: flexible modal vision transformers for face anti-spoofing. IEEE Trans. Inf. Forensics Secur. (2023)
7. Li, W., Lu, J., Feng, J., Xu, C., Zhou, J., Tian, Q.: Bridgenet: a continuity-aware probabilistic network for age estimation. In: IEEE/CVF CVPR, pp. 1145–1154 (2019)
8. Zhang, K., et al.: Fine-grained age estimation in the wild with attention LSTM networks. IEEE TCSVT **30**(9), 3140–3152 (2019)
9. Niu, Z., Zhou, M., Wang, L., Gao, X., Hua, G.: Ordinal regression with multiple output CNN for age estimation. In: IEEE CVPR, pp. 4920–4928 (2016)
10. Tan, Z., Wan, J., Lei, Z., Zhi, R., Guo, G., Li, S.Z.: Efficient group-n encoding and decoding for facial age estimation. IEEE Trans. Pattern Anal. Mach. Intell. **40**(11), 2610–2623 (2017)
11. Shin, N.-H., Lee, S.-H., Kim, C.-S.: Moving window regression: a novel approach to ordinal regression. In: IEEE/CVF CVPR, pp. 18760–18769 (2022)
12. Rothe, R., Timofte, R., Van Gool, L.: Deep expectation of real and apparent age from a single image without facial landmarks. Int. J. Comput. Vis. **126**(2), 144–157 (2018)
13. Zhang, C., Liu, S., Xu, X., Zhu, C.: C3ae: exploring the limits of compact model for age estimation. In: IEEE/CVF CVPR, pp. 12587–12596 (2019)
14. Shen, W., Guo, Y., Wang, Y., Zhao, K., Wang, B., Yuille, A.L.: Deep regression forests for age estimation. In: IEEE CVPR, pp. 2304–2313 (2018)
15. Shen, W., Guo, Y., Wang, Y., Zhao, K., Wang, B., Yuille, A.: Deep differentiable random forests for age estimation. IEEE Trans. Pattern Anal. Mach. Intell. **43**(2), 404–419 (2019)
16. Qin, L., Wang, M., Deng, C., Wang, K., Chen, X., Hu, J., Deng, W.: Swinface: a multi-task transformer for face recognition, expression recognition, age estimation and attribute estimation. IEEE Trans. Circ. Syst. Video Technol. **34**(4), 2223–2234 (2023)

17. Chen, C.-F.R., Fan, Q., Panda, R.: Crossvit: cross-attention multi-scale vision transformer for image classification. In: IEEE/CVF ICCV, pp. 357–366 (2021)
18. Guo, Y., Zhang, L., Hu, Y., He, X., Gao, J.: MS-Celeb-1M: a dataset and benchmark for large-scale face recognition. In: Leibe, B., Matas, J., Sebe, N., Welling, M. (eds.) ECCV 2016. LNCS, vol. 9907, pp. 87–102. Springer, Cham (2016). https://doi.org/10.1007/978-3-319-46487-9_6
19. Li, S., Deng, W., Du, J.: Reliable crowdsourcing and deep locality-preserving learning for expression recognition in the wild. In: IEEE CVPR, pp. 2852–2861 (2017)
20. Liu, Z., Luo, P., Wang, X., Tang, X.: Deep learning face attributes in the wild. In: IEEE ICCV, pp. 3730–3738 (2015)
21. Rothe, R., Timofte, R., Van Gool, L.: DEX: deep expectation of apparent age from a single image. In: IEEE ICCVW, pp. 10–15 (2015)
22. Levi, G., Hassner, T.: Age and gender classification using convolutional neural networks. In: IEEE CVPRW, pp. 34–42 (2015)
23. Ricanek, K., Tesafaye, T.: Morph: a longitudinal image database of normal adult age-progression. In: FGR 2006, pp. 341–345. IEEE (2006)
24. Panis, G., Lanitis, A., Tsapatsoulis, N., Cootes, T.F.: Overview of research on facial ageing using the FG-NET ageing database. IET Biometrics **5**(2), 37–46 (2016)
25. Escalera, S., et al.: Chalearn looking at people 2015: apparent age and cultural event recognition datasets and results. In: IEEE ICCVW, pp. 1–9 (2015)
26. Zhang, K., Zhang, Z., Li, Z., Qiao, Y.: Joint face detection and alignment using multitask cascaded convolutional networks. IEEE Signal Process. Lett. **23**(10), 1499–1503 (2016)
27. Shou, Y., Cao, X., Liu, H., Meng, D.: Masked contrastive graph representation learning for age estimation. Pattern Recogn. **158**, 110974 (2025)
28. Liu, X., et al.: Agenet: deeply learned regressor and classifier for robust apparent age estimation. In: IEEE ICCVW, pp. 16–24 (2015)

PGS-Net: Personalized Graph Structure Network with Self-Supervised Learning for Micro-Expression Recognition

Yujie Xu, Jie Hu, Zaiyu Pan, and Jun Wang[✉]

China University of Mining and Technology, Xuzhou , China
jrobot@126.com

Abstract. Micro-expressions (MEs) are subtle, involuntary facial muscle movements that occur without conscious awareness. Due to their fine-grained local variations and significant individual differences, micro-expression recognition (MER) remains a challenging task. To address this, we propose a novel recognition network (PGS-Net). First, we design a Self-Supervised Displacement Reconstruction Module (SDRM) that reconstructs and amplifies the displacement fields between the onset and apex frames, refining local motion information and enhancing the modeling of ME details. Then, we introduce a Displacement-Guided Personalized Graph Structure Module (DPGSM), which combines facial structure and displacement features to construct dynamic personalized graph topologies, adapting to differences in individual facial structures and motion patterns. Experiments on three public datasets—SMIC, CASME II, and SAMM—show that PGS-Net outperforms existing methods in three-class classification tasks in terms of UF1 and UAR, demonstrating strong recognition performance and generalization capability.

Keywords: micro-expression recognition · Self-Supervised Displacement Reconstruction · Displacement-Guided Personalized Graph Structure

1 Introduction

MEs are brief, involuntary facial muscle movements that typically last only 0.05 to 0.5 s [3]. These expressions are subtle in intensity, exhibit significant individual variation, and often occur outside of conscious awareness. Despite their fleeting nature, MEs can reveal a person's genuine emotions that they may attempt to conceal, making them a critical cue for inferring underlying emotional states. Owing to these characteristics, MER holds substantial application value in fields such as affective computing, human-computer interaction, and security surveillance.

Early MER approaches primarily relied on handcrafted spatiotemporal descriptors to extract features from facial sequences. Representative methods include Bi-WOOF [13], LBP-TOP [14]. While these techniques demonstrate

W. Jia et al. (Eds.): CCBR 2025, LNCS 16360, pp. 318–327, 2026.
https://doi.org/10.1007/978-981-95-6123-0_30

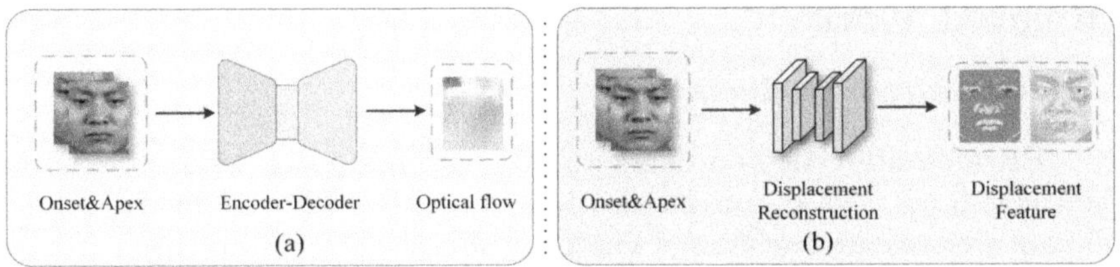

Fig. 1. (a): Existing method. (b): Our proposed method.

robustness under limited data conditions, their fixed encoding strategies are insufficient to capture the subtle and complex dynamics inherent in MEs. With the rise of deep learning, convolutional neural networks(CNNs) [9] and graph neural networks (GNNs) [8] have emerged as dominant solutions, leveraging optical flow estimation and facial graph modeling to improve recognition accuracy. However, existing optical flow methods, as shown in Fig. 1(a), often operate on the entire facial region across frames, making it difficult to localize fine-grained facial movements, which may lead to the loss of critical motion cues. Moreover, existing GCN-based methods typically depend on static, predefined facial landmark topologies, neglecting inter-individual differences in facial structure and expression patterns. This limitation hampers their generalization capability across diverse subjects.

To address the shortcomings of traditional optical flow in capturing subtle motion, we propose a Self-Supervised Displacement Reconstruction Module, as shown in Fig. 1(b). This module takes the onset and apex frames as input and learns to reconstruct and amplify the bidirectional (X and Y) displacement fields between them via a self-supervised learning objective. This design enhances the modeling of fine-grained motion features and helps capture critical expression dynamics. To overcome the lack of adaptability in current graph-based methods to individual differences, we further introduce a Displacement-Guided Personalized Graph Structure Module. By integrating each subject's displacement field features and facial structural information, we detect N most representative facial keypoints via local maxima selection and compute the similarity between keypoints using the $L2$ norm to construct a subject-specific dynamic graph topology. This personalized graph enables the model to better adapt to variations in facial structure and expression patterns, thereby improving generalization.

Based on the above, the contributions of this paper are as follows:

- We propose SDRM, which reconstructs and amplifies the displacement fields between onset and apex frames, effectively capturing fine-grained motion characteristics of MEs.
- We design DPGSM, which dynamically selects representative facial keypoints based on fine displacement and facial structure features, and constructs personalized graph topologies to accommodate inter-subject variability.
- Extensive experiments on public ME datasets demonstrate that PGS-Net achieves superior performance and strong generalization ability.

2   Related Work

2.1   Handcrafted Methods

Early MER methods relied on handcrafted spatiotemporal descriptors with traditional classifiers. Notable examples include LBP-TOP [14] by Huang et al., which captures texture variations via local binary patterns on three orthogonal planes, and Bi-WOOF [13], which uses optical flow to estimate facial motion direction and magnitude. These features are typically classified using SVMs [6] or Random Forests [1], and while robust under limited data, they depend heavily on manual tuning and fail to capture complex temporal dynamics and global context, limiting overall performance.

2.2   Deep Learning Methods

With the rise of deep learning, end-to-end feature learning has become central to MER. OFF-ApexNet [5], proposed by Gan et al., enhances motion representation by fusing forward and backward optical flow, while STSTNet [12] adopts a lightweight three-branch architecture for efficient and expressive feature extraction. RCN [17] integrates residual and recurrent structures to model short-term dynamics, and ICE-GAN [19] employs adversarial training for data augmentation and improved generalization. More recently, GCN [8]-based methods such as Graph-TCN [10] and OFVIG-Net [21] construct graphs from facial landmarks or optical flow patches to jointly capture local motion and global structure, leading to enhanced recognition performance.

3   Methods

3.1   Overall Architecture

We propose a novel MER network, PGS-Net, which consists of two key modules: SDRM and DPGSM (as shown in Fig. 2). SDRM extracts X and Y displacement features between the onset and apex frames. Based on these features, DPGSM detects keypoints and dynamically selects the top N with the most significant changes as graph nodes. These nodes, combined with displacement and facial structure features, are fed into the Graph Maker to construct a multi-branch personalized graph. The resulting graph is processed in parallel by a graph neural network (GNN) to extract structural representations. Finally, a classifier predicts the ME category based on the extracted features.

3.2   Self-Supervised Displacement Reconstruction Module

Extracting robust local subtle features is critical for MER. Traditional methods often rely on optical flow [7] estimation between two frames of the entire facial image, which overlooks the fine-grained local motion cues of MEs. To address this, we propose SDRM to reconstruct and amplify the X and Y displacements

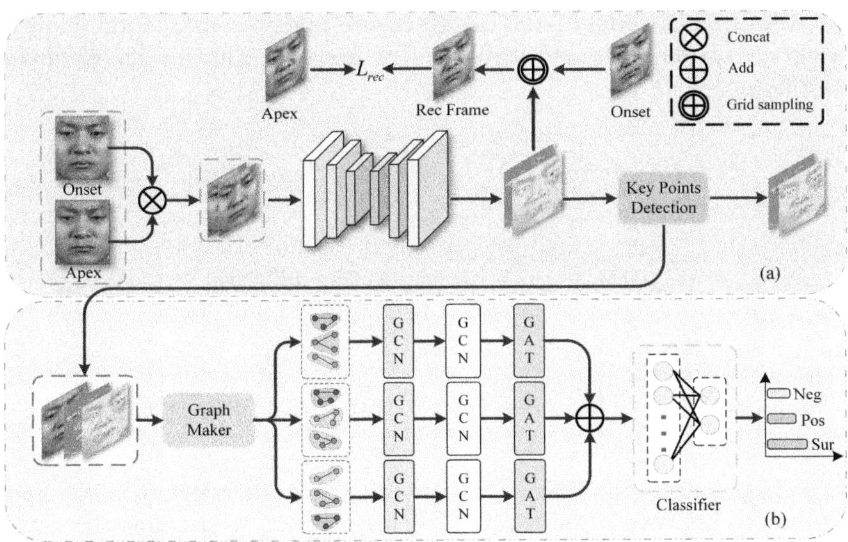

Fig. 2. The overall architecture of PGS-Net. (a): Self-Supervised Displacement Reconstruction Module (SDRM), (b): Displacement-Guided Personalized Graph Structure Module (DPGSM).

between the onset and apex frames, enabling more precise modeling of local motion features.

SDRM adopts a U-Net [15] architecture as an encoder-decoder network. First, the onset and apex frames are concatenated along the channel dimension and fed into the encoder, which performs downsampling to extract low-dimensional dynamic features. The decoder then upsamples these features to reconstruct precise X and Y displacement maps between the two frames. During this process, the displacement maps are amplified and reconstructed to refine the details of local motion, enabling the model to capture subtle motion variations in MEs.

To obtain accurate displacement maps, the onset and apex frames are concatenated along the channel dimension to form I_{in}, which is then passed through the encoder-decoder network to predict pixel-level displacement fields. The corresponding formulation is as follows:

$$D(x,y) = (d_x(x,y), d_y(x,y)) \in \mathbb{R}^2 \tag{1}$$

where $d_x(x,y)$ represents the displacement in the x direction, and $d_y(x,y)$ represents the displacement in the y direction for each pixel position. Through the sampling network $G \in \mathbb{R}^{B \times H \times W \times 2}$, we generate the reconstructed image $I_{rec} = G(I_{Apex}, D)$, as shown in the following sampling network:

$$G(x,y) = \left(\frac{2 \cdot d_x(x,y) - 1}{W - 1}, \frac{2 \cdot d_y(x,y) - 1}{H - 1} \right) \tag{2}$$

where W and H represent the image width and height, respectively.

We design multiple loss functions to ensure both reconstruction quality and the accuracy of the generated displacement features. The specific formulations are as follows:

$$L_{rec} = \frac{1}{N} \sum_{x=1}^{W} \sum_{y=1}^{H} \|I_{rec}(x,y) - I_{Apex}(x,y)\|^2 \tag{3}$$

$$L_{flow} = \frac{1}{N} \sum_{x=1}^{W} \sum_{y=1}^{H} \|G(x,y) - D(x,y)\|^2 \tag{4}$$

$$L_{smo} = \sum_{x=1}^{W} \sum_{y=1}^{H} (|D(x,y) - D(x+1,y)| + |D(x,y) - D(x,y+1)|) \tag{5}$$

where L_{rec} penalizes the difference between the reconstructed image and the apex frame to improve reconstruction accuracy; L_{flow} constrains the deviation between the generated sampling grid $G(x,y)$ and the actual flow field $D(x,y)$, enhancing displacement estimation; and L_{smo} enforces smoothness between neighboring pixels to ensure spatial consistency.

The total loss function is:

$$L_{total} = L_{rec} + \lambda_1 L_{flow} + \lambda_2 L_{smo} \tag{6}$$

where λ_1 and λ_2 are the hyperparameters for L_{flow} and L_{smo}, respectively.

3.3   Displacement-Guided Personalized Graph Structure Module

MEs exhibit significant individual variability, while existing GCN-based approaches typically rely on static, predefined facial landmark topologies, making it difficult to accommodate differences in facial structure and motion patterns across subjects. This limitation affects the generalization capability of such models. To address this, we propose DPGSM, which aims to design a personalized graph structure topology that can adapt to individual differences.

To capture subtle motion features of MEs from the fine-grained displacement fields generated by SDRM, we design a local maxima-based Keypoint Detection method to locate regions with prominent local motion, as described below:

$$\{(x_i, y_i)\}_{i=1}^{N} = \{(x,y) \in K \mid M(x,y)\} \tag{7}$$

where N is the number of keypoints, $M(x,y) = \sqrt{d_x(x,y)^2 + d_y(x,y)^2}$ is the magnitude of the displacement, and K is the set of keypoints in the region.

To incorporate both displacement and structural facial features, we concatenate the X and Y displacement maps with the grayscale apex frame. For each detected keypoint, a local patch of size $P \times P$ is extracted from each modality, centered at the keypoint, and flattened into vectors $p_i^x, p_i^y, p_i^g \in \mathbb{R}^{P^2}$. These vectors are used to construct the input feature tensors $F^x, F^y, F^g \in \mathbb{R}^{B \times N \times P^2}$.

To model topological relationships between keypoints, Graph Maker computes the L2 distance between keypoint features, yielding similarity measures $x_{b,i}$, as formulated below:

$$x_{b,i} = \frac{f_{b,i}}{\|f_{b,i}\|_2}, \quad b = 0, \ldots, B-1, \quad i = 1, \ldots, N \tag{8}$$

where $f_{b,i}$ represents the feature vector of the i-th keypoint from the b-th sample.

Then, based on the similarity relationship $x_{b,i}$, we construct the boundary graph $E^{(b)}$ and select the most similar keypoint pairs as follows:

$$E^{(b)} = \{(i,j) \mid S_{ij}^{(b)} > \tau, i \neq j\} \tag{9}$$

where $S_{ij}^{(b)} = x_{b,i}^T x_{b,j}$ is the similarity between the i-th keypoint and the j-th keypoint from the b-th sample, and τ is a threshold for the similarity value.

The feature tensors F^x, F^y, F^g are processed by Graph Maker to construct multiple personalized graph structures GR^x, GR^y, GR^g, which are then fed in parallel into a GNN [8] composed of multiple graph convolution and attention layers. The obtained features are summed and then fed into the classifier for MER.

4 Experiments

4.1 Dataset

We conducted experiments on three publicly available ME datasets: SMIC [11], CASMEII [18], and SAMM [2]. On each dataset, we performed a three-class classification task.

SMIC contains three camera modalities: HS (high speed camera), VIS (visible light camera), and NIR (near infrared camera). In our experiments, we use only the HS subset, which comprises recordings from 16 subjects and covers three emotion categories—positive, negative, and surprise.

CASME II comprises data from 26 subjects, with a total of 255 samples. It originally labels seven emotions—happiness, surprise, disgust, sadness, fear, repression, and others. For our three-class task, we merge them into positive, negative, and surprise.

SAMM contains recordings from 28 subjects, totaling 159 samples. It likewise defines seven categories—happiness, surprise, anger, disgust, sadness, fear, and others—which we collapse into the same three classes: positive, negative, and surprise.

4.2 Implementation Details

Our experiments are implemented in the PyTorch framework and trained on an NVIDIA GeForce RTX 3080 GPU. We use the Adam optimizer for 400 epochs with an initial learning rate of 1×10^{-4} and a batch size of 16. The SDRM module is configured with hyperparameters $\lambda_1 = \lambda_2 = 0.01$, and the DPGSM module uses $N = 50$ keypoints with a similarity threshold of $\tau = 80\%$.

To avoid performance bias caused by individual differences, we adopt the Leave-One-Subject-Out (LOSO) cross-validation protocol for both training and evaluation. Given the class imbalance in ME datasets, accuracy alone is insufficient to reflect model performance. Therefore, we report Unweighted F1-score (UF1) and Unweighted Average Recall (UAR) as complementary metrics.

4.3 Ablation Study

To evaluate the individual contributions of SDRM and DPGSM to MER performance, we conducted a three-class ablation study on the CASME II dataset, gradually assessing each module under various settings and then their combination. Table 1 reports UF1, UAR, and Accuracy for each configuration.

In M1, using FlowNet [7] as the opticalflow with a static graph yields UF1 = 0.8451, UAR = 0.7254. Replacing FlowNet with our SDRM (M2) raises these to UF1 = 0.8742, UAR = 0.7503, showing more precise capture of subtle facial motions. Further introducing our DPGSM with $N = 30$ keypoints and $\tau = 80\%$ (M4) boosts performance to UF1 = 0.8583, UAR = 0.7452. Increasing N to 50 (M6) yields UF1 = 0.9064, UAR = 0.8348, confirming improved interkeypoint structural modeling.

Table 1. The ablation experiment of the SDRM and DPGSM on CASME II.

Method	Feature	Graph	N	τ	UF1	UAR
M1(Baseline)	Optical flow	Static	-	-	0.8451	0.7254
M2	SDRM	Static	-	-	0.8742	0.7503
M3	SDRM	DPGSM	30	60%	0.8308	0.7413
M4	SDRM	DPGSM	30	80%	0.8583	0.7452
M5	SDRM	DPGSM	40	80%	0.8883	0.7750
M6	SDRM	DPGSM	50	80%	0.9064	0.8348

4.4 Comparison to State-of-the-Art Methods

In this section, we compare the proposed PGS-Net with various existing MER methods and evaluate them on three public datasets: SMIC, CASME II, and SAMM. UF1 and UAR are adopted as evaluation metrics to comprehensively assess the recognition performance of the models.

We include comparisons with representative state-of-the-art methods, including traditional handcrafted feature-based approaches (e.g., LBP-TOP [14], Bi-WOOF [13]), deep learning-based methods (e.g., CapsuleNet [16], STSTNet [12], OFF-ApexNet [5], RCN [17], MER-Supcom [22], DER-ViT [20], LAENet [4]), and GNN-based approaches (e.g., Graph-TCN [10], OFVIG-Net [21]). Experimental results show that PGS-Net consistently achieves superior performance across all datasets, outperforming existing methods. Specifically, it achieves UF1 = 0.8535 and UAR = 0.8023 on the SAMM dataset, and UF1 = 0.9064 and UAR = 0.8348 on the CASME II dataset. These results clearly demonstrate the excellent classification accuracy and generalization ability of PGS-Net (Table 2).

Table 2. Comparative Experimental Results for Three-Class Classification

Methods	SAMM		CASME II		SMIC	
	UF1	UAR	UF1	UAR	UF1	UAR
LBP-TOP (2007) [14]	0.3957	0.4102	0.7026	0.7429	0.2000	0.5280
Bi-WOOF (2018) [13]	0.5211	0.5139	0.7805	0.8026	0.5727	0.5829
CapsuleNet (2019) [16]	0.6209	0.5989	0.7068	0.7018	0.5820	0.5877
STSTNet (2019) [12]	0.6588	0.6810	0.8382	0.8686	0.6801	0.7013
OFF-ApexNet (2019) [5]	0.5409	0.5392	0.8764	0.8681	0.6817	0.6950
RCN (2020) [17]	0.7601	0.6715	0.8512	0.8123	0.6326	0.6441
Graph-TCN (2020) [10]	0.8050	0.7657	0.8648	0.8871	-	-
MER-Supcom (2022) [22]	0.8120	0.7125	0.8965	0.8806	-	-
DER-ViT (2023) [20]	0.7370	0.7470	0.9070	0.8980	0.7270	**0.7120**
LAENet (2024) [4]	0.6812	0.6620	**0.9101**	**0.9119**	0.6620	0.6523
OFVIG-Net (2025) [21]	0.7129	0.7195	0.6066	0.5787	0.6435	0.6400
Ours	**0.8535**	**0.8023**	0.9064	0.8348	**0.7922**	0.6685

4.5   Visualization for SDRM

To further verify the accuracy of the displacement features generated by SDRM, we designed a visualization experiment. By visualizing the displacement maps and the distribution of keypoint locations, the effectiveness of SDRM can be clearly validated.

We selected ME samples from different emotion categories for visualization, as shown in Fig. 3. In the figure, the color intensity represents the magnitude of displacement, and the markers indicate the detected keypoints. As illustrated, the displacement maps effectively capture the subtle motion variations where MEs occur. Meanwhile, the Keypoint Detection accurately identifies regions with significant changes, enabling the extraction of robust and fine-grained local features crucial for MER.

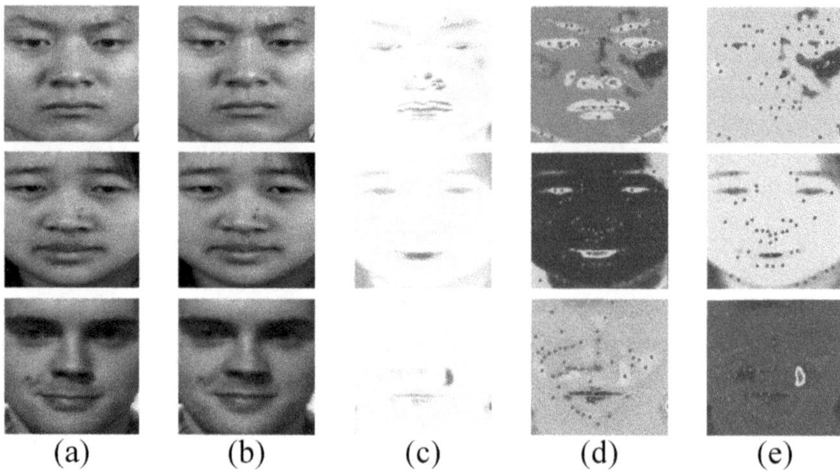

(a)   (b)   (c)   (d)   (e)

Fig. 3. Visualization of Displacement Maps and Keypoint Localization from SDRM. (a): Onset, (b): Apex, (c): Displacement Maps, (d): X keypoint, (e): Y keypoint

5 Conclusion

This paper addresses two key challenges in MER: the difficulty of modeling subtle local motion and the significant individual variability. We propose a novel network (PGS-Net), which leverages SDRM to reconstruct and amplify the X and Y displacement fields between onset and apex frames, enhancing fine-grained motion modeling. Additionally, DPGSM integrates facial structure and displacement features to construct dynamic, personalized graph structures that adapt to individual differences. On the SMIC, CASME II, and SAMM datasets, PGS-Net outperforms state-of-the-art methods across multiple metrics in three-class classification tasks, demonstrating superior recognition performance and generalization. In the future, we will extend SDRM to handle arbitrary frame pairs for richer feature diversity and explore lightweight graph structures to reduce complexity and mitigate overfitting.

References

1. Breiman, L.: Random forests. Mach. Learn. **45**(1), 5–32 (2001)
2. Davison, A.K., Lansley, C., Costen, N., Tan, K., Yap, M.H.: SAMM: a spontaneous micro-facial movement dataset. IEEE Trans. Affect. Comput. **9**(1), 116–129 (2018)
3. Ekman, P., Friesen, W.V.: Nonverbal leakage and clues to deception. Psychiatry Interpersonal Biol. Processes **32**(1), 88–106 (1969)
4. Gan, Y.S., Lien, S.-E., Chiang, Y.-C., Liong, S.-T.: Laenet for micro-expression recognition. Vis. Comput. **40**(2), 585–599 (2024)
5. Gan, Y.S., Liong, S.T., Yau, W.C., Huang, Y.C., Tan, L.K.: OFF-ApexNet on micro-expression recognition system. Signal Process. Image Commun. **74**, 129–139 (2019)

6. Hearst, M.A., Dumais, S.T., Osuna, E., Platt, J., Scholkopf, B.: Support vector machines. IEEE Intell. Syst. Appl. **13**(4), 18–28 (1998)
7. Ilg, E., Mayer, N., Saikia, T., Keuper, M., Dosovitskiy, A., Brox, T.: Flownet 2.0: evolution of optical flow estimation with deep networks. In: Proceedings of the IEEE Conference on Computer Vision and Pattern Recognition, pp. 2462–2470 (2017)
8. Kipf, T.N.: Semi-supervised classification with graph convolutional networks. *arXiv preprint*arXiv:1609.02907 (2016)
9. LeCun, Y., Bottou, L., Bengio, Y., Haffner, P.: Gradient-based learning applied to document recognition. Proc. IEEE **86**(11), 2278–2324 (2002)
10. Lei, L., Li, J., Chen, T., Li, S.: A novel graph-TCN with a graph structured representation for micro-expression recognition. In: Proceedings of the 28th ACM International Conference on Multimedia, pp. 2237–2245 (2020)
11. Li, X., Pfister, T., Huang, X., Zhao, G., Pietikäinen, M.: A spontaneous micro-expression database: inducement, collection and baseline. In: 2013 10th IEEE International Conference and Workshops on Automatic Face and Gesture Recognition (FG), pp. 1–6 (2013)
12. Liong, S-T., Gan, Y.S., See, J., Khor, H-Q., Huang, Y-C.; Shallow triple stream three-dimensional CNN (ststnet) for micro-expression recognition. In: 2019 14th IEEE International Conference on Automatic Face Gesture Recognition (FG 2019), pp. 1–5 (2019)
13. Liong, S.T., See, J., Wong, K., Phan, R.C.W.: Less is more: micro-expression recognition from video using apex frame. Signal Process. Image Commun. **62**, 82–92 (2018)
14. Pfister, T., Li, X., Zhao, G., Pietikäinen, M.: Recognising spontaneous facial micro-expressions. In: 2011 International Conference on Computer Vision, pp. 1449–1456 (2011)
15. Ronneberger, O., Fischer, P., Brox, T.: U-net convolutional networks for biomedical image segmentation (2015)
16. Van Quang, N., Chun, J., Tokuyama, T.: Capsulenet for micro-expression recognition. In: 2019 14th IEEE International Conference on Automatic Face & Gesture Recognition (FG 2019), pp. 1–7. IEEE (2019)
17. Xia, Z., Peng, W., Khor, H.-Q., Feng, X., Zhao, G.: Revealing the invisible with model and data shrinking for composite-database micro-expression recognition. IEEE Trans. Image Process. **29**, 8590–8605 (2020)
18. Yan, W.-J., et al.: Casme ii: an improved spontaneous micro-expression database and the baseline evaluation. PLOS ONE **9**(1), 1–8 (2014)
19. Yu, J., Zhang, C., Song, Y., Cai, W.: Ice-Gan: identity-aware and capsule-enhanced GAN with graph-based reasoning for micro-expression recognition and synthesis. In: 2021 International Joint Conference on Neural Networks (IJCNN), pp. 1–8 (2021)
20. Zhang, H., Zhang, H., Yin, L.: Data expansion and relabeling for improving the vision transformer-based micro-expression recognition. Authorea Preprints (2023)
21. Zhang, L., Zhang, Y., Sun, X., Tang, W., Wang, X., Li, Z.: Micro-expression recognition based on direct learning of graph structure. Neurocomputing **619**, 129135 (2025)
22. Zhi, R., Jing, H., Wan, F.: Micro-expression recognition with supervised contrastive learning. Pattern Recogn. Lett. **163**, 25–31 (2022)

Cross-Paradigm Facial Expression Recognition Based Emotional Category-Feature Prototypes

Yiluo Mao[1], Shasha Mao[1(✉)], Rui Wu[1], and Yimeng Zhang[2]

[1] School of Artificial Intelligence, Xidian University, Xi'an, China
`ssmao@xidian.edu.cn`
[2] Faculty of Integrated Circuit, Xidian University, Xi'an, China

Abstract. Due to emotional ambiguity and the subjectivity of annotators, noisy labels have become an unavoidable problem in facial expression recognition (FER). Most existing methods primarily employ supervised learning to address the noisy labels, which still tends to overfit them. In this paper, we propose a novel noise-tolerant FER model that integrates the prototypical classifier and the general classifier within a consistency-driven framework, to address the overfitting to noisy labels. In the proposed method, a prototypical classifier is designed based on emotional category-feature prototypes, replacing fully connected layers with a distance metric-based classification head. Furthermore, to eliminate emotional ambiguity in facial images, we propose an emotion consistency constraint between different classifiers, complementing our model to achieve the correction of noise labels, and meanwhile leveraging classifiers with varied metrics for improved detection and correction of noisy labels. Finally, experimental results illustrate that the proposed method outperforms the state-of-the-art methods on FER datasets with various noises.

Keywords: Deep Facial Expression Recognition · Label Noise · Label Correction

1 Introduction

Considering that facial expression is one kind of direct nonverbal signals that convey human emotions in communication, facial expression recognition (FER) has attracted considerable interest [1], and has been applied in many real-world fields, such as human-computer interaction, physical diagnosis, etc. Currently, numerous wild FER datasets have been collected, including AffectNet [2], RAF-DB [3], MsCeleb [4], FERPlus [5], etc., and contain abundant spontaneous facial expression images. Thanks to these publicly available datasets, deep learning-based methods [6–8] have become an important research direction in the field of FER. However, due to the inherent ambiguity [9] of emotions and the subjectivity of the annotators [10], some noisy labels inevitably appear in the data annotations for these wild FER datasets, challenging FER.

W. Jia et al. (Eds.): CCBR 2025, LNCS 16360, pp. 328–340, 2026.
https://doi.org/10.1007/978-981-95-6123-0_31

Consequently, many deep FER methods [11–14] have been introduced to mitigate the problem posed by label noises. Early, SCN [11] implements additional fully connected layers to learn the confidence of data samples and correct the labels of low-confidence samples. DMUE [12] employs a multi-branch model to assign multiple predicted labels to facial expressions, thereby exploring the potential distribution in the label space. Subsequently, EAC [13] models the noisy samples based on visual consistency. Recently, LA-Net [14] has integrated facial landmark information to assist in facial expression recognition and eliminate noise labels. Although existing methods have achieved promising results, most of them have been developed from the perspective of supervised learning paradigms. This means that the model is still trained based on the noisy labels in the dataset. For example, noisy labels were filtered by self-correction in SCN, but for some extreme noisy samples (especially for highly noisy datasets), SCN may not be able to exclude these samples completely efficiently, leading to a decrease in the accuracy of the model. Furthermore, it is difficult for the labeled noise to be definitely determined in practice, which fails to sufficiently distinguish between genuine noise and samples that are merely difficult to classify in the supervised learning model. Especially for FER, the model utilizes localized features to align facial expression images with noisy labels.

Unlike the supervised model, self-supervised learning [15,16] can extract the latent feature from the data itself without manual annotations, which benefits in filtering out inconsistencies caused by label noise [17]. Although self-supervised learning has been introduced into FER [18,19], most existing methods focus on the label-free characteristic of self-supervised learning to obtain superior model initialization parameters. In general, a contrastive model mainly focuses on learning the latent features of each image. However, for FER, expression datasets are collected only from human faces, which leads to a high degree of content homogeneity. It presents an unavoidable challenge when self-supervised learning is applied in FER. In addition, due to the complexity of facial expressions, individuals can exhibit significant variations in their expression for the same emotion. Therefore, maintaining consistency in feature representation during the learning process is essential to prevent individual differences from being misinterpreted as categorical information.

Based on this, in this paper we propose a cross-paradigm FER method, which effectively corrects the noisy label by uniting distinct paradigms of FER. In the proposed method, a class-prototypical classification module is first constructed by integrating self-supervised learning into FER, in which emotional category-feature prototypes are explored to achieve feature-to-class mapping by assessing the similarity between facial expression features and the category-feature prototypes. Meanwhile, inspired by [20], a class contrastive loss is designed for FER to enhance the focus of the contrastive model on extracting the latent emotional features of each facial image. Moreover, a cross-paradigm label-correction module is designed to unite the two distinct paradigms of FER and correct noisy labels by emotional consistency and label confidence evaluation. Extensive experiments are conducted to validate the effectiveness of the proposed method, and experiments involving noise addition based on emotional association are initiated for the first time.

2   Related Work

2.1   Deep Facial Expression Recognition

Currently, deep facial expression recognition has become the primary study of FER, since the deep model integrates feature learning and expression recognition to extract more discriminative representations. Numerous proposed methods have validated the effectiveness of deep learning in FER. Early, Zhang et al. [21] employed a deep neural network (DNN) to learn discriminative patterns and integrated facial features from various viewpoints. Furthermore, MA-Net [22] introduced an approach where an image feature pre-extractor is used to extract intermediate features from input images, a multi-scale module is employed to fuse features from various receptive fields, and a local attention module guides the network's focus towards locally salient features.

As is well-known, noisy labels present an unavoidable challenge in FER research, leading to the development of numerous related methods. SCN [11] and RUL [22] both divide the training dataset into clean and noisy samples, focusing on the information in the clean samples and relabeling the noisy ones. DMUE [12] introduces an auxiliary multi-branch learning framework that better uncovers and describes the latent distribution within the label space, maximizing the utilization of pairwise relationships among semantic features of instances to estimate uncertainty. EAC [13] generates new input by flipping the input image, thus mining noisy samples in the dataset based on visual consistency. Rather than correcting noisy labels, this model imposes consistency constraints on them. LA-Net [14] utilizes landmark information to reduce uncertainty in the emotional space and enhances training supervision quality by constructing a label distribution for each sample as supervisory information. Inspired by EAC and LA-Net, we recognize the importance of reducing uncertainty in Noise FER. Thus, our approach imposes consistency constraints at a different level compared to previous works, without necessitating additional auxiliary information.

2.2   Self-Supervised Learning

According to [23], self-supervised learning can be categorized into three main types based on the design of pretext tasks: context-based, temporal-based, and contrastive-based methods. In this paper, we focus primarily on the contrastive model. In contrastive learning, each sample is treated as a distinct category and compared with other samples to identify pairs of similar ones. This process enables contrastive learning to develop more discriminative feature representations, wherein the feature distance between similar samples is reduced, while it is increased for dissimilar samples, benefiting downstream tasks [24]. The study [25] introduced the Context Encoders method, which employs autoencoders for image inpainting as a pretext task in self-supervised learning. Autoencoders predict obscured regions in images, facilitating the learning of more intrinsic feature representations. The work [26] introduced data augmentation methods like rotation, cropping, and color transformations as pretext tasks in self-supervised learning. The researchers [17] innovatively introduced the concept of maximizing mutual information to train encoders for learning image feature representations. This approach involves maximizing both global and local information, ensuring alignment of the encoder's features with the assumed sample prior distribution. Whereafter, SimCLR [27] was proposed, which generated multiple views of the same input image through various data augmentations to construct positive and negative sample pairs. Its loss function encourages tighter representations for positive examples and greater separation for negative examples. Chuang et al. [28] proposed a novel contrastive loss function that was robust to noisy views, thereby expanding the applicability of contrastive learning methods.

3   The Proposed Method

This paper proposes a novel Cross-Paradigm FER method, which integrates different classification paradigms into a unified framework to overfitting of models to noisy labels. The proposed method framework is shown in Fig. 1 and consists of two main components: Class-Prototypical Classification Module and Cross-paradigm Label Correction Module. The class-prototypical classification module consists of a self-supervised contrastive module and a prototypical classifier. The prototypical classifier, combined with a conventional classifier, forms a Cross-Paradigm Label Correction Module. The prediction of one branch serves as a consistency constraint for the other branch. Label correction integrates the prediction results and confidence levels of each branch. These two components work together across different paradigms to improve the effectiveness of FER in noisy environments.

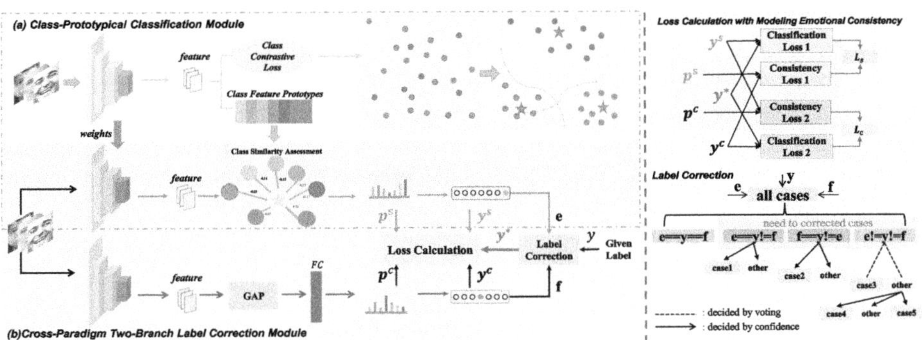

Fig. 1. The framework of the proposed method.

3.1   Class-Prototypical Classification Module

Since most existing methods are designed from the point of view of fully supervised learning, feature learning of FER models is still directly supervised by noisy labels. So we propose to decompose the noisy FER task into feature learning and distance-based classification. The former uses a self-supervised comparison module to extract noise-independent features, while the latter uses a prototype classifier to reduce the dependence on label accuracy by measuring the distance between the feature space and the category centroid. The first subtask involves learning the most discriminative features for each facial emotion class, while the second subtask involves obtaining facial expression recognition results based on the distances in the feature space between the sample features and the centers of various emotion categories [29].

In contrastive learning [27], a batch of N samples, undergoes data augmenta0tion, resulting in $2N$ samples. In traditional contrast learning, the loss function focuses on distinguishing different views of a single sample, but in the FER task, this strategy may neglect common features within the same emotion category. To better serve the properties of FER, we draw on the literature [20] and propose a category-based contrast loss, shown as

$$L_{s_f} = -\frac{1}{|P_{(i)}|} \sum_{p \in P_{(i)}} \log \frac{\exp\left(\mathrm{sim}(\mathbf{z}_i, \mathbf{z}_p)/\tau\right)}{\sum_{a \in A_{(i)}} \exp\left(\mathrm{sim}(\mathbf{z}_i, \mathbf{z}_a)/\tau\right)} \tag{1}$$

where $sim(\mathbf{a}, \mathbf{b}) = \frac{\mathbf{a} \cdot \mathbf{b}}{|\mathbf{a}||\mathbf{b}|}$, and $\mathbf{z}_i$ is the embedded representation of the sample $\mathbf{x}_i$ after passing through the feature extraction network. In that loss, we utilize label information to determine positive and negative samples: pairs of samples with identical labels are defined as positive samples, and pairs of samples with different labels are defined as negative samples. For each sample x_i in a batch containing $2N$ samples, $P_{(i)}$ expresses the set of its positive samples, and $A_{(i)}$ expresses the set of its negative samples. Unlike the traditional loss, the class contrast loss focuses on inter-class consistency and inter-class differentiation, which helps to form a more compact inter-class distribution and a more dispersed inter-class distribution in the feature space, and improves the ability to recognize subtle expression differences.

Inspired by the approach [30], we construct the feature prototypes of seven emotional categories, represented by $\mathcal{S}$. Seven prototypes encapsulate the latent emotional features identified across all images by our contrastive model and are expressed as $\mathcal{S} = \{\mathbf{s}_0, \mathbf{s}_1, ..., \mathbf{s}_c\}$. The feature prototype of each category is defined by the following formula

$$\mathbf{s}_k = \frac{1}{n_k} \sum_{i=1}^{n_k} f(\mathbf{x}_i). \tag{2}$$

where $f(\mathbf{x}_i)$ is the features of data samples following the implementation of contrastive learning, c is the number of emotional categories, and n_k denotes the count of samples within the k-th class, $k = \{0, ..., c\}$. Importantly, feature prototypes are generated based on the statistics of all samples within a category, thereby reducing the impact of individual noisy labels. During the training process, owing to the continuous correction of noisy labels, the prototypes of categorical features are recalculated. A momentum-based approach is adopted to update the category-feature prototypes by

$$\mathcal{S} = \alpha_p \mathcal{S} + (1 - \alpha_p)\mathcal{S}', \tag{3}$$

where $\mathcal{S}'$ denotes the recalculated category-feature prototypes following label correction, and α_p is a balancing parameter.

In the traditional classification paradigm, deep features are generally transformed into targets via a final fully connected layer. For example, 512-depth features are mapped to 7 emotional categories. This mapping enhances accuracy through the continuous optimization of parameters within a substantial nonlinear search space. However, the model can still fit noisy labels effectively, even when erroneous samples are present in the training set. To address this problem, we design a class-prototypical classification module that does not necessitate parameter optimization. In this paradigm, the classifier evaluates the similarity between depth features and the emotional-category prototypes, produced by the contrastive model.

The discriminative features, denoted as $f(\mathbf{x}_i)$, along with the generated feature prototypes of emotional categories $\mathcal{S}$, are employed to calculate the similarity. This similarity calculation assists in determining the probabilities $\mathbf{p}^s$ that a facial image $\mathbf{x}_i$ is predicted to belong to each class, represented as $\mathbf{p}^s_i = \{p^s_{i0}, p^s_{i1}, ..., p^s_{ic}\}$. Cosine similarity evaluation is utilized for this purpose, as demonstrated below

$$\mathbf{p}^s(\mathbf{x}_i) = sim(f(\mathbf{x}_i), \mathbf{s}_k), \tag{4}$$

Subsequently, the final classification prediction y^s_i is determined based on $\mathbf{p}^s_i$ using the formula

$$y^s_i = argmax(\mathbf{p}^s_i). \tag{5}$$

3.2   Cross-Paradigm Label Correction Module

In this part, we construct a cross-paradigm label correction module by designing jointly optimized dual-branches to integrate two distinct classification paradigms: the class-prototypical classification paradigm and the general classification paradigm (using an FC-layer). Specifically, considering the emotional consistency across different paradigms, the emotion consistency is modeled to constrain the feature learning of cross-paradigm and explore noisy labels. Subsequently, a label correction strategy is proposed to rectify the noisy labels. And the corrected labels are fed into two branches of cross classification paradigms, instead of the original given labels. Finally, the predictions are generated by the weighted fusion of two branches.

In the proposed method, the dual branches are initially loaded with different weights and utilize distinct classification paradigms. However, both branches essentially deal with the same facial expression images, and the expression in each image should remain consistent. Thus, we constrain the consistency of the dual branches to better explore the potential features of facial expressions and mitigate noisy labels. As mentioned previously, the class-prototypical classification branch provides the predicted probability vector $\mathbf{p}^s(\mathbf{x}_i)$ and the prediction y_i^s respectively. For the general classification branch, the prediction probability vector and the predictive label are represented by $\mathbf{p}^c(\mathbf{x}_i)$ and y_i^c, respectively. Based on these, the emotional consistencies are modeled as

$$Consist^s = entropy(\mathbf{p}_i^s(\mathbf{x}_i), y_i^c), \tag{6}$$

and

$$Consist^c = entropy(\mathbf{p}_i^c(\mathbf{x}_i), y_i^s), \tag{7}$$

where $entropy(\cdot)$ expresses the function of the cross-entropy loss. Then, the losses for two branches are formulated as

$$L_s = \alpha_s \cdot entropy(\mathbf{p}_i^s(\mathbf{x}_i), y_i^*) + (1 - \alpha_s) \cdot Consist^s, \tag{8}$$

and

$$L_c = \alpha_c \cdot entropy(\mathbf{p}_i^c(\mathbf{x}_i), y_i^*) + (1 - \alpha_c) \cdot Consist^c, \tag{9}$$

where α_s and α_c are hyper-parameters designed to balance the classification loss and the consistency loss, and y_i^* denotes the corrected label. Initially, y_i^* corresponds to the assigned label of the sample $\mathbf{x}_i$.

Meanwhile, a label correction mechanism is proposed to rectify noisy labels by leveraging the diversity between two classification paradigms. Based on the predictions obtained by the two branches, the samples can be broadly classified into four categories. Confidence assessments are combined to identify samples with noisy labels and simultaneously determine their potentially true labels. As shown in Fig. 1, four scenarios are defined as follows: 1) Both branches agree with the given labels; 2) Both branches differ from the given labels; 3) The class-prototypical paradigm branch agrees with the given label but differs from the other branch; 4) The general paradigm branch agrees with the given label but differs from the other branch. Utilizing the predicted probabilities, it is possible to identify and correct samples with noisy labels by the following formula

$$y' = \begin{cases} e, & \text{if } f = y \ \& \ e \neq y \ \& \ \mathrm{cof}(e) > th \\ f, & \text{if } e = y \ \& \ f \neq y \ \& \ \mathrm{cof}(f) > th \\ e \text{ or } f, & \text{if } e \neq y \ \& \ f \neq y \ \& \ e = f \\ f, & \text{if } f \neq y \ \& \ e \neq y \ \& \ \mathrm{cof}(f) > th \ \& \ \mathrm{cof}(e) < th \\ e, & \text{if } f \neq y \ \& \ e \neq y \ \& \ \mathrm{cof}(f) < th \ \& \ \mathrm{cof}(e) > th \\ y, & \text{otherwise} \end{cases} \tag{10}$$

where e, f, y and y' represent the results of the class-prototypical branch, the normal branch, the given label and the adjusted label, respectively. $cof()$ denotes the confidence function, which directly takes the maximum value of the predicted probability. th stands for the high confidence threshold, which is set to 0.7.

4 Experiments and Analyses

4.1 Experiment Setting

Datasets. RAF-DB contains 29,672 face images obtained from the Internet in real scenes under complex conditions such as natural lighting, different angles, and occlusion. The classification of emotions is typically divided into seven primary categories. The dataset includes 12,271 images used for training and 3,068 images used for testing. **FERPlus** is an extended dataset based on FER2013, which enhances the quality and accuracy of the dataset's sentiment labelling through re-labelling. The original FER2013, sourced through Google search, comprises 28,709 training images, 3,589 validation images, and 3,589 test images. **AffectNet** is currently the largest facial expression database. The dataset was compiled using three search engines and over a thousand emotion-related keywords. Of these images, 286,564 have been allocated for training purposes, while 4,000 have been designated for testing.

Implementation Details. To evaluate the performance of the proposed method, all face input images are uniformly sized at 224×224. The proposed method uses only flipping and erasing for data augmentation. We used the weights of Ms-Celeb-1M pre-trained on resnet-18. To ensure fair comparisons, consistent with the delineation method in previous studies, noise was added only to the training set. The Adam optimizer with a weight decay of 0.0001 and an exponential learning rate scheduler with a gamma of 0.9 are used. The contrastive model sets the initial learning rate at 0.0003 and conducts training for 200 epochs, with a final feature dimensionality of 300. The general classification model sets the initial learning rate at 0.0002 and performs training for 60 epochs. Two hyperparameters, α_s and α_c, are set to 0.3.

4.2 Comparisons with the State-of-the-Art

In this section, we evaluate the performance of the proposed method on the RAF-DB, FERPlus, and AffectNet datasets, each with different noise ratios, where noise labels are generated by randomly modifying sample labels, as described in [13], with the best results marked in bold. To ensure fairness, we directly use the noise label datasets provided in existing works. In addition to the artificial mislabeling in the FER dataset, poor facial image quality and the inherent ambiguity of emotions may introduce higher levels of label noise in the FER task. To simulate this scenario, we designed a novel experiment: adding noise labels to the dataset based on emotional associations. The fuzzy noise is generated based on the associations between emotional categories, better simulating the label noise problem in real-world scenarios.

From Table 1, in random noisy experiments our method improves by 0. 78%, 1. 38% and 1. 29% on RAF-DB, FERPlus and AffectNet, respectively, surpassing current state-of-the-art methods. Furthermore, it was observed that our method

Table 1. Performance (Accuracy%) Comparisons on Random Noisy Labels with different noise ratios (10%, 20% and 30%).

Methods	RAF-DB			FERPlus			AffectNet			Avg		
	10%	20%	30%	10%	20%	30%	10%	20%	30%	10%	20%	30%
Baseline	81.01	77.98	75.50	83.29	82.34	79.77	57.24	55.89	52.16	73.84	72.07	69.14
SCN (CVPR'20) [11]	82.15	79.79	77.45	84.99	83.35	82.20	58.60	57.51	54.60	75.24	73.55	71.41
RUL (NeurIPS'21) [22]	86.17	84.32	82.06	86.93	85.05	83.90	60.54	59.01	56.93	77.88	76.12	74.29
EAC (ECCV'22) [13]	88.02	86.05	84.42	87.03	86.07	85.44	61.11	60.29	58.91	78.72	77.47	76.25
LA-Net (ICCV'23) [14]	**88.75**	87.12	85.33	88.02	86.85	86.01	62.85	61.72	**60.82**	79.87	78.56	77.38
FAN (ICME'24) [31]	88.06	87.14	85.89	87.67	86.28	84.76	**64.92**	60.21	57.23	80.22	77.88	75.96
3WAUS (IS'24) [32]	88.17	86.90	84.71	87.15	86.59	85.46	61.53	61.19	60.08	78.95	78.23	76.75
Ours	88.26	**87.28**	**86.11**	**88.93**	**88.23**	**86.83**	64.14	**62.82**	59.79	**80.44**	**79.44**	**77.57**

exhibits greater performance improvements as the noise ratio increases. Specifically, on the AffectNet dataset with noises 10% and 30%, our model achieved improvements of 6.9% and 7.63%, respectively, compared to the baseline model.

Table 2. Performance (Accuracy%) Comparisons on Ambiguous Noisy Labels with different noise ratios (10%, 20% and 30%).

Methods	RAF-DB			FERPlus			AffectNet			Avg		
	10%	20%	30%	10%	20%	30%	10%	20%	30%	10%	20%	30%
Baseline	84.55	83.90	81.75	82.91	80.94	76.54	60.03	54.14	53.14	75.83	72.68	70.98
SCN (CVPR'20) [11]	86.70	84.09	81.06	83.84	80.49	79.15	60.17	56.43	53.26	76.90	73.67	71.15
RUL (NeurIPS'21) [22]	84.84	82.59	79.40	85.37	82.91	80.46	61.37	57.40	54.03	77.19	74.30	71.29
EAC (ECCV'22) [13]	84.74	83.83	82.59	88.55	87.72	86.51	**62.31**	**60.97**	**56.08**	77.68	77.50	75.06
LA-Net (ICCV'23) [14]	85.46	83.11	81.42	–	–	–	–	–	–	–	–	–
Ours	**88.16**	**86.66**	**86.14**	**89.09**	**88.49**	**87.75**	61.62	59.68	54.85	**79.62**	**78.27**	**76.24**

The Table 2 shows the results for ambiguous noise labels. It is obvious that the proposed method achieves higher accuracies than the compared methods for RAF-DB and FERPlus. However, in the AffectNet dataset, our model did not maintain its previously demonstrated advantage. Examining the label files, we discovered that in the dataset with ambiguous noise labels, the neutral and surprise classes had an additional 7,742 and 7,842 samples, respectively, compared to the dataset with random noise labels. The differences in the number of samples for the other categories were around 4,000, so we have good reason to believe that the performance degradation of our proposed model in the Affect-Net dataset is due to the skewed data distribution. In addition, since LA-Net networks require additional AU information in addition to facial keypoints, we only performed experiments with ambiguous noise on the RAF-DB dataset where the relevant data is publicly available, 3WAUS and FAN also did not make the relevant data public so we could not perform ambiguous noise experiments.

4.3   Visualization Analysis

To more intuitively demonstrate the effectiveness of the proposed method of learning emotional consistency, this study will present the visualization results of our model in label correction in Fig. 2, while the confusion matrix and the results of the loss distribution will be presented in Fig. 3 in the visualization section.

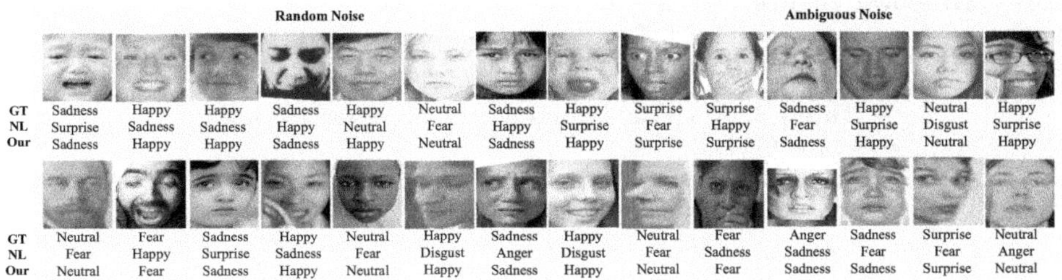

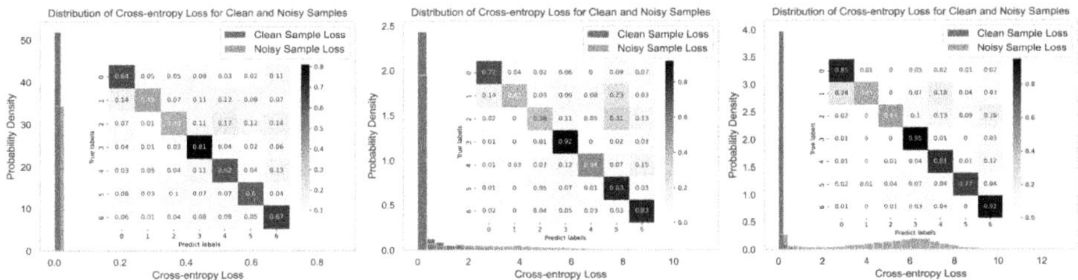

Fig. 2. Visualization of label correction. The left part pertains to random noise, while the right part refers to ambiguous noise.

Fig. 3. From left to right, the figures show confusion matrices and the distribution of losses generated by the baseline model, the SCN model, and our model, respectively.

As shown in Fig. 2, it is seen that our model performs well in label correction, does not overfit on noisy labels, and the prediction results are consistent with the true labels, where GT represents the true label, NL represents the noisy label, and Our represents the prediction result of our model.

Visualization of Confuse Matrix and Loss Distribution. From Fig. 3, the accuracy of our approach improves by 4% and 11% when dealing with the second and third classes with less data, respectively, compared to the previous model. In addition, we demonstrate the model's ability to distinguish between inaccurate and accurate labels by calculating the cross-entropy loss between the predictions of the training samples and their corresponding labels, as shown in Fig. The SCN model distinguishes between noisy samples and clean samples to a certain extent, but the cross-entropy loss distributions of the two still overlap considerably. In contrast, our model fits the clean samples better, as evidenced by the narrowest band of loss distribution for the clean samples. In addition, we can observe a significant difference in the loss distribution regions of the clean and noise samples.

4.4　Ablation Study

Table 3. Ablation studies on the proposed modules

Class-Prototypical	Consistency	Label-Correct	RAF-DB
×	×	×	75.5
✓	×	×	83.8
✓	✓	×	84.8
✓	✓	✓	**86.1**

To evaluate the effectiveness of the proposed method, we conducted an experiment on RAF-DB data with 30% noise, and the results are presented in Table 3. Ablation experiments were conducted on the class-prototypical classification module ('Class-Prototypical'), consistency assessment modules ('Consistency'), and label correction mechanisms ('Label-Correct'). Table 3 shows that each module effectively improves FER performance. From Table 3, it is obvious that three modules are effective in improving the performance of FER.

5　Conclusion

In this paper, we address the issue of noisy labels in FER using a proposed dual-branch consistent label correction approach that incorporates different classification paradigms. The introduced class-prototypical module successfully integrates a self-supervised model into FER, effectively mitigating the overfitting problem caused by both the data itself and noisy labels in FER. Furthermore, the designed class contrastive loss enables the model to more effectively extract the latent emotional features of each facial image. Ultimately, we employ emotional consistency between dual-branch networks with different classification paradigms to constrain feature learning and have designed a label correction strategy that combines voting with confidence assessment. Experimental results demonstrate that the proposed method achieves superior performance on three datasets with varying noise ratios, notably the first implementation of experiments based on ambiguous noise.

Acknowledgments. This work was funded by State Key Program of National Natural Science of China grant number 62234010, the National Natural Science Foundation of China 62576265.

References

1. Sariyanidi, E., Gunes, H., Cavallaro, A.: Automatic analysis of facial affect: a survey of registration, representation, and recognition. TPAMI **37**(6), 1113–1133 (2014)
2. Mollahosseini, A., Hasani, B., Mahoor, M.: Affectnet: a database for facial expression, valence, and arousal computing in the wild. TAFFC **10**(1), 18–31 (2017)
3. Li, S., Deng, W., Du, J.: Reliable crowdsourcing and deep locality-preserving learning for expression recognition in the wild. In: CVPR, pp. 2852–2861 (2017)
4. Guo, Y., Zhang, L., Hu, Y., He, X., Gao, J.: Ms-celeb-1m: a dataset and benchmark for large-scale face recognition. In: ECCV, pp. 87–102 (2016)
5. Barsoum, E., Zhang, C., Ferrer, C., Zhang, Z.: Training deep networks for facial expression recognition with crowd-sourced label distribution. In: ICML, pp. 279–283 (2016)
6. Li, S., Deng, W.: Deep facial expression recognition: a survey. TAFFC **13**(3), 1195–1215 (2020)
7. Khan, A.: Facial emotion recognition using conventional machine learning and deep learning methods: current achievements, analysis and remaining challenges. Information **13**(6), 268 (2022)
8. Shi, G., Mao, S., Gou, S., Yan, D., Jiao, L., Xiong, L.: Adaptively enhancing facial expression crucial regions via a local non-local joint network. MIR **21**(2), 331–348 (2024)
9. Mao, S., et al.: Multi-task hybrid conv-transformer with emotional localized ambiguity exploration for facial pain assessment. JBHI (2025)
10. Zhang, F., Xu, M., Xu, C.: Weakly-supervised facial expression recognition in the wild with noisy data. TMM **24**, 1800–1814 (2021)
11. Wang, K., Peng, X., Yang, J., Lu, S., Qiao, Y.: Suppressing uncertainties for large-scale facial expression recognition. In: CVPR, pp. 6897–6906 (2020)
12. She, J., Hu, Y., Shi, H., Wang, J., Shen, Q., Mei, T.: Dive into ambiguity: latent distribution mining and pairwise uncertainty estimation for facial expression recognition. In: CVPR, pp. 6248–6257 (2021)
13. Zhang, Y., Wang, C., Ling, X., Deng, W.: Learn from all: erasing attention consistency for noisy label facial expression recognition. In: ECCV, pp. 418–434 (2022)
14. Wu, Z., Cui, J.: La-net: landmark-aware learning for reliable facial expression recognition under label noise. In: ICCV, pp. 20698–20707 (2023)
15. Jing, L., Tian, Y.: Self-supervised visual feature learning with deep neural networks: a survey. TPAMI **43**(11), 4037–4058 (2020)
16. Gui, J., et al.: A survey on self-supervised learning: algorithms, applications, and future trends. TPAMI **46**(12), 9052–9071 (2024)
17. Hjelm, R., et al.: Learning deep representations by mutual information estimation and maximization. arXiv preprint arXiv:1808.06670 (2018)
18. Wang, J., Ding, H., Wang, S.: Occluded facial expression recognition using self-supervised learning. In: ACCV, pp. 1077–1092 (2022)

19. Chaudhari, A., Bhatt, C., Krishna, A., Travieso-González, C.: Facial emotion recognition with inter-modality-attention-transformer-based self-supervised learning. Electronics **12**(2), 288 (2023)
20. Khosla, P., et al.: Supervised contrastive learning. NeurIPS **33**, 18661–18673 (2020)
21. Zhang, T., Zheng, W., Cui, Z., Zong, Y., Yan, J., Yan, K.: A deep neural network-driven feature learning method for multi-view facial expression recognition. TMM **18**(12), 2528–2536 (2016)
22. Zhao, Z., Liu, Q., Wang, S.: Learning deep global multi-scale and local attention features for facial expression recognition in the wild. TIP **30**, 6544–6556 (2021)
23. Liu, X., et al.: Self-supervised learning: generative or contrastive. TKDE **35**(1), 857–876 (2021)
24. Jaiswal, A., Babu, A., Zadeh, M., Banerjee, D., Makedon, F.: A survey on contrastive self-supervised learning. Technologies **9**(1), 2 (2020)
25. Pathak, D., Krahenbuhl, P., Donahue, J., Darrell, T., Efros, A.: Context encoders: feature learning by inpainting. In: CVPR, pp. 2536–2544 (2016)
26. Lee, H., Hwang, S., Shin, J.: Rethinking data augmentation: self-supervision and self-distillation (2019)
27. Chen, T., Kornblith, S., Norouzi, M., Hinton, G.: A simple framework for contrastive learning of visual representations. In: ICML, pp. 1597–1607 (2020)
28. Chuang, C., et al.: Robust contrastive learning against noisy views. In: CVPR, pp. 16670–16681 (2022)
29. Bezdek, J., Kuncheva, L.: Nearest prototype classifier designs: an experimental study. IJIS **16**(12), 1445–1473 (2001)
30. Mao, S., et al.: Label distribution amendment with emotional semantic correlations for facial expression recognition. arXiv preprint arXiv:2107.11061 (2021)
31. Wang, W., Li, S.: Focusing on all refined attention regions for noisy label facial expression recognition. In: ICME, pp. 1–6 (2024)
32. Li, D., Xiong, W., Luo, T., Zhang, L.: 3waus: a novel three-way adaptive uncertainty-suppressing model for facial expression recognition. IS 120962 (2024)

Attribute-Driven Identity Disentanglement for Fine-Grained Face Anonymization

Zehui Song, Qian Yu, Yiqiang Wu, Jiao Feng, and Hao Liu$^{(\boxtimes)}$

School of Information Engineering, Ningxia University,
Yinchuan 750021, Ningxia, China
`liuhao@nxu.edu.cn`

Abstract. In this paper, we propose a unified face anonymization framework that integrates attribute-driven identity separation and spatial mask optimization, specifically designed to achieve an optimal balance between identity privacy protection and attribute utility preservation. Existing face anonymization methods are limited by insufficient disentanglement of identity and attribute features and lack of fine-grained control during image synthesis, making it challenging to simultaneously ensure privacy and attribute fidelity. To address these challenges, our framework consists of two main modules. Specifically, an attribute-guided separation mechanism is employed to achieve effective disentanglement of identity and attribute features, while differential privacy-based perturbation is used to enhance the irreversibility and security of identity information. Additionally, spatial region masks are introduced to guide the fine-grained optimization of latent representations, enabling precise and coordinated control over identity, attribute, and background regions during image synthesis. Experimental results show that the proposed method achieves better performance than existing approaches in terms of identity obfuscation, attribute preservation, and image quality, significantly enhancing the utility and robustness of anonymized faces.

Keywords: Face Anonymization · Attribute Disentanglement · Masked Latent Optimization

1 Introduction

With the rise of smart devices and facial recognition, facial data privacy has become a major global concern. Large-scale face image collection for analytics increases risks of identity leakage and misuse. Regulations such as GDPR mandate strict privacy protection for biometric data [15].

Early anonymization hides identities by pixelation or mosaic [4,6], but at the cost of recognition utility and image quality. Recent learning-based approaches for face anonymization [5,10,11,16] enhance realism but still encounter two major challenges: (1) limited generalization—defenses tuned to one model fail on

W. Jia et al. (Eds.): CCBR 2025, LNCS 16360, pp. 341–351, 2026.
https://doi.org/10.1007/978-981-95-6123-0_32

others [14]; (2) visible artifacts such as distorted edges [11]. Meanwhile, attribute-editing and GAN synthesis methods [13] focus on visual appeal but seldom address privacy; GAN outputs often exhibit domain gaps that lower matching accuracy [8]. Even advanced editors like InterFaceGAN and StyleGAN2 reduce verification scores while leaking sensitive attributes [13], underscoring the persistent privacy-utility trade-off.

To address these issues, we propose a unified high-resolution face anonymization framework that jointly optimizes privacy protection and attribute fidelity. Specifically, we introduce an attribute-driven identity separation mechanism at the identity feature extraction stage. This mechanism leverages attribute-aware constraints—such as those informed by expression, gender, and pose information—to provide targeted supervision signals during the construction of the identity representation. By incorporating such attribute guidance at this stage, our method ensures that both identity features and critical non-identity attributes are accurately disentangled and robustly represented. Building on this, our framework incorporates a differential privacy mechanism to introduce controlled perturbations into the identity features of face images, thereby making the reconstructed identity highly resistant to re-identification attempts and adversarial attacks. This process ensures that the original identity information cannot be recovered, providing a solid guarantee of privacy even under strong adversarial conditions. Furthermore, we design a spatially-aware masking scheme that divides the latent representation of the facial image into distinct regions corresponding to identity, attribute, and background information. By enabling region-wise, fine-grained optimization, this approach allows us to disentangle and independently control the identity features and non-identity attributes, leading to more natural and realistic synthesized results, and overcoming the over-entanglement problem seen in many prior methods. Collectively, these innovations provide a robust technical foundation for privacy-aware facial data processing.

The main contributions of this work are as follows:

1. We design an attribute-driven identity separation strategy to ensure the disentanglement and preservation of critical utility attributes.
2. We present a face anonymization framework that integrates differential privacy for identity obfuscation.
3. We introduce spatial region masks to achieve fine-grained, region-wise optimization of facial representations, enabling precise control over identity, attribute, and background regions.

2   Approach

In this section, we introduce a unified framework for face anonymization, as illustrated in Fig. 2(a).Initially, we invert the source image I into its latent representation via StyleGAN2. Subsequently, a Attribute-Driven Regularization identity encoder effectively disentangles identity features from non-identity attributes

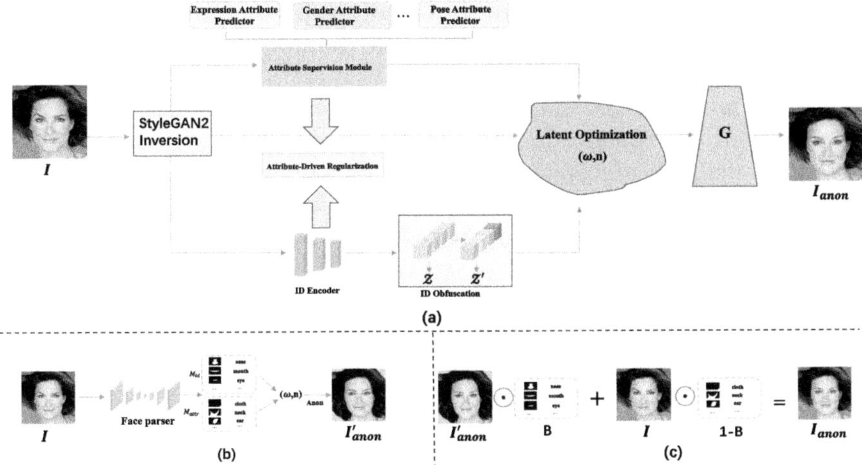

Fig. 1. (a) Overall pipeline of our face anonymization framework. The Attribute Supervision Module (ASM) and Mask-Guided Latent Optimization (MGLO) are the two principal modules. (b) MGLO enforces attribute-specific constraints in latent space via region masks. (c) The optimized anonymized region is seamlessly blended with the original image for high-fidelity results.

such as expression and hairstyle. Robust obfuscation of identity features is then achieved using a differential privacy-based perturbation module.

Finally, guided by spatial masks, the latent codes are optimized and fed into the generator G to produce high-quality anonymized images . Our method achieves a strong balance between privacy protection and attribute fidelity, with notable flexibility and controllability.

2.1   Identity Extraction

In face anonymization, a key challenge is balancing privacy protection with the preservation of useful attributes. Traditional approaches often use a single identity extractor, which can be influenced by model architecture and training data, leading to bias across age, gender, or ethnicity. Moreover, such extractors typically capture identity features together with non-identity attributes like expression, gender, and hairstyle, without separating them. Consequently, anonymization may inadvertently alter non-identity features, reducing image quality and failing to retain these attributes effectively.

To address these issues, we introduce an attribute-driven regularization strategy for identity extraction. Unlike traditional single identity extractors, our approach employs multiple attribute predictors, each focusing on different aspects of facial attributes, such as expression, gender, or pose. Through the collaborative supervision from these attribute predictors (via the attribute supervision module), we are able to extract and optimize identity features at a finer granularity, thus mitigating the bias of a single model. Attribute-driven constraints enable the model to learn identity features from various perspectives, reducing overfitting to specific data types and enhancing the disentanglement between identity and non-identity attributes.

To better integrate and optimize identity information extracted under different attribute-driven constraints, we apply a weighted summation of the output vectors from multiple attribute predictors and combine them through a nonlinear function. This produces a balanced identity representation that reduces bias and improves the robustness of the extraction process.

The formula $h_Z(I) = f\left(\sum_{i=1}^{k_Z} \phi_i(h_i(I))\right)$ describes the integration of multiple attribute predictors to extract identity features from an input image I. Here, $h_Z(I)$ is the final identity feature vector, obtained by aggregating outputs from k_Z attribute-driven predictors h_i, each capturing specific identity aspects under different attribute constraints. Before aggregation, each output $h_i(I)$ is processed by ϕ_i, typically a nonlinear activation or normalization, to enhance expressiveness and ensure scale consistency. The summation accumulates these processed features, which are then mapped by a nonlinear function f (e.g., ReLU or tanh) to the final identity feature space. This design leverages diverse attribute-driven perspectives while controlling redundancy and scale, producing a robust identity representation for downstream anonymization or perturbation tasks.

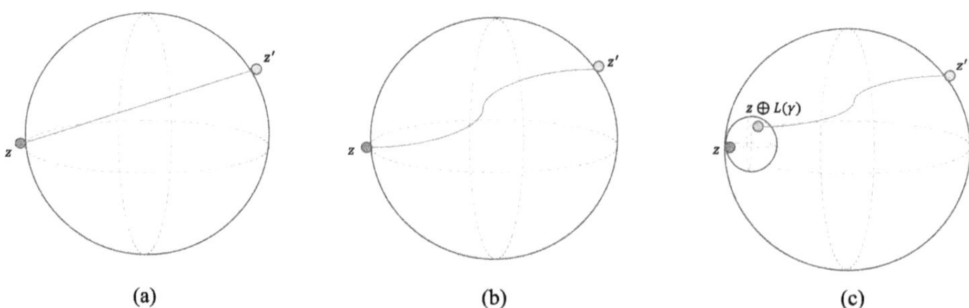

Fig. 2. Identity Perturbation Strategies. (a) Simply flipping z to $-z$ maximizes its distance from the original vector, yet the operation is easily reversible by another flip. (b) A learned MLP warps z along a non-linear path, making inversion harder. (c) Injecting Laplacian noise $z \oplus \mathcal{L}(\gamma)$ prior to the MLP enforces ε-LDP, markedly strengthening privacy and non-invertibility.

2.2   Identity Obfuscation

Traditional perturbation strategies—such as the opposite mapping in Fig. 2(a) and the multi-layer perceptron (MLP) method in Fig. 2(b)—provide some identity obfuscation but have inherent limitations. The opposite mapping perturbs identity information by negating the original identity vector, but this is reversible since an adversary can negate it again to recover the original identity. The MLP approach maps the identity vector to a new representation space through a trained multilayer perceptron, increasing perturbation complexity but remaining vulnerable if model parameters are exposed or subject to gradient-based attacks.

To improve perturbation robustness and ensure ε-local differential privacy (LDP), we add dimension-wise Laplacian noise during identity feature transformation, as shown in Fig. 2(c). Let $z = h_Z(I)$ be the aggregated identity feature from the attribute supervision module. A parameterized noise vector $L(\gamma)$ is generated, where γ is inversely proportional to the privacy budget ε and Λ is a sensitivity scaling factor. The noise is combined with z to obtain the perturbed identity representation: $z' = F_\theta(z \oplus L(\gamma))$, where F_θ is a parameterized nonlinear mapping function, typically a multilayer perceptron (MLP), that transforms and fuses the noisy identity features. This design allows privacy strength to be tuned via γ, balancing privacy protection with data utility. To measure perturbation effectiveness, we define a cosine distance-based identity discrepancy loss:

$$L_{id} = 1 - \frac{z \cdot z'}{\|z\|_2 \|z'\|_2} \tag{1}$$

where z represents the original identity feature vector, and z' denotes the identity feature vector after perturbation. By maximizing this loss during optimization, the method effectively prevents identity reconstruction, thereby achieving robust anonymization.

2.3 Latent Optimization

In face anonymization, our objective is to eliminate sensitive identity information while maximally preserving visual details and utility attributes of the

original image. We implement a mask-guided latent space optimization strategy using precomputed spatial masks. Specifically, we leverage a face parsing network to generate static masks that define identity-sensitive regions (M_{id}) and attribute-specific regions ($\{M_{attr}^{(k)}\}_{k=1}^{K}$) for distinct facial attributes. These masks are generated as:

$$M_{attr}^{(k)} = \text{FaceParser}(I, k) \tag{2}$$

where $\text{FaceParser}(\cdot)$ denotes the face parsing network, which produces binary or probabilistic masks for each attribute region.

The unified region-conditional loss $\mathcal{L}_{mask}$ guides spatial manipulation of identity and attribute features during latent space optimization through spatially constrained operations. In identity-sensitive regions defined by M_{id}, it maximizes identity feature differences between the original image I and anonymized output $G(w)$. In attribute-preserving regions, it minimizes variations in attribute-specific features to maintain semantic consistency, with operations confined to parser-designated facial areas:

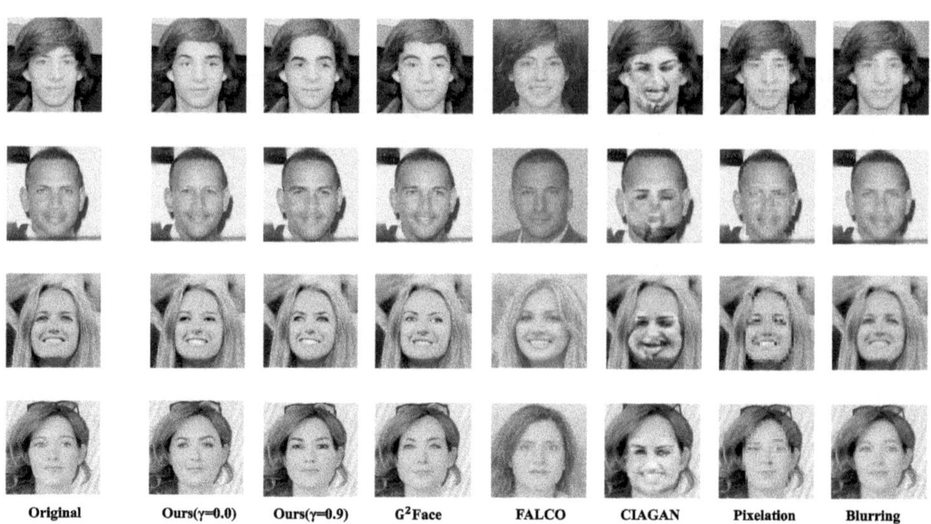

Fig. 3. Qualitative comparison of anonymization results between our method and previous approaches.

$$\mathcal{L}_{mask} = \lambda_{id} \left\| M_{id} \odot \left(h_Z(I) - h_Z(G(w)) \right) \right\|_2^2$$
$$+ \lambda_{attr} \sum_{k=1}^{K} \left\| M_{attr}^{(k)} \odot \left(\phi_k(I) - \phi_k(G(w)) \right) \right\|_2^2 \tag{3}$$

where M_{id} and $M_{attr}^{(k)}$ denote the identity mask and k-th attribute mask generated by the face parser, $\phi_k(\cdot)$ represents the k-th attribute prediction network in the attribute supervision module, $G(w)$ is the generator output during latent optimization phase, $\odot$ indicates element-wise masking operation, and $\|\cdot\|_2^2$ measures the squared L2-norm difference between features of the original image I and generated features.

To maintain structural integrity during optimization, we introduce a latent smoothness constraint, which ensures that the generated image retains consistent and natural facial structures:

$$L_{smooth} = \|\nabla_w \odot (w - w_0)\|_2^2 \tag{4}$$

where ∇_w is the Jacobian matrix of StyleGAN's mapping network, and w_0 is the initial latent code, effectively suppressing high-frequency artifacts while preserving facial geometry.

To ensure that the optimized face structure remains natural and that mask regions do not drift or deform, we introduce a target region shape loss, constraining the spatial distribution of target components in the anonymized image to match that of the input:

$$L_{shape} = \|Star(I) - Star(I'_{anon})\|_2^2 \tag{5}$$

where $Star(\cdot)$ denotes the spatial mask of facial structure components, automatically generated by the parser for the target region. This constraint is crucial for avoiding spatial misalignment, abnormal contours, or deformation of key regions after anonymization, thereby improving overall naturalness and visual consistency.

After latent space optimization, the anonymized image I'_{anon} obfuscates identity information. However, pixel-level optimization may introduce minor artifacts or alter non-identity regions, such as expression, background, or skin texture. To mitigate this and maintain visual fidelity, we apply a region-wise blending operation using spatial masks, as shown in Fig. 1(c). A binary or probabilistic mask B from the face parsing network marks identity-sensitive regions (e.g., eyes, nose, mouth) for replacement with the anonymized output, while other areas retain their original pixels. The final anonymized image is computed as:

$$I_{anon} = B \odot I'_{anon} + (1 - B) \odot I \tag{6}$$

where $\odot$ denotes the Hadamard product, B is the blending mask, I'_{anon} is the optimized anonymized result, and I is the original image. The operation ensures seamless integration between modified and unmodified regions, thereby preserving high-frequency details and achieving natural, artifact-free anonymization.

Finally, all the above losses are combined as a weighted sum to form the overall optimization objective:

$$L_{total} = \lambda_{id}L_{id} + \lambda_{mask}L_{mask} + \lambda_{smooth}L_{smooth} + \lambda_{shape}L_{shape} \tag{7}$$

where $\lambda_{id}, \lambda_{app}, \lambda_{smooth}, \lambda_{shape}$ are the weights for each loss, which are introduced to balance the contributions of different optimization objectives.

Table 1. Comparison of privacy protection results (ReID, IDS). Lower values correspond to better anonymization performance.

Method	ArcFace↓		FaceNet↓		
	$cos > 0.30$	$cos > 0.35$	$\ell_2 < 0.9$	$\ell_2 < 1.0$	$\ell_2 < 1.1$
CIAGAN	(1.7, 93.3)	(0.5, 51.4)	(**0.5**, 87.0)	(3.2, 99.9)	(11.3, **100**)
FALCO	(6.7, 81.8)	(2.7, 37.0)	(1.4, 83.7)	(1.7, 99.9)	(5.4, **100**)
G^{2}Face	(**0.0**, **72.9**)	(**0.0**, 26.2)	(0.6, **77.7**)	(**1.2**, 99.8)	(2.3, **100**)
Ours	(0.9, 82.1)	(**0.0**, **22.5**)	(1.2, 81.8)	(1.3, **99.7**)	(**2.1**, **100**)

Table 2. Evaluation of ReID and IDS performance with the AdaFace model.

	CIAGAN	FALCO	G^{2}Face	Ours
ReID ↓	0.7	8.0	0.6	**0.5**
IDS ↓	9.0	6.3	**5.0**	5.5

Table 3. Evaluation results on attribute preservation and image quality.

Method	Attribute ↑					LPIPS ↓	SSIM ↑
	Express	Ethnic	Gender	Age	Makeup		
CIAGAN	78.7	46.7	80.9	81.3	74.7	0.558	0.358
FALCO	82.6	**51.8**	84.8	**86.3**	77.6	0.307	0.475
G^2Face	77.9	41.8	81.0	84.4	68.9	**0.300**	0.530
Ours	**82.9**	49.3	**85.1**	82.3	**77.8**	0.342	**0.634**

Table 4. Evaluation results of our method for face anonymization on the LFW dataset.

Method	ArcFace ↓	FaceNet ↓	Attribute ↑	LPIPS ↓	SSIM ↑
CIAGAN	(0.6, **3.9**)	(1.5, **27.3**)	72.2	0.458	0.397
FALCO	(0.5, 7.6)	(8.7, 34.9)	78.2	**0.221**	0.672
G^2Face	(**0.0**, 8.5)	(**0.1**, 43.9)	61.7	0.460	0.428
Ours	(0.8, 4.6)	(**0.1**, 30.4)	**78.9**	0.367	**0.712**

Table 5. Evaluation results of key component ablation.

Method	ArcFace ↓	FaceNet ↓	Attribute ↑	LPIPS ↓	SSIM ↑
w/o ASM	(0.5, 22.1)	(0.6, 37.6)	71.8	**0.110**	0.773
w/o MGLO	(0.4, 25.8)	(**0.2**, 38.4)	74.1	0.123	0.623
Full Model	(**0.1**, **19.6**)	(**0.2**, **34.9**)	**75.4**	0.120	**0.799**

3 Experiments

3.1 Settings

Datasets. We use CelebA-HQ [9] (30K images with 40 attributes) and LFW [7] (13K images, 5,749 subjects), generating facial masks via a pretrained parser [1]. LFW evaluation uses a 5,000-image subset.

Implementation Details. The ID encoder is trained under the supervision of attribute predictors to disentangle identity and non-identity features. After identity extraction, differential privacy noise is injected to perturb the representation. During mask-guided latent optimization, the latent code is initialized with the mean and optimized for appearance preservation and semantic consistency. Adam optimizer ($\beta_1 = 0.5$, $\beta_2 = 0.999$), learning rate 1e-4, and batch size 16 are used, with random horizontal flipping for data augmentation.

Evaluation Metrics. We assess privacy via re-identification (ReID) and identity swapping (IDS) rates—lower values indicate stronger anonymization. ArcFace [3] and FaceNet [12] are used as verification models with cosine similarity and L2 distance, respectively. Detection accuracy is measured using a pretrained face alignment model. Visual quality is evaluated by LPIPS and SSIM [2], and attribute preservation is measured with pretrained classifiers on expression, gender, age, and makeup.

3.2 Main Results

Fig. 3 qualitatively compares our method with mainstream generative anonymization approaches (G^2Face, FALCO, CIAGAN). Compared to pixel-level methods, we directly compare with representative generative models. Existing approaches often show structural distortions or attribute loss, while our method better preserves facial structure and fine-grained attributes.

The figure also shows the effect of MLP+noise perturbation at different strengths (γ=0.0/0.9), where moderate noise improves privacy but excessive noise may reduce attribute fidelity. Figure 4 presents anonymization results on the LFW dataset, demonstrating effective generalization and practical applicability. Tables 1 and 2 show that our method achieves balanced or superior ReID and IDS results across ArcFace, FaceNet, and AdaFace, indicating lower identity leakage than previous approaches. As shown in Table 3, our method performs well in attribute preservation (e.g., expression, gender) and achieves competitive SSIM and LPIPS scores, indicating good attribute fidelity and image quality. Table 4 shows that, on the LFW dataset, our approach performs well across most metrics, particularly in SSIM and attribute accuracy.

Fig. 4. Anonymization results of our method on the LFW dataset.

3.3   Ablation Study

The ablation results in Table 5 show the effect of removing components from the proposed anonymization framework. Removing the Attribute Supervision Module (ASM) decreases the Attribute score, indicating its role in disentangling and regularizing identity and attribute features for better attribute preservation. Removing Mask-Guided Latent Optimization (MGLO) reduces SSIM, showing its importance in maintaining structural consistency. Without MGLO, the model loses fine details and facial structure, leading to lower visual quality.

4   Conclusion

In this work, we present an attribute-driven face anonymization framework that balances privacy protection and attribute fidelity. By combining identity disentanglement, differential privacy perturbation, and mask-guided latent optimization, our method achieves superior anonymization performance and better preserves visual quality compared with existing approaches.

Acknowledgments.. This work was supported by grants from the National Science Foundation of China (62476147), Ningxia Leaders in Innovation Fellowships (2024GKL-RLX17), and the Open Fund of the Key Laboratory of the Ministry of Education on Artificial Intelligence in Equipment (AAIE-2023-0403).

References

1. Bulat, A., Tzimiropoulos, G.: How far are we from solving the 2d & 3d face alignment problem? (and a dataset of 230,000 3d facial landmarks). In: Proceedings of the IEEE International Conference on Computer Vision, pp. 1021–1030 (2017)
2. Cao, J., Liu, B., Wen, Y., Xie, R., Song, L.: Personalized and invertible face de-identification by disentangled identity information manipulation. In: Proceedings of the IEEE/CVF International Conference on Computer Vision, pp. 3334–3342 (2021)
3. Deng, J., Guo, J., Xue, N., Zafeiriou, S.: Arcface: additive angular margin loss for deep face recognition. In: Proceedings of the IEEE/CVF Conference on Computer Vision and Pattern Recognition, pp. 4690–4699 (2019)
4. Du, L., Zhang, W., Fu, H., Ren, W., Zhang, X.: An efficient privacy protection scheme for data security in video surveillance. J. Vis. Commun. Image Represent. **59**, 347–362 (2019)
5. Gafni, O., Wolf, L., Taigman, Y.: Live face de-identification in video. In: Proceedings of the IEEE/CVF International Conference on Computer Vision, pp. 9378–9387 (2019)
6. Gerstner, T., DeCarlo, D., Alexa, M., Finkelstein, A., Gingold, Y., Nealen, A.: Pixelated image abstraction. In: Proceedings of the Symposium on Non-Photorealistic Animation and Rendering, pp. 29–36. Citeseer (2012)
7. Huang, G.B., Mattar, M., Berg, T., Learned-Miller, E.: Labeled faces in the wild: a database for studying face recognition in unconstrained environments. In: Workshop on Faces in 'Real-Life' Images: Detection, Alignment, and Recognition (2008)
8. Kan, M., Wu, J., Shan, S., Chen, X.: Domain adaptation for face recognition: targetize source domain bridged by common subspace. Int. J. Comput. Vision **109**, 94–109 (2014)
9. Lee, C.H., Liu, Z., Wu, L., Luo, P.: Maskgan: towards diverse and interactive facial image manipulation. In: Proceedings of the IEEE/CVF Conference on Computer Vision and Pattern Recognition, pp. 5549–5558 (2020)
10. Lopez, J., Hinojosa, C., Arguello, H., Ghanem, B.: Privacy-preserving optics for enhancing protection in face de-identification. In: Proceedings of the IEEE/CVF Conference on Computer Vision and Pattern Recognition, pp. 12120–12129 (2024)
11. Maximov, M., Elezi, I., Leal-Taixé, L.: Ciagan: conditional identity anonymization generative adversarial networks. In: Proceedings of the IEEE/CVF Conference on Computer Vision and Pattern Recognition, pp. 5447–5456 (2020)
12. Schroff, F., Kalenichenko, D., Philbin, J.: Facenet: a unified embedding for face recognition and clustering. In: Proceedings of the IEEE Conference on Computer Vision and Pattern Recognition, pp. 815–823 (2015)

13. Shen, Y., Yang, C., Tang, X., Zhou, B.: Interfacegan: interpreting the disentangled face representation learned by gans. IEEE Trans. Pattern Anal. Mach. Intell. **44**(4), 2004–2018 (2020)
14. Vakhshiteh, F., Nickabadi, A., Ramachandra, R.: Adversarial attacks against face recognition: a comprehensive study. IEEE Access **9**, 92735–92756 (2021)
15. Viorescu, R.: 2018 reform of EU data protection rules. Eur. J. Law Public Adm. **4**(2), 27–39 (2017)
16. Yang, H., et al.: G 2 face: high-fidelity reversible face anonymization via generative and geometric priors. IEEE Trans. Inf. Forensics Secur. (2024)

Emotional, Psychological, Physiological, and Health Intelligence Perception and Computing

AU-LLM: Micro-Expression Action Unit Detection via Enhanced LLM-Based Feature Fusion

Zhishu Liu[1], Kaishen Yuan[1], Bo Zhao[1], Yong Xu[2], and Zitong Yu[1(✉)]

[1] Great Bay University, Dongguan, China
yuzitong@gbu.edu.cn
[2] Harbin Institute of Technology, Shenzhen, Shenzhen, China

Abstract. The detection of micro-expression Action Units (AUs) is a formidable challenge in affective computing, pivotal for decoding subtle, involuntary human emotions. While Large Language Models (LLMs) demonstrate profound reasoning abilities, their application to the fine-grained, low-intensity domain of micro-expression AU detection remains unexplored. This paper introduces **AU-LLM**, the first framework to use an LLM for detecting AUs in micro-expression datasets, addressing subtle intensities and data scarcity. We address the vision-language semantic gap with the **Enhanced Fusion Projector (EFP)**. The EFP uses a Multi-Layer Perceptron (MLP) to fuse mid-level (local texture) and high-level (global semantics) visual features from a 3D-CNN backbone into a single, information-dense token. This compact representation effectively empowers the LLM to perform nuanced reasoning over subtle facial muscle movements. Extensive evaluations on CASME II and SAMM datasets, including LOSO and cross-domain protocols, show AU-LLM establishes a new state-of-the-art, validating the potential of LLM-based reasoning for micro-expression analysis. The codes are available at Link.

Keywords: Micro-Expression · Action Unit Detection · Large Language Model · Feature Fusion · Affective Computing

1 Introduction

Facial Action Units (AUs), from the Facial Action Coding System (FACS) [5], are atomic components of expressions, making their detection fundamental. Unlike macro-expressions, micro-expressions are brief, low-intensity, involuntary movements that betray concealed emotions. Their fleeting nature creates an extremely low signal-to-noise ratio, demanding exceptional model sensitivity to capture faint visual cues. While traditional models like CNNs and Transformers have advanced AU detection [15,29,32], they often lack the reasoning capacity for the complex interplay of AUs in such subtle conditions.

Z. Liu and K. Yuan—Equal contribution.

Large Language Models (LLMs) offer a new paradigm for complex reasoning [1,2], promising for interpreting the 'grammar' of facial movements. However, applying LLMs to micro-expression AU detection is challenged by the vision-language semantic gap [10]. A naive projection risks losing critical low-intensity signals, raising the question: how can we distill the essence of a fleeting facial movement into a representation an LLM can effectively reason about [34,35].

To bridge this gap, we introduce **AU-LLM**, the first framework to leverage LLM reasoning for micro-expression AU detection. Our approach features the **Enhanced Fusion Projector (EFP)**, an MLP-based module fusing mid-level (local) and high-level (global) visual features into one token. This gives the LLM a rich representation for reasoning, and we adapt the model efficiently with LoRA [7]. Experiments demonstrate AU-LLM significantly outperforms SOTA methods, showing its powerful generalization and reasoning. Our contributions are:

- We propose AU-LLM, the first framework to successfully apply LLM-based reasoning to the challenging task of micro-expression AU detection.
- We introduce the EFP module, an effective method for fusing multi-level visual features into a compact token to combine crucial local textural details with global semantic context, thereby bridging the vision-language gap more effectively.
- Our model outperforms state-of-the-art methods on the CASME II and SAMM datasets, validated through comprehensive experiments from both within-domain (LOSO) and cross-domain perspectives.

2   Related Work

Micro-Expression AU Detection. Automated AU detection is a core task in affective computing [24]. Micro-expression AU detection is significantly more challenging due to their fleeting, low-intensity, and involuntary nature [27]. Recent works enhance feature learning by improving the visual signal (e.g., LED [23], InfuseNet [9]) or learning discriminative representations via attention (e.g., SCA [11]) and advanced training like knowledge distillation (e.g., DVASP [12]) and contrastive learning (e.g., IICL [13]). Despite this, the focus is on refining visual representation for a simple classifier, limiting high-level reasoning. Their focus is on what features to extract, not how to reason about them. **AU-LLM** decouples feature extraction from reasoning, introducing a pre-trained LLM as a reasoning engine to address this.

Vision-Language Fusion for LLMs. Large Language Models (LLMs) are massive networks pre-trained on text, showing emergent reasoning capabilities foundational to modern AI [2]. A research frontier is extending their reasoning to multi-modal contexts like vision. This is made feasible by PEFT techniques like Low-Rank Adaptation (LoRA) [7], which we employ. A bottleneck is translating visual information into a format LLMs can process, as simply projecting a global feature discards details. Our proposed **enhanced fusion projector (EFP)** carves a distinct niche. By using an MLP to learn a non-linear mapping from concatenated multi-level visual features to a single, information-dense token, the EFP creates the high-quality representation necessary for robust LLM reasoning.

3   Methodology

This section presents our **AU-LLM** framework for micro-expression AU detection, which leverages LLM reasoning. As shown in Fig. 1, the architecture comprises a visual backbone for multi-level feature extraction, our novel Enhanced Fusion Projector (EFP), an LLM reasoning module, and a final classification head.

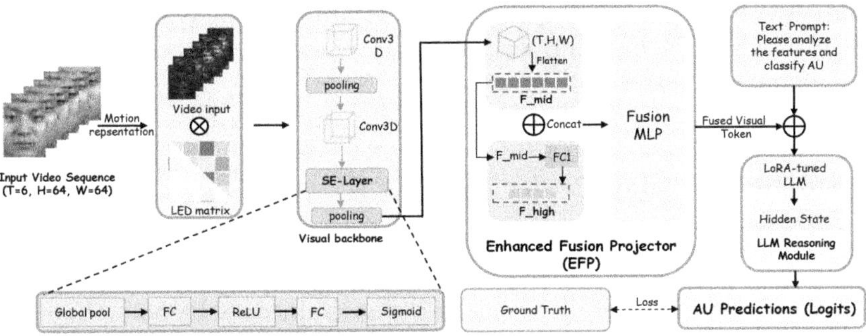

Fig. 1. The overall framework of our proposed AU-LLM. A video sequence is first processed by the visual backbone, which uses a LED matrix [23] and 3D-CNNs to extract multi-level features ($\mathbf{F}_{\mathrm{mid}}$ and $\mathbf{F}_{\mathrm{high}}$). The Enhanced Fusion Projector (EFP) then fuses these features via concatenation and an MLP into a single, information-dense visual token ($\mathbf{T_v}$). This visual token is combined with a text prompt and fed to a LoRA-tuned LLM for reasoning and final AU classification.

3.1   Visual Backbone

The visual backbone is engineered to extract a rich set of spatio-temporal features from an input video sequence $\mathbf{V} \in \mathbb{R}^{T \times H \times W}$, where $T = 6$ is the number of frames, and $H = W = 64$ are the spatial dimensions.

Temporal Filtering. To amplify subtle motion cues, we apply the Laplacian of Exponential of Difference (LED) module [23]. This module re-weights the temporal sequence by applying a learnable filter matrix $\mathbf{W} \in \mathbb{R}^{T \times T}$, computed as:

$$W_{i,j} = \begin{cases} \alpha\left((1-r_1)^{j-i}r_1^{\min(1,i)} - (1-r_2)^{j-i}r_2^{\min(1,i)}\right) & \text{if } j > i, \\ \alpha(r_1 - r_2) & \text{if } j = i, \\ 0 & \text{if } j < i, \end{cases} \tag{1}$$

where α, r_1, r_2 are learnable parameters initialized based on prior work to capture onset-apex-offset patterns [23]. The filtered video representation $\mathbf{V}'$ is obtained via a normalized matrix multiplication, enhancing transient changes.

Spatio-Temporal Feature Extraction. The temporally enhanced sequence $\mathbf{V}'$ is processed by a 3D-CNN. The network consists of 3D convolutional layers, batch normalization, and dropout. A Squeeze-and-Excitation (SE) Layer is integrated after the second convolution to perform channel-wise feature recalibration, allowing the network to focus on more informative channels for AU detection [8]. We extract features from two distinct stages of this backbone:

- **Mid-level Features** ($\mathbf{F}_{\mathrm{mid}}$): Extracted after the second 3D convolutional block and pooling layer, these features describe local textures and shapes [26].
- **High-level Features** ($\mathbf{F}_{\mathrm{high}}$): Extracted after a fully-connected layer that processes the flattened mid-level features, these more abstract features capture global semantics.

3.2 Enhanced Fusion Projector (EFP)

A challenge in leveraging LLMs for visual tasks is translating rich visual data into the compact token space LLMs use. Simply projecting final-layer features can discard vital mid-level details crucial for fine-grained tasks like AU detection. To address this, we designed the Enhanced Fusion Projector (EFP). It fuses multi-level visual features into a single, information-dense token for the LLM. The mid-level and high-level feature vectors are first flattened and concatenated:

$$\mathbf{f}_{\mathbf{cat}} = \mathrm{Concat}(\mathrm{Flatten}(\mathbf{F}_{\mathrm{mid}}), \mathbf{F}_{\mathrm{high}}). \tag{2}$$

This vector $\mathbf{f}_{\mathbf{cat}}$, containing a visual summary, is then passed through a dedicated fusion MLP. The MLP learns a powerful non-linear transformation to fuse the features and project them into the LLM's embedding space:

$$\mathbf{T}_{\mathbf{v}} = \sigma(\mathbf{W}_2(\mathrm{ReLU}(\mathbf{W}_1\mathbf{f}_{\mathbf{cat}} + \mathbf{b}_1)) + \mathbf{b}_2), \tag{3}$$

where $\mathbf{W}_1, \mathbf{b}_1, \mathbf{W}_2, \mathbf{b}_2$ are the weights and biases of the MLP, and σ is a non-linear activation. The resulting token, $\mathbf{T}_{\mathbf{v}}$, encapsulates both the local textural details (from $\mathbf{F}_{\mathrm{mid}}$) and the global semantic context (from $\mathbf{F}_{\mathrm{high}}$) of the facial movement. This single token acts as a soft prompt, prepended to a task-specific text prompt. The combined sequence is fed into the LLM for reasoning. This learned fusion is superior to a linear projection, as the MLP models complex interactions between mid- and high-level features, distilling salient AU information for the final classification [25].

3.3   LLM Reasoning Module

To steer the LLM, we provide visual evidence and analytical context. This is done by prepending the visual token $\mathbf{T_v}$, which serves as a soft prompt encapsulating the visual information, to a task-specific text prompt (e.g. Analyze the facial features to classify action units:). This multi-modal input is subsequently fed into a pre-trained LLM. We efficiently fine-tune the LLM using Low-Rank Adaptation (LoRA), which introduces low-rank matrices into the query and value projections of the self-attention layers. Finally, the hidden state of the last token from the LLM, encapsulating the model's unified reasoning over visual and textual cues, is passed to a linear classifier to produce the final logits $\mathbf{z} \in \mathbb{R}^{N_{AUs}}$ for each AU.

3.4   Loss Function and Optimization

To address class imbalance in multi-label AU detection, we employ the Asymmetric Loss (ASL) [17]. ASL mitigates the dominance of negative samples by applying different focusing parameters to positive and negative examples. The loss is formulated as:

$$\mathcal{L}_{\text{ASL}} = -\frac{1}{N}\sum_{i=1}^{N}\sum_{j=1}^{B}\left[y_{ij}(1-p_{ij})^{\gamma_+}\log(p_{ij}) + (1-y_{ij})(p_{m,ij})^{\gamma_-}\log(1-p_{m,ij})\right],$$

$$(4)$$

where p_{ij} is the predicted probability and y_{ij} is the ground truth label. The focusing parameters γ_+ and γ_- allow for flexible weighting of samples [29]. Based on our implementation, we set $\gamma_+ = 0$ and $\gamma_- = 4$.

4   Experiments

4.1   Datasets and Protocol

We validate our approach on two public, standard spontaneous micro-expression datasets. **CASME II** [28] contains 247 micro-expression samples from 26 subjects. Captured with a high-speed camera (200 fps), it is one of the most widely used datasets for micro-expression analysis. Following standard protocol, we detect 8 AUs: AU1, AU2, AU4, AU7, AU12, AU14, AU15, and AU17. **SAMM** [3] consists of 159 micro-expression samples from 32 subjects with diverse ethnic backgrounds. This dataset also utilizes a high-speed camera and provides a challenging testbed for model generalization. We conduct cross-dataset validation on SAMM, detecting 4 AUs common to its annotation: AU2, AU4, AU7, and AU12.

For robust, subject-independent evaluation, we use the Leave-One-Subject-Out (LOSO) cross-validation protocol [23]. The primary metric is the macro F1-score, suited for AU detection tasks with class imbalance as it treats each AU class equally [22]. The F1-score is the harmonic mean of precision and recall for each action unit class c:

$$\mathcal{F}_{1,c} = 2 \cdot \frac{\text{Precision}_c \cdot \text{Recall}_c}{\text{Precision}_c + \text{Recall}_c}.$$

$$(5)$$

Table 1. Micro-Expression AU Detection Performance Comparison (CASME II). F1-scores (%) are reported. Best results are in **bold**.

Method	AU1	AU2	AU4	AU7	AU12	AU14	AU15	AU17	Avg.
LBPTOP [31]	80.9	60.7	**89.8**	56.2	69.3	63.2	52.2	75.8	68.5
Resnet18 [6]	58.9	76.2	82.7	48.7	59.3	64.2	48.1	62.9	62.6
Resnet34 [6]	55.1	69.2	83.2	55.4	62.8	56.7	52.2	62.9	62.2
Fitnet [19]	65.5	74.3	79.1	46.8	61.7	62.4	53.9	57.6	62.7
SP [21]	69.0	68.5	77.7	51.1	57.0	65.3	56.6	61.3	63.3
AT [30]	65.0	62.7	83.1	57.6	58.6	62.5	46.6	65.6	62.7
SCA [11]	64.1	76.7	81.1	56.2	61.3	61.9	68.8	64.4	66.8
DVASP [12]	72.6	72.1	**89.8**	56.9	**79.6**	68.5	71.5	70.0	72.6
Resnet18 LED [23]	85.8	81.7	89.0	53.9	71.4	78.5	74.5	83.5	77.3
SSSNet LED [23]	**92.6**	83.7	88.6	63.7	76.6	74.4	71.5	76.1	78.4
AU-DeepSeek R1(1.5B)	92.2	**87.0**	89.5	**68.1**	79.0	75.1	**79.0**	81.0	**81.4**
AU-Qwen2(1.5B)	88.4	82.1	89.5	65.7	75.8	74.7	71.7	82.7	78.8
AU-Qwen2.5(1.5B)	89.1	86.6	89.5	65.2	74.4	**77.9**	67.6	**85.8**	79.5

The final reported score is the unweighted average of these individual F1-scores across all AU classes.

4.2   Implementation Details

AU-LLM is implemented in PyTorch. The visual backbone is trained from scratch for each cross-validation fold. We use the Adam optimizer with a learning rate of 3×10^{-5} and a weight decay of 0.005. The model is trained with a batchsize of 256. We utilize several 1.5B-parameter LLMs, including **Qwen2-1.5B**, **Qwen2.5-1.5B**, and **DeepSeek-R1-Distill-Qwen-1.5B**, loaded from Hugging Face [4] [20]. Parameter-Efficient Fine-Tuning is performed using Low-Rank Adaptation (LoRA) with a rank $r = 16$ and alpha $\alpha = 32$ applied to the query and value matrices of the attention blocks. All experiments are run on a single NVIDIA H100 GPU.

4.3   Comparison with State-of-the-Art Methods

We compare AU-LLM with several state-of-the-art (SOTA) methods on both datasets. As shown in Table 1, our model variants achieve superior performance on CASME II. Notably, **AU-deepseek R1(1.5B)** achieves a mean F1-score of **81.4%**, surpassing the previous best method SSSNet LED (78.4%) by a significant margin of 3.0%. Our method shows particularly strong performance on key AUs like AU2 (87.0%), AU4 (89.5%), and AU7 (68.1%), demonstrating its effectiveness in capturing diverse facial muscle movements.

Results on the SAMM dataset (Table 2) further validate our framework's generalization capability. In this cross-dataset setting, **AU-deepseek R1(1.5B)** again achieves the highest average F1-score of **61.9%**, outperforming all previous methods. This robust performance highlights the benefit of our EFP module in creating a rich, dataset-agnostic visual representation that enables the LLM to reason effectively even on unseen data distributions.

Table 2. Micro-Expression AU Detection Performance Comparison (SAMM). F1-scores (%) are reported. Best results are in **bold**.

Method	AU2	AU4	AU7	AU12	Avg.
LBP-TOP [31]	58.8	47.9	44.5	49.5	50.2
ResNet18 [6]	49.7	49.1	46.1	40.5	46.4
ResNet34 [6]	44.0	55.2	38.0	40.5	44.4
Fit-18 [19]	54.1	51.2	44.5	48.3	49.5
SP-18 [21]	42.8	64.2	38.1	49.5	48.7
AT-18 [30]	47.2	60.5	43.5	38.0	47.3
SCA [11]	45.7	59.2	43.9	53.2	50.5
DVASP-18 [12]	47.8	67.5	48.1	44.7	52.0
Resnet18 LED [23]	57.4	71.3	53.2	47.3	57.3
SSSNet LED [23]	61.5	62.4	45.2	47.8	54.2
AU-DeepSeek R1(1.5B)	**66.9**	**71.9**	**55.8**	52.8	**61.9**
AU-Qwen2(1.5B)	63.6	65.2	49.2	53.7	57.9
AU-Qwen2.5(1.5B)	63.2	67.6	50.7	**57.6**	59.7

Table 3. Ablation study on CASME II and SAMM datasets. Average F1-scores (%) are reported. Model names are abbreviated. Best results are in **bold**.

(a) CASME II				(b) SAMM			
Variant	D.R1	Q2	Q2.5	Variant	D.R1	Q2	Q2.5
F_{high}	80.1	79.8	78.8	F_{high}	54.5	55.5	54.3
F_{mid}	79.3	78.7	78.7	F_{mid}	54.7	55.6	55.5
EFP–	78.6	77.8	77.7	EFP–	58.2	56.3	55.3
Prompt Learning	80.4	78.6	79.3	Prompt Learning	59.6	56.4	57.6
all	**81.4**	**78.8**	**79.5**	all	**61.9**	**57.9**	**59.7**

4.4   Ablation Study

Ablation on Modules. To validate our design choices, we conducted ablation studies on the CASME II and SAMM datasets. We designed three variants to isolate the contributions of our core components: (1) using only high-level features ($\mathbf{F}_{\text{high}}$) or (2) only mid-level features ($\mathbf{F}_{\text{mid}}$) to test the necessity of fusing multi-level information, and (3) **EFP$-$**, which replaces the EFP's MLP with a simple linear layer, to verify the benefit of non-linear fusion. As shown in Table 3, the full model (all) consistently outperforms all ablated versions. The performance drop when using single-level features confirms that both local and global cues are vital. The superiority over the EFP$-$ variant highlights the importance of the MLP's non-linear fusion capability. These results are complemented by the visualizations in Fig. 2.

Ablation on Prompting Strategy. To further validate our dynamic visual prompting strategy, we introduce an ablation study that replaces our EFP module with a strong baseline: **Learnable Text Prompts** [33]. This variant uses a set of static, learnable embedding vectors optimized to act as a general textual instruction for the AU detection task, instead of generating a dynamic visual token for each sample. This experiment directly contrasts our "early fusion" approach, where rich visual information is integrated before reaching the LLM, with a "late fusion" approach. The expected superior performance of our EFP-based model would strongly demonstrate that for fine-grained visual tasks like micro-expression detection, dynamically generating an instance-specific visual prompt is more effective than using a static, task-level textual prompt, thus validating our EFP module.

Table 4. F1-scores (in %) for cross-domain evaluations between CASME II and SAMM.

Datasets	CASME II → SAMM					SAMM → CASME II				
AU	2	4	7	12	**Avg.**	2	4	7	12	**Avg.**
ResNet-18 [6]	**47.0**	15.7	**41.5**	45.1	37.3	47.8	**47.4**	47.9	46.4	47.4
LED SSSNet [23]	**47.0**	12.6	**41.5**	45.1	36.5	53.2	44.1	40.2	46.5	46.1
AU-LLM (Ours)	47.0	**62.4**	41.5	**48.8**	**49.9**	**67.8**	39.4	**50.4**	**53.6**	**52.8**

4.5   Cross-Domain Evaluation

To assess generalization, we conducted cross-domain evaluations between the CASME II and SAMM datasets on their shared AUs. As presented in Table 4, our model demonstrates superior generalization. Under the **CASME II →
SAMM** protocol (training on CASME II, evaluating on SAMM), our AU-LLM achieves an average F1-score of 49.9%, significantly outperforming the baseline

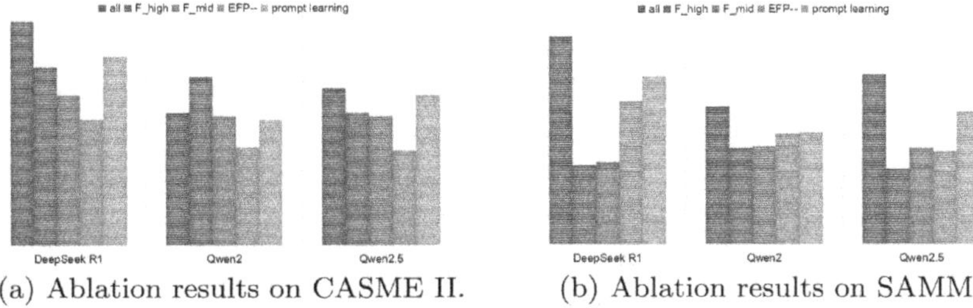

(a) Ablation results on CASME II.   (b) Ablation results on SAMM.

Fig. 2. Visualization of ablation studies on both datasets, showing the performance of the full model (all) versus variants lacking certain components.

LED SSSNet (36.5%) by **13.4** percentage points. Conversely, under the **SAMM → CASME II** protocol, our model achieves 52.8%, surpassing the baseline (46.1%) by **6.7** percentage points. These results validate our method's superior generalization.

4.6 Visualization and Analysis

To understand how our visual backbone works, we visualize the feature heatmaps and compare them against a baseline 3D-CNN. As shown in Fig. 3, our model demonstrates a superior ability to focus on the correct AU-related facial regions.

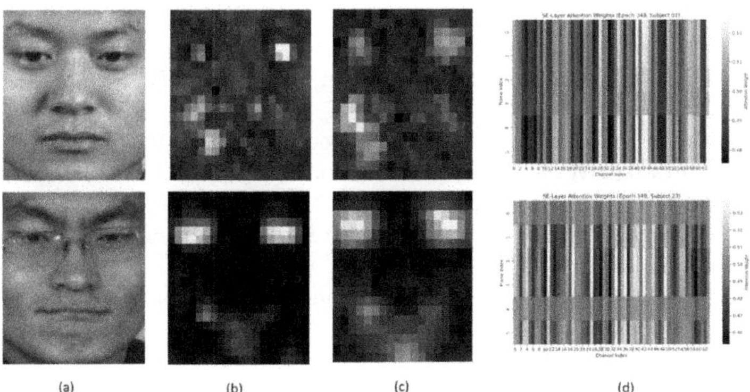

Fig. 3. Visualization of model attention. (a) Original micro-expression samples. (b) Heatmaps from a baseline 3D-CNN. (c) Heatmaps from our visual backbone, showing more precise focus. (d) SE-Layer channel attention weights over time. **Top row:** The ground truth is AU12 (Lip Corner Puller). **Bottom row:** The ground truth is a combination of AU4 (Brow Lowerer), AU15 (Lip Corner Depressor), and AU17 (Chin Raiser).

The qualitative analysis in Fig. 3 provides strong evidence for our model's effectiveness. For both a simple case (AU12, top row) and a complex combination (AU4+15+17, bottom row), our model's heatmaps (c) accurately localize the corresponding facial regions. In contrast, the baseline model (b) shows diffuse or incorrect attention. Furthermore, the SE-Layer's channel attention maps (d) illustrate the model's ability to dynamically re-weight feature channels to amplify the most informative signals. This confirms that our visual backbone learns a more precise and interpretable feature representation, providing high-quality input for the subsequent LLM reasoning.

5   Conclusion

We introduced **AU-LLM**, the first framework to successfully leverage Large Language Models for micro-expression Action Unit detection. Our **Enhanced Fusion Projector (EFP)** bridges the vision-language semantic gap by fusing multi-level visual features into a compact, information-rich token, empowering the LLM to perform nuanced reasoning over subtle facial cues. This work validates the potential of applying advanced reasoning engines to this fine-grained domain. Future work will focus on harnessing LLMs to develop systems for more complex micro-expression reasoning and interactive, context-aware question-answering, moving beyond simple classification to a deeper understanding of concealed emotions [14, 16, 18].

References

1. Alayrac, J.B., et al.: Flamingo: a visual language model for few-shot learning. In: NeurIPS (2022)
2. Brown, T.B., et al.: Language models are few-shot learners. In: NeurIPS (2020)
3. Davison, A.K., Lansley, C., Costen, N., Tan, K., Yap, M.H.: Samm: a spontaneous micro-facial movement dataset. In: IEEE TAFFC (2018)
4. DeepSeek-AI: Deepseek-r1: A 671b moe model with fine-grained sparsity (2024)
5. Ekman, P., Friesen, W.V.: Facial Action Coding System. Consulting Psychologists Press (1978)
6. He, K., Zhang, X., Ren, S., Sun, J.: Deep residual learning for image recognition. In: CVPR (2016)
7. Hu, E.J., et al.: Lora: low-rank adaptation of large language models. In: ICLR (2022)
8. Hu, J., Shen, L., Sun, G.: Squeeze-and-excitation networks. In: CVPR (2018)
9. Khor, H.Q., Li, Y., Jiang, X., Zhao, G.: Infused suppression of magnification artefacts for micro-au detection. In: SCIA (2025)
10. Li, G., Zhu, X., Zeng, Y., Wang, Q., Lin, L.: Semantic relationships guided representation learning for facial action unit recognition. In: AAAI (2019)
11. Li, Y., Huang, X., Zhao, G.: Micro-expression action unit detection with spatial and channel attention. Neurocomputing (2021)
12. Li, Y., Peng, W., Zhao, G.: Micro-expression action unit detection with dual-view attentive similarity-preserving knowledge distillation. In: FG (2021)
13. Li, Y., Zhao, G.: Intra-and inter-contrastive learning for micro-expression action unit detection. In: ICMI (2021)
14. Lin, X., et al.: Reliable and balanced transfer learning for generalized multimodal face anti-spoofing. PAMI (2025)

15. Jacob, G.M., Stenger, B.: Facial action unit detection with transformers. In: CVPR (2021)
16. Ye, Q., et al.: Cat+: investigating and enhancing audio-visual understanding in large language models. PAMI (2025)
17. Ridnik, T., et al.: Asymmetric loss for multi-label classification. In: ICCV (2021)
18. Cai, R., et al.: Rehearsal-free and efficient continual learning for cross-domain face anti-spoofing. PAMI (2025)
19. Romero, A., Ballas, N., Kahou, S.E., Chassang, A., Gkioxari, G., Bengio, Y.: Fitnets: hints for thin deep nets. arXiv preprint arXiv:1412.6550 (2014)
20. Team, Q.: Qwen2 technical report (2024)
21. Tung, F., Mori, G.: Similarity-preserving knowledge distillation. In: ICCV (2017)
22. Varanka, T., Li, Y., Peng, W., Zhao, G.: Data leakage and evaluation issues in micro-expression analysis. IEEE TAFFC (2023)
23. Varanka, T., Peng, W., Zhao, G.: Learnable eulerian dynamics for micro-expression action unit detection. In: Image Analysis (2024)
24. Xie, H.X., Lo, L., Shuai, H.H., Cheng, W.H.: Au-assisted graph attention convolutional network for micro-expression recognition. In: ACM MM (2020)
25. Xie, X., Cui, Y., Tan, T., Zheng, X., Yu, Z.: Fusionmamba: dynamic feature enhancement for multimodal image fusion with mamba. Visual Intell. **2**(1), 37 (2024)
26. Xie, Y., et al.: Physllm: harnessing large language models for cross-modal remote physiological sensing. arXiv preprint arXiv:2505.03621 (2025)
27. Xing, B., Yuan, K., Yu, Z., Liu, X., Kälviäinen, H.: Au-ttt: vision test-time training model for facial action unit detection. arXiv preprint arXiv:2503.23450 (2025)
28. Yan, W.J., et al.: CASME II: an improved spontaneous micro-expression database and the baseline evaluation. In: PLOS ONE (2014)
29. Yuan, K., Yu, Z., Liu, X., Xie, W., Yue, H., Yang, J.: Auformer: vision transformers are parameter-efficient facial action unit detectors. In: ECCV (2024)
30. Zagoruyko, S., Komodakis, N.: Paying more attention to attention: improving the performance of convolutional neural networks via attention transfer. arXiv preprint arXiv:1612.03928 (2016)
31. Zhao, G., Pietikainen, M.: Dynamic texture recognition using local binary patterns with an application to facial expressions. IEEE TPAMI (2007)
32. Zhao, K., Chu, W.S., De la Torre, F., Cohn, J.F., Zhang, H.: Joint patch and multi-label learning for facial action unit detection. In: CVPR (2015)
33. Zhou, K., Yang, J., Loy, C.C., Liu, Z.: Learning to prompt for vision-language models. IJCV (2022)
34. Zhu, Y., Lyu, Y., Yu, Z., Shao, R., Zhou, K., Nie, L.: Emosym: a symbiotic framework for unified emotional understanding and generation via latent reasoning. In: Proceedings of the 33nd ACM International Conference on Multimedia (2025)
35. Zhu, Y., Zhang, L., Yu, Z., Shao, R., Tan, T., Nie, L.: Uniemo: unifying emotional understanding and generation with learnable expert queries. arXiv preprint arXiv:2507.23372 (2025)

An EEG Depression Identification Model via Spatiotemporal Filtering

Zhijing Wu, Haomin Tan, Yinghao Zhang, Hao Zhang, and Dan Xu[✉]

School of Information Science and Engineering, Yunnan University,
Kunming 650091, China
{wuzhijing,12024215166}@stu.ynu.edu.cn, danxu@ynu.edu.cn

Abstract. EEG provides valuable biological information for BCI tasks. In the process of studying EEG, many complex preprocessing methods have been generated. These methods require researchers to manually select and process data and features, which takes a long time and has high professional requirements and is highly subjective. This paper proposes the TwoM model with a spatiotemporal filtering mechanism, which adaptively filters effective data by learning spatial and temporal features, addressing the overfitting problem caused by small samples and low signal-to-noise ratios. TwoM has been successfully validated on three EEG-based depression datasets, including MODMA, achieving strong results without preprocessing, demonstrating the model's robustness.

Keywords: EEG · Depression identification · CNN · Transformer

1 Introduction

According to the WHO, about 280 million people suffer from depression, and over 700,000 die by suicide annually [1]. EEG, as a biomarker of neural activity, is increasingly used for depression identification [2]. Recent studies have applied CNN and Transformer models to EEG data with promising results. Ding et al. [3] used multi-scale 1D CNN to classify emotions by exploiting spatial asymmetry. Researchers have also used signal processing methods like STFT, FFT, and Wavelet Transform to obtain spectrograms and PSD features, which are processed by 2D Conv [4–7]. While CNNs are effective in extracting local features, but struggle with global features and long range series.

EEG data, with its temporal and long-range dependencies, benefits from Transformers' self-attention mechanism. Combining CNN with Transformer improves feature extraction [8,9]. Ying et al. [10] improved model performance by calculating correlations between frequency and spatial domain features.

However, due to small samples and low signal-to-noise ratios, complex models risk overfitting [11]. Preprocessing methods include [12,13] bad channel removal, filtering, and artifact correction are widely used, but they rely on expert judgment and may not always benefit the model, as different methods show varying results [14]. High-dimensional data can also become redundant, affecting model

W. Jia et al. (Eds.): CCBR 2025, LNCS 16360, pp. 366–375, 2026.
https://doi.org/10.1007/978-981-95-6123-0_34

performance. Studies have shown that excess channels may lead to overfitting [15], while irrelevant channels reduce classification performance. This paper aims to reduce data processing requirements through deep learning methods [16], improving performance while reducing processing costs.

To address these issues, we propose the TwoM method with the following contributions:

(1) An end-to-end depression classification model (TwoM) that can automatically filter and fuse spatiotemporal features.
(2) A spatiotemporal filtering module (SCACF & CWTrans) that automatically extracts effective information and enhances model robustness without preprocessing.
(3) A feature fusion method (BPF) to achieve weighted fusion of channel and time features, improving classification accuracy.

2   Materials and Methods

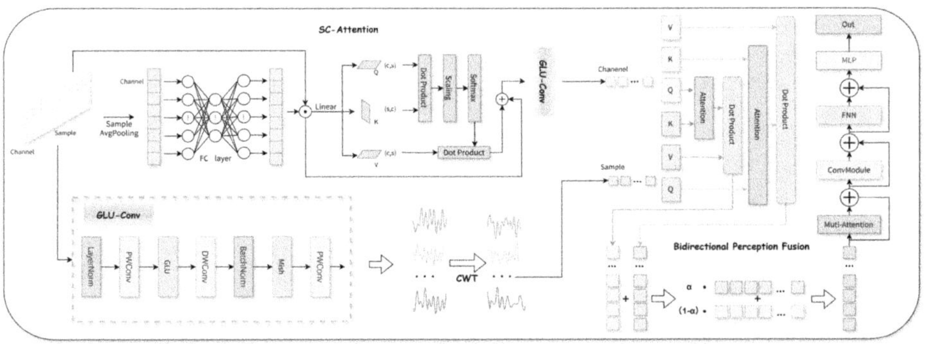

Fig. 1. The overall framework of the proposed TwoM model. It mainly consists of three parts: (1) SCACF based on SC-Attentionn; (2) CWTrans based on CWT; (3) Bidirectional Perceptual Fusion (BPF).

The original data is input into the SCACF and CWTrans modules respectively. The former extracts spatial features and the latter extracts time-frequency features. The two sets of features are fused by the BPF module and finally classified by the Multi-Attention & CNN network.

2.1   AGFC

This paper introduces a spatial filter combining GLU-Conv and SC-Attention to extract key spatial features. SC-Attention is an adaptive model, as shown in Fig. 1. The data is globally averaged along the sample dimension to capture spatial information. Two fully connected layers learn channel weights, with the spatial weight computed using a sigmoid function and applied to adjust the feature channels dynamically. Channel correlation is captured via attention queries, softmax normalization, and point multiplication, followed by a residual connection to the input data.

For shallow feature, a convolution module integrating the GLU mechanism is proposed. PWConv doubles the spatial dimensions, followed by Gated Linear Unit activation to regulate information flow. DWConv then applies independent convolutions to each spatial, preserving spatial independence while extracting feature relationships. Finally, PWConv fuses the spatial features to produce the output.

2.2   CWTrans

This study proposes a method to extract multi-scale time-frequency domain features of EEG signals using a learnable continuous wavelet transform (CWT).

What we are concerned about is the time-frequency characteristics of the signal. Therefore, only the real part is retained for calculation. Construct wavelet function:

$$\psi\left(t\right) = e^{-\frac{1}{2}t^2} \cdot \cos\left(\omega_0 t\right), \quad \omega_0 = 5 \tag{1}$$

The location and scale of the signal are controlled by the learnable parameters *translation* and *scale*:

$$t = \frac{x - translation}{scale} \tag{2}$$

By adding a learnable wavelet weight w to the wavelet function $\psi\left(t\right)$ and summing it in the time dimension, we can get the response of each channel after the weighted wavelet:

$$\text{Output}_{b,c} = \sum_t w\psi\left(x_{b,c,t}\right) \tag{3}$$

Similarly, add the same GLU-Conv as before CWT for shallow feature extraction.

2.3   Bidirectional Perceptual Fusion

To enhance the interaction between spatial and time-frequency features, we propose a Bidirectional Perceptual Fusion (BPF) module based on cross-attention.

Given spatial features $X_c \in \mathbb{R}^{B \times T \times d_c}$ and time-frequency features $X_s \in \mathbb{R}^{B \times T \times d_s}$, both are projected to query, key, and value vectors:

$$Q_c = W_Q^c X_c, \quad K_c = W_K^c X_c, \quad V_c = W_V^c X_c$$
$$Q_s = W_Q^s X_s, \quad K_s = W_K^s X_s, \quad V_s = W_V^s X_s$$

Then calculate the two attention results Att_c and Att_s respectively.

$$Att_c = softmax\left(\frac{(Q_c(K_s)^T)}{\sqrt{d}}\right), X'_c = Att_c \cdot V_s \tag{4}$$

$$Att_s = softmax\left(\frac{(Q_s(K_c)^T)}{\sqrt{d}}\right), X'_s = Att_s \cdot V_c \tag{5}$$

Project the spatial attention $X\prime_c$ and frequency domain attention $X\prime_s$ into the same embedding space:

$$Z = (\mathrm{W_c}\mathrm{X}'_\mathrm{c} + \mathrm{b_c}) + (\mathrm{W_s}\mathrm{X}'_\mathrm{s} + \mathrm{b_s}) \tag{6}$$

where $\mathrm{W_c}$ and $\mathrm{W_s}$ are trainable parameter matrices. Use tanh nonlinear activation and then perform softmax normalization to calculate the fusion weight α:

$$\alpha = \mathrm{softmax}(V^\top \tanh(Z)) \tag{7}$$

where V is the global score vector. The final feature fusion expression:

$$F_{fused} = \alpha \mathrm{X}'_\mathrm{c} + (1 - \alpha)\mathrm{X}'_\mathrm{s} \tag{8}$$

Through the above steps, the feature fusion sequence is obtained. The sequence is globally modeled through Multi-Head Attention, and then a simple deep separable module is used to extract local dependencies. Finally, it is output through the Feed Forward Module, and the modules are connected through the residual network.

3   Experiments and Results

3.1   Datasets and Experimental Details

Dataset I is the MODMA dataset from UAISL [17], consisting of 128-lead EEG data from 53 subjects (24 with MDD and 29 healthy controls) recorded during the emotional dot-probe task, with a sampling frequency of 250 Hz. No preprocessing was applied, except for data format adjustment, to avoid bias in model performance comparison. The data were then segmented independently using a 1 s time window.

Dataset II is the MDD Patients and Healthy Controls EEG from the University of Science Malaysia [18], including 34 depression patients and 30 healthy controls. It contains 19-lead EEG data recorded in both eyes-open and eyes-closed states at a 256 Hz sampling frequency. Data from the same subject in the eyes-closed state and the 4-minute interval were combined, followed by segmentation using a 1 s time window.

Dataset III is provided by a multidisciplinary team, including the Department of Biomedical Engineering at the University of the Andes [19]. It records changes in multimodal physiological indicators (EEG, EMG) and psychological indicators (VAS, HADS) under music stimulation in 9 severely burned patients. We selected 8-lead EEG data at a 256 Hz sampling frequency and divided the subjects into high (HADS-D $\geq$ 4) and low depression groups. Due to missing data for one patient, 8 subjects were selected, with 4 in each group.

For the classification performance evaluation of depression patients, we used 5-fold cross-validation with a 4:1 training-to-test ratio. The batch size was 80, the learning rate was 2e-4, and the Adam optimizer was applied, with β_1 and β_2 set to 0.9 and 0.9999, respectively. We use accuracy, specificity, precision, and F1 score as standard metrics.

Table 1. Performance comparison on Dataset I, Dataset II, and Dataset III.

Model	Dataset I				Dataset II				Dataset III			
	Acc	Prec	Rec	F1	Acc	Prec	Rec	F1	Acc	Prec	Rec	F1
DeepConvNet	71.97	68.56	70.58	74.24	82.45	81.95	80.74	84.86	94.78	89.98	94.22	99.07
EEGNet	65.73	46.52	57.20	75.41	73.89	53.70	61.24	91.56	97.96	97.20	97.89	98.64
DeprNet	93.97	94.72	94.06	93.98	81.57	80.04	79.55	80.86	96.40	99.51	96.61	94.42
Tsception	69.72	75.08	70.98	67.93	85.31	82.39	83.54	86.37	97.16	95.44	96.91	98.56
EEGConformer	73.02	68.51	71.51	75.42	81.07	66.97	77.12	92.81	98.86	98.47	98.83	99.22
EEGDeformer	75.22	72.40	74.15	76.53	87.38	75.50	84.71	99.23	98.20	98.15	98.10	98.18
MACTN	73.73	72.36	73.11	74.38	89.25	79.77	85.52	98.68	98.73	98.17	98.65	99.22
Ours	**99.12**	**98.68**	**99.11**	**99.57**	**98.68**	**98.38**	**98.66**	**98.98**	**99.41**	**99.42**	**99.38**	**99.35**

3.2 Baseline Comparison

To evaluate our model's performance, we compared it with seven recent state-of-the-art deep learning methods, including:

EEGNet [20]: A lightweight CNN designed for EEG data, using deep separable convolutions for efficient feature extraction and decoding.

DeepConvNet [16]: A deep CNN architecture with multiple convolution and pooling layers for spatiotemporal feature extraction

DeprNet [21]: Achieves good performance by using multiple 1D convolution kernels of different sizes, effectively capturing spatial and temporal data features.

TSception [3]: A multi-scale CNN with dynamic temporal, asymmetric spatial, and fusion layers for complex EEG pattern modeling.

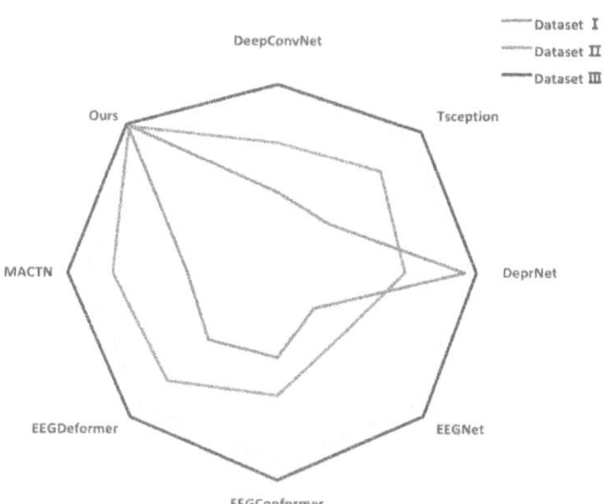

Fig. 2. Each circular line denotes a dataset, and points closer to the center indicate worse performance.

EEG Conformer [22]: Combines CNN and Transformer to improve context understanding while preserving CNN's ability to model local features.

EEG Deformer [23]: Combines CNN and Transformer, introducing a Hierarchical Coarse-to-Fine Transformer and Dense Information Purification to capture both long-term and short-term temporal dynamics in EEG signals.

MACTN [24]: An end-to-end model combining CNN and Transformer with channel and temporal attention mechanisms for stronger generalization ability.

Table 1 compares TwoM's performance across three datasets. Dataset I, with uncleaned EEG data and higher channel dimensions, introduces noise and redundancy, degrading baseline models' performance. Figure 2 visualizes the overall results. Due to its adaptive spatiotemporal filtering module, TwoM achieves an accuracy rate of 22.65% to 46% higher than other methods on the more complex Dataset I. Dataset II, containing noisy open-eye data, shows larger fluctuations in baseline accuracy, yet TwoM maintains a 9.43% to 24.79% advantage. Even on the small-sample Dataset III, TwoM resists overfitting and delivers stable results.

Table 2. Removed the SCACF and CWTrans parts of TwoM in turn, and removed SCACF, CWTrans, and BPF at the same time.

Model	Acc	Prec	Rec	F1
Base model	62.80	57.78	60.50	64.31
w/o SCACF	90.17	90.24	90.06	90.17
w/o CWT	94.25	93.53	94.02	95.06
TwoM	**97.39**	**97.63**	**97.36**	**97.16**

Table 3. Comparing BPF with TwoM[a](Cross-Attention) and TwoM[b](Concatenation) methods.

Model	Acc	Prec	Rec	F1
TwoM[a]	94.68	93.90	94.53	95.37
TwoM[b]	92.00	95.17	92.38	90.50
TwoM	**97.39**	**97.63**	**97.36**	**97.16**

3.3 Ablation Studies

Table 2 shows the effects of SCACF and CWTrans. We consider the portion excluding the three functional modules of CWT, SCACF, and BPF as the baseline model, with a basic accuracy of 62.80%.First, we add the SCACF module. The application of this module improves the accuracy of the model by 27.37%, which shows that channel selection has a positive effect on the performance of

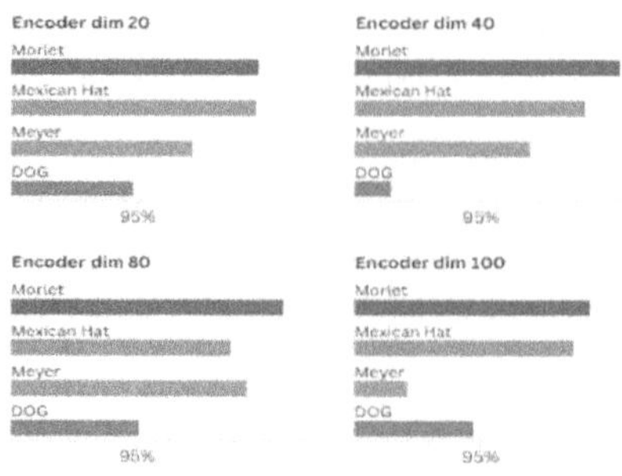

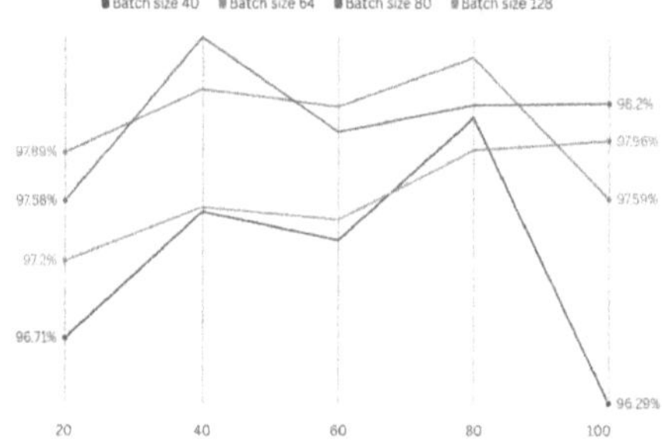

Fig. 3. These bar graphs show the accuracy of selecting different wavelet types under different Encoder dims.

Fig. 4. This line chart shows how different batch sizes change under the influence of different encoder dims.

the model, and too large a number of channels will easily affect the performance of the model if they are not selected. Similarly, we add the CWTrans module alone, and the accuracy of the model is also improved by 31.45%, verifying its value in extracting effective time-frequency features.

Table 3 shows the performance of using other common methods to replace BPF. In the comparison between BPF and Cross-attention and Concatenation, it can be found that BPF, a bidirectional attention and dynamic fusion method, improves the accuracy by 5.39% compared with simple Concatenation and 2.71% compared with the traditional Cross-attention method. This shows that BPF effectively dynamically selects features from different sequences and improves model performance.

3.4　Sensitivity Analysis

Figure 3 shows that the choice of wavelet basis will significantly affect the performance of the model, and its choice is crucial. EEG signal is a non-stationary time series signal. Compared with other wavelet bases, Morlet has good time-frequency locality and is suitable for the analysis of continuous oscillation waveforms. Morlet can be used to extract time-frequency features. The specific mathematical principles have been derived in the previous article and will not be described in detail here. In addition, Fig. 4 show that setting a larger encoder dim to strengthen the expression of features can indeed improve the performance of the model, but too large encoder dim will also cause the model to focus on irrelevant individual features, resulting in overfitting.

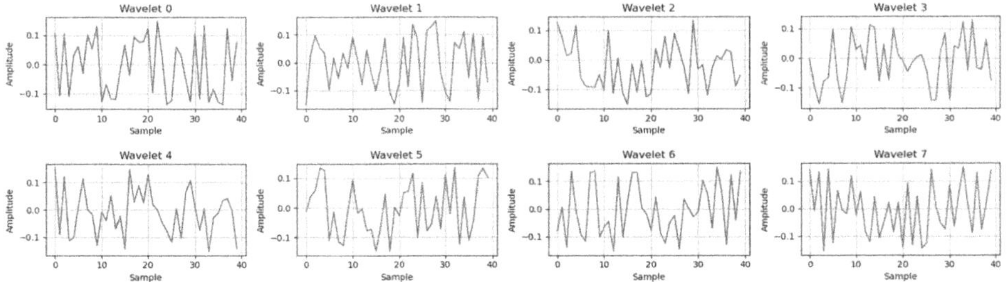

Fig. 5. Through learnable *translation* and *scale*, several wavelet functions can be generated, eight of which are shown here.

3.5   Visualization

Figure 5 shows the wavelet function learned by CWTrans. The learnable wavelet parameters break the limitation of a single wavelet basis and enrich the time-frequency features. Time-frequency sequence generated by the original data and the wavelet function operation, and the final feature is formed by summing up in the time dimension.

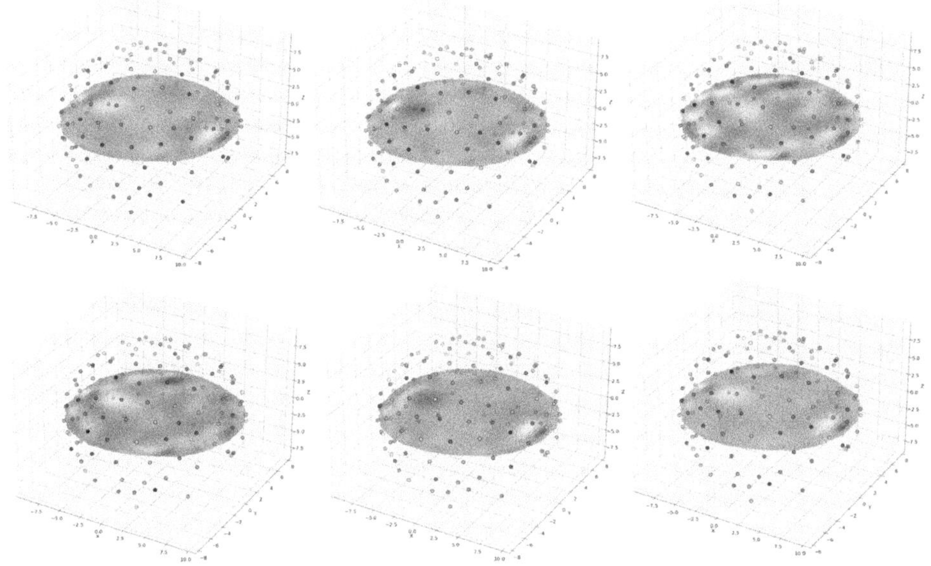

Fig. 6. Randomly drawn electrode weight maps with spatial topological information, from which it is found that the channels with relatively large changes are concentrated near the prefrontal and parietal lobes.

The SCACF module adaptively screens EEG channels to enhance discriminative spatial features for classification. Based on Dataset I's channel order, electrodes were mapped to 3D head coordinates via the 10-10 system [25], with normalized weights constructing a topologically informed electrode map. Figure 6 displays randomly sampled 3D channel weight maps, revealing that high-weight electrodes predominantly cluster in prefrontal and parietal regions-consistent with established neuroscience findings [26]. Specifically, SCACF's automatic emphasis on prefrontal channels aligns with known MDD-related prefrontal cortex alterations, theoretically validating its channel selection and enhancing model neurophysiological interpretability.

4 Discussion and Conclusions

EEG data preprocessing is complex and time-consuming, and the redundancy of high-channel data and noise and artifacts during the acquisition process will increase the risk of overfitting. This study proposes an end-to-end depression classification model, TwoM, which can automatically filter spatiotemporal features. Experimental results show that the SCACF and CWTrans modules automatically extract spatial and temporal features, reduce redundancy and suppress noise without complex preprocessing. TwoM shows performance advantages and good robustness, providing an effective solution for EEG signal decoding systems.

References

1. Collaborators, G.M.D., et al.: Global, regional, and national burden of 12 mental disorders in 204 countries and territories, 1990–2019: a systematic analysis for the global burden of disease study 2019. Lancet Psychiat. **9**(2), 137–150 (2022)
2. de Aguiar Neto, F.S., Rosa, J.L.G.: Depression biomarkers using non-invasive eeg: a review. Neurosci. Biobehav. Rev. **105**, 83–93 (2019)
3. Ding, Y., Robinson, N., Zhang, S., Zeng, Q., Guan, C.: Tsception: capturing temporal dynamics and spatial asymmetry from eeg for emotion recognition. IEEE Trans. Affect. Comput. **14**(3), 2238–2250 (2022)
4. Ieracitano, C., Mammone, N., Bramanti, A., Hussain, A., Morabito, F.C.: A convolutional neural network approach for classification of dementia stages based on 2d-spectral representation of eeg recordings. Neurocomputing **323**, 96–107 (2019)
5. Peng, P., Song, Y., Yang, L., Wei, H.: Seizure prediction in eeg signals using stft and domain adaptation. Front. Neurosci. **15**, 825434 (2022)
6. Shovon, T.H., Al Nazi, Z., Dash, S., Hossain, M.F.: Classification of motor imagery eeg signals with multi-input convolutional neural network by augmenting stft. In: 2019 5th International Conference on Advances in Electrical Engineering (ICAEE), pp. 398–403. IEEE (2019)
7. Roy, A.M.: An efficient multi-scale cnn model with intrinsic feature integration for motor imagery eeg subject classification in brain-machine interfaces. Biomed. Signal Process. Control **74**, 103496 (2022)
8. Xie, J., et al.: A transformer-based approach combining deep learning network and spatial-temporal information for raw eeg classification. IEEE Trans. Neural Syst. Rehabil. Eng. **30**, 2126–2136 (2022)

9. Yin, J., Liu, A., Li, C., Qian, R., Chen, X.: A gan guided parallel cnn and transformer network for eeg denoising. IEEE J. Biomed. Health Inf. (2023)
10. Ying, M., Shao, X., Zhu, J., Zhao, Q., Li, X., Hu, B.: Edt: an eeg-based attention model for feature learning and depression recognition. Biomed. Signal Process. Control **93**, 106182 (2024)
11. Keutayeva, A., Abibullaev, B.: Data constraints and performance optimization for transformer-based models in eeg-based brain-computer interfaces: a survey. IEEE Access (2024)
12. Bigdely-Shamlo, N., Mullen, T., Kothe, C., Su, K.M., Robbins, K.A.: The prep pipeline: standardized preprocessing for large-scale eeg analysis. Front. Neuroinform. **9**, 16 (2015)
13. Pedroni, A., Bahreini, A., Langer, N.: Automagic: standardized preprocessing of big eeg data. Neuroimage **200**, 460–473 (2019)
14. Delorme, A.: Eeg is better left alone. Sci. Rep. **13**(1), 2372 (2023)
15. Shen, J., et al.: An optimal channel selection for eeg-based depression detection via kernel-target alignment. IEEE J. Biomed. Health Inf. **25**(7), 2545–2556 (2020)
16. Schirrmeister, R.T., et al.: Deep learning with convolutional neural networks for eeg decoding and visualization. Hum. Brain Mapp. **38**(11), 5391–5420 (2017)
17. Cai, H., et al.: A multi-modal open dataset for mental-disorder analysis. Sci. Data **9**(1), 178 (2022)
18. Mumtaz, W., Xia, L., Mohd Yasin, M.A., Azhar Ali, S.S., Malik, A.S.: A wavelet-based technique to predict treatment outcome for major depressive disorder. PLoS ONE **12**(2), e0171409 (2017)
19. Cordoba-Silva, J., et al.: Music therapy with adult burn patients in the intensive care unit: short-term analysis of electrophysiological signals during music-assisted relaxation. Sci. Rep. **14**(1), 23592 (2024)
20. Lawhern, V.J., Solon, A.J., Waytowich, N.R., Gordon, S.M., Hung, C.P., Lance, B.J.: Eegnet: a compact convolutional neural network for eeg-based brain-computer interfaces. J. Neural Eng. **15**(5), 056013 (2018)
21. Seal, A., Bajpai, R., Agnihotri, J., Yazidi, A., Herrera-Viedma, E., Krejcar, O.: Deprnet: a deep convolution neural network framework for detecting depression using eeg. IEEE Trans. Instrum. Meas. **70**, 1–13 (2021)
22. Song, Y., Zheng, Q., Liu, B., Gao, X.: Eeg conformer: convolutional transformer for eeg decoding and visualization. IEEE Trans. Neural Syst. Rehabil. Eng. **31**, 710–719 (2022)
23. Ding, Y., et al.: Eeg-deformer: a dense convolutional transformer for brain-computer interfaces. IEEE J. Biomed. Health Inf. (2024)
24. Si, X., et al.: Temporal aware mixed attention-based convolution and transformer network for cross-subject eeg emotion recognition. Comput. Biol. Med. **181**, 108973 (2024)
25. Ferree, T.: Determination of the geodesic sensor nets' average electrode positions and their 10-10 international equivalents. Technical note (2000)
26. Zhang, F.F., Peng, W., Sweeney, J.A., Jia, Z.Y., Gong, Q.Y.: Brain structure alterations in depression: psychoradiological evidence. CNS Neurosci. Therapeut. **24**(11), 994–1003 (2018)

Learning to Decompose and Fuse: A Hybrid Approach for Noise-Robust Remote Photoplethysmography

Changchen Zhao[1], Shihan Sun[1], Ge Zheng[2], Shichao Cheng[1], and Jianhai Zhang[1(✉)]

[1] School of Computer Science, Hangzhou Dianzi University, Hangzhou 310018, China
`jhzhang@hdu.edu.cn`
[2] Department of Pediatrics, Ruian City People's Hospital, Wenzhou 325200, China

Abstract. Existing deep learning methods for remote photoplethysmography (rPPG) struggle with robust signal extraction due to a lack of explicit constraints for noise disentanglement. We propose a novel hybrid architecture that introduces a physics-informed reconstruction module to address this limitation. This module guides the network to decompose the signal by reconstructing the raw measurement traces using a fixed pulse and learnable motion basis vector. The architecture also integrates a temporal differencing front-end and is optimized with a hybrid time-frequency loss. Our model achieve superior performance on the PURE and UBFC-rPPG datasets, significantly improving SNR by over 2.5 dB on PURE, and secures top performance on UBFC-rPPG by over 0.26 dB.

Keywords: rPPG · Deep learning · Spatiotemporal feature fusion · Signal extraction · Noise suppression

1 Introduction

Remote photoplethysmography (rPPG) is a prominent non-contact technique for sensing physiological signs, such as heart rate, from subtle color changes in facial videos [4,12,15]. Its convenience and cost-effectiveness offer significant advantages over traditional contact-based methods. However, the primary challenge in rPPG lies in extracting the faint pulsatile signal, which is often contaminated by strong noise from motion artifacts and ambient illumination fluctuations [11].

While early signal processing methods like ICA [7] and CHROM [3] struggle in dynamic scenarios, modern deep learning models, such as PhysNet [13] and GLISNet [17], have achieved significant improvements. Nonetheless, two key limitations persist. Firstly, the disentanglement of pulse and noise signals often lacks explicit physical constraints, leading to ambiguity. Secondly, existing loss functions primarily focus on temporal fidelity, neglecting direct optimization of the signal's frequency-domain quality, which is crucial for achieving a high signal-to-noise ratio (SNR).

W. Jia et al. (Eds.): CCBR 2025, LNCS 16360, pp. 376–385, 2026.
https://doi.org/10.1007/978-981-95-6123-0_35

Addressing these limitations necessitates a hybrid framework that synergizes the feature-learning power of deep networks with the guiding principles of physics-based models. This philosophy is gaining traction as a powerful paradigm in computer vision. For instance, integrating a physical camera noise model has proven highly effective for extreme low-light image denoising [6], while employing a biophysical skin reflectance model has enabled more meaningful decomposition of face images [1]. Inspired by this trend, we propose a novel physics-informed, dual-branch network for robust rPPG. Our main contributions are threefold:

1. We propose a dual-branch architecture that explicitly models pulse and noise components for robust signal decomposition.
2. We introduce a physics-informed reconstruction module via RGB signal reconstruction, which uses fixed pulse and learnable motion vectors to regularize feature disentanglement.
3. We design a hybrid domain loss function that jointly optimizes for temporal accuracy and spectral purity, directly boosting the signal quality.

2   Related Work

2.1   Remote Photoplethysmography

Early rPPG research focused on unsupervised signal processing. Methods like ICA [7] and PCA [5] treat the problem as blind source separation, while others like CHROM [3] and POS [10] leverage properties of skin reflection in specific color spaces. However, these handcrafted approaches often lack robustness in uncontrolled, real-world conditions.

The field has since shifted towards supervised deep learning, with network architectures evolving to better capture spatio-temporal features. Initial end-to-end models like PhysNet [13] utilized 3D CNNs to directly process video clips. More recently, advanced backbones such as the Transformer have been introduced to model long-range temporal dependencies, as exemplified by Phys-Former++ [14], which integrates a SlowFast temporal difference transformer. Concurrently, other works have focused on multi-branch architectures to improve robustness and efficiency. For instance, GLISNet [17] introduced a dual-path network with local-global interaction. Our work extends this multi-branch paradigm by incorporating a distinct noise decomposition branch and enforcing physics-based supervision.

2.2   Hybrid and Physics-Informed Methods

An emerging approach in computer vision is to fuse data-driven methods with physics-based priors to overcome the limitations of purely learning-based systems. Moseley et al. [6] demonstrated this by creating a detailed physical camera noise model to generate realistic training data for lunar image denoising, a task where real ground-truth data is unavailable. In a different domain, Alotaibi and Smith [1] used a biophysical skin reflectance model as a differentiable decoder to enable self-supervised training for intrinsic face decomposition. From a broader perspective, the AI community increasingly advocates for evaluation frameworks that are more holistic and grounded in scientific principles, moving beyond task-specific metrics [8].

While these works validate the power of physics-informed learning, our method presents a unique formulation for the rPPG task. We are the first to combine a **physics-informed reconstruction loss**, which regularizes the decomposition, with a **dual-branch network** that explicitly learns to separate pulse and noise signals. Furthermore, our **hybrid domain loss** directly optimizes for the SNR, a critical metric for rPPG that is often overlooked by previous methods.

3   Methodology

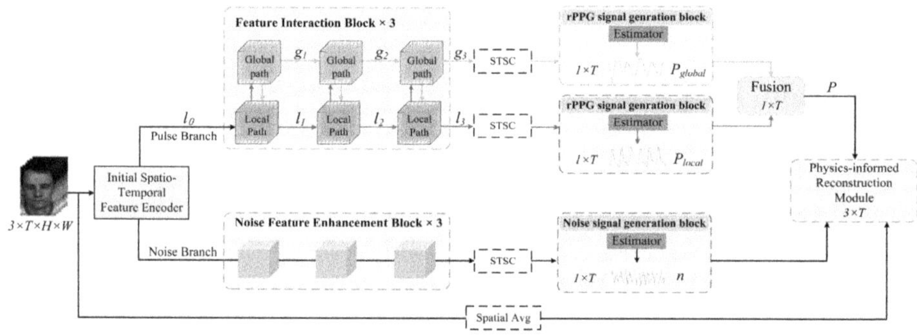

Fig. 1. Overall architecture of our proposed model.

To accurately extract the remote photoplethysmography (rPPG) signal from facial videos containing complex noise, we propose a novel network that fuses multi-scale interaction with physics-informed reconstruction module. As illustrated in Fig. 1, our framework primarily consists of three core components:

1. A **Initial Spatio-Temporal Feature Encoder** for early noise suppression and feature enhancement;
2. A **parallel core feature extraction network** comprising a pulse branch and a noise branch;
3. A **physics-informed reconstruction module** based on a biophysical skin reflectance model, along with a corresponding hybrid domain loss function.

In the following sections, we will elaborate on the design of each component.

3.1   Initial Spatio-Temporal Feature Encoder

The **Initial Spatio-Temporal Feature Encoder** is designed to suppress non-physiological noise and amplify pulse-related dynamics from the input video clip $x \in \mathbb{R}^{C \times T \times H \times W}$. It first performs a temporal shift operation to obtain x_{t-1} and x_{t+1} and then computes two difference videos that highlight inter-frame changes:

$$d_1 = x_t - x_{t-1}, \quad d_2 = x_{t+1} - x_t \tag{1}$$

These difference videos are concatenated and processed by a fusion block (2D Conv, BN, ReLU, Max Pooling) to produce a temporally-enhanced feature map. Subsequently, this map is passed through a series of 3D convolutional and spatial max-pooling layers to extract abstract spatiotemporal features. This entire process yields a final feature map where static information is suppressed and dynamic features are emphasized, providing a robust foundation for the subsequent parallel branches.

3.2   Core Feature Extraction Network

Following the Initial Spatio-Temporal Feature Encoder, we designed a dual-branch network architecture to learn pulse and noise features in parallel.

Pulse Branch: A Multi-scale Feature Interaction Network. The pulse branch, designed to extract physiological signals from multi-scale features, is fundamentally inspired by the local-global interaction paradigm of GLISNet. In this work, we adopt GLISNet's dual-path architecture due to its proven capability in separating and fusing features for remote PPG signals. Specifically, this branch consists of three Feature Interaction Module (FIMs), which are designed to progressively learn and separate local and global pulse representations.

As illustrated in Fig. 2, our pulse branch is constructed from a series of cascaded FIMs. Each FIM comprises a **Local Path** and a **Global Path**, with a bidirectional information flow established between them:

Local Path: This path operates at a larger spatial resolution, focusing on learning fine-grained spatial textures and short-range temporal dynamics through 3D convolutional layers. To progressively enlarge the spatial receptive field while preserving temporal resolution, this path interleaves convolutional blocks with purely spatial max-pooling layers. Its core objective is to retain the local details that are crucial for the rPPG signal.

Global Path: In parallel to the local path, the global path is designed to capture long-range dependencies and global contextual information. We argue that while the intensity of the pulse signal may vary across different facial regions, its periodicity should be globally consistent in time. The global path generates its features by applying adaptive spatial average pooling to the feature maps from the local path. This operation compresses the entire spatial information into a compact global feature vector, effectively filtering out local noise and extracting the mean color dynamic trend across the entire facial region.

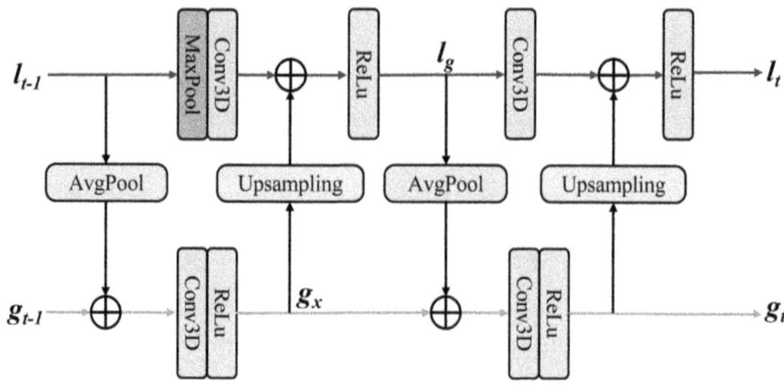

Fig. 2. Diagram of the feature interaction module.

Feature Interaction between Global and Local Paths: Within each FIM, a bidirectional information flow is established for mutual feature enhancement. Global features are upsampled to provide contextual guidance to the local path, while local features are downsampled via adaptive pooling to enrich the global path with fine-grained details.

Following the final FIM, features from both paths, $\boldsymbol{F}$, are refined by a **Spatio-Temporal Separable Convolution (STSC)** module. This module calculates spatial $(\boldsymbol{A}_S)$ and temporal $(\boldsymbol{A}_T)$ attention maps:

$$\boldsymbol{A}_S = \boldsymbol{\sigma}(\mathrm{f}_{\mathrm{spatial}}(\boldsymbol{F})), \quad \boldsymbol{A}_T = \boldsymbol{\sigma}(\mathrm{f}_{\mathrm{temporal}}(\boldsymbol{F})) \tag{2}$$

where $\mathrm{f}_{\mathrm{spatial}}$ and $\mathrm{f}_{\mathrm{temporal}}$ are $1\times3\times3$ and $3\times1\times1$ convolutions, respectively, and σ is the Sigmoid function. The refined feature $\boldsymbol{F}'$ is the element-wise product:

$$\boldsymbol{F}' = \boldsymbol{F} \otimes \boldsymbol{A}_S \otimes \boldsymbol{A}_T \tag{3}$$

These attention-weighted features are then directed to two separate rPPG signal generators, which use a sequence of 3D convolution, adaptive pooling, and a final projection layer to yield pulse signals $\boldsymbol{p}_{\mathrm{local}}$ and $\boldsymbol{p}_{\mathrm{global}}$. A learnable weight $\boldsymbol{\alpha}$ adaptively fuses these two signals to produce the final robust output:

$$\boldsymbol{p} = \boldsymbol{p}_{\mathrm{local}} + \boldsymbol{\alpha} \cdot \boldsymbol{p}_{\mathrm{global}} \tag{4}$$

Noise Branch. Operating in parallel to the pulse branch, the noise branch is designed to model non-pulse components, such as motion and illumination artifacts. Its architecture prioritizes spatial convolutions to capture textural information, followed by a temporal convolution layer that explicitly models inter-frame changes using a $3 \times 1 \times 1$ kernel. This design allows the branch to extract dynamic information related to subject movement. To process more abstract features without sacrificing the temporal sequence length, this branch maintains a constant temporal dimension while progressively downsampling the spatial dimensions. This design ensures that the noise branch is functionally complementary to the pulse branch, allowing the two pathways to specialize in capturing distinct aspects of the signal.

Similar to the pulse branch, the final features are refined by a STSC before being mapped to a one-dimensional n through a signal generator.

3.3   Physics-Informed Reconstruction and Loss Function

Our supervision strategy guides the network toward robust signal extraction using two key components: a physics-informed reconstruction loss that regularizes the decomposition process, and a complementary hybrid domain loss that directly optimizes signal quality.

Physics-Informed Reconstruction Loss. The cornerstone of our strategy is a **physics-informed reconstruction loss** ($\mathcal{L}_{\mathrm{rec}}$), which acts as a powerful regularizer. It enforces the physical constraint that the network's decomposed pulse (p) and noise (n) waveforms must coherently reconstruct the raw traces C_n (where $C_n \in \mathbb{R}^{3 \times T}$). Based on skin reflection models, this reconstruction is performed by combining the network outputs with basis vectors. The pulse waveform is projected onto a fixed pulse basis vector (u_p) representing blood volume changes, while the noise is projected onto a learnable motion basis vector (u_m). Furthermore, the model learns scalar weights (B and A) to modulate the intensity of the pulse and noise components before summation, allowing it to adaptively balance their contributions. $\mathcal{L}_{\mathrm{rec}}$ is then defined as the $\|\cdot\|_1$ distance between the final reconstructed signal $\hat{C}$ and C_n:

$$\mathcal{L}_{\mathrm{rec}} = \left\| \hat{C} - C_n \right\|_1 \tag{5}$$

Hybrid Domain Loss Function. To directly supervise the quality of the estimated pulse signal, we complement the reconstruction loss with a **hybrid domain loss function**, which provides direct supervision on the estimated pulse signal. Its calculation is structured to aggregate errors from the model's local, global, and combined pathways, defined as:

$$\mathcal{L}_{\mathrm{ppg}} = \mathcal{L}^{\mathrm{local}} + \alpha_{\mathrm{global}} \cdot \mathcal{L}^{\mathrm{global}} + \mathcal{L}^{\mathrm{p}} \tag{6}$$

where $\mathcal{L}^{\mathrm{p}}$ corresponds to the loss from the combined pathway and α_{global} is a balancing hyperparameter.

This formula serves as a template that is instantiated for three distinct metrics to ensure comprehensive signal fidelity. In the time domain, we apply this structure to calculate a negative Pearson loss ($\mathcal{L}_{\mathrm{np}}$) for waveform shape and an MSE loss ($\mathcal{L}_{\mathrm{mse}}$) for amplitude. In the frequency domain, it is applied to a Power Spectral Density (PSD) loss ($\mathcal{L}_{\mathrm{psd}}$) to enforce periodicity. The final PPG-related loss used in training is the weighted sum of these three instantiated components.

Total Loss Function. Finally, the total loss function for our model, $\mathcal{L}_{\text{total}}$, is a weighted sum of the two main components described above: the physics-informed reconstruction loss ($\mathcal{L}_{\text{rec}}$) and the hybrid domain PPG loss ($\mathcal{L}_{\text{ppg}}$). This is formulated as:

$$\mathcal{L}_{\text{total}} = \lambda_{\text{rec}}\mathcal{L}_{\text{rec}} + \lambda_{\text{ppg}}\mathcal{L}_{\text{ppg}} \tag{7}$$

where $\mathcal{L}_{\text{ppg}}$ is the composite loss combining the weighted np, mse, and psd metrics as defined previously. The λ terms are hyperparameters that balance the influence of the reconstruction and PPG supervision objectives.

4   Experiments

To comprehensively evaluate the performance of our proposed model, we conducted extensive experiments on two widely-used public rPPG datasets: PURE [9] and UBFC-rPPG [2]. This section details the characteristics of the datasets used, our data preprocessing pipeline, and the specific implementation details of our experiments.

4.1   Datasets

We evaluated our model on two public datasets: PURE and UBFC-rPPG. The PURE dataset contains 60 videos from 10 subjects, featuring diverse motion artifacts from six distinct scenarios, making it suitable for evaluating robustness. The UBFC-rPPG dataset includes 42 subjects in more naturalistic settings with slight head movements and illumination changes. For both datasets, a unified preprocessing pipeline was applied: facial regions were detected, the bounding box enlarged by a factor of 1.2, and each frame was subsequently cropped and resized to 192×128 pixels. The ground-truth PPG signals were resampled to match the 30 Hz video frame rate for strict temporal alignment.

4.2   Performance Evaluation Against Baseline Methods

To assess the effectiveness of our architecture, we conducted comparative evaluations against multiple baseline methods-encompassing both unsupervised and supervised categories-on the PURE and UBFC-rPPG datasets. It achieves over 50% reduction in MAE and RMSE compared to unsupervised methods (POS, CHROM, ICA) on PURE, while surpassing supervised counterparts (PhysNet, JAMSNet, GLISNet) with notable gains in SNR (2.3 dB higher than GLIS-Net) and Pearson correlation (0.979 on PURE). As detailed in Table 1, our model demonstrates significant improvements across all metrics. The advantage is particularly evident on the challenging PURE dataset, where our model improves the SNR by 2.3 dB over the GLISNet baseline. This gain highlights how our novel components—the physics-informed signal separation and initial spatio-temporal encoding—enhance robustness against motion artifacts. These results validate our architecture as a highly effective approach for robust rPPG signal extraction.

Table 1. Performance comparison with baseline methods on the PURE and UBFC-rPPG datasets. The best results for each metric are highlighted in **bold**.

	PURE				UBFC-rPPG			
	SNR (dB)	MAE (BPM)	RMSE (BPM)	R (Pearson)	SNR (dB)	MAE (BPM)	RMSE (BPM)	R (Pearson)
POS [10]	6.38	3.45	9.50	0.906	4.71	2.87	6.34	0.893
CHROM [3]	4.52	5.45	13.31	0.819	3.25	3.46	9.22	0.795
ICA [7]	4.62	5.89	14.54	0.781	1.52	11.76	22.28	0.524
PhysNet [13]	5.07	2.98	4.96	0.746	6.27	1.54	2.56	0.983
JAMSNet [16]	2.11	3.84	7.34	0.553	3.47	2.63	5.20	0.926
GLISNet [17]	6.87	1.45	2.99	0.902	5.57	1.58	3.91	0.960
Proposed	**9.24**	**0.97**	**1.45**	**0.979**	**6.54**	**1.10**	**2.46**	**0.984**

4.3   Ablation Study

To systematically validate the effectiveness of the key components in our proposed model, we designed a series of ablation experiments. This section separately investigates the impact of the temporal enhancement, and the reconstruction loss weight on the final model performance. All ablation studies were conducted on the both two datasets, using the same training, validation, and evaluation protocols as in the main experiments to ensure fair comparisons.

Impact of the Temporal Enhancement. To validate the effectiveness of the **temporal enhancement mechanism** within our Initial Spatio-Temporal Feature Encoder, we conducted an ablation study comparing the full model (**w/ Enhancement**) against a variant where this initial stage was removed (**w/o Enhancement**). As shown in Table 1 and Table 2, the results unequivocally demonstrate the mechanism's significant contribution. The inclusion of the temporal enhancement stage yields substantial performance gains across both datasets, improving MAE and RMSE by **27.6%** and **52.0%** respectively on the PURE dataset, and by **31.9%** and **23.0%** on the UBFC-rPPG dataset. This confirms that performing temporal differencing at the initial feature encoding stage is a crucial step, effectively suppressing low-frequency noise while enhancing pulse-related dynamic features, thereby boosting the overall accuracy and robustness of the network.

Table 2. Performance of the model without the temporal enhancement mechanism (w/o Enhancement configuration).

Dataset	SNR (dB) ↑	MAE (BPM) ↓	RMSE (BPM) ↓	R ↑
PURE	7.40	1.34	3.03	0.898
UBFC	5.54	1.61	3.20	0.972

Impact of the Reconstruction Loss Weight. The reconstruction loss weight, λ_{rec}, critically balances direct pulse supervision with the physics-based signal reconstruction. To investigate its impact, we conducted an ablation study varying $\lambda_{\text{rec}} \in \{0.05, 0.1, 0.2, 0.5\}$. As shown in Fig. 3, the optimal trade-off is achieved at $\lambda_{\text{rec}} = 0.05$, yielding the best performance across all metrics. Higher values lead to performance degradation, particularly in SNR and Pearson correlation, suggesting that an excessive weight prioritizes appearance patterns over the physiological signal. A small λ_{rec} of 0.05 thus serves as an effective regularizer, guiding decomposition without overpowering the primary task. Consequently, this value is adopted in our final configuration.

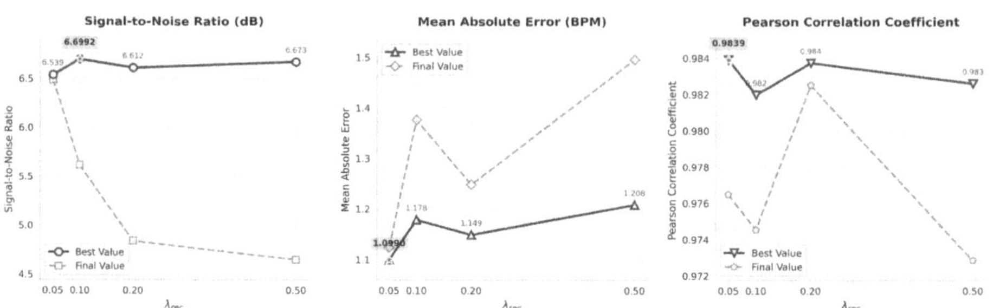

Fig. 3. Performance as a function of the reconstruction loss weight ($\boldsymbol{\lambda}_{\text{rec}}$). The model's performance on the UBFC-rPPG dataset is evaluated across three metrics for different values of $\boldsymbol{\lambda}_{\text{rec}}$.

5   Conclusion

In this paper, we proposed a novel hybrid architecture for robust rPPG that combines a temporal differencing front-end with a multi-scale global-local interaction backbone. Our physics-informed approach, leveraging a hybrid time-frequency loss, achieves state-of-the-art performance on PURE and UBFC-rPPG datasets, outperforming all baselines. Notably, it delivers over 2.5 dB SNR improvement on PURE and top-tier results on UBFC-rPPG (6.54 dB SNR, 2.46 BPM RMSE). Ablation studies confirm the effectiveness of our components. Future work will focus on real-time deployment and in-the-wild generalization.

References

1. Alotaibi, S., Smith, W.A.P.: Biofacenet: deep biophysical face image interpretation. In: Proceedings of the British Machine Vision Conference, Cardiff, UK (2019)
2. Bobbia, S., Macwan, R., Benezeth, Y., Mansouri, A., Dubois, J.: Unsupervised skin tissue segmentation for remote photoplethysmography. Pattern Recogn. Lett. **124**, 82–90 (2019)

3. De Haan, G., Jeanne, V.: Robust pulse rate from chrominance-based rppg. IEEE Trans. Biomed. Eng. **60**(10), 2878–2886 (2013)

4. Huang, P.W., Wu, B.J., Wu, B.F.: A heart rate monitoring framework for real-world drivers using remote photoplethysmography. IEEE J. Biomed. Health Inf. **25**(5), 1397–1408 (2020)

5. Lewandowska, M., Nowak, J.: Measuring pulse rate with a webcam. J. Med. Imaging Health Inf. **2**(1), 87–92 (2012)

6. Moseley, B., Bickel, V., López-Francos, I.G., Rana, L.: Extreme low-light environment-driven image denoising over permanently shadowed lunar regions with a physical noise model. In: Proceedings of IEEE/CVF Conference on Computer Vision and Pattern Recognition, Nashville, USA, pp. 6313–6323 (2021)

7. Poh, M.Z., McDuff, D.J., Picard, R.W.: Non-contact, automated cardiac pulse measurements using video imaging and blind source separation. Opt. Express **18**(10), 10762–10774 (2010)

8. Qu, Y., et al.: Integration of cognitive tasks into artificial general intelligence test for large models. iScience **27**(4), 109550 (2024)

9. Stricker, R., Müller, S., Gross, H.M.: Non-contact video-based pulse rate measurement on a mobile service robot. In: Proceedings of the IEEE International Symposium on Robot and Human Interactive Communication, Edinburgh, UK, pp. 1056–1062 (2014)

10. Wang, W., Den Brinker, A.C., Stuijk, S., De Haan, G.: Algorithmic principles of remote PPG. IEEE Trans. Biomed. Eng. **64**(7), 1479–1491 (2016)

11. Xi, L., Chen, W., Zhao, C., Wu, X., Wang, J.: Image enhancement for remote photoplethysmography in a low-light environment. In: Proceedings of the IEEE International Conference on Automatic Face and Gesture Recognition, Buenos Aires, Argentina, pp. 1–7 (2020)

12. Xiao, H., Liu, T., Sun, Y., Li, Y., Zhao, S., Avolio, A.: Remote photoplethysmography for heart rate measurement: a review. Biomed. Signal Process. Control **88**, 105608 (2024)

13. Yu, Z., Li, X., Zhao, G.: Remote photoplethysmograph signal measurement from facial videos using spatio-temporal networks. In: Proceedings of the British Machine Vision Conference, Cardiff, UK, p. 277 (2019)

14. Yu, Z., Shen, Y., Shi, J., Zhao, H., Torr, P.H.S., Zhao, G.: PhysFormer++: facial video-based physiological measurement with SlowFast temporal difference transformer. Int. J. Comput. Vision **131**(6), 1307–1330 (2023)

15. Zhao, C., Lin, C.L., Chen, W., Chen, M.K., Wang, J.: Visual heart rate estimation and negative feedback control for fitness exercise. Biomed. Signal Process. Control **56**, 101680 (2020)

16. Zhao, C., Wang, H., Chen, H., Shi, W., Feng, Y.: Jamsnet: a remote pulse extraction network based on joint attention and multi-scale fusion. IEEE Trans. Circuits Syst. Video Technol. **33**(6), 2783–2797 (2022)

17. Zhao, C., Zhou, M., Zhao, Z., Huang, B., Rao, B.: Learning spatio-temporal pulse representation with global-local interaction and supervision for remote prediction of heart rate. IEEE J. Biomed. Health Inf. **28**(2), 609–620 (2023)

Automatic Sleep Staging with Dynamic Hypergraph Neural Networks Using Spatiotemporal Features

Hailu Fan, Yubin Chen[(✉)], Lucong Wang, and Xinyang Li

School of Software, Nanchang Hangkong University, Nanchang, China
yubinchen@nchu.edu.cn

Abstract. In clinical medicine, the accuracy of sleep staging directly affects the diagnosis and treatment of sleep disorders. However, existing methods have significant limitations in characterizing dynamic spatiotemporal associations of the brain during sleep, especially in modeling nonlinear interactions across brain regions. To overcome these limitations, we develop STHGNN, a hypergraph-based neural network model that captures spatiotemporal features for automated sleep staging. The model fuses temporal and spatial features extracted from multi-modal data, and thus performs classification task effectively. In our experiments, we compared our method on the ISRUC-S1 and ISRUC-S3 datasets with the latest methods. Experimental results on the ISRUC-S3 dataset show that the overall classification accuracy of this method reaches 82.8%, F1-score and Cohen kappa reach 81.1% and 77.8%, respectively. Compared with existing baseline classification methods, this method has better classification performance.

Keywords: Sleep stage classification · Deep learning · Hypergraph neural networks · Bi-GRU

1 Introduction

Sleep is an important physiological process for maintaining internal environment homeostasis, and is the basis for tissue repair and energy metabolism [1]. To optimize the diagnosis of sleep disorders, the American Academy of Sleep Medicine (AASM) [2] established a sleep staging standard that utilizes physiological signals from polysomnography (PSG) to categorize sleep into five states: wakefulness, three non-rapid eye movement stages (N1, N2, N3), and rapid eye movement(REM) sleep. Figure 1 shows an example of an adult male sleep map. PSG signals include EEG, EOG, EMG, ECG and other physiological signals, where the interactions between channels and temporal dependencies are non-independent. Therefore, it is crucial to capture the interaction between channels during sleep and the heterogeneity of signals in frequency domain and amplitude characteristics by using multi-modal signals for achieving high-precision sleep staging.

© The Author(s), under exclusive license to Springer Nature Singapore Pte Ltd. 2026
W. Jia et al. (Eds.): CCBR 2025, LNCS 16360, pp. 386–394, 2026.
https://doi.org/10.1007/978-981-95-6123-0_36

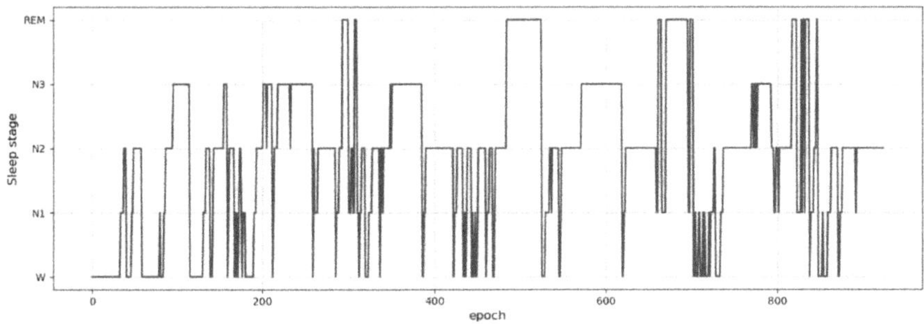

Fig. 1. The sleep map of a healthy adult male.

In recent years, deep learning methods represented by convolutional neural networks (CNNs) and recurrent neural networks (RNNs) have been widely used in sleep staging due to their powerful feature extraction and time series modeling capabilities, and their advantages are significant. However, deep learning technologies such as CNNs and RNNs require input features to be Euclidean data, and brain regions belong to non-Euclidean space, so their ability to model spatial features is insufficient. As deep learning models specifically designed for non-Euclidean data, GNNs explicitly model node-level topological relationships to extract spatial features. Therefore, Jia et al. [3] proposed SleepHGNN model, which fully combined the characteristics of interaction and heterogeneity, and considered the interaction between human organs, but the high-order relationship between modes was not obtained enough, and the dynamic spatial-temporal correlation of data was not included. Thus, hypergraph-based methods began to emerge [4]. Compared with traditional graph-based learning methods, hypergraphs introduce multiple hyperedges, each of which can connect more than two nodes, so that multimodal information can be combined into the same structure flexibly.

In this paper, we propose a dynamic sleep staging model based on heterogeneous hypergraph: STHGNN. The hypergraph representation is performed on the data after power spectral density calculation (Welch method). Bi-GRU is used to extract temporal features, which are combined with spatial features extracted by HMSG module. Then STFF module is used to fuse the spatio-temporal features progressively. Finally, conditional random fields (CRF) [5] are used to deal with label dependence. The main contributions of this work are summarized as follows: (1) A message aggregation and update algorithm for hypergraph nodes is proposed to model complex modal relationships. (2) A component STFF is designed to extract spatiotemporal fusion features. (3) Sleep stage classification experiments were performed on two public datasets ISRUC-S1 and ISRUC-S3 to test the performance of the STHGNN model between healthy subjects and sleep disordered subjects. The results show that the STHGNN model performs better than the baseline model on both datasets.

2   Related Work

Time series analysis is a crucial field within statistics and econometrics. As a classic example of non-stationary time series, physiological signals are revolutionizing medical diagnosis and health monitoring technologies through the continuous advancement of analytical methods. In the realm of sleep medicine, the application of sequential pattern recognition techniques to polysomnography data enables automated sleep stage classification, leading to a notable enhancement in the diagnostic accuracy of sleep disorders.

Early in the field of sleep staging, traditional machine learning classification algorithms like Support Vector Machines (SVM) [6], Random Forests (RF) [7], and Hidden Markov Models (HMM) [8] were commonly employed to address crucial healthcare requirements. However, in processing high-dimensional and nonlinear data like PSG signals, algorithms often require intricate feature extraction based on prior human expertise to streamline processes and prevent model overfitting. Additionally, they heavily depend on existing biomedical knowledge. With the development of deep learning, CNN and RNN show breakthrough advantages in the field of sleep staging. The DeepSleepNet model proposed by Akara et al. [9] employs CNNs to extract time-invariant features and incorporates a bidirectional long short-term memory (Bi-LSTM) network for sequence-level modeling. It automatically learns temporal, frequency-domain, and transition rules between adjacent sleep epochs, distinguishing itself from contemporary algorithms. Subsequently, Akara et al. designed a more efficient CNN model based on DeepSleepNet model, named TinySleepNet [10], which employs LSTM networks to capture transition patterns between sequences, while adopting a compact parameter design to mitigate the issue of excessive parameters in both multi-branch and bidirectional recurrent architectures, thereby reducing reliance on high-performance computing devices.

However, these methods rely on grid data and fail to explore brain spatial relationships during sleep. Some researchers have attempted to model the temporal and spatial relationships of sleep data. For example, GraphSleepNet model proposed by Jia et al. [11] adopts the dual architecture of graph convolutional network, innovatively models the interaction relationship of EEG signals from spatial topology and temporal dynamic dimensions, and automatically obtains key information in combination with spatiotemporal attention mechanism, thus significantly improving the accuracy of sleep classification. Following the improvement of GraphSleepNet, MSTGCN model [12] integrates space-time graph convolution based on self-attention mechanism and domain generalization by integrating physical topology structure and functional connection of brain regions, adaptively learns the inherent relationship between time domain and space domain of EEG signals, and enhances the generalization performance of the model. Liu et al.'s BSTT model [13], which integrates Bayesian inference with Transformer to acquire spatiotemporal features while emphasizing model interpretability. Despite their demonstrated efficacy, existing methods have some deficiencies in considering multimodality and fail to fully capture the spatiotemporal relationship.

3   Methodology

The overall architecture of STHGNN is shown in Fig. 2. Cut any channel data with a window of 30 s, and define the signal after power spectral density calculation as $\chi = \{X^1, X^2, ..., X^N\} \in R^{N \times L \times d}$, where N represents the number of channels, L is the number of time segments (number of sleep periods) after each channel is cut by 30 s, and d represents the sequence length of a single channel in a single sleep period. Mapping the data points of each window to a node, the hypergraph can be defined as $G = \{V, E\}$, where V is the set of nodes and E is the set of hyperedges. In Fig. 2, Bi-GRU is used to extract temporal features, and HMSG layer mainly includes two parts: message transfer mechanism for processing heterogeneity and message aggregation mechanism for processing interactivity, which are used to solve the correlation problem of multimodal data and capture spatial high-order relations. Then, the obtained spatiotemporal features are input to STFF module for fusion, and finally CRF is used to model temporal dependencies among labels and optimize global sequence prediction.

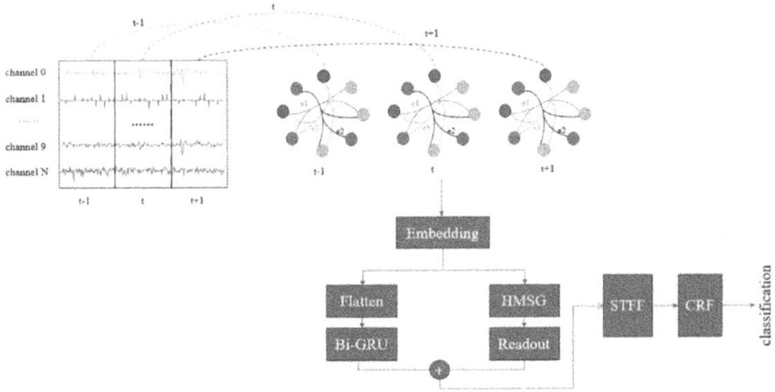

Fig. 2. The overall architecture of STHGNN model. The Readout layer comprises a tensor reshaping operation and a linear projection.

3.1   HMSG

To effectively capture high-order spatial correlations among multimodal physiological signals, we propose a hypergraph-based Type-Aware Message Mechanism (HMSG). This mechanism adeptly models intricate dependencies among diverse physiological signals by discerning distinct node interaction patterns across various hyperedge types. HMSG consists of two core components: a messaging unit for capturing heterogeneity and a node update unit for capturing interactivity.

390   H. Fan et al.

Message Passing. The hypergraph of the t-th sleep period can be defined as $G^t = \{V^t, E^t\}$. KNN algorithm is used to generate hyperedges, that is, each data sample is regarded as a central node, and hyperedges are constructed by connecting k nearest nodes in the feature space. So this paper introduces two kinds of nodes: master node and slave node [14]. There is only one primary node in each hyperedge, and any node can serve as the master node once. First, aggregate all node feature averages of each hyperedge into the master node:

$$MSG_{[\tilde{\nu}_i^t]} = \frac{1}{|S(\tilde{\nu}_i^t)|} \sum_{\nu \in S(\tilde{\nu}_i^t)} X_\nu \tag{1}$$

where $\tilde{\nu}_i^t$ denotes the primary node of the i-th hyperedge during the t-th sleep period, X_ν represents the characteristics of the node v, $S(\tilde{\nu}_i^t) = \{\tilde{\nu}_i^t\} \cup \{\nu \mid \nu \in KNN(\tilde{\nu}_i^t)\}$ is defined as the set of nodes belonging to the same hyperedge, and $G_{MSG} = \{MSG_{[\tilde{\nu}_i^t]} \mid t \in L, i \in N\}$ encompasses all primary node messages within the hypergraph G.

Accounting for heterogeneity across node types and hyperedge types, we design modality-specific feature projections for distinct physiological signals to capture their inter-signal specificity, while constructing dynamic relation matrices to model the evolving patterns of physiological interactions across different stages. The master node message is updated to:

$$MSG'_{[\tilde{\nu}_i^t]} = M_{\psi(\tilde{\nu}_i^t)} \cdot (U_{\phi(\tilde{\nu}_i^t)} \cdot MSG_{[\tilde{\nu}_i^t]})) \tag{2}$$

where ϕ is node type mapping function, ψ is a relation type (hyperedge type) mapping function, $U_{\phi(\tilde{\nu}_i^t)}$ represents the linear transformation matrix for node type $\phi(\tilde{\nu}_i^t)$, M defines a learnable message transformation matrix for each relation type, and performs relation adaptive feature mapping on node features in the message passing stage, $M_{\psi(\tilde{\nu}_i^t)}$ denotes the relation weight matrix for relationship type $\psi(\tilde{\nu}_i^t)$.

Thus, all master node messages in the hypergraph G can be updated to:

$$G'_{MSG} = \{MSG'_{[\tilde{\nu}_i^t]} \mid t \in L, i \in N\} \tag{3}$$

Node Feature Updating. After message transmission, attention weights are used to dynamically calibrate the interaction strength between master node features and aggregated neighborhood features.

$$Q_r = Lin_r[G'_{MSG}]_r, \quad K_r = Lin_r[G_{MSG}]_r \tag{4}$$

$$\alpha_r = sigmoid(Q_r \cdot K_r) \tag{5}$$

where r is the relationship type, Lin_r is a linear transformation of relation type r, $[G'_{MSG}]_r$ represents the primary nodes message with relation type r after message delivery and $[G_{MSG}]_r$ information transmitted by the hypergraph with the stability of the original features:

$$G_{out} = \Gamma_r[\alpha_r \cdot \sigma(Lin_r[G'_{MSG}]_r) + (1 - \alpha_r) \cdot [G_{MSG}]_r] \tag{6}$$

where σ is an activation function, Γ is a type-specific normalization operator.

3.2   STFF

Figure 3 shows the STFF module for progressive active fusion of spatiotemporal features, which aims to efficiently integrate the temporal dynamics and spatial dependencies of features.

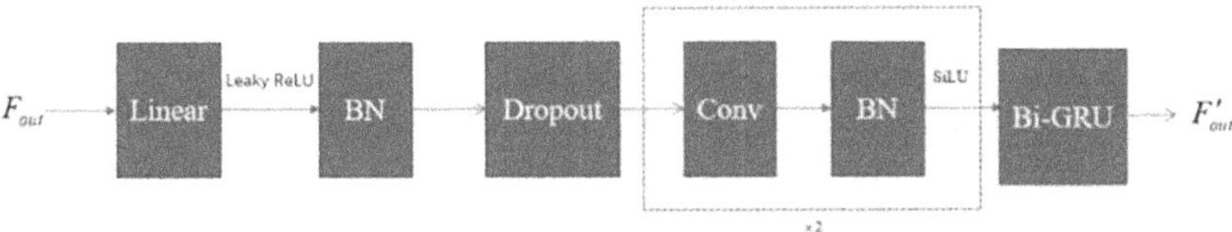

Fig. 3. The structure of the STFF.

F_{out} is the spatiotemporal feature of G_{out} combined with the temporal feature after it passes through the Readout layer. Linear layer and normalization layer are mainly used for linear projection and distribution normalization of original space-time features, eliminating modal differences and calibrating low-order features. Dropout is set to 0.2. To avoid neuronal death and enhance sensitivity to weak electrical signals, Leaky ReLU was used as the activation function with a negative slope of 0.01. Conv1D slides along the Timeline to capture local patterns in the waveform, supplemented by Batch Normalization to mitigate convolved feature distribution shifts. The Bi-GRU integrates features extracted from all preceding stages to model long-range dependencies. The output features F'_{out} are projected into the target output space, and then a CRF is employed to learn inter-stage transition probabilities, thereby optimizing the temporal coherence of final predictions.

4   Experiments

4.1   Datasets

In this study, experiments were performed on two subsets ISRUC-S3 and ISRUC-S1 from the ISRUC-SLEEP dataset [15] from the Portugal Foundation for Science and Technology (FCT). ISRUC-S3 collected data from 10 healthy subjects, nine men and one woman, aged 30 to 50. ISRUC-S1 collected data from 100 subjects with sleep disorders. For our experiments, we selected the first 50 subjects, including 31 men and 19 women, aged 22 to 85, and nearly half of the subjects had taken sleeping pills before going to bed. All data sets include EEG, EOG, ECG, EMG signals, data is sampled at 200 Hz, filtered through a 50 Hz notch filter to eliminate electrical noise, and 30 samples at the tail of each channel are removed to reduce noise.

4.2 Results

All experiments were performed on a computer equipped with an Intel i7- 12700H CPU, 16 GB of memory, and an Nvidia 3050 GPU. K-fold cross-theme validation was used to evaluate the model, k was set to 10, and accuracy (ACC), F1 Score and Kappa were selected as evaluation indicators to ensure the reliability and statistical significance of the experimental results.

Table 1 and Table 2 demonstrate that the proposed model achieves superior performance compared to other baseline methods on the two subsets of the ISRUC dataset. In particular, traditional machine learning methods are limited by shallow feature representation capabilities, and classification performance is relatively limited. DeepSleepNet focuses on the temporal characteristics of single-channel EEG signals, making it difficult to identify more complex sleep stages. SleepHGNN and MSTGCN model the spatiotemporal relationship during sleep and achieve better results, but the spatiotemporal features are not fully mined, which limits the classification performance to some extent. In contrast, the STHGNN model is more effective at modeling spatiotemporal features, but it performs slightly better than our model in N1 stage due to the domain generalization technique used in MSTGCN.

Table 1. Comparison of STHGNN with other deep learning methods on ISRUC-S3 dataset.

Method	Overall Metrics			Per-class F1-score(F1)				
	ACC	F1	Kappa	W	N1	N2	N3	REM
SVM [6]	69.7%	67.3%	61.1%	79.1%	40.3%	69.8%	79.7%	67.5%
RF [7]	74.1%	72.2%	66.4%	83.7%	46.5%	72.5%	81.9%	76.5%
DeepSleepNet [9]	71.3%	70.2%	64.1%	84.1%	53.0%	65.8%	84.5%	63.9%
SleepHGNN [3]	78.8%	76.9%	72.7%	85.4%	56.3%	79.3%	87.6%	75.9%
MSTGCN [12]	80.0%	78.7%	74.2%	87.4%	**57.1%**	78.3%	88.1%	82.6%
STHGNN (Our)	**82.8%**	**81.1%**	**77.8%**	**88.6%**	57.1%	**81.9%**	**90.3%**	**87.5%**

To validate the effectiveness of the multimodal spatial feature extraction and spatial-temporal feature fusion modules, we conducted ablation studies on the HMSG and STFF modules in STHGNN using the ISRUC-S3 dataset. As shown in Fig. 4, the performance of variant models degrades when specific modules are removed. These results demonstrate that hierarchical extraction of multimodal spatial features is crucial for sleep stage classification, while deep integration of spatial-temporal features can significantly improve classification performance.

Table 2. Comparison of STHGNN with other deep learning methods on ISRUC-S1-50 dataset.

Method	Overall Metrics			Per-class F1-score(F1)				
	ACC	F1	Kappa	W	N1	N2	N3	REM
SVM [6]	66.3%	64.0%	56.4%	73.1%	38.5%	66.5%	75.1%	66.7%
RF [7]	70.3%	66.1%	61.2%	85.3%	35.3%	67.8%	72.0%	70.3%
DeepSleepNet [9]	69.6%	67.1%	60.7%	75.8%	40.6%	69.9%	82.6%	66.7%
SleepHGNN [3]	71.4%	67.4%	62.7%	83.9%	36.6%	70.3%	75.9%	70.3%
MSTGCN [12]	75.3%	73.1%	68.2%	85.7%	**50.0%**	73.2%	82.3%	74.7%
STHGNN (Our)	**79.4%**	**76.5%**	**73.2%**	**89.5%**	48.2%	**77.2%**	**84.0%**	**83.6%**

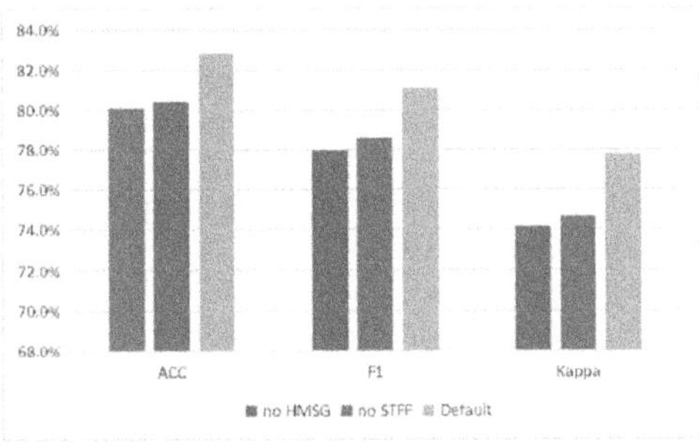

Fig. 4. Results of ablation experiments of STHGNN on ISRUC-S3 dataset.

5   Conclusion

In this paper, a spatiotemporal sleep staging model STHGNN based on heterogeneous hypergraph neural network is proposed. Experimental validation on public datasets shows that the proposed method performs well in sleep stage classification, especially in REM stage. However, the classification performance of this model in N1 still needs to be improved, which may be related to the relatively vague physiological characteristics and short duration of N1. It is worth emphasizing that STHGNN is essentially a general framework for learning spatiotemporal features of physiological signals, capable of modeling and reasoning spatiotemporal relationships of physiological data. In future studies, we will try our best to apply it to a wider range of tasks, such as mental load assessment, mood prediction, early screening for neurodegenerative diseases and other clinical applications. This series of explorations is expected to provide new methodological support for intelligent analysis of physiological signals.

References

1. Rangaraj, V.R., Knutson, K.L.: Association between sleep deficiency and cardiometabolic disease: implications for health disparities. Sleep Med. **18**, 19–35 (2016)
2. Berry, R.B., Brook, R., Gamaldo, C.E., et al.: The AASM manual for the scoring of sleep and associated events: rules, terminology and technical specifications. Am. Acad. Sleep Med. **176**, 2012 (2012)
3. Jia, Z.Y., Lin, Y.F., Zhou, Y.H., et al.: Exploiting Interactivity and Heterogeneity for Sleep Stage Classification via Heterogeneous Graph Neural Network. In: ICASSP 2023-2023 IEEE International Conference on Acoustics, Speech and Signal Processing (ICASSP), pp. 1–5 (2023)
4. Feng, Y.F., You, H.X., Zhang, Z.Z., et al.: Hypergraph Neural Networks. In: Proceedings of the AAAI Conference on Artificial Intelligence, pp. 3558–3565 (2019)
5. Lafferty, J.D., McCallum, A., Pereira, F.C.N.: Conditional random fields: probabilistic models for segmenting and labeling sequence data. In: Proceedings of the 18th International Conference on Machine Learning (ICML 2001), pp. 282–289 (2001)
6. Suykens, J.A.K., Vandewalle, J.: Least squares support vector machine classifiers. Neural Process. Lett. **9**, 29–300 (1999)
7. Breiman, L.: Random forests. Mach. Learn. **45**, 5–32 (2001)
8. Rabiner, L., Juang, B.: An introduction to hidden Markov models. IEEE ASSP Mag. **3**(1), 4–16 (1986)
9. Supratak, A., Dong, H., Wu, C., et al.: DeepSleepNet: a model for automatic sleep stage scoring based on raw single-channel EEG. IEEE Trans. Neural Syst. Rehabil. Eng. **25**(11), 1998–2008 (2017)
10. Supratak, A., Guo, Y.: TinySleepNet: an efficient deeplearning model for sleep stage scoring based on raw single-channel EEG. In: Proceedings of 42nd Annual International Conference of the IEEE Engineering in Medicine & Biology Society (EMBC), pp. 64–644 (2020)
11. Jia, Z.Y., Lin, Y.F., Wang, J., et al.: GraphSleepNet: adaptive spatial-temporal graph convolutional networks for sleep stage classification. In: Proceedings of 29th International Joint Conference on Artificial Intelligence (IJCAI), pp. 1324–1330 (2020)
12. Jia, Z.Y., Lin, Y.F., Wang, J., et al.: Multi-view spatial-temporal graph convolutional networks with domain generalization for sleep stage classification. IEEE Trans. Neural Syst. Rehabil. Eng. **29**, 1977–1986 (2021)
13. Liu, Y.C., Jia, Z.Y.: BSTT: a Bayesian spatial-temporal transformer for sleep staging. In: Proceeedings of 11th International Conference on Learning Representations (ICLR) (2023)
14. Liu, Y.Z., Zhao, Z.M., Zhang, T.H., et al.: Exploiting spatial-temporal data for sleep stage classification via hypergraph learning. arXiv. (2023)
15. Khalighi, S., Sousa, T., Santos, J.M., et al.: ISRUC-sleep: a comprehensive public dataset for sleep researchers. Comput. Methods Programs Biomed. **124**, 180–192 (2016)

Biometrics in Mobile Terminals, Healthcare, Banking, Internet of Things, Self-Driving, Intelligent Robots, etc

Research on DNA Storage Encoding Methods and Evaluation Standard System

Qianying Liu[⊠], Yao Liu, Li Geng, and Wenfeng Wang

China Electronics Standardization Institute, Beijing 100007, China
liuqy@cesi.cn

Abstract. DNA storage represents an innovative approach to information storage, leveraging the four nucleotide bases (A, G, C, T) to encode data. DNA encoding is a critical step in this process, determining how digital information is converted into DNA sequences and securely stored. This paper analyzes existing encoding methods and proposes a novel approach that demonstrates superior performance in terms,&of encoding density and compression efficiency. Furthermore, given the current diversity of encoding methods, poor system compatibility, and incomplete evaluation frameworks, we introduce a comprehensive performance evaluation standard system for DNA encoding. This work aims to support the advancement of DNA coding technology and the broader DNA storage industry through methodological research and technological system alignment.

Keywords: DNA storage · DNA encoding · performance evaluation standard system

1 Introduction

DNA storage technology is a revolutionary storage technology that focuses on the future. It uses artificially synthesized DNA as a storage medium. The biological DNA molecules are encoded using "A, T, G, C" (adenine, thymine, guanine and cytosine) to store information on the DNA sequence. DNA storage technology is the result of the joint development of biotechnology and information technology. It breaks through the bottleneck of information technology by using the principles of biotechnology and is one of the key technologies in biological digital fusion [1, 2].

DNA storage methods mainly include five major links: encoding, synthesis, storage, sequencing and decoding of DNA storage. The DNA synthesis and sequencing technology involved is also one of the key technologies supporting the development of biometric identification. It can be said that DNA storage came into being with the development of genome identification and has become a promising key technology for biological storage.

At present, there are many methods for biological storage in the information encoding and decoding step [3, 4], which can be mainly divided into two categories: the first category is the encoding algorithm based on the restricted basic mapping relationship, including but not limited to the Church encoding algorithm, Goldman encoding

W. Jia et al. (Eds.): CCBR 2025, LNCS 16360, pp. 397–403, 2026.
https://doi.org/10.1007/978-981-95-6123-0_37

algorithm, Grass encoding algorithm, Blawat encoding algorithm, etc. [5]. The second category is the encoding algorithm that adds screening and filtering steps on the basis of the basic mapping relationship, including DNA Fountain code and Yin-Yang dual encoding algorithm [6], which uses the combination diversity of binary information fragments in the file to generate more different DNA sequences. However, the current encoding has the following limitations: insufficient utilization of information capacity, traditional DNA storage methods are mainly based on the sequence arrangement of four bases (A, C, G, T), and each base position encodes 2 bits of information, which fails to fully explore the information carrying potential of DNA molecules. At the same time, due to the lack of special standard system research and standard support, the technical use and evaluation of each link of DNA storage lacks standardization, which hinders the high-quality development of technology and industry.

Based on this, this paper proposes an innovative information storage based on DNA encoding, and at the same time proposes an evaluation standard system for the encoding step to guide the development of the industry.

2   DNA Encoding Method

2.1   Code Design

The first step in encoding DNA is to convert stored information into base sequences. In order to better perform error correction and recognition, error correction codes and specific identification sequences are added to the base sequences [7]. Error detection and correction codes are inserted into the DNA sequence at every predetermined number of base positions, and the encoded DNA sequence is divided into multiple fragments of 100–150 bp in length, and specific identification sequences and index marks are added at both ends of each fragment (Fig. 1 shows an example).

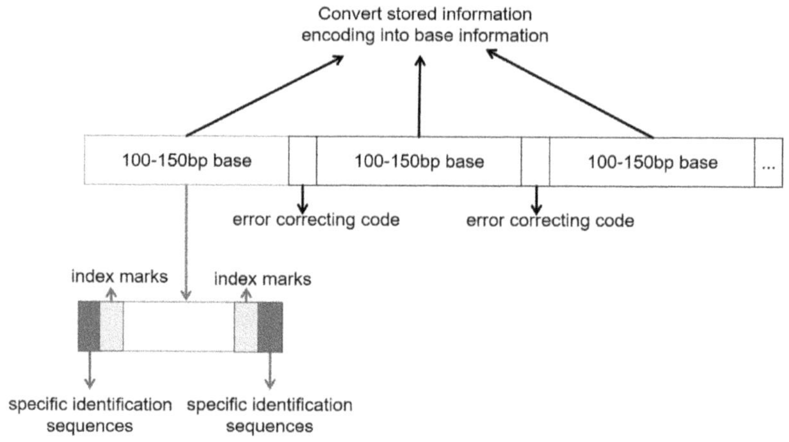

Fig. 1. Design of DNA coding sequence

2.2 DNA Encoding Methods Including Base Modification Status

The DNA encoding method proposed in this paper includes converting the digital information to be stored into a quaternary code, converting the quaternary code into a DNA sequence composed of adenine A, cytosine C, guanine G and thymine T according to the preset mapping rules, and using the chemical modification state of the nucleotide pair to represent the additional information dimension.

Specifically: 0 is mapped to A-unmodified or A-methylated, 1 is mapped to C-unmodified or C-methylated, 2 is mapped to G-unmodified or G-methylated, and 3 is mapped to T-unmodified or T-methylated.

For each quaternary value, the encoding scheme is determined based on the current position information:

If the position is available for additional modification (determined by the sequence context), then: quaternary $0 \rightarrow$ A (unmodified if the additional bit is 0, methylated if 1); quaternary $1 \rightarrow$ C (unmodified if the additional bit is 0, methylated if 1); quaternary $2 \rightarrow$ G (unmodified if the additional bit is 0, methylated if 1); quaternary $3 \rightarrow$ T (unmodified if the additional bit is 0, methylated if 1); If the position is not suitable for modification, only the base type is used to encode information (Fig. 2 shows an example).

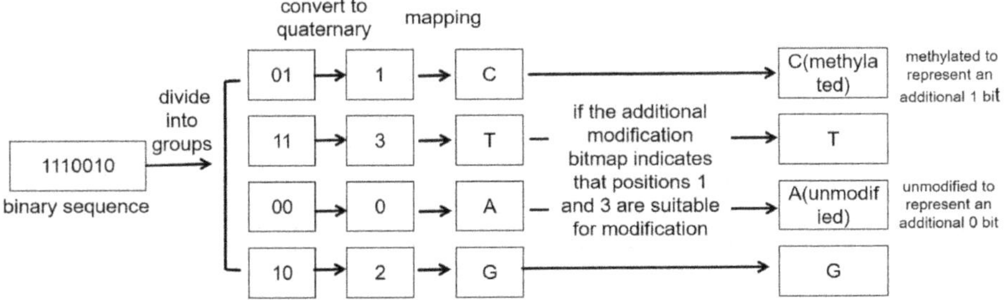

Fig. 2. Using "1110010" as an example, demonstrate the encoding rules

Traditionally, DNA storage uses only four bases (A, C, G, T) to represent information. Each position can only be one of the four bases A, C, G, T, and each position can store 2 bits of information (because $2^2 = 4$). The method proposed in this paper not only uses the type of base to store information, but also uses the chemical modification status of the base (whether it is methylated) to store additional information. This adds an additional information dimension to each position, through this method, the amount of information that can be carried by each base position is increased from 2 bits to 3 bits (2 bits from the base type+1 bit from the modification state), and the theoretical information density is increased by 50%.

2.3 DNA Coding Identification and Error Correction

The predetermined number of base positions for DNA coding identification and error correction has a value range of 10–30 bases, preferably 20 bases, this range is determined based on the error rate characteristics of DNA synthesis and sequencing technology. The error rate of DNA polymerase in the base synthesis process is about 10^{-3} to 10^{-5}, while the error rate of sequencing technology (such as Illumina sequencing platform) is about 10^{-2} to 10^{-3}; Therefore, setting an error correction code point every 20 bases can effectively capture and correct most errors without excessively occupying storage space [8].

The error detection and correction code adopts Reed-Solomon error correction code. This paper proposes an RS (15, 9) encoding scheme, that is, each codeword contains 15 symbols, 9 of which are data symbols and 6 are check symbols. This configuration can correct up to 3 random errors or 6 erasure errors at known positions, and further optimizes the encoding efficiency and error correction capability by grouping bases into quaternary symbols (two consecutive bases as one symbol). Figure 3 shows an example of a piece of encoded data and its corresponding Reed-Solomon error correction code.

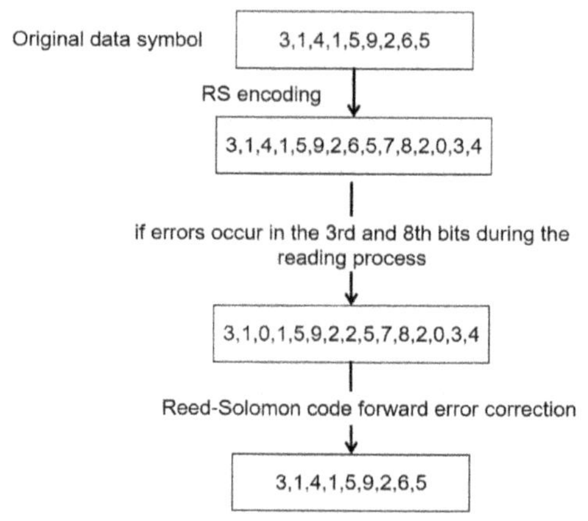

Fig. 3. An example of encoded data and its corresponding Reed-Solomon error correction code

The identification sequence is designed as follows:

(1) **Classification code sequence**: 8bp length, used to distinguish different types of data (such as text, images, audio, etc.), for example: "ATGCTAGC": represents text data.
(2) **Position index marks**: 12bp length, supports up to 16, 777, 216 unique position identifiers, and uses special encoding to maximize the Hamming distance to ensure that the position can be correctly identified even if an error occurs.
(3) **Homologous identifier**: 10bp length, as a unique identifier of the file, generated using a cryptographic hash function to ensure that the identifiers of different files are sufficiently different.
(4) **Protective sequence**: 8bp in length, rich in GC content and designed to be difficult to form secondary structures, such as "GCGCGCGC", to protect the core data area from degradation.

The total length of these recognition sequences is about 38bp, accounting for about 25%-38% of a 100-150bp DNA fragment; although this part of the sequence does not directly carry user data, it ensures reliable assembly and long-term preservation of data.

3 DNA Encoding Evaluation Standard System

Internationally, although the ISO/IEC JTCI/AG2 Emerging Technology and Innovation Advisory Group has proposed standardization requirements in the field of DNA storage for many years in identifying new technology direction standard requirements, the three major international standardization organizations ISO, IEC, and ITU have not yet launched DNA storage projects. In China, DNA storage also lacks relevant standards and specifications.

For the future development of the DNA storage industry, establishing a standard system for DNA storage and continuously improving it is of great significance. It is precisely because of the lack of current standards and diverse DNA encoding methods that compatibility issues exist between products, thereby affecting the development of DNA storage technology and industry.

In the encoding and decoding link, the programming languages and technical parameters used in the currently disclosed DNA storage coding algorithms are different, which is not conducive to subsequent development and optimization based on the existing research foundation [9]. There is also a lack of corresponding evaluation or selection criteria for the selection of the most suitable algorithm for different types of data files, which hinders the communication and development of this field. Therefore, the design of different developed coding algorithms should be consistent, and the evaluation criteria should form a clear consensus.

Based on the research and analysis of the domestic DNA storage encoding situation, this paper proposes the following evaluation standard system (see Fig. 4).

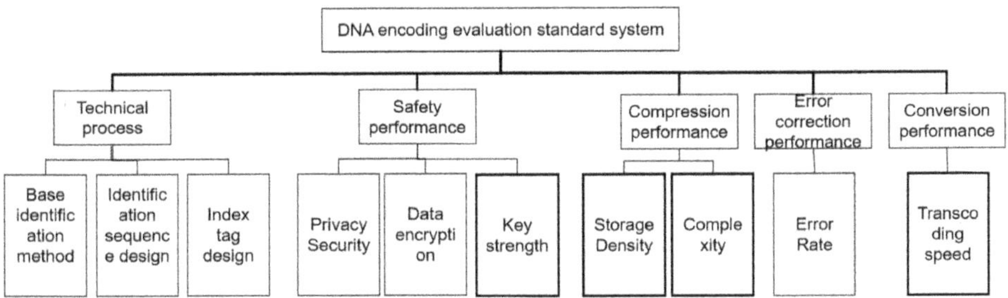

Fig. 4. DNA encoding evaluation standard system, the black bold box represents important parameters that must be evaluated

Key strength, storage density, complexity and transcoding speed are four major parameters that must be evaluated, the calculation method for these parameters is as follows:

1) **Key strength:**A performance parameter that characterizes the effectiveness of a password against guessing or brute force cracking, i. e. the average number of attempts an unauthorized visitor makes to obtain the correct password.

2) **Storage density:**A performance parameter that characterizes the ratio of the storage capacity (in bits) occupied by DNA storage data to the base number of the entire

DNA sequence library and is calculated by the following formula:

$$D = n/N * 100\% \tag{1}$$

Among them, n is the number of bases, N is the total number of bases contained in the DNA library.

3) **Complexity:**Used to describe the relationship between the amount of encoding and the scale of the problem being solved. Generally reflected by the combination of time complexity and space complexity.

Time complexity is calculated by the following formula:

$$C(t) = O(f(n))/n \tag{2}$$

Among them, n is the number of data, $f(n)$ is a function that processes a certain amount of data.

Space complexity is calculated by the following formula:

$$C(t) = O(f(n)) \tag{3}$$

Among them, $f(n)$ is a function that processes a certain amount of data.

4) **Transcoding speed:** The speed at which binary data is converted into DNA base sequences according to certain rules. Transcoding speed is calculated by the following formula:

$$S = N/t \tag{4}$$

Among them, N specify the bit value for time conversion, t is the time frame.

4   Conclusion and Future Prospects

With the development of the information and digital age, the requirements for information storage are getting higher and higher. The huge amount of data will cause the storage capacity of traditional storage media and the consumption of materials to face a serious imbalance with the demand for information storage. The introduction of the concept of DNA storage can effectively alleviate this problem, so the development of DNA storage technology is necessary and its potential is huge.

DNA coding standards are both the "codebook" that reveals the laws of life and the "common language" for technological innovation and clinical transformation. Its continuous optimization will profoundly affect the development boundaries of cutting-edge fields such as gene editing, synthetic biology, and nanomedicine. The coding method proposed in this paper provides a new method that is superior to traditional coding methods in compression and error correction. The proposed standard system can also provide a basic reference for the evaluation of coding methods.

DNA coding and DNA storage technology are developing rapidly. With the development of the industry, more effective coding methods will be derived. Based on the research in this paper, we will organize the construction of a DNA coding evaluation system, enter the current mainstream DNA coding methods into the system, and propose a set of evaluation systems through standard research to achieve objective evaluation of coding methods.

Acknowledgment. This work was supported by the National Key Research and Development Program "Base based DNA Storage Integrated Software and Hardware System for Massive Data Storage Applications" (Project No.: 2023YFF1206100).

References

1. Qi, S., Ding, C., Wu, X., Chen, F.: Analysis on the development strategies and trends of DNA storage technology. World SciTech R D **43**, 24–42 (2021)
2. Zhi, P., et al.: Carbon-based archiving: current progress and future prospects of DNA-based data storage. GigaScience (2019)
3. Goela, N., Bolot, J.: Encoding movies and data in DNA storage. In: Information Theory & Applications Workshop. IEEE (2017)
4. Kun, B., Gu, W., Lu, Z.: Coding algorithms in DNA storage. J. Bioinf. 76–85 (2020)
5. Garafutdinov, R.R. , Chemeris, D.A. , Sakhabutdinova, A.R., Kiryanova, O.Y., Mikhaylenko, C.I., Chemeris, A.V. : Encoding of non-biological information for its long-term storage in DNA. Bio Syst. 215–216 (2022)
6. Ping, Z., et al.: Towards practical and robust DNA-based data archiving using the yin-yang codec system. Nature Comput. Sci. 234–242 (2022)
7. Yim, A.K., et al.: The essential component in DNA-based information storage system: robust error-tolerating module. Front. Bioeng. Biotechnol. (2014)
8. Mortuza, G.M., et al.: In-vitro validated methods for encoding digital data in deoxyribonucleic acid (DNA). BMC Bioinf. **160** (2023)
9. Wei, Y., Liu, Q., Qi, H.: Integrated DNA storage system for massive data. Chem. Ind. Eng. 173–182 (2025)

MSPD-SAM: A Prompt-Free Framework for Cardiac Segmentation Using Multi-scale Adapters and Parallel Decoding

Chen Yin, Liwen Wang, Xingbo Dong$^{(\boxtimes)}$, and Zhe Jin

Anhui Provincial International Joint Research Center for Advanced Technology
in Medical Imaging, Anhui University, Hefei, Anhui, China
`xingbo.dong@ahu.edu.cn`

Abstract. Accurate segmentation of cardiac chambers from echocardiography is essential for assessing heart function. However, this task remains challenging due to blurred boundaries and the complex structure of the heart. While the Segment Anything Model (SAM) is promising, it requires manual prompts and performs poorly in capturing the heart's complex structures and indistinct boundaries. To address these limitations, we propose MSPD-SAM, a prompt-free framework for fully automatic cardiac segmentation. Specifically, our method enhances SAM's encoder with a multi-scale adapter to capture the complex anatomical structures of the heart. In addition, we propose a Parallel Mask Decoder to address the inherent trade-off in cardiac ultrasound segmentation between semantic coherence and boundary precision. We integrate these components into the MSPD-SAM framework and extensively evaluate our method on the public CAMUS and EchoNet-Dynamic datasets, achieving state-of-the-art performance and outperforming leading CNNs, Transformers, and other SAM-based adaptations.

Keywords: Medical image segmentation · SAM · Prompt-Free

1 Introduction

Accurate segmentation of cardiac chambers from echocardiography is a cornerstone of quantitative heart function analysis and is critical for clinical decision-making. However, this task is challenging for clinicians because the heart has a complex structure and its boundaries are often blurred by noise and low contrast [7,21]. Furthermore, manual annotation requires expert knowledge, making it both costly and time-consuming [12].

Deep learning has become the standard approach for automating this task [9, 11]. CNN-based models [28,29] like DW-Net [27] employed a multi-stage CNN for accurate segmentation of seven essential structures in the apical four-chamber view. On the other hand, Transformer-based models [24] such as TransFSM [30]

© The Author(s), under exclusive license to Springer Nature Singapore Pte Ltd. 2026
W. Jia et al. (Eds.): CCBR 2025, LNCS 16360, pp. 404–414, 2026.
https://doi.org/10.1007/978-981-95-6123-0_38

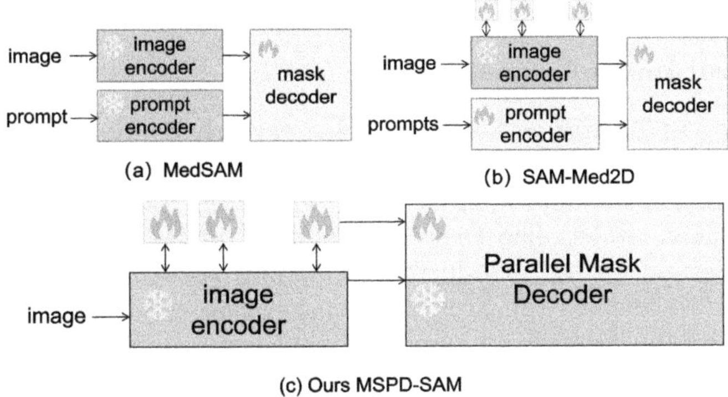

Fig. 1. Comparison of methods using SAM for medical image segmentation.

proposes a hybrid Transformer framework with deformable self-attention and a boundary-aware decoder for anatomy structure segmentation.

While CNNs and Transformers have led to significant improvements in structure segmentation, a paradigm shift is occurring with the advent of foundation models like SAM [15], which offer versatile zero-shot capabilities and prompting strategies, pushing the boundaries of generalization in medical image segmentation. Inspired by these strengths, recent studies have explored its application in cardiac ultrasound segmentation [2]. CAMUS [18] enhances its adaptability to ultrasound images by incorporating a CNN branch and adapter modules, enabling better representation of domain-specific features. Meanwhile, MemSAM [6] incorporates spatio-temporal memory to facilitate accurate segmentation, especially in complex temporal sequences such as cardiac cycles.

Despite the promising performance of existing SAM-based methods, they still face two limitations when applied to cardiac ultrasound. First, they struggle with the heart's intricate structures and indistinct boundaries. Second, they rely on external prompts, which prevent full automation in clinical practice. To address these challenges, our work introduces MSPD-SAM with the following main contributions:

- We introduce a Multi-Scale Adapter into the SAM encoder, enhancing its ability to capture the heart's varied anatomical scales, from large chambers to fine myocardial walls.
- We design a parallel mask decoder that resolves the common trade-off between accuracy and detail by synergistically fusing a semantic context path with a high-resolution boundary refinement path.
- We propose MSPD-SAM, a fully automatic framework for cardiac ultrasound segmentation that requires no manual prompting. Extensive experiments on CAMUS and EchoNet-Dynamic demonstrate that MSPD-SAM outperforms leading CNNs, Transformers, and SAM variants.

2   Related Work

2.1   Medical Image Segmentation

Medical image segmentation has become increasingly dominated by deep learning techniques. Classical Convolutional Neural Networks (CNNs), such as U-Net [25], established a solid foundation through their encoder-decoder architecture. Subsequent models like DeepLabv3plus [3] further enhanced multi-scale feature representation by introducing techniques such as atrous spatial pyramid pooling. To address the limited receptive field of CNNs, recent methods have adopted Transformers to capture global context. Representative models include SegFormer [26], which employs a lightweight transformer encoder and an MLP-based decoder for efficient and accurate segmentation. Recently, foundation models such as SAM [15] have emerged as a new paradigm for general-purpose segmentation, offering strong zero-shot capabilities across diverse domains.

2.2   Adapting SAM to Medical Image Segmentation

Although SAM demonstrates strong generalization on natural images, its direct application to medical imaging is limited due to significant domain differences such as low contrast and high noise [13]. To bridge this gap, existing methods like MedSAM [20] and SAM-Med2D [4] have explored effective adaptations through fine-tuning or integrating adapters. As illustrated in Fig. 1, these approaches generally rely on manual or semi-automatic prompts and still struggle to capture fine anatomical boundaries in complex scenarios like cardiac ultrasound. To address these challenges, we propose MSPD-SAM—a prompt-free, multi-scale framework designed for accurate and fully automatic segmentation.

3   Methodology

3.1   Overview

To address the challenges of cardiac ultrasound segmentation, we introduce three innovations to the SAM framework, as illustrated in Fig. 2. First, as described in Sect. 3.2, we embed a Multi-Scale Adapter (MSA) into the encoder to simultaneously capture both macroscopic anatomical structures and fine-grained details. Second, as detailed in Sect. 3.3, we designed a Parallel Mask Decoder that separates the segmentation task into two paths. A Semantic Path ensures structural consistency, while a Boundary Refinement (BR) Path refines the edges for accuracy. Finally, we adopt the two-stage training strategy detailed in Sect. 3.4 to efficiently adapt and fine-tune the model. This integrated design ensures accurate and robust segmentation under challenging ultrasound conditions.

3.2   Multi-scale Adapter

To better segment complex cardiac structures in ultrasound, we enhance the standard SAM image encoder. Its transformer architecture struggles to capture

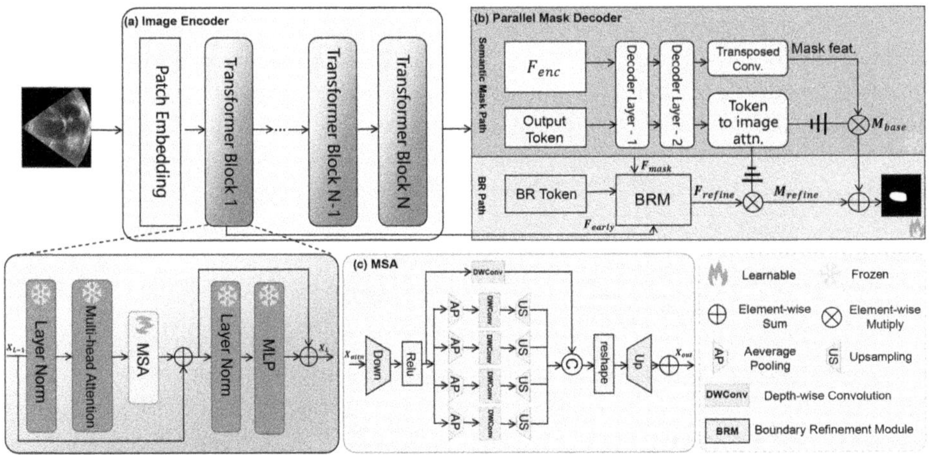

Fig. 2. Overview of the proposed MSPD-SAM.

the heart's multi-scale anatomy, from large chambers to thin myocardial walls, particularly amidst imaging noise. Inspired by [10], we propose an MSA module which integrated into each of the encoder's transformer layers. This design improves the extraction of multi-scale features without discarding the encoder's pre-trained knowledge.

As illustrated in Fig. 2, our MSA is positioned after the multi-head attention module to refine its output before the first residual connection. The complete data flow for a Transformer layer modified with our MSA, from an input token $X_{L-1} \in \mathbb{R}^{N \times D}$ to an output token $X_L \in \mathbb{R}^{N \times D}$, can be formalized as:

$$X' = X_{L-1} + \mathrm{MSA}(X_{attn}),$$
$$X_L = X' + \mathrm{MLP}(\mathrm{LN}(X')) \tag{1}$$

where MLP is a multilayer perceptron, and LN is layer normalization. We denote $X_{attn} \in \mathbb{R}^{N \times D}$ as the attention-enhanced feature that serves as the input to the MSA module. It is computed as:

$$X_{attn} = \mathrm{MHA}(\mathrm{LN}(X_{L-1})) \tag{2}$$

where MHA represents multi-head self-attention applied after normalization. The process within the MSA unfolds as follows. First, the input is prepared for spatial analysis. A linear projection layer reduces its feature dimension by a factor r, after which the token sequence is reshaped into a 2D spatial representation $X_s \in \mathbb{R}^{H \times W \times \left(\frac{D}{r}\right)}$. This initial step is formulated as:

$$X_s = \tau(\mathrm{ReLU}(X_{attn} W_{\mathrm{down}})) \tag{3}$$

where $W_{\mathrm{down}} \in \mathbb{R}^{D \times \left(\frac{D}{r}\right)}$ is the down-projection matrix and τ denotes the reshape operation which transforms the token sequence into a 2D feature map [8].

To encode contextual information at multiple scales, X_s is processed through four average pooling layers $AP_j(\cdot)$, each with different receptive fields. The downsampled features are then passed through depthwise separable convolutions and upsampled back to the original spatial resolution. Additionally, the original feature is also convolved and included in the fusion to generate the final fused feature map $X_{\text{fused}} \in \mathbb{R}^{H \times W \times (\frac{D}{r})}$, which is formulated as:

$$X_{\text{fused}} = \text{Conv}_{1\times1}\left(\left[\bigoplus_{j=1}^{4} \text{US}\left(\text{DWConv}\left(\text{AP}_j(X_s)\right)\right), \text{DWConv}(X_s)\right]\right) \quad (4)$$

Here, $\bigoplus$ denotes channel-wise concatenation, $DWConv(\cdot)$ denotes depthwise convolution [5], and $US(\cdot)$ denotes bilinear upsampling. Finally, X_{fused} is reshaped and projected by $\tau^{-1}(\cdot)$ and $W_{\text{up}} \in \mathbb{R}^{(\frac{D}{r}) \times D}$, then added to X_{attn} via residual connection to obtain the final output $X_{out} \in \mathbb{R}^{N \times D}$:

$$X_{\text{out}} = \tau^{-1}(X_{\text{fused}})W_{\text{up}} + X_{\text{attn}} \quad (5)$$

By weaving these spatial, multi-scale operations directly into the Transformer layers, the MSA equips SAM to perceive both global chamber structures and fine tissue details simultaneously, which is critical for accurate cardiac segmentation.

3.3 Parallel Mask Decoder

Cardiac ultrasound segmentation poses a unique challenge for standard decoders: prioritizing global semantic context often comes at the expense of boundary precision, while emphasizing fine-grained edges may compromise structural coherence in the presence of speckle noise. To overcome this trade-off, we adopt and adapt the parallel decoding architecture from [14], which comprises two specialized yet collaborative branches: a base Semantic Mask Path for semantic consistency, and a Boundary Refinement(BR) Path for precise boundary delineation as shown in Fig. 2(b).

Semantic Mask Path. This path aims to generate a semantically segmentation mask by leveraging the high-level global context from the final output of the Multi-Scale Feature Encoder. Specifically, the encoder's final-layer feature map $F_{enc} \in \mathbb{R}^{C \times (\frac{H}{4}) \times (\frac{W}{4})}$ serves as input to a SAM-style decoder. A set of learnable output tokens interacts with F_{enc} via cross-attention to capture semantic information, which is then refined through a lightweight MLP to produce dynamic mask weights. Meanwhile, the decoder upsamples its internal features to generate a high-resolution feature map, defined as $F_{mask} \in \mathbb{R}^{(\frac{C}{8}) \times H \times W}$. Finally, the dynamic weights are applied to F_{mask} to produce the base mask $M_{base} \in \mathbb{R}^{1 \times H \times W}$.

Boundary Refinement Path. Operating in parallel, this path is dedicated to correcting boundary-level inaccuracies in the initial mask generated by the semantic path. To this end, we adopt a token-based refinement strategy centered on a learnable Boundary Refinement Token (BR-Token) and a fused Boundary-Fusion Feature Map $F_{refine} \in \mathbb{R}^{\left(\frac{C}{8}\right) \times H \times W}$, generated by a dedicated Boundary Refinement Module (BRM). The BRM fuses early-layer encoder feature $F_{early} \in \mathbb{R}^{C \times \left(\frac{H}{4}\right) \times \left(\frac{W}{4}\right)}$ that preserves fine-grained edges, the final-layer encoder feature F_{enc} that provides global context and F_{mask} that contains a mask-shape prior. The fusion process is formally defined as:

$$F_{\text{refine}} = \phi_1(F_{\text{enc}}) + \phi_2(F_{\text{early}}) + \phi_3(F_{\text{mask}}) \tag{6}$$

Here, ϕ_1 and ϕ_2 are upsampling modules, each consisting of two ConvTranspose2d layers with a stride of 2. ϕ_3 contains two standard Conv2d layers with a stride of 1. These transformations ensure that all feature maps have the same spatial dimensions before summation. After decoding, the updated BR-Token is passed through a lightweight MLP to generate a dynamic convolution kernel, which is applied to F_{refine} to produce a high-resolution refinement mask M_{refine} This mask functions as an error correction map that complements the coarse prediction from the semantic path. The final output is computed by aggregating the logits of both masks:

$$M_{final} = M_{base} + M_{refine} \tag{7}$$

By explicitly decoupling semantic prediction and boundary refinement, our parallel design enables the model to maintain structural coherence while improving precision along complex or faint anatomical boundaries.

3.4   Training Strategy and Loss Function

We adopt a two-stage training strategy to integrate our proposed modules. In the first stage, the original SAM encoder and decoder are frozen, and only the newly introduced MSA are trained. Supervision is applied solely through the base mask path. To achieve this, we use the same Focal [17] and Dice [22] losses as SAM-Med2D. This enables the MSA modules to enhance feature representations without altering the pretrained backbone. In the second stage, the entire adapted encoder and base decoder path are frozen. Training is focused on the boundary refinement path, including the learnable BR-Token, its MLP head, and the BRM, using the same aforementioned composite loss function.

4   Experiments

4.1   Benchmark Dataset

We evaluate our method on two publicly available cardiac ultrasound datasets: CAMUS [16] and EchoNet-Dynamic [23]. The CAMUS dataset provides echocardiographic videos from 500 patients in apical two-chamber (2CH) and four-chamber (4CH) views, with pixel-level segmentation annotations for the left ventricle (LV), left atrium (LA), and myocardium (MYO). EchoNet-Dynamic is a dataset containing 10,030 videos, annotated with left ventricular (LV) contour points at end-diastole and end-systole, along with ejection fraction (EF) values, supporting segmentation and cardiac functional assessment tasks.

4.2 Implementation Details

All experiments were conducted on an NVIDIA RTX 3090 GPU, using the SAM-B architecture as the base model. The model was fine-tuned for 12 epochs on both the CAMUS and EchoNet-Dynamic datasets, following the two-stage strategy described in Sect. 3.4. We employed the AdamW [19] optimizer with a learning rate of 1e-4, and evaluated performance using Dice and IoU metrics.

4.3 Results and Evaluation

We selected multiple comparison methods spanning traditional and medical foundation segmentation models. Specifically, we evaluated CNN-based models such as U-Net [25] and DeepLabv3plus [3], transformer-based models such as SegFormer [26] and Swin-UNet [1], as well as medical foundation models including MedSAM [20] and SAM-Med2D [4].

As shown in Table 1, the quantitative results demonstrate that our proposed MSPD-SAM consistently outperforms all baseline models. On the CAMUS dataset, it achieves an mDice score of 90.59, surpassing both SAM-Med2D and MedSAM, with particularly notable improvements in fine structures such as the LA and MYO. Similarly, on the EchoNet-Dynamic dataset, MSPD-SAM achieves the best performance with an mDice score of 92.42, slightly outperforming strong models like Swin-UNet. These results strongly validate that by combining multi-scale adapters with a parallel decoding strategy, MSPD-SAM successfully enables high-quality cardiac segmentation.

As shown in the qualitative comparison in Fig. 3, MSPD-SAM produces smooth and accurate segmentation boundaries, with results (in yellow) showing a high degree of overlap with the ground truth. In contrast, U-Net and DeepLabv3plus generate coarser segmentations with evident false positives (in red) and false negatives (in green). While MedSAM and SAM-Med2D show improvements, they still exhibit uncertainty in boundary regions. This clear visual advantage intuitively demonstrates the effectiveness of our parallel decoding strategy in refining fine boundaries while preserving structural consistency.

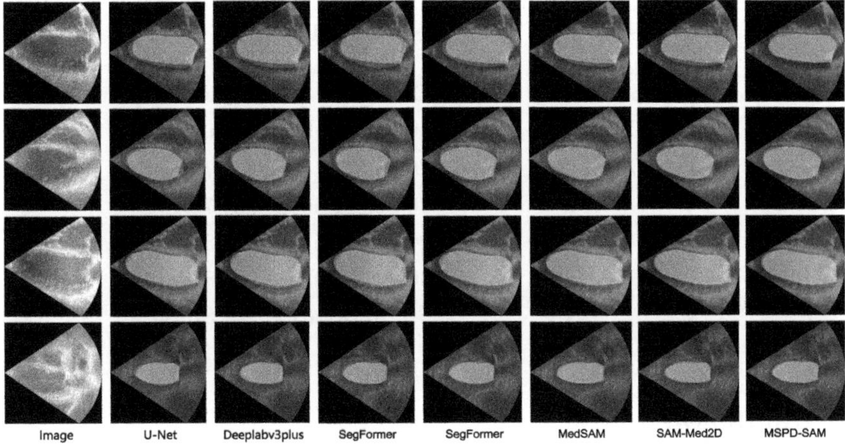

Fig. 3. CAMUS visualizations use green for ground truth, red for model output, and yellow for matched regions. (Color figure online)

Table 1. Comparative evaluation of MSPD-SAM and other models on CAMUS-LV, CAMUS-MYO, CAMUS-LA, and EchoNet-Dynamic datasets. Bold text indicates the best.

Method	CAMUS-LV		CAMUS-MYO		CAMUS-LA		CAMUS		EchoNet	
	Dice↑	IoU↑	Dice↑	IoU↑	Dice↑	IoU↑	mDice↑	mIoU↑	mDice↑	mIoU↑
U-Net [25]	94.03	88.73	86.38	76.02	90.77	83.10	90.39	82.62	67.28	50.69
Deeplabv3plus [3]	93.97	88.63	87.14	77.22	89.74	81.39	90.28	82.41	84.78	73.59
SegFormer [26]	91.98	85.14	85.98	75.41	89.35	80.75	87.91	78.55	87.37	77.58
Swin-UNet [1]	93.66	88.07	87.28	77.42	89.35	80.75	90.10	82.08	92.27	85.65
MedSAM [20]	91.76	85.81	82.48	70.64	90.41	82.69	88.22	79.71	86.47	79.19
SAM-Med2D [4]	93.85	88.55	86.39	76.33	89.64	81.60	89.96	82.16	90.69	83.46
MSPD-SAM	**94.32**	**88.91**	**87.30**	**77.45**	**91.03**	**84.23**	**90.59**	**83.48**	**92.42**	**85.84**

4.4   Ablation Studies

To validate the effectiveness of each component, we conducted ablation studies (Table 2). The results show that simply adding the MSA module to the baseline SAM model yields a significant mDice improvement of 7.89 on the CAMUS dataset, demonstrating the core value of multi-scale representation. Building upon this, we evaluated the components of the parallel decoder: using only the boundary details from F_{early} or the shape context from F_{mask} achieved mDice scores of 90.06 and 90.41, respectively. The full model, which fuses both feature streams, achieved the best performance of 90.59 on CAMUS and 92.42 on EchoNet-Dynamic, indicating that the combination of these two sources is crucial for correcting fine boundary errors and achieving high-precision segmentation.

Table 2. Ablation study on different component combinations on CAMUS and EchoNet-Dynamic datasets. Bold text indicates the best.

Components				CAMUS		EchoNet	
MSA	BRM	F_{early}	F_{mask}	mDice	mIoU	mDice	mIoU
✗	✗	✗	✗	78.63	72.45	80.41	72.32
✓	✗	✗	✗	86.52	81.50	85.25	78.16
✓	✓	✓	✗	90.06	82.57	91.20	84.59
✓	✓	✗	✓	90.41	82.98	91.39	84.23
✓	✓	✓	✓	**90.59**	**83.48**	**92.42**	**85.84**

5 Conclusion

The proposed MSPD-SAM is a prompt-free, fully automatic framework for cardiac segmentation, which enhances the perception of multi-level anatomical structures by introducing a MSA in the encoder stage. It further incorporates an parallel mask decoder that optimizes semantic consistency and boundary precision, effectively addressing core challenges in ultrasound imaging such as low signal-to-noise ratio and the difficulty of multi-scale feature extraction. Experimental results on CAMUS and EchoNet-Dynamic demonstrate that MSPD-SAM outperforms mainstream CNN, Transformer, and other SAM-adapted methods. Its success validates the proposed design and provides an example for specializing large foundation models in medical imaging.

Acknowledgments. This work was supported by the National Natural Science Foundation of China (Grant No. 62306003), the Open Research Fund of Guangdong Laboratory of Artificial Intelligence and Digital Economy (SZ) (Grant No. GML-KF-24-29), and the Open Foundation of Jiangxi Provincial Key Laboratory of Image Processing and Pattern Recognition (Grant No. ET202404437).

References

1. Cao, H., et al.: Swin-UNet: UNet-like pure transformer for medical image segmentation. In: European conference on computer vision, pp. 205–218. Springer (2022)
2. Chen, F.: The ability of segmenting anything model (SAM) to segment ultrasound images. Biosci. Trends **17**(3), 211–218 (2023)
3. Chen, L.C., Zhu, Y., Papandreou, G., Schroff, F., Adam, H.: Encoder-decoder with atrous separable convolution for semantic image segmentation. In: Proceedings of the European conference on computer vision (ECCV), pp. 801–818 (2018)
4. Cheng, D., et al.: Sam on medical images: a comprehensive study on three prompt modes. arXiv preprint arXiv:2305.00035 (2023)
5. Chollet, F.: Xception: Deep learning with depthwise separable convolutions. In: Proceedings of the IEEE conference on computer vision and pattern recognition, pp. 1251–1258 (2017)

6. Deng, X., Wu, H., Zeng, R., Qin, J.: Memsam: taming segment anything model for echocardiography video segmentation. In: Proceedings of the IEEE/CVF conference on computer vision and pattern recognition, pp. 9622–9631 (2024)

7. Dong, J., et al.: A generic quality control framework for fetal ultrasound cardiac four-chamber planes. IEEE J. Biomed. Health Inform. **24**(4), 931–942 (2019)

8. Dosovitskiy, A., et al.: An image is worth 16x16 words: Transformers for image recognition at scale. arXiv preprint arXiv:2010.11929 (2020)

9. Fiorentino, M.C., Villani, F.P., Di Cosmo, M., Frontoni, E., Moccia, S.: A review on deep-learning algorithms for fetal ultrasound-image analysis. Med. Image Anal. **83**, 102629 (2023)

10. Gao, S., Zhang, P., Yan, T., Lu, H.: Multi-scale and detail-enhanced segment anything model for salient object detection. In: Proceedings of the 32nd ACM International Conference on Multimedia, pp. 9894–9903 (2024)

11. Ghorbani, A.: Deep learning interpretation of echocardiograms. NPJ Digital Med. **3**(1), 10 (2020)

12. Guo, L.: Dual attention enhancement feature fusion network for segmentation and quantitative analysis of paediatric echocardiography. Med. Image Anal. **71**, 102042 (2021)

13. Huang, Y.: Segment anything model for medical images? Med. Image Anal. **92**, 103061 (2024)

14. Ke, L.: Segment anything in high quality. Adv. Neural. Inf. Process. Syst. **36**, 29914–29934 (2023)

15. Kirillov, A., et al.: Segment anything. In: Proceedings of the IEEE/CVF international conference on computer vision, pp. 4015–4026 (2023)

16. Leclerc, S., et al.: Deep learning for segmentation using an open large-scale dataset in 2D echocardiography. IEEE Trans. Med. Imaging **38**(9), 2198–2210 (2019)

17. Lin, T.Y., Goyal, P., Girshick, R., He, K., Dollár, P.: Focal loss for dense object detection. In: Proceedings of the IEEE international conference on computer vision, pp. 2980–2988 (2017)

18. Lin, X., Xiang, Y., Yu, L., Yan, Z.: Beyond adapting SAM: towards end-to-end ultrasound image segmentation via auto prompting. In: International Conference on Medical Image Computing and Computer-Assisted Intervention, pp. 24–34. Springer (2024)

19. Loshchilov, I., Hutter, F.: Decoupled weight decay regularization. arXiv preprint arXiv:1711.05101 (2017)

20. Ma, J.: Segment anything in medical images. Nat. Commun. **15**(1), 654 (2024)

21. Martins, J., et al.: Influence of maternal body mass index on interobserver variability of fetal ultrasound biometry and amniotic-fluid assessment in late pregnancy. Ultrasound Obstet. Gynecol. **58**(6), 892–899 (2021)

22. Milletari, F., Navab, N., Ahmadi, S.A.: V-net: fully convolutional neural networks for volumetric medical image segmentation. In: 2016 fourth international conference on 3D vision (3DV), pp. 565–571. IEEE (2016)

23. Ouyang, D., et al.: Echonet-dynamic: a large new cardiac motion video data resource for medical machine learning. In: NeurIPS ML4H Workshop: Vancouver, BC, Canada, vol. 5 (2019)

24. Pan, Y., Niu, L., Yang, X., Niu, Q., Chen, B.: EBTNet: efficient bilateral token mixer network for fetal cardiac ultrasound image segmentation. IEEE Access (2024)

25. Ronneberger, O., Fischer, P., Brox, T.: U-Net: convolutional networks for biomedical image segmentation. In: Navab, N., Hornegger, J., Wells, W.M., Frangi, A.F. (eds.) MICCAI 2015. LNCS, vol. 9351, pp. 234–241. Springer, Cham (2015). https://doi.org/10.1007/978-3-319-24574-4_28
26. Xie, E.: SegFormer: Simple and efficient design for semantic segmentation with transformers. Adv. Neural. Inf. Process. Syst. **34**, 12077–12090 (2021)
27. Xu, L., et al.: DW-Net: a cascaded convolutional neural network for apical four-chamber view segmentation in fetal echocardiography. Comput. Med. Imaging Graph. **80**, 101690 (2020)
28. Xu, L., Liu, M., Zhang, J., He, Y.: Convolutional-neural-network-based approach for segmentation of apical four-chamber view from fetal echocardiography. IEEE Access **8**, 80437–80446 (2020)
29. Yu, L., Guo, Y., Wang, Y., Yu, J., Chen, P.: Segmentation of fetal left ventricle in echocardiographic sequences based on dynamic convolutional neural networks. IEEE Trans. Biomed. Eng. **64**(8), 1886–1895 (2016)
30. Zhao, L.: TransFSM: Fetal anatomy segmentation and biometric measurement in ultrasound images using a hybrid transformer. IEEE J. Biomed. Health Inform. **28**(1), 285–296 (2023)

MGONet: An Optimized Segmentation Network for Esophageal Cancerous Lesions

Yuqi Guo[1], Fenglian Li[1(✉)], Ying Qiao[2], and Zelin Wu[1]

[1] College of Electronic Engineering, Taiyuan University of Technology, Taiyuan 030024, China
`lifenglian@tyut.edu.cn`
[2] The First Clinical Medical College, Shanxi Medical University, Taiyuan 030001, China

Abstract. Computed tomography (CT) enables precise esophageal cancer diagnosis through high-resolution lesion segmentation, supporting personalized treatment. Accurate segmentation supports precise diagnosis and personalized treatment. However, existing methods often fail to capture both small and large cancerous lesions simultaneously due to their complex morphology and size variations, resulting in suboptimal performance. To address this, we propose a multi-scale global optimization network with three key components: 1) An anatomical landmark masking module (ALMM) that localizes the esophageal region using anatomical priors;2) A multi-scale dynamic fusion module (MDFM) that integrates multi-scale dilated convolutions, dynamic convolution, and dual attention for robust feature extraction;3) A global attention fusion module (GAFM) that enhances feature discrimination via channel-spatial attention and channel shuffling. We establish the private esophageal cancer CT dataset to assess the segmentation performance of our method. Experiments show our network achieves state-of-the-art performance, with a 69.75% DSC score and 19.23px HD for esophageal cancerous lesions.

Keywords: Esophageal cancer · Medical image segmentation · Multi-scale dilated convolutions · Global attention · Dynamic feature fusion

1 Introduction

Esophageal cancer, the 7th most common global malignancy, has distinct pathological patterns [1]. It is predominantly squamous cell carcinoma in Asia and Africa [2], while adenocarcinoma is more common in western countries. CT imaging is an essential tool for clinical diagnosis and staging of esophageal cancer due to high resolution, rapid scanning, and wide applicability [3]. Accurate CT segmentation enables precise delineation of cancer lesion boundaries and disease progression assessment [4].

In recent years, the development of artificial intelligence has driven significant progress in medical image segmentation. Ronneberger et al. proposed U-Net [5] for fusing multi-scale encoder-decoder features via skip connections. Chen et al. proposed ASPP [6] to extract multi-scale features via dilated convolutions with different rates. However, both share a limitation: overemphasizing local detailed feature interaction in

W. Jia et al. (Eds.): CCBR 2025, LNCS 16360, pp. 415–424, 2026.
https://doi.org/10.1007/978-981-95-6123-0_39

single slices, under-modeling cross-slice global context, and thus struggling to balance local and global features. Hu et al. proposed SE-Net [7], which mainly enhances key features via channel-wise weight assignment but lacks optimization for the low pixel proportion of esophageal thin-walled tissue in channel weight logic—thus struggling to accurately focus on the region's effective features. 3D U-Net [8] can capture inter-slice information but needs to process massive 3D voxels, imposing extremely high requirements on hardware computing power.

CT segmentation of esophageal cancer remains challenging due to three key factors [9]: wide variation in lesion sizes, indistinct boundaries between cancerous and normal tissues, and complex lesion morphology. To overcome these challenges, we propose the multi-scale global optimization network (MGONet), an advanced framework integrating three core components: the anatomical landmark masking module (ALMM) for spine-guided anatomical constraints uses the spine to ensure longitudinally continuous distribution of esophageal regions in adjacent slices around it, indirectly compensating for inter-slice information loss in 2D segmentation. The multi-scale dynamic fusion module (MDFM) combining dynamic dilated convolutions with dual attention for adaptive multi-scale fusion, and the global attention fusion module (GAFM) employing channel attention and channel shuffling for boundary refinement. This integrated approach simultaneously addresses scale sensitivity and boundary ambiguity, achieving superior performance in esophageal cancerous lesions segmentation tasks.

2   Method

2.1   Multi-Scale Global Optimization Network (MGONet)

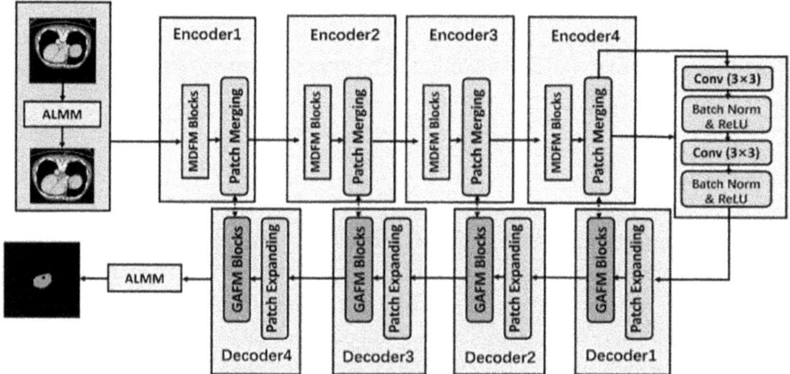

Fig. 1. The architectural overview of the multi-scale global optimization network, built on a U-Net backbone, is designed for esophageal cancer CT segmentation through three key modules.

MGONet, as shown in Fig. 1, the ALMM module first generates a binary esophageal mask to define the region of interest [10]. During encoding, the MDFM module extracts multi-scale features via parallel branches, then dynamically fuses and refines them through channel-spatial attention. In decoding, the GAFM module enhances feature interactions via channel attention and shuffle operations, followed by spatial attention focusing on cancer regions. The ALMM mask is reapplied to filter non-esophageal features before final segmentation. This integrated network effectively handles cancerous lesions of varying sizes and complex morphologies.

2.2 Anatomical Landmark Masking Module (ALMM)

We design a coarse segmentation network trained on annotated esophageal cancer CT data to generate initial lesion masks. These masks provide spatial priors to guide the fine segmentation network in focusing on relevant regions, boosting overall accuracy [11]. The spinal mask $S(x, y, z)$ is mathematically defined as follows:

$$S(x, y, z) = \begin{cases} 1, & \textit{if} HU(x, y, z) \cap Area(C(x, y, z)) \geq A_{spine} \\ 0, & \text{otherwise} \end{cases} \tag{1}$$

where A_{spine} is minimum cross-sectional area threshold of spine, $HU(x, y, z)$ represents the CT value at voxel coordinates (x, y, z), $Area(C(x, y, z))$ represents the cumulative cross-sectional area of the connected component formed by qualifying voxels. The cross-sectional area of the connected region formed by all adjacent voxels satisfying 300–500 HU is defined as the esophageal region. For each axial slice, the spinal centroid is calculated and automatically expanded 20 mm in anteroposterior and lateral directions to define a rectangular esophageal region. This efficiently constrains the esophageal region for precise segmentation in later models.

2.3 Multi-scale Dynamic Feature Fusion Module (MDFM)

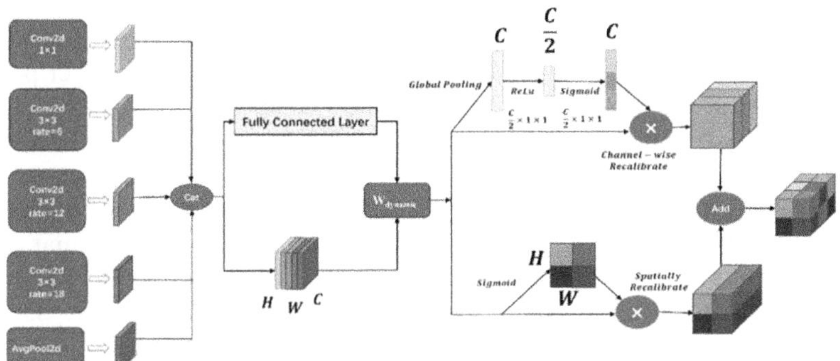

Fig. 2. The architectural diagram of the multi-scale dynamic feature fusion module.

As shown in Fig. 2, the MDFM employs adaptive convolution kernels to effectively combine multi-scale cancer features. The module's key innovation lies in its dynamic generation of fusion weights across five parallel processing branches, integrating detailed feature extraction through 1×1 convolutions, multi-scale contextual analysis via dilated convolutions, and global feature representation using pooling operations. This allows automatic, instance-specific feature integration tailored to each cancerous lesion characteristics, improving adaptability to diverse cancerous lesions morphologies while maintaining computational efficiency.

The dynamic kernel generation constitutes the core innovation of the MDFM, allowing automatic adjustment of feature fusion weights based on input characteristics, unlike traditional fixed convolution operations. This adaptive capability significantly enhances the network's ability to capture both local cancerous lesions details and global contextual relationships.

2.4 Global Attention Fusion Module (GAFM)

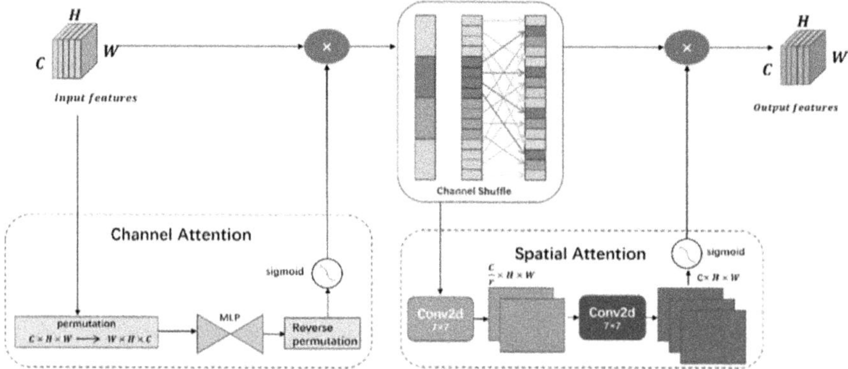

Fig. 3. The architectural diagram of the global attention fusion module.

As shown in Fig. 3, feature processing starts with channel attention. Input features are first permuted dimensionally and processed by a two-layer multi-layer perceptron (MLP). This MLP reduces then expands channels using rectified linear unit (ReLU) activation, finally producing channel weights through sigmoid. Weighted features then undergo channel shuffling—the module's core innovation. In this operation, features are split into 4 groups of C/4 channels each. A transpose operation then enables cross-group interaction while preserving original feature dimensions. For spatial attention, shuffled features pass through two 7×7 conv layers. These layers use channel reduction/expansion, batch normalization and ReLU, outputting spatial weights via sigmoid. Final features combine channel and spatial refinements via element-wise multiplication.

This dual attention mechanism with channel shuffling enhances feature discrimination while enabling effective cross-channel communication. The design strategically strengthens both local and global feature representations.

3   Experiments and Result Analysis

3.1   Datasets

We construct a private esophageal cancer CT dataset (ES-CTD) to evaluate the segmentation performance of our method. This dataset contains 204 DICOM-format CT scans obtained from a partner hospital. The first 120 cases were annotated by medical experts using ITK-SNAP, while the remaining 84 were labeled by trained researchers. All annotations were verified by clinical experts. We preprocess the dataset by splitting it into training, validation, and test sets at an 8:1:1 ratio. We convert all CT slices to 512 × 512 PNG format. Next, we apply standardized normalization to the converted images. This preprocessing step removes variations caused by different equipment and scanning parameters, ensuring stable and reliable network training and evaluation.

To validate the method's generalization, we conduct additional experiments on the liver cancer segmentation (LiTS 2017) benchmark [12]. The benchmark dataset includes 131 training cases and 70 test cases from seven medical centers.

3.2   Configuration

We conduct all experiments via Python 3.8 and PyTorch 1.12.0. Network training runs on an NVIDIA A800 GPU with 80 GB memory. We set max training epochs to 500, with early stopping triggered if no improvement is observed for 100 consecutive epochs. We use a batch size of 12 with the stochastic gradient descent optimizer, setting the initial learning rate to 0.01, momentum to 0.98, and weight decay coefficient to 1e-6. During model training, the optimal model is determined by cancerous lesion dice similarity coefficient (DSC) and validation loss on the validation set. After each epoch, if the current model has higher DSC and lower validation loss than historical bests, its parameters are saved as the optimal model.

3.3   Evaluation Metrics

We use five key metrics to comprehensively evaluate segmentation performance. The DSC and intersection over union (IoU) measure region overlap, where values closer to 1 indicate better performance. Precision quantifies the proportion of correctly predicted positives, while recall measures the proportion of actual positives that are correctly identified. The hausdorff distance (HD) quantifies boundary consistency through maximum boundary deviation, with smaller values being preferred. These metrics collectively evaluate segmentation quality from three perspectives including region matching classification reliability and boundary precision.

3.4   Comparative Experiments

We perform comparative experiments with representative segmentation methods including U-Net [5], TransUNet [13], UNETR [14], SwinUNet [15], TransResUnet [16], and PVTFormer [17] on the ES-CTD dataset. As these methods cover three core technical paradigms in medical image segmentation and are widely recognized as representative works in the field, enabling comprehensive verification of MGONet's competitiveness across different architectural frameworks. The classical U-Net architecture serves as our baseline implementation. TransUNet and TransResUnet represent hybrid methods combining Transformer and CNN structures, while UNETR and SwinUNet employ pure transformer architectures. PVTFormer demonstrates the latest vision transformer advancements for medical image segmentation. The comparison results of these methods are shown in Table 1.

Table 1. Performance comparison between the proposed and existing methods on the ES-CTD dataset.

Method	DSC(%)	Precision(%)	Recall(%)	HD(px)	IoU(%)
U-Net[5]	60.20	65.35	56.82	28.60	43.85
TransUNet[13]	69.52	**74.52**	66.03	26.45	53.92
UNETR[14]	68.46	73.81	63.23	23.18	51.63
SwinUNet[15]	64.28	66.75	62.05	21.52	47.87
TransResUnet[16]	67.69	70.12	65.51	21.08	51.32
PVTFormer[17]	66.10	69.58	62.97	20.65	50.86
MGONet(Ours)	**69.75**	72.36	**67.52**	**19.23**	**53.99**

MGONet demonstrates superior performance on the ES-CTD dataset, achieving a 9.55% DSC improvement and 9.37px HD reduction compared to U-Net. While TransUNet shows marginally higher precision, MGONet better balances the trade-off between recall and precision, with its ALMM module reducing HD by 1.42px versus PVTFormer through effective anatomical prior utilization.

The visualization results in Fig. 4 demonstrate MGONet's superior performance across different cases. In case 1, esophageal cancerous lesions are large and relatively regular in shape. While U-Net and TransUNet produce blurred boundaries and miss parts of the cancerous lesions, MGONet achieves clear segmentation margins against surrounding tissues. MGONet also handles small regions effectively. As shown in case 4, the esophagus is narrow and compressed by adjacent organs. Only MGONet correctly avoids misclassifying the tiny gaps between tissues as cancerous regions.

Experimental outcomes validate the effectiveness of MGONet's multi-module design, which integrates anatomical prior knowledge through the ALMM module while maintaining robust feature representation. The balanced performance across all evaluation dimensions suggests particular suitability for clinical deployment scenarios requiring both precision and reliability.

The experimental results of our method on the LiTS2017 dataset are presented in Table 2. The mIoU is calculated as the average of the IoU values for the liver and liver cancerous lesions. Our method achieves the second highest scores in Liver DSC and mIoU, performing slightly below TransUNet. In terms of Precision, it ranks third with 93.25 percent, following PVTFormer and TransResUnet. Our method achieves optimal

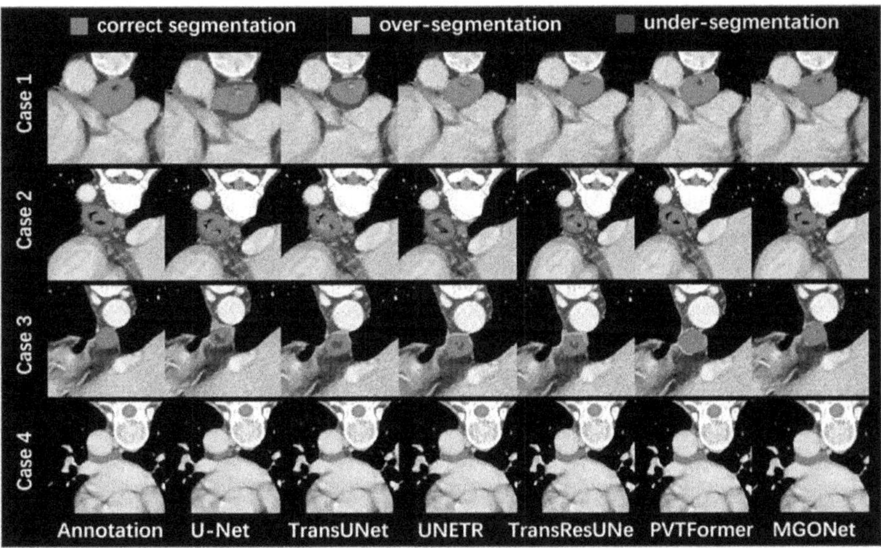

Fig. 4. Visual segmentation results of MGONet and five other high-performing methods on the ES-CTD dataset. Where, the red, blue, and green area mean correct segmentation, under-segmentation, and over-segmentation, respectively.

values across all other metrics, particularly in HD where it shows significant improvement from 12.65 pixels in U-Net to 7.80 pixels. These experimental results demonstrate our method's excellent generalization capability for segmenting cancerous lesions in different organs.

Table 2. Performance comparison between the proposed method and existing methods on the LiTS 2017 dataset.

Method	Liver DSC(%)	Lesions DSC (%)	Precision(%)	Recall(%)	HD(px)	mIoU(%)
U-Net [5]	82.65	79.45	91.10	77.23	12.65	73.56
TransUNet [13]	**95.17**	90.86	92.36	89.87	8.50	**90.57**
UNETR [14]	92.68	85.84	87.69	84.35	10.30	87.82
SwinUNet [15]	93.65	86.43	87.85	84.58	9.15	86.73
TransResUnet [16]	86.83	79.41	95.26	80.68	12.80	78.89
PVTFormer [17]	87.19	81.36	**96.18**	80.96	11.54	78.59
MGONet(Ours)	93.79	**90.96**	93.25	**91.12**	**7.80**	88.42

3.5 Ablation Study

We conduct ablation studies on the ES-CTD dataset to evaluate the individual contributions of each module to the segmentation of cancerous lesions. Using the U-Net method as backbone, we establish five experimental configurations: the baseline without any modules, the baseline with only ALMM, the baseline combining ALMM and MDFM, the baseline integrating ALMM and GAFM, and the baseline incorporating all three modules. For performance evaluation, we employ both DSC coefficient and HD metrics for esophageal cancer segmentation.

Table 3. Ablation study results on the ES-CTD dataset.

Backbone	Module			DSC(%)	HD(px)
U-Net	ALMM	MDFM	GAFM		
	–	–	–	60.20	28.60
	✓	–	–	63.42	25.85
	✓	✓	–	65.89	21.36
	✓	–	✓	68.65	22.96
	✓	✓	✓	69.75	19.23

Table 3 presents the quantitative results. The baseline U-Net achieves a DSC of 60.20% and an HD of 28.60 pixels without any additional modules. When incorporating the ALMM that leverages anatomical priors for esophageal region localization, performance improves to 63.42% DSC and 25.85px HD. Further adding the MDFM for adaptive multi-scale feature integration boosts the DSC to 65.89% and reduces HD to 21.36px. The combination of ALMM with the GAFM, designed to strengthen feature interactions through attention mechanisms, yields a higher DSC of 68.65%. The complete method integrating all three modules increases DSC to 69.75% while further decreasing HD to 19.23px, demonstrating the complementary benefits of anatomical guidance, multi-scale analysis, and global feature refinement for precise esophageal lesion segmentation.

4 Conclusion

This paper presents MGONet, an innovative three-module architecture for segmenting esophageal cancer in CT images. The proposed system combines an anatomical landmark masking module for cancer region localization using anatomical priors, a multi-scale dynamic feature fusion module with adaptive dilated convolutions and dual attention mechanisms for cancer feature representation, and a global attention fusion module that strengthens discriminative feature learning through integrated channel and spatial attention.

Experimental results show these components work together effectively to handle key challenges such as indistinct cancerous tissue boundaries and complex cancerous lesions morphology. Experiments on the LiTS 2017 dataset further demonstrate the system's robust generalization capability. MGONet not only provides an effective solution for esophageal cancer segmentation, but also demonstrates a flexible design paradigm that is generalizable to other medical image segmentation tasks. Future work will focus on refining segmentation accuracy for micro-lesions and enhancing overall precision.

Acknowledgments. This research was funded in part by the National Natural Science Foundation of China Grant Nos. 62171307.

References

1. Jiang, W., Zhang, B., Xu, J., et al.: Current status and perspectives of esophageal cancer: a comprehensive review. Cancer Commun. **45**(3), 281–331 (2025)
2. Morgan, E., Soerjomataram, I., Rumgay, H., et al.: The global landscape of esophageal squamous cell carcinoma and esophageal adenocarcinoma incidence and mortality in 2020 and projections to 2040: new estimates from GLOBOCAN 2020. Gastroenterology **163**(3), 649–658 (2022)
3. Lin, C., Guo, Y., Huang, X., et al.: Esophageal cancer detection via non-contrast CT and deep learning. Front. Med. **11**, 1356752 (2024)
4. Yang, R., Shi, Z., Ruan, J., et al.: Application of peritumoral radiomics based on simulated positioning CT images in the prognosis of intermediate-advanced esophageal cancer. Sci. Rep. **15**(1), 11865 (2025)
5. Ronneberger, O., Fischer, P., Brox, T.: U-net: convolutional networks for biomedical image segmentation. In: International Conference on Medical Image Computing and Computer-Assisted Intervention, pp. 234–241. Springer, Cham (2015)
6. Chen, L.C., Papandreou, G., Kokkinos, I., et al.: Deeplab: semantic image segmentation with deep convolutional nets, atrous convolution, and fully connected crfs. IEEE Trans. Pattern Anal. Mach. Intell. **40**(4), 834–848 (2017)
7. Hu, J., Shen, L., Sun, G.: Squeeze-and-excitation networks. In: Proceedings of the IEEE Conference on Computer Vision and Pattern Recognition, pp. 7132–7141 (2018)
8. Çiçek, Ö., Abdulkadir, A., Lienkamp, S.S., et al.: 3D U-net: learning dense volumetric segmentation from sparse annotation. In: International Conference on Medical Image Computing and Computer-Assisted Intervention, pp. 424–432. Springer, Cham (2016)
9. Jin, D., Guo, D., Ho, T.Y., et al.: DeepTarget: gross tumor and clinical target volume segmentation in esophageal cancer radiotherapy. Med. Image Analysis **68**, 101909 (2021)
10. Jin, J., Zhang, Q., Dong, B., et al.: Automatic detection of early gastric cancer in endoscopy based on Mask region-based convolutional neural networks (Mask R-CNN)(with video). Front. Oncol. **12**, 927868 (2022)
11. Kono, M., Ishihara, R., Kato, Y., et al.: Diagnosis of pharyngeal cancer on endoscopic video images by Mask region-based convolutional neural network. Dig. Endosc. **33**(4), 569–576 (2021)
12. Bilic, P., Christ, P., Li, H.B., et al.: The liver tumor segmentation benchmark (lits). Med. Image Anal. **84**, 102680 (2023)
13. Chen, J., Lu, Y., Yu, Q., et al.: Transunet: transformers make strong encoders for medical image segmentation. arXiv preprint arXiv:2102.04306, 2021
14. Hatamizadeh, A., Tang, Y., Nath, V., et al.: Unetr: transformers for 3d medical image segmentation. In: Proceedings of the IEEE/CVF Winter Conference on Applications of Computer Vision, pp. 574–584 (2022)

15. Cao, H., Wang, Y., Chen, J., et al.: Swin-unet: unet-like pure transformer for medical image segmentation. In: European Conference on Computer Vision, pp. 205–218. Springer, Cham (2022)
16. Tomar, N.K., Shergill, A., Rieders, B., et al.: TransResU-Net: transformer based ResU-Net for real-time colonoscopy polyp segmentation. arXiv preprint arXiv:2206.08985 (2022)
17. Jha, D., Tomar, N.K., Biswas, K., et al.: Ct liver segmentation via pvt-based encoding and refined decoding. In: 2024 IEEE International Symposium on Biomedical Imaging (ISBI), pp. 1–5. IEEE (2024)

Automatic Assessment of Facial Paralysis Severity from 3D Point Clouds

Liangchen Liu[1], Chengchao Li[1], Yue Yang[1(✉)], Qijun Zhao[1], Ziyu Li[2],
Shune Tan[2], Jicheng Zhang[2], Xin Shao[2], Ziyi Guo[2], Xing Tang[2],
Lanlan Wang[2], Chunlin Zhu[2], Chenman Zhang[2], Bingyu Chen[2], Yan Ai[2],
and Jing Wen[2]

[1] College of Computer Science, Sichuan University, Chengdu, China
`yueyang7@scu.edu.cn`
[2] Sichuan Integrative Medicine Hospital, Chengdu, China

Abstract. Facial paralysis seriously affects patients' quality of life, necessitating accurate severity assessment for effective treatment planning. Traditional House-Brackmann grading relies on subjective clinical evaluation, leading to low efficiency. Recent deep learning techniques offer the prospect of automatic facial paralysis assessment, but existing methods predominantly utilize 2D facial images, the accuracy is limited due to loss of spatial information. To address this, this paper presents the first study of automatic facial paralysis severity assessment using 3D point clouds. A novel facial paralysis dataset is collected, which comprises of 61 patients exhibiting eight clinically recommended facial expressions, resulting in 488 annotated samples across House-Brackmann grades II-V. We employ advanced 3D point clouds preprocessing techniques including landmark detection and spherical cropping. We evaluate SOTA 3D recognition models including PointNet++, PointMLP, and PointNN. Experimental results demonstrate the superiority of 3D-based assessment methods against 2D-based approaches. Specifically, Point-Net++, PointMLP and PointNN respectively achieve assessment accuracies of 35.00%, 40.13% and 37.50%, significantly surpassing 32.00% accuracy obtained from 2D-based approach. Our findings exhibit robust baselines for 3D facial paralysis severity assessment and validate the clinical potential of point cloud-based 3D recognition models.

Keywords: Facial paralysis severity assessment · 3D point clouds · 3D recognition models · Clinical diagnosis

1 Introduction

Facial paralysis is a medical condition that significantly affects patients' quality of life, causing asymmetrical facial movements and impaired facial expressions. Accurate assessment of facial paralysis severity is crucial for clinical diagnosis, treatment planning, and monitoring patient recovery progress. The House-Brackmann (H-B) grading system [1], which defines six grades (I-VI), has been

W. Jia et al. (Eds.): CCBR 2025, LNCS 16360, pp. 425–434, 2026.
https://doi.org/10.1007/978-981-95-6123-0_40

widely adopted as the international standard for facial paralysis severity assessment. However, traditional clinical evaluation methods rely heavily on subjective visual inspection by clinicians, leading to potential low efficiency, inconsistencies and inter-observer variability.

The advancement of deep learning technologies has opened new avenues for objective and automated facial paralysis severity assessment. While early approaches primarily focused on 2D image analysis using traditional machine learning techniques, such as those reported in previous studies [2] [3] [4], these methods often suffered from limitations related to the inherent loss of depth information, lighting conditions and pose variations. Recent studies [5] [6] have demonstrated that 3D facial analysis can provide more comprehensive and accurate assessments by capturing the complete geometric structure of facial expressions and quantifying volumetric asymmetries that are not present in 2D images. However, these methods didn't address the problem of facial paralysis severity assessment.

The emergence of 3D recognition models based on 3D point clouds, presents opportunities for facial paralysis severity assessment. These approaches can directly process 3D facial geometry without the need for intermediate representations, potentially capturing subtle facial asymmetries that are critical for accurate facial paralysis severity assessment. Inspired by these facts, this paper presents a comprehensive study on automatic facial paralysis severity assessment using 3D point clouds and 3D recognition models. We collect a novel dataset comprising 61 patients with facial paralysis, each exhibiting eight clinically recommended facial expressions, resulting in 488 annotated expression samples. Our dataset covers H-B grade II to grade V. We evaluate several state-of-the-art (SOTA) 3D recognition models, including PointNet++ [7], PointMLP [8], and PointNN [9], and compare their performance against 2D technique.

The main contributions of this work are threefold: (1) We collect a new 3D facial paralysis dataset with comprehensive clinical annotations according to the H-B grading system; (2) We demonstrate the superiority of point cloud-based 3D recognition models for facial paralysis severity assessment, showing significant improvements over the 2D technique; (3) We provide a thorough experimental evaluation using several performance evaluation metrics, establishing baseline results for future research in this domain. Experimental results demonstrate the superiority of 3D-based assessment methods against 2D-based approaches. Specifically, PointNet++ [7], PointMLP [8] and PointNN [9] respectively achieve assessment accuracies of 35.00%, 40.13% and 37.50%, significantly surpassing 32.00% accuracy obtained from 2D-based approach.

2   Related Work

2.1   2D Facial Paralysis Severity Assessment

In traditional machine learning approaches, researchers have quantified facial asymmetry through landmark-based features. For instance, studies like [10] employed simple mathematical operations on extracted facial landmarks to measure asymmetry, enabling binary classification between healthy and facial palsy states without requiring specific facial movements. Similarly, in [3], the authors introduced a new evaluation tool called the automatic facial evaluation system, which uses 68 facial landmarks on the face to select and segment static and dynamic features.

Deep learning offers the advantage of automatically learning features directly from data. For example, researchers proposed a hierarchical detection network consisting of three components for facial palsy detection [11]. Other work employed a cascaded encoder network architecture to automate diagnosis through a two main stage process [12], while Liu et al. developed a region-based parallel hierarchy convolutional neural network combined with an LSTM structure in [13].

2.2 3D Facial Paralysis Severity Assessment

To address the limitations of 2D facial paralysis severity assessment, researchers are exploring the 3D technique. For instance, the 3DPalsyNet model was proposed specifically to recognize mouth movements and grade facial palsy severity according to the H-B grading system [1]. Information derived from 3D face reconstruction or 3D facial landmarks also presents significant opportunities for facial paralysis severity assessment [14–18]. One study in [5]employed an objective grading method based on static 3D facial recordings, extracting radial curves to measure volumetric differences between the two sides of the face. Similarly, another study [6] described a method assessing 3D volumetric asymmetry in patients using advanced multi-view landmarks and radial curves.

3 Dataset Content

Facial data are acquired using the commercially available WS-BM321 high-precision 3D full-face acquisition device. The resulting dataset comprises facial expressions from patients with facial palsy, with each expression sample containing both a 3D point cloud and a 2D image. It includes 61 subjects exhibiting eight expressions: neutral expression, eyebrow raise, bared-teeth smile, eye closure, left corner-mouth movement, right corner-mouth movement, nose wrinkle, and cheek puff.

The H-B grades of facial palsy patients are annotated by clinicians. Patient distribution across H-B grades is summarized in Table 1. In reality, H-B grade I and H-B grade VI patients are clinically rare. Consequently, our dataset includes no H-B grade I and H-B grade VI cases, with all cases concentrated in H-B grades from II to V. In the following subsections, the facial paralysis data acquisition and expressions of facial paralysis patients are explained.

Table 1. Distribution of Facial Paralysis Patients and Expression Samples Across H-B Grades

Severity level	I	II	III	IV	V	VI
Patients numbers	0	19	22	11	9	0
Expression samples numbers	0	152	176	88	72	0

3.1   Facial Paralysis Data Acquisition

Due to the absence of a publicly available 3D dataset for facial paralysis severity assessment, we collect our own dataset at the Sichuan Integrative Medicine Hospital. As shown in Fig. 1, the WS-BM321 device, which is capable of reconstructing a 3D face in under 3 s, is used for data capture and subjects are seated approximately 0.45 m from the device. Uniform and diffuse indoor lighting conditions are maintained by avoiding intense sunlight sources.

Patients are instructed to remove glasses and earrings, and to keep hair away from their forehead to prevent occlusion. Minimal make-up is requested to reduce artifacts. Each patient sequentially exhibits the remaining seven expressions from the neutral expression: eyebrow raise, bared-teeth smile, eye closure, left corner-mouth movement, right corner-mouth movement, nose wrinkle, and cheek puff. Each face collection involves a licensed physician and a trained data collector. First, the data collector captures the patient's neutral expression. Then, the physician instructs the patient to produce each target expression, holding its peak for 35 s, during which the data collector captures the peak expression using the device.

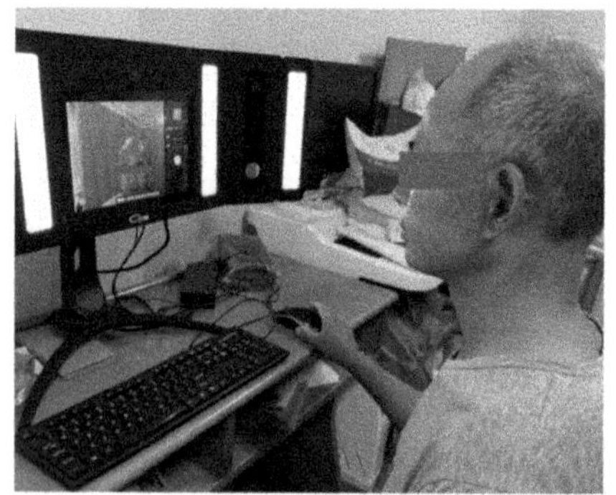

(a) 3D face collection scene

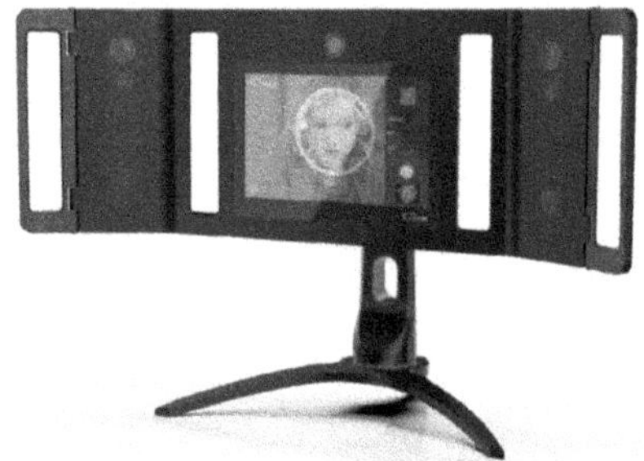

(b) WS-BM321 3D face collection device

Fig. 1. Face paralysis patients data collection scene and equipment.

3.2   Expressions of Facial Paralysis Patients

Eight facial expressions, recommended by clinicians and aligned with the internationally recognized H-B grading system, are acquired from each patient. Figure 2 shows representative 3D facial scans of patients exhibiting these expressions.

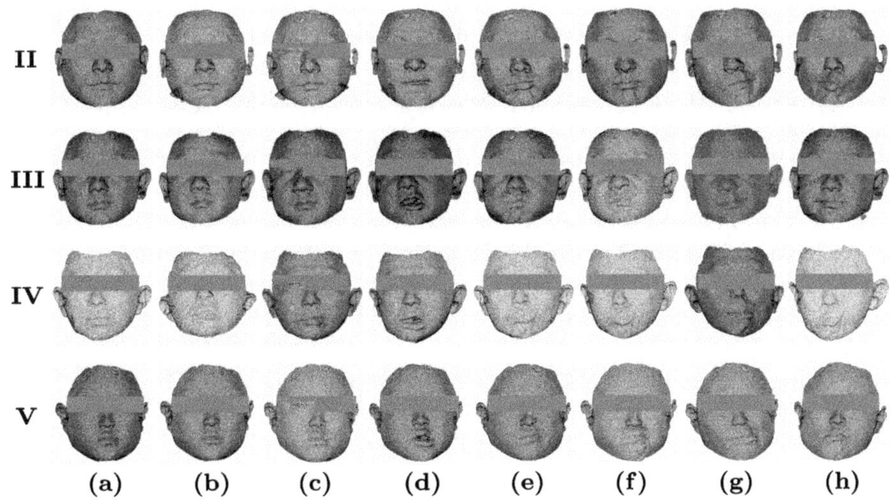

Fig. 2. Rows labelled "II", "III", "IV", and "V" correspond to H–B grades II–V, respectively. Columns (a)–(g) show the following facial actions: (a) neutral expression, (b) eyebrow raise, (c) eye closure, (d) bared-teeth smile, (e) nose wrinkle, (f) cheek puff, (g) left corner-mouth movement, and (h) right corner-mouth movement.

4   Methods

4.1   3D Point Clouds Pre-processing

Point clouds are acquired by using the WS-BM321 3D face collection device. The device captures frontal views of patients exhibiting prescribed facial expressions. As shown in Fig. 3, 68 3D facial landmarks are computed and placed on the face surface using the method described in [19]. The coordinate system origin is translated to the nose tip to simplify subsequent cropping. A cropping sphere, with a radius extending from the nose tip to the jaw tip, is defined, removing all points outside this sphere. This step, as shown in Fig. 3, eliminates extraneous points (e.g., hair and ears). If necessary, the point clouds can be rotated so that the nose point along the positive z-axis by using the 3D landmarks and the method described in [6].

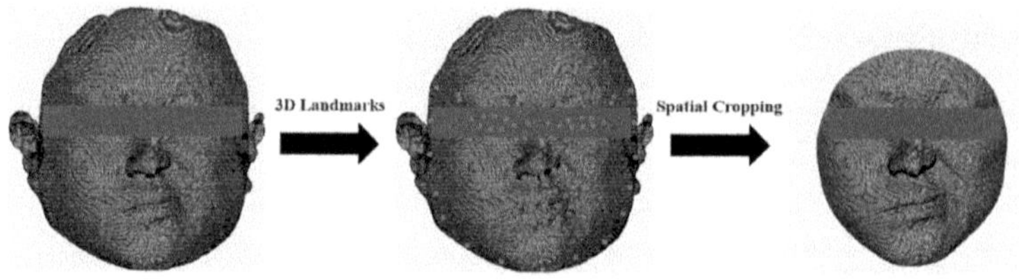

Fig. 3. 3D point clouds pre-processing steps.

4.2 Applying 3D Recognition Models for Severity Assessment

The high cost of 3D face collection devices and the lack of publicly available 3D dataset for facial paralysis severity assessment have limited the application of 3D recognition models based on 3D point clouds in this domain. To address this gap, we invest significant resources to procure hardware and dedicate substantial manual effort to 3D face collection and clinical annotations. The resulting dataset, annotated with H-B grades, aims to fill the current void of 3D training data for facial paralysis severity assessment and is planned for public release. We benchmark several SOTA 3D recognition models, including PointNet++ [7], PointMLP [8], and PointNN [9]. Notably, as our dataset contains no H-B grade VI facial palsy patients, the 3D recognition models are configured as four-class classification models (H-B grades II-V). Figure 4 shows the SOTA 3D recognition models, including PointNet++ [7], PointMLP [8], and PointNN [9].

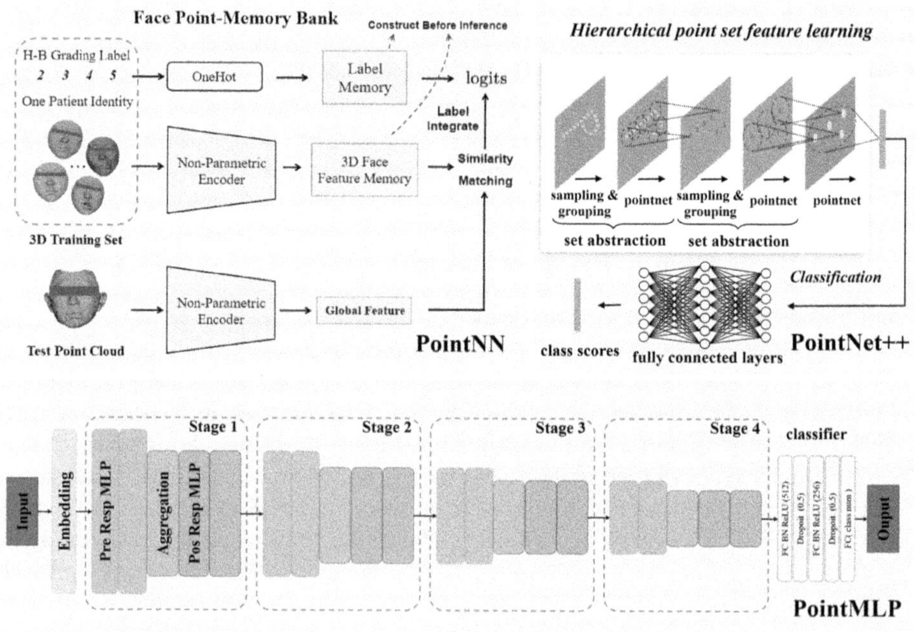

Fig. 4. SOTA 3D recognition models, including PointNet++ [7], PointMLP [8], and PointNN [9].

5   Experiments

5.1   Implement Details and Performance of Evaluation Metrics

In the experiments, for each category of patients, 70% are allocated to the training set, and 30% are allocated to the test set. To ensure a more reliable evaluation, we split the dataset such that the patients in the training set are completely different from those in the test set. This approach ensures that no patient appears in both training and testing sets, thereby preventing data leakage and providing a more realistic assessment of 3D recognition models. Each patient has a single H-B grade, which is applied to all eight expression samples. Table 2 summarizes the distribution of expression samples across the H-B grades.

Table 2. Expression Samples Distribution Across H-B grades in Training and Testing Sets

Dataset	II	III	IV	V	Total
Training Set	120	144	72	56	392
Testing Set	32	32	16	16	96
Overall		152	176	88	72	488

Table 3. Comprehensive evaluation metrics about SOTA 3D recognition models and 2D technique

Model	Accuracy	Precision	F1-Score	MAE	Kappa
LBP+SVM	0.3200	0.3200	0.31	1.1979	0.0732
PointNet++	0.3500	0.2398	0.2868	0.9474	0.0277
PointNN	0.3750	0.2079	0.1850	0.796	0.0185
PointMLP	0.4013	0.2864	0.3278	0.9671	0.099

We employ comprehensive evaluation metrics to assess the performance of the 3D recognition models. In this study, we report the weighted recall and weighted F1-score, which account for class imbalance by computing the per-class metrics and then averaging them according to the number of true instances in each H-B grade. Accuracy measures the overall proportion of correctly classified expression samples. Precision quantifies the proportion of correctly predicted expression samples for each H-B grade among all expression samples predicted at the same H-B grade. The Mean Absolute Error (MAE) quantifies the average absolute difference between predicted and ground truth H-B grade, with lower values indicating better performance. Cohen's Kappa coefficient measures inter-rater agreement while accounting for chance agreement, with values closer to 1.0

indicating better classification consistency. Additionally, we evaluate accuracy under specific disagreement conditions. Disagreement represents the percentage of test expression samples whose predicted H-B grade differs from the ground truth by no more than d levels. (e.g., $d = 1$ means the prediction is correct or off by one adjacent H-B grade).

Table 4. Disagreement about SOTA 3D recognition models and 2D technique

Model	Disagreement (d)				
	0	1	2	3	4
LBP+SVM	31.77%	57.29%	91.15%	100%	100%
PointNet++	35.0%	81.25%	91.12%	100%	100%
PointNN	37.5%	84.21%	100%	100%	100%
PointMLP	40.13%	85.s21%	95.395	100%	100%

Table 5. Weighted recall for each H-B grades about SOTA 3D recognition models and 2D technique

Model	Grade II	Grade III	Grade IV	Grade V
LBP+SVM	0.2656	0.4062	0.4375	0.1250
PointMLP	0.7500	0.3200	0.0800	0
PointNN	0.0724	0.1579	0.0066	0
PointNet++	0.2500	0.2500	0.2083	0

5.2   Performance Comparisons

To the best of our knowledge, this paper represents the first attempts at applying SOTA 3D recognition models for 3D facial paralysis severity assessment. As shown in Table 3, we benchmark three representative 3D recognition models based on 3D point clouds-PointNet++ [7], PointMLP [8], and PointNN [9]-on our novel dataset. In Table 3, to quantify the value information added by 3D point clouds, we conduct a comparative experiment with a 2D technique which uses 2D images extracted from the dataset. For the 2D technique, local binary pattern (LBP) features [20] are extracted from the 2D images and fed into a non-linear support vector machine (SVM) with a radial basis function (RBF) kernel for four-class classification. Table 4 shows the disagreement between the SOTA 3D recognition models and the 2D technique in the comparative experiment. Table 5 shows the weighted recall for each H-B grades for SOTA 3D recognition models3.

6   Conclusions

In this paper, we have made three major contributions. First, we collect a 3D dataset for facial paralysis severity assessment and manually annotate it with H-B grades. Second, we innovatively apply SOTA 3D recognition models for 3D facial paralysis severity assessment. Third, we carry out a comprehensive and comparative experiment using several performance evaluation metrics, providing baseline results for future research in this field. The experimental results show that the 3D recognition models significantly outperform the 2D technique, confirming that our initial attempt is promising. However, we have only conducted application-oriented experiments and have not improved the models themselves. Moreover, due to the lack of the 3D dataset for facial paralysis severity assessment, our method cannot be directly compared with others. We are currently working on collecting more data and plan to make this 3D dataset publicly available to the academic community in the future.

Acknowledgements. This work was supported by Sichuan Science and Technology Program under Grant No. 2024YFFK0040.

References

1. House, J.W.: Facial nerve grading systems. Laryngoscope **93**(8), 1056–1069 (1983)
2. Arora, A., Sinha, A., Bhansali, K., Goel, R., Sharma, I., Jayal, A.: Svm and logistic regression for facial palsy detection utilizing facial landmark features. In: Proceedings of the 2022 Fourteenth International Conference on Contemporary Computing, pp. 43–48 (2022)
3. Zhang, Y., et al.: The feasibility of an automatical facial evaluation system providing objective and reliable results for facial palsy. IEEE Trans. Neural Syst. Rehabil. Eng. **31**, 1680–1686 (2023)
4. Li, P., et al.: A two-stage method for assessing facial paralysis severity by fusing multiple classifiers. In: Sun, Z., He, R., Feng, J., Shan, S., Guo, Z. (eds.) CCBR 2019. LNCS, vol. 11818, pp. 231–239. Springer, Cham (2019). https://doi.org/10.1007/978-3-030-31456-9_26
5. Büchner, T., Sickert, S., Volk, G.F., Guntinas-Lichius, O., Denzler, J.: Automatic objective severity grading of peripheral facial palsy using 3d radial curves extracted from point clouds. In: Challenges of Trustable AI and Added-Value on Health, pp. 179–183. IOS Press (2022)
6. Büchner, T., Sickert, S., Volk, G.F., Guntinas-Lichius, O., Denzler, J.: Assessing 3d volumetric asymmetry in facial palsy patients via advanced multi-view landmarks and radial curves. Mach. Vis. Appl. **36**(1), 1 (2025)
7. Qi, C.R., Yi, L., Su, H., Guibas, L.J.: Pointnet++: deep hierarchical feature learning on point sets in a metric space. Adv. Neural Inf. Process. Syst. **30** (2017)
8. Ma, X., Qin, C., You, H., Ran, H., Fu, Y.: Rethinking network design and local geometry in point cloud: a simple residual mlp framework. arXiv preprint arXiv:2202.07123 (2022)
9. Zhang, R., et al.: Parameter is not all you need: starting from non-parametric networks for 3d point cloud analysis. arXiv preprint arXiv:2303.08134 (2023)

10. Parra-Dominguez, G.S., Sanchez-Yanez, R.E., Garcia-Capulin, C.H.: Facial paralysis detection on images using key point analysis. Appl. Sci. **11**(5), 2435 (2021)
11. Jison Hsu, G.S., Huang, W.F., Kang, J.H.: Hierarchical network for facial palsy detection. In: Proceedings of the IEEE Conference on Computer Vision and Pattern Recognition Workshops, pp. 580–586 (2018)
12. Wang, T., Zhang, S., Liu, L., Wu, G., Dong, J.: Automatic facial paralysis evaluation augmented by a cascaded encoder network structure. IEEE Access **7**, 135621–135631 (2019)
13. Liu, X., Xia, Y., Yu, H., Dong, J., Jian, M., Pham, T.D.: Region based parallel hierarchy convolutional neural network for automatic facial nerve paralysis evaluation. IEEE Trans. Neural Syst. Rehabil. Eng. **28**(10), 2325–2332 (2020)
14. Nguyen, D.P., Nguyen, T.N., Dakpé, S., Ho Ba Tho, M.C., Dao, T.T.: Fast 3d face reconstruction from a single image using different deep learning approaches for facial palsy patients. Bioengineering **9**(11), 619 (2022)
15. Ngo, T.H., Chen, Y.W., Seo, M., Matsushiro, N., Xiong, W.: Quantitative analysis of facial paralysis based on three-dimensional features. In: 2016 IEEE International Conference on Image Processing (ICIP), pp. 1319–1323. IEEE (2016)
16. Kim, J., Jeong, H., Cho, J., Pak, C., Oh, T.S., Hong, J.P., Kwon, S., Yoo, J.: Numerical approach to facial palsy using a novel registration method with 3d facial landmark. Sensors **22**(17), 6636 (2022)
17. Alagha, M.A., Ayoub, A., Morley, S., Ju, X.: Objective grading facial paralysis severity using a dynamic 3d stereo photogrammetry imaging system. Opt. Lasers Eng. **150**, 106876 (2022)
18. Banita, P.: Evaluation of 3d facial paralysis using fuzzy logic. Int. J. Eng. Technol. **7**(4), 2325–31 (2018)
19. Paulsen, R.R., Juhl, K.A., Haspang, T.M., Hansen, T., Ganz, M., Einarsson, G.: Multi-view consensus CNN for 3D facial landmark placement. In: Jawahar, C.V., Li, H., Mori, G., Schindler, K. (eds.) ACCV 2018. LNCS, vol. 11361, pp. 706–719. Springer, Cham (2019). https://doi.org/10.1007/978-3-030-20887-5_44
20. Ojala, T., Pietikainen, M., Maenpaa, T.: Multiresolution gray-scale and rotation invariant texture classification with local binary patterns. IEEE Trans. Pattern Anal. Mach. Intell. **24**(7), 971–987 (2002)

AM-UNet: Attention Mamba U-Net
for Medical Image Segmentation

Meiyun Wang[1], Changlu Guo[2], and Yugen Yi[3(✉)]

[1] School of Economics and Management, Jiangxi Normal University,
Nanchang 330022, China
[2] Department of Applied Mathematics and Computer Science,
Technical University of Denmark, Kgs. Lyngby, Denmark
[3] School of Artificial Intelligence, Jiangxi Normal University,
Nanchang 330022, China
`yiyg510@jxnu.edu.cn`

Abstract. Recently, architectures such as Mamba that leverage State Space Models (SSMs) have shown strong potential in rivaling conventional CNN and Transformer architectures. SSM is a deep sequence model known for its power to handle long sequence tasks, efficiently tracking intricate inter-sequence relationships with linear computational overhead. However, previous skip connection methods have not fully bridged the semantic gap across encoder and decoder features, which may lead to insufficient feature fusion and consequently affect fine-detail recovery. To address this problem, we propose the Attention Mamba UNet (AM-UNet), which integrates the traditional U-shaped architecture with Visual State Space (VSS) blocks to exploit richer contextual information. We further enhance the architecture by embedding a novel attention module into the skip connection framework, where dilated convolution broaden the perception range with no extra processing burden, while cross mechanism facilitates optimal feature fusion between the encoder and decoder, mitigating the semantic gap and enabling a more comprehensive understanding of spatial dependencies. Experiments on ISIC17, ISIC18, and ACDC datasets showing that AM-UNet delivers superior results compared to existing methods when applied to medical image segmentation tasks.

Keywords: Medical Image Segmentation · Mamba · Attention · Dilated Convolution

1 Introduction

Medical image segmentation is closely related to modern medical research. Medical images, through interaction with the human body via certain mediums (such as X-rays, ultrasound), present various tissues, organ structures, and densities within the body in image form. This allows diagnosing physicians to make judgments based on the information provided by the images. Automated medical image segmentation technology can assist physicians by quickly segmenting

W. Jia et al. (Eds.): CCBR 2025, LNCS 16360, pp. 435–445, 2026.
https://doi.org/10.1007/978-981-95-6123-0_41

the regions of interest, enabling rapid pathological diagnosis and thereby improving patient care efficiency [1].

In recent years, models based on CNNs [1] and Transformers [2] have demonstrated outstanding performance across various visual tasks. U-Net [3], a major representative of CNN-based models, utilizes a U-shaped architecture [4] with skip connections. This architectural approach enables the encoder and decoder to extract feature information across multiple levels, and its simplicity, ease of implementation, and ability to handle image segmentation of different sizes have made it widely adopted. TransUNet [5] pioneered the integration of the Transformer architecture into medical image segmentation, encoding image features as sequences to capture strong global context, while effectively leveraging low-level CNN features through a hybrid U-Net design. Following this, various Transformer-based models have been introduced, such as TransFuse [6] and Swin-Unet [7].

However, models based on CNN and Transformer structures have inherent limitations. CNN-based models, due to the presence of pooling layers, tend to lose valuable information and overlook the relationship between the whole and its parts. Moreover, constrained by the narrow spatial context, these models consistently struggle to recognize long-range interdependencies. Although Transformer-based models address the issue of capturing distant element relationships by leveraging the self-attention mechanism, which treats the image as a continuous patch sequence to capture global information, the inherent self-attention mechanism generates exponential processing demands, leading to pronounced computational resource consumption [8,9]. Furthermore, their effectiveness in capturing fine-grained details is limited. These limitations unders core the critical need for an innovative medical image segmentation framework capable of efficiently extracting remote contextual information while preserving linear computational efficiency.

In recent developments, State Space Models (SSMs) [10,11], with a particular emphasis on the structured State Space Sequence Model (S4) [12], have established themselves as a powerful method for long-sequence modeling, showcasing linear complexity and successfully bridging local and global dependency modeling. SSM-based models have been widely studied in many fields, such as Mamba. The Mamba [13] model advances S4 by implementing selective mechanisms and leveraging hardware optimization techniques. U-Mamba [14] first combined SSM-CNN in the context of medical image segmentation tasks to demonstrate its potential. VMamba [10] introduced Cross-Scanning Mechanism (CSM) to further improve Mamba's applicability to computer vision tasks. While VM-UNet [15] achieves superior medical image segmentation results through a pure SSM-based architecture, its reliance on conventional skip connections leads to unrefined feature propagation and unresolved semantic discrepancies between encoder and decoder representations.

To overcome these challenges, we propose a Spatial Attention Module (SAM) embedded in skip connections, which integrates spatial attention mechanisms [16] with cross-attention principles. SAM adaptively fuses multi-scale encoder-decoder features to generate attention maps, selectively enhancing low-level spatial details while suppressing misaligned features. To further strengthen semantic consistency, SAM employs dilated convolutions that expand receptive fields without computational overhead, thereby capturing hierarchical contextual dependencies for cross-stage feature alignment. Building on this foundation, we present Attention Mamba U-Net (AM-UNet), a hybrid architecture that synergizes attention-guided refinement with SSM's efficiency. AM-UNet introduces spatially-aware attention gates to resolve encoder-decoder semantic gaps and selective state transitions that preserve SSM's long-range dependency modeling while enabling adaptive feature recalibration, establishing a robust framework for medical image segmentation.

This research provides an in-depth assessment of AM-UNet through systematic experimentation on two critical medical imaging tasks: multi-class cardiac MRI segmentation and skin lesion segmentation. Rigorous validation is conducted across three benchmark datasets ACDC [17] for cardiac analysis, alongside ISIC17 [18] and ISIC18 [19] for dermatological applications where the proposed architecture consistently demonstrates state-of-the-art segmentation performance.

2   Method

2.1   AM-UNet

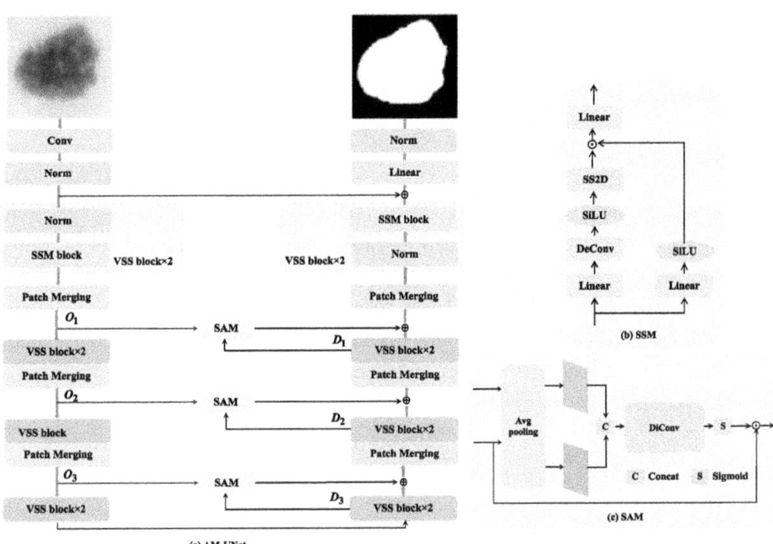

Fig. 1. The overview flowchart of our AM-UNet.

Figure 1(a) illustrates the overarching framework of AM-UNet. Initially, the input image $x \in R^{H \times W \times 3}$ is resized according to the scaling factor in both height and width, and the channel dimensions are modified to C (typically 96), producing an embedded image representation $x' \in \mathbb{R}^{\frac{H}{4} \times \frac{W}{4} \times C}$. Subsequently, x' using Layer normalization to standardize the statistical features of the input data before entering the backbone network, eliminating bias and variance in the input data, thus making it simpler for the backbone network to capture the patterns and regularities in the input data. The image is next processed by the encoder to obtain rich feature representations. The encoder is built with four stages, where the height and width of the input image are halved in the last three stages while the number of channels is increased. The network consists of four stages, each using 2 VSS blocks, with the corresponding output channels being $[C, 2C, 4C, 8C]$.

Similarly, the decoder also has four stages. During the initial three stages, spatial resolution is progressively upsampled while the channel dimensions are halved accordingly. The numbers of VSS blocks in the four stages are configured as $[2, 2, 2, 1]$, with corresponding output channels of $[8C, 4C, 2C, C]$, respectively. After decoding, a final projection layer is applied to recover the original feature resolution and adapt output channels to align the target segmentation classes.

For skip connections, we propose an attention mechanism to integrate the features from the encoder and decoder, providing optimized low-level detail features in the decoding stage, which helps to output higher-quality results. At the same time, we use dilated convolution techniques in the spatial attention, expanding the receptive field and capturing broader contextual information without increasing computational cost by enlarging the receptive field of the convolution kernel.

2.2   VSS Block

The Visual State Space (VSS) block serves as the core building component in our AM-UNet architecture, leveraging the efficiency of State Space Models (SSM) for medical image processing. Built upon the Mamba framework [13], VSS blocks enable linear-time sequence modeling while capturing long-range spatial dependencies essential for medical image segmentation.

As illustrated in Fig. 1(b), the VSS block employs a dual-branch design. The input features first undergo layer normalization, then split into two processing paths. The first branch applies a linear transformation followed by SiLU activation:

$$F_1 = \text{SiLU}(\text{Linear}(x)) \tag{1}$$

The second branch processes features through a linear layer ($Linear(\cdot)$), depth-wise convolution ($DeConv(\cdot)$), SiLU activation ($SiLU(\cdot)$), and SS2D module ($SS2D(\cdot)$):

$$F_2 = \text{SS2D}(\text{SiLU}(\text{DeConv}(\text{Linear}(x)))) \tag{2}$$

The output generated by the SSM is summarized as follows:

$$F = \text{Linear}(F_1 \odot F_2) \tag{3}$$

where $\odot$ denotes the element-wise multiplication operation.

2.3 SAM

The spatial attention module (SAM), originally introduced in the Convolutional Block Attention Module (CBAM) [20] and later adapted in SA-UNet's bottleneck blocks for state-of-the-art retinal vessel segmentation [21] has conventionally operated by deriving attention weights exclusively from encoder-generated feature maps. Although effective in bottleneck architectures, its direct application to skip connections fails to mitigate the persistent semantic imbalance between encoder and decoder features, as the unidirectional reliance on encoder-based spatial attention restricts dynamic feature refinement across hierarchical levels. This limitation disrupts cross-scale integration, amplifying inconsistencies between the encoder's localized structural patterns and the decoder's global contextual representations, ultimately compromising segmentation precision and model convergence.

To address this issue, as showed in Fig. 1(c), our proposed SAM framework synergistically processes multi-stage encoder features (from the first three stages) and their corresponding horizontally aligned decoder outputs. Specifically, these features undergo channel-wise global average pooling to compress channel dimensions, reducing computational complexity while preserving critical spatial dependencies. This preprocessing strategy that facilitates subsequent attention-driven spatial feature learning without information redundancy. Global average pooling can extract the overall information of each channel by averaging all spatial locations of the entire channel, effectively reducing the feature map's channel count while retaining comprehensive global information. The process can be represented as:

$$x_1 = \text{Avgpool}(O_i)$$
$$x_2 = \text{Avgpool}(D_i) \tag{4}$$

where $O_i \in R^{H \times W \times C}$ and $D_i \in R^{H \times W \times C}$ are the outputs of the i-th layer encoder and decoder. After performing global average pooling, we concatenate the global average pooled features from the encoder and decoder along the channel axis to create a two channel feature map. This strategy facilitates a synergistic combination of encoder's high-dimensional semantic features and decoder's granular-level features, allowing the model to simultaneously extract deep semantic context and shallow textural information, significantly improving the network's overall capabilities. Dilated convolution is applied to the concatenated feature map to capture multi-scale contextual information. By strategically expanding the receptive field, the model acquires broader context without increasing computational cost. Subsequently, a spatial attention weight matrix is generated using the Sigmoid activation function, and this matrix is element-wise multiplied with the encoder feature map to perform spatial feature weighting. The corresponding calculation is as follows:

$$F_{out}^i = S(DiConv_2^{7 \times 7}(\text{Concat}(x_1, x_2))) \odot O_i \tag{5}$$

where $S(\cdot)$ represents the Sigmoid activation function, and $DiConv_2^{7 \times 7}(\cdot)$ represents the dilated convolution with a dilation rate of 2 and kernel size of 7.

3   Experiments and Results

3.1   Datasets

ISIC17 and ISIC18 Datasets: ISIC17 [18] and ISIC18 [19] are openly accessible skin lesion segmentation datasets, comprising three lesion categories: melanoma, keratinocyte carcinoma, and benign nevi. Both datasets follow the standard train-validation-test split protocol to ensure rigorous model evaluation. ISIC17 consists of 2,750 images, including 2,000 for training, 150 for validation, and 600 for testing. ISIC18 is divided into 2,594 training images, 100 validation images, and 1,000 test images. Comprehensive evaluations were conducted using several metrics, including Mean Intersection over Union (mIoU), Dice Similarity Coefficient (DSC), Accuracy (Acc), Specificity (Spe), and Sensitivity (Sen).

ACDC Dataset: The ACDC dataset [17] contains five types of diseases: Normal, Hypertrophic Cardiomyopathy (HYP), Dilated Cardiomyopathy (DCM), Myocardial Infarction (MINF), and Right Ventricular Abnormalities (RV). And this dataset includes four segmentation labels: Background, Left Ventricle (LV), Right Ventricle (RV), and Myocardium (Myo). We performed detailed evaluations on four metrics: (Avg, RV, Myo, LV) Dice.

Table 1. Comparison of experimental results on the ISIC17 and ISIC18 datasets.

Dataset	Model	mIoU	DSC	Acc	Spe	Sen
ISIC17	UNet [3]	70.47	82.67	92.56	97.95	75.14
	Attention UNet [22]	69.73	82.17	92.32	97.69	74.93
	UNet++ [23]	71.21	83.18	92.63	97.40	77.18
	UNeXt [24]	74.03	85.08	93.40	97.62	79.71
	Rolling UNet [25]	71.01	83.04	92.55	97.26	77.28
	UKAN [26]	73.86	84.97	93.35	97.60	79.59
	UltraLight VM-UNet [27]	71.68	83.50	92.78	97.53	77.38
	VM-UNet [15]	73.20	84.53	93.26	**97.98**	77.98
	AM-UNet	**75.07**	**85.76**	**93.65**	97.60	**80.89**
ISIC18	UNet [3]	74.95	85.68	92.03	94.68	85.21
	Attention UNet [22]	76.78	86.86	92.74	95.45	85.76
	UNet++ [23]	76.76	86.85	92.69	95.19	86.25
	UNeXt [24]	78.08	87.69	93.21	95.84	86.42
	Rolling UNet [25]	77.74	87.47	92.82	94.11	89.51
	UKAN [26]	77.24	87.16	92.98	**96.02**	85.15
	UltraLight VM-UNet [27]	77.90	87.57	93.06	95.30	87.31
	VM-UNet [15]	80.39	89.13	93.81	95.04	90.64
	AM-UNet	**81.21**	**89.63**	**94.07**	95.09	**91.46**

3.2   Implementation Details

For both ISIC datasets, we first resized the images to 256 × 256 and performed normalization on both the images and labels. The data was subsequently transformed into NumPy (.npy) format for efficient storage and processing. The training epochs were set to 200, with an initial learning rate of 1×10^{-3} using the AdamW optimizer. For the ACDC dataset, the image size was set to 224×224, the training epochs were set to 400, and the learning rate was set to 1×10^{-3} using the AdamW optimizer. For the AM-UNet, we initialized the weights of the encoder and decoder using the pre-trained VMamba-S [10] on ImageNet-1k.

Table 2. Comparison of experimental results on the ACDC datasets.

Models	Dice	RV	Myo	LV
R50+UNet [5]	87.55	87.10	86.63	94.92
R50+AttUNet [5]	86.75	87.58	79.20	93.47
ViT+CUP [5]	81.45	81.46	70.71	92.18
R50+ViT+CUP [5]	87.57	86.07	81.88	94.75
SwinUNet [7]	88.07	85.77	84.42	94.03
MISSFormer [28]	90.86	89.55	88.04	94.99
UNEXt [24]	87.96	83.71	86.12	94.05
SSTransNet [29]	90.30	89.02	87.51	94.40
VM-UNet [15]	91.01	89.01	88.79	95.24
AM-UNet	**91.41**	**89.72**	**89.19**	**95.32**

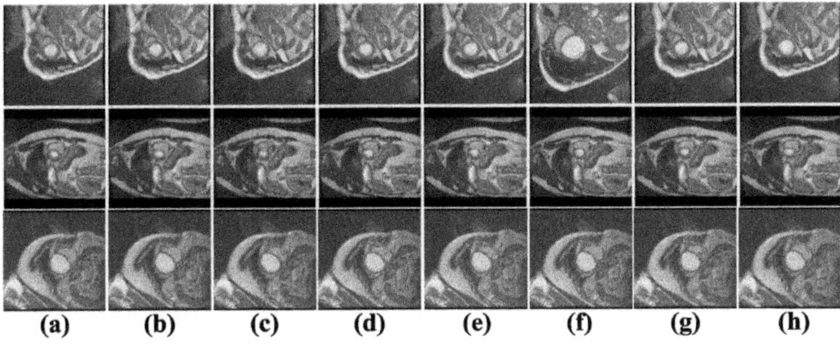

(a)   (b)   (c)   (d)   (e)   (f)   (g)   (h)

Fig. 2. Segmentation examples on the ACDC dataset. (a) Ground Truth; (b) AM-UNet; (c) VM-UNet; (d) R50+U-Net; (e) Swin-UNet; (f) SSTransNet; (g) MISSFormer; (h) UNeXt.

3.3   Results

We conducted a comparative evaluation between AM-UNet and several state-of-the-art models, with the results summarized in Table 1 and Table 2. On both the ISIC17 and ISIC18 datasets, AM-UNet consistently achieves superior performance across key metrics, including mIoU, DSC, Accuracy, and Sensitivity.

On the ACDC dataset, AM-UNet outperforms the other models in all metrics. Comparing to the VM-UNet model, AM-UNet outperform the Avg Dice, RV, Myo, and LV metrics by 0.4%, 0.71%, 0.4% and 0.08%, respectively. These results demonstrate the effectiveness and superiority of AM-UNet in medical image segmentation tasks.

The visualization results on the ACDC dataset are shown in Fig. 2, while those on the ISIC17 and ISIC18 datasets are presented in Fig. 3. It can be noticed that other models exhibit limitations in boundary delineation, whereas our model achieves the most accurate segmentation results.

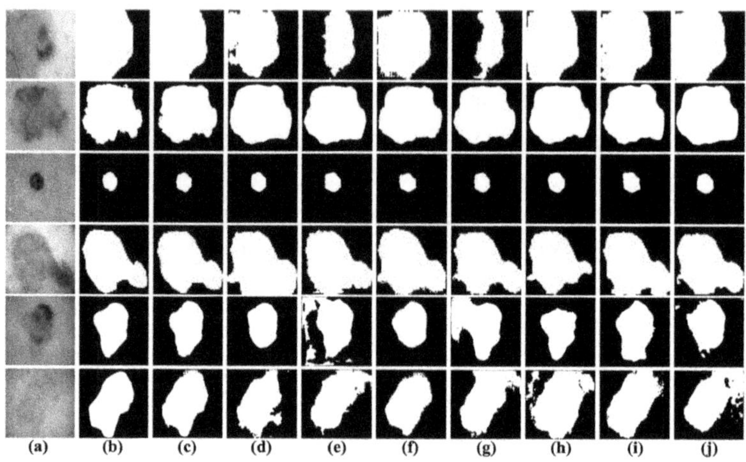

Fig. 3. Segmentation examples on the ISIC17 (row 1 to row 3) and ISIC18 (row 4 to row 6) dataset. (a) image; (b) Ground Truth; (c) AM-UNet; (d) UNeXt; (e) UNet++; (f) VM-UNet; (g) Attention UNet; (h) Ultralight VM-UNet; (i) Rolling UNet; (j) UKAN.

Table 3. Experimental results on the ISIC18 and ISIC17 datasets with different dilation rates.

Dataset	Rate	mIoU	DSC	Acc	Spe	Sen
ISIC18	1	78.66	88.06	93.32	95.39	87.99
	2	**81.21**	**89.63**	**94.07**	95.09	**91.46**
	3	77.20	87.13	92.92	**95.77**	85.60
ISIC17	1	74.22	85.20	93.42	97.50	80.23
	2	**75.07**	**85.76**	**93.65**	**97.60**	**80.89**
	3	74.34	85.28	93.45	97.48	80.38

3.4 Dilation Rate Analysis

We conduct comparative experiments on the AM-UNet adopting the ISIC18 and ISIC17 dataset, examining the influence of varied dilation rates on model performance. We set up experimental groups with dilation rates of 1, 2, and 3 for the SAM. According to the results in Table 3, AM-UNet achieves the highest accuracy when the dilation rate is set to 2.

4   Conclusions

This paper proposes AM-UNet, an innovative medical image segmentation framework that integrates Visual State Space (VSS) blocks with a dilated cross-scale spatial attention module in skip connections to bridge encoder-decoder semantic gaps and enhance spatial dependency modeling. Comprehensive experiments on ISIC17, ISIC18, and ACDC datasets show that AM-UNet achieves superior performance across skin lesion and cardiac MRI segmentation tasks.

Acknowledgments. This work is supported in part by grants from the National Natural Science Foundation of China (Nos. 62562039 and 62062040), the Major Discipline Academic and Technical Leaders Training Program of Jiangxi Province (No. 20212BCJ23017), the Outstanding Youth Project of Jiangxi Natural Science Foundation (No. 20212ACB212003), the Jiangxi Province Technological Innovation Base Program (20242BCC32021).

References

1. Aljabri, M., AlGhamdi, M.: A review on the use of deep learning for medical images segmentation. Neurocomputing **506**, 311–335 (2022)
2. Azad, R., Kazerouni, A., Heidari, M., et al.: Advances in medical image analysis with vision transformers: a comprehensive review. Med. Image Anal. **91**, 103000 (2024)
3. Ronneberger, O., Fischer, P., Brox, T.: U-net: convolutional networks for biomedical image segmentation. In: Navab, N., Hornegger, J., Wells, W.M., Frangi, A.F. (eds.) MICCAI 2015. LNCS, vol. 9351, pp. 234–241. Springer, Cham (2015). https://doi.org/10.1007/978-3-319-24574-4_28
4. Azad, R., Aghdam, E.K., Rauland, A., et al.: Medical image segmentation review: the success of U-net. IEEE Trans. Pattern Anal. Mach. Intell. **46**(12), 10076–10095 (2024)
5. Chen, J., Lu, Y., Yu, Q., et al.: TransUNet: transformers make strong encoders for medical image segmentation. arXiv preprint arXiv:2102.04306 (2021)
6. Zhang, Y., Liu, H., Hu, Q.: TransFuse: fusing transformers and CNNs for medical image segmentation. In: de Bruijne, M., et al. (eds.) MICCAI 2021. LNCS, vol. 12901, pp. 14–24. Springer, Cham (2021). https://doi.org/10.1007/978-3-030-87193-2_2
7. Cao, H., et al.: Swin-Unet: Unet-like pure transformer for medical image segmentation. In: Karlinsky, L., Michaeli, T., Nishino, K. (eds.) ECCV 2022. LNCS, vol. 13803, pp. 205–218. Springer, Cham (2022). https://doi.org/10.1007/978-3-031-25066-8_9

8. Dosovitskiy, A., Beyer, L., Kolesnikov, A., et al.: An image is worth 16×16 words: transformers for image recognition at scale. In: International Conference on Learning Representations, pp. 1–22 (2021)

9. Vaswani, A., Shazeer, N., Parmar, N., et al.: Attention is all you need. Adv. Neural. Inf. Process. Syst. **30**, 1–11 (2017)

10. Zhu, L., Liao, B., Zhang, Q., et al.: Vision mamba: efficient visual representation learning with bidirectional state space model. In: International Conference on Machine Learning, pp. 1–14 (2024)

11. Salam, A., Mahmud, R., Islam, T., et al.: A comprehensive survey on mamba: architectures, challenges, and opportunities. Computer **58**(8), 64–76 (2025)

12. Gu, A., Goel, K., Ré, C.: Efficiently modeling long sequences with structured state spaces. In: International Conference on Learning Representations, pp. 1–22 (2022)

13. Gu, A., Dao, T.: Mamba: linear-time sequence modeling with selective state spaces. arXiv preprint arXiv:2312.00752 (2023)

14. Ma, J., Li, F., Wang, B.: U-mamba: enhancing long-range dependency for biomedical image segmentation. arXiv preprint arXiv:2401.04722 (2024)

15. Ruan, J., Li, J., Xiang, S.: VM-UNet: vision mamba UNet for medical image segmentation. arXiv preprint arXiv:2402.02491 (2024)

16. Guo, M.-H., et al.: Attention mechanisms in computer vision: a survey. Comput. Vis. Media 1–38 (2022). https://doi.org/10.1007/s41095-022-0271-y

17. Janik, A., Dodd, J., Ifrim, G., et al.: Interpretability of a deep learning model in the application of cardiac MRI segmentation with an ACDC challenge dataset. In: Medical Imaging 2021: Image Processing, vol. 11596, pp. 861–872. SPIE (2021)

18. Berseth, M.: ISIC 2017-skin lesion analysis towards melanoma detection. arXiv preprint arXiv:1703.00523 (2017)

19. Codella, N., Rotemberg, V., Tschandl, P., et al.: Skin lesion analysis toward melanoma detection 2018: a challenge hosted by the international skin imaging collaboration (ISIC). arXiv preprint arXiv:1902.03368 (2019)

20. Woo, S., Park, J., Lee, J.Y., et al.: CBAM: convolutional block attention module. In: Proceedings of the European Conference on Computer Vision (ECCV), pp. 3–19 (2018)

21. Guo, C., Szemenyei, M., Yi, Y., et al.: SA-UNet: spatial attention U-net for retinal vessel segmentation. In: 2020 25th International Conference on Pattern Recognition (ICPR), pp. 1236–1242. IEEE (2021)

22. Oktay, O., Schlemper, J., Folgoc, L.L., et al. Attention U-net: learning where to look for the pancreas. In: Medical Imaging with Deep Learning Conference (2018)

23. Zhou, Z., Rahman Siddiquee, M.M., Tajbakhsh, N., Liang, J.: UNet++: a nested U-net architecture for medical image segmentation. In: Stoyanov, D., et al. (eds.) DLMIA/ML-CDS -2018. LNCS, vol. 11045, pp. 3–11. Springer, Cham (2018). https://doi.org/10.1007/978-3-030-00889-5_1

24. Valanarasu, J.M.J., Patel, V.M.: UNext: MLP-based rapid medical image segmentation network. In: Wang, L., Dou, Q., Fletcher, P.T., Speidel, S., Li, S. (eds.) MICCAI 2022. LNCS, vol. 13435, pp. 23-33. Springer, Cham (2022)

25. Liu, Y., Zhu, H., Liu, M., et al.: Rolling-UNet: revitalizing MLP's ability to efficiently extract long-distance dependencies for medical image segmentation. In: Proceedings of the AAAI Conference on Artificial Intelligence, vol. 38, no. 4, pp. 3819–3827 (2024)

26. Rege Cambrin, D., Poeta, E., Pastor, E., et al.: KAN you see it? KANs and sentinel for effective and explainable crop field segmentation. In: Del Bue, A., Canton, C., Pont-Tuset, J., Tommasi, T. (eds.) ECCV 2024. LNCS, vol. 15625, pp. 115–131. Springer, Cham (2024). https://doi.org/10.1007/978-3-031-91835-3_8

27. Wu, R., Liu, Y., Ning, G., et al.: Ultralight VM-UNet: parallel vision mamba significantly reduces parameters for skin lesion segmentation. Patterns (2024)
28. Huang, X., Deng, Z., Li, D., et al.: MissFormer: an effective medical image segmentation transformer. arXiv preprint arXiv:2109.07162 (2021)
29. Fu, L., Chen, Y., Ji, W., et al.: SSTrans-net: Smart swin transformer network for medical image segmentation. Biomed. Signal Process. Control **91**, 106071 (2024)

Multi-scale Channel Attention Vision LSTM Network for Optic Cup and Optic Disc Segmentation

Yu Duan, Bin Zhou, Hongyu Hua, and Yugen Yi[✉]

Jiangxi Normal University, Nanchang 330022, China
`yiyg510@jxnu.edu.cn`

Abstract. To enhance the precision and reliability of Optic Cup and Optic Disc Segmentation, we present a novel Multi-scale Channel Attention Vision LSTM (MCA-ViLSTM) Network. It integrates the encoder-decoder framework of U-Net with the sequential modeling capabilities of Long Short-Term Memory (LSTM) networks, thereby enabling the model to simultaneously capture local morphological features and long-range spatial dependencies while maintaining computational efficiency. Furthermore, we introduce a Multi-scale Channel Attention (MCA) module that enhances feature representation for small anatomical structures through adaptive channel weighting mechanisms, effectively addressing segmentation challenges arising from class imbalance. Comprehensive experiments conducted on publicly available datasets (DRIONS-DB and REFUGE) demonstrate that MCA-ViLSTM achieves superior segmentation performance in fundus image analysis.

Keywords: Optic Cup Segmentation · Optic Disc Segmentation · Vision LSTM · Multi-scale Channel Attention

1 Introduction

Glaucoma represents a chronic, progressive ocular pathology characterized by irreversible vision loss and potential blindness. Studies have shown that early and accurate diagnosis with timely intervention can reduce patients' risk of blindness by approximately 50%, making early detection crucial for mitigating disease progression [1]. Contemporary clinical diagnosis predominantly relies upon ophthalmologists' subjective assessment of fundus photography. However, with the rapidly growing demand for screening, the limitations of manual diagnosis in terms of efficiency, repeatability, and standardization have become increasingly apparent [1].

The conventional U-Net [2] architecture has been extensively employed across diverse medical image segmentation tasks. However, the model's reliance on convolutional operations with inherently local receptive fields limits its capacity to effectively capture long-range dependencies. Vision Transformer (ViT)

W. Jia et al. (Eds.): CCBR 2025, LNCS 16360, pp. 446–455, 2026.
https://doi.org/10.1007/978-981-95-6123-0_42

successfully introduced Transformers to computer vision by dividing images into patches and linearly embedding them as sequential representations, achieving breakthrough progress [3]. This global self-attention mechanism enables effective modeling of long-range spatial dependencies within medical images, considerably enhancing the model's capacity for global contextual understanding. However, existing Transformer architectures still face technical bottlenecks in practical applications. Their core limitation lies in the need to flatten two-dimensional medical images into one-dimensional sequences for global self-attention computation, which restricts their ability to process high-resolution images and leads to exponentially increasing computational costs [4]. Consequently, Transformer architectures show suboptimal performance in pixel-level dense prediction tasks, especially for high-resolution medical image segmentation. Recently, a novel extended LSTM (xLSTM) architecture was proposed that employs a bidirectional alternating feature traversal strategy, significantly enhancing the model's ability to process complex features [5]. Based on Vision Transformer's image serialization approach, Vision LSTM (ViL) [6] successfully applied xLSTM to computer vision. This architecture demonstrates excellent computational efficiency and segmentation accuracy while significantly reducing computational resource consumption, making it particularly well-suited for resource-constrained clinical environments.

This study proposes a Multi-scale Channel Attention Vision LSTM (MCA-ViLSTM) Network for precise semantic segmentation of optic disc (OD) and optic cup (OC) in fundus images. The proposed network integrates Vision LSTM (ViL) architecture into medical image segmentation by leveraging the structural advantages of U-shaped encoder-decoder networks alongside LSTM's sequential modeling capabilities, thereby achieving synergistic modeling of both local detail features and global contextual dependencies. This hybrid architecture design effectively reduces model complexity and computational requirements while maintaining segmentation accuracy. Furthermore, we propose a Multi-scale Channel Attention (MCA) module that significantly enhances feature representation for small target regions through adaptive weighting of encoder features, effectively mitigating the common class imbalance problem in medical image segmentation.

2   Related Work

Deep learning methodologies have achieved substantial advances in medical image processing over the past decade, with diverse approaches being successfully applied to medical image segmentation tasks. The introduction of U-Net established a foundational framework for medical image segmentation, and the majority of subsequent research has demonstrated remarkable success through architectural extensions and refinements of this seminal work [7]. However, constrained by the limited receptive field of convolutional operations, convolution-based methods struggle to effectively establish long-range dependencies. Due to the superior capability of Transformer in capturing long-range dependencies [8], it has been introduced from sequential data processing to computer vision, achieving success in multiple visual tasks. Researchers have subsequently adapted it for medical image segmentation model development. TransUNet [9] utilizes traditional convolutions to extract low-level features and employs Vision Transformer to obtain global perception. This architecture effectively combines the strengths of convolutions and multi-head self-attention mechanism, leading to improved model performance. However, the approach of flattening full-resolution images into sequences for self-attention computation incurs considerable computational overhead.

Building upon the image serialization framework introduced in the ViT architecture, numerous foundational techniques from large language models can be effectively transferred to the visual domain. For instance, Vim [10] and VMamba [11] have established foundational vision models for Mamba through bidirectional and quad-directional scanning methods, respectively. These approaches fully leverage the advantages of sequence modeling, enabling Vision Mamba to demonstrate outstanding performance across various tasks in fields such as remote sensing, medical imaging, and video understanding. Similarly, Vision LSTM (ViL) [6] employs image serialization techniques combined with alternating forward and backward scanning to enhance computational efficiency. However, image classification tasks rely relatively less on long-sequence modeling capabilities, making it difficult for ViL's strengths to be fully manifested in such tasks [12]. In contrast, segmentation and detection tasks depend more heavily on precise modeling of long sequences, thereby better evaluating visual models' ability to handle complex scenes. Therefore, this study aims to introduce ViL into medical image segmentation tasks, maintaining strong segmentation performance while effectively extracting global contextual dependencies.

Moreover, existing studies have investigated diverse feature fusion strategies aimed at effectively integrating multi-scale feature information while preserving critical detail features. U2-Net [13] incorporates multiple Residual U-blocks with different receptive field sizes to capture contextual information at various scales. TransAttUnet [14] utilizes multi-scale skip connections between decoder blocks to aggregate upsampled information at different scales, thereby enhancing semantic features containing diverse information. UCTransNet [15] proposes a channel-cross fusion Transformer module to replace the skip connections in U-Net architecture, establishing correlations between encoder and decoder by exploring multi-scale global context. However, none of these studies systematically integrate multi-scale information across all encoder stages, which may cause the network to overlook critical details. To address this limitation, we propose a Multi-scale Channel Attention (MCA) module that can adaptively adjust the channel-wise weight distribution of multi-scale features at each encoder stage. This approach effectively preserves more critical information and alleviates the class imbalance problem in medical images.

3   Method

The architecture of the proposed Multi-scale Channel Attention Vision LSTM Network (MCA-ViLSTM) comprises a Res-ViL-based encoder, a Multi-scale

Channel Attention (MCA) module and an ViL-Res-based decoder. The overall structure shown in Fig. 1.

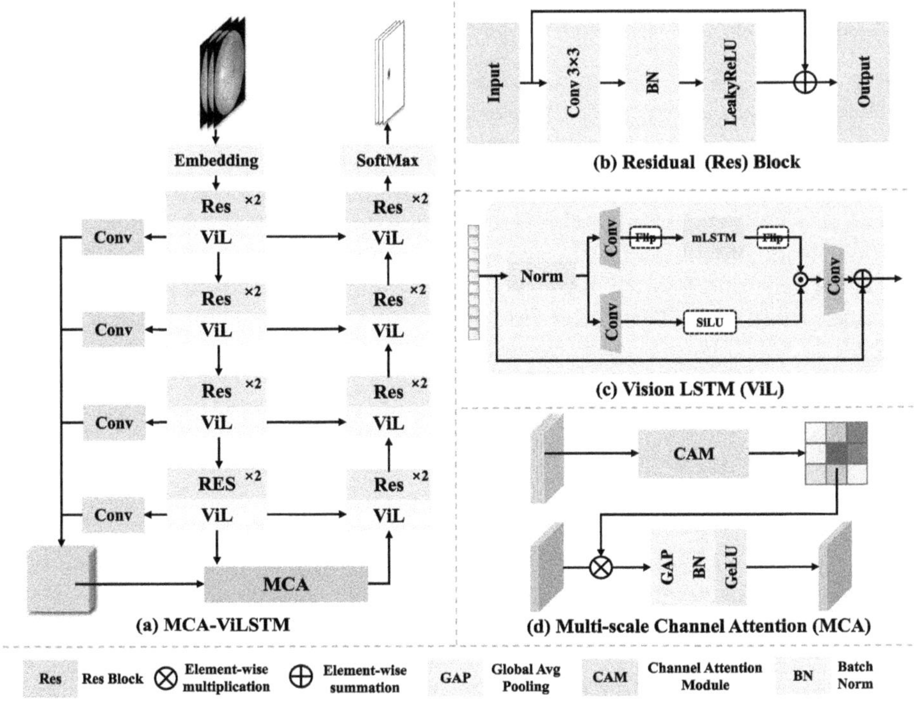

Fig. 1. The architecture of the proposed MCA-ViLSTM network.

3.1 Encoder and Decoder Architecture

The MCA-ViLSTM architecture comprises four encoder modules and four decoder modules. Each encoder consists of two consecutive residual (Res) blocks followed by a Vision LSTM (ViL) module, whereas each decoder consists of a ViL module followed by two consecutive Res blocks, as illustrated in Fig. 1(a). The process begins by partitioning the input feature map into non-overlapping patches of fixed size, which are then serialized via Embedding to obtain the feature vector (E^{out}), as formally expressed in Eq. (1).

$$E^{out} = Embedding(X_{img}) \qquad (1)$$

where X_{img} represents the input feature map.

Residual Block. The Residual (Res) block is designed to mitigate gradient vanishing issues while enhancing feature extraction capability and ensuring training stability and efficiency, as illustrated in Fig. 1(b). Each Res block consists of convolutional layers, normalization layers, and activation functions. The detailed computational process of the Res block is expressed by Eq. (2):

$$Res^{out} = (LeakyReLU(BN(Conv_{3\times3}(Res^{in}))) + Res^{in}) \tag{2}$$

where $Conv_{3\times3}(\cdot)$, $BN(\cdot)$, and $LeakyReLU(\cdot)$ denote the convolution, normalization, and activation operations, respectively. Res^{in} and Res^{out} represent the input and output of the Res block.

Vision LSTM Module. The structure of the Vision LSTM (ViL) model is shown in Fig. 1(c). Initially, the serialized image data (ViL^{in}) undergoes linear normalization, followed by the independent application of convolutional operations. Then, one branch flips the feature map and feeds it into alternately arranged Matrix LSTM (mLSTM) layers to obtain the output feature map ($mLSTM^{out}$). The process is described by Eqs. (3)–(5):

$$\overrightarrow{A} = mLSTM(Flip(Conv(LN(ViL^{in})))) \tag{3}$$

$$\overleftarrow{A} = mLSTM(Conv(LN(ViL^{in}))) \tag{4}$$

$$mLSTM^{out} = Flip(Concat(\overrightarrow{A}, \overleftarrow{A})) \tag{5}$$

where $Flip(\cdot)$ and $Conv(\cdot)$ represent the image feature flipping and convolutional operations, respectively. $LN(\cdot)$ is the linear layer and $Concat(\cdot)$ is the feature vector concatenation operation.

The other branch processes ViL^{in} by applying a convolutional operation with a SiLU activation function. Then, it performs element-wise multiplication with $mLSTM^{out}$, and finally incorporates a residual connection to produce the output of ViL module (ViL^{out}), as shown in Eq. (6):

$$ViL^{out} = ViL^{in} + mLSTM^{out} \odot \left(SiLU\left(Conv\left(LN\left(ViL^{in}\right)\right)\right)\right) \tag{6}$$

where $SiLU(\cdot)$ represents the activation function and $\odot$ denotes element-wise multiplication.

3.2   Multi-scale Channel Attention Module

Medical imaging applications frequently involve the detection and analysis of small yet clinically significant structures, including tumor lesions and vascular branches. Although medical images typically have high resolution, these small targets may occupy only a few pixels in actual size. Meanwhile, the shallow-layer feature representations of models contain large amounts of unscreened information, which often includes important features of these small targets. However, due to the inherently low resolution of small targets, their boundary and texture information is usually unclear, making it difficult to accurately locate and focus on these critical areas during decoding. To address these challenges, we propose a region-size normalization method that bridges the differences between features of different scales through bilinear interpolation and convolution, thereby obtaining multi-scale fused features (X_R). This procedure is detailed in Eqs. (7) and (8):

$$X_i^{EC} = Bilinear(Conv(ViL_i^{Eout})), i = 1, 2, 3, 4 \tag{7}$$

$$X_R = Concat(X_1^{EC}, X_2^{EC}, X_3^{EC}, X_4^{EC}) \tag{8}$$

where ViL_i^{Eout} represents the output feature map of the i-th ViL module in the encoder, X_i^{EC} denotes the feature map obtained by performing convolution and linear interpolation on ViL_i^{Eout}, $Concat(\cdot)$ indicates the channel-wise feature concatenation, and $Bilinear(\cdot)$ refers to the bilinear interpolation method.

Although the generated global features inherently encode comprehensive information from the encoder, this representation may contain spurious noise, and the significance of features across different layers exhibits considerable variation. To address this challenge, we propose a Multi-scale Channel Attention (MCA) mechanism that adaptively weights individual channels based on their relative importance, as illustrated in Fig. 1(d). First, Channel Attention Mechanism (CAM) [16] is applied to the extracted global features, as expressed in Eq. (9):

$$V_G = CAM(X_R) \tag{9}$$

where $CAM(\cdot)$ represents the channel attention mechanism.

Then, the extracted global regional feature (V_G) is element-wise multiplied with the output (ViL_4^{Eout}) from the final encoder layer to achieve feature enhancement. The resulting features then undergo global average pooling $(GAP(\cdot))$, normalization $(BN(\cdot))$, and activation function $(GeLU(\cdot))$ to obtain the final feature representation (MCA^{out}) as shown in Eq. (10):

$$MCA^{out} = GeLU(BN(GAP(V_G \odot ViL_4^{Eout}))) \tag{10}$$

where the symbol $\odot$ denotes the element-wise multiplication operation.

4   Experiments and Results

4.1   Datasets and Evaluation Metrics

This experiment uses publicly available optic cup and optic disc segmentation datasets DRIONS-DB [17] and REFUGE [18] to validate the performance of the proposed method. The DRIONS-DB dataset contains a total of 110 images, including 60 training samples and 50 test samples, with each image having a resolution of 600×400 pixels and all being color fundus images. However, due to the limited size of the DRIONS-DB dataset, to prevent overfitting, the experiment augments the data through rotation (within $45°$) and scaling (controlled at $\pm 10\%$ ratio), expanding the training dataset to 1,260 images. The training set, validation set, and test set of REFUGE dataset collectively contain 400 images. To mitigate the detrimental effects of extraneous noise on model performance, we implemented a preprocessing pipeline utilizing circular Hough transform for ROI extraction. We evaluate the segmentation performance using the Dice and IoU.

4.2 Ablation Experiments

To evaluate the efficacy of our proposed modules, we conducted an ablation study by systematically introducing each component individually and analyzing their respective contributions to overall performance. The MCA-ViLSTM contains three sub-modules: Residual (Res) block, Vision LSTM (ViL) module, and Multi-scale Channel Attention (MCA) module. The ablation experiment combinations are as follows:

- **Baseline:** The baseline network based on the U-Net model.
- **Baseline+Res:** Replaces the convolutional modules in U-Net with Res modules.
- **Baseline+ViL:** Replaces the convolutional modules in U-Net with ViL modules.
- **Baseline+Res+ViL:** Replaces the convolutional modules in U-Net with a combination of Res and ViL modules.
- **MCA-ViLSTM (Baseline+Res+ViL+MCA):** Based on the fourth configuration, adds the MCA module to the model.

The ablation experimental results are shown in Table 1. The experimental results demonstrate that incorporating residual blocks in place of the conventional convolutional modules in the baseline architecture yields improved performance across both datasets, attributable to enhanced transmission of fine-grained features. When the ViL module is added alone to the model, the performance improvement is still observed on the REFUGE dataset, but the improvement is limited on the DRIONS-DB dataset compared to the method with residual blocks. This is because the DRIONS-DB dataset has lower image quality than REFUGE, making it difficult for the globally-modeling-dependent ViL to capture effective spatial relationships. By combining RES blocks and ViL modules to form the encoder-decoder architecture of the model, the model retains local detailed features through residuals while utilizing ViL to capture contextual dependencies, leading to further performance improvement. Finally, with the addition of the MCA module, the optimal model MCA-ViLSTM in this section is constructed. The MCA first extracts features at different scales from the encoder and processes the multi-scale features using channel attention to enhance the perception capability of model for multi-scale features.

Table 1. Ablation study results on DRIONS-DB and REFUGE datasets.

Methods	DRIONS-DB		REFUGE			
	IoU	Dice	OD_{IoU}	OD_{Dice}	OC_{IoU}	OC_{Dice}
Baseline	0.9190	0.9566	0.8574	0.9288	0.7917	0.8529
Baseline+Res	0.9293	0.9655	0.8931	0.9446	0.8095	0.8751
Baseline+ViL	0.9257	0.9616	0.8977	0.9475	0.8114	0.8798
Baseline+Res+ViL	0.9369	0.9678	0.9112	0.9537	0.8186	0.8835
MCA-ViLSTM	**0.9422**	**0.9701**	**0.9226**	**0.9608**	**0.8271**	**0.9043**

4.3   Comparative Methods

In the process of reducing model complexity and improving operational efficiency, ensuring the stability and accuracy of segmentation performance is equally crucial. To address this challenge, we conducted comprehensive model training on both the DRIONS-DB and REFUGE datasets, with hyperparameters systematically optimized through iterative experimentation to achieve optimal performance.

As shown in the experimental results in Table 2, our method achieves IoU and Dice coefficients of 0.9422 and 0.9701 on the DRIONS-DB dataset, outperforming all current state-of-the-art methods. Compared to the second-best method C2FTFNet [21], it demonstrates improvements of 0.72% in IoU and 0.39% in Dice coefficient. Although the performance improvement may appear limited, when considering computational complexity, our model requires only 4.386 GFLOPs, approximately one-third of the computing power needed by the second-best method while achieving comparable or even superior segmentation performance.

Table 2. Comparison of methods on the DRIONS-DB dataset.

Methods	IoU	Dice	FLOPs(GB)	Param(MB)
PraNet [19]	0.9259	0.9572	12.11	14.25
DuAT [20]	0.9302	0.9635	10.48	**13.46**
C2FTFNet [21]	0.9350	0.9662	11.38	21.46
MCA-ViLSTM	**0.9422**	**0.9701**	**4.386**	13.60

Table 3 presents the performance of the MCA-ViLSTM method on the REFUGE dataset. Experimental results show that our proposed method achieves optimal performance in the optic cup (OC) segmentation task, significantly outperforming existing comparative methods. For the optic disc (OD) segmentation task, while slightly inferior to the top-performing method, it still delivers competitive segmentation results. Overall, MCA-ViLSTM achieves the highest average score among all compared methods, reflecting a balanced and robust performance across both OD and OC segmentation tasks.

Table 3. Comparison of methods on the REFUGE dataset.

Methods	OD_{IoU}	OD_{Dice}	OC_{IoU}	OC_{Dice}	Average
U-Net [2]	0.8554	0.9308	0.7921	0.8544	0.8582
Attention Unet [22]	0.8899	0.9411	0.8103	0.8814	0.8807
pOSAL [23]	0.8997	0.9460	0.8225	0.8750	0.8858
GDCSeg-Net [24]	**0.9310**	**0.9642**	0.8127	0.8938	0.9004
SeATrans [25]	0.9251	0.9608	0.8177	0.8974	0.9003
MCA-ViLSTM	0.9226	0.9608	**0.8271**	**0.9043**	**0.9037**

5   Conclusion

In this work, we employ the Vision LSTM (ViL) architecture, which balances computational efficiency with global information modeling, offering a novel method for image processing tasks. To address the class imbalance commonly encountered in medical imaging, we further propose a Multi-scale Channel Attention (MCA) module that preserves fine-grained features to improve model performance. Experimental results demonstrate that the proposed architecture offers significant advantages in medical image segmentation.

Acknowledgments. This work is supported in part by grants from the National Natural Science Foundation of China (Nos. 62562039 and 62062040), the Major Discipline Academic and Technical Leaders Training Program of Jiangxi Province (No. 20212BCJ23017), the Outstanding Youth Project of Jiangxi Natural Science Foundation (No. 20212ACB212003), the Jiangxi Province Technological Innovation Base Program (No. 20242BCC32021).

References

1. Iqbal, S., Khan, T.M., Naveed, K., et al.: Recent trends and advances in fundus image analysis: a review. Comput. Biol. Med. **151**, 106277 (2022)
2. Ronneberger, O., Fischer, P., Brox, T.: U-net: convolutional networks for biomedical image segmentation. In: Navab, N., Hornegger, J., Wells, W.M., Frangi, A.F. (eds.) MICCAI 2015. LNCS, vol. 9351, pp. 234–241. Springer, Cham (2015). https://doi.org/10.1007/978-3-319-24574-4_28
3. Dosovitskiy, A., Beyer, L., Kolesnikov, A., et al.: An image is worth 16×16 words: transformers for image recognition at scale. In: International Conference on Learning Representations, pp. 1–22 (2021)
4. Wang, W., Xie, E., Li, X., et al.: Pyramid vision transformer: a versatile backbone for dense prediction without convolutions. In: Proceedings of the IEEE/CVF International Conference on Computer Vision, pp. 568–578 (2021)
5. Beck, M., Pöppel, K., Spanring, M., et al.: xLSTM: extended long short-term memory. arXiv preprint arXiv:2405.04517 (2024)
6. Alkin, B., Beck, M., Pöppel, K., et al.: Vision-LSTM: XLSTM as generic vision backbone. In: International Conference on Learning Representations, pp. 1–22 (2025)
7. Azad, R., Aghdam, E.K., Rauland, A., et al.: Medical image segmentation review: the success of U-net. IEEE Trans. Pattern Anal. Mach. Intell. **46**(12), 10076–10095 (2024)
8. Vaswani, A., Shazeer, N., Parmar, N., et al.: Attention is all you need. In: Advances in Neural Information Processing Systems, vol. 30 (2017)
9. Chen, J., Mei, J., Li, X., et al.: TransUNet: rethinking the U-Net architecture design for medical image segmentation through the lens of transformers. Med. Image Anal. **97**, 103280 (2024)
10. Wang, H., Li, Z., Feng, L., et al.: VIM: out-of-distribution with virtual-logit matching. In: Proceedings of the IEEE/CVF Conference on Computer Vision and Pattern Recognition, pp. 4921-4930 (2022)

11. Liu, Y., Tian, Y., Zhao, Y., et al.: VMamba: visual state space model. Adv. Neural. Inf. Process. Syst. **37**, 103031–103063 (2025)
12. Yu, W., Wang, X.: MambaOut: do we really need mamba for vision?. In: Proceedings of the IEEE/CVF Conference on Computer Vision and Pattern Recognition, pp. 4484–4496 (2025)
13. Qin, X., Zhang, Z., Huang, C., et al.: U2-net: going deeper with nested U-structure for salient object detection. Pattern Recogn. **106**, 107404 (2020)
14. Chen, B., Liu, Y., Zhang, Z., et al.: TransAttUnet: multi-level attention-guided U-net with transformer for medical image segmentation. IEEE Trans. Emerg. Top. Comput. Intell. **8**(1), 55–68 (2023)
15. Wang, H., Cao, P., Wang, J., et al.: UCTransNet: rethinking the skip connections in U-Net from a channel-wise perspective with transformer. In: Proceedings of the AAAI Conference on Artificial Intelligence, vol. 36, no. 3, pp. 2441–2449 (2022)
16. Yi, Y., Zhou, B., Hu, Y., et al.: MACFNet: multi-attention cross-scale fusion network for OD and OC segmentation. Biomed. Signal Process. Control **110**, 108311 (2025)
17. Carmona, E.J., Rincón, M., García-Feijoó, J., et al.: Identification of the optic nerve head with genetic algorithms. Artif. Intell. Med. **43**(3), 243–259 (2008)
18. Orlando, J.I., Fu, H., Breda, J.B., et al.: Refuge challenge: a unified framework for evaluating automated methods for glaucoma assessment from fundus photographs. Med. Image Anal. **59**, 101570 (2020)
19. Fan, D.-P., et al.: PraNet: parallel reverse attention network for polyp segmentation. In: Martel, A.L., et al. (eds.) MICCAI 2020. LNCS, vol. 12266, pp. 263–273. Springer, Cham (2020). https://doi.org/10.1007/978-3-030-59725-2_26
20. Tang, F., et al.: DuAT: dual-aggregation transformer network for medical image segmentation. In: Liu, Q., et al. (eds.) PRCV 2023. LNCS, vol. 14429, pp. 343–356. Springer, Singapore (2024) . https://doi.org/10.1007/978-981-99-8469-5_27
21. Yi, Y., Jiang, Y., Zhou, B., et al.: C2FTFNet: coarse-to-fine transformer network for joint optic disc and cup segmentation. Comput. Biol. Med. **164**, 107215 (2023)
22. Oktay, O., Schlemper, J., Folgoc, L.L., et al.: Attention U-net: learning where to look for the pancreas. arXiv preprint arXiv:1804.03999 (2018)
23. Wang, S., Yu, L., Yang, X., et al.: Patch-based output space adversarial learning for joint optic disc and cup segmentation. IEEE Trans. Med. Imaging **38**(11), 2485–2495 (2019)
24. Zhu, Q., Chen, X., Meng, Q., et al.: GDCSeg-net: general optic disc and cup segmentation network for multi-device fundus images. Biomed. Opt. Express **12**(10), 6529–6544 (2021)
25. Wu, J., et al.: SeATrans: learning segmentation-assisted diagnosis model via transformer. In: Wang, L., Dou, Q., Fletcher, P.T., Speidel, S., Li, S. (eds.) MICCAI 2022. LNCS, vol. 13432, pp. 677–687. Springer, Cham (2022). https://doi.org/10.1007/978-3-031-16434-7_65

Anti-spoofing, Presentation Attack Detection

Deep Learning-Based Approaches for Iris Image Spoofing Prevention and Tamper Detection

Xiaodong Zhu, Ying Chen[✉], Junkang Deng, Zhijie Chen, and Changle He

Nanchang Hangkong University, Nanchang, China
c_y2008@nchu.edu.cn

Abstract. Iris recognition has become a crucial technology in modern security authentication systems. To effectively address the challenges of image anti-spoofing and tampering detection, this paper introduces the MNv4s-ECA (MobileNetV4Small-Efficient Channel Attention) model. The proposed architecture adopts MobileNetV4's Universal Inverted Bottleneck (UIB) as the backbone, which integrates variants including Inverted Bottleneck (IB), ConvNext-Like, and Extra Depthwise (ExtraDW). An Efficient Channel Attention (ECA) mechanism is incorporated to enhance feature extraction capabilities, selected based on experimental validation. The model is trained using the Adaptive Moment Estimation with Weight Decay (AdamW) optimizer, in conjunction with a composite learning rate scheduling strategy. Experimental results on the IIITD and CASIA-IrisV4 datasets demonstrate that the model achieves a classification accuracy of 99.96% and a perfect authenticity accuracy of 100%, with only 2.5 million parameters. Comparative analyses confirm that the proposed model outperforms existing state-of-the-art networks, maintaining a lightweight structure while achieving high accuracy in detecting forged and tampered iris images.

Keywords: Iris image anti-spoofing and tampering detection · lightweight network · convolutional neural network (CNN) · attention mechanism

1 Introduction

Iris recognition, a key biometric authentication method, remains vulnerable to presentation attacks. While traditional image processing techniques struggle against sophisticated spoofing, deep learning approaches excel by automatically extracting discriminative iris features. Recent studies show significant advances in deep learning-based iris anti-spoofing.

CNN-based methods learn discriminative iris features through multi-level feature extraction, improving detection accuracy. Tapia et al. [1] proposed a cascaded MobileNetV2 framework integrating contrast-limited adaptive histogram equalization enhancement, class weighting, and data augmentation to improve liveness detection accuracy. However, the architecture is computationally inefficient and shows limited generalization for unseen attack types.

Generative Adversarial Network (GAN)-based approaches improve model generalization by employing adversarial learning to synthesize realistic fake iris images.

© The Author(s), under exclusive license to Springer Nature Singapore Pte Ltd. 2026
W. Jia et al. (Eds.): CCBR 2025, LNCS 16360, pp. 459–469, 2026.
https://doi.org/10.1007/978-981-95-6123-0_43

Yadav et al. [2] introduced a style-transfer network based on cyclic GANs to generate diverse synthetic attacks by capturing domain-specific features, although they encounter challenges in maintaining output consistency and computational efficiency.

Domain adaptation aims to reduce the distribution gap between source and target domains to enhance model transferability. Li et al. [3] proposed a few-shot single-class framework based on frequency information, which consists of two core components: (1) a frequency attention module designed to capture key high-frequency features, and (2) a mixing module aimed at generating diverse target samples. Although effective in scenarios with limited target samples, the framework underutilizes low-frequency features and offers potential for improvement in cross-domain generalization.

Attention mechanisms dynamically emphasize discriminative features. Swarup et al. [4] integrated attention into DenseNet, allowing the model to focus on critical iris regions and improve spoof detection accuracy. However, the approach ignores inter-attack feature variations and adds computational overhead.

For iris anti-spoofing and tamper detection, this paper proposes the MNv4s-ECA, a lightweight yet efficient model combining MobileNetV4 [5] architecture with the ECA [6] mechanism. The model is designed to efficiently authenticate large-scale iris image datasets while ensuring compatibility with mobile platforms, thereby making it well-suited for high-throughput scenarios such as mobile authentication.

The main contributions of this work are threefold:

(1) The MNv4s-ECA model: A lightweight yet effective architecture for large-scale iris authentication, improving both computational efficiency and recognition reliability.
(2) An analysis of optimizer selection and learning rate scheduling strategies.
(3) Demonstrated superior performance on the IIITD and CASIA-IrisV4 datasets, thereby enhancing security against spoofing attacks.

2 Proposed Methods

2.1 Network Overall Structure

The MNv4s-ECA architecture (Fig. 1) consists of the following components: an input preprocessing layer, a multi-stage feature extraction layer, an ECA attention layer, and a classification head.

The input preprocessing stage employs a 3×3 3D convolution to expand channels from 3 to 32 while downsample the resolution from 224×224 to 112×112. This is followed by batch normalization and ReLU activation to enhance nonlinear feature representation and improve training stability.

In the multi-stage feature extraction layer, the network body is composed of five sequential stages that progressively abstract features using various types of UIB modules. The detailed operational procedure is described as follows:

(1) Stage 0 performs initial spatial downsampling using two consecutive Conv-BN-ReLU blocks: a 3×3 convolution reduces resolution from 112×112 to 56×56 (32 channels), followed by a 1×1 convolution that maintains the 56×56 resolution for channel adaptation.

(2) Stage 1 utilizes two sequential Conv-BN-ReLU blocks: first, a 3 × 3 convolution expands the channel count from 32 to 96 while reducing the resolution to 28 × 28; second, a 1 × 1 convolution compresses the channels to 64 to enable efficient feature integration.

(3) Stage 2 is the core feature enhancement layer, containing three module variants: (1) The ExtraDW module processes a 64-channel input with a 5 × 5 depthwise convolution (DWConv) for spatial mixing, expands channels to 192 via a 1 × 1 convolution, and reduces them to 96 using another 5 × 5 DWConv; (2) The IB module expands channels through a 1 × 1 convolution, applies a 3 × 3 DWConv, and restores the original dimension; (3) The ConvNext-Like module applies a 3 × 3 DWConv in low-dimensional space, expands channels to 384, and reduces them back to 96.

(4) Stage 3 enhances feature abstraction with three components: (1) An ExtraDW module uses a 3 × 3 depthwise convolution (DWConv) to expand channels to 576 and reduce resolution from 14 × 14 to 7 × 7 via strided convolution (output: 128 channels); (2) A second ExtraDW module applies a 5 × 5 DWConv at 7 × 7 resolution for spatial feature extraction, optimized for parallel architectures; (3) Three IB modules—the first two use 5 × 5 DWConvs for large receptive fields, while the last uses a 3 × 3 DWConv for local details, enabling multi-scale feature complementarity.

(5) The final stage employs a standard 1 × 1 convolution to expand the channel count from 128 to 960, followed by batch normalization and ReLU activation, thereby enhancing representational capacity while preserving computational efficiency.

The ECA module enhances deep features by first compressing the 7 × 7 feature maps into 1 × 1 representations through adaptive average pooling, followed by a dynamic 5 × 1 one-dimensional convolution (with kernel size adapted to the channel dimension) to capture local cross-channel dependencies.

The classification head first adjusts the feature channels to 1280 using a 1 × 1 convolution, followed by batch normalization (BN), ReLU activation, global average pooling, and a fully connected layer to generate the final prediction with minimal computational overhead.

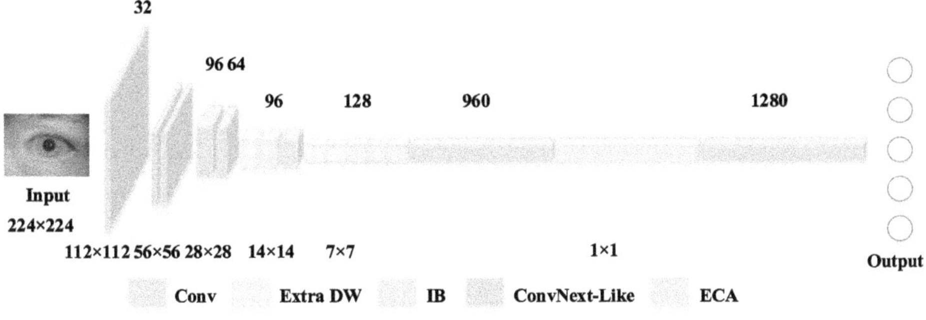

Fig. 1. The network structure of the MNv4s-ECA model

2.2 Instantiation of a Generic Anti-Bottleneck Module

The UIB integrates multiple architectural designs into a flexible framework, enabling the generation of four distinct variants. This study specifically adopts its IB, ConvNext-Like, and ExtraDW configurations for implementation and evaluation.

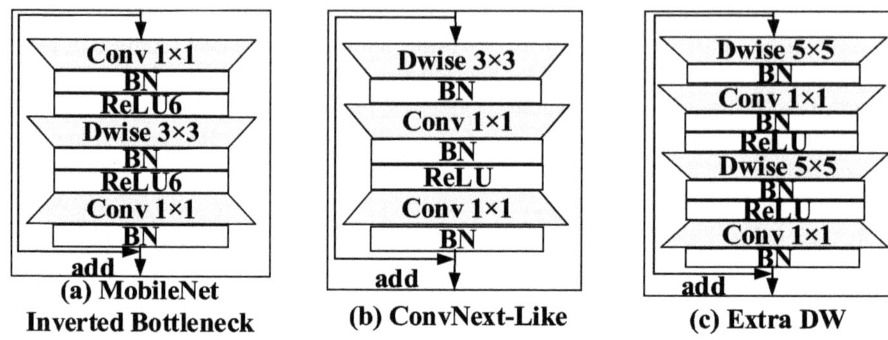

Fig. 2. Three instance structure diagrams of UIB

The IB block structure is shown in Fig. 2(a). In the MNv4s-ECA architecture, the inverted bottleneck (IB) replaces standard convolution with depthwise convolution (DWConv) to improve computational efficiency. It further incorporates high-dimensional feature transformations to enhance the model's expressive capacity, while promoting training stability through compressed linear outputs and residual connections. These mechanisms collectively achieve an effective trade-off between performance and efficiency in mobile-oriented models.

The ConvNext-Like block structure is shown in Fig. 2(b). In MNv4s-ECA, the ConvNext-Like module performs spatial mixing during channel expansion, employing larger kernel sizes with reduced computational complexity to enhance local feature extraction while maintaining efficiency.

The ExtraDW block structure is shown in Fig. 2 (c). In MNv4s-ECA, the ExtraDW module employs multi-stage depthwise convolutions to enhance multi-scale spatial feature extraction while preserving mobile-level efficiency, thereby achieving richer feature representations without incurring significant computational overhead.

2.3 Efficient Channel Attention

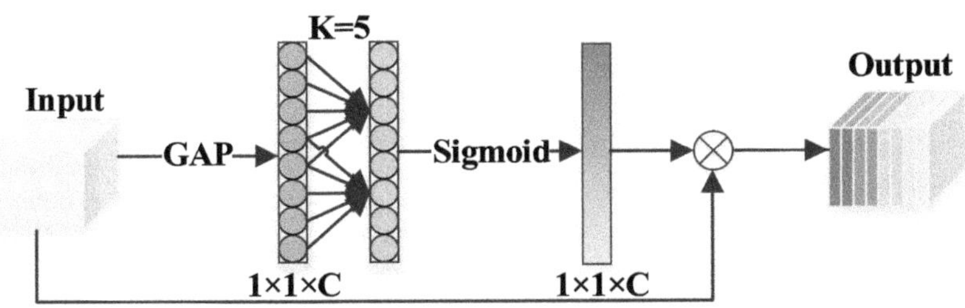

Fig. 3. Structural diagram of the ECA mechanism

The ECA module (Fig. 3) improves CNN feature representation using lightweight channel attention. In MNv4s-ECA, it applies global average pooling followed by an adaptive one-dimensional convolution with an optimized kernel size to capture channel dependencies and generates attention weights through sigmoid activation. This design maintains channel dimensionality while enhancing discriminative features with minimal computational cost, thus improving feature selection for mobile applications.

3 Experiments and Results

3.1 Preparation of Iris Image Dataset

For a comprehensive evaluation, two authoritative iris datasets are utilized: IIITD [7] and CASIA-IrisV4 [8], which are widely recognized as benchmark datasets in the field of iris recognition and provide diverse samples for experimental validation. Representative iris images from both IIITD and CASIA-IrisV4 are displayed in Fig. 4.

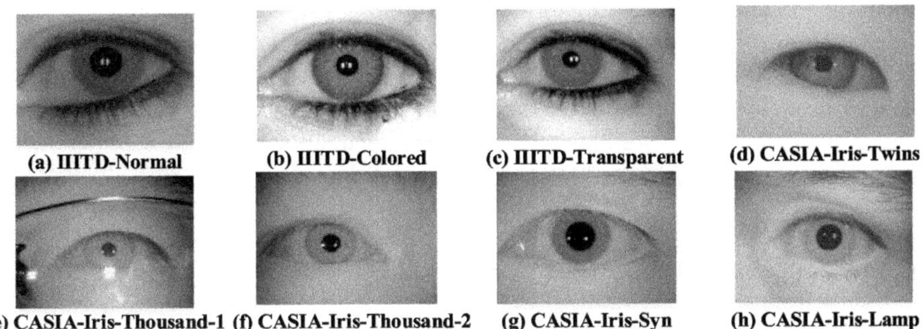

Fig. 4. Iris images from IIITD and CASIA-IrisV4

The experimental dataset (Table 1) was constructed using a total of 26,768 iris images selected from the available collections, excluding the Interval and Distance subsets from CASIA-IrisV4. The images are categorized into five distinct classes: (1) true_normal (natural iris), (2) true_glass (with regular glasses), (3) true_transparent (with clear contact lenses), (4) false_color (patterned contact lenses), and (5) false_syn (synthetic iris). This fine-grained classification scheme is intended to capture the distinct visual characteristics across various spoofing types and authentic imaging conditions, thereby facilitating more discriminative feature learning.

Table 1. Authentic and Spoofed Iris Image Dataset

Category		Source	Number
Authentic iris samples	true_normal	CASIA-Iris-Lamp, CASIA-Iris-Twins, IIITD	9106
	true_glass	CASIA-Iris-Thousand	5334
	true_transparent	IIITD	2153
Spoofed iris samples	false_color	IIITD	2175
	false_syn	CASIA-Iris-Syn	8000

3.2 Experimental Configuration

The model was developed in PyCharm 2024.2.4, utilizing an Intel Xeon Silver 4310 CPU and an NVIDIA A40 GPU (48GB VRAM), under the Linux 3.10.0 operating system with Python 3.9.21 and PyTorch 2.0.1.

The model was trained for 30 epochs with a batch size of 32 using the AdamW optimizer, configured with an initial learning rate of 0.0002, weight decay of 0.02, betas (0.9, 0.98), and epsilon 1e-6. The learning rate schedule included a 5-epoch linear warmup (start factor 0.01) followed by cosine decay. The dataset was split into 70% training, 10% validation, and 20% testing. During training, data augmentations—resizing, random rotation, translation, color jittering, and normalization—were applied. For validation and testing, only resizing, center cropping, and normalization were used. All augmentations were applied before tensor conversion (ToTensor).

The model utilized MobileNetV4-Small's ImageNet-1K pretrained weights, while the ECA module was trained from scratch. All comparative models similarly employed ImageNet-1K pretrained weights to ensure a fair evaluation.

3.3 Evaluation Metrics

The evaluation employs a multi-dimensional metric system, comprising classification accuracy for the five-class task and authenticity accuracy (binary true/false classification) for core performance assessment. The framework incorporates standard metrics—precision, recall, and F1-score—supplemented by confusion matrix analysis to provide a comprehensive characterization of model performance.

3.4 Optimization Algorithm Comparison

An evaluation compared Stochastic Gradient Descent (SGD) and AdamW. On the validation dataset, SGD achieved 99.74% classification accuracy and 100% authenticity accuracy at epoch 21, while AdamW reached 99.96% classification accuracy and 100% authenticity accuracy at epoch 24. As shown in Table 2, AdamW outperformed SGD in classification accuracy and F1-score during testing, with both maintaining perfect authenticity accuracy (100%). These results confirm AdamW's overall superiority.

Table 2. Comparative performance of SGD and AdamW on test dataset

Optimization Algorithm	Classification Accuracy (%)	Authenticity Accuracy (%)	F1 Score (%)
SGD	99.59	**100**	99.589
AdamW	**99.96**	**100**	**99.963**

The performance difference arises from the inherent characteristics of the two optimization algorithms: AdamW combines momentum with adaptive learning rates to stabilize large gradients while accelerating convergence in regions with small gradients, whereas SGD's fixed learning rate results in slower convergence in flat regions. Furthermore, AdamW's gradient normalization reduces sensitivity to noise and provides implicit regularization, while SGD is more susceptible to noise interference and tends to converge to sharp local minima. Therefore, AdamW was selected for its superior convergence rate and generalization capability.

3.5 Performance Evaluation of MNv4s-ECA

As shown in Table 3, MNv4s-ECA achieved a classification accuracy of 99.96% on the test dataset. Although the model demonstrated strong performance across four categories, it exhibited relatively lower detection accuracy for the true_transparent class. The confusion matrices in Fig. 5 illustrate the test performance of MNv4s-ECA: (a) the classification matrix shows that only two true_transparent samples were misclassified as true_normal, while (b) the authenticity matrix demonstrates perfect 100% accuracy in distinguishing real from spoofed samples.

Table 3. Evaluation results of MNv4s-ECA on test dataset

Classification Report	Precision	Recall	F1-score
false_color	1.0000	1.0000	1.0000
false_syn	1.0000	1.0000	1.0000
true_glass	1.0000	1.0000	1.0000
true_normal	0.9989	1.0000	0.9995

(continued)

Table 3. (*continued*)

Classification Report	Precision	Recall	F1-score
true_transparent	1.0000	0.9954	0.9977
accuracy	/	/	0.9996

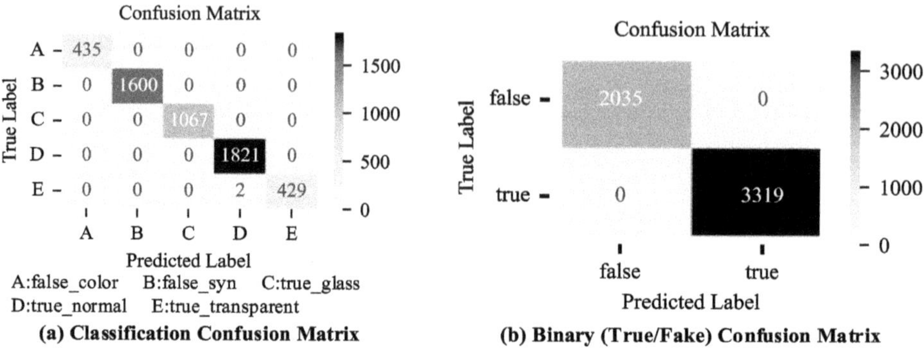

Fig. 5. Confusion matrix analysis of MNv4s-ECA on test dataset

The model exhibited relatively lower performance on the true_normal and true_transparent classes, likely due to two factors: (1) a limited number of training samples, particularly for the false_color and true_transparent classes, and (2) the presence of preserved iris patterns in transparent contact lenses, which introduced subtle feature ambiguities that led to classification confusion between these categories.

3.6   Comparative Experiments of Multiple Models

A comparative analysis was conducted between the proposed model and seven state-of-the-art architectures: MobileNetV3-Large, EfficientNet-B3, EfficientNetV2-S, MobileOne-S0, FastViT-T8 (a CNN-ViT hybrid), SHViT-S1 (another CNN-ViT hybrid), and StarNet-S1. All models were trained under identical experimental conditions, except for the adoption of a cosine annealing learning rate schedule. As shown in Table 4, our model achieved the highest classification accuracy (99.96%) and F1-score (99.963%) with a minimal number of parameters, while maintaining perfect 100% authenticity accuracy, which was also achieved by five other models. This demonstrates the superior lightweight design and classification performance of the proposed model.

Table 4. Performance of multiple models on test dataset

Model	Parameters(M)	Classification Accuracy (%)	Authenticity Accuracy (%)	F1 Score (%)
MobileNetV3-Large [9]	4.2	99.93	**100**	99.925
EfficientNet-B3 [10]	10.7	99.91	99.98	99.907
EfficientNetV2-S [11]	20.2	99.85	**100**	99.850
MobileOne-S0 [12]	4.3	99.89	**100**	99.888
StarNet-S1 [13]	2.7	99.85	**100**	99.850
FastVit-T8 [14]	3.3	99.89	**100**	99.888
SHViT-S1 [15]	6.0	99.89	**100**	99.888
ours	**2.5**	**99.96**	**100**	**99.963**

3.7 Ablation Study on Attention Mechanisms

To evaluate the effectiveness of the ECA module, ablation studies were carried out under five different configurations: (A) removing ECA, (B) replacing with coordinate attention [16], (C) replacing with squeeze-and-excitation network [17], (D) replacing with convolutional block attention module (CBAM) [18], and (E) retaining the original model.

Table 5. Performance of different attention mechanisms on the test dataset

Configuration ID	Parameters(M)	Classification Accuracy (%)	Authenticity Accuracy (%)	F1 Score (%)
A	**2.5**	99.91	**100**	99.906
B	2.6	99.85	**100**	99.850
C	2.6	99.83	99.98	99.832
D	22.8	99.93	**100**	99.925
E	**2.5**	**99.96**	**100**	**99.963**

As shown in Table 5, Scheme E (ECA) achieved optimal performance across all evaluation metrics, followed by Scheme D (CBAM). We hypothesize that although CBAM incorporates dual attention mechanisms across both channel and spatial dimensions, its significantly higher parameter count may introduce the risk of overfitting, resulting in marginally inferior performance compared to the lightweight ECA design. In contrast, ECA utilizes efficient one-dimensional convolution to capture cross-channel interactions without dimensionality reduction, thereby preserving more discriminative feature representations and demonstrating stronger generalization capability. These results provide strong evidence for the effectiveness of the ECA module in the proposed architecture.

3.8 Ablation Study on Learning Rate Strategies

Ablation studies were conducted to evaluate three learning rate scheduling strategies: (F) fixed-step decay, (G) 30-epoch cosine annealing, and (H) the approach adopted in this work, which consists of a 5-epoch warm-up followed by 25-epoch cosine annealing.

As shown in Table 6, Scheme H achieved optimal performance, which demonstrates the effectiveness of the phased learning rate strategy. The results indicate that the warm-up phase promotes stable convergence by starting with a reduced initial learning rate, thereby reducing training instability that can be caused by excessively large learning rates. Subsequently, cosine annealing enables finer optimization toward more favorable local minima, thus enhancing overall model performance.

Table 6. Performance of different learning rate schedules on the test dataset

Configuration ID	Classification Accuracy (%)	Authenticity Accuracy (%)	F1 Score (%)
F	99.63	99.89	99.627
G	99.74	99.89	99.738
H	**99.96**	**100**	**99.963**

4 Conclusion and Future Work

This study proposes MNv4s-ECA, a lightweight CNN-attention hybrid model for iris anti-spoofing and tamper detection, achieving state-of-the-art performance (99.96% classification accuracy, 100% authenticity accuracy) with minimal parameters.

Nevertheless, this study still has certain limitations, including class imbalance in the dataset and limited coverage of spoof iris types. Future work will focus on the following directions to improve the method: first, expanding the dataset's scale and diversity by emphasizing underrepresented categories and incorporating more iris forgery generation techniques, such as 3D prosthetic iris images, printed iris images, and screen-display-based iris attacks, thereby improving coverage; second, investigating the integration of the ECA attention mechanism with hybrid channel-spatial attention modules to enhance multi-scale feature fusion capabilities; finally, optimizing the fine-tuning strategy for pre-trained weights through cross-domain pre-training and layer-wise learning rate adjustment to fully exploit the potential of the pre-trained model.

Acknowledgements. This work was supported by the Natural Science Foundation of Jiangxi Province (Grant No.20242BAB26015, and Grant No. 20232BAB206129).

References

1. Tapia, J.E., Gonzalez, S., Busch, C.: Iris liveness detection using a cascade of dedicated deep learning networks. IEEE Trans. Inf. Forensics Secur. **17**, 42–52 (2021)
2. Yadav, S., Ross, A.: CIT-GAN: Cyclic image translation generative adversarial network with application in iris presentation attack detection. In: Proceedings of the IEEE/CVF Winter Conference on Applications of Computer Vision (WACV), pp. 2412–2421 (2021)
3. Li, Y., Lian, Y., Wang, J., et al.: Few-shot one-class domain adaptation based on frequency for iris presentation attack detection. In: Proceedings of the IEEE International Conference on Acoustics, Speech and Signal Processing (ICASSP), pp. 2480–2484 (2022)
4. Swarup, V.S., Sadhya, D., Patel, V., et al.: Presentation attack detection in iris recognition through convolution block attention module. In: Proceedings of the IEEE International Joint Conference on Biometrics (IJCB), pp. 1–8 (2022)
5. Qin, D., Leichner, C., Delakis, M., et al.: MobileNetV4: universal models for the mobile ecosystem. In: Proceedings of the 18th European Conference on Computer Vision (ECCV), pp. 78–96 (2024)
6. Wang, Q., Wu, B., Zhu, P., et al.: ECA-net: efficient channel attention for deep convolutional neural networks. In: Proceedings of the IEEE/CVF Conference on Computer Vision and Pattern Recognition (CVPR), pp. 11534–11542 (2020)
7. IIITD Contact Lens Iris Database. https://www.iab-rubric.org/resources/biometric-datasets/iris. Accessed 10 Jan 2025
8. CASIA-IrisV4. http://www.cbsr.ia.ac.cn/china/Iris%20Databases%20CH.asp. Accessed 10 Jan 2025
9. Howard, A., Sandler, M., Chu, G., et al.: Searching for MobileNetV3. In: Proceedings of the IEEE/CVF International Conference on Computer Vision (ICCV), pp. 1314–1324 (2019)
10. Tan, M., Le, Q.: Efficientnet: rethinking model scaling for convolutional neural networks. In: Proceedings of the 36th International Conference on Machine Learning (ICML), pp. 6105–6114 (2019)
11. Tan, M., Le, Q.: Efficientnetv2: smaller models and faster training. In: Proceedings of the 38th International Conference on Machine Learning (ICML), pp. 10096–10106 (2021)
12. Vasu, P.K.A., Gabriel, J., Zhu, J., et al.: MobileOne: an improved one millisecond mobile backbone. In: Proceedings of the IEEE/CVF Conference on Computer Vision and Pattern Recognition (CVPR), pp. 7907–7917 (2023)
13. Ma, X., Dai, X., Bai, Y., et al.: Rewrite the stars. In: Proceedings of the IEEE/CVF Conference on Computer Vision and Pattern Recognition (CVPR), pp. 5694–5703 (2024)
14. Vasu, P.K.A., Gabriel, J., Zhu, J., et al.: FastViT: a fast hybrid vision transformer using structural reparameterization. In: Proceedings of the IEEE/CVF International Conference on Computer Vision (ICCV), pp. 5785–5795 (2023)
15. Yun, S., Ro, Y.: SHViT: single-head vision transformer with memory efficient macro design. In: Proceedings of the IEEE/CVF Conference on Computer Vision and Pattern Recognition (CVPR), pp. 5756–5767 (2024)
16. Hou, Q., Zhou, D., Feng, J.: Coordinate attention for efficient mobile network design. In: Proceedings of the IEEE/CVF Conference on Computer Vision and Pattern Recognition (CVPR), pp. 13713–13722 (2021)
17. Hu, J., Shen, L., Sun, G.: Squeeze-and-excitation networks. In: Proceedings of the IEEE Conference on Computer Vision and Pattern Recognition (CVPR), pp. 7132–7141 (2018)
18. Woo, S., Park, J., Lee, J.Y., et al.: CBAM: convolutional block attention module. In: Proceedings of the European Conference on Computer Vision (ECCV), pp. 3–19 (2018)

Fingerprint Liveness Detection Based on EfficientNet and Adversarial Attacks

Kang Zhang, Ce Gao$^{(\boxtimes)}$, Xuhui Zhao, Linkai Niu, Zhicheng Cao, and Heng Zhao$^{(\boxtimes)}$

School of Life Science and Technology, Xidian University, Xi'an 710071, China
`gaoce55@stu.xidian.edu.cn`, `hengzhao@mail.xidian.edu.cn`

Abstract. With the rapid advancement of biometric technologies, fingerprint recognition has become one of the most widely used methods due to its low cost and ease of acquisition. However, it remains vulnerable to presentation attacks using forged fingerprints and faces challenges in generalization across different sensors and spoofing materials. To address this, we propose a robust fingerprint liveness detection (FLD) approach. The method applies efficient fingerprint foreground segmentation and local patch extraction as preprocessing, and generates adversarial perturbations to augment the training data, improving resilience against diverse attacks. An improved EfficientNet backbone, enhanced for lightweight structure and real-time performance, is then employed for classification. Experiments on the LivDet2015 dataset demonstrate that our method achieves high accuracy and superior robustness, particularly in cross-sensor scenarios.

Keywords: Fingerprint Liveness Detection · Fingerprint Recognition

1 Introduction

With the emergence of various emerging deceptive technologies in the field of biometric security recently, these biometric systems have also faced various security issues and challenges. As one of the main methods of biometric identification, fingerprint recognition is also the most popular and reliable identity authentication currently. Compared with other biometric identification, fingerprint recognition is regarded as highly reliable and practical due to its ease of acquisition, adaptability, strong privacy protection, non-invasiveness, and proven stability. But the security of fingerprint recognition systems has always been a problem that cannot be ignored. These systems are facing many serious security issues and new challenges. For example, in real-world applications, such systems are vulnerable to spoofing attacks using artificially fabricated fingerprints, which can effectively deceive recognition models [1]. These spoofed fingerprints—commonly created from materials such as Gelatine, Wood Glue, EcoFlex, and latex—pose severe risks to system security.

Fingerprint liveness detection is the primary countermeasure against such spoofing attacks. Current anti-spoofing methods are categorized into hardware-based and software-based approaches [2]. Hardware solutions rely on physiological signals (e.g., temperature, humidity) but suffer from high costs, complexity, and difficulty in adapting

W. Jia et al. (Eds.): CCBR 2025, LNCS 16360, pp. 470–481, 2026.
https://doi.org/10.1007/978-981-95-6123-0_44

to evolving attacks. Software-based methods, which analyze image features directly, have emerged as a flexible and cost-effective alternative. These are further divided into dynamic (e.g., sweat pore dynamics) and static feature detection (e.g., ridge patterns). Static methods, requiring only single or few images for verification, dominate current research due to their practicality and efficiency. Overall, our main contributions are summarized as follows:

(1) We propose a fingerprint liveness detection network based on an improved EfficientNet integrated with the Convolutional Block Attention Module (CBAM). This design not only reduces parameter count and computational complexity but also significantly enhances detection performance.
(2) We deceive state-of-the-art classifiers by adding specific perturbations to fingerprint images, causing the network to potentially misclassify them into different categories rather than their original predicted labels. These perturbed images, also known as adversarial examples, can significantly enhance model generalization capabilities when used to augment experimental data.

2 Related Work

Fingerprint liveness detection has evolved through two primary methodologies: handcrafted feature extraction and deep learning approaches.

Early research relied on engineered texture descriptors such as Local Binary Patterns (LBP), Local Phase Quantization (LPQ), and Weber Local Binary Descriptors (WLBD). Nikam et al. [3] pioneered LBP-based texture analysis for liveness detection, combining LBP histograms with wavelet energy features for hybrid classification. Subsequent enhancements included multi-scale LBP [4] and unified LBP [5], while LPQ [6] and WLBD [9] improved discriminative capabilities through short-time Fourier transforms and differential excitation components. Gragnaniello et al. developed Weber Local Descriptor (WLD) [7] and Local Contrast Phase Descriptor (LCPD) [8], integrating gradient and phase information for material differentiation. However, these handcrafted features exhibited limited generalization due to sensitivity to unknown spoofing materials and sensor variations [10], and primarily captured only superficial image characteristics [11].

The advent of convolutional neural networks (CNNs) brought a paradigm shift in FLD. Nogueira et al. [12] achieved 95.51% accuracy on LivDet2015 by fine-tuning VGG-19, demonstrating transfer learning efficacy. Chugh et al. [13] employed Inception-v3 with minutiae-centered patch voting but faced challenges in false fingerprint feature extraction and computational overhead. To address efficiency concerns, Zhang's team proposed lightweight CNN architectures such as Slim-ResCNN [14] and Light Dense CNN [15], which combined local patch selection with attention pooling to enhance both efficiency and discriminative feature learning.

Despite significant progress, existing methods still face three critical challenges: (1) Model overfitting caused by domain discrepancies between natural and fingerprint images; (2) Limited cross-material and cross-sensor generalization capability; and (3) Trade-offs between real-time detection requirements and computational complexity.

To mitigate these issues, recent studies have explored data augmentation and domain adaptation using Generative Adversarial Networks (GANs) [16–18]. While GAN-based augmentation has improved cross-domain generalization, adversarial attacks [19] remain an emerging security threat, exposing potential vulnerabilities in deep models. Consequently, developing robust, lightweight frameworks adaptable to multi-source data emerges as a pivotal direction for advancing biometric security systems.

3   Method

This paper proposes a fingerprint liveness detection method based on adversarial training. The core process is as follows: Firstly, the original fingerprint image is preprocessed (ROI extraction and block processing), and then adversarial samples are generated through the DeepFool algorithm to jointly build an enhanced dataset with the original data. The EfficientNet-b0 pre-trained on ImageNet is adopted as the basic model. Through structural lightweight transformation (reducing the computational load) and the introduction of the CBAM attention mechanism, the feature extraction ability is improved while maintaining high efficiency. Finally, the original images and adversarial samples are input into the improved network for joint training, and the classification results are output. This method effectively enhances the robustness and comprehensive performance of the liveness detection model through a goal-oriented adversarial data augmentation strategy. The overall architecture is shown in Fig. 1.

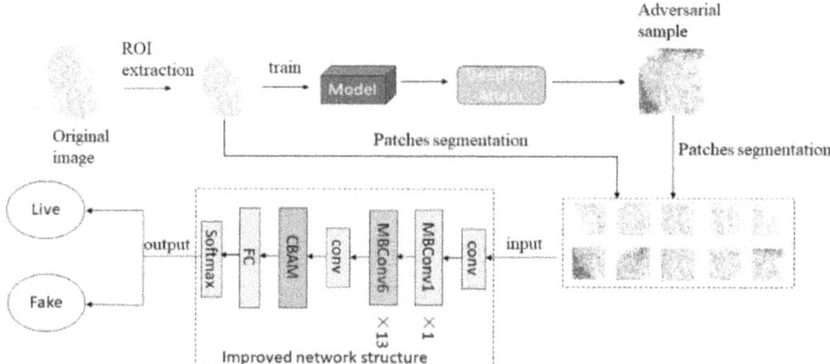

Fig. 1. The overall architecture of the proposed method.

3.1   Fingerprint Foreground Extraction and Patch Segmentation

Prior to fingerprint liveness detection, critical live/fake features reside in ridge-valley regions. As raw fingerprint images from sensors are large and contain substantial noise/background, we focus on effective areas through preprocessing: foreground extraction and patch segmentation. Early methods utilized full fingerprint images [12], but blank regions dominate and introduce noise. To eliminate background interference and improve network efficiency, we apply ROI extraction to isolate fingerprint regions from non-informative areas, ensuring maximal separation of fingerprint and background.

After foreground extraction, we perform patch segmentation by centering on the fin-gerprint core to extract local patches. A 224 × 224 patch is cropped from the foreground, with a stride of 56 pixels. Four additional patches are extracted from top/bottom/left/right positions relative to the core. This ensures uniform input size, reduces computational load, and excludes patches with insufficient fingerprint content. The proposed method augments data volume, mitigates overfitting in CNNs, and enables effective local texture learning. Figure 2 illustrates the process of fingerprint block segmentation.

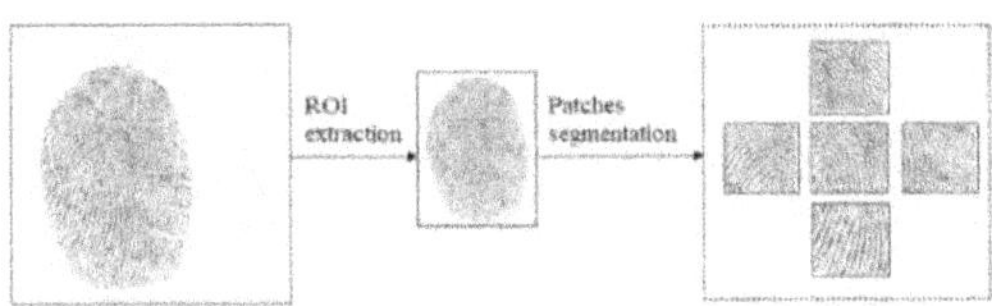

Fig. 2. The process of fingerprint block segmentation.

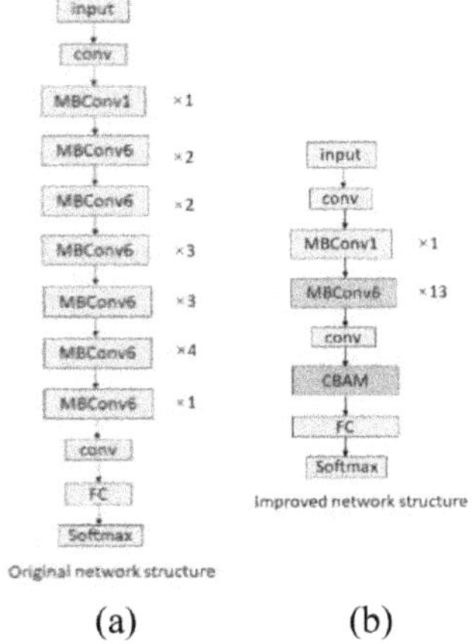

Fig. 3. The original network structure (a) and the improved network structure (b).

3.2 Network Architecture

Most of the existing fingerprint liveness detection (FLD) networks have the problems of high computational cost, complex network, operation and weak generalization ability. We chose the EfficientNet-b0 that has been trained on the ImageNet.

Due to the large computational load and slow speed of the original EfficientNet-b0 network, we modified its network structure, simplified the original network model archi-tecture, deleted some modules in the original network module, and replaced the original network module with the network composed of 16 large structural blocks was reduced to 14 structural blocks, retaining all 3 × 3 MBConv modules, and deleting the two 5 × 5 MBConv modules in the middle, while ensuring that the network-related parame-ters are reduced as much as possible. To achieve a higher recognition accuracy, while simplifying the computational complexity and network parameters of the convolutional network, the network can be lighter and more powerful. The original EfficientNet-b0 network structure diagram is shown in Fig. 3(a). By improving the original network structure, the improved network structure is shown of Fig. 3(b).

Meanwhile, we have also added the attention mechanism CBAM (Convolutional Block Attention) to the network. This module can perform attention mechanism on space and channel, infer the attention weight coefficient along the two dimensions of channel and space, and then multiply it with the feature map. The channel attention module and the spatial attention module are connected in series.

3.3 Adversarial Samples Generated

Deep neural networks have achieved remarkable results in many fields, but Szegedy et al. [19] first found that adding subtle perturbations to the original image may not detect changes in the image by the human eye. However, once input into the neural network, it may seriously affect the recognition performance of the network. With the exploration of this characteristic, many efficient and threatening attack methods are constantly being developed, and adversarial examples are to some extent universal, not just the result of overfitting to a specific model or specific training set selection.

Adversarial training enhances model robustness by incorporating adversarial examples into training, enabling learning of their feature distribution. Recent research has theoretically and practically advanced deep neural network security through adversarial example generation. Unlike natural images, biometric (e.g., fingerprint) images have unique characteristics; thus, we apply adversarial attacks to fingerprint data—using perturbation algorithms to generate adversarial samples that mislead CNN-based liveness detection systems. Integrating these samples into datasets improves detection robustness and model generalization.

Our main method is to use the DeepFool[20] to generate perturbations on fingerprint images. For sample x, label $\hat{k}(x)$, we use the following relationship to generate adversarial samples:

$$\Delta\left(x, \hat{k}\right) = min\|r\|_2 s.t. \hat{k}(x + r) \neq \hat{k}(x) \tag{1}$$

We call $\Delta\left(x, \hat{k}\right)$ the robustness of $\hat{k}$ at point x. E_X is the expectation of data distribution. The robustness of classifier $\hat{k}$ can be defined as follows:

$$\rho_{adv}\hat{k}(x) = E_X \frac{\Delta\left(x, \hat{k}\right)}{\|x\|_2} \tag{2}$$

DeepFool on a multivariate classifier can actually be seen as the aggregation of DeepFool on a binary classifier, and fingerprint liveness detection is always regarded as a binary classification problem, so we also use the DeepFool as a binary classifier. We suppose $\hat{k}(x) = sign(f(x))$, where f is an arbitrary scalar value image classification function, we record $\mathcal{F} = \{x : f(x) = 0\}$ as the boundary of the classifier, and analyze $f(x) = w^T x + b$ and derive a general algorithm, which can be applied to any differentiable binary classifier f. If f is a linear, we can easily see that f is at point x_0 x_0 robustness.

$\Delta\left(x, \hat{k}\right)$ is equal to the distance from x_0 to the classification boundary $\mathcal{F}$. It can also be expressed by $r_*(x_0)$.

An iterative process is used to estimate $\Delta(x; f)$. At each iteration, f is linearized around the current point x_i, where i is the current iteration number. The minimum perturbation of the linearized classifier is calculated by the following formula:

$$argmin\|r_i\|_2 subject to f(x_i) + \nabla f(x_i)^T r_i = 0 \tag{3}$$

In the binary classification problem, when the segmentation plane is not linear, we assume that when the moving distance is very small, the segmentation plane can still be considered a linear segmentation plane relative to the point. In each iteration, the point moves with a small amount. The distance continues to approach the splitting plane, and the algorithm terminates when x_i changes the sign of the classifier result or reaches the maximum iteration.

Adding subtle perturbations to the fingerprint image causes the model to give an erroneous output with high confidence by generating adversarial samples corresponding to it. Reusing the generated adversarial samples to enhance the experimental data can greatly enhance the generalization ability of the model.

4 Experiments

4.1 Dataset

This study utilizes the LivDet2015 [2] dataset for experiments, comprising images from four optical sensors: Green Bit, Biometrika, Digital Persona, and Crossmatch. Each sensor provides over 4,000 multi-modal fingerprint images (normal, wet, dry, high-pressure conditions) and spoof samples acquired via collaborative methods. The dataset is partitioned into training (algorithm configuration) and testing (performance evaluation) subsets, each containing live and fake fingerprints. To address size variability, we perform ROI extraction and segmentation on fingerprint foregrounds to standardize image dimensions.

Fake fingerprints on the LivDet2015 dataset are made from a variety of materials such as Playdoh, Ecoflex, gelatin, latex and wood glue. The test part contains unknown materials that are not present in the training part, such as liquid Ecoflex, OOMOO, artificial fingerprints produced by RTV. Table 1 summarizes the LivDet2015 dataset included in the study.

5 Results

5.1 Experimental Details

We evaluated our method on the LivDet2015 dataset containing live/spoof fingerprints from four sensors (Green Bit, Digital Persona, Biometrika, CrossMatch). Preprocessing involved ROI extraction, patch segmentation, and basic image enhancement, with fingerprint images further enhanced via DeepFool-generated adversarial perturbations to improve network robustness. The modified EfficientNet-B0 network was implemented in PyTorch using an Adam optimizer (lr $= 0.0001$, batch $= 32$, 200 epochs) on NVIDIA GTX 1660 Ti.

For performance evaluation, we followed the metrics used in LivDet to ensure consistency when comparing experimental results: Classification accuracy (Acc) and Classification Error (ACE) [13].

In this experiment, we first compared the accuracy of a single sensor. The accuracy of the Green Bit and Biometrika sensors reached 98.51% and 96.32% respectively. The accuracy of the Digital Persona sensor was lower at 94.92%. The accuracy of the CrossMatch sensor was 97.69%. At the same time, the method we proposed on the LivDet2015 data set was also compared with some other methods. Our experimental results achieved good results on LivDet2015. The experimental results are shown in Table 2.

Table 1. LiveDet2015 Datasets Information.

Sensor	Image Size	Resolution	Live Image(Train/Test)	Fake Image(Train/Test)	Spoof Materials
Green Bit	500 × 500	500	1000/1000	1000/1500	Ecoflex, Gelatine, Latex, WoodGlue, Liquid Ecoflex, RTVBodyDouble, PlayDoh,OOMOO
Biometrika	1000 × 1000	1000	1000/1000	1000/1500	
Digital Persona	252 × 324	500	1000/1000	1000/1500	
CrossMatch	640 × 480	500	1510/1500	1473/1448	

Table 2. Comparison Between the Results of the Proposed Method and the other Methods on LivDet2015 Dataset in terms of Classification Accuracy(Acc%).

Methods	Green Bit	Biometrika	Digital Persona	CrossMatch	Average
Mehboob [22]	96.55	**97.39**	91.18	96.55	95.42
Yuan [11]	91.10	92.48	91.32	94.30	92.30
Jomaa [23]	94.68	95.12	91.96	97.29	94.87
Zhang [14]	97.81	97.02	**95.42**	97.01	96.82
Nogueira [2]	95.40	94.36	93.72	98.10	95.40
Unina [2]	95.80	95.20	85.44	96.00	93.11
Proposed	**98.51**	96.32	94.92	**97.69**	**96.86**

Table 3. The Generalization Performance among different adversarial sample generation methods on LiveDet2015 database in terms of Average Classification Error (ACE).

Method	Sensor							
	Green Bit		Biometrika		Digital Persona		CrossMatch	
	Acc	ACE	Acc	ACE	Acc	ACE	Acc	ACE
DeepFool	94.43	5.35	93.63	7.29	90.9	12.62	95.63	3.43
FGSM	93.08	7.69	93.63	7.29	90.95	12.54	95.35	3.6
BIM	92.34	8.08	92.67	7.93	90.9	12.62	95.27	3.7
PGD	92.78	7.71	92.12	8.31	89.93	13.37	95.05	3.95

5.2 Generalized Comparison of Different Adversarial Samples

To evaluate the effect of adversarial samples generated by different adversarial perturbation algorithms on the generalization ability of our experimental database LivDet2015, we used several adversarial sample generation algorithms to conduct experiments on our experimental database LivDet2015, including adversarial samples generated by Deepfool, FGSM, BIM, PGD, etc.

Among different adversarial perturbation algorithms, the principle of FGSM algorithm is to generate adversarial perturbations based on the maximum direction of gradient changes in deep learning models, and add the perturbations to the image to generate adversarial examples. Usually, only one iteration is needed to obtain adversarial perturbations. BIM usually undergoes multiple iterative attacks, but it can also easily cause overfitting. Although PGD is simple and effective, its computational efficiency is not high. The DeepFool algorithm can generate more accurate perturbations in a shorter time, and the success rate of attacks is relatively higher. We have also evaluated and compared these methods, as shown in Table 3.

5.3 Cross-Sensor Fingerprint Spoof Generalization

We compared our experimental results with Sandouka [17, 18] when using original images from Green Bit, Digital Persona, Biometrika and CrossMatch as the training set and fingerprint images obtained by other different types of sensors as the test set. Have been significantly improved. Compared with using GAN networks to perform style transfer through a large number of different deception materials or fingerprint images collected by different sensors to improve model generalization capabilities, adversarial perturbations are used to generate adversarial methods in fingerprint activity detection. Fingerprint samples can also achieve the purpose of improving the generalization ability of the model.

We employed CycleGAN [24] to perform style transfer on fake fingerprint images fabricated from diverse materials across different capture devices, thereby augmenting training data and enhancing the model's generalization against spoofing attacks. Pairwise style transfer was applied to synthetic fingerprint materials from heterogeneous device datasets, generating cross-domain fake fingerprint samples.

We applied the DeepFool to generate adversarial versions of real fingerprint images from each sensor and synthesized fake prints via style transfer. Both sets were used to train our improved EfficientNet-b0 network to boost generalization. Experiments on LivDet2015 (Green Bit, Digital Persona, Biometrika, Crossmatch) are reported in Tables 4, 5, 6 and 7. While cross-sensor performance (e.g., training on Crossmatch and testing on Green Bit or Biometrika) still lags behind Sandouka [17, 18] and vanilla Deep-Fool, our approach consistently raises recognition accuracy and lowers average classification error. These results demonstrate that combining DeepFool adversarial samples with CycleGAN-generated fakes can improve fingerprint liveness detection and enhance cross-domain generalization despite sensor variability.

Table 4. The Generalization performance among cross-sensors (Green Bit in training) on LivDet2015 in terms of Classification Accuracy (Acc%) and Average Classification Error(ACE).

Method	Sensor					
	Biometrika		Digital Persona		CrossMatch	
	Acc	ACE	Acc	ACE	Acc	ACE
Sandouka [17]	91.20	10.20	81.20	23.21	76.96	23.06
Sandouka [18]	90.52	11.38	83.84	19.43	77.30	22.63
DeepFool	91.95	6.20	93.61	5.17	80.88	17.72
CycleGAN + DeepFool	91.58	8.40	97.31	4.19	91.05	10.22

Table 5. The Generalization performance among cross-sensors (Biometrika in training) on LivDet2015 in terms of Classification Accuracy (Acc%) and Average Classification Error(ACE).

Method	Sensor					
	Green Bit		Digital Persona		CrossMatch	
	Acc	ACE	Acc	ACE	Acc	ACE
Sandouka [17]	89.52	9.81	86.72	15.30	69.77	30.62
Sandouka [18]	89.68	8.75	87.52	14.00	69.84	30.60
DeepFool	94.27	4.42	82.11	15.99	82.56	15.63
CycleGAN + DeepFool	89.87	8.56	89.56	9.57	78.01	18.65

Table 6. The Generalization performance among cross-sensors (Digital Persona in training) on LivDet2015 in terms of Classification Accuracy (Acc%) and Average Classification Error(ACE).

Method	Sensor					
	Green Bit		Biometrika		CrossMatch	
	Acc	ACE	Acc	ACE	Acc	ACE
Sandouka [17]	85.36	13.05	84.96	14.28	69.02	31.36
Sandouka [18]	81.12	16.15	85.36	14.21	75.40	24.79
DeepFool	87.95	10.16	83.10	15.04	80.71	18.24
CycleGAN + DeepFool	91.79	7.16	89.13	8.87	82.21	15.93

Table 7. The Generalization performance among cross-sensors (CrossMatch in training) on LivDet2015 in terms of Classification Accuracy (Acc%) and Average Classification Error(ACE).

Method	Sensor					
	Green Bit		Biometrika		Digital Persona	
	Acc	ACE	Acc	ACE	Acc	ACE
Sandouka [17]	80.04	17.43	76.24	22.61	60.70	35.51
Sandouka [18]	84.44	13.90	78.04	18.40	62.31	30.25
DeepFool	81.13	16.87	80.32	17.93	76.98	23.02
CycleGAN + DeepFool	79.36	18.84	72.31	27.65	79.92	18.47

6 Conclusion

We propose a fingerprint liveness detection method based on an improved EfficientNet-b0 backbone. The approach incorporates a preprocessing pipeline for fingerprint foreground and local patch extraction, combined with targeted adversarial examples and style-transferred synthetic fakes to enrich training diversity. Experiments on the LivDet2015 dataset (Green Bit, Digital Persona, Biometrika, and Crossmatch) show that our method achieves higher accuracy and lower error rates compared with existing approaches. Moreover, it demonstrates strong cross-sensor robustness against unknown spoofing materials and sensor variations, highlighting its generalization capability. Future work will investigate advanced adversarial and generative strategies to further enhance cross-domain performance.

References

1. Marcel, S., Nixon, M.S., Li, S.Z.: Handbook of Biometric AntiSpoofing. Springer, London (2014)

2. Mura, V., Ghiani, L., Marcialis, G.L.: LivDet 2015 fingerprint liveness detection competition 2015. In: IEEE 7th International Conference on Biometrics Theory, Applications Systems (BTAS), pp. 1–6 (2015)
3. Nikam, S.B., Agarwal, S.: Texture and wavelet-based spoof fingerprint detection for fingerprint biometric systems. In: Proceedings of the 2008 First International Conference on Emerging Trends in Engineering and Technology, pp. 16–18 (2008)
4. Jia, X., Yang, X., Cao, K.: Multi-scale local binary pattern with filters for spoof fingerprint detection. Inf. Sci. **268**, 91–102 (2014)
5. Jiang, Y., Liu, X.: Uniform local binary pattern for fingerprint liveness detection in the gaussian pyramid. J. Electr. Comput. Eng. **2018**, 1–9 (2018)
6. Ghiani, L., Marcialis, G.L., Roli, F.: Fingerprint liveness detection by local phase quantization. In: Proceedings of the 21st International Conference on Pattern Recognition (ICPR), pp. 11–15 (2012)
7. Gragnaniello, D., Poggi, G., Sansone, C.: Fingerprint liveness detection based on Weber Local image Descriptor. In: Proceedings of the IEEE Workshop on Biometric Measurements and Systems for Security and Medical Applications (BIOMS), pp. 46–50 (2013)
8. Gragnaniello, D., Poggi, G., Sansone, C., Verdoliva, L.: Local contrast phase descriptor for fingerprint liveness detection. Pattern Recogn. **48**, 1050–1058 (2015)
9. Xia, Z., Yuan, C., Lv, R., Sun, X., Xiong, N.N., Shi, Y.Q.: A novel weber local binary descriptor for fingerprint liveness detection. IEEE Trans. Syst. Man Cybern. Syst. **50**, 1526–1536 (2018)
10. Marasco, E., Wild, P., Cukic, B.: Robust and interoperable fingerprint spoof detection via convolutional neural networks. In: Proceedings of IEEE Symposium Technol. Homeland Security (HST), pp. 1–6 (2016)
11. Yuan, C., Xia, Z., Sun, X., Wu, Q.M.J.: Deep residual network with adaptive learning framework for fingerprint liveness detection. IEEE Trans. Cogn. Dev. Syst. **12**(3), 461–473 (2019)
12. Nogueira, R.F., Alencar Lotufo, R., Machado, R.C.: Fingerprint liveness detection using convolutional neural networks. IEEE Trans. Inf. Forensics Secur. **11**, 1206–1213 (2016)
13. Chugh, T., Cao, K., Jain, A.K.: Fingerprint spoof buster: use of minutiae-centered patches. IEEE Trans. Inf. Forensics Secur. **13**(9), 2190–2202 (2018)
14. Zhang, Y., Shi, D., Zhan, X., Cao, D., Zhu, K., Li, Z.: Slim-ResCNN: a deep residual convolutional neural network for fingerprint liveness detection. IEEE Access **7**, 91476–91487 (2019)
15. Zhang, Y., Pan, S., Zhan, X., Li, Z., Gao, M., Gao, C.: FLDNet: light dense CNN for fingerprint liveness detection. IEEE Access **8**, 84141–84152 (2020)
16. Tarang, C., Jain, A.K.: Fingerprint spoof detector generalization. IEEE Trans. Inf. Forensics Secur. **16**, 42–55 (2020)
17. Sandouka, S.B., Bazi, Y., Alajlan, N.: Transformers and generative adversarial networks for liveness detection in multitarget fingerprint sensors. Sensors **21**, 699 (2021)
18. Sandouka, S.B., Bazi, Y., Alhichri, H., Alajlan, N.: Unified generative adversarial networks for multidomain fingerprint presentation attack detection. Entropy **23**, 1089 (2021)
19. Szegedy, C., et al.: Intriguing properties of neural networks. In: International Conference on Learning Representations (ICLR) (2014)
20. Moosavi, S.M., Fawzi, A., Frossard, P.: DeepFool: a simple and accurate method to fool deep neural networks. In: IEEE Conference on Computer Vision and Pattern Recognition (CVPR), pp. 2574–2582(2016)
21. Standard, I.; Information Technology–Biometric Presentation Attack Detection–Part 3: Testing and Reporting; International Organization for Standardization: Geneva, Switzerland (2017)

22. Mehboob, R., Dawood, H.: DEHFF–A hybrid approach based on distinctively encoded fingerprint features for live fingerprint detection. Biomed. Signal Process. Control **75**, 103572 (2022)
23. Jomaa, M.R., Mathkour, H., Bazi, Y., Islam, M.S.: End-to-End deep learning fusion of fingerprint and electrocardiogram signals for presentation attack detection. Sensors **20**, 2085 (2020)
24. Zhao, Y., Wu, R., Dong, H.: Unpaired image-to-image translation using adversarial consistency loss. In: Vedaldi, A., Bischof, H., Brox, T., Frahm, J.-M. (eds.) ECCV 2020. LNCS, vol. 12354, pp. 800–815(2020)

Bridging Synthetic and Real Domains for Face Presentation Attack Detection via Entropy-Regularized Alignment

Lin Li, Wenjun Wang, and Meiling Fang[✉]

College of Information and Artificial Intelligence (College of Industrial Software),
Yangzhou University, Yangzhou, China
`meiling.fang@yzu.edu.cn`

Abstract. Face presentation attack detection (PAD) is critical for securing face recognition systems against presentation attacks. Recent advances have explored synthetic data as a promising alternative to mitigate privacy concerns and the limited availability of real data. However, models trained solely on synthetic data often suffer from performance degradation due to distribution shifts when applied to real domains. In this work, we propose an entropy-regularized multi-level feature alignment framework that leverages labeled synthetic data and unlabeled real samples for domain-adaptive training. By encouraging feature consistency across domains and promoting confident predictions on real inputs, the proposed method effectively bridges the synthetic-to-real gap. Extensive experiments on public benchmarks demonstrate superior generalization performance compared to existing approaches, highlighting its potential for practical deployment in real-world face PAD systems.

Keywords: Face Presentation Attack Detection · Domain adaptation · Synthetic Data

1 Introduction

Face presentation attack detection (PAD) [1,2] is a fundamental component in securing face recognition systems against presentation attacks (PAs), such as printed photos, replayed videos, and 3D masks. With the increasing adoption of face recognition in sensitive applications including mobile payments, device authentication, and border control, the robustness and generalization ability of face PAD systems have become more important than ever. While deep learning has significantly advanced the face PAD performance, its effectiveness largely depends on the availability of large-scale, diverse, and well-annotated real-world data. Recent advances in data-centric machine learning [3] highlight the importance of improving model generalization through better data design rather than solely relying on model architecture. However, acquiring such datasets remains a major challenge. One key reason is that individuals are often unwilling to

W. Jia et al. (Eds.): CCBR 2025, LNCS 16360, pp. 482–492, 2026.
https://doi.org/10.1007/978-981-95-6123-0_45

share facial data due to growing concerns about privacy and the potential misuse of biometric information [4]. In addition, constructing attack samples such as printed photos, replayed videos, or 3D masks is time-consuming and requires considerable resources. As a result, existing face PAD datasets are often limited in scale, captured in controlled laboratory environments [5–8], or collected from the internet with uncertain provenance [9]. These limitations reduce data diversity and raise privacy concerns, constraining the development of models that generalize well to unseen domains and attack types.

To address the limited availability of real-world data, data augmentation has become a core strategy for enhancing the domain generalization of face PAD models. Recent works have proposed augmentation techniques at both the feature and image levels. To address the limited availability of real-world data, data augmentation has become a core strategy for enhancing the domain generalization of face anti-spoofing models. Recent works have proposed augmentation techniques at both the feature [10,11] and image levels [12,13]. At the feature level, Yang et al. [10] proposed a style transfer-based augmentation framework that generates intermediate samples across domains using the realistic stylization method. Chen et al. [11] decomposed images into statistical and spatial components and recombined them via a Cartesian product to produce samples that preserve bona fide identity cues while approximating the bona fide data distribution. At the image level, Wang et al. [12] introduced a negative sample augmentation strategy that converts bona fide face images into synthetic spoof samples by applying a combination of color jitter and color masking. Cai et al. [13] proposed a physics-based data augmentation framework that simulates realistic attack cues such as printing noise, color distortion, and moiré patterns to enhance cross-domain generalization. In addition, synthetic data generation has attracted increasing attention. Generative models are used to produce large-scale, photorealistic, and privacy-preserving datasets without relying on real user identities [14]. For example, recent work [15–17] has demonstrated the use of synthetic data to train models for different biometric tasks. Although synthetic data provides a scalable and privacy-friendly alternative, models trained exclusively on such data still suffer from noticeable performance drops when applied to real-world scenarios. This degradation is mainly caused by the domain gap between synthetic and real data. Differences in visual textures, scene complexity, and attack characteristics often result in models overfitting to synthetic patterns, limiting their effectiveness in authentic settings.

To mitigate this domain gap in PAD, we introduce a domain adaptation framework designed to enhance generalization from synthetic to real domains, named ERMLA (Entropy-Regularized Multi-level Alignment). ERMLA makes use of labeled synthetic data and unlabeled real samples to learn domain-invariant representations and improve prediction confidence on real inputs. By aligning features at multiple levels of the backbone network and applying entropy-based regularization to the prediction space, our method provides a simple yet effective solution for face PAD without requiring any real-world annotations.

Our main contributions are as follows: 1) we address the generalization challenge of synthetic-supervised face PAD and propose a unified framework that bridges the domain gap without relying on real-world annotations. 2) we introduce a multi-level feature alignment strategy that captures hierarchical PAD-related features, leading to more robust domain adaptation compared to single-layer approaches. 3) we propose an entropy-based regularization mechanism that promotes confident predictions on real samples, enhancing adaptation to real scenarios. 4) extensive experiments on several face PAD benchmarks validate the effectiveness of our method.

2   Methodology

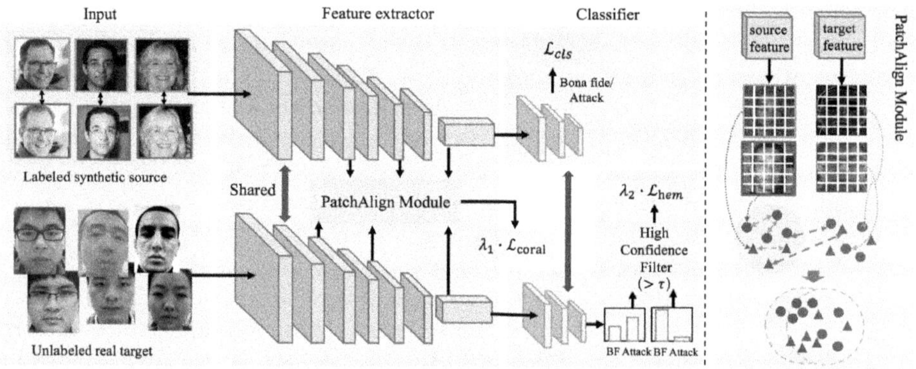

Fig. 1. An overview of the proposed ERMLA framework. It consists of a backbone encoder, class-conditional patch-level feature alignment, and entropy regularization on high-confidence target samples.

To address the domain gap between labeled synthetic data and unlabeled real images in face PAD, we propose a novel synthetic-supervised adaptation framework via Entropy-Regularized Multi-Level feature Alignment, i.e., **ERMLA**. As illustrated in Fig. 1, the framework is composed of a shared feature extraction backbone and two domain adaptation components: the class-conditional patch alignment (PatchAlign) module and the High-Confidence Entropy Minimization (HEM) module. The extracted hierarchical features from both source and target domains are first aligned at patch level across multiple layers to mitigate spatial discrepancies. In parallel, the prediction entropy of target samples is regularized based on confidence filtering, encouraging more reliable pseudo-labels. The entire system is optimized by jointly minimizing PAD classification loss, alignment loss, and entropy loss to achieve robust domain adaptation.

Class-Conditional Patch Alignment (PatchAlign). A key challenge in domain adaptation in our case arises from the complex structure of domain discrepancies under synthetic data training scenario. Specifically, two types of domain gaps co-exist: (1) the domain shift from synthetic to real-world data, and (2) the semantic gap between attack cues captured by using different sensors. Existing domain alignment methods, such as Maximum Mean Discrepancy (MMD) [18] and CORrelation ALignment (CORAL) [19], primarily perform global feature alignment by minimizing domain-level distributional shifts. However, these methods often overlook localized attack cues and class-conditional feature structures, which are essential for distinguishing subtle attack patterns. As a result, their generalization to real target domains is suboptimal.

To address the above challenge, we design a class-conditional patch alignment module that explicitly aligns local features between the source and target domains in a class-aware manner. Since the target domain lacks labels, we partition the source features into bona fide and attack classes and perform patch-level alignment between each source class and the target samples. This strategy relies on a soft class-consistency assumption across domains, enabling the model to align discriminative local semantic patterns that are indicative of attack. Although the source domain is fully labeled, class-wise patch processing also encourages intra-class local consistency, benefiting representation learning. By preserving class-specific structures during local alignment, our method mitigates the semantic gap between synthetic and real domains and improves robustness under real-world deployment scenarios.

Specifically, given intermediate feature maps $f^{(k)} \in \mathbb{R}^{B \times C_k \times H_k \times W_k}$ extracted from multiple backbone layers $k \in \mathcal{K}$, we partition them into non-overlapping local patches and flatten each patch into a 2D matrix $P^{(k)} \in \mathbb{R}^{N_k \times d_k}$, where N_k and d_k are the number and dimension of patches at layer k, respectively. In the source domain, we group patch features by bona fide/attack class $c \in \{0, 1\}$, using ground-truth labels. Each source class distribution is then aligned with the unlabeled target patch distribution via CORAL [19]. Compared to MMD [18], CORAL [19] offers a more memory-efficient solution for estimating distribution discrepancy, which fits well with our patch-level alignment setting.

$$\mathcal{L}_{\text{coral}}^{(k,c)} = \frac{1}{4d_k^2} \left\| \Sigma_s^{(k,c)} - \Sigma_t^{(k)} \right\|_F^2 , \tag{1}$$

where $\Sigma_s^{(k,c)}$ is the covariance matrix of source domain patch features for class c at layer k, and $\Sigma_t^{(k)}$ is the covariance matrix computed from all target domain patch features at the same layer. The final patch-level alignment loss aggregates over both class and layer dimensions with layer-specific weights:

$$\mathcal{L}_{\text{coral}} = \sum_{k \in \mathcal{K}} \alpha_k \sum_{c \in \{0,1\}} \mathcal{L}_{\text{coral}}^{(k,c)}, \tag{2}$$

where α_k denotes the importance weight for layer k, reflecting its semantic level. In our implementation, deeper layers are assigned larger weights (e.g., $\alpha_{\text{low}} < \alpha_{\text{mid}} < \alpha_{\text{high}}$) to emphasize more semantically informative features.

By performing class-aware patch alignment across multiple semantic levels, our method captures both fine-grained texture patterns and high-level discriminative cues. This multi-scale design improves the preservation of class-specific semantics and narrows the domain gap between synthetic and real distributions.

High-Confidence Entropy Minimization (HEM). Another critical challenge in the target domain is the absence of ground-truth labels, which prevents the direct application of supervised learning objectives. Although entropy minimization has been widely adopted to encourage confident predictions on unlabeled data, applying it uniformly across all target samples may amplify low-confidence or incorrect predictions, leading to negative adaptation. To overcome this limitation, we propose a high-confidence entropy minimization module that selectively applies entropy regularization only to target samples with sufficiently confident predictions.

Given the softmax output $p_i^t \in \mathbb{R}^C$ for a target image, we identify high-confidence samples by thresholding the maximum predicted class probability. Formally, the selected set is defined as:

$$\mathcal{M} = \left\{ i \,\middle|\, \max_j p_i^t(j) > \tau \right\}, \tag{3}$$

where τ is a confidence threshold. The entropy loss is then computed over this filtered set as:

$$\mathcal{L}_{\text{hem}} = -\frac{1}{|\mathcal{M}|} \sum_{i \in \mathcal{M}} \sum_j p_i^t(j) \log p_i^t(j). \tag{4}$$

By focusing on samples with confident predictions, the HEM module avoids reinforcing uncertain or noisy supervision signals. This confidence-aware filtering mechanism enables the model to sharpen decision boundaries based on reliable feedback, resulting in improved pseudo-label quality and more robust feature learning. Ultimately, this selective entropy minimization enhances the model's generalization ability under domain shift.

Training Strategy. During training, the source domain batches are constructed using balanced pairs of bona fide and attack samples from the same identity. This pairing strategy implicitly introduces a form of contrastive supervision, encouraging the model to capture identity-invariant yet PAD discriminative features. By comparing boan fide and attack samples from the same subject, the network learns to focus on subtle acttack artifacts while disregarding subject-specific variations. On the other hand, target domain samples are sampled randomly without label or identity constraints, reflecting the unlabeled and diverse nature of real-world deployment. This asymmetry in sampling mirrors the practical domain gap, while our loss design ensures that both domains contribute effectively to representation learning.

The full training objective integrates three components: the classification loss on labeled source data, the patch-level alignment loss between source and target domains, and the entropy minimization loss on confident target samples. The complete loss is defined as:

$$\mathcal{L}_{\text{total}} = \mathcal{L}_{\text{cls}} + \lambda_1 \cdot \mathcal{L}_{\text{coral}} + \lambda_2 \cdot \mathcal{L}_{\text{hem}}, \tag{5}$$

where λ_1 and λ_2 are trade-off hyperparameters controlling the contributions of alignment and entropy regularization. This joint optimization encourages the network to learn features that are both discriminative for attack detection and robust across domains.

3 Experiments

Datasets. To evaluate the effectiveness of our proposed ERMLA framework, we conduct extensive experiments using both synthetic and real-world face PAD datasets. Specifically, we utilize a large-scale synthetic dataset for training, and four widely-used real-world benchmarks for cross-domain evaluation. We adopt the publicly available SynthASpoof dataset [15] as the synthetic training source. SynthASpoof was originally introduced to promote the development of privacy-preserving face PAD techniques. It consists of 25,000 bona fide samples generated using StyleGAN2-ADA, and 78,800 attack samples acquired by presenting these synthetic identities through physical media (e.g., printed photos and replayed screens) to three different capture sensors. This setup enables realistic modeling of common attack scenarios while maintaining user privacy, as no real identities are involved in the dataset construction. To evaluate the generalization ability of models trained on synthetic data, we adopt four public face PAD datasets captured in real-world environments: Oulu-NPU [7], CASIA-MFSD [6], MSU-MFSD [5], and Idiap Replay-Attack [8]. These datasets cover a wide range of presentation attack types and acquisition conditions: Oulu-NPU [7] features high-resolution video clips collected under controlled lighting and different environments, including varied illumination and background. CASIA-MFSD [6] and MSU-MFSD [5]contain video-based recordings of printed photo and replay attacks, captured using diverse cameras and devices. Idiap Replay-Attack [8]includes both controlled and adverse scenarios, simulating realistic attack conditions through printed and video-based attacks. These datasets are widely used as target domains in synthetic-to-real generalization studies due to their overlap in attack types (e.g., print and replay) and the presence of potentially learnable attack-specific cues, making them suitable for evaluating the cross-domain transferability of synthetic-supervised methods.

Implementation Details. Following the protocols [15,20,21], we prepared training and testing data based on both synthetic and real-world datasets. For real-world datasets, 25 frames were uniformly sampled from each video to capture temporal diversity. All face regions were detected and cropped using the MTCNN detector, and resized to $224 \times 224 \times 224$ pixels. During training, we employed a balanced sampling strategy to maintain a 1:1 ratio between bona fide and attack samples. Data augmentation techniques including JPEG compression, Gaussian blur, color jittering, and random rotation were applied with a certain probability to improve generalization. We implemented our method

Table 1. Cross-domain performance comparison on four unseen target datasets: Replay-Attack, CASIA-FASD, OULU-NPU, and MSU-MFSD. We report AUC (%) ↑ and HTER (%) ↓ for each method. All models are trained on the same source domain.

Method	MSU-MFSD		CASIA-FASD		Replay Attack		OULU-NPU		AVG	
	AUC ↑	HTER ↓	AUC ↑	HTER ↓	AUC ↑	HTER ↓	AUC ↑	HTER ↓	AUC ↑	HTER ↓
ResNet [15]	79.54	25.48	62.00	39.22	96.96	8.90	71.48	31.48	77.50	26.27
PixBis [15]	63.87	38.33	64.79	38.44	96.88	7.50	67.71	35.77	73.31	30.01
CoDe-Lc [20]	71.45	37.14	69.08	37.11	95.31	12.10	66.30	37.58	75.54	30.98
CoDe-Lh [20]	70.58	39.05	63.70	39.33	93.84	13.90	68.33	38.11	74.11	32.60
OrthPADNet [20]	87.59	20.95	67.32	39.78	79.55	23.70	71.69	34.92	76.54	29.84
Co-Former A [20]	90.76	18.57	64.49	41.11	92.31	16.30	86.44	21.67	83.50	24.21
Co-Former B [20]	**91.61**	**16.67**	63.05	40.00	88.20	18.80	82.02	25.35	81.22	25.21
ViT-SIDE [20]	69.78	36.67	75.21	33.33	96.67	9.80	**94.04**	**13.26**	83.93	23.26
FoundPAD B [21]	66.18	47.14	83.03	27.33	90.79	16.15	73.56	33.12	78.39	30.94
FoundPAD L [21]	69.76	45.71	**96.03**	**9.89**	**98.58**	**6.40**	75.69	32.05	85.01	23.51
ERMLA (ours)	87.11	21.13	79.47	29.10	94.29	10.37	92.60	14.65	**88.37**	**18.81**

using PyTorch. The backbone of our model is a ResNet-18 [22], initialized with ImageNet-pretrained weights. The optimizer used was Adam with a learning rate of 1e-4. The batch size was set to 256, and the training lasted for 70 epochs. We set the confidence threshold $\tau = 0.8$ to select high-confidence target samples for entropy regularization. The weights for low-level, mid-level, and high-level patch alignment losses are set to 0.1, 0.3, and 0.6, respectively, reflecting the increasing relevance of deeper layers in capturing discriminative features for PAD. The trade-off coefficients for the patch alignment and entropy loss terms are set as $\lambda_1 = 0.3$ and $\lambda_2 = 0.1$, respectively. In the evaluation phase, video-level predictions were obtained by averaging the softmax scores of all frames from the same video. We used the mean score as the final PAD decision.

Evaluation Metrics. To evaluate the performance of our method in cross-domain scenarios, we adopt standard metrics used in face PAD studies [13,23–25]. We report the Area Under the Receiver Operating Characteristic Curve (AUC) and the Half Total Error Rate (HTER), where HTER is computed as the average of the Attack Presentation Classification Error Rate (APCER) and the Bona Fide Presentation Classification Error Rate (BPCER) [26]. These metrics reflect the model's ability to generalize from synthetic training data to real-world attack scenarios.

4   Results

Comparison with SOTA. Table 1 presents the PAD performance comparison on four unseen target datasets. All models are trained on a fixed source domain and evaluated without access to any target domain labels. We report both AUC (%) and HTER (%) as evaluation metrics. Our proposed method, ERMLA, achieves the best overall average performance across all target datasets, outperforming prior methods. Notably, ERMLA achieves a competitive AUC of 92.60% and a low HTER of 14.65% on OULU-NPU, while also maintaining strong generalization on the other datasets. These results validate the effectiveness of our class-conditional patch alignment and high-confidence entropy regularization, particularly in bridging the synthetic-to-real domain gap for face PAD.

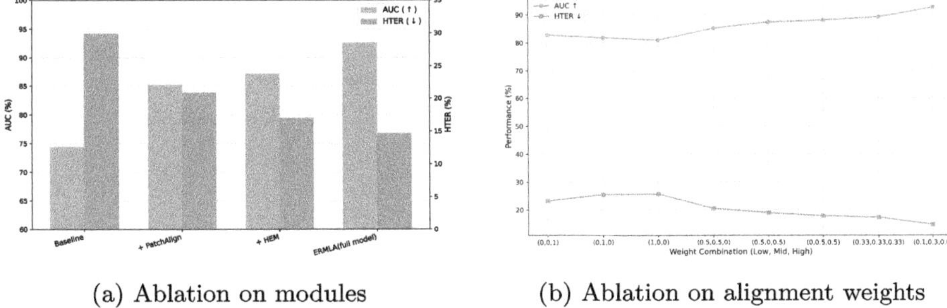

(a) Ablation on modules   (b) Ablation on alignment weights

Fig. 2. Ablation studies on modules and combination of feauture alignment weights. The blue is AUC (%) and the red is HTER (%). (Color figure online)

Ablation Studies. To investigate the contributions of each module in our framework, we conduct ablation studies on two modules and feature-level alignment weights on OULU-NPU dataset, as illustrated in Fig. 2. In the left plot, each component yields noticeable performance gains, and their combination achieves the best results. In the right plot, we analyze the impact of different alignment weight configurations across low-, mid-, and high-level features. We observe that giving higher weight to deeper features improves performance, and our default setting (0.1, 0.3, 0.6) achieves the best trade-off performance.

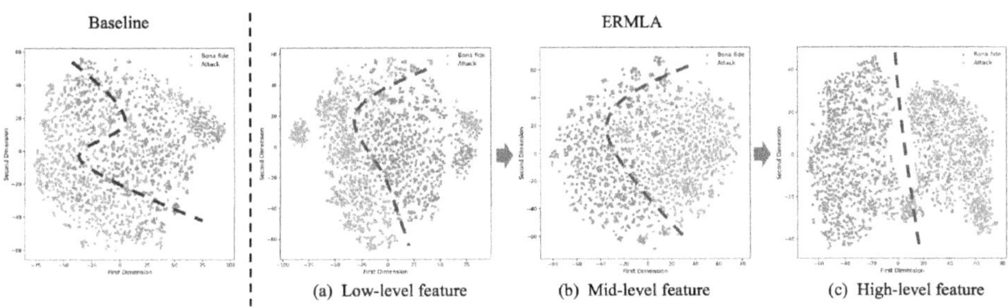

Fig. 3. t-SNE visualization of feature distributions for baseline (left) and our proposed ERMLA model (right). The right three plots correspond to features from multi-level layers of the proposed ERMLA method.

Visual Analysis. To further validate the effectiveness of our multi-level patch alignment strategy, we visualize the learned feature distributions using t-SNE on the target domain (OULU-NPU). We randomly sample 1500 bona fide and 1500 attack examples from the target domain and project their features onto a 2D space. As illustrated in Fig. 3, the baseline model without alignment exhibits overlap between the two classes, indicating weak discriminability. As patch alignment is applied at multi-level layers, the intra-class compactness improves while inter-class boundaries become more distinct. This gradual enhancement confirms the importance of aligning hierarchical features, especially those from higher layers that capture class-discriminative cues. The superior separation in the final stage suggests that our layer-weighted alignment strategy is critical for learning general and transferable PAD representations.

5   Conclusion

This paper introduced ERMLA, a novel face PAD framework that combines entropy-regularized multi-level alignment to mitigate the challenging domain gap between synthetic and real-world data. Built entirely on synthetic training data, our method advances a data-centric paradigm in which synthetic supervision serves as a practical and ethical foundation for training generalizable PAD systems. We proposed a class-conditional patch alignment module that performs second-order alignment of local features across multiple semantic levels, effectively preserving class-specific attack patterns while reducing cross-domain discrepancies. In addition, a high-confidence entropy minimization strategy is employed to selectively regularize target predictions, encouraging confident and discriminative decision boundaries. Extensive experiments on four public benchmarks demonstrate the effectiveness of our approach in real-world scenarios.

Acknowledgment. This work was supported by the China Postdoctoral Science Foundation under Grant No. 2024M762739 and the Yangzhou Green Yang Golden Phoenix Program Project under Grant No. YZLYJFJH2023YXBS131.

References

1. Yu, Z., Qin, Y., Li, X., Zhao, C., Lei, Z., Zhao, G.: Deep learning for face anti-spoofing: a survey. IEEE Trans. Pattern Anal. Mach. Intell. **45**(5), 5609–5631 (2023)
2. Hernandez-Ortega, J., Fierrez, J., Morales, A., Galbally, J. In: Introduction to Presentation Attack Detection in Face Biometrics and Recent Advances, 3rd edn. Springer (2023)
3. Zha, D., et al.: Data-centric artificial intelligence: a survey. ACM Comput. Surv. **57**(5), 129:1–129:42 (2025)
4. César Augusto Fontanillo López and Abdullah Elbi: On synthetic data: a brief introduction for data protection law dummies (2022)

5. Wen, D., Han, H., Jain, A.K.: Face spoof detection with image distortion analysis. IEEE Trans. Inf. Forensics Secur. **10**(4), 746–761 (2015)

6. Zhang, Z., Yan, J., Liu, S., Lei, Z., Yi, D., Li, S.Z.: A face antispoofing database with diverse attacks. In: ICB, pp. 26–31. IEEE (2012)

7. Boulkenafet, Z., Komulainen, J., Li, L., Feng, X., Hadid, A.: OULU-NPU: a mobile face presentation attack database with real-world variations. In: FG. IEEE Computer Society (2017)

8. Chingovska, I., Anjos, A., Marcel, S.: On the effectiveness of local binary patterns in face anti-spoofing. In: BIOSIG, LNI. vol. P-196, 1–7. GI (2012)

9. Zhang, Y., et al.: CelebA-spoof: large-scale face anti-spoofing dataset with rich annotations. In: Vedaldi, A., Bischof, H., Brox, T., Frahm, J.-M. (eds.) ECCV 2020. LNCS, vol. 12357, pp. 70–85. Springer, Cham (2020). https://doi.org/10. 1007/978-3-030-58610-2_5

10. Yang, B., Zhang, J., Yin, Z., Shao, J.: Few-shot domain expansion for face anti-spoofing. CoRR abs/2106.14162 (2021)

11. Chen, C., Li, Y., Zhang, J., Liu, J., Wang, C.: Generative data augmentation with liveness information preserving for face anti-spoofing. In: ICMR, pp. 302–310. ACM (2024)

12. Wang, W., Liu, P., Zheng, H., Ying, R., Wen, F.: Domain generalization for face anti-spoofing via negative data augmentation. IEEE Trans. Inf. Forensics Secur. **18**, 2333–2344 (2023)

13. Cai, R., Soh, C., Yu, Z., Li, H., Yang, W., Kot, A.C.: Towards data-centric face anti-spoofing: improving cross-domain generalization via physics-based data synthesis. Int. J. Comput. Vis. **133**(4), 1689–1710 (2025)

14. Qiu, H., Yu, B., Gong, D., Li, Z., Liu, W., Tao, D.: SynFace: face recognition with synthetic data. In: ICCV, pp. 10860–10870. IEEE (2021)

15. Fang, M., Huber, M., Damer, N.: SynthASpoof: developing face presentation attack detection based on privacy-friendly synthetic data. In: IEEE/CVF Conference on Computer Vision and Pattern Recognition, CVPR 2023 - Workshops, Vancouver, BC, Canada, 17–24 June 2023, pp. 1061–1070. IEEE (2023)

16. Boutros, F., Struc, V., Fierrez, J., Damer, N.: Synthetic data for face recognition: current state and future prospects. Image Vis. Comput. **135**, 104688 (2023)

17. Damer, N., López, C.A.F., Fang, M., Spiller, N., Pham, M.V., Boutros, F.: Privacy-friendly synthetic data for the development of face morphing attack detectors. In: IEEE/CVF Conference on Computer Vision and Pattern Recognition Workshops, CVPR Workshops 2022, New Orleans, LA, USA, 19–20 June 2022, pp. 1605–1616. IEEE (2022)

18. Gretton, A., Borgwardt, K.M., Rasch, M.J., Schölkopf, B., Smola, A.J.: A kernel two-sample test. J. Mach. Learn. Res. **13**, 723–773 (2012)

19. Sun, B., Feng, J., Saenko, K.: Return of frustratingly easy domain adaptation. In: AAAI, pp. 2058–2065. AAAI Press (2016)

20. Fang, M., et al.: Synfacepad 2023: Competition on face presentation attack detection based on privacy-aware synthetic training data. In: IEEE International Joint Conference on Biometrics, IJCB 2023, Ljubljana, Slovenia, 25–28 September 2023, pp. 1–11. IEEE (2023)

21. Ozgur, G., Caldeira, E., Chettaoui, T., Boutros, F., Ramachandra, R., Damer, N.: FoundPAD: foundation models reloaded for face presentation attack detection. In: IEEE/CVF Winter Conference on Applications of Computer Vision, WACV 2025 - Workshops, Tucson, AZ, USA, 28 February–4 March 2025, pp. 697–707. IEEE (2025)

22. He, K., Zhang, X., Ren, S., Sun, J.: Deep residual learning for image recognition. In: Proceedings of the IEEE Conference on Computer Vision and Pattern Recognition, pp. 770–778 (2016)
23. Liu, Y., Stehouwer, J., Jourabloo, A., Liu, X.: Deep tree learning for zero-shot face anti-spoofing. In: IEEE Conference on Computer Vision and Pattern Recognition, CVPR 2019, Long Beach, CA, USA, 16–20 June 2019, pp. 4680–4689. Computer Vision Foundation/IEEE (2019)
24. Yu, Z., Qin, Y., Zhao, H., Li, X., Zhao, G.: Dual-cross central difference network for face anti-spoofing. In: Proceedings of the Thirtieth International Joint Conference on Artificial Intelligence, IJCAI 2021, Virtual Event/Montreal, Canada, pp. 1281–1287. ijcai.org (2021)
25. Wang, G., Han, H., Shan, S., Chen, X.: Unsupervised adversarial domain adaptation for cross-domain face presentation attack detection. IEEE Trans. Inf. Forensics Secur. **16**, 56–69 (2021)
26. International Organization for Standardization: ISO/IEC DIS 30107-3:2016: Information Technology – Biometric presentation attack detection – P. 3: Testing and reporting (2017)

Adapting Vision Transformer with Dual Stream Token Difference for Mobile Face Anti-spoofing

Liepiao Zhang[1], Kun Liu[1], Junduan Huang[2], Zitong Yu[3], and Wenxiong Kang[1(✉)]

[1] South China University of Technology, Guangzhou, China
auwxkang@scut.edu.cn
[2] South China Normal University, Foshan, China
[3] Great Bay University, Dongguan, China

Abstract. In recent years, Vision Transformers (ViTs) have gained increasing attention in the field of face anti-spoofing. However, most methods use ViT-Base (over 86M parameters), which is unsuitable or inefficient for mobile/embedded deployment. While MobileViT reduces size vs. ViT-Base, its direct application to face anti-spoofing shows suboptimal generalization. To tackle this problem, we adopt MobileViT as a lightweight backbone and propose a novel dual-stream token difference adapter for fine-tuning. Our proposed adapter captures fine-grained information from dual directions, enhancing the model's adaptation ability. Extensive intra-domain and cross-domain experiments show our method's effectiveness.

Keywords: Face anti-spoofing · vision transformer · adapter

1 Introduction

Face recognition has been widely applied in various scenarios such as mobile access control, self-service terminals, and electronic payments. Despite its great success, face recognition systems remain vulnerable to presentation attacks [1,2], including printed photos, video replays, and 3D masks. To address these threats, researchers have developed a series of face anti-spoofing (FAS) algorithms.

With the rise of deep learning, numerous approaches [3,4] have employed convolutional neural networks (CNNs) for FAS tasks because of CNNs' capability in learning local features. However, some correlated spoofing artifacts may not be together in a local area. Thus, the features could be non-local. To further improve generalization capability, recent research works have been shifting to Vision Transformer [5–7]. With the self-attention mechanism [5,8], Vision Transformer (ViT) is able to learn non-local features from image tokens for classification.

However, existing works of using ViT for FAS mainly use the ViT-Base model, which contains 86 million parameters and requires over 700 MB of storage or

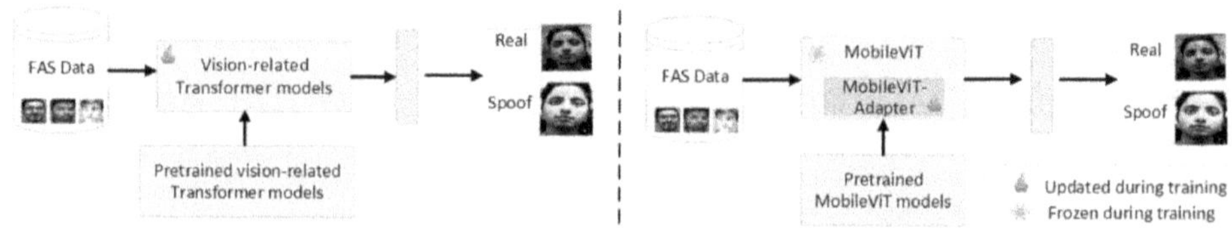

Fig. 1. *Left:* In traditional transfer learning, pretrained vision-related Transformer models are used for initialization, and the entire or most of the model parameters are fine-tuned. *Right:* Our proposed MobileViT-Adapter embedded in MobileViT with pretrained parameters fixed and only adapter parameters updated during training.

memory. Such computational and storage demands are difficult to meet in edge computing scenarios—such as mobile phones, smart door locks, and embedded systems—where hardware resources are often severely constrained. These devices typically have limited memory and computational capacity, and may not be equipped with dedicated GPUs or accelerators. Moreover, large models tend to consume more power and require longer inference times, which is particularly problematic for battery-powered devices where energy efficiency and real-time responsiveness are critical. Therefore, it is essential to design lightweight and efficient models that can maintain high accuracy while operating within the strict resource and latency constraints of edge environments.

To enable the deployment of lightweight Vision Transformer (ViT) on edge devices, we explore the use of MobileViT [9] for the face anti-spoofing (FAS) task. MobileViT is a light-weight variant of transformers. However, through our experiments, we observe that directly fine-tuning an ImageNet pre-trained MobileViT yields unsatisfactory performance on FAS benchmarks, especially when the dataset size is small. This is primarily due to the limited size of FAS data, whereas ViTs [10], as Transformer-based models, are typically more effective when trained on large-scale datasets. Consequently, directly training ViTs on small FAS datasets often leads to suboptimal convergence and poor task adaptation.

Inspired by recent research on parameter-efficient fine-tuning (PEFT), we propose to integrate adapter modules into MobileViT. As depicted in Fig. 1, during fine-tuning, the parameters of the pre-trained backbone are frozen, and only the lightweight adapter parameters are updated. This strategy mitigates overfitting on limited data and enables efficient domain adaptation with minimal computational cost. While prior works have explored convolution-based adapters for ViT [11], we observe that they often fail to capture sufficient fine-grained details. To address this, we introduce a **D**ual Stream Token **D**ifference Adapter (D^2-Adapter) tailored for MobileViT. Specifically, we extract token embeddings from intermediate layers and reconstruct the 1D tokens into spatial representations. The D^2-Adapter then computes first-order gradient information in both horizontal-vertical and diagonal directions from these spatial tokens. This enhances MobileViT's ability to capture non-local fine-grained features, promoting better generalization while maintaining a low computational footprint. To validate the effectiveness of the proposed D^2-Adapter for MobileViT, we conduct extensive intra-domain and cross-domain experiments. We show that our D^2-Adapter improves MobileViT significantly in both intra-domain experiments and cross-domain experiments. Our contribution involves: 1) we investigate the effectiveness of MobileViT for the face anti-spoofing in both intra-domain and cross-domain scenarios; 2) We propose D^2-Adapter for face anti-spoofing for efficiently adapting MobileViT for face anti-spoofing, significantly improving the generalization performance in both scenarios with very few extra computational cost.

2   Related Works

There have been various deep learning methods for Face anti-spoofing. Previous works are mainly about CNN. For example, Yu et al. [12] proposed the Central Difference Convolutional Network (CDCN) and the Bilateral Convolutional Network (BCN) [13], which leverage depth and reflection maps generated by auxiliary models [14,15] to enhance pixel-level supervision and improve discrimination in FAS. Liu et al. [16] introduced the Spoof Trace Disentanglement Network (STDN), consisting of a generator and multi-scale discriminators trained via adversarial learning to disentangle spoof traces from input images, thereby improving model interpretability. Wang et al. [17] further proposed a two-stage disentangled representation learning framework that effectively isolates spoof patterns and enhances training stability. To further enhance the generalization capability, specific optimization methods have been studied to enhance CNN methods, such as single-side contrastive learning [18], Adaptive Normalized Representation Learning [19], Shuffled Style Assembling [20], feature separability and Alignment [21], meta learning [22], and so on.

While CNNs are effective at extracting local features, another competitive architecture with non-local feature learning capabilities, the Vision Transformer (ViT) [5], has also been explored for face anti-spoofing. ViT employs a self-attention mechanism to compute token embeddings for subsequent layers. Unlike CNNs, each output token in ViT can attend to all input tokens, rather than just a local region. This ability to capture long-range dependencies is referred to as *non-local learning*. Although ViT has surpassed CNN in the ImageNet benchmark, previous works [7,23] found that directly fine-tuning a pretrained ViT for FAS is not satisfactory. To efficiently leverage pre-trained ViT models, prior works [7, 23] have introduced adapter modules for ViT. However, these methods primarily rely on ViT-Base as the backbone, which contains over 86 million parameters and is unsuitable for deployment on edge devices. In this work, we investigate the performance of lightweight ViT models and propose novel methods to enhance their effectiveness.

3   Methodology

To address the challenges of constrained computational cost on edge devices, we explore the effectiveness of using MobileViT as the backbone. Moreover, we propose and integrate D^2-Adapter with MobileViT to enhance the cross-domain generalization capability, while still maintaining the compact design.

In the remaining part of this section, we first introduce the structure of MobileViT. Then, we describe the design of D^2-Adapter tailored for MobileViT and face anti-spoofing.

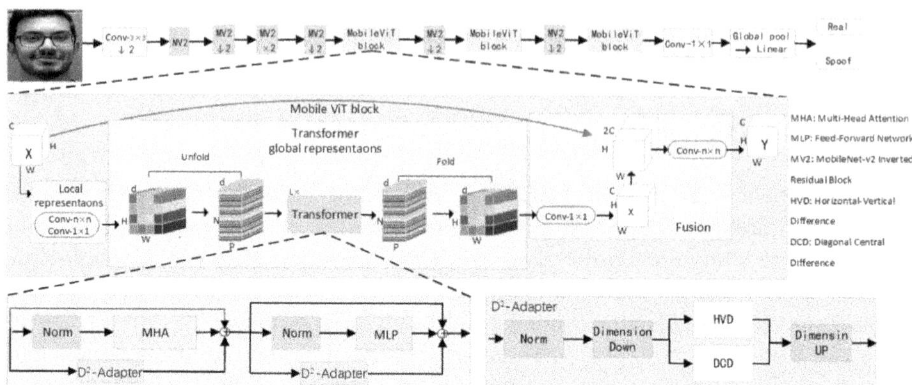

Fig. 2. MobileViT consists of L MobileViT blocks. In each block, our D^2-Adapter is inserted into the MHA and the MLP as a skip connection, sharing the same inputs. Within the D^2-Adapter, the input tokens are first projected into a lower-dimensional space, where they are processed by the HVD and DCD modules to extract horizontal-vertical and diagonal gradient information, respectively. The extracted features are then fused and projected back to the original dimensional space, forming the output of the MobileViT block.

3.1 Preliminary of MobileViT

Vision Transformer (ViT) is powered by the self-attention mechanisms, which help to extract non-local features. The self-attention layers involve abundant matrix multiplication, which is time-consuming and not friendly to edge devices. To reduce model size, the MobileViT [9] can maintain the self-attention mechanism but reduce multiplications by downsampling the feature maps.

The structure of MobileViT is illustrated in Fig. 2. The input feature map is first processed by convolution layers to encode local spatial information. Then, a point-wise convolution projects it into a high-dimensional space. The feature map is partitioned into a sequence of patches, which are fed into multiple Transformer modules to capture global dependencies. The transformed features are then projected back and fused to produce the output. For more details, please refer to [9].

In Vision Transformer (ViT) [10], there are typically N feed-forward Transformer blocks. The i-th block can be formalized as a feature extractor $\mathcal{W}_i^B$. Each block usually consists of a Multi-Head Attention (MHA) module $\mathcal{W}_i^{\text{MHA}}$

and a Multi-Layer Perceptron (MLP) module $\mathcal{W}_i^{\mathrm{MLP}}$, each followed by normalization and nonlinear activation layers. By omitting residual connections, normalization, and activation layers for clarity, the forward process of each Transformer block can be formalized as:

$$\mathbf{Y} = \mathcal{W}_i^{B}(\mathbf{X}) = \mathcal{W}_i^{\mathrm{MLP}}\left(\mathcal{W}_i^{\mathrm{MHA}}(\mathbf{X})\right),$$

where $\mathbf{X}$ denotes the input sequence to a Transformer block, and Y the corresponding output sequence.

3.2   Design of the Proposed $\mathbf{D}^2$-Adapter

In this work, we improve each MobileViT block by embedding the proposed D^2-Adapter module into the Transformer module. The overall modified framework is illustrated in Fig. 2. While we adopt MobileViT as the backbone for our method to maintain generality, it can be easily replaced with other lightweight Transformer-based architectures (e.g., ViT-Tiny from ViT [10]). In the experiments in Sect. 4, we present comparative results across different Transformer models to evaluate both domain generalization and model efficiency.

The structure of the D^2-Adapter module is shown at the bottom of Fig. 2. The D^2-Adapter module is inserted in parallel with the MobileViT block, sharing the same input tokens. This parallel connection allows the input to be simultaneously fed into the D^2-Adapter for a series of face anti-spoofing-related operations.

With the D^2-Adapter, the inference process in the i-th block is updated from Eq. (1) to Eq. (2):

$$\mathbf{Y} = \mathcal{W}_i^{\mathrm{MLP}}\left(\mathcal{A}_i^{\mathrm{MHA}}(\mathbf{X}) + \mathcal{W}_i^{\mathrm{MHA}}(\mathbf{X})\right) + \mathcal{A}_i^{\mathrm{MLP}}\left(\mathcal{A}_i^{\mathrm{MHA}}(\mathbf{X}) + \mathcal{W}_i^{\mathrm{MHA}}(\mathbf{X})\right), \quad (2)$$

where $\mathcal{A}_i^{\mathrm{MHA}}$ and $\mathcal{A}_i^{\mathrm{MLP}}$ denote the D^2-Adapter modules operating in parallel with the Multi-Head Attention (MHA) and Multi-Layer Perceptron (MLP) layers, respectively.

The pretrained weights of the MobileViT backbone based on ImageNet are readily available from open-source repositories. During implementation, $\mathcal{W}_i^{\mathrm{MHA}}$ and $\mathcal{W}_i^{\mathrm{MLP}}$ are initialized from the pretrained model and kept frozen during fine-tuning. In contrast, the inserted adapter modules $\mathcal{A}_i^{\mathrm{MHA}}$ and $\mathcal{A}_i^{\mathrm{MLP}}$ are randomly initialized and updated via backpropagation.

As shown in Eq. (2), the D^2-Adapter modules share the same input as the Transformer block. The D^2-Adapter first transforms the sequence token from the original embedding space into a new space that is more relevant for face anti-spoofing tasks.

To enhance feature discrimination for face anti-spoofing, we employ the Central Difference Convolution (CDC) [12], which integrates both standard convolution and a central difference term to capture subtle local variations. The CDC operation is defined as follows:

$$\mathbf{Z} = \sum_{P_n \in \mathcal{R}} \mathbf{w}(P_n) \cdot x(P_0 + P_n), \tag{3}$$

$$\mathbf{Z}_c = \sum_{P_n \in \mathcal{R}} \mathbf{w}(P_n) \cdot \left(x(P_0 + P_n) - x(P_0)\right), \tag{4}$$

$$\mathbf{Y}(P_0) = (1 - \theta) \cdot \mathbf{Z} + \theta \cdot \mathbf{Z}_c. \tag{5}$$

Equation (3) corresponds to standard convolution, Eq. (4) describes the difference convolution, and Eq. (5) is the generalized Central Difference Convolution (CDC) formulation. In the above equations, $\mathbf{x}$ denotes the input feature map, $\mathcal{R}$ represents the local receptive field, P_0 is the current spatial position in the input and output feature maps, and P_n enumerates the positions within the receptive field. The hyperparameter $\theta \in [0, 1]$ controls the relative contribution between standard convolution and central difference convolution when extracting features from the input map. Intuitively, θ balances the contribution of intensity-level and gradient-level information from the input image $\mathbf{x}$. Based on experimental results from [12], we set $\theta = 0.7$ in our implementation.

As MobileViT downsamples the tokens to reduce calculation, fine-grain information about subtle spoofing artifacts can be lost during the tokens downsampling. To tackle this problem, more fine-grain information extraction is needed. Inspired by [24], we design the D^2-Adapter by incorporating Horizontal-Vertical Difference (HVD) convolution and Diagonal Central Difference (DCD) convolution to extract Dual-stream central Difference information from tokens for MobileViT. For HVD, as shown in Eq. (3), the receptive field $\mathcal{R}$ is modified from a full square window to a "cross" shape, meaning that only the horizontal and vertical neighbors of P_n are used to compute the token difference. Similarly, DCD considers only the diagonal neighbors of P_n to compute the token difference. This design enables the model to capture directional gradient information from both horizontal-vertical and diagonal directions, thereby enriching the learned features for MobileViT. After applying HVD and DCD, we flatten the 2D feature map back into a 1D sequence. To preserve shape consistency, a nonlinear activation function is applied before the projection layer that restores the sequence dimension.

During training, we first utilize the pretrained weights to initialize the parameters. Then, we freeze the pretrained parameters by excluding them from the optimizer. We insert the D^2-Adapter into the backbone. The D^2-Adapter's parameters and the final classification head are randomly initialized and updated during the training.

4   Experiments

4.1   Experiment Setup

To validate the effectiveness of the proposed method, we conduct experiments on five publicly available face anti-spoofing datasets: OULU-NPU (O) [25], CASIA-MFSD (C) [26], Idiap Replay-Attack (I) [27], MSU-MFSD (M) [28], CelebA-Spoof [29]. For data processing, we use YOLO5Face [30] to localize faces. The localized faces are cropped and resized to 224×224 as input to the model.

All experiments are evaluated using Half Total Error Rate (HTER) and Area Under the Curve (AUC) as the performance metrics. We implement our method using the PyTorch 1.9 framework and conduct both training and testing on a single NVIDIA Tesla T4 GPU. The Adam optimizer is used with an initial learning rate of 0.0001.

4.2 Intra-domain Comparison

Although recent research works are mainly studying the cross-domain scenarios, the intra-domain experiments are still necessary for these scenarios. For example, in the scenario of self-service ATM machines, the model is put in a controlled indoor scenario, which can be considered as the intra-domain scenario. We conduct the intra-domain experiments to analyze the model performance. As can be seen from Table 1, the ViT-Base achieves an average HTER result of 1.62%, lower than two lightweight ViT backbones, CAS-ViT [31] and MobileViT. By inserting our D^2-Adapter with MobileViT, the average HTER result is significantly reduced from 2.52% to 0.58%. Also, our proposed adapter also works for other lightweight backbones and surpasses a larger ViT-Base model.

Table 1. Intra-domain experiments on the IDIAP Replay Attack, OULU-NPU, and CelebA-Spoof datasets. All results are in %.

Method	IDIAP Replay Attack		OULU-NPU		CelebA-Spoof		Avg.
	HTER	AUC	HTER	AUC	HTER	AUC	HTER
ViT-Base [5]	0.98	99.96	0.64	**99.98**	3.26	**99.56**	1.63
CAS-ViT [31]	1.02	99.78	0.46	**99.98**	4.36	98.94	1.95
MobileViT [32]	1.72	99.89	0.81	99.95	5.02	97.56	2.52
ViT-Tiny with CDC-Adapter (**Ours**)	0.55	99.86	0.45	99.97	2.10	99.52	1.03
MobileViT with CDC-Adapter (**Ours**)	0.56	99.98	0.41	**99.98**	1.25	98.76	0.74
ViT-Tiny with D^2-Adapter (**Ours**)	0.48	99.98	0.35	**99.98**	1.45	98.76	0.76
MobileViT with D^2-Adapter (**Ours**)	**0.24**	**99.99**	**0.26**	99.97	**1.24**	97.85	**0.58**

4.3 Cross-Domain Experiment

In Table 2, we compare our proposed D^2-Adapter and Mobile ViT with other existing methods. We can see that when directly finetuning MobileViT, the average HTER result is 22.93%. Although CAS-ViT [31] is more advanced than MobileViT, its average HTER is just about 1.5% lower than MobileViT, showing that the advanced lightweight design does not benefit much to the cross-domain generalization. By contrast, our D^2-Adapter can significantly improve the generalization performance with significantly lower HTER results over the 12 experiments.

Table 2. Cross-domain dataset comparison. "C" represents the CASIA dataset [26], "I" represents the IDIAP Replay Attack dataset [27], "M" represents the MSU dataset [28], and "O" represents the OULU-NPU dataset [25]. In the left of "to" is the training dataset and in the right is the testing dataset. The missing data is indicated by "–". "w/" is used to represent "with". All results are in %.

Method	C to I	C to M	C to O	I to C	I to M	I to O	M to C	M to I	M to O	O to C	O to I	O to M	Avg.
DRCN [33]	44.4	27.6	–	48.9	42	–	28.9	36.8	–	–	–	–	38.1
DupGAN [13]	42.4	33.4	–	46.5	36.2	–	27.1	35.4	–	–	–	–	36.8
KSA [34]	39.3	15.1	–	**12.3**	33.3	–	**9.1**	34.9	–	–	–	–	24
ADA [35]	**17.5**	9.3	29.1	41.5	30.5	39.6	17.7	**5.1**	31.2	19.8	26.8	31.5	25
CAS-ViT [31]	29.92	19.62	15.55	42.79	17.72	31.65	14.94	18.03	25.87	**4.37**	25.00	11.39	21.40
MobileViT [32]	29.23	16.14	18.17	35.38	15.51	40.53	17.10	15.00	31.08	15.80	25.87	15.35	22.93
MobileViT w/ CDC-Adapter (**Ours**)	23.65	11.65	17.18	30.55	11.23	**24.89**	18.69	12.00	25.36	9.36	15.36	5.68	17.13
MobileViT w/ D^2-Adapter (**Ours**)	25.00	**6.05**	**14.28**	17.09	**8.69**	26.31	12.36	15.69	**18.96**	6.43	**8.94**	**6.97**	**13.90**

Table 3. Computational cost comparison in terms of number of parameters (Params, million), FLOPs, and MACs. The missing data is indicated by "–". "w/" is used to represent "with". All results are in %.

Method	FLOPs(G)	MACS(G)	Params(M)
ViT-B [5]	33.73	16.94	85.65
DiVT-V(Tiny) [36]	1.26	–	5.52
DiVT-M [36]	2	–	4.94
CAS-ViT [31]	1.12	0.56	2.76
ViT-Tiny [5]	2.15	1.07	5.67
MobileViT [32]	**0.60**	**0.30**	**2.19**
MobileViT w/ D^2-Adapter (**Ours**)	0.80	0.4	2.56

4.4   Computation Cost

To show the advantage of our D^2-Adapter, we list the statistics of computational cost in Table 3. We compare the number of parameters, Floating Point Operations per Second (FLOPs), and Multiply-Accumulate Operations (MACs) between previous methods and our proposed approach.

Among all ViT-based methods, our MobileViT exhibits the lowest computational cost in terms of FLOPs, MACs, and parameter count compared to other ViT variants such as DiVT, ViT-Tiny, and CAS-ViT. When integrating our proposed D^2-Adapter into MobileViT, the increase in parameters is minimal and still remains lower than those of the other ViT variants. Considering the performance gains shown in Table 1 and Table 2, incorporating the D^2-Adapter with MobileViT is a worthwhile choice, especially in resource-constrained scenarios.

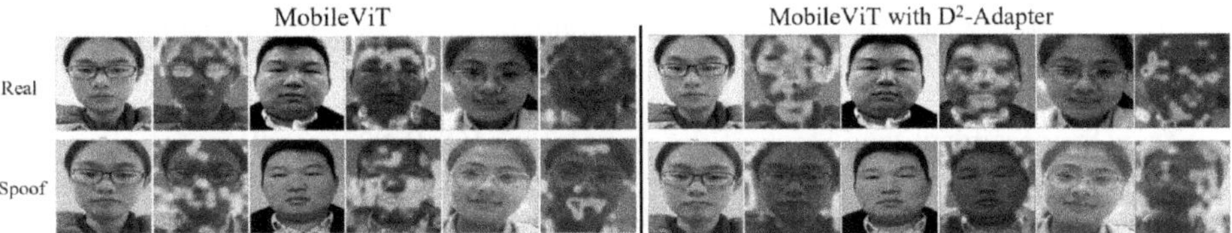

Fig. 3. The visualization of the attention heatmap. *Left*: the heatmaps extracted from the direct fine-tuning of MobileViT. *Right*: the heatmaps extracted from the efficient fine-tuning of MobileViT with our proposed D^2-Adapter.

4.5   Visualization Analysis

To further understand the effectiveness of the proposed D^2-Adapter, we randomly selected examples OULU-NPU dataset to visualize attention maps in Fig. 3. The first row is the real face samples, and the second row is the attack samples. In *left* side of Fig. 3, the attention maps of MobileViT are relatively scattered, corresponding to its higher error rate in experiments of "I to O" from Table 2. In the *right* side of Fig. 3, with our proposed D^2-Adapter, the attention distributions show clearer distinctions between real and fake faces. The model focuses more on the facial region for real faces, while it attends to contours and subtle differences in attack samples. This observation aligns with human visual perception, where regions outside the central face area are often used to identify spoofing attempts. These results further validate the effectiveness of the proposed D^2-Adapter.

5   Conclusion

This paper proposes a D^2-Adapter for efficiently adapting MobileViT for face anti-spoofing. Our extensive experiments show that our method can significantly improve MobileViT in both intra-domain and cross-domain scenarios compared with directly fine-tuning with very few extra parameters from the D^2-Adapter. For future work, we plan to further explore the more advanced adapter architecture by integrating additional processing mechanisms to enhance performance on face anti-spoofing tasks. Moreover, the proposed framework has the potential to be extended to related applications such as Deepfake detection, which could further improve algorithmic performance and advance the field.

References

1. Cai, C., Wang, Y., Zhang, L., et al.: Adversarial attacks on face recognition system in physical domain. J. Cyber Secur. **8**(2), 127–137 (2023)
2. Lin, C., Shen, C., Deng, J., et al.: Digitally forged face content creation and detection. Chin. J. Comput. **46**(3), 469–498 (2023)
3. Wang, Z., Wang, Q., Deng, W., et al.: Learning multi-granularity temporal characteristics for face anti-spoofing. IEEE Trans. Inf. Forensics Secur. **1**(1), 1–8 (2022)

4. Yang, J., Lei, Z., Li, S.Z.: Learn convolutional neural network for face anti-spoofing. arXiv preprint (2014)
5. Dosovitskiy, A., Beyer, L., Kolesnikov, A., et al.: An image is worth 16×16 words: transformers for image recognition at scale. In: ICLR 2021 (2021)
6. George, A., Marcel, S.: On the effectiveness of vision transformers for zero-shot face anti-spoofing. In: 2021 IEEE IJCB (2021)
7. Huang, H.-P., Sun, D., Liu, Y., et al.: Adaptive transformers for robust few-shot cross-domain face anti-spoofing. In: ECCV 2022 (2022)
8. Liu, Z., Lin, Y., Cao, Y., et al.: Swin transformer: hierarchical vision transformer using shifted windows. In: 2021 IEEE/CVF ICCV (2021)
9. Mehta, S., Rastegari, M.: MobileViT: light-weight, general-purpose, and mobile-friendly vision transformer. arXiv preprint arXiv:2110.02178 (2021)
10. Vaswani, A., Shazeer, N., Parmar, N., et al.: Attention is all you need. In: NeurIPS 2017 (2017)
11. Cai, R., Soh, C., Yu, Z., et al.: Towards data-centric face anti-spoofing: improving cross-domain generalization via physics-based data synthesis. Int. J. Comput. Vision **133**, 1689–1710 (2025)
12. Yu, Z. Zhao, C., Wang, Z., et al.: Searching central difference convolutional networks for face anti-spoofing. In: 2020 IEEE/CVF CVPR (2020)
13. Yu, Z., Li, X., Niu, X., et al.: Face anti-spoofing with human material perception. In: ECCV 2020 (2020)
14. Zhang, X., Ren, N., Chen, Q.: Single image reflection separation with perceptual losses. In: 2018 IEEE/CVF CVPR (2018)
15. Guo, J., Zhu, X., Yang, Y., et al.: Towards fast, accurate and stable 3d dense face alignment. In: 2020 ECCV (2020)
16. Liu, Y., Stehouwer, J., Liu, X.: On disentangling spoof trace for generic face anti-spoofing. In: 2020 ECCV (2020)
17. Wang, Y., Wang, C.-Y., Lai, S.: Disentangled representation with dual-stage feature learning for face anti-spoofing. In: 2022 IEEE/CVF WACV (2022)
18. Jia, Y., Zhang, J., Shan, S., et al.: Single-side domain generalization for face anti-spoofing. In: 2020 IEEE/CVF Conference on CVPR (2020)
19. Liu, S., Zhang, K., Yao, T., et al.: Adaptive normalized representation learning for generalizable face anti-spoofing. In: Proceedings of the 29th ACM International Conference on Multimedia (2021)
20. Wang, Z., Wang, Z., Yu, Z., et al.: Domain generalization via shuffled style assembly for face anti-spoofing. In: 2023 IEEE/CVF Conference on CVPR, pp. 6087–6096 (2023)
21. Sun, Y., Liu, Y., Liu, X., et al.: Rethinking domain generalization for face anti-spoofing: separability and alignment. In: IEEE Conference on Computer Vision and Pattern Recognition (CVPR), Vancouver, Canada (2023)
22. Cai, R., Li, Z., Wan, R., et al.: Learning meta pattern for face anti-spoofing. IEEE Trans. Inf. Forensics Secur. 1201–1213 (2022)
23. Cai, R., Yu, Z., Kong, C., et al.: S-adapter: generalizing vision transformer for face anti-spoofing with statistical tokens. IEEE TIFS (2023)
24. Yu, Z., Qin, Y., Zhao, H., Li, X., Zhao, G.: Dual-cross central difference network for face anti-spoofing. In: 2021 IJCAI (2021)
25. Boulkenafet, Z., Komulainen, J., Li, L., et al.: Oulu-NPU: a mobile face presentation attack database with real-world variations. In: 2017 12th IEEE International Conference on Automatic Face & Gesture Recognition (FG) (2017)
26. Zhang, Z., Yan, J., Liu, S., et al.: A face antispoofing database with diverse attacks. In: 2012 5th IAPR International Conference on Biometrics (ICB), pp. 26–31 (2012)

27. Chingovska, I., Anjos, A., Marcel, S.: On the effectiveness of local binary patterns in face anti-spoofing. In: 2012 International Conference of the Biometrics Special Interest Group (BIOSIG). IEEE (2012)
28. Wen, D., Han, H., Jain, A.K.: Face spoof detection with image distortion analysis. IEEE Trans. Inf. Forensics Secur. 746–761 (2015)
29. Zhang, Y., et al.: CelebA-spoof: large-scale face anti-spoofing dataset with rich annotations. In: Vedaldi, A., Bischof, H., Brox, T., Frahm, J.-M. (eds.) ECCV 2020. LNCS, vol. 12357, pp. 70–85. Springer, Cham (2020). https://doi.org/10.1007/978-3-030-58610-2_5
30. Qi, D., Tan, W., Yao, Q., et al.: YOLO5face: why reinventing a face detector. In: ECCV 2022 Workshops (2022)
31. Zhang, T., et al.: CAS-ViT: convolutional additive self-attention vision transformers for efficient mobile applications. arXiv preprint arXiv:2408.03703 (2024)
32. Sandler, M., Howard, A., Zhu, M., et al.: Mobilenetv2: inverted residuals and linear bottlenecks. In: IEEE Conference on CVPR, Salt Lake City, UT (2018)
33. Yu, Z., Qin, Y., Zhao, H., et al.: Dual-cross central difference network for face anti-spoofing. In: IJCAI 2021 (2021)
34. Torralba, A., Efros, A.A.: Unbiased look at dataset bias. In: CVPR 2011 (2011)
35. Johnson, J., Alahi, A., Fei-Fei, L.: Perceptual losses for real-time style transfer and super-resolution. In: ECCV 2016 (2016)
36. Liao, C., Chen, W., Liu, H.T., et al.: Domain invariant vision transformer learning for face anti-spoofing. In: IEEE/CVF WACV (2023)

Domain Generalization in Face Anti-Spoofing Based on Vision-Language Semantic Awareness

Fengmei Liang[1(✉)], Jin Zhang[1], Yanlong Jia[1], Hui Ma[2], and Yanyan Liang[2]

[1] College of Electronic and Information Engineering,
Taiyuan University of Technology, Jinzhong, China
fm_liang@163.com
[2] Macau University of Science and Technology, Macao, China

Abstract. Domain generalization-based face anti-spoofing has attracted the attention of researchers. Traditional domain generalization methods adopt adversarial training to explore domain-invariant feature spaces, but inevitably disrupt the semantic structure of the model. Instead of directly editing visual features, we propose a Semantic Guided-CLIP (SG-CLIP) based on the Contrastive Language-Image Pre-Training (CLIP) model. SG-CLIP uses language-guided classifier weights to re-calibrate visual features and boost generalization performance. Specifically, in the text branch, SG-CLIP uses content text prompts to describe the content information of each input sample, enhancing the model's understanding of content attributes. In the visual branch, C-Adapter is used to transfers the CLIP model to face anti-spoofing with a minimal set of trainable parameters, enabling the image encoder to perform fine-grained analysis of subtle facial differences. Experiments on multiple datasets show that the effect of SG-CLIP is better than the current advanced algorithms.

Keywords: Face anti-spoofing · Domain generalization · Semantic Guided-CLIP · C-Adapter

1 Introduction

Face recognition technology faces threats from presentation attacks such as photo, video replay, and 3D mask attacks. As a key technology for resisting attacks, the cross-domain generalization capability of Face Anti-Spoofing (FAS) has become a core challenge. Early deep learning methods [1–3] directly learn the mapping between live and fake faces, achieving impressive results in intra-domain. However, their performance degrades significantly in cross-domain settings due to overfitting to the training data distribution. To enhance model generalization, Domain Generalization Face Anti-Spoofing (DG-FAS) alleviates distribution discrepancies through multi-domain training. These methods typically employ adversarial training [4–6], meta-learning [7,8], or disentangled

W. Jia et al. (Eds.): CCBR 2025, LNCS 16360, pp. 504–514, 2026.
https://doi.org/10.1007/978-981-95-6123-0_47

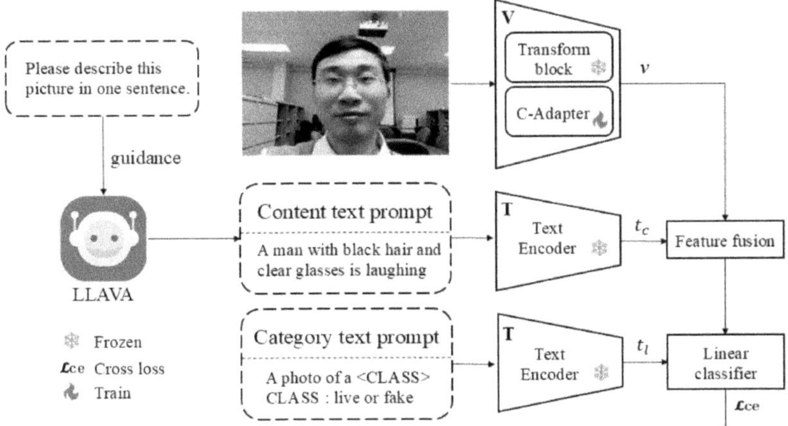

Fig. 1. Overall architecture of the SG-CLIP.

representation learning [9,10] to remove liveness-irrelevant features from the overall feature space. However, these methods lead to semantic feature distortion and limited generalization. ESCL [11] achieves cross-domain generalization by semantic consistency learning. Previous work has investigated model generalization based on data from a single source domain [12]. Adapter methods [13–16] introduce lightweight learnable modules to efficiently fine-tune pre-trained models, guiding them to focus on subtle spoof-relevant features while preserving their general knowledge, significantly improving cross-domain generalization and parameter efficiency.

In recent years, CLIP-based [23] multimodal methods [25–34] have improved generalization through vision-language alignment. CFPL-FAS [28] dynamically adjusts classifier weights using content and style features through category-agnostic prompt learning. CCPE [29] fuses inherent and learnable prompts to address the issue that single prompt forms cannot describe diverse spoof types. Although these CLIP-based methods have achieved promising results, two major problems remain when applying CLIP to FAS: (1) CLIP faces semantic barriers when distinguishing "live" from "fake". Although CCPE focuses on solving the semantic barrier of CLIP in FAS, its proposed composite prompt generation and multi-branch feature fusion inevitably increase model computational complexity. (2) There is a significant task gap between pre-trained CLIP and FAS. CLIP covers a wide range of general images, while FAS focuses on distinguishing subtle differences between live and fake faces. This essential task difference causes pre-trained CLIP difficult to directly adapt to FAS. Therefore, we proposes SG-CLIP, which optimizes the interaction between visual and language learning for DG-FAS. In the text branch, SG-CLIP uses additional content text and uses mean fusion to supplement category information, achieving vision-text semantic alignment. In the visual branch, we use a C-Adapter to enable more effective adaptation of the pre-trained CLIP model to face anti-spoofing, and use an adaptive attention mechanism to dynamically weight effective features. Additionally, subtle texture differences are captured through adaptive central difference convolution.

2   Methodology

2.1   Design of Content Prompts and Category Prompts.

The overall structure is shown in Fig. 1. FAS divides key information into domain-invariant content and domain-specific information. We utilize LLaVA (Large Language and Vision Assistant) [35] to generate content prompts T_c by asking "please describe what you see in short words", such as "A man with black hair and clear glasses is laughing". T_c guide the model to focus on facial regions with domain-invariant. Domain-specific information is represented by fixed template prompts T_l, such as "a photo of a < live/fake> face". T_l is used for authenticity discrimination, and joint learning is performed on T_c and T_l to achieve better generalization.

2.2   C-Adapter

As shown in Fig. 3, S-Adapter [13] uses histogram layers to capture statistical features of local textures for cross-domain generalization. However, due to the lack of constraints on semantic changes of image patches, it is relatively sensitive to data distribution and resolution variations. To adapt pre-trained CLIP for FAS, we utilize C-Adapter to adjust the visual features of the frozen image encoder. C-Adapter is placed in parallel with the Multi-Head Attention (MHA) blocks and Multi-Layer Perceptron (MLP) blocks in the image encoder, as shown in Eq. (1), where v_1 denotes the input visual features, v'' represents the Transformer output features, LN is the normalization layer, and r and r' represent the outputs processed by C-Adapter.

$$\begin{cases} v' = v_1 + \text{MHA}(\text{LN}(v_1)) + r \\ r = \text{Adapter}(\text{LN}(v_1)) \\ v'' = v' + \text{MLP}(\text{LN}(v')) + r' \\ r' = \text{Adapter}(\text{LN}(v')) \end{cases} \tag{1}$$

Yu et al. [3] proposed Central Difference Convolution (CDC), which captures detailed texture features by fusing intensity and gradient information. As shown in Fig. 2(b) and Fig. 2(c), inspired by CDC, C-Adapter adopt an improved adaptive central difference convolution (ACDC), which uses an adaptive attention mechanism to learn channel weights, thereby enhancing fine-grained features useful for liveness discrimination. Its calculation is shown in Eq. (2).

$$y(p_0) = \sum_{p_n \in D} w(p_n) \cdot x(p_0 + p_n) + \alpha \cdot \left(-x(p_0) \cdot \sum_{p_n \in D} w(p_n) \right) \tag{2}$$

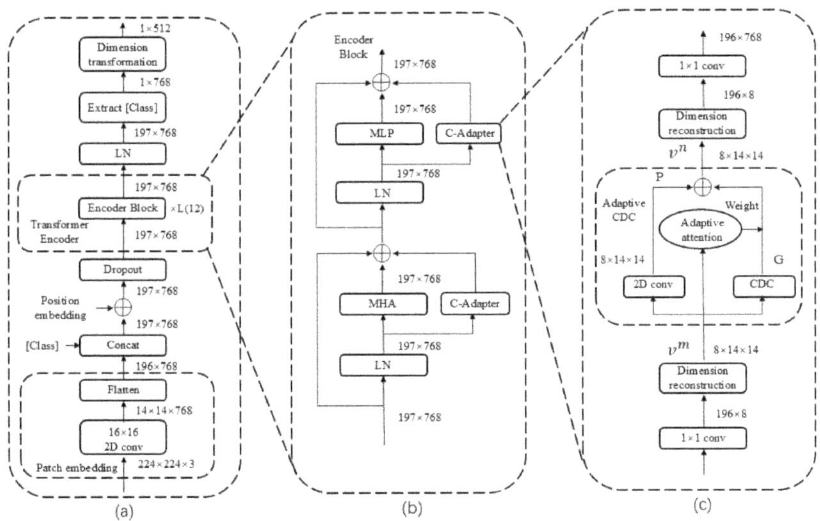

Fig. 2. Overall structure of the image encoder. (a) Image Processing Flowchart. (b) Encoding Block Structure Diagram. (c) C-Adapter Structure Diagram.

where x is the input, y is the output, p_0 is the current input position, p_n is the index of the neighborhood D centered at the current position, w is the convolution kernel, and α is the channel weight. It can be seen that the central difference convolution contains both high-level semantic information and feature gradient information. Specifically, after the image encoder flattens the image into a 1D structure $v_2 \in \mathbb{R}^{197 \times 768}$, to reduce model complexity and improve computational efficiency, v_2 reduces the feature dimension from 768 to 8 through a 1×1 convolution layer. To extract local information, we reconstruct the information dimension into a 2D structure $v^m \in \mathbb{R}^{14 \times 14 \times 8}$ and apply a 2D convolution w_{cov} to it to extract the mapping P in a learnable manner, as shown in Eq. (3).

$$P = w^{\mathrm{cov}}(v^m) \tag{3}$$

In addition, as shown in Eq. (4), considering that deceptive features are usually fine-grained, we extract gradients based on the central difference (CD) of tokens.

$$G = \sum_{q \in q_n} \omega(q) \times (P_q - P_n) \tag{4}$$

where p_n is the n-th element of P $(n < 196)$, q_n is the index set of the spatial neighborhood of p_n, and $\omega(q)$ is the kernel weight of w^{cov}.

As shown in Fig. 3, To enhance the model's sensitivity to key channels, a channel weight a is introduced, and the Squeeze-and-Excitation (SE) attention mechanism [36] as the adaptive attention mechanism.

First, global average pooling is performed on the input feature v_m to obtain a $1 \times 1 \times C$ feature vector Z. Then, a fully connected layer W_1 compresses the C channels into C/r channels, followed by a ReLU nonlinear activation layer. Next, a second fully connected layer W_2 restores the number of channels to C, and the output a is obtained through Sigmoid activation, with the process shown in Eq.s (5) and (6).

$$Z_c = \frac{1}{HW} \sum_{i=1}^{W} \sum_{j=1}^{H} v^m(i, j) \tag{5}$$

$$a = \sigma\big(W_2 \delta(W_1 Z)\big) \tag{6}$$

where Z_c is the feature value corresponding to the c-th channel of Z, i and j represent the indices of channels and spatial dimensions, respectively, δ denotes ReLU, σ denotes the Sigmoid activation function, the fully connected layer $W_1, W_2 \in \mathbb{R}^{\frac{C}{r} \times C}$, and a has a dimension of $1 \times 1 \times C$, representing the weight vector of each channel. The value of r is 4, representing the compression ratio. Then, the shape of a is expanded to $W \times H \times C$ to match G, and the final output of the adaptive central difference convolution is shown in Eq. (7).

$$v^n = P + a \times G \tag{7}$$

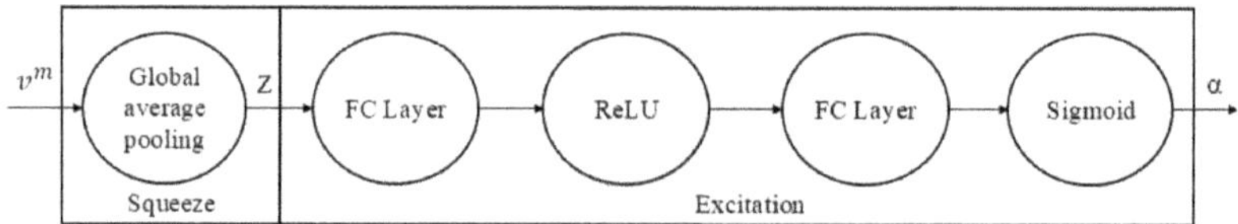

Fig. 3. Structure of the adaptive attention mechanism

2.3   Vision-Text Interaction

Unlike CCPE, which uses attention-based dynamic weighted fusion, SG-CLIP adopts mean fusion to achieve shallow interaction between text and vision, with lower computational complexity. Specifically, category prompts T_l and content prompts T_c are converted into embedding vectors E_l and E_c through the Tokenizer layer and Embed layer, then encoded into category text features t_l and content text features t_c by the text encoder T. The image I is encoded into visual features v by the image encoder V. We fuse content text features and visual features using mean fusion to obtain the fused feature f, which then pass through a linear classifier whose weights are the category text features to predict real or fake probabilities. The specific process is shown in Eq. (8).

$$
\begin{cases}
E_i = \text{Embed}(\text{Tokenizer}(T_i)), & i \in \{l, c\} \\
v = V(I), & v \in \mathbb{R}^{B \times 512} \\
t_c = T(E_c), & t_c \in \mathbb{R}^{B \times 512} \\
t_l = T(E_l), & t_l \in \mathbb{R}^{2 \times 512} \\
f = \text{AVE}(t_1, t_2), & f \in \mathbb{R}^{B \times 512} \\
\mathcal{L}_{\text{cls}} = \sum_{i=1}^{B} \mathcal{H}(y_i^{\text{cls}}; \mathcal{LC}^{\text{cls}}(f)), & f \in \mathbb{R}^{B \times 512}
\end{cases}
\tag{8}
$$

where $\mathcal{H}$ is a cross-entropy loss, $\mathcal{LC}^{\text{cls}}$ is a linear classifier synthesized from category prompts, AVE() represents the mean, $y_i^{\text{cls}} \in \{0, 1\}$ is the label of real or fake faces, and B represents the batch size.

2.4   Loss Function

In this paper, the binary cross-entropy loss function optimization model is adopted, which optimizes the model by measuring the distribution difference between the real label and the prediction probability, and the smaller the loss value, the closer the prediction result is to the real situation, and the better the model performance. The calculation formula is as follows:

$$
\mathcal{L}(y, p) = -\frac{1}{N} \sum_{i=1}^{N} \left[y_i \log(p_i) + (1 - y_i) \log(1 - p_i) \right]
\tag{9}
$$

where N is the number of samples, which y_i is the real label of the ith sample (1 represents the real face, 0 represents the fake face), and p_i denotes the probability predicted by the model that the i-th sample is real.

3   Experiments and Analysis

3.1   Datasets and Evaluation Metrics and Experimental Setup

We use four benchmark datasets for cross-dataset testing, including OULU-NPU (O) [37], MSU-MFSD (M) [38], Idiap-Replay-Attack (I) [39], and CASIA-FASD (C) [40]. These datasets are collected using different acquisition devices, attack methods, lighting conditions, backgrounds, and races, resulting in significant domain differences between datasets. We use HTER and AUC as evaluation metrics. All face images are center-cropped to $224 \times 224 \times 3$, then augmented with random rotations and normalized. Image and text encoders employ the pretrained ViT-B/16 from CLIP. Experiments are conducted on PyTorch using an NVIDIA GeForce RTX 2080 Ti GPU and Python 3.9. Training is performed with the Adam optimizer at an initial learning rate of 1e−5 and a batch size of 24. During training, the image and text encoders remain frozen; only the C-Adapter parameters are updated.

Table 1. Cross-domain experimental results

Methods	OCI→M		OMI→C		OCM→I		ICM→O		Avg
	HTER (%)	AUC (%)	HTER (%)	AUC (%)	HTER (%)	AUC (%)	HTER (%)	AUC (%)	HTER (%)
DR-MD-Net [4]	17.02	90.10	19.68	87.43	20.87	86.72	25.02	81.47	20.64
NAS-FAS [17]	19.53	88.63	16.54	90.18	14.51	93.84	13.80	93.43	16.09
D2AM [7]	12.70	95.66	20.98	85.58	15.43	91.22	15.27	90.87	16.09
SDA [4]	15.40	91.80	24.50	84.40	15.60	90.10	23.10	84.30	19.65
DRDG [18]	12.43	95.81	19.05	88.79	15.56	91.79	16.63	91.75	15.66
ANRL [19]	10.83	96.75	17.83	89.26	16.03	91.04	15.67	91.90	15.09
SSAN(R) [21]	6.67	98.75	10.00	96.67	8.88	96.79	13.72	93.63	9.81
PatchNet [21]	7.10	98.46	11.33	94.58	13.40	95.67	11.82	95.07	10.91
IADG [10]	5.41	98.19	8.70	96.44	10.62	94.50	8.86	97.14	8.39
SA-FAS [9]	5.95	96.55	8.78	95.37	6.58	97.54	10.00	96.23	7.82
DLIF [22]	3.75	98.33	6.67	97.27	5.82	98.13	8.89	96.36	6.28
S-Adapter [13]	3.43	99.50	6.32	97.82	7.16	97.61	7.21	98.00	6.03
CLIP [23]	2.86	99.30	4.21	**99.62**	8.21	96.52	5.01	97.19	5.07
CLIP-V [23]	2.86	98.82	4.55	99.11	9.56	95.13	5.14	98.26	5.52
Coop [24]	**2.70**	99.45	4.03	98.53	6.31	98.15	3.50	99.20	4.14
FLIP [25]	5.04	98.44	2.53	99.41	7.25	96.88	**3.01**	98.82	4.46
CFPL-FAS [28]	3.09	99.45	2.56	99.10	5.43	98.41	3.33	99.05	**3.60**
CCPE [29]	3.10	99.21	**1.33**	99.36	6.08	94.36	5.57	98.49	4.02
Ours(SG-CLIP)	4.05	**99.62**	2.93	98.50	**4.21**	**98.59**	3.26	**99.31**	3.61

3.2   Cross-Domain Comparison Experiments

To verify cross-domain generalization ability, this paper adopts the Leave-One-Out protocol on four datasets to construct four testing scenarios (OCI→M, OMI→C, OCM→I, ICM→O). As shown in Table 1, SG-CLIP outperforms various comparison methods. Compared with DLIF, a traditional domain generalization method, SG-CLIP achieves an average HTER improvement of 2.67%, with AUC metrics increasing by 1.29%, 1.23%, 0.46%, and 2.95% across the four scenarios respectively. This performance enhancement benefits from breaking the expression limitations of traditional methods that rely solely on image data and labels. In the low-resolution to high-resolution ICM→O scenario, S-Adapter exhibits an HTER of 7.21% due to histogram statistics being affected by drastic resolution changes, while SG-CLIP achieves an HTER of 3.26% in this scenario. Through the adaptive central difference convolution in C-Adapter, which aggregates intensity and gradient information, SG-CLIP better captures detailed information in feature maps. Compared with CLIP-based methods, SG-CLIP improves average HTER by 1.46%, 1.91%, 0.53%, and 0.85% respectively, verifying the effectiveness of supplementing with content text and fine-tuning the visual encoder via C-Adapter. Compared with CCPE, SG-CLIP achieves a lower average HTER (3.61% vs. 4.02% of CCPE). Particularly in the ICM→O scenario with large resolution differences, SG-CLIP's HTER (3.26%) is significantly superior to CCPE's (5.57%). This is because SG-CLIP's mean fusion enables more effective visual feature modulation, and its adaptive central difference convolution enhances sensitivity to spoof traces. Moreover, the way C-

Adapter adjusts visual features is better at capturing local spoof cues under drastic resolution changes compared to CCPE's Q-Former, which primarily refines global features, thus providing advantages in distinguishing subtle differences.

3.3 Ablation Experiments

We adopt four test protocols (OCI→M, OMI→C, OCM→I, and ICM→O) to assess the contribution of each module and report the average results in Table 2. Our baseline model uses the original CLIP, and we add content text prompts and C-Adapter to the baseline model respectively to verify the impact of each module. Experimental results show that compared with the baseline, adding only content text prompts reduces the average HTER by 0.72%, adding only C-Adapter reduces the average HTER by 0.70%, and adding both content text prompts and C-Adapter reduces the average HTER by 1.46%, proving that the proposed modules have significant effects on the model.

Table 2. Ablation experiments on OCIM datasets

base	content prompts	C-Adapter	Avg HTER (%)
✓	–	–	5.07
✓	–	✓	4.37
✓	✓	-	4.35
✓	✓	✓	**3.61**

To verify the impact of different positions of the C-Adapter on the encoder, we test on the OCI→M scenario, and the results are shown in Table 3, Experimental results indicate that the C-Adapter achieves optimal performance when placed in parallel with both MHA and MLP blocks.

Table 3. Experimental results of C-Adapter positions

MHA	MLP	OCI→M	
		HTER (%)	AUC (%)
–	✓	5.36	98.71
✓	–	4.33	98.90
✓	✓	4.05	**99.62**

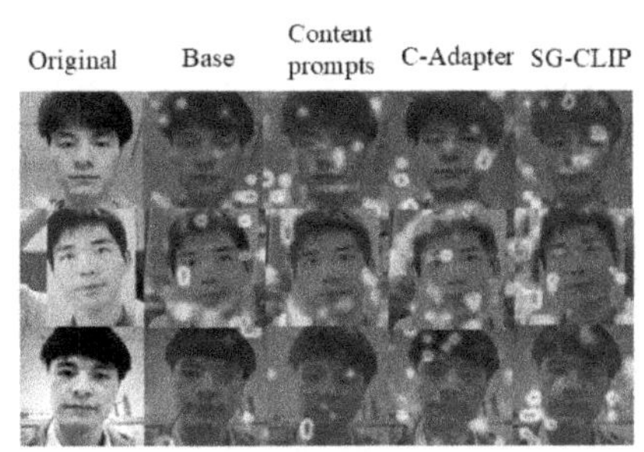

Fig. 4. Visual attention maps.

3.4 Attention Visualization

As shown in Fig. 4, To better verify the role of the proposed SG-CLIP model and its modules, we conduct visual analysis using an attention model interpretability tool [41]. The third column in the figure represents the baseline model with content text prompts. Our proposed content prompt module focuses on domain-invariant content information of the image. The fourth column represents the baseline model with C-Adapter. C-Adapter focuses on detailed features in the image: for print attacks, the model focuses on areas with brightness differences caused by light reflection; for replay attacks, the model focuses on contrast distortion in the eye area and bright spots from electronic screen reflection, not limited to the facial region.

4 Conclusion

We propose the Semantic Guided-CLIP (SG-CLIP), which uses content text features as additional text features to make up for the semantic deficiency of CLIP in face anti-spoofing, and introduces the C-Adapter in the visual branch to adaptively capture details in images. Our method achieves significant results in domain generalization face anti-spoofing.

References

1. Yang, J., Lei, Z., Li, S.Z.: Learn convolutional neural network for face anti-spoofing. Comput. Sci. **9218**, 373–384 (2014)
2. Deb, D., Jain, A.K.: Look locally infer globally: a generalizable face anti-spoofing approach. IEEE Trans. Inf. Forensics Secur. **16**, 1143–1157 (2020)
3. Yu, Z., Zhao, C., Wang, Z., et al.: Searching central difference convolutional networks for face anti-spoofing. In: Proceedings of the IEEE/CVF Conference on Computer Vision and Pattern Recognition, pp. 5295–5305 (2020)
4. Wang, G., Han, H., Shan, S., et al.: Unsupervised adversarial domain adaptation for cross-domain face presentation attack detection. IEEE Trans. Inf. Forensics Secur. **16**, 56–69 (2020)
5. Jiang, F., Li, Q., Liu, P., et al.: Adversarial learning domain-invariant conditional features for robust face anti-spoofing. Int. J. Comput. Vis. **131**(7), 1680–1703 (2023)
6. Yuan, S., Dong, J., Li, Y.: Where the devil hides: deepfake detectors can no longer be trusted. In: Proceedings of the IEEE/CVF Conference on Computer Vision and Pattern Recognition (CVPR), pp. 8764–8774 (2025)
7. Chen, Z., Yao, T., Sheng, K., et al.: Generalizable representation learning for mixture domain face anti-spoofing. In: Proceedings of the AAAI Conference on Artificial Intelligence, vol. 35, no. 2, pp. 1132–1139 (2021)
8. Wang, J., Zhang, J., Bian, Y., et al.: Self-domain adaptation for face anti-spoofing. In: Proceedings of the AAAI Conference on Artificial Intelligence, vol. 35, no. 4, pp. 2746–2754 (2021)
9. Sun, Y., Liu, Y., Liu, X., et al.: Rethinking domain generalization for face anti-spoofing: separability and alignment. In: Proceedings of the IEEE/CVF Conference on Computer Vision and Pattern Recognition, pp. 24563–24574 (2023)

10. Zhou, Q., Zhang, K., Yao, T., et al.: Instance-aware domain generalization for face anti-spoofing. In: Proceedings of the IEEE/CVF Conference on Computer Vision and Pattern Recognition, pp. 20453–20463 (2023)
11. Jiang, F., Liu, Y., Si, H., et al.: Cross-scenario unknown-aware face anti-spoofing with evidential semantic consistency learning. IEEE Trans. Inf. Forensics Secur. **19**, 3093–3108 (2024)
12. Jiang, F., Li, Q., Wang, W., et al.: Open-set single-domain generalization for robust face anti-spoofing. Int. J. Comput. Vis. **132**(11), 5151–5172 (2024)
13. Cai, R., Yu, Z., Kong, C., et al.: S-adapter: generalizing vision transformer for face anti-spoofing with statistical tokens. IEEE Trans. Inf. Forensics Secur. (2024)
14. Cui, X., Li, Y., Zhu, D., et al.: Forensics adapter: unleashing clip for generalizable face forgery detection. arXiv preprint arXiv:2411.19715 (2024)
15. Yu, Z., Cai, R., Cui, Y., et al.: Rethinking vision transformer and masked autoencoder in multimodal face anti-spoofing. Int. J. Comput. Vis. **132**(11), 5217–5238 (2024)
16. Cui, X., Li, Y., Luo, A., et al.: Forensics adapter: adapting CLIP for generalizable face forgery detection. In: Proceedings of the IEEE/CVF Conference on Computer Vision and Pattern Recognition (CVPR), pp. 19207–19217 (2025)
17. Yu, Z., Wan, J., Qin, Y., et al.: NAS-FAS: static-dynamic central difference network search for face anti-spoofing. IEEE Trans. Pattern Anal. Mach. Intell. **43**(9), 3005–3023 (2020)
18. Liu, S., Zhang, K., Yao, T., et al.: Dual reweighting domain generalization for face presentation attack detection. arXiv preprint arXiv:2106.16128 (2021)
19. Liu, S., Zhang, K., Yao, T., et al.: Adaptive normalized representation learning for generalizable face anti-spoofing. In: Proceedings of the 29th ACM International Conference on Multimedia, pp. 1469–1477 (2021)
20. Wang, C., Lu, Y., Yang, S., et al.: PatchNet: a simple face anti-spoofing framework via fine-grained patch recognition. In: Proceedings of the IEEE/CVF Conference on Computer Vision and Pattern Recognition, pp. 20281–20290 (2022)
21. Wang, Z., Wang, Z., Yu, Z., et al.: Domain generalization via shuffled style assembly for face anti-spoofing. In: Proceedings of the IEEE/CVF Conference on Computer Vision and Pattern Recognition, pp. 4123–4133 (2022)
22. Yang, J., Yu, Z., Ni, X., et al.: Generalized face anti-spoofing via finer domain partition and disentangling liveness-irrelevant factors. In: ECAI 2024, pp. 274–281. IOS Press (2024)
23. Radford, A., Kim, J.W., Hallacy, C., et al.: Learning transferable visual models from natural language supervision. In: Proceedings of the International Conference on Machine Learning, pp. 8748–8763 (2021)
24. Zhou, K., Yang, J., Loy, C.C., et al.: Learning to prompt for vision-language models. Int. J. Comput. Vis. **130**(9), 2337–2348 (2022)
25. Srivatsan, K., Naseer, M., Nandakumar, K.: Flip: Cross-domain face anti-spoofing with language guidance. In: Proceedings of the IEEE/CVF Conference on Computer Vision, pp. 19685–19696 (2023)
26. Fang, H., Liu, A., Jiang, N., et al.: VL-FAS: Domain generalization via vision-language model for face anti-spoofing. In: Proceedings of the IEEE International Conference on Acoustics, Speech, Signal Processing (ICASSP), pp. 4770–4774 (2024)
27. Guo, J., Liu, H., Luo, Y., et al.: Style-conditional prompt token learning for generalizable face anti-spoofing. In: Proceedings of the 32nd ACM International Conference on Multimedia, pp. 994–1003 (2024)

28. Liu, A., Xue, S., Gan, J., et al.: CFPL-FAS: class free prompt learning for generalizable face anti-spoofing. In: Proceedings of the IEEE/CVF Conference on Computer Vision and Pattern Recognition, pp. 222–232 (2024)
29. Guo, J., Liu, A., Diao, Y., et al.: Domain generalization for face anti-spoofing via content-aware composite prompt engineering. arXiv preprint arXiv:2504.04470 (2025)
30. Lin, X., Liu, A., Yu, Z., et al.: Reliable and balanced transfer learning for generalized multimodal face anti-spoofing. IEEE Trans. Pattern Anal. Mach. Intell. (2025)
31. Shi, Y., Gao, Y., Lai, Y., et al.: Shield: an evaluation benchmark for face spoofing and forgery detection with multimodal large language models. Vis. Intell. **3**(1), 9 (2025)
32. Liu, A., Yuan, H., Guo, X., et al.: Benchmarking unified face attack detection via hierarchical prompt tuning. arXiv preprint arXiv:2505.13327 (2025)
33. Li, Y., Li, N., Liu, A., et al.: FA^3-CLIP: frequency-aware cues fusion and attack-agnostic prompt learning for unified face attack detection. arXiv preprint arXiv:2504.00454 (2025)
34. Liu, A., Ma, H., Zheng, J., et al.: FM-CLIP: flexible modal CLIP for face anti-spoofing. In: Proceedings of the 32nd ACM International Conference on Multimedia, pp. 8228–8237 (2024)
35. Liu, H., Li, C., Wu, Q., et al.: Visual instruction tuning. Adv. Neural. Inf. Process. Syst. **36**, 34892–34916 (2023)
36. Hu, J., Shen, L., Sun, G.: Squeeze-and-excitation networks. In: Proceedings of the IEEE Conference on Computer Vision and Pattern Recognition, pp. 7132–7141 (2018)
37. Boulkenafet, Z., Komulainen, J., Li, L., et al.: OULU-NPU: a mobile face presentation attack database with real-world variations. In: IEEE International Conference on Automatic Face and Gesture Recognition, pp. 612–618 (2017)
38. Chingovska, I., Anjos, A., Marcel, S.: On the effectiveness of local binary patterns in face anti-spoofing. In: BIOSIG, pp. 1–7 (2012)
39. Wen, D., Han, H., Jain, A.K.: Face spoof detection with image distortion analysis. IEEE Trans. Inf. Forensics Secur. **10**(4), 746–761 (2015)
40. Zhang, Z., Yan, J., Liu, S., et al.: A face antispoofing database with diverse attacks. In: IAPR International Conference on Biometrics (ICB), pp. 26–31 (2012)
41. Chefer, H., Gur, S., Wolf, L.: Generic attention-model explainability for interpreting bi-modal and encoder-decoder transformers. In: Proceedings of the IEEE/CVF Conference on Computer Vision, pp. 397–406 (2021)

Human-Related Understanding

Distribution-Discriminative and Modality-Aware Test-Time Cross-Domain Adaptation for Text-Based Person Search

Liucun Shi[1,2] and Kai Niu[1,2(✉)]

[1] Shenzhen Research Institute of Northwestern Polytechnical University, Shenzhen, China
[2] School of Computer Science, Northwestern Polytechnical University, Xi'an, China
`shiliucun@mail.nwpu.edu.cn`, `kai.niu@nwpu.edu.cn`

Abstract. Text-based person search (TBPS) faces the severe problem of domain shifts in practical applications, which causes significant performance degradation and has to be carefully addressed. Test-time Adaptation (TTA) offers a feasible approach for quick adaptation during inference, but there are two major challenges when directly applying existing TTA approaches to TBPS: 1) Less Discriminative Cross-modal Distributions: the text-to-image prediction distributions are with flat characteristics and low discriminability caused by numerous irrelevant images inside the gallery. 2) Modality-specific Domain Shifts: domain shifts exist independently in textual and visual modalities. To address these challenges, we propose a novel test-time adaptation method named Distribution-discriminative and Modality-aware Domain Adaptation (DMDA). Firstly, the Discriminative Pairs Learning (DPL) module is proposed to discard irrelevant images and select a credible one for each text query based on cross-modal similarity, producing more discriminative distributions for cross-modal alignments. Secondly, the Modality-aware Stable Adaptation (MSA) module explicitly aligns domains within respective modalities by an anchor-based stable adaptation strategy. Finally, extensive experiments and analyses have been conducted to validate the effectiveness of our DMDA across three publicly available benchmarks for TBPS.

Keywords: Text-based Person Search · Test-time Adaptation · Cross-modal Retrieval · Domain Adaptation

1 Introduction

Text-based person search (TBPS) is a challenging task that aims to retrieve specific pedestrians from a large-scale image gallery through natural language descriptions. This task originates from the intersection of cross-modal retrieval and image-based person search. With its potential applications in public security, TBPS has seen substantial progress in recent years.

The majority of existing TBPS methods assume that the training and testing data are drawn from the same domain, *i.e.*, no significant domain shift between them. However, this assumption tends to break down in practical scenarios. The models trained on carefully collected image-text paired data in controlled laboratory environments are deployed in real-world unseen data from diverse scenarios. This significant and inevitable domain shift between training (source) and testing (target) data consequently leads to substantial performance degradation, making these laboratory-trained models unreliable for real-world applications.

Cross-domain adaptation is an important subfield of transfer learning that aims to address the model generalization problem caused by the data distribution discrepancy between the source and target domains. In this field, Test-Time Adaptation (TTA) does not need multiple rounds of intensive model fine-tuning. Instead, it performs a single-pass rapid adaptation using limited test data from the target domain before making final predictions, showing its great potential for tackling the domain shift problem and enabling the practical deployment of TBPS models in real-world scenarios.

However, the majority of existing TTA methods are designed based on unimodal tasks such as image classification, thus facing two main problems when directly applied to multi-modal TBPS. 1) **Less Discriminative Cross-modal Distributions**: Many existing TTA methods adapt the model by minimizing the entropy of prediction probabilities. However, directly formulating TBPS as a classification task based on text-image matching probabilities often results in flat and long-tail probability distributions. This problem arises because, in large-scale image galleries, a huge number of images are irrelevant to the text queries. Including these irrelevant images in the classification process introduces substantial noise, which leads to flat and long-tail prediction distributions with poor discriminability. Such flatness characteristics lead to inaccurate entropy estimation, and ultimately hinder the entropy minimization adaptation process. 2) **Modality-specific Domain Shifts**: TBPS is a multi-modal task, where different ways of domain shift exist in different modalities. Specifically, sentences exhibit style variations in terms of word choice, length, *etc.*, while images vary in lighting, pedestrian poses, clothing, and so on. These diverse variations lead to inconsistent domain shifts between modalities, which need to be further bridged for more accurate cross-modal alignments in the target domain.

To address the problems, we propose a novel TTA approach for TBPS, named **D**istribution-discriminative and **M**odality-aware **D**omain **A**daptation (DMDA), guiding models to quickly adapt to unseen domains during inference.

Firstly, to address the Less Discriminative Cross-modal Distributions problem, we design the **Discriminative Pairs Learning** (DPL) module, which discards numerous irrelevant images and only selects a credible one for each text query based on the cross-modal similarities, producing more discriminative distributions for accurate entropy estimation and learning. Secondly, to solve the Modality-specific Domain Shifts problem, we present the **Modality-aware Sta-**

ble Adaptation (MSA) module, which explicitly aligns domains within respective modalities by an anchor-based stable adaptation strategy. Specifically, MSA adaptively splits the testing image-text pairs to source- or target-like ones, and simultaneously constructs visual and textual anchors for these two kinds of pairs. The anchors within each modality in different domains serve as bridges for conducting domain adaptation, and are momentum updated to ensure stability.

To our knowledge, this is one of the earliest works that introduces TTA to TBPS, providing a new paradigm for domain adaptation for this cross-modal retrieval task. Our DMDA outperforms existing TTA approaches and achieves state-of-the-art domain generalization performance across three datasets, CUHK-PEDES [1], ICFG-PEDES [2], and RSTPReid [3]. The main contributions are:

- To our knowledge, this work is among the first studies to explore TTA approach specifically for the TBPS task.
- We propose the DMDA solution, which firstly constructs discriminative pairs in DPL module for effective cross-modal alignments, and then conducts modality-aware adaptation in MSA module for achieving a stable cross-modal domain adaptation process.
- Extensive experiments and analyses demonstrate the effectiveness of our proposed DMDA method, and it has achieved the state-of-the-art domain generalization performance across three public benchmarks for TBPS.

2   Related Work

2.1   Text-Based Person Search

Text-based person search (TBPS) [4] is first proposed in [1]. Many recent approaches [5–10] are dedicated to facilitating more fine-grained alignments between the text and image modalities. Jiang *et al.* [5] propose a cross-modal Implicit Relation Reasoning and Aligning (IRRA) framework that learns relations between local visual-textual tokens, and aligns the global representations between text and image by a novel KL divergence loss. Unlike these works that focus on facilitating cross-modal alignments within the same domain, our work is dedicated to addressing the domain shift in more practical TBPS scenarios.

2.2   Cross-Domain Adaptation

Cross-domain adaptation aims to address the model's poor generalization ability when facing the the domain shift. In this field, Source-Free Domain Adaptation (SFDA) strategy only uses unlabeled data from target domain to adapt model. As a special case of SFDA, Test-Time Adaptation (TTA) [11–15] performs a single-pass rapid adaptation using limited test data. Most of these works focus on the image classification task. For example, Wang *et al.* propose the Tent [11] method, which optimizes the model by minimizing the entropy of its predictions, leading the model to produce more confident predictions in the target domain. Unlike previous works that mainly focus on applying TTA to uni-modal tasks, our work focuses on establishing a new TTA paradigm for cross-modal TBPS.

3   Method

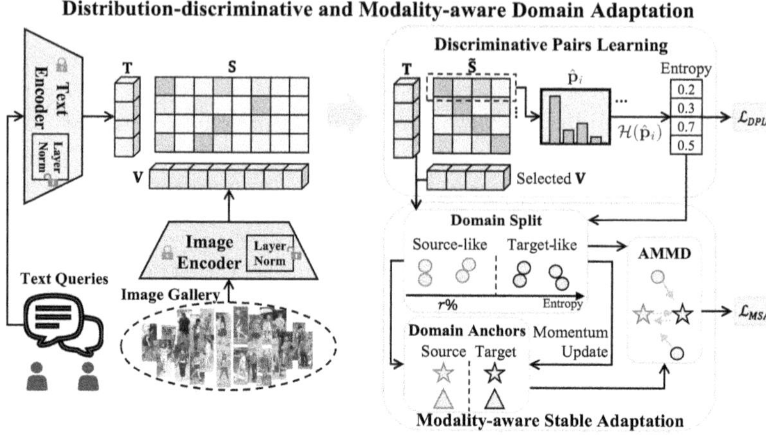

Fig. 1. The framework of our proposed Distribution-discriminative and Modality-aware Domain Adaptation (DMDA) method.

Considering a practical scenario for TBPS, the model is first trained in the source domain includes a textual encoder f^t and a visual encoder f^v. And it is then used to retrieve images of pedestrians from a pre-collected image gallery $\{v_j\}_{j=1}^m$ based on a set of user-generated text queries $\{t_i\}_{i=1}^n$. Both the testing texts and images are from another unseen domain, which we denote as target domain. Parameters n and m are the sizes of text query set and image gallery, respectively. To address the cross-domain TBPS, we propose the novel TTA approach named Distribution-discriminative and Modality-aware Domain Adaptation (DMDA). As shown in Fig. 1, there are two major modules in DMDA, *i.e.* Discriminative Pairs Learning (DPL), and Modality-aware Stable Adaptation (MSA).

3.1   Discriminative Pairs Learning

We introduce a naive transfer scheme based on Tent [11] as our baseline. In order to apply the entropy minimization learning strategy, we convert the retrieval task into a text classification task, where each image in the gallery is treated as an individual class. Specifically, we first compute the cross-modal cosine similarities between texts and images as

$$\mathbf{S} = [S_{i,j}]_{n \times m} = [cos(\mathbf{T}_i, \mathbf{V}_j)]_{n \times m}, \tag{1}$$

where $\mathbf{T}_i = f^t(t_i)$, $\mathbf{V}_j = f^v(v_j)$, are the representations of text and image. Afterwards, the prediction probabilities $\hat{\mathbf{p}}$ for texts are obtained by applying the softmax operation on cross-modal similarities:

$$\hat{\mathbf{p}} = [\hat{p}_{i,j}]_{n \times m}, \text{ where } \hat{p}_{i,j} = \frac{exp\left(S_{i,j}/\tau\right)}{\sum_{k=1}^{m} exp\left(S_{i,k}/\tau\right)}, \tag{2}$$

and τ is the temperature coefficient. Finally, the entropy loss is computed by

$$\mathcal{L}_{Ent}(\hat{\mathbf{p}}) = \sum_{i=1}^{n} \mathcal{H}(\hat{\mathbf{p}}_i) = -\sum_{i=1}^{n}\sum_{j=1}^{m} \hat{p}_{i,j} \log \hat{p}_{i,j}. \tag{3}$$

We conduct this naive TTA approach as our baseline. However, as shown in Table 4 (Baseline), less discriminative cross-modal distributions result in poor performance, since many irrelevant images introduce substantial noise.

To address this issue, our Discriminative Pairs Learning (DPL) module discards numerous irrelevant images according to cross-modal relation, for accurate entropy estimation and learning. Specifically, since higher cross-modal similarity often indicates stronger semantic relevance, for each text query t_i, we select the image $v_{j'_i}$ with the highest similarity and treat them as credible positive pairs.

$$j'_i = \arg\max_{j \in \{1,2,\ldots,m\}} S_{i,j}. \tag{4}$$

Then we can obtain the similarity matrix $\tilde{\mathbf{S}}$ between text queries and all of the selected images by reorganizing $\mathbf{S}$ as

$$\tilde{\mathbf{S}} = [\tilde{S}_{i,k}]_{n \times n}, \text{ where } \tilde{S}_{i,k} = S_{i,j'_k}. \tag{5}$$

Afterwards, we compute the prediction probabilities $\mathbf{p}$ and entropy loss $\mathcal{L}_{Ent}(\mathbf{p})$ using the similarity matrix $\tilde{\mathbf{S}}$, similar to Eq. 2 and Eq. 3. In this way, we discard numerous images that are irrelevant to the current text queries, retaining only those that are semantically relevant. This prevents the prediction distribution from becoming overly flat and long-tailed due to the presence of too many irrelevant images, and enables accurate entropy estimation and learning on a discriminative distribution constructed by credible samples only. We use $\mathcal{L}_{Ent}(\mathbf{p})$ as the optimization objective of the DPL module, denoted as $\mathcal{L}_{DPL}$.

3.2 Modality-Aware Stable Adaptation

Traditional TTA approaches [11,12,14] usually adopt entropy minimization for uni-modal domain adaptation. However, in TBPS, inconsistent domain shifts exist in respective textual and visual modalities. And this modality-specific domain shifts problem, caused by different intra-modal variations, needs to be further bridged. To solve this problem, we propose the Modality-aware Stable Adaptation (MSA) module, which explicitly aligns domains within respective modalities by an anchor-based stable adaptation strategy.

Since the source-domain data are unavailable during the TTA process, we begin with identifying source-like samples to approximate the distribution of source-domain data. Specifically, we split samples with low prediction entropy as source-like samples, and those with high entropy as target-like ones. And the reason is that samples with low entropy are typically better aligned with the source-domain distribution, while high-entropy samples indicate greater uncertainty and are more likely to come from an unseen domain. We rank all texts t_i by their entropy scores $\mathcal{H}(\hat{\mathbf{p}}_i)$ in ascending order, and split the top $r\%$ texts with the lowest entropy together with their paired images to construct source-like sample sets $\mathcal{S}^t$ and $\mathcal{S}^v$, while the rest of the samples are used to form target-like sample sets $\mathcal{T}^t$ and $\mathcal{T}^v$. After that, we can align domains in each modality by measuring and minimizing the maximum mean discrepancy (MMD) between the distributions of source-like and target-like samples.

However, this widely-used vanilla MMD is unsuitable for TTA, since using limited samples in a mini-batch to estimate the overall distribution of a domain may cause severe estimation bias. To address this issue, we introduce four domain anchors for both the source and target domains as well as the textual and visual modalities, respectively. Each domain anchor acts as the central representation for the modality and domain it belongs. These domain anchors are updated dynamically across mini-batches in a momentum manner to ensure accuracy and stability. Taking the textual modality as an example, for each domain, we maintain a domain anchor that is updated across mini-batches by

$$\mathbf{a}_d^{(t)} = (1 - \beta) \cdot \mathbf{a}_d^{(t-1)} + \beta \cdot \bar{\mathbf{T}}_d^{(t)}, \tag{6}$$

where $\mathbf{a}_d^{(t)}$ denotes the domain anchor for domain $d \in \{\text{source}(s), \text{target}(t)\}$ at the t-th mini-batch. $\bar{\mathbf{T}}_d^{(t)}$ is the mean representation of texts from the same domain, and β is momentum coefficient. Finally, by incorporating these anchors, the anchor-based maximum mean discrepancy (AMMD) loss is obtained by

$$\mathcal{L}_{AMMD}^t(\mathcal{S}^t, \mathcal{T}^t) = \frac{1}{a} \sum_{p=1}^{a} \mathbf{s}_p \left(\mathbf{a}_s - \mathbf{a}_t\right) + \frac{1}{b} \sum_{q=1}^{b} \mathbf{t}_q \left(\mathbf{a}_t - \mathbf{a}_s\right), \tag{7}$$

where $\mathbf{s}, \mathbf{t}$ denote the representations of two domains, a, b are their corresponding amounts in a mini-batch, and $\mathbf{a}_s$, $\mathbf{a}_t$ represent the anchor of source and target domain, respectively. Facilitating domain alignments in both textual and visual modalities, our Modality-aware Stable Adaptation (MSA) loss is computed by

$$\mathcal{L}_{MSA} = \mathcal{L}_{AMMD}^t(\mathcal{S}^t, \mathcal{T}^t) + \mathcal{L}_{AMMD}^v(\mathcal{S}^v, \mathcal{T}^v). \tag{8}$$

3.3   Overall Objective

The overall objective of our DMDA method is formulated as

$$\mathcal{L}_{DMDA} = \mathcal{L}_{DPL} + \mathcal{L}_{MSA}. \tag{9}$$

Only LayerNorms inside the model are optimized while other layers are frozen, following previous TTA works [11,12,14]. After adaptation for only one epoch in inference, all text queries obtain final retrieval results using the adapted model.

4 Experiments and Analyses

4.1 Experimental Settings

To validate the effectiveness of our DMDA, we conduct experiments across three widely-used benchmarks. **CUHK-PEDES** [1] is the first public benchmark for TBPS, containing 40,206 images of 13,003 pedestrians, and each image is annotated with two sentences. **ICFG-PEDES** [2] annotates each image with one detailed sentence, and consists of 54,522 images from 4,102 identities. **RST-PReid** [3] consists of 20,505 images from 4,101 identities in total, and each image is annotated using two sentences. For performance evaluation and comparisons, we adopt four widely-used metrics of Rank@1 (R@1), Rank@5 (R@5), Rank@10 (R@10), and mean Average Precision (mAP).

As for the base models used to apply our DMDA method, we adopt the ALBEF [16] backbone pretrained by the CADA [6] approach, on CUHK-PEDES, ICFG-PEDES, and RSTPReid datasets. We adopt the Adam optimizer, with a batch size of 128, and set the learning rates to 0.002 for all cross-domain directions, except that it is set to 0.0005 for the CUHK-PEDES to ICFG-PEDES and RSTPReid to ICFG-PEDES directions. The temperature coefficient τ is set to 0.05. The split ratio $r\%$ is 50%, and the momentum β is set to 0.2.

4.2 Comparison with State-of-the-Art (SOTA) Approaches

Table 1. Cross-domain performance comparisons with SOTA TBPS approaches. The best and second-best results are shown in bold and underlined, respectively.

Methods	Venue	ICFG→CUHK				CUHK→ICFG			
		R@1	R@5	R@10	mAP	R@1	R@5	R@10	mAP
DCEL [17]	ACMMM 23	32.35	54.86	65.51	–	43.31	62.29	70.31	–
IRRA [5]	CVPR 23	33.42	56.21	66.20	31.39	42.55	62.19	69.68	21.84
RDE [8]	CVPR 24	37.88	59.00	68.39	33.99	48.15	66.26	73.68	25.03
CFAM [18]	CVPR 24	40.48	63.48	72.68	37.38	46.21	65.18	72.65	24.77
APTM [19]	ACMMM 23	48.67	68.75	77.06	–	46.20	65.13	72.59	–
RaSa [7]	IJCAI 23	50.70	72.40	79.58	–	50.59	67.46	74.09	–
CADA [6]	TMM 24	54.18	73.68	80.48	<u>46.48</u>	<u>52.60</u>	<u>69.03</u>	<u>75.22</u>	<u>25.36</u>
AUL [20]	AAAI 24	<u>56.79</u>	<u>76.14</u>	<u>83.14</u>	–	49.29	67.46	74.42	–
DMDA (Ours)	–	**58.58**	**77.11**	**83.30**	**50.91**	**52.92**	**70.13**	**76.44**	**26.76**

We comprehensively compare the domain generalization performance of our proposed DMDA method with previous SOTA TBPS approaches. As shown in Table 1, our DMDA outperforms all of the previous SOTA TBPS approaches in both CUHK to ICFG (C→I) and ICFG to CUHK (I→C) cross-domain directions, clearly demonstrating its effectiveness. For instance, in I→C direction, our

DMDA achieves the new SOTA performance with 58.58% on R@1, which surpasses the current SOTA AUL by 1.79%. As for the C→I direction, our DMDA obtains improvements over the current SOTA CADA by 0.32% on R@1.

4.3   Comparison with Other TTA Approaches

We evaluate the cross-domain performance of our DMDA method in comparison with other existing representative TTA approaches, including Tent [11] and SAR [12]. As shown in Table 2, these methods obtain poor retrieval performance when applied to TBPS. The reason is that these methods have been proposed mainly for the uni-modal image classification tasks, which cannot address the severe problems of less discriminative cross-modal distributions and modality-specific domain shifts when directly applied to TBPS. In contrast, our DMDA obtains significant performance gains, demonstrating its effectiveness.

Table 2. Performance comparisons with representative TTA methods for other tasks. The best and second-best results are shown in bold and underlined, respectively.

Methods	Venue	ICFG→CUHK				CUHK→ICFG			
		R@1	R@5	R@10	mAP	R@1	R@5	R@10	mAP
CADA (Test)	TMM 24	54.18	73.68	80.48	46.48	52.60	69.03	75.22	25.36
Tent [11]	ICLR 21	49.35	63.35	66.55	38.79	36.34	45.76	48.55	11.83
SAR [12]	ICLR 23	54.21	73.70	80.52	46.48	52.61	69.14	75.26	25.40
DMDA (Ours)	-	**58.58**	**77.11**	**83.30**	**50.91**	**52.92**	**70.13**	**76.44**	**26.76**

4.4   Evaluation on Multiple Cross-Domain Directions

To further validate the effectiveness of our DMDA under different domain generalization situations, we conduct experiments on all possible cross-domain directions. As shown in Table 3, 4.40%, 14.40%, 0.32%, 4.50%, 2.40%, and 1.07% improvements can be obtained on R@1 criterion for different cross-domain directions among the three available benchmarks, respectively.

4.5   Ablation Study

In Table 4, we perform an ablation study to evaluate the effectiveness of modules in our DMDA method. We take the I→C direction for detailed explanations. It can be observed that: **1)** Applying DPL module (No. 1) makes significant performance improvements compared to the Baseline. Specifically, we observe performance gains of 7.96% in terms of R@1 metric. This result demonstrates that, under the premise of discarding numerous irrelevant images with DPL, the entropy minimization learning is more effective. **2)** When further using the MSA

Table 3. Cross-domain performance comparisons of our DMDA across benchmarks for TBPS. The 'C', 'I', and 'R' denote CUHK-PEDES, ICFG-PEDES, and RSTPReid.

Methods	R@1	R@5	R@10	mAP
I→C Test	54.18	73.68	80.48	46.48
I→C DMDA	58.58 (4.40↑)	77.11	83.30	50.91 (4.43↑)
I→R Test	51.65	72.55	81.95	39.03
I→R DMDA	66.05 (14.40↑)	84.95	90.35	50.74 (11.71↑)
C→I Test	52.60	69.03	75.22	25.36
C→I DMDA	52.92 (0.32↑)	70.13	76.44	26.76 (1.40↑)
C→R Test	60.20	82.30	87.90	44.02
C→R DMDA	64.70 (4.50↑)	83.55	89.35	46.28 (2.26↑)
R→C Test	50.96	71.28	78.22	44.22
R→C DMDA	53.36 (2.40↑)	72.27	79.39	47.00 (2.78↑)
R→I Test	46.03	62.04	68.02	25.22
R→I DMDA	47.10 (1.07↑)	63.61	69.98	26.00 (0.78↑)

Table 4. Ablation study of our DMDA method.

Methods	$\mathcal{L}_{Ent}$	DPL	MSA	ICFG→CUHK			
				R@1	R@5	R@10	mAP
Baseline	✓			49.35	63.35	66.55	38.79
1	✓	✓		57.31	76.02	82.13	49.78
2	✓	✓	✓	58.58	77.11	83.30	50.91

module, our DMDA (No.2) can outperform the Baseline and only DPL (No.1) by 9.23% and 1.27% on R@1, respectively, since our MSA can effectively bridge the domain gap between source and target domains. These experimental results effectively demonstrate the collaboration of our DPL and MSA modules.

4.6 Retrieval Results Comparisons

As shown in Fig. 2, we provide the retrieved images for comparisons among Baseline, DPL, and the DMDA, corresponding to the results in Table 4. Taking the left case for instance, the DMDA retrieves four correct images at 1st, 2nd, 4th, and 7th places, significantly outperforming the above two rows. These results demonstrate that our proposed DMDA, as well as the DPL solely, can effectively improve the retrieval results.

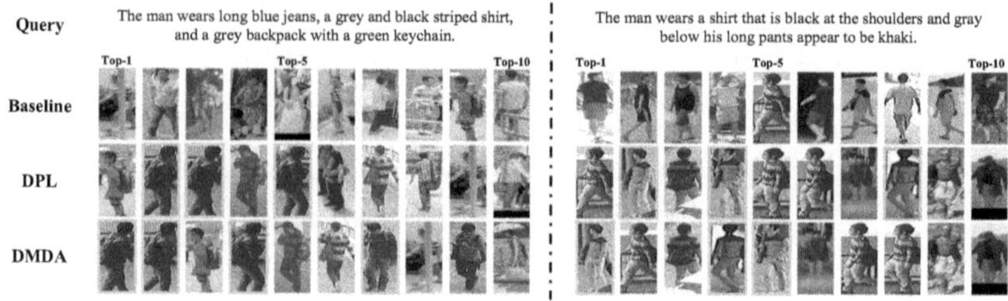

Fig. 2. Retrieval results comparisons. Correctly retrieved images are in green boxes. (Color figure online)

5 Conclusions

In this paper, we have proposed the Distribution-discriminative and Modality-aware Domain Adaptation (DMDA) method, which can quickly achieve domain adaptation only using unsupervised test data, for addressing the domain shift problem when applying text-based person search (TBPS) technique to real-world scenarios. Our DPL module discards irrelevant images and selects a credible one for each text query, producing more discriminative distributions for cross-modal alignments learning. And our MSA module explicitly aligns domains within respective modalities by an anchor-based stable adaptation strategy. Extensive experiments and analyses have validated the effectiveness of our DMDA method, and it has obtained the SOTA retrieval performance for cross-domain TBPS.

Acknowledgements. This work is jointly supported by the Key Research and Development Program of Shaanxi (2024GX-YBXM-117), Guangdong Basic and Applied Basic Research Foundation (2023A1515011427), National Natural Science Foundation of China (62571445), China National Post-doctoral Program for Innovative Talents (BX20230498), Young Talent Fund of Association for Science and Technology in Shaanxi (20240150), China Post-doctoral Science Foundation (2024M754224), and Shaanxi Post-doctoral Research Project (2024BSHSDZZ088).

References

1. Li, S., Xiao, T., Li, H., Zhou, B., Yue, D., Wang, X.: Person search with natural language description. In: CVPR (2017)
2. Ding, Z., Ding, C., Shao, Z., Tao, D.: Semantically self-aligned network for text-to-image part-aware person re-identification. arXiv:2107.12666 (2021)
3. Zhu, A., Wang, Z., Li, Y., Wan, X., Jin, J., Wang, T., Hu, F., Hua, G.: DSSL: deep surroundings-person separation learning for text-based person retrieval. In: ACM MM (2021)
4. Niu, K., Liu, Y., Long, Y., Huang, Y., Wang, L., Zhang, Y.: An overview of text-based person search: recent advances and future directions. TCSVT **34**(9), 7803–7819 (2024)

5. Jiang, D., Ye, M.: Cross-modal implicit relation reasoning and aligning for text-to-image person retrieval. In: CVPR (2023)
6. Lin, D., Peng, Y., Meng, J., Zheng, W.S.: Cross-modal adaptive dual association for text-to-image person retrieval. TMM **26**, 6609–6620 (2024)
7. Bai, Y., et al.: RaSa: relation and sensitivity aware representation learning for text-based person search. In: IJCAI (2023)
8. Qin, Y., Chen, Y., Peng, D., Peng, X., Zhou, J.T., Hu, P.: Noisy-correspondence learning for text-to-image person re-identification. In: CVPR (2024)
9. Niu, K., Huang, L., Long, Y., Huang, Y., Wang, L., Zhang, Y.: Comprehensive attribute prediction learning for person search by language. TIP **33**, 1990–2003 (2024)
10. Niu, K., Huang, T., Huang, L., Wang, L., Zhang, Y.: Improving inconspicuous attributes modeling for person search by language. TIP **32**, 3429–3441 (2023)
11. Wang, D., Shelhamer, E., Liu, S., Olshausen, B., Darrell, T.: Tent: fully test-time adaptation by entropy minimization. In: ICLR (2021)
12. Niu, S., et al.: Towards stable test-time adaptation in dynamic wild world. In: ICLR (2023)
13. Niu, S., et al.: Efficient test-time model adaptation without forgetting. In: ICLR (2022)
14. Lee, J., et al.: Entropy is not enough for test-time adaptation: from the perspective of disentangled factors. In: ICLR (2024)
15. Zhou, X., et al.: Test-time adaptation on noisy data via model-pruning-based filtering and flatness-aware entropy minimization. In: AAAI (2025)
16. Li, J., Selvaraju, R., Gotmare, A., Joty, S., Xiong, C., Hoi, S.C.H.: Align before fuse: vision and language representation learning with momentum distillation. In: NeurIPS (2021)
17. Li, S., et al.: Deep cross-modal evidential learning for text-based person retrieval. In: ACM MM (2023)
18. Zuo, J., et al.: UFineBench: towards text-based person retrieval with ultra-fine granularity. In: CVPR (2024)
19. Yang, S., Zhou, Y., Zheng, Z., Wang, Y., Zhu, L., Wu, Y.: Towards unified text-based person retrieval: a large-scale multi-attribute and language search benchmark. In: ACM MM (2023)
20. Li, S., He, C., Xu, X., Shen, F., Yang, Y., Shen, H.T.: Adaptive uncertainty-based learning for text-based person retrieval. In: AAAI (2024)

MFNet: Mamba-Driven Feature Fusion for Human Parsing

Xinyu Liu[1], Xiaomei Zhang[2,3(✉)], Jing Gu[4], Ajian Liu[2,7], Fengmei Liang[1(✉)], Hongsen Bi[5], and Zhen Lei[2,3,6,7]

[1] Taiyuan University of Technology, College of Electronic Information Engineering, Jinzhong, Shanxi, China
`fm_liang@163.com`
[2] MAIS, Institute of Automation, Chinese Academy of Science, Beijing, China
`zhangxiaomei2016@ia.ac.cn`
[3] School of Artificial Intelligence, University of Chinese Academy of Sciences, Beijing, China
[4] Guangzhou Pixel Solutions Co., Ltd., Guangzhou, China
[5] Department of Plastic Surgery, Peking University Third Hospital, Beijing, China
[6] CAIR, HKISI, Chinese Academy of Sciences, Hong Kong, China
[7] School of Computer Science and Engineering, the Faculty of Innovation Engineering, M.U.S.T., Macau, China

Abstract. Human parsing, which classifies each pixel in human images into predefined classes of human parts or clothing, faces challenges in efficient modeling complex scenarios involving pose variations and occlusion. While existing methods have shown that pose estimation benefits human parsing via multi-task learning, most of them use simplistic feature fusion strategies, making it difficult to achieve efficient parsing-pose interaction. In this paper, we propose Mamba-Driven Feature Fusion Network (MFNet), leveraging Mamba's global modeling capabilities to establish deep bidirectional parsing-pose interaction, enhancing fused features for joint human parsing and pose estimation. MFNet employs a shared backbone for initial feature extraction. Central to the framework, we introduce a cross fusion mamba module, enabling efficient parsing-pose interaction while capturing comprehensive global information. Simultaneously, an attention atrous spatial pyramid pooling module refines parsing features using dual channel-spatial attention to adaptively enhance multi-scale context. Through the combination of the two modules, MFNet effectively integrates parsing and pose features while capturing comprehensive global information. Results on two datasets demonstrate MFNet's superiority in various metrics.

Keywords: Human parsing · Mamba-driven feature fusion · Attention atrous spatial pyramid pooling

1 Introduction

Human parsing aims to classify each pixel in human images into predefined classes of human parts or clothing (e.g., head, coat, etc.). It has been widely

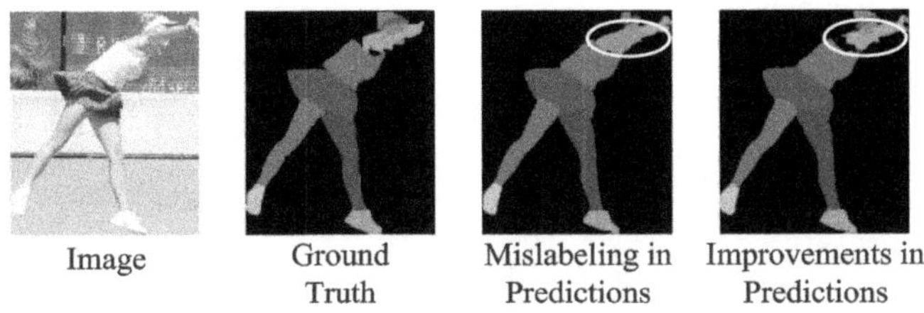

Image   Ground   Mislabeling in   Improvements in
Truth   Predictions   Predictions

Fig. 1. Examples of the challenges in human parsing. In the third image, SCHP [5] fails to parse the right-arm and left-arm due to the lack of pose and global information. In the fourth image, our method has better performance.

used in multiple challenging fields, such as person re-identification [1] and human-computer interaction [2]. However, human parsing still faces challenges of how to parse human body parts accurately under complex scenarios (e.g., diverse human poses, occlusions, etc.) (Fig. 1).

Utilizing contextual information is one of the most effective methods to improve the performance of human parsing. Existing approaches fuse multi-scale features to capture contextual information [3,4], for example, by using pyramid pooling module or atrous spatial pyramid pooling module. However, these methods struggle to model long-range dependencies across human body parts, resulting in poor performance in human parsing.

The human body has a fixed skeletal structure, hence, we can introduce pose estimation to predict the locations of keypoints on human body, providing valuable information about human structure. The information can assist in generating better parsing results. Some attempts that combine human parsing and pose estimation [6,7] have been made to improve the performance of human parsing via multi-task learning. However, most of the methods use simplistic feature fusion strategies such as concatenation, making it difficult to achieve efficient parsing-pose interaction.

In this paper, we propose Mamba-Driven Feature Fusion Network (MFNet) for human parsing. MFNet comprises two branches: the parsing branch and pose branch, along with two main components, namely the attention atrous spatial pyramid pooling module and the cross fusion mamba module. The parsing and pose branch are used to extract features for two respective tasks. The attention atrous spatial pyramid pooling module extracts multi-scale features for the parsing branch through dilated convolutions and the extracted multi-scale features are refined by attention mechanism. As for the cross fusion mamba module, we utilize the innovative architecture Mamba [8] to capture global information for both branches separately and get sufficient parsing-pose interaction, obtaining parsing features guided by pose information.

The main contributions of this paper are summarized as follows: (1) We propose MFNet, a novel framework that integrates local and global information for human parsing. (2) We introduce the pose branch to assist in human parsing, coupled with a cross fusion mamba module for deep bidirectional parsing-pose

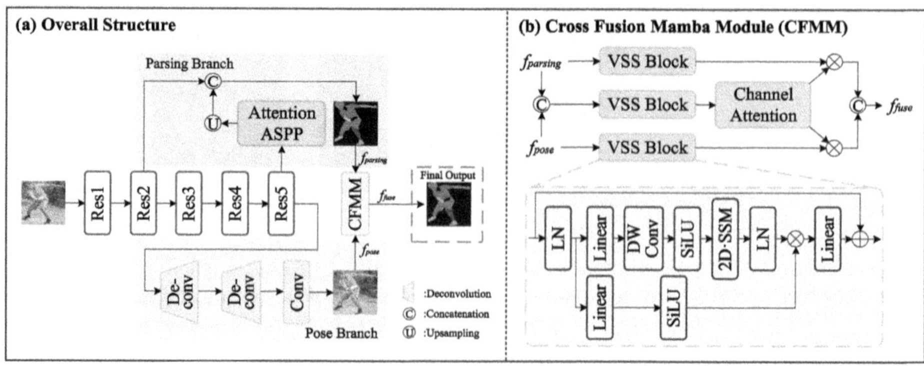

Fig. 2. Framework of the MFNet. (a) Overall structure. Attention ASPP indicates our attention atrous spatial pyramid pooling module. (b) Cross fusion mamba module. VSS block indicates visual state space module, the application of Mamba in visual tasks.

interaction and global information extraction. Simultaneously, we introduce an attention atrous spatial pyramid pooling module to capture and adaptively refine multi-scale contextual information. (3) Extensive experiments are conducted on the LIP and Pascal-Person-Part datasets. Results show the superiority and validity of the proposed MFNet.

2　Methodology

2.1　Overall Structure

The overall structure of our network is illustrated in Fig. 2(a), we leverage human pose information to benefit human parsing via multi-task learning. Human parsing and pose estimation are closely related and complementary, with their features being learnable by a shared model. Therefore, we adopt a shared backbone to extract features for both tasks. For the parsing branch, we adopt a parsing pipeline to predict a coarse parsing map, then introduce the attention atrous spatial pyramid pooling module to capture contextual information. To prevent the loss of details in the process of downsampling, we employ the features from Res2 and upsample the output of the attention atrous spatial pyramid pooling module to the same scale as Res2 and concatenate them as $f_{parsing}$. Inspired by [5, 18], Res2 features are chosen for their optimal balance between spatial resolution and semantics. For the pose branch, inspired by [10], we only deploy two deconvolution layers to extract human keypoints information. Specifically, two deconvolution layers process Res5 features, upsampling them by 4 times to yield pose feature f_{pose} at the same scale as $f_{parsing}$. Ultimately, both features are fed into cross fusion mamba module to produce a refined parsing feature map. The detailed information about the two modules will be explained in subsequent content.

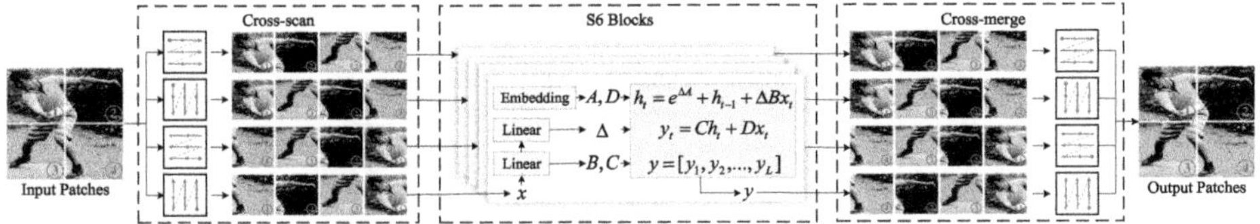

Fig. 3. Illustration of 2D selective scan module.

2.2   Cross Fusion Mamba Module

Human parsing benefits from models that integrate both global and local information processing capabilities [12]. In recent advancements, Transformer-based models have demonstrated excellent performance in various visual tasks [14,15]. However, these models are often constrained by the quadratic time complexity, posing challenges to scalability.

Mamba [8] is an extension of the selective structured state space model, which efficiently capture long-range dependencies via linear-time state transitions without Transformer's quadratic complexity. The S6 module, as the core of Mamba, maintains the linear complexity of the state space model while introducing input dependency, enabling the model to dynamically adjust parameters to capture contextual key information.

The visual state space module [16] represents an application of Mamba in visual tasks, which introduces the 2D selective scan module derived from the S6 module. As illustrated in Fig. 3, processing comprises three steps: cross-scan, selective scanning with S6 blocks, and cross-merge. For a given input, the module initially unfolds the input patches into sequences along four distinct traversal paths (cross-scan). Subsequently, each resulting patch sequence undergoes independent processing by a dedicated S6 block in parallel. Finally, the processed sequences are reshaped and merged to reconstruct the output feature map (cross-merge). By leveraging complementary 1D traversal paths, the module enables each pixel aggregate contextual information from all other pixels across different directions, thereby establishing comprehensive 2D receptive fields.

Inspired by the success of Mamba in long-range modeling and its linear complexity, we introduce the visual state space module to the human parsing. As illustrated in Fig. 2(b), we adopt the visual state space block as the main component of cross fusion mamba module. The entire process for the visual state space block can be formulated as follows:

$$x_1 = LN(2D \cdot SSM(SiLU(DWConv(Linear(LN(x)))))), \tag{1}$$

$$x_2 = SiLU(Linear(LN(x))), \tag{2}$$

$$x_{out} = Linear(x_1 \otimes x_2) \oplus x, \tag{3}$$

where x is input feature, LN is LayerNorm, 2D·SSM is the 2D selective scan module, DWConv represents depthwise convolution, $\otimes$ denotes Hadamard product and $\oplus$ denotes element-wise addition. Following [16], the 2D selective scan

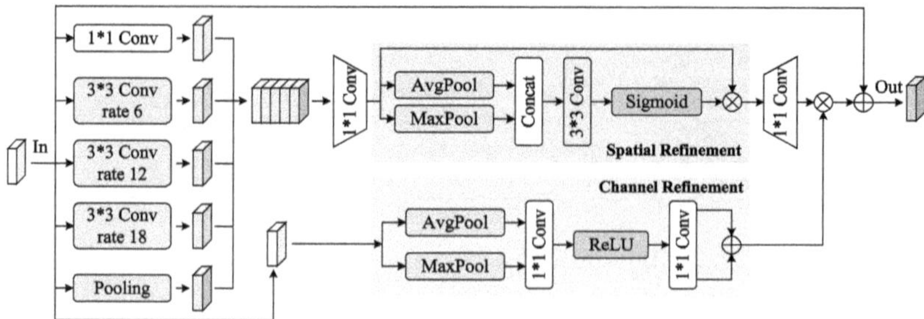

Fig. 4. The attention atrous spatial pyramid pooling module. $\otimes$ denotes Hadamard product, $\oplus$ indicates element-wise addition.

module has been applied to image segmentation, so we adopt the visual state space block as the core component of cross fusion mamba module.

As illustrated in Fig. 2(b), our proposed cross fusion mamba module fuses parsing feature $f_{parsing}$ and pose feature f_{pose} to obtain the final parsing feature f_{fuse}. Our cross fusion mamba module can be divided into three branches. In the first and third branches, features are processed through visual state space blocks to capture global information. In the second branch, original features are concatenated, then sequentially passed through a visual state space block and a channel attention block to capture global information and enrich channel information. The channel attention map from the second branch then performs Hadamard product with the processed features from the first and third branches, respectively. Ultimately, we concatenate the resulting features to obtain the final features f_{fuse}:

$$f'_{parsing} = VSS(f_{parsing}), \tag{4}$$

$$f'_{pose} = VSS(f_{pose}), \tag{5}$$

$$f'_{com} = CA(VSS(concat(f_{parsing}, f_{pose}))). \tag{6}$$

The equations above represents the process of extracting global information for parsing, pose, and combined features. VSS is the visual state space block, CA represents channel attention block, $concat$ means concatenation. $f'_{parsing}$, f'_{pose} and f'_{com} represent parsing, pose, and combined features, respectively. The following equations represent the process of interaction between parsing and pose features. $f''_{parsing}$ and f''_{pose} represent parsing features with pose information and pose features with parsing information, respectively, f_{fuse} denotes the final parsing features.

$$f''_{parsing} = f'_{com} \otimes f'_{parsing}, \tag{7}$$

$$f''_{pose} = f'_{com} \otimes f'_{pose}, \tag{8}$$

$$f_{fuse} = concat(f''_{parsing}, f''_{pose}). \tag{9}$$

where $concat$ means concatenation and $\otimes$ denotes Hadamard product.

2.3   Attention Atrous Spatial Pyramid Pooling Module

Contextual information is leveraged in many previous tasks in semantic segmentation [4,11], and it is also crucial in human parsing. Therefore, we introduce the attention atrous spatial pyramid pooling module for the parsing branch to enlarge receptive fields and acquire more valuable contextual information.

As illustrated in Fig. 4, output from Res5 is fed into the attention atrous spatial pyramid pooling module for refinement. We first extract multi-scale features through atrous convolution (dilation rates 6, 12 and 18) [11] and concatenate them. After that, spatial refinement starts with channel projection via a 1×1 convolution reducing channel, followed by mean and max pooling, 3×3 convolution and sigmoid activation to generate spatial attention map. The spatial attention map is combined with the feature map prior to spatial refinement through Hadamard product to acquire spatial refined features. In parallel, channel refinement uses global average pooling and global max pooling to reduce dimensions, followed by 1×1 convolution and ReLU activation to generate channel attention map. The channel attention map is expanded to match the input dimensions and combined with the refined spatial feature map. By incorporating the module, the resulting feature maps are enriched with spatial and channel information.

2.4   Loss Function

The total loss function of our method is defined as Eq. (10),

$$L = L_p + L_{up} + \alpha L_{ps}. \tag{10}$$

where L is the total loss, L_p is the loss between the coarse parsing results and the annotations, L_{up} is the loss between the final parsing results and the annotations, L_{ps} is the loss of the pose branch and α is the loss weight parameter for pose branch. The cross entropy loss is adopted as L_p and L_{up}, and the mean square error loss is used for L_{ps}.

3   Experiments

3.1   Experimental Settings

Datasets and Metrics. We evaluate the performance of the proposed method on two human parsing datasets:

LIP. The LIP dataset [6] is a large-scale benchmark dataset focusing on single human parsing. There are 50462 human images in total, including 30462 for training, 10000 for testing, and 10000 for validation. It contains coordinates of 16 body keypoints and 19 semantic human parts.

Pascal-Person-Part. The Pascal-Person-Part dataset [26] is one of the most representative and widely used datasets in the human parsing task. There are 3533 human images in total, including 1716 for training and 1817 for validation

Table 1. Experimental results on the LIP validation set.

Method	hat	hair	glove	s-glass	clot	dress	coat	sock	pant	suit	scarf	skirt	face	l-arm	r-arm	l-leg	r-leg	l-shoe	r-shoe	bkg	**mIoU**
MuLA [17]	-	-	-	-	-	-	-	-	-	-	-	-	-	-	-	-	-	-	-	-	49.30
JPPNet [6]	63.55	70.20	36.16	23.48	68.15	31.42	55.65	44.56	72.19	28.39	18.76	25.14	73.36	61.97	63.88	58.21	57.99	44.02	44.09	86.26	51.37
CE2P [18]	65.29	72.54	39.09	32.73	69.46	32.52	56.28	49.67	74.11	27.23	14.19	22.51	75.50	65.14	66.59	60.10	58.59	46.63	46.12	87.64	53.10
BraidNet [19]	66.84	72.04	42.54	32.14	69.84	33.74	57.44	49.04	74.94	32.44	19.34	27.24	74.94	65.54	67.94	60.24	59.04	47.44	54.54	88.04	54.40
PCNet [20]	69.32	73.08	44.72	34.21	72.59	36.02	60.84	51.03	76.66	38.78	31.60	33.94	76.65	67.07	68.74	60.22	60.16	47.65	48.67	88.68	57.03
CNIF [21]	69.55	73.45	45.17	**41.45**	70.57	38.52	57.94	54.02	75.07	28.00	31.92	30.20	76.38	68.28	69.49	65.52	65.51	52.67	53.38	87.99	57.74
NPPNet [22]	66.43	72.34	51.98	31.59	71.88	40.88	60.54	49.81	77.07	27.55	26.58	33.54	75.31	71.04	71.50	**71.75**	**70.55**	56.66	55.84	88.38	58.56
SCHP [5]	69.96	73.55	50.46	40.72	69.93	39.02	57.45	**54.27**	76.01	32.88	26.29	31.68	76.19	69.65	70.92	67.28	66.56	55.76	56.50	88.36	58.62
PRM [23]	**70.83**	**74.22**	50.32	40.02	73.12	38.52	63.81	53.64	**78.51**	40.05	**32.51**	35.13	**77.26**	68.52	68.92	62.32	61.35	49.64	49.75	88.82	58.86
DTML [27]	68.07	73.86	43.62	34.27	**75.23**	**53.63**	**66.34**	49.56	77.72	**43.45**	30.78	**38.29**	76.45	67.21	68.80	62.32	62.22	49.37	50.19	**89.11**	59.02
MFNet(ours)	70.03	73.67	**52.16**	40.89	71.39	41.15	58.16	53.09	77.49	33.63	27.17	32.42	77.05	**71.88**	**72.27**	71.53	70.29	**56.69**	**57.07**	88.71	**59.84**

Table 2. Experimental results on the Pascal-Person-Part validation set.

Method	head	torso	u-arm	l-arm	u-leg	l-leg	bkg	**mIoU**
MuLA [17]	-	-	-	-	-	-	-	65.10
PGN [24]	**90.89**	**75.12**	55.83	64.61	55.42	41.57	95.33	68.40
CNIF [21]	88.02	72.91	64.31	63.52	55.61	54.96	96.02	70.76
SCHP [5]	87.41	73.80	64.98	64.70	57.43	55.62	**96.26**	71.46
NPPNet [22]	86.78	72.50	66.33	63.95	58.06	58.58	95.88	71.73
MTMamba [25]	-	-	-	-	-	-	-	72.62
MFNet(ours)	88.47	74.87	**67.34**	**66.92**	**59.24**	**58.78**	96.17	**73.11**

and it contains 6 semantic human parts. On account of no human pose annotations in Pascal-Person-Part, we utilize the pose estimator trained on COCO [10] to obtain 14 human body keypoints locations as ground truth.

Metrics. We mainly report three standard metrics, including pixel accuracy (Pixel Acc), mean accuracy (Mean Acc) and mean intersection over union (mIoU). The mIoU is the main metrics to judge the overall parsing performance of the method.

Implementation Details. We conduct all experiments on three NVIDIA 2080Ti GPUs. We choose ResNet101 pre-trained on ImageNet [9] as the backbone. We employ SGD optimizer with a base learning rate of 7e-3 and the 'Poly' learning rate policy is adopted to adjust the learning rate. We set the momentum at 0.9 and the weight decay at 5e-4. The weight of pose loss α is 70 based on [7]. Training is done with a total batch size of 8. Following previous work [1], we train our network for 150 epochs in total, the first 100 epochs serve as initialization, while the subsequent 50 epochs are divided into 5 cycles with each cycle consisting of 10 epochs dedicated to self-correction process. As for two datasets (LIP and Pascal-Person-Part), we resize images to 473×473 and 512×512 as the input size, respectively. For data augmentation, we apply random scaling (from 0.5 to 1.5) and left-right flipping during training. In the inference process, following the general protocol [18], we average the per-pixel classification scores at multiple scales with flipping; the scale is 0.5 to 1.5 times the original size.

3.2   Model Comparison

Performance on LIP. As illustrated in Table 1, MFNet achieves superior performance with a higher mIoU of 59.84%, surpassing all other methods listed in table. Notably, MFNet outperforms other methods on the classes contain prominent human keypoints such as glove, l-arm, r-arm, l-shoe and r-shoe, indicating that incorporating pose information provides substantial auxiliary benefits for the complex task of human parsing. Furthermore, the results underscore the inherent strength of the cross fusion mamba module itself in sufficient feature fusion and capturing comprehensive contextual information. However, as we can see, performance varies across different categories of human body parts, primarily resulting from the complexity of certain classes and the specific strengths of different modules. MFNet excels in keypoint-rich areas (e.g., arms and legs) attributed to its pose-guided global fusion. Conversely, classes with complex textures or loose contours (e.g., coat and scarf) that rely on local recognition show modest gains. Although MFNet's attention atrous spatial pyramid pooling module enhances multi-scale local feature extraction, texture regions benefit less from pose and global information. Thus, MFNet excels in structured regions but poorly in areas with complex textures and loose contours.

Performance on Pascal-Person-Part. As illustrated in Table 2, MFNet outperforms other competitors. MFNet achieves mIoU of 73.11%, surpassing all comparative methods documented in the table. Detailed analysis of per-class performance further reveals MFNet's pronounced advantages in several critical anatomical segments. Specifically, the model exhibits its strongest gains over alternatives in u-arm, l-arm, u-leg, and l-leg. Importantly, these specific regions encompassing the arms and legs are precisely where human keypoints are most prominent. This pattern of excellence is highly consistent with the previously reported results on the LIP dataset. The performance of the model is superior to other models in these keypoint-rich areas, which once again provides strong empirical verification for the core components of MFNet.

Visualization of Results. The visual comparison of parsing results on LIP are visualized in Fig. 5. There are two human parsing methods, SCHP and our network. As illustrated in Fig. 5, SCHP has the problem of misjudgment. In the first and second columns, SCHP mistakenly categorizes the right shoe as a sock, and SCHP confuses the left and right arm in the second column. In contrast, our network achieves the correct result, demonstrating the effectiveness of the pose information. From the last three columns, our method achieves better performance in extracting more complete human parts because the pose information provides more complete human structures and our cross fusion mamba module captures more comprehensive global information while enabling sufficient interaction between the parsing and pose information.

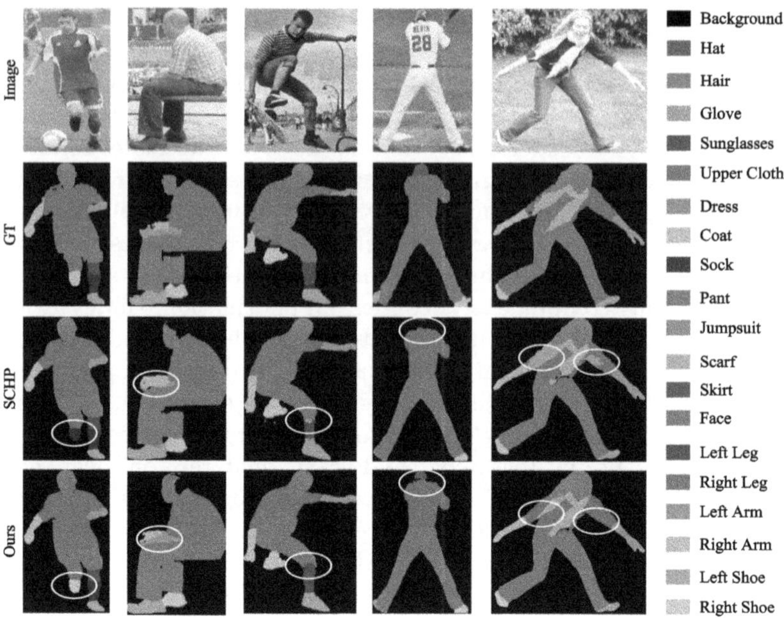

Fig. 5. Visual comparisons on the LIP dateset.

3.3   Ablation Study

To verify the effectiveness and the design of our modules, we evaluate Pixel Acc, Mean Acc and mIoU for ablation study on the LIP validation dataset.

Effectiveness of the Attention Atrous Spatial Pyramid Pooling Module and Cross Fusion Mamba Module. To validate the effectiveness of the two modules, we conduct experiments using the basic atrous spatial pyramid pooling module and the fusion strategy of concatenation separately to replace our modules. As illustrated in Table 3, our network outperforms the baseline model for all metrics. Specifically, using the attention atrous spatial pyramid pooling module alone leads to improvements, demonstrating its effectiveness in feature refinement. Similarly, using the cross fusion mamba module further enhances the performance, demonstrating its effectiveness in extracting global information and feature fusion. Notably, the combination of them yields the best results across all metrics, demonstrating their synergistic effect and the superiority of our method.

Design of the Cross Fusion Mamba Module. To verify the effectiveness of each subcomponent of the cross fusion mamba module, we sequentially remove channel attention block, visual state space blocks, and multi-branch design respectively while retaining the attention atrous spatial pyramid pooling module. Table 4 shows that removing multi-branch design severely degrades performance, confirming the necessity of posture guidance. Removing the visual state space

Table 3. Ablation results on the designed modules. Attention ASPP indicates atrous spatial pyramid pooling module and CFMM indicates cross fusion mamba module.

Attention ASPP	CFMM	Pixel Acc	Mean Acc	mIoU
✗	✗	88.10	72.76	58.62
✔	✗	88.19	73.42	59.06
✗	✔	88.33	73.97	59.38
✔	✔	**88.45**	**74.58**	**59.84**

Table 4. Ablation results on the design of the cross fusion mamba module. Experimental configurations include CA+VSS (removing the multi-branch design); Multi-branch+CA (removing the visual state space blocks); Multi-branch+VSS (removing the channel attention block); and Multi-branch+VSS+CA (retaining all components).

Subcomponents	Pixel Acc	Mean Acc	mIoU
CA+VSS	87.92	71.87	58.11
Multi-branch+CA	88.21	73.45	58.97
Multi-branch+VSS	88.29	74.01	59.68
Multi-branch+VSS+CA	**88.45**	**74.58**	**59.84**

blocks causes significant performance degradation, proving their critical role of global modeling. The removal of the channel attention block leads to a minor mIoU drop but is retained for dynamically adjusting salient channel weights after feature fusion. The complete MFNet achieves substantial gains, demonstrating the value of all three components.

4 Conclusion

In this paper, we propose MFNet, a novel framework leveraging mamba for human parsing via multi-task learning. To improve parsing performance, we integrate pose estimation as an auxiliary task, providing structural priors via a shared backbone. A key innovation is the cross fusion mamba module, which employs mamba's selective state space mechanism to scan features bidirectionally across four directions, enabling efficient global modeling and deep interaction between parsing and pose information. We also introduce an attention atrous spatial pyramid pooling module with dual channel-spatial attention to adaptively refine multi-scale context. MFNet has been validated on the LIP and Pascal-Person-Part datasets and the results show the superiority of our method.

Acknowledgment. This work was supported in part by Chinese National Natural Science Foundation Projects 62206280, U23B2054 and 62276254, 62376265, Young Scientists Fund of the State Key Laboratory of Multimodal Artificial Intelligence Systems ES2P100113, Beijing Natural Science Foundation 7252151 and L221013, Science and Technology Development Fund of Macau Project 0140/2024/AGJ.

References

1. Kalayeh M., Basaran E., Gökmen M., et al.: Human semantic parsing for person re-identification. In: IEEE CVPR, pp. 1062–1071 (2018)
2. Qi S., Wang W., Jia B., et al.: Learning human-object interactions by graph parsing neural networks. In: ECCV, pp. 401–417 (2018)
3. Liang X., Xu C., Shen X., et al.: Human parsing with contextualized convolutional neural network. In: IEEE ICCV, pp. 1386-1394 (2015)
4. Chen, L., Papandreou, G., Kokkinos, I., et al.: Deeplab: semantic image segmentation with deep convolutional nets, atrous convolution, and fully connected CRFs. IEEE TPAMI **40**(4), 834–848 (2017)
5. Li, P., Xu, Y., Wei, Y., et al.: Self-correction for human parsing. IEEE TPAMI **44**(6), 3260–3271 (2020)
6. Liang, X., Gong, K., Shen, X., et al.: Look into person: joint body parsing & pose estimation network and a new benchmark. IEEE TPAMI **41**(4), 871–885 (2018)
7. Zhang Z., Su C., Zheng L., et al.: Correlating edge, pose with parsing. In: IEEE CVPR, pp. 8900–8909 (2020)
8. Albert, G., Tri, D.: Mamba: linear-time sequence modeling with selective state spaces. arXiv preprint arXiv:2312.00752 (2023)
9. He, K., Zhang, X., Ren, S., et al.: Deep residual learning for image recognition. In: IEEE CVPR, pp. 770–778 (2016)
10. Xiao, B., Wu, H., Wei, Y.: Simple baselines for human pose estimation and tracking. In: ECCV, pp. 446–481 (2018)
11. Chen, L., Zhu, Y., Papandreou, G., et al.: Encoder-decoder with atrous separable convolution for semantic image segmentation. In: ECCV, pp. 801–818 (2018)
12. Song, J., Shi, Q., Li, Y., et al.: Enhanced context learning with transformer for human parsing. Appl. Sci. **12**(15), 7821 (2022)
13. Zhang, J., Liu, H., Li, Y., et al.: Tkformer: typed keypoints guided transformer for human parsing. In: 7th ACAIT, pp. 1468–1477 (2023)
14. Dosovitskiy, A., Beyer, L., Kolesnikov, A., et al.: An image is worth 16x16 words: transformers for image recognition at scale. arXiv preprint arXiv:2010.11929 (2020)
15. Liu, Z., Lin, Y., Cao, Y., et al.: Swin transformer: hierarchical vision transformer using shifted windows. In: IEEE ICCV, pp. 10012–10022 (2021)
16. Liu, Y., Tian, Y., Zhao, Y., et al.: Vmamba: visual state space model. NeurIPS **37**, 103031–103063 (2024)
17. Nie, X., Feng, J., Yan, S.: Mutual learning to adapt for joint human parsing and pose estimation. In: ECCV, pp. 502–517 (2018)
18. Ruan, T., Liu, T., Huang, Z., et al.: Devil in the details: towards accurate single and multiple human parsing. In: AAAI, pp. 4814–4821 (2019)
19. Liu, X., Zhang, M., Liu, W., et al.: Braidnet: braiding semantics and details for accurate human parsing. In: ACM MM, pp. 338–346 (2019)
20. Zhang, X., Chen, Y., Zhu, B., et al.: Part-aware context network for human parsing. In: IEEE CVPR, pp. 8971–8980 (2020)
21. Wang, W., Zhang, Z., Qi, S., et al.: Learning compositional neural information fusion for human parsing. In: IEEE ICCV, pp. 5703–5713 (2019)
22. Zeng, D., Huang, Y., Bao, Q., et al.: Neural architecture search for joint human parsing and pose estimation. In: IEEE ICCV, pp. 11385–11394 (2021)
23. Zhang, X., Chen, Y., Tang, M., et al.: Human parsing with part-aware relation modeling. IEEE TMM **25**, 2601–2612 (2022)

24. Gong, K., Liang, X., Li, Y., et al. : Instance-level human parsing via part grouping network. In: ECCV, pp. 770–785 (2018)
25. Lin, B., Jiang, W., Chen, P., et al.: MTMamba: enhancing multi-task dense scene understanding by mamba-based decoders. In: ECCV, pp. 314–330. Springer (2024)
26. Chen, X., Mottaghi, R., Liu, X., et al.: Detect what you can: detecting and representing objects using holistic models and body parts. In: CVPR, pp. 1971–1978 (2014)
27. Liu, Y., Wang, C., Lu, M., et al.: From simple to complex scenes: learning robust feature representations for accurate human parsing. IEEE TPAMI **46**(8) (2024)

Automatic Visual-Language Aligning Network for Visible-Infrared Person Re-identification

Qihan Chen, Guifang Zhang$^{(\boxtimes)}$, Dingyue Liu, and Yuming Fang

School of Information Technology, Jiangxi University of Finance and Economics,
Nanchang, Jiangxi, China
1439402142@qq.com

Abstract. Visible-infrared person re-identification focuses on matching identities across visible and infrared images, with the key challenge being extracting discriminative features across modalities. To tackle this, we propose an Automatic Visual-Language Aligning Network (AVLA). It leverages a multi-modal pre-trained model to automatically generate text descriptions for pedestrians during training, and incorporates an Image-Text Dynamic Attention (ITDA) module to categorize and fuse features by modality. Additionally, we design weighted distribution matching (WDM) to align visual and textual embeddings globally. Extensive experiments on public datasets demonstrate that our method outperforms existing approaches.

Keywords: Person Re-identification · Multi-modal · Automatic text generation · Weighted distribution matching

1 Introduction

Visible-infrared person re-identification (VI-ReID) aims to match people's identities in different imaging modalities. However, the unique modality of infrared images produces significant domain differences and more complex environments, such as the loss of color, texture, and detail information that are common in images. These make previous single-modality methods based only on visible images less efficient for the VI-ReID task.

The definition of visible-infrared person re-identification was proposed by Wu [1]; they proposed a cross-modal person re-identification framework and a large-scale RGB-infrared multi-modal pedestrian database named SYSU Multiple Modality Re-ID (SYSU-MM01). Inspired by this groundbreaking work, a multitude of related studies [2–10] have been proposed, which can generally be categorized into two types, including feature-level-based and image-level methods. Feature-level-based methods [2–5] are based on the original modal data and strive to map images from different modalities into a shared embedding space to reduce their differences. Image-level methods [7–10] aimed to minimize the

W. Jia et al. (Eds.): CCBR 2025, LNCS 16360, pp. 540–549, 2026.
https://doi.org/10.1007/978-981-95-6123-0_50

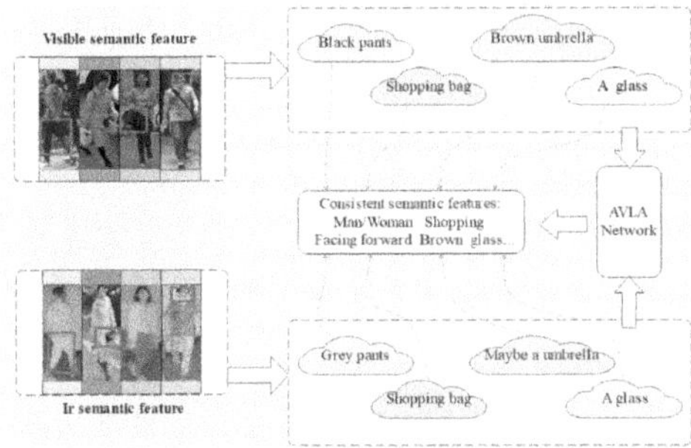

Fig. 1. The potential of multi-modality in VI-ReID: The consistency of semantic information across different modalities provides a crucial bridge, allowing us to mine and utilize information at various scales to extract more comprehensive and precise individual features. Our AVLA effectively achieves this objective.

differences between two modalities at the image level by using Generative Adversarial Networks (GANs) [6] to transform images from one modality to another or by creating intermediate modality images for training. However, the cross-modal images often contain noise, which compromises the output quality and presents a significant challenge to the stability of the training process.

Recently, visual-language learning has received extensive attention, in the VI-ReID, as depicted In Fig. 1, despite the significant disparity between the images of the two modalities of pedestrians, the semantic consistency enables us to delve deeper and harness the information more effectively across various levels. However, the great potential of multi-modality in promoting feature learning for Visible-infrared ReID has not been fully explored. CSDN [11] was the first to apply CLIP to Visible-infrared ReID. By using language as a bridge, CSDN successfully establishes the matching of high-level semantic features between infrared and visible images. However, the model still has room for improvement in terms of perfection. YYDS [12] provided a new perspective on the field of Visible-infrared ReID by introducing manually depicted text to assist the person retrieval process. However, the manual text description method has certain limitations regarding versatility.

To address the issues above, we design a visual-language person re-identification model capable of automatically generating textual descriptions (AVLA). The method employs a ViLT pre-trained model to generate text during training. Then, it uses both the features of the image and the text description to enhance the accuracy and robustness of VI-ReID. We adopt an ITDA module [13]. This module specializes in separating and aligning features, segregating visual and textual data into visible and infrared categories, and integrating the corresponding modality features with weighted consideration. In addition, we designed cross-modal matching loss (WDM) to handle visual-text features better. Our improvements enhance the generalization ability of the model, enabling the model to capture and fuse visual and semantic features more effectively. Ultimately, it improves the model's performance in complex scenarios and provides a new perspective on multi-modal learning. The contributions of this paper are summarized as follows:

- We introduce a new Automatic Visual-Language Aligning Network for Visible-Infrared Person Re-Identification.
- We adopt an ITDA module that automatically categorizes features into visible and infrared groups and combines the text features with the visual features by weight.
- We design a novel cross-modal matching loss (WDM), which incorporates the attention distribution of image and text feature interactions into the KL divergence to relate the representations of different features.
- Extensive experiments are conducted on SYSU-MM01, RegDB, and LLCM to demonstrate the effectiveness of our approach.

2   Proposed Method

An overview of our proposed AVLA is shown in Fig. 2. Our network comprises a text generation module, an image encoder, a text encoder, and an ITDA module. The text generation module uses ViLT [14] to act as our multi-modal model. The image encoder is responsible for processing visible and infrared images and extracting their key visual features. At the same time, the text encoder processes visible and infrared images to generate corresponding text features. The ITDA module aims to categorize and integrate visual and textual information between different images and finally feeds the integrated interactive features into the WDM loss for optimization. In the following sections, we will comprehensively describe our network, detailing the role and impact of these encoders and modules in the network.

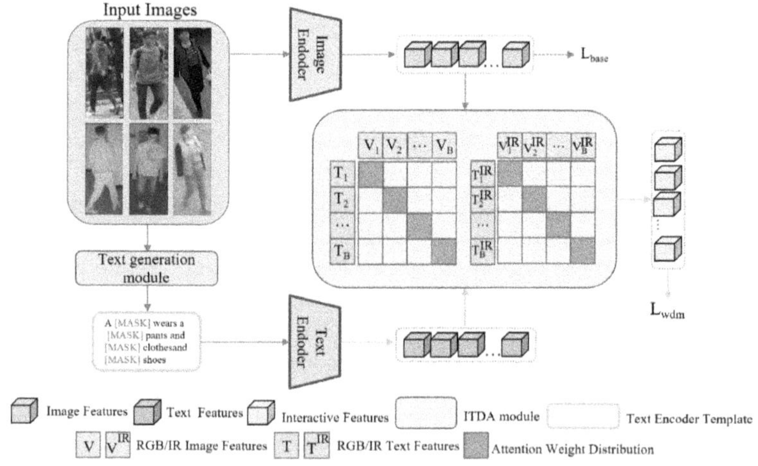

Fig. 2. The overview of our proposed network. It comprises a text generation module, an image encoder, a text encoder, and an ITDA module. The text encoder uses a preset text template to generate text features. Text and image features are classified and integrated into a comprehensive feature to calculate the loss.

2.1 Encoders

The image encoder is built upon the baseline established by the diverse embedding expansion network DEEN [5] for visible-infrared person re-identification. It utilizes a two-stream ResNet-50 architecture pre-trained on large-scale datasets to extract robust features from visible (VIS) and infrared (IR) images. The encoder is designed to handle the modality gaps between VIS and IR images by incorporating a diverse embedding expansion (DEE) module and a multi-stage feature aggregation (MFA) block. Finally, the global image features are output: f_I. To facilitate the integration with the features of the text encoder and enable the subsequent loss calculation, batch normalization (BN) blocks are used for normalization.

The text encoder processes textual inputs and produces features corresponding to the input image, denoted as x_o. We employ a set of predefined text templates, represented by $\mathbb{T}$, to extract semantic insights. For instance, the template might read: "A [MASK] is wearing [MASK] pants and [MASK] sneakers, facing [MASK] direction, and donning a [MASK] garment." To maintain the uniformity and coherence of text representations across various images, we designate the [MASK] as the element to be predicted. We then supply $\mathbb{T}$ and x_o to ViLT, a model that extends the transformer architecture to handle visual and textual data, processing information from both domains in tandem. By harnessing the capabilities of ViLT, the text encoder automatically deduces the content of the [MASK] element based on the details present in x_o. It then substitutes the predicted content back into the template, resulting in an updated template $\mathbb{T}'$. Subsequently, we derive a suite of text features, f_T, that are intricately linked to the input image and encapsulate the semantic essence of the image within the prediction template $\mathbb{T}'$. It is essential to highlight that the dimensionality of f_T is synchronized with that of f_I, which ensures compatibility within the network and simplifies subsequent integration processes.

2.2 Image-Text Dynamic Attention Module

Due to the inherent differences between visible and infrared modalities, the text features extracted from these two modalities also show significant differences. If these two modalities' image and text features are directly combined and calculated, it may cause interference from invalid information. To address the above situation, we adopt an ITDA module [13], classify the features, integrate them according to their respective modalities, and feed the integrated features into WDM. This approach can ensure the effectiveness and accuracy of the feature fusion process, thereby improving the performance of Visible-infrared pedestrian re-identification.

First, the modules process the visual features f_I and text features f_T from different modal images. Together, they serve as the Attention Weight Controller (AWC) input. The AWC module calculates the attention weights of the image and text features and dynamically assigns the weights to the features that best describe the pedestrian. The attention weights between the text and image features using the AWC module can be expressed as follows:

$$\omega_{\mathrm{TI}} = \mathrm{softmax}\left(\frac{f_T \cdot f_I^T}{\sqrt{d_T}}\right) \cdot S_{\mathrm{TI}}$$
$$\omega_{\mathrm{IT}} = \mathrm{softmax}\left(\frac{f_I \cdot f_T^T}{\sqrt{d_I}}\right) \cdot S_{\mathrm{IT}} \tag{1}$$

where ω_{TI} denotes the attention weights for the text-to-image (TI) mapping, which signifies the degree of relevance between each text feature element and its corresponding image feature element. In a parallel manner, ω_{IT} denotes the attention weights for the image-to-text (IT) attention mechanism. The term d_T refers to the dimensionality of the text features, while d_I corresponds to the dimensionality of the image features. The notation f_I^T represents the transpose of signifies the transpose of the f_I tensor, and similarly, f_T^T represents the transpose of the f_T tensor. The symbol $\cdot$ denotes the dot product operation. S_{TI} and S_{IT} are tensor matrices that are capable of being learned for the TI and IT attention mechanisms, respectively.

2.3   Loss Functions

This paper designed a novel cross-modal matching loss termed weighted distribution matching (WDM) to optimize the integrated features better. WDM combines the attention weight distributions of image and text feature interactions into Kullback-Leibler(KL) divergence to correlate representations of different modalities. KL divergence loss is responsible for Interactive Features. The objective function of our AVLA can be summarized as follows:

$$\mathcal{L}_{total} = \mathcal{L}_{base} + \mathcal{L}_{wdm} \tag{2}$$

where $\mathcal{L}_{base}$ represents the loss derived from the image features, $\mathcal{L}_{wdm}$ represents the weighted distribution matching loss between images and text. Bidirectional WDM loss is calculated by:

$$\mathcal{L}_{wdm} = \mathcal{L}_{i2t} + \mathcal{L}_{t2i} \tag{3}$$

Similarly, Triple-weighted distribution matching loss is calculated by:

$$\mathcal{L}_{twdm} = \mathcal{L}_{i2i} + \mathcal{L}_{t2t} + \mathcal{L}_{i2t} \tag{4}$$

$\mathcal{L}_{i2t}$ represents the weighted distribution matching loss from image to text. Symmetrically, the $\mathcal{L}_{t2i}$ represents the weighted distribution matching loss from text to image. The formula can be expressed as:

$$\mathcal{L}_{i2t} = KL(\omega_{TI} \parallel \omega_{IT}) = \frac{1}{N}\sum_{i=1}^{N}\sum_{j=1}^{N} \omega_i \log\left(\frac{\omega_i}{\omega_j + \epsilon}\right) \tag{5}$$

where N represents the number of image-text feature pairs, ω_i is the matching weight between the image-to-text feature, and ω_j is the corresponding matching weight from text-to-image. ϵ is a small number to avoid numerical problems. Symmetrically, the $\mathcal{L}_{t2i}$ can be formulated by exchanging ω_{TI} and ω_{IT} in Eq. 5.

3   Experiments

3.1   Datasets and Implementation Details

We compare the performance of our proposed AVLA on three datasets, SYSU-MM01 [1], RegDB [15], and LLCM [5], which include a large number of images and identity information to verify the effectiveness of our proposed method. We use comparable evaluation metrics mAP and Rank-1(R1) to evaluate the metrics. In our experiments, all images are uniformly resized to 3x384x144, and a series of enhancements are performed to improve the robustness of the model. These enhancements include random horizontal flipping, padding, random cropping, random erasing [16] and random grayscale conversion [17]. In the training stage, we used a batch size of 6. The SGD optimizer is used with a momentum of 0.9 and weight decay of 1e-4. Due to the high efficiency of the visual-semantic pre-trained model, the training process is adjusted to 80 epochs, with a starting learning rate of 0.01, which is then increased to 0.1 after 20 epochs through a warm-up strategy. After that, we decay the learning rate to 0.01 in 40 epochs and 0.001 in epoch60. To optimize the learning process, we choose a cosine learning rate decay schedule is applied to optimize the learning process. All experiments are performed on a single NVIDIA GeForce RTX 4090 GPU.

3.2   Comparison with State-of-the-Arts

We compare our AVLA model with state-of-the-art VI-ReID methods published in recent years on public VIReID datasets SYSU-MM01, RegDB, and LLCM.

The comparison results based on the SYSU-MM01 dataset can be demonstrated from Table 1. The dataset results show that the proposed AVLA performs best compared to all other state-of-the-art methods. Specifically, for All-Search on SYSU-MM01, AVLA achieves 77.36% Rank-1 accuracy and 71.80% mAP. For indoor search mode, AVLA achieves 83.11% Rank-1 accuracy and 84.56% mAP. The results verify the effectiveness of our method. It demonstrates its robustness and effectiveness on different datasets. Our method exhibits more satisfactory performance than other methods. The results also show that the proposed AVLA can effectively reduce the modality gap between VIS and IR modalities.

The experimental results based on RegDB and LLCM datasets are shown in Table 2. In the RegDB dataset, AVLA achieves a Rank-1 of 93.66%, and a mAP of 85.11%, which is higher than the top score of DEEN's Rank-1 of 89.5%, and the top score of mAP of 83.4%. In the LLCM dataset, our method AVLA achieves a Rank-1 of 57.12%, and a mAP of 63.34%, which is higher than the top score of DEEN's Rank-1 of 54.9%, and the top score of mAP of 62.9%. The result demonstrates the effectiveness of the proposed AVLA in reducing the modality gap between RGB and IR images.

Table 1. Comparison with the state-of-the-art on the SYSU-MM01 dataset.

| Method | Reference | SYSU-MM01 | | | | | | | |
| | | All Search | | | | Indoor Search | | | |
		Rank-1	Rank-10	Rank-20	mAP	Rank-1	Rank-10	Rank-20	mAP
DML [18]	TCSVT2022	58.4	91.2	96.9	56.1	62.4	95.2	98.7	69.5
FMCNet [8]	CVPR2022	66.3	-	-	62.5	68.2	-	-	74.1
SPOT [19]	TIP2022	65.34	92.73	97.04	62.25	69.42	96.22	99.12	74.63
DCLNet [20]	ACM MM2022	70.8	-	-	65.3	73.5	-	-	76.8
DSCNet [21]	TIFS2022	73.8	96.2	98.8	69.4	79.3	98.3	99.7	82.6
MSCLNet [3]	ECCV2022	76.99	97.63	99.18	71.64	78.49	**99.32**	**99.91**	81.17
GUR [22]	ICCV2023	63.51	-	-	61.63	71.11	-	-	76.23
CMTR [23]	TMM2023	65.4	94.4	98.1	62.9	71.4	97.1	99.2	76.6
MRCN [4]	AAAI2023	68.9	95.2	98.4	65.5	76.0	98.3	99.7	79.8
DEEN [5]	CVPR2023	74.7	**97.6**	99.2	71.8	80.3	99.0	99.8	83.3
MFCS [24]	IEEE2024	70.59	96.22	98.77	67.49	75.98	98.12	99.62	80.24
AVLA	Ours	**77.36**	97.50	**99.42**	**71.8**	**83.11**	98.73	99.46	**84.56**

Table 2. Comparison with the state-of-the-art on the RegDB and LLCM dataset.

| Method | Reference | RegDB | | LLCM | |
		Rank-1	mAP	Rank-1	mAP
DDAG [25]	ECCV2020	68.1	61.8	41.0	49.6
AGW [26]	TPAMI2021	70.05	66.37	46.4	54.8
LbA [27]	ICCV2021	67.5	72.4	44.6	53.8
CAJ [28]	ICCV2021	84.8	77.8	48.8	56.6
MMN [10]	MM2021	87.5	80.5	52.5	58.9
DART [28]	CVPR2022	82.0	73.8	52.2	59.8
DEEN [5]	CVPR2023	89.5	83.4	54.9	62.9
AVLA	Ours	**93.66**	**85.11**	**57.12**	**63.34**

3.3   Ablation Study

In this study, our core motivation is to learn visual representations with semantic information and effectively integrate visual and textual features to alleviate the challenges of modality alignment in VIReID. We conducted several ablation studies to verify the effectiveness of our network structure. Specifically, we first evaluated the impact of each component module on the performance of AVLA, the effect of cross-modal pre-trained models on different image inputs, and the performance of different loss function selections. All experiments were conducted under All-search and single-shot.

Ablation Study of Different Components of AVLA. To evaluate the effectiveness of each module on the AVLA network, we conduct ablation experiments to compare the modules. The results of the comparative study are summarized in Table 3. Base: only uses an image encoder. Vilt: uses vilt pre-trained model. ITDA: uses the ITDA module to integrate features. WDM: adds WDM loss function.

First, we tried directly applying the pre-trained Vilt model without deep integration of visual-language features. Although this method caused a slight decrease of 4.42% and 4.57% in Rank-1 accuracy and mAP, respectively, it significantly accelerated the training process. The number of epochs required to achieve the best performance dropped sharply from 123 to 27, significantly reducing the training time. This phenomenon verifies the efficiency of multi-modal pre-trained models and shows that the training efficiency can be improved considerably without sacrificing too much performance. Then, by introducing the ITDA module, we observed that the Rank-1 accuracy and mAP indicators increased by 2.69% and 3.44%, respectively. This result not only confirms the rationality of the integration of visual semantic features but also fully proves the effectiveness of this technology. Subsequently, by introducing the WDM loss function, our model's performance in Rank-1 and mAP further surpassed the baseline, increasing by 2.29% and 0.78%, respectively. Overall, these improvements enhance the model's performance and demonstrate the potential of multi-modal learning in pedestrian re-identification tasks.

Table 3. Ablation study of different components of AVLA on SYSU-MM01 and Comparative experiments on different loss functions.

Method				SYSU-MM01				
Base	Vilt	ITDA	WDM	R-1	R-10	R-20	mAP	Epoch(Best/total)
✓				75.07	97.32	99.18	71.02	123/150
✓	✓			70.65	96.13	98.84	65.55	27/150
✓	✓	✓		74.07	96.71	99.37	69.42	23/150
✓	✓	✓	✓	**77.36**	**97.50**	**99.42**	**71.8**	70/80
Id Loss+Tri Loss				74.07	93.56	96.89	69.42	-
Softmax				75.02	94.47	97.12	69.77	-
KL				75.15	96.27	98.18	70.78	-
TWDM				75.97	96.24	98.40	71.09	-
WDM				**77.36**	**97.50**	**99.42**	**71.8**	-

Comparative Experiments on Different Loss Functions. This ablation experiment aims to ensure that the integrated visual-language features can be correctly and effectively optimized through a carefully designed loss function, thereby improving the model's discriminative ability and overall performance.

The experimental results are shown in the Table 3. KL refers to KL divergence, WDM is the bidirectional WDM loss, and TWDM is the triple WDM loss, which is introduced explicitly in Sect. 2.3. From the chart results, it can be seen that different loss functions significantly impact optimizing the image-text integrated features. The traditional identity loss and triple loss methods or softmax methods are not satisfactory, with the highest mAP reaching 69.77%. Although the triple loss helps to bring the feature representation of the same identity closer and push the feature representation of different identities further, it may not be enough to fully capture the details in the image-text integrated features that help distinguish pedestrians.

The loss function using KL divergence and its variants has improved Rank-1 accuracy and mAP, especially the WDM method, which shows the best performance. The symmetric loss function may more effectively optimize the model's learning process of visual semantic integration features and improve the model's ability to distinguish different pedestrians.

4 Conclusion

In this paper, we proposed a novel automatic vision-language aligning network for ReID. Our network automatically captures rich semantic representations from images and text and integrates image-text features from different modalities. The ITDA module and WDM loss play a core role in our network, aiming to incorporate information from images and texts from different modalities while mitigating bias in feature integration. We conducted extensive experiments on the three datasets, including SYSU-MM01, RegDB, and LLCM. The experimental results demonstrate the superior performance of our method, achieving state-of-the-art results on three datasets. It proves the feasibility of leveraging language modality for feature integration in VI-ReID tasks and provides a basis for further research by others.

References

1. Wu, A., Zheng, W. S., Yu, H. X., Gong, S., Lai, J.: RGB-infrared cross-modality person re-identification. In: 2017 IEEE International Conference on Computer Vision (ICCV) (2017)
2. Hao, Y., Wang, N., Li, J., Gao, X.: HSME: hypersphere manifold embedding for visible thermal person re-identification. In: Proceedings of the AAAI Conference on Artificial Intelligence, pp. 8385–8392 (2019)
3. Zhang, Y., Zhao, S., Kang, Y., Shen, J.: Modality synergy complement learning with cascaded aggregation for visible-infrared person re-identification. In: European Conference on Computer Vision, pp. 462–479. Springer (2022)
4. Zhang, Y., Yan, Y., Li, J., Wang, H.: MRCN: a novel modality restitution and compensation network for visible-infrared person re-identification. In: Proceedings of the AAAI Conference on Artificial Intelligence, vol. 37, pp. 3498–3506 (2023)
5. Zhang, Y., Wang, H.: Diverse embedding expansion network and low-light cross-modality benchmark for visible-infrared person re-identification. In: Proceedings of the IEEE/CVF Conference on Computer Vision and Pattern Recognition, pp. 2153–2162 (2023)
6. Goodfellow, I., et al.: Generative adversarial networks. Commun. ACM **63**(11), 139–144 (2020)
7. Wang, G.A., Zhang, T., Cheng, J., Liu, S., Yang, Y., Hou, Z.: RGB-infrared cross-modality person re-identification via joint pixel and feature alignment. In: IEEE Conference Proceedings (2019)
8. Zhang, Q., Lai, C., Liu, J., Huang, N., Han, J.: Fmcnet: feature-level modality compensation for visible-infrared person re-identification. In: Proceedings of the IEEE/CVF Conference on Computer Vision and Pattern Recognition, pp. 7349–7358 (2022)
9. Li, D., Wei, X., Hong, X., Gong, Y.: Infrared-visible cross-modal person re-identification with an x modality. In: Proceedings of the AAAI Conference on Artificial Intelligence, pp. 4610–4617 (2020)
10. Zhang, Y., Yan, Y., Lu, Y., Wang, H.: Towards a unified middle modality learning for visible-infrared person re-identification. In: Proceedings of the 29th ACM International Conference on Multimedia, pp. 788–796 (2021)
11. Yu, X., Dong, N., Zhu, L., Peng, H., Tao, D.: Clip-driven semantic discovery network for visible-infrared person re-identification, arXiv preprint arXiv:2401.05806 (2024)
12. Du, Y., Zhao, Z., Su, F.: YYDS: visible-infrared person re-identification with coarse descriptions, arXiv, vol. abs/2403.04183 (2024)
13. Zhang, G., Tan, S., Ji, Z., Fang, Y.: Dynamic attention vision-language transformer network for person re-identification. Int. J. Comput. Vision 1–13 (2024)
14. Kim, W.-J., Son, B., Kim, I.: Vilt: vision-and-language transformer without convolution or region supervision. Cornell University - arXiv, Cornell University (2021)

15. Nguyen, D., Hong, H., Kim, K., Park, K.: Person recognition system based on a combination of body images from visible light and thermal cameras. Sensors 605 (2017)
16. Zhong, Z., Zheng, L., Kang, G., Li, S., Yang, Y.: Random erasing data augmentation. In: Proceedings of the AAAI Conference on Artificial Intelligence, pp. 13001–13008 (2020)
17. Gong, Y., Zeng, Z., Chen, L., Luo, Y., Weng, B., Ye, F.: A person re-identification data augmentation method with adversarial defense effect. Cornell University - arXiv, Cornell University - arXiv (2021)
18. Zhang, D., Zhang, Z., Ying, J., Wang, C., Xie, Y., Yanyun, Q.: Dual mutual learning for cross-modality person re-identification. IEEE Trans. Circuits Syst. Video Technol. **32**(8), 5361–5373 (2022)
19. Chen, C., Ye, M., Qi, M., Jingjing, W., Jiang, J., Lin, C.-W.: Structure-aware positional transformer for visible-infrared person re-identification. IEEE Trans. Image Process. **31**, 2352–2364 (2022)
20. Sun, H., et al.: Not all pixels are matched: dense contrastive learning for cross-modality person re-identification. In: Proceedings of the 30th ACM International Conference on Multimedia, pp. 5333–5341 (2022)
21. Zhang, Y., Kang, Y., Zhao, S., Shen, J.: Dual-semantic consistency learning for visible-infrared person re-identification. IEEE Trans. Inf. Forensics Secur. **18**, 1554–1565 (2022)
22. Yang, B., Chen, J., Ye, M.: Towards grand unified representation learning for unsupervised visible-infrared person re-identification. In: Proceedings of the IEEE/CVF International Conference on Computer Vision, pp. 11069–11079 (2023)
23. Liang, T., Jin, Y., Liu, W., Li, Y.: Cross-modality transformer with modality mining for visible-infrared person re-identification. IEEE Trans. Multimedia **25**, 8432–8444 (2023)
24. Yang, X., Dong, W., Li, M., Wei, Z., Wang, N., Gao, X.: Cooperative separation of modality shared-specific features for visible-infrared person re-identification. IEEE Trans. Multimedia (2024)
25. Ye, M., Shen, J., J. Crandall, D., Shao, L., Luo, J.: Dynamic dual-attentive aggregation learning for visible-infrared person re-identification. In: Vedaldi, A., Bischof, H., Brox, T., Frahm, J.-M. (eds.) ECCV 2020. LNCS, vol. 12362, pp. 229–247. Springer, Cham (2020). https://doi.org/10.1007/978-3-030-58520-4_14
26. Ye, M., Shen, J., Lin, G., Xiang, T., Shao, L., Hoi, S.C.H.: Deep learning for person re-identification: a survey and outlook. IEEE Trans. Pattern Anal. Mach. Intell. 2872–2893 (2022)
27. Park, H., Lee, S., Lee, J., Ham, B.: Learning by aligning: visible-infrared person re-identification using cross-modal correspondences. In: Proceedings of the IEEE/CVF International Conference on Computer Vision, pp. 12046–12055 (2021)
28. Ye, M., Ruan, W., Du, B., Shou, M.Z.: Channel augmented joint learning for visible-infrared recognition. In: Proceedings of the IEEE/CVF International Conference on Computer Vision, pp. 13567–13576 (2021)

Temporally-Aware Multi-task Representation Learning for Compositional Action Recognition

Peng Huang[1], Wenxuan Ge[1], He Yan[2], Henghao Zhao[1], and Xiangbo Shu[1]($\boxtimes$)

[1] School of Computer Science and Engineering, Nanjing University of Science and Technology, Nanjing 210000, China
{penghuang,gwx,henghaozhao,shuxb}@njust.edu.cn

[2] College of Information Science and Technology and Artificial Intelligence, Nanjing Forestry University, Nanjing 210000, China
yanhe@njfu.edu.cn

Abstract. Compositional Action Recognition (CAR) aims to identify unseen verbnoun combinations during training, yet complex human-object interactions, diverse spatiotemporal dynamics, and distributional shifts pose significant challenges to compositional generalization. Although existing approaches have achieved notable progress, mainstream video baseline methods still suffer from performance bottlenecks, particularly in distinguishing fine-grained action categories, which reflects their limited capacity for temporal structure modeling. To address this issue, we propose a Temporally-Aware Multi-task Representation Learning (TAM) framework, by employing multi-task co-optimization, to encourage the model to actively construct temporal semantic structures. Specifically, three auxiliary tasks are introduced: (1) Forward-Reversed Discriminator (FRD), to enhance global temporal direction awareness; (2) Frame-Stage Classifier (FSC), to capture the fine-grained temporal structure within the action; (3) Temporally-Semantic Alignment (TSA), to further improve representations of temporal semantic and dynamic structural evolution. Extensive experiments on CAR benchmarks demonstrate the effectiveness of the proposed method.

Keywords: Action recognition · compositional generalization · multi-task

1 Introduction

Compositional Action Recognition (CAR) [1–4] has garnered increasing interest in the video understanding community for its emphasis on the compositional generalization problem. In contrast to conventional action recognition tasks [5–7] that operate within a closed set of atomic labels, CAR introduces a more challenging out-of-distribution paradigm, wherein models are expected to generalize from observed atomic concepts to novel verbnoun compositions. This setting necessitates a fine-grained understanding and systematic disentanglement

W. Jia et al. (Eds.): CCBR 2025, LNCS 16360, pp. 550–561, 2026.
https://doi.org/10.1007/978-981-95-6123-0_51

of the semantic constituents of a compositional action, such as motion patterns (verbs) and interacting objects (nouns). The inherent complexity of humanobject interactions, along with substantial distributional shifts, further compounds the difficulty of the task, rendering CAR a compelling yet relatively underexplored direction in video understanding research [8–10].

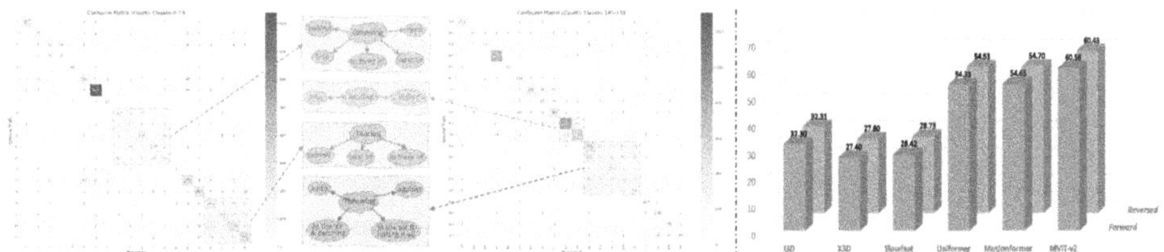

Fig. 1. Most misclassified samples by baseline models are concentrated in fine-grained compositional clusters (left); Existing baselines show similar predictions for forward and reversed sequences (right).

Recent advances in the CAR domain have explored various strategies to enhance compositional generalization, including semantic decomposition [3], trajectory modeling [4], and dual-branch architectures [10] that separately model verbs and nouns. These approaches have shown promise in alleviating feature entanglement and improving recognition performance on novel compositions. However, most of them rely heavily on object appearance cues and precise data annotations, while overlooking the temporal structures inherent in human actions. A notable issue lies in the tendency of many widely adopted video baseline models [11–13] to struggle with actions or scenarios characterized by fine-grained temporal dynamics. The lack of temporal sensitivity weakens the model's ability to understand actions precisely. It also makes it difficult to distinguish between actions that are semantically similar but differ in temporal structure.

A complementary observation, as shown in Fig. 1(left), indicates that misclassified samples often cluster within action categories requiring fine-grained temporal understanding. Moreover, Fig. 1(right) shows that mainstream models produce similar predictions for both forward and reversed videos, despite the semantic implausibility of the latter. These observations indicate that current baselines may place greater emphasis on appearance-level cues or static correlations between features and labels, while insufficiently capturing the temporal semantics and dynamic structures essential to compositional action understanding.

To mitigate this issue, a promising discussion is how to explicitly guide models to attend to the dynamic temporal properties of actions. To this end, we propose a novel Temporally-Aware Multi-task (TAM) Representation Learning framework, which introduces three complementary auxiliary tasks designed to supervise the model from three distinct perspectives: global temporal direction, local structural stages, and semantic consistency. Specifically, TAM comprises: 1) a Forward-Reversed Discrimination (FRD) task to enhance sensitivity to global temporal orientation; 2) a Frame-Stage Classification (FSC) task to capture fine-grained temporal progression within actions; and 3) a Temporally-Semantic Alignment (TSA) task to enforce cross-modal consistency between visual features and temporally coherent textual descriptions. By encouraging the model to actively construct temporal semantic structures, the proposed baseline systematically improves its capacity for compositional action discrimination and generalization.

Overall, the contributions of this work are summarized:

- 1) We propose a novel Temporally-Aware Multi-task (TAM) Representation Learning framework to mitigate the challenge of fine-grained temporal understanding in compositional action recognition.
- 2) Three complementary auxiliary tasks: Forward-Reversed Discrimination (FRD), Frame-Stage Classification (FSC) and Temporally-Semantic Alignment (TSA), are designed to collaboratively supervise the model from global, local, and semantic perspectives, thereby strengthening its temporal structure understanding.
- 3) Extensive experiments on the CAR task demonstrate that the proposed novel baseline consistently outperforms existing methods and provides new insights into the role of temporal structure in video understanding.

2   Related Work

Action Recognition. As a fundamental task in computer vision, action recognition (AR) [14–17] has undergone a paradigm shift from handcrafted features [18,19] to deep representations [20–23]. Early approaches based on shallow motion descriptors exhibited limited scalability and generalization on large-scale benchmarks, whereas CNN-based models significantly advanced the field: 2D CNNs [24,25] primarily capture spatial patterns, while 3D CNNs [26,27] jointly model spatiotemporal dynamics. More recently, Transformer-based [11,28,30] architectures have gained prominence due to their capacity for modeling long-range dependencies, and ViT-based adaptations (e.g., TimeSformer [29], Motionformer [11], Uniformer [12], MViT [30], and VideoMAE [31]) have demonstrated strong performance on standard video benchmarks. Nonetheless, these methods remain challenged in compositional scenarios, particularly in recognizing novel combinations with fine-grained semantic distinctions. In this work, we investigate how to improve temporal understanding in complex scenarios and introduce a novel baseline to enhance model generalization in CAR.

Compositional Generalization. Real-world activities are inherently compositional [1,4], and humans, with their remarkable capacity for conceptual disentanglement and compositional reasoning, can rapidly understand and generalize to unseen combinations. However, such compositional generalization remains a major challenge for existing video understanding models. To evaluate compositional generalization, Materzynska *et al.* [1] proposed the Compositional Action Recognition (CAR) task, which requires models to recognize novel actionobject combinations during testing. Existing approaches [3, 32–36] often rely on explicit object annotations, but at the cost of introducing pronounced appearance bias, making models overly dependent on visual co-occurrence patterns rather than the underlying action semantics. To address this issue, Yan *et al.* [2] proposed an instance mutation strategy that perturbs annotated object regions to weaken spurious correlations, while Huang *et al.* [4] introduced an appearance-agnostic modeling approach to improve the robustness of compositional reasoning. In this work, we revisit compositional generalization from the perspective of fine-grained temporal structure modeling, without resorting to additional region-level computations or bounding box encoding.

3   Methods

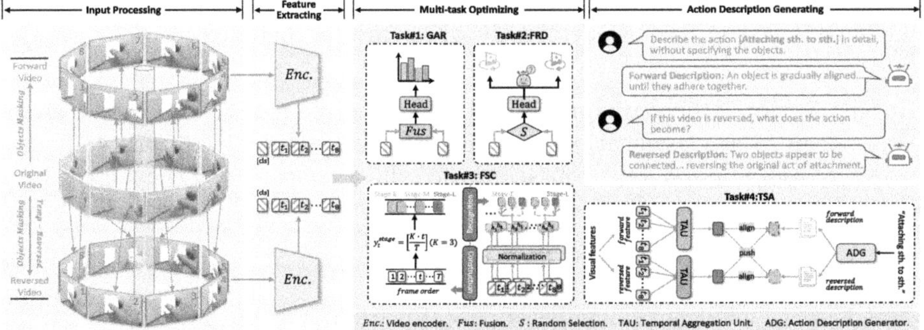

Fig. 2. Overview of the proposed TAM framework. Given an input video X, we construct forward and reversed sequences with object-related appearance masked to mitigate visual bias. Both sequences are encoded by a shared video encoder and jointly optimized via four tasks: (1) GAR, global compositional recognition; (2) FRD, forward-reverse discrimination for directional awareness; (3) FSC, frame-stage classification for local temporal structure modeling; and (4) TSA, temporally-semantic alignment bridging visual dynamics with language.

3.1   Input Processing and Feature Extracting

To encourage temporal modeling beyond static patterns, we begin by constructing temporally augmented input sequences. Given the raw video $X \in \mathbb{R}^{T \times 3 \times H \times W}$, we first generate its forward and reversed versions with object-masking by,

$$X_{\mathrm{FD}}, X_{\mathrm{RD}} = Mask((X, \Phi(X))|_{\mathsf{SAM}}), \tag{1}$$

where $\Phi(\cdot)$ denotes temporal reversal and SAM applies Segment Anything [37] for fine-grained object masks. The operator $Mask(\cdot)$ occludes salient regions to encourage motion-aware learning. Both $\boldsymbol{X}_{\mathrm{FD}}$ and $\boldsymbol{X}_{\mathrm{RD}}$ are then passed through the processing of feature extracting, specifically formulated as,

$$\hat{\boldsymbol{X}}_* = [\boldsymbol{C}_*^{\mathrm{cls}}, \, [\boldsymbol{H}_*, \mathcal{P}(\boldsymbol{X}_*)]] + \varUpsilon_*, \quad \boldsymbol{F}_* = Enc._*(\hat{\boldsymbol{X}}_*), \tag{2}$$

where $*$ indicates FD or RD. Here, $\boldsymbol{C}^{\mathrm{cls}}$ and $\boldsymbol{H}_* = \{\boldsymbol{h}^t\}_{t=1}^T$ denote global and temporal classification tokens, respectively. $\mathcal{P}(\cdot)$ is the patch embedding function, $\varUpsilon_*$ represents the learnable position encoding, and $Enc._*(\cdot)$ identifies the parameter-shared video encoder. As a result, the extracted feature $\boldsymbol{F}_*$ consists of global classification feature $\boldsymbol{f}_*^{\mathrm{cls}}$ (obtained from $\boldsymbol{C}_*^{\mathrm{cls}}$) and frame-level prediction feature $\boldsymbol{h}_*^t$. The resulting features are then optimized in a multi-task framework to capture both global and local temporal semantics.

3.2   Multi-task Optimizing

To effectively guide the model toward understanding temporal semantics beyond surface appearance, we introduce four complementary tasks within a unified multi-task learning framework. Details are presented below,

Global Action Recognition (GAR). As the main task of our framework, GAR targets the classification of compositional actions by learning discriminative spatiotemporal representations. We first concatenate the forward and reversed classification tokens and aggregate them via a lightweight MLP:

$$\boldsymbol{f}_{\mathrm{cls}} = MLP(Concat(\boldsymbol{f}_{FD}^{\mathrm{cls}}, \, \boldsymbol{f}_{RD}^{\mathrm{cls}})), \tag{3}$$

where $Concat$ denotes channel-wise concatenation. The output is then fed into a classification head $(Head_{\mathrm{GAR}})$ and trained with a standard smoothing cross-entropy loss,

$$\mathcal{L}_{\mathrm{GAR}} = CE(Head_{\mathrm{GAR}}(\boldsymbol{f}_{\mathrm{cls}})). \tag{4}$$

where $Concat$ denotes concatenation along the channel dimension, and MLP is a lightweight projection module implemented with a linear layer followed by a non-linear activation. The classification head then maps the aggregated feature to a predicted label, supervised by a cross-entropy loss, here $Head_{\mathrm{GAR}}$ is the global classifier and $CE(\cdot)$ is the standard smoothing cross-entropy loss.

Forward-Reversed Discrimination (FRD). This auxiliary task is designed to enhance temporal sensitivity by classifying whether a video is played forward or reversed, encouraging learning of motion-consistent dynamics.

Specifically, the global features $\boldsymbol{f}_{\mathrm{FD}}^{\mathrm{cls}}$ and $\boldsymbol{f}_{\mathrm{RD}}^{\mathrm{cls}}$ are fed into two separate binary classifiers,

$$\boldsymbol{S}_{\mathrm{FD}} = Head_{\mathrm{FRD}}^{FD}(\boldsymbol{f}_{\mathrm{FD}}^{\mathrm{cls}}), \; \boldsymbol{S}_{\mathrm{RD}} = Head_{\mathrm{FRD}}^{RD}(\boldsymbol{f}_{\mathrm{RD}}^{\mathrm{cls}}), \tag{5}$$

Then, the overall FRD loss is computed as,

$$\mathcal{L}_{\text{FRD}} = \frac{1}{2}(CE(S_{\text{FD}}, Y_{\text{FD}}) + CE(S_{\text{RD}}, Y_{\text{RD}})). \tag{6}$$

here $Y_{\text{FD}} = 1$ and $Y_{\text{RD}} = 0$ are corresponding labels.

Frame-Stage Classification (FSC). To model fine-grained temporal structure, FSC assigns each frame to a coarse temporal stage, guiding the model to capture intra-action dynamics.

We begin by dividing the full sequence into K temporal stages. Given a total of T frames, the stage label $y^t \in \{1, 2, ..., K\}$ for the t-th frame is calculated as $y^t = \lfloor (t - 1) \cdot K/T \rfloor + 1$, where $\lfloor \cdot \rfloor$ denotes the floor operation. This simple yet effective strategy yields a stage-wise pseudo-label for each frame that reflects its coarse temporal position. Next, for each frame feature $\boldsymbol{h}_*^t \in \boldsymbol{H}_*$ (with $* \in \{\text{FD}, \text{RD}\}$), a shared classifier $Head_{\text{FSC}}$ is applied to obtain stage prediction,

$$\hat{y}_*^t = \text{Head}_{\text{FSC}}(\boldsymbol{h}_*^t), \quad \forall t \in 1, ..., T. \tag{7}$$

Thus the loss for this task can be formulated as the average cross-entropy over all frames in both forward and reversed sequences,

$$\mathcal{L}_{\text{FSC}} = \frac{1}{2T} \sum_{t=1}^{T} \left[CE(\hat{y}_{\text{FD}}^t, y^t) + CE(\hat{y}_{\text{RD}}^t, y^t) \right]. \tag{8}$$

This auxiliary task provides localized temporal supervision, promoting sensitivity to intra-action dynamics and enabling the model to distinguish stages of motion, which is especially beneficial for understanding compositional and multi-phase actions.

Temporally-Semantic Alignment (TSA). This auxiliary task aims to align video dynamics with compositional action descriptions in both forward and reversed directions, encouraging the model to learn semantically grounded temporal representations.

To construct temporally-aware, object-agnostic textual supervision, we employ a language model in conjunction with carefully designed prompt templates,

- **Forward prompt**: *Describe the action [Attaching sth. to sth.] in detail, without specifying the objects.*
- **Reversed prompt**: *If this video is reversed, what does the action become?*

These prompts yield a pair of temporally inverse language descriptions that abstract away from object identities while preserving the core motion semantics. Next, we aggregate frame features $\boldsymbol{h}_*^t$ into sequence-level representations $\boldsymbol{v}_* \in \mathbb{R}^{1 \times d}$, and encode textual descriptions via a frozen text-encoder obtain embeddings l_*. A symmetric alignment loss is applied to pull aligned pairs together and push apart the misaligned ones,

$$\mathcal{L}_{\text{TSA}} = \sum_{(i,j)\in\mathcal{P}} (1 - \cos(\boldsymbol{v}_i, \boldsymbol{l}_j)) + \lambda \sum_{(i,k)\in\mathcal{N}} \max(0, \ \cos(\boldsymbol{v}_i, \boldsymbol{l}_k) - m), \qquad (9)$$

where $\mathcal{P}$ and $\mathcal{N}$ are sets of positive and negative video-text pairs. λ is a balancing hyperparameter, m is the contrastive margin, and $\cos(\cdot)$ is cosine similarity.

To jointly optimize the model across multiple temporal comprehension tasks, we formulate the total training objective as a weighted sum of the individual loss terms:

$$\mathcal{L}_{\text{total}} = \mathcal{L}_{\text{GAR}} + \lambda_{\text{FRD}}\mathcal{L}_{\text{FRD}} + \lambda_{\text{FSC}}\mathcal{L}_{\text{FSC}} + \lambda_{\text{TSA}}\mathcal{L}_{\text{TSA}}, \qquad (10)$$

where each λ_* is a task-specific balancing weight to control the relative contribution of its corresponding loss. This multi-task design allows the model to learn complementary temporal signals from different perspectives: global action discrimination ($\mathcal{L}_{\text{GAR}}$), directional sensitivity ($\mathcal{L}_{\text{FRD}}$), stage-level structure modeling ($\mathcal{L}_{\text{FSC}}$), and semantic alignment with language supervision ($\mathcal{L}_{\text{TSA}}$).

Table 1. Comparisons with the state-of-the-art methods. "$bbox^{\S}$" indicates whether or not bounding boxes encoding is used.

Method	$bbox^{\S}$	Accuracy	
		Top-1	Top-5
I3D [26]		42.8	71.3
SlowFast [40]		45.2	78.4
TSM [41]		55.4	83.6
TimeSformer [29]		44.2	76.8
Motionformer [11]	✗	62.3	86.7
UniFormer-v2 [12]		61.8	85.7
MViT-v2 [13]		65.8	89.9
VideoMAE [31]		66.3	89.1
A^{2}RL [4]		71.6	91.8
Ours	✗	**72.5**	**92.4**

Method	$bbox^{\S}$	Accuracy	
		Top-1	Top-5
STIN [1]		51.4	79.3
STIN+I3D [1]		54.6	79.4
IF [32]		59.6	85.8
CDN [42]		64.5	88.2
MGAF [43]		60.5	84.3
MGAF (DP) [43]		68.0	88.7
Motionformer [11]	✓	67.6	89.9
ORViT [34]		69.7	91.0
ObjectLearner [35]		73.6	93.5
DeFormer [3]		74.3	93.7
ObjectViViT [44]		74.5	—
A^{2}RL [4]		75.1	94.0
Ours	✓	**75.9**	**94.1**

4   Experiments

4.1   Dataset and Implementation

Dataset. We evaluate on STH-ELSE [1], a compositional benchmark derived from Something-Something V2 (SSV2) [38]. Each video is annotated with verbnoun pairs, where test combinations are unseen during training. The dataset contains $54,919$ training and $57,876$ testing samples.

Implementation Details. For ablation, we adopt divided-attention Motionformer [11] pre-trained on Kinetics-400 [39], trained with 8 frame inputs for 25 epochs using AdamW (lr: 2×10^{-4}, weight decay: 5×10^{-2}), with decay at epochs 10 and 20. For SOTA comparison, we switch to VideoMAE [31], use 16 frame inputs, 35 epochs, and lr of 1×10^{-4}. Action descriptions are generated via ChatGPT and encoded by a frozen RoBERTa [50] model. All experiments are implemented in PyTorch 2.0 and run on 4×NVIDIA RTX 3090 GPUs.

4.2   Comparison to State-of-the-Arts

To validate the effectiveness of our proposed method, we compare it against recent state-of-the-art approaches on the STH-ElSE [1] benchmark for CAR, covering both popular baselines (without bounding boxes) and object-centric models (with bounding boxes), as summarized in Table 1.

Our method achieves state-of-the-art performance in both the presence and absence of bounding box. In the setting without "$bbox^\S$", it surpasses the strong baseline VideoMAE by a notable margin of 6.2% in Top-1 accuracy. Furthermore, despite employing only a simple box embedding and ensemble, our approach attains a competitive accuracy of 75.9%, underscoring the effectiveness and robustness of the proposed temporally-aware multi-task framework even in object-centric contexts.

4.3   Ablation Studies

Ablation Study About Forward/Reversed Streams and Object-Masking. Table 2 demonstrates that bidirectional modeling (F+R) significantly outperforms single-stream baselines, verifying the importance of temporal complementarity. Object-masking (O-M) consistently yields additional gains by suppressing appearance bias. The full configuration achieves the highest Top-1 accuracy (62.6%), confirming the synergy between temporal diversity and visual debiasing.

Ablation Study About Different Sub-Task. Table 3 evaluates the contribution of each auxiliary task. Individually, FRD, FSC, and TSA all lead to consistent improvements over the GAR-only baseline (62.6%), with TSA showing the most notable gain (2.9%). Combining any two tasks further enhances performance, and the full integration of all four components achieves the highest Top-1 accuracy of 65.8%, confirming their complementary effects in facilitating temporal and compositional understanding.

Ablation Study About Different Text-Encoders. As shown in Table 4, several language encoders, including CLIP and GPT2, exhibit performance degradation, likely due to overfitting or suboptimal alignment with temporal semantics.

Table 2. Ablation study about forward/reversed streams and object masking.

Method	Stream F	Stream R	O-M	Accuracy Top-1	Accuracy Top-5
Baseline	✓	✗	✗	54.6	80.5
	✗	✓	✗	54.7	80.6
	✓	✓	✗	58.8	84.0
	✓	✗	✓	59.3	84.7
	✗	✓	✓	59.4	94.9
	✓	✓	✓	**62.6**	**86.5**

Table 3. Ablation study about different sub-task.

Method	GAR	FRD	FSC	TSA	Accuracy Top-1	Accuracy Top-5
Baseline	✓	✗	✗	✗	62.6	86.5
	✓	✓	✗	✗	63.4	87.2
	✓	✗	✓	✗	63.5	87.4
	✓	✗	✗	✓	64.2	87.6
	✓	✓	✓	✗	64.3	88.0
	✓	✓	✗	✓	65.1	88.2
	✓	✗	✓	✓	65.1	88.3
	✓	✓	✓	✓	65.8	88.7

Table 4. Ablation study on the impact of different language encoders for TSA.

Method	Text Encoder	Accuracy Top-1	Accuracy Top-5
Baseline	–	62.6	86.5
	CLIP [45]	54.3	75.1
	GPT2 [46]	56.8	77.4
	DistillBERT [47]	59.7	82.6
	DeBERTa [48]	55.9	76.0
	ALBERTa [49]	63.1	86.9
	RoBERTa [50]	**64.2**	**87.6**

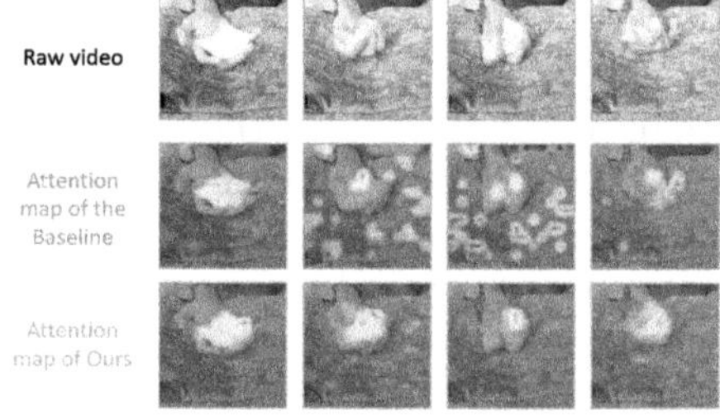

Fig. 3. Visualization of attention maps between the Baseline and our method.

In contrast, RoBERTa achieves the best results, highlighting its strong contextual modeling capability. This discrepancy warrants further investigation in future work.

4.4 Visualization Analysis

As illustrated in Fig. 3, the attention maps of the baseline model tend to scatter across irrelevant background regions, indicating poor localization and weak temporal consistency. In contrast, our method produces more compact and semantically aligned attention responses, focusing primarily on the hand-object interaction area across frames. This demonstrates that our framework facilitates more precise and temporally coherent feature learning, which is essential for compositional action understanding.

5 Conclusion

We propose TAM, a Temporally-Aware Multi-task representation learning framework tailored for Compositional Action Recognition (CAR). To overcome the limitations of existing baselines in temporal structure modeling, TAM integrates three auxiliary objectives: Forward-Reverse Discrimination, Frame-Stage Classification, and Temporally-Semantic Alignment, to jointly enhance global temporal awareness, local temporal precision, and semantic alignment over time. By leveraging multi-task co-optimization, the framework facilitates the construction of structured temporal representations conducive to compositional generalization. However, the framework design of TAM still relies on manually designed auxiliary tasks and fixed temporal partitions. Future work will explore adaptive temporal segmentation strategies and data-driven task discovery methods to improve the flexibility and generalization capability. In addition, we plan to evaluate TAM on a broader range of compositional and real-world video datasets to further assess its robustness and scalability.

Acknowledgments. This work is supported in part by the National Natural Science Foundation of China under Grant 62306142.

References

1. Materzynska, J., Xiao, T., Herzig, R., et al.: Something-else: compositional action recognition with spatial-temporal interaction networks. In: IEEE Conference on Computer Vision and Pattern Recognition (CVPR), pp. 1049–1059 (2020)
2. Yan, R., Huang, P., Shu, X., et al.: Look less think more: rethinking compositional action recognition. In: ACM International Conference on Multimedia (ACM MM), pp. 3666–3675 (2022)
3. Huang, P., Yan, R., Shu, X., et al.: Semantic-disentangled transformer with noun-verb embedding for compositional action recognition. IEEE Trans. Image Process. **33**, 297–309 (2023)
4. Huang, P., Shu, X., Yan, R., et al.: Appearance-agnostic representation learning for compositional action recognition. IEEE Trans. Circuits Syst. Video Technol. (2024)
5. Shu, X., Yang, J., Yan, R., et al.: Expansion-squeeze-excitation fusion network for elderly activity recognition. IEEE Trans. Circuits Syst. Video Technol. **32**(8), 5281–5292 (2022)
6. Xu, B., Shu, X., Zhang, J., et al.: Spatiotemporal decouple-and-squeeze contrastive learning for semisupervised skeleton-based action recognition. IEEE Trans. Neural Netw. Learn. Syst. **35**(8), 11035–11048 (2023)
7. Zhu, X., Shu, X., Tang, J., et al.: Motion-aware mask feature reconstruction for skeleton-based action recognition. IEEE Trans. Circuits Syst. Video Technol. **34**(11), 10718–10731 (2024)
8. Zhao, H., Lin, K., Yan, R., et al.: DiffusionVMR: diffusion model for joint video moment retrieval and highlight detection. IEEE Trans. Neural Netw. Learn. Syst. 1–14 (2024)
9. Zhao, H., Ji, G., Yan, R., et al.: VideoExpert: augmented LLM for temporal-sensitive video understanding. arXiv preprint arXiv:2504.07519 (2025)
10. Li, R., Feng, Z., Xu, T., et al.: C2C: component-to-composition learning for zero-shot compositional action recognition. In: European Conference on Computer Vision (ECCV), pp. 369–388 (2024)

11. Patrick, M., Campbell, D., Asano, Y., et al.: Keeping your eye on the ball: trajectory attention in video transformers. In: Advances in Neural Information Processing Systems (NeurIPS), pp. 12493–12506 (2021)

12. Li, K., Wang, Y., He, Y., et al.: UniformerV2: Spatiotemporal learning by arming image ViTs with video Uniformer. arXiv preprint arXiv:2211.09552 (2022)

13. Li, Y., Wu, C.-Y., Fan, H., et al.: MViTv2: improved multiscale vision transformers for classification and detection. In: IEEE Conference on Computer Vision and Pattern Recognition (CVPR), pp. 4804–4814 (2022)

14. Qu, H., Yan, R., Shu, X., et al.: MVP-shot: multi-velocity progressive-alignment framework for few-shot action recognition. IEEE Trans. Multimedia (2025)

15. Tu, Z., Shu, X., Huang, P., et al.: Leveraging frame- and feature-level progressive augmentation for semi-supervised action recognition. ACM Trans. Multimedia Comput. Commun. Appl. **21**(4), 1–21 (2025)

16. Wei, R., Yan, R., Qu, H., et al.: SVMFN-FSAR: semantic-guided video multimodal fusion network for few-shot action recognition. Big Data Min. Anal. **8**(3), 534–550 (2025)

17. Yan, R., Wang, J., Qu, H., et al.: TEST-V: TEst-time Support-set Tuning for Zero-shot Video Classification. arXiv preprint arXiv:2502.00426 (2025)

18. Wang, H., Schmid, C.: Action recognition with improved trajectories. In: International Conference on Computer Vision (ICCV), pp. 3551–3558 (2013)

19. Peng, X., Zou, C., Qiao, Y., et al.: Action recognition with stacked fisher vectors. In: European Conference on Computer Vision (ECCV), pp. 581–595 (2014)

20. Yan, R., Xie, L., Shu, X., et al.: Progressive instance-aware feature learning for compositional action recognition. IEEE Trans. Pattern Anal. Mach. Intell. **45**(8), 10317–10330 (2023)

21. Yan, R., Xie, L., Tang, J., et al.: HiGCIN: hierarchical graph-based cross inference network for group activity recognition. IEEE Trans. Pattern Anal. Mach. Intell. **45**(6), 6955–6968 (2020)

22. Chen, Q., Liu, Y., Huang, P., et al.: Linguistic-driven partial semantic relevance learning for skeleton-based action recognition. Sensors **24**(15), 4860 (2024)

23. Wang, J., Guo, J., Wang, R., et al.: Parameter disentanglement for diverse representations. Big Data Min. Anal. **8**(3), 606–623 (2025)

24. Wang, L., Qiao, Y., Tang, X.: Action recognition with trajectory-pooled deep-convolutional descriptors. In: IEEE Conference on Computer Vision and Pattern Recognition (CVPR), pp. 4305–4314 (2015)

25. Wang, L., Xiong, Y., Wang, Z., et al.: Temporal segment networks: towards good practices for deep action recognition. In: European Conference on Computer Vision (ECCV), pp. 20–36 (2016)

26. Carreira, J., Zisserman, A.: Quo vadis, action recognition? A new model and the Kinetics dataset. In: IEEE Conference on Computer Vision and Pattern Recognition (CVPR), pp. 6299–6308 (2017)

27. Feichtenhofer, C.: X3D: expanding architectures for efficient video recognition. In: IEEE Conference on Computer Vision and Pattern Recognition (CVPR), pp. 203–213 (2020)

28. Dosovitskiy, A., Beyer, L., Kolesnikov, A., et al.: An image is worth 16x16 words: transformers for image recognition at scale. arXiv preprint arXiv:2010.11929 (2020)

29. Bertasius, G., Wang, H., Torresani, L.: Is space-time attention all you need for video understanding? In: International Conference on Machine Learning (ICML), pp. 813–824 (2021)

30. Fan, H., Xiong, B., Mangalam, K., et al.: Multiscale vision transformers. In: International Conference on Computer Vision (ICCV), pp. 6824–6835 (2021)

31. Tong, Z., Song, Y., Wang, J., et al.: VideoMAE: masked autoencoders are data-efficient learners for self-supervised video pre-training. In: Advances in Neural Information Processing Systems (NeurIPS), pp. 10078–10093 (2022)
32. Yan, R., Xie, L., Shu, X., et al.: Interactive fusion of multi-level features for compositional activity recognition. arXiv preprint arXiv:2012.05689 (2020)
33. Radevski, G., Moens, M.F., Tuytelaars, T.: Revisiting spatio-temporal layouts for compositional action recognition. In: British Machine Vision Conference (BMVC), p. 110 (2021)
34. Herzig, R., Ben-Avraham, E., Mangalam, K., et al.: Object-region video transformers. In: IEEE Conference on Computer Vision and Pattern Recognition (CVPR), pp. 3148–3159 (2022)
35. Zhang, C., Gupta, A., Zisserman, A.: Is an object-centric video representation beneficial for transfer? In: Asian Conference on Computer Vision (ACCV), pp. 1976–1994 (2022)
36. Huang, P., Qu, H., Shu, X.: Revisiting few-shot compositional action recognition with knowledge calibration. IEEE Signal Process. Lett. (2025)
37. Kirillov, A., Mintun, E., Ravi, N., et al.: Segment anything. In: International Conference on Computer Vision (ICCV), pp. 3992–4003 (2023)
38. Goyal, R., Kahou, S.E., Michalski, V., et al.: The "something something" video database for learning and evaluating visual common sense. In: International Conference on Computer Vision (ICCV), pp. 5842–5850 (2017)
39. Kay, W., Carreira, J., Simonyan, K., et al.: The Kinetics human action video dataset. arXiv preprint arXiv:1705.06950 (2017)
40. Feichtenhofer, C., Fan, H., Malik, J., et al.: SlowFast networks for video recognition. In: International Conference on Computer Vision (ICCV), pp. 6202–6211 (2019)
41. Lin, J., Gan, C., Han, S., et al.: TSM: temporal shift module for efficient video understanding. In: International Conference on Computer Vision (ICCV), pp. 7083–7093 (2019)
42. Sun, P., Wu, B., Li, X., et al.: Counterfactual debiasing inference for compositional action recognition. In: ACM International Conference on Multimedia (ACM MM), pp. 3220–3228 (2021)
43. Kim, T.S., Jones, J., Hager, G.D.: Motion-guided attention fusion to recognize interactions from videos. In: International Conference on Computer Vision (ICCV), pp. 13076–13086 (2021)
44. Zhou, X., Arnab, A., Sun, C., et al.: How can objects help action recognition? In: IEEE Conference on Computer Vision and Pattern Recognition (CVPR), pp. 2353–2362 (2023)
45. Radford, A., Kim, J.W., Hallacy, C., et al.: Learning transferable visual models from natural language supervision. In: International Conference on Machine Learning (ICML), pp. 8748–8763 (2021)
46. Radford, A., Wu, J., Child, R., et al.: Language models are unsupervised multitask learners. OpenAI Blog **1**(8), 9 (2019)
47. Sanh, V., Debut, L., Chaumond, J., et al.: DistilBERT, a distilled version of BERT: smaller, faster, cheaper and lighter. arXiv preprint arXiv:1910.01108 (2019)
48. He, P., Liu, X., Gao, J., et al.: DeBERTa: decoding-enhanced BERT with disentangled attention. arXiv preprint arXiv:2006.03654 (2020)
49. Lan, Z., Chen, M., Goodman, S., et al.: ALBERT: a lite BERT for self-supervised learning of language representations. arXiv preprint arXiv:1909.11942 (2019)
50. Liu, Y., Ott, M., Goyal, N., et al.: RoBERTa: a robustly optimized BERT pre-training approach. arXiv preprint arXiv:1907.11692 (2019)

CGDRF-YOLO: A Lightweight and Efficient UAV-Based Pedestrian Detection Algorithm

Binbin Gui, Fang Dong, Wenjie Fan, Rihui Yuan, and Wenfeng Wang[✉]

School of Information Engineering, Jiangxi University of Water Resources and Electric Power, Nanchang 330099, China
Wangwf@nit.edu.cn

Abstract. Addressing challenges in UAV-based pedestrian detection, including small target sizes, complex backgrounds, and computational constraints of resource-limited devices, this study proposes an improved pedestrian detection algorithm, CGDRF-YOLO. First, the algorithm proposes a downsampling module to aggregate multi-scale receptive field and context information, which mitigates feature loss and strengthens anti-interference capabilities. Secondly, a content-aware feature reassembling operator is integrated to dynamically generate adaptive kernels and reorganize features, thus enhancing feature utilization efficiency. Finally, the Inner-WIoU loss function is incorporated to improve localization precision and optimize loss calculation. Experimental results from the VisDrone2019 pedestrian detection sub-dataset demonstrate that, compared with the baseline algorithm, CGDRF-YOLO not only improves mAP50, mAP50:95 and FPS by 3.6%, 2.2% and 5%, but also reduces the FLOPs and Params by 10% and 5%, respectively. This clearly demonstrates that CGDRF-YOLO can effectively meet the requirements of pedestrian detection tasks in UAV scenarios.

Keywords: Context information · Feature reassembling operator · Inner-WIoU · Pedestrian detection

1 Introduction

Unmanned aerial vehicle (UAV) has been widely applied in object detection, due to its unique advantages such as exceptional flexibility, extensive coverage, and easy deployment. These images play a pivotal role in various fields, including traffic monitoring [1], agricultural surveillance [2], and disaster rescue [3]. As UAV technology continues to advance at a remarkable pace, the application prospects of UAV image in object detection are growing increasingly promising, with its potential application scope expanding into more emerging domains.

However, UAV images present unique challenges for pedestrian detection. Captured pedestrian images often contain dense small targets and complex backgrounds. Additionally, given the unique nature of UAV-based pedestrian detection, it often requires deployment on devices with limited computational resources, thus demanding lightweight algorithms and reduced computational demands. These limitations severely hinder the

© The Author(s), under exclusive license to Springer Nature Singapore Pte Ltd. 2026
W. Jia et al. (Eds.): CCBR 2025, LNCS 16360, pp. 562–571, 2026.
https://doi.org/10.1007/978-981-95-6123-0_52

practical application of UAV-based pedestrian detection, making the development of UAV-adapted algorithms highly significant.

Deep learning-based object detection methods exhibit significant advantages, as they autonomously learn hierarchical features from datasets to achieve higher detection accuracy and stronger generalization capabilities. Among deep learning-based frameworks, two-stage algorithms (e.g., Faster R-CNN [4]) generate candidate regions prior to classification and regression, offering high accuracy but relatively slow inference. In contrast, one-stage algorithms such as the YOLO series [5–8] and SSD [9] directly predict object categories and locations in a single iteration. Compared to other object detection algorithms, YOLO series algorithms are more suitable for pedestrian detection in drone imagery due to their superior real-time performance.

To address the various issues posed by UAV image, numerous scholars have proposed improvements to the YOLO algorithm. Zhu et al. [10] incorporated an additional small object detection layer to enhance the detection accuracy of small objects in images with dense small objects. However, this modification significantly increases the algorithm's computational load. Removing the large object detection layer to reduce the computational burden of the small object detection layer further exacerbates the problem of significant object scale variations. Zhao et al. [11] boosted the algorithm's feature extraction capability by combining Space-to-Depth and receptive field attention convolutions, thereby improving small object detection accuracy. This method, however, inevitably increases computational load and parameter count. To tackle issues of complex backgrounds and significant target scale variations, Qiu et al. [12] leveraged multi-scale feature fusion to balance shallow-level features and high-level semantic information. Ma et al. [13] adopted a feature fusion module integrating re-parameterization and ELAN strategies to extract more precise and abundant features, thus reducing interference from complex background noise. In terms of algorithm lightweighting, Wang et al. [14] reduced computational complexity and parameter count by pruning channels with low information content and small scaling factors, which inevitably led to a decline in detection accuracy. Weng et al. [15] introduced lightweight GhostConv to replace the convolutional module in feature extraction, effectively reducing computational burden while slightly lowering detection accuracy.

Although some improvements have been proposed to address issues in drone images, they often struggle to balance detection accuracy and algorithm lightweighting. Additionally, pedestrians in UAV images are mostly small targets, leading to more detailed feature loss during downsampling and further increasing detection difficulty. Moreover, in feature upsampling, existing algorithms often only focus on neighborhood features while overlooking the rich semantic features critical for the task. To address these issues, built upon the YOLO11 [16] algorithm, we propose an improved algorithm based on Context Guided Downsampling and Reassembly of Feature, named CGDRF-YOLO for short. The main contributions and innovations are as follows:

(1) This study proposes a Context Guided Downsampling (CGD) module based on the improved Context Guided block. This module reduces computational complexity and parameter count through lightweight local feature extraction and downsampling operations. It can learn joint features of local features and surrounding contextual information, and further combine them with global features to achieve efficient

feature extraction and reduce feature information loss during the downsampling process.

(2) This study introduces CARAFE [17] to upsample a feature map. This operator enables instance-specific content-aware processing, dynamically generates adaptive kernels, and facilitates context information aggregation across a wide receptive field, thereby enhancing the receptive field and acquiring richer semantic information.

(3) This study replaces CIoU in YOLO11 with Inner-WIoU [18], aiming to enhance the algorithm's accuracy in complex localization tasks. Inner-WIoU can more accurately quantify localization errors when objects have irregular shapes or their positions are offset, thereby significantly boosting target localization accuracy.

2 CGDRF-YOLO: Integration of Context Guided Downsampling and Feature Reassembling Operators

The YOLO11 algorithm includes five versions spanning from small to large-scale: YOLO11n, YOLO11s, YOLO11m, YOLO11l, and YOLO11x. Among these, considering the real-time requirements and computational resource constraints inherent in drone image detection tasks, we selected YOLO11n as the baseline algorithm. Building on this baseline, in this study we propose an improved algorithm based on YOLO11, whose architectural diagram is presented in Fig. 1.

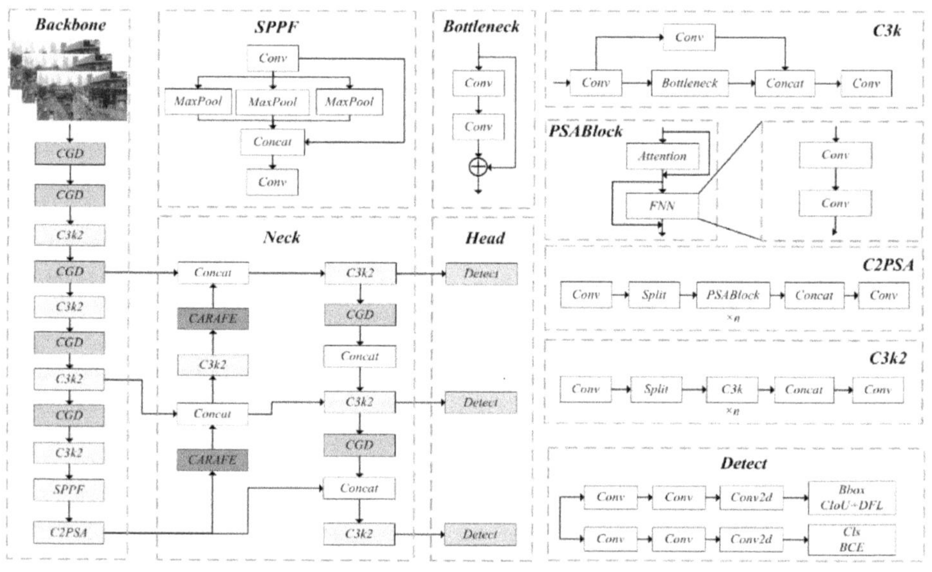

Fig. 1. Architecture of CGDRF-YOLO

2.1 Context Guided Downsampling

In the UAV-based pedestrian detection tasks, downsampling operations reduce the resolution of feature maps, potentially causing partial loss of detailed feature information in the process, this may lead to lower detection accuracy for small objects. Additionally, most existing downsampling operations focus solely on features within the current receptive field, resulting in biased detection outcomes due to the incompleteness of feature information within the current receptive field. To address these issues, we propose a context-aware downsampling module called CGD, whose structure is shown in Fig. 2. CGD comprises five components: a Downsampling module, a Surrounding Context Extractor, a Local Feature Extractor, a Joint Feature Extractor and a Global Context Extractor.

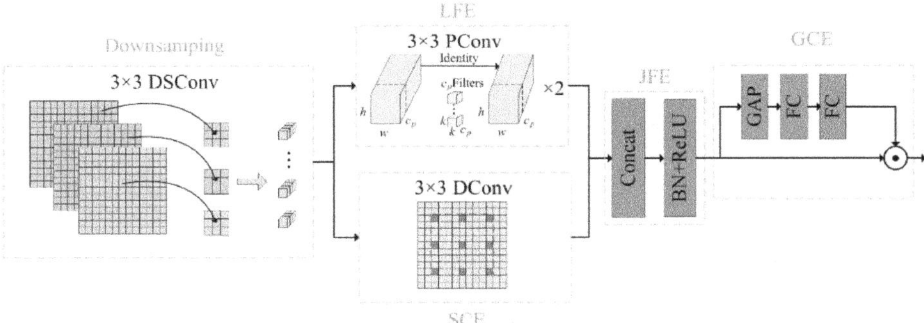

Fig. 2. Structure of CGD, which consist of Downsampling, Surrounding Context Extractor (SCE), Local Feature Extractor (LFE), Joint Feature Extractor (JFE), Global Context Extractor (GCE).

CGD consists of three main steps: (1) we adopt lightweight depth-wise separable convolution for downsampling to reduce the overall computational load and parameter count of the module. (2) LFE and SCE respectively learn local features and corresponding surrounding context, while JFE acquires their joint features. Specifically, for local feature extraction, 3 × 3 standard convolution is replaced with successive partial convolutions for lightweight module design without compromising extraction efficiency. For surrounding context extraction, dilated convolution with a large receptive field is used to effectively learn context information. Finally, JFE employs a concatenation layer, followed by batch normalization and ReLU activation. (3) Global context information serves as a weighting vector to fuse with joint features, enhancing useful information while reducing complex background interference. In the GCE, global average pooling is first used to aggregate global context, followed by successive fully connected operations for further extraction. Finally, the extracted global context and joint features are re-weighted.

2.2 Content-Aware Reassembly of Feature

Feature upsampling is an indispensable component in modern convolutional neural networks. Traditional upsampling methods, such as bilinear interpolation and nearest-neighbor interpolation, focus solely on predicting subpixels within the current receptive field and its adjacent regions, while neglecting the semantic information of the feature map. Unlike these traditional methods, CARAFE not only aggregates contextual information within a larger receptive field but also dynamically generates adaptive convolutional kernels based on the input feature content, thereby achieving superior detection performance. The structure of its module is shown in Fig. 3.

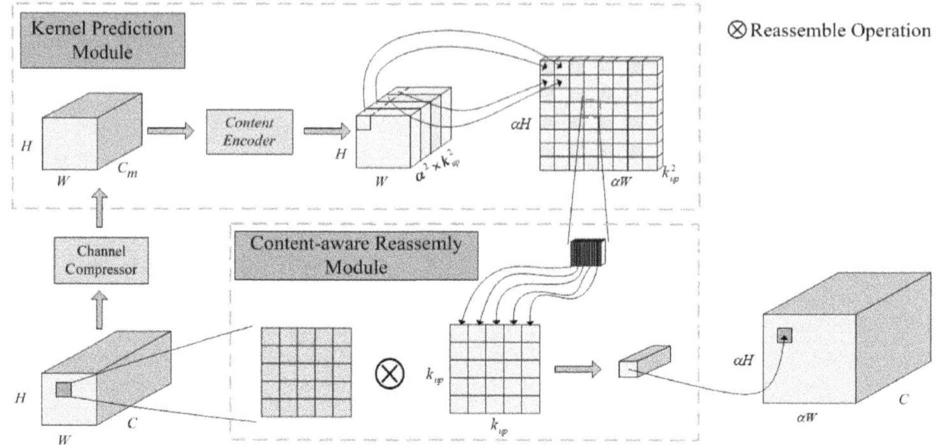

Fig. 3. Structure of CARAFE.

CARAFE comprises two core components, namely the Content-aware Reassembly Module and the Kernel Prediction Module. In the Kernel Prediction Module, channel compression is first performed to reduce the computational overhead of subsequent operations, thereby achieving module lightweighting. Subsequently, a content-aware reassembly kernel is predicted for each feature element. In the Content-aware Reassembly Module, features are reassembled based on the predicted adaptive kernels. Taking Fig. 3 as an example, given an input feature map of size $C \times H \times W$ and an upsampling rate α, the content encoder in the Kernel Prediction Module employs a convolution with kernel size $k_{encoder}$ to generate adaptive kernels. Thus, increasing $k_{encoder}$ can expand the receptive field of the encoder, ultimately producing a set of adaptive kernels with size $k_{up}^2 \times \alpha H \times \alpha W$, where k_{up} denotes the adaptive kernel size. The method of feature reassemble operation as shown in Eq. (1):

$$F'_l = \sum_{n=-r}^{r} \sum_{m=\{-\}r}^{r} K(n, m) \cdot F_l(i + n, j + m). \tag{1}$$

where $F_{l'}$ donates the feature corresponding to the position l of the output feature map. $r = \lfloor k_{up}/2 \rfloor$, $K(n, m)$ represents the local position of adaptive kernel, $F_l(i+n, j+m)$ donates the feature map at location (i, j) and its neighborhood features.

2.3 Improved Loss Function

In object detection, the loss function is designed to measure the discrepancy between an algorithm's predictive results and ground-truth annotations. Since its introduction, IoU

(Intersection over Union) has established itself as the dominant metric for evaluating the loss of predicted bounding boxes in the detection field. The original YOLO11 algorithm adopts CIoU as the loss function for its predicted bounding boxes. Nevertheless, in the context of small object detection, the penalty term associated with centroid distance may be exaggerated, which could impede the optimization process, thus leading the algorithm to overprioritize centroids at the expense of optimizing overlapping regions.

In response to the above issues, we introduce Inner-WIoU. it introduces an inner bounding box mechanism that defines a relatively small inner bounding box centered on the target box. Compared to the entire target box, this inner bounding box more accurately covers the target's actual region, thereby effectively reducing the interference of outer bounding box noise during loss calculation. By optimizing the IoU between the inner bounding box and the ground-truth target bounding box, the algorithm's localization accuracy no longer excessively depends on the position of the outer bounding box.

Additionally, through the introduction of a dynamic weight adjustment mechanism, Inner-WIoU adaptively assigns weights based on the degree of overlap between the predicted bounding box and the ground-truth bounding box. For samples where the outer bounding box exhibits minimal overlap with the target and suffers from significant noise interference, the weights are reduced to minimize the negative impact of low-quality bounding boxes on algorithm training. Conversely, for high-quality predicted boxes, the inner bounding box mechanism strengthens the focus on the actual target region, enabling the algorithm to more precisely capture the target's position. The specific calculation method of Inner-WIoU is shown in Eq. (2)–(10):

$$L_{inner-WIoU} = r \times R_{WIoU} \times \left(1 - IoU^{inner}\right). \tag{2}$$

$$R_{WIoU} = exp\left([(x_c^p - x_c^{gt})^2 + (y_c^p - y_c^{gt})^2]/(W_g^2 + H_g^2)^*\right). \tag{3}$$

$$IoU^{inner} = inter/union. \tag{4}$$

$$inter = [min(b_r^{gt}, b_r^p) - max(b_l^{gt}, b_l^p)] \times [min(b_b^{gt}, b_b^p) - max(b_t^{gt}, b_t^p)]. \tag{5}$$

$$union = (w^{gt} \times h^{gt}) \times ratio^2 + (w^p \times h^p) \times ratio^2 - inter. \tag{6}$$

$$b_l^{gt} = x_c^{gt} - (w^{gt} \times ratio)/2, b_r^{gt} = x_c^{gt} + (w^{gt} \times ratio)/2. \tag{7}$$

$$b_l^p = x_c^p - (w^p \times ratio)/2, b_r^p = x_c^p + (w^p \times ratio)/2. \tag{8}$$

$$b_t^{gt} = y_c^{gt} - (h^{gt} \times ratio)/2, b_b^{gt} = y_c^{gt} + (h^{gt} \times ratio)/2. \tag{9}$$

$$b_t^p = y_c^p - (h^p \times ratio)/2, b_b^p = y_c^p + (h^p \times ratio)/2. \tag{10}$$

where r donates a non-monotonic focus factor. (W_g, H_g) represents the size of the smallest enclosing box. (x_c^{gt}, y_c^{gt}) and (x_c^p, y_c^p) donate the centroids of the ground-truth and prediction box, (w^{gt}, h^{gt}) and (w^p, h^p) donate the width and height of the ground-truth and the prediction box, respectively. *Ratio* is in the range of [0.5, 1.5] [19].

3 Experiment

3.1 Experimental Environment and Parameter Configuration

Environmental parameter settings for the experimental platform utilized in this study are presented in Table 1.

Table 1. Experimental Environment Parameters

Name	Parameters
Operating System	Windows11
CPU	Intel@ Core™ i7-13650HX
Memory Size	16G
Graphics Card	RTX 4060 8G
Programming Language	Python3.9
Deep Learning Framework	PyTorch 2.1.1 + Cuda 12.1

The experiment is configured with 300 training epochs, and Stochastic Gradient Descent (SGD) is employed as the optimizer. Input images are sized 640×640, and the batch size is set to 8. In terms of learning rate, the initial value is 0.01, while the momentum weight is 0.9. Additionally, we conducted experiments on sub-datasets extracted from Visdrone2019 and BUU-SARD to validate the algorithm's effectiveness. Mean Average Precision (mAP), Parameters (Params), frames per second (FPS) and Floating-point Operations (FLOPs) were used as evaluation metrics.

3.2 Ablation Experiments

To validate the effectiveness of each improvement module in the proposed algorithm, we integrated CGD, CARAFE, Inner-WIoU, and their respective combinations into the baseline algorithm to develop a series of new algorithms. Subsequently, we conducted ablation experiments on the validation and test sets using these algorithms and CGDRF-YOLO. The experimental results are summarized in Table 2.

From the data in the tables, first, after adding the CGD module to the baseline algorithm, mAP50 on the validation and test sets increased by 1.6% and 1.1%, respectively, while the algorithm's computational complexity and parameter count both decreased by 9% and 13%, respectively. Additionally, FPS increased by 7%. This indicates that the CGD module can effectively retain shallow feature information during downsampling and incorporate contextual information to help the algorithm better identify targets, thereby effectively suppressing interference from complex backgrounds in drone images.

Subsequently, after integrating CARAFE module into the algorithm, we found that the increases in computational complexity and parameter count were negligible, mAP50 on the validation and test sets improved by 1.2% and 0.7%, respectively. This suggests that the CARAFE module can effectively predict adaptive kernels and reorganize features through feature content awareness.

Finally, after incorporating Inner-WIoU, mAP50 rose by 0.7% and 0.4% on the validation and test sets. Meanwhile, FPS increased by 3%, computational complexity and parameter count unchanged. This indicates that Inner-WIoU enables more accurate target localization, thus boosting both detection accuracy and inference speed.

Table 2. Ablation experiments on the VisDrone2019 sub-dataset

Algorithms	mAP50%		mAP50:95%		Params(M)	FLOPs(G)	FPS
	val	test	val	test			
YOLO11n	39.7	22.8	19.5	11.3	2.58	6.6	560
+ CGD	41.3	23.9	20.6	12.1	**2.35**	**5.8**	601
+ CARAFE	40.9	23.5	20.1	11.6	**2.72**	**6.8**	498
+ Inner-WIoU	40.4	20.2	19.8	11.4	2.58	6.6	576
+ CGD + Inner-WIoU	41.9	24.4	21.0	12.3	**2.35**	**5.8**	**617**
+ CGD + CARAFE	42.4	24.5	21.4	12.4	2.49	6.0	565
+ CARAFE + Inner-WIoU	41.4	23.7	20.4	11.8	2.72	6.8	518
CGDRF-YOLO	**43.3**	**24.7**	**21.7**	**12.5**	2.49	6.0	585

Overall, compared to YOLO11n, Algorithms incorporating various combinations of improvements exhibits superior detection performance. CGDRF-YOLO maintains algorithm lightweightness while improving mAP50 by 3.6% on the validation set and 1.9% on the test set.

3.3 Experimental Comparison with Other Algorithms

To further validate the superiority of the proposed algorithm, we performed a comparative experimental analysis between it and classical object detection algorithms on the validation set. The results of these experiments are summarized in Table 3.

As evident from the table above, compared with other algorithms, CGDRF-YOLO exhibits superior detection performance. Specifically, on the BUU-SARD sub-dataset, when benchmarked against the baseline methods, it achieves respective improvements of 2.4% and 1.9% in mAP50 and mAP50:95. These results indicate that CGDRF-YOLO possesses strong generalization capabilities.

Table 3. Comparative experiments with other algorithms

Algorithms	VisDrone2019 sub-dataset		BUU-SARD sub-dataset	
	mAp50%	mAP50:95%	mAP50%	mAP50:95%
SSD	24.6	12.2	89.8	61.2
YOLOv5n	38.7	18.4	92.9	63.5
YOLOv6n	37.9	18.1	91.6	62.5
YOLOv7-tiny	38.4	18.6	93.9	62.1
YOLOv8n	40.4	19.7	95.1	63.9
YOLOv9-t	39.1	18.9	92.2	62.4
YOLOv10n	39.4	19.1	93.5	62.9
YOLO11n	39.7	19.5	93.8	63.6
CGDRF-YOLO	**43.3**	**21.7**	**96.2**	**65.5**

4 Conclusion and Future Work

To address the challenges in UAV-based pedestrian detection, this study proposes an efficiently improved algorithm, CGDRF-YOLO. First, we incorporate CGD module, which achieves lightweight processing via depth-separable convolutions. This module aggregates both the current receptive field and contextual information of input features, reducing feature loss during downsampling and enhancing the algorithm's robustness against interference. Second, we integrate CARAFE module, which employs content-aware generation mechanisms to generate adaptive kernels and reorganize features, enabling the algorithm to leverage feature information more efficiently. Finally, we introduce Inner-WIoU loss function to improve the algorithm's target localization accuracy and optimize its inference speed. Experiments on both Visdrone2019 and BUU-SARD sub-datasets demonstrate that CGDRF-YOLO outperforms both baseline and other comparative algorithms in detection performance. It achieves enhanced detection accuracy while maintaining the lightweight nature of the algorithm, thus making it suitable for pedestrian detection in drone images.

Acknowledgments. This work was supported in part by the Jiangxi Provincial Department of Water Resources Science & Technology Program Foundation (Grant NO. 202325ZDKT17, 202426ZDKT13).

References

1. Byun, S., Shin, I.-K., Moon, J., et al.: Road traffic monitoring from UAV images using deep learning networks. Remote Sens. **13**(20), 4027 (2021)
2. Wu, J., Yang, G., Yang, H., et al.: Extracting apple tree crown information from remote imagery using deep learning. Comput. Electron. Agric. **174**, 10554 (2020)

3. Lei, T.J., Li, C.C., He, X.Y.: Application of aerial remote sensing of pilotless aircraft to disaster emergency rescue. J. Nat. Disast. **20**(1), 178–183 (2011)
4. Ren, S.Q., He, K.M., Girshick, R., et al.: Faster R-CNN: towards real-time object detection with region proposal networks. IEEE Trans. Pattern Anal. Mach. Intell. **39**(6), 1137–1149 (2017)
5. Redmon, J., et al.: You only look once: unified, real-time object detection. In: Computer Vision & Pattern Recognition. IEEE (2016)
6. Redmon, J., Farhadi, A.: YOLOv3: an incremental improvement. arXiv preprint arXiv:1804.02767 (2018)
7. Glenn, J.: YOLOv5 release v7.0 (2022). https://github.com/ultralytics/YOLOv5/tree/v7.0
8. Zhao, L., Zhu, M.: MS-YOLOv7: YOLOv7 based on multi-scale for object detection on UAV aerial photography. Drones **7**, 188 (2023)
9. Liu, W., Anguelov, D., Erhan, D., et al.: SSD: single shot multibox detector. CoRR (2015)
10. Zhu, G., Wang, Z., Zhu, F.: HCAC and MWFN based small object detection algorithm. Electron. Optics Control 1–8 (2024)
11. Zhao, S., Chen, H., Zhang, D., et al.: SR-YOLO: spatial-to-depth enhanced multi-scale attention network for small target detection in UAV aerial imagery. Remote Sens. **17**(14), 2441 (2025)
12. Qiu, X., Chen, Y., Sun, C., Li, J., Niu, M., et al.: DMFF-YOLO: YOLOv8 based on dynamic multiscale feature fusion for object detection on UAV aerial photography. IEEE Access **12**, 125160–125169 (2024)
13. Ma, C., Fu, Y., Wang, D., et al.: YOLO-UAV: object detection method of unmanned aerial vehicle imagery based on efficient multi-scale feature fusion. IEEE Access **11**, 126857–126878 (2023)
14. Wang, X., Zhuang, X., Zhang, W., et al.: Lightweight real-time object detection model for UAV platform. In: International Conference on Computer Communication and Artificial Intelligence, pp. 20–24 (2021)
15. Weng, S., Wang, H., Wang, J., et al.: YOLO-SRMX: a lightweight model for real-time object detection on unmanned aerial vehicles. Remote Sens. **17**(13), 2313 (2025)
16. Jocher, G., Qiu, J.: Ultralytics YOLO11 (2024). https://github.com/ultralytics/ultralytics
17. Wang, J., Chen, K., Xu, R., Liu, Z., Loy, C.C., Lin, D.: CARAFE: content-aware reassembly of features. In: IEEE/CVF International Conference on Computer Vision, pp. 3007–3016 (2019)
18. Wang, H., Xu, S., Chen, Y., et al.: LFD-YOLO: a lightweight fall detection network with enhanced feature extraction and fusion. Sci. Rep. **15**(1), 1–18 (2025)
19. Zhang, H., Xu, C., Zhang, S.: Inner-IoU: more effective intersection over union loss with auxiliary bounding box. arXiv preprint arXiv:2311.02877 (2023)

Region-Level Cross-Modal Matching Framework for Text-Based Geo-Localization

Yanhe Yu, Quan Zhang$^{(\boxtimes)}$, Qihua Ou, and Hongbo Chen$^{(\boxtimes)}$

School of Systems Science and Engineering, Sun Yat-sen University,
Guangzhou, China
{yuyh53,ouqh}@mail2.sysu.edu.cn, {zhangq689,chenhongbo}@mail.sysu.edu.cn

Abstract. Text-based geo-localization, which aims to identify a target location in an aerial image using a natural language description. Existing methods often rely on global feature matching and local spatial information for alignment. However, fine-grained semantic matching between specific textual phrases and their corresponding visual regions is not effectively utilized. To this end, we propose the Region-level Cross-modal Matching Framework (RCMF), which forges robust correspondences across multiple levels of detail. Furthermore, we propose a novel Dual-stream Cross-Attention Fusion module (DCAF) that facilitates deep, reciprocal information exchange between image and text modalities. Finally, extensive experiments demonstrate that our approach achieves state-of-the-art performance on the GeoText-1652 benchmark, improving localization accuracy.

Keywords: Cross-modal Learning · Fine-grained Alignment · Geo-localization · Text-based Geo-localization

1 Introduction

Guiding drones with natural language commands is gaining traction due to their increasing use in social services, urban monitoring, and remote sensing applications [1–3]. Earlier work formulates drone navigation as an image-retrieval problem that matches a query image to a gallery to localize the target [4]. This scheme fails whenever a query image is unavailable—a common situation in practice. Natural language descriptions therefore provide a more natural and flexible interface for human-drone interaction while eliminating the need for visual queries.

Cross-view geolocalization research was significantly accelerated by large-scale imagery across ground, drone, and satellite views [4]. The recent introduction of the GeoText-1652 dataset [5] further advanced the frontier by incorporating dense, region-level textual annotations, enabling sophisticated tasks like

Q. Zhang and H. Chen—This work was supported by the Postdoctoral Fellowship Program and China Postdoctoral Science Foundation (GZC20252314).

W. Jia et al. (Eds.): CCBR 2025, LNCS 16360, pp. 572–582, 2026.
https://doi.org/10.1007/978-981-95-6123-0_53

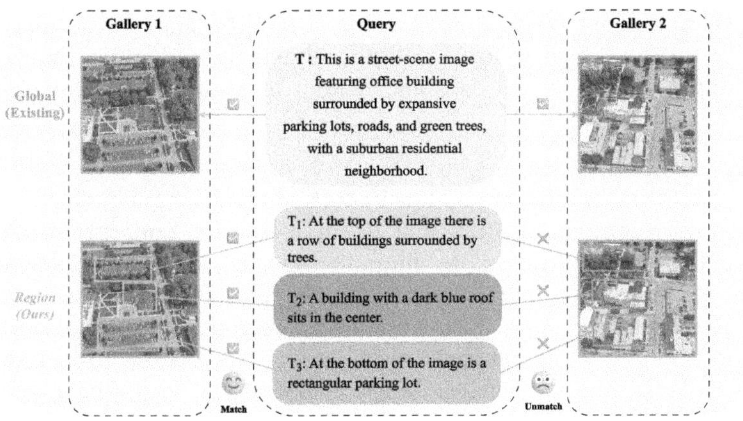

Fig. 1. Overview of text-based Geo-localization. The system needs to understand natural language descriptions and locate corresponding regions in aerial images.

language-guided drone navigation. However, this progress also highlighted a critical limitation of existing methods: they typically rely on global feature matching, which aligns an entire image with a full text description. This coarse-grained approach may not fully leverage the fine-grained correspondences between specific visual regions and textual phrases, a capability that could be beneficial for enhanced semantic understanding and localization performance.

To tackle this limitation, we propose the Region-level Cross-modal Matching Framework (RCMF), which establishes fine-grained alignments between visual regions and textual descriptions through hierarchical supervision and novel cross-attention mechanisms. Extensive experiments on the GeoText-1652 benchmark confirm the effectiveness of our approach. Our contributions are:

- We propose the RCMF, which employs a hierarchical supervision strategy that moves beyond global-only matching to enforce fine-grained, region-level alignment between visual and textual modalities.
- We propose a novel dual-stream cross-attention fusion module within our RCMF framework that facilitates deep, reciprocal information exchange to learn highly contextualized representations.
- We establish new state-of-the-art performance on the GeoText-1652 benchmark, providing comprehensive empirical evidence for the effectiveness of our region-centric approach.

2   Related Work

Cross-view Geolocalization. Cross-view geolocalization identifies the same geographic location from images captured at different viewpoints [4,6]. The challenge is appearance shift caused by viewpoint variations, addressed by image-level alignment (geometric transformations [7,8] or generative synthesis [9]) and feature-level alignment (region-partitioning [10,11] to Transformer-based architectures [12]). While effective for aerial-ground person re-identification [13], these methods rely solely on visual cues and cannot leverage natural language guidance.

Text-Based Geo-localization. Leveraging natural language for guidance in geolocalization represents a promising research frontier, conceptualized as fine-grained text-to-image retrieval to pinpoint specific locations from candidate images using descriptive text queries. The GeoText-1652 dataset [5] has been a key catalyst in this domain, providing dense region-level textual annotations for the University-1652 benchmark and enabling challenging tasks like natural language-guided drone navigation. While foundational vision-language models such as CLIP [14], ALBEF [15], and XVLM [16] have shown remarkable success in learning joint image-text representations, advances in multi-modal learning [17] demonstrate the potential for cross-modal understanding, yet they often lack the granularity to capture detailed spatial relationships required for precise geolocalization. Motivated by this limitation, our work introduces a framework that shifts from global feature matching to explicit region-level alignment to tackle the fine-grained understanding challenge posed by benchmarks like GeoText-1652.

Fine-Grained Visual Understanding. Fine-grained visual understanding is a critical capability for tasks that involve distinguishing between visually similar categories or localizing specific object details. In related domains such as object detection and segmentation, region-based methods like Mask R-CNN [18] and DETR [19] have established the efficacy of an object-centric approach. By processing information at the level of object proposals or queries, these frameworks underscore the importance of analyzing specific image regions to extract detailed semantic information. Recent advances in transformer-based uncertainty modeling [12,20] and separable spatial-temporal residual graphs [21] provide insights for constructing robust region-level features in scenarios with appearance variations.

3   Method

3.1   Problem Formulation

Text-based geo-localization requires establishing fine-grained correspondences between specific image regions and textual fragments, a task that demands precise semantic understanding beyond global image-text alignment. Given an aerial image I, a global description T, and corresponding regions I_1, I_2, I_3 with their region-level descriptions T_1, T_2, T_3, we formulate this as a region-level cross-modal matching problem where the goal is to learn discriminative representations that enable accurate localization of described objects or regions through hierarchical supervision at both global and fine-grained levels.

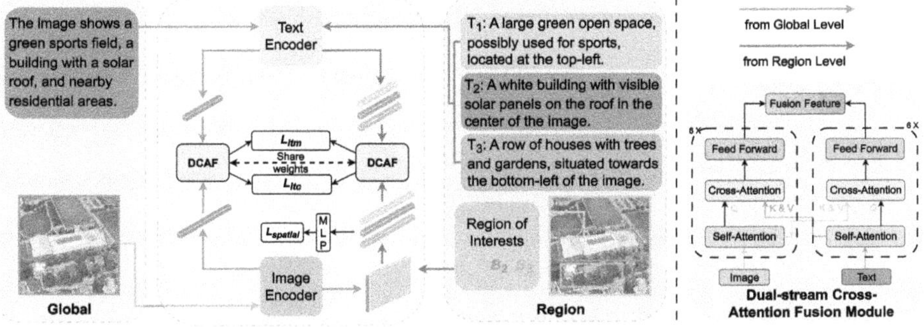

Fig. 2. Overview of our Region-level Cross-modal Matching Framework (RCMF). The framework consists of three main components: (1) Dual-stream Cross-Attention Fusion (DCAF) module with parallel image and text streams, (2) hierarchical supervision strategy processing both global and region-level information through shared-weight attention modules, and (3) multi-objective training with contrastive learning, matching objectives, and spatial relation matching.

3.2   Region-Level Cross-Modal Matching Framework (RCMF)

Our Region-level Cross-modal Matching Framework (RCMF) tackles the fine-grained alignment challenge through a hierarchical supervision strategy that enforces correspondences at both global (image-to-text) and local (region-to-fragment) levels, enabling precise cross-modal alignment and improved localization performance, as illustrated in Fig. 2.

3.3   Dual-Stream Cross-Attention Fusion (DCAF)

The core of our framework is a novel DCAF module that enables deep bidirectional information exchange between visual and textual modalities. As illustrated in the right part of Fig. 2, this module consists of two parallel processing streams that operate iteratively over multiple layers.

Each stream processes its respective modality through a sequence of self-attention and cross-attention operations. In the image stream, visual features first undergo self-attention to capture intra-modal dependencies, followed by cross-attention where the self-attended image features serve as queries (Q) while receiving keys and values (K&V) from the text stream's self-attention output. Similarly, in the text stream, textual features are processed through self-attention, then cross-attention with keys and values derived from the image stream.

Formally, given input visual features $F_v \in \mathbb{R}^{N \times d}$ and textual features $F_t \in \mathbb{R}^{M \times d}$, the dual-stream cross-attention fusion is formulated as:

$$\mathrm{DSCF}(F_v, F_t) = \frac{\mathrm{CA}_{V \to T}(F_v, F_t) + \mathrm{CA}_{T \to V}(F_t, F_v)}{2}, \tag{1}$$

where the cross-attention from visual to textual modality is:

$$\text{CA}_{V \to T}(F_v, F_t) = \text{SoftMax}\left(\frac{(\mathbf{W}_Q^{V \to T} F_v)(\mathbf{W}_K^{V \to T} F_t)^{\top}}{\sqrt{d}}\right)(\mathbf{W}_V^{V \to T} F_t), \qquad (2)$$

and the cross-attention from textual to visual modality is:

$$\text{CA}_{T \to V}(F_v, F_t) = \text{SoftMax}\left(\frac{(\mathbf{W}_Q^{T \to V} F_t)(\mathbf{W}_K^{T \to V} F_v)^{\top}}{\sqrt{d}}\right)(\mathbf{W}_V^{T \to V} F_v), \qquad (3)$$

where $\mathbf{W}_Q, \mathbf{W}_K, \mathbf{W}_V$ are learnable parameters.

This bidirectional cross-attention mechanism facilitates mutual information exchange, allowing visual representations to integrate relevant textual semantics and textual tokens to selectively focus on corresponding image regions. The process is repeated across multiple layers (6× in our implementation) to progressively refine the cross-modal representations.

3.4   Optimization

Image-Text Contrastive Learning (ITC). To establish effective cross-modal alignment, we employ contrastive learning at both global and region levels. The region-level ITC loss $\mathcal{L}_{\text{itc}}^{\text{R}}$ enforces fine-grained correspondences between image regions and their corresponding textual fragments. Given the visual features V derived from image I and textual features T, the region-level loss is formulated as:

$$\mathcal{L}_{\text{itc}}^{\text{R}} = \sum_i - \log \frac{\exp(\text{sim}(V_i^R, T_i^R)/\tau)}{\sum_k \exp(\text{sim}(V_i^R, T_k^R)/\tau)}. \qquad (4)$$

where $\text{sim}(V_i^R, T_j^R) = \frac{(V_i^R)^{\top} T_j^R}{\|V_i^R\|\|T_j^R\|}$ computes the cosine similarity between region feature V_i^R and fragment T_j^R, and τ is a learnable temperature parameter.

Complementing this fine-grained objective, we employ a global-level contrastive loss $\mathcal{L}_{\text{itc}}^{\text{G}}$ that aligns the overall image representation V^G with the complete text description T^G:

$$\mathcal{L}_{\text{itc}}^{\text{G}} = - \log \frac{\exp(\text{sim}(V^G, T^G)/\tau)}{\sum_k \exp(\text{sim}(V^G, T_k^G)/\tau)}. \qquad (5)$$

This hierarchical contrastive learning strategy ensures that the model learns both coarse-grained global correspondences and fine-grained regional alignments simultaneously.

Image-Text Matching Learning (ITM). Complementing the contrastive learning objectives, we employ image-text matching as a binary classification task to explicitly verify the semantic correspondence between regions and fragments. The region-level ITM loss $\mathcal{L}_{\text{itm}}^{\text{R}}$ operates on region-text fragment pairs to determine whether they represent the same semantic entity:

$$\mathcal{L}_{\text{itm}}^{\text{R}} = \mathbb{E}\left[\text{H}(y_{ij}, p_{ij}(V_i^R, T_j^R))\right], \qquad (6)$$

where $y_{ij} \in \{0,1\}$ indicates whether region V_i^R and fragment T_j^R are semantically matched, p_{ij} is the predicted matching probability computed through cosine similarity, and $\mathrm{H}(y,p) = -y\log(p) - (1-y)\log(1-p)$ is the binary cross-entropy loss function:

$$p_{ij} = \sigma(\mathrm{sim}(V_i^R, T_j^R)/\tau), \tag{7}$$

where σ is the sigmoid function, $\mathrm{sim}(V_i^R, T_j^R) = \frac{(V_i^R)^\top T_j^R}{\|V_i^R\|\|T_j^R\|}$ is the cosine similarity, and τ is a learnable temperature parameter.

Similarly, the global-level ITM loss $\mathcal{L}_{\mathrm{itm}}^{\mathrm{G}}$ assesses the overall semantic coherence between the complete image and text description:

$$\mathcal{L}_{\mathrm{itm}}^{\mathrm{G}} = \mathbb{E}\left[\mathrm{H}(y_g, p_g(V^G, T^G))\right], \tag{8}$$

where $p_g = \sigma(\mathrm{sim}(V^G, T^G)/\tau)$ is computed using the same cosine similarity approach with the same learnable temperature parameter τ, and $\mathrm{H}(y,p)$ is the same binary cross-entropy loss function as defined above.

Spatial Relation Matching. To enhance the framework's understanding of spatial configurations, we introduce a spatial relation matching objective $\mathcal{L}_{\mathrm{spatial}}$ that captures the relative spatial relationships between image regions. This is formulated as a 9-class classification task, where the model predicts the spatial relationship between pairs of regions based on their bounding box geometries.

The spatial relationships are defined using a 3×3 grid pattern: left-above, above, right-above, left, center, right, left-below, below, right-below. Given two regions V_i^R and V_j^R, the spatial relationship is determined by comparing their bounding box centers and computing the relative position. Let y_{rel}^{ij} denote the ground-truth spatial relationship label derived from the bounding box geometries. The loss is formulated as:

$$\mathcal{L}_{\mathrm{spatial}} = \mathbb{E}\left[-\sum_{k=1}^{9}(y_{\mathrm{rel}}^{ij})_k \log((\hat{p}_{\mathrm{rel}}^{ij})_k)\right], \tag{9}$$

where $\hat{p}_{\mathrm{rel}}^{ij}$ is the predicted probability distribution over the 9 spatial relationships, computed as:

$$\hat{p}_{\mathrm{rel}}^{ij} = \mathrm{SoftMax}(\mathrm{MLP}([V_i^R; V_j^R; V_i^R \odot V_j^R])). \tag{10}$$

This spatial awareness enables the model to understand complex spatial configurations, which is crucial for accurate geo-localization in aerial imagery.

Overall Training Objective. Our framework integrates all objectives into a unified training objective. The total loss function combines global and region-level objectives:

$$\mathcal{L} = (\mathcal{L}_{\mathrm{itc}}^{\mathrm{G}} + \mathcal{L}_{\mathrm{itm}}^{\mathrm{G}}) + \mu(\mathcal{L}_{\mathrm{itc}}^{\mathrm{R}} + \mathcal{L}_{\mathrm{itm}}^{\mathrm{R}}) + \lambda\mathcal{L}_{\mathrm{spatial}}, \tag{11}$$

where μ controls region-level objectives and λ balances spatial awareness. We empirically set $\lambda = 0.1$ and $\mu = 0.3$. The global-level losses ensure semantic coherence, while region-level losses enforce precise local correspondences. The spatial loss enhances understanding of spatial configurations crucial for geo-localization.

4   Experiments

Dataset. We evaluate on the GeoText-1652 dataset with 1,652 locations and dense region-level text annotations. The dataset is split into training, validation, and test sets with 1,152, 250, and 250 locations respectively, with an average of 3.2 region-level annotations per location.

Table 1. Performance comparison on GeoText-1652 dataset, including settings of text query (text-to-image) and image query (image-to-text). Recall@K (R@K) have been reported.

Method	Text Query			Image Query		
	R@1	R@5	R@10	R@1	R@5	R@10
UNITER [22]	10.6	20.4	26.1	21.4	43.4	59.5
METER-Swin [23]	11.3	21.5	27.3	22.7	46.3	60.7
ALBEF [15]	12.5	22.8	28.5	23.2	49.7	62.4
XVLM [16]	13.2	23.7	29.6	25.0	52.3	65.1
Baseline	13.6	24.6	31.2	26.3	53.7	66.9
RCMF (Ours)	**13.7**	**24.8**	**31.2**	**27.6**	**54.7**	**67.4**

Implementation Details. Our implementation is built upon PyTorch. Following GeoText [5] as our baseline, we adopt XVLM [16] pre-trained on 16M images as backbone. Visual and textual features are extracted using Swin Transformer [24] and BERT [25] respectively. We train with AdamW optimizer [26] (learning rate $3e^{-5}$), 384×384 image resolution, and set $\lambda = 0.1$, $\mu = 0.3$.

Comparisons with Competitive Methods. We compare our RCMF framework with several state-of-the-art cross-modal learning methods, including UNITER [22], METER-Swin [23], ALBEF [15], and XVLM [16]. To ensure fair comparison, all baseline methods are fine-tuned on the GeoText-1652 dataset using the same training protocols and evaluation metrics. Table 1 presents the comprehensive comparison results on the GeoText-1652 dataset.

Our RCMF framework achieves state-of-the-art performance on GeoText-1652, with R@1/R@5/R@10 of 27.6%/54.7%/67.4% for image-to-text and 13.7%

Table 2. Ablation study results on GeoText-1652 dataset. $\mathcal{L}^R$ means the sum of $\mathcal{L}^{\mathrm{R}}_{\mathrm{itc}}$ and $\mathcal{L}^{\mathrm{R}}_{\mathrm{itm}}$.

Method	Text Query			Image Query		
	R@1	R@5	R@10	R@1	R@5	R@10
RCMF	**13.7**	**24.8**	**31.2**	**27.6**	**54.7**	**67.4**
RCMF w/o $\mathcal{L}_{\mathrm{spatial}}$	13.5	24.5	31.1	26.6	54.0	67.1
RCMF w/o $\mathcal{L}^{\mathrm{R}}$	13.6	24.6	31.2	26.3	53.7	66.9

/24.8%/31.2% for text-to-image retrieval. The results demonstrate that region-level supervision enhances the accuracy of image query tasks while improving the performance of text query tasks, indicating that fine-grained correspondences provide complementary benefits across different retrieval directions.

Ablation Study. Table 2 reveals several important insights. First, removing the spatial loss component results in performance degradation, with R@1 dropping from 13.7% to 13.5% for text-to-image retrieval and from 27.6% to 26.6% for image-to-text retrieval. Second, removing the region-level losses ($\mathcal{L}^{\mathrm{R}}$) leads to more significant performance drops, with image-to-text R@1 decreasing from 27.6% to 26.3%, demonstrating the critical importance of fine-grained region-level supervision. This observation indicates that the region-level contrastive and matching objectives are the primary drivers of performance improvement, while spatial consistency provides additional benefits.

Table 3. Parameter analysis of different μ values on GeoText-1652 dataset.

μ	R@1	R@5	R@10	R@1	R@5	R@10
0.9	8.8	17.5	18.5	20.2	40.4	59.2
0.5	10.2	22.5	27.8	24.7	51.2	65.1
0.3	**13.7**	**24.8**	**31.2**	**27.6**	**54.7**	**67.4**
0.1	13.1	24.5	30.8	27.1	54.2	66.9

Parameter Analysis. Table 3 shows that $\mu = 0.3$ achieves the optimal performance across all evaluation metrics. Performance degrades when μ is set too high (0.9) or too low (0.1), indicating the importance of balanced supervision between global and region-level objectives. The optimal μ value of 0.3 suggests that region-level supervision should be weighted appropriately to complement global alignment without overwhelming the global semantic understanding.

Visualization. Figure 3 compares retrieval results between our RCMF and baseline methods. Our approach consistently retrieves more relevant images (green borders) compared to incorrect baseline results (red borders), demonstrating the effectiveness of region-level supervision for fine-grained cross-modal alignment.

Fig. 3. Visual comparison of text-to-image retrieval results. Green borders indicate correct matches, red borders indicate incorrect ones. (Color figure online)

5   Conclusion

This paper proposes the Region-level Cross-modal Matching Framework (RCMF) to tackle fine-grained cross-modal alignment in text-based geo-localization. Our framework employs hierarchical supervision at global and region levels with a dual-stream cross-attention fusion module for bidirectional information exchange. Experiments on GeoText-1652 achieve state-of-the-art performance across all metrics. Ablation studies validate the effectiveness of region-level supervision and spatial relation matching. Future work will explore multi-modal extensions and real-world applications.

References

1. Liu, S., Zhang, H., Qi, Y., Wang, P., Zhang, Y., Wu, Q.: Aerialvln: vision-and-language navigation for uavs. In: IEEE/CVF International Conference on Computer Vision, pp. 15384–15394 (2023)
2. Rashid, M.T., Zhang, D.Y., Wang, D.: Socialdrone: an integrated social media and drone sensing system for reliable disaster response. In: IEEE Conference on Computer Communications, pp. 218–227 (2020)

3. Lyu, R., Zhang, J., Pang, J., Zhang, J.: Modeling the impacts of 2d/3d urban structure on pm2. 5 at high resolution by combining uav multispectral/lidar measurements and multi-source remote sensing images. J. Clean. Prod. 140613 (2024)
4. Zheng, Z., Wei, Y., Yang, Y.: University-1652: a multi-view multi-source benchmark for drone-based geo-localization. In: ACM International Conference on Multimedia, pp. 1395–1403 (2020)
5. Chu, M., Zheng, Z., Ji, W., Wang, T., Chua, T.: Towards natural language-guided drones: Geotext-1652 benchmark with spatial relation matching. In: European Conference on Computer Vision, pp. 213–231 (2024)
6. Lin, T., Cui, Y., Belongie, S., Hays, J.: Learning deep representations for ground-to-aerial geolocalization. In: IEEE Conference on Computer Vision and Pattern Recognition, pp. 5007–5015 (2015)
7. Shi, Y., Liu, L., Yu, X., Li, H.: Spatial-aware feature aggregation for image based cross-view geo-localization. Adv. Neural. Inf. Process. Syst. **32**, 1–11 (2019)
8. Wang, X., Xu, R., Cui, Z., Wan, Z., Zhang, Y.: Fine-grained cross-view geo-localization using a correlation-aware homography estimator. Adv. Neural. Inf. Process. Syst. **36**, 1–19 (2023)
9. Ju, H., Huang, S., Liu, S., Zheng, Z.: Video2bev: transforming drone videos to bevs for video-based geo-localization. In: IEEE/CVF International Conference on Computer Vision (2025)
10. Zhang, Q., Lai, J., Feng, Z., Xie, X.: Seeing like a human: asynchronous learning with dynamic progressive refinement for person re-identification. IEEE Trans. Image Process. 352–365 (2021)
11. Zhang, Q., Lai, J., Xie, X.: Learning modal-invariant angular metric by cyclic projection network for vis-nir person re-identification. IEEE Trans. Image Process. **30**, 8019–8033 (2021)
12. Zhang, Q., Lai, J., Feng, Z., Xie, X.: Uncertainty modeling for group re-identification. International Journal of Computer Vision, pp. 3046–3066 (2024)
13. Zhang, Q., Wang, L., Patel, V.M., Xie, X., Lai, J.: View-decoupled transformer for person re-identification under aerial-ground camera network. In: IEEE/CVF Conference on Computer Vision and Pattern Recognition, pp. 22000–22009 (2024)
14. Radford, A., et al.: Learning transferable visual models from natural language supervision. In: International Conference on Machine Learning, pp. 8748–8763 (2021)
15. Li, J., Selvaraju, R., Gotmare, A., Joty, S., Xiong, C., Hoi, S.: Align before fuse: vision and language representation learning with momentum distillation. **34**, 9694–9705 (2021)
16. Zeng, Y., Zhang, X., Li, H.: Multi-grained vision language pre-training: aligning texts with visual concepts. In: International Conference on Machine Learning, pp. 25994–26009 (2022)
17. Zhang, Q., Liao, Z., Huang, Y., Lai, J.: Multi-modal face anti-spoofing based on a single image. In: Chinese Conference on Pattern Recognition and Computer Vision, pp. 424–435. Springer, Heidelberg (2021)
18. He, K., Gkioxari, G., Dollár, P., Girshick, R.: Mask r-cnn. In: IEEE International Conference on Computer Vision, pp. 2980–2988 (2017)
19. Carion, N., Massa, F., Synnaeve, G., Usunier, N., Kirillov, A., Zagoruyko, S.: End-to-end object detection with transformers. In: European Conference on Computer Vision, pp. 213–229 (2020)
20. Zhang, Q., Lai, J.H., Feng, Z., Xie, X.: Uncertainty modeling with second-order transformer for group re-identification. In: Proceedings of the AAAI Conference on Artificial Intelligence, vol. 36, pp. 3318–3325 (2022)

21. Zhang, Q., Lai, J., Xie, X., Jin, X., Huang, S.: Separable spatial-temporal residual graph for cloth-changing group re-identification. IEEE Trans. Pattern Anal. Mach. Intell. 5791–5805 (2024)
22. Chen, Y., et al.: Uniter: universal image-text representation learning. In: European Conference on Computer Vision, pp. 104–120. Springer, Heidelberg (2020)
23. Dou, Z., et al.: An empirical study of training end-to-end vision-and-language transformers. In: IEEE/CVF Conference on Computer Vision and Pattern Recognition, pp. 18166–18176 (2022)
24. Liu, Z., et al.: Swin transformer: hierarchical vision transformer using shifted windows. In: IEEE/CVF International Conference on Computer Vision, pp. 10012–10022 (2021)
25. Devlin, J., Chang, M.W., Lee, K., Toutanova, K.: Bert: pre-training of deep bidirectional transformers for language understanding. In: North American Chapter of the Association for Computational Linguistics, pp. 4171–4186 (2019)
26. Loshchilov, I., Hutter, F.: Decoupled weight decay regularization. In: International Conference on Learning Representations, pp. 1–18 (2019)

Basic Theory of Biometric Recognition

Exponential Non-negative Matrix Factorization for Image Data Representation

Mingze Gao[1,2], Wen-Sheng Chen[1,2(✉)], and Binbin Pan[1,2]

[1] School of Mathematical Sciences, Shenzhen University, Shenzhen 518060, China
`chenws@szu.edu.cn`
[2] Guangdong Provincial Key Laboratory of Intelligent Information Processing,
Shenzhen University, Shenzhen 518060, China

Abstract. This paper proposes an Exponential Non-negative Matrix Factorization (ExpNMF) model for extracting discriminative non-negative features to achieve robust image representation. To solve the optimization problem, we develop a novel gradient descent algorithm with theoretically guaranteed convergence. Rigorous mathematical analysis derives a valid step size range, ensuring stable convergence behavior. Compared with most NMF-based algorithms, ExpNMF offers key advantages, including automatic step size adjustment along the negative gradient, inherent capability to handle mixed-sign data, and effective support for zero-value initialization. Experimental validation on diverse image datasets confirms consistent convergence within the theoretical step size bounds while demonstrating superior classification accuracy for both non-negative and mixed-sign data. These results demonstrate that Exp-NMF provides an effective feature extraction framework for real-world data applications.

Keywords: Non-negative matrix factorization · gradient descent · feature extraction · image representation

1 Introduction

Feature extraction is a core component of image data processing and analysis, directly impacting the effectiveness of subsequent tasks. Among various methods, Non-negative Matrix Factorization (NMF) [1,2] is a non-negative feature extraction approach that has gained significant popularity. By expressing a high-dimensional non-negative data matrix as the product of two low-rank non-negative matrices—a basis matrix and a feature matrix—NMF constructs a representation framework based on linear superposition. This matrix decomposition not only effectively uncovers latent structural features within image data but also enhances part-based representations through non-negativity constraints. As a result, NMF demonstrates unique advantages for the representation of non-negative image data and has been widely applied in domains including hyperspectral unmixing [3,4], image processing [5,6], data classification [7,8] and data

W. Jia et al. (Eds.): CCBR 2025, LNCS 16360, pp. 585–595, 2026.
https://doi.org/10.1007/978-981-95-6123-0_54

clustering [9–12]. The standard NMF methods [2] are solved using the gradient descent method, where multiplicative update rules are derived by selecting specific step sizes to preserve non-negativity during iterations. For NMF variants, Cai *et al.* [10] proposed graph-regularized NMF (GNMF) by incorporating manifold learning into nonnegative matrix factorization. It preserves the geometric structure of data through a graph Laplacian regularizer, thereby enhancing clustering and representation performance on nonlinear manifolds. Li *et al.* [11] developed an orthogonal subspace-based NMF using multiplicative updates. By embedding orthogonality directly into the objective function, it eliminates explicit constraints to enhance efficiency. Ding *et al.* [12] presented Semi-NMF to generalize NMF for mixed-sign data. Experiments demonstrate its superiority over standard NMF in clustering task.

However, most NMF-based methods suffer from three limitations: reliance on specific step sizes in gradient descent, inability to handle mixed-sign data, and failure with zero-initialization. To address these limitations, this paper proposes a novel Exponential Non-negative Matrix Factorization (ExpNMF) model that imposes a column-sum-to-one constraint on the basis matrix. This enforcement eliminates scale ambiguity and provides direct coefficient interpretability as proportional weights in ExpNMF. The ExpNMF optimization problem is addressed through optimality conditions that utilize derivatives of the step-size function. A theoretically derived optimal range for the step size is established to ensure convergence of the algorithm. Rigorous proofs confirm a strict monotonic decrease in the objective function throughout the process. Experimental results show that the proposed ExpNMF method converges effectively on facial image datasets, achieves better recognition performance, exhibits enhanced robustness when handling mixed-sign data, outperforms traditional NMF variants, and maintains its effectiveness even when initialized with zero values.

The rest of this paper is organized as follows. Section 2 will briefly introduce some related NMF algorithms, providing a foundational understanding of the existing techniques in this field. Section 3 creates the ExpNMF model and theoretically derives the optimal range for the step size parameter to ensure the convergence of this model. Section 4 reports the experimental results of our algorithms. Finally, the conclusion is given in Sect. 5.

2   Related Work

This section will describe NMF [2] and Semi-NMF [12] algorithms briefly.

2.1   NMF

NMF seeks to decompose a given nonnegative matrix $V \in R_+^{d \times n}$ into two lower-rank nonnegative factor matrices $W \in R_+^{d \times r}$ and $H \in R_+^{r \times n}$, such that $V \approx WH$, where matrices W and H are called basis matrix and feature matrix, respectively. The optimization problem for NMF is $\min_{W, H \geq 0} \|V - WH\|_F^2$, where $\| \cdot \|_F$ is the Frobenius norm. Based on the gradient descent method, NMF specifically chooses the step sizes as $\rho_H = \frac{H}{W^T W H}$ and $\rho_W = \frac{W}{W H H^T}$, yielding the multiplicative update rules for W and H as follows:

$$H \leftarrow H \odot \frac{W^T V}{W^T W H}, \quad W \leftarrow W \odot \frac{V H^T}{W H H^T},$$

where $A \odot B$ and $\frac{A}{B}$ denote the Hadamard product and element-wise division between matrices A and B, respectively.

2.2 Semi-NMF

Semi-NMF is designed for mixed-sign data. Semi-NMF model is $\min_{H \geq 0} \|V - W H\|_F^2$, where the data matrix V and the basis matix W are mixed-sign matrices, while the feature matrix H is required to be nonnegative. The Semi-NMF algorithm is shown below:

$$H \leftarrow H \odot \sqrt{\frac{[(W^T V)^+] + [(W^T W)^-]H}{[(W^T V)^-] + [(W^T W)^+]H}}, \quad W \leftarrow V H^T (H H^T)^{-1},$$

where for a mixed-sign matex A, the operators A^+ and A^- are defined by $A^+ = (|A| + A)/2$ and $A^- = (|A| - A)/2$, respectively.

It can be seen that the update rule for NMF is derived by choosing specific step sizes in gradient descent. Altering these step sizes results in modified update rules; however, such modifications cannot guarantee the non-negativity and convergence of NMF algorithm. Furthermore, NMF is unable to handle mixed-sign data, and most variants inherit these limitations. While Semi-NMF accommodates mixed-sign data, both standard NMF-based methods and Semi-NMF are ineffective under zero-value initialization. To overcome these limitations, we propose a novel exponential NMF algorithm in the following section.

3 Exponential Non-negative Matrix Factorization Algorithm

In this section, we will establish the ExpNMF model and present the solution method for the ExpNMF model along with determining the optimal step size.

3.1 ExpNMF Model Establishing

For a matrix $A = (a_{ij}) \in R^{m \times n}$, we define its exponential type matrix e^A by $e^A = (e^{a_{ij}})_{m \times n}$. So, e^A is always a non-negative matrix for any matrix A.

The proposed exponential NMF (ExpNMF) model with unit column sum constraints is given by:

$$\min_{W,H} F(W, H) = \frac{1}{2} \|V - e^W e^H\|_F^2 + \frac{\alpha}{2} \|1_{1 \times m} e^W - 1_{1 \times r}\|_F^2, \tag{1}$$

where $V \in \mathbb{R}_+^{m \times n}$, $W \in \mathbb{R}^{m \times r}$, $H \in \mathbb{R}^{r \times n}$, with $1_{s \times t}$ denoting a $s \times t$ all-ones matrix, and $\alpha > 0$ a regularization parameter controlling constraint enforcement.

The optimization problem (1) is hard to solve directly. Hence, we turn to convert the original problem into the following two optimization sub-problems (2) and (3):

$$\min_{H} F_1(H), \quad \text{where } F_1(H) = F(W, H), \text{ with } W \text{ fixed.} \tag{2}$$

$$\min_{W} F_2(W), \quad \text{where } F_2(W) = F(W, H), \text{ with } H \text{ fixed.} \tag{3}$$

The optimization sub-problems (2) and (3) will be resolved using the gradient descent method, along with finding the optimal step size to ensure convergence. Details are given in the next subsection.

3.2   ExpNMF Model Solving

Let D_H and D_W be the negative gradient directions of $F_1(H)$ and $F_2(W)$, respectively. From (1), we obtain

$$D_H = -\frac{\partial F_1(H)}{\partial(H)} = e^H \odot [(e^{W^T} V) - (e^{W^T} e^W e^H)] \tag{4}$$

and

$$D_W = -\frac{\partial F_2(W)}{\partial(W)} = W \odot [V e^{H^T} - e^W e^H e^{H^T} - \alpha 1_{m \times m} e^W + \alpha 1_{m \times r}]. \tag{5}$$

Therefore, the update rules for W and H using the gradient descent method are as follows:

$$H \leftarrow H + \Lambda \odot D_H, \quad W \leftarrow W + \Phi \odot D_W, \tag{6}$$

where the step sizes $\Lambda = (\lambda_{ij})$ and $\Phi = (\eta_{ij})$ are matrices.

The update rules (6) constitute the ExpNMF algorithm. While these rules do not guarantee the nonnegativity of the matrices H and W, the resulting matrix factorization $V = \tilde{W} \tilde{H}$ is a nonnegative decomposition. This is because $\tilde{H} = e^H > 0$ and $\tilde{W} = e^W > 0$. In the following sections, we will focus on how to determine the iterative step size matrices Λ and Φ such that the ExpNMF algorithm converges.

3.3   Convergence Analysis for ExpNMF

In this section, we will discuss how to determine the optimal range of the step sizes, ensuring the ExpNMF algorithm is convergent.

Convergence Analysis on H. We analyze the scalar step size λ_{pq} in $H_{pq} \leftarrow H_{pq} + \lambda_{pq} D_{H_{pq}}$, such that the objective function $F_1(H_{pq})$ decreases strictly monotonically. To this end, we first need to prove Lemma 1.

Lemma 1. *Given* $G_1(\lambda_{pq}) = F_1(H_{pq} + \lambda_{pq} D_{H_{pq}})$, *where* F_1 *is defined in (2),* $D_{H_{pq}} \neq 0$ *and* $\lambda_{pq} \geq 0$, *then there exists an optimal interval* $[0, \lambda_{pq}^*)$ *on which* $G'(\lambda_{pq}) < 0$.

Proof. From (2) and (4), we derive that

$$G_1(\lambda_{pq}) = \frac{1}{2} \sum_i O_{pqi}^2 - \sum_i O_{pqi} e^{W_{ip}} e^{H_{pq} + \lambda_{pq} D_{H_{pq}}} + \frac{1}{2} \sum_i e^{2W_{ip}} e^{2(H_{pq} + \lambda_{pq} D_{H_{pq}})},$$

where $O_{pqi} = V_{iq} - \sum_{s \neq p} e^{W_{is}} e^{H_{sq}}$. Differentiating $G_1(\lambda_{pq})$ with respect to λ_{pq} yields that

$$G_1{}'(\lambda_{pq}) = D_{H_{pq}} \cdot e^{H_{pq}} \cdot e^{\lambda_{pq} D_{H_{pq}}} \left(\sum_i e^{2W_{ip}} \cdot e^{H_{pq}} \cdot e^{\lambda_{pq} D_{H_{pq}}} - \sum_i O_{pqi} \cdot e^{W_{ip}} \right). \quad (7)$$

If we replace $e^{\lambda_{pq} D_{H_{pq}}}$ with $\Delta_{H_{pq}}$ in Eq. (7), the derivative function $G_1{}'(\lambda_{pq})$ can be expressed as the following quadratic function $\tilde{G}_1$ in the variable $\Delta_{H_{pq}}$:

$$\tilde{G}_1(\Delta_{H_{pq}}) = G_1{}'(\lambda_{pq}) = \kappa_1 \Delta_{H_{pq}}^2 - \kappa_2 \Delta_{H_{pq}}, \quad (8)$$

where $\kappa_1 = D_{H_{pq}} e^{2H_{pq}} \sum_i e^{2W_{ip}}$ and $\kappa_2 = D_{H_{pq}} e^{H_{pq}} \sum_i O_{pqi} \cdot e^{W_{ip}}$. Obviously, the equation $\tilde{G}_1(\Delta_{H_{pq}}) = 0$ has two real roots given below:

$$\Delta_{H_{pq}} = \begin{cases} 0 \\ \Delta_{H_{pq}}^* = \dfrac{\kappa_2}{\kappa_1} = \dfrac{\sum_i O_{pqi} \cdot e^{W_{ip}}}{\sum_i e^{2W_{ip}} \cdot e^{H_{pq}}} \end{cases}.$$

Next, we will determine the range of $\Delta_{H_{pq}}$ satisfying $\tilde{G}_1(\Delta_{H_{pq}}) < 0$, and then derive the corresponding interval for λ_{pq} such that $G_1'(\lambda_{pq}) < 0$ holds, using the substitution $\Delta_{H_{pq}} = e^{\lambda_{pq} D_{H_{pq}}}$.

First, when $\lambda_{pq} = 0$, we have $\Delta_{H_{pq}} = 1$. From (7), we have

$$\tilde{G}_1(1) = G_1{}'(0) = D_{H_{pq}} \cdot \left[e^{H_{pq}} \cdot \left(\sum_k e^{W_{kq}} V_{kq} - \sum_s \sum_i e^{W_{ip}} e^{W_{is}} e^{H_{sq}} \right) \right]$$

$$= D_{H_{pq}} \cdot (-D_{H_{pq}}) = -(D_{H_{pq}})^2 < 0. \quad (9)$$

1) When $D_{H_{pq}} > 0$: From (4), we obtain $\Delta_{H_{pq}}^* = \dfrac{\sum_i O_{pqi} \cdot e^{W_{ip}}}{\sum_i e^{2W_{ip}} \cdot e^{H_{pq}}} > 1$. Since $\kappa_1 > 0$ and $\tilde{G}_1(1) < 0$, the quadratic function $\tilde{G}_1(\Delta_{H_{pq}})$ (with $\Delta_{H_{pq}} = e^{\lambda_{pq} D_{H_{pq}}} > 0$) is illustrated in Fig. 1(a). The function $\Delta_{H_{pq}}(\lambda_{pq}) \geq 1$ for $\lambda_{pq} \geq 0$ is shown in Fig. 1(b). From these figures, $\tilde{G}_1(\Delta_{H_{pq}}) < 0$ holds for $\Delta_{H_{pq}} \in [1, \Delta_{H_{pq}}^*)$, while $\tilde{G}_1(\Delta_{H_{pq}}^*) = 0$. Equivalently, $G_1{}'(\lambda_{pq}) < 0$ for $\lambda_{pq} \in [0, \lambda_{pq}^*)$ with $G_1{}'(\lambda_{pq}^*) = 0$, where $\lambda_{pq}^* = \dfrac{\ln \Delta_{H_{pq}}^*}{D_{H_{pq}}} > 0$.

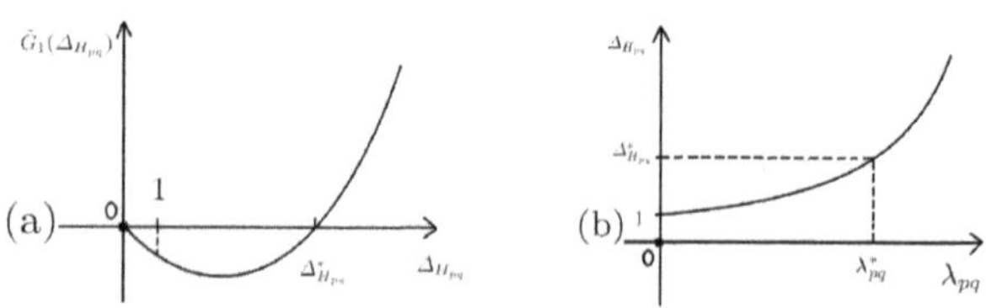

Fig. 1. (a) The curve of $\tilde{G}_1(\Delta_{H_{pq}})$; (b) The curve of $\Delta_{H_{pq}}$ against λ_{pq}.

2) When $D_{H_{pq}} < 0$: $\kappa_1 < 0$ and from (4), we derive $\Delta^*_{H_{pq}} = \frac{\sum_i O_{pqi} \cdot e^{W_{ip}}}{\sum_i e^{2W_{ip}} \cdot e^{H_{pq}}} < 1$.

(i) $D_{H_{pq}} < 0$ and $\Delta^*_{H_{pq}} \leq 0$: The relationship between $\tilde{G}_1(\Delta_{H_{pq}})$ and $\Delta_{H_{pq}} (= e^{\lambda_{pq} D_{H_{pq}}} > 0)$ is illustrated in Fig. 2(a). The function $\Delta_{H_{pq}}(\lambda_{pq}) = e^{\lambda_{pq} D_{H_{pq}}}$ is strictly decreasing with respect to λ_{pq}, as shown in Fig. 2(b). It can be seen form these figures that $\tilde{G}_1(\Delta_{H_{pq}}) < 0$ as $\Delta_{H_{pq}} \in (0, 1]$. This implies that $G'_1(\lambda_{pq}) < 0$ when $\lambda_{pq} \in [0, \infty)$.

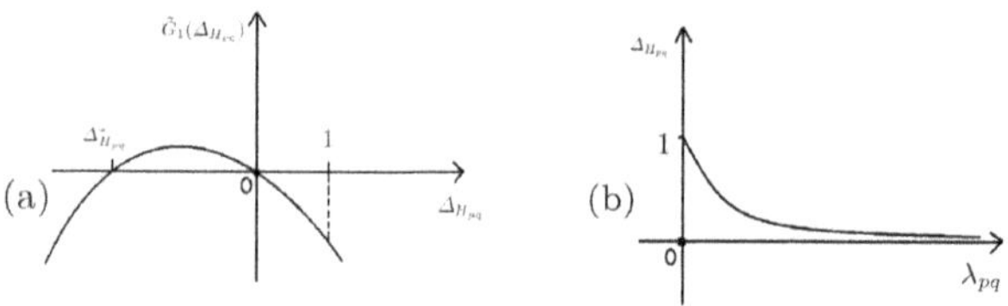

Fig. 2. (a) The curve of $\tilde{G}_1(\Delta_{H_{pq}})$; (b) The curve of $\Delta_{H_{pq}}$ against λ_{pq}.

(ii) $D_{H_{pq}} < 0$ and $0 < \Delta^*_{H_{pq}} < 1$: The function $\tilde{G}_1(\Delta_{H_{pq}})$ for $\Delta_{H_{pq}}$ is plotted in 3(a). We conclude $\tilde{G}_1(\Delta_{H_{pq}}) < 0$ as $\Delta_{H_{pq}} \in (\Delta^*_{H_{pq}}, 1]$ with $\tilde{G}(\Delta^*_{H_{pq}}) = 0$. Therefore, from Fig. 3(b) it yildes that $G_1'(\lambda_{pq}) < 0$ as $\lambda_{pq} \in [0, \lambda^*_{pq})$ with $G_1'(\lambda^*_{pq}) = 0$, where $\lambda^*_{pq} = \frac{\ln \Delta^*_{pq}}{D_{H_{pq}}} > 0$.

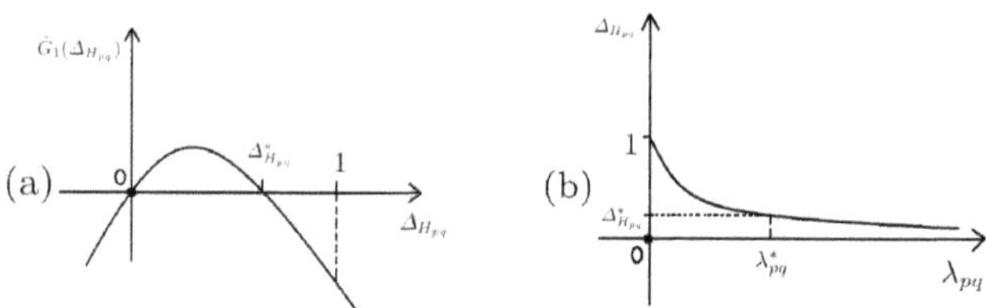

Fig. 3. (a) The curve of $\tilde{G}_1(\Delta_{H_{pq}})$; (b) The curve of $\Delta_{H_{pq}}$ against λ_{pq}.

In summary, if we set

$$\lambda^*_{pq} = \left| \frac{\ln |\Delta^*_{H_{pq}}|}{D_{H_{pq}}} \right|, \tag{10}$$

where $\Delta^*_{pq} = \frac{\sum_i O_{pqi} \cdot e^{W_{ip}}}{\sum_i e^{2W_{ip}} \cdot e^{H_{pq}}}$, then $G'(\lambda_{pq}) < 0$ as $\lambda_{pq} \in [0, \lambda^*_{pq})$.

Theorem 1. *If the conditions in lemma 1 are satisfied, then the objective function $F_1(H)$ defined by (2) will strictly monotonically decrease under the gradient descent update rule of H when the step size λ_{pq} is chosen within the interval $(0, \lambda^*_{pq}]$, where λ^*_{pq} is the optimal step size given by (10).*

Proof. Lemma 1 shows that $G(\lambda_{pq})$ is strictly monotonically decreasing in the interval $[0, \lambda^*_{pq}]$. Hence, it exhibits that

$$G_1(\lambda^*_{pq}) = F_1(H_{pq} + \lambda^*_{pq} D_{H_{pq}}) < G_1(\lambda_{pq}) < G_1(0) = F_1(H_{pq}), \forall \lambda_{pq} \in (0, \lambda^*_{pq}).$$

Therefore, we conclude that if the step size λ_{pq} is chosen within the interval $(0, \lambda^*_{pq}]$, then the objective function $F_1(H)$ strictly monotonically decrease. Here, the largest admissible step size λ^*_{pq} ensuring this property.

Based on Lemma 1, we have the following update rule for H:

$$H \leftarrow H + t \cdot \Lambda^* \odot D_H = H + t \cdot sign[D_H] \odot |\ln|\Delta^*_H||, \ t \in (0, 1], \qquad (11)$$

where

$$\Delta^*_H = \frac{e^{W^T} \cdot (V - e^W e^H) + (e^{W^T} e^W \odot I_r) \cdot e^H}{e^{2W^T} \cdot 1_{m \times n} \odot e^H}.$$

Theorem 1 guarantees that (11) is convergent.

Convergence Analysis on W. For the matrix W, Lemma 2 and Theorem 2 hold analogously to those for H. The proofs are omitted here.

Lemma 2. *Given $G_2(\eta_{pq}) = F_2(W_{pq} + \eta_{pq} D_{W_{pq}})$, where F_2 is given by (3), $D_{W_{pq}} \neq 0$ and $\eta_{pq} \geq 0$, then there exists an optimal interval $[0, \eta^*_{pq})$ such that $G'_2(\eta_{pq}) < 0$ holds for all $\eta_{pq} \in [0, \eta^*_{pq})$, where*

$$\eta^*_{pq} = \left| \frac{\ln|\Delta^*_{W_{pq}}|}{D_{W_{pq}}} \right| \quad \text{and} \quad \Delta^*_{W_{pq}} = \frac{\sum_j (V_{pj} - \sum_{k \neq q} e^{W_{pk}} e^{H_{kj}}) \cdot e^{H_{qj}} - \alpha U_{pq}}{[(\sum_j e^{2H_{qj}}) + \alpha] \cdot e^{W_{pq}}}.$$

Theorem 2. *If the conditions in Lemma 2 are satisfied, then the objective function $F_2(W)$ defined by (3) strictly monotonically decrease under the gradient descent update rule of W when the step size η_{pq} is chosen within the interval $(0, \eta^*_{pq}]$, where η^*_{pq} is the optimal step size.*

The following update rule for W can be obtained from Lemma 2. Theorem 2 guarantees it convergence.

$$W \leftarrow W + t \cdot sign[D_W] \odot |\ln|\Delta^*_W||, \quad t \in (0, 1). \qquad (12)$$

where

$$\Delta^*_W = \frac{(V - e^W e^H) e^{H^T} + e^W (e^H e^{H^T} \odot I_r) - \alpha[(1_{m \times m} - I_m) e^W - 1_{m \times r}]}{(1_{m \times n} \cdot e^{2H^T} + \alpha 1_{m \times r}) \odot e^W}.$$

The update rules (11) and (12) constitute the proposed ExpNMF algorithm.

4 Experimental Results

In this section, we would like to assess the performance of the proposed Exp-NMF algorithm. The NMF-based algorithms, such as NMF [2], NMFOS [11], GNMF [10], SemiNMF [12], are selected for comparison. We employ the optimal step size matrices $\Lambda^* = (\lambda_{ij}^*)$ and $\Phi^* = (\eta_{ij}^*)$ for the proposed ExpNMF algorithm. Two publicly available face databases, ORL and Yale databases, are chosen for evaluation. In the experiments, all compared algorithms utilize 150 features and run for a maximum of 300 iterations. In our proposed ExpNMF algorithm, the hyperparameter α is set to 10 for the ORL database and 0.01 for the Yale database. In NMFOS, the weight for orthogonality constraint is set to 80. For GNMF, the k-nearest-neighbor graph is constructed with $k = 3$, a Gaussian kernel bandwidth $\sigma = 5$, and a graph-regularization weight of 10^{-3}. For each dataset, we randomly select TN images per individual to construct the training set and use the remaining images as the testing set. To reduce statistical variability, every experiment is run ten times for all compared methods under the identical conditions. The average accuracies are used for comparision. The best results highlighted in bold.

Experiments on Non-negative Data. The mean accuracies for the ORL and Yale databases are recorded in Tables 1 and 2, respectively.

It can be seen from Table 1 that the average accuracies of ExpNMF, NMF, NMFOS, GNMF, and SemiNMF algorithms rise from 80.00%, 79.09%, 79.09%, 79.03%, and 72.94% (when $TN = 2$) to 96.13%, 94.63%, 94.88%, 95.13%, and 80.00% (when $TN = 8$), respectively. We also observe that the proposed Exp-NMF algorithm achieves the best performance across all training numbers. The NMF, GNMF and NMFOS algorithms yield comparable results. In contrast, SemiNMF consistently shows the lowest accuracy, indicating limited ability to capture discriminative features from the non-negative data. These findings demonstrate that ExpNMF significantly improve learning effectiveness over traditional matrix factorization methods.

Table 1. Mean accuracy (%) on the ORL database under different training numbers

TN	2	3	4	5	6	7	8
ExpNMF	**80.00**	**83.96**	**88.79**	**92.10**	**93.94**	**95.00**	**96.13**
NMF	79.09	83.00	87.83	91.10	91.75	92.83	94.63
NMFOS	79.09	82.32	87.13	90.75	92.44	93.08	94.88
GNMF	79.03	82.82	88.08	91.05	92.00	92.67	95.13
SemiNMF	72.94	72.43	72.63	75.20	77.69	78.33	80.00

The results from Table 2 indicate that the average accuracies of Exp-NMF, NMF, NMFOS, GNMF, and SemiNMF algorithms increase from 94.22%,

Table 2. Mean accuracy (%) on the Yale database under different training numbers

TN	5	6	7	8	9	10
ExpNMF	**94.22**	**96.00**	**97.17**	**96.22**	**98.33**	**98.00**
NMF	89.11	89.33	92.67	92.44	95.00	94.00
NMFOS	91.22	92.53	94.50	92.89	97.00	96.67
GNMF	89.11	89.07	93.17	92.00	95.00	94.00
SemiNMF	81.78	79.60	77.83	71.11	70.33	64.67

89.11%, 91.22%, 89.11%, and 81.78% (when $TN = 5$) to 98.00%, 94.00%, 96.67%, 94.00%, and 64.67% (when $TN = 10$), respectively. It is evident that Exp-NMF consistently achieves the highest accuracy across all training sample sizes, demonstrating its superior performance on the Yale database. NMFOS achieves the second-highest accuracy. NMF and GNMF demonstrate comparable performance. Semi-NMF, however, exhibits a notable decline in performance as TN increases, indicating its limited robustness and generalization ability in handling non-negative image data. These results further validate the effectiveness of Exp-NMF in extracting discriminative features and enhancing classification accuracy.

Experiments on Mixed-Sign Data. To validate the robustness of ExpNMF with mixed-sign data, we preprocess the ORL database using zero-mean normalization and compare recognition rates against SemiNMF as the baseline. NMF, NMFOS, and GNMF are excluded as they cannot process mixed-sign inputs. Critically, our method preserves non-negativity through exponential mapping ($V \rightarrow e^V$). As shown in Table 3, ExpNMF consistently outperforms SemiNMF while maintaining competitive accuracy under mixed-sign conditions.

Table 3. Mean accuracy (%) on the ORL database under different training numbers

TN	2	3	4	5	6	7	8
ExpNMF	**71.47**	**78.50**	**83.92**	**87.00**	**88.25**	**89.08**	**90.88**
SemiNMF	71.03	74.43	74.08	76.35	76.19	78.25	81.75

Experiments on Convergence. While the theoretical convergence of the Exp-NMF algorithm has been established, we now empirically validate it through experiments under three crucial conditions: non-negative data, mixed-sign data, and zero-value initialization. Figure 4 plots the relative reconstruction error versus iteration number for these cases. It is evident that our ExpNMF algorithm converges consistently across all scenarios. However, NMF, NMFOS, and GNMF fail to converge with mixed-sign data. Additionally, these three methods, along with SemiNMF, will get stuck with $W = 0$ and $H = 0$ when initialized with zero values.

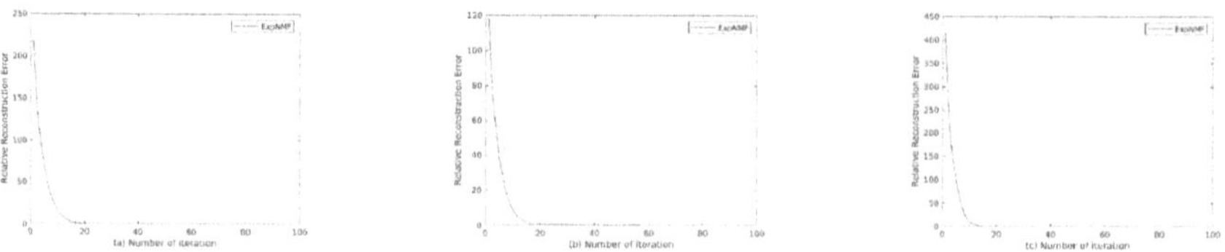

Fig. 4. The convergence curves of ExpNMF algorithm: (a) using nonnegative data; (b) using mixed-sign data; (c) Zero-Initialization.

5   Conclusion

This paper presents a framework called Exponential NMF (ExpNMF), designed to extract robust non-negative features for representing image data. The main contribution of ExpNMF lies in its convergence-guaranteed gradient descent algorithm, which is supported by mathematical foundations that establish an optimal admissible step size range for stable optimization. Notably, ExpNMF surpasses traditional NMF by automatically enabling gradient-based step adaptation, effectively processing mixed-sign data, and allowing for reliable initialization from zero values. Empirical results indicate that the convergence behavior of ExpNMF consistently matches theoretical predictions. The features extracted using this method demonstrate superior classification performance for both nonnegative and mixed-sign inputs. Overall, the results are promising.

Acknowledgment. This work is supported by National Natural Science Foundation of China (62573298) and Guangdong Provincial Key Laboratory with (Grant 2023B1212060076). We would like to thank the Olivetti Research Laboratory, and Yale University for the contributions of the ORL and Yale face databases, respectively.

References

1. Lee, D.D., Seung, H.S.: Learning the parts of objects by nonnegative matrix factorization. Nature **401**, 788–791 (1999)
2. Lee, D.D., Seung, H.S.: Algorithms for nonnegative matrix factorization. In: Advances in Neural Information Processing Systems (NIPS), pp. 535–541 (2000)
3. Li, X., Zhang, X., Yuan, Y., Dong, Y.: Adaptive relationship preserving sparse NMF for hyperspectral unmixing. IEEE Trans. Geosci. Remote Sens. **60**, 1–16 (2022)
4. Leplat, V., Gillis, N., Févotte, C.: Multi-resolution beta-divergence NMF for blind spectral unmixing. Signal Process. **193**, 108428 (2022)

5. Ye, M.C., Qian, Y.T., Zhou, J.: Multitask sparse nonnegative matrix factorization for joint spectral-spatial hyperspectral imagery denoising. IEEE Trans. Geosci. Remote Sens. **53**, 2621–2639 (2015)
6. Hu, L.Y., Guo, G.D., Ma, C.F.: Image processing using Newton-based algorithm of nonnegative matrix factorization. Appl. Math. Comput. **29**, 956–964 (2015)
7. Lu, Y., Yuan, C., Zhu, W., Li, X.: Structurally incoherent low-rank nonnegative matrix factorization for image classification. IEEE Trans. Image Process. **27**(11), 5248–5260 (2018)
8. Lu, G., Leng, C., Li, B., Jiao, L., Basu, A.: Robust dual-graph discriminative nonnegative matrix factorization for data classification. Knowl.-Based Syst. **268**, 110465 (2023)
9. Li, H., Zhou, Y., Zhao, P., Yu, C.: Class-driven nonnegative matrix factorization with manifold regularization for data clustering. Neurocomputing **548**, 127751 (2024)
10. Cai, D., He, X., Han, J., Huang, T.S.: Graph regularized nonnegative matrix factorization for data representation. IEEE Trans. Pattern Anal. Mach. Intell. **33**, 1548–1560 (2011)
11. Li, Z., Wu, X., Peng, H.: Nonnegative matrix factorization on orthogonal subspace. Pattern Recognit. Lett. **31**, 905–911 (2010)
12. Ding, C., Li, T., Jordan, M.: Convex and semi-nonnegative matrix factorizations. IEEE Trans. Pattern Anal. Mach. Intell. **32**(1), 45–55 (2010)

Orthogonal-Bidirectional Pose Anchoring Model for Micro-expression Recognition

Zunxiao Xu, Yunpeng Yao, Xinyue Wang, Xiaotong Li, and Xianye Ben[✉]

School of Information Science and Engineering, Shandong University,
Jinan 250100, China
benxianye@126.com

Abstract. Micro-expressions, fleeting and involuntary facial movements, are crucial for revealing concealed emotions but pose significant recognition challenges due to their subtlety and brief duration. Traditional methods, including handcrafted features and deep learning, often struggle with residual pose misalignments from imperfect facial alignment during preprocessing. This paper proposes a Facial Pose-Constrained Micro-Expression Recognition (MER) framework featuring a lightweight Orthogonal Bidirectional Long Short-Term Memory (O-BiLSTM) module. The module extracts fixed pose features from reference frames along orthogonal directions, providing spatial constraints to mitigate misalignment effects in the primary 3D ResNet network. Experiments on CASME II, SAMM, and SMIC datasets demonstrate state-of-the-art performance, with accuracies of 80.9%, 73.7%, and 70.1%, respectively. Ablation studies confirm the module's efficacy in enhancing recognition by modeling global facial geometry. The method outperforms existing techniques, offering a robust solution for MER in applications like security and clinical diagnosis.

Keywords: Micro-expression recognition · Pose constraint ·
O-BiLSTM · Deep learning · Facial alignment

1 Introduction

Deception is a pervasive aspect of human communication. Two independent studies on everyday lying revealed that young adults lie on average twice per day, while middle-aged adults average one lie per day [1]. Despite such prevalence, humans are generally poor at detecting deception, often performing no better than chance [2].

Micro-expressions, first identified by Paul Ekman in the 1960s [1], are subtle, involuntary facial expressions that typically last less than half a second. Although fleeting, they can reveal genuine emotional states that individuals attempt to conceal [3]. Accurate recognition of micro-expressions is therefore of great value in domains such as security interrogation, clinical diagnosis, business negotiation, and daily social interaction.

W. Jia et al. (Eds.): CCBR 2025, LNCS 16360, pp. 596–605, 2026.
https://doi.org/10.1007/978-981-95-6123-0_55

However, micro-expression recognition is inherently challenging. These expressions are extremely brief and subtle in appearance, making them difficult to detect even for trained experts. In controlled experiments, professionally trained human observers achieved only 47% recognition accuracy [4], underscoring the difficulty of manual detection.

Advances in computer vision have enabled the development of automatic micro-expression recognition (MER) algorithms. Early approaches relied on handcrafted features [5–7], designed based on prior knowledge of micro-expression patterns. While capable of capturing certain variations such as facial texture or illumination changes [8], these methods struggled to fully represent the spatiotemporal dynamics of micro-expressions, often leading to incomplete features and limited performance.

The success of deep learning in visual feature extraction has motivated the adoption of deep neural networks for MER [9–11]. These methods significantly improve feature learning, yet MER remains difficult due to the transient nature of micro-expressions and the scarcity of available data. In laboratory settings, eliciting micro-expressions often requires carefully designed scenarios, which may introduce irrelevant variations such as background noise and head movement. Although facial landmark detection and alignment can mitigate some of these effects, intrinsic differences among subjects (e.g., gender, ethnicity, facial morphology) hinder perfect normalization, leaving residual pose misalignments that degrade recognition accuracy.

To address this issue, we propose a lightweight Orthogonal Bidirectional Long Short-Term Memory (O-BiLSTM) network as a Facial Pose Constraint (FPC) module. The FPC module extracts pose information along orthogonal directions from calibrated reference frames, constraining the training of the primary MER network and reducing the impact of residual pose variation. Specifically, our contributions are as follows:

- A standard-framebased constraint is designed to align pose information of features during training.
- An O-BiLSTM model is introduced to effectively model low-resolution micro-expression pose information, enabling the extraction of comprehensive global facial features.

2   Preliminary

The Bidirectional Long Short-Term Memory (Bi-LSTM) network is an extension of the traditional Long Short-Term Memory (LSTM) architecture, designed to process sequential data by incorporating both past and future contextual information. Unlike a conventional unidirectional LSTM, which processes a sequence only from beginning to end, a Bi-LSTM comprises two independent LSTM layers: one operating in the forward direction and the other in the backward direction. The outputs from both directions are then combined, effectively eliminating sequence order bias and yielding a more comprehensive representation of sequential features.

When static images are serialized into sequences (e.g., by scanning pixel rows or columns), the bidirectional modeling capability of Bi-LSTM becomes particularly advantageous. Facial attributes such as the eyes, nose, and mouth are characterized not only by their individual shapes and sizes but also by their spatial relationships with surrounding regions. Through bidirectional processing, Bi-LSTM can simultaneously capture each facial component and its contextual dependencies, enabling the extraction of subtle expression variations that might otherwise be overlooked. Moreover, its modeling capacity extends beyond localized keypoint analysis to encompass broader facial areas, such as the forehead and chin, thereby supporting a holistic facial representation.

By capturing global dependencies in both temporal directions, Bi-LSTM serves as a powerful module for high-precision face analysis and emotion recognition. In practical applications, it can be seamlessly integrated with other deep learning components to jointly model inter-feature relationships via Bi-LSTM and intra-feature dependencies via FC layers. This integration enhances both the accuracy and the robustness of the overall recognition or classification framework.

3   Facial Pose-Constrained Micro-expression Recognition Model

The proposed micro-expression recognition framework is designed to extract discriminative spatiotemporal features from preprocessed micro-expression video sequences for accurate classification. The standard preprocessing pipeline consists of three main stages: *video frame extraction*, *face detection and alignment*, and optional *data augmentation*. In the face detection and alignment stage, the detected facial region is cropped and aligned according to predefined facial landmarks, ensuring that the primary facial components occupy consistent spatial positions across all frames. However, due to inter-subject variations in facial appearance and motion patterns, such as differences in interpupillary distance, nose size, head pose, and natural movement, perfect alignment is inherently difficult to achieve. As shown in Fig. 1, examples from CASME II, SAMM, and SMIC demonstrate that even minor inaccuracies in cropping and alignment can introduce spatial misalignments. These subtle shifts result in the same facial region being mapped to different pixel coordinates, thereby reducing the network's ability to precisely localize and analyze the subtle motion patterns characteristic of micro-expressions. Moreover, such alignment errors can propagate and accumulate during subsequent processing stages, ultimately diminishing recognition performance.

To mitigate these effects, we introduce a Facial Pose Constraint (FPC) module based on an Orthogonal Bidirectional Long Short-Term Memory (O-BiLSTM) network. Acting as an auxiliary sub-branch of the main recognition network, this module learns fixed facial pose embeddings from reference frames

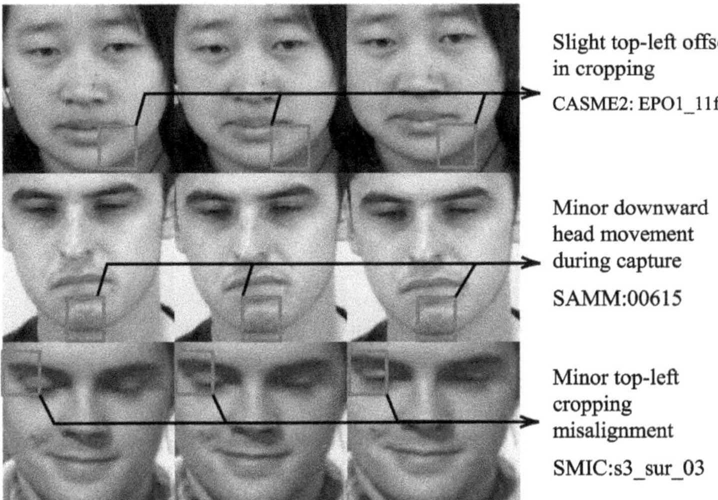

Fig. 1. Subtle offsets introduced during preprocessing of micro-expression videos.

and constrains the training of the primary network, thereby reducing the impact of residual pose variation and improving recognition accuracy.

3.1   Anchor Sample Frame Selection and Preprocessing

The construction of anchor sample frames for pose constraint learning consists of three key steps:

1) Reference Frame Selection. The first frame I_0 of each video sample is selected as the reference facial pose frame. Using the initial frame as the standard helps minimize cumulative positional misalignment introduced by head motion or imperfect face alignment in subsequent frames.
2) Scaling to Thumbnail Size. The selected reference frame is resized to match the spatial resolution of the final feature map in the primary recognition network, producing a low-resolution thumbnail. Since the aim is to capture pose geometry rather than fine-grained texture or identity-specific details, high-resolution input is unnecessary. This step also reduces the number of trainable parameters and the overall computational cost.
3) Orthogonal Direction Serialization. The low-resolution thumbnail is serialized along the horizontal and vertical directions to form a horizontal pose calibration sequence S_H and a vertical pose calibration sequence S_W. These sequences, collectively referred to as anchor sample frames, encode fixed facial pose information to be used by the O-BiLSTM.

The processed anchor sample frames $\{S_W, S_H\}$ are subsequently fed into the O-BiLSTM model to extract facial pose constraint features.

3.2 Orthogonal-Bidirectional Long Short-Term Memory Model

The O-BiLSTM model processes the anchor sample frames to extract fixed-pose features that can be used to correct pixel displacements introduced during pre-processing. Specifically, the vertical sequence S_W and the horizontal sequence S_H are separately processed by two BiLSTM networks operating along orthogonal directions. Each BiLSTM models sequential dependencies between pixels, effectively capturing spatial relationships of facial components in its respective orientation.

A cross-direction computation strategy is employed to enhance sensitivity to spatial interactions between orthogonal dimensions. The outputs from the two BiLSTMs are concatenated along the channel dimension and then passed through a Multi-Layer Perceptron (MLP) for channel mixing, yielding the final facial pose constraint feature F_{pc}.

Because S_W and S_H are relatively short sequences after downsampling, the LSTM units can efficiently learn both long- and short-range dependencies. Compared with CNN-based approaches, this method captures global spatial relationships across the entire face rather than focusing solely on local regions. Compared with Transformer-based methods, the LSTM is computationally lighter, easier to train, and well-suited to the compact input sequences in this task.

The computation process is given by:

$$Y_{:H,:}^{hor} = BiLSTM_H(F_H) \tag{1}$$

$$Y_{W,:}^{ver} = BiLSTM_W(F_W) \tag{2}$$

$$Y_{pc} = FC\left(\text{concatenate}\left(Y_{W,:}^{ver}, Y_{:H,:}^{hor}, \dim = c\right)\right) \tag{3}$$

where F_H and F_W are the serialized horizontal and vertical feature sequences obtained from the anchor frames, $BiLSTM_H(\cdot)$ and $BiLSTM_W(\cdot)$ denote the BiLSTM operations along horizontal and vertical directions, and $FC(\cdot)$ denotes the MLP transformation.

3.3 Spatial Constraint Features for Assisting Micro-Expression Recognition

The facial pose constraint feature F_{pc} generated by the O-BiLSTM is fused with the micro-expression feature F_{me} extracted by the primary classification network (Fig. 2).

The model input consists of the preprocessed micro-expression video sequence and the initial frame I_0:

$$V_{sub}^e = [F(1), F(2), \ldots, F(T)]_{sub}^e \in \mathbb{R}^{T \times W \times H \times C} \tag{4}$$

$$F_{onset} = F(1) \in \mathbb{R}^{W \times H \times C} \tag{5}$$

where T is the number of frames, W and H are the frame width and height after preprocessing, and C is the number of channels.

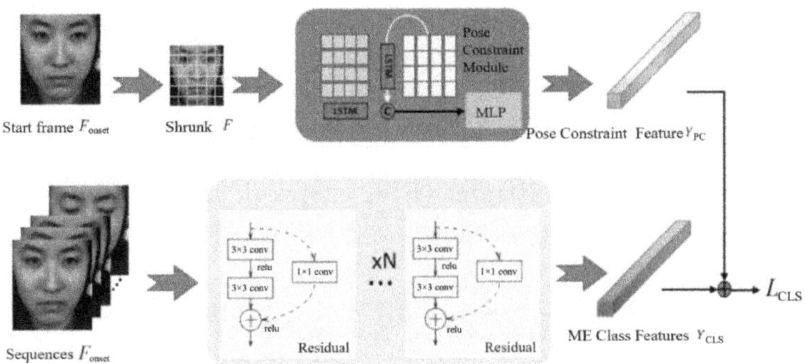

Fig. 2. Facial pose constraint feature F_{pc} assisting the main micro-expression recognition network in mitigating the effects of residual pose misalignment.

Within the FPC module, F_{onset} is orthogonally serialized into S_W and S_H and processed by the two orthogonal BiLSTM networks. After channel fusion via the MLP, the final pose constraint feature Fpc is obtained. In parallel, the primary classification network, implemented as a 3D ResNet, processes the sequence $V^e{sub}$ to extract micro-expression features F_{me}. The two feature sets are combined by element-wise summation:

$$Y_{cls} = Resblock\left(V_{sub}^e\right)_{\times N} \tag{6}$$

The entire network is trained using the cross-entropy loss:

$$L_{cls} = -\frac{1}{N}\sum_{n=1}^{N}\sum_{c=1}^{C} y_{gt} \log\left(Y_{cls} + Y_{pc}\right) \tag{7}$$

where N is the number of samples, y_{gt} is the one-hot encoded ground truth, and C is the number of expression classes.

Through this, the FPC module provides fixed-pose priors derived from reference frames to guide the recognition network, effectively reducing the impact of residual misalignments and enhancing micro-expression recognition accuracy.

4   Experimental Results and Analysis

This section reports experiments conducted on three widely used micro-expression datasets: CASME II, SAMM, and SMIC. All experiments follow the three-class classification setting to ensure consistency across performance evaluation, ablation analysis, and interpretability studies.

4.1   Experimental Environment and Parameter Settings

Experiments were conducted on Ubuntu using PyTorch. Model generalization was evaluated via Leave-One-Subject-Out (LOSO) cross-validation.

Models were trained for 100 epochs using the Adam optimizer, with the best checkpoint selected based on validation performance. Batch size was 34, dropout rate 0.1, and learning rate 1×10^{-4}. Data preprocessing included two pipelines, Data-Transforms and Data-Transforms-Norm, with random horizontal flipping (50%), rotation ($\pm 4°$), and cropping to $H \times W$. The architecture comprises two modules: the Facial Pose Constraint (FPC) network and the primary classification network.

Table 1. Performance Comparison of MER on CASME II, SAMM, and SMIC.

Method	Dataset								
	CASME II			SAMM			SMIC		
	Acc.	UF1	UAR	Acc.	UF1	UAR	Acc.	UF1	UAR
LBP-TOP [12]	40.9	36.9	/	41.5	40.6	/	45.7	46.1	/
LBP-SIP [5]	42.1	42.2	/	41.7	40.2	/	42.1	42.2	/
FDM [13]	41.7	29.7	/	/	/	/	60.4	54.0	/
MODO [14]	51.0	41.8	/	/	/	/	61.5	40.6	/
Sparse MODO [15]	48.9	41.7	46.6	44.2	24.6	32.3	46.1	42.7	46.8
ESCSTF [16]	51.1	50.4	53.4	46.9	49.1	52.1	50.5	49.8	50.1
ELRCN [17]	55.6	53.4	51.9	56.1	48.1	54.4	46.7	42.3	39.5
RCN-X [18]	58.8	47.2	53.0	51.9	41.4	46.4	45.2	33.7	41.5
G-TCN [19]	50.8	45.0	44.8	51.7	45.0	44.8	43.6	40.1	40.6
AU-GACN [20]	71.2	35.6	57.5	70.2	43.3	60.7	72.3	55.4	56.7
TSCNN [21]	79.2	77.7	78.1	73.4	70.3	72.6	**70.4**	69.3	**72.0**
3D ResNet [22]	73.7	60.0	69.2	70.5	62.5	60.9	64.4	63.9	70.0
*Triple-ATFME [23]	/	81.6	81.0	/	66.8	65.0	/	63.9	63.1
*PASTFNet [24]	/	**83.2**	**82.7**	/	68.5	67.2	/	65.9	65.3
Proposed Method	**80.9**	77.5	81.1	**73.7**	**71.4**	**72.9**	70.1	**69.9**	71.8

* Methods marked with * report results from [25]

4.2 Performance Evaluation Experiments

The effectiveness of the proposed method was assessed against several representative micro-expression recognition algorithms, as summarized in Table 1.

From Table 1, the proposed method consistently outperformed classical MER algorithms across CASME II, SAMM, and SMIC. Specifically, it achieved accuracies (Acc.) of 80.9%, 73.7%, and 70.1%, unweighted F1-scores (UF1) of 77.5%, 71.4%, and 69.9%, and unweighted average recalls (UAR) of 81.1%, 72.9%, and 71.8%, respectively. The confusion matrices of the proposed method on these three datasets are shown in Fig. 3.

For 3D ResNet, the FPC module provided an average Acc. gain of 5.3% across the three datasets, reflecting the compatibility between pose-calibrated inputs and raw-frame sequences.

Traditional handcrafted feature-based methods (e.g., LBP-TOP, LBP-SIP, FDM) exhibited lower performance, as they are less sensitive to subtle, localized muscle movements. Overall, the FPC module enhances various MER architectures by providing explicit spatial pose priors, mitigating residual misalignments, and promoting more discriminative deep feature learning from raw micro-expression sequences.

4.3   Ablation Study

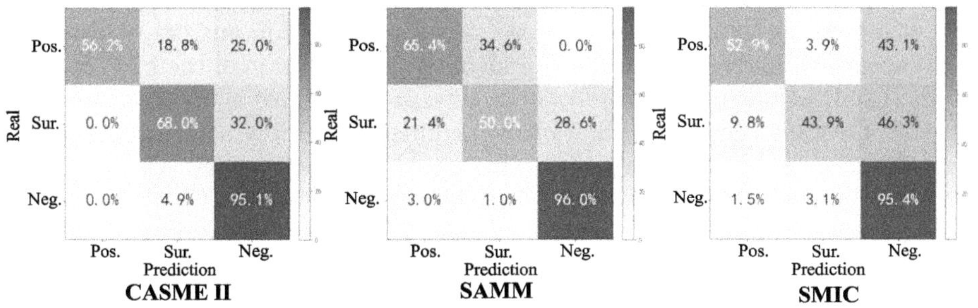

Fig. 3. Confusion matrices showing the classification performance across three benchmark micro-expression datasets: CASME II, SAMM, and SMIC.

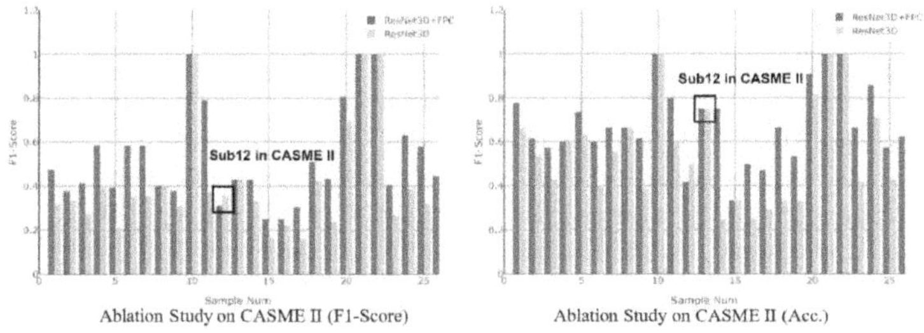

Fig. 4. Ablation results of the FPC module on individual subjects across CASME II, SAMM, and SMIC datasets. Results are reported as F_1-score and accuracy (Acc.) under the LOSO cross-validation protocol.

To quantify the FPC module's contribution, ablation experiments were conducted on CASME II, SAMM, and SMIC under the three-class setting, with per-subject F_1-scores and Acc. shown in Fig. 4.

Overall, 3D ResNet with FPC achieved higher F_1 and Acc. In rare cases, such as `Sub12` in CASME II, FPC slightly reduced F_1 without affecting Acc., indicating limited impact on certain facial configurations.

5   Conclusion

This work addresses pose misalignment in micro-expression video preprocessing and proposes a facial pose-constrained recognition framework. We introduce a lightweight Facial Pose Constraint (FPC) module based on an Orthogonal-Bidirectional LSTM, which extracts pose information along orthogonal directions from reference frames. By capturing spatial relationships between facial regions, the FPC provides auxiliary guidance to the primary 3D ResNet network, mitigating residual pose variations and enhancing recognition accuracy.

Extensive experiments on CASME II, SAMM, and SMIC demonstrate that the proposed method consistently outperforms classical and state-of-the-art MER approaches. Ablation studies confirm the contribution of the FPC module, while visualizations of its outputs offer interpretability of the pose calibration process. Overall, the proposed framework effectively integrates pose priors to improve micro-expression recognition from raw video sequences.

Acknowledgments.. This research was funded in part by the National Natural Science Foundation of China (62322111, 62271289), the Natural Science Fund for Outstanding Young Scholars of Shandong Province (ZR2022YQ60), the Research Fund for the Taishan Scholar Project of Shandong Province (tsqn202306064), Jinan "20 Terms of New Universities" Funding Project (202333035), and the Natural Science Fund for Distinguished Young Scientists of Shandong Province (ZR2024JQ007).

References

1. Bond, C.F., Omar, A., Mahmoud, A., et al.: Lie detection across cultures. J. Nonverbal Behav. **14**, 189–204 (1990)
2. DePaulo, B.M., Kashy, D.A., Kirkendol, S.E., et al.: Lying in everyday life. J. Pers. Soc. Psychol. **70**(5), 979 (1996)
3. Bhushan, B.: Study of facial micro-expressions in psychology. In: Understanding Facial Expressions in Communication, pp. 265–286. Springer (2015)
4. Frank, M., Herbasz, M., Sinuk, K., et al.: I see how you feel: training laypeople and professionals to recognize fleeting emotions. In: Int. Commun. Assoc. Annu. Meet., pp. 1–35 (2009)
5. Huang, X., Wang, S.J., Liu, X., et al.: Discriminative spatiotemporal local binary pattern with revisited integral projection for spontaneous facial micro-expression recognition. IEEE Trans. Affect. Comput. **10**(1), 32–47 (2017)
6. Zhou, L., Mao, Q., Huang, X., et al.: Feature refinement: an expression-specific feature learning and fusion method for micro-expression recognition. Pattern Recognit. **122**, 108275 (2022)
7. Takalkar, M.A., Thuseethan, S., Rajasegarar, S., et al.: LGAttNet: automatic micro-expression detection using dual-stream local and global attentions. Knowl.-Based Syst. **212**, 106566 (2021)

8. Li, Y., Wei, J., Liu, Y., et al.: Deep learning for micro-expression recognition: a survey. IEEE Trans. Affect. Comput. (2022)
9. Patel, D., Hong, X., Zhao, G.: Selective deep features for micro-expression recognition. In: ICPR 2016, pp. 2258–2263. IEEE (2016)
10. Peng, M., Wang, C., Chen, T., et al.: Dual temporal scale convolutional neural network for micro-expression recognition. Front. Psychol. **8**, 1745 (2017)
11. Li, Y., Huang, X., Zhao, G.: Joint local and global information learning with single apex frame detection for micro-expression recognition. IEEE Trans. Image Process. **30**, 249–263 (2020)
12. Ben, X., Ren, Y., Zhang, J., et al.: Video-based facial micro-expression analysis: a survey of datasets, features and algorithms. IEEE Trans. Pattern Anal. Mach. Intell. **44**(9), 5826–5846 (2021)
13. Wang, Y., See, J., Phan, R.C.W., et al.: Efficient spatio-temporal local binary patterns for spontaneous facial micro-expression recognition. PLoS ONE **10**(5), e0124674 (2015)
14. Wang, Y., See, J., Phan, R.C.-W., Oh, Y.-H.: LBP with six intersection points: reducing redundant information in LBP-TOP for micro-expression recognition. In: Cremers, D., Reid, I., Saito, H., Yang, M.-H. (eds.) ACCV 2014. LNCS, vol. 9003, pp. 525–537. Springer, Cham (2015). https://doi.org/10.1007/978-3-319-16865-4_34
15. Fan, X., Chen, X., Jiang, M., et al.: SelfME: self-supervised motion learning for micro-expression recognition. In: IEEE/CVF Conference on Computer Vision and Pattern Recognition (CVPR), pp. 13834–13843 (2023)
16. Pfister, T., Li, X., Zhao, G., et al.: Recognising spontaneous facial micro-expressions. In: International Conference on Computer Vision (ICCV), pp. 1449–1456. IEEE (2011)
17. Hochreiter, S., Schmidhuber, J.: Long short-term memory. Neural Comput. **9**(8), 1735–1780 (1997)
18. Zhang, S., Zheng, D., Hu, X., et al.: Bidirectional long short-term memory networks for relation classification. In: Pacific Asia Conference on Language, Information and Computation (PACLIC), pp. 73–78 (2015)
19. Liong, S.T., Gan, Y.S., See, J., et al.: Shallow triple stream three-dimensional CNN (STSTNet) for micro-expression recognition. In: IEEE International Conference on Automatic Face & Gesture Recognition (FG), pp. 1–5 (2019)
20. Sun, B., Cao, S., Li, D., et al.: Dynamic micro-expression recognition using knowledge distillation. IEEE Trans. Affect. Comput. **13**(2), 1037–1043 (2020)
21. Wang, Y., Huang, Y., Liu, C., et al.: Micro expression recognition via dual-stream spatiotemporal attention network. J. Healthc. Eng. 2021 (2021)
22. Nie, X., Takalkar, M.A., Duan, M., et al.: GEME: dual-stream multi-task gender-based micro-expression recognition. Neurocomputing **427**, 13–28 (2021)
23. Li, F., Nie, P., You, M., Chen, Z., Wang, G.: Triple-ATFME: triple-branch attention fusion network for micro-expression recognition. Arab. J. Sci. Eng. **50**(2), 807–823 (2025)
24. Tian, H., Gong, W., Li, W., Qian, Y.: PASTFNet: a paralleled attention spatiotemporal fusion network for micro-expression recognition. Med. Biol. Eng. Comput. **62**(6), 1911–1924 (2024)
25. Zhao, H., Kim, B.-G., Slowik, A., Pan, D.: Temporal-spatial correlation and graph attention-guided network for micro-expression recognition in English learning livestreams. Discov. Comput. **27**(1), 47 (2024)

Gesture, Action

A Unified Transformer with a Parametric Activation Function for Robust Gesture Recognition Across Sparse and Dense EMG Signals

Chenyan Ge, Jun Li[✉], Tao Hu, and Haifeng Huang

College of Intelligent Systems Science and Engineering, Hubei Minzu University,
Enshi, China
lijun72213@163.com

Abstract. Deep learning has advanced electromyography (EMG) based gesture recognition, yet existing models face robustness challenges. We propose a novel Transformer-based framework to enhance classification accuracy. Our architecture introduces two key innovations: a customized Patch Embedding module to adapt 1D time-series EMG signals for self-attention, and a novel Parametric Tanh Activation Function (DyT) that replaces conventional Layer Normalization to improve training stability and generalization. We evaluated our model on two public datasets representing distinct modalities: a sparse sEMG dataset (NinaPro DB2 Exercise B) and a high-density EMG dataset. The framework achieved high classification average test accuracies of 85.18% and 86.69%, respectively. These results confirm the effectiveness of our architecture, demonstrating its significant potential for real-world applications such as prosthetic control and human-computer interaction.

Keywords: Hand Gesture Recognition · Electromyography (EMG) · Transformer · Parametric Activation Function · Deep Learning

1 Introduction

Electromyography (EMG) signals, which are electrophysiological recordings of muscle activity [1], can directly reflect human motor intent. Consequently, they have been widely utilized in diverse fields such as human-computer interaction (HCI), prosthetic control [2], and medical rehabilitation. High-accuracy and computationally efficient gesture recognition based on EMG signals is a cornerstone technology for enabling these applications. With the rapid advancement of deep learning, its superior capability in handling complex pattern recognition tasks has positioned EMG-based gesture recognition as a prominent research area [3].

Prevailing research has largely focused on separate modeling paradigms for high-density EMG (HD-EMG) and surface EMG (sEMG). HD-EMG provides richer spatial information, enabling the extraction of high-resolution muscle

W. Jia et al. (Eds.): CCBR 2025, LNCS 16360, pp. 609–618, 2026.
https://doi.org/10.1007/978-981-95-6123-0_56

activity features for gesture recognition. However, its high acquisition cost and limited range of application scenarios restrict its widespread use. In contrast, sEMG offers superior wearability and practicality, but its signals are often sparse and noisy, which makes it challenging for conventional methods to achieve consistently stable performance. Therefore, constructing a unified framework that demonstrates both robustness and high accuracy on dense and sparse EMG data alike has become a critical research objective for addressing multi-scenario adaptation and lowering the barrier to deployment [4].

To address these challenges, we propose DyT-HGR, a unified and normalization-free framework that demonstrates both robustness and high accuracy on dense and sparse EMG data alike [5]. Instead of relying on a fixed normalization scheme, our core innovation is to replace LayerNorm with a Parametric Tanh Activation Function (DyT). This function introduces learnable parameters that allow the network to dynamically adapt the shape of the non-linear transformation, thereby enhancing its ability to model the non-stationary dynamics of EMG signals and improving training stability.

The main contributions of this work are as follows:

- A unified, normalization-free Transformer architecture, DyT-HGR, is proposed. Its core innovation is a Parametric Tanh Activation Function (DyT) that replaces conventional Layer Normalization. By adaptively modeling the non-stationary dynamics of EMG signals through learnable parameters, DyT significantly enhances training stability and generalization.
- The architecture's unified nature is achieved through a convolutional patch embedding strategy. This strategy effectively transforms EMG inputs of varying channel counts (both sparse and high-density) into a uniform sequence representation, eliminating the need for modality-specific architectural modifications.
- Extensive experiments on two public benchmark datasets validate the model's effectiveness. The results demonstrate that DyT-HGR achieves state-of-the-art performance and a superior accuracy and complexity trade-off compared to existing models.

2 Related Work

This section reviews prior work on EMG-based gesture recognition, which can be broadly categorized into two primary research directions: learning methods, deep learning-based approaches, and the recent integration of Transformer architectures.

With the advent of deep learning, architectures such as Convolutional Neural Networks (CNNs) and Recurrent Neural Networks (RNNs) have been widely applied to EMG analysis, achieving notable improvements in accuracy and feature representation. However, these models often face limitations in modeling long-range temporal dependencies, which are critical for complex gesture under-standing [6]. Additionally, EMG signals are inherently non-stationary, with statistical properties that vary over time due to factors like electrode displacement, muscle fatigue, and inter-subject variability. Such variability poses significant challenges for model robustness and domain generalization, often requiring sophisticated regularization or adaptation strategies.

Transformers [7], originally introduced in the domain of natural language processing and later extended to computer vision, have recently garnered attention in EMG-related research due to their strong capacity for modeling long-range dependencies via self-attention mechanisms [8]. These properties make them well-suited for biosignals, where global context and long-term structure play a crucial role. Nonetheless, applying standard Transformer architectures to EMG signals is non-trivial. A key limitation arises from their reliance on Layer Normalization (LayerNorm), which, while effective in many domains, may be suboptimal for noisy, highly variable, and non-stationary physiological signals. This limitation motivates the investigation of alternative normalization strategies that can better accommodate the dynamic nature of EMG data and enhance training stability.

Despite notable progress in EMG-based gesture recognition, existing methods still face critical limitations. Traditional approaches depend heavily on hand-crafted features, which are difficult to generalize across varying recording conditions. Deep learning models, while more flexible, often struggle with the non-stationary and noisy nature of EMG signals, especially under cross-subject and cross-session scenarios. Furthermore, Transformer-based architectures, though powerful in modeling long-range dependencies, typically rely on Layer Normalization, which may be suboptimal for physiological signals due to their high variability and dynamic distributions. To address these challenges, we propose a unified Transformer framework enhanced by a parametric activation function (DyT) that replaces conventional normalization layers. Our design aims to improve training stability, generalization, and adaptability across both sparse and dense EMG modalities, thereby advancing the robustness and practical deployment of gesture recognition systems.

3   DyT-HGR Architecture

We introduce a Transformer-based framework designed for EMG gesture recognition, with emphasis on cross-domain adaptability. This architecture is capable of handling both sparse (sEMG) and dense (HD-EMG) acquisition modalities without modification. It incorporates a patch-based input strategy, a lightweight dynamic normalization module, and a streamlined encoding structure tailored to the time-varying and noisy nature of biosignals (Fig. 1).

3.1   Data Preprocessing

The performance and robustness of EMG-based recognition models are strongly influenced by the quality and consistency of input signals. To this end, we employ

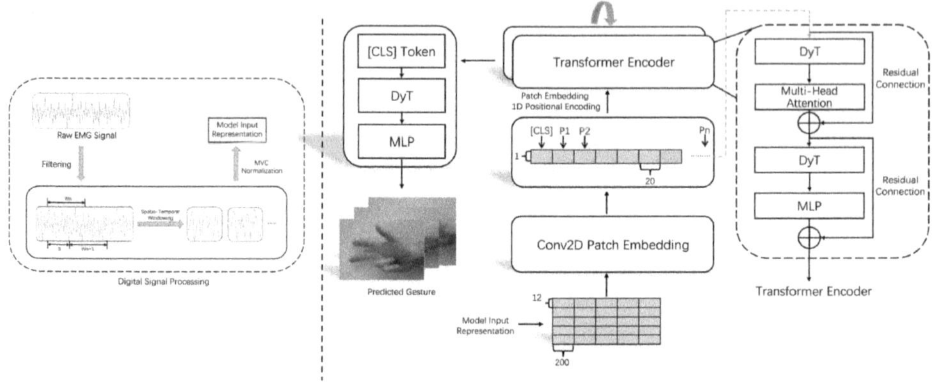

Fig. 1. Overview of the proposed DyT-HGR framework. The system consists of two components: a digital signal preprocessing pipeline, and a Transformer-based classification model.

a structured preprocessing pipeline designed to enhance signal fidelity, suppress nuisance variability, and ensure statistical coherence across training and evaluation.

Origin EMG signals are first subjected to temporal filtering to suppress low-frequency motion artifacts and high-frequency electronic noise. A 4th-order Butterworth bandpass filter with a passband of 20300 Hz is adopted, which preserves the physiologically relevant frequency components associated with voluntary muscle contractions while attenuating spectral outliers. In indoor recording environments, powerline interference at 50 Hz is further removed using a narrowband notch filter.

Window Segmentation. Filtered EMG sequences are partitioned into overlapping temporal windows using a sliding window strategy. Let $\mathbf{X} \in \mathbb{R}^{T \times C}$ denote an EMG sequence with T time steps and C channels. Each segment $\mathbf{x}_i \in \mathbb{R}^{w \times C}$ is extracted using a window of width $w = 400$ and stride $s = 200$, such that the total number of windows per gesture instance is given by Eq. (1):

$$N = \left\lfloor \frac{T - w}{s} \right\rfloor + 1 \tag{1}$$

This window length corresponds to a 200ms receptive field at 2 kHz sampling rate [9], balancing temporal resolution with gesture dynamics. Overlap between windows ensures continuity and reduces sensitivity to gesture boundaries.

MVC Normalization. EMG amplitudes are subject to large inter-subject and intra-session variability due to electrode positioning, skin impedance, and physiological differences. To reduce these confounding factors, we apply Maximum Voluntary Contraction (MVC) normalization independently on each channel.

For each channel c, the normalization is defined as Eq. (2):

$$x^{(c)}_{\mathrm{norm}} = \frac{x^{(c)}}{\max \left| x^{(c)} \right|} \tag{2}$$

where the denominator is computed only from the training set. This approach preserves within-channel relative activation patterns while ensuring that all inputs lie within a bounded dynamic range [10].

Compared to z-score or minmax normalization, MVC provides better physiological interpretability and improved empirical stability in EMG-based recognition tasks.

3.2   Input Representation

Let $\mathbf{X}_{\mathrm{raw}} \in \mathbb{R}^{T \times C}$ denote the raw multi-channel EMG signal, where T is the number of time steps and C the number of channels. The raw signal is processed through the pipeline described in Sect. 2.2 to generate normalized data windows, which serve as the input to our model.

3.3   Patch Tokenization

Each normalized window $\mathbf{S} \in \mathbb{R}^{L \times C}$ is processed into a sequence of tokens. This is achieved using a patch embedding layer implemented via a 2D convolution. Specifically, we apply a convolutional layer with a kernel size and stride equal to the patch size ($P \times 1$, where $P = 20$). This operation efficiently partitions the input window into a grid of patches and linearly projects each patch into a D-dimensional embedding space (e.g., $D = 128$) [11]. The output is then flattened and rearranged to form a sequence of N_p patch tokens, as the Eq. (3):

$$\{\mathbf{z}_1, \ldots, \mathbf{z}_{N_p}\} \subset \mathbb{R}^D, \quad \text{where } N_p = (L/P) \times C \tag{3}$$

A learnable class token $\mathbf{z}_{\mathrm{cls}} \in \mathbb{R}^D$ is prepended to the sequence, and a trainable 1D positional encoding $\mathbf{E}_{\mathrm{pos}} \in \mathbb{R}^{(N_p+1) \times D}$ is added, as the Eq. (4):

$$\mathbf{Z}_0 = [\mathbf{z}_{\mathrm{cls}}; \mathbf{z}_1; \ldots; \mathbf{z}_{N_p}] + \mathbf{E}_{\mathrm{pos}} \tag{4}$$

This patching scheme abstracts the input regardless of the electrode count, enabling a unified representation across sEMG and HD-EMG formats.

3.4   Parametric Tanh Activation Function (DyT)

The sequence $\mathbf{Z}_0$ is passed through a stack of $M = 6$ Transformer encoder blocks. Each block applies multi-head self-attention (MHSA) and a feed-forward MLP, both preceded by our novel parametric activation function (DyT) as shown in Eq. (5):

$$\mathrm{DyT}(x) = \gamma \cdot \tanh(\alpha x) + \beta \tag{5}$$

Here, $\alpha \in \mathbb{R}$ is a learnable scalar gain parameter, and $\gamma, \beta \in \mathbb{R}^D$ are learnable per-channel scaling and shifting parameters. This formulation is a specific instance of a broader class of adaptive activation functions. Unlike LayerNorm [12], which computes statistics over the features, DyT requires no layer statistics and provides stable adaptive transformations for non-stationary EMG inputs by learning the optimal activation shape directly from data [13]. Our choice of a parametric activation function, with its globally learned parameters (α, β, γ), is motivated by the unique characteristics of EMG signals. Unlike dynamic, input-dependent functions, a globally optimized activation shape is more robust to the high local noise inherent in non-stationary EMG signals and is more computationally efficient, allowing the model to learn the signal's general dynamics without overfitting to instance-level variations.

From the final encoder output $\mathbf{Z}_M \in \mathbb{R}^{(N_p+1) \times D}$, the token is selected, passed through a final DyT layer, and projected into logits via a linear classifier, as the Eq. (6):

$$\text{Logits} = \text{Linear}(\text{DyT}(\mathbf{z}_{\text{cls}}^{(M)})) \in \mathbb{R}^K \tag{6}$$

where K is the number of gesture classes.

3.5   Objective Function

For model training, we employ the standard Cross-Entropy Loss, a conventional choice for multi-class classification tasks like gesture recognition. The model's raw output, the logits, are first converted into class probabilities using the Softmax function. The Cross-Entropy Loss then measures the discrepancy between the predicted probability distribution and the one-hot encoded true label.

The loss function $\mathcal{L}$, is defined in Eq. (7):

$$\mathcal{L} = -\sum_{k=1}^{K} y_k \log(p_k) \tag{7}$$

where K is the total number of classes, y_k is the ground truth (1 if k is the correct class, 0 otherwise), and p_k is the predicted probability for class k obtained from the Softmax function. The model is trained by minimizing this loss across all training samples using the AdamW optimizer.

4   Experiments and Results

To evaluate the proposed DyT-HGR framework, we conduct experiments on two EMG datasets with differing signal densities: NinaPro DB2 (sEMG) and a high-density EMG (HD-EMG) dataset. The first, NinaPro DB2 (Exercise B) [14], contains 17 gestures from 40 subjects, with each gesture repeated six times (a 5-s contraction and a 3-s rest). For this 12-channel sEMG dataset, we utilize the first four repetitions for training, the fifth for validation, and the sixth for testing. The second, a 128-channel HD-EMG dataset [15], comprises 65 gestures from 20 subjects, each repeated five times with 5-s intervals. To ensure fair and direct comparisons, our evaluation protocols strictly align with the established benchmarks for each dataset. Consequently, for the NinaPro DB2 dataset, we adopt the intra-subject protocol consistent with prior works. For the HD-EMG dataset, we employ an inter-subject, subject-based cross-validation scheme to maintain methodological consistency with its primary baseline. For this dataset, a five-fold cross-validation approach is adopted, where four repetitions serve as the training set and the remaining one as the test set in each fold. The model is trained using the AdamW optimizer with a cross-entropy loss [16].

Table 1. Comparison of classification accuracy across models on the NinaPro DB2 (Exercise B) dataset.

Model	Source	Dataset	Windowlength	Classes	Avg. Acc.(%)
LST-EMG-Net [17]	Front. Neurorob. 2023	ExerciseB	300 ms	17	81.47
Deep-LSTM [18]	RA-L 2021	ExerciseB	300 ms	17	79.19
CNN-VIT [19]	Biomed Signal Proces 2024	ExerciseB	300 ms	17	83.05
CNN-VIT [19]	Biomed Signal Proces 2024	ExerciseB	200 ms	17	82.76
LDA [20]	Appl. Sci. 2021	ExerciseB	200 ms	17	70.53
Ours	**This work**	**ExerciseB**	**200 ms**	**17**	**85.18**

Table 1 compares our model with several baselines on the NinaPro DB2 dataset. Despite using a shorter input window (200 ms), DyT-HGR achieves the highest accuracy (85.18%), outperforming both conventional and deep learning methods. These results demonstrate the model's effectiveness under limited temporal context and its suitability for real-time EMG-based gesture recognition.

Table 2. Comparison of model performance on the HD-EMG dataset.

Model	Embed dim	Parameters	Acc. F1(%)	Acc. F2(%)	Acc. F3(%)	Acc. F4(%)	Acc. F5(%)	Avg. Acc.(%)
ViT-HGR-1 [21]	192	340,886	75.92	87.97	88.47	87.71	83.22	**84.62**
ViT-HGR-2 [21]	96	78,210	75.21	87.34	88	87.88	82.78	**84.24**
ViT-HGR-3 [21]	48	25,314	73.92	87.09	87.56	87.09	81.65	**83.46**
Ours	64	**222,479**	74.19	**90.42**	**91.59**	**90.53**	**86.72**	**86.69**

As summarized in Table 2, our model achieves an average accuracy of 86.69% on the HD-EMG dataset, outperforming three variants of ViT-HGR under consistent training protocols. Although ViT-HGR-1 uses a larger embedding dimension (192) and more parameters (340k), it achieves only 84.62% average accuracy. In contrast, DyT-HGR reaches higher accuracy with fewer parameters (222k) and a lower embedding dimension (64), demonstrating a more efficient accuracy-complexity trade-off. This performance gain is attributed to the improved stability and modeling capacity provided by the DyT activation function, which enhances representation quality without increasing model size.

Table 2 compares our model with several baselines on the HD-EMG dataset. Our model achieves the highest average accuracy (86.69%) while maintaining fewer parameters than ViT-HGR-1, and significantly outperforming smaller variants ViT-HGR-2 and ViT-HGR-3. This demonstrates a favorable trade-off between accuracy and model complexity. "Embed Dim" denotes the token embedding dimension, and "Parameters" is the total number of trainable weights. Accuracy is reported for five cross-validation folds (F1F5), and the mean accuracy is listed as Avg. Acc. Our method achieves the best overall accuracy with moderate model complexity. This performance gain is attributed to the improved temporal encoding and the use of dynamic normalization, which enhance representation quality without increasing model size.

To validate our primary design choices, we conducted a series of comparison experiments, with all other settings held constant. The results, summarized in Table 3, confirm the superiority of both our proposed DyT module over standard LayerNorm and our 2D patch embedding strategy over a 1D temporal alternative. This validates their crucial contributions to the framework's overall effectiveness.

Table 3. Analysis of Model Components on the Ninapro DB2 dataset.

Model	Dataset	Windowlength	Classes	Average Accuracy(%)
ViT(DyT+1D Patch)	DB2	200	17	**63.78**
ViT(LayerNorm+GELU)	DB2	200	17	**74.27**
DyT-HGR	**DB2**	**200**	**17**	85.18

Confusion matrices for both datasets are presented in Fig. 2, illustrating consistent performance across diverse gesture classes. Notably, the model maintains robust accuracy under both sparse (sEMG) and dense (HD-EMG) conditions without requiring architectural changes or extensive dataset-specific tuning. These results highlight the model's scalability and generalization capability. We attribute the improvements to the combination of a patch-based temporal embedding and the Parametric Tanh (DyT) activation, which together enhance temporal modeling and training stability across heterogeneous EMG signals.

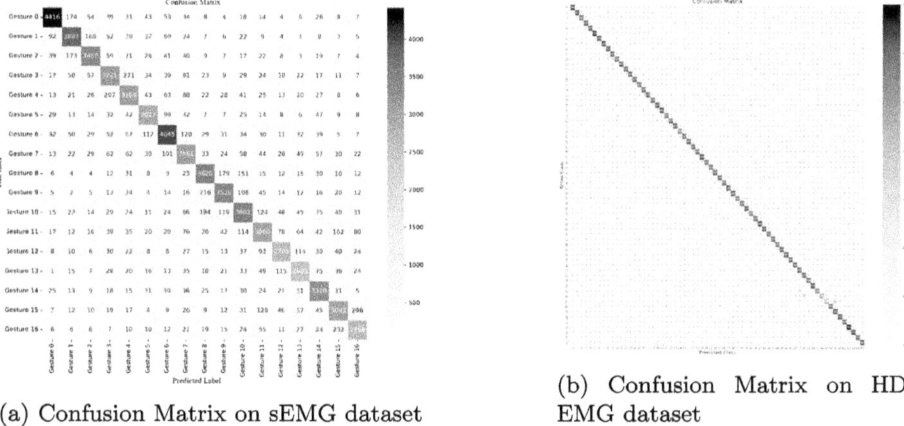

(a) Confusion Matrix on sEMG dataset

(b) Confusion Matrix on HD-EMG dataset

Fig. 2. Classification performance on sparse and dense EMG signals.

5   Conclusion

This work addresses a critical challenge in EMG-based gesture recognition: achieving robust, high-accuracy classification across both sparse and dense signal modalities without relying on dataset-specific architectural tuning. To this end, we propose a unified Transformer-based framework enhanced by two key innovations: a Parametric Tanh activation function (DyT) and a patch-based temporal embedding strategy that together enable more effective and stable learning from non-stationary biosignals. Extensive experiments on two representative datasets demonstrate the versatility and efficiency of our approach. Without altering the architecture or requiring modality-specific adjustments, our model achieves state-of-the-art performance on both sparse sEMG (85.18%) and high-density EMG (86.69%) datasets. Compared to existing ViT-based and recurrent models, DyT-HGR delivers a more favorable accuracy-complexity trade-off, maintaining a moderate parameter count while achieving superior generalization. Qualitatively, we also observed that the training process with DyT was more stable, exhibiting smoother convergence compared to the LayerNorm-based baseline. We attribute this enhanced stability to the adaptive nature of the parametric activation function, which avoids the per-instance statistical computation of normalization layers. Future work will explore integrating domain adaptation mechanisms to improve inter-subject generalization, and extending the framework to accommodate multi-modal biosignal fusion (e.g., EMG + IMU), enabling more robust intent inference in dynamic environments.

Acknowledgments. This work was supported by Hubei Provincial Key Research and Development Project under Grant 2025BEB003, Hubei Province Natural Science Foundation of China under Grant 2023AFD061, the Outstanding Youth Science and Technology Innovation Team Project for Colleges and Universities of Hubei Province of China under Grant T2023013

References

1. Mills, K.R.: The basics of electromyography. J. Neurol. Neurosurg. Psychiatry **76**(suppl 2), ii32–ii35 (2005)
2. Lee, S., Saridis, G.: The control of a prosthetic arm by EMG pattern recognition. IEEE Trans. Autom. Control **29**(4), 290–302 (1984)
3. Xiong, D., et al.: Deep learning for EMG-based human-machine interaction: a review. IEEE/CAA J. Automatica Sinica **8**(3), 512–533 (2021)
4. Du, Y., et al.: Surface EMG-based inter-session gesture recognition enhanced by deep domain adaptation. Sensors **17**(3), 458 (2017)
5. Rasamoelina, A.D., Adjailia, F., Sinčák, P.: A review of activation function for artificial neural network. In: 2020 IEEE 18th World Symposium on Applied Machine Intelligence and Informatics (SAMI). IEEE (2020)
6. Atzori, M., Cognolato, M., Müller, H.: Deep learning with convolutional neural networks applied to electromyography data: a resource for the classification of movements for prosthetic hands. Front. Neurorobot. **10**, 9 (2016)
7. Vaswani, A., et al.: Attention is all you need. In: Advances in Neural Information Processing Systems, vol. 30 (2017)
8. Wen, Q., et al.: Transformers in time series: a survey. arXiv preprint arXiv:2202.07125 (2022)
9. Shen, S., et al.: Gesture recognition using MLP-mixer with CNN and stacking ensemble for semg signals. IEEE Sens. J. **24**(4), 4960–4968 (2024)
10. Hudgins, B., Parker, P., Scott, R.N.: A new strategy for multifunction myoelectric control. IEEE Trans. Biomed. Eng. **40**(1), 82–94 (1993)
11. Dosovitskiy, A., et al.: An image is worth 16x16 words: transformers for image recognition at scale. arXiv preprint arXiv:2010.11929 (2020)
12. Ba, J.L., Kiros, J.R., Hinton, G.E.: Layer normalization. arXiv preprint arXiv:1607.06450 (2016)
13. Zhu, J., et al.: Transformers without normalization. In: Proceedings of the Computer Vision and Pattern Recognition Conference (2025)
14. Atzori, M., et al.: Electromyography data for non-invasive naturally-controlled robotic hand prostheses. Sci. Data **1**(1), 1–13 (2014)
15. Malešević, N., et al.: A database of high-density surface electromyogram signals comprising 65 isometric hand gestures. Sci. Data **8**(1), 63 (2021)
16. Zhou, P., et al.: Towards understanding convergence and generalization of AdamW. IEEE Trans. Pattern Anal. Mach. Intell. (2024)
17. Zhang, W., et al.: LST-EMG-net: long short-term transformer feature fusion network for sEMG gesture recognition. Front. Neurorobot. **17**, 1127338 (2023)
18. Sun, T., et al.: Temporal dilation of deep LSTM for agile decoding of sEMG: application in prediction of upper-limb motor intention in NeuroRobotics. IEEE Robot. Autom. Lett. **6**(4), 6212–6219 (2021)
19. Liu, X., et al.: Integration of convolutional neural network and vision transformer for gesture recognition using sEMG. Biomed. Signal Process. Control **98**, 106686 (2024)
20. Kang, K., Shin, H.-C.: EMG based gesture recognition using the unbiased difference power. Appl. Sci. **11**(4), 1526 (2021)
21. Montazerin, M., et al.: ViT-HGR: vision transformer-based hand gesture recognition from high density surface EMG signals. In: 2022 44th Annual International Conference of the IEEE Engineering in Medicine & Biology Society (EMBC). IEEE (2022)

Multimodal Higher-Order Statistical Adapter For Video Action Recognition

Meng Li, Bingbing Zhang[(✉)], and Jianxin Zhang[(✉)]

Dalian Minzu University, Dalian 116650, Liaoning, China
icyzhang@dlnu.edu.cn, jxzhang0411@163.com

Abstract. Recently, Contrastive Language-Image Pre-Training(CLIP) and Parameter-Efficient Fine-Tuning(PEFT) have attracted significant attention in the field of video action recognition. Nevertheless, effectively capturing both temporal dynamics and spatial local variations remains essential. Previous methods either concentrated on modeling long-term dependencies in video-level features while ignoring intra-frame spatial details, which frequently contain crucial discriminative information, or captured lower-order features in spatial details. In this paper, a multimodal higher-order statistical adapter (MHoS-Adapter) approach for CLIP is proposed, introducing a visual-branch Higher-Order Statistical Adapter (HS-Adapter) and a textual-branch Parallel Text Adapter (Para-Adapter). To drastically cut down on computational expense and time overhead, both employ adapter tuning, which involves freezing the initial two-branch structure and adjusting just a few parameters. Higher-order statistics of feature maps, including long-term and higher-order data, are modeled by HS-Adapter to improve local detail discrimination and capture long-term dependencies with minimal temporal complexity. Para-Adapter improves text-visual feature alignment by using Video Caption to produce video-level text descriptions for labels. Comprehensive tests on standard benchmarks like Kinetics-400, Mini Kinetics-200, UCF101, and HMDB51 validate the method's effectiveness and show that MHoS-Adapter outperforms most full fine-tuning approaches, achieving 83.2% Top-1 fully-supervised performance on Kinetics-400 with just 19M trainable parameters.

Keywords: Video Action Recognition · Parameter-Efficient Fine-Tuning · Higher-Order Statistical Adapter

1 Introduction

Full fine-tuning techniques have long been the primary modeling architecture for the translation of CLIP [1] models to video action recognition applications. One of the simplest methods is integrating a temporal modeling module in the visual coder, such as ActionCLIP [4] or X-CLIP [3], and then fine-tuning the entire network. The Parameter-Efficient Fine-Tuning (PEFT) approach has been widely adopted by many researchers since the proposal of Adapters [5] in 2019.

W. Jia et al. (Eds.): CCBR 2025, LNCS 16360, pp. 619–628, 2026.
https://doi.org/10.1007/978-981-95-6123-0_57

This approach involves freezing most of the parameters of a pre-trained model and adding only trainable components, such as additional adapters (e.g. Adapt-Former [6]) or Prompts (e.g. Vita-CLIP [7]).

The contextual relevance in video action recognition tasks is not sufficiently captured by Adapter Tuning, despite the fact that it successfully minimizes the number of parameters to be trained. Techniques for long-term dependency capture have primarily fallen into two categories in recent years: self-attention mechanisms and Graph Convolution Networks (GCNs [8]). Although these methods have gained considerable success in long-time dependency capture, they still have problems in differentiating small changes, which are critical for the recognition of comparable actions. In essence, the previously described approaches concentrate on first-order data and are inherently ineffective at capturing higher-order data, which hinders the model's ability to adapt to certain downstream tasks.

In this paper, a novel multimodal high-order statistical adapter (MHoS-Adapter) framework is proposed to overcome the aforementioned issues. In particular, it introduces a high-order statistical adapter (HS-Adapter) in the visual branch. The HS-Adapter comprises two modules: Spatio-Temporal Enhancement (STE) and High-Order Statistical Modeling (HoSM). The STE models spatial features in the first order while capturing long-range temporal correlations. High-Order Statistical Attention (HS-Attention) is the core component of HoSM, which learns precise different information by projecting features into a higher-order space, where minor differences between comparable features are greatly magnified. Para-Adapter enhances text-vision alignment by leveraging Video Caption to generate semantic-rich text descriptions for action labels. Overall, the contributions of this paper are as follows:

I. By introducing particular Adapters in the visual and text branches of CLIP [1], respectively, we propose the MHoS-Adapter to optimize the network architecture for certain downstream tasks.

II. To capture long-range relationships and different information, we design an HS-Adapter for the visual branch. For the textual branch, we suggest a Para-Adapter that is based on category labels and descriptions, improving descriptor discriminability through visual-text fusion.

III. Using standard datasets including Kinetics-400, Mini Kinetics-200, HMDB51, and UCF101, we verify the accuracy and generalizability of our approach.

2   Related Work

The PEFT architecture has improved the constraints of complete fine-tuning of large-scale language-image models since its introduction in NLP in 2019 [5]. EVL [9] initially suggested using frozen CLIP [1] image characteristics with a lightweight spatio-temporal transformer decoder to enhance video representations. An effective spatio-temporal adapter, ST-Adapter [10], demonstrated CLIP's strong modeling capabilities in the action recognition domain. While SOTA performance is attained by all of these approaches, the text branch of

CLIP [1] is ignored and only a unimodal transformation is implemented. In order to execute the transition, Vita-CLIP [7] tries to add cues to both branches; nevertheless, it has performance issues when handling intricate scenes or particular tasks.

Although Wang et al.'s Non-local [11] is good at capturing long-term dependencies, it is expensive since it involves a lot of redundant calculations. In the meanwhile, deep learning-based higher-order modeling techniques demonstrate notable benefits in video action recognition: TCP [12] uses global covariance pooling; GSoP [13] uses global second-order pooling of the pre-convolutional layer's 3D tensor output to obtain the covariance matrix. ViSoT [14] further integrates covariance modeling into the Transformer framework for cross-token interaction. These methods nevertheless have difficulties when it comes to fine-grained integration with adaptive fine-tuning tactics. Important insights for this work are provided by SANet [15], which notably uses an adaptive distribution method of statistical data to capture the fine-grained differences.

3   Method

A video encoder and a text encoder are the two main components of the model architecture suggested in this study, which is based on the two-branch paradigm of CLIP [1] and is seen in Fig. 1(a).

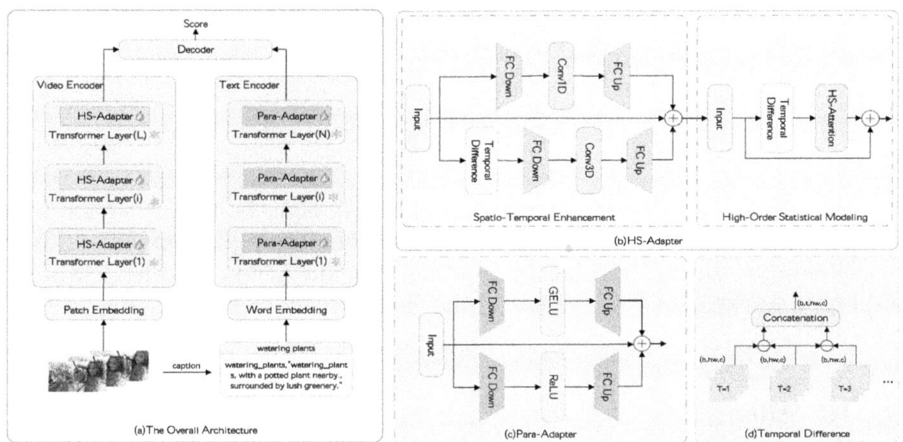

Fig. 1. (a) The overall architecture of MHoS-CLIP: The proposed trainable HS-Adapter in the video encoder and Para-Adapter in the text encoder help to stabilize the frozen backbones of the two encoders. (b) The proposed HS-Adapter's detailed structure: Its two sub-modules are STE and HoSM. (c) The proposed Para-Adapter's detailed structure. (d) Temporal Difference: This section describes how to compute temporal differences from input data for adapter operations within the overall framework.

Video Encoder: $\mathbf{E}_v$ consists of L_v Vision Transformer layer $\left\{\mathcal{E}_v^{(i)}\right\}_{i=1}^{L_v}$ and HS-Adapter $\left\{\mathcal{H}_v^{(j)}\right\}_{j=1}^{L_{H_v}}$. Given a video $V \in \mathbb{R}^{T \times H \times W \times 3}$, where T represents the video frame, H represents the height and W represents the width. We divide the video frame into non-overlapping patches with spatial size $(P \times P)$ and channel dimension 3. The Patch Embedding yields $E_t \in \mathbb{R}^{N \times d_v}$ ($t \in \{1, 2, \ldots, T\}$), $N = HW/P^2$ is the number of patches divided by an image frame. Splice it with a learnable class label $c_t^{(0)}$ and add positional encoding. The t-th frame is constructed as:

$$\mathbf{Z}_t^{(0)} = \left[c_t^{(0)}, E_t^{(0)}\right] + e_t^{pos} \tag{1}$$

We then input the entire video into the Transformer layer and the output is:

$$\mathbf{Z}_v^{(i)} = \mathcal{E}_v^{(i)}\left(\mathcal{H}_v^{(i)}\left(\mathbf{Z}_v^{(i-1)}\right)\right), \quad i = 1, 2, \ldots, L_v \tag{2}$$

Text Encoder: Similarly, $\mathbf{E}_l$ consists of L_l the Transformer layer $\left\{\mathcal{E}_l^{(i)}\right\}_{i=1}^{L_l}$ and Para-Adapter $\left\{\mathcal{P}_v^{(j)}\right\}_{j=1}^{L_{T_v}}$. The input words are tokenized and projected into Word Embedding $W_l^{(0)} = [w_1, w_2, \ldots, w_n] \in \mathbb{R}^{n \times d_v}$, where n is the number of sequence lengths of word tokens and d_v is the dimension size of the word tokens. The input structure of the text encoder is:

$$\mathbf{X}_l^{(0)} = W_l^{(0)} + e_l^{pos} \tag{3}$$

The text features of each Transformer layer are:

$$\mathbf{X}_l^{(i)} = \mathcal{E}_l^{(i)}\left(\mathcal{P}_l^{(i)}\left(\mathbf{X}_l^{(i-1)}\right)\right), \quad i = 1, 2, \ldots, L_l \tag{4}$$

Decoder: We create a decoder with a multi-task constraint mechanism based on the output properties of the two encoders. This technique maximizes feature discriminability during training by guiding text and video encoder features to attain accurate semantic alignment in the shared space and improving interclass differentiation.

3.1   HS-Adapter

The overall basic architecture of HS-Adapter is illustrated in Fig. 1(b). To capture long-term spatio-temporal dependencies, we design the STE module to learn the local inter-frame differences and the global temporal enhancement features of video frames. The HoSM is designed to model the higher-order statistical information in order to model high-order detailed information.

As shown in Fig. 2, HS-Attention is the innovative and successful module that is suggested in this paper. The Statistics Calculation computes and normalizes the higher-order statistical scores for the input feature maps. The Statistics

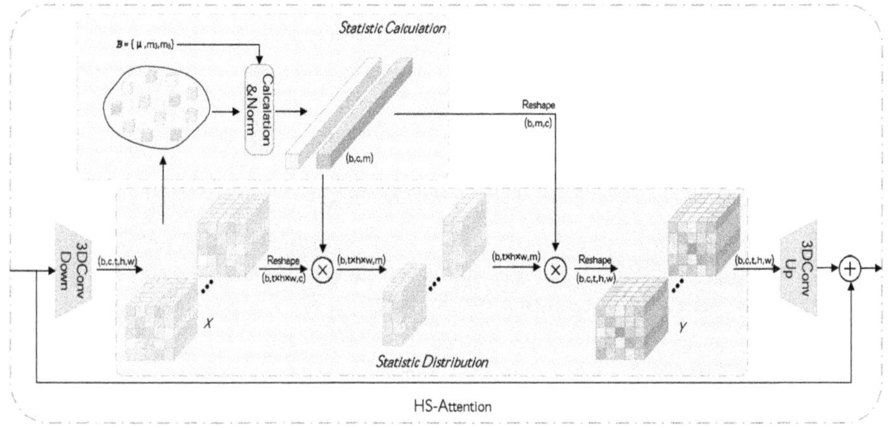

Fig. 2. Detailed HS-Attention diagram. Within the blue box, the statistical score computation processes are carried out, while the pink portion allocates the statistical scores to different locations based on similarity. (Color figure online)

Distribution module then distributes the normalized statistical scores to the entire feature maps according to the feature affinities while also introducing residual connections to stabilize the training process.

Statistics Calculation

The higher-order statistics for a particular feature map are calculated as the first step in the HS-Attention module. For the inter-frame difference information $\mathbf{X}$ output by the Temporal Difference module, we first reorganize the $\mathbf{X}$ vector into $[\mathbf{x}_1, \ldots, \mathbf{x}_{THW}] \in \mathbb{R}^{C \times THW}$. Inspired by Non-local [11], the location information is temporarily ignored to construct the feature map ensemble:

$$S = \{\mathbf{x}_i \mid i = 1, ..., THW\}. \tag{5}$$

The statistics of the vectors can be reduced to statistics for each dimension. The k-th standard moment is defined as:

$$m_k = \frac{1}{|S|\sigma^k} \sum_{\mathbf{x} \in S} (\mathbf{x} - \mu)^k, \quad k = 3, 4, 5... \tag{6}$$

where $\mu, \sigma \in \mathbb{R}^C$ is the mean and standard deviation of the set S and $|S|$ is the number of elements of the set S. For simplicity, we define $\mathcal{B}$ as a subset of statistical scores to represent selected statistical information. Further, a functional function $\mathcal{M}(S, \mathcal{B})$ is used to compute the required statistical scores for $\mathcal{B}$ in the set S:

$$\mathcal{M}(S, \mathcal{B}) = \{\mathcal{F}_s(S) \mid \forall s \in \mathcal{B}\} \tag{7}$$

where $\mathcal{F}_s(S)$ is the statistical score of s in S, e.g., $\mathcal{F}_\mu(S)$ is the mean value of S.

Statistics Distribution

After the statistical scores are computed and normalized, they need to be distributed to the original feature maps. We use the statistical scores as weights and attach them to the feature maps as a way to differentiate the primary and secondary information in the feature maps. The feature after statistical distribution is known as:

$$\mathbf{Y}^T = \text{softmax}(\mathbf{X}^T\mathbf{S})\mathbf{S}^T \tag{8}$$

where $\mathbf{Y} = [\mathbf{y}_1, \ldots, \mathbf{y}_{THW}] \in \mathbb{R}^{C \times THW}$ is the splice of the output features, $\mathbf{S} = [\mathbf{s}_1, \ldots, \mathbf{s}_{|\mathcal{B}|}] \in \mathbb{R}^{C \times |\mathcal{B}|}$ is the splice of the statistics vector in $\mathcal{M}(\mathcal{S}, \mathcal{B})$, where $|\mathcal{B}|$ is the size of the number of elements in $\mathcal{B}$.

3.2   Para-Adapter

In action recognition, text labels are typically brief (e.g., "watering flowers", "hitting the ball"), limiting CLIP [1] text encoders' ability to distinguish them. We introduce a Para-Adapter to optimize the learning of semantic representations. Para-Adapter is presented in Fig. 1(c). Specifically, given that the text tokens input to the Para-Adapter layer are $\mathbf{z}_l$, the output of the Para-Adapter is:

$$\mathcal{P}_l(\mathbf{z}_l) = \mathbf{z}_l + \text{ReLU}(\mathbf{z}_l\mathbf{w}_{dn})\mathbf{w}_{up} + \text{GeLU}(\mathbf{z}_l\mathbf{w}_{dn})\mathbf{w}_{up} \tag{9}$$

where $\mathbf{w}_{dn}$ and $\mathbf{w}_{up}$ denote the down-sampling and up-sampling layers, respectively, and ReLU and GeLU are nonlinear activation functions. In addition, in order to fully utilize category label semantics, we integrate Video Caption, which enhances behavioral label understanding, captures richer semantic information, and improves text-visual representation alignment.

4   Experiments

In this study, we perform ablation experiments on Kinetics-200 (K200), test the scheme's generalization on HMDB51 and UCF101, and assess the scheme's supervised learning capability and accuracy on Kinetics-400 (K400). The backbone network was the ViT-B/16 in the CLIP [1] framework, and only the added HS-Adapter and Para-Adapter components were parameterized, the fundamental model parameters were frozen. The K-400 dataset consists of four hundred human body movement categories, which includes 240k training videos and 20k validation videos. Mini-K200 is a subset of K400, which includes a total of 200 categories. HMDB51 and UCF101 are two small datasets, containing 5k videos across 51 classes and 13k videos across 101 classes, respectively. The AdamW optimizer was used for training, with 15 epochs of training rounds, a base learning rate of 3e-4, and a weight decay of 0.01. With a spatial resolution of 224×224 and a sparse frame sampling strategy, 8 frames were evenly sampled at 16-frame intervals. Data enhancement techniques included short-edge scaling jitter (range 1.0–1.15) and random horizontal flipping. The assessment approach is a 4 clips × 3 crops multi-view strategy, and the training batch sizes are 64 (K200) and 16 (K400). Every experiment was conducted using a single NVIDIA RTX 4090-24G GPU and implemented with PyTorch.

4.1 Fully Supervised Experiments

Table 1 compares the performance of the MHoS-Adapter with other SOTA methods on the fully supervised performance comparison. Our method outperforms an end-to-end fine-tuned CLIP model using the same ViT-B/16 backbone network in the visual unimodal PEFT approach. The performance is inversely 0.3% better and only 22% of the 86M parameters of EVL-B/16 [9] are needed. It should be highlighted that, despite the slight difference, contemporary ideal approaches like BIKE [18] use a significantly larger network architecture (ViT-L) and twelve times as many configurable parameters as ours. Lastly, our method also performs significantly among multimodal PEFT methods: we achieve higher performance using an adapter architecture with only about 49% of trainable parameters (19M) compared to the cue learning-based multimodal method Vita-CLIP [7] (39M). By adding only roughly 18% more parameters, we reach 83.2% performance compared to the Top-1 accuracy of M2-CLIP-B/16 (82.6%).

Table 1. Comparison with other video action recognition methods SOTA on Kinetics-400.[†]Reproduced by us.

Model	Pre-training	Tunable Param	frames×crops ×clips	Top-1 (%)	Top-5 (%)	GFLOPs
Full Finetuning						
Swin-B [16]	IN-21k	88	$32 \times 4 \times 3$	82.7	95.5	282
MViTv2-B [17]	×	52	$32 \times 5 \times 1$	82.9	95.7	225
ActionCLIP-B/16 [2]	CLIP-400M	142	$32 \times 10 \times 3$	83.8	96.2	563
X-CLIP-B/16 [3]	CLIP-400M	132	$16 \times 4 \times 3$	84.7	96.8	287
BIKE-L/14 [18]	CLIP-400M	230	$16 \times 4 \times 3$	88.1	97.9	830
PEFT: unimodal visual framework (frozen CLIP)						
EVL-B/16 [9]	CLIP-400M	86	$8 \times 1 \times 3$	82.9	–	444
ST-Adapter-B/16 [10]	CLIP-400M	7	$32 \times 1 \times 3$	82.7	96.2	607
AIM-B/16 [19]	CLIP-400M	11	$32 \times 1 \times 3$	84.7	96.7	809
PEFT: multimodal framework (frozen CLIP)						
Vita-CLIP-B/16 [7]	CLIP-400M	39	$8 \times 4 \times 3$	81.8	96.0	97
M2-CLIP-B/16 [20][†]	CLIP-400M	16	$8 \times 4 \times 3$	82.6	95.9	127
MHoS-Adapter (Ours)	CLIP-400M	19	$8 \times 4 \times 3$	**83.2**	**96.2**	117

4.2 Zero-Shot Experiments

Table 2 presents zero-shot results on HMDB51 and UCF101. Leveraging weights reused from K400, MHoS-Adapter follows the official three-split protocol. It achieves 50.4% (HMDB51) and 69.2%, outperforming many state-of-the-art methods like ActionCLIP (40.8% ± 5.4/58.3% ± 3.4).

4.3 Ablation Experiments

Using the basic video and text encoders as our Baseline, we construct a CLIP [1] two-branch structure in Table 3. Adding our HS-Adapter to the Baseline achieves a 6.9% accuracy boost. Further adding the Para-Adapter to the text branch increases accuracy from 86.3% to 86.6%. We assess the impact of HS-Adapter's included STE and HoSM positions in the Transformer layer in Table 4. We find that only 85.8% Top-1 accuracy is obtained when using both STE and HoSM, which adds 34.5M parameters. With only half the parameters needed, the accuracy is 85.9% Top-1 when STE is used initially, followed by HoSM. The best Top-1 accuracy of 86.6% is achieved by using HoSM first, then STE. Table 5 shows the outcomes of adding Para-Adapter either behind the feedforward layer or behind the attention layer. The down-sampled linear layer is initialized using the Kaiming initialization and the up-sampled linear layer is initialized using the Xavier initialization. To stabilize the training process, all bias terms are initialized to 0. We employ a whole-to-local approach for layer ablation, as indicated in Table 6. After adding HS-Adapter to every layer of the Transformer, we inserted it at the beginning, middle, and end, and then only in a small number of them. According to the results, an optimal accuracy of 86.6% is obtained by inserting the HS-Adapter at layers 4, 8, and 12 of the encoder, respectively. As indicated in Table 7, we increase the higher-order moments of HS-Attention sequentially from low order to high order in order to more effectively evaluate the higher-order modeling ability of HS-Adapter. The best Top-1 accuracy of 86.6% is achieved when the combination of high-order moments is [1, 3, 5].

Table 2. Zero-Shot performance comparison on the HMDB51 and UCF101 datasets.

Method	HMDB51 (%)	UCF101 (%)	CLIP FT
ActionCLIP [2]	40.8 ± 5.4	58.3 ± 3.4	✓
X-CLIP-B/16 [3]	44.6 ± 5.2	72.0 ± 2.3	✓
CoOp [21]	–	66.6	✗
MHoS-Adapter(Ours)	**50.4**	**69.2**	✗

Table 3. Ablation of components on K200 dataset

Components	Top-1 (%)
Baseline(CLIP zero-shot)	56.5
Baseline	79.4
+HS-Adapter	86.3
+HS-Adapter+Para-Adapter	**86.6**

Table 4. Location and structural ablation of HS-Adapter in the Transformer layer on the k200 dataset

Attention	STE	HoSM	MLP	STE	HoSM	Params (M)	Top-1 (%)
Attn	✓	✓	MLP	✓	✓	34.5	85.8
Attn	✓	✗	MLP	✗	✓	17.9	85.9
Attn	✗	✓	MLP	✓	✗	17.9	**86.6**

Table 5. Positional ablation of Para-Adapter in the Transformer layer on the k200 dataset

Attention	Para-Adapter	MLP	Para-Adapter	Params (M)	Top-1 (%)
Attn	✓	MLP	✓	18.3	86.0
Attn	✓	MLP	×	17.9	86.1
Attn	×	MLP	✓	17.9	**86.6**

Table 6. HS-Adapter layer ablation on the k200 dataset

Visual encoder layer K	Params (M)	Top-1 (%)
[1,2,...,12]	28.6	82.2
[2,4,6,8,10,12]	21.5	85.3
[1,3,5,7,9,11]	22.6	85.2
[1,6,12]	17.9	86.0
[4,8,12]	17.9	**86.6**
[12]	15.5	85.9
[1]	16.7	86.0

Table 7. Higher order moments ablation on k200 dataset

Higher-order moments	Top-1 (%)
[1]	86.2
[1,2]	86.0
[1,2,3]	86.1
[1,2,3,4]	86.5
[1,2,3,4,5]	86.2
[1,3,5]	**86.6**
[1,2,...,6]	86.2

5 Conclusion

MHoS-Adapter is proposed in this paper to improve CLIP's adaption to video action recognition, addressing issues in higher-order feature modeling and video temporal information mining. The HS-Adapter in the visual branch uses HoSM for higher-order statistical modeling and STE to capture intra-frame or inter-frame spatio-temporal dependencies, while the Para-Adapter in the text branch enhances label semantic understanding. The joint development of HS-Adapter and Para-Adapter improves spatio-temporal feature modeling and multimodal alignment. Experimental results show our framework performs better than the majority of baselines in terms of generalization and recognition.

References

1. Radford, A., et al.: Learning transferable visual models from natural language supervision (2021)
2. Wang, M., Xing, J., Mei, J., Liu, Y., Jiang, Y.: ActionCLIP: adapting language-image pretrained models for video action recognition. IEEE Trans. Neural Netw. Learn. Syst. 2023
3. Ni, B., et al.: Expanding language-image pretrained models for general video recognition (2022)
4. Houlsby, N.: Parameter-efficient transfer learning for NLP', arXiv e-prints/, Art. no. arXiv. 1902.00751 (2019). https://doi.org/10.48550/arXiv.1902.00751.

5. Houlsby, N.: "Parameter-Efficient Transfer Learning for NLP", arXiv e-prints. Art. no. arXiv. **00751**, 2019 (1902). https://doi.org/10.48550/arXiv.1902.00751

6. Chen, S., et al.: AdaptFormer: adapting vision transformers for scalable visual recognition (2022). https://doi.org/10.48550/arXiv.2205.13535

7. Wasim, S.T., Naseer, M., Khan, S., Khan, F.S., Shah, M.: Vita-CLIP: video and text adaptive CLIP via multimodal prompting (2023). https://doi.org/10.48550/arXiv.2304.03307.

8. Defferrard, M., Bresson, X., Vandergheynst, P.: Convolutional neural networks on graphs with fast localized spectral filtering. 10.48550/arXiv.1606.09375 (2016)

9. Lin, Z., et al.: Frozen CLIP models are efficient video learners (2022). https://doi.org/10.48550/arXiv.2208.03550

10. Pan, J., Lin, Z., Zhu, X., Shao, J., Li, H.: ST-Adapter: Parameter-efficient image-to-video transfer learning (2022). https://doi.org/10.48550/arXiv.2206.13559

11. Wang, G., Gupta,H.: Non-local neural networks (2018). https://doi.org/10.1109/CVPR.2018.00813

12. Gao, Z., Wang, Q., Zhang, B., Hu, Q., Li, P.: Temporal-attentive covariance pooling networks for video recognition. In: Advances in Neural Information Processing Systems, vol. 34, pp. 13587–13598 (2021)

13. Gao, Z., Xie, J., Wang, Q., Li, P.: Global second-order pooling convolutional networks (2018)

14. Zhang, B., Dong, W., Wang, Z., Zhang, J., Sun, Q.: Second-order transformer network for video recognition. Alexandria Eng. J. **114**, 82–94 (2025). https://doi.org/10.1016/j.aej.2024.11.067

15. Bai, S., Ma, B., Chang, H., Huang, R., Shan, S., Chen, X.: SANet: statistic attention network for video-based person re-identification. IEEE Trans. Circ. Syst. Video Technol. **32**(6), 3866–3879 (2022). https://doi.org/10.1109/TCSVT.2021.3119983

16. Liu, Z., et al.: Swin transformer, Hierarchical vision transformer using shifted windows. arXiv (2021)

17. Li, Y., Wu, C-Y., Fan, H., Mangalam, K., Xiong, B., Malik, J., Feichtenhofer, C.: MViTv2: Improved multiscale vision transformers for classification and detection (2022)

18. Wu, W., Wang, X., Luo, H., Wang, J., Yang, Y., Ouyang, W.: Bidirectional cross-modal knowledge exploration for video recognition with pre-trained vision-language models (2023)

19. Yang, T., Zhu, Y., Xie, Y., Zhang, A., Chen, C., Li, M.: AIM: Adapting Image Models For Efficient Video Action Recognition. arXiv (2023) https://doi.org/10.48550/arXiv.2302.03024.

20. Wang, M., et al.: M2-CLIP: a multimodal, multi-task adapting framework for video action recognition (2024). https://doi.org/10.48550/arXiv.2401.11649.

21. Zhou, K., Yang, J., Loy, C.C., Liu, Z.: Learning to prompt for vision-language models. Int. J. Comput. Vis. **130**(09), 2337–2348 (2022). https://doi.org/10.1007/s11263-022-01653-1

Individual Characterization
and Human-Computer Interaction

Context and Visibility-Aware Part Learning for Aerial-Ground Person Re-identification

Cang Yuan[1,4], Hongxu Chen[2], Xiaohua Xie[3], and Jianhuang Lai[1,2,3,4]($\boxtimes$)

[1] School of Computer Science and Engineering, Sun Yat-sen University,
510006 Guangzhou, China
`yuanc9@mail2.sysu.edu.cn`
[2] Guangdong Province Key Laboratory of Information Security Technology,
Sun Yat-sen University, Guangzhou 510006, China
`chenhx87@mail2.sysu.edu.cn`
[3] Key Laboratory of Machine Intelligence and Advanced Computing,
Ministry of Education, Sun Yat-sen University, Guangzhou 510006, China
`xiexiaoh6@mail.sysu.edu.cn`
[4] Pazhou Lab (Huangpu), Guangzhou, China
`stsljh@mail.sysu.edu.cn`

Abstract. Aerial-Ground Person Re-Identification (AGPReID) aims to match pedestrians from drastically different views. Part-based person re-identification methods have proven effective in capturing fine-grained details which are critical for better discrimination. However, applying part-based methods to AGPReID faces several challenges. First, the large view gap makes it difficult to properly align the feature of the parts. Second, view variation often causes some part features to be missing or invisible across views. To address these challenges, we propose a Context- and Visibility-Aware Part Learning (CVPL) framework which consists of Context-Aware Part Learning (CPL) and Visibility-Aware Part Learning (VPL). Specifically, for CPL, we observe that corresponding parts usually share similar context information. Therefore, we leverage such context to aid in the part feature extraction and alignment. Additionally, for VPL, we use the similarity values obtained during part extraction to estimate the visibility of each part, and further incorporate visibility into the training loss and part feature distance computation. Experiments on the CARGO and AG-ReID datasets demonstrate the effectiveness of our method.

Keywords: Aerial-Ground Person Re-Identification(AGPReID) · Part Feature · Context · Visibility

1 Introduction

The Aerial-Ground Person Re-identification (AGPReID) [11,12,21] aims to match images of the same individual captured from cameras with different views.

Supplementary Information The online version contains supplementary material available at https://doi.org/10.1007/978-981-95-6123-0_58.

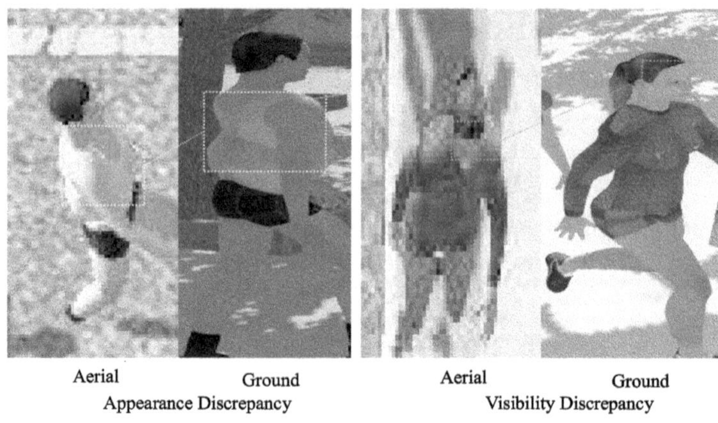

Aerial   Ground   Aerial   Ground

Appearance Discrepancy   **Visibility Discrepancy**

Fig. 1. Appearance and visibility discrepancy caused by the view discrepancy.

AGPReID remains highly challenging due to the substantial domain gap between aerial and ground views, including the appearance discrepancy and the visibility discrepancy. As shown in Fig. 1, due to the view discrepancy, the same part in the left image pair exhibits different appearance and in the right image pair, the same part is invisible in the aerial view while visible in the ground view.

Part-based methods achieve great success by extracting fine-grained features which are useful for better discrimination facing great view discrepancies. Most existing attention-based methods(SAAI [4], PAT [7], CAL [18]) adopt part prototypes to extract part features. They typically compute the similarity between learnable part prototype and pixel-wise features in the feature map to aggregate part features. However, such similarity is often calculated at the pixel level, neglecting context information. This limitation becomes critical in aerial-ground scenarios, where large view differences lead to drastic changes in appearance, making the extracted part features difficult to align reliably. In practice, we observe that the same parts not only share similar visual appearance but also exhibit similar contextual semantics. Therefore, incorporating context information can facilitate more stable and accurate part feature alignment. Moreover, due to the significant view variation between aerial and ground perspectives, some parts may be visible in one view but not the other. Blindly enforcing alignment on these invisible parts can degrade performance.

To address these challenges, we propose a Context- and Visibility-Aware Part Learning (CVPL) framework, which considers both context information and part visibility for more robust part learning. Specifically, CVPL comprises Context-Aware Part Learing (CPL) and Visibility-Aware Part Learning (VPL). For CPL, we adopt context-aware part prototypes to extract part features, specifically, when calculating similarities, we not only consider the content of the pixel-wise feature itself in the feature map, but also incorporate the context information of the pixel-wise feature. We take the neighbors and the pixel-wise feature itself in order as the context information, after transforming and concatenating it, we get the context feature and concatenate it with the pixel-wise feature as context-aware pixel-wise feature. Then we calculate similarities between context-aware part prototypes and context-aware pixel-wise features. After incorporating the context information, the extracted part features that belong to the same part are not only similar in contents, but also similar in context information, making the alignment more stably. As for VPL, we take the average of the top-k similarity values of one part as the visibility of the part. It is natural in that if one part is visible, the similarity value is high, the same holds in reverse. We employ the visibility to weight the loss, making model to focus on visible part features in the training stage. In the inference stage, we reconstruct the part distance using visibility, making the distance between shared parts dominate the part feature distance. Extensive experimental results on two aerial-to-ground datasets, CARGO and AG-ReID, suggest that our CVPL efficiently improves the part learning.

Our main contributions are summarized as follows:

- We propose a novel framework CVPL for AGPReID, addressing the misalignment and invisibility of part features caused by the view discrepancy, facilitating the part learning.
- We propose CPL to leverage the context information to establish in the part alignment and VPL to make model foucs on the visible parts.
- Extensive experimental results have shown that our CVPL is effective in part learning.

2   Related Work

2.1   Aerial-Ground Person Re-Identification

Most existing ReID methods concentrate on view-homogeneous scenarios, relying on images captured either from ground-only [1,20] or aerial-only camera networks [2,17]. In comparison, view-heterogeneous ReID, particularly aerial-ground person ReID (AGP-ReID) [11,12,21], has been less studied, mainly due to the significant view gap. To address this, Nguyen et al. [11] released an AG-ReID dataset featuring both aerial and ground views, along with an interpretable model leveraging attribute information for training. Zhang et al. [21] later introduced a larger and more comprehensive dataset, CARGO, and proposed the View-Decoupled Transformer (VDT), which disentangles pedestrian and view-related features. Nevertheless, these works neglect the importance of part features that provide fine-grained information.

2.2   Part-Based Person Re-Identification

Part-based person ReID methods extract local features from distinct body regions to improve the model's discriminative power and robustness. Existing methods can be broadly categorized into three groups: splitting-based, auxiliary-model-based, and attention-based approaches. Splitting-based methods [13,15,16] extract part features from uniformly divided horizontal stripes, which have become a strong baseline for part feature learning. However, simple divisions often suffer from poor semantic alignment due to inaccurate detections, pose variations, and occlusions. Auxiliary-model-based methods [5,8,10] utilize pre-trained models such as human parsing or pose estimation networks to obtain semantically meaningful body parts. These approaches, however, incur extra computational cost and are vulnerable to noise, especially when faced with domain shifts. Attention-based methods [4,7,18] aim to learn discriminative part features through attention mechanisms and have shown impressive performance. They usually adopt part prototypes to extract part features. Nevertheless, they are not directly applicable to AGPReID tasks, as great view discrepancy poses a significant challenge.

3 Method

3.1 Preliminaries and Problem Formulation

We denote $X = \{(x_i, y_i^{id}, y_i^{vid}) | i = 1, \ldots, N\}$ as the training dataset, where x_i is the i-th image, N is the total number of images, y_i^{id} represents the corresponding identity label, and y_i^{vid} corresponds to the view label. For one image x_i, we input it into the vision transformer which is our backbone F_v to get the global feature $f_g^i \in \mathbb{R}^c$ and feature map $f_{map}^i \in \mathbb{R}^{h \times w \times c}$,

$$f_g^i, f_t^i = F_v(x_i). \tag{1}$$

For the global feature f_g^i, we calculate the loss of identification L_{id} and the loss of the triplet L_{tri} to maintain discrimination. For the feature map f_{map}^i, we aim to extract part features from it. Most of attention-based methods adopt learnable part prototypes $P = [P_1, P_2, \ldots, P_l] \in \mathbb{R}^{l \times c}$ as references of latent semantic part features. They calculate similarities between part prototypes P and pixel-wise features $f_{m,n}^i \in \mathbb{R}^c$ in the feature map f_{map}^i, where $m \in [1, h]$ and $n \in [1, w]$ and similarities are used to aggregate pixel-wise features to form part features. However, they neglect context information and visibility of part features, making the alignment unstable and inappropriate (Fig. 2).

3.2 Context-Aware Part Learning

Different with former methods, we do not calculate the similarities between part prototypes and pixel-wise features in the feature map directly. We first transform the feature map f_{map}^i into context-aware feature map $f_{map_{ca}}^i$. Specifically, for each pixel-wise feature $f_{m,n}^i$ in the feature map f_{map}^i, we select its r neighbors and itself, supposing r is 8, to form $N_{m,n}^i = [f_{m-1,n-1}^i, \ldots, f_{m,n}^i, \ldots, f_{m+1,n+1}^i] \in \mathbb{R}^{r \times c}$ as its context information. Then, we transform $N_{m,n}^i$ with a projection $J_1 \in \mathbb{R}^{c \times s}$ and concatenate it to be the context feature $f_{m,n_c}^i \in \mathbb{R}^{(r \times s)}$. f_{m,n_c}^i

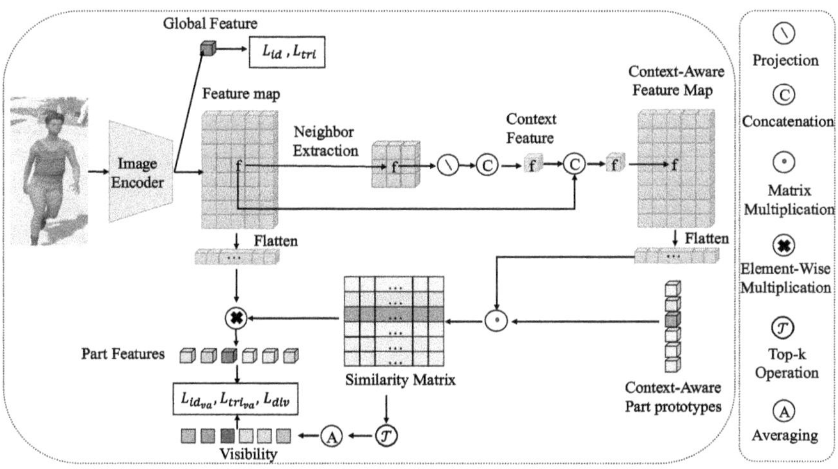

Fig. 2. The overview of our method.

is concatenated with $f^i_{m,n}$ to form the context-aware pixel-wise feature $f^i_{m,n_{ca}} \in \mathbb{R}^{c+r\times s}$, thus we get the context-aware feature map $f^i_{map_{ca}}$. Then we flatten the $f^i_{map_{ca}}$ as $T_{ca_i} = [T^1_{ca_i}, T^2_{ca_i}, ..., T^{h\times w}_{ca_i}] \in \mathbb{R}^{(h\times w)\times(c+r\times s)}$ where T^t_i represents the t-th context-aware pixel-wise feature. We calculate similarities between learnable context-aware part prototypes $P_{ca} = [P_{ca_1}, P_{ca_2}, ..., P_{ca_l}] \in \mathbb{R}^{l\times(c+r\times s)}$ and T_i to get the similarity matrix $S^i \in \mathbb{R}^{l\times(h\times w)}$. Similarly, we flatten the original feature map f^i_{map} into $T_i = [T^1_i, T^2_i, ..., T^{h\times w}_i] \in \mathbb{R}^{(h\times w)\times c}$ and S_i is used to aggregate part features $f^i_p = [f^i_{p_1}, f^i_{p_2}, ..., f^i_{p_l}] \in \mathbb{R}^{l\times c}$ from T_i as a high similarity between the pixel-wise feature and a learnable prototype suggests that the pixel likely corresponds to a specific part. The process can be expressed by the following equation:

$$S^i = \sigma(P_{ca} \odot T^\top_{ca_i}), \tag{2}$$

$$f^i_{p_j} = \frac{1}{h \times w} \sum_{z=1}^{h\times w} S^i_{j,z} \otimes T^z_i, \quad (j = 1, 2, \ldots, l) \tag{3}$$

where $\odot$ represents the matrix multiplication, σ denotes the Sigmoid activation function, $\otimes$ denotes element-wise multiplication and $S^i_{j,z}$ represents the similarity between the j-th context-aware part prototype and the z-th pixel-wise feature in the feature-map.

We employ shared prototypes P_{ca} for both the aerial and ground views. The shared prototypes enable the aggregation of part features with similar content and context information across both views into the same parts.

3.3 Visibility-Aware Part Leaning

Views discrepancy between aerial and ground will make some part features invisible across views. Aligning visible part with invisible part will lead to bias in the training stage and the inference stage. We leverage visibility to adjust the training progress and the distance between pedestrians. The visibility value for each part of the i-th image $V^i = [V_1^i, V_2^i, \ldots, V_l^i] \in \mathbb{R}^l$ can be obtained from the similarities between part prototypes and pixel-wise features. We first take the top-k values from the similarities of each part and calculate the mean values of them to obtain the visibility of each part.

$$\hat{S}_j^i = \mathcal{T}(S_j^i, k), \tag{4}$$

$$V_j^i = mean(\hat{S}_j^i), \tag{5}$$

where $\mathcal{T}$ denotes the top-k operation, k is the num of the selected elements, $mean(\cdot)$ refers to the extraction of the mean value and S_j^i denotes the j-th row of S^i.

It is natural because if one part is invisible, the similarities are low as no pixel-wise features are similar with the part prototype. For the part features, we calculate the visibility-aware id loss $L_{id_{va}}$ and triplet loss $L_{tri_{va}}$ for part features as shown in equation (6), (7), (8).

$$L_{id_{va}} = \sum_{n=1}^{l} V_n \cdot L_{id}^n(f_{p_n}), \tag{6}$$

$$L_{tri_{va}} = [D_{va}^{a,p} - D_{va}^{a,n} + \alpha]_+, \tag{7}$$

$$D_{va}^{i,j} = \frac{\sum_{n=1}^{l} V_n^i \cdot V_n^j \cdot D_n^{i,j}}{\sum_{n=1}^{l} V_n^i \cdot V_n^j}, \tag{8}$$

where L_{id}^i and V_i indicates the n-th id loss and the n-th visibility value of the n-th part feature f_{p_i}. We use the visibility to weight the $L_{id_{va}}$, guiding the model to pay more attention to visible parts. For $L_{tri_{va}}$, we use the $D_{va}^{i,j}$ to measure the visibility-aware part-feature distance of the i-th and the j-th sample. $D_n^{i,j} = \|f_{p_n}^i - f_{p_n}^j\|_2$ is the n-th part-to-part euclidean distance between two samples. By weighting the distance of each part with the visibility, the distance between visible parts constitutes the major part of the overall distance.

4   Training and Inference

Training. For training, we first apply the id loss L_{id} and triplet loss L_{tri} on the global feature f_g. As for part features, visibility-aware id loss $L_{id_{va}}$ and triplet loss $L_{tri_{va}}$ are used to ensure the discrimination of part features. As for diversity, lacking the human part annotations, we apply the diversity loss L_{div} [4] to force each prototype to extract different part features as shown in equation (9).

$$L_{div} = -\frac{2}{l(l-1)} \sum_{i=1}^{l-1} \sum_{j=i+1}^{l} \|P_{ca_i} T_{ca}^T - P_{ca_j}^T T_{ca}^T\|_2 \tag{9}$$

Table 1. A performance comparison of the leading methods is presented on the CARGO dataset and AG-ReID dataset. Rank-1 and mAP are reported (%). The best performance is shown in **bold**.

Method	Publication	CARGO								AG-ReID			
		Protocol 1: ALL		Protocol 2: G↔G		Protocol 3: A↔A		Protocol 4: A↔G		Protocol 1: A→G		Protocol 2: G→A	
		Rank-1	mAP	Rank-1	mAP	Rank-1	mAP	Rank-1	mAP	Rank-1	mAP	Rank-1	mAP
SBS [6]	ACM MM-23	50.32	43.09	72.31	62.99	67.50	49.73	31.25	29.00	73.54	59.77	73.70	62.27
PCB [14]	TPAMI-2021	51.00	44.50	74.10	67.60	55.00	44.60	34.40	30.40	–	–	–	–
BoT [9]	TMM-19	54.81	46.49	77.68	66.47	65.00	49.79	36.25	32.56	70.01	55.47	71.20	58.83
OSNet [22]	TPAMI-22	–	–	–	–	–	–	–	–	72.59	58.32	74.22	60.99
MGN [16]	ACM MM-18	54.81	49.08	83.93	71.05	65.00	52.96	31.87	33.47	–	–	–	–
AGW [19]	TPAMI-22	60.26	53.44	81.25	71.66	67.50	56.48	43.57	40.90	–	–	–	–
ViT [3]	ICLR-21	61.54	53.54	82.14	71.34	80.00	64.47	43.13	40.11	81.28	72.38	82.64	73.35
Explain [11]	ICME-23	–	–	–	–	–	–	–	–	81.47	72.61	82.85	73.39
VDT [21]	CVPR-24	64.10	55.20	82.14	71.59	82.50	66.83	48.12	42.76	82.91	74.44	86.59	78.57
Ours		**67.63**	**62.69**	**84.82**	**80.73**	**82.50**	**74.36**	**53.75**	**50.08**	**83.10**	73.95	85.24	76.45

The total loss L for training is as follows:

$$L = L_{id} + L_{tri} + \lambda_p(L_{id_{va}} + L_{tri_{va}}) + \lambda_{div}L_{div}, \tag{10}$$

where λ_p and λ_{div} are hype-parameters to balance the loss items.

Inference. For inference, we use the global feature f_g and part features $f_p = [f_{p_1}, f_{p_2}, \ldots, f_{p_l}]$ to measure the distance between pedestrians. For the i-th image and the j-th image, the distance $D^{i,j}$, shown in equation (11), consists of global-feature distance $D_g^{i,j} = \|f_g^i - f_g^j\|_2$ and visibility-aware part-feature distance $D_{va}^{i,j}$ as shown in equation (8).

$$D^{i,j} = (1 - W_p)D_g^{i,j} + W_pD_{va}^{i,j}, \tag{11}$$

where W_p is a hype-parameter to balance the distance items.

5 Experiments

5.1 Datasets and Evaluation Metrics

CARGO [21]. CARGO has gathered a total of 5,000 identities and 108,563 images from 13 cameras containing five aerial cameras and eight ground cameras, which exhibit considerable view discrepancy along with various challenges such as differences in resolution, lighting, occlusion, and more. It supports four test protocols ('ALL', 'A↔A', 'G↔G', and 'A↔G') where 'ALL' emphasizes overall retrieval performance, 'A↔A' only includes data captured from the aerial camera in the test set for evaluation, and the same applies to 'G↔G', 'A↔G'.

AG-ReID [11]. For AG-ReID, the training set consists of 11,554 images with 199 identities, while the test set contains 12,464 images with 189 identities. AG-ReID features two evaluation protocols, 'A→G', and 'G→A'.

Evaluation Metrics. We adopt the cumulative matching characteristic at Rank-1 and mean Average Precision (mAP) to evaluate our method (Table 1).

5.2   Experimental Settings

Our method is implemented using PyTorch and all experiments are conducted on a single NVIDIA RTX 3090 GPU. The backbone of our model is a Vision Transformer [16] pre-trained on ImageNet [5]. During both training and inference, input images are resized to 256×128. In the tokenization process, the patch and stride sizes are set to 16×16, with a token embedding dimension of 768. Data augmentation techniques such as random cropping, color jittering, and random erasing are applied during training. The batch size is 64, consisting of 16 identities with 4 images each. We adopt the soft version of triplet loss [19] to avoid manually tuning the margin parameter. The model is trained for 120 epochs using the Stochastic Gradient Descent (SGD) optimizer, with a cosine learning rate decay from 8×10^{-3} to 1.6×10^{-6}. The part num l is set to 6, the num of neighbors r is 6, s is 1 and k is 3. The λ_p, λ_{div} and W_p are set to 0.5. No data augmentation or re-ranking is used during inference.

5.3   Comparison with State-of-the-Art Methods

In this section, we compare our method with state-of-the-art methods on two datasets: CARGO and AG-ReID, including CNN-based (BoT [9], SBS [6], MGN [16], AGW [19]) and transformer-based methods (ViT [3]), and interpretable model Explain [11] and VDT [21]. On the CARGO dataset, our method achieves the state-of-the-art performance, reaching 67.63%/62.69% (Rank-1/mAP) under the 'ALL' protocol, and 53.75%/50.08% under the 'A↔G' protocol, outperforming another vit-based method VDT by a large margin. On the AG-ReID dataset, our method achieves a comparable result. Compared with the baseline ViT, our method achieves a great improvement.

5.4   Ablation Study

To test the effectiveness of our proposed CPL and VPL, we perform ablation studies on the CARGO and AG-ReID datasets. The 'Baseline+part' refers to extracting part features without introducing the context information and incorporating the visibility. The results are shown in Table 2.

Effectiveness of Part Features. The comparison between the 'Baseline' and 'Baseline+part' shows that incorporating part features brings great improvement. However, facing part misalignment and invisible parts caused by the great view discrepancy in the AGPReID, the potential of local features has not been fully explored.

Effectiveness of CPL. Compared with the 'Baseline+part', 'Baseline+CPL' incorporating context information for better part alignment so that part features extracted by the same part prototype not only are similar in the content, but also have similar context information, ensuring that they belong to the same part. The results shows that the context information improve the performance.

Effectiveness of VPL. VPL leverage the visibility to adjust the leaning process and the distance between pedestrians. With the visibility, the model can

Table 2. Performance comparisons under different settings on the CARGO and AG-ReID datasets. Rank-1 and mAP are reported (%).

Method	CARGO								AG-ReID			
	Protocol 1: ALL		Protocol 2: G↔G		Protocol 3: A↔A		Protocol 4: A↔G		Protocol 1: A→G		Protocol 2: G→A	
	Rank-1	mAP	Rank-1	mAP	Rank-1	mAP	Rank-1	mAP	Rank-1	mAP	Rank-1	mAP
Baseline	61.54	53.54	82.14	71.34	80.00	64.47	43.13	40.11	81.28	72.38	82.64	73.35
Baseline+part	65.38	60.66	83.04	79.82	77.50	71.58	50.00	46.83	81.89	73.93	84.20	76.12
Baseline+CPL	66.67	61.03	83.93	79.57	82.50	73.26	51.88	47.75	83.29	73.86	84.82	76.25
Baseline+VPL	67.31	61.53	83.04	78.62	85.00	74.57	53.12	48.77	82.63	73.92	85.03	76.03
CVPL	**67.63**	**62.69**	**84.82**	**80.73**	82.50	74.36	**53.75**	**50.08**	83.10	**73.95**	**85.24**	**76.45**

focus on the visible parts, avoiding the bias caused by misalignment between visible and invisible parts. Compared with the 'Baseline+part', 'Baseline+VPL' achieves better performance.

6 Conclusions

In this paper, we propose a novel framework called Context- and Visibility-Aware Part Learning (CVPL) for AGPReID. To address the misalignment caused by appearance discrepancy and visibility discrepancy we propose CPL to extract context information and VPL to incorporate visibility for more stable and appropriate alignment. Experiments on CARGO and AG-ReID datasets show that our method efficiently facilitating the part learning.

Acknowledgement. This project was supported by the National Natural Science Foundation of China (U22A2095) and the Project of Guangdong Provincial Key Laboratory of Information Security Technology (2023B1212060026).

References

1. Chen, H., Zhang, Q., Lai, J.H., Xie, X.: Unsupervised group re-identification via adaptive clustering-driven progressive learning. In: Proceedings of the AAAI Conference on Artificial Intelligence, vol. 38, pp. 1054–1062 (2024)
2. Chen, H., Zhang, Q., Xie, X., Lai, J.: Unsupervised group re-identification from aerial perspective via strategic member harmonization. Pattern Recogn. **164**, 111508 (2025)
3. Dosovitskiy, A., et al.: An image is worth 16x16 words: transformers for image recognition at scale (2021)
4. Fang, X., Yang, Y., Fu, Y.: Visible-infrared person re-identification via semantic alignment and affinity inference. In: Proceedings of the IEEE/CVF International Conference on Computer Vision, pp. 11270–11279 (2023)
5. Gao, S., Wang, J., Lu, H., Liu, Z.: Pose-guided visible part matching for occluded person ReID. In: Proceedings of the IEEE/CVF Conference on Computer Vision and Pattern Recognition, pp. 11744–11752 (2020)
6. He, L., Liao, X., Liu, W., Liu, X., Cheng, P., Mei, T.: FastReID: a PyTorch toolbox for general instance re-identification. In: Proceedings of the 31st ACM International Conference on Multimedia, pp. 9664–9667 (2023)

7. Li, Y., He, J., Zhang, T., Liu, X., Zhang, Y., Wu, F.: Diverse part discovery: occluded person re-identification with part-aware transformer. In: Proceedings of the IEEE/CVF Conference on Computer Vision and Pattern Recognition, pp. 2898–2907 (2021)
8. Lin, Y., et al.: Exploring part-informed visual-language learning for person re-identification. arXiv preprint: arXiv:2308.02738 (2023)
9. Luo, H., Gu, Y., Liao, X., Lai, S., Jiang, W.: Bag of tricks and a strong baseline for deep person re-identification. In: Proceedings of the IEEE/CVF Conference on Computer Vision and Pattern Recognition Workshops, pp. 0–0 (2019)
10. Miao, J., Wu, Y., Liu, P., Ding, Y., Yang, Y.: Pose-guided feature alignment for occluded person re-identification. In: Proceedings of the IEEE/CVF International Conference on Computer Vision, pp. 542–551 (2019)
11. Nguyen, H., Nguyen, K., Sridharan, S., Fookes, C.: Aerial-ground person Re-ID. In: 2023 IEEE International Conference on Multimedia and Expo (ICME), pp. 2585–2590. IEEE (2023)
12. Nguyen, H., Nguyen, K., Sridharan, S., Fookes, C.: AG-ReID. v2: bridging aerial and ground views for person re-identification. IEEE Trans. Inf. Forensics Secur. **19**, 2896–2908 (2024)
13. Sun, Y., et al.: Perceive where to focus: learning visibility-aware part-level features for partial person re-identification. In: Proceedings of the IEEE/CVF Conference on Computer Vision and Pattern Recognition, pp. 393–402 (2019)
14. Sun, Y., Zheng, L., Li, Y., Yang, Y., Tian, Q., Wang, S.: Learning part-based convolutional features for person re-identification. IEEE Trans. Pattern Anal. Mach. Intell. **43**(3), 902–917 (2019)
15. Sun, Y., Zheng, L., Yang, Y., Tian, Q., Wang, S.: Beyond part models: person retrieval with refined part pooling (and a strong convolutional baseline). In: Proceedings of the European conference on computer vision (ECCV), pp. 480–496 (2018)
16. Wang, G., Yuan, Y., Chen, X., Li, J., Zhou, X.: Learning discriminative features with multiple granularities for person re-identification. In: Proceedings of the 26th ACM International Conference on Multimedia, pp. 274–282 (2018)
17. Wang, L., Zhang, Q., Qiu, J., Lai, J.: Rotation exploration transformer for aerial person re-identification. In: 2024 IEEE International Conference on Multimedia and Expo (ICME), pp. 1–6. IEEE (2024)
18. Wu, J., Liu, H., Su, Y., Shi, W., Tang, H.: Learning concordant attention via target-aware alignment for visible-infrared person re-identification. In: Proceedings of the IEEE/CVF International Conference on Computer Vision, pp. 11122–11131 (2023)
19. Ye, M., Shen, J., Lin, G., Xiang, T., Shao, L., Hoi, S.C.: Deep learning for person re-identification: a survey and outlook. IEEE Trans. Pattern Anal. Mach. Intell. **44**(6), 2872–2893 (2021)
20. Zhang, Q., Lai, J., Feng, Z., Xie, X.: Uncertainty modeling for group re-identification. Int. J. Comput. Vision **132**(8), 3046–3066 (2024)
21. Zhang, Q., Wang, L., Patel, V.M., Xie, X., Lai, J.: View-decoupled transformer for person re-identification under aerial-ground camera network. In: Proceedings of the IEEE/CVF Conference on Computer Vision and Pattern Recognition, pp. 22000–22009 (2024)
22. Zhou, K., Yang, Y., Cavallaro, A., Xiang, T.: Learning generalisable omni-scale representations for person re-identification. IEEE Trans. Pattern Anal. Mach. Intell. **44**(9), 5056–5069 (2021)

Adversarial Attack and Proactive Defense

Adversarial Prompt Increment for Robust Vision-Language Models

Zhouchen Yang and Zhongchen Ma[✉]

School of Computer Science and Communication Engineering, Jiangsu University, Zhenjiang, China
zhongchen_ma@ujs.edu.cn

Abstract. Pre-trained visual language models (VLMs) like CLIP excel at cross-modal reasoning but remain vulnerable to adversarial attacks. This paper introduces Adversarial Prompt Increment (API) learning to enhance VLMs' adversarial robustness. Our approach starts with a base prompt (P_{base}) optimized on clean data, then adds an adversarially trained residual vector (ΔP) to form a robust prompt: $P_{\text{robust}} = P_{\text{base}} + \Delta P$. This design allows ΔP to counter adversarial perturbations while P_{base} preserves semantic integrity, achieving robustness without extensive parameter training or architectural changes. To enhance generalization, we use dynamic parameter tuning by varying perturbation budgets during training. Experiments on 8 benchmark datasets show that our approach improves clean accuracy by +1.64% and adversarial robustness by +1.42% over baselines under PGD attacks ($\varepsilon = 4/255$), with notable effectiveness also demonstrated at ($\varepsilon = 1/255$).

Keywords: Vision-Language Models · Adversarial Robustness · Prompt Adaptation

1 Introduction

Vision-language models such as CLIP [1] and ALIGN [2] have emerged as important components of multimodal AI, demonstrating strong capabilities across various tasks. These models leverage the relationship between visual and textual modalities through contrastive learning to help bridge the semantic gap between images and natural language descriptions. However, despite their impressive performance, VLMs have been shown to be susceptible to adversarial examples—imperceptible perturbations to the visual or textual inputs that can lead to incorrect predictions.

Current adversarial defense strategies for VLMs predominantly adopt model-centric approaches that fine-tune billions of parameters with fixed perturbations [3,4]. These methods tend to be computationally intensive, and their optimization for specific attack patterns may limit effectiveness against diverse adversarial threats. To address these challenges, we propose a parameter-efficient prompt-centric defense that operates within the prompt embedding space.

© The Author(s), under exclusive license to Springer Nature Singapore Pte Ltd. 2026
W. Jia et al. (Eds.): CCBR 2025, LNCS 16360, pp. 643–652, 2026.
https://doi.org/10.1007/978-981-95-6123-0_59

Our approach is motivated by two key observations from recent literature: (1) textual prompts can serve as efficient update targets for modifying model behavior with minimal parameter changes; and (2) prompt-based methods show varying robustness characteristics under different configurations [4]. Based on these insights, we introduce **A**dversarial **P**rompt **I**ncrement (API), which augments a base prompt (P_{base}) optimized on clean data with an adversarially trained residual vector (ΔP), forming $P_{\mathrm{robust}} = P_{\mathrm{base}} + \Delta P$. By delegating perturbation defense to ΔP while P_{base} preserves semantics, this design achieves robustness without major parameter or architectural changes. To enhance generalization to different attack scenarios, we implement a dynamic parameterization approach during training, where attack configurations vary within controlled ranges to improve robustness across multiple attack patterns (see Fig. 1). Our contributions are as follows:

- We propose the Adversarial Prompt Increment mechanism, which aims to improve prompt robustness through learnable residual augmentation while maintaining semantic consistency.
- We develop a dynamic parameterization strategy to enhance defense generalization against varying attack strengths by exposing the model to different perturbation budgets during training.
- Experiments on eight benchmark datasets demonstrate that API can achieve an improved balance between clean accuracy and adversarial robustness compared to existing prompt-based defenses.

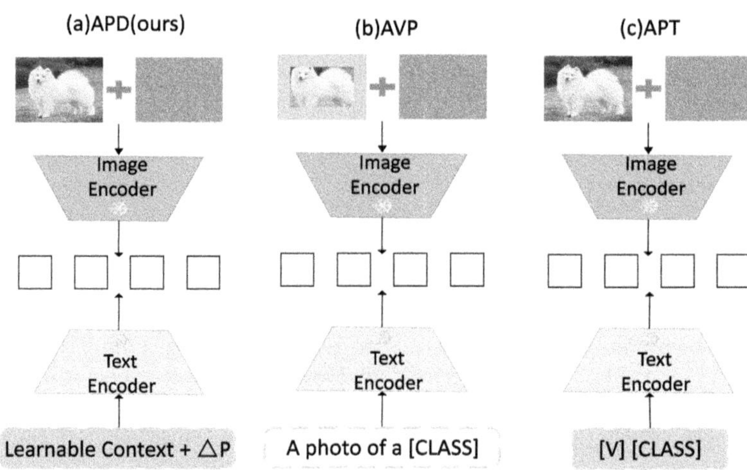

Fig. 1. High-level architecture comparison of our methods Adversarial Prompt Increment (API), Adversarial Visual Prompt (AVP), and Adversarial Prompt Fine-Tuning (APT). Learnable parameters are highlighted in yellow. (Color figure online)

2 Related Work

2.1 Prompt Learning for Vision-Language Models

Contextual Optimization (CoOp) [5] introduces learnable continuous context vectors to replace hand-crafted prompts, achieving superior performance while optimizing only a small number of parameters in CLIP. CoCoOp [6] extends this approach by conditioning the prompts on the input image, leading to better generalization, while Visual Prompt Tuning (VPT) [7] introduces learnable visual cues. However, recent studies have suggested that prompt-based methods can be particularly vulnerable to adversarial attacks [3], with different prompt configurations exhibiting varying robustness characteristics. This sensitivity highlights the need for parameter-efficient defense mechanisms specifically designed for prompt-based VLMs.

2.2 Adversarial Training for Vision-Language Models

Adversarial training for vision-language models introduces complexity due to their multimodal nature, requiring consideration of perturbations in both visual and textual domains. Standard approaches like PGD-based adversarial training [8] have been adapted to VLMs but often require extensive parameter updates throughout the model. Effective VLM adversarial training requires careful balancing of perturbations across modalities to avoid performance degradation [9]. The computational complexity increases as generating adversarial examples requires simultaneous optimization of image pixels and text embeddings. Additionally, most existing methods employ fixed perturbation budgets during training, potentially limiting their generalization to diverse attack strengths. These limitations motivate our exploration of parameter-efficient prompt-centric defenses with dynamic training strategies.

3 Methodology

3.1 Preliminaries

CLIP employs dual encoders to compute image features $z_v^i = f(x_i; \theta_v)$ and text features $z_t^j = f(t_j; \theta_t)$, with classification based on cosine similarity.

CoOp revolutionizes prompt engineering by learning continuous context vectors to replace hand-crafted prompts. Instead of using discrete text templates like "a photo of a [CLASS]", CoOp parameterizes the prompt context as learnable vectors $\mathbf{v}_1, \mathbf{v}_2, \ldots, \mathbf{v}_M$ in the embedding space:

$$t_j = [\mathbf{v}_1][\mathbf{v}_2]\ldots[\mathbf{v}_M][C_j] \tag{1}$$

where $[C_j]$ represents the class embedding. This achieves remarkable parameter efficiency by optimizing only prompt-related parameters while freezing the backbone encoders (θ_v and θ_t).

However, adversarial attacks against VLMs exploit this dependency on text prompts. The goal is to find a perturbation δ_i that maximizes the classification loss, conditioned on a specific prompt t':

$$\arg \max_{|\delta_i|_p \leq \epsilon} L(x_i + \delta_i, t', y_i; \theta_v, \theta_t) \tag{2}$$

Here, t' can be any prompt, including the learnable vectors from CoOp. Recent studies [4] have found that VLMs' robustness is highly sensitive to the choice of t': attack strength varies greatly with different prompt choices, lowest robustness occurs when attack and inference prompts match, and simple prompt changes can substantially alter worst-case robustness. These findings show that traditional CoOp, while effective for clean performance, lacks inherent robustness against adversarial perturbations and motivates our adaptive defense to address these prompt-specific vulnerabilities.

3.2   Adversarial Prompt Increment Learning

Our core insight is that standard context vectors P_{base} learn rich semantic knowledge on clean data but lack robustness against adversarial perturbations. Therefore, we introduce a learnable adversarial prompt increment ΔP, which aims to inject defensive capabilities into prompts without compromising the original semantic knowledge (see Fig. 2).

Our method consists of two stages. First, we train the base context vectors $P_{\text{base}} = [v_1, v_2, \ldots, v_M]$ on clean data following the standard CoOp protocol. Specifically, we initialize these context vectors according to CoOp's initialization strategy and optimize them using the cross-entropy loss on the clean dataset $D_{\text{clean}} = \{(x_i, y_i)\}_{i=1}^{N}$:

$$\mathcal{L}_1 = \mathbb{E}_{(x,y) \sim \mathcal{D}_{\text{clean}}}[\mathcal{L}_{\text{CE}}(f(x, P_{\text{base}}), y)] \tag{3}$$

During this stage, only the context vectors are updated while keeping both the image encoder θ_v and text encoder θ_t frozen. We train with the same hyperparameters as specified in CoOp to obtain the optimized P_{base}, which captures high-quality semantic knowledge for clean data classification.

Subsequently, the method enters the adversarial training stage. In the adversarial training stage, for each clean sample $(x_i, y_i) \in D_{\text{clean}}$, we generate a corresponding adversarial image $x_{i,\text{adv}}$. Parallel to this process on the image side, on the text side, we introduce an increment vector ΔP with the same dimensionality as P_{base}. Formally, ΔP is defined as:

$$\Delta P = [\Delta p_1, \Delta p_2, \ldots, \Delta p_M] \tag{4}$$

where each $\Delta p_i \in \mathbb{R}^d$ has the same dimensionality as v_i in P_{base}, and d is the feature dimension. To ensure training stability and learning from the original semantics, ΔP is initialized to zero. The final robust prompt P_{robust} is constructed through element-wise addition and concatenated with class embeddings $[C_j]$:

$$P_{\text{robust}} = [v_1 + \Delta p_1][v_2 + \Delta p_2] \ldots [v_M + \Delta p_M][C_j] \tag{5}$$

Crucially, during the adversarial training process, we simultaneously update both P_{base} and ΔP through backpropagation. This joint optimization design enables P_{base} to undergo fine-tuning while maintaining core semantics, while ΔP focuses more on learning defensive patterns against adversarial perturbations. The two components complement each other, jointly constituting a complete prompt that is both accurate and robust.

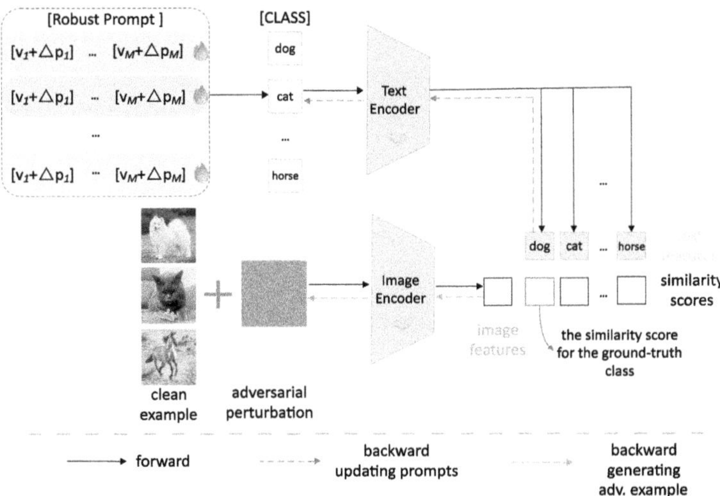

Fig. 2. Overview of the proposed Adversarial Prompt Increment (API) defense framework for CLIP-like VLMs. The method introduces learnable residual vectors ΔP to enhance contextual prompts against adversarial perturbations, while keeping both image and text encoders frozen.

3.3   Dynamic Parameter Modulation Strategy

Traditional adversarial training uses fixed attack parameters, causing models to overfit to specific attack configurations. We propose dynamic parameter modulation that introduces controlled stochasticity during training to prevent overfitting to fixed attack patterns and expose the model to diverse threat intensities.

As shown in Algorithm 1, we apply dynamic random scaling to the base attack parameters at each training iteration. This stochastic modulation improves defense generalization across different attack strengths and enhances transferability to unseen attack methods while maintaining computational efficiency.

3.4   Loss Function for Robust Prompt Optimization

The core objective of our Adversarial Prompt Increment (API) learning is to train a prompt that is resilient to adversarial attacks while maintaining high

---

Algorithm 1. Adversarial Prompt Increment (API) Learning

Require: Dataset $\mathcal{D}$, ε_{base}, α_{base}, steps K, learning rate lr
1: Initialize and train P_{base} on clean data $\mathcal{D}$ following CoOp protocol to optimize $\mathcal{L}_1$
2: Initialize $\Delta P = 0$
3: **for** $(x, y) \in \mathcal{D}$ **do**
4:     $\varepsilon = \varepsilon_{base} \times (1 + 0.1 \times \mathcal{U}(-1, 1))$ ▷ Dynamic perturbation budget
5:     $\alpha = \alpha_{base} \times (1 + 0.1 \times \mathcal{U}(-1, 1))$ ▷ Dynamic step size
6:     $\delta = \mathcal{U}(-\varepsilon, \varepsilon)$ ▷ Adversarial attack generation
7:     **for** $k = 1$ to K **do**
8:         $P_{\text{robust}} = P_{\text{base}} + \Delta P$
9:         $\delta = \text{Clip}(\delta - \alpha \cdot \text{Sign}(\nabla_\delta \mathcal{L}_{CE}(f(x + \delta, P_{\text{robust}}), y)), -\varepsilon, \varepsilon)$
10:     **end for**
11:     $P_{\text{robust}} = P_{\text{base}} + \Delta P$ ▷ Robust prompt learning
12:     $\mathcal{L}_{adv} = \mathcal{L}_{CE}(f(x + \delta, P_{\text{robust}}), y)$
13:     $P_{\text{base}} = P_{\text{base}} - lr \cdot \nabla_{P_{\text{base}}} \mathcal{L}_{adv}$ ▷ Joint optimization of P_{base} and ΔP
14:     $\Delta P = \Delta P - lr \cdot \nabla_{\Delta P} \mathcal{L}_{adv}$
15: **end for**
16: $P_{\text{robust}} = P_{\text{base}} + \Delta P$
17: **return** P_{robust}

---

accuracy on clean data. This is achieved by optimizing the prompt parameters using a carefully defined loss function within an adversarial training paradigm. Our goal is to minimize the classification error on adversarially perturbed images.

For a given input image x and a set of K classes, the Vision-Language Model computes the similarity scores between the image embedding and the text embeddings for each class prompt. The probability of the image belonging to class j is calculated via a softmax function over these similarity scores:

$$p(y = j | x, P) = \frac{\exp(\text{sim}(f_v(x), f_t(P, C_j))/\tau)}{\sum_{k=1}^{K} \exp(\text{sim}(f_v(x), f_t(P, C_k))/\tau)} \tag{6}$$

where f_v and f_t are the image and text encoders, $\text{sim}(\cdot, \cdot)$ denotes the cosine similarity, (P, C_j) represents the full prompt for class j, and τ is a temperature parameter.

Our method enhances robustness by following the min-max formulation of adversarial training. The objective is to find a robust prompt, P_{robust}, that minimizes the cross-entropy loss under worst-case adversarial perturbations. Therefore, the adversarial loss $\mathcal{L}_{\text{adv}}$ is defined by optimizing the prompt against these challenging examples:

$$\mathcal{L}_{\text{adv}} = \mathbb{E}_{(x,y) \sim \mathcal{D}_{\text{clean}}} [\mathcal{L}_{\text{CE}}(p(y | x_{\text{adv}}, P_{\text{robust}}), y)] \tag{7}$$

4   Experiments

Datasets and Evaluation Protocol. We conduct our study mainly on 8 high-resolution vision datasets: Pets [10], Flowers [11], ImageNet [12], Food [13], SUN [14], DTD [15], EuroSAT [16], and UCF [17]. For training on each dataset, we use a few-shot protocol where N samples per class are randomly selected from the official training set. N can be 1, 4, 16, or "all", where "all" means the entire training set is used. Due to space constraints, the main results presented in this paper are based on $N=16$ samples per class, which represents a balanced few-shot learning scenario that demonstrates the effectiveness of our method across different domains. For ImageNet, due to computational constraints, we use 100 samples per class instead of the full training set when $N=$ "all". Regardless of the training data scheme used, all methods are evaluated on the entire test set.

Model Architecture. We use the standard CLIP ViT-B/32 [18] pre-trained weights as our image encoder backbone, following common practice in prompt learning literature [5]. We compare our method, API, against several representative baselines: Hand-Engineered Prompts (HEP) [1], which is the standard zero-shot CLIP setting that uses manually crafted text prompts such as "a photo of a [CLASS]" and serves as a fundamental baseline without any prompt learning; Adversarial Visual Prompt (AVP) [19], which is a defense method that learns a small, universal adversarial perturbation to add to images, effectively creating a "visual prompt" to enhance robustness; and Adversarial Prompt Tuning (APT) [20], which is a strong baseline that directly fine-tunes the entire learnable prompt context on adversarial examples, similar to standard adversarial training in the prompt space.

Adversarial Training and Evaluation. We use the torchattacks library and adopt PGD attack for adversarial robustness evaluation. For PGD attack generation, we use 10 steps with step size $\alpha = \varepsilon/4$, following standard practices. During training, we use the same configuration to generate adversarial examples. To assess performance across different threat levels, we evaluate all methods under multiple perturbation budgets, primarily $\varepsilon = 4/255$ and $\varepsilon = 1/255$, following Croce et al. [21].

4.1   Main Results and Analysis

We compare API with baseline methods under both $\varepsilon = 4/255$ and $\varepsilon = 1/255$ PGD attacks. As shown in Tables 1 and 2, our method consistently achieves a superior balance between clean and robust accuracy. Under the attack ($\varepsilon = 4/255$), API outperforms the best baseline (APT) in robust accuracy across all 8 datasets while maintaining highly competitive clean accuracy. This advantage is preserved under the attack ($\varepsilon = 1/255$), where API again demonstrates state-of-the-art performance. This highlights the effectiveness of our method in generalizing defense across different attack intensities.

Table 1. Performance comparison on 8 benchmark vision datasets. HEP refers to Hand-Engineered Prompts using the default CLIP template. The context length $M = 16$, $\varepsilon = 4/255$. The **best** and <u>second best</u> results are highlighted under each metric.

		Flowers	Pets	Food	SUN	DTD	EuroSAT	UCF	ImageNet
HEP [1]	Clean	30.09	62.14	21.53	32.06	26.12	20.08	36.06	39.10
	PGD	9.50	14.75	3.05	6.42	12.48	8.45	6.13	10.50
AVP [19]	Clean	31.11	61.15	20.83	32.56	24.11	19.09	35.65	39.11
	PGD	11.32	15.28	3.20	6.50	11.73	7.33	6.50	11.25
APT [20]	Clean	**70.60**	<u>66.17</u>	**28.95**	<u>43.57</u>	**45.44**	<u>43.79</u>	<u>50.14</u>	<u>40.99</u>
	PGD	<u>31.26</u>	<u>21.17</u>	<u>8.24</u>	<u>10.50</u>	<u>19.62</u>	<u>23.91</u>	<u>16.07</u>	<u>12.13</u>
API	Clean	<u>70.40</u>	**67.10**	<u>28.38</u>	**44.34**	<u>45.09</u>	**55.51**	**50.96**	**41.05**
	PGD	**32.93**	**22.98**	**8.35**	**11.38**	**21.82**	**27.95**	**16.57**	**12.34**

Table 2. Performance comparison under a weaker perturbation budget ($\varepsilon = 1/255$). The context length $M = 16$. The **best** and <u>second best</u> results are highlighted under each metric.

		Flowers	Pets	Food	SUN	DTD	EuroSAT	UCF	ImageNet
HEP [1]	Clean	48.84	75.43	44.67	46.85	32.47	22.56	47.96	55.29
	PGD	32.19	59.72	25.14	35.29	25.83	15.34	34.73	38.76
AVP [19]	Clean	49.67	75.18	43.38	46.17	21.19	24.91	46.82	56.41
	PGD	33.25	59.91	26.82	36.44	22.72	18.25	35.15	39.53
APT [20]	Clean	<u>84.36</u>	<u>85.09</u>	**56.00**	<u>62.03</u>	**57.21**	<u>64.25</u>	<u>68.78</u>	<u>58.16</u>
	PGD	<u>69.58</u>	<u>68.60</u>	<u>34.24</u>	<u>42.07</u>	<u>41.66</u>	<u>44.66</u>	<u>50.06</u>	<u>40.80</u>
API	Clean	**85.58**	**85.20**	<u>55.65</u>	**62.13**	<u>56.26</u>	**68.81**	**68.99**	**58.21**
	PGD	**70.97**	**68.92**	**34.49**	**42.17**	**41.67**	**46.51**	**50.69**	**41.17**

4.2   Ablation Study and Analysis

To validate the effectiveness of our dynamic parameter modulation strategy, we conduct an ablation study comparing it against training with a fixed perturbation budget. As shown in Table 3, using a dynamic budget (based on $\varepsilon = 4/255$) improves the average robust accuracy by $+0.67\%$ across the eight datasets compared to using a fixed budget, with a negligible impact on clean accuracy. This demonstrates that exposing the model to varied threat intensities during training effectively prevents overfitting to a specific attack configuration and enhances generalization.

Table 3. We present the key findings from our ablation experiments, comparing the defensive performance of fixed and dynamic perturbation budget training strategies on eight benchmark datasets.

ε		Flowers	Pets	Food	SUN	DTD	EuroSAT	UCF	ImageNet
4/255	Clean	70.42	68.54	28.17	44.08	45.32	48.19	50.10	41.14
	PGD	31.32	21.64	8.23	11.07	20.57	27.40	16.46	12.25
Dynamic ε (based on 4/255)	Clean	71.40	67.10	29.38	44.34	46.09	55.51	50.96	41.05
	PGD	32.93	22.98	8.35	11.38	21.82	27.95	16.57	12.34

5   Conclusion

This work addresses the critical challenge of adversarial robustness in VLMs by developing a parameter-efficient, adaptive prompt-based defense mechanism. To tackle the common trade-off between robustness and accuracy, our proposed API method employs a functional decoupling design. It leverages a base prompt (P_{base}) as a strong semantic anchor, which is then synergistically fine-tuned with a learnable residual vector (ΔP) to specifically counter adversarial perturbations. Furthermore, to enhance generalization against diverse threats, we introduce a dynamic parameter modulation strategy that exposes the model to varying attack strengths during training. Extensive experiments validate that our parameter-efficient API method achieves a superior balance between adversarial robustness and clean accuracy, proving its effectiveness across different attack intensities and in few-shot scenarios. While this work demonstrates strong performance against PGD-based attacks, we acknowledge that comprehensive robustness evaluation requires assessment against diverse attack types. Future research should validate API's resilience against more sophisticated adaptive attacks, such as AutoAttack and multimodal attacks targeting both visual and textual modalities simultaneously, to further establish its practical reliability.

Acknowledgements. This work was supported in part by the National Natural Science Foundation of China (NSFC) under the Grant No. 62006098 and the Fellowship of China Postdoctoral Science Foundation under the Grant No. 2020M681515.

References

1. Radford, A., et al.: Learning transferable visual models from natural language supervision. In: International Conference on Machine Learning, pp. 8748–8763. PMLR (2021)
2. Jia, C., et al.: Scaling up visual and vision-language representation learning with noisy text supervision. In: International Conference on Machine Learning, pp. 4904–4916. PMLR (2021)
3. Mao, C., Geng, S., Yang, J., Wang, X., Vondrick, C.: Understanding zero-shot adversarial robustness for large-scale models. arXiv preprint: arXiv:2212.07016 (2022)

4. Zhang, J., et al.: Adversarial prompt tuning for vision-language models. In: European Conference on Computer Vision, pp. 56–72. Springer (2024)
5. Zhou, K., Yang, J., Loy, C.C., Liu, Z.: Learning to prompt for vision-language models. Int. J. Comput. Vision **130**(9), 2337–2348 (2022)
6. Zhou, K., Yang, J., Loy, C.C., Liu, Z.: Conditional prompt learning for vision-language models. In: Proceedings of the IEEE/CVF Conference on Computer Vision and Pattern Recognition, pp. 16816–16825 (2022)
7. Jia, M., et al.: Visual prompt tuning. In: European Conference o Computer Vision, pp. 709–727. Springer (2022)
8. Madry, A., Makelov, A., Schmidt, L., Tsipras, D., Vladu, A.: Towards deep learning models resistant to adversarial attacks. arXiv preprint: arXiv:1706.06083 (2017)
9. Wu, J., Gan, W., Chen, Z., Wan, S., Yu, P.S.: Multimodal large language models: a survey. In: 2023 IEEE International Conference on Big Data (BigData), pp. 2247–2256. IEEE (2023)
10. Parkhi, O.M., Vedaldi, A., Zisserman, A., Jawahar, C.: Cats and dogs. In: 2012 IEEE Conference on Computer Vision and Pattern Recognition, pp. 3498–3505. IEEE (2012)
11. Nilsback, M.E., Zisserman, A.: Automated flower classification over a large number of classes. In: 2008 Sixth Indian Conference on Computer Vision, Graphics & Image Processing, pp. 3498–3505. IEEE (2008)
12. Deng, J., Dong, W., Socher, R., Li, L.J., Li, K., Fei-Fei, L.: ImageNet: a largescale hierarchical image database. In: 2009 IEEE Conference on Computer Vision and Pattern Recognition, pp. 248–255. IEEE (2009)
13. Bossard, L., Guillaumin, M., Van Gool, L.: Food-101–mining discriminative components with random forests. In: Computer vision–ECCV 2014: 13th European Conference, Zurich, Switzerland, 6–12 September 2014, Proceedings, Part VI 13, pp. 446–461. Springer (2014)
14. Xiao, J., Hays, J., Ehinger, K.A., Oliva, A., Torralba, A.: Sun database: large-scale scene recognition from abbey to zoo. In: 2010 IEEE Computer Society Conference on Computer Vision and Pattern Recognition, pp. 3485–3492. IEEE (2010)
15. Cimpoi, M., Maji, S., Kokkinos, I., Mohamed, S., Vedaldi, A.: Describing textures in the wild. In: Proceedings of the IEEE Conference on Computer Vision and Pattern Recognition, pp. 3606–3613 (2014)
16. Helber, P., Bischke, B., Dengel, A., Borth, D.: EuroSAT: a novel dataset and deep learning benchmark for land use and land cover classification. IEEE J. Sel. Top. Appl. Earth Observations Remote Sens. **12**(7), 2217–2226 (2019)
17. Soomro, K., Zamir, A.R., Shah, M.: UCF101: a dataset of 101 human actions classes from videos in the wild. arXiv preprint: arXiv:1212.0402 (2012)
18. Dosovitskiy, A., et al.: An image is worth 16x16 words: transformers for image recognition at scale. arXiv preprint: arXiv:2010.11929 (2020)
19. Chen, A., Lorenz, P., Yao, Y., Chen, P.Y., Liu, S.: Visual prompting for adversarial robustness. In: ICASSP 2023-2023 IEEE International Conference on Acoustics, Speech and Signal Processing (ICASSP), pp. 1–5. IEEE (2023)
20. Li, L., Guan, H., Qiu, J., Spratling, M.: One prompt word is enough to boost adversarial robustness for pre-trained vision-language models. In: Proceedings of the IEEE/CVF Conference on Computer Vision and Pattern Recognition, pp. 24408–24419. (2024)
21. Croce, F., Hein, M.: Reliable evaluation of adversarial robustness with an ensemble of diverse parameter-free attacks. In: International Conference On Machine Learning, pp. 2206–2216. PMLR (2020)

Template Protection and Cryptosystems

A Highly Secure Biometric Template Protection Method Based on Householder Matrices and Absolute Value Equation Transform

Naiquan Wang, Linkai Niu, Ce Gao, and Heng Zhao$^{(\boxtimes)}$

School of Life Science and Technology, Xidian University, Xi'an 710071, China
hengzhao@mail.xidian.edu.cn

Abstract. With the widespread adoption of biometric recognition technology, the protection of biometric templates has become crucial for safeguarding user biometric data. However, while protection methods based on random projection can effectively preserve matching performance, they are vulnerable to the reconstruction of original biometric features when multiple projected templates are compromised. To address this issue, a cancellable template protection method, termed Householder-AVET, which is based on Householder matrices and the Absolute Value Equation Transform. It leverages the precise similarity-preserving property of Householder matrices to overcome the matching performance deficiencies inherent in AVET methods that rely on Gaussian random projection. This design allows the key advantage of AVET-its irreversibility-to be fully exploited. Experimental results demonstrate that the proposed Householder-AVET achieves matching performance superior to the conventional AVET on both face and fingerprint databases. Furthermore, it completely surpasses methods that employ random projection on the challenging FVC2004 fingerprint database, highlighting the algorithm's excellent matching performance and robustness.

Keywords: Householder Matrix · Absolute Value Transformation · Revocable Biometric Template Protection

1 Introduction

Biometric recognition technology has been widely adopted due to its significant convenience, but it has also significantly increased the risk of biometric information leakage. Therefore, Biometric Template Protection (BTP) has become an urgent and essential security measure. A revocable biometric template protection method needs to satisfy the following four characteristics: Revocability, Irreversibility, Unlinkability, and Performance Preservation. Currently, the random mapping method supported by the Johnson-Lindenstrauss lemma [1] is widely applied in most revocable biometric template protection methods due to its excellent similarity-preserving properties. However, when multiple templates and their corresponding projection matrices are simultaneously exposed, the original biometric features can be reconstructed. Therefore, methods employing random mapping suffer from the issue of original biometric feature leakage

W. Jia et al. (Eds.): CCBR 2025, LNCS 16360, pp. 655–662, 2026.
https://doi.org/10.1007/978-981-95-6123-0_60

[2]. In response to the aforementioned issues, this paper proposes the Householder-AVET revocable template protection method, which can transform original fixed-length features into highly secure and accurate transformed templates, effectively addressing the reversibility problem inherent in template protection methods based on random mapping.

The main contributions of this paper are as follows: The introduction of Householder matrices preserves the distance relationships among original biometric features post-transformation, thereby effectively enhancing the matching accuracy of the transformed templates. By integrating the irreversible property of the AVET transformation, the irreversibility of the revocable templates is significantly enhanced. Experiments conducted on face and fingerprint databases indicate that the proposed method achieves different modality versatility and offers a favorable trade-off between security and matching performance.

2 Related Works

With the advancement of biometric recognition technology, biometric template protection techniques based on feature transformation have witnessed rapid development. Ratha et al. [3] first proposed the concept of revocable biometric template protection. Jin et al. [4] first proposed the BioHashing template protection method based on random mapping. This method generates a random vector using a built-in random seed and performs iterative inner products with the biometric feature vector to ultimately produce a binary template. However, when an attacker steals the user's random vector, the security of the system will be significantly compromised. Jin et al. [5] proposed the Index of Max Hashing (IoM Hashing), which can effectively conceal biometric information and enhance feature robustness. However, this method is susceptible to similarity attacks [6]. Li et al. [7] introduced the One-Permutation Hashing (OPH) method, which generates fixed-length binary feature templates and can be combined with fuzzy commitment systems to further enhance template security. In another work, Li et al. [8] designed the Indexing-Min-Max Hashing (IMM Hashing) method. This demonstrates only slight, or even improved, matching accuracy after transformation. However, both of these methods exhibit certain limitations in fault tolerance when applied to fingerprint databases with poor image quality. Gao et al. [9] proposed generating revocable binary face templates based on partial Walsh matrices and the Simhash. However, this method lacks different modality versatility. Dang et al. [2] addressed the reversibility issue in random mapping by proposing an Absolute Value Equations Transform (AVET) method. It maps the original feature vector to another region through a nonlinear transformation function, thereby eliminating the reversible security risks associated with random projections. Although the AVET method has achieved remarkable improvements in security, its suboptimal recognition performance necessitates careful consideration of the trade-off between security and accuracy.

3 Proposed Method

The Householder-AVET template protection method offers a favorable trade-off between security and matching performance by leveraging the irreversibility of the AVET transform and utilizing the superior biometric feature preservation capability of Householder matrices.

3.1 Householder Matrix

The Householder matrix, also known as the reflection matrix, is capable of mapping any vector to its symmetric counterpart with respect to a certain hyperplane and has extensive applications in high-dimensional data processing [10]. Moreover, unlike the probabilistic preservation of geometric properties in Gaussian matrix projection, the Householder matrix can precisely control the target subspace onto which a vector is projected, thereby accurately preserving the geometric properties of the projected vector and ultimately enhancing the matching performance of the template protection method. The method for generating the Householder matrix used in this paper can produce square matrices of arbitrary size (Fig. 1).

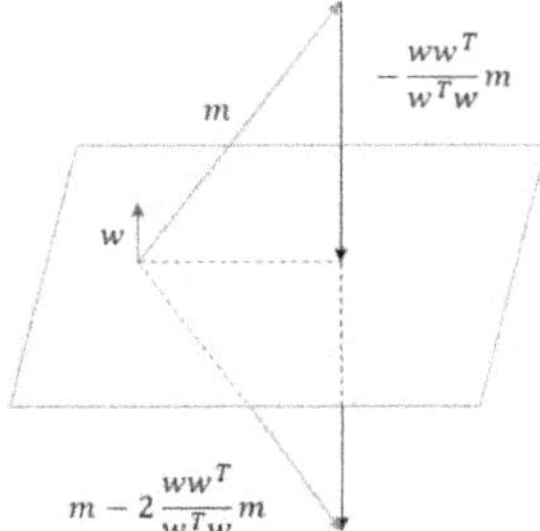

Fig. 1. Schematic diagram of mirror transformation

The specific implementation process is as follows: First, a random vector m of dimension n is randomly generated (the dimension of this vector determines the size of the matrix to be generated), and the norm $||m||$ of the random vector m is calculated. Simultaneously, a standard basis vector e of the same dimension as vector m is randomly generated. The plane normal vector w is constructed using the formula $w = m + G(m_1)||m||e$, where $G(m_1)$ denotes taking the sign of the first element of the random vector m, thereby determining the direction of the plane normal vector. Once the plane normal vector w is selected, the Householder matrix is rapidly constructed using formula (1). The final generated Householder matrix is of size $n \times n$. In Sect. 3.2, this Householder matrix generation method will be employed to produce matrices of various sizes to meet the projection requirements of original feature vectors of different dimensions.

$$H = I - 2\frac{ww^T}{w^Tw} \tag{1}$$

3.2 Householder-AVET

The Householder-AVET method proposed is based on the Absolute Value Equations Transform (AVET) formula presented in reference [2]:

$$X = A \cdot u + B \cdot |R \cdot v| \tag{2}$$

Here, matrices A, B, and R are all generated using the Householder matrix generation method introduced in Sect. 3.1, with the same size but different internal elements. Furthermore, templates are revocable, as these matrices are deterministically generated from a user-specific secret key, allowing re-issuance by changing the key. In this equation, following the AVET framework for maximizing non-linear security, the original feature vectors $x \in \mathbb{R}^n$ is split into two halves, $u \in \mathbb{R}^{n/2}$ and $v \in \mathbb{R}^{n/2}$. The vector X then represents the transformed feature. Figure 2 presents a simplified schematic diagram of the fixed-length feature extraction methods for face and fingerprint used in this paper, as well as the Householder-AVET transformation process. In the experimental section (Sect. 4.1), a performance comparison are conducted between Householder-AVET and AVET.

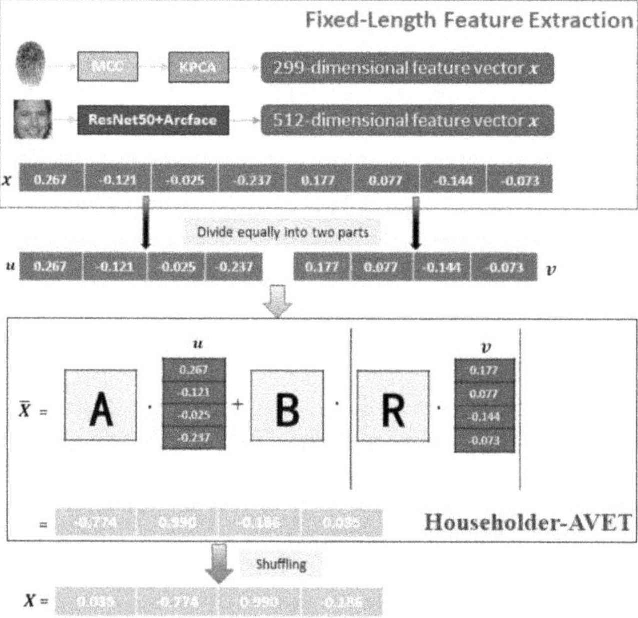

Fig. 2. The purple-boxed area illustrates the extraction process of fixed-length feature vectors for face and fingerprint, while the black-boxed area demonstrates the simplified transformation process of Householder-AVET.

4 Experiments

In the experiments of this paper, the FVC matching protocol was uniformly adopted for both the face database and the fingerprint database. For face images, the LFW database (with 127 individuals, each having 12 images) [11], the Color FERET database (with 154 individuals, each having 12 images, hereinafter abbreviated as FERET) [12], and the FEI database (with 200 individuals, each having 14 images) [13] were utilized. The Arcface [14] deep neural network model for face image recognition was employed, and the MS-Celeb-1M database [15] was used for pre-training. The pre-trained model was then applied to extract face features from the images in the databases used for the matching experiments, generating 512-dimensional feature vectors. For fingerprint images, the FVC2002 (DB1-DB3) [16] and FVC2004 (DB1-DB3) [17] databases from fingerprint recognition competitions were used. A 299-dimensional fixed-length feature vector for fingerprints was generated by combining the fingerprint MCC feature descriptor [18] with the KPCA algorithm [19].

4.1 Matching Performance Analysis

Table 1 presents the matching performance of different template protection methods on face and fingerprint databases (where the last column indicates whether the template generation method addresses the reversibility issue of random mapping). The Householder-AVET aims to resolve the reversibility problem of random projection. It employs a nonlinear transformation by equally dividing the original biometric features to achieve the irreversibility of random projection transformation.

Table 1. Comparison of EER (%) among Different Template Protection Methods

Method	LFW	FERET	FEI	FVC2002			FVC2004			Reversibility Addressed
				DB1	DB2	DB3	DB1	DB2	DB3	
Baseline	0.73	0.05	0.51	0.20	0.19	2.30	4.70	3.13	2.80	NO
IoM [5]	0.83	0.15	0.82	0.22	0.47	3.07	4.74	4.10	3.99	NO
OPH [7]	0.95	0.12	0.92	0.19	0.51	3.44	1.49	3.80	4.15	NO
IMM [8]	0.96	0.12	1.05	**0.09**	**0.23**	3.02	1.99	3.89	3.90	NO
Simhash [9]	**0.75**	**0.08**	**0.70**	0.31	0.81	4.02	2.01	3.63	3.91	NO
AVET [2]	1.19	0.37	1.46	0.20	0.51	**2.35**	2.28	4.77	3.42	YES
Householder-AVET	0.94	0.11	1.02	0.10	0.40	2.41	**0.71**	**3.40**	**3.20**	YES

Consequently, in terms of matching performance, there is a slight disparity compared to methods [5, 7–9] that utilize the complete feature vector for linear random projection on certain databases, and it has comparable performance, especially on FVC2004. Meanwhile, compared to the AVET, which also addresses the reversibility issue of random projection, the Householder-AVET achieves significantly better matching performance on both face and fingerprint databases. This is because it utilizes the Householder matrix, which can better preserve the biometric features before and after transformation compared to the Gaussian matrix. Therefore, the Householder-AVET provides effective performance enhancement and is capable of different modal application.

4.2 Analysis of Security and Template Protection Characteristics

Irreversibility Analysis. Irreversibility refers to the inability of attackers to restore the original biometric information by analyzing or reversely deducing the transformed biometric template. The inverse solution of the absolute value equation transformation is an NP-hard problem, ensuring that attackers cannot infer the original biometric feature information from the transformed features. Additionally, the method employs a shuffling algorithm to randomly permute the real-valued features after transformation, effectively disrupting the biometric features that have undergone the absolute value equation transformation.

Brute Force Attack Analysis. The Householder-AVET template protection method converts fixed-length face features into 256-dimensional real-valued protected templates and fixed-length fingerprint features into 149-dimensional real-valued protected templates. Given that these values are real numbers, and assuming each digit can take on k possible values, the complexity of a brute-force attack would be k^{256}, which is computationally infeasible. Therefore, the possibility of a successful Brute force attack on the protected templates is virtually 0. Taking FVC2002DB1 as an example, with a maximum real value of 0.10 and a minimum real value of $-$ 0.07, if an attacker guesses that each element can take on 17 possible values, the complexity of guessing a 149 $-$ dimensional protected template would be 17^{149}, which is computationally impossible to achieve. Hence, the Householder-AVET exhibits strong resistance to Brute force attack.

Revocability Analysis. In the experiment, 100 different sets of matrices A, B, and R were randomly generated for each image in the FERET face and FVC2002DB1 fingerprint databases to construct 100 protected templates. These "mated-imposter" templates were then matched against genuine and imposter users. Figure 3 show the score distributions for mated-imposter, genuine, and imposter matching. As shown, the distribution of mated-imposter scores largely overlaps with that of imposter scores, while the distribution of genuine scores shows a significant deviation from these two. Therefore, the Householder-AVET method satisfies the revocability criterion.

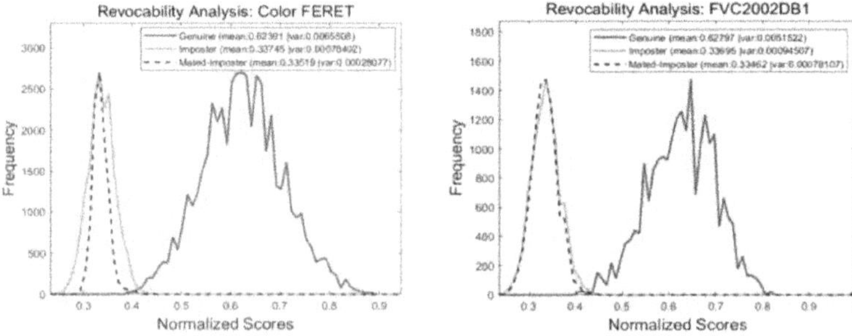

Fig. 3. Experimental results on revocability for the face database and the fingerprint database

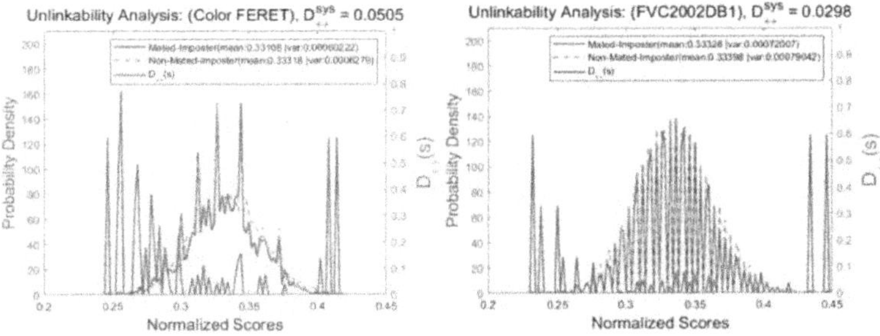

Fig. 4. Experimental results on unlinkability for the face database and the fingerprint database

Unlinkability Analysis. In the experiment, this paper adopts the methodology of Gomez-Barrero et al. [20]. This approach introduces two metrics—a global measure $D_{\leftrightarrow}^{sys}$ and a local measure $D_{\leftrightarrow}(s)$—derived from mated-imposter and non-mated imposter scores. The closer the global measure $D_{\leftrightarrow}^{sys}$ is to 0, the stronger the method's unlinkability. Figure 4 illustrates a significant overlap between the mated-imposter and non-mated imposter score distributions for both the FERET face and FVC2002DB1 fingerprint databases. The resulting global measure $D_{\leftrightarrow}^{sys}$ values are 0.0505 and 0.0298, respectively. Thus, the Householder-AVET meets the unlinkability requirement.

5   Conclusion

The Householder matrix is capable of mapping any vector to its symmetric counterpart with respect to a certain hyperplane and accurately preserving the geometric properties of the projected vector. The Householder-AVET template protection offers enhanced security compared to methods based on random projection, and it achieves comparable matching performance on face and fingerprint database. Moreover, it exhibits superior performance compared to the AVET method. The experimental section provides a detailed analysis of the algorithm's irreversibility, revocability, unlinkability, and resistance to Brute force attack. These analyses confirm that the Householder-AVET achieves a favorable trade-off between security and recognition accuracy. Additionally, the Householder-AVET offers versatility, allowing it to conveniently replace existing methods that utilize random projection transformations in practical applications, thereby enhancing the security of the system.

References

1. Dasgupta, S., Gupta, A.: An elementary proof of a theorem of Johnson and Lindenstrauss. Random Struct. Algor. **22**(1), 60–65 (2003)
2. Dang, T.M., Nguyen, T.D., Hoang, T., Kim, H., Teoh, A.B.J., Choi, D.: AVET: a novel transform function to improve cancellable biometrics security. IEEE Trans. Inf. Forensics Secur. **18**, 758–772 (2023)
3. Ratha, N.K., Connell, J.H., Boll, R.M.: Enhancing security and privacy in biometrics-based authentication systems. IBM Syst. J. **40**(3), 614–634 (2001)

4. Jin, A.T.B., et al.: BioHashing: two factor authentication featuring fingerprint data and tokenised random number. Pattern Recogn. **37**(11), 2245–2255 (2004)

5. Jin, Z., Hwang, J.Y., Lai, Y.-L., Kim, S., Teoh, A.B.J.: Ranking-based locality sensitive hashing-enabled cancelable biometrics: index-of-max hashing. IEEE Trans. Inf. Forensics Secur. **13**(2), 393–407 (2017)

6. Dong, X., Jin, Z., Teoh, A.B.J., et al.: On the reliability of cancelable biometrics: revisit the irreversibility. arXiv preprint arXiv:1910.07770 (2019)

7. Li, Y., Zhao, H., Cao, Z., Liu, E., Pang, L.: Compact and cancelable fingerprint binary codes generation via one permutation hashing. IEEE Signal Process. Lett. **28**, 738–742 (2021)

8. Li, Y., Pang, L., Zhao, H., Cao, Z., Liu, E., Tian, J.: Indexing-min–max hashing: relaxing the security-performance tradeoff for cancelable fingerprint templates. IEEE Trans. Syst. **52**(10), 6314–6325 (2022)

9. Gao, C., Zhang, K., Wang, W., et al.: Protected face templates generation based on multiple partial Walsh transformations and Simhash. IEEE Trans. Inf. Forensics Secur. **19**, 4100–4113 (2024)

10. Sangwine, S.J., Le, B.N.: Quaternion singular value decomposition based on bidiagonalization to a real or complex matrix using quaternion Householder transformations. Appl. Math. Comput. **182**(1), 727–738 (2006)

11. Huang, G.B., Ramesh, M., Berg, T., et al.: Labeled faces in the wild: a database for studying face recognition in unconstrained environments. Workshop on faces in 'Real-Life' Images: detection, alignment, and recognition (2008)

12. Phillips, P.J., Moon, H., Rizvi, S.A., et al.: The FERET evaluation methodology for face recognition algorithms. IEEE Trans. Pattern Anal. Mach. Intell. **22**(10), 1090–1104 (2000)

13. Thomaz, C.E., Giraldi, G.A.: A new ranking method for principal components analysis and its application to face image analysis. Image Vis. Comput. **28**(6), 902–913 (2010)

14. Deng, J., Guo, J., Xue, N., et al.: Arcface: additive angular margin loss for deep face recognition. Proceedings of the IEEE/CVF Conference on Computer Vision and Pattern Recognition, pp.4690–4699 (2019)

15. Guo, Y., Zhang, L., Hu, H., et al: MS-Celeb-1M: a dataset and benchmark for large-scale face recognition. 14th European Conference, Amsterdam, The Netherlands, Proceedings, Part III 14, pp. 87–102. Springer, Heidelberg (2016)

16. Maio, D., Maltoni, D., et al.: FVC2002: Second fingerprint verification competition. 2002 International conference on pattern recognition. IEEE, pp.811–814(2002)

17. Maio, D., et al.: FVC2004: third fingerprint verification competition. In: International Conference on Biometric Authentication. pp. 1–7. Springer, Heidelberg (2004)

18. Cappelli, R., Ferrara, M., et al.: Minutia cylinder-code: a new representation and matching technique for fingerprint recognition. IEEE Trans. Pattern Anal. Mach. Intell. **32**(12), 2128–2141 (2010)

19. Jin, Z., Lim, M.H., Teoh, A.B.J., et al.: Generating fixed-length representation from minutiae using kernel methods for fingerprint authentication. IEEE Trans. Syst. Man Cybern. Syst. **46**(10), 1415–1428 (2016)

20. Gomez-Barrero, M., et al.: General framework to evaluate unlinkability in biometric template protection systems. IEEE Trans. Inf. Forensics Secur. **13**(6), 1406–1420 (2018)

Datasets, Evaluation, Benchmarking, Performance Modelling and Prediction

Study on the Construction of a Biometric Database of Parasites in Cattle and Sheep

Huikai Qin[1], Xiangqing Sui[1], Yongqi Sui[2], Liangliang Liu[2]([✉]), and Longxian Zhang[1]([✉])

[1] College of Veterinary Medicine, Henan Agricultural University, Zhengzhou 450046, People's Republic of China
zhanglx8999@henau.edu.cn
[2] College of Information and Management Science, Henan Agricultural University, Zhengzhou 450046, People's Republic of China
liangliu@henau.edu.cn

Abstract. Cattle and sheep farming play a pivotal role in agricultural economies, yet parasitic diseases significantly impede industry development. Traditional manual diagnostic methods suffer from low efficiency and subjectivity. While art ificial intelligence (AI) based detection shows promise, its advancement is constrained by limited data availability. This study aims to integrate microscopic images, morphological characteristics and genomic data of bovine and sheep parasites, and establish a multimodal biometric database of bovine and sheep parasites. Standardized protocols were implemented to collect blood, fecal, and ectoparasite samples. Expert teams conducted cross-validated annotations following unified protocols to ensure data integrity. The database system, developed based on MySQL, comprises a structural design, a user front-end module, and an administrator back-end module. This database provides comprehensive data support for AI model development and validation, promising enhanced efficiency and accuracy in parasitic disease detection, which facilitates the healthy development of the animal husbandry industry.

Keywords: Parasites · Database · Microscopic images · Genome · Artificial intelligence

1 Introduction

In recent years, the cattle and sheep farming industry has become a crucial pillar of the agricultural economy. Data from 2024 shows that beef and mutton consumption accounted for 18.7% of total meat consumption [1]. However, parasitic diseases in cattle and sheep have emerged as a key bottleneck constraining the further development of this industry, causing significant economic losses and posing public health risks [2]. Epidemiological investigations reveal that the incidence of parasitic infections commonly exceeds 40% in large-scale cattle and sheep farms across China [3]. Traditional methods for detecting parasites in livestock suffer from numerous limitations, including high

W. Jia et al. (Eds.): CCBR 2025, LNCS 16360, pp. 665–675, 2026.
https://doi.org/10.1007/978-981-95-6123-0_61

technical expertise requirements, poor reproducibility, inability to perform rapid and simple on-site nucleic acid testing, and susceptibility to cross-reactivity. These drawbacks hinder their widespread adoption on farms [4–6]. With the rapid advancement of Artificial Intelligence, particularly the revolutionary capabilities of Deep Learning in processing diverse data types, more accurate, rapid, cost-effective, and intelligent solutions for pathogen detection are now emerging [7].

Deep learning methods based on parasitic microscopic images have demonstrated promising efficacy in screening, diagnosing, and quantitatively assessing parasitic diseases [8, 9]. However, the effectiveness of deep learning is highly dependent on the scale and quality of training data, which constitute the core foundation of AI-powered parasitic diagnosis. Currently, the development of parasitic image databases, both domestically and internationally, remains in its nascent stages. Commonly used datasets for parasitic detection include: ICIP 2022 Challenge: Detection and Classification of Parasitic Eggs in Microscopy Images (https://icip2022challenge.piclab.ai/) and The Eimeria Image Database for Eimeria detection (http://www.coccidia.icb.usp.br/imagedb/). Nevertheless, these datasets suffer from small sample sizes and insufficient diversity and representativeness. Within China, data sources are predominantly limited to small-scale, self-constructed datasets. Crucially, there is a lack of cross-institutional and cross-regional data-sharing mechanisms, resulting in datasets with pronounced regional-specific characteristics. Furthermore, no industry-consensus data annotation standards have been established. Significant discrepancies exist among research teams regarding key dimensions such as morphological identification criteria for eggs and taxonomic hierarchy systems. These inconsistencies directly limit the generalization capabilities of trained models when applied across different scenarios, rendering the resulting diagnostic models lacking in universality and practical utility [10, 11].

Based on current research needs, this study will establish a large-scale, diverse, and high-quality multimodal biometric database of livestock parasites. This resource will provide comprehensive and multidimensional data to support the development and validation of AI models and products for parasite screening, diagnosis, and quantitative assessment.

2 Sample Collection and Processing

To comprehensively assess parasitic infections in livestock within the farm, blood samples, fecal samples, and ectoparasite samples were collected from cattle and sheep. The samples were immediately placed in pre-labeled sterile sealed bags, with simultaneous recording of key information including collection time, animal ID, and clinical symptoms.

During the sample collection phase, the diversity and representativeness of standard data sources must be considered. At least five representative large-scale cattle and sheep farms from different regions should be selected. Sampling should be conducted using a stratified random sampling method based on the total population and distribution of animals within each farm. This ensures samples cover animals across different age groups and genders. Detailed records must include the breed, age group, identification number, collection time, and clinical symptoms of each sampled animal [12].

2.1 Blood Sample Processing

Freshly collected anticoagulated bovine and ovine blood samples were placed in centrifuge tubes. Separation was performed using centrifugation: Centrifuge parameters were set to 3000 rpm at room temperature (approximately 25 °C) for 15 min. After centrifugation, the sample was used for subsequent smear preparation. During blood smear preparation, an appropriate volume of the sample was placed at one end of a clean glass slide. A clean-edged slide was then used to prepare a uniformly thick blood film using standard techniques [13]. After allowing the smears to air-dry completely, modified Giemsa staining was performed. Before staining, the blood smears were fixed with absolute methanol for 5 min. Following fixation, freshly prepared 10% Giemsa working solution was applied to cover the blood film and allowed to stain at room temperature under light-protected conditions for 30 min. After staining, the slides were gently rinsed by directing a stream of phosphate-buffered saline (PBS, pH 7.0–7.2) or distilled water across the back and edges of the slide to remove excess stain, avoiding direct flow over the blood film surface. The stained slides were then vertically air-dried in a dust-free environment.

2.2 Fecal Sample Processing

Freshly collected cattle and sheep fecal samples were processed for parasite egg or oocyst enrichment using the saturated sucrose solution flotation method. Approximately 2 g of feces per sample was thoroughly mixed with an appropriate volume of saturated sucrose solution in a centrifuge tube. The mixture was filtered through double-layered gauze or a sieve to remove coarse debris. The filtrate was then transferred to a specialized flotation tube or a narrow-mouthed container. Saturated sucrose solution was slowly added along the tube wall until a convex meniscus formed. The sample was allowed to stand for 15–20 min. Following enrichment, a clean 18 × 18 mm coverslip was gently touched to the surface film of the enriched solution. This film was then completely transferred onto a glass slide pre-prepared with a small drop of distilled water or 50% glycerol solution [4]. To aid identification, 1% Lugol's iodine solution was applied to the edge of the coverslip for staining, allowing the iodine to seep into the sample area.

2.3 Ectoparasite Sample Processing

Collected samples of ectoparasitic ticks and mites are first subjected to preliminary morphological observation and identification under a stereomicroscope. To preserve specimen integrity and facilitate examination, individual ticks/mites are carefully transferred onto clean glass slides or transparent Petri dishes. To prevent desiccation and shrinkage, which can obscure the observation of fine structures, a small volume of distilled water or a 50–70% glycerin aqueous solution is applied around or onto the specimen surface. Maintaining a suitable humidified environment, key taxonomic identification features-such as the mouthparts, scutum, spiracular plates, anal groove, leg segments, and setal arrangements-are clearly and meticulously observed, photographed, and documented. This utilizes the stereomicroscope's three-dimensional imaging capabilities and adjustable illumination (e.g., oblique lighting, transmitted light) in conjunction with objectives of varying magnifications. The identification process adheres to established morphological taxonomic keys for ticks and mites [14].

Regarding sample handling, strict quality control of samples and careful attention to technical procedures are essential during specific operations. Standardized reagents and consumables should be employed to minimize batch-to-batch variation and ensure the quality of subsequent imaging. Regarding instrumentation, primary considerations include the manufacturer and model of the equipment, as well as the various imaging parameters available on the same instrument. The microscopy equipment includes a Zeiss Axio Observer inverted fluorescence microscope system and an Olympus upright microscope.

3   Construct a Dataset

Multimodal data enables more comprehensive and precise analysis and interpretation by integrating information from diverse sources. This study integrates microscopic image data, morphological data, and genomic data of parasites to establish a standardized multimodal dataset.

3.1   Microscopic Image Data

Microscopic images of parasite eggs were acquired using a Zeiss Axio Observer inverted fluorescence microscope system operating in bright-field imaging mode. To balance species identification accuracy with clinical application requirements, a dual-magnification imaging strategy was employed at $200 \times$ ($20 \times$ objective/$10 \times$ eyepiece) and $400 \times$ ($40 \times$ objective/$10 \times$ eyepiece) to obtain high-resolution microscopic image data. As shown in Fig. 1, representative microscopic images of common ruminant parasites are presented, forming the basis of the constructed Ruminant Parasite Microscopic Image Dataset. The current database contains 12,000 parasite microscopic images.

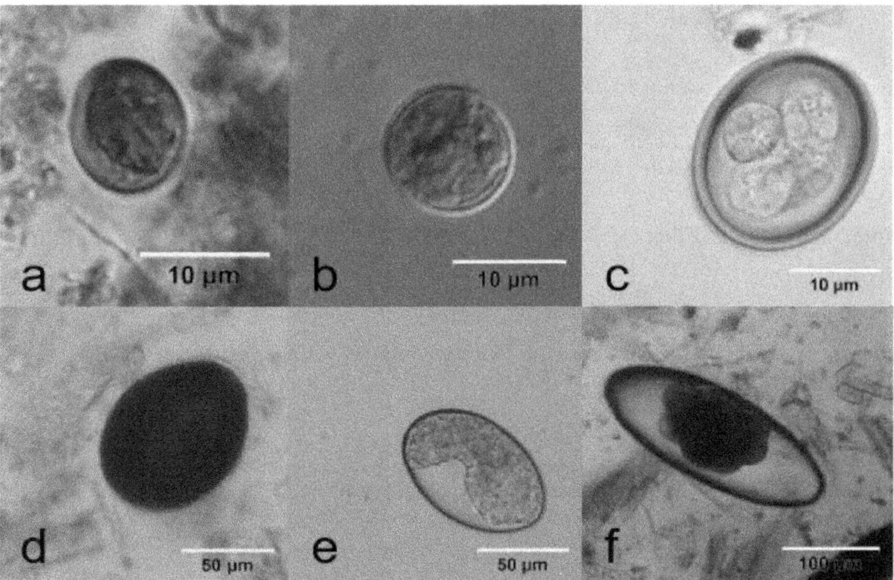

Fig. 1. Microscopic image data of selected common parasites in cattle and sheep a: *Giardia duodenalis*; b: *Entamoeba histolytica*; c, d: *Eimeria spp.*; e: *Strongyloides ova*; f: *Nematodirus spp.*

3.2 Morphological Data

In this study, in addition to utilizing traditional microscopic image data, we engaged two experts in animal parasitology to provide detailed morphological descriptions for each parasite specimen. This aimed to generate precisely corresponding morphological information. These descriptions comprehensively cover fundamental characteristics such as parasite size, shape, color, internal structural composition, structure of mouthparts, leg morphology, and location of genital openings, among other fundamental features. Concurrently, we systematically correlated these morphological characteristics with clinical diagnostic information and corresponding drug treatment regimens. This integration provides richer and more practical data support for subsequent research and practical applications. Specific details of these correlations can be found in Table 1. Currently, the database contains 12,000 entries of morphological descriptions derived from parasite microscopic images.

Table 1. Extract quantitative indicator data of parasites

Text Data	Remarks			
Parasite Type	☐ Helminth	☐ Protozoan	☐ Arthropod	
Developmental Stage	☐ Adult	☐ Larval stage	☐ Egg	
Morphology	☐ Elliptical	☐ Ovoid	☐ Flattened	☐ Fusiform
Size (μm)	-			
Common Host	☐ Cattle	☐ Sheep		
Site of Parasitism	☐ Body surface	☐ Internal tissues	☐ Bloodstream	
Pathogenic Potential	☐ Strong	☐ Weak	☐ None	
Clinical Symptoms	☐ Gastrointestinal dysfunction	☐ Developmental impairment	☐ Periodic fever	☐ allergy
Prevention & Treatment	-			

3.3 Genomic Data

Genomic data holds transformative significance in animal parasitology research. It reveals the biological characteristics, evolutionary relationships, pathogenic mechanisms, and key targets for control of parasites at the molecular level, driving multifaceted breakthroughs in both research and application. Consequently, corresponding genetic data have also been incorporated into this database. We acquired the omics data through a multi-source bioinformatics database federated retrieval strategy. Whole-genome sequencing data for parasites were downloaded from the NCBI GenBank database (https://www.ncbi.nlm.nih.gov/), RNA-seq transcriptome data were obtained from the NCBI SRA database, and validated protein sequence data with clearly defined functions were extracted from the UniProtKB/Swiss-Prot database. All collected omics data are stored in text files (.txt format). As shown in Fig. 2 (depicting the *Cryptosporidium gp60* sequence) [15], this sequence can be used to identify *Cryptosporidium* subtypes, thereby providing robust support for parasitic vaccine research. Currently, the database contains 9000 genomic datasets for parasites.

> *Cryptosporidium parvum* glycoprotein (*gp60*) gene, partial cds

CTGTTGTCTGTTGAGGGTTCATCAGTCATCATCATCATCATCATCATCATCATCATCATCA
TCGTCATCATCATCATCATCAACATCGACTGTAGCACCAACTCCAAAGAAAGAAAGAAC
TGGAGAGGAAGTAGGTAATCCAGGTTCTGAAGGTCAGGACGGTAAAGGAGACACTGA
AGAAACAGAAGACAATCAGACCGAGAGTACTGTTTCTCAAAATACTCCAGCTCAAACT
GAAGGCACAACTACCGAAACCACAGAAGCTGCTCCAAAGAAAGAGTGCGGTACTTCA
TTTGTTATGTGGTTCGGAGAGGGTGTTCCAGTTGCATCTTTGAAGTGTGGCGACTATACT
ATGGTCTATGCACCAGAAAAGGACAAAACAGATCCCGCACCAAGATATATCTCTGGTGA
AGTTACATCTGTAACCTTTGAAAAACAAGAGAGCACAGTTACAATCAAGGTTAATAATG
TAGAGTTCAGCACTCTTTCTACTAGCTCAAGTAGTCCAACTGAAAATAGCGCATCTGCA
GGTCAGGTTCCATCAAGATCAAGAAGATCACTCTCAGAGGAGGCTAGTGAAACTGCAA
CCGTCGATTTGTTTGCCTTCACCCTTGATGGTGGTAAAAGAATTGAAGTTGCTGTACCA
AGCGACGAAGATGCATCTAAAAGAAACCAGTACAGTTTGGTTGCAGACGATAAACCTT
TCTATACCGGCTCAAATAGCGGCGCCACTGATGGCATCTTCAGGTTGAATGAGGACGGA
GACTTGGATGACAAGGACAACAAAGTTCTTTTGAAGATGTGTGTTCTC

Fig. 2. The nucleotide sequence of the Cryptosporidium gp60 gene (830 bp)

3.4 Data Labeling

We engaged two experienced parasitologists from our team to annotate the micro-scopic images. Both annotators possess extensive taxonomic knowledge of parasites and demonstrated proficiency in microscopic morphological identification capabilities. Before annotation, we established detailed annotation standards for parasite microscopic images. These standards encompass specifications for labeling parasite species, morpho-logical characteristics (size, shape, color, structure), and pathological features, ensuring annotation consistency and accuracy. Following the established standards, both experts independently annotated the parasites using the VOTT annotation software (https://git hub.com/microsoft/VoTT). The resulting annotations underwent a double-blind cross-review process. A randomly selected subset of 30% of the samples was subjected to inter-annotator consistency validation, achieving a Kappa coefficient of ≥ 0.85. Sub-sequently, the two experts conducted a comprehensive review to verify the accuracy, completeness, and compliance of the annotations with the predefined standards. Any identified issues during the review were promptly communicated back to the annota-tors for necessary revisions and refinements, thereby ensuring the overall quality of the annotated dataset.

4 Database System Development

4.1 Front-End System Design and Implementation

The system frontend utilizes Vue.js 3.4 as the core development framework, integrated with the Vite 6.0 build tool, significantly enhancing both development and compila-tion efficiency. Through component-based and modular design, the system architecture achieves greater clarity, facilitating functional extensibility and long-term maintainability. For interface construction, the Element Plus UI component library is implemented, enabling rich interactive elements and responsive design. This ensures a consistent and optimal user experience (UX) across diverse terminal devices.

Regarding frontend-backend data interaction, Axios is employed to uniformly encapsulate the network request module, guaranteeing communication consistency. To achieve centralized state management and efficient inter-component communication, the system integrates the Pinia state management library. Concurrently, Vue Router enables dynamic route control and lazy loading, optimizing page rendering performance. For style management, SCSS is adopted in conjunction with the BEM (Block, Element, Modifier) naming convention, enhancing the structural organization and reusability of stylesheets. Within the data presentation layer, ECharts is utilized to construct multi-dimensional data visualizations. These visualizations provide intuitive insights into system data characteristics, supporting rapid analysis and decision-making.

4.2   Backend System Design and Implementation

The backend service system is developed using the Java programming language, built upon the Spring Boot 2.7.0 framework, and adopts a RESTful architectural style. It comprehensively supports core functional modules, including user authentication, access control, data management, and log monitoring. Employing a modular and decoupled architecture design significantly enhances system scalability (supporting ≥ 50 concurrent requests) and maintainability (achieving an average fault recovery time of < 15 min). For security mechanisms, the system integrates Spring Security to implement fine-grained access control. This is combined with JSON Web Tokens (JWT) to enable stateless user authentication, ensuring secure system communication and flexible access control.

At the data layer, the system employs MyBatis-Plus to simplify database access logic and enhance database operation efficiency. MySQL serves as the primary data storage, integrated with Druid to provide high-performance data source management and runtime monitoring. Redis is utilized for caching frequently accessed (hotspot) data and distributed session management, thereby boosting system responsiveness and concurrent processing capabilities. To further strengthen platform security and practicality, the system implements email notifications via Spring Mail, captcha validation using Easy-Captcha, and password strength enforcement leveraging Passay.

Regarding system monitoring, the backend incorporates a dedicated logging module that records critical behavioral information such as user operation logs and login audit trails. Concurrently, real-time server health monitoring is achieved through integration with the OSHI library. The overall backend architecture exhibits a well-organized structure and comprehensive functionality, enabling stable support for diverse frontend operations and efficient handling of high-concurrency data requests.

4.3   Database Structure Design and Implementation

The persistence management of backend data in this system employs MySQL 8.0 as the core Relational Database Management System (RDBMS) solution. It fully leverages MySQL 8.0's functional advantages, including its transaction processing capabilities, full-text indexing support, and JSON data type handling, thereby providing a robust foundation for the multi-dimensional storage and efficient retrieval of parasitological data. The interface of the database management is shown in Fig. 3.

Fig. 3. Database Management Interface

The database schema is centered around parasitological information, encompassing core thematic domains such as host data, parasite characteristics, omics data, and diagnostic, preventive, and therapeutic information. This structure constitutes a comprehensive data support framework. Relationships between different entities are established through primary-foreign key associations, composite indexes, and junction tables, effectively supporting requirements for complex queries and aggregate analyses.

Furthermore, the database schema incorporates predefined extensible fields at the database level to accommodate future functional expansions, such as the integration of model prediction results, recording of image storage paths, and multi-language annotations. In practical operation, the database ensures data security, stability, and sustainable evolvability through strategies including master-slave replication, regular backups, and slow query analysis. These measures provide a solid data infrastructure foundation for the system's overall stable operation and long-term maintenance.

4.4 Operation and Maintenance

The system was deployed and operates within Tencent Cloud server instances, utilizing CentOS 7.6 as the operating system. The website employs a frontend-backend separation deployment architecture. The frontend, built using Vite, is compiled into static files and hosted on an Nginx server to provide external access. The backend, developed with Spring Boot, is packaged as an executable JAR file running as a background service process. Nginx is configured to handle routing between the frontend and backend, load optimization, and HTTPS support, thereby enhancing system security and response performance.

In terms of continuous integration and automated deployment, the system was integrated with the Alibaba Cloud CloudEffect platform. Combined with the Git version control tool, an automated CI/CD pipeline was established: Upon code commit to the remote repository, the CloudEffect platform automatically triggers build and deployment tasks. This process completes source code compilation, testing, packaging, and remote deployment, significantly reducing the need for manual intervention and the potential for deployment errors. Consequently, this enhances both the efficiency of system iteration and the quality of releases.

5 Conclusion

This study establishes a multimodal biometric parasite database for cattle and sheep, providing comprehensive and multidimensional data resources for developing and validating artificial intelligence models and products. This progress will contribute to the advancement of artificial intelligence-assisted research on parasitic diseases in livestock, enhance the efficiency and accuracy of parasitic detection, and support the sustainable development of the cattle and sheep breeding industry.

References

1. Ryan, U.M., Feng, Y., Fayer, R., Xiao, L.: Taxonomy and molecular epidemiology of Cryptosporidium and Giardia - a 50 years perspective (1971–2021). Int. J. Parasitol **51**(13–14), 1099–1119 (2021)
2. Burke, J.M., Miller, J.E.: Sustainable approaches to parasite control in ruminant livestock. The veterinary clinics of North America. Food Anim. Pract. **36**(1), 89–107 (2020)
3. Zhao, Q., et al.: Cryptosporidium spp. in large-scale sheep farms in China: prevalence and genetic diversity. Sci. Rep. **14**(1), 11218 (2024)
4. Lang, J., et al.: Molecular characterization and prevalence of Cryptosporidium spp. in sheep and goats in western Inner Mongolia, China. Parasitol. Res. **122**(2), 537–545 (2023)
5. Liang, Y., et al.: A novel cross-priming amplification technique combined with lateral flow strips for rapid and visual detection of zoonotic Toxoplasma gondii. Vet. Parasitol. **334**, 110402 (2025)
6. Li, S., et al.: Host specific Eimeria genus diagnosis and qPCR development in Ovis aries and Capra hircus. J. Microbiol. Methods **220**, 106910 (2024)
7. Naskar, S., et al.: The biomedical applications of artificial intelligence: an overview of decades of research. J. Drug Target. **33**(5), 717–748 (2025)
8. Li, Y., et al.: Deep learning-based detection of bacterial swarm motion using a single image. Gut Microbes **17**(1), 2505115 (2025)
9. Şener, A., Ergen, B.: Automatic detection of gastrointestinal system abnormalities using deep learning-based segmentation and classification methods. Health Inf. Sci. Syst. **13**(1), 37 (2025)
10. Xiao, J., et al.: Improved pine wood nematode disease diagnosis system based on deep learning. Plant Dis. **109**(4), 862–874 (2025)
11. Bai, S., Shi, L., Yang, K.: Deep learning in disease vector image identification. Pest Manag. Sci. **81**(2), 527–539 (2025)
12. Wang, H.Y., et al.: Prevalence and population genetics analysis of enterocytozoon bieneusi in dairy Cattle in China. Front. Microbiol. **10**, 1399 (2019)
13. Pandey, O., Hona, E., Shrestha, E., Khadka, V., Ghising, T.: Unusual presentation and difficult to diagnose: a case of malaria with negative thick and thin giemsa stain smear tests. Cureus **15**(5), e39675 (2023)

14. Li, J., et al.: Survey of tick species and molecular detection of selected tick-borne pathogens in Yanbian, China. Enquête sur les espèces de tiques et détection moléculaire de certains agents pathogènes transmis par les tiques à Yanbian, en Chine. Parasite (Paris, France) **29**, 38 (2022)
15. Chen, Y., Huang, J., Qin, H., Wang, L., Li, J., Zhang, L.: Cryptosporidium parvum and gp60 genotype prevalence in dairy calves worldwide: a systematic review and meta-analysis. Acta Trop. **240**, 106843 (2023)

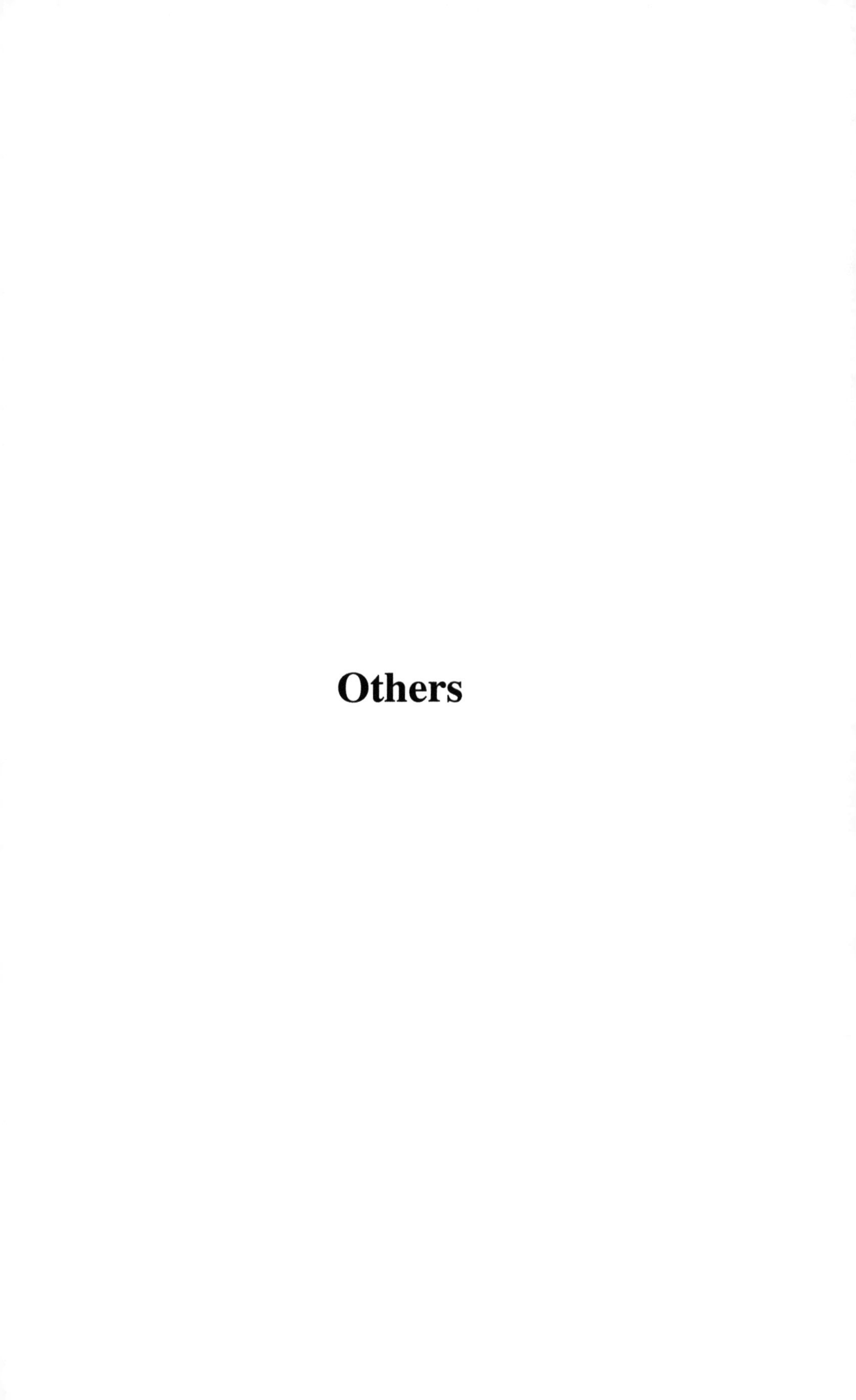

Others

Disentangled Representation Learning for Single-Domain Generalization in PPG Biometric Recognition

Ran Yi[1], Yuwen Huang[2(✉)], Gongping Yang[3], and Yilong Yin[3]

[1] School of Information Science and Engineering, Linyi University, Linyi 276000, China
[2] School of Computer, Heze University, Heze 274015, China
`huangyuwen@hezeu.edu.cn`
[3] School of Software, Shandong University, Jinan 250101, China

Abstract. Due to physiological and environmental influences, PPG signal distributions dynamically change over time, potentially impairing model generalization. To address this, we propose a single-domain generalization disentangled representation learning framework (PPGDRL) for PPG biometrics. First, data augmentation via discrete Fourier transform (DFT) enriches distribution diversity. Then, a deep disentangled learning framework (D1DViT) based on a 1D vision Transformer is built, comprising local and disentangled encoders. The local encoder extracts PPG features into sequences, while the disentangled encoder separates them into domain-invariant and domain-specific features, capturing discriminative and environmental information, respectively. Finally, the recognition results of overall features and invariant features are predicted through a dual-branch classifier. Experimental results on public PPG databases demonstrate that PPGDRL achieves strong generalization performance under distribution shift.

Keywords: PPG biometrics · 1D-vision transformer · distribution shift · disentangled representation learning · single-domain generalization

1 Introduction

Photoplethysmography (PPG) signals have attracted increasing attention as inherent biometric traits for identity recognition. Compared to extrinsic biometric traits, PPG signals offer several distinctive advantages: 1) Intrinsic liveness detection. PPG signals capture dynamic changes in blood volume, thereby providing inherent verification of physiological activity and preventing spoofing attacks. 2) Low-dimensional representation. As one-dimensional waveforms, PPG signals have significantly lower dimensionality than image-based biometric traits, which reduces computational complexity and facilitates real-time processing. 3) Rich physiological information. PPG data inherently support a wide range

W. Jia et al. (Eds.): CCBR 2025, LNCS 16360, pp. 679–689, 2026.
https://doi.org/10.1007/978-981-95-6123-0_62

of applications beyond biometric recognition, such as blood pressure monitoring, emotion recognition, and physiological state assessment. 4) Convenient and non-invasive acquisition. PPG signals can be easily collected from various body locations using wearable devices such as smartwatches or wristbands, enabling continuous and user-friendly biometric authentication.

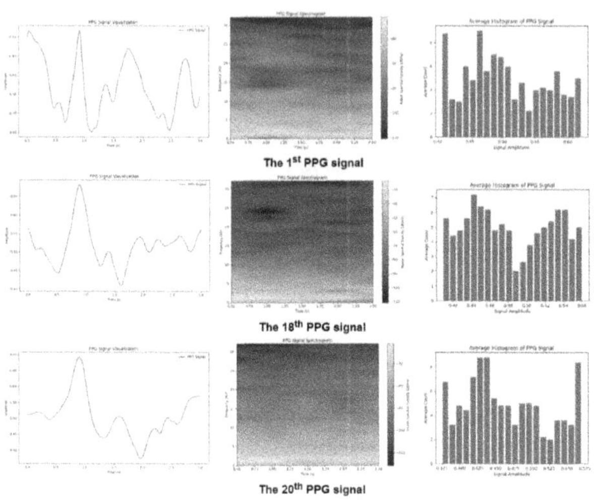

Fig. 1. Distribution of PPG signals for the same subject at different moments.

In recent years, identification methods based on the unique advantages of PPG signals have gained increasing attention [1] [2] [3]. However, PPG signal waveforms are influenced by factors such as temporal variations, physiological differences, motion artifacts, and device variations [4], leading to changes in signal distribution, as illustrated in Fig. 1. These changes can significantly reduce model performance and generalization on unseen data. Such variations are commonly referred to as domain shifts caused by changing conditions [5]. Among these, covariate shift, defined as a change in input feature distribution, is the most common. Compared with image data, obtaining domain labels for PPG datasets is more costly [6], making it important to explore domain generalization methods for PPG-based recognition.

To address the aforementioned issues and challenges, we propose PPGDRL, a disentangled representation learning framework inspired by single-domain generalization. It can learn invariant representations applicable to PPG biometrics under distributional shifts. Figure 2 provides an overview of the proposed IRL-PPG architecture. At the core of PPGDRL is a disentangled 1D Vision Transformer (D1DViT). In D1DViT, locality mechanisms are integrated into the feedforward network of the vision transformer architecture. The progressive disentanglement module decomposes the overall features of PPG signals into domain-invariant and domain-specific features. During the training phase, a classifier correction loss is used to reinforce the dual-branch classifier to ensure the generalization ability of PPGDRL. Crucially, these learned domain-invariant features are directly used for PPG biometric recognition.

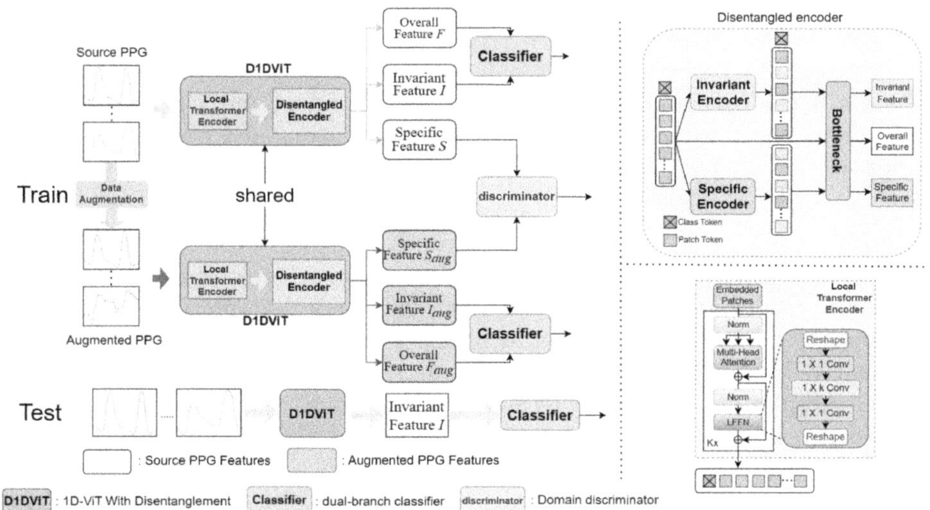

Fig. 2. The structure of PPGDRL and the sub-module structure in D1DViT.

Overall, the main contributions of PPGDRL for biometric recognition are summarized as follows:

(1) We propose a model called PPGDRL for learning disentangled representations for PPG biometric recognition under distributional shifts.
(2) We propose a phase spectrum perturbation-based data augmentation method tailored for PPG signals, enhancing diversity by generating synthetic samples that preserve biometric invariants while simulating distribution shifts.
(3) We propose a Disentanglement 1D Vision Transformer (D1DViT), which integrates a locality-aware transformer encoder with a dual-branch disentanglement encoder to decompose the extracted features into domain-invariant and domain-specific features.

2   Disentangled Representation Learning Framework

In this section, we first describe the method for generating augmented samples, then introduce the proposed Disentangled 1D Vision Transformer (D1DViT), and finally outline the loss functions employed.

2.1   Data Augmentation

The preprocessed PPG signals $x[n](n = 0, 1, \cdots, N-1)$ are first transformed into frequency-domain data $X[m]$ using the Discrete Fourier Transform (DFT) as [7]:

$$X[m] = \sum_{n=0}^{L-1} x[n]e^{-j2\pi\frac{n}{L}m}, \quad m = 0, 1, 2, \ldots, L-1 \tag{1}$$

where n is the spatial index, m is the frequency index, and j is the imaginary unit. From $X[m]$, we obtain the amplitudes value $A(m)$ and phases value $P(m)$ as follows:

$$X[m] = |X[m]|e^{j\cdot\arctan\left(\frac{I(m)}{R(m)}\right)} = A(m)e^{jP(m)}, \tag{2}$$

where $I(m)$ and $R(m)$ denote the imaginary and real parts of DFT.

Phase perturbation changes the waveform shape but preserves the energy distribution, while amplitude perturbation is more likely to destroy the discriminative information in the signal. By perturbing the phase, we can generate diverse samples, thereby achieving signal data augmentation. And random Gaussian noise is introduced to mitigate the influence of high-quality data. Formally, the mixed phase is defined as:

$$P_{\text{Aug}}(m) = R \cdot P(m) + (1-R) \cdot P_{\text{rand}}(m) + \mathcal{N}\left(0, (0.2\pi)^2\right), \quad R \sim U(a, b) \tag{3}$$

where $P_{rand}(m)$ is the phase spectrum of a separately obtained random signal, a, b are the upper and lower bounds of the random range.

At last, we reassemble the augmented signal X_{aug} via the inverse DFT (IDFT) as:

$$X_{aug} = \frac{1}{L}\sum_{m=0}^{L-1} A(m)e^{j(2\pi\frac{m}{L}n + P_{Aug}(m))} \tag{4}$$

2.2   Disentangled 1D Vision Transformer

To enhance the features of adjacent PPG signals that contribute more significantly to biometric recognition [8], we propose a Local Transformer Encoder (LTE), which consists of a multi-head self-attention module (MSA) and a Local Feed-Forward Network (LFFN) [9].

Local Transformer Encoder. First, the raw PPG signal X is divided and projected into N d-dimensional patch tokens through a PatchEmb layer. It is then augmented with a learnable class token and combined with positional encodings to form the Transformer input Z_0.

Then, the hidden state sequence Z_{k-1}, which is the output of the kth encoder layer, is updated as follows:

$$Z'_k = MSA\left(LN\left(Z_{k-1}\right)\right) + Z_{k-1} \tag{5}$$
$$Z_k = LFFN\left(Z'_k\right) + Z'_k \tag{6}$$

where Z'_k is the intermediate state and Z_k is the output of the kth encoder layer. LN denotes Layer Normalization, and MSA represents the standard multi-head attention mechanism in Transformers.

In LFFN, local receptive fields are introduced to capture spatially correlated features and enhance local perception. The process includes:

(1) Separating the class token from the patch tokens:

$$\left(Z_k^{cls}, Z_k^{patch} \right) \leftarrow Split\left(Z'_k \right), \tag{7}$$

$$Z_k^r = Reshape\left(Z_k^{patch} \right), \tag{8}$$

where $Z_k^r \in R^{d \times N}$ is the reshaped patch token, and $Reshape(\cdot)$ denotes the reshaping operation.

(2) A depth-separable 1D convolution with kernel size 3 is applied to extract local features. Pointwise convolutions are used before and after the depth-wise convolution to adjust the hidden dimensions. The computation of the local feature S_k is:

$$S_k = \sigma\left(\sigma\left(Z_k^r \circledast W_1 \right) \circledast W_D \right) \circledast W_2 \tag{9}$$

(3) Projecting S_k back to the source dimension and concatenating it with the class token to produce the final output:

$$LFFN\left(Z'_k \right) = [Z_k^{cls}; Reshape\left(S_k \right)]. \tag{10}$$

Finally, the output after the K-layer Transformer encoder can be expressed as:

$$Z = \left[Z^{CLS}, Z^1, Z^2, \ldots, Z^N \right] = Encoder\left(Z_0 \right) \tag{11}$$

where Z^{CLS} is the class token and Z^i (for $i = 1, 2, \ldots, N$) are the patch tokens.

Disentangled Encoder. In the disentangled encoder [10], the patch token $Z_{local} = \left[Z^1, Z^2, \ldots, Z^N \right]$ is fed into two structurally different encoders to extract local invariant and local specific features, respectively:

$$\begin{cases} Z_{inv} = Enc_{inv}\left(Z_{local} \right) \\ Z_{spe} = Enc_{spe}\left(Z_{local} \right) \end{cases} \tag{12}$$

where Z_{inv} represents local domain-invariant features, and Z_{spe} contains local domain-specific features.

Subsequently, the global feature Z^{CLS}, along with Z_{inv}, and Z_{spe}, are integrated through output blocks. The resulting outputs are expressed as:

$$\begin{cases} F = Block_{overall}\left(Z_k^{CLS} + Z_{inv} + Z_{spe} \right) \\ I = Block_{inv}\left(Z_k^{CLS} + Z_{inv} \right) \\ S = Block_{spe}\left(Z_{spe} \right) \end{cases} \tag{13}$$

where $Block_{overall}\left(\cdot\right)$, $Block_{inv}\left(\cdot\right)$, and $Block_{spe}\left(\cdot\right)$ denote the bottleneck operation functions.

Accordingly, for the input data X and its augmented version X_{aug}, the outputs from D1DViT are:

$$\begin{cases} F, I, S = D1DViT(X) \\ F_{aug}, I_{aug}, S_{aug} = D1DViT\left(X_{aug}\right) \end{cases} \tag{14}$$

where F, F_{aug} are overall features; I, I_{aug} are domain-invariant features; S, S_{aug} are domain-specific features.

2.3   Overall Loss

Our optimization objectives consist of a task prediction loss, a domain discrimination loss, a contrastive loss, and classifier correction loss.

$$\mathcal{L} = \mathcal{L}_{classifier} + \mathcal{L}_{domain} + \mathcal{L}_{Contra} + \mathcal{L}_{Cls} \tag{15}$$

Task Prediction. We employ the dual-branch classifier $Cls(\cdot)$ to predict both the overall features and the invariant features, and compute the cross-entropy loss ℓ_{CE} with respect to the true label Y:

$$\mathcal{L}_{classifier} = \sum \ell_{CE}\left(Cls\left(F_{set}\right), Y\right), F_{set} \in \{F, F_{aug}, I, I_{aug}\} \tag{16}$$

Domain Discrimination. By utilizing a discriminator $Dis(\cdot) \rightarrow [0, 1]$ to distinguish the domain specific features, the information can be disentangled [11]. The domain discrimination is defined by binary cross-entropy loss ℓ_{BCE} as follows:

$$\mathcal{L}_{domain} = \sum \ell_{BCE}\left(Dis\left(F_1\right), 1\right) + \sum \ell_{BCE}\left(Dis\left(F_2\right), 0\right) \tag{17}$$

where $F_1 \in \{F, S\}$ and $F_2 \in \{F_{aug}, S_{aug}\}$.

Contrastive Loss. To preserve domain invariance and ensure the discriminability of domain-specific features, we use contrastive loss to maximize the separation between features:

$$\mathcal{L}_{Contra} = -\frac{1}{N} \sum_{i=1}^{N} \left(\frac{e^{I \cdot I_{aug}}}{e^{I \cdot I_{aug}} + e^{I \cdot S} + e^{I_{aug} \cdot S_{aug}}} \right) \tag{18}$$

Classifier Correction Loss. Inspired by domain adaptation methods [12], we improve classifier adaptability to distribution shifts using the classifier correction loss. First, we compute the mean μ_c and covariance matrix Σ_c for each class:

$$\mu_c = \frac{1}{N_c} \sum_{i=1}^{N} f_i \cdot \mathbb{I}\left(y_i = c\right) \tag{19}$$

$$\Sigma_c = \frac{1}{N_c} \sum_{i=1}^{N} \left(f_i - \mu_c\right)\left(f_i - \mu_c\right)^T \cdot \mathbb{I}\left(y_i = c\right) \tag{20}$$

where $\mathbb{I}\,(y_i = c)$ denotes the number of samples of class c, f_i is the feature vector of the ith sample ,and N is the total number of samples.

Then, the prediction for sample i belonging to class c is corrected as follows:

$$\tilde{y}_{i,c} = y_{i,c} + \lambda(\frac{\Delta W_{i,c}^T \Sigma_{a,c} \Delta W_{i,c}}{2} + \Delta W_{i,c}^T (\mu_{a,c} - \mu_{s,c})) \tag{21}$$

where $\tilde{y}_{i,c}$ denotes the corrected output corresponding to the source prediction of $y_{i,c}$, λ is a hyperparameter, $\Delta W = W_c - W_{y_i}$ represents the weight difference matrix for each sample, $\Sigma_{a,c}$ is the covariance matrix of class c in the augmented data. $\mu_{a,c}$ and $\mu_{s,c}$ denote the mean features of class c in the augmented and source data, respectively.

Finally, the classifier correction loss is calculated:

$$\mathcal{L}_{Cls} = -\frac{1}{N} \sum_{i=1}^{N} \log \left(\frac{e^{\tilde{y}_{i},y_i}}{\sum_{c=1}^{C} e^{\tilde{y}_{i},c}} \right) \tag{22}$$

3   Experiment

We tested DRLPPG on three public datasets to evaluate its recognition performance and generalization. BIDMC [13] is widely used for identity recognition, while PPG-DaLiA [14] and PTT-PPG [15] are designed for analyzing physiological signals during motion. We focused on sitting and walking states in PTT-PPG. For each participant in the BIDMC and PTT-PPG datasets, 300 pulse signals were used, while 400 pulse signals were used for each participant in the PPG-DaLiA dataset. The data were partitioned into training and test sets, with 80% allocated for training and 20% for testing.

Table 1. Pulse recognition rate of ablation studies on three databases.

Method	BIDMC	PTT-PPG	PPG-DaLiA
PPGDRL with Amplitude Augmentation	97.42%	91.06%	82.08%
PPGDRL with clstoken Disentangled	97.42%	90.76%	82.83%
PPGDRL without Correction Loss	97.64%	91.52%	82.83%
PPGDRL without LFFN	97.01%	90.45%	77.50%
PPGDRL	**97.77%**	**92.27%**	**83.25%**

Overall Performance. We first conducted experiments on the PPGDRL model using three datasets and compared it with ablated versions lacking certain modules. Experimental results show that under single-pulse conditions, PPGDRL achieved 97.77% accuracy on the BIDMC, dropped to 92.27% in the sitting-and-walking scenario of PTT-PPG and further decreased to 83.25% under the complex motion in PPG-DaLiA. As shown in Table 1, phase information contains more environment-related features than amplitude, local features can provide details that are helpful for recognition. In addition, the classifier correction loss has a certain positive effect on data distribution shifts.

We then selected several representative baseline methods for comparison. PPGDRL outperformed the best baseline methods on the three datasets by 1.96%, 2.57%, and 0.92%, respectively. These results demonstrate that PPGDRL exhibits improved robustness under distribution shifts, and each module contributes effectively to the overall performance.

Table 2. Pulse recognition rate of different methods under the Hilbert transform.

Method	BIDMC	PTT-PPG	PPG-DaLiA
CNN	73.08%	78.48%	73.83%
GIN	72.39%	59.39%	65.08%
GraphSAGE	70.97%	53.18%	53.67%
LSTM	72.92%	80.45%	77.17%
GRU	75.41%	**85.30%**	75.08%
1D-ViT	76.45%	76.21%	67.17%
PPGDRL	**79.09%**	83.18%	**78.58%**

Performance Under Domain Shifts. To validate the generalization and robustness of the proposed method across different domains, we employ the Hilbert transform to artificially induce signal distribution changes that simulate domain shift. We then compare the performance of PPGDRL with six baseline methods. As shown in Table 2 and Fig. 3, PPGDRL still maintains a certain degree of generalization capability.

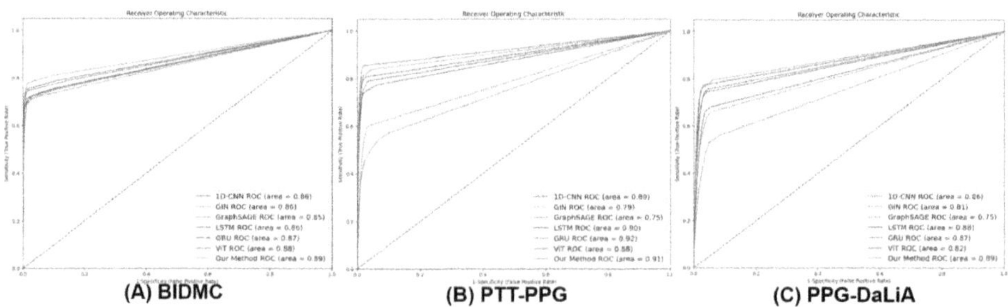

Fig. 3. ROC curves of pulse recognition rates for different approaches under the Hilbert transform.

Table 3. Subject recognition rate of comparison with state-of-the-art methods.

Database	Method	Subject Recognition Rate	EER
BIDMC	[1]	97.2%	2.5%
	[2]	99.5%	~
	[16]	99.3%	~
	[17]	97.8%	2.8%
	[18]	99.3%	0.6%
	Our method	**99.6%**	1.6%
PPG-DaLiA	[3]	87.0%	~
	[8]	75.0%	10.7%
	[19]	75.8%	12.2%
	Our method	**90.0%**	**5.6%**
PTT-PPG	[3]	93.0%	~
	[8]	91.8%	5.9%
	[19]	79.0%	7.4%
	Our method	**97.2%**	**3.4%**

To evaluate the effectiveness of PPGDRL, we applied majority voting for continuous authentication to assess the legitimacy of the current user, and compared it with several state-of-the-art PPG recognition methods, including both traditional non-deep learning approaches and deep learning techniques. As shown in Table 3, PPGDRL achieved higher recognition accuracy than most of the compared methods. Due to limitations in its data augmentation strategy, the performance improvement of PPGDRL is not significant when handling high-quality datasets like BIDMC. It performs more effectively in extracting domain-invariant features when faced with datasets that have significant distributional differences.

4   Conclusion and Future Work

In this paper, we propose a single-domain generalized disentangled representation learning framework (PPGDRL) for PPG biometric recognition, aimed at addressing distribution shifts caused by non-individual factors. PPGDRL treats non-semantic signal information as domain information and learns domain-invariant features from source and augmented data, improving generalization across diverse distributions. Experiments on three public PPG datasets show that the method performs competitively with state-of-the-art approaches. However, PPGDRL may overfit high-quality datasets, which remains a challenge. Notably, D1DViT's feature extractor is modular and replaceable, allowing for future improvements. We plan to explore lightweight designs to reduce model parameters and enhance practicality and efficiency.

Acknowledgments. This work was supported in part by the National Natural Science Foundation of China 62276093 and in part by the Natural Science Foundation of Shandong Province under Grant ZR2022MF286

References

1. Zhang, L., Li, A., Chen, S., Ren, W., Choo, K.K.R.: A secure, flexible, and ppg-based biometric scheme for healthy IoT using homomorphic random forest. IEEE Internet Things J. **11**(1), 612–622 (2023)
2. Wan, L., Liu, K., Mengash, H.A., Alruwais, N., Al Duhayyim, M., Venkatachalam, K.: Deep learning-based photoplethysmography biometric authentication for continuous user verification. Appl. Soft Comput. **156**, 111461 (2024)
3. Ghorbani, R., Reinders, M.J., Tax, D.M.: Personalized anomaly detection in ppg data using representation learning and biometric identification. Biomed. Signal Process. Control **94**, 106216 (2024)
4. Ho, Y.C., Lin, T.S., Wang, S.C., Chang, C.H., Lin, Y.T.: Variability of morphology in photoplethysmographic waveform quantified with unsupervised wave-shape manifold learning for clinical assessment. Physiol. Meas. **45**(9), 095005 (2024)
5. Sun, T., et al.: SHIFT: a synthetic driving dataset for continuous multi-task domain adaptation. In: Proceedings of the IEEE/CVF Conference on Computer Vision and Pattern Recognition, pp. 21371–21382 (2022)
6. Lu, W., Wang, J., Sun, X., Chen, Y., Xie, X.: Out-of-distribution representation learning for time series classification. arXiv preprint: arXiv:2209.07027 (2022)
7. Lee, I., Lee, W., Myung, H.: Domain generalization with vital phase augmentation. In: Proceedings of the AAAI Conference on Artificial Intelligence, vol. 38, pp. 2892–2900 (2024)
8. Xu, P., Zhang, L.: A fault diagnosis method for rolling bearing based on 1D-ViT model. IEEE Access **11**, 39664–39674 (2023)
9. Li, Y., et al.: LocalViT: analyzing locality in vision transformers. In: 2023 IEEE/RSJ International Conference on Intelligent Robots and Systems (IROS), pp. 9598–9605. IEEE (2023)
10. Jia, L., Chow, T.W., Yuan, Y.: Causal disentanglement domain generalization for time-series signal fault diagnosis. Neural Netw. **172**, 106099 (2024)
11. Peng, D., Wu, J., Han, T., Li, Y., Wen, Y., Yang, G., Qu, L.: Disentanglement-inspired single-source domain-generalization network for cross-scene hyperspectral image classification. Knowl.-Based Syst. **303**, 112413 (2024)
12. Wang, S., et al.: Disentangled representation learning with causality for unsupervised domain adaptation. In: Proceedings of the 31st ACM International Conference on Multimedia, pp. 2918–2926 (2023)
13. Pimentel, M.A., et al.: Toward a robust estimation of respiratory rate from pulse oximeters. IEEE Trans. Biomed. Eng. **64**(8), 1914–1923 (2016)
14. Reiss, A., Indlekofer, I., Schmidt, P., Van Laerhoven, K.: Deep PPG: large-scale heart rate estimation with convolutional neural networks. Sensors **19**(14), 3079 (2019)
15. Mehrgardt, P., Khushi, M., Poon, S., Withana, A.: Pulse transit time PPG dataset. PhysioNet **10**, e215–e220 (2022)
16. Xiong, G., Ye, Y., Lu, L., Dong, Q., Zhang, B.: A stable ppg-based biometric method using dynamic time warping and deep learning. In: 2021 3rd International Academic Exchange Conference on Science and Technology Innovation (IAECST), pp. 517–520. IEEE (2021)

17. Wei, R., Xu, X., Li, Y., Zhang, Y., Wang, J., Chen, H.: PulseID: multi-scale photoplethysmographic identification using a deep convolutional neural network. Biomed. Signal Process. Control **88**, 105609 (2024)
18. Wang, D., Hu, Q., Yang, C.: Biometric recognition based on scalable end-to-end convolutional neural network using photoplethysmography: a comparative study. Comput. Biol. Med. **147**, 105654 (2022)
19. Aslan, H.İ, Choi, C.: VisGIN: visibility graph neural network on one-dimensional data for biometric authentication. Expert Syst. Appl. **237**, 121323 (2024)

Author Index

J
Jia, Congcong   79
Jia, Wei   237
Jia, Yanlong   504
Jiang, Shuangtia   47
Jiang, Yue   226
Jin, Dongyang   293
Jin, Zhe   79, 90, 404

K
Kang, Wenxiong   14, 282, 493
Kong, Xiangyu   183

L
Lai, Jianhuang   631
Lai, Qi   57
Lei, Zhen   195, 307, 528
Leng, Fuyou   90
Li, Annan   260
Li, Chengchao   425
Li, Fenglian   415
Li, Haiyang   3, 161
Li, Huayang   101
Li, Jijie   195
Li, Jun   609
Li, Lin   482
Li, Meng   619
Li, Wei   112
Li, Xiaotong   596
Li, Xinyang   386
Li, Xueshuang   131
Li, Ya   173
Li, Ziyu   425
Li, Zongpeng   249
Liang, Fengmei   307, 504, 528
Liang, Yanyan   504
Liao, Xiaochuan   282
Lin, Junheng   173
Liu, Ajian   307, 528
Liu, Dingyue   540
Liu, Hao   204, 341
Liu, Kun   282, 493
Liu, Liangchen   425
Liu, Liangliang   665
Liu, Longfa   25
Liu, Qianying   397
Liu, Xianghuai   161
Liu, Xinyu   528
Liu, Xinyue   90

Liu, Yao   397
Liu, Zhishu   355
Lyu, Yueming   226

M
Ma, Hui   142, 504
Ma, Tianxiang   226
Ma, Zhongchen   643
Mahmood, Arif   14
Mao, Shasha   328
Mao, Yiluo   328
Marin-Jimenez, Manuel J.   293
Meng, Qingguo   79

N
Niu, Kai   517
Niu, Linkai   470, 655

O
Ou, Qihua   572

P
Pan, Binbin   585
Pan, Zaiyu   47, 68, 150, 318
Peng, Bo   226
Peng, Guozhen   260

Q
Qian, Yanhong   90
Qiao, Ying   415
Qin, Huafeng   3, 161
Qin, Huikai   665

R
Ren, Yani   101

S
Shakeel, M. Saad   282
Shao, Huikai   101
Shao, Xin   425
Shen, Linlin   183
Shen, Zhengwen   68
Shi, Liucun   517
Shu, Xiangbo   550
Song, Siyang   183
Song, Zehui   341
Su, Fei   36
Sui, Xiangqing   665
Sui, Yongqi   665